THE CAMBRIDGE
ANCIENT HISTORY

VOLUME III
PART 2

THE CAMBRIDGE
ANCIENT HISTORY

SECOND EDITION

VOLUME III
PART 2

The Assyrian and Babylonian Empires and other States of the Near East, from the Eighth to the Sixth Centuries B.C.

Edited by

JOHN BOARDMAN F.B.A.
Lincoln Professor of Classical Archaeology and Art, in the University of Oxford

I. E. S. EDWARDS F.B.A.
Formerly Keeper of Egyptian Antiquities, The British Museum

N. G. L. HAMMOND F.B.A.
Professor Emeritus of Greek, University of Bristol

The Late E. SOLLBERGER F.B.A.
Formerly Keeper of Western Asiatic Antiquities, The British Museum

With the assistance of C. B. F. WALKER
Department of Western Asiatic Antiquities, The British Museum

*The right of the
University of Cambridge
to print and sell
all manner of books
was granted by
Henry VIII in 1534.
The University has printed
and published continuously
since 1584.*

CAMBRIDGE UNIVERSITY PRESS

CAMBRIDGE

NEW YORK   PORT CHESTER
MELBOURNE   SYDNEY

Published by the Press Syndicate of the University of Cambridge
The Pitt Building, Trumpington Street, Cambridge CB2 1RP
40 West 20th Street, New York, NY 10011, USA
10 Stamford Road, Oakleigh, Melbourne 3166, Australia

© Cambridge University Press 1991

First published 1991

Printed in Great Britain at the University Press, Cambridge

British Library cataloguing in publication data
The Cambridge ancient history. – 2nd edn.
Vol. 3
Pt. 2, The Assyrian and Babylonian empires and other states
of the Near East, from the eighth to the sixth centuries B.C.
1. World, ancient period
1. Boardman, John
930

Library of Congress catalogue card number: 75-85719

ISBN 0 521 22717 8   hardback

SE

CONTENTS

v

PART II   THE EASTERN MEDITERRANEAN AND THE BLACK SEA

BIBLIOGRAPHY

MAPS

TEXT-FIGURES

PREFACE

The first part of this volume deals with the rivalries and triumphs of the Assyrians and the Babylonians in the period of their greatest achievements and fame. Babylonia slowly recovered from a long economic decline and under the leadership of Chaldaean tribal chieftains began the attempt to assert its independence from the overshadowing power of Assyria, but while Assyria's energy remained, the struggle was an unequal one.

Assyria appeared to move from strength to strength. The old enemy in the north, Urartu, was defeated by Sargon in a spectacular campaign. Expansion in the west led to the capture of Samaria and the elimination of Israel by Sargon in the eighth century, and to the invasion of Egypt by Ashurbanipal in the seventh century. In the east, Elam was crushed. The great palaces built by Tiglath-pileser III at Calah (Nimrud), by Sargon at Dur-Sharrukin (Khorsabad), and by Sennacherib and Ashurbanipal at Nineveh (Kouyunjik) are public monuments to Assyrian success, and the libraries, sculptures and ornament found in them are the epitome of Mesopotamian culture. In contrast, the internecine struggle between Ashurbanipal and his brother Shamash-shuma-ukin, appointed as King of Babylon, proved to be the beginning of a fatal weakness. The sudden arrival on the international scene of the Medes and the Scythians and their alliance with the Babylonians led to the unexpected defeat and collapse of Assyria in 612 B.C., and its almost total disappearance from the historical record.

Babylonia under a new dynasty was at first quick to fill the void and take over much of the Assyrian domain, further expanding in the west with the destruction of Jerusalem and the subjugation of Judah. In terms of sheer scale the building undertaken by the triumphant Nebuchadrezzar II at Babylon outstrips anything attempted by the Assyrian kings. Of other contemporary cultural achievements there are fewer traces. Much of what is told here of Babylonian literature is derived from the Assyrian libraries and represents the culmination of centuries of tradition. Once again internecine strife, this time between Nabonidus and his priesthood, seems to have weakened the empire, and with the onslaught of the

xv

Persian king Cyrus in 539 B.C. Mesopotamia's independence was at an end and its culture went into decline. There remained, however, one last flash of Babylonian genius, with the flowering of mathematical and observational astronomy from the fifth century B.C. onwards, the fruits of which continued to be enjoyed, through their transmission to the Greeks, down to the Middle Ages.

The chapters on the history of Israel and Judah down to the end of the Exile in Babylonia tell a story which has become an intimate part of the western cultural heritage. The constant struggles, internally for religious purity and externally for freedom first from Assyria and then from Babylonia, the disaster of the destruction of Jerusalem, and the despair of the Exile hardly need to be rehearsed. In this field the addition of new written documentation is sparse by comparison with Mesopotamia, but the high level of archaeological exploration in the land of the Bible continues to throw new light on the details of the story and to enrich its background.

In the setting of imperial struggles between Assyria, Babylonia, and Egypt the Phoenicians found themselves forced ever further west for trade and room to live. The importance of new discoveries in Phoenician archaeology is easily underestimated by comparison with the more familiar record of Greece and Italy. Archaeological work in the west Mediterranean, especially in Tunisia and Spain, continues to enhance our picture of these tough, enterprising people. Carthage became their most important focus, but they spread even wider. Persistently they forced their way into most parts of the Mediterranean world, sailing along every coast and exploring the river valleys, until their expansion was halted geographically by the Atlantic Ocean and politically by Greek colonialism and the rise of Rome.

Very different from the Phoenicians were the Scythians and the Thracians, who had no interest or skill in seafaring but excelled in raiding and horsemanship. The Scythian raids in Asia contributed to the downfall of the Assyrian empire, and some of their tribes, migrating from their homeland in southern Russia, were in conflict with the peoples of the lower Danube valley, who belonged linguistically to the Thracian group. In Chapter 33 the identification and the distribution of the named Scythian and Thracian tribes in the Early Iron Age are described by the masters of the subject, the late Professor T. Sulimirski and Professor G. Mihailov. Recent archaeological discoveries have shed new light on the tribal systems and the burial customs of both peoples. In this chapter the scene is set for the arrival on the coasts of Thrace and Scythia of the Greek colonists (Volume III Part 3) and for the Persian invasion of Thrace and Scythia (Volume IV).

The fertile crescent and its history do not monopolize this volume. In Anatolia, successor states to the Hittites, the Phrygian and then the Lydian, developed a distinctive culture which has become better known to us in the last forty years from excavations in their capitals at Gordium and Sardis. Not the least of their interest lies in their relations with the growing strength of the Aegean Greeks, exemplified by adoption of alphabets that seem to owe not a little to Greek example. Lydia especially is to play a major role in Greek Ionia and is the major western centre of Persian power.

The conquest of Egypt by Py in *c.* 728 B.C. resulted in a period of Kushite (Nubian) domination over the country without involving any fundamental political or religious change. Local chiefs retained their former positions, while owing allegiance to the Kushite king, and the kings themselves were already adherents of the cult of Amun, the centre of which in Nubia lay at Gebel Barkal, close to their capital, Napata, in the vicinity of the Fourth Cataract. The new dynasty, the Twenty-fifth, consisted of four kings besides Py: Shabako (his brother), Shebitku and Taharqa (his sons), and Tantamani (a nephew of Taharqa). Egypto-Nubian armies battled on a number of occasions with Assyrian forces operating in Palestine and Syria, as the Old Testament records, but the results did little to enhance Egypt's military reputation. Taharqa, in *c.* 674 B.C., was able to resist Esarhaddon's first attempt to invade Egypt, but not his second attack three years later. A further, and more destructive, Assyrian invasion in 664–663 B.C., in the time of Ashurbanipal, brought the Kushite rule over Egypt to an end. It was followed by a dynasty, the Twenty-sixth, of native kings under whom the arts prospered. Foreign mercenaries, mostly Carian and Lydian, strengthened the Egyptian army and, with their help, a successful expedition was conducted in Nubia in the reign of Psammetichus II, but against the Babylonian forces in the Levant they fared no better than their predecessors had done against the Assyrian armies. A Babylonian invasion of Egypt by Nebuchadrezzar II in 568 B.C., when Amasis was on the throne, seems to have soon been forgotten. The dynasty came to an end with the defeat of Psammetichus III in 525 B.C. by Cambyses.

It was decided not to set close chronological limits for all the material in this volume. Where chronological data exist, the connexions with previous volumes were easy to make; but in other subjects, such as the Scythians and the Thracians, we were dealing with the penumbra between prehistory and history. At the lower end it proved to be in the nature of the subjects that a writer should sometimes round off his account with a preview, for instance, of the restoration of the Jews from Exile or the afterlife of Assyrian traditions.

The publication of this volume was delayed sadly by the illness of Dr E. Sollberger, who had planned much of the contents and chosen some of the contributors before he withdrew in 1982. We express our deep sorrow at the news of his death on 21 June 1989. He was a most friendly and helpful colleague. Very fortunately Mr C. B. F. Walker, who was working with Dr Sollberger in the same department in the British Museum, came to the rescue of the Editors. He has co-ordinated the work of the contributors to Chapters 21–32, edited their texts and helped with the compilation of the bibliographies. We are immensely grateful to him. Invaluable assistance has been given to him and the Editors by Mrs Stephanie Dalley, who has helped with the final stages of some texts, prepared chronological tables and suggested suitable subjects for line-drawings.

The death of Professor W. Culican on 24 March 1984 deprived us of a leading authority on a fast-changing subject and of access to his enviable command of the archaeology of Phoenicians east and west. His chapter here, lightly revised by Mr Walker and with some added bibliography, is his fullest and last statement on the subject to which he devoted his life as a scholar.

The writing of Chapter 33a, 'Scythians and Cimmerians', was undertaken first by Professor E. D. Phillips of The Queen's University of Belfast, and then on his death by Professor T. Sulimirski who completed his typescript in 1979. Since the death of Professor Sulimirski the updating and the revision of this section with the title 'The Scythians' has been most generously undertaken by Mr T. F. Taylor, Lecturer in Archaeology, Bradford. He has written the Prolegomena and footnotes 1–24, and he has made additions to footnotes 25–124 (his additions being enclosed in square brackets) and to the Bibliography. It should be borne in mind that Mr Taylor is not necessarily in agreement with the late Professor Sulimirski on some matters, as is indeed to be expected in a field in which there have been so very many discoveries in recent years. The Editors are particularly grateful to Mr Taylor for his care in this delicate task.

Mr T. G. H. James wishes to express his thanks to the many colleagues whose studies have done so much to increase our knowledge of the Twenty-fifth and Twenty-sixth Egyptian Dynasties, and in particular to Professor K. A. Kitchen, Professor J. Leclant, Professor A. B. Lloyd, Professor H. De Meulenaere, Dr A. Spalinger and Professor J. Yoyotte.

Despite the inevitable delay in the completing of this volume it has been possible for the bibliographies to be kept generally up to date.

The Staff of the Cambridge University Press have given the greatest possible help throughout the preparation of this volume, and the Editors wish to express their gratitude. Mrs T. Minorsky translated Professor Dandamaev's chapter from the Russian. Mrs Henrietta McCall compiled the Index. The maps have been drawn by Euromap Ltd. Marion Cox prepared the illustrations.

With the publication of this volume Dr I. E. S. Edwards and Professor N. G. L. Hammond complete their work as Editors. Dr Edwards has been Editor-in-Chief for Volumes I.1, I.2, II.1 and II.2, and Professor Hammond for Volumes III.1, III.2, III.3 and IV.

February 1990 J.B.
I.E.S.E.
N.G.L.H.

NOTE ON FOOTNOTE REFERENCES

Works cited in the various sections of the Bibliography are referred to in footnotes by the appropriate section letter followed by the number assigned to the work in the sectional bibliography, followed by volume number, page references etc. Thus A 137 II, 5 is a reference to p. 5 of vol. II of M. E. L. Mallowan's *Nimrud and its Remains* – no. 137 of Bibliography A: Assyria and Babylonia.

CHAPTER 21

BABYLONIA IN THE SHADOW OF ASSYRIA
(747–626 B.C.)

J. A. BRINKMAN

I. BACKGROUND AND GENERAL TRENDS

Babylonia in the early centuries of the first millennium B.C. reached a
nadir in its history. Political power was effectively fragmented between
a weak central government, semi-independent cities, and vigorous tribes
who controlled substantial portions of the hinterland. The older settled
population had declined significantly in size as well as influence,
although the cities continued as religious and intellectual centres. Long
stretches of watercourses, the lifelines of irrigation agriculture, were
abandoned or had fallen into disuse. Recorded economic life had all but
ceased, and there is no evidence for significant foreign trade being
carried on by the settled population. Because of her political and
economic debility, Babylonia's international horizons during this period
were considerably narrowed; almost all known contacts were with her
immediate neighbours to the north and east: Assyria, Luristan, and
Elam.

In the six score years between 747 and 626 B.C.,[1] Babylonia underwent
a substantial but gradual transformation from political and economic
weakness to reinvigorated national strength on the threshold of territorial expansion. The Late Assyrian empire dominated most of south-west
Asia during these decades. For Babylonia, Assyrian military and political
oppression served in effect as a catalyst: it stimulated the people of the
land to develop new social institutions, to heal political fragmentation,
and to transcend military backwardness. The stabilization of the Babylonian monarchy under Assyrian occupation enhanced the economic
environment and prepared the way for revitalization of urban structures.
It is the purpose of this chapter to chart the career of Babylonia over
these crucial decades and to probe the reasons behind the transforma-

---

[1] Year dates in this chapter are given according to the Julian calendar. Years cited simply as '747'
stand for 747/6, since the Babylonian New Year fell in the early spring. In accordance with
Babylonian custom, regnal dates for monarchs are considered to begin with the first full year of
reign and exclude the accession year (except when the king's reign did not extend beyond the
accession year); thus Shamash-shuma-ukin, whose reign is listed as 667–648, came to the throne in
668. The chronology followed here is based on A 543.

2

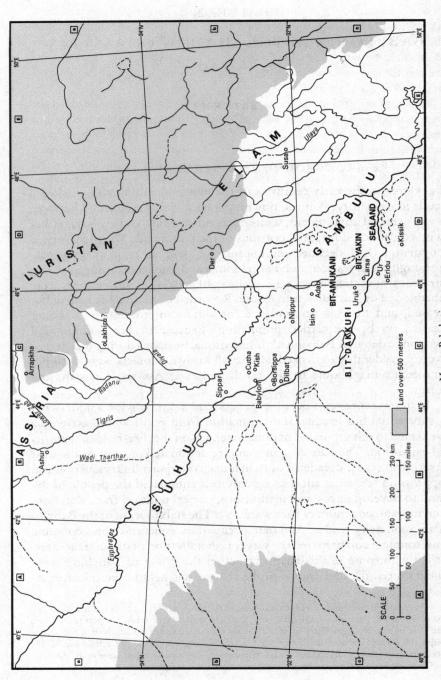

Map 1. Babylonia.

tion.[2] We shall begin in the present section with a general discussion of the institutional landscape in which these changes took place; we shall then deal chronologically with the events through which these trends manifested themselves (Sections II–VII), discuss the textual and archaeological sources (Section VIII), and conclude with an overall perspective (Section IX).[3]

Recently published archaeological surface surveys provide data for appraising the demographic base of Babylonian society over the longer time span between 1150 and 626 B.C.[4] Despite their methodological and practical limitations,[5] these surveys help to compensate for an absence of adequate contemporary documentation, especially pertaining to the economy and to rural society.[6] The detailed surveys concerned with this time[7] cover less than one-third of the settled area in the alluvium between the lower Tigris and Euphrates; the surveyors chose to concentrate along the main course or courses of the lower Euphrates as known in the fourth and third millennia B.C.[8] Thus a comparatively narrow belt (c. 40–70 km wide) around the former Euphrates channels from about 45 km north west of Nippur down to the vicinity of Ur has been subjected to at least limited survey, as has the southern end of the lower Diyala basin. For these regions, the coverage may at present be presumed to be reasonably representative.[9]

Statistics for all intensively surveyed regions point to a significant drop in population in the late second and early first millennia B.C. Compared with the preceding period (c. 1600–1150), the gross settled area[10] in each region declined, progressively more severely as one moves from south to north. The extreme proportions vary from Ur, where the settled area was 78 per cent as large as it had been in Kassite times, to the lower Diyala, where the area was only 23 per cent of its former size. Though we are not as yet in a position to make due allowance for possible diachronic shifts in population-density ratios, the raw figures suggest that relative losses in population in the early stages of the 1150–626 period may have ranged from about one person in four in the far

---

[2] For the geographical and institutional background of Babylonia in this period, the reader is referred to *CAH* III².1, 285–95.

[3] Footnote documentation in this chapter is intended to be illustrative rather than exhaustive, especially in the case of Assyrian royal inscriptions (which are treated more fully in chapters 22–4 below). Additional documentation for many of the subjects discussed here may be found in A 551.

[4] I.e., from about the end of the Kassite dynasty to the beginning of the Neo-Babylonian dynasty under Nabopolassar.

[5] A 513, chapter 2; A 705. Discussion: A 551, 3 n. 4.   [6] A 551, 3 n. 5; A 552, 177.

[7] A 511; A 513; A 514; A 783. Supplementary material in A 568, 1–13 and plan 1; A 599, 20–4; A 624; A 625; A 726.

[8] A primary research interest for the surveyors was the origins and early development of urbanism in Mesopotamia; hence they tended to focus in areas where settlement was heaviest between 4000 and 2000 B.C.

[9] Discussion: A 551, 4 and n. 8.   [10] Discussion: A 551, 4 n. 9.

Table 1. *Percentage of settled surface area occupied by settlements of ten hectares or less,*[11] *2700–626 B.C.*

	B.C.	Lower Diyala	Nippur–Uruk
Early Dynastic II–III	2700–2350	52.9	9.9
Akkadian	2350–2100	57.8	18.4
Ur III–Larsa	2100–1800	61.9	25.1
Old Babylonian	1800–1600	74.5	29.6
Kassite	1600–1150	81.5	56.8
Post-Kassite	1150–626	100.0[12]	64.3

south (Ur) to three persons in four in the north-east (lower Diyala). It must be stressed that these ebbs in population size are not to be viewed as a unique sharp decline brought on by catastrophic events, but rather as part of a secular trend toward lower population levels which had begun in most areas of southern Mesopotamia after the Ur III period (*c.* 2000 B.C.) and reached its climax at this time.[13]

Also typical of this period is a further decline in urbanism: proportionately more people were living in small towns or villages, that is, settlements that were ten hectares or less in area. This too is part of a long-term trend, in most areas going back to the Early Dynastic periods (*c.* 2700–2350), whereby the percentage of the population concentrated in small settlements gradually increased. Here, too, regional variations may be noted (Table 1). Thus, both the lower Diyala and the Nippur–Uruk regions, though starting from substantively different patterns of urbanism or hierarchical settlement distribution, gradually became more village-oriented. In contrast, the area around Ur, according to Henry Wright's survey,[14] stood out sharply: after 2900 B.C. the distribution of smaller settlements (here 9.5 ha or less) fluctuated in no regular pattern between 40 per cent and 49 per cent of the total settled area, reaching a maximum in Old Babylonian times and a minimum under the Kassite dynasty. Thus the tendency for a growing percentage of the population to live in small settlements was pronounced, but not universal. This ruralization movement reached its apogee in the early first millennium, but was clearly being reversed by 600 B.C., except in the Diyala.[15]

Also of interest in the early first millennium B.C. are the geographical patterns of abandonment, continuity, and new settlement within each region. In the lower Diyala basin, the only extended watercourse that

---

[11] Sources of data: A 511, 39–57; A 513, 142 table 13 (cf. p. 138 table 12).
[12] As emended in A 513, 179 table 16 (81.1 per cent in A 511, 56 table 15).   [13] A 552, 173.
[14] A 783.   [15] Where the reversal began only in Seleucid times (A 513, 179).

definitely remained in use in the period was on the far eastern edge of the surveyed zone;[16] moreover, only 5.7 per cent of the settled area was occupied by new settlements – the abnormally low percentage presumably reflecting the inability or unwillingness of the population to assume new risks in the sparsely settled countryside. Along the Nippur–Uruk axis, there was extensive abandonment on the east side of the surveyed region and in the central area between Ishan al-Howa on the north and Qal'a Dulu' on the south. Only the western part of the Uruk area south of Qal'a Dulu' had a significant percentage of stable, continuing communities. It is striking that in the Nippur–Uruk region there were no new settlements south of Isin and Adab and only about 18 per cent of the gross settled hectarage in the northern sector represented fresh settlement.

In the southernmost region around Ur, abandonment was particularly pronounced in the northern zone: the former Ur channel of the Euphrates was reduced to a small canal supporting only a few villages besides Ur itself. But in the Ur survey region as a whole more than half the settlements were new, and these represented 22 per cent of the total settled area. It is difficult to estimate how much of this overall relocation may have been due primarily to hydrological factors (such as the drying up or shifting of watercourses) and how much to political disruption. But the decline in the western part of the lower Diyala basin and in the eastern section of the Nippur–Uruk region occurred where one would expect pressures from newly arrived Aramaean tribesmen to have been greatest; and one could make a similar case for Chaldaean–Aramaean stress (especially from the Bit-Yakin and Puqudu tribes) in the northern Ur area. The rise in small undefended settlements on the southernmost fringe of the Ur region could indicate sedentary linkage with neighbouring Arab tribes who were moving through the area.[17] The low proportion of investment in new settlements was probably dependent on several factors, including reduced population size and unreliable defence mechanisms in times of political unrest.

Thus from the surface surveys one gains a general picture of population decline, dispersal into smaller settlements, and relocation out of vulnerable areas. From the jejune textual evidence, especially for the period from 1100 to 750 B.C., one can detect complementary background hints of climatic irregularity, crop failure, outbreaks of plague,[18] and disruptive tribal population movements. But there remain questions about whether the broad picture of decline applies with equal validity to all of Babylonia and for all of the time span between 1150 and 626 B.C.

---

[16] A 551, 7 and n. 19.
[17] Compare the data in A 534, 258; A 583; A 783, 333; A 829, no. 167.
[18] A 535, 389 n. 2180; A 763, 430 and 432; cf. A 25, 76.

Although generally unnoticed, there is evidence which indicates that: (1) by the early first millennium B.C. the intensively surveyed regions may no longer have been typical for Babylonia as a whole, and (2) the general decline in Babylonia may have been substantially arrested before 720 B.C., rather than a century later. The detailed surveys did not touch several crucial areas where major economic and political activity is documented in the eighth and seventh centuries, particularly the north-west section of the alluvium (where urban centres were concentrated)[19] and the principal tribal homelands of the Chaldaeans in the west[20] and south east.[21] According to the longer accounts of Sennacherib's first campaign, these tribal areas held a large number of cities and fortified settlements.[22] Also, in the early first millennium B.C., two additional factors must be taken into account. First, the major Euphrates courses had by then shifted considerably to the west of the old Nippur–Uruk axis (and so outside the area covered by the intensive surveys) and thus the principal band of contemporaneous Euphrates-based settlements would be expected to lie to the west of the surveyed zone.[23] Secondly, much of the Nippur–Uruk hinterland would have been controlled by Aramaean tribal groups at a comparatively low level of urbanism, that is, groups whose impermanent quarters would not leave traces that are readily identifiable by traditional surface reconnaissance techniques. Thus the major scene of action in lower Mesopotamia from at least the middle of the ninth century[24] would not be expected to lie in the former urban 'heartland', but outside the intensively surveyed areas, especially to the north west, west, and south east. In addition, the substantial documentation – administrative, legal, and epistolary – that commences about 747 and increases significantly after 722 suggests by both its quantity and contents that the depths of the prior dark age were over in the third quarter of the eighth century.[25] Thus, while the broad picture of population decline may be generally valid for central lower Mesopotamia in the early first millennium B.C., there is evidence indicating that:

(1) the period of worst decline ended in the second half of the eighth century rather than one hundred years later
(2) a primary focus of urban activity after the mid-ninth century lay outside the intensively surveyed regions, that is, to the north west of the Nippur–Uruk corridor
(3) the major tribal areas – including fortifications and towns – lay along the unsurveyed banks of the contemporary Euphrates to the west of

---

[19] Notably Babylon, Borsippa, Dilbat, and Sippar. This area was covered principally by an early survey which is considered inadequate by present standards (see A 551, 4 and n. 6).
[20] Especially Bit-Dakkuri.   [21] Bit-Yakin. Topography of this area: A 726; A 783.
[22] A 270, 52–4.   [23] Cf. A 551, 9 n. 30.
[24] And perhaps from the mid-twelfth century on.   [25] Discussion: A 551, 10 n. 33.

Nippur and Uruk and in the marshy territories to the east of Uruk and Ur.[26]

Therefore the general picture of population decline should be modified to reflect local variations as well as adjustments in periodization.[27]

For the late eighth and seventh centuries, written sources supplement and add depth to the rough demographic portrait drawn from archaeological surveys. Contemporary letters and economic records, as well as the campaign narratives of Assyrian royal inscriptions, help to fill in details about the population of the towns and countryside of Babylonia. The inhabitants of Babylonia in the late eighth century were composed of two principal groups: the older 'Babylonian' native stock (an amalgam of descendants of the Sumerians and Akkadians and such assimilated later immigrants as the Amorites and Kassites), and relatively recently arrived tribesmen, such as Aramaeans and Chaldaeans, who were as yet unassimilated. By 750 B.C., the constituent elements of the older population had lost their political and ethnic identity and shared a common Babylonian culture. This group formed the majority of the population in the urban centres in the north-west alluvium[28] and in the south west.[29] Because of the urban focus of the extant documentation, we do not yet know whether significant numbers of this population group resided in the countryside, for instance in northern Babylonia. The dominant social unit among the older Babylonians was the family (nuclear or extended), although under the hectic political conditions of the seventh century smaller family units in the cities increasingly came to align themselves into broader kin-based groups that traced descent from common eponymous ancestors or bore distinctive family names.[30] The most important larger kin-groups eventually came to dominate the civil and religious hierarchy in several towns, particularly in northern Babylonia.[31]

The tribesmen, who are distinguished primarily by their social structure,[32] controlled substantial portions of the countryside. There were two major tribal groups, the Aramaeans and the Chaldaeans,[33] both of West Semitic origin.[34] It should be stressed that the dichotomy between the diverse populations in Babylonia was not based on place or type of residence (urban versus rural, sedentary versus non-sedentary), but on social organization (tribal versus non-tribal). Many tribesmen lived in towns, and some even in large urban centres.[35]

---

[26] Note the qualifying statements in A 513, 152–4 and the reservations in A 601, 40.

[27] Discussion: A 551, 10 n. 35. [28] Notably at Babylon, Borsippa, Sippar, Dilbat, and Nippur.

[29] Particularly at Uruk and Ur. [30] Discussion: A 551, 11 n. 38.

[31] A 545, 237–8; A 590. [32] Discussion: A 551, 12 n. 40.

[33] For Arabs in Babylonia, see p. 17 below. Further discussion: A 551, 12 n. 41.

[34] I.e., their basic linguistic affiliation lay with Semitic groups outside the East Semitic (Assyro-Babylonian) language family.

[35] Towns: A 185, 44 and 58–60; A 270, 52–4. Large urban centres: A 270, 54.

The Aramaeans had been in Babylonia longer than the Chaldaeans, but were on the whole more fragmented and less sedentary.[36] Aramaeans had begun arriving in lower Mesopotamia in large numbers at the beginning of the eleventh century[37] and had settled principally across the northern end of the alluvium, around Nippur, and on both sides of the lower Tigris. There were more than forty Aramaean tribes, some of which were under the simultaneous leadership of as many as eight sheikhs (nasīku).[38] The most prominent of these tribes in the late eighth and seventh centuries were: (1) the Gambulu, living in a marshy region (perhaps centred around modern Wasit) near the Elamite border;[39] (2) the Puqudu, active both along the Babylonian–Elamite frontier and in the vicinity of Uruk in south-western Babylonia;[40] and (3) the Ruʾua near Nippur. The Aramaeans had generally resisted assimilation to Babylonian ways; they had retained their distinctive personal names and tribal structure and had not taken an active role in the Babylonian political system.[41] Individual Aramaeans were usually identified in texts not by a Babylonian two-tier genealogy (such as 'Nadinu son of Zakir-shumi'), but simply by their own personal name plus a gentilic adjective referring to their tribe – 'Samunu, the Gambulian' (Samunu Gambūlayu). The Aramaeans had few large towns,[42] and their economy was primarily pastoral. Their principal impact on Babylonia seems to have been in the realm of language, where in this period Aramaic was fast replacing Babylonian as the vernacular; by the late eighth century, the use of Aramaic in Babylonia may have become so widespread that officials had to be dissuaded from using it in government correspondence.[43] It is unfortunate that we are not better informed about the Aramaeans in Babylonia and Assyria at this time because the widespread language changes may already have been symptomatic of an incipient Aramaiza-tion of Mesopotamian culture; at maturity, this trend was to impart a distinctive character to Mesopotamian civilization, especially in the centuries between the demise of independent Babylonia (539 B.C.) and the coming of Islam (c. A.D. 637).

[36] On the Aramaeans in Babylonia, see A 535, 267–85; A 574 (with adjustments noted in A 544); A 683; A 733; A 755.
[37] Earlier contacts with the Aramaeans (under the name Akhlamu) date back to at least the fourteenth century and perhaps as early as the eighteenth century B.C.
[38] A 185, 45 n. 9; A 545, 226.
[39] A 755, 218–23; Streck in The Encyclopaedia of Islam II (2nd edn. Leiden, 1965) 357, s.v. Djabbul; cf. A 603, 8.
[40] A 551, 13 n. 49.
[41] The theory that an eleventh-century king of Babylonia (Adad-apla-iddina) was Aramaean has now been shown to be based on a textual misreading: C. B. F. Walker in A 54, 414.
[42] Discussion: A 551, 13–14 n. 52.
[43] A 570, 90; A 575, no. 10. Further discussion of Aramaean influence in Babylonia at this time: A 551, 14 n. 53.

The Chaldaeans, although later arrivals,[44] were both more sedentary and more unified than the Aramaeans. There were three major and two minor Chaldaean tribes, each named the 'House of So-and-so' (after an eponymous ancestor), and each under the control of a single chieftain.[45] The major tribes were: (a) Bit-Amukani, on the lower Euphrates above Uruk; (b) Bit-Dakkuri, on the central Euphrates south of Borsippa but occasionally active around Babylon itself;[46] and (c) Bit-Yakin, the most powerful of the Chaldaean tribes, dominating the land around Ur and the marshes to the east (the 'Sealand').[47] Of lesser importance were the Bit-Sha²alli and the Bit-Shilani, smaller tribes which are mentioned only infrequently in the sources.[48] By the late eighth century, the Chaldaeans – although preserving their basic tribal structure – were becoming Babylonized: many of them bore Babylonian names, were settled in fortified towns and villages, and were engaged in cultivating date palms and raising cattle. Individual Chaldaeans cited their genealogy in most cases simply by calling themselves 'son' of their tribe's eponymous ancestor (thus: Ea-zera-iqisha 'son' of Amukanu).[49] Because they controlled most of the course of the Euphrates through Babylonia as well as the marshes at the head of the Persian Gulf, the Chaldaeans were in a position to regulate a substantial portion of international and domestic trade. Beginning in the early eighth century, they also entered actively into Babylonian political life; before the year 730, each of the three principal Chaldaean tribes had in turn furnished at least one occupant of the Babylonian throne.[50]

The king of Babylon presided over this heterogeneous population,[51] though his power was in effect limited by independent actions of both the larger cities and the tribes. Some of the weaker kings were unable to police dissident elements, and uncontrolled civil unrest and disruption of trade routes are probably what attracted the initial Assyrian military intervention in Babylonia in 745 B.C. Following the political collapse of Babylonia at the end of the ninth century, the hereditary principle for monarchical succession had been undermined in practice: there is only one known instance of Babylonian father–son succession between 810 and the rise of the Neo-Babylonian empire in 626.[52] The monarchy was

---

[44] They are first attested in Babylonia about the year 878 B.C. (A 535, 260).

[45] Powerful chiefs of Chaldaean tribes were sometimes styled 'kings' in Assyrian royal inscriptions, e.g., A 234, 52 Episode 12; A 532, 12.

[46] This included the town of Marad (A 270, 52).

[47] This included Larsa, Eridu, and Kissik (A 270, 53). Location of Bit-Yakin: A 726. Geography of the Chaldaeans: A 296, 19–25.

[48] Discussion: A 551, 15 n. 59.   [49] Discussion: A 551, 15 n. 60.

[50] General literature on the Chaldaeans: A 535, 260–7 (with reference to earlier treatments); A 582.

[51] Discussion: A 551, 16 n. 62.

[52] When Nabu-nadin-zeri (Nadinu) succeeded Nabonassar in 734 (discussion: A 551, 16 n. 64).

further destabilized by a rapid turnover in rulers, especially in the years from 733 to 689 (when there were no less than fourteen reigns averaging just 3.2 years each).[53] Although weakened, the Babylonian monarchy endured as an institution and served as a focus of contention in the late eighth and seventh centuries, when Chaldaeans and Assyrians vied with each other to ensure succession of their own candidates to the throne.[54]

Local government in Babylonia was administered through a province (*pīhatu*) system, with most major cities and many minor towns serving as capitals of their own small provinces. The far south-eastern section of the country, which had extensive marshes and no large cities, was treated as a separate larger province under its old name, the 'Sealand'. Most provinces were under the jurisdiction of a royally appointed governor, the *šakin ṭēmi* (an older title which had taken on an elevated function about the middle of the ninth century); a few provinces, such as Nippur and the Sealand, had governors who bore traditional titles, such as *šandabakku* (Nippur) and *šaknu* (Sealand).[55] Occasionally local rulers with dynastic pretensions affected a more ambitious titulary; thus various members of the Ningal-iddin family, which held the governorship at Ur between 680 and 648, styled themselves *šaknu* or even *šakkanakku*.[56]

The Babylonian city remained a strong political and cultural institution. The historical picture is undoubtedly skewed by the urban origins of most surviving documentation, but the elitist bias of the sources is not unrepresentative: cities dominated the economic and intellectual life of the country. Retaining an aura of tradition that in some instances dated back to the golden era of city states in preceding millennia, the city was still a provincial seat of government and had an assembly of citizens which functioned as a law court in trying contested cases.[57] Temples in the large cities remained powerful institutions with their splendid liturgical ceremonies, prestigious officials, lucrative prebends, and extensive properties. Citizens in major cult cities, especially in the north-west alluvium, held privileges of exemption from taxes, corvée, and army service.[58] Urban centres such as Nippur and Babylon were distinguished for their pluralist, cosmopolitan society, which included foreigners as well as tribal residents;[59] cities were not only the home of intellectuals and scribal schools, but contained a broad spectrum of

---

[53] Statistics: A 551, 16 n. 65.

[54] Studies of the royal titulary in the eighth and seventh centuries: A 535, 167–8; A 895, v. 9, 53–65 and 99–100; A 541, 412–13 n. 25. Discussion of the powers and duties of the king: A 535, 289–96; A 541; *CAH* III².1, 290.

[55] Discussion: A 551, 17 n. 68.   [56] A 551, 17 n. 69.

[57] See provisionally A 729, 146–7.

[58] Particularly in Sippar, Nippur, Babylon, and Borsippa; see *CAH* III².1, 291. Note also the general right of Babylonian citizens to appeal directly to the king (A 714).

[59] Discussion: A 551, 18 n. 73.

classes from merchants and temple officials to settled agriculturalists and pastoralists. The line between town and country population was not so sharply drawn as in some modern Western societies. Cities drew their economic support from a range of sources: temple endowments, private landed property, international and domestic trade, the skilled crafts, and the agricultural and stock-raising activities of the hinterland. Despite the demographic trend toward ruralization in the early first millennium, urbanism remained the norm: successful or prosperous tribes built cities and towns and fortified them with walls.[60] Because of their wealth and prestige, cities were obvious targets for Assyrian aggression; yet they were not always as vulnerable as one might expect in a non-militaristic society. The walled cities of the north-west alluvium proved formidable obstacles to the Assyrians in the time of the Great Rebellion (652–648), and Babylon itself long held out against two sieges: for more than fifteen months in 690–689 and for more than two years in 650–648.[61] It is surely significant that the most ambitious building programme in Babylonia during this period was carried out by a city governor (Sin-balassu-iqbi of Ur)[62] rather than a king; and another city governor dated by his own regnal years.[63] Cities were the focus of local government, society, and economy and remained critical factors in the political and cultural life of the land.

The tribes seem generally to have remained outside the province system and to have operated under their own leaders. The Chaldaean tribes Bit-Yakin and Bit-Dakkuri and the Aramaean tribes Gambulu and Puqudu were politically the most powerful groups in the land; what prevented them from dominating the entire country was that they seldom agreed to work under common direction for a common purpose. When an exceptional leader such as Merodach-baladan or Mushezib-Marduk appeared and personally won their allegiance, the disparate tribes could work together with the rest of Babylonia and offer surprisingly effective resistance to the militarily superior Assyrians. Occasionally there were strained relations or hostile incidents between tribe and tribe or between a tribe and the older population. This seems seldom to have developed into long-lasting or deep-seated enmity; but, in the case of Ur and the Bit-Yakin tribe (which controlled much of Ur's hinterland),[64] there was continuing friction that erupted into warfare several times during the period.

Though politically weak and internationally insignificant in the mid-

---

[60] A 185, 44 and 58–60; A 270, 52–4; A 234, 52–3 Episode 13; A 337, 70.

[61] Borsippa and Ur also endured long sieges in the seventh century; see A 551, 18 n. 75.

[62] A 537, 336–9; A 534, 249–51.   [63] A 829, nos. 27 and 90.

[64] Including (at various times) the towns of Eridu, Larsa, and Kissik (A 270, 53; cf. A 185, 58 and 64).

eighth century, Babylonia nonetheless enjoyed a limited regional importance. It formed the vulnerable southern border of Assyria and stood astride several important trade routes: the southern section of the Euphrates (which was a crucial link in commerce between the Persian Gulf and the Mediterranean), the beginning of the Baghdad–Kermanshah–Hamadan road to the east, the overland route to Elam via Der, and the developing caravan tracks west onto the Arabian desert. Assyria, as it grew into an imperial power, could not afford to ignore disruptive tribesmen close to its southern frontier; they not only menaced the outskirts of Assyria itself but threatened the Babylonian hub of international trade. Assyria thus made a concerted effort to neutralize destabilizing influences in Babylonia, and this it did primarily by launching a series of massive strikes against Babylonia's tribal population. The ensuing struggle between the Assyrians and the tribesmen dominated the political history of Babylonia from 745 to 626.

Assyrian initiatives in Babylonia took a variety of forms, including campaigns into tribal areas, wholesale deportation of tribal populations, diplomatic efforts to secure the allegiance of the non-tribal urbanites, and direct intervention in government through the installation of Assyrian or pro-Assyrian rulers on the Babylonian throne (in effect, making Babylonia a client state). Campaigns into tribal regions tended to focus on fortified towns, which were unable to withstand aggressive Assyrian siege techniques.[65] The effectiveness of this strategy varied in direct proportion to the percentage of the tribal population found in these towns; the tactic was essentially a failure in the case of the relatively nonsedentary Aramaeans and only a qualified success in the case of the Chaldaeans, who took somewhat longer to regroup. Deportation was another technique much in favour with the Assyrians; it was employed several times on a large scale in Babylonia in the second half of the eighth century, both to export insurgent tribesmen and to import potentially more docile inhabitants from other lands.[66] According to official if tendentious Assyrian statistics, almost half a million people were removed from Babylonia between 745 and 702; more than half of these were Chaldaeans.[67] The combined tactics of repeated military campaigns and deportations were responsible for the eclipse of the Bit-Yakin tribe in the seventh century and for the temporary ascendancy of the Bit-Dakkuri among the Chaldaeans between 693 and 675.[68]

For most of the period under consideration (85 out of 121 years), Assyria controlled the Babylonian throne either by having the Assyrian monarch personally rule also as king of Babylonia or by installing one of

---

[65] E.g., A 185, 44 and 58–60; A 270, 52–4; A 337, 70.
[66] Discussion: A 551, 20 n. 80.   [67] Statistics and discussion: A 551, 20 n. 81.
[68] Discussion: A 551, 20 n. 82.

its own nominees (sometimes a member of the Assyrian royal family) as king.[69] The latter method eventually proved more successful; and the two long reigns from 667 to 627 stabilized the Babylonian monarchy and provided support for the burgeoning economy – despite the notable interruption of the Great Rebellion (652–648). Assyria did not always respect the territorial integrity of Babylonia, especially east of the Tigris; at various times it incorporated such centres as Der, Lakhiru, Khilimmu, and Pillatu within its own borders, albeit with only mixed success.[70] In the area of local administration within Babylonia, Assyria in the late eighth century attempted to override the structure of small provincial units when Sargon divided the land into two large provinces with one governor in Babylon and another in the eastern region of Gambulu.[71] The new system did not succeed and may have been abandoned already in the next reign.[72] Assyria conducted local administration either by appointing Babylonians on whom it could rely or by installing Assyrian emissaries, the latter usually in minor positions and for shorter periods.[73] Officials serving in Babylonia from the king down to local temple stewards were required to take a loyalty oath (adû) to the Assyrian monarch and to promise that they would faithfully report to the Assyrian court any subversive actions or plots.[74] The Assyrians did not maintain control in Babylonia by stationing large garrisons on Babylonian soil, but relied on an efficient intelligence network to direct army units based in Assyria to major trouble spots.[75] The local Assyrian military policy was one of defence-in-depth: quickly suppressing insurgence with forces from outside rather than laying an extensive internal network to forestall revolt.[76]

Assyrian relations with the older urban centres of Babylonia deserve further comment. Previous Assyrian rulers in the ninth and early eighth centuries had had a special relationship with the venerable religious cities of the north-west alluvium, notably Babylon, Borsippa, and Cutha; they had bestowed gifts on the major temples and had sponsored sacrifices there.[77] Shalmaneser III (858–824) had fêted the citizens of Babylon and Borsippa at lavish banquets and presented them with festal garments and other gifts.[78] In the late eighth and seventh centuries, when the Assyrian monarchs came to rule either directly or through intermediaries in southern Mesopotamia, they increased efforts to establish solidarity between themselves and Babylonian city-dwellers. They pursued a tactic of attempting to separate this urban population from the tribesmen; in times of unrest, they appealed directly to the men of Babylon for support

[69] A 540, 90–2. [70] E.g., A 535, 240; A 676, no. 70. Discussion: A 551, 21 n. 84.
[71] A 185, 66. Discussion: A 551, 21 n. 85. [72] A 551, 21 n. 86.
[73] A 545, 232–3. [74] A 674, 31–40; cf. A 72, nos. 287 and 327; A 344, 28–30.
[75] Cf. A 551, 21 n. 89. [76] A 545, 235.
[77] A 535, 197 and 217. [78] A 535, 197.

against Chaldaean and other rebels, such as Mukin-zeri and Shamash-shuma-ukin.[79] To secure this political allegiance, the Assyrians offered political and economic advantages to the city-dwellers and to their temples. Most Assyrian monarchs of this time sent generous offerings to the major deities of Babylonia, particularly to Marduk and Nabu.[80] They renewed the traditional privileges of the citizens of the old religious centres, including freedom from certain taxes.[81] Sargon attempted to broaden his base of support by extending comparable privileges to such southern cities as Uruk, Ur, Kissik, and Eridu, which do not seem to have had them previously.[82] But, except in the far south,[83] acceptance of Assyrian rule seems generally to have been lukewarm; and cities that sided with Assyria ran the risk of finding themselves isolated from their countrymen. As the governor of Nippur wrote to the Assyrian court:

The king knows that people everywhere hate us because of our allegiance to Assyria. We are not safe anywhere; wherever we might go, we would be killed. People say, 'Why did you submit to Assyria?' We have now locked our city gates tight and do not go out . . .[84]

Even under Esarhaddon, who made a show of restoring Babylon and reinstating its privileges, there were tax protests in the capital and obvious signs of Assyrian unpopularity.[85] In times of major revolt,[86] cities in the north west supported the anti-Assyrian side, even though they were particularly vulnerable to Assyrian reprisals.[87] Thus the Assyrian policy of cultivating Babylonian urban centres for religious and political reasons yielded marginal results that on the whole were not favourable to Assyria, especially after the accession of Sennacherib.[88]

Anti-Assyrian resistance in Babylonia was generally led by the Chaldaeans. Revolts which brought a member of the older Babylonian population to the throne were invariably taken over and the Babylonian candidate displaced in favour of a Chaldaean within a few weeks or months.[89] Before the time of Sennacherib, the Chaldaeans chose tribal areas as sites for their military engagements against the Assyrians, perhaps because they were unsure of the support of the older urban population. After Sennacherib's accession, many of the battles took place in northern Babylonia near cities,[90] and the Chaldaeans drew on

---

[79] A 72, no. 301 (= A 698, no. 115); A 79, no. 1.

[80] A 185, 58; A 204 II, pl. XXXIV 9–10; A 234, 24 Episode 33; A 344, 226–48; A 689, no. 132. Also A 72, no. 1241 + A 575, no. 112; cf. A 72, no. 339 (= A 73, no. 293; A 77, 511).

[81] A 663, 1; A 234, 25–6 Episode 37; A 551, 22 n. 95.   [82] A 185, 64.

[83] Where cities such as Uruk and Ur, which were situated in enclaves in tribal territory, saw an advantage in having an Assyrian defender.

[84] A 72, no. 327 (= A 698, no. 121).   [85] A 72, nos. 327 and 340 (= A 73, no. 276).

[86] Notably in 703, 694–689, and 652–648.   [87] Cf. A 551, 23 n. 101.

[88] Discussion: A 551, 23 n. 102.   [89] Examples: A 551, 23 n. 103.

[90] Perhaps because Sennacherib even early in his reign was perceived as anti-Babylonian.

urbanites, Aramaean tribesmen, and foreign contingents for assistance. Not all Chaldaeans were consistently anti-Assyrian. The Assyrians may occasionally have manipulated the accession of well-disposed chieftains, and Chaldaean soldiers served with the Assyrian army.[91] By the middle of the seventh century, Bit-Amukani had effectively fallen under Assyrian domination and was itself subject to Aramaean raids.[92] But in general, especially between 732 and 646, the Chaldaeans were the mainstay of anti-Assyrian politics in Babylonia, and occasional extraordinary tribal leaders were able to combine the political strength of their unified tribes, economic power based on their animal husbandry and trade, and tactical benefits of their environment[93] to good advantage in harrying the Assyrians.[94]

Over the years, repeated Assyrian attacks on the tribal countryside and Assyrian interference in Babylonian government stimulated the growth of more effective political and military strategies among both the older Babylonians and the tribal populations. Babylonia under Assyrian stress became more adept in utilizing its natural resources – especially its hydrological features – for offensive and defensive strategy. Use of marshes[95] as bases for mobile raiding parties and the deliberate shifting of watercourses (either to put pressure on unsympathetic cities or for defensive flooding around tribal towns)[96] evince a heightened awareness of the tactical potential of the environment in resisting a militarily superior enemy. In addition, Babylonians and Chaldaeans broadened anti-Assyrian resistance into a regional movement by bringing in their nearby trading partners, the Elamites and Arabs, to furnish auxiliary troops for hostilities in Babylonia. This inevitably expanded the theatre of conflict into neighbouring lands, which presented formidable natural obstacles for Assyrian armies: hills and mountains in Elam, desert in Arabia, and extremes of climate in both areas. Furthermore, in times of stress, there appeared, especially from the Chaldaean Bit-Yakin tribe, a remarkable series of leaders, who commanded substantial strength from the various parts of Babylonia: Merodach-baladan, Mushezib-Marduk, and Nabu-bel-shumati, to name only the most prominent.[97] These leaders, with a core of support from their native tribe, learned to rally widespread anti-Assyrian forces from other tribes and the older population of Babylonia, as well as from foreign lands. Eventually these

---

[91] A 234, 52 Episode 12; A 497, nos. 105 and 139. Cf. A 551, nn. 106, 185, 188.

[92] A 72, no. 275; cf. A 72, no. 896 and A 497, no. 139.

[93] Particularly the marshy terrain and the dispersed population.

[94] A 539, 279; A 588, chapter 5. The Chaldaean economic base (especially agriculture and trade) would have been particularly vulnerable to Assyrian military moves.

[95] A 551, 24 n. 110.   [96] A 551, 25 n. 111.

[97] The older Babylonian population produced few leaders who were able to survive even a short time. See A 551, 23 n. 103.

traditional alliances were available to assist even the Assyrian arch-rebel, Shamash-shuma-ukin, who led Babylonia and its allies in a devastating blow to the unity of the Assyrian empire. Unquestionably, the perennially interfering presence of a strong Assyria spurred the political and military development of Babylonia in the eighth and seventh centuries.

Despite the focus of much of the extant documentation, Babylonian–Assyrian contacts at this time were not entirely political or military. The venerable culture of Babylonia with its flourishing traditions of scholarship, *belles lettres*, and ancient religion exerted a strong attraction for Assyria. From the beginning of the second half of the eighth century, Babylonian astronomy experienced a significant revival, and astronomical observations were again recorded with great care.[98] There is also evidence for at least a passing interest in horticulture.[99] Babylonian scribes cultivated the tradition of Mesopotamian lexical scholarship,[100] and the stylistic quality of longer royal inscriptions under Merodach-baladan and Shamash-shuma-ukin shows that scribal authors were striving with mixed success to emulate literary models.[101] Babylonian literary and scientific works occupied a prominent place in Assyrian libraries; and Ashurbanipal, when augmenting his own palace collection of cuneiform tablets, sent emissaries to search through Babylonian temple archives as well as collections in private houses.[102] Individual Babylonians were brought to Assyria to be educated as scribes and courtiers, in the hope that they would one day prove loyal to Assyria.[103] Even the landscape of the south held a fascination for the Assyrians: Sennacherib, when planning amenities for his renovated capital at Nineveh, laid out a park imitating the Chaldaean countryside with its distinctive trees, marshes, and wild life.[104] It is difficult to estimate the cultural impact of Babylonia on Assyria in the sphere of religion; Assyrian kings proudly recorded their offerings to Babylonian temples[105] and celebrated a New Year's Festival (*akītu*) in Assyria, but we do not know how much of this was due to Babylonian influence and how much may have been reshaping of native Assyrian customs. In the realm of law, there was a mingling of Babylonian and Assyrian traditions in a few legal documents dated early in the reign of Esarhaddon,[106] but it is unclear whether this ever went beyond the adoption of a few superficial traits of style.[107] In material culture, notably in the few surviving examples of contemporary Babylonian architecture, in glyptic, and in

[98] A 535, 227; A 532, 49 under 44.3.12; A 772, 20–1. Cf. A 551, 26 n. 114.
[99] A 532, 48 under 44.3.5. Cf. A 204, 60–2 (= A 35, 1 § 794).   [100] A 551, 26 n. 116.
[101] A 595; A 651 II, 6–8; A 676, no. 37. Cf. A 551, 49 n. 230.
[102] A 508; A 632 XXII no. 1 (A 88 IV, 212–14 no. 6).
[103] A 270, 54 and A 703, 33–4.   [104] A 270, 97; cf. *ibid.*, pp. 115–16.
[105] Note especially the lavish gifts of Sargon (A 226 I, 124–6).
[106] Cf. A 551, 27 n. 122.   [107] Cf. A 551, 27 n. 123.

ceramics, there were new aesthetic and stylistic developments, perhaps influenced by Assyrian advances,[108] but this has yet to be satisfactorily studied. One would not expect that after 625 the architectural and artistic achievements of the dynasty of Nabopolassar and Nebuchadrezzar came to fruition without relation to their native predecessors.

When viewed from a broader regional perspective, Babylonia was involved in a close network of relationships with nearby lands. Ties with Assyria were traditional, but now unavoidably heightened because of Assyria's direct political involvement in the south. Relations with the Elamites and Arabs developed more spontaneously as a result of geographical proximity, commercial ties, mingling of populations, and shared political interests (usually anti-Assyrian). Fleeting Babylonian contact with the state of Judah in Palestine may have been motivated by common antipathy to Assyrian encroachments.

Babylonian–Arab relations in the late eighth and seventh centuries are sparsely attested; but there is a general pattern of commercial and social interaction, light Arab settlement on the outskirts of Babylonia, and occasional Arab military assistance to Babylonia in its anti-Assyrian struggles.[109] In the time of Sennacherib, the queen of the Arabs sent her brother with troops to assist Merodach-baladan in the rebellion of 703.[110] Half a century later, Arab chieftains and their men endured considerable hardship in Babylon with Shamash-shuma-ukin when the city was under Assyrian siege.[111] There is also scattered and occasionally ambiguous evidence for penetration of Arabs or Arab influence into Babylonia: Arab toponyms in western Chaldaea in the late eighth century,[112] small population movements of Arab tribesmen between Eridu and Qedar territory on the desert,[113] the visit of a merchant from Tema to the king of Babylon,[114] an Arab raid on Sippar,[115] new small settlements just off the desert to the south of Ur,[116] and a growing number of Arab or Phoenician trade objects – as well as inscriptions in a script akin to early epigraphic South Arabic – found in first-millennium levels in excavations in southern Mesopotamia (principally at Nippur, Uruk, and Ur).[117]

Babylonia's most valued ally was Elam, its eastern neighbour, which also possessed a literate urban civilization. Babylonia and Elam had close trade relations, shared religious interests,[118] and often pursued a

---

[108] A 551, 27 n. 124; cf. *ibid.*, pp. 120–1.
[109] General treatment of the early Arabs: A 19. Onomastic evidence in Mesopotamia: A 784.
[110] A 270, 51.   [111] A 344, 68.
[112] A 583; discussion: A 551, 28 n. 128.   [113] A 829, no. 167.
[114] A 72, no. 1404.   [115] A 72, no. 88.
[116] A 783, 333; cf. A 551, 28 n. 132.
[117] A 522; A 534, 258 n. 1; A 583, 109–10; A 631, 43–4; cf. A 784. The exact date of the objects and inscriptions has yet to be determined.   [118] Discussion: A 551, 28 n. 134.

common anti-Assyrian policy. The eastern tribal regions of Babylonia abutted on the Elamite border; and the nearby large tribes of Gambulu and Bit-Yakin traditionally had close ties with the Elamite monarchs and people.[119] During the period of most co-ordinated Chaldaean resistance to Assyria, first under Merodach-baladan and later under Mushezib-Marduk, Elamite troops became heavily involved in fighting in Babylonia. Chaldaean leaders in time of major crisis sent substantial gifts (ṭaʾtu)[120] to secure Elamite support; and large Elamite armies took part in decisive field battles in or near northern Babylonia.[121] Elamite generals played prominent roles at the battle of Kish in 703 and at Khalule in 691.[122] Besides providing direct military aid to Babylonia, Elam on occasion harboured political fugitives from Assyrian wrath – notably Merodach-baladan (after 700) and Nabu-bel-shumati (after 648).[123] Relations between Elam and Bit-Yakin were particularly strong and undoubtedly accounted for some of the staying power in the lengthy Chaldaean resistance movement in southern Mesopotamia.[124]

But Babylonia's eastern alliance could not always be relied on. The Elamite monarchy, especially after 693, was subject to periods of instability because of the uncertain health of some kings and because of frequent revolutions.[125] There were also times of political fragmentation, when two or more kings ruled simultaneously in such centres as Susa, Madaktu, and Khaidalu.[126] After 670, Elam was beset by vagaries of climate: drought led to famine and caused people to flee the country.[127] On occasion, Elam drew diplomatically closer to Assyria, especially in the quarter century between 690 and 665; in the time of Esarhaddon a formal peace agreement was concluded between the two lands, and Assyria later provided sustenance and shelter for Elamites hard pressed by food shortages.[128]

Generally, however, Elam backed Babylonia in its struggle against Assyria. Between 652 and 648, although three Elamite kings were deposed in quick succession, each new ruler soon adopted the country's anti-Assyrian and pro-Babylonian stance.[129] This policy on occasion led to Elamite invasions of southern Mesopotamia when the Babylonian throne was occupied by an Assyrian monarch,[130] and such incursions occasionally resulted in the harsh treatment of Babylonian cities such as

---

[119] Discussion: A 551, 29 n. 135.   [120] Discussion: A 551, 29 n. 136.

[121] Note particularly the battles of Der (720), Cutha and Kish (703), and Khalule (691). Cf. A 751, 45–8.

[122] A 270, 45 and 51. The evidence for 691 is unclear.   [123] Discussion: A 551, 29 n. 139.

[124] Discussion: A 551, 29 n. 140.   [125] A 25, 77–81; A 344, 32–4, etc.

[126] A 8, chapters 9 and 11 (the discussion there requires revision).

[127] A 337, 56–8; cf. A 72, no. 295.

[128] A 234, 58–9; A 337, 56–8; A 688, 102. Cf. A 703, 34 n. 66.

[129] A 344, 32–62.   [130] Examples: A 551, 30 n. 146.

Sippar.[131] But, in general, Elamite–Babylonian relations were cordial and not just between the tribal populations and the Elamites; there were also direct contacts between the older, urban inhabitants – especially the family of Gakhal – and Elam.[132] Elam was intimately involved in the political fate of Babylonia, especially in the three-quarters of a century between 720 and 646;[133] and Elamite support or lack thereof was often decisive in determining the political strength of such anti-Assyrian movements as the Chaldaean resistance (721–689) and the Great Rebellion (652–648). Had Elam itself enjoyed greater political stability, the hegemony of the Assyrian empire might not have been so long-lived.[134]

The Babylonian economy too should be placed in regional perspective, although documentary evidence is sparse and much essential research in this area remains to be done. It would be anachronistic to regard Babylonia throughout the late eighth and seventh centuries as merely a desiccated shadow of its former self, possessing a high culture of venerable antiquity, but seriously underpopulated, politically weak, and generally poverty-stricken. In the seventh century, as the Babylonian monarchy gradually stabilized and longer reigns provided greater continuity in governance, there are signs of increasing economic prosperity: a significant rise in the number of economic records, growing concern with land-tenure and the maintenance of irrigation networks, developing technology and trade, and more ambitious construction programmes (both monumental and residential).[135] Babylonian temples remained important economic institutions; and projects requiring major capital expenditures, such as securing the intervention of Elamite armies, were on occasion financed from temple treasuries.[136] The Babylonian economy continued to rest on the twin pillars of agriculture and animal husbandry, which provided the internal basis for extensive trade relations. Although the present state of research does not permit a detailed analysis of the Babylonian economy, we can at this juncture offer a few preliminary observations.

Babylonian agriculture in this period concentrated primarily on producing barley and dates, which were grown extensively even in tribal areas. Most surviving real-estate transactions involving rural land concerned date-palm orchards, often located in places described as 'swamps' near large cities. Wine was produced locally in hilly regions east of the Tigris such as Khirimmu, but was not a significant

---

[131] A 25, 78 and 83. See A 551, 78–9 n. 380.   [132] Discussion: A 551, 30 n. 148.

[133] Discussion: A 551, 31 n. 149. For a general appraisal of Babylonian–Elamite relations at this time, see A 552A.

[134] Discussion: A 551, 31 n. 150.

[135] An even more significant indication of prosperity may be the wealth of ordinary people, reflected in the richness of contemporary grave gifts at Nippur (A 664, 147).

[136] A 234, 13 Episode 4; A 270, 42.

commercial item. Atypically, Babylonia in the early first millennium appears as a producer of timber; the southern and eastern sections of the country (especially Chaldaea and Khararatu) grew *musukkannu* trees,[137] which were prized for palace and temple construction. There are many and varied references to agricultural land in legal contracts; and the introduction of revised toponymic terminology indicates shifting patterns at the lower levels of rural society. There was a new unit of local agricultural administration called the 'Fifty' (*ḫanšu*) presided over by the 'Commander of the Fifty' (*rab ḫanše*).[138] Local canals and irrigation works were often named the *ḫarru* (or *ḫarri*) of So-and-so (for example, the canal 'Ḫarri-of-Merodach-baladan'), and various Commanders of Fifties were allocated responsibility for the maintenance of segments of local irrigation systems. These new developments and their ramifications have yet to be studied in detail.

Animal husbandry, practised by both the older settled population and the tribesmen, raised a variety of beasts: sheep, goats, bovines, donkeys, mules, and even horses and camels. Transport animals were much in demand for the movement of goods and for military service; sheep's wool and goat-hair were used in the manufacture of textiles, a traditional Babylonian high-quality export.

Agriculture and livestock-raising thus created a local resource base to support trade. Babylonia, as observed earlier, was the crossroads of many trade routes reaching west to the Mediterranean and to the Arabian desert, north into Assyria, north east into the Zagros mountains, east into Elam, and south east by the Persian Gulf. Within this broad network, Babylonia not only exported its own products and imported necessities as well as luxury goods for its own consumption, but also served as an entrepôt for transshipment of goods from and to many foreign lands. Along these radiating routes moved substantial amounts of cargo, some of it requisitioned by way of booty and tribute (an economic dimension of the Neo-Assyrian empire). In the late eighth and seventh centuries, Babylonia's most important export was people, removed in large numbers from tribal areas as well as from cities, especially over the six decades from 745 to 685.[139] Although these deportations are described in the Assyrian royal inscriptions primarily as political or military manoeuvres,[140] they nonetheless had an economic side. Subject peoples, including Chaldaeans and Aramaeans, were pressed into working on Sennacherib's massive urban renewal project for Nineveh and its environs;[141] and Babylonian Aramaeans were set to

---

[137] Botanical identification not yet established.
[138] Discussed in more detail in A 706; A 551, 32–3 and nn. 157–61.
[139] A 545, 227 and 234–5; further discussion: A 551, 34 n. 166.
[140] See p. 12 above.   [141] A 270, 95.

agricultural tasks in western Mesopotamia near Harran and in Syria.[142] The second most important export from Babylonia was animals, known mostly through Assyrian booty lists; these included transport and draught animals (oxen, donkeys, mules, horses, and camels), produce animals (cows, sheep, and goats), and to a much lesser extent exotic beasts such as wild boar.[143] Grain, dates, and wine were also taken from Babylonia as spoil; and Chaldaeans and Aramaeans were reckoned among the principal suppliers of wood for the decoration of the palace of Tiglath-pileser III.[144] Durand has recently made a case for interpreting certain enigmatic Babylonian tags found in Assyria as 'wool dockets', that is, labels attached to packets of wool at the time of shearing and then taken with other captured goods to Assyria after the fall of Dur-Yakin.[145] Textiles, especially garments with multicoloured trim, were also obtained from the south.[146] Reeds were cut down in the Chaldaean marshes and brought to Assyria for use in construction.[147] Other items imported into Babylonia were captured by the Assyrians, including silver, gold, precious stones, and luxury woods such as ebony;[148] the magnificence of such spoil conveys an impression of significant wealth among the ruling classes in Babylonia, particularly among the tribal chieftains. As yet most movement of goods to and from Babylonia in this period must be reconstructed largely from forced transactions documented in the Assyrian booty and tribute lists;[149] we have no systematic information about the scale and scope of such exactions, much less of their impact on the Babylonian economy. It is possible that the geographical spread of the Assyrian empire expanded the market for Babylonian trade or at least facilitated the movement of Babylonian goods.[150]

By the seventh century, the technology of the Iron Age was making inroads in Babylonia.[151] In addition to iron tools found at Nippur,[152] there is an increasing number of references in account texts to iron objects: nails, daggers, razors, bedsteads, and pot-stands. There is also the first specific mention in a Babylonian document of an ironsmith (LÚ.SIMUG AN.BAR), which seems to be a new occupation in the land. At least some of the iron used in Babylonia was imported from Cilicia (*māt Ḫumê*).[153]

Another topic about which we should like to be better informed for this period is the Babylonian military. The conquering armies of

---

[142] Examples: A 551, 34 n. 169.   [143] Discussion: A 551, 34 n. 170.

[144] E.g., A 185, 46; A 270, 26, 55, and 57; A 204 I, 74 (= A 35 I, § 804). Cf. A 93 II (1901), no. 1013 rev. 12–14.

[145] A 578, 258–9.   [146] A 204 I, 62 (= A 35 I, § 794).

[147] A 270, 95.   [148] A 185, 60; A 204 I, 62 (= A 35 I, § 794); A 270, 56–7; A 337, 70.

[149] Cf. A 551, 35 n. 176.   [150] Cf. A 551, 35 n. 177.

[151] Cf. A 551, 36 n. 178.   [152] A 601, 43.

[153] A 551, 36 nn. 180–3.

Nabopolassar, which in the two decades after 625 B.C. put an end to the Assyrian empire and then pushed west to win Carchemish and Syria, were not without their Babylonian forerunners, despite the relative silence of the texts. Nor should the heavy reliance of the Chaldaeans on Elamite generals, officers, and soldiery (especially archers) obscure the fact that the Chaldaeans, Aramaeans, and older Babylonians had troops of their own and occasionally fought battles without substantial foreign aid. At Dur-Atkhara in 710, Merodach-baladan's forces are said to have included 600 cavalrymen (*pēthallū*) and 4,000 garrison soldiers (*ṣābē šulūti*).[154] In the following year, at the Assyrian siege of Dur-Yakin, Merodach-baladan's capital in the south, Chaldaean forces included a central contingent under the king (*kiṣir šarrūti*) and horses trained for chariot use.[155] Ashurbanipal claimed that he had given Shamash-shuma-ukin infantry, cavalry, and chariotry,[156] the three major components of contemporary armed forces. Babylonian armies by themselves proved capable of capturing major cities such as Nippur (693) and Cutha (651).[157] Southern Mesopotamians were apparently not devoid of military skills, since the Assyrian army in the time of Ashurbanipal included troops recruited from among Babylonians, Chaldaeans, and Aramaeans;[158] but we have as yet discovered practically no documentation concerning the Babylonian army itself. Although the army in the eighth and seventh centuries was generally not a match for the Assyrian forces and their more advanced techniques, it was able to face the Assyrians in the field and on several occasions to check Assyrian moves.[159]

These then are some of the factors in the transformation of Babylonia between 747 and 626 B.C. To what at the beginning of this period had been a sparsely populated, impoverished, and unstable land with rival tribal and traditional groups, Assyrian military intervention and governance meant oppression and limited economic exploitation. But the Assyrian presence aroused local resistance, helped to heal political fragmentation, and led Babylonia to develop regional alliances with Elam and the Arabs. A series of political leaders, mostly Chaldaean but culminating in the disaffected Assyrian prince Shamash-shuma-ukin, organized a series of national and international coalitions to oppose Assyrian encroachment. Although Babylonian forces inevitably succumbed in each protracted encounter, their perennial struggles revealed Assyrian vulnerability[160] at the height of the Late Assyrian empire. The Babylonian metamorphosis under Assyrian stress was not simply politi-

---

[154] A 185, 44.   [155] A 185, 60; cf. A 185, 72 and A 226 I, 118.
[156] Literally 'men, horses, chariots' (A 344, 28).
[157] A 25, 78 and 129.   [158] A 497, no. 105; cf. A 100, 38 ND 2619.
[159] A 551, 37 n. 189.   [160] And the inadequacy of imperial bureaucratic methods.

cal and military; its social and economic dimensions were also impressive. With the eventual stabilization of the Babylonian monarchy under Assyrian domination, the Babylonian economy showed signs of increasing growth, even after diversion of goods and services for Assyrian use. Babylonian cities prospered financially and, under royal or gubernatorial patronage, also architecturally. The older Babylonian settled population increased in size and, in order to survive in a world dominated by Assyrians and tribesmen, developed broader kinship-based groups with a more effective voice than the isolated family unit. The great families of the urban north west – the Gakhal, the Egibi, the Arka(t)-ilani-damqa – rose to prominence. Babylonia's pluralist population with its long-standing capacity to absorb heterogeneous newcomers, at length, found its language and, to a lesser extent, its culture giving way under growing Aramaean influence.

In these decades, the shadow of the Assyrian empire meant compromised independence and a muted political career for Babylonia; but it also meant relative stability, prosperity, and protection from outside foes. In the words of Sargon, subject peoples were advised to enjoy the protective benefits of the *pax assyriaca*: 'Eat your bread [and] drink your water [under] the shadow of the king my lord, [and] be glad.'[161] Under these conditions, political and social institutions underwent substantial transformation, and Babylonia expanded its international horizons. Although thwarted in its attempts to assert its freedom, Babylonia in the course of its struggle created new mechanisms that would – in the two decades after 625 B.C. – not only dispel the Assyrian shadow but eradicate the empire that cast it.

II. INITIAL ASSYRIAN INVOLVEMENT IN BABYLONIA, 747–722 B.C.[162]

Around 750 B.C., the major states of Mesopotamia were beset by debilitating political lassitude. Effective power in both Assyria and Babylonia was segmented among weak monarchs, quasi-independent governors, and aggressive tribal groups. The population of Assyria had suffered from two severe outbreaks of plague in the preceding fifteen years.[163] East of the Tigris, the borderland between the two countries, most of which had been taken over by Assyria in campaigns in the late ninth century,[164] had gradually fallen away from Assyrian control and had resisted Assyrian attempts to retake it.[165] Chaldaean and Aramaean

---

[161] A 82, 182–4; A 198, 22–3; cf. *CAH* III².1, 421.
[162] Detailed documentation for Section II may be found in A 535, 226–45.
[163] A 763, 430 and 432.   [164] Cf. A 719.
[165] Discussion: A 551, 39 n. 194.

tribesmen in northern and eastern Babylonia and in the adjacent borderland were posing serious problems for the major states.

Against this general background, Nabonassar came to the throne in Babylonia in 748 or 747,[166] and Tiglath-pileser III acceded in Assyria in 745.[167] Although later ages were to view Nabonassar's accession as a turning point in Babylonian history,[168] it is difficult to discern qualities in Nabonassar or his reign that were epoch-making. Babylonia continued to suffer from weak central government: a local revolt in Borsippa had to be forcibly repressed, and officials in Uruk were obliged to usurp the usually royal prerogative of temple-building and reconstruct an *Akitu* shrine that had fallen into disrepair.[169] Although Babylonia was beginning to stabilize economically during this reign (if one can judge from the relative number of economic texts surviving),[170] such stabilization seems to have taken place because Tiglath-pileser was propping up the Babylonian throne against domination by the Chaldaeans.

The forceful character of Tiglath-pileser III overshadows all of Mesopotamia at this time. Most likely of non-royal parentage, he had come to the Assyrian throne after a revolt in Calah, the political capital. He quickly brought order to Assyria; and, in three vigorous campaigns in the opening years of his reign (745–743), he moved against bothersome trouble spots of the preceding decades – his south-eastern borderlands (extending into tribal areas of Babylonia), Namri, and Urartu – and asserted Assyrian dominance on these fronts. His first campaign (745) concentrated on northern and eastern Babylonia.[171] In the north he reached the cities of Dur-Kurigalzu and Sippar and perhaps went as far as the vicinity of Nippur,[172] but his armies did not touch the metropolitan regions near Babylon. In the east he defeated several Aramaean tribes, including the Adile, Dunanu, Hamranu, and Rabilu, and resettled captives in a newly constructed city named Kar-Ashur.[173] In effect, he secured his southern flank and neutralized troublesome Aramaean tribes in Nabonassar's realm.[174]

Tiglath-pileser after 745 turned his attention elsewhere and left the Babylonians to shift for themselves. Nabonassar, though not a strong ruler, managed to hold the throne for fourteen years and, at his death in 734, to pass his kingdom on to his son Nabu-nadin-zeri. In the latter's second regnal year (732), a Babylonian provincial official deposed him

[166] Discussion: A 551, 39–40 n. 195.
[167] A 551, 40 n. 196.
[168] For the use of a 'Nabonassar Era' by the 'Ptolemaic Canon', see A 551, 40 n. 197.
[169] Borsippa: A 25, 71; cf. *CAH* III².1, 311–12. Uruk: A 536.
[170] Discussion: A 551, 40 n. 199.
[171] Discussion of source problems for events of 745: A 551, 41 n. 200.
[172] A 204 II, pl. XI; cf. *ibid.*, pls. XXXII–XXXIII.
[173] A 25, 71; A 204 II, pl. XI. Cf. A 759, 203 n. 21.   [174] Discussion: A 551, 42 n. 203.

and took the throne as Nabu-shuma-ukin II. The new king ruled for just over a month before being displaced by a Chaldaean, Mukin-zeri (731–729), chief of the tribe of Bit-Amukani.[175]

In 732, the year of the Babylonian revolts, Tiglath-pileser was off campaigning in Syria. He reacted quickly to the presence of a Chaldaean on the Babylonian throne, returned to Assyria, and over the next three years concentrated his military and diplomatic skill on removing Mukin-zeri. He dispatched an envoy to Babylon in an attempt to convince its citizens to reject the Chaldaean and to support the Assyrian side. He had retained the loyalties of some Aramaean tribes and of a few Babylonian cities such as Dilbat and Nippur. The Chaldaeans, on the other hand, failed to maintain a united front and engaged in petty intrigues. In a show of force, Tiglath-pileser went south, campaigned against Bit-Amukani and Bit-Sha'alli, and effectively confined Mukin-zeri to his local capital, Shapiya; this induced other Chaldaean chieftains to submit and pay substantial tribute. The description of this payment, in contrast to most prosaic booty lists recorded by Tiglath-pileser's scribes, shows the wealth of the Chaldaean leaders and particularly of Merodach-baladan of Bit-Yakin, who is given prominence by the title 'King of the Sealand' in the Assyrian account. Merodach-baladan, though now portrayed as submissive, was to prove the main antagonist of the Assyrians in Babylonia in the decades after 722 B.C.

After the containment of Mukin-zeri and the neutralization of the tribesmen,[176] Tiglath-pileser himself ascended the Babylonian throne.[177] This personal assumption of the dual Assyro-Babylonian monarchy was to set a precedent for his successors over the next century. The arrangement had the advantage of preserving a nominal independence for Babylonia rather than simply relegating it to vassal status. Tiglath-pileser personally participated in the pre-eminent rite of the Babylonian monarchy and escorted the statue of the god Marduk in the New Year's procession at Babylon. He also weakened potential local opposition by deporting numerous Chaldaeans from the conquered areas.

After Tiglath-pileser's death in 727, his son Shalmaneser V succeeded to the dual monarchy and reigned for five years.[178] His reign is poorly documented, and the only known major activity relating to Babylonia is his deportation of Chaldaeans from Bit-Adini (probably a section of Bit-Dakkuri).[179]

These twenty-five years, 747–722, witnessed the initial involvement of the nascent Late Assyrian empire in securing its southern flank in and

[175] A longer form of his name may be Nabu-mukin-zeri (A 535, 235 n. 1492).
[176] Cf. A 551, 43 n. 208.   [177] Cf. A 551, 43 n. 209.
[178] Cf. A 551, 43 n. 210.   [179] Cf. A 551, 43 n. 211.

around Babylonia. At first Tiglath-pileser invaded only to pacify Aramaean and Chaldaean tribesmen; and, though claiming nominal suzerainty, he left the Babylonian king undisturbed. Later, when confronted by the prospect of a Chaldaean on the Babylonian throne, he campaigned more extensively and eventually assumed personal control of the Babylonian monarchy. The Assyrians also attempted to avert future troubles in the south by deporting or resettling substantial numbers of tribesmen.

III. THE CHALDAEAN STRUGGLE FOR INDEPENDENCE, 721–689 B.C.

The Assyrian hold on Babylonia proved to be ephemeral, ceasing after the death of Shalmaneser V in 722 when the Assyrians became preoccupied with a power struggle in their own land. Although the sequence of events at this juncture must be reconstructed from scattered and often ambiguous clues, it appears that Shalmaneser lost his throne as the result of a revolution and the emergent monarch proved to be a usurper from outside the direct line of succession who took the wishful but assertive throne name Sargon (Assyrian *Šarru-kēnu*, 'legitimate king').[180] While Sargon was consolidating his power in Assyria, Merodach-baladan, the Chaldaean who had paid tribute to Tiglath-pileser in 729, took the opportunity to make himself king of Babylonia. Thus began a period of three decades in which Chaldaeans and Assyrians were to struggle for control over the Babylonian throne.

To place in perspective the history of Babylonia during these years, it is important to consider the political situation in south-west Asia as a whole. Under Sargon and Sennacherib, the military apparatus of the Late Assyrian empire overshadowed the whole of the Fertile Crescent from Palestine in the south west to Babylonia in the south east. The Assyrians controlled or actively meddled in the government of each significant polity in this zone. In greater Syria, they put an end to the last of the Neo-Hittite states east of the Taurus (Kummukhu). In Palestine, they deported the inhabitants of Samaria and later reduced Judah and its neighbour kingdoms to the status of tribute-paying vassals. Assyrian armed forces campaigned in the mountains and plains on the outer rim of the Crescent: Anatolia, Urartu, the Zagros highlands, and Elam. In pointed contrast to the general pattern of military successes throughout the core of this area were the perennial troubles at the south-east end of

---

[180] This is a traditional meaning of the name, but variant writings in Sargon's royal inscriptions reflect more than one scribal tradition and interpretation of the name's meaning.

the Crescent, where a recalcitrant Babylonia resisted Assyrian encroachment with frequent assistance from its neighbour Elam.[181]

The three decades from 721 to 689 marked a turning point for both Babylonia and Assyria. Although the Late Assyrian empire was still expanding through the unrivalled power of its armies, Babylonia was quick to take advantage of perceived imperial weaknesses: excessive dependence on the person of the monarch and inadequate local deployment of troops to enforce the allegiance of subject populations. The removal of Shalmaneser V by revolution (722) and the death of Sargon II in battle (705) showed the Assyrian imperial structure as vulnerable at the apex, despite its vast territories. In addition, after Assyria had installed vassal kings in Babylonia,[182] it did not provide sufficient local forces to give these rulers firm control of their territory and their throne. The Chaldaeans in particular took advantage of opportunities unwittingly provided by Assyria, and on several occasions their tribal leaders took over the Babylonian monarchy. The older, non-tribal population of Babylonia actively joined the anti-Assyrian opposition, particularly after the accession of Sennacherib; they twice revolted (703, 694) and put their own nominees on the throne. But overall the Chaldaeans orchestrated the struggle against Assyria; their tribes united behind a single leader and gradually built up a wider base of support consisting of most Aramaeans, the majority of Babylonian urbanites, and Elamite and Arab allies. As time went on and local resistance grew stronger, Assyria found itself channelling more and more of its military resources against its southern neighbour. As will be seen below, this crystallization of opposition in Assyria and Babylonia took place over thirty years with widespread consequences for both countries.

Merodach-baladan, the new Chaldaean king of Babylonia in 721, was a worthy opponent for the Late Assyrian empire (Pls. Vol., pl. 32).[183] As chief of Bit-Yakin, the most prestigious and wealthy of the Chaldaean tribes, he controlled extensive territories along the south-east course of the lower Euphrates – terrain of strategic importance as well as the source of significant revenue from trade routes. In addition he demonstrated considerable personal skill as a political leader and diplomat. He managed to weld together the usually discordant Aramaean and Chaldaean tribes into a united anti-Assyrian front and to retain their loyalty despite military reverses. He gradually reached outside Babylonia to both east and west to combine or co-ordinate efforts with strong anti-

---

[181] Anatolia and especially Tabal were also troublesome areas, but on the north-west fringes of the empire – thus geographically more remote and generally of less concern than Babylonia. See *CAH* III².1, 416–22.

[182] Bel-ibni (702–700) and Ashur-nadin-shumi (699–694).

[183] Sources for the reign of Merodach-baladan II: A 532; A 649; A 533, 8–13.

Assyrian movements in Elam, northern Arabia, and Judah. Many of the older Babylonians in urban centres eventually found him acceptable as monarch, and their attachment may have been influenced by his lineage: his ascendant Eriba-Marduk had occupied the Babylonian throne with distinction some decades earlier and had earned a reputation for fair dealing with his non-tribal subjects.[184]

There are, however, major source problems in reconstructing Mero-dach-baladan's political career. Most pertinent texts are Assyrian; and, in addition to the customary propagandistic distortion of their narratives, they express an unwonted degree of personal vituperation against Merodach-baladan, perhaps because he for so long managed to frustrate Assyrian punitive expeditions. Sargon's scribes in particular took great pains to portray Merodach-baladan as an outsider: a Chaldaean who occupied the Babylonian throne against the will of the gods, an illegitimate monarch rejected by the religious elite of his capital, and an oppressor who maltreated the non-tribal population by taking hostages from the major cities of the north and by removing divine statues from the cult centres of the south.[185] In part, of course, Merodach-baladan was set up in these inscriptions as an elaborate literary foil for Sargon himself, who was praised as fulfilling the divine will and championing the political and religious rights of venerable Babylonian temples and cities. By contrast, the few contemporary Babylonian royal sources paint a different picture: Merodach-baladan, as eldest son of the earlier great monarch Eriba-Marduk, dutifully revered the shrines built by his remote royal predecessors;[186] he expelled the 'wicked enemy, the Subarian' (the Assyrians) from Babylonia; he preserved and extended the ancient privileges of the major cult cities of Babylonia.[187] These self-serving claims and counter-claims of partisan royal inscriptions, both Babylo-nian and Assyrian, have to be viewed critically; and due weight must be placed on independent evidence of a more prosaic type – particularly legal and administrative documents – which indicates that Babylonia and its economy prospered under Merodach-baladan.[188] Keeping in mind these parameters, we may attempt a diachronic perspective of Merodach-baladan's career.

After Shalmaneser's death in 722, Babylonia and Assyria drifted apart under the separate governments of their new rulers. Assyria was preoccupied by internal troubles in 721,[189] and the first contact between the two countries came only in the following year when the Assyrian garrison at Der was attacked as the result of a joint Babylonian–Elamite initiative. The ancient town of Der, near modern Badrah in eastern Iraq,

[184] Discussion: A 551, 47 n. 216.   [185] E.g., A 185, 40–64; cf. A 532, 13.
[186] Shulgi and Anam (A 595, 133).   [187] A 595, 133–4; A 676, no. 37.
[188] A 532, 15–18; A 553, 8–13.   [189] A 209, 37–8 and 94.

was in former Babylonian territory that had been annexed by Assyria; it lay at the northern end of the principal access road to Elam. The city was to have been assaulted by the combined forces of Babylonia and Elam; and its capture would have meant for Babylonia the regaining of an old possession and for Elam enhanced protection from Assyrian aggression. The Babylonian contingent of Merodach-baladan was delayed, so the Elamites, under their king Khumban-nikash I (Ummanigash), invaded the area by themselves and fought the Assyrians on a plain outside the city. The immediate result of the battle was a stalemate; the Elamites bested the Assyrian army in the field and gained some territory south of Der,[190] but the Assyrians retained the city itself. The aftermath, however, was significant: the Assyrians directed their military attentions elsewhere, and the Babylonians and Elamites were left in peace for a full ten years.[191]

This decade free from Assyrian interference allowed Babylonia to prosper, even with a Chaldaean on the throne.[192] Merodach-baladan, despite his tribal background, seems to have conscientiously performed the duties of a Babylonian monarch. He repaired and endowed temples for the traditional gods of Mesopotamia;[193] he acknowledged the tax-exemption privileges of the citizens of the old sacred cities such as Babylon, Borsippa, and Sippar. He kept provincial administration functioning and saw to the maintenance of canals, irrigation systems, and bridges; one of the major waterways near Uruk came to bear his name.[194] The legal and administrative documents surviving from his time show a significant rise in the number of economic transactions, reaching the highest level in five centuries.[195] There is also evidence for cultural and scientific activity. Merodach-baladan's scribes wrote passable Sumerian as well as Akkadian, and some of his royal inscriptions have decided literary overtones.[196] Later traditions mention a garden (*gannatu*) of Merodach-baladan filled with exotic plants, and formal records being kept of astronomical observations during his reign. The impression gained from contemporary and later documentation is hardly that of a tribal interloper alternately terrorizing or neglecting the urban populations, as Sargon's inscriptions would have us believe.

In the year 710 the picture changed abruptly. Sargon, who for a decade had been campaigning extensively in the western and northern portions of the Fertile Crescent, turned his attention to the south east.[197] His decision was to prove fateful for both Assyria and Babylonia and to have

---

[190] A 250, 90; A 270, 39; cf. A 551, 48 n. 223.
[191] A 532, 13; A 533, 161–2; A 606, 340–2.
[192] A 532, 15–18, 37, 48–9. [193] Discussion: A 551, 49 n. 226.
[194] Bridge text: A 771, 64 no. 75; cf. A 567. Uruk waterway: A 532, 17 and n. 89; cf. A 654, 14.
[195] Statistics: A 551, 49 n. 229. [196] A 551, 49 n. 230.
[197] Discussion: A 551, 50 n. 231.

effects that lasted well beyond the term of his own reign. Babylonia
became engaged in a determined struggle to preserve its independence, a
struggle which in its early phases was dominated almost exclusively by
Chaldaean leaders and which relied heavily on Elamite support. Assyria
found itself gradually absorbed in a series of often protracted campaigns
which consumed a disproportionate amount of its military and economic
energy; between 710 and 678, from the twelfth year of Sargon until well
into the reign of his grandson Esarhaddon, most major Assyrian
campaigns were directed at Babylonia or its immediate neighbours.[198] It
is significant that the Assyrian empire almost at its apogee proved unable
to cope decisively with militarily inferior forces who were relatively
nearby. One of the reasons for Chaldaean and Elamite successes –
however ephemeral – was that these peoples were capable of exercising a
resilient, environmentally based defence, since they were able to withdraw into swamps and rugged highlands in which regular Assyrian
forces could not be deployed to advantage.

In 710 Sargon forestalled the Babylonian–Elamite coalition that had
engineered the Assyrian defeat ten years earlier.[199] In an astute tactical
move, he sent his principal fighting forces along the eastern frontier of
Babylonia to drive a wedge between the erstwhile allies. He himself set
up headquarters at Kish in northern Babylonia and received the
submission of cities such as Nippur.[200] Merodach-baladan did not
attempt to defend the Babylonian urban centres, but instead made his
stand at fortified sites on the tribal periphery, first (in 710) in the east at
Dur-Atkhara among the Gambulu (the principal Aramaean group in the
region) and then (in 709) in the south at Dur-Yakin, his own native
capital among the Chaldaeans. On each occasion he relied on limited
contingents of his own troops, allied forces (mainly Aramaean), and a
defensive strategy that included extensive flooding of the surrounding
terrain.[201]

The Assyrian campaigns were successful in that they effectively
deprived Merodach-baladan of his tribal base and deterred the untried
Elamite monarch, Shutur-nahhunte, from offering assistance to the
Chaldaeans.[202] The capture of Dur-Atkhara and the ensuing mop-up
operations neutralized most of the major Aramaean tribes in eastern
Babylonia by the end of 710. Before the next campaign commenced early
in the following year, several major developments had taken place.
Sargon brought most of his troops into Bit-Dakkuri, just south of
Babylon. Merodach-baladan fled the capital by night, and Babylon and
Borsippa then submitted to Sargon,[203] who formally ascended the

[198] Examples: A 551, 50 n. 232.　　[199] Discussion: A 551, 50 n. 233.
[200] A 551, 51 n. 234.　　[201] Cf. the relief in A 134, 60 fig. 72.
[202] Discussion: A 551, 51 n. 236.　　[203] A 185, 54–6.

Babylonian throne. Merodach-baladan requested asylum in Elam from Shutur-nahhunte, who forbade him to enter the country.[204] Shutur-nahhunte withdrew to the highlands and tried to escape being drawn into the conflict. Without Elamite support, Merodach-baladan was constrained to make a stand in 709 at his tribal capital of Dur-Yakin, where he was soon defeated in the countryside and eventually forced to yield the town itself.[205]

After Sargon had won Babylonia, he took decisive steps to consolidate his conquest. He centralized the myriad small centres of provincial and tribal government by placing them under the jurisdiction of two principal governors, one stationed in the eastern region of Gambulu and the other in the west at Babylon. In the tribal areas, according to his official accounts, Sargon resorted to wholesale relocation of populations: more than 108,000 Aramaeans and Chaldaeans were deported into various sections of western Asia.[206] In return, Sargon later brought many people from Commagene (Kummukhu) to be settled in southern Babylonia. He also transformed the towns that had been centres of tribal resistance. The Aramaean stronghold of Dur-Atkhara he turned into an Assyrian fortification and renamed Dur-Nabu. Dur-Yakin, Merodach-baladan's local capital, he despoiled and then destroyed in 707.[207] Sargon remained in Babylonia almost continuously from 710 to 707 and supervised these operations from close at hand.[208]

Sargon's inscriptions give an official, if idealized, account of his relations with the non-tribal population of Babylonia. Even before the conclusion of his campaigns against Merodach-baladan, leading citizens of Babylon and Borsippa, including high temple officials and scribes, had come to Sargon's camp, offered him remnants from cultic meals (a perquisite of Babylonian royalty), and invited him to enter the capital. Sargon accepted the invitation and assumed the responsibilities of the Babylonian monarchy. He participated as king in the New Year's rites at Babylon, presented lavish gifts to Babylonian temples,[209] and added Babylonian royal titles to his official titulary. He remedied specific problems caused by Merodach-baladan's abuse or neglect: he released urban hostages, restored purloined statues of deities, and extended tax-exemption privileges to major southern cities (notably Ur, Uruk, Eridu, Larsa, Kissik, and Nemed-Laguda).[210] He turned his attention to the neglected countryside of north-west Babylonia, which one of his more colourful inscriptions depicts as having lapsed from cultivation, with

[204] A 185, 54; revised translation in A 533, 163.

[205] Sargon's final campaigns against the Chaldaeans: A 766. For the location of Dur-Yakin, see the sources cited in A 551, 52 n. 240.

[206] A 551, 52 n. 242.   [207] A 766.

[208] Foreign tribute was delivered to him in Babylon during this time (A 185, 70).

[209] Cf. A 551, 53 n. 246.   [210] A 185, 64.

settlements in ruin and roads impassable, overgrown with dense underbrush, and infested with wild beasts – an abandoned area inhabited only by Aramaeans and Sutians, tent dwellers, who preyed on travellers.[211] Sargon cut down trees, burned underbrush, slew both wild beasts and Aramaeans, and resettled the region with captives from other lands. He put a stop to Aramaean raids on caravans in the vicinity of Sippar.[212] He reopened the old Babylon–Borsippa canal and sponsored extensive construction in the Eanna precinct at Uruk (though in the latter case he may in part have been taking credit for work done by Merodach-baladan).[213] Thus Sargon's texts claimed that he had significantly improved the lot of the non-tribal Babylonians, and the five years of his reign in lower Mesopotamia (709–705) seem to have been free from major disorders.[214]

Babylonian relations with Assyria underwent a substantial readjustment after 705 B.C., when Sargon lost his life on campaign.[215] In the late eighth and seventh centuries, much of Assyrian policy toward Babylonia seems to have been determined personally by the Assyrian monarch, and a new king often meant a radical change in direction. Sennacherib in particular seems to have been anxious to distance himself from his father. His attitude was probably conditioned by the inauspicious death of the otherwise successful Sargon; a text of Sennacherib inquires what crime his father had committed to merit such an end.[216] Sennacherib took care to chart new courses: he shifted the seat of government from the recently inaugurated capital of Dur-Sharrukin (which his father had built) south to the old city of Nineveh;[217] contrary to the long-standing Assyrian royal custom of genealogical citation, he did not mention his father's name in his inscriptions; and he did not authorize the incorporation of Babylonian royal titles into his titulary.[218] To judge from the royal inscriptions of Sargon and Sennacherib, whereas the father had courted Babylonian favour and basked in signs of acceptance, there is little indication that Sennacherib valued Babylonian opinion or that he ever performed the minimal ceremonial duties required of a Babylonian monarch.[219]

Did Sennacherib have to contend with a revolt or unsettled conditions in Assyria or Babylonia at the beginning of his kingship (705–704)? This has sometimes been inferred because various texts from later in his reign indicate conflicting dates (705, 704, or 703) for his first regnal year.[220] It is

---

[211] A 170, 192.   [212] A 185, 56; A 72, no. 88 (Arab raid on Sippar).
[213] A 551, 53–4 n. 250.   [214] Cf. A 551, 54 n. 251.
[215] A 763, 435. Cf. A 77, 235; A 209, 97; *CAH* III².1, 422.   [216] A 756.
[217] Cf. A 551, 54 n. 254.   [218] Cf. A 551, 55 n. 255.
[219] This conclusion is based on negative evidence and comparison with Sargon; for comparative purposes, there is an ample number of royal inscriptions surviving from both rulers.
[220] A 551, 55 n. 257.

possible to explain these discrepancies in dating by presuming political upheaval or contested succession to the throne; but it is also conceivable that Assyrian scribes did not always achieve precision when calculating according to the varying calendrical systems then in use.[221] Sargon's scribes made similar mistakes in calculation.[222] At present, there is no clear evidence for political unrest in Assyria or Babylonia in 705 or 704, even though such unrest often attended a monarch's unexpected demise.[223]

Sennacherib's political relations with Babylonia seem to have had predominantly military overtones. Our knowledge is of course conditioned by the nature of the source material, which consists principally of formal royal inscriptions composed by Sennacherib's scribes;[224] as regards Babylonia, these inscriptions concentrate on Assyrian military efforts to cope with the perennial widespread resistance to Assyrian rule. There is one notable exception that shows Sennacherib in an unaccustomed light as benefactor of Babylonia; this is the text on the splendid breccia pavement that he installed in the central Processional Street (*Ayibur-shabu*) in Babylon.[225] Sennacherib tried various modes of governance in southern Mesopotamia; at different times he himself, his crown prince (Ashur-nadin-shumi), and a native Babylonian (Bel-ibni) ruled there as king.[226] None of these solutions proved entirely successful, though Ashur-nadin-shumi served six years (apparently without major disturbance) until an Assyrian expedition provoked the Elamites into breaking the peace. Time and again, through most of Sennacherib's reign, successful urban–tribal coalitions in Babylonia rallied against Assyria and won considerable support from neighbouring powers, notably the Elamites but also occasionally the Arabs. In the case of Elam, the assistance was sometimes furnished after a substantial payment had been sent from the Babylonians to the Elamite ruler.[227] Elam dispatched large numbers of troops and high-ranking military officers, who took command of allied forces in the major pitched battles. As long as Babylonia and Elam worked together, Assyria continued to have serious difficulties in the south.

As far as we know at present, Sennacherib's troubles in Babylonia began in 703.[228] Early in that year, a provincial official from a prominent scribal family led a revolt and succeeded in making himself king as

---

[221] For experiments in the Assyrian calendar at this time, see A 551, 55 n. 258.

[222] A 551, 55 n. 259.

[223] *CAH* III².1, 426 deals with possible disturbances in the north-west provinces of the empire near where Sargon met his death. Cf. A 551, 55–6 n. 260.

[224] A 76, 119 n. 1 (*contra*: A 570, 98–100; A 571, 192–206). Cf. A 549.

[225] A 636, 52–3 and 187; A 762, 109; A 634, 10 and pl. 4 v (A 762, 279 no. 19).

[226] A 540, 91–2; A 717.   [227] A 533.   [228] Cf. A 551, 57 n. 266.

Marduk-zakir-shumi II.[229] He was replaced after one month by the indefatigable Merodach-baladan, who in a nine-month reign assembled a powerful group of supporters: urban Babylonians, Chaldaeans, Aramaeans, Elamites, and Arabs.[230] Yatiʾe, queen of the Arabs, sent her brother Basqanu with an army. The Elamite king, Shutur-nahhunte, after receiving a massive payment, sent eighty thousand archers and thirteen high-ranking commanders.[231] Merodach-baladan split these forces into two groups, stationing them at Cutha and his capital, Babylon; he himself remained in the capital.

Sennacherib left the city of Ashur in late 703.[232] He sent an advance party to Kish, just east of Babylon, while he concentrated his main forces against the allied army at Cutha. Merodach-baladan moved against the Assyrian contingent at Kish and forced them to send to Sennacherib for help; Sennacherib stayed long enough to defeat the allies at Cutha and then descended on Kish. In advance of the Assyrian arrival, Merodach-baladan himself withdrew and took refuge in the marshes.[233] Sennacherib vanquished the allied forces remaining at Kish[234] and then proceeded to Babylon, where he captured Merodach-baladan's wife and other female family members, the royal treasury, and many courtiers.[235] Sennacherib attempted to set up a stable government in Babylon by installing as king a Babylonian commoner, Bel-ibni, whom Sennacherib's annals describe as a man 'who had grown up in my palace like a young dog'.[236]

Sennacherib then moved against Merodach-baladan's supporters in tribal regions of Babylonia. The Assyrian army despoiled most major towns and many villages in the territory of four Chaldaean tribes: Bit-Dakkuri, Bit-Shaʾalli, Bit-Amukani, and Bit-Yakin. Urban rebels, both tribesmen and native Babylonians, were taken off as prisoners, as were many representatives of the principal Aramaean tribes. Particular mention is made in Sennacherib's annals of Khararatu and Khirimmu, old border towns east of the Tigris:[237] the former submitted voluntarily and was let off with the payment of a heavy tribute; the latter had to be subdued by force and was required to make annual payments in cattle and produce to the Assyrian temples. This first campaign of Sennacherib stretched over into a second year (702) and was followed almost immediately by a short expedition into adjacent Iranian mountain regions occupied by Kassite and Yasubigalli tribes.

When Sennacherib departed from southern Mesopotamia, he left

---

[229] A 532, 24 and n. 137.   [230] Cf. A 551, 57 n. 268.
[231] A 270, 49. The number of archers is likely to be an exaggeration.
[232] Discussions of the date: A 551, 57 n. 271; A 658, 29–35.
[233] Assyrian forces subsequently made an unsuccessful search for him there.
[234] Cf. A 551, 58 n. 273.   [235] A 270, 51–2.
[236] A 270, 54. Discussion: A 551, 58 n. 275.   [237] Cf. A 551, 58 n. 276.

Bel-ibni as monarch over the whole of Babylonia.[238] Economic texts dated under the latter's reign show that he was recognized as ruler in the northern cities of Dilbat, Nippur, and Babylon;[239] and a damaged tax-exemption document indicates that he was exercising authority in Chaldaean territory at some point during these years.[240] But by early 700 his jurisdiction had been officially restricted to northern Babylonia, and Assyrian officials were said to be administering the south.[241] In fact, however, there is evidence that it was the Chaldaeans, rather than the Assyrians, who were now in control of the south.[242] In any case, in 700 Sennacherib regarded the situation in Babylonia as sufficiently out of hand that he mounted another campaign against the region.[243] He removed Bel-ibni and his officials to Assyria – whether for disloyalty or incompetence is not known – and installed as king in Babylon someone in whom he placed more confidence: his own eldest son, Ashur-nadin-shumi (Fig. 1). The Assyrian forces campaigned briefly against the Chaldaeans, defeating Mushezib-Marduk[244] in Bit-Dakkuri; but their most important achievement was driving Merodach-baladan, the thirty-year political veteran, out of Babylonia permanently. Merodach-baladan seems to have been caught by surprise; he fled across the ancient equivalent of the Hor el-Hammar to Nagitu, a settlement in the marshes on the Elamite side, where he died within the next few years.[245] The Assyrians gradually reasserted their control over the south.[246]

With Merodach-baladan out of the way, Ashur-nadin-shumi's stewardship in Babylonia (699–694) seems to have been the most peaceful and successful interval in Sennacherib's early dealings with that country. Six years went by with no recorded revolts or disturbances. It is unfortunate that the reign is as yet so little documented,[247] since it might have shown what this type of Assyrian administration could achieve under favourable conditions.

In 694, Sennacherib decided to follow up on the successes of his campaign six years earlier and to attack the Yakinite exiles and the

---

[238] For letters that have sometimes been attributed to Bel-ibni, see A 549.

[239] A 553, 14–15; A 553A, 99.

[240] A 773, no. 1; cf. A 553, 15 En. 1.

[241] A 521, 114–15 variant, as pointed out in A 657, 63; contrast the interpretation in A 660, 256. Cf. A 658, 40.

[242] Cf. A 829, no. 206 (A 532, 16).

[243] A 270, 34–5 (cf. A 251, 140–4 and A 632, XXVI, pls. 12–13); for further sources, see A 532, 26–7 and chapter 23 n. 14 below.

[244] The future king of Babylon (692–689).

[245] At least, he is not mentioned again in Assyrian sources when military action in this area resumed in 694.

[246] Ashur-nadin-shumi was recognized as king at Uruk on 5/VIII/700 (A 956, 202–3 no. 3; for the date see A 538, 245).

[247] Sources: A 538; A 703; A 553, 15–16; A 553A, 99; A 553B; A 536A, 129–30 no. 555. Cf. A 551, 60 n. 289.

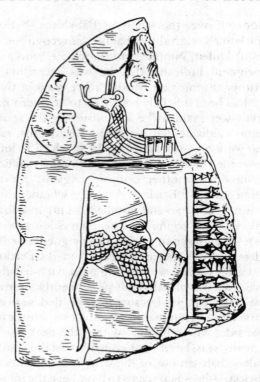

Fig. 1. Kudurru of Ashur-nadin-shumi. (After A 737, pl. 32a.)

Elamites who had granted them refuge.[248] He sent a naval expedition across the marshes to the Elamite side, where it supposedly defeated both Elamites and Chaldaeans and then took many of them as prisoners to Assyria.[249] The Elamites subsequently launched a counter-attack against northern Babylonia,[250] capturing Sippar and carrying off Ashur-nadin-shumi, who was betrayed by a group of Babylonians.[251] The Elamite king, Khallushu-Inshushinak (699–693), then installed Nergal-ushezib, a member of the prominent Babylonian family of Gakhal, on the throne in Babylon. An Assyrian army came against the Elamites and rebellious Babylonians, but suffered a reverse; and so the Elamites and Nergal-ushezib's forces were left in control of northern Babylonia.

One wonders at this point which cities were supporting what cause, since both sides subsequently seem to have taken military action against areas that one might have expected would be allied with them. The first

---

[248] Fullest account of this campaign: A 270, 73–6.
[249] A 270, 87.
[250] Discussion: A 551, 61 n. 293.   [251] A 703.

events recorded by the Babylonian Chronicle for the next year (693) were Nergal-ushezib's capture and plundering of Nippur (dated 16/IV). Then an Assyrian army pushed south, entered Uruk (1/VII), and took as spoil the statues of the principal gods of Uruk and Larsa. Finally the Assyrian army and that of Nergal-ushezib clashed on open ground in the province of Nippur (7/VII); Nergal-ushezib was taken prisoner and removed to Assyria. In the same month (26/VII) the Elamites deposed Khallushu-Inshushinak and replaced him with Kudur-nahhunte. The Assyrians took advantage of political vicissitudes in Elam and campaigned there until the onset of winter forced them to withdraw. At this time they managed to regain for Assyria territory that Sargon had lost almost three decades before.[252] The Assyrians, however, did not attempt to regain control of north-western urban Babylonia; and the Chaldaean, Mushezib-Marduk of Bit-Dakkuri, succeeded Nergal-ushezib as king.

In the following year, 692, another revolt in Elam removed Kudur-nahhunte and brought his younger brother, Khumban-nimena (Menanu) to the throne. Instability in throne tenure in both Elam and Babylonia had little immediate impact on the external politics of the two countries. Mushezib-Marduk, the new Chaldaean king in Babylonia, had lived in Elam as an exile and so turned to Elam for military assistance. According to Assyrian accounts, the Babylonians under Mushezib-Marduk sent to the new Elamite ruler a substantial present of gold and silver taken from the treasury of the Marduk temple in Babylon. Together Babylonia and Elam assembled a wide array of troops, including Aramaeans, Chaldaeans, and men from such diverse places in western Iran as Ellipi, Anshan (*Anzan*), and Fars (*Parsuas*). Probably in 691,[253] the allied forces marching north along the Tigris from Babylonia met the Assyrian army in a fiercely contested battle at the site of Khalule.[254] The Assyrian sources claimed a victory of stunning proportions, whereas the Babylonian Chronicle stated that the allies forced the Assyrians to withdraw. The latter may be literally true, but the Babylonian–Elamite coalition probably achieved either a pyrrhic victory or one without significant lasting effects.[255] By the next year, 690, the Assyrians were in a sufficiently strong position to erect a stela on the battle site and to press forward a siege of Babylon itself. A legal text dated at Babylon on 28/V/690 describes conditions in the city at that time:

The land was gripped by siege, famine, hunger, want, and hard times. Everything was changed and reduced to nothing. Two *qa* of barley [sold for] one shekel of silver. The city gates were barred, and a person could not go out in

---

[252] A 250, 90; A 270, 39.
[253] Date: A 551, 63 n. 306.
[254] Discussion: A 551, 63 n. 307.
[255] A 540, 93; this is argued in more detail in A 658, 48–51.

any of the four directions. The corpses of men, with no one to bury them, filled the squares of Babylon.[256]

Despite its desperate state, Babylon held out for fifteen more months; but at the end of that time, Mushezib-Marduk could no longer count on the country's traditional sources of support from either east or west. The Assyrians had campaigned against and neutralized the Arabs at Adummatu in the western desert, probably in the year 690.[257] In Nisan, the first month of 689, Khumban-nimena, the Elamite king, suffered a stroke and lingered incapacitated for almost eleven months. During this interval of dislocation in Elam, the city of Babylon fell to the Assyrians, just before the onset of winter (1/IX).

Thus ended the concerted Chaldaean-led struggle for Babylonian independence. Three decades of revolts against Assyrian control had gradually united the tribal and non-tribal populations of Babylonia and schooled them in the value of outside alliances. Although the forces of Babylonia and its allies had eventually been subdued, their several successes in the face of Assyrian military superiority provided encouragement for future resistance movements. But in the meantime, with the collapse of Babylon in 689, Sennacherib was free to reap the fruits of victory.

IV. BABYLON: DESTRUCTION AND REBIRTH, 689–669 B.C.[258]

Sennacherib's treatment of Babylon in defeat was unexpectedly harsh. His forbearance had been taxed by several lengthy campaigns, by a protracted siege of the capital, and not least by the death in captivity of his eldest son, Ashur-nadin-shumi. According to an official Assyrian account, the destruction of Babylon was brutal and systematic.[259] Assyrian soldiers put the defenders to death and left their corpses in the city's squares. They took away the defeated king, Mushezib-Marduk, and his family as prisoners to Assyria. Assyrian troops were allowed to loot the temples and other local property and to smash the statues of the city's gods. They razed the city, including the residential quarters, the temples, the ziggurat, and the city walls, and dumped the debris into the Arakhtu river.[260] They removed even the surface soil from the site, hauling it off to the Euphrates which carried it downstream to the Persian Gulf;[261] the Assyrians also put some of this soil on display in the *Akitu* temple in Ashur.[262] To obliterate even the memory of the city,

---

[256] A 551, 64 n. 311.   [257] Date: A 551, 64 n. 312.

[258] This period is dealt with in detail in A 588, chapter 4, sections 1–2.

[259] A 270, 83–4; cf. *ibid.*, pp. 137–8.   [260] Discussion: A 551, 67 n. 318.

[261] Cf. A 270, 137 (the debris was visible as far away as Dilmun).

[262] A 270, 138.

they dug canals to flood the ruins and turned the area into a swamp. The treatment of Babylon was exceptionally ruthless and vindictive, well beyond the retribution usually exacted of a rebel city and far in excess of the punishment expected for a revered religious centre, no matter what its offences.[263]

Sennacherib's graphic account of the city's destruction has yet to be substantiated from independent sources. Lengthy excavations at Babylon by the Deutsche Orient-Gesellschaft at the beginning of this century found various destruction levels, but none clearly assignable to the time of Sennacherib.[264] The Babylonian Chronicle records the capture of the city in 689, but says nothing about subsequent plundering or destruction. Later texts of Esarhaddon describe in detail how the city was destroyed and turned into a swamp, how the gods deserted it, and how its population went into slavery in foreign lands; but these say nothing about the date of the destruction or Assyrian involvement and identify the destructive agency as a flood caused by the wrath of Marduk.[265] In general, Babylonian writers seem to have avoided the topic except to record that the Marduk cult had been interrupted for two decades.[266] Later Assyrian scribes, when they mentioned the affair at all, tastefully omitted any reference to participation on the part of their countrymen.[267]

Sennacherib's brutal actions against the old capital and the enforced suspension of the land's primary religious cult[268] would have profoundly shocked the urban Babylonians. This is reflected in later traditions, including the Babylonian Chronicle and the 'Ptolemaic Canon', which refused to recognize Sennacherib's second reign over the land (688–681) and officially described the period as 'kingless'. Sennacherib himself does not seem to have been overly concerned with the governance of the country. In north-west Babylonia, Chaldaeans were permitted to take over agricultural land which had belonged to citizens of Babylon and Borsippa. During these eight years, economic activity in Babylonia sank to the lowest level in six decades: there are only three known economic texts from this time, two of them dated at Nippur and one at Khursagkalama (the twin city of Kish).[269] Southern Babylonia may have fared better than the north during this interval. Toward the very end of Sennacherib's reign, in 681, the gods of Uruk, stolen twelve years earlier, were restored to their city.[270] Also in the south, it is likely that governors who were subsequently prominent, Nabu-zer-kitti-lishir of the Sealand and

---

[263] The avowed ferocity of the treatment may reflect the personal character of Sennacherib's anger against the betrayers of his eldest son.

[264] For possible evidence from the residential quarter Merkes in Babylon see A 588, 65–6; A 551, 68 n. 322.

[265] A 234, 14–15; A 550, 39.   [266] Cf. A 551, 68 n. 325.   [267] A 551, 68–9 n. 326.

[268] Because of the absence or destruction of Marduk, the tutelary deity.

[269] A 553, 14. Cf. A 72, no. 327.   [270] A 551, 70 n. 334.

Ningal-iddin of Ur, were appointed in the second half of Sennacherib's reign;[271] but, as with so many other subjects pertaining to this time, adequate attestation is lacking. There is very little documentation in either Assyria or Babylonia for these years.[272]

The assassination of Sennacherib and the accession of Esarhaddon in late 681 marked a turning point in Babylonian history.[273] Whereas the preceding decades had been characterized by repeated Assyrian invasions and by the instability of the Babylonian crown (ten changes of monarch in twenty-nine years),[274] Esarhaddon's reign stabilized throne tenure and brought enlightened policies of rule. He restored the Babylonian capital as a political and commercial centre and took an interest in the reallocation of agricultural resources.[275] This new stability and concern fostered a gradually increasing material prosperity and initiated a major cycle of sustained economic growth that was to last, with only one minor recession, for the next fifty years.[276] Although it is difficult to articulate chronologically many of the events of Esarhaddon's reign (his royal inscriptions generally eschew the numbered campaigns of his immediate predecessors), major trends may be discerned, and these mark a sharp reversal of previously prevailing policies. In general, to judge from the official stance conveyed in his royal inscriptions,[277] Esarhaddon fostered a policy of peaceful relations with both Babylonia and its immediate neighbours, Elam and the Arab tribes. His non-confrontational politics bore fruit in that Babylonia as a whole never united against Esarhaddon's rule, and local disturbances did not attract widespread support from either inside or outside the country.

It is difficult to determine forces and motives behind the Assyrian change of direction. The time-honoured explanation of a pro-Babylonian party in Assyria may have some merit, but is in need of detailed critical re-examination.[278] One should not underestimate the impact of Sennacherib's violent death on the impressionable and valetudinarian Esarhaddon, who seems in any case to have been excessively preoccupied with manifestations of divine will. Nor should one neglect social and economic factors which may have been conducive to change. But, however great our ignorance of the underlying causes, it is plain that Esarhaddon in effect abandoned Sennacherib's harsh anti-Babylonian

---

[271] A 234, 46–7 Episode 4; A 25, 82.

[272] Other than Assyrian legal and administrative documents.

[273] A 550, 35 n. 1; A 551, 72 n. 346; A 704.

[274] Including the violent deaths of the last two monarchs who had ruled simultaneously in Assyria and Babylonia (Sargon in 705 and Sennacherib in 681).

[275] A 234, 25–6 Episode 37 Fassung a; ibid., p. 52 Episode 12. Cf. A 72, no. 327.

[276] At which point it was absorbed in the rising fortunes of the Neo-Babylonian empire.

[277] A 644, 16 expresses doubts about the sincerity of Esarhaddon's Babylonian policy.

[278] Cf. A 551, 71 n. 343 for the alleged Babylonian connexions of the women of the Assyrian royal family.

stance and returned to the more conciliatory attitude of his grandfather.
Esarhaddon, however, was unable to proceed with his programme
directly after his accession. With the assassination of Sennacherib and the
ensuing civil disturbances in Assyria,[279] the uncertainties in the royal
succession there were perceived in Babylonia as signs of political
weakness and grasped by some as an opportunity for revolt. Inchoate
rebels looked for support to Elam, the erstwhile backer of Babylonia. A
Babylonian conspirator wrote to the Elamite king, Khumban-khaltash
II, pointing out Assyria's vulnerability in the wake of Sennacherib's
death and sending generous gifts to enlist Elamite support.[280] The
governor of the Sealand, Nabu-zer-kitti-lishir[281] of the Yakin tribe, took
more direct action. He moved his men into siege positions around Ur,
the only major city in south-eastern Babylonia not under direct Yakinite
control. After Esarhaddon had gained the upper hand in the delicate
political situation in Assyria, he dispatched troops south to relieve Ur.
Anticipating their arrival, Nabu-zer-kitti-lishir withdrew to the supposed safety of Elam, where he was put to death. His brother, Na'id-
Marduk, who had accompanied him, realized that the old Elamite–
Yakin alliance was not to be revived and fled to Nineveh to submit to
Esarhaddon. The Assyrian king installed Na'id-Marduk as governor of
the Sealand in his brother's stead and imposed a heavy annual tribute on
the province. Thus Esarhaddon, with the co-operation of Elam, was able
both to preserve the anti-Yakinite enclave at Ur and to gain an acceptable
Chaldaean governor to preside over the strategic Sealand territories.[282]

Having circumvented these early troubles, Esarhaddon proceeded to
implement his policy of reinstating Babylon as the political and commercial capital of southern Mesopotamia.[283] His description of the restoration is worth summarizing, since it gives a detailed statement of what
Esarhaddon intended to accomplish for Babylon as well as an Assyrian
'theological' interpretation of Babylon's misfortunes and their redress.
In Esarhaddon's Babylon inscriptions, attention is focused on the divine
framework within which the destruction and resurrection of Babylon
occurred: malportent omens, the iniquitous conduct of the Babylonians
(including misappropriation of temple funds), the destruction of the city
by a severe flood,[284] Marduk's decision to shorten the years of desolation
(from seventy to eleven),[285] auspicious omens, and restoration. The
Assyrians assembled a large group of skilled workmen drawn (according
to various versions) from all of Babylonia, from Assyria, and/or from

[279] A 25, 81; cf. A 551, 70 n. 337 and 72 n. 346.   [280] A 304.
[281] Son of the old rebel Merodach-baladan II.
[282] A 25, 82; A 234, 46–7 Episode 4. Cf. A 760, 46–7.   [283] Discussion: A 551, 73 n. 351.
[284] The role of the Assyrian military is conspicuously absent from the narrative.
[285] Cf. A 551, 73 n. 354.

conquered lands;[286] and Esarhaddon claimed to have taken part in the work personally.[287] Babylonian workers prepared the site, clearing reeds and trees and restoring the Euphrates to its old bed.[288] Craftsmen supervised massive contruction works in the city, including the rebuilding of Esagila (the Marduk temple), Etemenanki (the ziggurat), and the inner and outer city walls. Statues of gods and goddesses that had been taken as spoil were returned from Assyria and from Elam.[289] Enslaved or impoverished exiles were brought back to the city and provided with clothing, housing, orchards, and even canals (presumably for irrigation of crops). The citizens' old privileges, including tax exemptions, were reinstated. Babylon was restored as the mercantile hub of the region, with routes opened up in all directions and commercial relations reestablished. These were Esarhaddon's avowed intentions for Babylonia, according to his inscriptions.[290] Details can be added from other sources: agricultural lands around Babylon and Borsippa were taken from Chaldaean encroachers and restored to their rightful owners; a new governor of Babylon was appointed to supervise the resettlement of the city; and the local assembly of citizens was again convened to hear legal cases.[291]

Esarhaddon's statement was programmatic; not all the work he describes was done at once, and some of it may not have been done at all. The material remains at Babylon have not permitted detailed verification of his claims. Though there are bricks bearing his inscriptions, none of these has been recovered in unmistakably contemporary context; they were either found loose in rubble or reused in later construction.[292] Correspondence preserved in the Nineveh archives includes a letter from Ubaru, Esarhaddon's new governor at Babylon, reporting to the king on his arrival in the city. Although we must allow for a generous dose of courtly obsequiousness, Ubaru states that he had been welcomed by the men of Babylon and that the king had been praised for restoring stolen property to the city; even the Chaldaean leaders are said to have blessed the king for resettling the capital.[293] To round out the rosy picture, one should also note that Esarhaddon used the spoils of his Egyptian campaign to sponsor temple reconstruction (also at Borsippa, Nippur, and Uruk)[294] and returned divine statues to Der, Uruk, Larsa, and

---

[286] A 234, 20 Episode 19.   [287] A 234, 20 Episode 21.

[288] A 234, 19 Episode 18. Note, however, that the wandering river was described elsewhere as the Arakhtu (A 234, 14 Episode 7 Fassung a).

[289] This did not include the images of the principal deities of Babylon, Marduk and his wife Zarpanitu. Cf. A 551, 74 n. 359.

[290] A 234, 10–30; A 678; updated textual apparatus in A 550, 38. Cf. A 551, 74 n. 363; A 644.

[291] A 72, no. 418; A 234, 52 Episode 12; A 753, no. 4. Babylonian economic texts from Esarhaddon's reign: A 553, 17–20; A 553A, 99–100.

[292] A 635; A 724; cf. A 636.   [293] A 72, no. 418.   [294] A 551, 75–6 n. 368.

Sippar-Aruru.[295] Later, booty from an Assyrian campaign in Shubria near Lake Van was said to have been sent as a gift to Uruk.[296] The Assyrians under Esarhaddon actively sought reconciliation with Babylonia.

Assyrian policies, however enlightened, did not elicit unanimous support from Babylonian officialdom or from local populations. In the central and northern alluvium, Nippur and Bit-Dakkuri did not welcome the resurgence of Babylon, a regional rival: there were severe disturbances in these areas, particularly in the first half of the reign when the resettlement of Babylon was still under way.[297] The chief bone of contention may have been access to primary agricultural resources, namely land and water.[298] In addition, increased supervision by the central government may not have appealed to local officials who had fattened their purses in the looser conditions prevalent under Sennacherib; officials at Borsippa, Cutha, and Dur-Sharrukin were accused of collusion with local financial interests and of blatant peculation with temple revenues.[299] Even at Babylon, matters were not as straightforward as official texts would have us believe. A heavy tax was levied on the impoverished – and supposedly tax-exempt – citizens, and stories circulated of a protest in which the governor's messengers were pelted with clods.[300]

Esarhaddon dealt benevolently with Babylonia's erstwhile allies, the Arabs and the Elamites, with mutually favourable results. For the Arabs, Esarhaddon was in part reversing the harshness of Sennacherib; he returned stolen statues of deities to the ruler Hazael and only modestly increased his tribute. He appointed Tabua, a young Arab woman raised at Sennacherib's court, as queen of the Arabs, and restored missing divine statues to her people. Later he confirmed Yauta², son of Hazael, as king after his father's death. Although the Arab west was not totally quiet during Esarhaddon's reign, it was often preoccupied with internal squabbles; only a few sections of it were visited by Assyrian campaigns in the time of Esarhaddon.[301]

Esarhaddon's relations with Elam were surprisingly peaceful and on occasion even cordial. After decades of active Elamite–Assyrian hostility (720–691), there followed a significant quiet interval (690–665)

---

[295] A 234, 84; cf. A 25, 82 and 125. See also A 551, 76 n. 369.

[296] A 25, 84–5 (with inconsistent dates). The text from which the chronicle was copied was damaged at this point, and the booty may have had no connexion with Uruk (A 552C, 94).

[297] A 25, 82–4 and 126 (entries for 680, 678, and 675).

[298] A 72, no. 327 (= A 698, no. 121) and A 75, no. 75 (= A 73, no. 284).

[299] A 72, nos. 339 and 1202 (= A 73, nos. 293 and 281); A 75, no. 75 (= A 73, no. 284). Cf. A 77, 273–5 and A 551, 75 n. 366.

[300] A 72, no. 340 (= A 73, no. 276). For discussion of alleged instances of Assyrian conscription of troops in Babylonia between 679 and 652, see A 551, 77 n. 375.

[301] A 19, 125–42; cf. A 77, 514.

which Esarhaddon undoubtedly fostered. As noted above, the Elamite
king Khumban-khaltash II resisted Babylonian attempts to involve him
in anti-Assyrian resistance in Esarhaddon's early years. The Assyrians,
however, did not place unquestioning trust in the peaceful intentions of
the Elamites; Esarhaddon reached an understanding with the paramount
Aramaean tribe on Babylonia's eastern frontier, the Gambulu (under
their sheikh Bel-iqisha), so that their chief city Sha-pi-Bel could monitor
Elamite movements across the frontier.[302] The only obvious Elamite act
of hostility that can be unambiguously assigned to Esarhaddon's reign is
their raid on Sippar in the year 675.[303] This stands out as an isolated
event, the only apparent disruption in a quarter-century of otherwise
good relations between Assyria and Elam. There are at least two
divergent ways of explaining it: either (a) as Elamite conjuncture with
contemporaneous disturbances in Bit-Dakkuri and Nippur,[304] or (b) as a
lapse of the chronicler, who inserted for the sixth year of Esarhaddon an
entry originally composed for the sixth year of his similarly named
brother who reigned two decades earlier.[305]

In any case, Khumban-khaltash II died in the same year (675) and was
succeeded by his brother Urtak.[306] Early in his reign Urtak sent
messengers to conclude a peace agreement with Esarhaddon[307] and then
returned to Babylonia some statues of Babylonian deities which had been
in Elam.[308] There followed several more years of friendly relations
between the two powers, lasting into Ashurbanipal's reign; there is even
an indication – far from certain – that during this time Assyrian princes
and princesses were being brought up at the Elamite court, and young
members of the Elamite royal family resided at Nineveh.[309] Assyrian–
Elamite relations remained peaceful during most of Esarhaddon's reign;
Esarhaddon's diplomatic endeavours generally met with more success in
Elam than they did in Babylonia.[310]

Esarhaddon's policies toward Babylonia and her neighbours did not
eliminate urban and tribal unrest, but diffused its effects. New leaders of
anti-Assyrian movements such as the Chaldaean chieftain Shamash-ibni
of the Bit-Dakkuri were unable to garner widespread support in
southern Mesopotamia or to invoke Elamite or Arab assistance from
abroad. Consequently Assyria under Esarhaddon had to deal only with

---

[302] A 234, 52–3 Episode 13. Cf. A 72, nos. 541 and 336.   [303] A 25, 83.

[304] All taking place in 675, according to the chronicles.

[305] This alternative must be regarded as less likely; see A 551, 78–9 n. 380.

[306] Reading of the name Urtak: A 551, 79 n. 381.

[307] A 234, 58–9 Episode 19; A 551, 79 n. 382.

[308] A 25, 84 and 126; cf. A 234, 25 Episode 36.

[309] A 703, 34 n. 66 (a theory based principally on the interpretation of personal pronominal
suffixes in A 72, no. 918).

[310] See the qualifying statements in A 551, 79 n. 385.

localized disruptions rather than with broad-based revolts carried out by urban–tribal coalitions assisted by foreign troops (as had been the case under Sennacherib). Nonetheless political conditions in Babylonia remained volatile. Reaction to Assyrian rule varied sharply from one locale to another; and, in some places, power oscillated between anti-Assyrian and pro-Assyrian factions. Assyria did not attempt to over-whelm the populace by stationing large garrisons within the cities or by leaving heavy troop concentrations in the countryside; her military control was generally loose and depended on an efficient system of intelligence reports to locate trouble spots and call for outside aid when necessary.[311]

The political fragmentation of Babylonia, with its local and vacillating reactions to Assyrian rule, led to internecine as well as anti-Assyrian conflicts. Chaldaeans were almost uniformly anti-Assyrian. Thus Nabu-zer-kitti-lishir of Bit-Yakin attacked pro-Assyrian Ur and was put to flight only by the advance of an Assyrian army;[312] and Shamash-ibni of Bit-Dakkuri had to be removed because of his penchant for appropriat-ing agricultural land belonging to the inhabitants of Babylon and Borsippa.[313] Other tribal leaders were willing to co-operate with the Assyrians: Na'id-Marduk (Bit-Yakin) acted for them as governor of the Sealand, and Bel-iqisha (Gambulu) agreed to let his city serve as a check on the Elamites.[314] Nippur, despite a rapid turnover of governors early in Esarhaddon's reign,[315] at one point had a pro-Assyrian administration which frankly admitted to Esarhaddon that the city was detested by its neighbours and in mortal danger because of its Assyrian sympathies.[316] Ur at this time was governed by a stable and staunchly pro-Assyrian gubernatorial dynasty, founded by Ningal-iddin; its various governors adopted an elevated titulary, and Ningal-iddin himself dated documents by his own regnal years. The governor's office at Ur stayed in this family for more than thirty years and was passed down in succession to at least three of Ningal-iddin's sons.[317] But Ur had become a frontier town on the limits of cultivation, serving not only as the local bastion against the Chaldaeans of Bit-Yakin but also keeping a close watch on Arab movements to and from the desert;[318] its very survival depended on Assyrian favour, and it was fiercely loyal to its benefactors. The Assyrians monitored unrest and potentially disruptive Elamite contacts in Babylonia,[319] although their officials were not always competent in dealing with problems. On at least four occasions during Esarhaddon's

[311] A 545, 235.   [312] A 25, 82; A 234, 46–8 Episode 4.
[313] A 234, 52 Episode 12. Cf. A 560, no. 43 and A 749, nos. 81–2.
[314] A 234, 47 Episode 4 and 52–3 Episode 13.
[315] A 25, 82–4 and 126; A 575, no. 22 reverse 10.   [316] A 72, no. 327 (= A 698, no. 121).
[317] A 534, 246–55; A 579.   [318] A 551, 81 n. 395; A 829, no. 167.
[319] A 72, nos. 266–9 (from the reign of Ashurbanipal) and *passim*.

reign (680, 678, 675, 674), Assyrian military or disciplinary action had to be undertaken against sections of Babylonia, always at least partly against the Chaldaeans and in the final instance specifically against the town of Shamele in Bit-Amukani.[320] We have no significant details for any of these operations, perhaps because Esarhaddon's scribes showed an almost Babylonian affinity for recounting his munificence and piety rather than particulars of his campaigning. There are also many tantalizing references in the Assyrian court correspondence to an individual named Sillaya[321] fomenting discontent in several sections of Babylonia over these years; but the evidence is still too fragmentary and uncertain to yield more than a sketchy portrait of a revolutionary entrepreneur disconcerting and eluding the Assyrian authorities. At this time, urban Babylonia was generally under Assyrian control, but within broad limits.

Toward the end of Esarhaddon's reign, events in Egypt and in Assyria came to dominate his attention, and Assyrian affairs eventually had a major impact on Babylonia. At this time perhaps late in 673, Esharra-khamat, the principal wife of Esarhaddon, died.[322] Two months after-wards, with the inevitable realignment of female personnel at court, Esarhaddon designated one of his younger sons, Ashurbanipal, as heir to the Assyrian throne and at the same time named Shamash-shuma-ukin as future king of Babylonia.[323] As crown prince Shamash-shuma-ukin seems to have taken up residence in lower Mesopotamia and to have served as an administrator there for Esarhaddon.[324] In these later years of Esarhaddon's reign, increasing use was made of the substitute-king (šar pūhi) ritual, whereby commoners were temporarily installed as surro-gates on the Assyrian or Babylonian thrones to absorb the effects of evil omens and were then put to death.[325] One of these substitute kings was the son of a major Babylonian religious official, and there was consider-able unrest in Babylonia after his death.[326] It is not clear whether Babylonia was involved in the great revolt in Assyria that led to the execution of so many of Esarhaddon's officials in 670.[327] In any case, we have no knowledge of major anti-Assyrian disruptions in Babylonia between 673 and Esarhaddon's death in 669.

The two decades from 689 to 669 witnessed significant changes in the

---

[320] A 25, chronicles 1 and 14. Cf. A 551, 81 n. 397.
[321] Discussion: A 551, 82 n. 398.
[322] A 25, 85 and 127. Discussion: A 551, 82 n. 400; A 552C, 94–5 (which raises doubts about the reliability of the date).
[323] A 307; A 773A; cf. A 551, 82 n. 401.
[324] Evidence of Babylonian residence (uncertain): A 77, 32, 78–81, 271, and passim: A 703, 27. Supposed Babylonian origin of Shamash-shuma-ukin or his mother: A 550, 36 n. 5.
[325] A 74, 54–65; A 77, xxii–xxxii, 35–7, etc. Followed by A 238.
[326] A 72, no. 437 (= A 73, no. 280).
[327] A 25, 86 and 127; A 77, 238–40, 262, 429, etc.; A 266, 22; cf. A 544, 312–15 (vs. A 574, 50–6).

fortunes of Babylonia. Unfortunately, to reconstruct the political vicissitudes of the time, we are often dependent on the tendentious testimony of Assyrian royal inscriptions; we know only what the chancelleries of Sennacherib and Esarhaddon chose to record. The royal scribes of these two rulers paint sharply contrasting pictures: Babylon in 689 was captured and systematically destroyed, with its gods taken away and their cults suspended, its population dispersed into slavery and their agricultural holdings taken over by tribesmen; Babylon after 681 was revived and rebuilt, with its gods returned and their cults resumed, its population freed and resettled in the city, and its fields reclaimed by their former owners. Neither of these descriptions has been independently verified to a significant extent; and, while there is little reason to doubt the general maltreatment of the city and the removal of the cult statues, there are grounds for suspecting hyperbole in other details.[328] Nonetheless it seems clear that Babylonia was regarded with unmistakable hostility in the closing years of Sennacherib's reign, that its capital was severely punished and that, some years later, Esarhaddon implemented a policy of reconciliation and did much to repair former ravages. The inhabitants of Babylonia, who seem to have been largely anti-Assyrian in the time of Sennacherib, were in part reconciled to Esarhaddon; and Assyrian rule, while never popular with the bulk of the population, came to be accepted at least passively in most areas and with enthusiasm by such partisans as Ningal-iddin at Ur, who perceived that his own survival depended on Assyrian favour. Babylonia seems generally to have prospered under the stable government provided by Assyrian rule, commencing a long period of economic growth and benefiting from sponsored construction programmes. Discontent was sporadic, local, and readily contained.

V. SIBLING MONARCHS: SHAMASH-SHUMA-UKIN AND ASHURBANIPAL, 669–653 B.C.[329]

Esarhaddon's design to divide his royal powers between his sons Ashurbanipal (for Assyria) and Shamash-shuma-ukin (for Babylonia) was carried out after his death. Although it is not known whether Esarhaddon had determined in detail the jurisdiction to be exercised by each monarch, it soon turned out that Ashurbanipal not only assumed full control of Assyria and the empire at large but closely supervised Babylonia as well. Shamash-shuma-ukin became in fact a dependent monarch, not only subject to Ashurbanipal in the areas of military defence and foreign policy, but also overshadowed in local political and

---

[328] A 551, 83 n. 407.
[329] Detailed discussion of the political history of this period: A 588, 96–115.

Fig. 2. Shamash-shuma-ukin and Ashurbanipal, the appointed heirs, shown on the sides of the stela of Esarhaddon from Zincirli. For the front see Pls. Vol., pl. 51. (Berlin, Staatliche Museen (East) VA 2708; after J. Börker-Klähn, *Altvorderasiatischen Bildstelen* (Mainz, 1982), pl. 219.)

religious matters. Shamash-shuma-ukin was obliged to swear an oath of fealty to Ashurbanipal, and his letters to his brother show him accepting a subordinate role.[330] Since the relations between the two brothers were eventually to develop into a bloody civil war that would weaken the foundations of the Assyrian empire, it is worth inquiring into the antecedents of their quarrel and scrutinizing the ostensibly peaceful relations during the first sixteen years of their reigns. It is impossible to evaluate hidden reserves of sibling rivalry or fraternal jealousy that may have fuelled their animosity,[331] but one can observe patterns of overt action on each side, especially Ashurbanipal's alternating procrastination and interference which must inevitably have caused tension between the brothers.

Ashurbanipal's dilatory conduct seems to have begun soon after his father's death (10/VIII/669 B.C.). Ashurbanipal succeeded to the throne in the next month, but Shamash-shuma-ukin's installation was delayed so

---

[330] A 551, 85 n. 411.   [331] Discussion: A 551, 85 n. 412.

long (until late I or II/668) that his official accession year (668) fell a full
year behind that of Ashurbanipal (669). Furthermore, even though the
prized statue of Marduk was returned to Babylon at the beginning of
Shamash-shuma-ukin's reign, major items of its cult furniture were
retained in Assyria for at least fourteen years.[332] Ashurbanipal was also
slow to move his troops in response to an Elamite invasion of
Babylonia,[333] and Assyrian revenge for that invasion was delayed for
more than a decade.[334] It is difficult to determine in individual instances
whether Ashurbanipal was unable or unwilling to act promptly on
Shamash-shuma-ukin's behalf; but these incidents were clearly detri-
mental to Shamash-shuma-ukin and as a result he was unlikely to have
been more kindly disposed toward Ashurbanipal.

The military defence of Babylonia may have been a continuing source
of friction between the brothers. Although Ashurbanipal states that he
had given armed forces, including infantry, cavalry, and chariotry, to
Shamash-shuma-ukin,[335] these were insufficient to deal with significant
troubles; and Assyria remained essentially responsible for Babylonia's
defence.[336] In 668, when raiders from Kirbitu in the eastern mountains
were harassing trans-Tigridian Babylonia (Yamutbal), Assyrian forces
had to be sent to the area to crush the offenders.[337] But on occasion the
quality and promptitude of Assyrian defence coverage were not all that
was desired. When in about 664 the Elamites under Urtak invaded
Babylonia,[338] Ashurbanipal delayed dispatching troops until he had
received word that the Elamites had spread out over northern Babylonia. Even then the Assyrians did not attempt to punish the local
fomenters of the invasion, Nabu-shuma-eresh the governor of Nippur
and Bel-iqisha the chief of the Gambulu tribe; they and their descendants
escaped Assyrian retribution for more than ten years, until the campaign
of 653. Ashurbanipal contemplated an action against the Gambulu as
early as 658,[339] but this was not undertaken. Thus Babylonia's defence
needs were not always well served by Assyrian troops; and perhaps in
recognition of that fact, the city walls of both Babylon and Sippar were
rebuilt during these years.[340]

Ashurbanipal intervened actively in Babylonian internal affairs that
should have been within the jurisdiction of the Babylonian ruler. In his
inscriptions Ashurbanipal claims sole credit for completing his father's
reconstruction of the Marduk temple in Babylon (Pls. Vol., pl. 33), for
re-establishing the tax-exemption privileges of Babylon's citizens, and

---

[332] A 25, 129.   [333] Specifically Urtak's invasion about 664 B.C.
[334] Discussed in more detail in the succeeding paragraph.
[335] A 344, 28.   [336] Cf. A 551, 86 n. 421.
[337] A 337, 48 and parallels; cf. A 551, 86 n. 422.
[338] Date of this campaign: A 551, 87 n. 423.
[339] A 498, no. 153; cf. A 230, 117. Cf. A 72, no. 269.   [340] A 344, 236–8; A 651 II, 6–9.

for installing Shamash-shuma-ukin as king (he makes no mention of Esarhaddon's testamentary instructions).[341] Ashurbanipal also repaired major sanctuaries in Sippar, Babylon, Borsippa, and Uruk in his own name.[342] Moreover, Ashurbanipal communicated directly with local officials in Babylonia, who reported to him on internal matters as well as on foreign affairs (especially concerning Elam).[343] Despite the nominal allegiance of the Babylonian realm to Shamash-shuma-ukin, there were cities such as Uruk and Ur which seemed to be more in touch with the Assyrian than the Babylonian government. At Ur, economic texts were dated under Shamash-shuma-ukin as king; but Sin-balassu-iqbi, the local governor,[344] undertook a massive reconstruction programme for the monumental buildings of the city and dedicated his work 'for the life of Ashurbanipal' rather than for his nominal sovereign.[345] Spies resident in Shamash-shuma-ukin's capital, Babylon, reported to Ashurbanipal on the Babylonian king's activities.[346] In fact, for the greater part of Shamash-shuma-ukin's reign, it is difficult to determine just what powers he was allowed to exercise as Babylonian king: apart from the use of his name in date formulae, he is known principally for his jurisdiction in cases involving land ownership and water traffic.[347] The only provincial governors who were clearly subject to him were Sin-sharra-usur at Ur (who made a dedication for the life of Shamash-shuma-ukin) and Shula at Dilbat;[348] both of these are poorly attested and may have been appointed only in the days of the civil war (652–648). Although the evidence – and our perspective – may be far from balanced, one gains the impression that Shamash-shuma-ukin for most of his reign may have been simply a figurehead.

Nonetheless, however nominal his royal power, Shamash-shuma-ukin's reign marks a period of increasing economic prosperity and governmental stability in Babylonia. The number of economic texts per year rises significantly, beginning in Shamash-shuma-ukin's tenth year; and the geographical distribution of the texts is impressive, encompassing most major urban centres in the central Mesopotamian floodplain.[349] In addition, significant building programmes were undertaken at Babylon, Borsippa, Sippar, Uruk and Ur, perhaps supported from Assyrian

[341] A 344, 226, etc. Cf. A 551, 87 n. 426.

[342] A 344, 228–48; A 662; A 630, 60. Cf. A 551, 87 n. 427.

[343] A 534, 252–3; A 588, 102. Discussion: A 551, 88 n. 428.

[344] Or 'viceroy' (*šakkanakku*), as he styles himself. For the titulary of the seventh-century governors of Ur, see p. 10 above.

[345] A 593, nos. 168 and 170; A 744, no. 102. Cf. A 72, no. 426 (see A 579, 183); A 534, 248–53; A 537, 336–42; A 771, nos. 81–6.   [346] A 72, no. 119.

[347] A 633, no. 10. A 72, no. 1385.

[348] A 565, no. 13 (duplicate: A 581, no. 144); bibliography: A 551, 117 n. 566. A 72, no. 326.

[349] Sippar, Cutha, Kish, Babylon, Borsippa, Dilbat, Nippur, Uruk, and Ur. Cf. A 553, 25–39; A 588, 252; A 590.

resources (if Ashurbanipal's sponsorship was more than nominal).[350] There is also evidence for considerable scribal activity in both the religious and scientific spheres: composition and editing of prayers and rituals,[351] copying of lexical and diagnostic texts,[352] recording of astronomical observations, and the earliest known astronomical diary text.[353] Regardless of underlying political tensions, the stability in throne tenure from 669 to 653, following as it did the two preceding stable decades, provided a solid foundation for the growth of the Babylonian economy.

The beginning of Shamash-shuma-ukin's reign was marked by considerable confusion. First, there was an interregnum prior to his installation; after Esarhaddon's death, the year 669 was not officially ascribed to any king of Babylonia. Economic texts in the latter part of that year were dated according to the accession year of Ashurbanipal, and later chronological texts assigned it variously to Esarhaddon and Shamash-shuma-ukin.[354] In 11/668 the Marduk statue made a triumphal return from Ashur to Babylon; Shamash-shuma-ukin and an Assyrian army escorted the statue by boat amidst splendid ceremonies down the Tigris and eventually to Babylon, where the cult images of Shamash, Nergal, and Nabu from Sippar, Cutha, and Borsippa had gathered to welcome Marduk home.[355] In the same year, an Assyrian army was sent against the region of Kirbitu, which was harassing eastern Babylonia. In x/668, a 'judge of Babylon', one Bel-etir, was executed; but his fault, presumably treason, was not recorded.[356]

It is hard to speak of a distinctive foreign policy for Babylonia in the years 669–653, since Assyria managed foreign relations on behalf of both lands. The former principal allies of Babylonia, the Elamites and Arabs, are not known to have maintained ties with Shamash-shuma-ukin during these years; practically nothing is known about the Arabs (their major hostilities with Ashurbanipal commence after 652),[357] and the Elamites were aligned primarily with the Gambulu in opposition to both the Assyrians and the central government in Babylonia. In this case we should not over-interpret the silence of the texts, since both the Arabs and Elamites rallied round Shamash-shuma-ukin once the rebellion had begun.[358]

The history of relations over these years between Elam, Assyria, and Babylonia is worth reviewing. As noted above, a radical shift in the

[350] A 344, 226–48; A 72, no. 119 (cf. A 75, no. 60 and A 77, 283 n. 522); A 651 11, 6–12 (cf. A 712, no. 6); A 771, no. 77. Cf. A 551, 89 n. 438.
[351] List of sources: A 551, 89 n. 439.
[352] A 551, 89 n. 440.   [353] A 1045, nos. 1414–17; A 1046, 48 and pl. 3.
[354] FGrH 680 F 7; A 553, 21; A 770, 305.
[355] A 25, 86, 127, and 131; A 344, 262–8. Cf. A 684 and A 551, 90 n. 444.
[356] A 25, 86 and 127; A 588, 99.   [357] A 19, 142–69.
[358] A 344, 30–4, 64, and 68.

traditional alignment of Elam and Babylonia versus Assyria took place around 691 B.C. After the battle of Khalule, Babylonia no longer had the support of Elam and was unable to organize effective large-scale resistance against Assyria. With the exception of one or another minor incident of hostilities, Elam and Assyria generally had peaceable relations during the quarter-century between 690 and 665. The high point seems to have been reached when Esarhaddon and Urtak, the Elamite king, entered into a pact around 674. Afterwards, in the early 660s, when patterns of severe climatic disruption caused drought in Elam and exceptionally bountiful rainfall in Assyria,[359] the Assyrians not only sent grain as famine aid to Elam but provided temporary homes in Assyria for hard-pressed Elamites.[360] Assyrian beneficence, however, had no lasting effect; for in 664 Elam unexpectedly turned hostile. The governor of Nippur and the chief of the Gambulu tribe had persuaded Urtak to invade Babylonia. Ashurbanipal, reacting slowly to news of the invasion,[361] sent out only a reconnaissance mission, which confirmed that the Elamites were in northern Babylonia and that they had set up a camp which menaced Babylon itself. Only then did Ashurbanipal dispatch an army. According to Assyrian sources, the Elamite forces withdrew without resistance and were subsequently defeated as they neared their own land. Before the end of the year Urtak died; a revolution brought a new anti-Assyrian ruler, Teumman, to the Elamite throne and drove the families of Urtak and his predecessor Khumban-khaltash II into exile at the Assyrian court,[362] where they later served as pawns in Assyrian manoeuvres to dominate the Elamite monarchy.[363]

Assyria, however, proved unable to punish most of the main actors in this invasion, though it eventually avenged itself on the areas involved. Marduk-shuma-eresh, the governor of Nippur, kept his office[364] but died soon after of natural causes, as did Bel-iqisha, chief of the Gambulu tribe.[365] But it was only eleven years afterwards (653) that campaigns against Elam and the Gambulu were undertaken. At that time an Assyrian army invaded Elam, defeated and killed Teumman in a battle at Tell Tuba on the Ulaya river, and installed in his place two Elamite princes who had been in exile at the Assyrian court.[366] Then the Assyrians proceeded against the Gambulu, devastating their land and removing Dunanu and Samgunu, two of Bel-iqisha's sons, for punishment in Assyria.[367]

At this point, just before the civil war broke out, Assyria should have been in a strong position. It had recently crushed Elam and Gambulu,

---

[359] A 337, 56–8; A 344, 6; cf. A 551, 91 n. 450.   [360] A 337, 58; A 688, 102 iii.
[361] Cf. A 551, 91 n. 452.   [362] Cf. A 551, 92 n. 453.   [363] A 337, 56–60.
[364] Cf. A 551, 92 n. 455.   [365] A 337, 60.
[366] A 312, 38–40; A 337, 60–70; A 346, 178ff nos. 5–17, 30–3, 35, etc. Cf. A 551, 92 n. 457.
[367] A 337, 70–6; cf. A 346, 182–6 nos. 18–26, 29, 34, 36–8; A 312, 40–2.

two of the major trouble spots in the south east, and had divided jurisdiction in Elam between two princes who had lived in Assyria for more than a decade. But the flaw this time lay in central Babylonia: Shamash-shuma-ukin was no longer content with his subordinate role nor with Ashurbanipal's interference and inadequate defence policies. His resolution to set an independent course was to have fateful consequences both for Babylonia and for the Assyrian empire.

VI. THE GREAT REBELLION (652–648 B.C.) AND ITS AFTERMATH: ASHURBANIPAL VERSUS SHAMASH-SHUMA-UKIN AND HIS ALLIES[368]

In the middle of the seventh century, a bitter struggle between the two most prominent members of the Assyrian royal family shook the base of the Assyrian empire. Shamash-shuma-ukin led Babylonia in a full-scale rebellion against Ashurbanipal and won support from Elam, Arabia, and elsewhere in western Asia.[369] Assyrian military energies were absorbed for four years in dealing with the revolt in urban Babylonia and then for several additional years in cleaning up pockets of resistance in the Sealand and exacting vengeance from Babylonia's foreign supporters. These massive military efforts severely strained the resources of the Assyrian empire, for in its final three decades (after 640 B.C.) it launched few if any significant initiatives. The purpose of the present section is to describe the events of this revolt, which formed a watershed in Mesopotamian political history.

To assess the impact of the rebellion on Assyria, we should be better informed of the empire's status c. 653 B.C., just before the outbreak of hostilities. It seems likely that Assyrian power had already begun to decline after the early years of Ashurbanipal. Assyria's control over Egypt had been slipping since about 660, Cimmerians were menacing Syria by 657,[370] and some associated states such as Lydia had renounced their connexions with Assyria.[371] A major difficulty in interpreting the history of Ashurbanipal's reign is that reconstruction of the sequence of events often depends on vague statements in documents with little or no chronological perspective. We simply do not know how weak the Assyrian empire may have been, especially in the west, by around 653, and this seriously diminishes our ability to appraise events from a regional perspective.

In the preceding section of this chapter, we discussed the background for Shamash-shuma-ukin's discontent – Ashurbanipal's interference in

---

[368] A detailed discussion of the political and military events of this period may be found in A 588, 115–68.

[369] Cf. A 551, 93 n. 460.   [370] Thus A 77, 307–8.   [371] Cf. A 317.

Babylonian internal affairs and his inadequate military protection of the realm. When this was added to the general restlessness of Babylonia under the Assyrian yoke (evident from the preceding decades of political turmoil), it provided the occasion for concerted rebellion by the local population and their Assyrian-born leader. Whether there was a single cause which sparked the conflagration, such as Ashurbanipal's Elamite–Gambulu campaign(s) of 653, or his rumoured plans for treating Babylon more harshly,[372] we do not know. In any case, Shamash-shuma-ukin's intention to raise the standard of rebellion had become known by 23/II/652 B.C., for on that date Ashurbanipal wrote to the citizens of Babylon in a standard Assyrian manoeuvre to detach them from allegiance to their king.[373]

Although Ashurbanipal weighed the possibility of a quick move into Babylon as early as 17/IV/652,[374] almost eight months were to elapse between the discovery of Shamash-shuma-ukin's plot and the formal outbreak of hostilities (19/X/652).[375] One of the reasons for the delay may have been that Ashurbanipal could not count on the wholehearted support of Assyria (where there may have been insurrections in the very next year, 651).[376] By the time that battle was joined in Babylonia between the forces of Ashurbanipal and Shamash-shuma-ukin, the lines of adherence to the two monarchs seem to have been clearly drawn. Shamash-shuma-ukin could rely on the cities of northern and central Babylonia (with the possible exception of Cutha),[377] as well as on Chaldaean and Aramaean tribal areas, with some exceptions in the far south to be noted presently. The Assyrians had their chief support in the non-tribal urban south – Uruk, Ur, Kissik, Kullab, Eridu, and Shat-iddin – plus a few local tribal adherents such as the Gurasimmu and some of the Puqudu. We do not know who had the support of the countryside in northern Babylonia; forces from both sides marched through it apparently without opposition, and it may have been effectively neutralized by its open and vulnerable position. To some extent this line-up within Babylonia reflects long-standing pro- and anti-Chaldaean sentiment, with the principal opposition coming from southern cities which were enclaves struggling to survive in a predominantly Chaldaean landscape.[378]

Outside Babylonia, the Elamites and Arabs seem generally to have supported the cause of Shamash-shuma-ukin, occasionally to the extent of participating in the fighting.[379] Ashurbanipal claimed that Shamash-

[372] A 72, no. 301 (= A 698, no. 115).

[373] A 72, no. 301 (= A 698, no. 115). Cf. A 551, 94 n. 465.

[374] A 497, no. 102.   [375] A 25, 131.

[376] A 25, 132; cf. A 551, 94–5 n. 468.

[377] A 551, 95 n. 470.   [378] Cf. A 551, 95 n. 471.

[379] E.g., A 19, 153–6; A 344, 30–4, 64, 68; A 337, 76.

shuma-ukin had induced the 'kings of Gutium, Amurru, and Meluhha' (archaic names for such places as the middle Zagros, northern Syria, and Egypt–Nubia) to rebel and side with the Babylonian king;[380] but we have no independent evidence that any of these regions actively assisted the Babylonian effort. Foreign support does not seem to have been a significant factor in determining the outcome or even the course of the fighting, except in so far as Elam assisted Chaldaean dissidents in prolonging hostilities in the south east for more than a year after the fall of Babylon and the death of Shamash-shuma-ukin.

The principal actions of the war may be divided into two theatres, north and south. In each of these regions, from 652 to 648, major urban areas were particularly vulnerable and often under attack. Their hinterlands eventually came under enemy control, and though urban defenders could hold out under siege-like conditions – for periods of two years or more in such cities as Ur and Babylon – isolated cities were clearly at a disadvantage in these long-drawn-out fights. In the north, after hostilities commenced on 19/x/652,[381] Shamash-shuma-ukin's forces were quickly checked; in less than three weeks (8/xi/652) he was forced to make a strategic withdrawal into Babylon 'in front of the enemy'.[382] The Babylonian decline, however, was only temporary. In the next month there were two major battles between the Assyrian and Babylonian armies; in the latter of these, at Khirit in the province of Sippar on 27/xii/652, the Babylonian army suffered a serious defeat.[383] Early in the war, Elamite troops sent to help Shamash-shuma-ukin were defeated at Mankisu (on the Tigris near modern Baghdad);[384] and Arab troops arrived in Babylon, probably in 651 or the first months of 650.[385] Despite setbacks in early engagements, the Babylonian army continued to fight actively in both urban and rural areas[386] and on 9/via/651 succeeded in capturing Cutha.[387] But within a few months (before the end of xi/651) the Assyrians gained Nippur in central Babylonia,[388] and an Assyrian army put Babylon itself under siege on 11/iv/650.[389] Thus, in the northern theatre, most military action in the field took place in an eighteen-month period between x/652 and iv/650; after that time the Assyrians were in control of the countryside and had settled down to reducing urban strongholds such as Babylon, Borsippa, Cutha, and Sippar by siege.

The early course of the war in the south may have been similar, but there it was the pro-Assyrian cities that were under attack. (It should be

---

[380] A 344, 30. See also A 551, 93–4 nn. 460 and 463.   [381] A 25, 131.
[382] A 25, 129 and 131. Cf. A 551, 96 n. 475.
[383] A 25, 132; A 588, 266–70; A 1046, 48 and pl. 3.
[384] A 337, 76; cf. A 588, Appendix C.   [385] A 344, 68. Date: A 19, 154.
[386] A 344, 32.   [387] A 25, 129; A 72, no. 1117 (A 19, 153–4).
[388] A 551, 97 n. 481.   [389] A 25, 130; A 729, no. 19.

noted that most available evidence concerning the southern theatre comes from letters and their chronological vagueness permits many possible interpretations.) Uruk, Kullab, Ur, Kissik, Eridu, and a few other cities seem early to have declared their adherence to Ashurbanipal;[390] but only Uruk seems to have been reinforced with Assyrian troops to the extent that it was never in serious danger from Chaldaean forces and the generally hostile countryside. In fact, Uruk seems to have served as a staging area for Ashurbanipal's forces in the south; and the Assyrian governors of Arrapkha, Lakhiru, and Zame exercised military commands there.[391] Early in the war, the Sealanders and the Puqudu tribe controlled the south and seriously pressed the pro-Assyrians; Eridu, Kullab, and the Gurasimmu tribe eventually defected to the side of Shamash-shuma-ukin.[392] Ur under its governor Sin-tabni-uṣur found itself in dire straits, but held out against famine and the enemy for at least two years.[393] Eventually a letter was dispatched to Ashurbanipal pleading for troops and warning that the wealth which his ancestors had bestowed on the temple of Sin, patron deity of Ur, would fall into enemy hands.[394] Legal texts found at Ur and dated in 650 and 649 show men selling property rights and a prebend to raise money for food.[395] Ur was subjected to extreme stress, and a damaged letter suggests that Sin-tabni-uṣur may have been forced to submit to Shamash-shuma-ukin before relief came.[396] But, if Ur actually was lost, it was only for a brief period; Assyrian troops eventually arrived with the governor of Uruk to rescue the city.[397]

As noted above, the southern theatre of war was dominated at first by tribal forces, especially the Sealanders[398] and the Puqudu. The Sealanders were under the control of Nabu-bel-shumati, a grandson of Merodach-baladan, who was a symbol of anti-Assyrian resistance from early in the revolt[399] until his death five years later. The Sealanders and Puqudu were closely allied with Elam; they drew military support from there, occasionally conducted raids from Elamite bases, and eventually – after the Assyrians had gained the upper hand in southern Babylonia – made Elam their permanent refuge.[400] Nabu-bel-shumati was allied with

[390] A 551, 97 n. 483.

[391] A 72, no. 754 + A 575, no. 250; A 72, nos. 543 and 1108. Cf. A 72, no. 1028. J. C. L. Gibson, *Textbook of Syrian Semitic Inscriptions* II (Oxford, 1975), no. 20 (= A 15, no. 233) may also date from Uruk about this time.

[392] A 72, no. 1241 + A 575, no. 112.

[393] A 72, no. 290; cf. A 72, no. 523 and A 497, nos. 129 and 135.

[394] A 72, no. 1241 + A 575, no. 112.   [395] A 551, 98 n. 489.

[396] A 72, no. 1274 (interpretation uncertain).

[397] A 72, no. 754 + A 575, no. 250 (interpretation uncertain).

[398] The name may at this time designate primarily members of the Chaldaean tribe of Bit-Yakin.

[399] A 551, 98 n. 492.

[400] A 588, chapter 4 section 4; A 751, 51. Cf. A 72, nos. 942 and 1241 + A 575, no. 112.

four Elamite kings, Khumban-nikash II, Tammaritu, Indabibi, and Khumban-khaltash III,[401] who ruled in quick succession; the first three of them were deposed in revolts, but each new king sooner or later embraced the tradition of opposition to Assyria. Nabu-bel-shumati seems to have been unusually successful in his anti-Assyrian manoeuvres; the frequent occurrence of his name joined with slanderous epithets in the Assyrian court correspondence indicates not only his crucial role in undermining the Assyrian cause in the south, but also the violent antipathy that he aroused in his opponents. To stem the tide, Ashurbanipal in the middle of the war (5/11/650) sent Bel-ibni, the son of a former Babylonian official, as military commander to the Sealand.[402] He struggled bitterly, if not always successfully, against Nabu-bel-shumati; but, after Assyria had gained the upper hand in the north and had the major cities there under siege, Ashurbanipal's cause came to prevail in the south as well.[403] By the second half of 649, legal documents were being dated under Ashurbanipal in parts of Bit-Amukani and Bit-Dakkuri.[404]

We do not know the sequence of events that led to the collapse of the revolt in either the north or the south. Babylon, Borsippa, Cutha, and Sippar continued under siege – Babylon itself for more than two years – with food ever scarcer and plague becoming endemic.[405] During this time, Arab auxiliaries who were serving in Babylon under Abiyateʾ and Ayamu fought their way out of the besieged town, but suffered heavy losses.[406] The last known documents dated under Shamash-shuma-ukin come from Babylon and Borsippa in the summer of 648;[407] within the next few months the northern cities fell and Shamash-shuma-ukin perished in the conflagration at Babylon.[408] Ashurbanipal reimposed his rule over the land and removed the surviving urban population of Cutha and Sippar to the capital city.[409]

After the suppression of rebellion in the north in 648, fighting in the south may have continued. Nabu-bel-shumati remained at large until 646; and, although details are far from clear, he seems to have been harassing the Assyrian side either from headquarters in the south east or from refuge in Elam. Elam continued to be a major problem for Assyria. After the defeat and death of Teumman at the hands of the Assyrians in 653, Ashurbanipal had apportioned the rule of Elam between two monarchs, Khumban-nikash II (with capitals at Madaktu and Susa) and Tammaritu I (with his capital at Khaidalu), both exiled princes who had

---

[401] A 344, 60. For the reading of the name as Indabibi (rather than Indabigash), see A 551, 101 n. 506.   [402] A 72, no. 289.

[403] Cf. A 497, no. 139.   [404] A 551, 99 n. 499.

[405] A 344, 32. Cf. A 19, 154; A 162, no. 34; A 258, 55–7; A 344, 36–40; A 553, 34–6; A 563.

[406] A 344, 68; A 19, 154–6.   [407] A 551, 100 n. 502.

[408] Cf. A 551, 100 n. 503.   [409] A 344, 40; cf. A 551, 100 n. 504.

been living at the Assyrian court. This division may have further destabilized what was already a highly volatile political environment. Khumban-nikash was overthrown by Tammaritu II, who was in turn dethroned by Indabibi[410] and fled to the Assyrian court. Indabibi was killed and replaced by Khumban-khaltash III.[411] These three revolutions took place in less than five years; and, as noted above, each new king – regardless of previous Assyrian benefactions – came eventually to support the Babylonian rebels against Ashurbanipal.

Thus, after reducing the cities of northern Babylonia, Ashurbanipal turned his attention to the next most troublesome region, south-eastern Babylonia and western Elam. Probably in 647 and 646, the Assyrian army conducted at least two campaigns reaching widely into Elam. The first of these punitive expeditions began in Aramaean territory in the eastern borderlands of Babylonia. Several prominent tribal towns there, including Khilimmu and Pillatu, submitted voluntarily rather than face a full-scale Assyrian assault. The Assyrian army then marched to Bit-Imbi, a local capital in western Elam, captured and despoiled it. Khumban-khaltash fled from Madaktu into the highlands; and Ashurbanipal set up Tammaritu II again as king in Susa. Tammaritu objected to the plundering of Elam by Assyrian armies and promptly lost his throne.[412] Ashurbanipal claimed to have concluded this campaign with the capture, spoliation, and destruction of most of the major cities of western Elam, including Susa, Madaktu, and Dur-Untash; but, since some of these cities were still flourishing on the occasion of his next campaign, his scribes may have been indulging in Assyrian narrative licence.[413]

In the second campaign, Assyrian troops ranged widely over western Elam, conquering and supposedly devastating extensive areas but never managing to engage in battle with Khumban-khaltash, who once again escaped to the highlands. In his anger, Ashurbanipal decided to make an object lesson of Susa, the venerable political and religious capital. He took up residence there in the royal palace and stripped it of treasure, furniture, vehicles, and animals. He had his soldiers destroy the temples and sanctuaries, pull down the ziggurat, and set fire to the sacred groves reserved for secret rites. The Assyrians took away the cult images of the principal gods and goddesses, their priests and sacred vessels, and the statues of earlier Elamite kings. They also desecrated the tombs of former monarchs:

I exposed [them] to the sun and took their bones away to Assyria. I imposed restlessness upon their shades [and] deprived them of food-offerings and of people to pour libations for them.[414]

[410] A 551, 101 n. 506.   [411] A 344, 26, 32–6, 142–4; cf. A 312, 40–4.
[412] A 312, 46; A 344, 44–6. Cf. A 551, 101 n. 508.   [413] A 312, 44–8; A 344, 40–6; A 757.
[414] A 312, 56.

Ashurbanipal then proceeded to devastate the Elamite plain, destroying cities, deporting the population, and driving off to Assyria the vast flocks of animals that constituted Elam's chief source of wealth. He sowed salt and thorn-bearing plants over the fields and returned the land to a primeval state:

In a month of days I levelled the whole of Elam. I deprived its fields of the sound of human voices, the tread of cattle and sheep, the refrain of joyous harvest songs. I turned it into a pasture for wild asses, gazelles, and all manner of wild animals.[415]

The effect was decisive. Elam was never again a major political power, though Khumban-khaltash and other highland rulers would continue to prove a minor annoyance to Assyria.[416]

But, in the short term, Khumban-khaltash in his devastated capital at Madaktu[417] agreed to comply with the wishes of Ashurbanipal and to extradite Nabu-bel-shumati. The latter, preferring to evade the grisly fate accorded most notorious anti-Assyrian leaders, had himself slain by his personal attendant (*kizû*). Khumban-khaltash, fearing Ashurbanipal's further displeasure, packed the body in salt and dispatched it to Nineveh.[418]

A direct benefit to Babylonia from Ashurbanipal's Elamite campaigns was the return of a statue of the goddess Nanaya from Susa to its original home in Uruk. When the statue had been removed, we do not know; the texts of Ashurbanipal mention that it had been absent for 1,635 years, but such figures are usually exaggerated.[419]

After Ashurbanipal's revenge on Elam, the last target of retribution remaining from the days of the Great Rebellion was the dissident Arab tribes in the western desert. In 645 or shortly thereafter,[420] in order to punish these tribes both for their assistance to Shamash-shuma-ukin and for their continuing raids on Assyrian territories (probably on the middle Euphrates and in the neighbourhood of Palmyra), Ashurbanipal launched a lengthy and arduous summer campaign, designed to catch the nomads and their animals in the season when they would have to remain closest to their water supplies.[421] The Assyrians pursued a strategy of quick marches and seizure of critical oases and watering points. Some of the Arab chieftains, notably Abiyate° and Ayamu, surrendered. Uaite°, chief of the Qedarites, was deposed and handed over to the Assyrians by his own people; and a later campaign resulted in the submission of the Nabayatu.[422] Thus not only were pro-Babylonian actions punished, but the desert frontier was at least temporarily quieted.

[415] A 344, 56–8.   [416] A 312, 48–60; A 344, 46–60. Cf. A 551, 102 n. 512.
[417] Perhaps to be identified with Tepe Patak (A 679, 174).
[418] A 344, 60–2; cf. A 551, 103 n. 514.   [419] A 312, 58; A 344, 58.
[420] Date: A 19, 157.   [421] A 19, 157–65; A 344, 64–80.   [422] Cf. A 72, no. 1117.

Thus the Great Rebellion and its aftermath occupied the Assyrians for at least seven years, and the Assyrian royal inscriptions record no great campaign conducted thereafter by the imperial armies. Although Assyria had succeeded in recapturing Babylonia and in disciplining Babylonia's allies on both the Elamite plain and the Arabian desert, these actions had entailed disproportionate expenditures of time, manpower, and financial resources. Assyria had reasserted its hegemony; but the empire had declined in both power and geographical extent, and the long-drawn-out struggle had highlighted Assyrian vulnerability. More serious was the fact that, in decimating Elam, Ashurbanipal had removed a buffer state which had insulated Assyria from strong tribal groups in the Iranian interior.[423] The next enemies of the empire who arose in south-west Iran and southern Babylonia would be more formidable and would not repeat their predecessors' mistakes.

VII. KANDALANU AND THE DECLINE OF ASSYRIAN POWER, 647–626 B.C.

The two decades of the reign of Kandalanu (647–627) mark a period of relative quiet in Babylonia between two major anti-Assyrian upheavals. During the early years of this time, probably before 640, Ashurbanipal's armies were occupied in settling scores with the principal foreign supporters of Shamash-shuma-ukin's rebellion, that is the Elamites and Arabs.[424] For the later years there were no major military campaigns recorded by Assyria; and this silence has generally been interpreted as indicating a decline in Assyrian strength. The history of Babylonia during this time must at present be reconstructed almost entirely from economic texts (administrative and legal); very little is known about political history.[425]

Kandalanu himself is practically unknown.[426] Although he presided over Babylonia for twenty-one years at a time when the country fully regained its economic strength, his name is known only from chronological texts (king lists and a chronicle)[427] and from date formulae in documents referring to his reign. There is no contemporary evidence about his origin[428] or about any action that he took as king. Because he is such a shadowy figure and because he and Ashurbanipal seem to have died in the same year (627),[429] it has sometimes been suggested that 'Kandalanu' is simply a throne name for Ashurbanipal.[430] This hypothe-

---

[423] Cf. A 551, 104 n. 519.
[424] These campaigns are discussed in Section VI above.
[425] The period has been treated in detail in A 588, 168–82.   [426] A 546, 368.
[427] A 25, 132.   [428] A 551, 105 n. 525.   [429] A 551, 106 n. 527.
[430] Or even that Kandalanu was a statue that represented Ashurbanipal at the New Year's festival (A 393, 1).

sis, however, has little to recommend it. Other alleged cases of Assyrian kings bearing Babylonian throne names have been shown to be spurious.[431] Furthermore, there seems little reason, if Kandalanu and Ashurbanipal were identical, to preserve two entirely different systems of chronological reckoning for one and the same king (dating at Nippur under the name Ashurbanipal with a reign officially beginning in 668 and elsewhere in Babylonia under the name Kandalanu with a reign starting in 647).

Kandalanu was appointed to the Babylonian throne by Ashurbanipal probably within a year after the suppression of the revolt of Shamash-shuma-ukin. It appears, however, that Babylonia was only gradually placed in his charge. Babylon itself was under his control by 6/x/647 and Uruk by 11/vii/646;[432] but at some cities in the heartland of north-west Babylonia texts were still being dated under Ashurbanipal in Kandalanu's first and second regnal years: at Borsippa as late as 18/ix/647 and at Dilbat on 29/1/646.[433] After 646, only Nippur remained under the explicit control of Ashurbanipal, and elsewhere texts were uniformly dated under Kandalanu.[434]

The opening years of Kandalanu's reign saw Babylonia only slowly recovering from the effects of the Great Rebellion. Economic activity for his first five years dropped back to the level of some twenty-five years earlier.[435] As for the rehabilitation of the Babylonian civil administration, Ashurbanipal stated: 'I imposed upon them [the people of Babylonia] the yoke of the god Ashur which they had cast off; I established over them governors [šaknūti] and officials [qīpāni] whom I had selected'[436] – with no explicit mention of the installation of Kandalanu. In the south, Kudurru served as governor at Uruk after the revolt;[437] and Bel-ibni continued his activity in the Sealand, which included raids against Elam.[438] Elam also served as a refuge for fugitive Babylonians and Chaldaeans from Uruk, Nippur, Larak, Bit-Dakkuri, and Bit-Amukani, those who had withheld taxes from Ashurbanipal during the rebellion and later fled into exile; many of these people were eventually captured on the Assyrian campaigns into Elam and then taken off to Assyria.[439] Nippur, the most persistently rebellious of the Babylonian cities from 680 to 651, was kept under direct Assyrian supervision, perhaps as a garrison town strategically located in central Babylonia.[440]

By 642 economic activity had returned to its former pace before the

---

[431] A 535, 61–2.   [432] A 551, 106 n. 530.

[433] A 646, 321 (now published in A 667A, no. 399); A 957, no. 13.

[434] For Ur, see A 551, 106–7 n. 532.

[435] I.e., the last few years of Esarhaddon's reign. Cf. A 553, 19, 39–40; A 553A, 99–101.

[436] A 344, 40. Cf. A 551, 107 n. 534.   [437] A 551, 107 n. 535.

[438] E.g., A 72, no. 280; cf. A 72, no. 462 (A 588, 178 n. 1).

[439] A 258, 59 (text damaged); A 588, 175–6.   [440] A 588, 169.

Rebellion. It then remained at a high level throughout the rest of Kandalanu's term in office. More than 200 dated economic texts are known from this reign, representing the heaviest concentration (texts per year) for any Babylonian king since the thirteenth century. Almost half of these texts (48 per cent) come from the principal cities in the north west: Babylon, Borsippa, Sippar, Dilbat, and Khursagkalama.[441] In the far south Uruk is well represented in the first six years of the reign (28 per cent of the texts from 647 to 642), but then declines drastically (only 6 per cent of the texts from the whole reign).[442] The texts embrace a wide range of activities; but livestock accounts (especially for sheep and goats), purchases of real estate, and promissory notes are most common. Particularly noteworthy are accounts dealing with oil and with iron (especially large quantities of iron, which was sometimes imported from Cilicia), and purchases of prebends. The only traces of active Assyrian intervention in the land are in Ashurbanipal's building activities at the religious centres of Babylon, Borsippa, Cutha, Nippur, and Sirara.[443]

Events at the close of Kandalanu's reign show Assyria rapidly losing control over Babylonia. In 627, Kandalanu died at some point between 8/III and 1(+)/ VIII.[444] Ashurbanipal may have died in the same year, according to evidence from the next century.[445] About the same time as Kandalanu's death,[446] civil disorder broke out in Babylon;[447] and the Assyrian Sin-sharra-ishkun, who was later to govern parts of Babylonia, fled to Assyria.[448] The Assyrian army subsequently entered the city of Shaznaku and set fire to its temple (12/VI/627); for protection, the gods of Kish were sent to Babylon. In VII/627, an Assyrian army forced Nabopolassar, the new Babylonian leader, to withdraw from Nippur and pursued him as far as Uruk, but was itself then compelled to retreat. The situation was clearly unstable.

The year 626 saw further upheaval. Even in later historical tradition there was no agreement as to who was even nominally in control of the land. A Seleucid king list records that in this year the government of Babylonia was in the hands of two Assyrians, Sin-shumu-lishir and Sin-sharra-ishkun; but a Babylonian chronicle refers to 626 as 'the first year in which there was no king in the land'.[449] Early in the year (II/626), an Assyrian army came down to Babylonia and five months later attacked Babylon itself. In contrast to earlier occasions on which Babylon had first been besieged and later overwhelmed by the Assyrians, the men of Babylon sallied forth and plundered the Assyrian army. In the next

---

[441] Cf. A 551, 108 n. 540.

[442] The accidents of discovery may significantly influence these statistics.

[443] A 551, 108 n. 543.   [444] A 551, 108 n. 544.

[445] Cf. A 551, 108 n. 545.   [446] For this dating, see A 551, 109 n. 546.

[447] Cf. A 551, 109 n. 547.   [448] Cf. A 551, 109 n. 548.   [449] A 551, 110 n. 550.

month (26/VIII/626), Nabopolassar officially mounted the throne in Babylon, inaugurating a new era.[450]

It is unfortunate that these decades, 647–627, immediately antedating the rise of the Neo-Babylonian empire in Mesopotamia, are not better attested. It is clear that Babylonia's economy quickly recovered from the effects of the civil war; but Babylonia's king, Kandalanu, is at present known only as a name in dating formulae or in chronological documents. We cannot as yet appraise the factors which shaped the course of Babylonian history during this time. We do not know whether the economic recovery took place under stricter Assyrian occupation or whether stability was achieved because urban Babylonians and Chaldaeans temporarily abandoned their unsuccessful struggle for independence and acquiesced in Assyrian rule; and there are obviously other alternatives that might be considered. The silence of the sources permits myriad interpretations.

VIII. NOTE ON SOURCES

For the history of Babylonia between 747 and 626 B.C. there is a broad range of epigraphic and archaeological evidence and, in some parts of the documentary record, significant amounts of extant material. But, as is common in Mesopotamian studies, much of this evidence remains unpublished; and there has been little critical appraisal of either the published or unpublished sources. Thus the historian is faced with substantial data, almost all in very raw form; much basic research has yet to be done before the full potential of this material can begin to be realized.

The following pages present a brief survey of the major types of sources, written and non-written, pertaining to this period. No attempt has been made at bibliographical completeness, which would expand this chapter well beyond the desired scope.

We shall begin with the most illuminating and also the most voluminous of the written materials, the correspondence of the Assyrian court. In the imperial archives at Calah and Nineveh, more than 3,200 documents have been found which date between 735 and 645 B.C.; and a substantial portion of this material deals with affairs in Babylonia: reports from local officials on events of political or diplomatic significance, requests for economic or military aid, and comments on the unpopularity of the Assyrian regime, to name a few topics. The letters are not spread evenly over this period, but are concentrated principally in three phases (in 720–717 and 713–705 under Sargon II and in 673–664

---

[450] To be discussed in Chapter 25 below. For Nabopolassar's supposed Chaldaean origin, see A 551, 110–11 n. 551.

under Esarhaddon and Ashurbanipal) with sparser coverage of certain years under Tiglath-pileser III (735–727) and Ashurbanipal (655–645).[451] Of particular significance is the dearth of letters under Sennacherib (705–681) and late in the reign of Ashurbanipal (645–627), since this skews the source materials available for these decades.[452] The extensive court correspondence furnishes insights into the inner workings of the administrative system of the Assyrian empire and, apart from occasional self-serving statements by officials, gives a private, non-propagandistic view of Assyrian successes and failures. These letters contain a wealth of incidental detail on life in Babylonia: tribal disputes, irrigation problems, regional rivalries, the rhythm of the economy. But there are serious difficulties in using these archives: (1) many of the tablets containing the letters are broken or heavily damaged; (2) their language tends to be highly idiomatic and is therefore not always readily comprehensible; (3) the historical context of the message is often unclear, since a writer seldom rehearses well-known background for his correspondent; and (4) the date of each document must usually be inferred (less than ten of the letters are explicitly dated).[453] There are few letters from this period which were found in Babylonia itself, and only two of these have been plausibly dated to the early seventh century.[454] Also to be placed here is the so-called Ashur Ostracon, a letter written in Aramaic and found at Ashur, which was sent as a report from southern Babylonia about the middle of the seventh century.[455]

Another significant corpus of material is the scattered group of more than six hundred indigenous economic texts (legal and administrative) dating from between 747 and 626. More than 60 per cent of these documents come from the major urban centres of Sippar, Babylon, Borsippa, Dilbat, Nippur, and Uruk, which have been subjected to controlled and uncontrolled excavations.[456] Most of the texts are legal documents, and they are concerned principally with financial transactions or with income-producing property: purchases of land (agricultural and urban), loans, and acquisition of prebends. There are various types of account texts, many of them dealing with herds of sheep or cattle, allocation of foodstuffs, or disbursement of metal (silver, gold, and iron). Of particular interest for future study will be two common features of legal texts: the witness lists with their individual genealogies and the detailed descriptions of real estate (house plots, fields, and date-

---

[451] See the chart in A 76, 136 for the Assyrian material. The distribution of comparable Babylonian letters conforms to the same general pattern.

[452] The years from 664 to 655 are only slightly represented.

[453] Bibliography of letters found in Assyria: A 551, 113 n. 552.

[454] A 551, 114 n. 556.

[455] J. C. L. Gibson, *Textbook of Syrian Semitic Inscriptions* II, no. 20 (= A 15, no. 233).

[456] Cf. A 551, 115 n. 558.

palm groves). As yet, only about one-third of these texts have been published in any form, and no systematic attempt has been made to utilize them for historical purposes. These documents should prove a mine of information for researchers interested in demography, social institutions, economic history, and even ancient technology.[457]

Also of considerable interest is the extensive corpus of Assyrian royal inscriptions, which contain detailed accounts of the Babylonian campaigns of Tiglath-pileser III, Sargon II, Sennacherib, and Ashurbanipal.[458] The Assyrian scribes recorded much information that is invaluable to the modern historian – details about the topography, flora, fauna, and social and economic institutions of the inhabitants. If one prescinds from the tendentious style glorifying the Assyrian monarchy and military, one quickly strikes a core of usable data. For example, statistics given by these texts for people deported to various parts of the empire are among the few numbers available for Babylonian and tribal populations, even though they are difficult to use critically. The figures seem uniformly too high, probably because greater magnitude was perceived as ideologically desirable.

Babylonian royal inscriptions are a much smaller and duller lot. There are a few short texts written in the name of Merodach-baladan II and Shamash-shuma-ukin; but, except for a veiled reference to an Assyrian military reversal in 720, most of the texts are either conventional expressions of pious sentiments or laconic records of repair to religious structures.[459]

Inscriptions written by or for local officials or dignitaries present a more interesting and variegated picture. From the reign of Nabonassar there is a text written in the name of two private individuals who describe how they repaired the *Akitu* temple at Uruk because this duty had been neglected by those responsible (the king and local officials).[460] Three decades later, a governor of Kish recorded his construction of a bridge over the principal local waterway (the Banitu canal).[461] Toward the close of the eighth century, a local temple official restored plundered statues of the gods to the town of Sha-uṣur-Adad and secured tax exemptions from Bel-ibni, the reigning monarch.[462] From Ur about 665– 650 date several monumental building inscriptions in the name of the local governor Sin-balassu-iqbi[463] as well as a votive text of his brother and successor, Sin-sharra-uṣur.[464]

Contemporary texts of at least incidental value include formal omen inquiries from the Assyrian court, soliciting information from the gods

[457] Bibliography of these texts: A 553, A 553A. For technology, see A 552B.
[458] A 35; A 185; A 204; A 226; A 234; A 270; A 312; A 313; A 337; A 344; A 663.
[459] A 551, 116, n. 561.   [460] A 536, with duplicates noted there.
[461] Latest edition: A 771, no. 75.   [462] A 773, no. 1 (cf. A 553, 15 En. 1).
[463] A 593, nos. 168–83; A 744, no. 102.   [464] Bibliography: A 551, 117 n. 566.

on how current crises were to be resolved.[465] Also of interest are scholarly texts, including lexical series (Erimkhush), a compendium listing flora associated with Merodach-baladan's garden (*gannatu*), and prayers and rituals written down in the time of Shamash-shuma-ukin;[466] these represent various scribal traditions that flourished in this period. In addition there are passing references to Babylonia and its inhabitants in contemporary economic texts in Assyria; these have yet to be systematically collected and evaluated.

Providing an essential chronological framework for the overall historical picture are the king lists and chronicles, which are concerned primarily with chronology and with military and religious event-history. The king lists, Babylonian and Assyrian, give the names and sequence of monarchs who ruled during this period and sometimes their lengths of reign.[467] The heterogeneous Babylonian chronicles furnish an indispensable chronological listing of the beginnings and ends of reigns for kings in Babylonia, Elam, and Assyria, especially for the years from 747 to 668; they also mention and often date major events of political or religious significance.[468] The Assyrian Eponym Chronicles record the destination of the principal annual campaigns of the Assyrian army between 747 and 699 (with some lacunae) and give supplementary details for the years 745, 729–728, 710–709, 707, 704, and 700.[469] Additional chronological information is provided by other texts: an astronomical diary[470] and nineteen-year cycle texts,[471] astronomical records including later references in Ptolemy's *Almagest*,[472] and the so-called 'Ptolemaic Canon' (which includes a list of Babylonian monarchs and the lengths of their reigns, beginning with Nabonassar).[473]

Later texts of interest include sections from the writings of the Hellenistic historian Berossos,[474] from Biblical books,[475] and from Josephus' *Antiquities of the Jews*.[476] These late traditions are frequently garbled and sometimes difficult to interpret chronologically. They add incidental details to the historical picture, but must be used with considerable caution.

Turning now to the extensive non-epigraphic materials, we note first the regional evidence reconstructed from surface surveys: location of watercourses and settlements, urban and village hierarchies, and synchronic and diachronic patterns of expansion and abandonment.[477] For

---

[465] A 497.   [466] A 532, 48 under 44.3.5; see also A 551, 89 nn. 439–40.
[467] A 607, nos. 3.3, 3.5, 3.12, 3.17.   [468] A 25, nos. 1, 2, 14–16.
[469] A 763, 428–35.   [470] A 1046, pl. 3.
[471] E.g., BM 33809, mentioned in A 588, 19–20.
[472] A 1045, nos. 1414–18 (and possibly 1413); cf. A 551, 89 n. 441. A 772. *Almagest*: A 675; A 1049.
[473] A 770, 304–6.   [474] *FGrH* 680 (A 7; A 735).
[475] II Ki. 17:24 and 20:12–21; II Chron. 32:31 (cf. 33:11); Is. 39:1–8; Ezra 4:9–10.
[476] IX.xiv.3; X.ii.2. For additional late texts, see A 551, 118–19 n. 582 and A 745A.
[477] A 511; A 512; A 513; A 514; A 568; A 597; A 783. Cf. A 625; A 726.

the lower Diyala basin and the ribbon of settlement extending along the older course of the Euphrates from just above Nippur down to Ur, we now have preliminary statistics for a local history of urbanism. Excavations at Babylon, Kish-Khursagkalama, Nippur, Uruk, and Ur, as well as in the Hamrin, have revealed monumental buildings and residences in use in this period; but, except at Ur in the massive reconstruction undertaken by Sin-balassu-iqbi,[478] there are few of these buildings which can be seen to have originated – rather than simply to have been repaired – at this time.[479] In most instances, we know more about major building projects from inscriptions than we do from excavations.[480]

The material culture of this age, whether reconstructed from archaeological evidence or from texts, has not been seriously studied and remains a prime area for future research. A satisfactory typology for the pottery of eighth- and seventh-century Babylonia has yet to be worked out, though there seem to be distinctive ceramic remains from this time, including vessels in use at Nippur which have decoration akin to Assyrian palace ware.[481] We note also Porada's pioneering typology of early Neo-Babylonian glyptic,[482] although in this regard studies of seals and seal impressions from stratified excavations will remain an essential desideratum. It will be of particular importance to determine possible cultural influences between contemporary Babylonian and Assyrian art styles,[483] as well as between Babylonian and Elamite art.[484]

Another archaeological area of high potential interest is the use of wall reliefs from Assyrian palaces as pictorial sources for Babylonian history. The systematic interpretation of Assyrian reliefs as historical evidence is in its infancy. The most recent detailed study of the portrayal of non-Assyrians in the reliefs unfortunately excluded Babylonians (including Aramaeans and Chaldaeans) and Elamites from consideration.[485] It is to be regretted that primary publications of Assyrian reliefs have on occasion been insufficiently critical in identifying specific historical persons and places in particular scenes. This area of research is still underdeveloped, but with improving methodology one may anticipate significant advances in historical and ideological interpretation.[486]

This brief survey has outlined the principal indigenous and external sources, epigraphic and archaeological, that are presently available for the history of Babylonia from 747 to 626 B.C. It is important that we be

---

[478] Summarized in A 534, 249–51; A 537, 336–42.
[479] Bibliography in A 551, 119–20 n. 586.   [480] Cf. A 551, 120 n. 587.
[481] A 551, 120 n. 588.   [482] A 713.   [483] Cf. A 601.
[484] Note the preliminary comments in A 680. The archaeological material from this period in Babylonia is discussed in more detail in A 551, 119–21.
[485] A 155.
[486] A 115; A 116; A 117; A 118; A 126; A 127; A 132; A 133; A 135; A 147; A 153. Cf. A 136, 123–30 and Bagh. Mitt. 10 (1979), 17–49, 52–110; and 11 (1980) 71–87.

aware of inevitable distortions in the material. First, the bulk of the textual sources (correspondence and royal inscriptions) originates in the Assyrian or Assyrian-dominated bureaucracy. The letters reflect the interests of that bureaucracy and tend to be obscure to the modern reader (because of background obvious to the correspondents and thus unexpressed); the royal texts are intended primarily to glorify the achievements of the ruler, and literal truth is on occasion sacrificed to ideological preferences. Second, the native Babylonian source material is composed principally of legal and administrative documents, concerned chiefly with property rights of the urban population and with temple offices, especially in the north-west alluvium; non-economic and rural affairs are seriously underrepresented. In the archaeological surveys, the bias is reversed; and well-known areas tend to be rural and along the old bed of the Euphrates and in the lower Diyala. The extent of urban centres such as Nippur and Uruk in this period is very poorly known, and the main band of settlements and larger cities along the contemporary course of the Euphrates has barely been touched. Excavations, however, have concentrated on cities and their public edifices; little is known of smaller sites or even of residential quarters within the larger centres. The presently available source material is rich, and much work remains to be done on relatively untapped data. But it is also desirable that future fieldwork be directed to redressing current biases in the distribution of sources: to seek out more Babylonian native materials – textual as well as archaeological – in rural areas and in urban residential quarters; and to extend survey coverage to deal effectively with larger towns and cities and with settlements along the contemporary Euphrates and in north-eastern and south-eastern Babylonia.

IX. CONCLUSION

This chapter has presented a survey of Babylonian history over the turbulent decades between 747 and 626 B.C., from the beginning of the reign of Nabonassar to the accession of Nabopolassar. These years saw the transformation and revitalization of Babylonia on many levels – demographic, political, socio-economic, and cultural – despite almost constant pressure from the Late Assyrian empire. Although critical appraisal of the voluminous source materials is still at a primitive stage, it may be useful to offer here a provisional synthesis of presently observable trends, if for no other reason than to help formulate questions which should be asked as research progresses.

Babylonia in the mid-eighth century was underpopulated, impoverished, and politically fragmented. Disruption caused by its uncontrolled tribal populations soon attracted Assyrian military intervention; but occasional Assyrian repression of the tribes did not suffice to stabilize the land, and Assyria was eventually drawn into direct administration of the Babylonian government. This brought Assyria into almost continual conflict with the Chaldaeans, who over a period of four decades (732–689) alternated with Assyria in control of the Babylonian monarchy. Against the constant threat of Assyrian domination, the Chaldaeans forged far-reaching internal and external alliances, uniting previously discordant tribesmen (Aramaeans as well as Chaldaeans) and the non-tribal populations of Babylonia in a common anti-Assyrian movement and joining to them their eastern and western neighbours, the Elamites and Arabs. This transformation of anti-Assyrian elements within Babylonia into a political coalition was to provide the effective power base for the later Neo-Babylonian state after 626 B.C.

The political dimension, however, was only one aspect of Babylonia's growth during these decades. Paradoxically, despite frequent disruptions by war and the damage wrought on cities and countryside, there are hints that Babylonia generally prospered, both economically and culturally. With the stabilizing of the monarchy after 689 under Assyrian aegis, the rise in the volume of financial transactions and the monumental building projects betoken a strengthening of the Babylonian economy. Despite occasional military interruptions, Babylonian agriculture, livestock-raising, and international trade seem to have thrived, and it is likely that the alliances with Elam and the Arabs brought commercial advantages as well. As population density increased, urbanites whose social organization had previously centred on the family gradually aligned themselves into broader kin-based groups that achieved more effective economic and political recognition. Urban centres, though vulnerable to Assyrian devastation and deportation, nonetheless boasted cosmopolitan populations with upper strata of considerable wealth and prestige; and, even after depopulation, the number of residents seems to have been quickly replenished, perhaps by implosion from the hinterlands. The cultural florescence of the land in both science and literature continued a long scholarly tradition that was not impaired by the rise of Aramaic as the vernacular. Babylonia in 626, on the eve of the Neo-Babylonian empire, had not only achieved political unity, but had reached a stage of socio-economic and cultural development that could benefit from territorial expansion and augmented international horizons.

Nonetheless there are other significant factors in the history of these decades that we are as yet unable to assess, given the present state of research. In a land where the ecological balance was fragile, the vagaries of climate and demography, still so seldom examined, would have had a profound impact. The shifting status of basic topography – wandering rivers, seasonal marshes, and migratory dunes – must have significantly affected the population. We also know little about the essential features of the rural landscape: its inhabitants, their society and mode of life, their relation to the land, and the precariousness of urban authority in the countryside. We are ill informed about even the more prominent tribes among the Chaldaeans and Aramaeans, their social (or socio-political) structure, their economy, their internal development and change under pressure of Assyrian political power, much less their culture or their inter-relations with the older Babylonian population. Much remains to be investigated about the urban population: their cultural and economic status, their living conditions, their lack of involvement in politics, their gradual reorientation from small family units to larger kin-based groups that would gain them more effective recognition in a world dominated by tribes and Assyrians. We should also take into consideration local history and urban particularism, exemplified in such features as the Babylon–Uruk rivalry. In addition, Babylonia itself should be scrutinized as a national state; it does not seem to have been a 'well-defined territorial polity' and it seems to have lacked internal cohesion for much of the period under consideration. One may at least begin to look forward to holistic historical treatment for both Babylonia and the Assyrian empire, a treatment that will integrate intellectual and cultural history into the political, social, and economic dimensions of the presently available presentations. It is plain that much work remains to be done on many levels and on topics other than those adumbrated here.

Finally, the role of Assyria as catalyst in the eighth- and seventh-century transformation of Babylonia should not be underestimated. Anti-Assyrianism provided a rallying cry for the heterogeneous Babylonian populations and stimulated political unity. Assyrian governance in Babylonia eventually strengthened the local monarchy and, especially after 689, created a climate for economic prosperity. But in its Babylonian involvement, the Assyrian empire revealed its own weaknesses and especially the ineffectiveness of its methods for controlling territories that it had won by aggression. The political drama in seventh-century Babylonia highlighted Assyrian inability to effect long-term consolidation of political gains and demonstrated why massive military expenditure would not suffice to keep the empire intact. Despite geographical proximity and strong cultural ties, Assyria with all its armed might could not achieve lasting political control over Babylonia.

The history of these decades illustrates the rise of Babylonia to the threshold of its greatest political successes and the paradoxical role of Assyria in facilitating that rise.

CHAPTER 22

ASSYRIA: TIGLATH-PILESER III TO SARGON II

(744–705 B.C.)

A. K. GRAYSON

The rebirth of the Assyrian empire after the dark days of 'the Interval' is the main theme during the period covered by this chapter. Tiglath-pileser III devoted his entire career to fighting on foreign campaigns and, after a brief interlude under Shalmaneser V, Tiglath-pileser's mantle fell upon Sargon II, who not only continued the extensive offensive but also began to find time for non-military matters. By the end of the era with which this chapter is concerned the Assyrian empire had become the largest political power the world had ever seen, and the conquest of Egypt was a tantalizing possibility.

I. TIGLATH-PILESER III (744–727 B.C.)

The eclipse of Assyria during the Interval came to an end with the accession of Tiglath-pileser III, who achieved his goal of restoring Assyrian fortunes by a series of campaigns of exceptional intensity; the west was reconquered, Urartu was intimidated, and the Babylonian crown was placed on the Assyrian king's head.[1] Sources for the reign are more numerous than for the preceding decades and consist of royal inscriptions,[2] chronographic texts,[3] letters,[4] legal and administrative documents,[5] and sculptured reliefs found at Calah (below, pp. 83–4). The annals of Tiglath-pileser are in a very bad state of preservation and there are many problems and gaps in our knowledge, although a study being prepared by Tadmor is making great strides forward with this material. A curious feature of the chronology is that Tiglath-pileser's annalists numbered the years of his reign (*palû*) according to his campaigns, and

---

[1] For a detailed although dated history of the reign see A 156.

[2] For the moment cf. A 212. The royal inscriptions of Tiglath-pileser III are being edited by H. Tadmor and I wish to thank Professor Tadmor for allowing me to read a preliminary manuscript of his work while writing this chapter. Unfortunately, until his corpus is published one must use the unsatisfactory work by P. Rost, A 204. In this chapter, reference to Tiglath-pileser III's royal inscriptions will normally be made to the translations in A 35. Further bibliography will be found in A 25, 248, to which add A 116, A 179, A 183, and A 199; see also A 5 under relevant authors.

[3] For all references see A 25, 248f. Also note the Eponym Chronicles Cᵇ 1 and Cᵇ 3 (A 763, 430–2).

[4] See A 72–88. [5] See A 89–109.

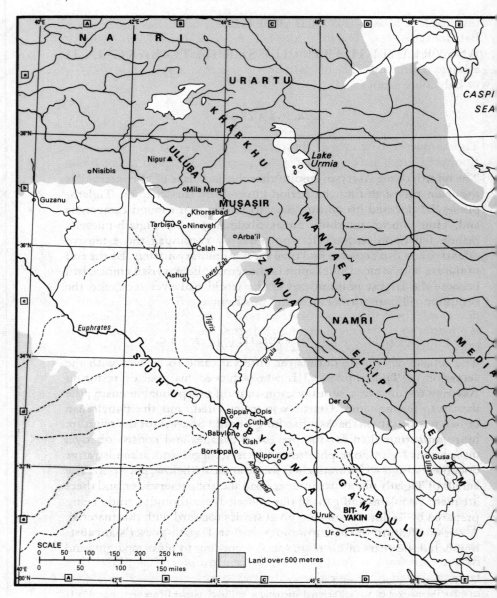

Map 2. Assyria and its neighbours.

thus the first *palû* is actually his accession year, since he campaigned in Babylonia that year. Tiglath-pileser bore a second name, Pulu (Pul in the Bible), which may have been a hypocorism derived from the second element of his name. The old assumption that Pulu was his name as king of Babylonia is not valid.[6]

1. *The accession*

Tiglath-pileser III came to the throne as a result of revolution: the Eponym Chronicle for 746 states that there was rebellion in Calah and two months later (11/745) Tiglath-pileser became king.[7] No details are available regarding these events, but it is of interest that there is some doubt about the king's origins. Most significant is the fact that there are two conflicting witnesses as to his parentage. On an inscribed brick from Ashur, Tiglath-pileser records that he is the 'son of Adad-nirari, king of Assyria', and this can only be Adad-nirari III.[8] The other witness is one exemplar, the latest in date, of the Assyrian king list in which Tiglath-pileser III appears and is said to be the 'son of Ashur-nirari', clearly the fifth king of this name who was Tiglath-pileser III's immediate predecessor.[9] There are two possible solutions to the contradiction: either it is a matter of scribal error, or it is deliberate misrepresentation. If it is only scribal error, then almost certainly the Assyrian king list is at fault, for it is unlikely that one of Tiglath-pileser's own scribes would be so careless. Assuming so much, Tiglath-pileser III would be the son of Adad-nirari III and a brother of Ashur-nirari V, his immediate predecessor. This is chronologically feasible; if Tiglath-pileser had been born towards the end of Adad-nirari III's reign, he would have been in his early forties when he ascended the throne and about sixty when he died. It is not necessary to postulate that 'son of' means 'grandson of' or even 'descendant of' in this case. The assumed error in the Assyrian king list involves only one cuneiform sign (either 'son' instead of the correct 'brother', or 'Ashur' instead of the correct 'Adad').

Scribal error does not, however, fully explain some other phenomena. Thus one must consider the alternative solution, deliberate misrepresentation. It is a curious fact that there is not a single royal inscription, apart from the brick quoted earlier, in which the name of Tiglath-pileser III's father is given. One questions why this brick inscription should be unique and whether its testimony is valid. Moreover, if the royal inscriptions were totally silent as to Tiglath-pileser's parentage, this would be suspicious enough, but the fact is alluded to in an unusual way. The epithet 'offspring of Baltil' (an ancient quarter of the city Ashur) first

---

[6] See A 535, 61f.   [7] Cᵇ 1 (A 763, 430).   [8] A 35 I, 822, 1.
[9] Assyrian King List iv, 24f. (A 607, §3 King List 9, §76).

appears in the royal epithets of Tiglath-pileser III, and one wonders why Tiglath-pileser makes such an amorphous claim to ancient Assyrian lineage rather than a specific statement of his parentage.[10] The evidence of the Assyrian king list can also be called in question. This document portrays the descent of Assyrian sovereignty within a single dynastic line and rarely recognizes, particularly in the later period, any disruption in this line. While one cannot prove that such a portrayal is false at any point, it remains dubious. In sum, there is good reason to question whether Tiglath-pileser was in the direct royal line, and there is reason to believe that he was a usurper who took advantage of the chaotic times to stage a *coup d'état* and win the Assyrian crown for himself.

2. *The war with Urartu*

The major foreign power with which Tiglath-pileser III had to contend was the kingdom of Urartu, which, during the years preceding this reign, had grown at Assyria's expense to be the greatest state in south-west Asia. Tiglath-pileser's reassertion of Assyrian imperialism meant direct confrontation with the young kingdom. The conflict took place both in the north and in the west, for Urartu had expanded westward into the Taurus range and the region of the upper Euphrates. Tiglath-pileser regarded the kingdoms and peoples in these areas as belonging to the Assyrian empire, although they, through lack of Assyrian presence, had long since changed their political ties. Arpad (Bit-Agusi), once a vassal state of Adad-nirari III and a treaty partner with Ashur-nirari V, was independent; Gurgum, once friendly to Assyria or at least to the Assyrian king's representative, Shamash-ili, was now anti-Assyrian; Kummukhu had recently become a vassal state of Urartu, but it is uncertain if Carchemish suffered the same fate;[11] and even the various peoples along the middle Euphrates were lost to the central monarchy. There is no information about how Tiglath-pileser regained control over the middle Euphrates, but one may assume that he was unopposed in his march through this region, and that the inhabitants more or less automatically resumed their dependent status.

The first resistance, according to the extant sources, was led by Arpad. Mati'el of Arpad had organized an anti-Assyrian alliance consisting of himself, Sarduri III of Urartu, Sulumal of Melid, Tarkhulara of Gurgum, and Kushtashpi of Kummukhu. It was this formidable coalition which Tiglath-pileser III faced when he invaded the area in 743.[12] The

[10] See A 51, 225; A 183, 16 i 23; cf. A 417, 27.

[11] See A 210, 240 and the bibliography there. Also cf. A 177, 72f (Carchemish) and 80 (Kummukhu); *CAH* III².1, 406f.

[12] C^b 1 (A 763, 430, and cf. A 210, 252–4); A 35 1, §§769, 785, 797, 813, 821; A 116, xx–xxiv and pls. XLV–LV, LVIII–LIX, LXIV–LXVII. Cf. A 210, 239–58, A 177 and *CAH* III².1, 410; A 157.

major battle was fought with the Urartian army, led personally by
Sarduri, in Kummukhu. Assyria won the day and the Urartian king fled
the battlefield. Tiglath-pileser proceeded to Gurgum, subdued it,
accepted the tribute of Tarkhulara, and made him an Assyrian vassal.
Despite this initial success, Arpad itself remained a staunch centre of
resistance, and for the next three years (742–740) Tiglath-pileser continued his offensive against it until its fall in or about 740, when the area
became an Assyrian province.[13] Thus Urartu's hold on the west was
considerably weakened early in the reign, and Tiglath-pileser could
temporarily turn his attention to another border with that kingdom, to
the north.

Assyria was even more vulnerable on the northern frontier, for
Urartian influence had crept south into a region called Ulluba on the very
edge of the Assyrian heartland.[14] Ulluba, which ancient geographers
regarded as part of Khabkhu, was approximately 100 km north of
Nineveh and was divided from Assyria by a range of mountains called
Mount Nal. The modern location of the area is provided by an inscribed
rock relief found at Mila Mergi, in which Tiglath-pileser records his
campaign against Ulluba in 739. This campaign was prompted by an
intended invasion of Assyria by the Ullubaeans and their allies, and one
suspects that Urartu had a hand in this in an attempt to relieve pressure
on the western front. Tiglath-pileser successfully conquered Ulluba and
organized it into an Assyrian province. A year later (738) he transported
people to the district from Tushkha. The area was still not secure,
however, for three years later (736) Tiglath-pileser, according to the
Eponym Chronicle, once again marched to Mount Nal. There is nothing
preserved in the fragmentary annals regarding this campaign, but the
building of a provincial capital called Ashur-iqisha, described in display
texts, may date to this later occasion. With the conquest and annexation
of Ulluba, Tiglath-pileser had not only secured this part of his northern
frontier but also gained an excellent bridgehead for the invasion of
Urartu in 735. Before describing this daring deed, however, it is
necessary to recount activities that had been taking place in the west
since the fall of Arpad in 740.

A new anti-Assyrian coalition appeared on the scene while Tiglath-
pileser was occupied with Ulluba. The alliance was led by a man called
Azriyau (not to be confused with Azariah, king of Judah).[15] The
coalition included a number of north Syrian coastal cities and part of the
kingdom of Hamath. As is so often the case with Tiglath-pileser, the

[13] C^b I (A 763, 430); the relevant portion of the annals is not preserved. Regarding the question of
741 or 740 as the date of the fall, see most recently A 208, which argues for 741.

[14] C^b I (A 763, 431); A 199; A 35 I, §§770, 785, 796, 814.

[15] A 210. But see now A 23, 111 n. 1; A 187, 228–39; A 274; J. D. Hawkins, 'Izrijau', in A 16, 5, 227.

fragmentary sources provide no details about how Assyria defeated these armies and occupied their lands, but this was done in 738.[16] It is significant that a number of important kingdoms were not involved in the alliance, and as soon as Tiglath-pileser had achieved his victory the non-belligerent states that paid tribute included Carchemish, Melid, Kummukhu, Gurgum, Tabal, Tuna, Sam'al, Kaska, and Que. On the same occasion tribute was received from southern regions such as Damascus, part of Hamath, Byblos, Tyre, and Samaria. Perhaps Kullani (also known as Kinalua, Unqi, or Patinu) was a member of Azriyau's league; for on the same campaign this state was taken and made a province.[17] It was also in this year that Tushkha was recaptured and, as mentioned earlier, people of Tushkha were transported to Ulluba. This was part of a massive resettlement project by which Tiglath-pileser hoped to bring peace and security to his western and northern frontiers with Urartu. Groups of people were shunted back and forth, and Assyrian contingents carried out raids in Babylonia to capture Aramaeans, who were removed to the newly formed provinces in Syria.

By 735 Tiglath-pileser felt that his military victories and provincial organization had sufficiently prepared the ground for a direct attack on Urartu.[18] Information about this campaign is scarce and disjointed because of the mutilated state of the annals, so that unfortunately very little is known about one of the most significant accomplishments of the reign. The Assyrians marched right through Urartu and laid siege to its capital, Turushpa (Tushpa, modern Van). The city did not fall, but Tiglath-pileser boasts that he defeated Sarduri at the city gate and erected a stela to commemorate the victory. That an Assyrian king could strike such a blow against Urartu only a decade after the period of Assyria's eclipse is remarkable. Clearly Tiglath-pileser had planned and acted with consummate skill. The campaign included the acquisition of more northern territories, and these were added to various provinces, such as those of Ashur-iqisha (Ulluba) and Nairi. This bold thrust into Urartu brought to an end Tiglath-pileser's war with Urartu, and in subsequent years the Assyrians concentrated on other areas. As for the kingdoms in the Taurus range, there is record of one further disturbance; at some unknown date Wassurme (Uassurme) of Tabal was deposed by Tiglath-pileser and replaced by Khulli.[19] Thus Tiglath-pileser III's war with

---

[16] C^b 1 (A 763, 431); A 35 1, §§770–2, 801; A 183, 18 ii 1–23; II Ki. 15: 19f. See A 177, 81–3; A 210, 266–71; A 225; A 274; *CAH* III².1, 59–64; and cf. A 208 and A 182.

[17] See J. D. Hawkins, 'Izrijau', in A 16, 5, 227. Cf. A 116, xxivf and plates. On the identification of Unqi, Patinu and Kinalua/Kullani as referring to the same place, see A 177, 81f and A 274, 37 n. 51. Cf. A 182.

[18] C^b 1 (A 763, 431); A 35 1, §§775, 785, 813, 814. Cf. A 82, 187–90 and 208f.

[19] A 35 1, §802; cf. *CAH* III².1, 415.

Urartu gained advances on both the northern and western fronts and paved the way for Sargon's invasion.

3. Southern Syria, Palestine, Egypt, and the Arabs

The war with Urartu having been brought to a successful conclusion, Tiglath-pileser was free to pursue another ambition, the conquest of territory right up to the Egyptian border.[20] After the defeat of Azriyau in 738, the major southern kingdoms, Hamath, Damascus, Byblos, Tyre, and Samaria, had voluntarily paid tribute to Tiglath-pileser. In 734 Tiglath-pileser, believing he had firm control over key areas in Syria, Phoenicia, and Palestine, marched right through these lands and captured Gaza in the south.[21] The city was plundered, and an Assyrian divine image, together with a golden statue of Tiglath-pileser, was erected. The ruler of Gaza, Khanunu (Hanno in Greek), abandoned his city in the face of the Assyrian onslaught to take refuge in Egypt, but eventually he came back, presumably after some negotiation, and was allowed to resume his seat as an Assyrian vassal. Tiglath-pileser says that he created an Assyrian trading-centre (*bīt kāri*), apparently at Gaza, and he also states that he erected his statue on the Egyptian border at Nakhal Muṣri ('Brook of Egypt').[22] Further attempts to establish an Assyrian presence on the border with Egypt were delayed, however, by a rebellion in Syria and Palestine. For the next two years (733–732) Assyria was embroiled in conflict with the insurgents; only towards the end of that interval could the original plan be resumed.

The chief rebel was Rakhianu (Rezin of the Bible) of Damascus, and he was supported by Tyre, Samaria, some Arabs, and probably others whose names are not preserved in the fragmentary sources;[23] all of these had paid tribute in 738. In 733 Tiglath-pileser defeated the army of Rakhianu, who fled from the battlefield and slipped inside the gate of Damascus. The Assyrians laid siege to the city for forty-five days, but Damascus did not fall and the frustrated besiegers, as in the time of Shalmaneser III, vented their wrath by cutting down the surrounding orchards. The ancestral home of Rakhianu, Bit-Khadara, was taken and people were transported from various parts of the kingdom. In 732 the Assyrian army was back in Damascus and, although the annals are

---

[20] In addition to the sources quoted throughout this section note the letters published in A 80 and A 84, 70, 79f, no. LXX. Also cf. A 165 and A 193.

[21] Cᵇ 1 (A 763, 431); A 35 1, §§801, 815. Cf. A 155, 24–7. On Tiglath-pileser III's relations with Judah see A 214.

[22] On Tiglath-pileser III's relations with Egypt see A 171 and A 188. Nakhal Muṣri has generally been identified as modern Wadi el-Arish but A 188, 74–80 proposes Nakhal Besor farther north.

[23] Cᵇ 1 (A 763, 431); A 35 1, §777; II Ki. 15: 37–16: 10; Isaiah 7.

missing for this year, it was doubtless on this campaign that the city fell. The kingdom of Damascus (Bit-Hazael) was made an Assyrian province, the territory of which stretched from the Lebanon in the north to Gilead in the south.[24]

Other events recorded in display texts must have occurred in 733–732 in connexion with the Assyrian suppression of Damascus, and among these the attack on Hiram of Tyre should be included. Tiglath-pileser did not take Tyre itself, but he did capture one of its fortified cities, forcing Hiram to submit and pay tribute.[25] The Assyrians also attacked Pekah, king of Israel, for he had been in league with Rakhianu against Assyria, and Pekah was defeated. Subsequently he was killed, possibly by a conspiracy led by Hoshea, who replaced him but now became an Assyrian vassal.[26] No account of other military action in Palestine and Syria during this time is preserved, but there is a list (of uncertain date) of rulers who paid tribute: Matan-bi'il of Arvad, Sanipu of Ammon, Salamanu of Moab, Metinti of Ashkelon, Jehoahaz of Judah, Qaush-malaku of Edom, and Khanunu of Gaza are the names preserved. At some later date a rather large payment, according to a display text, was received from Metenna of Tyre.[27]

As a result of the suppression of the revolt and the added vassalship of several other states, Tiglath-pileser was able some time in 732 to return to his original purpose, which was to gain control over the Sinai, the road to Egypt. He appointed an Arab sheikh called Idi-bi'il as his representative in the area and installed him in a newly formed office with the appropriate title 'Gatekeeper on the border of Egypt'.[28] It was probably about this time that tribute was received from the Meunites, a people whose land is said to have been 'below Egypt', which possibly means south of Nakhal Muṣri.[29]

A clash with Arab tribes is recorded for this time, and it is appropriate to complete this aspect of Tiglath-pileser's campaigns with an account of his relations with the Arabs. In a recent study of the ancient Arabs, Eph ʿal has pointed out that the Assyrians and Babylonians in the first millennium relied upon the Arab nomads to maintain important trade routes across the northern Arabian peninsula and to provide auxiliary forces on the borders of the empire.[30] This arrangement lies behind the reference in Assyrian records to the Arabs paying 'tribute' to Assyria. In 738 after the defeat of Azriyau, Tiglath-pileser counted among the many

[24] See A 116, xxiv and pl. LXIX; A 155, 119–24; A 211.

[25] See A 163. Cf. A 84, 70 and 76–8, no. LXIX; A 116, xxivf and pl. LVII.

[26] II Ki. 15: 29–31, 37; 16: 5.

[27] A 35 I, §801. Regarding A 80, 134f and 152f, no. XVI, see A 11, 118, which dates the letter to the reign of Sargon II (see below, n. 77). For Metenna see A 35 I, §803. Cf. A 163, 98.

[28] A 35 I, §§778–9, 800, 818–19.

[29] Information courtesy of Tadmor, and see now the reference in A 19, 91.   [30] A 19.

states which paid tribute that of Zabibe, queen of the Arabs.[31] In 733 the Assyrian fought with Samsi, another queen of the Arabs, who, he said, had broken her oath.[32] Thus it seems that Samsi had joined Rakhianu of Damascus against Assyria. Her Arabs were defeated and she fled the scene of battle. However, at a later date she travelled to Assyria bearing tribute, and Tiglath-pileser allowed her to resume her leadership, although with Assyrian officials at her side. It was doubtless during the same general period, 734–732, that Tiglath-pileser received 'tribute' from a variety of Arab tribes, such as Tema and Saba, from north Arabia and the Sinai.[33]

4. Namri and Media

The eastern frontier was not a top priority in the foreign policy of Tiglath-pileser III, but he did conduct two major military expeditions in the area, one early in his reign (744) and the other in 737, the year after he had driven the Urartians out of Syria and Anatolia.[34] On these campaigns he concentrated upon the Zagros in the region along and between the upper Diyala and Ulaya (modern Karun) rivers, and this brought him into direct contact with the Medes. The Mannaeans, who occupied the mountains a little to the north near Lake Urmia, are mentioned only briefly in the campaign narratives, and Urartu, which would play the leading role on this frontier in Sargon II's reign, is not referred to at all. The inhabitants fiercely resisted Tiglath-pileser III's invasion, for they had been free of Assyrian intervention since the days of Shalmaneser III and Shamshi-Adad V. Virtually the same tale is told of each people conquered: they either stood their ground and were overwhelmed and plundered, or they fled and were pursued and caught with the same terrible results. Rarely did anyone submit to the Assyrians without a fight. As a sufficiently large and cohesive area was captured it was organized into a province with a governor.

On the first campaign (744) Tiglath-pileser marched to Namri and adjacent regions of the Diyala valley.[35] Among the many states conquered were Bit-Zatti and Bit-Abdadani; the city of Nikur was designated provincial capital and captives from other areas resettled there. Bit-Kapsi and neighbouring regions were overrun and put under the authority of the king of Bit-Kapsi, Batanu, as an Assyrian vassal. Bit-Khamban and Parsua were taken and formed into Assyrian provinces. The terror spread by the Assyrian assault stretched as far as Ellipi, along

---

[31] A 35 I, §772; A 183, 18 ii 19–23. Cf. A 19, 83.
[32] A 35 I, §§778, 817; A 116, xviif and pls. XIII–XXX. Cf. A 19, 83–7.
[33] A 35 I, §§799, 818. Cf. A 19, 87–92.
[34] On the historical geography of the region in this reign see A 33.
[35] Cᵇ 1 (A 763, 430); A 35 I, §§766–8, 795, 807; A 183, 18–21 ii 24–36.

the Ulaya river, and its ruler, Dalta, sent his tribute to Tiglath-pileser in token of his submission. On the return march to Assyria a Mannaean ruler, Iranzu, came in person to Tiglath-pileser bearing tribute and submitting to vassalship.

The Assyrians came back to this frontier in 737 and penetrated Median territory.[36] Suzerainty was reasserted over states previously taken, such as Bit-Kapsi, and the army proceeded into Media as far as Zakruti, Mount Bikni (modern Alwand?), and a salt desert called Ushqaqqana. The Assyrians also pushed south east to conquer territory up to the Elamite border and in the east Tigris area. Among the cities captured were Tupliash and Bit-Ishtar, and at the latter place Tiglath-pileser erected an inscribed iron 'arrow' by a spring to commemorate his victory. Other cities seized included Sibur, Til-Ashur, Bit-Sagbat, and Silkhazi. The last three were fortresses of the Babylonians, according to Tiglath-pileser, and it is known from Sargon's inscriptions that Bit-Sagbat was on the Elamite border. A fragmentary stela of Tiglath-pileser III, said to have been found in western Iran, was almost certainly erected on the occasion of this campaign.[37]

Given the fragmentary state of the sources for these two campaigns and the lack of knowledge about the precise location of the geographic names listed, it is impossible to give more than a general assessment of the extent of Tiglath-pileser III's conquests. It is clear that he gained direct control over Namri, Bit-Khamban and Parsua, for these states were still in Assyrian hands in the reign of Sargon II. In addition, Dalta of Ellipi and Iranzu of Mannaea had become Assyrian vassals and they later played an important role in Sargon's campaigns. Thus Tiglath-pileser had established a major bridgehead in Media and Mannaea, which would provide an excellent base for Sargon II's offensive against the eastern frontier of Urartu. Furthermore, he had secured his border with Elam and captured from Babylonia territory in the east Tigris region.

5. Babylonia

The fortunes of Assyria depended upon her relations with Babylonia, and Assyrian monarchs, fully conscious of this axiom, tried various policies in an effort to achieve a secure southern border. Tiglath-pileser III was no exception to this rule, and a great deal of his time and energy was absorbed by Babylonian affairs.[38] It will be recalled that Adad-nirari III claimed to have the upper hand over Babylonia through a treaty

[36] C^b 1 (A 763, 431); A 35 1, §§784, 787, 795, 811–12. Also note A 116, xixf and pls. XXXV–XLIV and cf. A 173.
[37] A 183, 16–21.
[38] On Tiglath-pileser III's relations with Babylonia see A 535, 228–43.

arrangement; but in 'the Interval' Babylonia had turned the tables and through a series of attacks had gradually encroached upon Assyrian territory. This state of affairs was totally unacceptable to Tiglath-pileser, and a bare five months after he ascended the throne (11/745) he launched a campaign against Babylonia (VII/745).[39] The territory invaded was that traditionally disputed between the two powers, the extreme north of Babylonia and the east Tigris area. In the latter region a number of places were taken as the Assyrian invasion pushed east and south as far as the Ulaya river and the Persian Gulf. This advance brought under Assyrian control numerous cities over which the Babylonians had hegemony, and Aramaean tribes, which were transported to various areas. The conquered domains were divided up and apportioned to neighbouring provinces in the Zagros, such as (Ma)zamua. A new city called Kar-Ashur was built, a canal dredged to provide irrigation, and people settled there.

Concerning the activities of the Assyrians between the Tigris and Euphrates on this campaign, there is a problem: it is uncertain which Babylonian cities were conquered by Tiglath-pileser on his first campaign and which on his later campaigns. In the display texts the place names are all listed together and the annals, which could solve the problem, are badly broken in the relevant sections. There is no doubt that he captured important centres in the extreme north, such as Dur-Kurigalzu and a suburb of Sippar called Sippar of Shamash, but how far beyond this did Tiglath-pileser go?[40] The generally accepted view is that he achieved little between the two rivers beyond the conquests in the extreme north just named. In the annals for 745 he boasts of capturing a suburb of Nippur, Qin-Nippur, but none of the major cities south of Dur-Kurigalzu is mentioned in the preserved narrative, and it seems as though he merely made a quick raid into the heart of Babylonia.

The purpose of this raid is of special interest. There is reason to believe that it was intended to make secure the position of the Babylonian king, Nabonassar, in fulfilment of a treaty obligation. There is no explicit reference to such a treaty, but it is a reasonable assumption given the circumstantial evidence. Such treaties existed between Babylonia and Assyria during the previous century, and on one occasion Shalmaneser III was called upon to invade Babylonia and restore the kingdom to its legitimate monarch, Marduk-zakir-shumi I (*CAH* III².1, 270). The situation in 745 may have been quite similar. This would explain the total lack of reference to any confrontation between Tiglath-pileser and the Babylonian king, Nabonassar, and the fact that Nabonassar remained on the throne after the Assyrians withdrew. Thus one might assume that Tiglath-pileser invaded Babylonia to support Nabonassar against Chaldaean and Aramaean tribes, the latter possibly allied to Aramaeans in Syria, in accordance with a pact concluded between the two leaders either just after Tiglath-pileser seized the throne or possibly even earlier when he was plotting his *coup d'état*.

Many years later, in 731, Tiglath-pileser once again intervened in Babylonia for this very reason. When Nabonassar died (734) the reign of his son was cut short by a revolution which led ultimately to a successful attempt by a Chaldaean, Mukin-zeri, to capture the throne in 732. Tiglath-pileser would not allow a hostile group to control Babylonia and in 731 he marched south. The suppression of the rebellion required two campaigns, the first in 731 and the second in 729, and during the intervening year Tiglath-pileser did not conduct a military expedition anywhere.[41] The sources for these events fortunately include a number of letters found at Calah, which provide numerous and occasionally dramatic details.[42] Tiglath-pileser adopted the strategy of attempting to alienate the native Babylonians from the Chaldaean rebels by rhetoric and offers of favours. An intriguing letter reports to the king how two Assyrian officials stood under the walls of Babylon haranguing the citizens, exhorting them to expel the Chaldaeans and open the gates to the Assyrians.

It is unknown how effective the strategy was, but eventually the Assyrians had to use force. They captured one Babylonian city after another and laid siege to Shapiya, Mukin-zeri's capital. In the course of the war a number of Aramaean tribes were subdued. The crowning achievement came in 729 when Tiglath-pileser III triumphantly entered Babylon, where he was crowned king of Babylon. By assuming the sovereignty of Babylonia himself the Assyrian king began a new phase of Assyria's Babylonian policy and, in the short term, it was successful, for Tiglath-pileser was recognized by the Babylonians as their legitimate king and his successor, Shalmaneser V, won the same recognition. But, with the accession of Sargon II, Assyria's right to rule Babylonia was challenged by another Chaldaean, Merodach-baladan. Merodach-baladan became a serious threat to Assyria's control over Babylonia in the reigns of Sargon II and Sennacherib, and it is interesting to note, by way of conclusion to this treatment of Tiglath-pileser's relations with Babylonia, that Merodach-baladan had submitted to the Assyrian monarch on his campaign of 729.[43]

---

[41] Cᵇ 1 (A 763, 431); Cᵇ 3 (A 763, 432); A 25, no. 1 i 19–23; A 35 1, §§792–4, 806. Also note A 15, no. 233.

[42] A 79; A 84, 70–3, no. LXV.   [43] Cf. A 532, 7–12.

Tiglath-pileser III ranks as one of the most industrious Assyrian kings for, with the exception of one year (730), he campaigned every year that he was on the throne, including both his accession year and the year of his death. Unfortunately it is not known where he campaigned in his last two regnal years, 728 and 727, since the Eponym Chronicles are broken and there are no royal inscriptions for these last days.[44] Much of Tiglath-pileser's success is to be ascribed to this assiduity, but there were other factors as well. The organization and manoeuvring of the army were considerably improved in his reign, and weapons and military equipment also underwent substantial changes for the better. The provincial system of administration which was born in the ninth century now became more rigorous, with the inevitable result that the empire was not only more efficiently and profitably managed but also was more secure from foreign invasion. Of particular note is the policy of massive transportation of peoples which began in Tiglath-pileser's reign. Before his time groups of people had been transported, but mainly to Assyria to work on the land and on building projects. Tiglath-pileser, on the other hand, systematically exchanged population groups, in order to forestall future attempts at rebellion in the regions involved. Another innovation which may be ascribed to him is the practice of putting the crown prince in charge of the administration of the empire while the reigning monarch was on campaign. It seems that Shalmaneser, while crown prince, was assigned this task, and the custom was commonly followed in subsequent reigns.

6. Building

Given the fact that Tiglath-pileser's main concern was the resurrection of the Assyrian empire, and that this entailed his being on campaign for almost the entire length of his reign, it is little wonder that he can be credited with very few building projects. The main monument which he left was a new palace at Calah; its first excavator, Layard, called this the Central Palace.[45] The structure was raised on a platform of limestone blocks, which rested in the water at the edge of the Tigris. A variety of imported woods was employed in the palace, and it was decorated with various objects of precious metals. There was a pillared portico, called a *bīt-hilāni*, in the Syrian fashion, and the entrances were flanked by lion and bull colossi. Huge stone slabs, upon which Tiglath-pileser's victor-

---

[44] C^b 1 (A 763, 431); C^b 3 (A 763, 432).
[45] A 35 1, §804; A 116; A 150, 314f, §§20–1; A 155, 302–8; A 200, 307f; A 201.

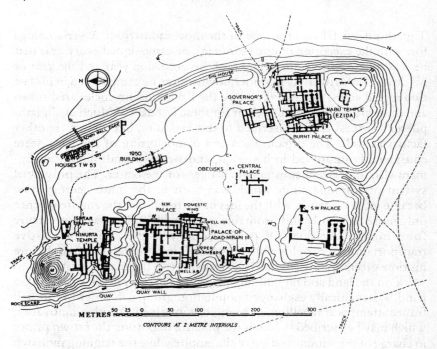

Fig. 3. Plan of Calah (Nimrud). (After A 137 I, 32, fig. 1.)

ies were depicted in sculptured relief and incised cuneiform, lined the palace walls and many of these were recovered by modern archaeologists (Pls. Vol., pl. 57). In these reliefs one sees the first attempt to portray a sequence of events in pictorial and written narrative, although the sad state of preservation of the stones makes it difficult to reconstruct many of the sequences. The reason for the poor condition of the objects is that Tiglath-pileser's palace was looted in antiquity by Esarhaddon in order to build his own residence, the South-West Palace at Calah. Esarhaddon never finished his work, with the result that modern excavators found reliefs of Tiglath-pileser III at both sites, many of them lying flat and stacked in piles. There is evidence also of Tiglath-pileser's interest in the Nabu temple in Calah.[46] At Ashur there is a record of work on the Ashur temple and on the Adad temple.[47] Otherwise it is only known that Tiglath-pileser built a palace at Ashur-iqisha (above p. 75) and did some construction at Khadatu (Arslan Tash) near Carchemish.[48]

[46] Cf. A 137 I, 237–9.

[47] A 35 I, §822.1. Tadmor kindly drew my attention to a brick from the Adad temple which he is editing.

[48] A 217, 61–3, 85–7; A 219. Cf. A 218 and A 435, 88f.

7. Conclusion

The reign was a brilliant beginning to a new and final era in the history of the Neo-Assyrian empire. Tiglath-pileser concentrated upon territorial aggrandizement and administrative reforms and did so with such success that his heirs, besides adding to these achievements, had opportunity to encourage their subjects in cultural pursuits, a matter for which there was little time to spare in the reign of Tiglath-pileser III.

II. SHALMANESER V (726–722 B.C.)

Shalmaneser V, also known by the nickname Ululaya, was on the throne for five years, but almost nothing is known of him and his time. There are no royal commemorative inscriptions, only a few royal labels on some weights and possibly a brick;[49] there is a brief statement in the Babylonian Chronicle;[50] and the relevant portion of the Eponym Chronicle is almost totally missing.[51] The absence of major royal inscriptions can be explained by the brevity of the reign; there was scarcely time to complete a major building project and prepare the accompanying commemorative inscriptions. But the scant reference to this king in the Babylonian Chronicle indicates that, apart from the siege of Samaria which it records, nothing of importance happened in this period.

Crown prince Shalmaneser may have been entrusted with the administration of Assyria and the empire, in order to free Tiglath-pileser III for campaigning. This was the role later assigned to Sennacherib by his father, Sargon II, as we know from Sennacherib's letters of the period addressed to his father. Letters with similar greeting formulae written to the king by a certain Ululayu may, as Brinkman has observed, be letters from Shalmaneser while crown prince to Tiglath-pileser.[52] In the correspondence he reports on various administrative matters and assures the monarch that all is well in the state. When Tiglath-pileser III died, the crown passed to Shalmaneser (25/x/726) without any opposition.

The most significant achievement of Shalmaneser was the conquest of Samaria. It is a sorely debated point among modern historians which king, Shalmaneser V or Sargon II, captured Samaria, but the evidence certainly is in favour of Shalmaneser V.[53] The exact date of the siege,

---

[49] Weights: A 221, 1–12, nos. 2–7, 11–12. Brick: unpublished, cf. Laessøe *apud* A 192, 73. A 35 1, §§828–30 is almost certainly an Esarhaddon text; see A 234, 32.

[50] A 25, no. 1 i 27–30. For further references in chronographic texts see A 25, 242b.

[51] Cᵇ 3 (A 763, 432).

[52] A 81, 47, no. XXXI; A 83, 159–63, nos. L, LI, LIII. Cf. A 535, 243 n. 1564.

[53] See A 209, 33–9.

which lasted from two to three years according to the Bible, is more difficult to determine.[54] The entry, 'He ravaged Samaria', appears in the Babylonian Chronicle under Shalmaneser V's accession year, but this cannot be the date of the fall; the chronicle was no doubt merely recording the most important event of the reign without intending a specific date.[55] Tadmor dates the fall of Samaria to 722.[56] After the capture of the city the inhabitants were transported, and this operation actually took place mainly during the reign of Sargon II.

In addition to a siege of Samaria, Josephus (*Antiquities* IX.xiv) credits Shalmaneser with a siege of Tyre, but no other source mentions this. One suspects that there has been confusion with a later king, possibly Esarhaddon or Ashurbanipal.[57] It is sometimes assumed that the Anatolian states Que and Sam'al became Assyrian provinces during the reign of Shalmaneser V, since they are under Assyrian control early in the reign of Sargon II; but our scant sources for the period are silent on how this came about (cf. *CAH* III². 1, 415-16).

Shalmaneser continued the Babylonian policy adopted by Tiglath-pileser III by ascending the Babylonian throne himself, and he was universally recognized by the Babylonians as their rightful monarch. It is commonly assumed that the other name by which Shalmaneser was known, Ululayu, was his official name as king of Babylonia, but the evidence is definitely against such an assumption and Brinkman has suggested that Ululayu was a nickname derived from the date of Shalmaneser's birth (presumably in the month of Ululu).[58] Chaldaean opposition to Assyrian rule in Babylonia continued in this reign and there is reference in an Aramaic document of a later date to Shalmaneser's transportation of people from Bit-Adini in southern Babylonia (not to be confused with the Syrian province of the same name).[59] There is a fragmentary Akkadian letter in which Shalmaneser may be mentioned in connexion with the special status (*kidinnūtu*) of Babylon.[60] If one can believe the testimony of Sargon, Shalmaneser incurred displeasure by imposing tax and corvée on the traditionally free cities, Ashur and Harran, and thus precipitated a revolution in which his throne was seized by Sargon.

III. SARGON II (721–705 B.C.)

Whether or not Sargon had a legitimate claim to the Assyrian throne, he was certainly a worthy successor to Tiglath-pileser III and emulated that sovereign through intensive campaigning, by which he not only

[54] II Ki. 18: 9–10.   [55] A 25, no. I i 27f.   [56] A 209, 37.
[57] Cf. A 535, 244f and n. 1569; A 203.   [58] A 535, 62 n. 320.
[59] A 15, no. 233: 15. Cf. A 535, 244 n. 1567.   [60] A 570, 68.

regained lost territory but also added new holdings to the empire.[61] Not content to be remembered only as a staunch soldier, Sargon created a new Assyrian city and named it Dur-Sharrukin ('Fort Sargon') after himself (Pls. Vol., pls. 48, 69). The reign is well documented, there being an abundance of royal inscriptions,[62] chronographic texts,[63] letters,[64] legal and administrative documents,[65] astrological reports,[66] and sculptured reliefs unearthed by modern excavators at Dur-Sharrukin (Pls. Vol., pl. 49, and see below pp. 100–1). The internal chronology of the period and in particular of the military campaigns is a difficult problem which has been treated in an excellent study by Tadmor.[67]

1. The accession

The accession of Sargon II to the throne is shrouded in mystery and there is good reason to wonder whether he was a usurper. He never mentions his father in all the preserved royal inscriptions, with the exception of a glazed plaque bearing a label in which he records that he is the son of Tiglath-pileser III.[68] A similar situation raised the same suspicion concerning Tiglath-pileser. If Sargon was Tiglath-pileser's son, why was he so reluctant to acknowledge such an illustrious parent? His name raises doubts too, for *Šarru-kēnu* means 'legitimate king'. Of further relevance is this king's creation of a new royal city, Dur-Sharrukin, where there had never been a city before. Why did he do this in preference to living in the old centre, Calah? One could provide plausible answers to each of these questions, and even analogies from other reigns of Assyrian monarchs, but there is room for reasonable doubt and this doubt is heightened by the circumstances surrounding his accession.

The evidence regarding Sargon's enthronement and its immediate aftermath is very meagre. The main source is a document commonly called the Ashur Charter, in which Sargon related that Shalmaneser V (the name is actually missing in a lacuna but clearly this is the king involved) wrongfully imposed corvée on the city of Ashur, with the result that the gods deposed him and appointed Sargon as legitimate king.[69] There are two important facts implicit in this view: Shalmaneser was deposed by a revolution, and Sargon was not the heir designate. Another important statement in the Ashur Charter is: 'Because they [the

---

[61] For a valuable, although dated, history of the reign see A 39.

[62] Unfortunately there is no up-to-date corpus of editions of Sargon's royal inscriptions. For a brief bibliography see A 25, 236f. In the discussion of the military campaigns the sources quoted do not include general geographic descriptions such as those found in the great Display Inscription.

[63] Babylonian King List A iv 11 (A 607, §3 King List 3); A 25 no. 1 i 31 – ii 6'; C[b] 4 and C[b] 6 (see A 209, 84–7).   [64] See A 72–88.

[65] See A 89–109. Also note A 676, no. 70.   [66] See A 1032 and A 1040.

[67] A 209. Also cf. A 169 and A 183, 28.   [68] A 220.   [69] A 206.

citizens of Ashur] . . . came to my help.' Although not explicitly stated, the help the city of Ashur provided was obviously support to Sargon in his bid for the throne. As a reward for this assistance Sargon abolished the illegal obligations imposed upon Ashur by his predecessor, thus restoring the city's privileged status. In his royal inscriptions Sargon boasts that he restored this special exempt status (*kidinnūtu*) to both Ashur and Harran, which indicates that the latter city also sided with Sargon in the revolution.[70] On the other hand those who opposed Sargon were punished after his accession, '6,300 Assyrian criminals' being transported to Hamath.[71] To this data one can add the observation that no foreign campaigns were conducted until Sargon's second regnal year, and it is apparent that he was embroiled in domestic strife securing his right to rule during the accession and first regnal years.[72]

Before drawing any conclusions it is relevant to note the obvious link of Sargon's name with that of Sargon of Akkad, one of the greatest of all ancient Mesopotamian kings. During the Sargonid period in Assyria there is evidence of a revival of interest in this older monarch, in that several literary texts (chronicles, omen collections, legends, epics, and a treatise on the geography of the empire) are attested, some for the first time.[73] Thus one is justified in believing that Sargon was not in the direct royal line, and that he gained the throne through violence, as did his predecessor, Tiglath-pileser III. Unlike Tiglath-pileser, however, he felt very insecure, perhaps because he was not of royal birth, and therefore adopted the unusual name by which he is known, and encouraged research into the mighty deeds of his namesake. Afraid of the old nobility in Calah, he founded a new city named after himself.

2. *The west: Syria, Palestine, Egypt, Arabia*

The confusion which attended the accession of Sargon II was the occasion for a major rebellion in Syria and Palestine. Damascus, Ṣimirra, Arpad, Samaria and perhaps Khatarikka were incited to rebellion by Yau-bi'di of Hamath. As soon as Sargon had secured his domestic position, and after an initial clash with Babylonia and Elam, he launched a campaign into Syria, where he met the allied rebel forces at Qarqar (720), scene of the famous battle fought by Shalmaneser III more than a century earlier.[74] Sargon won the day, and then proceeded south to

---

[70] A 35 II, §§54, 78, 92, 99, 102, 104, 107, 182; A 162, 86–9: 2.   [71] See *CAH* III².1, 417.

[72] Cf. A 209, 25b, 30f, and 37f.

[73] For the chronicles and omen collections see A 25, 43–9; for the King of Battle Epic see *ibid.* 57 n. 60; for the Birth Legend see A 26, 8 n. 11; for the geographical text see A 175. Cf. A 39, 27–9.

[74] Cᵇ 4 (A209, 94); A 35 II, §§55, 125; A 80, 137f and 153, no. XVIII; A 113; A 166, 9, 35–47 and 10, 26f; A 183, 34f r. 4–13 (cf. p. 46); A 185, 23–57; A 202, 99–104, Room 5; A 206 lines 16–28; A 216; a new stela (see O. Muscarella, *Ladders to Heaven* (Toronto, 1981) 125 no. 83). See A 209, 37–9.

reconquer Gaza and to defeat an Egyptian army at Raphia on the border of Egypt.[75] These major victories were followed by massive operations in which the rebel states were reoccupied and the offenders punished; large numbers of people were transported to Assyria and captured peoples from other regions settled in their place. Although the resettlement of people is specifically mentioned for only two cities, Samaria and Hamath, the operation was probably more widespread and no doubt required several years to complete.

Sargon's initial contact with Egypt at Raphia in 720 was followed a few years later (716) by the posting of an Assyrian garrison on the Egyptian border at Nakhal Muṣri, a point reached previously by Tiglath-pileser III.[76] The fortress was settled with transported peoples, who were put under the authority of a local Arab sheikh loyal to Assyria. The Egyptians, in face of Assyria's strong position, opted to seek friendly relations; the pharaoh Osorkon IV sent gifts to Sargon, and Assyrians and Egyptians mixed freely in exchanging trade goods. It was probably in this same year that Sargon received tribute from various Arabs, including Shamshi (Samsi), queen of the Arabs, who had also paid tribute to Tiglath-pileser III; and transported some Arabs to Samaria.

One other part of Palestine received special attention from Sargon and this was Philistia.[77] Ashdod had remained outside the Assyrian orbit until its king, Aziru, conspired, according to Sargon, with surrounding kings against Assyria. Sargon therefore deposed him and replaced him by his brother, Akhimetu (c. 713). But the Assyrian appointee was disliked by the people of Ashdod, who replaced him with Yamani. The moment news of this second rebellion at Ashdod reached Sargon, the Assyrian ordered his troops to Philistia (712). Yamani fled to Egypt, where he was eventually put in irons by the pharaoh and sent to Assyria as a gesture of goodwill. Ashdod, Gath and Asdudimmu were besieged and conquered, their populations transported and peoples from the east settled in their place. There is no further reference to troubles in Palestine during the reign, and it may be assumed that the vigorous campaigns and extensive pacification measures were successful. The major gains on this front were, then, the extension of Assyrian power in Philistia to embrace three more city states, Ashdod, Gath and Asdudimmu, and the intimidation of Egypt, by establishing a bridgehead at Nakhal Muṣri, resulting in friendly and profitable exchanges.

[75] See A 160; A 174.

[76] A 35 II, §55; A 185, 123–5; Nineveh Prism (see A 209, 95a). See A 19, 101–11; A 171, 42–8; A 188; A 209, 77f and see below, p. 692.

[77] A 35 II, §§62f, 79f; A 80, 134f, 152f, no. XVI and cf. A 11, 118; A 185, 249–62; A 224, 49f; Nineveh Prism (see A 209, 95b). See A 155, 27–41; A 180; A 181; A 209, 25, 79f, 83f, 92–4; A 213.

A word at this point on Sargon's relations with Cyprus is appropriate.[78] In the royal inscriptions it is recorded that seven kings of Ya', a district of Yadnana (Cyprus), sent precious gifts to Sargon. He in return sent them an inscribed stela to be erected in their land, and this very object was discovered in Cyprus in the middle of the nineteenth century. It may be that people as well as gifts came to Sargon from Cyprus, for men called Papu were present in Sargon's court, and one is inclined to identify them with the name of the Cypriot city, Paphus.[79] The Papu in Sargon's palace eventually caused some disturbance in league with peoples to the north of Assyria.[80]

3. The west: the upper Euphrates and Anatolia

Sargon's activity on the Anatolian frontier was essentially that of consolidation and fortification against two major powers, the Mushki (Phrygians) led by Mita (Midas) and the Urartians under Rusa I and later Argishti II. The campaigns of Tiglath-pileser III had established the Assyrian frontier in the Taurus range in dangerous proximity to the domain of Midas, who felt threatened. The war between Midas and Sargon resulted in some territorial gains for Assyria, but the most significant achievement was peace with Midas after bitter and prolonged animosity. Midas always avoided open conflict with Assyria, preferring like Urartu to form alliances with the various small states in the buffer zone of eastern Anatolia and to encourage them to rebel against Sargon. It is these states that bore the brunt of Assyria's hostility, for they became the battlefield.

Before describing these events a word about the historical geography is needed; for both the political and the geographical scene in this region are extremely confusing, not only because of the intrigues and changing alliances, but also because of uncertainty about the territory covered by a given place name.[81] By the beginning of Sargon's reign the frontier of Assyria in Anatolia stretched westwards to include a number of eastern Anatolian kingdoms: Que was ruled both by the local prince and by an Assyrian governor; Melid, Atuna (Tuna), and Tabal (a name which included several kingdoms) were still governed by indigenous kings who held allegiance to Assyria. On the map these states form a diagonal line running south west through the Taurus mountains from Melid on the upper Euphrates to Que on the Cilician coast. This frontier was fairly flexible when Sargon began to rule, but he would gradually strengthen it as Midas endeavoured to break it.

---

[78] A 35 II, §§70, 179–89; A 170, 191–4 vii 25–44; A 185, 457–67. See A 126, 214.
[79] See A 41, 369; A 344 III, 802; A 234, 60 v 66.   [80] A 185, 76–8.
[81] See *CAH* III².1, chapter 9. See also A 155, 190–5; A 198, 29–34.

The Phrygian first tried to weaken the centre by plotting with one of the kings of Tabal, Kiakki of Shinukhtu. Sargon launched a campaign against Kiakki in 718, defeated him, looted his city, and added it to the holdings of Kurti of Atuna.[82] Undeterred by this failure, Midas initiated intrigue even farther within Assyria, inciting Pisiri of Carchemish to rebel. This was an excellent excuse for Sargon to annex Carchemish, whose loyalty had always wavered, as a province: the Assyrians recaptured the city (717), carried off Pisiri with his family and other people to Assyria, and replaced him with an Assyrian governor.[83] So ended indigenous rule in Carchemish; eventually Assyrians were settled in the area. This first phase of Midas' anti-Assyrian strategy ended in 715, when Assyria took the offensive and recaptured some border towns of Que which the Phrygians had seized earlier.[84]

In subsequent years Urartu allied with the Phrygians against Assyria, and another king of Tabal, Ambaris of Bit-Burutash, was persuaded to join them. This defection particularly vexed Sargon, for when Khulli, father of Ambaris, had died the Assyrian had sanctioned Ambaris' accession to the throne and had even given him his own daughter in marriage, and suzerainty over Khilakku. In 713 Sargon despatched an army to seek vengeance and Ambaris, with his family and leading men, was taken prisoner.[85] It is at this point, Urartu having been effectively silenced on the north-eastern frontier by the campaign of 714, that the Assyrian king recognized the need to defend his Anatolian front more effectively. He constructed ramparts and fortifications in Bit-Burutash and Khilakku, settled there peoples transported from other regions, and installed his own governor, thus making the area a province.[86] It would appear that the loyalty of Kurti of Atuna, which was once a vassal state of Tiglath-pileser III, was in doubt during this period, but Kurti promptly ended suspicion by paying homage to Sargon when he heard of the fate of Ambaris.[87]

The scene now shifts to the northern extreme of the boundary, Melid on the upper Euphrates. At some earlier date the Assyrian had set a new king on the throne of Melid, Tarkhunazi by name, but this ruler together with Tarkhulara of Gurgum, a state which had paid tribute to Tiglath-pileser III, had been lured into the Phrygian camp. Sargon's punishment of the defectors seems to have stretched over two years, Melid in 712 and Gurgum in 711.[88] Melid was captured and when Tarkhunazi took refuge

---

[82] Cᵇ 4 (see A 209, 94b); A 35 II, §55; A 170, 179–82 iv 50–5; A 183, 36f r. 17–19; A 185, 68–71. For the reading 'Kurti' (rather than 'Matti') see *CAH* III².1, 418.

[83] Cᵇ 4 (see A 209, 94b); A 170, 179–81 iv 13–24; A 183, 36f r. 20–2; A 185, 72–6; A 209, 22f. See A 177, 72f and *CAH* III².1, 418.

[84] A 170, 182–4 v 34–40; A 185, 118–20, 125f.

[85] A 35 II, §55; A 170, 182–4 v 13–33; A 185, 194–204; Nineveh Prism (see A 209, 95).

[86] Cf. J. D. Hawkins, 'Hilakku', in A 16, 4, 402f.

[87] Nineveh Prism (see A 209, 95).   [88] Cf. A 177, 79; A 209, 92–4.

in another city, Til-Garimmu, its citizens opened their gates to the Assyrians; the luckless fugitive was transported with his family and followers to Assyria.[89] Gurgum was also taken, but there is some confusion in the sources as to whether Tarkhulara, its ruler, was murdered by his son, Mutallu, or transported by the Assyrians.[90] Following the practice recently adopted in Tabal, Sargon organized the area as a province with a governor and fortified it; defences were strengthened in old cities, new garrison towns constructed, and Sutian bowmen stationed inside. Melid was handed over to Mutallu of Kummukhu.

A dramatic turn of events occurred about 709, when Assyria once again went on the offensive against the Phrygians.[91] By this time the Cimmerian invasion of Anatolia may have begun, thus forcing Midas to seek an end to hostilities with Assyria.[92] In any event, the Assyrian governor of Que carried out border raids on provinces under Midas and was so successful that the Phrygian king sued for peace. He sent a message to Sargon by way of the Assyrian governor at Que, and the message was relayed to the king, who was in Babylonia at the time. Sargon was delighted and, in a letter recently discovered, instructed his governor to agree to peace.[93] He further directed him to return Phrygian captives to Midas as a gesture of goodwill, and to keep an Assyrian envoy at his court. Subsequently a formal Phrygian delegation travelled to Sargon in Babylonia, and peace was established between the two powers. This marks the close of hostilities between Assyria and the Phrygians but not of rebellions in eastern Anatolia.

Some of the kingdoms of Tabal were restless in this period, as is evident from statements in Sargon's letter to the governor of Que just mentioned, and Mutallu of Kummukhu, once a trusted vassal, now changed his allegiance to Argishti II, king of Urartu. Mutallu fled in the face of an Assyrian punitive campaign, but his city was captured in 708 and his family and people carried off.[94] They were eventually settled in southern Babylonia, in the area occupied by the tribe of Bit-Yakin, and people of Yakin, who had recently been subdued, were resettled in Kummukhu.[95] Kummukhu was now organized into an Assyrian province with a governor and militia. The last regnal year of Sargon, 705, saw one final expedition against troublesome Tabal. On this campaign Sargon was killed in action, but unfortunately no details of the event are

[89] C[b] 4 (see A 209, 96a); A 35 II, §§60f; A 170, 182–5 v 41–76; A 185, 204–49; Nineveh Prism (see A 209, 96a).   [90] A 170, 185; A 177, 75; *CAH* III².1, 420.

[91] A 35 II, §71; A 185, 444–54. Regarding the date cf. A 198, 33.

[92] See *CAH* III².1, 420f.   [93] A 198, 22–5; cf. A 172.

[94] C[b] 4 and C[b] 6 (see A 209, 96b); A 35 II, §64; A 170, 179–81 iv 1–12; A 177, 80; A 178; A 185, 70: 467–71: 12.

[95] In addition to the sources in n. 94 see: A 35 II, §69; A 185, 65: 13–16.

preserved.[96] His death was the signal for the rebellion of Tabal to be joined by Que, Khilakku and Melid (*CAH* III².I, 426).

4. *The north and north east* [97]

The kingdom of Urartu still sat atop Assyria with limbs stretched out west and east into Anatolia and Mannaea. Assyro-Urartian contacts occurred at these two extremities and were inevitably interrelated, the scene of major action shifting back and forth from west to east, while Sargon, with a network of informants on the Urartian border, was kept aware of events in the enemy capital, Tushpa.[98] Sargon's dealings with Urartu in Asia Minor have already been discussed, and it is now time to describe events on the eastern frontier.

When the reign began, Assyria claimed control over the western Mannaeans from the headwaters of the lower Zab (Uishdish and Zikirtu) across Namri, Lullumu (formerly Zamua), Karalla, and Allabria to the Diyala river. From there it was the Median sphere of influence, although Assyria held sway over Ellipi, Parsua, and Kharkhar in the upper reaches of the Ulaya river. But only three of these provinces, Lullumu, Parsua, and Namri, remained loyal during Sargon's early and difficult years, the Mannaeans being wooed to the Urartian side and the Median states denying allegiance and tribute to any outside power. In addition the Cimmerians were now on the scene; and while their primary impact was felt by the Urartians and Mannaeans, the Assyrians were justifiably concerned.[99] By means of campaigns concentrated in the years 719 to 713, Sargon retrieved the territory temporarily lost, added new domains to the empire, and dealt a crippling blow to Urartu.

The disaffection of the Mannaean states was high on Sargon's list of priorities, for as soon as he had looked to the more pressing problems on the western and southern fronts, he began in 719 to campaign to the north east.[100] His first objective was to relieve a faithful Mannaean vassal from the days of Tiglath-pileser III, Iranzu, who was being hard pressed by two neighbouring rulers. These rebels were being supplied with troops and cavalry by another Mannaean, Mitatti of Zikirtu, who had renounced allegiance to Assyria in favour of Urartu. The rebels were defeated, their cities captured, the fortifications torn down, and people and property carried off. Sargon continued the campaign to subdue the Sukkaeans, Balaeans, and Abitiknaeans, who had joined with Urartu against Assyria. These people were uprooted and transported to Syria.

---

[96] C^b 6 (see A 209, 97 and n. 311); A 25, no. I ii 6′ (cf. p. 238a).

[97] On the geography of this region during Sargon's campaigns see A 33; A 158; A 159. Regarding the reliefs relevant to these campaigns see A 155, 266–82.

[98] Cf. A 164; A 168.   [99] Cf. A 72, no. 112.   [100] A 183, 34f r. 13–16; A 185, 58–68.

The north-eastern offensive had barely begun, however, before Sargon was forced to return to the west to cope with the intrigues of Midas in Anatolia, and he could not resume the offensive until three years later, in 716.[101] By this time the Urartian conspiracy had grown and blossomed. The traitor Mitatti of Zikirtu had been joined by Bagdatti of Uishdish in rejecting Assyrian vassaldom, and the allied forces had fought and won a pitched battle with Mannaeans loyal to Assyria on Mount Uaush, slaying the defeated leader Aza. An Assyrian raid, concerning which there are no details, had managed to capture one of the insurgents, Bagdatti, and his flayed skin had been displayed on Mount Uaush, scene of his former victory. Aza had been succeeded by his brother, Ullusunu, who joined the alliance with Urartu and managed to persuade two other rulers, Ashur-le'u of Karalla and Itti of Allabria, to join him. This was the dangerous state of affairs in 716 when Sargon returned to this front.

In 716 Ullusunu was Sargon's first target. Izirtu, his capital, was captured and burnt and Ullusunu, according to Assyrian sources, begged for mercy. Sargon spared his life and re-established him on the throne as an Assyrian vassal. Ashur-le'u and Itti did not fare so well: both were taken in irons to Assyria and Karalla was added to the province of Lullumu, while Allabria was put under the authority of Bel-apla-iddina of Pattira. But the campaign had only started. Sargon now turned his face to the south east and conquered some cities which he added to the loyal province of Parsua. Another city, Kishesim, was captured, its ruler abducted and replaced by an Assyrian governor, the city renamed Kar-Nergal, and several captured regions added to it to form a province.

At this stage Sargon approached Kharkhar. Four years previously the people of Kharkhar had expelled their ruler, a faithful Assyrian vassal, and pledged allegiance to Dalta of Ellipi, who had, apparently, temporarily strayed from the Assyrian fold since the days of Tiglath-pileser III. Sargon took Kharkhar, renamed it Kar-Sharrukin, appointed his own governor, added territory to the province, and eventually resettled people there from another area. The campaign concluded with a deep thrust into Median territory, and on his return Sargon formally received in Kharkhar tribute from twenty-eight rulers of the land of the Medes.[102]

In the face of Assyrian aggression Rusa I now stepped up his involvement in the east, seized several fortresses belonging to Ullusunu and persuaded another Mannaean governor, Daiukku, to side with him.[103] In 715 Sargon returned to the area, recaptured the fortresses, and

---

101 C^b 4 (see A 209, 94b); A 166, *Sumer* 9, 47–59 and *Sumer* 10, 27–35; A 170, 176f ii; A 183, 36–45 r. 23–71; A 185, 78–100; A 224, 41; cf. A 202, 102–4, Room 2. Cf. A 82, 191–3 and 209f, no. 42. See A 194.

102 The geography of this part of the campaign has been discussed by A 183, 29–33.

103 The name Daiukku has been regarded as the Assyrian form of the name Deioces, the first Median king. See Hdt. 1, 96–102 and cf. A 41, 243–9; A 207; *CAH* III¹, 51 n. 1. But Daiukku is called a Mannaean, not a Mede, and the theory is very doubtful.

carried off Daiukku with his family.[104] Now he invaded Urartian territory and captured several fortresses including those in Andia. Yanzu, king of Nairi in Khubushkia, sent him tribute. In the south east the Assyrian army pacified the areas which had been joined the previous year to the province of Kharkhar and went on to conquer more Median territory. Once again Sargon concluded his penetration of Media with a ceremonial receipt of tribute in Kharkhar (Kar-Sharrukin). The campaign was a great success; for, in addition to re-establishing his control over Uishdish and Kharkhar, Sargon had expanded his holdings in Media, seized Andia on the Urartian border, and even captured some Urartian border points.

The year 714 witnessed the greatest campaign on this frontier and one of the most significant achievements of Sargon's career.[105] A unique narrative of this expedition is preserved in the form of a letter to the god Ashur and, while the chronological and geographical sequence of the text is not totally trustworthy, the abundant detail is most welcome. The Assyrian army marched to the province Lullumu, where Sargon inspected the troops and then led them on the way to Zikirtu and Andia. At some point in the march tribute was received from several rulers: Ullusunu of Uishdish, Bel-apla-iddina of Allabria, Dalta of Ellipi, and the rulers of Parsua, Namri and Median areas. Ullusunu came out to meet Sargon, crawling on all fours like a dog, and pleaded with the Assyrian for vengeance against Rusa I who had taken Uishdish, forcing Ullusunu to flee.

After a splendid banquet to celebrate the meeting the Assyrian army advanced. Gizilbundi, an area which had been lost to Assyria since the reign of Adad-nirari III, quietly submitted to Sargon. Upon arrival at the borders of Zikirtu and Andia the Assyrians reinforced a fortress and then invaded Zikirtu. It will be recalled that Mitatti of Zikirtu, an Urartian ally, had for years been instigating anti-Assyrian hostilities in Mannaea, and in face of the invasion he fled.

The Assyrians left Zikirtu and proceeded to Uishdish, where one of the most dramatic incidents in Assyrian history occurred. The Urartian army led by Rusa and joined by the troops of Zikirtu had assembled in Uishdish to avenge Mitatti. Reports reached Sargon that the enemy was lying in wait for him in the mountains and, rather than pause to allow his troops time to rest after their arduous march, Sargon pushed forward to catch the enemy by surprise. The scene is dramatically depicted in the letter to the god. The Assyrians, tired, hungry, and thirsty from a long route march were momentarily dismayed to find the full force of Urartu

[104] Cb 4 (see A 209, 95a); A 166, *Sumer* 9, 214–24; A 185, 101–17; A 202, 98f and 104 Room 14; A 224, 46f; Nineveh Prism (see A 209, 95a).
[105] Cb 4 (see A 209, 95a); A 166, *Sumer* 9, 225–8; A 170, 177f iii 1–41; A 185, 127–65; A 191; A 202, 98, Room 13; A 215; A 222; A 223; A 224, 47f; Nineveh Prism (see A 209, 95). See A 33; A 184; A 195; A 196; A 197.

before them, but Sargon acted with lightning speed. Without waiting for his whole army to file out of the mountains, he led an immediate attack in person with his household cavalry. The Urartians were caught off guard and the charge broke their ranks. Sargon spotted Rusa in his chariot in the midst of the *mêlée* and rode straight for him. Rusa's horses were slain and the terrified king, leaping upon a mare, fled the battlefield. His ally, Mitatti, was caught and killed. The Urartian host panicked and ran after their fleeing king. The Assyrians pursued them into the mountains where, Sargon boasts, those they did not kill perished in the snow.

It was a total rout of the Urartian army, if one can believe the Assyrian sources, and the invaders ravaged the border areas of Urartu up to the shores of the 'rolling sea' (Lake Urmia). The letter to the god, the major source for this campaign, provides unusual detail about the areas conquered. It describes the method of training horses in Ushqaia and the elaborate waterworks in Ulkhu. The Assyrians also penetrated the region of Yanzu, king of Nairi, who came with tribute to meet Sargon. The final achievement of the campaign was the sack of Muṣaṣir, the sacred city of Urartu which was located near the source of the upper Zab.

Urzana, king of Muṣaṣir, had for years been torn between loyalty to Urartu and to Assyria. This is apparent not only from letters of the period but also from an Urartian royal inscription in which the Urartian king boasts of the conquest of Muṣaṣir.[106] Sargon's decision to attack Muṣaṣir was taken, according to the letter to the god, after the Assyrians had begun the homeward march. Ominous signs appeared and the diviners, who regularly accompanied the Assyrian army on campaign, interpreted them to mean that Sargon would attack, capture and destroy Muṣaṣir. One of the portents is of particular interest, for it was a lunar eclipse which can be dated to the evening of 24 October 714 B.C., thus happily providing a precise date for the campaign. It is also significant to note that a lunar eclipse was usually regarded as an unfavourable omen, but on this occasion it was twisted around to be unfavourable for Muṣaṣir. Here is an excellent illustration of both the intricacies of Assyrian divination and the cunning of Sargon. When the eclipse occurred on that evening, a sudden dread must have befallen the camp. Sargon, faced with troops ready to panic, probably personally influenced the diviners to allay everyone's fears by declaring that the portent meant disaster for Muṣaṣir, not Assyria, thus swiftly turning the cause for fright into incitement to further conquest and plunder.[107] A little more than two centuries later a similar deft interpretation of a solar eclipse was said to have inspired Xerxes' army to cross the Hellespont to conquer Greece.[108]

---

[106] A 72, nos. 409, 768, 891, 1079; A 186, no. 264; cf. A 168, 77f.
[107] Cf. A 195, 137f.   [108] Hdt. VII, 39.

The Assyrian army stormed down upon Muṣaṣir, the terrified people opened the gates without attempt at resistance, and Sargon marched in to thoroughly plunder the city. The list of spoil is long and lavish and includes the image of the god Khaldi. Muṣaṣir became an Assyrian possession with the obligation to pay taxes and perform corvée. Rusa was so overcome by the sack of Muṣaṣir that, according to an Assyrian account, he killed himself with his sword. Thus this campaign not only added considerably to the territorial extent of the Assyrian empire, it also precipitated a change of monarch in Urartu. The new king, Argishti II, refrained from hostile acts on the north and north-eastern frontier, and so Sargon could turn his attention to the damage done by Urartian intrigues in Anatolia (see above pp. 91–2).

The absence of Urartian activity on the north-eastern front did not mean the immediate end of trouble after 714. In 713 Assyria had to deal with insurrections in two states, Karalla and Ellipi.[109] Karalla, as noted above, had been forcibly annexed to the province of Lullumu in 716. Now the people had rebelled, expelled the Assyrian officials and put over them Amitashi, brother of the unfortunate Ashur-leʾu. In 713 the Assyrians defeated the rebel forces and organized Karalla as a province in its own right. As for Ellipi, its ruler Dalta had remained loyal but some of his districts rebelled and drove him out. The Assyrian army stormed into the insurgent areas, slaughtering and plundering, and restored Dalta as their ruler. Sargon boasts that he received tribute from forty-five Median rulers on this campaign, in addition to the tribute of his loyal vassals, Ullusunu and Bel-apla-iddina. Both Ellipi and Karalla continued recalcitrant, however. When Dalta of Ellipi died, two of his sons (by different wives) fought over the throne and this resulted in a division of the kingdom. One claimant, Nibe, allied himself to Elam, while the other, Ispabara, turned to Assyria for help. Sargon despatched an army in 708 which defeated Nibe, supported by an Elamite army, and confirmed Ispabara's right to rule.[110] Disturbances in Karalla are known to have taken place, since the Eponym Chronicle, in a badly broken section, has this laconic entry for the year 706: 'The officers in Karalla'.[111] Obviously an Assyrian army had been sent to pacify the province once again, but further details are wanting.

5. Babylonia and Elam

The question of control over Babylonia was a more serious problem in the reign of Sargon II than it had been in that of Tiglath-pileser III, for Assyria lost Babylonia at Sargon's accession and it was not recaptured

---

[109] Cᵇ 4 (see A 209, 95b); A 170, 177f iii 42–56; A 185, 165–94; Nineveh Prism (see A 209, 95).
[110] A 35 II, §65; A 185, 73: 13–75: 8. [111] Cᵇ 4 and Cᵇ 6 (see A 209, 97a).

until near the end of the reign. Probably Sargon had intended to continue direct rule over his southern neighbour, but he was forestalled in his intention by the wily leader of the Chaldaean tribe Bit-Yakin, Merodach-baladan II, who first appeared in the time of Tiglath-pileser III.[112] Merodach-baladan seized Babylon during the confusion surrounding the accession to the throne of Sargon II, and he maintained his control, using bribes to purchase Elamite assistance, for twelve years (721–710). In 720, the same year in which the Syrian rebellion occurred (see above, pp. 88–9), the Assyrian garrison at Der was attacked.[113] The outcome of this conflict is described in three different ways in the three main sources: Sargon claimed a victory in his royal inscriptions, Merodach-baladan did the same for Babylonia in his cylinder inscription, and the Babylonian Chronicle recorded that the Elamite army, led by king Khumban-nikash, defeated the Assyrians before Merodach-baladan even arrived on the battlefield. The last version is, no doubt, closest to the truth and Sargon, occupied with other military matters, was forced to leave Merodach-baladan to rule unchallenged until 710.

It was in 710 that the Assyrian launched his major offensive against Merodach-baladan and his ally, Shutur-nahhunte of Elam.[114] Although Assyria had lost the battle of Der in 720, she had retained control over the city itself, so Sargon directed his attack into the east Tigris region first where he secured a hold over Gambulu. The role of Gambulu as a buffer zone between Assyria, Babylonia and Elam thus begins and continues for much of the Sargonid period. In 710 the city of Dur-Atkhara was the focus of attention, since Merodach-baladan had stationed here large numbers of Gambulaean troops and strengthened its defences by heightening the walls and cutting a canal from the River Surappu, so that the water flooded the plain, turning the city on its *tell* into an artificial island. Despite these precautions Dur-Atkhara fell to the Assyrians. Sargon organized the city as the administrative centre of the province of Gambulu, renamed it Dur-Nabu, appointed a governor, and imposed upon the inhabitants the obligation to pay taxes and perform corvée. The surrounding region was conquered and brought under the authority of the governor at Kar-Nabu.

Stubborn resistance was encountered in the marshes of the River Uqnu, where Gambulaean and Aramaean refugees had hidden. The Assyrians dammed one of the tributaries of the Uqnu with the result that the area was flooded and the fugitives forced out of hiding. They were

---

[112] See A 532.

[113] A 25, no. 1 i 33–7; A 185, 19–23, 262–9; A 206, lines 16f; A 595, 123: 16–18. Cf. A 72, no. 1127. See A 25, 237a and 292a; A 532, 12f; A 606, 340–2.

[114] Cᵇ 4 (see A 209, 96); A 25, no. 1 ii 1–5 and 1′; A 185, 43: 269–59: 14; A 191; A 209, 99f. See A 209, 96 regarding letters and also note A 72, no. 899; A 570, 69, 77–82, 84. See A 25, 237a and A 532, 18–20.

taken prisoner, while those who lingered in the marshes were attacked and defeated and the region added to the province of Gambulu. At this point the Assyrians were on the edge of Elamite territory, and to secure this border they captured a number of Elamite fortresses. Sargon proceeded to surround Merodach-baladan by crossing the Tigris and Euphrates and working his way up the Euphrates through territory occupied by the Chaldaean tribe, Bit-Dakkuri. When news of the trap reached Merodach-baladan, he fled Babylon by night and escaped to Elam. There, according to the Assyrian account, the fugitive offered all his precious possessions in a vain attempt to persuade Shutur-nahhunte to attack Assyria. Back in Babylonia, Sargon was invited by the priests and people of Babylon to enter their city, which he did, and there took up residence for the next few years (until 707).

Sargon's policy towards Babylonia was conciliatory, since he did not hold the Babylonians responsible for the hostile activity of the Bit-Yakin under Merodach-baladan. He sacrificed to the gods of Babylonia, he ordered an army to eliminate some Aramaean brigands who had been plundering Babylonian caravans, and he had a new canal dug for the annual procession of Nabu from Borsippa to Babylon. At the beginning of the New Year (709) he grasped the hand of the statue of Marduk as a Babylonian king in the *Akitu* (New Year) ritual. But the war with Merodach-baladan was not finished.

The month following the festivities in Babylon (11/709), Sargon was back in the south attacking Merodach-baladan, who had appeared in Dur-Yakin (modern Tell al-Lahm) in the marshes.[115] In preparation for the Assyrian assault the walls of Dur-Yakin had been strengthened and a canal dredged from the Euphrates to flood the surrounding plain, a tactic used the previous year at Dur-Atkhara. Undaunted, the Assyrians laid earthen banks across the streams of water and rushed upon the enemy host, which included Aramaean and Sutian auxiliaries, drawn up on high ground outside the city walls. While the Assyrians victoriously fought and plundered, Merodach-baladan was wounded in the hand by an arrow and slipped back inside the city. Dur-Yakin was put under siege, but by some means Merodach-baladan once again eluded capture and was not heard of again until the reign of Sennacherib. The Assyrians eventually captured Dur-Yakin, plundered it, and tore down its fortifications. The people of Yakin were led away, and a year or so later, after a rebellion in Kummukhu had been suppressed in 708 (see above p. 92), they were settled in Kummukhu and the people of Kummukhu settled in the region of Yakin. The area was divided in two with one portion under Babylonian jurisdiction and the other under the governor of Gambulu.

[115] A 25, no. 1 ii 2'; A 35 II, §§54, 66–70, 78, 92, 117, 184; A 162, 86–9:1; A 170, 185–93 vi and vii; A 185, 59: 15–67: 444 (cf. A 209, 96b); A 224, 50. See A 25, 237b and A 532, 20–2.

Until 707, the year in which Sargon left his residence in Babylon,[116] the king personally supervised conciliatory endeavours. Political prisoners who had been incarcerated by Merodach-baladan were freed and their fields in Sippar, Nippur, Babylon, and Borsippa restored to them. The Sutians who had seized these lands were massacred, as were Aramaean and Sutian robbers who lurked in the abandoned wilderness around Babylon. Statues of gods, which had been carried off from Ur, Uruk, Eridu, Larsa, Kullab, Kissik, and Nemed-Laguda were returned. For the remainder of his life Sargon ruled Babylonia directly and he was almost universally recognized by the Babylonians as their rightful sovereign. His fame spread thence as far as Dilmun in the Persian Gulf and two of its kings, Uperi and Akhundra (presumably his successor) sent gifts.[117]

The net gains of the campaigns were impressive. On all fronts Sargon had consolidated and expanded his empire; he had established good relations with two major powers, Egypt and Phrygia; he had seriously intimidated two other powerful opponents, Urartu and Merodach-baladan; and he had taken a firm hold of Babylonia. Sargon preferred to lead campaigns in person and while away from home left the administration of the empire in the hands of the crown prince, Sennacherib. Indeed Sargon was slain on the battlefield, and this led to interesting results as will be seen in the next chapter. A curious fact is that, although Sargon indulged in the hunt as a good Assyrian king should, the only game he is known to have sought, according to present evidence, was small creatures, birds and rabbits.[118] Finally, a feature of the royal inscriptions of Sargon is that they contain more detail concerning battles and military tactics than the royal inscriptions of any other Assyrian. Some of the more dramatic scenes are found, of course, in the letter to the god about the eighth campaign (714), but even in the other royal inscriptions it is not unusual to find descriptions of incidents in other than stereotyped phraseology.[119]

6. Building

As a builder Sargon II is virtually unparalleled, for he created a totally new Assyrian city, Dur-Sharrukin (Khorsabad) (Pls. Vol., pl. 69). While Ashurnasirpal II and Sennacherib are justly famous for their extensive development of Calah and Nineveh respectively, these had been major Assyrian cities before their time, and the only achievement comparable

---

[116] For Sargon's residence in Babylon see the Eponym Chronicle and the Babylonian Chronicle as quoted by A 209, 96.

[117] A 35 II, §§70, 81, 185; A 170, 191–4 vii 20–4 (cf. p. 194); A 185, 67: 1–444 and 69: 454.

[118] Cf. A 176.   [119] See A 481.

to Sargon's is the building of Kar-Tukulti-Ninurta by Tukulti-Ninurta
I. It has already been suggested that Sargon's creation of a new city was
the act of a usurper wishing both to enhance his image and to escape
hostile elements in the old cities. But, apart from this possibility, the
revival of the Assyrian empire which was well under way provided the
necessary impetus to create a new centre, and it is even possible that
Tiglath-pileser III had already entertained such an idea, it being
postponed because of more urgent affairs. Work began on the site very
early in the reign, the foundations being laid in 717.[120] The location was
approximately 25 km north of Nineveh in the foothills of the Jebel
Maqlub (Muṣri). Sargon discovered that the inhabitants of a local
village, Magganuba, held claim to the ground under a royal grant issued
by Adad-nirari III, and he compensated the villagers by providing them
with other fields, in the same general area, and issued a revised
proclamation to certify the exchange (5/VIII/713).[121]

The central structure in the new metropolis was the palace (Pls. Vol.,
pl. 48) in which were employed various exotic materials, all kinds of
wood, metals, precious stones and ivory.[122] A pillared portico in the
Syrian fashion (bīt ḫilāni) formed the grand entrance with numerous
columns of cedar and animal colossi in bronze and limestone. The walls
of the palace were lined with huge stone slabs, on which Sargon's
conquests were depicted both in sculptured relief and in cuneiform
inscriptions (rediscovered in modern excavations). A splendid ceremony
celebrated completion of the palace: the Assyrian gods were brought
inside to receive their sacrifices in an appropriate ritual, and when they
had departed the king, his nobles, and 'the princes of all lands' sat down
to a magnificent feast. A park was laid out with imported trees; shrines
for several deities including Ea, Sin, Ningal, Shamash, Nabu, Adad,
Ninurta and the Sibitti were erected; a residence for Sin-akha-uṣur, chief
vizier and brother of Sargon, was built; and a wall with eight gates
surrounded the city. People transported from all areas conquered by
Sargon were settled inside and taught 'to revere god and king'.

Despite the special attention paid to the building of Dur-Sharrukin
Sargon did not neglect other Assyrian centres. At Ashur he refurbished
the temple of the god Ashur, Ekhursaggalkurkurra, restored the
processional way of the forecourt, and did some repairs to the palace and
the Sin-Shamash temple.[123] His main work at Nineveh was reconstruction of the temple of Nabu (Sargon calls it the 'temple of Nabu and

120 Cᵇ 4 (see A 209, 94b).   121 A 102, no. 32.
122 Cᵇ 4 and Cᵇ 6 (see A 209, 96); A 35 II, §§72–5, 83–90, 93–4, 97–114, 119–23, 127a, 128–31, 228; A
72, nos. 138, 452, 480–4, 757, 813–14, 1432, 1442; A 81, 47f and 55f, nos. xxxi and xxxii; A 84, 70, and
73–5, no. LXVIII; A 86, 178 and 190f no. xciv; A 162, 86–9: 8–11; A 170, 196–8 viii; A 185, 75: 8–81: 1; A
189, 85–8; A 226, pl. 49, nos. 7, 9. See A 118; A 134; A 148; A 166; A 202, 95–104; A 205.
123 A 35 II, §§224–5; A 72, no. 91; A 128, 89–92; A 162, 86–9; A 170, 175 i 24–32; A 222. See A 507, 21.

Marduk'), which Adad-nirari III had earlier renewed.[124] He also restored the *Akitu* (New Year) House, according to Ashurbanipal.[125] The foundation of the North-West Palace of Ashurnasirpal II at Calah was in bad condition. Sargon cleared the site, laid a new terrace of limestone, and restored the building.[126] Upon completion he invited the gods inside to receive their offerings and then he staged a banquet. The spoil taken from Pisiri of Carchemish (717) was stored inside. Sargon made some repairs to the palace at Ekallatu[127] and also did some work on a temple at Der.[128]

Given the short period of time during which Sargon controlled Babylonia, one would not expect much building to be done there under his rule. In fact there is record of restoration of the Eanna temple at Uruk, and work on the walls of Babylon, and of an endowment for Ishtar of Uruk and Nanaya.[129] In the provinces there is evidence of Sargon's building activities at Harran, Til-Barsib, Carchemish, Malatya, and Arslan Tash.[130]

7. Conclusion

Tiglath-pileser III and Sargon II are the pioneers of the greatest phase of Neo-Assyrian history; they blazed the trail on all fronts, opening new paths for the Assyrian armies and for the trade and culture which followed in their steps, and they added new domains to what was already the most extensive kingdom the world had ever known. After this burst of glory the course of events becomes a little more involved, albeit no less dramatic, as Sargon's heirs are drawn into situations and problems not of their own making.

---

[124] A 35 II, §226; A 102, no. 54; A 122, nos. 29, 41, 69–71; A 123, 103f; A 190, 18, no. VIII. See A 124, 66–9.

[125] A 161, 35f V 33–42.   [126] A 35 II, §138. See A 137 I, 93–183.   [127] A 72, no. 99.

[128] A 72, no. 157.   [129] A 560, no. 38; A 596; A 689, no. 132.

[130] Harran: A 72, no. 489; A 162, 86–9: 6f. Til-Barsib: A 167. Carchemish: A 228, 211 and 265. Malatya: cf. A 167, 164 n. 3. Arslan Tash: cf. A 218.

CHAPTER 23

ASSYRIA: SENNACHERIB AND ESARHADDON
(704–669 B.C.)

A. K. GRAYSON

The history of Assyria during the reigns of Sennacherib and Esarhaddon is slightly different in character from that of the reigns of Tiglath-pileser III and Sargon II in that military achievements, although still of major significance, do not totally dominate the scene. Indeed, apart from the invasion of Egypt under Esarhaddon, there are no further extensive conquests to be recorded. Rather the emphasis gradually shifts to cultural enterprises, especially great building projects, and this development is illustrated by the fact that for Esarhaddon there are virtually no annalistic records preserved, although there is a vast number of display texts in which construction and religion have the centre stage. One must not make too much of this transformation, however, for it is gradual and subtle; both kings, but particularly Sennacherib, still sent out their vast armies to maintain and occasionally expand the frontiers of the empire.

I. SENNACHERIB (704–681 B.C.)

Of the two monarchs, Sennacherib was certainly the more warlike and therefore a son of whom Sargon could be proud. Among the deeds of Sennacherib, the most creditable is his work at Nineveh, which he transformed into the great metropolis to be known by posterity as the Assyrian capital. Paradoxically, the other event of his time which would long be remembered in Mesopotamia was the destruction of the sister capital, Babylon.[1]

1. Sources and chronology

Sources for the reign of Sennacherib are both abundant and informative. Of the large number of royal inscriptions a substantial proportion are annalistic and the information they provide is further elucidated by chronographic texts, particularly the Babylonian Chronicle and the

---

[1] For a detailed, albeit dated, history of the reign see A 40.

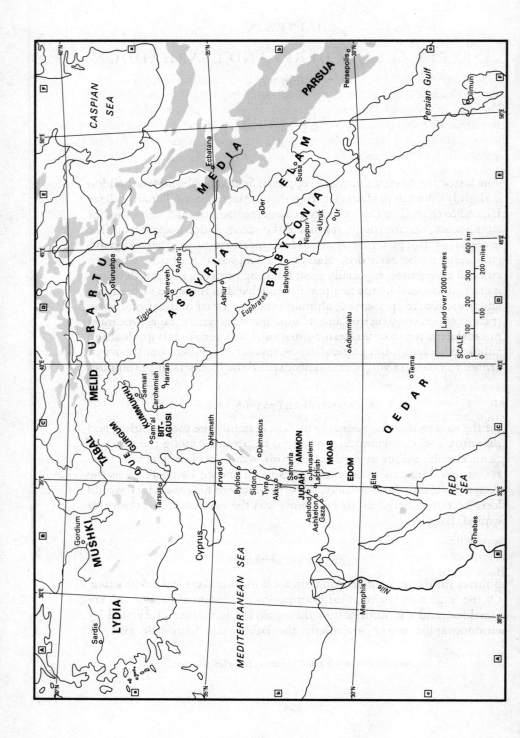

Eponym Chronicle.[2] At least some letters, in the archives of the royal chancellery which have been recovered, should date to this period,[3] and there are astrological reports[4] which bear on political and administrative affairs. There are also a number of legal and administrative documents.[5] The bulk of the inscribed material comes from Nineveh, and this is also the source of a rich quantity of sculptures in the round and in relief, these being among the spectacular finds of the early days of Assyrian archaeology.[6] Foreign sources, especially the Bible, are of some significance for the history of this reign.[7]

The chronology of Sennacherib's reign is unfortunately not as certain as one would like. In the chronology followed by our ancient sources there are three different dates used as the first regnal year, 705, 704, or 703, and it is manifest from this curious state of affairs that there was considerable confusion during the period from Sargon's death on the battlefield to his son's general acceptance as the new monarch.[8] In passing, it should be noted that despite this confusion Sennacherib was able to carry out substantial construction at Nineveh during these early years. To return to the chronology, there is also difficulty about the precise years of the royal campaigns and even about how many there were. The problem of the dates arises out of the fact that in the royal annals, as in the immediately preceding reigns, the campaigns are not dated by eponyms but merely numbered as first, second, third, etc. In the standard editions of the campaigns the accepted number is eight, but it is known that there were at least four additional expeditions, and there could have been more, since there are many years for which no record of military activity is preserved. It is a pity that the Eponym Chronicle, which could have shed light on this problem, is missing for all but the beginning of this reign.

2. *The Babylonian question*

One theme is predominant in the military and administrative policies of Sennacherib and that is the Babylonian question.[9] It is an axiom of Assyrian foreign policy that special privilege must be accorded to Babylonian affairs, and no better illustration of this could be found than in the time of Sennacherib. Throughout his reign Sennacherib wrestled

---

[2] Most of the royal inscriptions were edited by Luckenbill in A 270 and translated by him in A 35 II, §§231–496. To this add A 250. Bibliography of additional texts will be found in A 250, 84 n. 5 and in A 25, 238–40 and 292; A 285. The annalistic texts have been edited in A 4, 59–80, which also provides an extensive bibliography of published and unpublished texts. The relevant references in chronographic texts have been listed in A 25, 238b, and note especially Chronicle 1 ii 19 – iii 36. For the Eponym Chronicles, Cᵇ 6 and Cᵇ 7, see A 763, 435.

[3] See A 72–88. Cf. A 76, 119f and n. 1.

[4] See A 1032 and A 1040.   [5] See A 89–109.   [6] A 147.

[7] Regarding Berossus see A 7, 34f.   [8] See A 269 and A 532, 22–4.   [9] See A 540.

with the problem, attempting various solutions, but ultimately resorting to the most drastic action of all, the capture and destruction of Babylon. The resistance to Assyria centred around the figure of the Chaldaean Merodach-baladan II, who was eventually succeeded in this role by his son, but much of the actual fighting was conducted by Elamite troops under the direction of their king, who was persuaded by bribes to assist.[10] The first formal campaign of the reign was directed against Babylonia, and fortunately we have a detailed annalistic account written shortly after the event, as well as later more concise versions.[11] The campaign began late in the year 703 and was instigated by Merodach-baladan, who had seized the Babylonian throne and gathered a large force of Chaldaeans, Aramaeans, and Elamites to support his claim. The revolt against Assyria was far-flung; it included Judah, if we may date to this period the visit of ambassadors of Merodach-baladan to Hezekiah as described in the Bible and Josephus.[12] Presumably the allies were hoping to reap great advantage from the fact that there had been so much confusion about Sennacherib's accession.

When the army departed from Ashur, Sennacherib sent ahead to Kish a contingent which immediately engaged the enemy stationed there. The king in the interval proceeded to attack another enemy force at Cutha; he captured the city and then rushed to the aid of his embattled troops in the plain of Kish. Merodach-baladan fled the scene of battle and the allied army was defeated. Sennacherib went on to Babylon, where he plundered the palace but otherwise did not harm the inhabitants. He continued farther south to hunt for Merodach-baladan in the marshes and left behind him a smoking trail of burnt towns. Nonetheless, the search was in vain; Merodach-baladan was not found. Sennacherib turned his attention to exterminating rebel factions in large cities: Uruk, Nippur, Kish, Khursagkalama, Cutha, and Sippar. On the Babylonian throne he put Bel-ibni, a man of Babylonian descent but raised at the Assyrian court, in other words a puppet king. On Sennacherib's return march (by this time the year 702 had begun) he captured and plundered numerous Aramaeans; he forcibly extracted tribute from Khirimmu; and he received voluntary tribute from Nabu-bel-shumati of Khararate.

For two years Assyria, busy elsewhere, left Babylonia undisturbed and Merodach-baladan took the opportunity, as we know from a number of reports to the Assyrian court which presumably date to this period, to make his presence felt in Babylonia.[13] In 700 Sennacherib led a campaign,

[10] See A 533.

[11] Cᵇ 6 r. 12–15 (A 763, 435). A 25 no. 1 ii 12–25. A 270, 24 i 20 – 26 i 64; 48–55; 56f: 5–19; 66f: 3–9; 76f: 7–11, 13–15; 85f: 6f, 12. A 162, 94f; A 251, 118–25 i 23–79; A 241, 59. Possibly A 270, 157 no. xxx and A 72, no. 1452 date to this or the fourth campaign; A 15, no. 233: 16. See A 296 and A 532, 22–6.

[12] II Ki. 20: 12–19; Is. 39: 1–8; II Chron. 32: 31; Jos. *Ant. Jud.* x.ii 2. See A 532, 31–3.

[13] A 570, 98; A 571, 194–202.

his fourth in the official reckoning, into the Babylonian marshes to crush the Bit-Yakin tribe of Merodach-baladan.[14] First he hunted down a new leader of the rebellious Chaldaeans, who is merely called Shuzubu (a hypocorism) but must be identical with the later king of the name Mushezib-Marduk. Shuzubu was defeated and fled. The victorious army then marched against the Bit-Yakin. Merodach-baladan fled by ship across the Persian Gulf, abandoning his brothers and people to the Assyrians, who devastated their settlements. Merodach-baladan eventually died in exile in Elam. The Assyrians now punished Bel-ibni, who had been false to the Assyrian cause, taking him captive to Assyria. Ashur-nadin-shumi, Sennacherib's son, was installed on the Babylonian throne. But the Babylonian question was far from resolved.

The major confrontation with the rebels and their Elamite allies began six years later, in 694, and continued almost unremittingly until the sack of Babylon in 689.[15] In 694 Sennacherib launched a campaign, the sixth in the official numbering, to destroy the Elamite base of the fugitive Bit-Yakin on the shore of the Persian Gulf.[16] To accomplish this task he had Syrian craftsmen build boats of Phoenician design, to be manned by sailors from Tyre, Sidon, and Cyprus. The ships were brought down the Tigris to Opis and dragged overland to the Arakhtu canal. Assyrian troops, horses, and impedimenta were loaded onto the ships, and they sailed down the Euphrates, while Sennacherib marched with another body of men along the bank. Making camp near the sea-shore, they were suddenly overwhelmed by waves and forced to huddle in the boats for five days and nights. It seems that the Phoenician sailors, accustomed to the virtually tideless Mediterranean, were caught unawares by the gulf tide. Eventually they were able to sail across the water where, after a difficult landing, they engaged the Chaldaeans in a pitched battle on the river Ulaya. The Assyrians won the day, plundered the area, and sailed their spoil-laden craft back to the king who awaited them on the shore. But Sennacherib had been outwitted.

While the Assyrians had been busy on the Persian Gulf, the Elamites had invaded Babylonia in the north, through the Diyala valley, and occupied Sippar. It was a brilliant stroke and caught the Assyrians completely off guard. The Babylonians handed over Ashur-nadin-shumi, the Assyrian prince whom Sennacherib had imposed upon them as king, to the Elamites and he was carried off to Elam.[17] His place on the

[14] C^b 7 (A 763, 435) 2–9(?). A 25, no. 1 ii 26–31. Synchronistic King List (A 607, §3 King List 12) iv 3–6. A 270, 34f iii 50–74; 71: 33–7; 76–8: 11f, 25–7; 85f: 7–12; 87: 27; 89: 4–6. A 295, 306–8 iv 40 – v 16; A 251, 140–5 iv 10–48; A 570, 100, K. 13071; Berossus, see A 7, 24; A 122, pl. LVIII, fig. 6 (cf. A 115, 26). See A 532, 26f.   [15] See A 524, 116–23; A 534, 244–6; A 574, 9–18.

[16] A 25, no. 1 ii 36 – iii 6. A 270, 38f iv 32–53; 73–6: 48–106; 78: 28–32; 86–8: 19–36 (cf. A 162, 95 no. 7 col. B); 89f: 1–15 (cf. A 234, §91); 156: 14–7(?). A 250, 88–91: 16–19. Cf. A 115, 25a.

[17] See A 703, lines 26f.

Babylonian throne was taken by Nergal-ushezib. Few details of the subsequent events are preserved but it is apparent that a fierce struggle began as Sennacherib worked his way north, desperately attempting to recoup his losses. The conflict continued into the next calendar year, 693. On the sixteenth of Duʾuzu (IV) Nergal-ushezib captured Nippur and on the first of Tashritu (VII) the Assyrians took Uruk. Six days later a major battle was fought near Nippur, and Nergal-ushezib was taken prisoner and transported to Nineveh.

But Sennacherib was far from done. In the same year, 693, he launched an offensive (officially the seventh campaign) against Elam, where his son had been taken into exile.[18] He recaptured Bit-Khairi and Raṣa on the border and made them garrison towns under the control of the governor of Der. He then sacked and destroyed numerous cities, and when news reached the new king of Elam, Kudur-nahhunte, he abandoned his capital, Madaktu, and hid in the mountains. Sennacherib ordered a march to Madaktu, but winter suddenly set in and the Assyrians returned to Nineveh. Thus the final conflict with Elam was postponed.

The last great battle between Sennacherib and the Elamite–Babylonian coalition was fought at Khalule on the Tigris, probably in 691, during the course of the eighth campaign (according to the official numbering).[19] Mushezib-Marduk, whom Sennacherib had forced to flee to Elam in 700, returned to claim the Babylonian throne and won Elamite support through, according to Assyrian claims, payment of bribes from the treasure of Esagil. The Assyrians marched south and met a large force of Elamites and Babylonians at Khalule. There are two conflicting accounts about the outcome. The Babylonian Chronicle records, in its laconic fashion, that the Assyrians retreated, but Sennacherib claims, in one of the longest descriptions of a battle scene in Assyrian annals, that he won. It is a fact that Mushezib-Marduk remained on the Babylonian throne for two regnal years after the battle, and this, taken together with the greater reliability of the Babylonian source, would indicate that Sennacherib, far from winning a major victory at Khalule, probably suffered a setback or at least a check to his advance. But he would not stop here.

The allies had won, at best, a brief respite; within a very short time the Assyrians were able to apply considerable pressure on Babylonia, and this eventually led to the fall of Babylon itself in 689. Unfortunately we do not have a coherent narrative of the events.[20] By the middle of the year after the battle of Khalule, which is to say the fifth month of 690, it is

---

[18] A 25, no. 1 iii 9–15. A 270, 39 iv 54 – 41 v 16; 88: 36–44 (cf. A 162, 95 no. 7 col. B); 90f: 16–24 (cf. A 234, §91); A 250, 90f: 19–41.

[19] A 25, no. 1 iii 16–18. A 270, 41 v 17 – 47 vi 35; 82f: 34–43; 88f: 44–55; 91f: 25 – r. 21. A 250, 88–95: 11–16, 47–114. See A 606, 342 and A 540, 92f.

[20] A 25, no. 1 iii 19–24. A 270, 83f: 43–54; 137f: 36–47. See A 540, 93–5.

apparent from a contemporary description that life in Babylonia and especially in Babylon was grim; the Assyrian siege had begun and famine, starvation, and death were everywhere.[21] Tenaciously the Babylonians refused to submit for another fifteen months after the date of this scene; but on the first day of Kislimu (IX) of 689 Babylon was captured. Sennacherib boasts, in a description reeking with hatred for Babylon and Babylonians, that he utterly destroyed the city; he diverted water from the canals in order to flatten not only the buildings but the very mound upon which Babylon stood. As usual allowance must be made for the extravagance of Assyrian prose and the actual destruction was probably not nearly as bad as the description.

The serious catastrophe was the traumatic effect this outrage had on the Babylonians themselves, for it marks a turning point in Babylonian history and in Assyro-Babylonian relations. Far from solving the Babylonian question by this decisive deed, Sennacherib had kindled a spark in the south that would eventually burst into the flames of a war of independence. For the remainder of this reign the Babylonians suffered in silence although they did not recognize Sennacherib or anyone else as king after Mushezib-Marduk was taken to exile in Assyria; in their official chronicles they spoke of these eight years as a period 'of there not being a king in Babylon'.[22]

3. Palestine

Next to Babylon the most important area in Sennacherib's foreign policy was in the west, especially Palestine and Egypt. The centre of interest was the kingdom of Judah under Hezekiah. Hezekiah had been drawn into intrigue with Merodach-baladan, as noted earlier, and with Egyptian and Nubian encouragement he had renounced Assyrian allegiance. But Sennacherib, once he had driven Merodach-baladan out of Babylon, was prepared to assert his authority in Palestine, which he did beginning with a campaign in 701. The history of Sennacherib's military actions in Palestine is a problem for modern scholars. The two main accounts of the relevant events are found in the Assyrian royal inscriptions and in the Bible.[23] In both the Assyrian texts and in the Old Testament the narrative concerns an invasion by Sennacherib of Palestine during the reign of Hezekiah of Judah and an Assyrian siege of the city of Jerusalem. Beyond these basic similarities, however, the descriptions are not identical, and, while some of this can be attributed to the different

---

[21] YBC 11377. See A 540, 93.

[22] A 25, no. 1 iii 28. Cf. the Ptolemaic Canon (A 607, §3 King List 8): ἀβασίλευτα.

[23] A 270, 29–34 ii 37 – iii 49; 60f; 68–70: 18–32; 77: 17–22; 86: 13–15 (cf. A 162, 94f no. 7). A 251, 130–41 ii 60 – iv 9; II Ki. 18: 13–19: 37; II Chron. 32: 1–23; Is. 36: 1–37: 38; Jos. Ant. Jud. x.i 1–5. Cf. also below, pp. 110–11.

outlook and purpose of the authors, not all the difficulties can be resolved in this way. Let us briefly outline the events in each narrative and then consider the problems.

Sennacherib's annals state that the third campaign (701) was directed against Syria. Sidon and Ashkelon were taken by force but other states, including Arvad, Byblos, Samsimurun, Ashdod, Ammon, Moab, and Edom paid tribute without resistance. The citizens of Ekron (Amqarruna) became frightened, for they had handed over their king, Padi, as a prisoner to Hezekiah, and they called on Egypt and Nubia for aid. The Assyrians met this allied force at Eltekeh and claimed a victory. Eltekeh and Timna were plundered, the rebellious nobles of Ekron were slain, and Padi was returned from Jerusalem to sit once again on his throne. Now Sennacherib laid siege to Jerusalem. During the siege the surrounding towns were sacked and put under the authority of Ashdod, Ekron, and Gaza. At this point one expects a statement in the Assyrian annals regarding the manner in which the siege of Jerusalem was ended, but instead there is a long list of booty which we are told was sent from Jerusalem to Nineveh. These are the events as narrated in Sennacherib's annals, and there is no doubt that all of this had happened by 700 since the fullest account, the Rassam Cylinder, is dated in that year. There can, however, be no certainty about the two other pieces of Assyrian evidence: the reliefs upon which is portrayed the looting of Lachish;[24] and a fragmentary text, which may be of Sennacherib, in which is described the conquest of two Palestinian towns, one of them being Azekah (the name of the other is broken).[25] Neither Lachish nor Azekah is mentioned in any annalistic narrative of the third campaign.

Turning to the Biblical account, in the Book of Kings it is stated that Sennacherib took all the fortified cities of Judah and then, while at Lachish, he received from Hezekiah a vast amount of tribute (II Ki 18: 13–19: 37).[26] In the Book of Chronicles, where this passage does not appear, there is a detailed narration of the measures taken by Hezekiah to fortify Jerusalem against a siege (II Chron. 32: 1–21). The Assyrian sent an army to Jerusalem where the *rab-šaqēh* harangued the people, trying to persuade them of their foolishness in relying upon Egyptian aid. Hezekiah, on the advice of the prophet Isaiah, stood his ground. When the *rab-šaqēh* reported back to Sennacherib, whom he found at Libnah, a message came that Taharqa of Nubia had set out for battle. The Assyrian now sent an ultimatum to Hezekiah, but Isaiah assured his king that Sennacherib would never approach Jerusalem. The Biblical narrative proceeds: 'That night the angel of the Lord went forth and slew a

---

[24] A 147, pls. 68–76. Cf. A 155, 44–67, and below, fig. 14.

[25] A 274, 25–39. Na'aman believes that the fragment is a description of the campaign in 701 and that the missing name is Gath (also not mentioned in the annals of the third campaign).

[26] Cf. Jos. *Ant. Jud.* x i 1.

hundred and eighty-five thousand in the camp of the Assyrians.' Sennacherib returned to Nineveh where he was slain by his sons.

Unless we dismiss one or both of these sources as unreliable, we are faced with an interesting, albeit intricate, task of historical research. There is no scope in these pages to discuss the problem in detail, nor to do justice to the voluminous pages written by numerous scholars on this matter;[27] rather I shall present very briefly my own view. It seems obvious that the two sources are describing essentially different events, and that we must reckon with at least one further Palestinian campaign after 701. This second campaign probably took place late in the reign (688–681), a period for which no Assyrian annalistic narratives are preserved.[28] Assuming this much, let us outline a hypothetical reconstruction.

Sennacherib's first invasion of Palestine took place more or less as he describes it in his annals. He probably won the day at Eltekeh, for he went on to plunder this and other towns. It is extremely unlikely that he suffered any severe defeat or slaughter on this campaign, since he was able to carry out a major attack on Babylonia the following year. The siege of Jerusalem ended in Hezekiah paying a huge bribe to Sennacherib (perhaps this same incident is referred to in II Kings 18: 14–16), but otherwise the city was not harmed. During subsequent years, while Assyria was busy with other problems, Hezekiah resolved to resist any future Assyrian invasion by allying himself to Egypt and by fortifying Jerusalem to face a siege. Until 689 Sennacherib was busy with the Babylonian problem, but after this date he was free to launch a new campaign to the west. To this late Palestinian campaign one might assign the conquest of Azekah and the siege of Lachish. Presumably it was on this occasion that the *rab-šāqēh* made his abortive trips to Jerusalem and that the report of Taharqa's advance was brought to Sennacherib. Before fighting commenced, however, a catastrophe befell the Assyrian camp; the Biblical narrative speaks of a slaughter by the angel of the Lord, and Josephus recalls in this connexion a story of Herodotus about mice gnawing through the bowstrings of Sennacherib's army.[29] Whatever happened, Sennacherib withdrew in confusion and disgrace. How close this interpretation of our sources is to reality must await the test of future discoveries.

4. *Other military matters*

The remaining campaigns of Sennacherib are over-shadowed by his Elamite–Babylonian and Syro-Egyptian offensives and are not dis-

---

[27] See A 302; A 254; A 240; A 249; A 245; A 299; A 276; and the bibliography of older works in these references.

[28] The years 699–7, allowing one of these for the fifth campaign, cannot be entirely ruled out.

[29] Hdt. II.141f and Jos. *Ant. Jud.* x.i 4. See A 232, 89–92.

tinguished by any significant territorial gains. Two campaigns, the second (702) and fifth (somewhere in the period 699–697) according to the official numbering, were directed to the mountains east of Assyria. On the first of these Sennacherib attacked troublesome Kassites and Yasubigallians in the Zagros.[30] He captured Bit-Kilamzakh, garrisoned it, and transported conquered peoples to settle in it. Kassites and Yasubigallians were settled in Khardishpi and Bit-Kubatti, which were put under the authority of the governor of Arrapkha. Sennacherib moved on to Ellipi. Its king, Ispabara, once a vassal of Sargon II, had obviously changed heart, for he fled. The Assyrians swept over the area, adding Şişirtu, Kummakhlum, and the province of Bit-Barru to their holdings. Elenzash was made the capital, the name changed to Kar-Sennacherib, and it was put under the authority of the governor of Kharkhar. On his return Sennacherib received tribute from the Medes. On the fifth campaign the army attacked the people on Mount Nipur (Herakul Dağ), and devastated their cities.[31] Sennacherib then attacked Maniyae, king of the city of Ukku of the land of Daiye. The king fled and his city was captured and plundered.

Turning to Anatolia, as we noted earlier, several states had rebelled at Sargon II's death and Sennacherib was too occupied with other frontiers to do much about this. None the less he did send two expeditions into Anatolia in successive years, 696 and 695. The first was against Cilicia and its allies, who are said to have blocked the road to Que.[32] Hawkins has suggested that in fact Que was once again friendly to and possibly a vassal state of Assyria and the purpose of this campaign was to assist Que (cf. *CAH* III[2].1, 426–7). Be that as it may, the rebel cities of Ingira, Tarsus, and Illubru were captured and the leader, Kirua, taken with much spoil to Nineveh. The campaign of 695 was directed against Tabal but was far from successful, the plunder of only one border city, Til-Garimmu, being recorded.[33]

One further campaign is known from a fragmentary text of Sennacherib, as well as from allusions in inscriptions of Esarhaddon and Ashurbanipal.[34] This was against Arabs in the north Arabian desert and involved the conquest of the oasis settlement of Adummatu (Biblical Dumah, modern Dumat al-Jandal), where the queen of the Arabs had taken refuge. There can be no certainty about the date of this event,

---

[30] A 270, 26–9 i 65 – ii 35; 58–60: 20–33; 67f: 9–17; 77: 15f; 86: 12f (cf. A 162, 94f no. 7); 157, no. XXVII. A 251, 124–9 i 80 – ii 59. See A 33, 11, 26; D.–O. Edzard, 'Jasubu', in A 16, 5, 271; A 286, 97–9.

[31] A 270, 35–8 iii 75 – iv 31; 63–6; 71f: 37–47; 77: 22f; 86: 16f (cf. A 162, 94f no. 7). A 251, 144–7 iv 49–91. See A 287, 60.

[32] A 270, 61f iv 61–91; 77: 24; 86: 17f (cf. A 162, 94f no. 7). A 251, 146–51 iv 92 – v 28; Berossus, see A 7, 24. Cf. A 178, 155f; A 172.

[33] A 270, 62f v 1–22; 77: 24f; 86: 19. A 251, 150–3 v 29–52.

[34] A 270, 92f r. 22–7; A 234, 53: 1–5; A 344, 11, 216–19 and 222–5. See A 236, 8–11; A 19, 117–23.

although some have suggested 690 since the narrative in Sennacherib's text follows immediately upon a description of the eighth campaign.[35]

In the realm of military strategy and tactics there are some features in the reign of Sennacherib which should be noted. On his first campaign he employed two separate contingents, one initially to engage the enemy at Kish while the main body of the Assyrian army attacked Cutha in force. The manoeuvre was successful; the first contingent was just able to hold its own until Sennacherib had been victorious at Cutha and could rush to its aid. An ingenious strategy was the use of Phoenician boats on the sixth campaign to transport troops across the Persian Gulf, although Sennacherib was outwitted on this occasion by the Elamites who cut off the Assyrians by an invasion of northern Babylonia. Sennacherib clearly understood the power of propaganda as illustrated by the *rab-šāqēh*'s attempt, so vividly described in the Bible, to persuade the king and inhabitants of Jerusalem to submit without a struggle. As mentioned earlier, a similar method was employed by Tiglath-pileser III at Babylon. Finally, the texts of Sennacherib contain more details about siege techniques than are usually found in Assyrian royal inscriptions, but whether this indicates a great advance in siege methods in his reign or is to be attributed to some other cause must remain an open question.

5. Building

The most outstanding achievement of this reign was a great urban development, the transformation of Nineveh into the leading metropolis of the empire.[36] Sennacherib began this project almost as soon as he ascended the throne, and as early as 703 he had already expanded the size of the city and constructed a palace complete with park and artificial irrigation. During the remainder of his reign he not only embellished and enlarged these works but constructed new city defences and a fortress. The labour for these endeavours was provided by Chaldaeans, Aramaeans, Mannaeans, and people of Que, Cilicia, Philistia, and Tyre, who were pressed into service. Remains of Sennacherib's great palace, which he called 'Palace Without a Rival' and which modern excavators have labelled the 'South-West Palace', were found on the larger of the two mounds of Nineveh, Kouyunjik. Sennacherib tore down the ruins of an old palace, diverted the course of a stream which had flooded the area, and erected a huge terrace. On this foundation rose the palace, decorated with all manner of exotic woods, stones, metals, and ivory,

[35] Cf. A 285, 194.
[36] On Nineveh's topography, its environs, and Sennacherib's construction there see A 124, 106–41 and A 287.

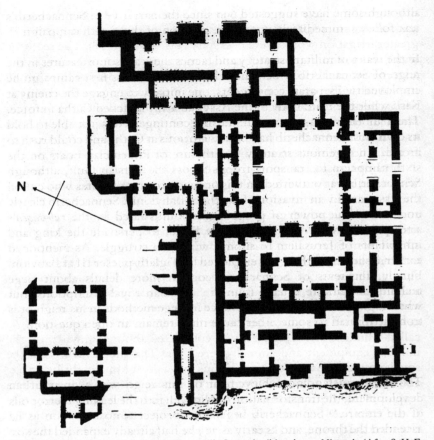

Fig. 4. Plan of the South-West Palace, Kouyunjik, Sennacherib's palace at Nineveh. (After S. H. F. Lloyd, *Archaeology of Mesopotamia* (London, 1978), 199, fig. 142.)

and a tremendous number of sculptures in the round (including the bull colossi) and in relief, many of which were recovered in modern excavations. These were described by Layard as 'two miles of bas-reliefs' (Pls. Vol., pls. 47, 67, 73).[37] The palace included a pillared portico in the style of a Syrian structure called a *bīt-ḫilāni*. Beside the palace Sennacherib created a large park, planted with a variety of imported herbs and fruit trees, and elsewhere he provided a number of small garden plots for the citizens of Nineveh.[38]

These gardens required water and Sennacherib devoted a great deal of time and expense to artificial irrigation. Early in his reign he had a canal

---

[37] A full publication of the reliefs has never appeared (cf. A 115, xif),but see A 147 and A 115, 1–27.
[38] A 270, 94–127: 152f; A 295, 308; A 162, 89; A 251, 152–67 v 53 – vii 63 and 170f viii 20–8. Cf. A 121, 103.

dug to bring water from the River Khosr through Nineveh, but as his park and gardens were expanded, some time between 700 and 694, greater irrigation works were necessary (Pls. Vol., pl. 73). The requisite water was found in mountain springs to the north east of Nineveh, and sixteen new canals were excavated to conduct this supply to the city and its suburbs. To carry off the excess water during the flood season Sennacherib formed a large marsh, which was stocked with the flora and fauna of the Babylonian marshes. These extensive water works are known both from descriptions in Sennacherib's royal inscriptions and from a study of the remains still visible in and near Nineveh.[39]

At the accession of Sennacherib Nineveh was an ancient settlement with dark, narrow alleys winding through a maze of buildings; Sennacherib widened the squares, cleared the streets, and constructed a royal road, an avenue which crossed a bridge on its approach to the park gate and which was lined on both sides with stelae to prevent further urban sprawl from encroaching upon its width.[40] The construction of the city's external defences was completed by about 694; there was a moat surrounding a wall with no less than eighteen gates. The modern visitor to Nineveh can still see the outline of the walls and moat, and some of the ancient gates have been excavated and restored in recent years.[41] After completion of the palace Sennacherib built an arsenal (*ekal māšarti*) called 'Hinder Palace' (*ekal kutalli*), completed about 689, where all the military equipment and animals were kept. The site, which is on the smaller mound now called Nebi Yunus, has a great Muslim shrine on top and has not been excavated. But from the details in the royal inscriptions it appears that the fortress was similar in design to Fort Shalmaneser (see *CAH* III².1, 268). It was built on a terrace, on land reclaimed from the river, and had a wing in the Syrian style and a wing in the Assyrian style. There was a large paved courtyard where the horses and other animals could be exercised and, in addition to the military quarters, there were state apartments and a throne room.[42]

Sennacherib was responsible for other building enterprises at Nineveh, but there is as yet scant evidence of these works. A fragmentary text which might be ascribed to Sennacherib tells us of activity at shrines of deities of which only two names are preserved, Sin and Ishtar of Nineveh.[43] A number of bricks bear inscriptions indicating that they came from a house which Sennacherib built for his son; these bricks were

---

[39] The early waterworks are described in texts cited in n. 38. For the later works see: A 270, 79–82: 6–34; 114–16 viii 31–64; 124f: 43–8; A 162, 89f and 93f; A 130; A 241; A 251, 170–5 viii 29–70; A 287.

[40] The squares and streets are described in texts cited in n. 38. For the royal road see: A 270, 102: 90; 153: 15–27; 154: 9f.

[41] A 270, 79: 5f, 111–13 vii 58 – viii 12, 153f. A 122, nos. 79, 99; A 251, 166–71 vii 64 – viii 19. See A 162, 90–3; A 287, 47–54.   [42] A 270, 128–34. See A 154.

[43] A 239, 95–8 and pl. 18 no. 16. Cf. A 5, 1, 526.

Fig. 5. Reconstruction of the *Akitu* temple of the New Year's festival, built by Sennacherib at Ashur. (After A 112, 66, fig. 44.)

found on the flats just below Kouyunjik.[44] Remnants of two other buildings of this period have been uncovered in modern times, one (*bīt-nakkapti*) on the east side of Kouyunjik overlooking the Khosr,[45] and the other on the east side of the city roughly equidistant from the two mounds and south of the Khosr.[46]

The chief work of Sennacherib at Ashur concerned two buildings, the Temple of the New Year (*akītu*) and the Ashur temple. Extensive reconstruction was carried out on the Ashur temple, including the opening of a new doorway facing east.[47] The ancient practice of celebrating the *Akitu* in the temple outside the city walls had long since been abandoned, Sennacherib tells us, and the building fallen into ruin. He built a new temple on the site (Fig. 5), decorated it with images and inscriptions depicting the myth of Ashur (not Marduk) conquering Tiamat, and symbolically deposited inside it a pile of rubble from the destruction of Babylon.[48] Other structures erected or improved by Sennacherib at Ashur were the temple of Zababa,[49] a house for his first-born son Ashur-nadin-shumi,[50] a house for his younger son Ashur-ili-

[44] A 292; A 293, 22, 37d; A 122, 125 and pls. 45f nos. 85, 97, 98, 101. See A 121, 103; A 124, 83–8; A 115, 2, 5f, 26.

[45] A 122, 135 and pl. 52 no. 122N. See A 121, 103 and A 124, 64–6.   [46] A 284, 60.

[47] A 270, 144–51; A 128, 52–73; and cf. A 507, 21–9. Also note A 90, 23–8 and cf. A 507, 65f. See now A 248.

[48] A 270, 135–43; A 128, 74–80. Also note A 90, 3–9 and cf. A 102, 121f. See A 507, 57–9.

[49] A 229, 29; A 102 no. 40 and 122f, 4b. See A 242, 467.   [50] A 270, 151f, xv.

muballiṭsu,[51] the royal sepulchre,[52] the *mušlalu*,[53] the Sin-Shamash temple,[54] and the palace.[55] The only other important Assyrian city at which Sennacherib did some construction is Arbaʾil, for which he provided water by a system of new canals,[56] but it is possible that he did work at Calah.[57] Other building projects of this reign include the Nergal temple at Tarbiṣu,[58] the wall of Kalizi,[59] a palace at Tell Billa,[60] and the wall at Sur-marriti (modern Samarra?).[61]

6. *Character*

Although it is singularly difficult to find clues to individual characteristics of most kings of Assyria, there are some indications of the personality and character of Sennacherib. Of course he was bellicose and boastful as any true Assyrian monarch should be, but it is in his building projects, in his attitude towards his father, and in his treatment of Babylonia that there is a glimpse of some individuality on his part. All kings of Assyria liked to build, but only a few built on a scale anywhere near that of Sennacherib's work at Nineveh. However, it is not even the enormity of the work which interests us here, it is the monarch's personal interest in it. He is portrayed supervising gangs of labourers moving a bull colossus;[62] he was interested in engineering techniques, such as the system of drawing water from his well;[63] and he proudly boasted that he had devised a new method of casting bronze monuments.[64]

Sennacherib's attitude towards his father provides another glimpse of his character. While crown prince, Sennacherib had held a very responsible position within the empire, for he seems to have been left in charge of the state while Sargon conducted campaigns in person. The son reported to his father by means of letters, and it is to be presumed that these reports were frequent and related to all important affairs of state. Certainly the few that survive are relatively detailed and cover a wide range of subjects.[65] After a standard introduction in which Sennacherib

---

[51] A 270, 150f, X and XI; A 151, 32. See F. H. Weissbach, 'Aššuriliabulliṭsu', in A 16, 1, 211b; A 347, 215 n. 70.   [52] A 270, 151, XIII and XIV.

[53] A 270, 151, XII. See A 110, 86–91; A 507, 29–31.   [54] A 128, 89–92.

[55] A 151, 27.   [56] A 290. Cf. A 262, 29f.

[57] Two fragmentary inscriptions of Sennacherib (ND 5414 and 5416) were found at Calah: see A 308, 122 and A 258, 67 and pl. XXII. Further note A 137 1, 239.

[58] A 270, 155; A 301, 41f and 93.   [59] A 270, 155, XXIII; A 246; A 247.   [60] A 300, 12.

[61] A 250, 94–6: 115–25. Further note the inscribed tile from Babylon published in A 634, 10 and pl. 4, and cf. A762, 279. Also note the fragmentary clay tablet from Kouyunjik on which is described work on the temple of the god Khani; see A 270, 147f. It is unknown if the endowment of a temple at Shabbu (A 102, nos. 34–6) by Sennacherib involved construction.

[62] A 147, pl. 32f.   [63] A 270, 110 vii 45–9 and 124: 37–9.

[64] A 270, 108–10 vi 80 – vii 30 and 122f: 14–33.

[65] A 72, nos. 196–9, 730–1, and possibly 568, 1079, and 1083. See A 257 and A 540, 90. Regarding the Nimrud letter mentioned by A 540, 90 n. 5, see now A 198, 21–34.

reports that all is well in Assyria, he proceeds to relate reports that have
come to him from various sources regarding events in Urartu, Anatolia,
activities on Assyria's borders, flood conditions in the area of Kurba'il,
and the receipt of tribute from Kummukhu and Phoenicia. Obviously
Sennacherib was highly trusted by his father and performed his administrative duties capably.

Suddenly the report came that Sargon had been killed in battle.
Sennacherib's reaction to this news is what concerns us here. The
circumstances of Sargon's death haunted the son. It was most unusual
for an Assyrian king to die in battle and it was inevitably interpreted by
the Assyrians as a bad omen, particularly because the royal corpse could
not be buried at home. A fragmentary text, which is usually attributed to
Sennacherib, concerns an inquiry to the gods to discover what terrible
sin Sargon had committed to deserve such a fate.[66] Unfortunately,
neither the circumstances of the inquiry nor its results are known. The
ominous dread surrounding the fallen king manifested itself in other
forms. Sennacherib, in contrast to usual practice, never mentioned his
parent's name in his royal inscriptions, nor did he waste any time in
abandoning Sargon's city of Dur-Sarrukin, which was left uncompleted.

The character of Sennacherib is further illuminated by his treatment of
Babylonia, since this problem eventually became a very personal affair
for the king. The constant unrest in Babylonia was undoubtedly a source
of vexation, indeed exasperation, to the monarch but the cruelest blow
was the kidnapping of his son, Ashur-nadin-shumi, in 694. The prince,
who is never mentioned again, presumably was killed in exile, and so the
war with the Babylonians and their Elamite allies became a blood feud.
The Babylonians were the chief culprits; for, as we know from a letter of
a later period, they had actually handed over Ashur-nadin-shumi to the
Elamites.[67] The vengeful father was, therefore, not satisfied until he had
destroyed Babylon.[68] This act ended the vendetta as far as Sennacherib
was concerned, but it confronted him with a new problem.

When the Assyrians were pillaging and ravaging Babylon, they went
so far as to destroy not only the temples of the gods, but the divine
statues as well, although the statue of Marduk apparently escaped and
was removed to Assyria. These actions were the height of sacrilege, not
only to Babylonians but also to many Assyrians who had great reverence
for the Babylonian deities. Thus Sennacherib had to ponder how to
justify these acts to many of his countrymen. He began by dissociating
himself personally from the deed; in the passage where the event is
described, first-person narration by the king is abandoned and the crucial
sentence reads: 'The hands of my people seized and smashed them [the

---

[66] K. 4730 published in A 306, 2, 52f and edited in A 756. Cf. A 422, 193–6.
[67] A 703. Cf. A 540, 92 n. 18.   [68] Cf. A 422, 195f. Also note A 717; A 524.

divine statues]'.[69] But this word play was not enough; there is some evidence that Sennacherib resorted to religious propaganda. The background for this was provided by a theological change developing in Sargonid Assyria, whereby Marduk was regarded as the son of Ashur and therefore subordinate to him.[70] Sennacherib, in his dilemma, pushed this movement dramatically forward. When he rebuilt the *Akitu* House at Ashur (cf. above, p. 116) he replaced Marduk with Ashur in images portraying victory over the dragon, and he made it manifest that this was directly related to the desecration of the Babylonian shrines by heaping up rubble from the city's destruction inside the temple. To an ancient Mesopotamian this was a clear statement that Marduk had been conquered by Ashur.

Even more explicit is a curious composition that seems to be specifically related to this occasion.[71] The badly preserved text is written in the style of a learned commentary but in the Assyrian rather than the Babylonian dialect. From it one gleans a bizarre tale: Bel (Marduk) has been imprisoned and subjected to trial by ordeal with numerous gods, the chief of which seems to be Ashur, presiding. Because of Bel's imprisonment the *Akitu* festival cannot be celebrated in the normal way, and there is allusion to two battles, one among men in Babylonia and one among the gods. There are many uncertainties about this composition but, as two commentators have suggested, it appears to be an Assyrian parody or piece of propaganda regarding the Marduk cult, the purport of which is to show that Bel (Marduk) had committed some terrible offence. It seems that the period under discussion would be the obvious occasion for such a text. The celebration of the *Akitu* festival in Babylonia was actually cancelled for twenty years after 689, and the two battles mentioned in the composition could refer to the Assyrian capture of Babylon and the mythological conflict which this would imply. Thus what had begun as a personal vendetta of the king came to have serious implications for a major theological movement in Assyria.

7. *Assassination*

On the twentieth of Tebet (x) 681, Sennacherib was murdered and his son Esarhaddon ascended the throne. The identity of the murderer or murderers is not certain, and the circumstances of the assassination remain one of the great mysteries of ancient history.[72] The most detailed account of the relevant events is found in a royal inscription of Esarhaddon, written almost ten years later; some vital facts are also

---

[69] A 270, 83: 48. See A 540, 94f. [70] See A 526, 36.
[71] A 739; A 741; A 283; A 104 no. 268. Cf. A 644, 15f and n. 9.
[72] For bibliography see A 44, 288 n. 1, to which add: A 265, 65–73; A 56, 70–3; A 303; A 282.

found in the Babylonian Chronicle, a text of Nabonidus, Berossus, the Bible, and Josephus.[73] Esarhaddon tells us that he was chosen by his father as heir to the throne, although he had elder brothers, and the choice was announced to a great assembly of all Assyrians, including Esarhaddon's brothers, who swore to respect the appointed successor's right to the throne. Afterwards the brothers plotted against Esarhaddon, slandering him to their father, who was thus turned against the crown prince, and Esarhaddon withdrew to an unnamed abode for safety's sake; in Nineveh the brothers took to arms. But the rebellion was not supported by the people of Assyria and Esarhaddon returned to Nineveh, meeting on the way rebel forces which had gathered in Khanigalbat. The insurgents were overwhelmed by fear and the troops, far from resisting, joined forces with Esarhaddon, while their leaders fled the scene to seek refuge in an 'unknown land'. Esarhaddon entered Nineveh and ascended his father's throne. Such is Esarhaddon's version of this momentous period.

Turning to the other sources, under the year 681 it is recorded in the Babylonian Chronicle that Sennacherib was killed by his son in a rebellion, and that the rebellion continued in Assyria from the day of the murder, the twentieth of Tebetu (x), until the second of Addaru (XII), some forty-two days later; shortly thereafter Esarhaddon ascended the throne in Assyria. In the three relevant passages of the Bible the narrative follows immediately upon the description of the great catastrophe which befell the Assyrian army while on campaign in the west (see above, p. 111). According to the Biblical narrative (II Ki. 19: 37), and a similar account in Josephus, Sennacherib was worshipping in the house of his god 'Nisroch' when his sons, 'Adrammelech and Sharezer', slew him with the sword. The assassins escaped to the land of Ararat and Esarhaddon reigned in his father's stead. Berossus says the culprit was Sennacherib's son, 'Ardumuzan', and Nabonidus simply says it was 'his natural son'.

The information in the Babylonian Chronicle, Berossus, Nabonidus, and the Bible is complementary to the narrative of Esarhaddon and, in fact, solves one mystery, the fate of Sennacherib, for nowhere does Esarhaddon state that his father was assassinated. But beyond this there is considerable controversy among modern scholars about these events and particularly about the identity of the assassin or assassins. All the evidence points to one or more of Sennacherib's sons and two different theories have developed: that the chief assassin was an elder brother of Esarhaddon called Arda-Mulissi, or that the chief assassin was Esarhad-

[73] (a) Esarhaddon's texts: A 234, 40–5 i 8 – ii 10 (cf. A 487, 466–88); A 234, 16, Episode 11; cf. A 234, 109f §71. (b) A 25, no. 1 iii 34–8. (c) Nabonidus: A 856, 272 i 35–40. (d) Berossus: A 7, 24f. (e) II Ki. 19: 37; II Chron. 32: 21; Is. 37: 37f. (f) Jos. *Ant. Jud.* x.i 5. The *ša arki* date discussed in A 266, 22 is not directly relevant. The method of murder seems to be described by Ashurbanipal in A 344 II, 38 iv 70f (cf. A 44, 288). For another interpretation see A 265, 215–21 and A 231, 180f.

don himself. Before deciding which theory seems the more credible, let us consider some other facts.

As a general background it must be remembered that regicide, which is endemic in a military autocracy, was not unknown in Assyria. Tukulti-Ninurta I fell victim to a plot and Shalmaneser III may have met a similar fate. As to the immediate cause, it is a fact that Esarhaddon was not the first-born son (his name means 'Ashur has given a brother') and yet somehow he won his father's throne. Esarhaddon claims that Sennacherib designated him as his successor, and this is certainly true. It is corroborated, for example, by the fact that during the father's reign Esarhaddon's name was officially changed, obviously at the time he was appointed successor, to Ashur-etel-ilani-ka²in-apla which means 'Ashur, noblest of the gods, confirm the heir'.[74] Herein lies sufficient reason for a revolt by the disappointed and jealous siblings.

The cause of the rebellion then points to the elder brothers of Esarhaddon as the most likely leaders of the insurrection and murderers of Sennacherib. Parpola has argued on the basis of a fragmentary letter that in fact the chief assassin's name was Arda-Mulissi, the eldest surviving son before Esarhaddon's appointment as heir, and that this is the name preserved in the garbled forms 'Adrammelech' and 'Ardumu-zan' in other sources.[75] There is much to be said for this theory, but, given the broken state of the letter, it cannot be definitively proven.

As to the possible complicity of Esarhaddon in the murder, if his brothers had turned Sennacherib against Esarhaddon by their slander, as Esarhaddon tells us they did, here again is sufficient motive. Other elements possibly related to the causes of the rebellion are strong resentment towards Sennacherib because of his sack of Babylon eight years before, and the role of the harem in political affairs under the leadership of Esarhaddon's mother, Naqia, who will be discussed presently. But most of this is conjecture and it must be confessed that the murder of Sennacherib, the circumstances surrounding it, and the causes leading up to it, are unsolved puzzles.

8. Conclusion

Looking back over the events of Sennacherib's reign there are two or three features which stand out against the busy background. In both Babylonia and Palestine the Assyrian military machine was extremely vigorous and, on the home front, the building of Nineveh is equally impressive in its own way. While the latter phenomenon was the result of a policy decided upon and personally directed by Sennacherib, in the military sphere the motivation is not so clear. How much of Sennacherib's activity in Palestine and Babylonia can be attributed to long-range

[74] A 72, no. 1452; cf. A 234, §7 and 70.   [75] A 282.

policy? In the case of Palestine it is fairly obvious from the circumstances that Sennacherib envisaged the conquest of Egypt, and that all his efforts in the west came to be dictated by this overriding goal, a goal that his son would pursue almost as soon as he took the crown. In the case of Babylonia, however, one setback after another was heaped upon the king's head and, in a sense, he became the victim of fate; where he started out to find a suitable administrative scheme for Babylonia, he was trapped in a vendetta which compelled him to destroy the sacred city itself. It was a black deed that ruined his own reputation for posterity and was the starting-point for the ruin of the empire.

II. ESARHADDON (680–669 B.C.)

The reign of Esarhaddon (Pls. Vol., pl. 51), as mentioned at the beginning of this chapter, is unusual in that more emphasis in the official records is placed on cultural than on military endeavours. Nonetheless one of the greatest achievements of the Assyrian military machine, the invasion of Egypt, was enacted during this time.[76]

1. Sources and chronology

The sources for the reign of Esarhaddon, although as abundant as the sources for the reign of Sennacherib, are rather different in character. This is particularly so with the royal inscriptions which are largely of the 'Display' type rather than of the annalistic type and thus very uninformative with regard both to the details of the campaigns and to their chronology.[77] Fortunately the Babylonian Chronicle is of considerable help with the date of the campaigns and, because of its greater objectivity, it also provides important information omitted by the royal inscriptions.[78] This is in contrast to another document, the Esarhaddon Chronicle, which is a version of the reign written to shed a more favourable light on Esarhaddon and therefore as unreliable a source as the royal inscriptions. The portion of the royal archives found at Nineveh, which has been mentioned earlier, includes a large number of letters and astrological reports[79] from this reign, and from the same site come a significant quantity of legal and administrative documents.[80]

Our knowledge is further enriched by a group of texts, oracle inquiries and answers, which date to the reigns of Esarhaddon and Ashurbanipal; these inscriptions shed considerable light on political,

---

[76] For a brief but useful history of the reign see F. H. Weissbach, 'Aššuraḫiddin', in A 16 1, 198–203.

[77] The royal inscriptions have been edited in A 234 and see A 5 11, 18f for additions to this work.

[78] The relevant references in chronographic texts have been listed in A 25, 217–19. Note especially A 25, no. 1 iii 38 – iv 33 and no. 14 (the Esarhaddon Chronicle).

[79] For letters, see A 72–88. For astrological reports, see A 1032 and A 1040.   [80] See A 89–109.

administrative, and military events of the period.[81] They are involved
with the practice of extispicy, prediction of the future by observation of
animal entrails. Each of the oracle inquiries contains a request for an
answer, either yes or no, to a specific question. The inquiries are
presented in a fixed, formal style and, when the animal entrails are
examined, the omina are recorded at the end of the document. Unfortunately it is not clear from these whether the answer was favourable or
unfavourable. From Ashurbanipal's time we actually have replies to the
inquiries and these give explicit answers. Both the inquiries and the
replies are a mine of historical information and many of them describe
the details of projected military campaigns. Unfortunately none of the
inquiries is dated, although occasionally the day and month are given,
and thus they are of no help in the vexed problem of the chronology of
Esarhaddon's reign. From the point of view of reliefs and architecture
the most productive site has been Calah, although some information is
available from other excavated cities, notably Nineveh and Ashur.

A large number of campaigns were conducted during the twelve years
that Esarhaddon occupied the throne, but there are problems with both
the relative and absolute chronology of these expeditions. Indeed, it is
not even certain how many campaigns there were although later texts
speak of 'ten', the second invasion of Egypt (671) being the tenth
campaign. As with Sennacherib, this official numbering ignored some
campaigns; there were certainly more than ten military expeditions
before this date and there were others after it. There is no record of
campaigns for two regnal years: the ninth year (672) is omitted by the
chronicles, which means that either there was no campaign, or else there
was one but it was of no interest to the Babylonian chronicler; in the
eleventh year (670) there was a domestic crisis during which the king
executed a number of his officers, and this would account for the failure
to launch a foreign expedition. Briefly stated, while some campaigns can
be given absolute dates, for others one can only provide a *terminus ante
quem*, the date of the earliest text in which it is included.

2. Egypt, Phoenicia, and the Arabs

The political concerns of Esarhaddon were really a continuation of those
of the previous reign, the western offensive and Babylonia. To this was
added, however, the threat of various belligerent peoples on the north
and north-eastern frontiers and military activity in Anatolia. We shall
first concern ourselves with the invasion of Egypt.[82] The friendly
relations which were established between Egypt and Assyria when
Tiglath-pileser III and Sargon II reached her borders had been dispelled
by Egypt's anti-Assyrian activities in Palestine during Sennacherib's

---

[81] A 498; A 497; A 230.   [82] See A 298; A 299. Cf. A 310. See also below, pp. 378, 699–700.

reign, and it is a reasonable surmise that Sennacherib had hoped to invade Egypt himself, to punish the people, Kushites, responsible. After his assassination, his son wasted little time in launching the Egyptian offensive. In his second regnal year, 679, an Assyrian army pushed right to the borders of Egypt, where they captured the city of Arza and carried off its king, Asukhili, to Nineveh.[83] Five years passed before Esarhaddon could follow up this initial bid, years in which Phoenician cities became troublesome thanks to Egyptian agents, and the follow-up was a major disaster. The Assyrian army, according to the Babylonian Chronicle, was defeated in Egypt on the fifth of Addaru (XII) 674.[84] Nothing else is known of this event, which is ignored in the royal inscriptions; in the Esarhaddon Chronicle a minor campaign to Babylonia has been substituted for it.[85]

Only two years elapsed before the next attack on Egypt. No military campaigns are recorded for the immediately preceding year, 672, the year in which Esarhaddon gathered his subjects together to swear allegiance to his heirs, but this important event did not occupy the entire year and it may be assumed that much of the year was devoted to preparation for the next invasion of Egypt. We have an oracle request in which Esarhaddon asks whether this campaign is advisable and whether he will return from it in safety.[86] At the beginning of 671 the Assyrians marched to Egypt[87] and *en route* they laid siege to Tyre, an incident to be discussed presently. The Assyrian army was assisted in its progress across the Sinai Desert by camels commandeered from the Arabs to carry skins of water.[88] Upon arrival in Egypt they successfully fought three pitched battles with Egyptian forces, all in the month of Du'uzu (IV). Four days after the third battle, on the twenty-second of the same month, Memphis was captured; Taharqa, the pharaoh, fled but his family, including the crown prince, was caught. Esarhaddon appointed kings, governors, and other officials to rule Egypt and to collect the tribute for Assyria and the god Ashur.

The penetration of Egypt marks the high point in Assyria's imperialist expansion. Yet it was an ephemeral accomplishment; for Egypt, although temporarily forced out of Palestinian affairs, was far from subdued, as Esarhaddon himself must have realized. Certainly he wasted little time in returning. After a year fraught with domestic difficulties, the Assyrians launched a new Egyptian expedition in 669.[89] This

[83] A 25, no. 1 iii 48–50 and no. 14: 6–8. A 234, 33: 16f; 50, Ep. 7; 86 §57: 3f; 110f §72: 14f r. 12. A 252, 14 i 57–63. See A 25, 219b. Cf. A 275, 72–4 and 77 identifying Arza as modern Tel Gamma.

[84] A 25, no. 1 iv 16.   [85] A 25, no. 14: 20, and see 219 and 291a.

[86] A 498, no. 68.

[87] A 25, no. 1 iv 23–8, no. 14: 25f; A 234, 65f §28, 70 §§36f, 86 §57: 8f, 96–100 §65, 101f §67, 111–14 §§75–81. See A 25, 219b. Cf. A 275, 73f.   [88] Cf. A 19, 137–42.

[89] A 25, no. 1 iv 30f, no. 14: 28f; A 497, no. 36.

campaign was, however, abortive, for Esarhaddon died on the way to Egypt and his son and heir, Ashurbanipal, was left to deal with the unresolved issue of the conquest of Egypt.

A successful invasion of Egypt depended upon control of Syria–Palestine; Sennacherib had prepared the way by his activities in Palestine and he had done this so effectively that, apart from Phoenicia, no state in this region is known to have given Esarhaddon any trouble. Thus as early as 676 Esarhaddon could list all the coastal states of Syria–Palestine as having supplied him with exotic building materials for work at Nineveh; this list included Tyre, Judah (king Manasseh is named), Edom, Moab, Gaza, Ashkelon, Ekron, Byblos, Arvad, Samsimurun, Ammon, and Ashdod.[90] Tyre and Ashkelon were to cause trouble after this time, as we shall see, but the omission of Sidon from the list is significant.

The first source of trouble in Phoenicia was Sidon. Sidon had been captured by Sennacherib in 701 but early in Esarhaddon's reign its king, Abdi-milkutti, renounced Assyrian vassalship.[91] In 677 Esarhaddon captured the coastal city and, according to his account, tore down both the wall and the town, but Abdi-milkutti escaped by boat. The sequel to this action took place in the following year, 676, according to the Babylonian Chronicle. Esarhaddon caught Abdi-milkutti in the sea 'like a fish' and had him beheaded in the month Tashritu (VII). His family and people were transported to Assyria and a new city, called Kar-Esarhaddon, was erected and settled with people transported from the east. An ally of Abdi-milkutti, Sanduarri, who was king of Kundu and Sissu (presumably in Cilicia), was also captured and decapitated (XII/676), and the heads of the two kings were hung around the necks of their nobles who were paraded through the streets of Nineveh.[92] Two cities of Sidon were handed over to Baal, king of Tyre.

The relations between Tyre and Assyria during this period deserve further attention. Baal, king of Tyre, had signed a vassal treaty with Esarhaddon, a copy of which is extant.[93] The provisions preserved in the broken text concern the trading rights of the Tyrians and salvage rights in the event of shipwreck. The events leading up to the conclusion of this treaty are unknown; no specific reference to a conquest of Tyre appears in the sources for Sennacherib's reign and it is extremely unlikely that such a victory had been achieved. Nevertheless Sennacherib boasted that he had forced Tyrians, among others, to man his boats on the expedition

---

[90] A 234, 60 §27 v 54–63. These exemplars are dated 673 but the duplicate A 252, 28 iv 54f (actually it only has 'the twenty-two kings of Hatti-land' instead of the list of names) is dated 676.

[91] A 25, no. 1 iv 3–8, no. 14: 12–14; A 234, 8 §5, 48f Ep. 5, 86 §57: 2f; A 252, 10–13 i 14–37. See A 25, 218f; A 235, 115 n. 2. See also below, pp. 469–70.

[92] See *CAH* III².1, 427–8 and n. 454. A 25, no. 1 iv 5–8, no. 14: 13f; A 234, 49f Ep. 6; A 252, 12–15 i 38–56. See A 25, 219a.   [93] A 234, 107–9 §69; A 44, 533f.

across the Persian Gulf,[94] and Tyrians appear in the list of peoples transported to Nineveh for his great building projects.[95] But both these acts must have been by mutual agreement rather than unilateral coercion. Be that as it may, Baal later chose to revoke the treaty with Esarhaddon and ally himself to Taharqa. Thus, when Esarhaddon launched his Egyptian campaign in 671, he laid siege to Tyre before proceeding to Egypt.[96] The result of the siege is not recorded, apart from Esarhaddon's grandiose claim that he conquered Tyre and deprived Baal of all his cities and possessions. Tyre probably did not actually fall but the siege may have been continued by an Assyrian contingent, while the bulk of the troops proceeded to Egypt. There were also problems with Ashkelon which involved Egyptians, as we know from two oracle requests, and these probably occurred about the same time.[97]

The attack on Egypt depended, as we have seen, upon co-operation with the Arabs in the Sinai peninsula. This was not the only contact with the Arabs during Esarhaddon's reign, for he was concerned to maintain control over the oasis of Adummatu which Sennacherib had captured. Hazael, its king, paid homage to Esarhaddon and brought rich presents to Nineveh. The Assyrian restored to him the statues of his gods, but not before inscribing his own name thereon. A certain Tabua, who had been raised in the Assyrian court, was appointed queen of the Arabs and permitted to return to her people. When Hazael died, Yauta˒ his son succeeded to the throne and his position was recognized by Esarhaddon. The oath of subservience of the Arabs to Assyria, which is implied by these events, suddenly became important when a rebellion broke out against Yauta˒. Esarhaddon despatched an expedition which suppressed the rebels.[98] Subsequently Yauta˒ rebelled against Esarhaddon and escaped, after a defeat at the hands of the Assyrians, to remain free of the Assyrian yoke until the reign of Ashurbanipal, from whose account this event is known.[99]

A campaign against Bazza in 676 should also be mentioned in this context, since it is now generally assumed, although it is still very uncertain, that Bazza was in the east or north east of the Arabian peninsula.[100] Esarhaddon describes Bazza as a salty area and a place of thirst. On this campaign he claims to have killed eight kings and carried off their booty and people. Subsequently he installed a certain Layale, king of Yadi˓, as king of Bazza after this man had come to Nineveh for help.[101]

[94] A 270, 73: 59.   [95] A 270, 104: 53.   [96] A 234, 86 §57: 7f, 112 §76: 12–14.

[97] A 498, no. 70; A 497, no. 41. See A 497, LXI. Also note A 234, 102 §67: 31.

[98] A 234, 53f Ep. 14, 100f §66, 110f §72; A 252, 18–21 ii 46 – iii 8; A 344, 216–19, 222–5. See A 236, 8–11; A 19, 125–30.   [99] A 777, 73–85 Episode 2.

[100] See A 535, 160 n. 970; A 19, 130–7.

[101] A 25, no. 1 iv 5f, no. 14: 13; A 234, 33 §21: 24–7, 56f Ep. 17, 86 §57: 4f; A 252, 20–3 iii 9–36; A 235, 116a.

3. Anatolia

There is much uncertainty about Esarhaddon's activities in Anatolia, due largely to the nature of our sources, and it may be that more occurred on this frontier than our bits of information would indicate.[102] Esarhaddon's expansive boast that all kings in the sea from Yadnana (Cyprus) and Yaman (Ionia) to Tarsisi (Tarsus) were submissive and paid tribute would support this suggestion, although such claims can never be accepted uncritically.[103] Another boast of Esarhaddon is also of interest in this regard; the Assyrian lists the names of ten kingdoms in Cyprus which provided him with exotic building materials, and this list of largely Greek names is significant: Idalium (Edi'il), Chytri (Kitrusi), Salamis? (Sillua), Paphus (Pappa), Soli? (Silli), Curium (Kuri), Tamassus (Tamesi), Citium (Qartikhadasti), Ledra (Lidir), and Nuria (Nuriya).[104]

Perhaps the most serious threat to Assyrian influence in Anatolia was now the Cimmerians led by Teushpa, and Esarhaddon was able to defeat him at Khubushna (in the vicinity of modern Kara Hüyük?).[105] This event is probably to be dated to 679, since the Esarhaddon Chronicle records a slaughter of the Cimmerians for this year.[106] Between 679 and 676 there was at least one and possibly two further Anatolian campaigns against states which had once been Assyrian dependencies. Khilakku and Tabal were attacked but the expedition was unsuccessful, and it remained for Ashurbanipal to win them back.[107] Another event of significance had to do with Sanduarri, king of Kundu and Sissu. The identity of this king has long been a mystery, but since Kundu and Sissu seem to have been in the region of Cilicia, Winter and Hawkins have suggested that Sanduarri is identical with Azatiwatas, known from hieroglyphic Hittite inscriptions, and that his area of control included Que.[108] In any event, Sanduarri joined with Sidon in a naval alliance against Assyria, a fact mentioned earlier. In 676 the Assyrians defeated the allies and Sanduarri was captured and decapitated.

An ominous enemy was one Mugallu who, although he had at one point sought friendship with Esarhaddon, made alarming inroads into Assyrian holdings, sometimes in collusion with Ishkallu of Tabal, and besieged and captured Melid. In 675 the Assyrians launched an expedition against Mugallu at Melid, but the result of the attack is not recorded

---

[102] See A 279, 290f, and A 233; see also *CAH* III².1, 427–8.   [103] A 234, 86 §57: 10f.

[104] A 234, 60 §27 v 63–72; A 252, 28 iv 54f; cf. *CAH* III².3, 57–9.   [105] A 256, 66f.

[106] A 25, no. 1 iii 48–50, no. 14: 6–9; A 234, 33 §21: 18f, 51 Ep. 8, 86 §57: 1f, 100 §66: 23f, 110 §71: 18; A 252, 14 ii 1–4. Cf. A 244, 112f. A 72 no. 1026, a letter from Ashurbanipal while crown prince to Esarhaddon regarding Cimmerians is of later date. See also below, p. 559.

[107] A 234, 33 §21: 20, 51 Ep. 9; A 252, 14–17 ii 5–15.

[108] A 306A, 145–7; A 178, 155–7.

and the entire incident is missing from the royal inscriptions, a strong indication that the offensive failed.[109]

4. The north and north east

Assyria under Sennacherib had a short respite from any serious threat on the north and north-eastern frontier, but by the reign of Esarhaddon new dangers had appeared which directed Assyrian attention once again to these regions.[110] The scene is confused because, as usual with this reign, there is no coherent account of the events. A variety of peoples, most of whom spoke Indo-Aryan languages, are named in our sources; some (the Sapardaeans, Medes, Mannaeans, and Cimmerians) had been encountered by the Assyrians of earlier periods, while the Scythians were newcomers. In general these peoples had a common cause in their ambition to wrest territory and wealth from the empire of Assyria, but in practice they were rarely united in order to achieve this end, and on occasion a group, or sub-group, might even align itself with an Assyrian monarch. The Assyrians, for their part, were concerned both for the security of their borders and for a continuous supply of horses from this area, a supply route which was constantly harassed by these people.[111] In many ways the most informative documents are the oracle requests. As observed earlier, these texts concern various matters, but the bulk of them deal with questions about the hostile groups under discussion.[112] Whether or not this imbalance is a coincidence must remain an open question.

The Mannaeans and Scythians sometimes operated as allies, and Esarhaddon boasts of a victory over the Mannaeans and the army of Ishpaka, their Scythian ally, which possibly occurred in 676.[113] An oracle request, which probably dates after this event, speaks of Scythians who dwell in Mannaea; the query is whether they will emerge from the pass of Khubushkia, south of Lake Urmia, and plunder cities on the Assyrian border.[114] One of the most interesting oracle requests records that Bartatua (usually identified with the Protothyes of Herodotus), king of the Scythians, has sent messengers to Esarhaddon requesting an Assyrian princess in marriage; it asks whether, if Esarhaddon agrees, the Scythian will honour the bond forged.[115] This incident should probably

---

[109] A 497, no. 29; A 498, nos. 54, 55, 56a, 57; A 497, no. 30 joined to A 498, no. 21 (see A 230, 116); BM 99108 (A 230, 116). A 25, no. 1 iv 9f, no. 14: 15. Also note A 73, no. 279.

[110] See A 243; A 244; A 307.

[111] A 498, no. 31; A 497, nos. 15, 21, 22. See A 464, 117. Also note A 72, no. 1237.

[112] See A 497, LVI–LXII.

[113] A 234, 34 §21: 30, 52 Ep. 11; A 252, 16 ii 20–3; A 72, nos. 434, 1109, 1237; A 571, 233–7 (which presents the evidence for the date 676).

[114] A 498, no. 35. Also note A 498; nos. 25, 30, 36 and A 497, no. 20.

[115] A 497, no. 16; Hdt. 1.103.

be dated after 676 as well but possibly before the other oracle requests about the Scythians.[116] It is unknown if Esarhaddon agreed to the proposal. Mannaean aggression achieved the capture of Assyrian fortresses, some of which were regained by Ashurbanipal.[117]

The Medes were rather a special people during the reign of Esarhaddon, for many of them became sworn vassals of Assyria. An Assyrian expedition against the land of Patusharri (location uncertain), described as on the border of the salt desert in the midst of Media by Mount Bikni, brought back the rulers Shidirparna and Eparna together with their people and booty.[118] Because of this various rulers of the Medes came to Nineveh with gifts of horses and lapis lazuli, in order to win an alliance with Assyria (before 676), and Esarhaddon sent his eunuchs as governors of their districts.[119] A few years later, in 672, Esarhaddon gathered representatives of all his subject peoples to swear allegiance to his appointed successors, and the few copies of the record of this oath which were recovered in modern times concern Median princes.[120] But relations were not always peaceful. The Medes were ever regarded as a potential threat and in many oracle requests they are regularly listed as a possible enemy.[121]

The chief foe in these oracle requests was a man called Kashtaritu who is described as the 'city ruler' of Kar-Kashshi. It is generally assumed by modern historians that this ruler was identical with Phraortes, king of the Medes, whose history is briefly described by Herodotus; but, as Labat has observed, this identification is by no means certain.[122] In any case, Kashtaritu was a dangerous enemy and the oracle requests, which probably date to the period 676–672, indicate that he was attacking one Assyrian border fortress after another. In these texts Kashtaritu usually appears in a list of various potential attackers, a list which also regularly includes the Sapardaeans, Cimmerians, Mannaeans, and Medes. It should be observed that these enemies are regarded as alternative possibilities, and there is no indication that Kashtaritu was at the head of an alliance which embraced them all.

By chance we have a detailed narrative of one military action in the region of ancient Urartu, the conquest of Shubria in 673.[123] Shubria and its capital Ubumu were on the shore of Lake Van. Our main source for this campaign is a letter to a god, a genre of text already noted in the

---

[116] See A 230, 114.   [117] A 498, nos. 19, 20; A 497, no. 10; A 337, 52–5: 71–7.

[118] A 234, 34 §21: 31–6, 55 Ep. 16, 100 §66: 22f, 111 §75: 1–11; A 252, 24 iii 53–61; A 497, no. 21. See A 33, 118f.

[119] A 234, 54f Ep. 15; A 252, 24–7 iv 1–20; A 72, no. 434.   [120] A 307.

[121] A 497, nos. 1–8, 12–14; A 498, nos. 1, 2, 5–7, 10 and possibly 72. See A 230, 113–15.

[122] A 261. See CAH IV² 18f.

[123] A 25, no. 1 iv 19–21, no. 14: 23–5; A 234, 86 §57: 6f, 102–9 §68. See A 235, 114f. Also note A 498, no. 48. See A 291.

chapter on Sargon. Esarhaddon's letter is very similar to Sargon's, even to the point of listing the same casualties at the end. The beginning of the text is missing, and the first preserved portion concerns Assyrians who have fled to Shubria for refuge. We are not told of what crime these people were guilty, but it has been suggested that they included the conspirators who killed Sennacherib. According to the text, Esarhaddon wrote to the ruler of Shubria asking him to send heralds through the land exhorting people to produce the political refugees. The document is badly broken at this point but obviously the reply from Shubria was unsatisfactory. A series of messages were now exchanged between the two rulers but to no avail; although the Shubrian finally pleads with Esarhaddon to accept his submission, he had delayed too long, according to the Assyrian account. Having established a *casus belli*, Esarhaddon invaded Shubria to lay siege to Ubumu. The Assyrians built a siege wall which the besieged tried to burn down, but the wind shifted and the flames destroyed the city's defences. Ubumu was plundered and the political refugees were caught and mutilated. Urartian fugitives, which the king of Shubria had refused to surrender to Urartu, were also discovered and sent back to their land. Obviously Esarhaddon was willing to renew friendship with Urartu, a state which, however weakened, might be of some support against the multitude of peoples moving into this region. Esarhaddon rebuilt the city, renamed it, settled transported peoples in it, and appointed two of his eunuchs as governors.

5. Elam

Relations between Assyria and Elam fluctuated during Esarhaddon's sovereignty. There is no record of any Elamite interference during the later years of Sennacherib, nor during the turmoil surrounding the accession of Esarhaddon, despite the attempt of a group of dissident Babylonians to persuade Elam to wage war with Esarhaddon upon the death of Sennacherib.[124] Nevertheless, the Elamites were not favourably disposed towards Assyria after Sennacherib's treatment of them. Early in Esarhaddon's reign a certain Bel-iqisha, a Gambulaean, brought gifts including cattle and mules to the Assyrian court; his gifts were accepted, the man and his people became Assyrian vassals, and they were used to garrison a fortress, Sha-pi-Bel, on the Elamite border.[125] An Assyrian expedition against the Barnakkeans (perhaps identical with Bit-Burnakki in northern Elam) may have occurred about this time, the

---

[124] See A 304.
[125] A 234, 52f Ep. 13, 110f Frt. B: 6–13; A 252, 22–5 iii 37–52; A 72, nos. 336, 541; A 571, 222f and 242–4.

intention being to enforce Assyria's hold on the Elamite frontier.[126] It was probably after, and possibly as a result of these actions, that the Elamites and 'Gutians' (i.e. barbarians of the mountains) sent ambassadors to conclude a peace treaty in Nineveh.[127] This agreement was concluded in or before 676, and it may have been no more than a ruse to lull Assyrian vigilance on the Elamite border.

In any case in 675, according to the Babylonian Chronicle, the Elamites suddenly invaded Babylonia, probably swooping down the Diyala valley, and captured Sippar.[128] Since this is the same year for which the chronicles record the Assyrian campaign against Melid, the result of which is not noted, it is possible that there was a connexion between the two events. The Elamites may have been prompted to attack by the absence of the main Assyrian army in Anatolia, and the expedition against Melid may have been suddenly abandoned, so that the army might rush back to deal with the alarming situation. The Elamites had used such a strategy with devastating effect in 694, when they fell upon Sippar while Sennacherib was busy on the Persian Gulf. But it cannot be certain that this is how events evolved in 675, since no precise dates are given in our sources and, indeed, in the Babylonian Chronicle the Elamite raid is narrated first. Incidentally, the capture of Sippar, being a disgrace to Esarhaddon, is not mentioned in the Esarhaddon Chronicle or the royal inscriptions.

No further direct information is available for the raid of 675, but other items recorded in the chronicles are almost certainly relevant: in this same year the Elamite king, Khumban-khaltash II, died and was succeeded by his brother, Urtak; two prominent figures in Babylonia were taken as prisoners to Assyria, and at the end of the following year, 674, the divine images of Agade were returned to Babylonia from Elam.[129] One can reconstruct the events of 675 from these circumstantial details and show that the Elamite coup had missed its mark. The unexpected death of the king of Elam was probably the occasion for the Elamite withdrawal from Sippar, for if Esarhaddon had driven them out he would have boasted of the fact in his inscriptions, and the two prisoners taken to Assyria from Babylonia must have been implicated in the Elamite attack on Sippar. The Elamites suddenly found themselves in a bad position; they had deliberately provoked hostilities with Assyria but with no tangible gain. Thus they made a conciliatory gesture to Esarhaddon, who was actively restoring Babylon, by returning some divine statues to Babylonia which they had carried off on some previous

[126] A 234, 34: 28f, 51 Ep. 10; A 252, 16 ii 16–19. See A 307, 12f, and regarding Bit-Burnakki see F. W. König, 'Bît-Bunak(k)u/i', in A 16, 2, 38; A 309, 13 and n. 21.   [127] A 234, 58f Ep. 19.
[128] A 25, no. 1 iv 9–15, no. 14: 15–19; A 571, 237f.
[129] A 25, no. 1 iv 11–18, no. 14: 16–22; A 571, 249.

occasion, perhaps in 694. Esarhaddon accepted the gesture and a treaty was formed, as we know from letters which refer not only to the treaty but to the fact that the two monarchs exchanged children to be raised in each other's courts.[130]

6. *Other military matters and prominent men*

Apart from Babylonian affairs there is not much more to be said about military events during Esarhaddon's reign. Esarhaddon claims, in an undated text, to have imposed tribute upon Dilmun and its king Qana, but we have no other information on this.[131] There is a tantalizing scrap of information for the year 670 in the chronicles: 'In Assyria the king put his numerous officers to the sword.'[132] Unfortunately no further details are known of this affair, but the cause of the massacre must have been the discovery of a treasonable plot.

Very little is known about Assyrian army officers as individuals, since they are rarely mentioned in the royal inscriptions, and the texts of this reign are no exception; but fortunately more information in this regard is available in the oracle requests. Some of these documents concern expeditions to be led by Sha-Nabu-shu, chief eunuch, and the expeditions cover a wide geographic spectrum which included Ellipi, Melid, and Tabal, as well as the third expedition to Egypt.[133] This general may be identical with the eponym of the same name in the reign of Ashurbanipal (658). In speaking of notable men it is as well to remember Aba-Enlil-dari, the *ummânu* or vizier of Sennacherib and Esarhaddon, who was called Ahiqar in Aramaic and to whom a wisdom text in Aramaic (cf. *CAH* III². 1, 243–4) was attributed, which enjoyed popularity long after this era.

7. *Babylonia*

Esarhaddon's policy towards Babylonia was diametrically opposed to the hostile and vengeful treatment meted out by Sennacherib in his later years; where the father had raided and ravaged, the son attempted appeasement through a re-building programme and good government. In these pages only the Assyrian side of Babylonian affairs concerns us, for domestic events in Babylonia belong in Chapter 21, although Esarhaddon was king of Babylonia for his entire reign. In view of the dramatic difference between the Babylonian policies of Sennacherib and Esarhaddon, historians have suggested that there were two groups or

---

[130] A 72, no. 918 and cf. A 703, 34 n. 66; A 571, 245f.
[131] A 234, 86 §57: 5.   [132] A 25, no. 1 iv 29, no. 14: 27.
[133] A 498, nos. 57, 75; A 497, nos. 9, 34, 36; A 72, no. 1119.

parties in Assyria, one pro-Babylonian and the other anti-Babylonian, and, although this is probably an over-simplification, there is much to be said for the idea.[134] The opposing views were undoubtedly prompted by various motives: political, economic, sociological, religious, and cultural; and it would be a mistake on the basis of our present evidence to single out any one of these as the prime aim. As to the personal attitude of Esarhaddon we are completely ignorant.

Of course Esarhaddon's policy of appeasement could be explained, without resort to a two-party theory, as a natural reaction to the harsh and disastrous course which Sennacherib had followed. Such a reaction might have been behind Sennacherib's assassination, as we suggested earlier, and this could have occurred with or without a pro-Babylonian party of Assyrians. In passing it should be noted that the theory that Esarhaddon was governor of Babylonia during Sennacherib's reign lacks any supporting evidence.[135]

Esarhaddon, it appears, was more concerned than any of his predecessors who ruled Babylonia with the actual administration of that land, and letters of the period to the Assyrian court are full of reports and complaints regarding disputes among his officials in Babylonia.[136] These documents leave a firm impression that Esarhaddon kept a close personal eye on the details of Babylonian administration. In later years he was assisted in this by his son, Shamash-shuma-ukin, who was appointed crown prince of Babylonia. The king reaped his reward in that, while some anti-Assyrian resentment is always evident, there were few serious political disturbances in this part of his realm during his sovereignty, and even those few were in no way comparable to the problems which had beset his father.

The first instance of a real challenge to Esarhaddon's authority in Babylonia occurred during the confusion surrounding the accession. Nabu-zer-kitti-lishir, son of the notorious Merodach-baladan II and governor of the Sealand, revoked his oath of fealty to Assyria, and marching up the Euphrates laid siege to Ur and its governor Ningal-iddin.[137] As soon as Esarhaddon had won the throne, he despatched a force to relieve Ur; the siege was lifted and Nabu-zer-kitti-lishir fled to Elam, where he was murdered. Esarhaddon eventually appointed the fugitive's brother, Na'id-Marduk, in his stead as governor of the Sealand.

Two years later, in 678, a Chaldaean called Shamash-ibni, of the Bit-Dakkuri tribe, seized agricultural land belonging to Babylon and

[134] See A 265, 65–73; A 644, 13–16; A 756, 150–4; A 526, 34–6.
[135] See A 260; A 526, 33.   [136] A 644 (cf. A 526); A 574, 19–68 (cf. A 544).
[137] A 25, no. 1 iii 39–47, no. 14: 1–5; A 234, 33: 21, 46–8 Ep. 4; A 252, 16 ii 24–33; A 571, 247–9. See A 534, 246–8; A 574, 19–28; A 544; A 25, 218a and 291a.

Borsippa.[138] An Assyrian expedition caught Shamash-ibni and he, together with the *šandabakku*-official of Nippur, who must have been involved in this crime, was transported to Assyria and executed. Nothing further of major military significance happened until the Elamite raid on Sippar in 675, an event discussed earlier. The deportation and execution of two officials, a Dakkurian and the *šandabakku*-official of Nippur, which followed this event suggests that some important people in Babylonia were not guiltless with regard to the Elamite attack. For the following year it is recorded in the Esarhaddon Chronicle, in lieu of the Assyrian defeat in Egypt noted in the Babylonian Chronicle, that the Assyrians marched against Sha-amile, a town in southern Babylonia; the circumstances surrounding this raid are not recorded. These are the most important military engagements which are known to have taken place in Babylonia during the reign of Esarhaddon.

There is one sour note in Esarhaddon's conciliatory policy towards Babylonia: on two occasions the Babylonian Chronicle records that an Assyrian officer conscripted troops in Babylonia.[139] No doubt Esarhaddon felt that this was only a fair exchange for the protection afforded by his army, but the Babylonians would not have viewed it in that light, and the practice is not mentioned again after 677.

Esarhaddon's policy of appeasement called for the reconstruction of Babylon, which Sennacherib claimed to have completely destroyed. While there is reason to be sceptical of Sennacherib's boast, Esarhaddon's building programme at Babylon was extensive.[140] In a group of inscriptions recording this work there is a long prologue in which Esarhaddon presents his view of the circumstances surrounding the sack of Babylon in 689.[141] According to this narrative, because the evil people of Babylonia used temple property to bribe the Elamites, Marduk became angry with them and the result was chaos in the city: the Arakhtu canal overflowed its banks, so that the temples were flooded and the gods fled, followed by the people who fell into slavery. But then Marduk's anger abated, and he changed the period of time fixed for this 'bad' period from seventy to eleven years (a simple transposition of two cuneiform signs).[142] Good omens appeared and Esarhaddon in obedience to these set about the reconstruction of the city. It is, of course, not surprising that the Assyrians put all the blame for the catastrophe on the Babylonians; but what is unusual is the lengthy elaboration of this theme.

[138] A 25, no. 1 iv 1f, no. 14: 10–11; A 234, 33: 22f, 52 Ep. 12; A 252, 16–19 ii 34–45; A 571, 215f, 218f. See A 25, 218b.   [139] A 25, no. 1 iii 48–50 = no. 14: 6; A 25, no. 1 iv 3f = no. 14: 12.

[140] A 234, 10–30, 78–95; A 277; A 237; A 571, 215f. See A 526.

[141] A 234, 12–19 Ep. 3–17. See A 288, 9f.

[142] An oracle states that the period was reduced from sixty to ten years. See A 278, 158f.

The building projects involved the Esagila temple with its ziggurat Etemenanki, the processional way leading up to it, and the walls of the city. Esarhaddon's programme also included restoring to Babylonians who had been carried off into slavery their freedom, property, and right to return to Babylon, where they were encouraged to rebuild their houses, plant trees, and dig canals. The city's special status (*kidinnūtu*) and freedom (*zakûtu*) from levies of various kinds were reaffirmed. Further illustration of Esarhaddon's desire for reconciliation with the Babylonians is provided by a distinctive group of royal inscriptions which narrate the building of Marduk's temple at Babylon and Ashur's temple at Ashur in a comparative manner (see below, p. 136). The comparison was obviously intended to prove to gods and men that Esarhaddon was concerned for both projects equally.

The focal point of the restoration programme was the return of the statues of the gods from their captivity in Assyria and Elam, a symbol of divine appeasement, and in particular the restoration of the statue of Marduk. Marduk's statue was not returned from Ashur until the end of Esarhaddon's reign, and the reason for the delay, which some modern scholars have regarded as a curious mystery, is simply that the shrine was not ready until then. In fact the reconstruction of Babylon and the redecoration of its temples, launched at the very beginning of Esarhaddon's sovereignty, continued for the entire length of his reign, and even in the time of Shamash-shuma-ukin cult objects were being brought to Babylon from Ashur. The Babylonians were acutely aware that the statue was missing and carefully recorded this fact in their chronicles, noting also that this meant the *Akitu* festival could not be celebrated for twenty years.[143]

8. Building

The building projects of Esarhaddon were rather diverse, covering a number of sites in both Assyria and Babylonia. At Nineveh his main work was an extension of the arsenal (*ekal māšarti*) built by his father on the mound now called Nebi Yunus (Fig. 9).[144] Esarhaddon had one wing torn down, the terrace extended, and a number of large wings built with materials imported from a great variety of western lands. In conjunction with this he created a splendid garden full of exotic vegetation. Completion of this work was celebrated by a great banquet with the statues of the gods present. Fragmentary texts from Nineveh indicate that other building was carried out in this city, but it is uncertain just which structures were involved and no details of the work are preserved.

[143] A 25, no. 1 iv 34–6, no. 14: 31–7, no. 16: 1–8.
[144] A 234, 59–64 Ep. 21–5; A 252, 26–37 iv 32 – vi 43. See A 124, 132f; A 280; A 154; A 115, 2.

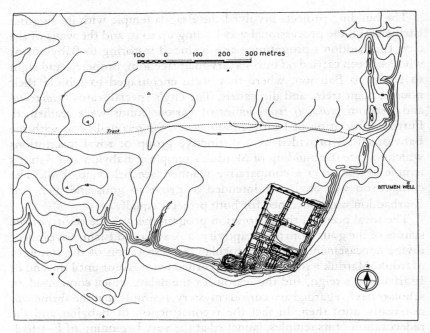

Fig. 6. Plan of Fort Shalmaneser, Nimrud. (After A 137 II, 370, fig. 301.)

The Emashmash temple, the temple of Sin, Ningal, Shamash, and Aya, and the temple of Nabu, are the names which are legible.[145]

A major work was the reconstruction of the temple of Ashur at Ashur, which is described in great detail in various inscriptions including the distinctive group, already mentioned, in which is narrated the building of this temple and Marduk's temple in Babylon in a comparative manner.[146] Other construction at Ashur included a palace, the *mušlālu*, and the *Akitu* house.[147] Calah received considerable attention from Esarhaddon, beginning as early as 676, and he had work done on Fort Shalmaneser, the Nabu temple, and the canal which carried water from the upper Zab.[148] He also began the construction of a palace (the South-West Palace) and transported a number of reliefs of Ashurnasirpal II and Tiglath-pileser III to be reused for this purpose, but the building was never completed.[149] At Arbaʾil Esarhaddon devoted some attention to

---

[145] A 234, 66–70, 94f r. 5–9. The work on the *Akitu* temple described *ibid.* r. 20–46 may have been at Nineveh.   [146] A 234, 1–6 iii 16 – viii 19, 6f §3, 78–91; A 235, 113f §10a. See A 507, 29.

[147] Palace: A 234, 8 §6. *mušlālu*: A 234, 9 §8; A 110, 86–91. Uncertain: A 234, 7f §4 (cf. A 5 11, 18), 9 §9.

[148] Fort Shalmaneser: A 234, 32–5 §21; A 273; A 255; A 308, 122 no. 5 i; A 137 II, 369–470. Nabu temple: A 137 I, 239–56. Canal: A 234, 35f §23. Cf. A 150.

[149] See A 116, 20–4; A 271, 5f. The new cylinder published by Wiseman (see now A 234, 32–5 §21), mentioned in A 116 and A 271 concerns Fort Shalmaneser, not the South-West Palace (see n. 148). Inscriptions of Esarhaddon from the South-West Palace are: A 267, 19 no. 1 (A 234, 36 §24) and A 267, 83 c (A 234, 69 §33). See A 150, 315 §§22–3.

the decoration of the temple of Ishtar.[150] The palace at Tarbiṣu (Sharif Khan) was enlarged as a residence for Ashurbanipal when he was designated crown prince.[151]

In Babylonia, the centre of attention was Babylon itself, which has already been described, but building projects in other cities were sponsored by Esarhaddon and materials supplied from the spoils of the campaigns. Restoration of Eanna, the temple of Anu and Ishtar, at Uruk was undertaken;[152] at Nippur the temple of Enlil and the temple of Inanna were restored;[153] and the temples of Nabu and Gula at Borsippa were refurbished.[154]

9. *Substitute king*

A curious phenomenon in the reign of Esarhaddon is the use of a substitute king.[155] A number of letters of the period inform us of this practice but our knowledge is still very sparse.[156] A substitute king was put on Esarhaddon's throne during the later years of his reign for short periods of time (a period of one hundred days is mentioned) on at least three different occasions. One of these occasions revolved around the lunar eclipse of the fifteenth of Tebetu (x) 671; indeed it was the prediction of this eclipse, which meant the king's death according to the astrologers, that occasioned the installation of the substitute king to divert the fatal blow from the real monarch. A ritual for the substitute king is fragmentarily preserved from this period and describes eclipses of various planets and stars, which would necessitate its use.[157] From the ritual it is clear that at the end of the period of danger the substitute king must die. Nothing is known from our sources about the duties and privileges of the substitute, nor is there any information about the abode of the genuine king during this period. He was in touch with his officials, however, for a number of letters addressed to 'the peasant' are clearly to the king, and these epistles must come from a time when a substitute king was on the throne.[158] Affairs of state are never mentioned in this correspondence, which suggests that these were beyond the king's prerogative during such a period.

There is allusion in the letters to the institution of the substitute king as having existed in former times, and in this regard a chronicle entry about two ancient kings of Isin, Erra-imitti (1868–1861) and Enlil-bani (1860–1837), is relevant:

---

[150] A 234, 33 §21: 8–11, 95 §64 r. 16–18.
[151] A 234, 71–3 §§43–6; A 72, nos. 628, 885. See A 280.
[152] A 25, no. 1 iv 19–21; A 234, 73–8 §§47–51; A 689, no. 132 (cf. A 235, 116f; A 5 1, 216).
[153] A 234, 70f §§39–42; A 605.   [154] A 234, 32 §20, 95 §64 r. 10–15.
[155] See A 644, 45–51; A 259, 169–87, and the literature cited there, to which add A 238.
[156] See A 297.
[157] A 263.   [158] A 73, nos. 25, 30, 31, 77, 137–9, 162, 166–7; A 72, no. 735.

Erra-imitti, the king, installed Enlil-bani, the gardener, as substitute king on his throne. He placed the royal tiara on his head. Erra-imitti died in his palace when he sipped a hot broth. Enlil-bani, who occupied the throne, did not give it up (and) so was sovereign.[159]

Leaving aside the question of the historicity of this passage, the explicit reference to the 'substitute king' has been accepted by many modern historians as confirmation that the institution was ancient.[160] It must be stressed, however, that this chronicle is known only from late Babylonian copies, and that the date of composition of the original work and the sources for this section are unknown.[161] On the other hand, it would be unwarranted to suggest that the story was fabricated in the seventh century in order to persuade Esarhaddon of the authenticity of the device; the fate of the real king, Erra-imitti, would hardly be reassuring! But it does raise the question whether an obscure custom was not revived and transformed to suit some sinister purpose of Esarhaddon's officers, particularly if it is true that they had absolute control of state affairs during such a period. An attempt was made in Ashurbanipal's reign to continue the practice but perhaps with little success.[162] The idea of a substitute king survived the Assyrians, for there are tales told in classical sources which seem to be garbled versions of the oriental custom, and the institution existed in Safavid (seventeenth-century) Persia.

10. *Naqia and the harem*

The mother of Esarhaddon, Naqia, was mentioned in the discussion of Sennacherib's assassination, but it is now time to say more about her. This woman bore both an Aramaic name, Naqia, and an Assyrian name, Zakutu, and she was obviously of Aramaean lineage. She was married to Sennacherib while he was crown prince and rose during his subsequent reign to become chief lady in the royal harem, when her son, Esarhaddon, was appointed crown prince.[163] The fortuitous rise in status, occasioned by the tragic fate of Sennacherib's first-born son Ashurnadin-shumi, was an opportunity which Naqia used to gain unprecedented authority. Her new position brought wealth, for the lands of the queen mother, now either deposed as chief lady or dead, were transferred to her.[164] She celebrated her success by building a palace for the new king at Nineveh, and had a text exactly like a royal inscription inscribed to

[159] A 25, no. 20 A 31–6 = B 1–7.
[160] Also *CAH* III². 1, 274 n. 208, to which add A 96, pl. 41: 1 and pl. 45: 12, 14, 16; and cf. A 253, 215f; A 281, 173.   [161] See A 25, 48a.
[162] Cf. A 73, nos. 298–9, 334. References courtesy of Parpola.
[163] A 293 (20), 200 no. 8, (26), 28 no. 1; A 272; A 268, 272 n. 41. Cf. A 111, no. 4 (see A 5 1, 8).
[164] A 102, nos. 34–6.

commemorate this deed.[165] She behaved like a king in other ways: she dedicated cult objects;[166] reports and oracles on cultic and military matters were addressed to her;[167] a sculptor was commissioned to create her statue;[168] and she was portrayed in a relief standing behind the king.[169] When she became ill, Esarhaddon resorted to extispicy to discover if she would recover, and copies of his anxious inquiries have survived.[170] These scattered bits of evidence fail to provide a full picture of Naqia's character and actions, but there is sufficient to indicate that her position was at least as influential as that of Semiramis, if not more so, and it may be that the late legends of Semiramis incorporated tales of Naqia.[171]

There are references to other women in Esarhaddon's harem. One of his more important wives, Esharra-khamat, had a mausoleum erected in Ashur, in which she was buried in 673.[172] She was a Babylonian and no doubt the mother of Shamash-shuma-ukin, which explains her high status. Ashurbanipal's mother, on the other hand, lived to see her son reign.[173]

11. *The succession*

Esarhaddon was very concerned over the succession, which is not surprising when we consider the circumstances of his own accession to the throne, and he laid careful plans. In the month Ayyaru (11) of 672 the king assembled representatives from all parts of the empire and had them swear by the gods to carry out his wishes with respect to the succession. The numerous oaths taken on this occasion were recorded on large clay tablets, one tablet for each group of people. Some of these texts have survived, all concerning the Medes as we mentioned earlier.[174] The manner of succession was totally new: Ashurbanipal was appointed heir to the throne in Assyria and Shamash-shuma-ukin heir to the throne in Babylonia. Thus the Babylonian question had become so important that it was a major factor in the succession to the throne. Whether or not this decision to split the crown was wise is questionable. At the time Esarhaddon was congratulated by at least one eminent Assyrian on his wisdom,[175] but the roots of the civil war to be waged between Ashurbanipal and Shamash-shuma-ukin lie here.

---

[165] A 234, 115f §86.   [166] A 93, no. 645 = A 97, no. 14.
[167] A 72, nos. 324, 368, 917, 1216 (see A 260); A 44, 605.   [168] A 72, no. 114.   [169] A 278.
[170] A 498, nos. 101–2.   [171] See A 268; A 278; A 289, 128.
[172] A 25, no. 1 iv 22, no. 14: 23; A 234, 10 §10; A 90, 18–20; A 264; A 526, 34.
[173] A 344, 392–5.
[174] A 307 (bibliography in A 5 1, 640 and 11, 325, to which add A 305), translated in A 44, 534–41; A 347, 215; A 234, 8 §6, 40 of Ep. 2 i 15–22, 72: 40; A 255, 116; A 344, 2–4 i 11–23, and 258–63 i 29 – ii 25; A 72, no. 213; A 73, nos. 1 and 3.   [175] A 73, no. 129.

Both successors were sons of Esarhaddon, although by different mothers, and Shamash-shuma-ukin seems to have been the older of the two.[176] The mother of Shamash-shuma-ukin was a Babylonian, which accounts for his designation to the Babylonian crown. Ashurbanipal, as heir to Assyria, entered the 'House of Succession' (*bīt-redûti*) at Tarbiṣu. The palace at Tarbiṣu was the traditional residence of the Assyrian heir apparent: Sennacherib had lived there before his succession and it was during this period that Esarhaddon was born there.[177] As previously noted, Esarhaddon enlarged the palace for Ashurbanipal. Both princes were assigned major administrative duties, directly under the king, a custom of the Sargonid age. One of the stipulations of the loyalty oaths to the crown princes was that all seditious matters must be reported to them, a provision to which there is frequent reference in the correspondence.[178] It appears that Shamash-shuma-ukin's responsibility was Babylonia, while Ashurbanipal had authority over the rest of the empire.[179]

Esarhaddon had other sons and at least one daughter.[180] Sin-nadin-apli was the eldest son, but the total silence of our sources, apart from an oracle request, with regard to this prince suggests that he died young. It was fortunate that Esarhaddon had made such elaborate preparation and given his heirs training in the administration of the empire, for otherwise his sudden death might have resulted in chaos. The succession followed smoothly although the precaution was taken, after his death, of having the oaths of loyalty reaffirmed both by the other brothers and by the people in general. It was Naqia who had a record of these renewed vows drawn up, evidence that her influence increased even farther with the accession of her grandson.[181]

12. *Character*

A salient characteristic of Esarhaddon is his almost fanatical devotion to divination. Of course all ancient Mesopotamians firmly believed in the arts of the diviner, but Esarhaddon, like his son Ashurbanipal, had more than his share of this faith. The king was persuaded of the efficacy of the substitute king ritual to avoid ominous harm, despite the fact that this

---

[176] See A 344, CCXLII–CCXLVI; A 347, 213f; A 268, 280f; A 307, 6f.

[177] A 234, 8 §6, 40f Ep. 2 i 15–22; A 344, 2–4 i 11–23, 258–63 i 29 – ii 25.

[178] See A 703, 31.

[179] See the following letters: (a) Ashurbanipal: (1) from him: A 72, nos. 430, 1026, 1257; A 571, 245. (2) to him: A 72, nos. 65, 187, 189, 445, 500, 885, 948, 950; A 73, no. 130. (3) about him: A 72, nos. 308, 1216; A 73, no. 70. (b) Shamash-shuma-ukin: A 72, nos. 534–6; A 73, nos. 140, 258; A 703. (c) also note: A 72, nos. 113, 434; A 73 no. 249; A 234, 87 §57 r. 4, 90 §59.

[180] A 344, CLXXXV, CCXLI–CCXLIX.

[181] A 72, no. 1239, and note no. 1105. See A 268, 282–5.

involved some loosening of his control over the kingdom. He was constantly seeking prognostic reports of every kind and would complain to his diviners if they did not keep him informed about any ominous occurrence.[182] There are numbers of astrological reports from his reign, and oracle requests have been frequently referred to in this narrative. These latter texts first appear in Assyria in the reign of Esarhaddon, and it is possible, although by no means certain, that this was an innovation inspired by Esarhaddon's penchant for prognostication.[183]

Another practice which was apparently introduced to Neo-Assyrian culture at this time was the oracle pronounced by an ecstatic. Devotees of the cult of Ishtar of Arbaʾil collected oracular utterances from people, mainly women, in various areas and copies of these oracles have been preserved.[184] The utterances were addressed to Esarhaddon by Ishtar of Arbaʾil and were words of comfort and reassurance that he would have a long and happy life, and that his kingdom and offspring would prosper. No doubt the cult profited from these oracles by receiving royal reward in such concrete forms as temple offerings. Yet another indication that Esarhaddon was unusually concerned about supernatural phenomena is the important place granted to such topics in the royal inscriptions. Given the nature of our sources, it is impossible to be positive about the reason for this extreme emphasis on divination in state affairs, but in the general context of the Assyrian state the most obvious explanation is that it reflects a personal characteristic of the monarch.

13. *Conclusion*

Despite his short rule and untimely death Esarhaddon was the king who added the most decorative jewel to the Assyrian tiara, Egypt. Of course the way had been prepared by his father but this does not detract from the son's achievement. At the other end of the empire, in Babylonia, Esarhaddon inherited quite a different state of affairs, and he had the good sense to do his utmost to mend the horrible wound inflicted by Sennacherib. In Anatolia he lost ground to new invaders, Cimmerians, and the Medes and Scythians on the north and north-eastern frontiers had become a serious problem, a foretaste of the final blow to come.

---

[182] A 72, no. 1409; A 73, nos. 50, 278–9. See A 294.
[183] See A 230, 112; A 1040, 124f; A 1082, 188 n. 217.   [184] A 44, 605. See A 26, 13f and n. 4.

CHAPTER 24

ASSYRIA 668–635 B.C.: THE REIGN OF
ASHURBANIPAL

A. K. GRAYSON

The reign of Ashurbanipal begins in what appears to be the hey-day of
Assyrian imperialism and ends in a dark period of confusion, followed
shortly by the fall of Assyria itself. It is the task of the present chapter
both to describe the great days of Ashurbanipal's reign and briefly to
reflect upon the reasons for the catastrophe which brought to an end one
of the great empires of the ancient world.[1] The end of the reign of
Ashurbanipal is part and parcel of the history of the foundation of the
Neo-Babylonian empire which will be treated in the next chapter.

1. Sources and chronology

The reign of Ashurbanipal is the best attested of all periods in the history
of Assyria in terms of quantity of material, but it is extremely difficult to
use much of this documentation to write history because of its unusual
nature and because of the lack of a chronology. Chief among the sources
are Ashurbanipal's royal inscriptions; these are more numerous and
lengthier than those preserved for any earlier monarch, and include a
group of texts which are commonly called 'annals' but which are really a
curious combination of the annalistic form and the 'display' form.[2] They
are rather like small historical novels and have behind them a complex
textual history. Considerable care must be exercised in studying these to
unravel the true course of events. Turning to the other sources, as with
Ashurbanipal's immediate predecessors, there are a large number of state
letters, astrological reports, and legal and administrative documents.[3] In
addition there are the oracle texts which have already been described
under Esarhaddon. The bulk of the inscribed material comes from
Nineveh, which is also a source of a rich quantity of sculptured reliefs.

---

[1] Specialized histories of the reign are A 344, CCXXX–CDLXXII; F. H. Weissbach, 'Aššurbânapli', in
A 16, 1, 203–7.

[2] There is no comprehensive edition or bibliography of the royal inscriptions of Ashurbanipal.
Many sources in English translation will be found in A 35 II, §§ 762–1129. The more important text
editions are: A 344; A 313; A 337; A 162; A 312; A 258; A 335. Further see the bibliography in A 5 under
the relevant entries, to which add A 563. For the references in chronographic texts see A 25, 208.

[3] See A 72–109.

Chronologically oriented sources for the period are unusually sparse, and the internal chronology of the reign is one of the more uncertain areas in Neo-Assyrian history. There is no Eponym Chronicle for the entire reign; the eponym list breaks off at 649; no Babylonian Chronicles are preserved beyond 667; and the so-called 'annals' of Ashurbanipal confuse rather than contribute to a solution of the chronological problems. No eponyms are quoted in the text of the annals, but rather the compaigns are numbered in order of their appearance in the narrative, and this order is not necessarily according to chronological sequence. Moreover, the order varies from one edition of the annals to another, so that the same campaign can have two or more different numbers in the various editions. The recently proposed reconstruction of the chronology of the reign will be followed in these pages.[4]

2. Egypt and the west

Ashurbanipal's relations with Egypt are highlighted by two military campaigns; the first, against Taharqa, culminated in the recapture of Memphis (667) (Pls. Vol., pl. 56); the second, against Tantamani, was crowned by the capture of Thebes (c. 663).[5] The death of Esarhaddon while en route to Egypt in 669 meant that Assyrian ambition in Egypt was suspended while the new king, Ashurbanipal, consolidated his domestic position. Taharqa took advantage of the situation by occupying Memphis and launching an attack against the Assyrian garrison stationed there by Esarhaddon. When news of this action reached Nineveh, Ashurbanipal promptly despatched an Assyrian force to Egypt, which met and defeated at Kar-baniti an army sent out by Taharqa. As soon as word of the disaster reached Memphis, Taharqa abandoned the city and fled up the Nile to take refuge in Thebes. The Assyrians, whose numbers were augmented by auxiliaries contributed by a number of kingdoms in the Mediterranean region and by Egyptian vassals, commandeered ships to pursue the enemy up the Nile. Taharqa abandoned Thebes and prepared to defend himself on the opposite bank of the river.

The narrative of the proposed pursuit, preserved only in early editions of the annals, stops abruptly at this point and is followed by a description of treachery on the part of Assyrian vassals in Egypt. Thus, as Spalinger

---

[4] See A 326.
[5] Sources for the Egyptian campaigns – A 25, no. 14: 40–4. Edition A: A 344, 6–17 i 52 – ii 48. Edition B: A 337, 30–41 i 50 – ii 40. Edition C: A 344, 138–43; A 313, 14f; A 258, 52f; A 335, 105. Edition D: A 337, 97. Edition E: A 337, 10–15; A 335, 99–101. Edition F: A 312, 30–3. Edition H: A 688, 102f. Annals tablet: A 344, 158–67, and cf. A 313, 56 (82–5–22, 10). Other royal inscriptions: A 313, 54; A 162, 106f; A 120, 84: 80. Reliefs: A 115, 47b and pl. xxxvi. Letter: A 72, no. 923 (A 73, 117 and see A 341). See also A 25, 208b. For a thorough exposition of the sources, including the Egyptian material, see A 340 and A 324. Also cf. A 30. See below, pp. 700–2.

has suggested, one suspects that the Assyrian march to Thebes was prevented or interrupted by the discovery of the treachery.[6] Necho, Sharru-lu-dari, and Pakrur, Egyptian princes whom Esarhaddon had earlier recognized, communicated secretly with Taharqa, seeking an alliance. The messengers were caught and the plot revealed to the Assyrians. Presumably it was in this emergency that the army abandoned its expedition to Thebes, although this is not stated in our sources, and promptly crushed the rebellion. The Assyrians punished in their inimitable fashion all those implicated in the plot with the exception of Necho, who was reinstated with much honour as a vassal prince at Kar-bel-matati (Saïs), and his son, who would eventually become known as Psammetichus I. Memphis was reoccupied by the Assyrians, who restored order to their holdings in Egypt, strengthened their defences, and brought back prisoners and booty to Assyria.

Eventually Taharqa was replaced by his nephew Tantamani, who carried on his uncle's attempt to win Egypt. Tantamani secured Thebes and then marched down the Nile to Memphis, where he met in battle the Egyptian princes of the Delta, including Necho. Tantamani won the day but a subsequent invasion of the Delta itself foundered. By this time the news had reached Nineveh and an Assyrian army once again invaded Egypt. In face of this attack Tantamani abandoned Memphis but his army was overtaken by the Assyrians and defeated. Tantamani escaped to Thebes, from whence he had to flee when the Assyrians captured the city and looted it. The fall of Thebes (c. 663) marks the pinnacle of Assyrian achievement in Egypt and, in more practical terms, it ended Kushite interference with Assyrian holdings in Syria–Palestine. Under Psammetichus I, who was installed as king at Saïs and Memphis, Egypt caused Assyria no further trouble and Ashurbanipal was free to concentrate his efforts elsewhere.[7]

Since the days of Sennacherib Assyria had enjoyed a strong position in Syria–Palestine and, with the exception of Tyre, Ashurbanipal had no difficulties with this region. Indeed the state of Arvad was more effectively embraced within Assyria's sphere of influence during his reign.[8] Ashurbanipal's firm hold is illustrated by a long list of his western vassals, although the reliability of the list is suspect, since it is copied verbatim from a list in the royal inscriptions of Esarhaddon.[9] But Tyre remained the centre of resistance which it had been in the previous reign, and Ashurbanipal laid siege to the island stronghold (c. 662) after

---

[6] See A 340.   [7] See A 342.
[8] Sources for relations with Arvad – Edition A: A 344, 18–21 ii 63–7 and 81–94. Edition B: A 337, 44–7 ii 71–92. Edition D: A 337, 97. Edition F: A 312, 34f i 70 – ii 9. Annals tablet: A 344, 168f r. 27–31. Other royal inscriptions: A 120, 84: 83f. On the date of these events see A 326.
[9] See A 4, 85.

Egyptian affairs had been settled.[10] Ashurbanipal's siege was more
successful than that of Esarhaddon, for, although Tyre did not actually
fall, it is claimed that its ruler, Baal, submitted and Ashurbanipal
accepted his daughter and nieces along with much treasure in token of
his vassalship. But Tyre did not remain subservient, and later in the reign
(c. 644), on his return from a campaign against the Arabs, Ashurbanipal
attacked the mainland suburb of Tyre, called Ushu, and plundered it.[11] It
seems that it was on this same occasion that he took Akku (Acco, Acre)
by force and a number of men whom he carried off he added to his
army.[12]

3. Anatolia

The suppression of Tyre brought in its wake offers of friendship from
major Anatolian states, Tabal, Khilakku, and Lydia, for Asia Minor was
by this time sorely pressed by the Cimmerians. Although Esarhaddon
had claimed a victory over a Cimmerian band, by the reign of Ashurbanipal the Cimmerians had effectively ended Assyrian control in this area
and were threatening states as far west as Lydia. Ashurbanipal's victories
in Egypt and against Tyre caused the beleaguered ruler of Khilakku to
seek Assyrian support by sending his daughter with a dowry to
Nineveh.[13] As for Tabal, Mugallu, the old enemy of Esarhaddon, was
now its ruler and presumably the ruler of Melid as well, although Melid
is not mentioned by Ashurbanipal.[14] Mugallu is said to have brought his
daughter with a dowry to Nineveh, but, true to his wily nature, he then
began to intrigue with Dugdamme (the Lygdamis of classical authors) of
the Ummanmanda (an Akkadian literary term applied to various enemies
including the Cimmerians and Scythians) against Assyria.[15] Dugdamme
attempted two invasions of Assyria (c. 640)[16] but calamity befell him
both times before he could actually attack; on the first occasion fire broke
out in his camp and on the second he was struck by illness and died.

[10] Sources for Tyre – Edition A: A 344, 16–19 ii 49–62. Edition B: A 337, 40–5 ii 41–70. Edition D:
A 337, 97. Edition F: A 312, 32–5 i 56–69. Edition H: A 688, 102f ii 14–24. Other royal inscriptions: A
120, 84: 81f. Regarding the date see A 326.

[11] Edition A: A 344, 80f ix 115–21.

[12] Edition A: A 344, 82f ix 122–8.

[13] Sources for Khilakku – Edition A: A 344, 18f ii 75–80. Edition B: A 337, 44f ii 71–9. Edition D:
A 337, 97. Edition F: A 312, 34f. Other royal inscriptions: A 120, 84: 83f.

[14] Sources for Tabal – Edition A: A 344, 18f ii 68–74. Edition B: A 337, 44f ii 71–9. Edition D: A
337, 97. Edition F: A 312, 34f i 71–7. Annals tablet: A 344, 168f r. 22–6. Other royal inscriptions A
120, 88: 138–45.

[15] Sources for Dugdamme – Edition H: A 775, 4: 1–6; A 162, 109; A 335, 109f. Other royal
inscriptions: A 120, 88f 138–62; A 344, 276–87: 20–6; A 162, 106f. For discussion and bibliography see
A 342, 136 and n. 19; A 317, 80 n. 26.   [16] See A 326; and see below, p. 559.

Dugdamme was succeeded by his son Sandakshatru, concerning whom no further narrative is preserved.

The third ruler who is recorded as having sought friendly relations with Assyria in the face of the Cimmerian threat was Gyges (Gugu) of Lydia.[17] Prompted by a dream, says Ashurbanipal, Gyges sent a messenger with gifts to Nineveh and from that day he began to be successful in his war with the Cimmerians. The Cimmerians were not so easily repelled, however, and in 657 an astrologer predicted, in a report to Ashurbanipal, that the Cimmerians would overrun the west, although Assyria would be spared.[18] Several years after this report Lydia was overrun by the Cimmerians and Gyges was killed (c. 645). He was succeeded by his son who, Ashurbanipal says, resumed good relations with Assyria.[19] From these incidents it is clear that Assyria was still on the defensive on the Anatolian frontier, worried by the Cimmerian hordes and anxious to ally itself with any Anatolian state that would resist and hamper Cimmerian progress.

4. The north and north east

The scene on this frontier is much the same as during the reign of Esarhaddon, with the Mannaeans, Medes, and Urartians being the leading antagonists, and there is no need to repeat the description of the intricate relationships and primary goals of the participants. The highlight of the action, from the Assyrian point of view, was a brilliantly successful campaign against the Mannaeans.[20] Before Ashurbanipal's time the Mannaeans had made inroads into territory claimed by the Assyrians, capturing one city after another. Early in his reign (c. 660), Ashurbanipal launched an attack against the Mannaeans, crashed through their domain as far as Izirtu, and by means of vigorous excursions regained numerous districts for Assyria. This operation precipitated a revolution; Akhsheri, king of the Mannaeans, was assassinated and his son Ualli took the throne. Ualli sent his son and daughter to Ashurbanipal's court and agreed to supply the Assyrians with horses.

The Medes, many of whom had been vassals of Esarhaddon, had by now become aggressive, but Ashurbanipal boasts of only one expedition

[17] Edition A: A 344, 20f ii 95–110. Edition B: A 337, 46–9 ii 93 – iii 4. Edition D: A 337, 97. Edition E: A 337, 16f; A 335, 102. Edition F: A 312, 34–7 ii 10–20. Annals tablet: A 344, 166–9 r. 13–21. See A 339; A 317; A 244, 113–18; A 325. See below, p. 559.   [18] A 72, no. 1391; and see A 327.

[19] Edition A: A 344, 20–3 ii 111–25. See A 342, 133–7 and n. 6. The date of Gyges' death is usually given as 652 B.C. but this must be lowered. See A 317, 78f n. 25; A 343; A 326.

[20] Edition A: A 344, 22–7 ii 126 – iii 26. Edition B: A 337, 50–7 iii 16 – iv 2. Edition C: A 313, 15 iv 31–62. Edition D: A 337, 97. Edition F: A 312, 36–9 ii 21–52. Edition H: A 688, 102f. Other royal inscriptions: A 120, 85: 87–90; A 313, 83 r. 10.

against them, during which he captured alive some Median rulers who had previously been subject to Assyria.[21] The king of Urartu, Rusa, sent a peaceful envoy to Ashurbanipal early in the latter's reign, which was in keeping with Urartu's long avoidance of confrontation with Assyria.[22] Nonetheless, in about 657 an Urartian governor attacked Ubumu, the capital of Shubria, which Esarhaddon had added to his empire. Ashurbanipal's troops managed to capture the Urartian leader of this expedition, Andaria, and his head was brought back to Nineveh.[23] Many years later (*c.* 643), when the Shamash-shuma-ukin rebellion had been crushed and Ashurbanipal had won a major victory over Elam, Sarduri, king of Urartu, sought friendly relations with Assyria.[24] The paucity of praiseworthy deeds in the Assyrian records is indicative of the vulnerability of Ashurbanipal's northern and north-eastern frontier, for during this time the enemies of Assyria were creeping closer and closer to the centre of the empire.

5. *Elam and Babylonia*

Babylonia and Elam were natural allies during the long period of Assyrian ascendancy, and this fact had interesting results during Ashurbanipal's reign. Babylonian affairs are treated in detail in Chapter 21, and here the main emphasis will be upon Elam with only a synopsis of the Shamash-shuma-ukin rebellion. The good relations between Elam and Assyria established by the treaty during Esarhaddon's reign continued into the early part of Ashurbanipal's sovereignty; when there was famine in Elam, Ashurbanipal not only allowed some starving Elamites to take refuge in Assyria but also sent grain to Elam.[25] Given the long bitter struggle with Elam that preceded Ashurbanipal's time, however, it is not surprising that in due course hostilities broke out. According to Ashurbanipal, three leading figures instigated Urtak, king of Elam, to invade Babylonia; these men were Bel-iqisha, the Gambulaean and former vassal of Esarhaddon, Nabu-shuma-eresh, the *guenna* of Nippur, and Marduk-shuma-ibni, a Babylonian general in the service of Urtak.[26] The occasion for the invasion was Assyria's involvement with Egypt in 667; the Elamites very quickly overran Babylonia and laid siege to Babylon. Despite his preoccupation, Ashurbanipal eventually despatched troops to the south and the invaders fled back across the border.

[21] Edition B: A 337, 56f iv 3–8. Edition D: A 337, 97.

[22] A 346, 188, and cf. A 115, 6f; A 155, 251–8. Cf. A 337, 102 iii 21–4. See A 326.

[23] Edition B: A 337, 56f iv 9–17. Edition C: A 313, 15f v 9–23. Edition D: A 337, 97. Cf. A 569, 344 n. 9.   [24] Edition A: A 344, 84f x 40–50. Other royal inscriptions: A 120, 87: 121–3.

[25] Edition B: A 337, 56–9 iv 18–26. Edition H: A 688, 102f. Also see A 72, no. 295.

[26] Edition B: A 337, 56–9 iv 18–53. Edition D: A 337, 97. Edition H: A 688, 102f. Other royal inscriptions: A 313, 87–9: 28f.

A few years later, in 664, there was a dynastic upset in Elam and Teumman seized the throne. Urtak's sons, together with many of the royal family and retainers, fled Elam to seek asylum with Ashurbanipal.[27] The presence in Nineveh of a rival claimant to the Elamite throne meant that good relations between Ashurbanipal and Teumman were out of the question, particularly when the Assyrian rejected Teumman's demand for the extradition of the fugitives. The hostile atmosphere became absolutely stormy when Shamash-shuma-ukin began, perhaps as early as 653, to form an anti-Assyrian alliance into which Elam was drawn. Teumman invaded the east Tigris region in this year and the move may well have been intended to support Shamash-shuma-ukin's bid for power, a bid which was not actually made until the following year.[28] Be that as it may, the attack was unsuccessful, for Ashurbanipal's army promptly occupied Der and the Elamites fled back to Susa without a confrontation. The Assyrians pursued their enemies and a pitched battle was fought at Tell Tuba on the banks of the River Ulaya. The conflict is vividly portrayed in a series of reliefs with cuneiform captions from Nineveh, in which the Assyrian troops are shown cutting down the Elamites.[29] Thus Assyria defeated the Elamite army on home ground. Teumman was beheaded, and Ashurbanipal appointed one of the Elamite princes who had been living at his court, Khumban-nikash II, as king at Susa and another such prince, Tammaritu I, as king at Khaidalu.

The success of this Elamite campaign provided an excellent opportunity to regain dominance over the buffer state of Gambulu.[30] Ashurbanipal had not forgotten that Bel-iqisha had been implicated in Urtak's invasion of Babylonia and, although Bel-iqisha had now been replaced by his son Dunanu as leader of the Gambulaeans, the Assyrian wanted vengeance. He stormed through Dunanu's lands and captured, sacked, and destroyed the capital Sha-pi-Bel. Dunanu was taken captive to Nineveh, where he was displayed to the people with the head of Teumman hanging from his neck. The bones of Nabu-shuma-eresh, the *guenna* of Nippur, who like Bel-iqisha had urged Urtak to invade Babylonia, were brought back from Gambulu and crushed in a gate of Nineveh.

[27] A 25, no. 15: 2f. Edition B: A 337, 6of iv 58–86. Other royal inscriptions: A 313, 87–9: 29 – r. 1. See A 677, 19; A 326.

[28] Edition A: A 344, 26f iii 27–51. Edition B: A 337, 60–77 iv 87 – vii 2. Edition C: A 313, 16 vi 37 – vii 9. Edition D: A 337, 97. Edition F: A 312, 38–41 ii 53–71. Other royal inscriptions: A 344, 188–95: 7 – r. 13; A 313, 45f, 51: 5–8, 67, 83f.

[29] A 115, 14f, 42f, and pls. xxiv–xxvi; A 147, pls. 68–70 (and cf. A 115, 20 and 42a). Also note A 344, 322–33; A 346, 176–91; A 313, 91–105; and cf. A 314; A 155, 287–97.

[30] Edition A: A 344, 26–9 iii 52–69. Edition B: A 337, 70–7 vi 17 – vii 2. Edition C: A 313, 16 vii 10–120. Edition D: A 337, 97. Edition F: A 312, 40–3 ii 72 – iii 5. Other royal inscriptions: A 120, 85: 105–7; A 313, 83: 10–13; A 346, 176–91 and A 313, 91–105. Also note A 313, 85 r. 1–4; A 72, no. 269.

These early clashes with Elam are a mere prologue to the serious situation which developed with the outbreak of the Shamash-shuma-ukin rebellion, and it is necessary to go back for a moment and outline the beginnings of the war with Babylonia.[31] Although Esarhaddon had stipulated that at his death Shamash-shuma-ukin was to become king of Babylonia, this did not happen automatically, as it did with Ashurbanipal in Assyria, and Ashurbanipal claims that he actually appointed his brother to the southern monarchy.[32] He further claims that during the period of the dual monarchy he was friendly and generous towards Babylonia and Shamash-shuma-ukin. But the very fact that two brothers wore the crowns of two lands which were ancient rivals was sufficient reason for jealousy and hostility to erupt and, despite Ashurbanipal's boasts of friendly acts, the record speaks against him.

At the beginning of Ashurbanipal's reign the statues of Marduk and other Babylonian deities were taken back to Babylon from Ashur (668), thus continuing Esarhaddon's policy of restoring Babylon after Sennacherib's destruction,[33] but the practice stopped abruptly with this event and was not resumed for thirteen years, until 655–653, when further cult objects were returned.[34] This may possibly indicate a lapse in the restoration programme as a whole. Whether the lapse of the restoration policy was by design or mere casual neglect, it could not but have caused dissatisfaction in Babylonia; and the resumption of the policy in 655, three years before the revolt broke out, was an eleventh-hour attempt by Assyria to quell disaffection. It is to this period that one should probably date an incident related by Ashurbanipal: Babylonian envoys came to the court at Nineveh.[35] The purpose of the mission is not stated, and this is not surprising, since they had probably been sent to complain of neglect by the Assyrian court. Ashurbanipal records that he treated the delegation handsomely, and it was his policy throughout the subsequent tumult to regard the Babylonians as innocent dupes of Shamash-shuma-ukin's cunning.

Shamash-shuma-ukin gradually built up support for his ambitious aims in a wide circle which embraced a number of foreign nations, including the Elamites and Arabs, and, as we suggested earlier, one may regard Teumman's attack in 653 as the first move on the part of this alliance, although this is not stated in any of the sources. As the clouds of war gathered on the horizon, Ashurbanipal attempted to undermine Shamash-shuma-ukin's position by seeking to win the Babylonians to his side. This was a favourite Assyrian strategy, attempting to alienate an

---

[31] Cf. A 574, 74–8.
[32] A 344, 28 iii 72, 230: 11f, 234: 14f, etc. Cf. A 574, 72f and A 544, 319 no. 33.
[33] A 25, no. 1 iv 34–6 = no. 14: 35f = no. 16: 5–7; A 498, no. 149.
[34] A 25, no. 15: 4f; K.2411 in A 677, 21f (and cf. pp. 19–23).
[35] Edition A: A 344, 28–31 iii 82–95.

enemy ruler from his people; Sennacherib's *rab-šāqēh* had tried this under the walls of Jerusalem and Tiglath-pileser III's officers did the same at the gates of Babylon during the Mukin-zeri rebellion.

In the present instance there is actually a letter preserved from Ashurbanipal to the citizens of Babylon, dated Ayyaru (II) of 652, in which the king emphasizes the privileges which the Babylonians enjoyed and would continue to enjoy under the *pax Assyriaca* so long as they were loyal to Ashurbanipal.[36] One may presume that the Babylonian response to this ploy was silence, for in the same month that the letter was despatched the major-domo began to conscript troops in Babylonia.[37] Events moved rapidly. Two months later (17/IV/652) Ashurbanipal considered but then rejected a plan to force an entrance into Babylon in the hope that Shamash-shuma-ukin would be captured and the revolt nipped in the bud.[38] The conscription of troops continued in Babylonia until open warfare erupted towards the end of the year (19/X/652), the immediate cause probably being the conscription.[39]

The war raged for four years (652–648) and, while the issue hung in the balance for the first half of this period, after the middle of 651 it became just a matter of time before Shamash-shuma-ukin succumbed.[40] At the end of 652 there were two battles, one on 12/XII and the second on 27/XII, when the Assyrians defeated a Babylonian force at Khirit.[41] Elam, of course, was another of Shamash-shuma-ukin's allies and in the early days of the war Khumban-nikash II of Elam sent a contingent to assist Shamash-shuma-ukin, but the Elamite troops were defeated by the Assyrians.[42] The abortive attack probably precipitated the revolution in Elam, in which Khumban-nikash was replaced by Tammaritu II.[43] The usurper continued the Elamite policy of support for Shamash-shuma-ukin and advanced once again to participate in the war.[44] Suddenly mutiny broke out in the ranks; Indabibi seized the sovereignty and Tammaritu II fled with his family for asylum, but not as one would expect to Shamash-shuma-ukin; rather he fled to Ashurbanipal! This is indicative of a change in the relative fortunes of Ashurbanipal and

---

[36] A 72, no. 301.   [37] A 25, no. 16: 9f.   [38] A 497, no. 102.   [39] A 25, no. 16: 11.

[40] Edition A: A 344, 28–41 iii 70 – iv 109. Edition C: A 313, 16f; A 258, 55–7. Other royal inscriptions: A 120, 86: 110–13. Also note A 313, 79–81, 86 r. 14–17. Further see A 497, LXII–LXVI; A 677, 24–9; A 572; A 574, 78–125.   [41] A 25, no. 16: 13–16.

[42] Edition B: A 337, 76f vii 3–35. Edition C: A 313, 17 viii 3–16. Edition D: A 337, 97. Edition F: A 312, 42f iii 6–9. Other royal inscriptions: A 313, 51f 9–12; A 344, 180f: 30–4; A 346, 198–201. Also note A 72 no. 1380.

[43] That this Tammaritu and the Tammaritu (II) mentioned earlier are two different men has been shown by A 313, 52 n. 5.

[44] Edition B: A 337, 76–81 vii 36–92. Edition C: A 313, 17 viii 17–52. Edition D: A 337, 97. Edition F: A 312, 42–5 iii 10–32. Edition G: A 337, 102f iv 1–22; A 563, 229–37. Other royal inscriptions: A 344, 180–3: 35–9; A 313, 46f: 13 – r. 8, 51f: 13 – r. 7, 54 (K.6358), 67f, 86: r. 9–21, 91–105; A 346, 191–203; A 35 II, § 1087; A 72, no. 1195.

Shamash-shuma-ukin, for this narrative has dashed ahead of other events which must now be considered.

During the first half of 651 there was considerable chaos both in Babylonia and Assyria,[45] chaos compounded by the fact that Nabu-bel-shumati, son of the notorious Merodach-baladan II and ruler of the Sealand, had come in on the side of Shamash-shuma-ukin. Doubts about Nabu-bel-shumati's loyalty were voiced at the Assyrian court at the beginning of 651 (4/I), when a report came to Nineveh that he was gathering troops in Elam.[46] But Ashurbanipal, believing Nabu-bel-shumati still to be loyal, sent troops to assist him on the southern front, and Nabu-bel-shumati, in a cunning move worthy of his father, trapped these Assyrian auxiliaries by night and made them prisoners.[47] A few months later (9/VIa) Assyria lost Cutha to Shamash-shuma-ukin.[48] This was the last victory of Shamash-shuma-ukin, however, for immediately afterwards the balance swung in favour of Ashurbanipal. Although there is no record of what brought about this alteration, it may have been the mutiny in the attack force of Tammaritu II. With the Elamite army out of action the Assyrians would have had a free hand to concentrate on Shamash-shuma-ukin and, if this is so, one wonders whether Ashurbanipal had a clandestine hand in the mutiny.

In any event, a month after the Babylonian victory at Cutha, Shamash-shuma-ukin's luck had so altered that there was a real possibility, as known from an oracle request, that the Babylonian king might flee the country to seek refuge in Elam (15/VII/651).[49] Ashurbanipal, on the other hand, was growing in confidence and success, as is manifest from further oracle requests, including one about a proposed attack on Shamash-shuma-ukin's army at Bab-same (near Babylon).[50] Early in 650 (5/II) the Sealand was back in the Assyrian camp and Ashurbanipal sent Bel-ibni with an army to take charge of Nabu-bel-shumati's old domain.[51] The Assyrians could now apply pressure on Babylonia from all sides, and on the eleventh of Du'uzu (IV) they pressed up to the gates of Babylon and laid siege to the city.[52] The Babylonians endured the siege for two years, suffering terrible hardships and famine, until the city fell in 648.

The maintenance of the siege would have occupied only a portion of Ashurbanipal's fighting forces, and thus most of the army was free to carry out campaigns against the Arabs and Elamites as retribution for their support of Shamash-shuma-ukin. The Arabian campaigns will be

[45] A 25, no. 15: 11, no. 16: 17–19.   [46] A 497, no. 105.

[47] A 25, no. 15: 12–18. Edition B: A 337, 8of vii 81–8. Edition D: A 337, 97. Cf. A 677, 26–8 and A 574, 77f.

[48] A 25, no. 15: 7–10.   [49] A 497, no. 109.

[50] A 497, no. 118 and cf. nos. 107, 113, 115; further cf. nos. 126, 129, 135, 139.

[51] A 72, no. 289.   [52] A 25, no. 15: 19.

treated later. It is now time to return to Assyria's relations with Elam. Elam's position had altered considerably with the change in the fortunes of war, and when Tammaritu II fled to Ashurbanipal's court, rather than using this as a pretext for further hostilities, Indabibi sought and gained good relations with the Assyrian king. Ashurbanipal, in a letter to Indabibi, addresses him as 'my brother', which is an indication of a treaty between the two.[53] Although the treaty has not been recovered, one of its provisions or preliminary stages involved Indabibi's voluntary release to Ashurbanipal of the Assyrian troops which Nabu-bel-shumati had treacherously seized.[54] The Elamite–Assyrian accord continued until 649, the year in which the aforementioned letter is dated, and it was probably in this same year that Indabibi was overthrown by Khumban-khaltash III.

In passing one should note a late and garbled version of these events in Ashurbanipal's annals, in which it is related that Ashurbanipal demanded of Indabibi the surrender of the Assyrian troops captured by Nabu-bel-shumati and of Nabu-bel-shumati himself; but before Ashur-banipal's messengers could reach Indabibi, he was deposed by Khum-ban-khaltash.[55] This story is obviously Assyrian rationalization of the overthrow of Indabibi and conflates two separate incidents, the return of the Assyrians by Indabibi and Ashurbanipal's demand to Khumban-khaltash for the extradition of Nabu-bel-shumati (646).[56] The sequel to the second incident was dramatic: when the demand was delivered at the Elamite court, Nabu-bel-shumati committed suicide (he and his shield-bearer fell on one another's swords) and Khumban-khaltash could only send back with Ashurbanipal's messenger his corpse.[57] Friendship towards Elam was a temporary expedient during the latter days of the Shamash-shuma-ukin rebellion, but with the rebellion crushed Assyria could dispense with the expedient and launch a campaign against Elam.

The purpose of the campaign (648) was to win back the buffer states between Elam and Assyria, to seek revenge for Elam's earlier role as an ally of Shamash-shuma-ukin, and to replace Khumban-khaltash with Tammaritu II, who had been living in exile at Ashurbanipal's court.[58] The people of the border states of Khilimmu and Pillatu fled to Assyria in face of the conflict, but Bit-Imbi resisted and was taken by force. When news of the invasion reached Khumban-khaltash, he abandoned Madaktu and fled to the mountains. Ashurbanipal once again put his

[53] A 72, no. 1151. Cf. A 574, 106f.   [54] Edition B: A 337, 8of vii 77–92.
[55] Edition C: A 344, 142–5 'viii'.   [56] A 72, no. 879.
[57] Edition A: A 344, 60–3 vii 25–50. Other royal inscriptions: A 120, 85f: 107–10; A 313, 68f; A 72, no. 879.
[58] Edition A: A 344, 40–5 iv 110 – v 22. Edition F: A 312, 44–7 iii 33–71. Cf. A 326.

own choice, this time Tammaritu II, on the throne at Susa. Tammaritu's tenure of office was short-lived, however, for he was forced a second time to flee to Ashurbanipal for asylum when Khumban-khaltash made a successful bid to reclaim the crown. Ashurbanipal attempted another attack in the same year to re-establish Tammaritu, but his army succeeded only in capturing and plundering a number of towns, including Khamanu (depicted in reliefs), and Khumban-khaltash remained in control of the Elamite throne.[59]

Elam had consumed a considerable quantity of Assyrian time and effort with no benefit to Assyria, and even the attempts to control Elam through a puppet king had been frustrated; it is not surprising that Ashurbanipal now felt compelled to take drastic steps. The Assyrian monarch called for a massive effort, an effort that would virtually crush Elam once and for all.[60] In 647 the Assyrian forces thundered through the border regions recapturing Bit-Imbi, Rashi, and Khamanu, and Khumban-khaltash once again fled, this time to take up a defensive position at the Idid river. Ashurbanipal pursued him there, and as the invading army crossed the river the Elamite abandoned his position and fled to the mountains.

The Assyrians swarmed through Elam taking one city after another (one of these cities, Din-sharri, is pictured in the reliefs), killing, looting, and even smashing cult images. But the capital, Susa, took the brunt of this rampage. While Ashurbanipal sat in state in the Elamite palace his soldiers destroyed temples and the ziggurat, desecrated the sacred groves and royal tombs, seized cult statues and royal statues, emptied the royal treasury, and carried off numbers of people and valuable booty and animals to Assyria. The devastation even included the spreading of salt over the fields, and Ashurbanipal boasted that henceforth no human cry would be heard throughout Elam for the land had reverted to wilderness. Back in Assyria the best of the plunder was dedicated to the gods, the skilled soldiers were added to the royal guard, and the remaining people and goods were distributed among the nobles and cities. The statue of the goddess Nanaya, which had been stolen by the Elamites in antiquity, was restored with great celebration to its proper abode in Uruk.[61] The might of Elam was destroyed, for however sceptical one

[59] Edition A: A 344, 44–7 v 23–62. Edition F: A 337, 46–9 iii 72 – iv 16. Reliefs: A 115, 14, 20, 39–41, 46, 58f and pls. XVI–XXI, LXVI.

[60] Edition A: A 344, 46–61 v 63 – vii 8. Edition F: A 312, 48–61 iv 17 – vi 21. Edition T: A 161, 34f iv 37 – v 32. Other royal inscriptions: A 344, 186f r. 15–20; A 313, 43f, 51f r. 7–14; A 120, 85: 96–105. Reliefs: A 115, 20, 59–61, and pls. LXVII (Din-sharri), LXX, and Fragment g (Bit-Burnakki). Cf. A 326.

[61] Opinions on the date of the statue's abduction by the Elamites vary. Cf. A 328, 97f; A 8, 59, 111, 206; A 41, 486. On the return of Nanaya note A 318, 9f, which may be a hymn to celebrate this occasion. Also cf. A 313, 74f, 82: 9–13.

might be of the details of the Assyrian rampage, in subsequent history Elam appears rarely and modestly until the Khuzistan plain is finally occupied by the Persians.[62]

6. The Arabs

It has already been observed that the presentation of military and political events found in the various editions of Ashurbanipal's annals is very confused, and this is perhaps best illustrated in the diverse narratives regarding relations with the Arabs.[63] Fortunately two recent studies, by Epha꜄l and Weippert respectively, have dealt with this problem in detail, although there is some discrepancy between them, and the following synopsis relies heavily upon the results of their investigations.[64] The oath of subservience which had been imposed upon Uaite꜄ of Qedar by Esarhaddon was renewed under Ashurbanipal, but some time before 652 this ruler, together with Ammuladdin, carried out border raids in Palestine and Syria, areas subject to Assyria. Ashurbanipal despatched troops which skirmished with the Arabs and burnt and looted their tents. However, Uaite꜄ escaped and took refuge with Natnu of the Nabayatu. Ashurbanipal installed Abiyate꜄ in place of Uaite꜄ as king of Qedar and imposed upon him an oath of subservience.[65] Eventually Natnu submitted to a similar oath. Ammuladdin, on the other hand, was captured by the Moabites and sent as a prisoner to Nineveh.

Difficulties with the sources for relations with the Arabs become even more pronounced in treating their role in the Shamash-shuma-ukin rebellion, and the following synthesis is rather uncertain. When Shamash-shuma-ukin formed his alliance, his Arab allies included Qedarites, led by Abiyate꜄ and Ayamu, and a people called the Shumu꜄ilu (not to be confused with Ishmael). These groups invaded Babylonia, and when the tide of war turned against Shamash-shuma-ukin in the middle of 651, Ashurbanipal despatched an army against the Arab contingent, probably either late in 651 or in 650. The Arabs suffered two defeats. A few years after the suppression of the Shamash-shuma-ukin rebellion, beginning c. 644, the Assyrian army again campaigned against the Arabs, namely Abiyate꜄ of Qedar, Uaite꜄ of Shumu꜄ilu, and Natnu of the

---

62 Edition A: A 344, 60–3 vii 9–81, 82–5 x 6–39. Reliefs: A 115, 16, 19f, 45–7, 54–8, and pls. xxxiv–xxxv, lx–lxv.

63 Edition A: A 344, 64–83 vii 82 – x 5. Edition B: A 337, 80–7 vii 93 – viii 63. Edition C: A 344, 144f; A 313, 18; A 258, 54. Edition D: A 337, 97. Other royal inscriptions: A 344, 216–19, no. 15; A 313, 35, 45; A 120, 86f: 113–29; A 777, 74–85. Reliefs: A 346, 200f nos. 79–82; A 115, 15f, 45, and pls. xxxii–xxxiii; A 155, 152–7. Letters: A 72, nos. 260, 262, 305, 1117. Cf. A 326.

64 A 19, 142–69; A 777.

65 In addition to the sources given above in n. 63 see A 321; A 316; A 777, 51 n. 57; A 315.

Nabayatu, in retaliation for raids which they had conducted against Palestine and Syria. The Assyrians used Damascus as their base and had a number of encounters with the nomads, destroying and looting their camps. Abiyate᾽ was captured, but Natnu seems to have escaped and it was probably on a subsequent campaign that he was caught. Nukh-khuru, his son, escaped on this occasion but subsequently came with tribute to Ashurbanipal, who crowned him king in his father's stead.

7. Other political events

The people of the city of Kirbitu had made border raids in the east Tigris region, plundering and harassing the inhabitants of Der, who appealed to Ashurbanipal for help. In 668 the king ordered his local governors to send a force to punish the trouble makers; Kirbitu, along with other cities, was besieged and captured.[66] It was probably in the following year, after the first campaign in Egypt, that the people carried off from Kirbitu were transported to Egypt and other people were settled in Kirbitu.

Apart from the events thus far narrated no other campaigns are recorded, although Ashurbanipal boasts of some exotic peoples and places which sent messengers and gifts to him on hearing of his great deeds. Khundaru, king of Dilmun, is said to have sent annual tribute; Shikhum, king of an island near Dilmun, came in person with tribute;[67] the kings of both Kuppi and Qade sent messengers who travelled six months to Ashurbanipal;[68] and two kings in Iran, one of them none other than Cyrus I, sent 'tribute' after Ashurbanipal's great victory over Elam.[69]

8. Building

The untimely death of Esarhaddon left a number of building projects and related enterprises unfinished and Ashurbanipal assumed the responsibility for their completion as well as initiating a number of enterprises himself. Nineveh continued to be the chief royal residence, and among the various works of Ashurbanipal here the most spectacular was the North Palace on the mound now called Kouyunjik.[70] This was erected on the site of 'The House of Succession' (bīt-redûti) of Nineveh,

---

[66] A 25, no. 1 iv 37 = no. 14: 38. Edition B: A 337, 48f iii 5–15. Edition C: A 313, 15. Edition D: A 337, 97. Edition E: A 337, 14f; A 335, 101f. Annals tablet: A 344, 166f r. 6–12. Other royal inscriptions: A 344, 206–9.

[67] A 120, 87f: 129–31, 135–8; A 72, no. 458. Cf. A 120, 99–105; A 345, 22.

[68] A 120, 87: 131–5; A 162, 106f. Cf. A 345, 24f.

[69] A 775, 4f: 7–25; A 120, 86: 115–18. Cf. A 775, 1–7; A 120, 98f; A 338.

[70] Edition A: A 344, 84–91 x 51–120. Edition F: A 312, 60–5 vi 22–73. See A 334; A 115.

the palace in which Ashurbanipal had grown up and to which he had, therefore, a special attachment. The ruined portions were torn down, the terrace rebuilt, the processional approach widened, a pillared portico in the Syrian style (*bīt-ḫilāni*) was added, and a garden planted with exotic trees. Inside, the walls of the numerous rooms were lined with miles of sculptured reliefs depicting the exploits of the king. Many of these magnificent carvings were recovered by nineteenth-century excavators and have recently been studied and re-published by Barnett (Pls. Vol., pls. 53–4, 56, 59–60).

Ashurbanipal also did some work on Sennacherib's South-West Palace, to which he added some sculptured reliefs portraying his own achievements.[71] The palace built by Sennacherib on the east side of Nineveh roughly equidistant between Kouyunjik and Nebi Yunus and south of the River Khosr received attention from Ashurbanipal, as is indicated by inscribed remains recently found there.[72] As noted in the preceding chapter, Esarhaddon had made additions to the arsenal (*ekal māšarti*) of Sennacherib in Nebi Yunus and Ashurbanipal continued restoration work there, but no details are preserved of the extent of his work.[73] Similarly Ashurbanipal carried on the restoration of the temple of Ishtar, Emashmash; he enlarged the forecourt, dedicated and deposited a number of precious objects in Ishtar's shrine, and installed the statue of Sharrat-Kidmuri in an appropriate cella.[74] Further, he restored the ziggurat and the Temple of the New Year (*bīt-akīti*).[75] Work on two other temples which had been initiated by Esarhaddon was brought to completion: the forecourt of Nabu's shrine, Ezida, was enlarged[76] and the restoration of the temple of Sin, Ningal, Shamash, and Aya finished.[77] As if these activities at Nineveh were not sufficient, Ashurbanipal repaired the dilapidated portions of the city wall.[78]

Arba'il is the only chief city of Assyria which has never been excavated, since the modern city sits atop the *tell*, and its history and the building activities of Assyrian kings there remain almost a complete

---

[71] See A 147 and cf. A 115, 2.

[72] A 284, 60. The following fragmentary texts cannot presently be identified with any particular palace: Edition C (A 313, 18); A 313, 35–7.

[73] Edition B: A 337, 86–9 viii 64–96. See A 154.

[74] Edition B: 337, 28f i 19–26. Edition C: (A 344, 146–51; A 313, 13f; A 258, 51f) i 63–89. Edition D: A 337, 97. Edition T: A 161, 29–33 ii 7–24. Other royal inscriptions: A 120, 81f: 30–6, 89f: 166–85; A 344, 274–7; A 313, 44–7, 54. Also note A 72, no. 1092; A 331, 68–70; A 332, no. 15. Cf. A 123, 71–3 and A 115, 26.

[75] Ziggurat: A 120, 82: 36. *Bīt-akīti*: Edition T (A 161, 35f; A 337, 4–6 n. 17; A 335, 105f) v 33 – vi 22. Cf. A 503, 72 n. 19.

[76] Edition T: A 161, 32 iii 15–17. Other royal inscriptions: A 120, 82: 39f; A 344, 272–5; A 313, 51–3. Also note A 344, 342–51 no. 2; A 322, no. 122. See A 124, 67–79, 117f, and cf. A 115, 26a.

[77] Edition T: A 161, 32 iii 18–35. Other royal inscriptions: A 120, 82: 40f.

[78] Edition D: A 337, 98f viii 64–83 and the improved edition in A 335, 102–5 viii 64–102. Edition E: A 337, 16 and A 335, 102 vi 1–14.

blank. This great gap in our knowledge is particularly unfortunate in relation to Ashurbanipal, for he had a special interest in this city, and the frequent references in sources of the period to the cult of its tutelary deity, Ishtar of Arbaʾil, suggest that much building activity must have gone on there. Indeed, although almost no inscribed remains have come from this mound, there are a significant number of texts from other sites which concern Ashurbanipal's construction at Arbaʾil and the dedication of precious objects to Ishtar of Arbaʾil.[79]

Little other work in Assyria is known to have been done by Ashurbanipal. The great rebuilding of the temple of Ashur at Ashur, which had been begun and largely completed by Esarhaddon, was finished by Ashurbanipal,[80] who also made some repairs to the city wall of Ashur.[81] At Calah he restored the temple of Nabu which Adad-nirari III had built,[82] and he may have done some work on the North-West Palace.[83] Although Ashurbanipal as crown prince had resided in the palace at Tarbiṣu after Esarhaddon had enlarged it for him, there is no record that Ashurbanipal himself did any work on the structure. He did dedicate an object to Nergal of Tarbiṣu.[84]

It fell to Ashurbanipal's lot to finish the great restoration programme at Babylon which had been one of the chief concerns of his father, Esarhaddon. As indicated earlier in this chapter in connexion with the Shamash-shuma-ukin rebellion, there were two phases to this restoration, one at the very beginning of the reign (668) and the other (655) shortly before the outbreak of the Shamash-shuma-ukin rebellion; it may be that nothing was done during the intervening gap of thirteen years, and this would have been a serious source of Babylonian discontent. In 668 the statutes of Marduk and other Babylonian deities were returned to Babylon from Ashur, and in 655 and following years further cult objects were returned; the restoration of Esagila was completed.[85] Other activities by Ashurbanipal at Babylon included the rebuilding of Eturkalamma, temple of Ishtar of Babylon;[86] the rebuilding of Emakh, temple of Ninmakh;[87] the rebuilding of Esabad, temple of Gula;[88] and repair of the city walls.[89] As to construction in Babylonia in general,

[79] A 313, 46f; A 344, 188–95, 248–53. See A 115, 15. Also note A 331, 68–70.

[80] Edition B: A 337, 28f i 19–26. Edition C: (A 344, 146–51; A 313, 13f) i 26–32. Edition D: A 337, 97. Edition T: A 161, 29f i 14–20. Other royal inscriptions: A 120, 81: 27–30; A 335, 111. Also note A 313, 83f; A 332, no. 16.   [81] A 347, 206 r. 3–23 and see pp. 204–18.

[82] Edition C: A 258, 60–3 iii 1–19. A 137 I, 231–88.   [83] Cf. A 137 I, 119.

[84] Edition T: A 161, 31f ii 25–30. Other royal inscriptions: A 344, 248–51: 10f.

[85] A 25, no. 1 iv 34–6 = no. 14: 35f = no. 16: 5–7; A 25, no. 15: 4f; A 344, 232–5, 244–9, 262–71, 276–87 (cf. A 313, 48f on K.3412),292–303; A 313, 49f; A 331, 70–2; A 347, 204–7, 217f: 13–18; A 35 II, § 1118–20. Also note A 498, nos. 104, 105, 106, 149 (cf. A 497, LXII and n. 4); A 72, nos. 119, 120, 951. See A 677, 19–23.   [86] A 344, 226–9.   [87] A 344, 238–41.

[88] Edition H: A 688, 102f viii 1–13 (the name of the structure is missing but the curses are all related to Gula).   [89] A 344, 234–9.

Fig. 7. Royal stamp seal (one of many with similar device) from a bale sent to Shalmaneser III at Nimrud. Width 4.5 cm. (After A 681, 41, pl. 27.)

Ashurbanipal had work done on Ebabbar, temple of Shamash at Sippar;[90] Emeslam, temple of Nergal at Cutha;[91] Ezida, temple of Nabu at Borsippa, and the city wall of Borsippa;[92] Ekur, temple of Enlil at Nippur, and the ziggurat;[93] and Eanna, temple of Ishtar at Uruk.[94] Restoration was even carried out on Edimgalkalama, temple of Anu *rabû* at Der on the Elamite-Babylonian border.[95]

The city of Harran and the cult of its tutelary god Sin had a privileged position in Sargonid Assyria, and this fact is well illustrated by Ashurbanipal's undertakings here. He rebuilt, enlarged, and refurbished Ekhulkhul, the temple of Sin; he restored the New Year's temple (*bīt-akīti*), and Emelamana, temple of Nusku.[96]

9. Special features

Next to military campaigns hunting was the favourite sport of Assyrian kings, and Ashurbanipal seems to have particularly enjoyed it. The greater portion of the reliefs recovered from the North Palace present hunting scenes, and while the figures of the king and his subjects are stereotyped, the artists have sculpted the animals in a strikingly life-like style.[97] The victims of the hunt were deer, gazelles, onagers, and most especially lions. At least one lion hunt was artfully contrived with

[90] A 344, 228–33. Cf. A 322, nos. 55, 105 and 361; A 323, no. 31.

[91] Edition H: A 688, 98f i 13–25. Other royal inscriptions: A 344, 176–89.

[92] Edition C: (A 344, 146–51; A 313, 13f) i 59–62. Edition H: A 688, 98f i 4–6. Edition T: A 161, 29–33 ii 1–6. Other royal inscriptions: A 344, 240–5; A 120, 83: 49–55; A 347, 217f; A 311; A 330.

[93] A 344, 352f.   [94] A 560, no. 42; A 72, no. 476.   [95] A 120, 84: 69–72.

[96] Edition B: A 337, 28f i 19–26. Edition C: (A 344, 146–51; A 313, 13f) i 90–107. Edition D: A 337, 97. Edition T: A 161, 31f ii 31 – iii 14. Other royal inscriptions: A 120, 83f: 60–9; A 344, 168–75; 286–93; A 336, no. 6; A 313, 35–44, 90 (cf. A 464, 2).

[97] A 115, 11–14, 19, 36–9, 48–54 and pls. II–XV, XXXIX–LIX, A and E; A 344, 304–11; A 313, 30, 82–5–22, 2: 1′–9′.

spectators on a hill ringed by a protecting band of warriors with shields and dogs (Pls. Vol., pl. 54); the king in his chariot fired arrows at lions which were released from cages, while mounted soldiers kept a wary eye on the proceedings. At the end of the slaughter the dead animals were brought to Ashurbanipal who, in the course of a religious ritual, poured a libation over the corpses (Pls. Vol., pl. 53). On another occasion the lions were hunted down in their native environment, in this case the marshes of southern Iraq. According to Ashurbanipal, lions had become so numerous there that they were a menace, killing not only livestock but also people.[98] On this exotic expedition, which included hunting the beasts from boats, Ashurbanipal took in his entourage the Elamite princes who had sought asylum in his court. From this brief reference to the exiles it would appear that they enjoyed the privileges of royalty while in Assyria, and Ashurbanipal describes, both in a relief and in a text, how he saved the life of one of them when attacked by a lion.[99]

Because of the abundant everyday documents preserved for this reign there is substantial information on the names and careers of many important men, including Adad-shuma-uṣur, scholar and political adviser; Bel-ibni, general; Mar-Ishtar, astrologer; and Balṭaya, a wealthy bureaucrat.[100] The appointment of someone to high office, which involved intensive lobbying and intrigue, depended upon the monarch's decision, which was conditional upon approval of the gods through extispicy.[101] But even a successful candidate could never be secure, for he was subject to sedition and slander and could be deposed and even executed if he failed to satisfy his king.

More is also known about the education and activities of Ashurbanipal as crown prince than about any other monarch. In the 'House of Succession' (*bīt-redûti*) he was taught how to ride horses, drive chariots, throw the spear, shoot the arrow, and how to bear the various kinds of shields. He also learned how to behave and to rule as a king, and as crown prince he gained practical experience of this, as we noted in the preceding chapter. An exceptional part of his education was reading, for most of his royal ancestors were probably illiterate. There is no doubt that he could read, since there is reference to this ability of the king both in letters and in the colophons of tablets. This atypical interest led Ashurbanipal to be actively involved in the acquisition of great numbers of tablets for the libraries at Nineveh, a subject to be treated in Chapter 26.[102]

[98] A 313, 87–9.　　[99] See n. 98 above and cf. A 115, 53 and A 72, nos. 943 and 1400.

[100] Adad-shuma-uṣur: see A 320 and A 73, nos. 119–70. Bel-ibni: see J. Schawe, 'Bêlibni', A 16, 1, 477–9 and A 574, 99–110. Mar-Ishtar: see A 73, nos. 275–97 and A 644, 37–57. Balṭaya: see A 102, nos. 9–12. Also note A 319.　　[101] See A 497 nos. 122, 124, 139 and cf. p. LXV.

[102] Edition A: A 344, 2–7 i 1–40; 84–7 x 57–74. Edition B: A 337, 28f. i 8. Edition D: A 337, 97. Edition E: A 335, 99f. Edition F: A 312, 28–31 i 1–34. Other royal inscriptions: A 344, 252–61 i 1–ii 8. Also see A 72, nos. 255 and 334; A 621, nos. 318, 319, 323–31, 336–8, 345. Cf. A 329.

The almost fanatical devotion of Esarhaddon to divination is also a characteristic of Ashurbanipal. Like his father, Ashurbanipal constantly sought prognostic reports and submitted requests for oracular decisions on state matters. The oracular utterances of ecstatics, particularly those associated with the cult of Ishtar of Arbaʾil, were carefully reported to the king and commonly mentioned in the royal inscriptions in connexion with major political and military events.[103] Another vehicle of divine utterance, the oracular dream, was favoured by Ashurbanipal. Ominous dreams were a well-known phenomenon in ancient Mesopotamia, and Tiglath-pileser III, among others, was concerned with them, but with Ashurbanipal there are several reports of such phenomena, including the famous dream of Gyges.[104] The influence of the soothsayers on state affairs during the latter days of the Assyrian empire obviously must not be underestimated.

Another illustration of continuity between the successive rulers is in the important role allowed the chief women of the harem. Naqia not only survived her son Esarhaddon, but also seems to have enjoyed greater influence, as noted in the preceding chapter. It was probably at her death that Ashurbanipal's wife, Ashur-sharrat, came to the fore; there is a stela inscribed with her name and she is probably the woman portrayed in the banquet scene with Ashurbanipal (Pls. Vol., pl. 50).[105] As for the rest of the king's family, it is known that Ashurbanipal dedicated two of his brothers to the priesthood.[106]

10. *Conclusion and reflection*

The early part of the reign of Ashurbanipal was brilliant, with military victories in the field, economic prosperity, great building projects, cultural achievements, and a general feeling of security and well-being. This state of affairs is a common theme in contemporary sources, in which the king is credited with bringing all this about. But as time wore on conflict and confusion evolved, and it is probably safe to say that Assyria never recovered from the effects of the Shamash-shuma-ukin rebellion, which, although it was a victory, in the long run turned out to be a pyrrhic victory. Other dangers which beset the land came nearer to the fore in this reign, as the Cimmerians occupied more of Anatolia and more losses were suffered at the hands of such peoples as the Mannaeans and Medes on the north-eastern frontier.

In this chapter the history of Ashurbanipal has been carried as far as 635, since subsequent events and in particular the fall of Assyria are best

---

103 In addition to the relevant passages in royal inscriptions see: A 313, 79–82; A 318 1, 26f; A 348.
104 For Tiglath-pileser III see A 323, no. 36 and cf. A 1145, 354.
105 A 111, no. 1. Cf. A 333; A 344, CCXVI–CCXXII and 390f; A 115, 20a, 56–8, and pls. LXIII–LXV; also note A 72, no. 308.   106 A 344, CCXLVII–CCXLIX, 250f: 16–18; cf. A 73, no. 150.

dealt with separately (Chapter 25) because of their close relationship to events in Babylonia. Before leaving the political history of the Assyrian empire, however, it is fitting to consider briefly the reasons for the fall of this great power. If the term 'fall' suggests total collapse followed by chaos, then this is a totally false impression; Assyria's demise was not like that of the Third Dynasty of Ur or of the Roman empire. The event was more a transfer of power from Nineveh to Babylon. The geography of the empire and its administration remained basically the same and there was no prolonged period without a central authority – Nineveh fell in 612, Harran in 609, and Nebuchadrezzar won the day at Carchemish in 605. The term 'Assyrian empire' might also be misleading, for until the reign of Tiglath-pileser III (744–726) any hold which Assyria had over surrounding areas and peoples was insecure and any serious attempt to throw off Assyrian bondage commonly succeeded. Only with Tiglath-pileser III did the Assyrians enforce their control and arrange their administration effectively. Thus, in speaking of the 'Fall of the Assyrian empire', one is actually referring to a power which flourished for little more than a century, before its centre was moved to an adjacent and ethnically related kingdom.

The reasons for the event itself should by now be apparent from the narrative of the preceding chapters and it is merely necessary to highlight the chief factors, always keeping in mind that the evolution of events is a complex affair with various elements intermixed at any given point in time. One of the basic problems in Assyrian foreign policy was that while a system of provincial administration slowly evolved over the centuries it was still a rather makeshift affair even in the latter days. If chance had allowed the Assyrians more time, perhaps they would have developed a more effective system; the Achaemenids did and their organization was based upon that of the Assyrians.

The most problematic sphere in Assyria's foreign policy was its relations with Babylonia. Because of the firm cultural links between the two nations Assyria could never treat its southern neighbour as it treated any other territory. Over the centuries various strategies were tried but they all foundered, and the irony was that in the end non-militaristic Babylonia conquered the great warrior nation. Assyria was governed by an absolute monarch, and the advantages and dangers of such a political structure are well known from numerous historical examples. In the Assyrian case the character and personality of the monarch was a crucial factor. While a capable man was on the throne, the empire enjoyed stability and prosperity. But the reign of an incompetent king meant disaster, for immediately the Assyrian nobility made inroads upon royal prerogative and possessions. This is what happened in the mid-eighth century and again at the end of the reign of Ashurbanipal.

CHAPTER 25

THE FALL OF ASSYRIA (635–609 B.C.)

J. OATES

This period includes the final years of the reign of Ashurbanipal, and
those of his three successors in Assyria, his sons Ashur-etel-ilani and Sin-
sharra-ishkun, and Ashur-uballiṭ II for whose affiliation we have no
evidence. Ashurbanipal is perhaps the best known of Late Assyrian
kings, and his reign is in some respects the best documented. Yet of his
final years we know little beyond the fact that he continued to be
recognized at Nippur until his thirty-eighth year (631). Even the length
of his reign remains in dispute, although one later inscription attributes
to him a total of forty-two years, i.e. until 627. His sons are even more
shadowy figures, of whose reigns in Assyria we are certain of neither
their length nor their date, while the last king of the once great empire is
attested solely in the Babylonian Chronicle recording his defeat (609).
Indeed the extant evidence for the chronology of the final years of the
Assyrian empire is so sparse and problematic that attempts to resolve the
difficulties have included the suggestion of Ashurbanipal's (perhaps
forced) abdication or retirement to Harran sometime before 627, for
which there is no direct evidence, and the hypothesis, now clearly
unacceptable, that Sin-sharra-ishkun and Ashur-etel-ilani were one and
the same person. These chronological problems are discussed in more
detail below (pp. 166ff).

The other major historical figure within this time span is Nabopolassar, a Chaldaean who first comes to our notice as an Assyrian-appointed
official in the Sealand. It is clear that he revolted against his erstwhile
sponsors, since he was recognized as king of the Sealand before his
accession to the throne of Babylon in 626. Although in his early years –
and probably as late as 616 – the Assyrians continued to contest the
control of Babylonia, Nabopolassar was successful in establishing
himself as the first of the distinguished line which ruled in Babylon, and
indeed as far as Egypt, from 626 until 539, when this short-lived empire
fell to Cyrus. This Neo-Babylonian dynasty is the proper subject of
Chapter 27, but the affairs of Nabopolassar are so involved with those of
the last Assyrian kings that he cannot be ignored here. One other major

SOURCES   163

personality concerns us, the Assyrian Sin-shumu-lishir, the 'chief eunuch' (GAL.SAG, *rab ša rēši*), whose protégé Ashur-etel-ilani was king of Assyria after the death (or abdication) of Ashurbanipal, and who himself claimed the Assyrian throne and was recognized briefly in Babylon in the same year as Sin-sharra-ishkun, brother of Ashur-etel-ilani and the penultimate Assyrian king.

I. SOURCES

1. King lists[1]

The king lists, which together with the so-called chronicles provide the backbone of Mesopotamian chronology, unfortunately fail adequately to document the span of time which concerns us here. Indeed, had the breaks in the few surviving tablets been deliberately designed to obscure this period they could hardly have been better placed. The Assyrian king list, preserved in four versions, unfortunately survives only in copies of which the latest date to the eighth century. However, since the Assyrian list was designed to perpetuate the concept of a hereditary and uncontested monarchy, even the fortunate discovery of a later copy might fail to resolve the complications of post-Ashurbanipal chronology, at which time we know from other sources that there were rival claimants to the kingship of both Babylonia and Assyria. The most extensive Babylonian document, Babylonian King List A, is of course concerned solely with the kingship of Babylon, but together with a new text found at Warka in 1959/60 it provides important if regrettably incomplete information for this period. King List A is broken just after the name of Kandalanu, king of Babylon 647–627, contemporary with the latter half of the reign of Ashurbanipal, the period in which Assyrian chronology becomes obscure. The Warka King List, a fragment of a Seleucid copy, is preserved from the name Kandalanu onwards, and attests the contemporaneity of the accession years in Babylon of Sin-shumu-lishir and Sin-sharra-ishkun.

A second form of king list, the so-called Synchronistic List, provides the names of Assyrian and Babylonian kings, side by side in parallel columns, presumably indicating their contemporaneity. Yet again, the best-preserved version ends with Ashurbanipal and Kandalanu. A further tantalizing fragment includes the name of Ashurbanipal's successor Ashur-etel-ilani, but his Babylonian contemporary, whose identity is of great importance for chronology, is again regrettably missing.

[1] A 607; A 767, 53.

2. *Eponym lists*[2]

The Assyrians dated by *limmū*, eponymous officials of whom lists are preserved only as late as 648 B.C. We know the names of a large number of *limmū* who do not appear on the extant lists and must therefore almost certainly date from the years after 648. Unfortunately the order of these 'post-canonical' eponyms is not known. Indeed there now exist more names than there are possible years, and it has been proposed that at least in some periods of the final decades of the empire disputing factions (perhaps in Nineveh and Ashur) appointed their own officials, who were not everywhere recognized.

3. *Chronicles*[3]

These texts, closely related to the king lists, are our other major source of chronographic information. Most important is the Babylonian Chronicle, at present thirteen known texts, which spans the period from the middle of the eighth to the third century B.C. Of these, seven tablets have so far been discovered, which constitute a sequential if selective history from the reign of Nabonassar (747–734) to the fall of Babylon in 539. The first of the extant texts ends in 668; there follows a gap, presumably of several tablets, before the next surviving document which begins in 627, after the death of Ashurbanipal. The latter text is our most important source for this confused and confusing period; it covers the first four years of the reign of Nabopolassar (from his accession to 623), while Chronicle 3 begins in 616 and provides an invaluable if sparse historical framework for the last years of Assyria. Yet again there is an unfortunate gap (622–617).

The Berossus and Ptolemaic traditions should also be mentioned, although they are of little direct value. Berossus was a priest of the temple of Marduk in Babylon, who dedicated to Antiochus I (281–261) a 'history' of Babylonia from before the Flood to Alexander the Great, a work which unfortunately survives only at third or fourth hand. The Canon of Kings of the second century A.D. by the scholar Claudius Ptolemaeus of Alexandria is a list of Babylonian, Persian, Greek, and Roman kings. This has proved a reliable source, but it omits kings whose reigns lasted less than a full year. Thus for the period discussed here we find only Kandalanu and Nabopolassar, with no mention of those brief claimants to the Babylonian throne whose dating remains a problem.

---

[2] A 361; A 763; additional post-canonical names can be found in the Nimrud economic texts (cf. n. 8 below) and A 356.   [3] A 25.

Biblical sources of course provide background to the fall of Assyria, especially with regard to the role of the Egyptians and Josiah in the west.

4. Royal inscriptions[4]

Comment on the extensive nature of Ashurbanipal's annals and other historical documents can be found in the preceding chapter. A number of these are dated by post-canonical *limmū*, i.e. after 648, but for the most part probably before 639, the year of Ashurbanipal's latest precisely datable inscription, a commemorative text recording the restoration of the Gula temple in Babylon and attributed, following the Babylonian dating system, to his thirtieth regnal year.[5] Some religious texts referring to the king's ill-health and old age have been assumed to date from his later years, but this is far from certain. The formal inscriptions of Ashur-etel-ilani and Sin-sharra-ishkun are few in number and rarely historically informative,[6] as are those of Nabopolassar. The royal records of the Neo-Babylonian kings reveal a pious preoccupation with prestigious building programmes and lack the campaign records of their Assyrian rivals. In fact there exist no 'historical' annals in the Assyrian sense, a lack which is to some extent compensated for by the less biased chronicles.

5. Letters; economic, legal and administrative texts

Only a very few of the letters preserved from the royal capitals date from this period; two royal letters, from Ashur-etel-ilani to his father and one to an unidentified son of Ashurbanipal, are known.[7] Economic texts are potentially a major source, not only for chronology, since many are dated, but for more general information. Our most important evidence for the troubled accession of Ashur-etel-ilani, for example, derives from a land charter. The Assyrian documents, which are dated by post-canonical *limmū*, have yet to be systematically studied, though many are available in transliteration and translation.[8] Since the Babylonians dated by regnal years, the economic texts from major southern centres such as Babylon, Nippur, Uruk, and Sippar not only attest the oscillating control of these cities in the final conflict between Assyria and Babylon,

[4] A new edition of the Assyrian royal inscriptions is being prepared by Grayson, but the volume containing the texts of Ashurbanipal and his successors has yet to appear. For references see A 25, appendix B. An English edition of the texts known before 1927 can be found in A 35 II.

[5] A 688.   [6] A 25, appendix B; A 353; A 360.

[7] A 72, nos. 469 and 1444; no. 1444 can be dated to Sin-sharra-ishkun on astronomical grounds (A 73, 70–1 no. 105 and A 77, 90–3). Private letters are preserved also from Ashur, Calah and Dur-Sharrukin.

[8] *Inter alia*, A 93; A 97; A 98; A 99; A 100; A 102; A 103; A 105; A 108; A 198; A 729.

but also provide such chronology as survives for the reigns of Ashur-
etel-ilani and his brother, of whose regnal years the extant Assyrian and
chronographic sources fail to inform us.[9]

II. ASHURBANIPAL AND KANDALANU (635–627 B.C.)

These years constitute a minor dark age in the history of Assyria. Official
sources are silent, while our inadequate understanding of the system(s)
of post-canonical *limmū* makes difficult any coherent assessment of the
rich mine of information contained in the surviving economic texts. We
have more than a dozen too many *limmū* officials for the number of years
available after 648, but the reasons for this remain a matter for
speculation. Precise chronology is not the only problem. The other
defect in our knowledge unfortunately applies not only to the last years,
but to the Late Assyrian empire as a whole, for we have no prosopo-
graphic knowledge of its high officials, even though we sometimes know
a great deal about their private and public affairs. The custom of
identifying a man by his patronymic disappeared in the Middle Assyrian
period and may perhaps be associated with the insistence on the role of
the king as the sole source of power and the author of all achievement,
which is particularly marked from the mid-eighth century onwards,
notably following a period when certain provincial governors had
trespassed on royal prerogatives. Yet we know that the king depended
on the nobility for both military and civil service. What we cannot
reconstruct are the factions that must have existed within a society that
was, in all but the most technical sense, feudal. It seems possible that the
transfer of the seat of government from Ashur to Nimrud, to Dur-
Sharrukin, and finally to Nineveh may reflect the king's desire to be with
his friends, or at least to escape from his enemies. It is also worth
recalling, in this connexion, that the consulate in Rome, an annual office
whose holders gave their name to the year, was commonly under the
empire held in the same year by more than two persons whose tenure of
high office was essential to the administration, and whose loyalty the
emperor wished to ensure. It may be that the last Assyrian kings
employed the same political device. This is pure speculation, but affords
a plausible explanation for the number of Assyrian eponyms whose
names have survived, especially at Calah (Nimrud). Certainly the

---

[9] A 553. I am indebted to D. Kennedy for providing me with the new lists of Nabopolassar year-
dates from his forthcoming publication of this material (see now A 367). Note that although
Babylonian years should be written, for example, 626/625 to conform with the Julian calendar, the
convention of writing the single year, 626, is followed here. Moreover, in order to avoid confusion,
the convention of using Babylonian months is retained even when citing Julian years. For example,
the accession date of Nabopolassar (26/VIII/acc.) is written here 26/VIII/626, despite the fact that the
appropriate Julian date is 23/XI/626 (see A 877, 27).

geographical distribution of the known *limmū* according to the provenance of the texts does not immediately reveal the existence of any
consistent or clear-cut factions.

It is widely assumed that at least in Assyria the final years of
Ashurbanipal were ones of unrest and dissension. The superfluity of
limmū and the absence of official documentation contribute to this view,
as does our hindsight knowledge of the imminent collapse of the empire.
Moreover, the difficulties inherent in the chronology of his immediate
successors, of whose reigns neither the lengths nor the dates are directly
attested, have led to a variety of historical reconstructions, none of
which has met with immediate acceptance.[10] A widely held view is that
Ashurbanipal abdicated in or sometime after 631, his last attested
Babylonian year date, and retired to Harran, where he had consecrated
his youngest brother as *urigallu* priest of the famous temple of the moon-
god, and where an inscription of the next century attests his forty-two-
year reign. This is seen as an old man's response to an escalation of
trouble at home and a crumbling empire abroad. This hypothetical
abdication, for which there is no direct evidence, has a superficial appeal
as the simplest solution to the apparent contradictions in chronology
(discussed below). However, another interpretation of the evidence is
possible, indeed probable. The chronology proposed here assumes that
Ashurbanipal ruled in Assyria until his death in 627. Because both
general and specialist literature disagree in their conclusions and differ
from the view presented here, it will be necessary briefly to review the
following basic sources.

Source 1. During the reign of Kandalanu in Babylon the city of Nippur,
alone among the cities of Babylonia, maintained direct allegiance to the
monarch in Assyria and continued to date by the regnal years of
Ashurbanipal. Whether this custom was a reflection of Nippur's strategic importance or a special privilege of the pre-eminent religious
centre in Babylonia is not clear, but in the absence of chronicle and king
list evidence these dates are our most important single source for the
chronology of the Assyrian kings during this period. The latest of the
Ashurbanipal tablets is dated 20/III/631. Year dates from Nippur also
inform us that Ashurbanipal's successor Ashur-etel-ilani reigned in
Assyria for at least four years and eight months, not including the year of
his accession which is so recorded.

Source 2. No official source provides us with the length of Ashurbanipal's reign, but an inscription on a stela from Harran commemorating
the mother of Nabonidus, the lady Adda-Guppiʾ, who herself lived to
the impressive age of 102 (or perhaps 104), attributes to Ashurbanipal a

---

[10] *Inter alia*, A 353; A 390; A 393; A 401.

reign of forty-two years, i.e. until 627. Adda-Guppi' was born in the 20th
year of Ashurbanipal (649) and lived

until the 42nd year of Ashurbanipal, the 3rd year of Ashur-etel-ilani, his son, the
21st year of Nabopolassar, the 43rd year of Nebuchadrezzar, the 2nd year of
Amel-Marduk, the 4th year of Neriglissar, and died in the 9th year of Nabonidus
[547].

The arithmetic of the inscription requires Ashur-etil-ilani to have ruled
in Assyria for at least one year after 627; thus he is the Assyrian king in
626.[11]

Source 3. Two texts recording grants of land by Ashur-etel-ilani
provide information about his accession:

After my father and begetter had 'departed' [died], no father brought me up or
taught me to spread my wings, no mother cared for me or saw to my education.
Sin-shumu-lishir, the chief eunuch [GAL.SAG], who had led me constantly like
a father, installed me safely on the throne of my father and begetter, and made
the people of Assyria, great and small, keep watch over my kingship during my
minority . . . Afterwards, Nabu-rehtu-usur . . . who had made a revolt and
rebellion . . . assembled the people of the city and the land of Assur . . .[12]

Uncertainty over the meaning of the word here translated 'departed', but
according to the *Chicago Assyrian Dictionary* a euphemism for 'died', has
encouraged the abdication theory.[13]

Source 4. Ashurbanipal ascended the Assyrian throne in 669 and
whatever his age on accession he must have been far from young in the
620s. Another argument for his retirement or banishment to Harran lies
not only in his undoubted age but more specifically in the royal
disillusion and ill-health assumed from another oft-quoted text:

Why have sickness, ill-health, misery and misfortune befallen me? Enmity in the
land and dissensions in my family remain with me. Disturbing scandals
continually oppress me. Misery of mind and of flesh bow me down. I spend my
days in lamentation [*lit.*, in oh's and ah's] . . .[14]

This passage is from a religious text, an introduction to an incantation in
which the wording may have followed some prescribed convention.
Moreover, the appointment of Shamash-shuma-ukin in Babylonia is
referred to in this same text without comment, which strongly suggests
that this particular document – and the troubles it purports to describe –
pre-dates the latter's insurrection (652).

---

[11] A 362. The inscription gives the age at death of Adda-Guppi' as 104. Unless there is an error of
two years in our overall chronology, which at this time is unlikely, she died at 102. A simple scribal
error is responsible for the discrepancy, cf. A 390, 142, and A 370, 218 n. 4.

[12] A 102, 44; also A 97, nos. 20, 21.

[13] Even if read *šimat mūši-šu*, the implication is the same, 'he died'.

[14] A 35 II, §§981–4 (K 891).

Source 5. The evidence of the Warka King List is crucial to the chronology of this period, but its interpretation is also far from straightforward:

... years [ ]	
'alias' [ ]	
(or, 'for a second time')	
21 years	Kandalanu
1 year	Sin-shumu-lishir
and	Sin-sharra-ishkun
21 years	Nabopolassar
43 years	Nebuchadrezzar, etc.[15]

This text provides the important information that Sin-shumu-lishir and Sin-sharra-ishkun were recognized in Babylon only briefly, and in the same year. Taken literally it would place the accession of Sin-sharra-ishkun, Ashur-etel-ilani's successor on the Assyrian throne, between the death of Kandalanu, which we know occurred in 627, and the accession of Nabopolassar, according to the chronicle 26/VIII/626. However, it cannot be assumed that this single year lies necessarily in 627/626. The inscription of Adda-Guppi' implies that in 626 the Assyrian king was Ashur-etel-ilani, and other evidence suggests that he was still in control of Nineveh as late as 623 (below, p. 174). Moreover, Chronicle 2 states explicitly that before the accession of Nabopolassar 'for one year there was no king in the land',[16] while posthumous Kandalanu dates (*arki, lit.* 'after' Kandalanu) are found as late as the month of Nabopolassar's accession.

Source 6. One last text should be mentioned, a tablet probably from Nippur and now in the Hilprecht collection in Jena, which lists a number of contracts dated to Babylonian years of Sin-sharra-ishkun or Ashur-etel-ilani, one of which provides an important synchronism between the third year of a king whose name is unfortunately broken and the accession year of Sin-sharra-ishkun:

year 3 of [   ], that is to say the accession year of Sin-sharra-ishkun[17]

The unknown king can only be Ashur-etel-ilani or Nabopolassar.

There is no immediately obvious resolution of the contradictions inherent in a literal reading of these texts. It is certain that both Ashurbanipal and Kandalanu died in 627, and that their deaths precipitated struggles for the succession in both countries, though on this evidence alone it remains uncertain whether in 627 Ashurbanipal was

---

[15] A 767, 53.

[16] Or perhaps this is a year formula, 'the first year there was no king in the land', but the implication is the same.   [17] A 729, no. 63 = A 638, no. 35.

everywhere still recognized as king. The assumption, based on the Warka King List, that the recognition in Babylon of both Sin-shumu-lishir and Sin-sharra-ishkun should be dated to 627 requires the restoration of the name Ashur-etel-ilani in Text 6 above, and his accession in 630. In itself such a recognition on the same document of rival Assyrian claimants is inherently unlikely on the part of any Assyrian scribe, and the little that survives of the name virtually rules out such a reading.[18] A further and almost insuperable difficulty in such a reconstruction is that it not only presupposes three claimants to the throne of Assyria in 627/626, all of whom were recognized in Nippur and two of whom are attested in Babylon in addition to Nabopolassar, but that in the same year(s) we have in Babylon the posthumous '*arki Kandalanu*' dates and the chronicle reference to the year in which no king was recognized. That Ashur-etel-ilani contested the throne (or that Sin-shumu-lishir did so for him) with his brothers is certain, but in any case the evidence of Text 3 makes it highly improbable that Sin-shumu-lishir revolted against his young protégé and claimed the Assyrian throne in the middle of Ashur-etel-ilani's reign. This is perhaps an argument for placing the death of Ashur-etel-ilani in 627 (accession 631), but such a reconstruction is not compatible with the evidence of either Adda-Guppi' or Text 6. Thus there is no unequivocal nor indeed persuasive argument for the abdication or retirement of Ashurbanipal before his death in 627. Indeed the land charters support the view that Ashur-etel-ilani acceded to the throne (in his minority) following the death of his father in 627 and amidst the insurrections in both Babylonia and Assyria attested by the chronicle.

That Babylonia was both peaceful and prosperous under Kandalanu, that is, during the final years of Ashurbanipal, seems beyond doubt. The evidence is discussed in Chapter 21, but it is necessary to return here to the subject of Kandalanu, since the interpretation of these years in Babylonia has implications for the history of Assyria. Kandalanu is described in the previous chapters as the Babylonian 'monarch', but he is known solely from the Babylonian year dates, king lists and a single chronicle reference. There is no Assyrian inscription that mentions his name, nor does he appear as a personality in any letter or in any economic or legal document.[19] Nor are there dates from an 'accession year'. Given the large number of economic texts from Babylonia at this time, this is indeed strange. Moreover, we know that during Kandalanu's 'reign' it

---

18 All that remains of the name is a single vertical wedge at the end; A 401, 246.

19 I am indebted to G. Frame for calling my attention to CT 53 no. 966, in which the name Kandalanu appears (line 10). However, there is no reason to suppose that this is the king of Babylon, despite a mention of 'the king' in the text. I am also indebted to Dr I. Finkel for collating the text for me.

was Ashurbanipal who appointed officials in Babylonia, even in Babylon itself, and who reconstructed, refurbished and made dedications in the temples of Babylon and other southern cities.

Tradition identifies Kandalanu as a brother of Ashurbanipal (and conceivably Ashurbanipal himself).[20] That Ashurbanipal appointed his brothers to a number of major posts in both Babylonia and Assyria is well attested, but nowhere is Kandalanu mentioned; nor does Kandalanu figure among the nine known sons of Esarhaddon.[21] The name itself is puzzling – it derives from some form of kitchen utensil – perhaps more appropriate to a child than a ruling monarch![22] The view, long held, that Kandalanu was but a throne name for Ashurbanipal is now rejected by many scholars (pp. 60–1 above). However, if he was a real individual, and on present evidence this cannot be demonstrated, he is curiously elusive, appearing as, at most, an eponymous official after whom the Babylonian years were designated. Neither case can be proved, but on present evidence the throne-name theory cannot be rejected out of hand and there is much among the circumstantial evidence to lend it credence.

Historical experience would suggest that after his difficulties with Shamash-shuma-ukin, Ashurbanipal might have appointed in Babylon a loyal Chaldaean sheikh to appease the tribal opposition, but also that no such personality – nor indeed an ambitious brother – would have resisted the temptation to revolt in the final years of a weak and ageing king. The one fact that seems certain is that during the Kandalanu years Babylonia remained not only prosperous but peaceful. The corollary, that Assyria under Ashurbanipal was also peaceful, suggests itself, and there is no unequivocal evidence to the contrary. Biblical references tell of Josiah's revival of the anti-Assyrian policies of Hezekiah sometime after 630, but it was the death of Ashurbanipal that ensured their success.[23] Ashurbanipal is often described as a vain and cruel tyrant, perhaps best epitomized in the idyllic garden scene on the Nineveh reliefs, with the head of Teumman hanging in a tree near the banquet table. But this is also the monarch to whom we owe the preservation of much of the literary heritage of Mesopotamia. His reign was one of the longest in Assyrian history and in his later years his savage policies achieved peace, if perhaps an uneasy one, in the cities of Assyria and Babylonia. From an Assyrian point of view, his crime was not his ruthless success but his seemingly arrogant disregard for the future, both in failing to secure the succession and in expending the empire's not unlimited resources. The price was paid by his successors.

[20] A 551, 105 n. 525.   [21] A 77, 117–19.
[22] The possible parallel with Ululaju/Shalmaneser V cannot entirely be dismissed (see A 535, 62 n. 320).   [23] II Chron. 34: 3; also II Ki. 23.

III. THE YEARS OF CONFLICT (627–623 B.C.)

We have no knowledge of Ashurbanipal's designated heir, although economic texts dated to his reign imply the existence of a crown prince. One such document is witnessed by a *turtān ša mār šarri*, the 'commander-in-chief of the crown prince'.[24] We know from earlier periods that the crown prince had military responsibilities, and Chronicle 2 places Sin-sharra-ishkun, presumably himself a general, with the Assyrian army in Babylonia in 627. Sin-sharra-ishkun was ultimately to succeed Ashur-etel-ilani, but on the evidence for chronology presented above and the chronicle account, discussed below, not until 623. The mention of his name early in the chronicle (627) is certainly not evidence that he was then king, as some authorities have assumed, since the chronicle practice, more often than not, was to refer to the king, whether of Akkad or Assyria, by his title and not his name. From the evidence of Text 3 we learn that insurrection, at least in Ashur, followed the death of the monarch and that the throne was secured for Ashur-etel-ilani by Sin-shumu-lishir, his chief eunuch and presumably the head of the young prince's household.

Assyrian sources reveal little of the events of Ashur-etel-ilani's reign. Brick inscriptions attest his reconstruction of Ezida, the great temple of Nabu in Calah (Fig. 8), work which we know to have been continued by Sin-sharra-ishkun. Large numbers of economic texts survive, but their precise dating to Ashur-etel-ilani or Sin-sharra-ishkun is in most cases uncertain. They contain much invaluable social and economic information, but they have yet to be systematically studied. Of particular interest are the texts involving Sin-shumu-lishir, who secured the young king's accession with his private army ('the battle troops of his own estate'), in itself suggestive of the breakdown of royal authority at this time. Sin-shumu-lishir's reward was not merely a position of influence as the royal mentor, but the gift of property, and its exemption from tax, for members of his own household and presumably others who had sided with him in support of the new king. It is unfortunate that we know nothing of the background or family of Sin-shumu-lishir, the one eunuch to have claimed the throne of Assyria, albeit briefly. The role of the eunuchs – loyal servants who themselves could have no dynastic ambitions and whose major responsibility was the welfare of the king and his family – seems to have become increasingly important in the later years of Assyria. But Sin-shumu-lishir's extraordinary status as the orchestrator of Ashur-etel-ilani's succession must reflect the extent to which the old order had died with Ashurbanipal and, in the ensuing

---

[24] A 97, no. 659 (= A 93, no. 321). Although a *mār šarri* is any son of the king, such a reference to the *turtānu* of the *mār šarri* almost certainly implies the designated heir.

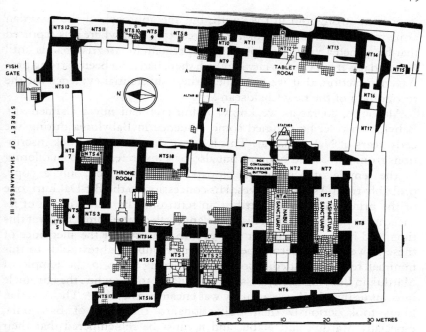

Fig. 8. Plan of the Nabu temple at Nimrud. (After A 137, folder VI.)

period of weakness and dissension attested in the chronicle, the royal prerogative was assumed by ambitious officials. The position of Sin-shumu-lishir is particularly emphasized in a text once thought to have been an edict of Sin-sharra-ishkun but now to be interpreted as a treaty guaranteeing the sovereignty of Ashur-etel-ilani, imposed by Sin-shumu-lishir on three individuals, otherwise unknown.[25] A 'treaty oath' is also mentioned in Text 3, in this instance apparently administered by another of Ashur-etel-ilani's official eunuchs.

The historical framework for the remaining years of the Assyrian empire is derived almost entirely from the Babylonian Chronicle. We learn that in 627/626 there were battles in both Assyria and Babylonia, of which the Ashur rebellion was certainly a part, and that from the time of Kandalanu's death until the accession of Nabopolassar 'no king was recognized' in Babylon. Indeed two battles are attested there, the first fought 'all day within the city' (627). Nabopolassar must thereafter have enjoyed a measure of success against the Assyrian armies. This can be seen in his recognition already in 22/VI/626, probably in Sippar. The year 626 finds him also in Nippur, throughout this period Assyria's most

[25] A 398; see also A 353, 76. I am indebted to A. K. Grayson for permission to refer to his new interpretation of this important text.

important stronghold in the south, but the approach of the Assyrian army forced the Babylonian king's retreat to Uruk, where it is reported that he gained a victory. Nippur was to remain in Assyrian hands until 616, and it is from Uruk, a city in which there had long been a strong pro-Assyrian faction, that we have the earliest substantial evidence for the recognition of the new Chaldaean king.

Although, so far as we know, Ashur-etel-ilani never claimed any Babylonian title, he retained some influence in Babylonia during the early years of Nabopolassar. This is attested not only by brick inscriptions from Dilbat and Nippur, but also by a text referring to an offering to the temple of Marduk in Sippar-Aruru, of which only a copy, probably from Ashur, survives. His concession to the Bit-Dakkuri, one of the principal Chaldaean tribes, in returning the body of one of its sheikhs for proper burial in his homeland, reflects the competition at this time, and indeed throughout the seventh century, for the allegiance of these powerful southern tribes. A recently published text adds to this minimal record the dedication of an offering table in the temple of Marduk in Babylon itself, possibly to be dated to 624 when the chronicle informs us that the Assyrian army was encamped nearby.[26] The Assyrian kings took seriously their obligations to the gods of Babylonia, especially Marduk and Nabu, and it must be remembered that their 'wars', though often devastating in their immediate and local effects, involved normally only seasonal campaigns and as such were not a permanent impediment to the proper demands of ritual and commerce, in Babylonia far more likely to have been interrupted by tribal depredations and their legacy of insecurity in the countryside.

The control of Babylonia was contested between Nabopolassar and Ashur-etel-ilani until 623, with the former recognized in Babylon and Uruk for much of this time. In 623, however, events take a new turn. In that year the chronicle records the revolt of Der, a strategically important outpost on the eastern foothills route from Assyria to Babylonia and Elam. This provoked a response from Ashur-etel-ilani himself, who marched with his army to Babylonia. Whether the instigator of the Der rebellion was Sin-sharra-ishkun or Sin-shumu-lishir cannot be established with certainty, though the latter is the more likely candidate. That he must finally have rebelled against his king and erstwhile protégé, possibly provoked by the threat of Sin-sharra-ishkun's activities in the south, is certain both from his own claim to the kingship of Assyria and his recognition in Assyrian Nippur in the early months of 623. After 15/v in that year (and possibly as late as 14/vi),[27] at which time he was

---

[26] A 370.
[27] BM 54153 (A 553, 54: N.5) is probably to be dated 14/vi/acc; I am indebted to Dr I. Finkel for this information.

recognized briefly in Babylon, we know no more of this distinguished eunuch, though he is very possibly the 'rebel king' of this same chronicle, who is referred to in the context of '100 days'. Unfortunately the end of the chronicle is badly damaged. There is mention of an otherwise unknown Itti-ili, who ravaged some city of which the name is broken and stationed a garrison in Nippur, presumably removing Sin-shumu-lishir, since we know that Ashur-etel-ilani was recognized there again in 1/VIII/623, his last preserved date. It is conceivably Ashur-etel-ilani who 'marched against Syria' at this time, but it is perhaps more likely to have been the ultimately successful Sin-sharra-ishkun. The broken final lines of the chronicle are especially frustrating, as mention is made of someone who set out for Nineveh, where 'those who had come to do battle against him [i.e. supporters of Ashur-etel-ilani?] . . . when they saw him bowed down before him'. That this is the newly acclaimed Sin-sharra-ishkun is probable, again suggesting Sin-shumu-lishir as the most plausible identification for the final reference to a 'rebel king'. Certainly his is the only other name to appear on any king list. Sin-sharra-ishkun claimed the kingship of both Assyria and Babylonia in this, his accession year, but he was recognized in Babylon – and then briefly – only at the end of the year, following Sin-shumu-lishir's short-lived success.

The accession of Sin-sharra-ishkun in 623, argued here, is not widely accepted. But it is the only interpretation that accords with all the sources, including the year dates and chronicles. Moreover, in Text 6, cited above, the synchronism plausibly becomes 'Year 3 of Nabopolassar, that is to say the accession year of Sin-sharra-ishkun'. This reading, in fact, is the only logical interpretation of such a scribal translation, that is, from a Babylonian to an Assyrian year date. Only the Warka King List appears to support a 627 accession date for Sin-sharra-ishkun, but scribal tradition could not accommodate the insertion of one reign within the years attributed to another. Thus the brief recognition of the two kings in 623 would inevitably have been recorded as found in the text, between Kandalanu and Nabopolassar, and we have here a late example of a tradition long apparent in the Sumerian king list. That the 623 accession year makes sense of the evidence from both the chronicle and the synchronism must be more than coincidence.

IV. SIN-SHARRA-ISHKUN (623–612 B.C.)

The reign of Assyria's penultimate king is better attested than that of his brother. Several commemorative inscriptions survive, recording the restoration of 'the building of alabaster' at Nineveh, probably the west wing of Sennacherib's South-West Palace, the Nabu temple at Ashur and the Tashmetum shrine in Ezida at Calah;[28] we know also that he had a palace in Calah, possibly the North-West Palace where a number of economic texts dated to his reign were found. The commemorative inscriptions refer to 'the enemies of Assyria who would not accept my sovereignty' – presumably a reference to the contested succession in 627 as well as 623 – and inform us that the new king was chosen by the gods for sovereignty 'instead of his twin brother', or perhaps 'from amongst his (real) brothers',[29] a phrase often used by those whose right to the throne was dubious. That Sin-sharra-ishkun was the rightful crown prince must remain a possibility, however, and we cannot be certain of the identity of the 'twin' or 'real brother' referred to. Indeed if the two kings were twins, it is difficult to understand Ashur-etel-ilani's reference to his 'minority' in 627, when Sin-sharra-ishkun was a general in Babylonia. We know that Ashurbanipal was married while he himself was crown prince, that is, before 669, making it unlikely, though of course not impossible, that his wife Ashur-sharrat was the mother of Ashur-etel-ilani, still 'in his minority' in 627, perhaps itself a reason for the contested succession and the intervention of the ambitious Sin-shumu-lishir. This is entirely speculative, but in the Late Assyrian period we are denied information about the relatives of the wife (or wives) of the king, or indeed other members of the royal family,[30] and there can be little doubt that such information would help to explain many a troubled path to the throne. Another indication of Sin-sharra-ishkun's relative age can be found in the economic texts dated by *limmū* which can be attributed to his reign because they date his commemorative inscriptions. These texts, some of which must be dated before 620, contain numerous references to officers of a son of the king, in this case undoubtedly a son of Sin-sharra-ishkun.[31]

The chronicle tablet for the years 622–617 has yet to be found, and we are forced for the history of the early years of Sin-sharra-ishkun to rely once again on the Babylonian year dates. Admittedly, the date assumed for his accession, in this case 623, affects their interpretation, but whatever system is followed this Babylonian evidence reveals a pro-

[28] A 308, 123–4; A 353, 76–8; A 354; A 357, nos. 236–48; A 360; A 363; A 399, 45f. I am indebted to A. K. Grayson for information about recent references. The cylinder Ass. 13158 mentioned in A 360, 305 remains unpublished.

[29] A 353, 67: 5, *ina birīt maš-ši-su . . . ippalsušu*: 'whom the gods have chosen instead of his twin brother'; A 363, Cylinder C, line 5, *ina birīt maš-ši-ia*: 'instead of *my* twin brother'; cf. *CAD māšu* (*maššu*), 'twin'. Perhaps, however, to be translated, 'from among my brothers' in the sense of 'full brother' rather than 'twin'.

[30] A 72, no. 308 provides an amusing sidelight on this veiled subject (see also A 698, 158). A 72, no. 2 (= A 698, 149–50) reveals another way in which families gained influence at court.

[31] A 360, 309; A 361; and especially the contracts in which Kakkulanu, the *rab kiṣir ša mār šarri*, appears as witness or as an involved party (A 361, 107). A 'treaty oath' of the time of Sin-sharra-ishkun refers only in general to 'his sons' and 'his sons' sons' (A 347, 215 n. 69).

tracted struggle for Uruk and Nippur.[32] At times both cities were under siege, their inhabitants in desperate straits. For the first few years Sin-sharra-ishkun continued to hold Sippar, an important religious centre and the northern gateway to Babylonia, strategically important for its control both of the Euphrates upstream from Babylon and of land routes from Assyria. After 11/1/620 there is evidence for his recognition in Uruk and Nippur only, both cities with a long pro-Assyrian history.

After 623 Nabopolassar's hold on north-central Babylonia seems more secure and is attested by year dates from Babylon, Borsippa, Dilbat, and Cutha. However, there is no evidence that he controlled the south. Indeed the prolonged struggle for Uruk in 621–616 undoubtedly reflects a major preoccupation of Assyrian policy in the seventh century, the control – to which Uruk was the key – of the Sealand with its access to the rich Gulf trade.[33] The only tablets of this date recovered from Ur, loan transactions for the years 624–617, comprise a family archive written in northern Babylonia, for the most part in Babylon itself.[34] These documents were presumably moved to Ur only after the cessation of hostilities in Babylonia, that is, sometime after 616.

The variety of dated contracts which have survived from this period reveal that in 621 Uruk, at that time under the control of a pro-Babylonian faction, was under siege. By 620 the tide was turning in favour of the Babylonians, and early in the year Assyrian Nippur was itself besieged. Severe famine, the legacy of the seven-year conflict, is vividly attested in a group of contracts from Nippur dated to this time. These record not only exorbitant market prices but the sale of young children by their starving parents, in order to obtain food.[35] The Assyrians held Nippur until late 617 (the earliest Nabopolassar document is dated 9/x/617), but the struggle for Uruk was more complex. In 618 the Assyrians again held the city, but from then until the final siege in 616 Uruk oscillated between Babylonian and Assyrian control.

Throughout the seventh century the cities of Babylonia had preferred the prosperity of Assyrian subjugation – and the privileged status they were accorded – to the unreliability of tribal control.[36] But by 616 the devastation of the ten-year struggle must have made the prospect of

---

[32] The scheme proposed in A 390 remains essentially unaltered by the newly available year dates (see n. 9 above), though it should be noted that of the six dated tablets now extant for Nabopolassar Year 3 (A 367, 181), one is certainly from Uruk (pace A 390, 147, 151 no. 2), while the last attested document of Sin-sharra-ishkun from Sippar is dated 11.i.3. The scheme proposed in A 393 is further complicated by the new dates, especially in the years 621 and 620.

[33] A 385.   [34] A 829; A 534, 255–7; A 390, 155–6.

[35] A 391. The chronology followed here resolves the 'problem' of the severity of the famine; cf. A 391, 86.

[36] Kidinnūtu or tax-exempt status was granted to the citizens of the major religious centres such as Babylon, Borsippa, Sippar, and Nippur in northern Babylonia, while similar privileges had been extended by Sargon to many southern cities, including Ur and Uruk.

Chaldaean rule seem a positive blessing. A number of letters from an earlier period reveal the insecure situation of those Babylonians professing loyalty to Assyria, for instance the following letter from an official in Nippur to Esarhaddon:

The king well knows that people hate us everywhere on account of our allegiance to Assyria. We are not safe anywhere; wherever we might go we would be killed. People say, 'Why did you submit to Assyria?' We have now locked our gates tight [a phrase used to indicate sieges] and do not go out of town . . .[37]

Certainly Uruk paid heavily for its divided loyalties, suffering sieges on a number of occasions between 620 and the last attested pro-Assyrian coup in 616.

In 616 we return to the evidence of the Babylonian Chronicle series with Chronicle 3, the so-called Fall of Nineveh text. It was now, coinciding with the final collapse of Assyrian pretensions in Babylonia, that Nabopolassar took the offensive against the Assyrians on their home ground, although his initial strategy may have been little more than an attempt to adjust the boundaries, a recurring subject of dispute between the two nations. Certainly the idea of a territorially weakened Assyria is not supported by the evidence of the economic texts; *limmū* which can be unequivocally attributed to the reign of Sin-sharra-ishkun are found on texts as far west as Harran and Tell Halaf, and on the upper Tigris to the north of the Tur-Abdin, while one of these officials is a 'commander-in-chief of the left' and almost certainly the governor of Kummukhu (Commagene).[38] This identification has been questioned, but it is difficult to envisage the successful retreat to Harran in 612 had the Assyrians not retained control of this north-western province.

According to the Babylonian Chronicle, in 616 Nabopolassar campaigned up the Euphrates, defeating an Assyrian army with its Mannaean allies (from north-west Iran) at Gablini, and continuing upstream as far as the river Balikh. Such was the new Babylonian threat that, although less than fifty years had passed since Ashurbanipal's sack of

---

[37] A 72, no. 327 (see A 698, 175). See also a letter from Nimrud, A 79, 23–4.

[38] Cf. A 97, no. 57 (= A 93, no. 308), dated by the *limmū* Salmu-šarru-iqbi, the '*turtānu* of the left', and A 97, no. 376 (= A 93, no. 446), dated by a man of the same name who is *turtānu* of Kummukhu. That the *turtānu* of the left *is* the *turtānu* of Kummukhu is known from earlier texts (*inter alia*, A 420, 78, 84). An examination of the witnesses on A 97, nos. 56–7, both dealing with the affairs of Kakkulanu, demonstrates that these tablets cannot be far apart in time from documents dated by *limmū* known to have been appointed by Sin-sharra-ishkun (*inter alia*, A 97, no. 118, *limmū* Ashur-matu-taqqin). A 97, no. 56 is dated Salmu-šarru-iqbi '*turtānu* of the land . . .' (for the reading of the name see A 361, 106 n. 21), while A 97, no. 57 is dated Salmu-šarru-iqbi '*turtānu* of the left'. It is inconceivable that the post-canonical *turtānu* of Kummukhu, who bears the same name, is not the same man; the latter text too deals with the affairs of Kakkulanu. See also A 356, no. 31. Certainly under Sin-sharra-ishkun there are governors of Upummu, Tushhan, and possibly also Simirra; cf. also A 99, 135–6 (ND 5550) and A 105, no. 15.

Thebes, the Egyptians now joined their former enemy in an alliance of which the immediate effect was the withdrawal of Nabopolassar. While the fate of Uruk – and Assyrian power in the south – remained in the balance, the Assyrians and Egyptians gathered their armies in pursuit of Nabopolassar, failing at Gablini to catch the Babylonian forces on their way home. Later in the year another battle was fought near Arrapkha (Kirkuk) – perhaps instigated by the Medes who had succeeded to Elamite power in Iran, with the Babylonians again victorious. In 615, with Babylonia at last secure, Nabopolassar mustered an army and marched to Ashur, failed to capture the city and was forced by an Assyrian army again to retreat, this time down the Tigris to Tikrit. In a ten-day battle Sin-sharra-ishkun failed to wrest the fortress city from Nabopolassar, and the chronicle records another Babylonian victory. Yet in the following year (614) it was the Medes and not the Babylonians who attacked Nineveh and Calah, captured Tarbiṣu (modern Sherif Khan, just north of Nineveh where Ashurbanipal had resided as crown prince), and destroyed Ashur. Nabopolassar was quick to take advantage of the Median victory – perhaps conveniently his troops had arrived just too late to take part – and on the battlefield made a formal alliance with the Median king Cyaxares. Both armies returned home, and in 613 Sin-sharra-ishkun again took the offensive, with his Scythian allies, if Greek accounts are to be believed, protecting his eastern flank by engaging the Medes. He marched south, forcing Nabopolassar to abandon Anat, which the latter had besieged after a revolt, almost certainly encouraged by the Assyrians, of the Suhu on the middle Euphrates. There is no indication at this time that the Assyrian king saw any serious threat to his position. Not only did he lead his army far from Assyria to attack Nabopolassar, but the authorities at home were so complacent, despite the destruction of Ashur the previous year, that they dismantled the defences of one of their strongest fortresses in order to carry out extensive repairs.[39]

It is often remarked that in retrospect the Assyrian campaign of 613 is puzzling. Although Ashur had already fallen, and in the next year the empire itself was to disappear, the Assyrians in 613 were sufficiently confident to take offensive action against the Babylonians. The chronology advocated here, however, makes this operation more comprehensible in view of Nabopolassar's lack of success against the Assyrians in Babylonia during the first ten years of his reign, that is, as late as 616. There must certainly have been an Assyrian garrison at Nippur during these years, which could hardly have survived without the support of regular Assyrian campaigns, although these must eventually have had to by-pass the northern cities in which Nabopolassar's control was

[39] A 383, 12–13.

effectively established. The campaign of 613 thus falls into perspective as one of what were probably annual Assyrian forays southwards.

The end came in 612, and without doubt unexpectedly. The combined armies of Nabopolassar and Cyaxares, together with the Ummanmanda (a term simply denoting 'tribal hordes', of which the Scythians were now almost certainly a part), attacked Nineveh. After a siege of three months the walls were breached and the city looted: in the words of the chronicle, 'turned into a ruin heap'. The fate of Sin-sharra-ishkun is less certain. The chronicle is broken at this point, and it is not clear whether he died (in the flames of his palace in the tradition concerning Sardanapalus, Diodorus II.27), or whether it is the Assyrian king who 'escaped from the enemy and grasped the feet of the king of Akkad to plead for his life'.[40] Certainly he was never heard of again.

The Assyrian was perhaps unlucky in his fate. He was a conventionally pious king and no doubt a more able general than many of his predecessors. The roots of Assyria's collapse lay not in his own policies but in the limited resources of the Assyrian homeland and the strain on these resources imposed by his more illustrious and ambitious predecessors. Nineveh must have seemed impregnable, and we know that Sin-sharra-ishkun himself had repaired the massive walls. Later tradition suggests that the walls were breached by flooding, presumably by the destruction of Sennacherib's dams on the Khosr, which river must in the seventh century have been diverted around the walls. Although no evidence for such a breaching now remains,[41] it is difficult to imagine in what other manner this great fortress city could have been destroyed.

This was not the end of Assyria. The chronicle informs us that an otherwise unknown Ashur-uballit II (conceivably Sin-sharra-ishkun's crown prince) fled ignominiously westwards to Harran, where an exiled Assyrian government was established. This ancient religious and commercial centre, whose inhabitants enjoyed the royal favours and tax-exempt status that ensured their loyalty, was the site of one of the most famous temples of the moon-god, where Ashurbanipal had appointed his younger brother and where the long-lived mother of Nabonidus, perhaps herself a member of the Assyrian royal family, was a votaress. Whether Ashurbanipal's attention was a reflection solely of his concern for the ancient gods or a political move to strengthen his support in the west cannot be ascertained, but the latter is likely. Certainly the city remained loyal to the Assyrian cause in 612.

Although what survived of the government had moved to Harran and

---

[40] A 25, no. 3: 44–6, and p. 281. See also S. Zawadski, *The Fall of Assyria and Median-Babylonian Relations*. Poznan, 1988.

[41] Nahum 2: 5–7; A 287, 68. The breach in the main wall mentioned in A 41, 637 is no longer visible.

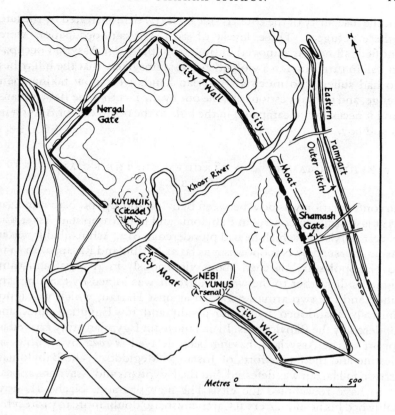

Fig. 9. Plan of Nineveh. (After S. H. F. Lloyd, *Archaeology of Mesopotamia* (London, 1978), 198, fig. 141.)

the great metropolitan cities were never to recover, the local population of the Assyrian homeland did not simply disappear. The excavations at Calah show that at least some of the inhabitants returned after the 612 sack, to seek shelter in the ruins. The character of this temporary settlement is, however, significant. It was confined to the fortified areas, and in the case of the *ekal mašarti* (the great arsenal in the outer town, Fig. 9) an attempt was made to put the building in a posture of defence by rebuilding the north gate, which had been dismantled for repair in 614 and had not been re-erected at the time of the final onslaught in 612.[42] We have no means of knowing what authority was responsible for this work, but it was not the Assyrian government, which lingered on in Harran until 608 but never again exercised control over the homeland. How-

[42] A 66, 58–9; A 381; A 382, 10–11; A 383, 11–13; A 389.

ever, the insecurity of the countryside is clearly demonstrated by the fate of these refugees. Three levels of post-Assyrian occupation were identified, all not far removed in time from the latest Assyrian occupation. All in turn came to a violent end. It seems likely that the hill tribes who had suffered so much at Assyrian hands were now taking their revenge, and the suggestion is borne out by the fact that the Babylonians found it necessary to campaign in the hills to the north east of Assyria in 608 and 607.

V. ASHUR-UBALLIṬ AND CARCHEMISH: THE FINAL YEARS (612–605 B.C.)

The confrontation was now between Babylon and Egypt. Nabopolassar was at last firmly in control in Babylonia and in metropolitan Assyria as far west as Nisibis, which he had plundered in 612. Ashur-uballiṭ was in Harran, pursued by Nabopolassar as far as Nisibis and Raṣappa. In 611–610 Nabopolassar 'marched about victoriously in Assyria' and campaigned still further to the west. In 610 he was joined by the Ummanmanda and the two armies marched against Harran, which was ignominiously abandoned by Ashur-uballiṭ and his Egyptian allies and plundered by the Babylonians. In 609 the main Egyptian army arrived in support of the Assyrians, having been delayed *en route* by troubles in Palestine and the fatal efforts of Josiah at Megiddo.[43] The Babylonian garrison in Harran was defeated, but the Egyptians and Assyrians appear not to have reoccupied the city. The new pharaoh, Necho II, now established his headquarters at Carchemish, no doubt more to protect his own long-standing interests in Syria than to provide support for the beleaguered Assyrians. Ashur-uballiṭ is not heard of again, at least the chronicle does not deem him worthy of further mention, and we are ignorant of his fate. Trouble for the Babylonians now erupted on the north-eastern front, an area Assyria had expended much effort to contain, and in 609–607 Nabopolassar was forced to turn his attention towards Urartu.

In 607 one of the most justly celebrated figures in ancient history appears on the scene, Nabopolassar's son, the crown prince Nebuchadrezzar. In that year both king and crown prince mustered their armies for the Urartian campaign, the king alone marching thereafter to the Euphrates where he sacked Kimuhu, near Carchemish, and stationed there a Babylonian garrison. In 606 the Egyptians retaliated and battles were fought at Kimuhu and several other Syrian cities, with the Egyptians eventually forcing Nabopolassar's retreat. In 605 Nabopolassar remained in Babylon, perhaps then already ill, and the crown prince assembled his army and marched to Carchemish. Here was fought one of

---

[43] II Ki. 23: 29–30. For the date of the battle see A 861. See also below, pp. 715–20.

the great battles of antiquity, of which we read in Jeremiah (42: 12), 'for the mighty man has stumbled against the mighty, they are fallen both of them together'.

Both sides obviously suffered heavy losses, but it was Nebuchadrezzar who emerged victorious, pursuing the retreating Egyptians to Hamath, where a second engagement took place from which, according to the not entirely unbiased Babylonian account, 'not a single Egyptian returned home'. Fortunately for Egypt news of the death of Nabopolassar then reached Nebuchadrezzar, who hastened back to Babylon to claim the throne which he was to occupy with such distinction for the next forty-two years. Babylon was now the uncontested successor of Nineveh and the new capital of the world.

The reasons for the sudden collapse of Assyria have been much debated. Ashurbanipal controlled the greatest empire the world had known, yet within two decades of his death the country was overrun, its cities destroyed, and Assyria as a significant political entity had disappeared forever. The reasons for this collapse are certainly complex, but the fundamental seeds of failure lay simply in the very small size of metropolitan Assyria. A study of the population and resources of the homeland suggests that their inadequacy dictated the policies which created the empire and compelled its maintenance, while their exhaustion contributed to its collapse.[44] The royal grandeur, of which the great cities were an expression, indeed the prosperity of the country, could only be supported by the tribute of territories far beyond the natural borders of Assyria, and tribute could only be exacted by the threat, and at least intermittently the presence, of overwhelming military force. Subject populations proved loyal as long as the military success of Assyria assured their prosperity, but they had no reason to risk their lives in its defence in times of trouble. Assyrian policies demanded huge resources in manpower, and the practice of deportation provided not only a method of controlling potentially rebellious populations but of ensuring labour for the vast building programmes and military enterprises of the Neo-Assyrian kings. But it also left a growing legacy of subject peoples, both in metropolitan Assyria and in its garrisons abroad, whose loyalty in times of weakness the state could not ensure.

This relentless imperialism proved in the end too costly. In the seventh century the invasions of Egypt, though prestigious, had not been born of common sense, while the destruction of Elam and the repetition of campaigns against Urartu and tribal coalitions to the north east had been a severe drain on manpower and resources. Most damaging of all, however, was the time and energy spent in attempting to maintain control in Babylonia,[45] where the countryside was an ideal setting for guerrilla warfare and where the privileges accorded to its

[44] A 66, 42–66.   [45] A 540; A 545; A 658.

ancient cities encouraged the growth of the urban prosperity that was in
the end to prove more of an asset to Babylon than to Assyria. Until the
620s the Assyrians had been victorious, but it was a pyrrhic victory.
Assyria was destroyed not so much by the powerful military coalition
that sacked Nineveh – it had met such opposition before – but by the vast
wealth of the southern tribes allied with the successful commercialism of
the Babylonian cities, which Assyrian policies had fostered. In the
seventh century the imperial ambitions of the Sargonids had imposed an
intolerable strain on Assyrian resources, and the failure of the ageing
Ashurbanipal to secure the succession was a mortal blow to the royal
authority, on which the Assyrian system depended. Inroads on this
authority at the time of Ashur-etel-ilani are clear signs of severe internal
weakness. It has been suggested that the fall of Assyria was not so much
the collapse of an empire but a shift of power southwards, but it would
certainly not have appeared so to the inhabitants of the great Assyrian
capitals, devastated in 612 and now largely abandoned. Sin-sharra-
ishkun was not an incompetent monarch, but Assyria was soon to be
taken over by the Achaemenids, whose imperial administration was a
more effective development of his own, and whose success ensured that
the centre of power never again returned to the north.

VI. THE ARAMAEANS[46]

The Aramaeans were a tribal people who are first attested in Mesopotamia at the end of the second millennium B.C. By this time they had
already occupied a substantial portion of Syria and had encroached on
Assyria itself. By the eighth century the inscriptions of Tiglath-pileser
III list the names of thirty-six Aramaean tribes settled in Babylonia along
the Tigris and Euphrates and as far as the shores of the Gulf. The West
Semitic language of these tribes had a considerable influence on
Assyrian,[47] and its much simpler alphabetic script began to be used
alongside Assyrian cuneiform from about the middle of the eighth
century, at which time the Egyptian and the Aramaean scribes appear on
wine-ration tablets found in the arsenal at Calah,[48] perhaps in this early
period as court officials in charge respectively of Egyptian and Aramaean
affairs. Stone reliefs of Tiglath-pileser III (Pls. Vol., pl. 57) show two
scribes, the first writing on a clay tablet, presumably in cuneiform, and
the second on a scroll of some perishable material like parchment or
papyrus, probably in Aramaic. Indeed a letter of the time of Sargon II
tells of the receipt by a palace scribe of rolls of papyrus.[49]
    The Aramaean scribe is often identified as such in economic and legal

---

[46] See also *CAH* III².1, 239f.   [47] A 742.
[48] A 96, 2 and no. 9; for the date see now A 356, 22.
[49] A 72, no. 568; see also the Til-Barsib fresco, which clearly differentiates in colour the clay and
the papyrus documents (A 146, fig. 348); for a different interpretation see A 136, 122.

texts of the seventh century, by this time almost certainly serving a growing Aramaean element in the population. At the same time it has been suggested that the dearth of letters from provincial governors after the time of Sargon II reflects a shift to the use of Aramaic in their correspondence.[50] But this may equally be an accident of archaeological discovery, as unfortunately all archives are. Certainly there are large numbers of economic and administrative documents in cuneiform preserved from the last years of Assyria, at Calah, Ashur, and Nineveh, though letters are rare. At Calah, moreover, the few cuneiform letters of palace officials in the post-canonical period show plainly that the Assyrian dialect of Akkadian was still spoken and written by these officials.[51]

At Nineveh cuneiform documents have been found with brief annotations scratched in Aramaic on the edges of the tablet, almost certainly 'filing instructions'.[52] The existence of such notes implies that some clerks or officials involved in the administration could read only Aramaic. A small number of contracts written wholly in Aramaic are known from several sites, while it has been proposed that some cuneiform dockets served to seal Aramaic scrolls.[53] There are occasional Aramaic ostraca and at Calah Layard discovered weights inscribed in Aramaic characters (Pls. Vol., pl. 75).[54] The precise date of most of these documents cannot be ascertained, but some are certainly from the time of Sin-sharra-ishkun.[55]

A letter of Sargon II to the governor of Ur is revealing:

As to what you wrote, 'if it is acceptable to the king, let me write down and send [my message] to the king in Aramaic letter-scrolls', why wouldn't you write and send [your messages] in Akkadian on clay-despatches? Really, the despatches which you write . . . should be drawn up for safety(?) in this very manner.[56]

It has been suggested that this letter may imply that already at the end of the eighth century Akkadian was less widely read than Aramaic, but the fact that such records are more secure in the sense of less destructible may well be the true sense. Certainly by the seventh century the language which was to replace Akkadian as the *lingua franca* of the Near East was already widely spoken in both Assyria and Babylonia, and its easier script was in use at least for mercantile purposes. However, cuneiform was to remain the preferred script for literary and religious works for some

[50] A 76, 122–3.

[51] A 356, 2. Over 30 cuneiform letters of this period are known also from Ashur.

[52] For references to texts in Aramaic see A 375; A 403; A 659.   [53] A 105, 5–6, 11.

[54] A 400; J. C. L. Gibson, *Textbook of Syrian Semitic Inscriptions*, II: *Aramaic Inscriptions*, nos. 20, 98–110 (Oxford, 1975). There are also a number of mace-heads inscribed in Aramaic; see A 355; A 375.

[55] A 374, no. 7 is dated by one of the known Sin-sharra-ishkun *limmū*. The Nimrud ostracon probably dates from the earliest known post-612 occupation of the *ekal māšarti*.

[56] CT 54 no. 10; A 76, 123 n. 9.

centuries to come, at least in Babylonia, and it is of interest that the few preserved catalogue texts from the Nineveh library fail to mention copies of texts on papyrus (*niāru*) or parchment (*mašku*), though large numbers of writing boards are mentioned, presumably inscribed on wax in cuneiform, together with the conventional clay tablets.[57] That in 612 Aramaic had not entirely replaced the Assyrian dialect of Akkadian as the spoken language can be seen in the post-canonical letters from Nimrud, but it was clearly soon to do so, and both the Greeks and the Egyptians were to come to view the Aramaic script as the 'writing of the Assyrians'.[58]

VII. THE ARCHAEOLOGY

Although it is clear from the dated tablets found within them that the major buildings of Nineveh, Calah and Ashur continued in use through the time of Sin-sharra-ishkun,[59] there is relatively little direct archaeological evidence for the activities of the latest Neo-Assyrian kings. We know that Ashur-etel-ilani honoured the ancient shrines of northern Babylonia, and pavement bricks bearing his name attest at least minor repairs in the temple of Nabu at Calah. Sin-sharra-ishkun worked on the shrine of Tashmetum in the same complex, and restored the twin temples of Nabu and Tashmetum and of Ishtar at Ashur. But lack of manpower or money, or both, prevented major building projects, and no new monumental buildings of this date are known. Indeed, it would appear that Sin-sharra-ishkun, in repairing Sennacherib's palace at Nineveh, actually recut some of the earlier stone reliefs,[60] a miserly enterprise that would have been unthinkable earlier in the seventh century.

Particularly informative for this latest phase of Assyrian history are the cuneiform texts from a building at Calah known as the *ekal māšarti* (the 'palace of the muster'), which reveal the operation of this royal arsenal at the time of Sin-sharra-ishkun.[61] The *ekal māšarti* was a standard feature of the imperial capitals, and its purpose is described in a prism of Esarhaddon from Nineveh – 'for the ordinance of the camp, the maintenance of the stallions, chariots, weapons, equipment of war, and the spoil of the foe of every kind' – and it was here every year that the annual 'stock-taking' was carried out, of the army, its animals and equipment, and of the booty taken from the enemy.[62] This description is

---

[57] A 508.   [58] A 375, 107.

[59] Including the famous North-West Palace at Calah; see A 100, 15; also A 98, 33 (ND 2076).

[60] A 394, 109–10.   [61] A 356.

[62] Hence Parpola's term 'Inventory Palace'. There is no evidence that it was specifically a 'Review Palace' (A 356, 2), except in the sense of an annual muster, since it is unlikely that the throne dais in the south-east corner is *in situ*. 'Arsenal' remains the best translation of *ekal māšarti*, encompassing as it does the two-fold purpose described by Esarhaddon. Both functions of the building (the palace of

most amply borne out by the archaeological discoveries at Calah, in the building referred to by its excavators as 'Fort Shalmaneser' because of its foundation by Shalmaneser III.[63]

Fort Shalmaneser comprised a large open area within the south-east corner of the city wall, marked off from the city on the west and north by a rampart (Fig. 6). Troops of the annual levy were probably housed and exercised here, together with chariots and horses – indeed the arsenal at Nineveh was enlarged by Esarhaddon because 'it had become too small for the training of horses and chariot manoeuvres', and there would have been room for the bulk storage of supplies. A second smaller fortress stood in its south-east corner, broadly divided into northern and southern sectors. On the north were two outer courtyards, surrounded by workshops and store rooms, and two inner courts with no direct access from outside, one surrounded by barrack rooms, which may have housed the royal bodyguard, the other subdivided into ranges of magazines, one a wine store, others packed with thousands of pieces of carved ivory that had originally decorated furniture or horse-harness – the tribute and booty of Esarhaddon's inscription, and one of the major archaeological discoveries at Calah.[64] The whole northern sector centred on the residence of the *rab ekalli*, the palace superintendent. In the southern sector there were two basic units. In the extreme south-east corner, and approached through the barracks court, was a vast throne room with other reception suites, obviously designed for ceremonial occasions. Finally, and most inaccessible of all, in the south-west corner of the building were private residential suites with their service areas. In a storeroom here were found the archives of the *šakintu*, the 'lady housekeeper', and this whole area may have been the harem.

The military functions of Fort Shalmaneser were predominant when Calah was the capital, that is, down to the reign of Sargon, but by the time of Sin-sharra-ishkun the cuneiform tablets largely reflect the city administration. However, Calah remained an important provincial capital and garrison city, and although its arsenal was no longer the site of the annual levy and the major repair depot, it continued in use as a large storehouse for the imperial revenues in kind, such as grain, wine, and oil, evidence for which was found both in the excavations and in the surviving cuneiform texts. The presence in one of the workshops of the broken statue of Shalmaneser from Kurbaʾil, brought in for repair, shows also that its practical functions were still more than local, and a single text attests its continued military use.[65] Odd weapons, armour, and other military equipment were found in many of the workshops and

---

the muster and the place where booty was stored) are well illustrated by Fort Shalmaneser. See also A 154. For the Esarhaddon inscription see A 365, 26–7 iv 32–5; also A 234, 59 v 40–1.

[63] A 137; A 381; A 382; A 383.   [64] A 138; A 139; A 141.

[65] A 356, no. 12; A 369; A 383.

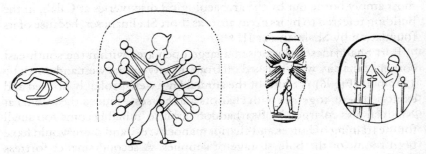

Fig. 10. Late Assyrian stamp seals. (After A 143, 37ff, figs. 3–6.)

magazines, probably salvaged and stored indiscriminately during the rehabilitation of the building after the 614 sack. Indeed, the sequence of destruction levels at Fort Shalmaneser provides important archaeological confirmation of the historically attested Median and Babylonian campaigns of 614 and 612, together with the only substantial evidence for the nature of post-612 occupation in the Assyrian heartland (above, pp. 181–2), although Calah itself is not mentioned in the chronicle account. Perhaps also relevant to the final years of Assyria are a group of undated inventories, found in the same workshop as the Kurbaᵓil statue, of objects destined to embellish the Nabu temple, which we know to have been restored by Sin-sharra-ishkun.[66]

Of archaeological interest are the numerous seal impressions found on tablets of the late seventh century (Fig. 10). These show clearly that the stamp seal, which was virtually to replace the cylinder seal in succeeding centuries, was already in common use. This prehistoric seal form reappears in Late Assyrian times, at first as a royal seal,[67] but increasingly after the time of Sargon in more general use. By the time of Sin-sharra-ishkun some two-thirds of the total number of seals attested were stamp seals, and indeed at this time even the cylinder seals are used as though they were stamps.[68] Some of these stamp seals are Babylonian in style while many display Egyptian or Syrian motifs, a clear reflection not only of late seventh-century political involvement with the west, but of the transportation of Syrian populations and craftsmen.[69]

---

[66] A 356, nos. 93–7. There is no direct evidence for the date of these texts, but on archaeological grounds the fish-men at the gate of Ezida, mentioned in no. 95, are no earlier than the time of Sargon, who, like Sin-sharra-ishkun, restored the temple.

[67] A 152, pl. XIX.

[68] A 143, 27, and *inter alia*, pl. XX.4 ND 7070 and pl. XXI ND 7080.

[69] For Egyptian motifs see A 142; *inter alia*, p. 119 and pl. XXVI (ND 3424, 3425), and p. 106 (ND 3301); for Neo-Babylonian see A 143, 38 and pl. XX (ND 7086). Note also the possible papyrus impression on the back of ND 7039 (A 143, 37).

VIII. ASSYRIA AFTER THE FALL

The history of northern Mesopotamia after the destruction of Assyria must be reconstructed almost entirely from archaeological evidence, in itself sparse, occasionally supplemented by mostly uninformative literary references. This evidence reveals a significant change in settlement pattern following upon the breakdown of authority in 612. No longer did ambitious Assyrian kings maintain the great cities; this artificial stimulus removed, the local population seems to have reverted to a condition dictated to a greater extent by its immediate environment. This fact in itself has served to limit our archaeological knowledge, and only in recent years have archaeologists begun to take an interest in the less spectacular remains of the post-empire settlements. The evidence for the squatter reoccupation of Calah has been discussed above (pp. 181–2), but there was no serious attempt at reconstruction and when Xenophon passed by in 401 this city at least was wholly abandoned.

We remain uncertain of the degree to which the Chaldaean kings of Babylon maintained control in metropolitan Assyria, but we know that the capitals were not rebuilt and that the Medes held Harran when Nabonidus was instructed in his famous dream to rebuild Ehulhul, the great temple of the moon-god which had lain in ruins since its destruction at the time of Assur-uballiṭ.

Marduk said to me, 'Nabonidus, king of Babylon, bring bricks on your own chariot, rebuild the temple of Ehulhul and let Sin take up his dwelling there.' I [Nabonidus] said to Marduk, 'The Ummanmanda are laying siege to the very temple which you have ordered me to rebuild and their armed might is very great!' But Marduk said to me, 'The Ummanmanda, of whom you spoke, they, their country and all the kings, their allies, shall cease to exist.' And indeed . . . Marduk made rise against them Cyrus, king of Anshan, his young servant, and Cyrus scattered the numerous Ummanmanda and captured Astyages, king of the Ummanmanda, and brought him in fetters into his land.[70]

The young servant was of course the Achaemenid Cyrus, who in 539 was to put an end to the Neo-Babylonian dynasty of Nabopolassar.[71] Harran, however, survived as an important centre of the moon-god, whose crescent symbol still appeared there on Roman coins minted in the third century A.D., and whose 'pagan ceremonial' is attested even as late as the Abbasid caliphate.

From northern Mesopotamia we have up to now very little post-612 archaeological evidence until Hellenistic times. To some extent this must reflect the security and stability re-established under Achaemenid rule, for the huge mounds of ruins which now represented the citadels of

---

[70] A 856, 218–21 no. 1 i 18–33; A 1145, 250.
[71] For a general discussion of this later history see A 694, 134f.

Assyrian cities were unattractive to later settlers except in time of danger. Since it is these sites that have been excavated, we lack knowledge of the distinguishing features of Achaemenid pottery, the tool most useful to archaeologists in settlement-pattern studies. At Calah somewhat ephemeral traces of possible Achaemenid date were identified in the area of the Nabu temple, but these are not informative. Indeed the political position of Assyria under the Achaemenids is not entirely clear, but it seems under Cyrus to have been included in the satrapy of Babylon, despite the inclusion of the name Athurā in the Old Persian *dahyāva* (lands or districts) lists. Later sources suggest that Erbil, Assyrian Arbaʾil, was the one major centre to have escaped destruction in 612 and a document found in Egypt identifies it as an Achaemenid centre of administration. This refers to one Nehtihur, who was travelling to Egypt on business from Babylon and was provided with a letter authorizing the issue of rations along his route.[72] It not only informs us that a Persian nobleman owned estates in northern Mesopotamia at this time, but also identifies a number of administrative centres of the fifth century, together with Arbaʾil. The existence of estates belonging to members of the Achaemenid royal house is also recorded by Xenophon.[73]

Xenophon's account of his march through Assyria provides an interesting description of the state of the country at this time, for its resources were of immediate concern to him and are frequently mentioned. Passing the site of Calah, he refers to the local villagers who took refuge on the top of the ziggurat at the approach of the Greek army, although the city itself was deserted and Xenophon knew neither its name nor its former inhabitants, whom he describes as Medes. Nineveh too was identified as a ruined Median city, but here he reports the existence of a town, Mespila, nearby, possibly on the Mosul side of the Tigris. The countryside at this time seems to have been prosperous, since he comments on the plentiful supplies, and in one case a 'kind of palace' where flour, wine, and barley for horses had been stored for the satrap. The recent archaeological salvage project in the region of Eski Mosul has resulted in the identification of several sites which may possibly be Achaemenid,[74] and it is hoped that their publication will assist in the further identification of material of this date from metropolitan Assyria.

Alexander also passed through Assyria, and the battle named after the city of Arbaʾil, at which he finally defeated the last Achaemenid king, Darius III, was fought on the plain of Keramlais, 23 km east of Nineveh. For the Hellenistic period we have isolated fragments of archaeological evidence, and it is perhaps a reflection of contemporary insecurity that at Calah and Nineveh, and indeed on many sites to the west, we find

---

[72] A 358, 28; also A 66, 59f.   [73] *Anabasis* II.iv – III.v.
[74] For a list of sites and summary information see A 368, 216f, especially on Khirbet Qasrij.

settlement again on the citadel mounds. At Nineveh the settlement must have been quite large and had acquired at least the superficial forms of Hellenistic city organization. An inscription found there during the excavation of the Nabu temple in 1904 records a dedication by one Apollophanes who is described as *strategos* and *epistates* of the city, to the *theoi epekooi*.[75] An Assyrian altar inscribed with a later Greek dedication, probably by this same Apollophanes, was discovered during more recent excavations at the city.[76] Whether the citadel was continuously occupied in Hellenistic times is difficult to say, for the strata and architectural remains associated with the pottery of this date are too confused to permit analysis, but it seems probable that by now the greater part of the town lay in the plain below, where a small shrine of Hermes, the travellers' patron peculiarly appropriate to a bridge-head site, was identified in 1954.[77] It is interesting that the Greek shrine was of a plan very reminiscent of Assyrian prototypes, a raised cella approached by steps from the ante-cella and with a door leading into a small lateral chamber.

Two other sites afford isolated but significant additions to the general pattern, although in the first case the evidence is negative. At Ashur no traces of Seleucid occupation were identified, and very little that can be confidently assigned to the Achaemenid period. Indeed Andrae remarks that the period from the fall of Ashur in 614 to the appearance of Parthian buildings, which he dates to the first century B.C., has no history.[78] The apparent decline of Ashur, economically vulnerable at the edge of the zone of viable rain-fed agriculture, was complemented by another significant foundation, that of Hatra on the Wadi Tharthar about 55 km to the north west. Recent excavations there have shown that the great Parthian shrines were preceded by temples of purely Hellenistic aspect, themselves founded on the trodden surfaces of the campsites of nomads from the Jezirah, attracted by the brackish springs in the Tharthar nearby.[79]

The post-war excavations at Calah provide perhaps the most informative archaeological data for the period of Alexander and his Seleucid successors. Here a small village, of which six building levels were identified, was founded sometime around 250 B.C.[80] After the relative peace of Achaemenid domination, it would appear that the rise of the Arsacid dynasty of Parthia provided a new threat from the east, and the resulting insecurity seems likely to account for the foundation of this new village on the relative safety of the citadel mound. By 130 B.C. the

---

[75] A 122, 140–2.   [76] A 392.
[77] A 376, 280–3 (Arabic). More recent excavations have identified five levels of 'Hellenistic' and Islamic occupation; A 372.
[78] A 112, 169.   [79] A 395; A 396.   [80] A 386.

Parthians were in control of all Mesopotamia to the banks of the Euphrates. At what stage they conquered the northern plain we do not yet know, but it seems reasonable to assume that their advent in the area is reflected at Calah by the destruction of level 2 of this village, some time after 146 B.C., and the appearance of their distinctive pottery in the short-lived upper level. The final establishment of their authority, which was to last more than three centuries, presumably brought with it the conditions of peace and order in which villages could once more exist in safety on the plain. It was at this time that Ashur was rebuilt, and the German excavations have revealed a large Parthian city with a palace, agora and temple precinct.[81] Here and at Hatra the influence of Assyrian tradition and symbolism can sometimes still be seen in architecture and art.[82]

With the advent of the Romans as successors to Hellenistic power in Asia Minor, control of Assyria was now contested between Rome and Parthia, though until c. A.D. 200 Rome's influence east of the Khabur was never more than brief. Recognizing that control of Assyria was crucial to control of the Euphrates route, in A.D. 114 the emperor Trajan, following the subjugation of Armenia, attacked and captured Nisibis (modern Nusaybin). Singara was occupied and Hatra appears to have submitted to the Romans; indeed a bust of Trajan has recently been found at the site.[83] In A.D. 116 Trajan, following an ancient custom, led his army to the Gulf, sacking Ctesiphon en route. A revolt in the north, now joined by the Hatrenes, forced the emperor to withdraw, and the attempt to extend the frontier to the Tigris was abandoned by the more prudent Hadrian. Trajan's presence is archaeologically attested not only by the Hatra bust, but by a milestone and the traces of a remarkable road terraced down the precipitous north slope of Jebel Sinjar.[84] A fragment of a stone inscription, now lost, from the bank of the Tigris at Nineveh, the preserved portion of which read 'occuli [sic] legionum', attests the deliberate choice of the Tigris frontier.[85]

Although Singara may have been a colonia under the Antonines, it was Septimius Severus who next conquered the northern plain, and pottery of this period has been found at a number of sites. Hatra was attacked, but held out against the Romans, according to Dio Cassius (LXXV. 10–11), with the aid of a number of highly advanced defensive devices, including the use of bituminous naphtha and elaborate torsion-artillery of which an example was recently found at the site.[86] Coins from an excavated Roman barracks and castellum at Ain Sinu, ancient Zagurae,

[81] A 349.   [82] A 396; A 397.
[83] A 402, 231–5.   [84] A 66, 67–71 and pl. v.
[85] The inscription was found in 1940, by the river just south of Kouyunjik; I am indebted to D. Oates for this information.   [86] A 350.

east of Singara, span the period from Septimius Severus to Severus Alexander, who we know was welcomed by the Arab king of Hatra.[87] Again the Roman presence in this desert city is commemorated by a portrait bust. The castellum at Ain Sinu appears to have been destroyed by the Sasanian Ardashir I (A.D. 237), who also besieged Hatra. A number of coins purporting to come from a new mint at Singara attest the presence of Gordian III, whose Moorish cohort was based in Hatra, where the Arab rulers appear to have accepted Roman help in the final struggle against the Sasanians. Indeed a consular date of A.D. 235 survives on the earliest of three Latin inscriptions recovered at the site.[88] The little evidence available suggests that the area east of Singara was surrendered once more by Philip the Arab, while Diocletian's acceptance of the Singara–Nisibis line in his frontier settlement implies that the Tigris frontier had long been abandoned. After the death of Julian (363), Rome was forced to give up Nisibis and Singara, but the Roman walls of the latter, presumably built earlier in the fourth century, still remain an impressive sight today.[89]

While some occupation of Nineveh and Calah is attested under the Seleucids and Parthians, it is under the latter dynasty that Ashur once again became a city of note, almost certainly, like Hatra, reflecting its importance as a tribal rather than a metropolitan centre. Arbaʾil and Kirkuk, which alone remained major centres of administration under the Achaemenids, retained their importance under the Sasanians and were indeed seats of Nestorian metropolitans. By now Nineveh was again abandoned, as we know from the great battle fought over its ruins between Heraclius and Chosroes.[90]

[87] A 66, 80f; A 387.   [88] A 66, 75 and n. 1; A 373.
[89] A 66, pls. VII–XII; A 378.
[90] E. Gibbon, *The Decline and Fall of the Roman Empire* II, 800.

CHAPTER 26

ASSYRIAN CIVILIZATION

A. K. GRAYSON

Many topics have been lightly touched upon in the preceding chapters which merit special attention, and it is the purpose of this chapter to fulfil that need. A synthesis of our knowledge of a given aspect of Assyrian civilization is full of lacunae and surmise, and I advise the reader of this now, for I have spared him endless repetitions of such phrases as 'It would seem that' or 'Possibly so'. These topics are usually treated for Assyria and Babylonia together in secondary works, and I have therefore stressed some of the major contrasts with Babylonian civilization.

I. THE MONARCHY

The idea of monarchy was born with the emergence of the Assyrian state and the two grew to maturity together like twins. The seed for these developments may be found in the ancient city state of Ashur and its ruler who was called a vice-regent (*iššʾakku*) of the city god Ashur. When Shamshi-Adad I captured this city state, he sought acceptance by the indigenous population of himself as the legitimate ruler and at the same time, by conquering other city states in the region and assuming the imperialistic title *šarru* ('king'), dramatically altered the previous course of Ashur's history and set for its people and their heirs highly ambitious goals. The idea of an Assyrian state under an absolute monarch was conceived at that moment but lay dormant until the time of Ashur-uballiṭ I (1363–1328 B.C.), who not only won Assyrian independence but laid the foundations of an Assyrian nation and an Assyrian monarchy. In subsequent centuries, as the political and military power of Assyria grew, so too did the authority and accoutrements of majesty until its full fruition with the great kings of the Middle Assyrian period, Tukulti-Ninurta I (1243–1207 B.C.) and Tiglath-pileser I (1114–1076 B.C.). This then set the pattern and, although changes and developments can be noted from time to time, the idea of monarchy and its practical expression stayed substantially the same for the remainder of Assyrian history. It was clearly an indigenous development but with many individual customs and practices borrowed from the culture in the Babylonian plain.

The political theory of monarchy is not described for us in any ancient Assyrian text, but there is much incidental evidence that allows us to formulate a statement on the Assyrians' view of kingship. Of fundamental importance was the intimate link between the supernatural powers, the gods, and the Assyrian king, who was the earthly representative of the supreme god Ashur. In Sumerian political ideology kingship was believed to have descended from heaven to earth and the Assyrians certainly subscribed to this view. In contrast to Sumerian and Babylonian belief, where rule of the land passed from one city state to another as the fortunes of the respective patron deities waxed or waned in heaven, in Assyria the supreme god was always the same (Ashur), and the family tree to which the supreme earthly ruler belonged was also, in theory, always the same. Both of these tenets, like all absolute doctrines, seemed to be contradicted by facts from time to time. The popularity in Assyria of Marduk, king of the gods in the Babylonian pantheon, caused some embarrassment, and in Chapter 23 we saw how Sennacherib attempted to suppress the cult. As to the theory of an unbroken royal line, the frequent *coups d'état* resulted in the gaining of the throne by usurpers whose royal lineage is highly suspect, and the compilers of the Assyrian king list attempted to resolve these situations by ingenious genealogical complexities.

The monarch was the supreme human being in Assyrian thought, since he was god's anointed, but he was a mere mortal all the same, and this is in contrast again to Sumer and Babylonia where deification of the ruler was known. The Assyrians were, of course, aware of this southern phenomenon, and they flirted with the idea of the apotheosis of their own king, but it never achieved full official recognition in Assyria. It surfaces, nonetheless, in various forms. In the royal epithets there is sometimes ambiguity as to whether the king or the deity is described, and there were titles and adjectives (such as *dandannu*, 'almighty') which were applied only to god or monarch. The royal images (*ṣalmu*), statues and reliefs of the king, are another case in point; in texts where these images are mentioned the word *ṣalmu* is preceded by the divine determinative,[1] and the personal name 'The-Divine-Image-of-the-King-Has-Commanded' (^dṢalam-šarri-iqbi) is well attested.[2] This last fact brings to mind the custom practised at Guzanu (Tell Halaf) of concluding contracts before the images of gods including the 'divine image of the king'.[3] None of this evidence justifies a conclusion that official

---

[1] See A 495, 112.   [2] See A 443A, 205.   [3] See A 92, 58f n. 21.

sanction was given to the worship of the Assyrian king or his images,[4] but it does underline the fact that he was generally regarded as being on a plane closer to the gods than other mortals. In popular thought no doubt people went one step further and regarded the king as at least partially divine, and uneducated Assyrians probably believed that the offerings placed on a table before a royal image in a temple were offerings to the image itself rather than offerings to be presented by the king portrayed to the god.[5]

The supreme, god-like position of the Assyrian monarch was promoted and enhanced in a variety of practical ways. Access to the king by individuals was, at best, extremely difficult, and the long walk through the gates and corridors flanked by bull and lion colossi and stone reliefs depicting the king slaying and mutilating his enemies would overwhelm the visitor, as it was intended to do, with 'awesome splendour' (*puluḫti melemmī*).[6] The only mortal who could be regarded as an equal of the Assyrian king was a foreign king, whom the Assyrian monarch addressed as 'my brother',[7] but even he was a potential subject of the 'king of kings' (*šar šarrāni*).[8]

The Assyrian king enjoyed absolute power over the state, there being only three checks to his autocratic rule, religion, legal precedent, and the temper of his nobles and officials. The monarch was subject to religious belief and practice, and examples of royal attempts to depart therefrom are extremely rare. As to legal precedent, the king had to respect the traditional rights of individuals, such as property ownership, and of groups or institutions, such as tax exemptions granted to privileged cities. Finally he had to respect the mood of the upper classes or run the risk, as a few kings did, of revolution and regicide. Apart from these considerations, however, the king's will was supreme in all affairs of state. Indeed, in the legislative sphere he was not only the supreme but the sole legislator, his 'law-making' consisting of royal decrees. There was not even an assembly, as in Sumer, with which he might discuss a proposal, although he did seek advice from his various officials and sanction from the gods by means of omens. The king was presumably supreme judge, and he was definitely commander-in-chief of the army. In religion, although he was subject to commonly accepted beliefs and practices, as already mentioned, he was the high priest (*šangû*) of the god Ashur. This is in contrast to Babylonia where the high priest was not the same person as the king. Finally, even the economy was subject to his will, for in theory he owned all the land, and trade, both domestic and foreign, depended upon his sanction.

Given the sweeping authority of the Assyrian king it is pertinent to

4 See A 11, 56–61.   5 See A 41, 600f, and A 412, 319 n. 51.
6 See A 9, 65–82.   7 E.g. A 72, no. 918.   8 See A 51, 318f.

inquire how extensive, in practice, his knowledge of these various spheres of activity was and to what extent he was personally involved in their direction. This would vary with the individual character and personality of the reigning monarch at a given time, but there was one activity which was traditionally the central concern of the monarch, the military. The king did not always lead his army in person, so much is clear, but it was assumed that he did, and in the official presentations, the commemorative inscriptions and sculptured reliefs, events are usually portrayed as though the king were present and fighting personally. The fact that the king was principally involved with the direction of the armed forces is a reflection of the militaristic manner in which the Assyrian state was organized, for there were not many state affairs which were not either directly involved with the war department or at least affected by it. As to legislation, there was no need for formal laws similar to the Justinian Code followed in Western civilization; Assyrian society was so traditionally conservative that most legal matters were regulated by custom and the judicial system operated without the king's personal intervention. In religion the priests carried out their duties without royal involvement, except on occasions when the king's presence was prescribed by a particular rite; but they kept the king regularly informed of their activities. As to land-ownership, the highly complex system of land-tenure (Section V below) required no direct involvement on the part of the monarch, and trade, about which we know virtually nothing, would always go forward so long as no one made a determined effort to control or stop it. In addition to the income which the king enjoyed by right of being the supreme land-owner, he had income from land held by personal right, as did individual members of the royal family, such as the crown prince, the queen, and the queen-mother.[9]

The world in which the monarch spent his days and nights was the palace and the harem. Since our knowledge of the Assyrian court is derived, to a certain extent, from incidental evidence we naturally look to other, better known, Oriental courts (such as the seraglio at Constantinople in the Ottoman period) for analogies, a procedure which has much to recommend it since the later courts have their historical foundation in the Assyrian. To Western eyes the most striking characteristic is the harem. The Assyrian royal harem was undoubtedly large, although we have no information about the numbers of wives, concubines, serving maids, and eunuch guards. Within the harem there was a hierarchy of which the queen-mother was the head, and she had her own court. The next in line, and also with a court of her own, was the chief wife of the reigning monarch, her status being determined by the fact

[9] See A 102, no. 36 and A. K. Grayson, *JNES* 31 (1972) 47*b*.

that she was the first wife to give the king a male offspring. There is one example of a departure from this normal ranking and that is the case of Naqia, wife of Sennacherib, who continued supreme in the harem during both the reign of her son, Esarhaddon, and the early years of her grandson, Ashurbanipal.

Princes normally spent their early years in the harem, but while still fairly young were removed to be educated and trained for their future role in life. In the Sargonid period (and possibly earlier), the crown prince, once he had been officially so designated, entered the 'House of Succession' (bīt-redûti), where he was surrounded by his own court and personal bodyguard. In this milieu he was prepared for his eventual elevation to the supreme position in the Assyrian state. Ashurbanipal tells us that it was in the House of Succession that he was trained both in military arts and intellectual pursuits, learning not only to ride and shoot but also to read and write. When the prince 'graduated' he was assigned to responsible duties in the empire, and in the Sargonid period, at least, the crown prince became the king's representative at home with regal authority while the father was campaigning. As to the rule of succession, we lack sufficient information both about the principle and about the practice, but it would appear that primogeniture was the guiding rule and in the odd case where it is known that the actual successor was not the eldest son, one may assume that his elder brother or brothers had died young, or been killed in a revolution led by the successful usurper.

Returning for a moment to the court itself, something must be said about palace protocol and the daily conduct of affairs. From the Middle Assyrian period there is a group of royal edicts which lays down rules with regard to court and harem etiquette, and, given the conservative character of Assyrian society, the general picture provided is probably applicable to the Neo-Assyrian court.[10] It was similar to the seraglio of the sultan in the Ottoman period, as already mentioned; the women of the harem were jealously guarded and every effort made to contain and control the disputes which frequently erupted. In order to prevent seditious plots, of which harems were a notorious source, there was a strict ban on any woman giving a present to a servant. All persons admitted to the court were carefully examined by senior officials, and if someone unsuitable was mistakenly admitted, the officials responsible for the error were mutilated as punishment. The court and harem travelled with the king when he moved about the country and even on the road there were strict rules of procedure. Officially only one courtier had the right of direct and continuous access to the king, and all news

---

[10] See E. F. Weidner, 'Hof- und Harems-Erlasse assyrischer Könige aus dem 2. Jahrtausend v. Chr.', AfO 17 (1954–6), 257–93; A. K. Grayson, Assyrian Royal Inscriptions (Records of the Ancient Near East) I, §§304–6, 335–41, 517, 681–3, 850–9, 928, 989 and II, §§184–93 (Wiesbaden, 1972–6).

and petitions had to be transmitted through him or at least by his sanction. Patronage was the rule in Assyria, both in the palace and the country at large, and no one could succeed who did not have an influential friend who would accept bribes in order to plead a cause.[11] The king was formally addressed in letters in the third person as 'the king my lord' and replied in the first person singular, rather than in the plural (the 'royal we' of other traditions), and it may be assumed that this reflects oral practice in the court.

The public image presented for the king is coldly impersonal, and a superficial look at his portrayal in art or writing would lead to the conclusion that one Assyrian king was much like another; each was a strong, fearless warrior with unswerving faith in god and himself. Such was not always the case and in preceding chapters glimpses have been gained of individual personality traits of certain kings, such as Esarhaddon. But for many kings we have no personal details at all; we do not even know the age of any of them since Mesopotamians never recorded this fact. Among the symbols of majesty were the crown (agû), the sceptre (ḥaṭṭu), the throne (kussû), and the royal standard (urigallû). The king rode in a magnificent ceremonial chariot on state occasions and was surrounded by his personal bodyguard (qurbūtu). There were various state and religious ceremonies in which the king participated and chief among these was the New Year's (Akitu) festival. This rite may have included a great ritual banquet (called the tākultu), the text for which is also known, and one of the principal purposes of the ceremony was to confirm the rule of the king for another year. Since no separate coronation ritual is known, it is reasonable to assume that this same rite served officially to proclaim the rule of a new king who had succeeded to the throne after the preceding New Year's festival. This assumption is supported by the fact that Assyrian chroniclers dated the first year of a king as beginning at the first New Year after his actual accession.[12]

II. THE BUREAUCRACY

Assyrian bureaucracy can be viewed as a pyramid with the king at the pinnacle and the working population at the base with graduated layers of officials in between, the number of officials at each level increasing as one descends. It is convenient to keep this image in mind, although there are problems with such a neat schema, since the system was not theoretically thought out in advance but simply developed to meet demands as they arose. Particularly relevant to this point is the fact that the Assyrian state, including the administration, was essentially militaristic in organization and there was usually little distinction between military service and civil

[11] E.g. A 72, no. 2.   [12] See A 495; A 496; A 507; A 412, 318f and n. 50.

service. Another consideration is that the chain of command was not always from one level to that immediately adjacent; the crown gave direct orders to some officials far down the pyramid and the king had the right to intervene at any level in any matter. But for clarity it is useful to have the image of a pyramid in mind as one goes through the various levels of officials and describes their position, function, and responsibilities. Only the upper echelons will be discussed, since they are of most importance and our sources provide more information about them than about the lower orders.

At the top of the pyramid sat the king and immediately under him was a trio of officials, the major-domo (*akil/rab/ša muḫḫi ekalli*), the vice-chancellor (*ummânu*), and the field-marshal (*turtānu*). The major-domo was the only person who officially had direct access to the monarch, his position being comparable to the Black Eunuch of the sultan's court in Ottoman Turkey. The power and influence of this individual was immense. Roughly on an equal footing with this officer was the vice-chancellor, whom the king consulted frequently on the various affairs of state and whose importance is illustrated by a legend (see above, p. 132) that surrounds one of them, Ahiqar, and the fact that their names are enshrined beside the names of their monarchs in ancient lists. The field-marshal completes the trio of officers directly under the king, his high status being confirmed by the lists of Assyrian eponyms (*limmū*), wherein he appears immediately after the king.

A second group of three which, if not equal in rank to the aforementioned trio, was a close second, consisted of the palace herald (*nāgir ekalli*), the chief cup-bearer (*rab šāqe*), and the steward (*abarakku*). Although these officers bore titles related originally to domestic service in the court and they may have performed these services on ceremonial occasions, in practice they were entrusted with duties of state of a very high order. The palace herald was the chief administrative officer of the realm. The chief cup-bearer acted as the king's plenipotentiary on great occasions such as, it will be remembered, at the siege of Jerusalem in the time of Sennacherib. The steward of the king (there was also a steward for each of the crown prince, the queen-mother and the chief wife) carried out special royal commissions, such as the direction of the transportation of precious items.

The offices of most of the officials mentioned so far included governorships over certain provinces, and the remaining provincial governors come immediately after them in rank. The governors (*šaknu* or *bēl piḫāti*), including the governors of the chief Assyrian cities, were arranged in a hierarchy, as is evident from the eponym lists, with the governor of Assyria (i.e. the Assyrian heartland) first. Each governor had his own palace and court, located at the provincial capital, and there was a standing army at his disposal.

Next in seniority was a series of officials with diverse functions. There were the viziers (*sukallu*), of which one was called the grand vizier (*sukallu rabû*), and whose position was so prestigious that occasionally one of their number served as an eponym, and they commonly occur high in lists of witnesses in legal documents. In view of the name of the office, one suspects that they were advisers to the king. There was a chief eunuch (*rab ša rēši*) attached to the king's court and also one to the court of the crown prince; the title implies that they had control over the eunuchs who permeated the Assyrian court and bureaucracy. The chief justice (*sartennu*) (an official whose duties included acting as a judge on occasion), who might serve as an eponym, belongs at this level as well as, probably, the high priests (*šangû*) of the many temples and the mayors (*ḫazannu*) of Assyrian cities. The mayor of a city was lower than the governor of the same city and the latter's jurisdiction included the immediate environs of the city.

Descending further, within the court itself there were a number of officers, such as the chief baker (*rab nuḫatimme*), responsible for the daily needs of the numerous courtiers (*manzāz pāne*), and such offices existed at the courts of the crown prince and the governors as well as at that of the king. At about this rank in the bureaucratic pyramid we encounter a large group of people who fulfilled one of the most important functions in the empire, the collection of taxes. Land and its taxation were divided into two jurisdictions, those lands under the authority of the crown and those under the authority of the provincial government. Each collected its own taxes from those lands and the king's tax collectors (*ša qurbūti* or *qēpu*) took orders directly from him. There was another type of official (*mušarkisu*) who, working in pairs or small groups assigned to a specific province, collected horses for the central government and communicated directly with the crown. It was noted earlier that most Assyrian officials had military functions, and this was certainly true of the tax gatherers.

At about this point in the pyramid we should probably place the army captains (*rab kiṣri*) and charioteers (*ša mugerre?*), the latter group including the driver (*mukīl appāte*) and the 'third man' or shield-bearer (*tašlišu*). Indeed the status of the charioteers was rather special since each of the highest officials, including the king, had his own chariot and crew who were commonly entrusted with important missions by their superiors. There is one person, a woman called the *šakintu*, whose position and function is unclear but who was obviously an eminent individual with substantial wealth. Below these high-ranking officers there were still several levels in the state bureaucracy which included everything from the palace kitchen to the flocks of shepherds, but a catalogue of these would become tedious. The mass of unskilled labourers was called *ṣābū*, a term which can be translated both as 'soldiers' and as 'labourers', since there was no distinction between them and the work they performed, whether military or public works, was called *dullu*.

There seems to have been no training programme for potential bureaucrats nor were the officials literate, since an army of scribes bolstered up the entire system. The son of an official learned his father's job by watching him at work, occasionally helping, and not infrequently the son succeeded the father in the post. This meant that families and social groups tended to regard certain offices as theirs, or at least as primarily within their sphere of influence. Patronage was the rule of the day, and no one could get a good position without an influential relative or friend.

The scribes were a special segment of the bureaucracy and were the products of a lengthy and rigorous educational system. Scribes were attached to every level in the official hierarchy, beginning at the very top with the vice-chancellor (*ummânu*), who was the king's chief scribe. Another special group which permeated the system consisted of eunuchs (*ša rēše*), for eunuchs were regarded, as in Byzantine and Ottoman times, as the most trustworthy of servants. The proportion of eunuchs in the bureaucracy was substantial, and a collective term for the king's officers was 'eunuchs and bearded ones' (*ša rēše u ša ziqne*).[13]

An official kept his position indefinitely, that is until he fell from favour, was promoted, or died. It is unlikely that rapid 'progress through the ranks' was possible, but gradual elevation of a social group over several generations was known, a good example being the rise of the Aramaeans to the highest levels during the ninth and eighth centuries. A second-in-command (*šanû*) was attached to most offices and he, together with offspring of the principal office-holder, would probably be one of the first to be considered as a replacement. Appointments had to be approved by the gods through omens and thus the diviners were in an influential position with regard to promotion. Each office and particularly the more eminent had distinctive symbols such as uniforms, badges, standards, bodyguards, and chariots. The ceremonies of installation included the swearing of an oath of loyalty to the king.

Officers were paid from the resources of the jurisdiction, central or provincial, in which they were employed and the remuneration took various forms such as food and clothing allowances (especially for those

---

[13] *ša rēše* does not always literally mean 'eunuch' however. See A 431A.

at court), or income from specified land-holdings. On occasion the king would add a special reward such as clothing, jewelry, tax exemption, or residence for life at the palace. Officials constantly complained that they were underpaid, and it was accepted practice that they would augment their pay by surreptitious means, bribes, 'special' taxes, and the like. Inefficiency and corruption if detected were punished, however, and the punishments ranged over a wide number of possibilities including imprisonment, mutilation, and execution. The vast and complex nature of the empire meant that there was a great deal of work to do and, on the whole, the Assyrian officers seem to have been a hard-working lot who travelled where and when it was necessary and relayed regular reports to their superiors. The king, in some instances at least, set a good example by accompanying the army on campaign and by personally supervising building projects.

As to the territory administered by this large bureaucracy, there were two major units, the land of Assyria proper and Greater Assyria. In contemporary records the term 'Land of Ashur' (*māt Aššur*) can refer to the two together or to Assyria proper, and the latter can also simply be called 'The Land' (*mātu*). Assyria proper, or the 'Assyrian heartland', was roughly a triangle with its apex at the city Ashur on the Tigris, and its base stretching from Arbaʾil in the east to Nineveh in the west. This area consisted of four major cities (Ashur, Arbaʾil, Nineveh and Calah) which were surrounded by fertile agricultural land. The entire area was under a governor (*šakin māt Aššur*) and each city had its own governor (*šaknu*) and mayor (*ḫazannu*) with a hierarchy of administrators beneath them. The cities had special privileges (exemption from various taxes and impositions), which each jealously guarded; the most privileged of all was the city of Ashur whose governor reported directly to the king.

Beyond Assyria proper was 'Greater Assyria' (there is no ancient equivalent for this term), a name which denotes territory outside of the Assyrian heartland and directly ruled or indirectly manipulated by the Assyrian king. The size of this area and its administrative divisions changed considerably during the three centuries of the Neo-Assyrian empire, and two distinct methods of administration, treaty arrangements and provincial administration, are evident. The treaty arrangement was the first to evolve, as Assyrian foreign policy slowly graduated in the late second millennium from staging razzias on neighbouring states to arranging more permanent and still profitable relations with these states. Two basic kinds of treaty relations emerged, treaties with equal partners and treaties with vassals. While vassal treaties, which involved keeping foreign princes and nobles hostage at the Assyrian court, continued to be arranged throughout Neo-Assyrian history, treaties with equal partners were gradually replaced in the ninth century by quite another device, conquest and imposition of provincial administration. A major reform of the entire administrative system for Greater Assyria was instituted by Tiglath-pileser III, who reduced the size of the provinces and thus reduced the power of the individual provincial governors. He thereby thwarted the ambitious expansion of authority by some of these men, a phenomenon which had plagued Assyria immediately preceding his accession.

One part of Greater Assyria, Babylonia, could not be treated like any other part and Assyria tried various methods of control without success. In the ninth century there were treaty arrangements between Assyria and Babylonia, arrangements which included Assyria's guarantee of the Babylonian king's position, and a similar agreement seems to have existed between Tiglath-pileser III and Nabonassar in the eighth century. In the face of repeated troubles with maintaining an acceptable monarch on the Babylonian throne, however, Tiglath-pileser finally abandoned the policy and ascended the Babylonian throne himself. This new method of treating Babylonia was adopted by subsequent Assyrian kings, with the exception of Sennacherib who tried to rule through puppet kings, but it still did not provide the ideal means of controlling Babylonia, which remained the most fractious part of the empire.

The centre of the Assyrian administrative system was, in theory, the royal court, but since kings tended to travel the administrative structure found a more permanent headquarters in the palace of one of the major cities; this we call the 'capital', although there is no Assyrian equivalent for this word. Calah served as the administrative headquarters during the ninth and eighth centuries B.C., while Nineveh filled this role in the seventh century. At these sites have been found the state archives, consisting of voluminous correspondence with the king, and administrative records, from the respective periods just mentioned. The absence of such archives at Dur-Sharrukin should probably not be attributed to the chance of discovery but to the fact that there had not been time to move the administrative headquarters before Sargon II's sudden death. There was a standing order to all officials to report to the king 'whatever you see and hear', and to ensure rapid communication there was a corps of messengers which enjoyed the use of a network of roads and posting stations.[14] Messages could be relayed even more quickly in emergencies by a system of observation towers and fire signals. Borders were carefully guarded by a series of fortresses and garrison-troops, who permitted the passage of individuals and small groups on business, after due payment of tariffs, but stood in the way of attempted border raids or foreign invasions.

---

[14] See A. L. Oppenheim, 'The eyes of the Lord', *JAOS* 88 (1968) 173–80; A 703, 30f.

Before leaving the subject of the administrative headquarters of the empire, a word should be said about the move from Calah to Nineveh. This change was part of a much larger operation which involved massive building programmes, major theological developments, and social and economic upheavals. The factors lying behind this major shift in royal policy were varied and included the changing political, economic, and social scene. That the Assyrian monarch should wish to move his capital away from the city of Ashur near the vulnerable southern border with Babylonia is not surprising. Nor was the economic position of Ashur ideal, since it was located at the extreme south of the fertile Assyrian heartland. Calah and Nineveh were more ideally situated from both points of view. Other factors which probably played a part were the ancient rights of the nobility of Ashur and the ancient accumulation of buildings, both of which an Assyrian monarch would have found inhibiting and oppressive. Finally, a leading desire of an Assyrian monarch was to do something gigantic and unique which would be remembered for all time, and what better fits that aim than building a totally new city or at least completely rebuilding an old one?

In Chapter 25, weaknesses in the Assyrian monarchy and administrative system were cited as causes contributing to the fall of Assyria, and here one must delineate these together with some general remarks on this subject by way of conclusion. The chief advantage of an autocracy is that decisions can be made quickly since they come from only one individual, and if the autocrat makes decisions rapidly and wisely there is great benefit to the state, which is saved the waste and divisiveness of protracted debate. This was certainly true in Assyria, where such decisive figures as Ashurnasirpal II and Sargon II brought great glory to the country. But not all kings were so effective and, while outside elements played against some of them, for others, such as Shamshi-Adad V and Adad-nirari III, the fault must surely be found with weakness in the character and capabilities of the monarch himself. The removal of such a weak king was possible only by revolution for there was no constitutional means. At the monarch's death he was succeeded by his own offspring, which meant that hereditary weaknesses, as well as strengths, would continue. New blood flowed into the royal line from the female side through marriage but the only chance of a totally new infusion was a usurper, such as Sargon II possibly was. Even an aged monarch could not retire, at least there is no clear evidence of abdication, although there is one instance, in the reign of Shalmaneser III, where the affairs of state were gradually managed by others as the king grew older.

Thus the burden of running the state sometimes fell heavily on the bureaucracy, and the system, which depended upon a firm hand at the helm, was found wanting. The entire structure was permeated by patronage and bribery, and even one who succeeded in gaining a post was open to slander and disgrace, for the standing order to all officials to report to the king whatever they saw and heard drove them zealously to inform on their colleagues. The higher the official, the larger the bribe, so that the most powerful were also the most wealthy, and in two periods, 784–745 and after 635, a small number of exceptionally strong and rich individuals made serious encroachments upon the royal prerogative.

III. SOCIAL STRUCTURE

Assyrian society was conservative in nature but flexible enough to manage the stresses and strains to which it was subjected by the emergence of the state as a great empire. In fact it was the stability of the social structure which gave the Assyrian state such strength. The focus of social relations was tribal and family affiliation, and a fundamental motivation in every Assyrian's life was the protection and propagation of his family and tribe. This phenomenon is amply illustrated by the various types of personal names expressing a prayer to a god to preserve the family (e.g. *Aššur-šumu-līšir* 'Oh-Ashur-May-the-Name-be-Well!') or to protect the heir (e.g. *Aššur-apla-uṣur*, 'Oh-Ashur-Protect-the-Heir!') and expressing thanks to a god for granting an heir so that the family name will endure (e.g. *Aššur-zēra-ibni*, 'Ashur-Has-Created-Seed'). It is also apparent from the frequent occurrence of adoption, a practice which not only provided a childless couple with care for their old age but ensured the future of the family. Even the dead were kept within the home for they were buried under the floor.

Beyond the family and tribal groupings there were social classes. Since the criteria for class division were power and wealth, the social strata corresponded more or less to the bureaucratic hierarchy outlined in the preceding section, and no distinction can be made between social standing and rank in state service. At the top of the scale was the king and at the bottom were the slaves, with various levels of society in between. The royal court represented the height of society and it was immediately followed by the courts of the crown prince and the governors. Following these in the social scale were the nobles or officers (*rabûtu*) with their families and relations and the 'heads' (*qaqqadu*) of the major cities.[15] Members of the upper classes were distinguished by the external marks of office, already mentioned, their entourage of dependents, guards, and servants, and by their grand houses if they were not palace residents. The mode of address found in letters, which was probably also used in

15 See A 72, no. 2; A 319.

speech, was formal and included the use of 'my lord' (*bēlī*) for one of superior rank while the speaker referred to himself as 'your servant' (*uradka*). Social equals addressed one another as 'my brother' (*aḫī*). Obsequiousness characterizes letters from an inferior to a superior, again no doubt reflecting oral practice. Letters to the king contain fawning phrases, and occasionally the writer goes so far as to call himself a 'dog' (*kalbu*) in the king's service.

Ignoring the various lower orders of free men, about which little is known, one comes to the non-free or slaves. Slavery was not so extensive in Assyria as one might expect; certainly it was not as common as in the Roman empire, nor did the economy of Assyria, if one excludes the monumental building works, rely heavily upon this institution. A possible source of misunderstanding is the term *urdu*, which in Assyrian is used both for a person who is the property of another and for anyone, free or not, in describing his relation to his superior; for example even the field-marshal (*turtānu*) could be referred to as the *urdu* of the king. Another consideration is the fact that, while people were attached to land and households and were sold with them, it is unknown whether all such people were technically slaves or if some were half-free.

As for slavery proper, there were both debt slaves and foreign captives. The debt slave was better off, for he enjoyed a number of privileges. He could marry a free person, appear as a witness in a court case, conduct business transactions with other slaves and their masters, and he could even own property to which people were attached. There was also the prospect that some day his debts would be paid and freedom restored, although in practice manumission was rare, since it would not be encouraged by the master and the debt slave's incentive to seek it would be attenuated by the aforementioned privileges. The lot of the foreign captive was entirely different; he was given the meanest of manual labour to perform with little hope for the future apart from escape or death.

The position of women in Assyrian society was quite inferior, being even lower than that in Babylonia. One rarely encounters a woman acting in a legal or business transaction on her own behalf, for she had virtually no status or rights as an individual. She was entirely dependent upon her male relations, father, husband, sons, and brothers, and their position in society. She was confined to separate quarters, the harem, and apart from male relatives she could have social intercourse only with other females. Marriage, the rearing of children, and the care of the home were her established roles in life.

An individual Assyrian belonged to a particular class because of his kinship and not because of personal merits or achievements. If he were a particularly capable and successful man, any promotion and distinction he might gain would involve all his relations, and thus a family and tribe blessed with a series of successful members would gradually rise in the class structure. An outstanding example of this phenomenon is the Aramaeans, who were forcibly brought to Assyria in the ninth century B.C. to do corvée, but by the late eighth century B.C. there were people bearing Aramaean names at very high levels in the class structure. While the general pattern of this phenomenon is apparent, it is impossible to document the rise of a particular family or group in detail because of our lack of continuous sources over a sufficient length of time. One can, however, single out names of individuals who were advancing rapidly at certain times and places. Such, for example, is the case with Kakkulanu (or Akkulanu), the 'captain of the crown prince' (*rab kiṣir ša mār šarri*), who bought up a great deal of land and was very much involved in business transactions of various kinds at Nineveh during the Sargonid period.[16] A caveat to this and similar examples, however, is that sometimes these individuals might have been acting on behalf of their office rather than their personal interests.

Most of what has been said so far applies only to native Assyrians, but there were foreigners living in the state as well. There were the foreign captives, already mentioned, who generally did forced labour on building projects or were otherwise employed in menial capacities in temples and palaces. There were also free foreigners within Assyria proper, some of whom had very high positions. The fact that many of these people were known by their gentilics alone ('The Babylonian', 'The Arab', 'The Tabalaean') rather than by real personal names shows that, despite their accepted position in the state, their foreign extraction had not been forgotten, and suggests that they were subjected to social sanctions. Possible support for this proposal is found in a unique marriage contract, wherein a mother purchases a woman to become the bride of her son.[17] This was not normal Assyrian practice, for a wife was not considered a slave, and the irregular procedure may have been the only means whereby a wife could be found for the son, who belonged to an Egyptian family living in Assyria.

Another group of foreigners comprised the princes and nobles of other lands who were kept at the Assyrian court, hostages in effect, to assure the observance of treaties by their countries of origin. These foreign dignitaries could cause problems as, for example, the people of Papu, living in Sargon's court, who conspired with some other foreigners (see Chapter 22). Even a foreign king, such as a king of Elam in

---

[16] See the references in A 443A, 110f. For other individuals see A 444, 169f; A 104, 12–15; A 23, 263–7.

[17] A 93, no. 307. See A 105, no. 13; V.A. Jakobsen, 'Studies in Neo-Assyrian law', *AOF* 1 (1974) 115–21.

Ashurbanipal's reign (see Chapter 24), might seek asylum at the Assyrian court. Thus there were many foreigners of every social class in Assyria, a fact which made the Assyrians aware of different lands and manners.

As to the Assyrian attitude towards countries and peoples beyond their homeland, they were reasonably interested and knowledgeable. Not only could they learn from the foreigners in their midst but also they heard the accounts of returned soldiers, officials, and business men. Other languages would not intimidate a people who were already familiar with both Akkadian and Aramaic, the latter being the *lingua franca* in any case, and great surprise was expressed on one occasion when a foreign emissary (from Gyges of Lydia) reached the Assyrian court and no one could understand his tongue.[18] Another illustration of the fact that foreign manners piqued the curiosity of the Assyrians is the portrayal of Urartian institutions in a text of Sargon II (Letter to the God) which was read out to the people of the city of Ashur.[19] In it were described, with a keen eye to detail, the ingenious water works, the methods of horse-training, and the coronation practices. Thus an Assyrian was reluctant to have a foreigner as a son-in-law, but he was willing to learn from him and tolerate him. Indeed, Assyrians could afford to tolerate foreigners, since they ruled most of those they knew.

Family and class were mainstays of Assyrian society, but another significant social unit was the community, be it city or village. There were four major cities, Ashur, Calah, Arba'il and Nineveh, and a number of lesser centres such as Kurba'il, Tarbiṣu, and Kalizi. Calculation of population figures for the major urban centres is difficult, but one study has suggested that Calah contained about 63,000 people while Nineveh, which covered an area twice the size of that of Calah, contained about 120,000.[20] The city streets were narrow and dark, being flanked by the blank walls of houses which had all their openings (apart from the street entrance) facing into an enclosed courtyard. The inhabitants were conscious of themselves both as citizens of Assyria proper and as citizens of a particular city. The term 'city' is used to translate the Assyrian *ālu* and a much smaller social unit, a 'village' (*kapru*), existed as well. The villages were scattered throughout Assyria and contained the dwellings of the local farmers and officials. Often one or more villages with their agricultural lands belonged to a large land-owner, whose holdings might be scattered over a wide area. Virtually nothing is known of the way of life of the population of ancient Assyria outside the city walls, and thus it is impossible to say whether the upper classes lived entirely in cities or whether some of them were landed gentry who spent at least part of their time on their estates.

Whatever social problems existed in Assyria, they were not suffi-

[18] A 337, 16f v.   [19] A 35 II, §§139-78. See A 195.   [20] A 66, 43-9.

ciently serious to cause social unrest. There was never a Peasants' Rising, for example, and the revolutions which shook the throne from time to time were palace affairs with no direct bearing on the majority of the population. The poor – widows, orphans, and cripples – were regarded as a corporate responsibility, and everyone from the king down was expected to protect and support those who lacked families to do this for them. Prostitution seems to have been an accepted but limited phenomenon in society, and drunkenness was known but frowned upon. Crimes of violence, including murder and the vendettas they sparked, are rarely mentioned in our documentation and theft was not a serious problem. In general the picture we have is of a stable, secure, rather spartan society in which men, other than the priests and scribes, engaged in the vigorous exercise of manual labour, arms, and hunting, while the women minded the children and the home. The steadying force was the community, the tribe, and especially the family.

IV. LAW

The ultimate legal authority in Assyria was the king, but in practice judicial powers were exercised by the bureaucracy. The legal system was an integral part of the administrative structure and not, as developed in Western civilization, a separate institution with its own officers and a code of laws to enforce. In passing one may note that the 'Middle Assyrian Laws' (cf. *CAH* $\text{II}^2.2$, 475f) were more literary than legal documents and, in any case, bear little relation to legal theory or practice in the first millennium. The law of the land was custom and precedent, and the occasional legal disputes which could not be settled by the people directly involved were adjudicated by administrative officials. Since most of our knowledge of Neo-Assyrian law is derived from the everyday legal documents which have survived, it is as well to describe these first.

Neo-Assyrian legal documents have been recently analysed by J. N. Postgate, and the following description relies heavily upon his excellent treatment.[21] A 'legal document' is the record of a transaction between two or more parties, including the names of witnesses, the scribe, and the date. A common feature of such texts is the inclusion of seal impressions as proof that those who impressed their seals upon the tablet subscribed to the statements therein. If an individual was too poor to own a seal, be it cylinder seal or stamp seal, he pressed his fingernail into the moist clay, and it was duly recorded on the tablet that this was the mark of the relevant person. Not infrequently tablets were enclosed in a case or

---

[21] A 105, 1–72.

envelope of clay and a version of the transaction was written on this cover and duly sealed. There were also legal documents written in Aramaic on parchment or papyrus, and, although these have all perished, the *bullae* (lumps of clay with brief notes in Assyrian) which were squeezed over the cord binding them are known.

There are four general types of legal documents: conveyances, contracts, receipts, and court documents. The term 'conveyance' covers all texts which record the transfer of property, and most of these are, therefore, sale documents, although rentals, marriages, adoptions, and inheritance also come under this general heading. Sale documents concerned only the transfer of people and real estate; and sales of any other property, such as crops or animals, did not require a legal record or 'deed'. Provision was made in the conveyances against future litigation, and while the normal penalty for instigating a false claim was a heavy fine, occasionally some bizarre penalties were prescribed. Thus the guilty party might be required to present a number of white horses to a god, to burn his eldest son, or even to swallow an enormous amount of wool! The inclusion of such curious penalties was a mere formality, for there is no evidence that they were ever enforced. In the case of sales of people the seller is customarily required to guarantee the slaves against illness for one hundred days and against any litigation involving the slave at any time in the future.

Contracts involve an obligation on one party in favour of another ('bond' is the technical term) and thus cover all kinds of loans and promissory notes. The amount of the debt might be stated in kind or in terms of silver or copper as the standard of exchange, although frequently the sum did not actually change hands at that point. Indeed, 'true loans' were not all that common and most debts were incurred in a variety of ways, such as inability to pay rent, or crop failure. Interest, when stipulated, was very high (interest rates of more than 100 per cent per annum are attested), but frequently the creditor took a pledge, fields or people, from the debtor and made use of the pledge for the period of the debt in lieu of interest (an 'antichretic' loan). When the debt was paid, the tablet upon which the contract was inscribed was smashed, thus effectively destroying all evidence that such an obligation existed. On occasion, however, it was necessary to have concrete proof that the obligation had been met, and so a receipt, another type of legal document, was drawn up. This did not happen very often and few receipts are known. Similarly there are few of the last type of legal texts, the court documents, since disputes were normally handled privately. Despite their small number, however, these court documents are of special interest, since they provide an insight into the manner in which legal arguments were settled on a formal basis.

There were no law courts and certainly no court houses in ancient Assyria, but parties who were involved in a dispute which they were unable to resolve by themselves could go before a high administrative official to seek a settlement. Appeal was made normally only to certain officials, the 'mayor' (*ḫazannu*), the 'chief justice' (*sartennu*), and the 'vizier' (*sukallu*), although in some instances another high official (for example, the 'steward', *abarakku*) might be asked. They could act singly or in a group of two or more. If the official or officials could not come to a decision, the disputants were sent to the ordeal. The little which is known about the ordeal in Neo-Assyrian times can be stated briefly: under the supervision of appointed officers the litigants would declare their respective claims orally before the god and the ultimate verdict would be pronounced by the god. How the deity came to a decision and announced it is unknown. The ordeal was the final court of appeal and the decision binding. It is interesting that there is no record of an appeal being made to the king in such cases, for in other administrative realms an Assyrian subject could apply directly to the monarch.

The entire proceedings of the judicial settlement, whether an ordeal was involved or not, were recorded, together with the names of the participants and witnesses and the ultimate decision. The settlement usually called for the imposition of a payment or fine on one party, since most such disputes concerned the ownership of property. Among the settlements known to us there are no examples of litigation stretching over long periods of time, in contrast to Babylonia, and this may be a reflection of the greater political stability in Assyria.

Cases involving bodily injury and murder were normally settled by private agreement or vendetta. Prisons existed and there are recorded instances of people claiming to have been kept in jail for many years but these, on the whole, seem to have been political prisoners. It is not clear whether people were ever incarcerated by the state for legal infractions, although it was possible for an individual forcibly to detain a person who had wronged him, until he had been redressed either privately or in a judicial case.

The Assyrian legal system changed little over the centuries, being impervious to foreign influence and the stresses brought to bear by imperialistic expansion. It was, then, another steadying influence in Assyrian civilization.

V. THE ECONOMY

The economic structure of Assyria was considerably transformed by the evolution of the state into an imperial power; it will be the aim of this section not only to analyse the structure which evolved but also to highlight features of it which are relevant to the fall of the empire. Given that the economic system was gradually altered, it is necessary to consider separately the economy in the two areas, the Assyrian heartland and the empire. In Assyria proper the economic base was agriculture, animal husbandry, and trade. All three of these activities were practised from ancient times, since they were natural pursuits in an area with the geographic features of the Assyrian heartland.

The southern border of this area, where the city state of Ashur was located, coincided with the southern limit of dependable annual rainfall, so that Assyria's meadows could be cultivated with considerably more ease and profit than those farther south in Babylonia, where artificial irrigation was vital. The position of the city of Ashur, at the point where the Jebel Hamrin fades into the Jezirah, was also significant for trade, since it was a strategic point for crossing the Tigris on the east–west trade route as well as being on the north–south route along the Tigris. The inhabitants of the Assyrian heartland were compelled to trade from earliest times because, apart from the produce of their fertile land and some stone for building in the north, the area had no natural resources. This statement seems ludicrous today, since one of the world's great oilfields is located on the very edge of the ancient Assyrian heartland.

The main cereal grown was barley although other grains, such as wheat and emmer, were known. Barley was used for bread, sesame was grown for oil, and flax for linen. While the beer brewed from barley was the staple drink, vineyards produced wine, the supply of which was augmented from immediately adjacent areas in the mountains. Orchards and gardens yielded fruit, nuts, leeks, onions, and cress. The most common animals bred were cattle, sheep, goats, donkeys, mules, and various kinds of fowl such as ducks. The fowls produced eggs, the goats provided milk, with its by-products of butter and cheese, and the sheep were raised for wool. Cattle, donkeys, and mules were used as draught animals and beasts of burden. On special occasions an animal was slaughtered for its meat and hide. The shepherd worked on a contract basis, whereby he paid the owner a fixed portion of the flock's yield and kept the remainder. In the Neo-Assyrian period all animals were subject to a state tax.

In theory all land belonged to the god, represented by the crown, while in practice the state owned only a certain portion, the remainder being held by the temples, wealthy families, and private individuals. In addition to outright private possession, land could be held under an arrangement called *ilku*. By this method, the client had the use of the land in return for performing state service, both civil (road building, canal repairs, and so on) and military. It should be noted that a few scholars believe the *ilku* was not associated with land tenure but simply with the fact of being an Assyrian; however, most believe that originally the *ilku* was applicable only to land-holding and by Neo-Assyrian times the proportion of the population not working on the land had increased to such a point that it was necessary to impose *ilku* on citizens throughout the state. The more important and wealthy were allowed to make payments in lieu of service, and in the case of large estates where *ilku* was involved the owner was expected to produce a certain number of men for *ilku* and would not himself perform the service. The absence of an *ilku* obligation on a piece of land was an asset and was duly noted in sale documents. It is unknown what proportion of the entire land area of the state was held under *ilku*, but all cultivated areas, whether subject to *ilku* or not, were assessed a grain and straw tax (*šibšu u nusāḫē*).

As for trade, because of lack of natural resources the list of imports was extensive and included metals, timber, precious stones, ivory, horses, camels, wine, aromatics, and possibly silk from China.[22] The principal export was manufactured goods, particularly textiles, but of equal importance with the export of goods was the fact that Assyria was a crossroads for major trade routes, including those to and from Babylonia and the Persian Gulf. In practice trade was conducted not by the Assyrians themselves but by Aramaeans, Phoenicians, and Arabs, to name some, and this fact accounts for the lack of cuneiform documentation on trade. The state reaped profits from the trade through the imposition of customs duties (quay tax, gate tax, and so on) and through the indirect benefits of a thriving economy.

Crafts in Assyria were conducted in the palace and possibly also in the temples and large estates. Before Neo-Assyrian times the crown issued raw materials to the craftsmen and they returned all finished products to the crown, their subsistence being provided extra. But in Neo-Assyrian times the craftsmen worked on a contract basis, whereby they repaid the crown for the raw materials in other forms, not necessarily in manufactured goods, and kept a certain portion of the raw materials as commission.

Going beyond the confines of Assyria proper, the economy of the areas ruled varied according to local conditions, but the empire profited from each and every one of them by the receipt of tax and tribute. Taxes were imposed upon the provinces proper, while tribute was collected from the regimes which were under obligation to Assyria by treaty. Both taxes and tribute were rendered in kind and included exotic imports as well as the animals which were used to support local administration and armies. Tribute was paid annually at an appointed time, when the representatives of each government paraded before the Assyrian king with their contributions borne in state. On this occasion the Assyrians required the ambassadors to renew their treaty oaths (*adû*) on behalf of their rulers. Bulky items, such as grain and animals, were delivered to an Assyrian centre close by rather than being brought to the capital.

Tribute came under the direct jurisdiction of the crown, regardless of where it was deposited, while taxes in the provinces were collected by the local governor and his bureaucracy. The *ilku* and the grain and straw taxes mentioned earlier also applied to the provinces but, of course, not to the vassal states. In addition, in the provinces there were agents (*mušarkisu*) directly responsible to the king who gathered horses and raised levies of troops for the royal armies. The booty taken on foreign campaigns consisted of luxury items and became the property of the palace to dispose of at will. Some was kept but some was distributed to the temples, to provincial governors, and to the nobility.

The leading economic institution in the state was the palace, but it did not have a monopoly, for industry and commerce were conducted by the large estates and by smaller units and individuals. The temples still had independent revenues from their land, but the increase in their size in the Neo-Assyrian period had made them dependent upon royal favour in the form of transferred taxes, *ilku*, and a portion of the booty, in order to survive economically. It was possible, as noted in Section II above, for a man and his family slowly to build a fortune by acquiring land and its revenue through skilful management and clever transactions.

The standard of exchange in business deals was silver or copper, both being used contemporaneously, but copper being more common in the eighth century and silver in the seventh century. The metal was only a standard and did not actually change hands except in the few instances where it was the substance involved. This is in contrast to Babylonia in a later period, where regular statements about the form and quality of the metal indicate that it did change hands. There is no clear evidence that coinage was used in Assyria. Of equal importance with a standard of exchange was a standard of weights and measures, and it is commonly stated in the documentation which standard was being followed, both the 'mina of Carchemish' and the 'royal mina' being in common use. Official weights, of stone or metal in the shape of ducks or lions and with a cuneiform label indicating weight and royal name (where applicable), were available for checking and some of these have been recovered in modern times. A careful account was kept of business transactions and hundreds of administrative tablets, mainly from palaces, have been recovered. The main types of documents represented are debenture lists, credit lists, inventories, accounts, tax assessments, census lists, and notes and memoranda of all kinds.

Prices fluctuated according to supply and demand, and there is no suggestion that the state ever fixed or controlled prices. A fitting illustration of this is Ashurbanipal's boast that he brought back so many camels from his Arabian campaigns that the price of camels in Assyria plummeted to a ridiculously small sum.[23] Given the nature of our sources, we cannot assess the standard of living in the Assyrian empire, although it is clear that it would have fluctuated with the fortunes of the state as a whole, and there is every indication that the upper classes enjoyed many exotic luxuries during the great days of Assyrian power. It is equally apparent that in such a highly centralized system the outlying regions of the empire were relatively economically depressed areas.

This last observation leads to some concluding remarks on the problems and weaknesses in the Assyrian economy. The concentration of supplies and wealth in the large cities gave great strength and authority to the crown, a necessary adjunct to a political structure based on royal absolutism, but, as Postgate has pointed out, it meant that Assyria was vulnerable to disruptions of supplies from its outlying regions and these regions were, in addition, deprived of their internal viability and strength.[24] Garelli has suggested that there is evidence of increasing inflation with the devaluation of silver brought about by the large quantities of that precious substance flowing into Assyria.[25] Another problem was the continual increase in the number of people not directly engaged in food production, members of the state bureaucracy and most of the urban dwellers. As early as the reign of Tiglath-pileser I (1114–1076 B.C.) Assyrian kings were expanding the area of land under cultivation and forcibly transporting peoples to work on it, in order to supply food for this growing segment of the population. Such a process could not go on indefinitely.

While the expansion of the Assyrian empire in its initial phases stimulated the economy by bringing a great deal of wealth and manpower under the sway of the Assyrian state, the stimulus could not have permanent effects without some major readjustments to the economic structure. Conquered regions could produce only so much, even with the best will in the world, and the inhabitants of these areas were naturally reluctant to work hard only to see the greater portion of the fruits of their labours carted off to a foreign country. They were hesitant to engage vigorously in foreign trade under Assyrian eyes since the more wealthy they became the more attractive their assets were to Assyria's covetous eyes. The Assyrian state's only answer to apathy and resistance was to use the iron fist, and it never occurred to the crown to replace this heavy-handed technique with attempts to encourage local initiative and industry. Assyria's view of the economy of the empire was

[23] A 344, 76f ix 46–9.   [24] A 464, 200–2.   [25] A 23, 273–5.

simplistic: the ruled territories were there to supply the central state with as much wealth and labour as could be squeezed out of them, and no thought was given to long-range schemes and profits. Here lies one of the basic flaws in the Assyrian imperial structure, a flaw which would reappear in subsequent empires formed after the Assyrian model.

VI. WARFARE

The chief occupation of the Assyrian king and state was warfare. All other interests were subordinate to this central concern and over the centuries Assyria developed military expertise far surpassing that of any other contemporary nation. A supplement to knowledge gleaned from contemporary sources is provided by the fact that the armies of the succeeding Oriental powers, the Babylonian and Persian, were in many respects modelled after the Assyrian, so that information generally applicable to Assyrian warfare can be gained from Greek accounts of the Persians during their wars with the Greeks in the fifth century B.C. Developments and changes were taking place in Assyrian armed might throughout her history, but the reign of Tiglath-pileser III must be highlighted, since this king was responsible for a number of alterations and improvements including, it would seem, the organization of a proper standing army.

The Assyrian army in the Sargonid period had a potential magnitude of several hundreds of thousands of troops, although a call-up of the entire force for a campaign was extremely rare. Supreme command of the army rested with the king and, immediately under him, the 'field marshal' (*turtānu*). The army was divided into units of various sizes and types; but the basic division was the 'company' (*kiṣru*) of fifty men under a 'captain' (*rab kiṣri* or *rab ḫanšê*) and this unit was in turn broken down into files of ten men. An officer carried a mace as a symbol of his authority.

The majority of the troops were infantry and these were supported by chariotry, cavalry, and engineers. The common weapons of the footmen were the spear, bow, sling, dagger, sword, mace, and battle-axe, and they carried shields of various types. Among the infantry units were special groups of archers, each archer with a bow as tall as himself and carrying his own quiver. The archer was accompanied by a spearman and protected by an enormous shield carried by a third man. Chariot types varied over the centuries, but they were essentially two-wheeled with an open back and drawn by one or more horses. In the ninth century B.C. each vehicle had a driver and an archer, and later one or two shield-bearers were added. The bow used was smaller than that employed by the foot archer, as was the bow of the cavalry.

The cavalryman had, besides the bow, a short sword, and in the ninth century he was usually accompanied by a second mounted man with a shield who protected the archer and held his horse's reins when he shot. In the later period this companion disappeared. The engineering units consisted of men who operated and maintained the siege engines, a subject to which we shall return in a moment. Whether or not these units also included men who performed the other special tasks of siege operations (such as scaling and sapping) is not clear, nor do we know who was specifically responsible for the mechanics of crossing rivers and making roads. If possible rivers were forded but, when necessary, timbers were stretched across or pontoon bridges of rafts constructed. Sometimes troops and horses swam across, the men with the assistance of inflated goatskins, while equipment and supplies were ferried over on rafts floated on goatskins. In mountainous terrain new paths were hacked out as required by pick men, and old paths widened and improved.

The clothing of troops in battle was protective, the lower orders wearing leather and the higher ranks scale armour. Professional Assyrian soldiers wore pointed helmets in battle, while in peace they replaced them with braided headbands. Provincial troops wore native dress. In the reliefs soldiers are portrayed as smartly and uniformly dressed; and the stalwart figures give the impression that they were highly disciplined, the orderly ranks suggesting that parade ground drill was not unknown. These representations may, however, be idealistic.

Originally troops were raised under *ilku* and were required only for limited periods of time during the year. Veterans were settled in military colonies in newly acquired territory. As Assyria's foreign expansion was stepped up, more troops were required and even an extension of *ilku* beyond land-holding arrangements could no longer satisfy this demand, particularly with the creation of a standing army. Eventually there came to be three kinds of soldier, the permanent professional, the man fulfilling his *ilku* obligation, and the extraordinary soldier called up for a specific campaign.

The levying of troops was the primary responsibility of the captains, each of whom had a certain number of villages under his command, and the captains were in turn responsible to the provincial governor. By the Sargonid age there was also a standing army which was under the direct authority of the king, no doubt created as a counter-balance to the potential misuse of military power by the provincial governors. The king also had his own bodyguard of infantry and cavalry. The troops recruited within Assyria proper were spread around the empire as much as possible, since they were the most loyal, and they constituted the chariotry and cavalry divisions. The infantry consisted largely of foreigners, mainly Aramaeans. Some foreign groups became specialized units. For example, the Ituaeans, an Aramaic people, were entrusted with special tasks such as escort duty throughout the empire.

Garrisons and barracks were scattered over the empire, but the military headquarters was a massive armoury in the Assyrian capital. Here was stationed a large portion of the troops, animals, and equipment of the standing army, and there were, in addition, royal apartments for the king to occupy when he wished. At each New Year there was a grand inspection at the armoury when the king reviewed his troops and their equipment. The architecture of the armoury is known since that at Calah in the ninth century, Fort Shalmaneser, was excavated in recent years; that at Nineveh, the *ekal māšarti* or *ekal kutalli*, is still known only from descriptions in royal inscriptions.

In Assyria's early days warfare was conducted sporadically, in the form of quick raids, but by the Neo-Assyrian period the institution of annual campaigns of longer duration was well established. The king, in theory, personally led the yearly campaign but in practice he did not always do so, nor, in fact, did a campaign actually take place every year, but royal annals and eponym chronicles usually assumed that they did. The motives and aims of the campaigns were multiple and complex involving, as they did, economic greed, the imperialistic idea, national pride, the egotism of the Assyrian monarch, and religious fervour, and it is reasonably apparent that there was a long-range policy behind them, a policy which altered from reign to reign.

A campaign normally started in the spring, as soon as the rains of winter were past, and the beginning was a great occasion. The core of the army was gathered at the starting point, which was not necessarily the capital, where the monarch inspected the troops and the priests and diviners performed the customary rites. As the army marched off it was preceded by the standards, accompanied by the priests and diviners, and the king with his bodyguard. These were followed in order by the chariotry, cavalry, infantry, and the impedimenta. Further levies would be picked up at gathering points in the regions of the empire through which the army marched on its way to the frontier. When the army set out it carried some food supplies, mainly barley, which were issued in daily rations, but it lived mainly off the land and this determined the routes followed. In each territory it traversed the local governor or ruler was required to provide sustenance as long as the army was within his territory. If, as happened occasionally, the duration of a campaign stretched over a year, the army would normally wait out the winter in a suitable camping spot. At the successful conclusion of a campaign the hostages and booty were paraded through the streets of the Assyrian capital. The king was driven in state in his ceremonial chariot with the conquered princes and nobles plodding in chains behind him.

Assyrian military strategy involved pitched battles, siege warfare, and psychological warfare. The Assyrians did not use guerrilla methods, apart from the occasional ambush, although their enemies sometimes did with success. Being a land-locked nation it depended upon foreign sailors, usually Phoenicians, when a navy was required. In open battles most of the fighting was hand-to-hand combat by the infantry, under fire cover from the archers, chariotry, and cavalry. Special tactics known were midnight attacks, damming rivers to flood the enemy camp, and taking a position which cut the enemy off from his water supply. A central aim in all battles was the enemy's leader and the signal of victory was his death, flight, or surrender. This being so, a lightning attack led by the king and his bodyguard on the enemy commander in the midst of the foray was a proven tactic.

Siege warfare became a highly specialized technique in the Neo-Assyrian period and many of the skills developed by the Assyrians were subsequently adopted, improved upon, and expanded by later imperial powers including the Romans. Against the moats and ramparts of the well-fortified garrisons the Assyrian engineers brought a variety of engines and skills. There were the enclosed battering rams on wheels, in effect primitive tanks, with archers ensconced in turrets on top to pick off defenders on the wall who would attempt to burn the machine with torches or dislodge the battering rams with 'wolves', looped chains lowered from the walls. As for scaling techniques, in addition to using ladders, earthen ramps were sometimes heaped up against the wall for battering rams to roll up and demolish the upper defences and allow the infantry to rush up and over. The Assyrians also used sappers to burrow under or through the walls and fires were set with torches at wooden gates. Engineers engaged in these various activities were under constant threat from the defenders who shot arrows and spears at them, dropped rocks and scalding liquid. Cover was provided by the archers who took up strategic positions with their shield-bearers.

If the initial attempts at taking a city by siege failed, the Assyrians usually withdrew, but not before ravaging the surrounding countryside, burning and destroying crops, trees and houses. Only on occasion would they settle down for a long siege. When they did this, they stationed small groups of men in redoubts and siege towers near the wall, particularly near the gates, in order to prevent any traffic in or out of the city and to warn of any planned sortie from the gates. Once ensconced, the Assyrians were willing to wait many months or even a year or more, until the starved inhabitants capitulated.

But siege warfare was a prolonged and costly business and even pitched battles could not be indulged in too frequently, so that the Assyrians preferred psychological warfare. They used a variety of tactics to persuade the people of target areas to surrender without resistance, these tactics involving initial overtures of peace. One such method was to surround a city and then have one or more high-ranking Assyrian officers stand near the walls to address the population, presenting arguments why they should disobey their leaders and open the gates. This tactic was employed at the siege of Babylon during the reign of Tiglath-pileser III and at the siege of Jerusalem in the time of Sennacherib. If the enemy resisted peaceful overtures, then Assyria's tactics changed dramatically. One or more groups of cities were singled out for a major onslaught, be it pitched battle or siege, and once they were defeated the population was horribly mutilated and slaughtered, while their houses and towns were torn down and burnt. The skins of flayed people were prominently displayed and corpses erected on stakes on the spot as gruesome testimony to what the Assyrians could do. Surrounding people, once they heard of these acts, commonly surrendered to the Assyrian army without further resistance; indeed there were campaigns which met no hostilities, so widely had Assyrian terror spread. This 'calculated frightfulness' or psychological warfare is what has won the Assyrians such a notorious reputation in world history. The practice was extremely effective, and it is important to remember that the terror was selective. While an Assyrian king boasts of wholesale slaughter and devastation, in practice only certain pockets of resistance were subjected to this treatment.

Another tactic which was employed selectively and for which Assyria also became notorious was the transportation of people. Populations of a given region were uprooted and moved to areas completely foreign to them, where they were forced to settle and work. The reasons for this were to provide labour on major building projects, such as a new palace, or to develop uncultivated land and increase the food supply. But an equally important administrative and military reason was to remove particularly rebellious groups from their home territory, thereby depriving them of their effectiveness, and also presenting an admonitory example to other potential rebels.

Assyrian warfare was supremely successful, witness the great empire it won and maintained, and the collapse of that empire cannot be attributed to any major advance in military techniques on the part of Assyria's conquerors, the Medes and Babylonians. If there was any weakness at all in the Assyrian fighting arm it was the increasing dependence upon foreign troops rather than native militias, but this was a relatively unimportant factor in light of the more substantial political and economic forces which caused the collapse.

VII. THE HUNT

A common recreation of a warlike people is hunting and the Assyrians were no exception to this rule. Already in the Middle Assyrian period the

pursuit and killing of animals as sport was a popular royal pastime, and
this continued into the Neo-Assyrian era, when the royal hunt developed
into a national institution similar in many respects to the annual
campaign. Indeed in the reign of Ashurbanipal the lion hunt was
performed, as we know from the reliefs and their captions, with great
attention to organization and ceremony and was staged in such a way
that the general populace could watch as the king despatched one lion
after another. The end of the hunt was celebrated by a religious
ceremony, for the gods Ninurta and Palil were patron deities of the hunt.

Any wild creature, bird, beast, or fish, was fair game for an Assyrian
royal hunt but those which presented the greatest challenge were
preferred. Most commonly chased were the elephant, lion, and wild bull
which at that time roved the Syrian steppes, a favourite hunting ground
for Assyrian kings. Beasts were also captured alive and brought back to
Assyria to be released at will for the purposes of a hunt. Assyrian interest
in wild beasts was not confined to killing, however, for kings collected
animals and kept them in zoological gardens and exotic creatures such as
apes were prized as pets. Wild animals were hunted in a variety of ways,
pursued from a chariot, stalked on foot, surprised in ambush, and
stampeded towards the hunting party by *battue*. Most of our information
about the hunt concerns the king's exploits, but presumably Assyrian
males in general pursued this pastime both for enjoyment and for the
maintenance of their military skills. The uncontrolled slaughter of
animals in Syria by the Assyrians led to the elephant becoming extinct in
that area in antiquity.

VIII. RELIGION

Any account of Assyrian religion is necessarily a discussion of the great
state cults, since we have much information about them, whereas very
little is known about the religious beliefs and practices of the individual
Assyrian. Polytheism and cult are salient features of the religion of
Assyria although, on the highest level at least, there were not nearly so
many gods as there were in Babylonia. The reason for this is that deities
in both civilizations were associated with cities, and the Babylonian plain
had many more large urban centres than Assyria, where one finds only
Ashur, with the god of the same name, Nineveh and Arba'il, each with
Ishtar, and Calah with Ninurta. In addition, there was Shamash, the sun-
god, Adad the storm-god, and Sin, the moon-god, who was also the
tutelary deity of the provincial city of Harran, which played an
interesting role in the latter days of the Assyrian empire.

Ashur was the king of gods, a reflection of the ancient beginnings of
Assyria in the city state of Ashur. He was the official god of the Assyrian

nation, all of which belonged to him, and he appointed the Assyrian monarch as his vice-regent to rule on his behalf. The king attributed all his accomplishments, and especially his military victories, to the god Ashur, for not only his authority but his intelligence and resources were granted to him by divine favour. Ashur ruled the gods, mankind, and the universe as sovereign, lord, father, creator, sage, and warrior, these being the general categories into which his epithets fall. He was not a deity of the people at large and his presence was manifest only on state occasions and in official documents.

Ninurta was the first-born son of Ashur and was the god of warfare and hunting. There was a shrine dedicated to him at Ashur but Calah was his chief centre, at least from the time of Ashurnasirpal II. The goddess Ishtar combined two main spheres of activity, battle and love, and she was the tutelary deity of two cities, Nineveh and Arbaʾil, as well as being highly revered in Ashur; our sources regularly speak of 'Ishtar of Nineveh', 'Ishtar of Arbaʾil', and 'Assyrian Ishtar'. Ninurta, Ishtar, Shamash, Adad, and Sin all had counterparts of the same name in Babylonian religion where, thanks to extensive Babylonian literature, their activities are much more widely attested than are those of Ashur. While the figure of Ashur appears static and austere, like that of an Assyrian king, the personalities of the other chief Assyrian deities are quite colourful. All of these deities, with the exception of Ishtar, are males, and while each of them had a spouse, her role was so subordinate that she was rarely mentioned, a reflection of the male-oriented nature of Assyrian society. Ishtar is the only exception, and her importance goes back to prehistoric times at Nineveh before Assyrian domination.

Babylonian influence on Assyrian religion was immense, and this may be aptly illustrated at the outset by noting the penetration of three Babylonian deities, Ellil, Marduk, and Nabu into Assyria. Ellil appeared first, as early as the reign of Shamshi-Adad I (1813–1781 B.C.), and eventually came to be virtually identical with Ashur, who assumed his epithets including the name Ellil itself. Evidence for the cult of Marduk in the city of Ashur appears in the fourteenth century B.C. and Marduk's popularity among Assyrians grew apace thereafter. Nabu's presence in Assyria came to the fore in the ninth century B.C., when great temples were built in his honour in Assyrian cities.

Babylonian influence was not confined to the gods worshipped but stretched out to the religious rites as well. Most ceremonies and in particular the *Akitu* seem to have been affected by Babylonian ideas and practices. This was all part and parcel of the continuous cultural penetration of Babylonian civilization into Assyria. There were attempts, however, to reject this influence. In the reign of Sennacherib Marduk's supreme position in the pantheon was challenged, as noted in a previous chapter (see above, p. 119), and his name was replaced by Ashur's name in some Assyrian copies of the Babylonian 'Poem of Creation' (*enūma eliš*).

Cult was a characteristic of Assyrian religion, as mentioned earlier, and the centre of the cult was the temple and the divine statue. The temple was a monumental building with a central shrine, where the cult image stood, several lesser chapels, and a multitude of rooms and corridors. Cities normally had a number of temples, the chief being the temple of the tutelary deity, and a given temple could include, besides the central shrine, any number of ancillary chapels dedicated to deities who nevertheless might have their own temple elsewhere. Thus, for example, the temple of Ashur at Ashur, Ekhursaggalkurkurra, embraced shrines dedicated to, among others, Ninurta and Dagan. The same deity might have a temple in more than one city, such as Nabu, who had temples in both Calah and Nineveh. While a god normally shared his temple with his spouse, occasionally two male deities were equally honoured by a temple; at Ashur there was the temple of An and Adad and the temple of Sin and Shamash.

A temple was a self-contained community with its own hierarchy of personnel and its own economic resources, although in the Neo-Assyrian period it began to lose control over its own affairs as it became more dependent upon royal benefits. The head of the temple was the '(chief) priest' (*šangû*), who was responsible to the king as the representative on earth of Ashur, king of the gods. In theory the king's presence was in heavy demand, for his participation was required in large numbers of religious celebrations; in practice, however, substitution was possible and necessary since the monarch had so many other demands on his time. Under the (chief) priest was a variety of priests who were responsible for the various rites and activities of the temple. The temple personnel also included artisans, scribes, kitchen staff, and domestic servants.

Traditionally the temple derived its income from land which it owned, but in the Neo-Assyrian period this income was supplemented by royal benefits in the form of offerings in perpetuity, of which there were different types, and extraordinary gifts granted on special occasions, such as a portion of the booty after a successful campaign. Renovation or expansion of the temple building was done under the authority of and at the expense of the crown. Thus the Assyrian cult by the Neo-Assyrian period depended very much on royal favour and loss of that favour meant serious depletion of revenue and gradual deterioration of the temple building itself. Relations between palace and temple were not all one-sided, however, for the king depended upon the priests for advice and assistance in religious matters. Given the pervasive presence of religion in Assyrian society, this was a highly influential position for the priests. They told the king when he must fast, when he must be present to participate in a religious ceremony, when he might travel, and so on. That this is not just theory is illustrated by letters of the Sargonid period wherein matters of this kind are commonly discussed with the monarch.

Of all the religious ceremonies in the Assyrian calendar by far the most important was the *Akitu*, which could be celebrated at any time of the year, although one thinks of it as a New Year's festival. Much of the ceremony was performed in the *Akitu* temple, there being one in each major Assyrian city. According to ancient custom this structure was outside the city walls, but by the reign of Sennacherib it had been moved inside the walls and Sennacherib decreed a return to the old ways. The ritual involved an elaborate procession and a great banquet (*tākultu*) of considerable ceremony, wherein the king's right to rule for another year was granted by the god and his princes and nobles renewed their loyalty oaths to him. Little is known about the other Assyrian rituals apart from some of their names and fragments of their ceremonies. The care of the gods, their feeding and washing, involved frequent rites but none of these has survived in written form.

The official Assyrian attitude towards foreign gods and cults was one of tolerance, and Assyria did not attempt to impose upon conquered peoples the worship of Ashur or of any other Assyrian deity. They did, however, carry off divine statues and emblems of conquered peoples; but these were regarded as hostages, similar to the young nobles taken into exile, and were returned when Assyria was assured that the people would remain loyal to them. Thus, for example, Esarhaddon returned to the Arab sheikh Hazael the statues of his gods captured by Sennacherib. Far from suppressing local cults of conquered people, the Assyrian king sometimes presented them with offerings and sponsored building work for them.

The extent to which the individual Assyrian, apart from temple and court personnel, would have been involved in the religious life of the cults was probably minimal. Presumably crowds gathered to watch the great processions which took place in connexion with such a ceremony as the *Akitu*, but unauthorized people were not allowed into the temple. There is no direct information about how an individual Assyrian satisfied his religious needs, for what textual information we have regarding personal gods, magic, and incantations is Babylonian in origin. These texts were kept, however, in the Assyrian libraries, and so the picture we have of popular religion in Babylonia may be generally valid for Assyria.

Related to religion is the matter of divination. Every Assyrian believed that the gods communicated their plans through various signs and it was up to mankind to learn to read such signs. These omens were presented through different media, such as smoke patterns or deformed animal or human births. In the Neo-Assyrian period the two most common types of divination were astrology and extispicy. A massive literature developed explaining the multitude of signs which might appear, and this documentation represents the beginning of science, for the whole foundation of ancient Mesopotamian divination depended upon accurate observation of natural phenomena. Thus, if one ignores the interpretations, one has a mine of accurate scientific information on the movements of heavenly bodies in the case of astrology, or on the physiology of animals in the case of extispicy.

But of course this was not the intent of the diviners, whose profession was dedicated to predicting the future. While all Assyrians believed in their art and would avail themselves of it if possible, it was practised in its most elaborate form only by the court, which could maintain a whole school of diviners. The mechanics of prognostication can best be illustrated by extispicy, for which we have relevant records from the reigns of Esarhaddon and Ashurbanipal, as mentioned in a preceding chapter (see above, p. 122). When the king wished to undertake a major enterprise such as a royal campaign, his scribes and diviners would outline the details of the proposal in an 'oracle request', of which many on clay tablets have survived. This request was then presented to the gods of extispicy, Shamash and Adad, accompanied by the appropriate ritual, and one or more lambs were sacrificially slaughtered. The entrails of the carcase were minutely examined according to the dictates of the diviner's profession and ominous features duly noted. These features were multitudinous but centred upon the liver and lungs, of which the ancient Assyrians had intimate knowledge, and for every deformity and discolouration a special meaning was recorded in their reference works. As the diviners performed their *post mortem* all the significant signs were noted on a clay tablet and the interpretation added. Interpretations took a variety of forms but essentially had three meanings, 'good', 'bad', or 'confused'. At the end of the examination a total was made of the number of each kind of interpretations and an opinion expressed as to whether or not the proposal was auspicious. A record of the entire examination and the result was sent back to the king as an 'oracle response'.

Astrological procedures were quite different from those of extispicy, for, rather than being induced, the astrological signs could only be observed as they happened to occur and interpreted accordingly. Astrological observers were stationed throughout Assyria and Babylonia and every night they watched the heavens, carefully writing down what they saw. Over the centuries the diviners developed such expertise that they had plotted the paths of many heavenly bodies with minute accuracy and could predict various phenomena, including the possibility of lunar eclipses. Events such as an eclipse were ominous and thus when a lunar eclipse was forecast during the reign of Esarhaddon, as we have seen (see above p. 137) it caused a great deal of consternation, for it was interpreted to mean that the king would die. Esarhaddon's extreme reaction is perhaps not typical of the extent to which the Assyrian monarch was subject to the dictates of divination, but there is no question that every Assyrian, king or commoner, had great regard for prognostication.

IX. LIBRARIES

Literature and learning were highly prized in Assyria, where libraries existed as early as Middle Assyrian times. These libraries contained largely Babylonian texts, for the Assyrians, while they admired literary talent in others, were not themselves commonly inspired by the muse. There were, of course, Assyrian scribes and these occasionally put forth literary efforts, such as the Epic of Tukulti-Ninurta I, but such works are notable for their scarcity. The idea of a library was imported from Babylonia and serious acquisition of Babylonian written lore in Assyria probably began with the sack of Babylon by Tukulti-Ninurta I (1243–1207), and libraries were developed over the centuries at the different Assyrian cities. The assiduity with which Assyrian kings sought Babylonian writings for their libraries is illustrated by a royal letter, probably from Ashurbanipal, in which the monarch instructs his agents in Babylonia: 'Collect every last tablet in their establishments and all the tablets which are in Ezida! Gather together the entirety of . . . [a long list of text types] and send them to me. . . . If you see any tablet which I have not mentioned and it is fitting for my palace . . . send it to me!'[26]

Nabu, as god of the scribal craft, was the patron deity of the libraries, which were commonly called, at least in the temples, 'Ezida' after the name of Nabu's shrine in his city of Borsippa. Indeed the term 'library' may be misleading, since so little is known about these collections and nothing about the physical arrangements, staffing, and purpose of the depositories in which they were stored. They are collections of large numbers of compositions of literary, learned and religious content and the tablets in such collections are distinguishable from everyday documents by the extra care with which they are written, the inclusion of colophons, the better quality of clay, and often the size and shape of the tablet.

There were probably many libraries in ancient Assyria, in palaces,

[26] CT 22 no. 1. See A 88 IV, 212–15. See also A 508.

temples, and houses of the wealthy, but to date there is firm evidence about only a few of them. A library, commonly called the Library of Tiglath-pileser I because so many texts in it can be dated to his reign, was found in the Ashur temple at Ashur. This collection probably had ancient antecedents, almost certainly as early as the reign of Ashur-uballiṭ I (1363–1328), and there was no doubt a continuation of it in later centuries. Another, smaller collection of library tablets was found in Ashur dating from the reign of Sargon II (721–705).[27] The library of the Nabu temple at Calah, uncovered recently, was presumably created in the ninth century B.C. when Ashurnasirpal II made Calah a great city. Another fairly recent discovery has been the library at Khuzirina (Sultantepe), which dates to the Sargonid period. Since Khuzirina was only a minor provincial town, this find indicates that libraries were much more widely scattered through the Assyrian empire than one would have imagined. But the greatest of all libraries were those developed at Nineveh by the Sargonid kings, among which that of Ashurbanipal has principally and justly become famous.

The libraries at Nineveh are both the best known and the largest, and they serve as an example of what a library should contain and in what proportion. It is impossible to give an accurate statement of the numbers of tablets because of the broken and incomplete state of the recovered material. A. Leo Oppenheim estimated that originally there were about fifteen hundred tablets, and, although the discovery in recent years of many more uncatalogued fragments in the British Museum will push that figure higher, Oppenheim's calculations with regard to the proportions are probably still valid.[28] He concluded that the greatest portion of library tablets were prognostic texts and the next largest group were lexical works. In decreasing size there followed religious texts, scientific texts, and literary compositions. Modern man's knowledge of both Babylonian and Assyrian culture is still largely based upon the tablets in these collections, and full credit must be given to the Assyrians for valuing, seeking out, and preserving such a treasury of literature and learning.

---

[27] Cf. A 223, 147 and n. 25.   [28] A 43, 16f.

CHAPTER 27

BABYLONIA 605–539 B.C.

D. J. WISEMAN

I. THE DEFEAT OF EGYPT

The so-called 'Chaldaean' dynasty of Babylon inaugurated by Nabopolassar has also been designated the dynasty of Bit-Yakin or the Third Dynasty of the Sealand. It was not, however, the first occasion the southern tribes had dominated the whole of southern Iraq, for Nebuchadrezzar I, Eriba-Marduk, and Marduk-apla-iddina II had each, for a time, united the leading families against their more powerful northern neighbours. Nabopolassar, aware of the dangers of any lack of central control, followed up the unity shown against their former enemy Assyria with a new alliance with the Medes before taking his army further afield. The treaty arrangements were perhaps intended also to guard the eastern frontier of Babylonia, and were sealed by the marriage of Nabopolassar's eldest son to Amytis of Media.[1] At an early stage Nabopolassar began renovation work on the palace, ziggurat, and walls of Babylon to make the city of Babylon the capital of the newly independent state.[2] His son Nabu-kudurri-uṣur (Nebuchadrezzar, Biblical Nebuchadnezzar, classical Nabuchodonosor, 'O Nabu, protect my lineage') was present at the foundation ceremonies and soon thereafter was proclaimed 'the chief son, the crown prince'.[3] Since there was no principle of dynastic succession in Babylonia, the king by this means indicated his wish and brought the crown prince into public affairs. They were together in operations near Harran before the king departed from the field, more from the need to have a responsible member of the ruling family in Babylon than necessarily because of the king's ill-health or old age, as Berossus later surmised.[4] Meanwhile the prince led his own army into the mountains of Za[mua],[5] seizing forts, setting them on fire and gaining much loot from a three-month campaign, the aim of which might have been to thwart incursions from Elamite territory. Then, while his father marched to Kimuhu (Samsat) on the upper Euphrates,

---

[1] A 7, 25–6.   [2] A 856, 60–5 no. 1.   [3] A 856, 62–3 ii 71 – iii 3.
[4] Quoted in Jos. *Contra Apionem* 1.135–6 (A 7, 26; A 626, 389 §135–6).
[5] A 789, 29 (reading Za[mani]); A 932, 64–5.

setting up garrisons against expected Egyptian attacks, Nebuchadrezzar remained at home. If he were the author of a letter reporting the king's earlier operations with the Medes in the Harran area, he was active in raising support from the temple authorities for these operations.[6] The Babylonian Chronicle affords a precise and reliable source for the major events until 594/3.[7] The Egyptians soon retaliated, besieging the Babylonians who were garrisoning Kimuhu, thus preventing their use of Carchemish as a forward base, and pressing the Babylonians to withdraw from Quramati and posts further south on the Euphrates.

In 605 B.C. Nebuchadrezzar took personal command of the whole army and marched direct to Carchemish, where the Egyptians had fallen back from Quramati. Near his objective he crossed to the west bank to cut the Egyptians off from their direct line of retreat and force them out to battle. The tactic worked and a contest ensued in which the retreating Egpyitians were completely overwhelmed. Those who escaped were overtaken in the Hamath area and 'not a single man escaped to his own country'.[8] If the primary aim was the annihilation of Necho's forces this was successfully brought about in the victory in August, enabling the Babylonian king to impose his hold swiftly over the former Assyrian provinces and vassal territories in the west. Sensitive opinion there, as in Judah, advocated submission (Jer. 25: 1–14; 36: 29; 46: 1–12). These operations were notable for the presence of Greek mercenaries on both sides, attested by finds from Carchemish,[9] pottery evidence from a fort at Meṣad Ḥashavyahu on the Mediterranean coast,[10] and the statements about Antimenidas, brother of Alcaeus, fighting for Nebuchadrezzar.[11] As far as the Egyptian border, hostages were taken as pledges to the new regime, among them Daniel and his companions from Judah.[12]

II. NEBUCHADREZZAR'S CAMPAIGNS IN THE WEST

Nebuchadrezzar, as crown prince, was still in the west when, according to the Babylonian Chronicle, Nabopolassar died in his twenty-first regnal year (8/v/605). Berossus records that when Nebuchadrezzar shortly after heard the news,

he arranged affairs in Egypt and the remaining territory. He ordered some of his friends to bring the Jewish, Phoenician, Syrian, and Egyptian prisoners together with the bulk of the army and the rest of the booty to Babylon. He himself set out with a few companions and reached Babylon by crossing the desert.[13]

[6] A 941, 12–13.   [7] A 25, 99–102; A 932, 64–75.   [8] A 932, 68:7.
[9] A 942 I, 128 and pl. 24.   [10] A 791, 149.   [11] A 802, 22; A 882.
[12] A 938, 336 (possibly in 603/2 B.C.).
[13] Quoted in Jos. Contra Apionem 1.136–7 (A 7, 27; A 626, 389 §137).

This rings true, for he reached Babylon in less than two weeks and 'sat on the royal throne' on 1/vi/605. The phrase implies that he took it in his own right and was supported by the agreement of the leading tribes and palace officials. There is no basis for the view that the date of the succession was made retrospective,[14] for documents were dated in Babylon by his accession within twelve days.[15] Nor is there any indication of schism following the introduction of the new regime, for Nebuchadrezzar was sufficiently confident of his position to return to Syria (Khatti) almost immediately. If the procedures adopted for the coronation of Nabopolassar were used, the new appointment may have involved a double ceremony within the palace and before an assembly of the princes and palace officials who made their loyalty oaths outside for public acclamation.[16] In Khatti the Chronicles record Nebuchadrezzar's intentions almost annually for the next ten years: 'he marched about victoriously', an expression implying the regular enforcement of law and order in the dominions he had inherited from his father rather than specific military mopping-up operations.[17] In his first year this required a six months' absence during which 'all the rulers of Khatti came before him and he received their heavy tribute'. Among these was Jehoiakim of Judah who entered into a vassalage he was to keep for three years.[18] Ashkelon presumably refused to pay tribute, for its king was captured and thereafter Babylon reinforced key places to the south such as Arad (level VII) to thwart any possible Egyptian response. Judah was allowed to reinforce its own southern border and thereafter 'the king of Egypt did not march out of his country again because the king of Babylon had taken all his territory, from the Wadi of Egypt (Nahal Muṣur) to the Euphrates River' (II Kings 24: 7).

Opposition in the west was, however, not fully overcome, for in the following year the Babylonians had to call up stronger military forces and siege equipment for use against an unknown city.[19] A seventh-century Aramaic letter found at Saqqara is an appeal from one Adon to his overlord in Egypt for help, since Babylonian forces had reached Afek.[20] Their ultimate target is not specified and has been variously judged to be Gaza, Ekron, Ashdod, Lachish, or even Sidon or Tyre.[21] Nebuchadrezzar sought to eliminate pro-Egyptian support in the coastal cities, and 'the hostile alien king' named in his Wadi Brissa and Nahr el-Kelb inscriptions could well have been a dependent of the pharaoh from whom he took timber in the Lebanon for his works in Babylon during these early expeditions there.[22]

[14] A 922, 105 n. 28a.   [15] A 877, 12.   [16] A 26, 78–86; A 798; A 799.
[17] A 941, 21–2.   [18] II Ki. 23: 36–24: 1. A 25, 100: 15–20; A 932, 68: 15–20.
[19] A 25, 100: 21–2; A 932, 70–1 21–2; A 941, 24–5.   [20] A 823.
[21] Gaza: A 920, 87–8; A 863. Ekron: B 269, 43–5. Ashdod: B 301, 229 n. 21. Lachish: A 883, 55–6. Sidon or Tyre: A 859, 239; A 941, 24–9.   [22] A 928.

During 601 B.C. the Babylonian garrisons in Khatti were reinforced, but towards the end of the year word reached them that Necho II had called out his army. In the month of Kislimu (December) Nebuchadrezzar took personal command of the Babylonian army, which clashed with the enemy south west of Pelusium on the road from Egypt to Gaza. In an open battle, favourable for the manoeuvring of chariots, cavalry, and archers, both sides 'inflicted a major defeat on each other'. Losses were so heavy that the Babylonians had to devote the whole of the next year to re-equipment and retraining at home.[23] Though the Egyptians may have penetrated as far as Gaza,[24] the battle effectively ended any Saite control by land in Asia. Jehoiakim of Judah interpreted the outcome as favourable to Egypt and abrogated the ties imposed by Babylon. The Babylonian response was to march yet again to Syria and from the garrison base at Hamath and Riblah to begin a series of raids against the Arabs to the south east in order to safeguard their flank when they later moved south.[25] Soon thereafter the Babylonians encouraged Aramaeans,[26] Moabites and Ammonites to raid across Judah's borders (II Ki. 24:2). This was probably a holding operation until due punishment could be meted out, and it depended for its efficacy on the response to the recently invoked loyalty oaths imposed on these tribes. Retribution was not long delayed, for in his seventh year Nebuchadrezzar called out his army, marched to Khatti and besieged the city of Judah. 'On the second day of Adar he captured the city and seized its king. He appointed there a ruler of his own choice, took heavy tribute and sent it back to Babylon.'[27] The Babylonian Chronicle makes it clear that Jerusalem was the planned target, though there seems hardly sufficient time for the action to have been initiated as a reaction to Jehoiakim's death a month before departure. The insertion of a precise date for the capture of Jerusalem (15/16 March 597 B.C.) indicates the importance of this event in Babylonian eyes. Similarly the appointment of Mattaniah (Zedekiah) as regent to replace the captured Jehoiachin shows the desire to have a member of the ruling house subservient to Babylon on oath while the existing head of state was taken off hostage with his immediate family for the victory celebrations. Their presence in Babylon and dependence on the palace there is attested by ration lists dated to 592–569 found in the southern citadel, naming 'Ya'ukīn king of Judah'.[28] The heavy tribute taken included the temple vessels which were to be dedicated to Marduk in Babylon (II Chron. 36: 10; Daniel 1: 1–2; 5: 2). While Jehoiachin's

---

[23] A 932, 70: r. 7. See below, pp. 398 and 717.

[24] Known to the Egyptians as ḳdt, to Herodotus (II. 159) as Kadytis; A 859, 237–8.

[25] Jer. 49: 28–33. A 25, 101: 9–10; A 941, 30–1.

[26] A 941, 31; rather than read Edomites (Jer. 35: 11, Peshitta); cf. A 795.

[27] A 25, 102: 11–13; A 932, 72–3: 11–13.   [28] A 923, 925–6; cf. Ezekiel 17: 12.

submission appears to have saved Judah from the severest destruction, its subordination to Babylon marked a watershed in the affairs of Judah, which was destined to be dominated by foreign powers, with but a few years' respite, for the next fourteen centuries.

In his eighth year (597–596) Nebuchadrezzar made a sortie as far as Carchemish, from where he ordered affairs in Syria for a month before returning home. In the following year a new threat arose from the hill people to the east, perhaps Elam, later claimed as subjects by Cyrus.[29] Alternatively the enemy may have lain further to the north west where the Babylonians included Marhashi in their dominions.[30] The Babylonian army encamped on the bank of the Tigris a day's march from the enemy, whose king panicked and turned home. This may have been part of a co-ordinated action in support of dissident groups, for in the next year (595–594) 'numerous leading officials' took part in a rebellion in Babylonia which lasted a month before it was suppressed, the leader being captured by Nebuchadrezzar personally.[31] Some light on this is afforded by the account of the confiscation and disposal of the property of Babu-aha-iddina, son of Nabu-ahhe-bulliṭ, following a summary trial in which he was found guilty of breaking his official loyalty oath and so was condemned to death.[32] His father had been granted lands near Borsippa by Nabopolassar, so he could have been one of a group of landed gentry whose rise in opposition contributed to the Jews Ahab ben Kolayah and Zedekiah ben Maʾaseyah seeing a possible end to their exile at that time (Jer. 29: 21–2). If the disturbances were widespread they may have lain behind Nebuchadrezzar's later reference to the time when people 'devoured one another like dogs and the strong robbed the weak', which led to his inaugurating legal reforms and taking action against corruption.[33] Nebuchadrezzar gained the upper hand, for within a few months he was again with his forces in Syria to receive the tribute brought him once more by vassals and officials there. The extant Babylonian Chronicle for this reign finishes after the note that in 594/3 the army was mustered once more for operations in Khatti. This could have been a reaction to the elevation of a new pharaoh Psammetichus II to the throne in Egypt.

III. THE FALL OF JERUSALEM

Zedekiah of Judah now became the focus of opposition to Babylon by the city states in the west. Despite warnings from the pro-Babylonian elements, for whom the prophet Jeremiah was spokesman, he sum-

---

[29] A 26, 25, 32–3 ii 17–24. [30] A 854, 2. [31] A 25, 86: 29.
[32] A 924, 1–5; cf. I Ki. 21: 1–16 for confiscation of a traitor's property. [33] A 854, 4 ii 2–3.

moned representatives from Tyre and Sidon, Edom, Moab, and Ammon
to Jerusalem (Jer. 27: 1–11). Significantly none came from the coastal
cities of Philistia, which was still influenced by Egypt. Lacking internal
historical sources it can only be surmised that this action provoked
Nebuchadrezzar. Once again subordinate states were encouraged to
exert pressure on Judah, for there was an Edomite threat when a border
post, Ramat-Negeb, and Arad fell about this time.[34] The Babylonians
began large-scale siege operations against Jerusalem on the tenth of
Tebet in Zedekiah's ninth year (II Ki. 25: 1; Jer. 39: 1). Judah's appeal to
the new pharaoh Apries led only to a modest response by a small force,
whose approach caused the besiegers but a temporary diversion a year
after they had initiated the siege by building circumvallating walls (Jer.
37: 5).[35] This appeal to the Egyptians may have been undertaken by one
Koriah, possibly the Judaean army commander, named in the Lachish
ostraca.[36] Jerusalem itself was initially surrounded by a number of
defensive watch-posts from which smoke or fire signals passing between
Lachish and Azekah and as far north as Khirbet et-Twein could be
observed. The Babylonians drew the net tighter with an inner siege wall
and were able to breach the northern wall on the ninth of Tammuz; they
sacked the city and the temple in the following month (25 August 587 by
the Nisan-year dating);[37] the interval is perhaps attributable to protracted negotiations, for there is no sure evidence that the final outcome
resulted from starvation (II Ki. 25: 2–10). Zedekiah's attempted escape
through the Royal Gardens to the east could have been made during the
parleying. Archaeological evidence from the City of David (stratum 10A)
shows total destruction of buildings and a fierce conflagration which
consumed the wooden parts of houses. The contents are marked by large
quantities of weapons but no human remains. The collapse of structures
on the east slope seems to have followed their abandonment during the
following winter.[38] Except to the north in the territory of Benjamin,
cities and villages elsewhere in Judah were destroyed, among them
Ramat Raḥel (V), Lachish (II), Gezer (V), Tell el-Ḥeṣi (VII/VI), Arad
(VI), and En-gedi (V).[39] At the earlier capture of the city, in 597 B.C., the
Babylonians had removed numerous leaders, fighting personnel, craftsmen, and artisans; fewer captives were taken at this time.[40] The majority
of the survivors fled into the hills, while the poorer peasants were left to
maintain the royal estates north of the city and around Tell Beit Mirsim,
which supplied wine to Babylon. The estates were under 'Eliakim,

---

[34] B 17, 46–9, 149–51, no. 24.

[35] Cf. Ezekiel 17: 15–17; Jos. *Ant. Jud.* x.108–10; A 839. See below, pp. 718 and 725.

[36] A 832, 480; A 862, 151.

[37] A 941, 36–7; Malamat (A 862, 150–5) and others follow the Tishri New Year dating for the fall
on 15 August 586 B.C.   [38] A 847. 596; A 899, 29.   [39] A 896; A 918.

[40] II Ki. 24: 14 (10,000 in 597 B.C.); cf. Jer. 52: 28 (3,023 in 597 B.C.), 29 (832 in 587 B.C.).

assistant of Jehoiachin', whose seal impression on jars may imply a reorganized tax system in this area.[41] Mizpah (Tell en-Naṣbeh) was chosen as the headquarters of Gedaliah, the Babylonian nominee for the governorship of Judah, either because of its proximity to the loyal provincial capital of Samaria or because it lay in the virtually untouched zone between Jerusalem and Bethel. Smaller settlements in the Negeb and Shephelah borderlands seem to have been left intact.[42] Seal impressions of a number of dispersed Judaean bureaucrats, including those of the king's son, Jerahmeel, and Berahiah (Baruch) the scribe, show that influential persons were among the survivors left in the land.[43] Any attempt to regain control by supporters of the old royal house was dashed after the assassination of Gedaliah and the Babylonian garrison. In 582 B.C. the Babylonian Imperial Guard under Nabuzaradan carried off a further 745 Judaeans (Jer. 52: 30) and even this last small measure of Judaean independence came to an end. This punitive expedition also ended the independence of Ammon, whose ruler Baalis harboured the murderers from Judah, and of Moab, allowing Edomites under Nabatean pressure to infiltrate into southern Judah.

Meanwhile, further north, at his main base at Riblah where he punished Zedekiah by slaying his sons in front of him and then putting out his eyes, Nebuchadrezzar was pressing the siege of Tyre. Since this operation lasted, according to Menander of Ephesus, for thirteen years it could have been one of containment rather than of continuous determined attack. Josephus (*Contra Apionem* 1.156) dates the commencement of the siege to Nebuchadrezzar's seventh year (the Babylonian Chronicle makes no reference to it), and its duration as running for thirteen years during the reign of Ethbaʿal. The dates of Ethbaʿal III are disputed, and the majority opinion makes the siege fall in the reign of Baʿal II, *c.* 587–572 B.C. Certainly Tyre was under Babylonian jurisdiction in Nebuchadrezzar's fortieth year, when a contract dated there (assuming it to be the same Ṣurru) implies that it came within the province of Kadesh governed by Milki-eṭeri.[44] Further afield Nebuchadrezzar also claimed to control lands from Humē and Piriddu (Cilicia) and Luddu (Lydia) in the north west to Egypt in the south west. This claim appears to be justified, since the king, or his representative Nabonidus, called Labynetos by Herodotus (1.74), was a mediator and witness, with Syennesis of Cilicia, in the pact between the Medes and Lydia made after their battle by the river Halys had ended following a solar eclipse on 28 May 585. The former Assyrian provinces in Cilicia thus appear to have been incorporated into the Neo-Babylonian empire, and subsequent operations there by Neriglissar confirm this.[45]

---

[41] B 20, 77–106.   [42] B 16, 409–10.   [43] A 793.
[44] A 941, 27–9; on the contract from Ṣurru see A 815A, 142.   [45] See p. 244 below.

The claim that Nebuchadrezzar invaded Egypt itself rests mainly on
Old Testament references, which imply an attack on Egyptian temples in
Heliopolis (On) and Tahpanhes (Tell Defenna) (Jer. 43: 8–13). No
inscriptions of this reign have yet been found in Egypt.[46] A fragmentary
Babylonian text with a hymnic preface refers to Nebuchadrezzar's thirty-
seventh year and may indicate a campaign against Amasis in 568/7. Its
precise genre is uncertain, and though it mentions marching to do battle
with Egypt, the objectives, including Putu-Yaman and 'remote territories amid the sea', are uncertain.[47] Megasthenes, in a text preserved by
Abydenus and Eusebius,[48] later refers to a Babylonian invasion of Libya
and even Iberia, but this could be a confusion with the campaign by
Cyrus. The Babylonian fragment may be part of a list of foreign
mercenaries in Babylonian service. In his so-called 'Court List',[49]
Nebuchadrezzar claimed that the kings of Tyre, Gaza, Sidon, Arvad,
Ashdod and Mir . . . (and probably others whose titles are now lost,
including the Kings of Judah and Ashkelon who are known to have been
in Babylon at the time), had participated in a ceremony marking some
major restoration work there, possibly the opening of the new royal
palace. Thus his claim to have ruled 'from the Upper to the Lower seas'
(the Mediterranean to the Persian Gulf) was no mere traditional
formula. In less than thirty years he had taken over an 'empire' larger
than that lost by the last major king of Assyria, Ashurbanipal, and had
reordered his provincial system of government with supporting measures to enforce law and order. Largely because of the Biblical narratives,
Nebuchadrezzar came to be remembered in the West, through later
Hebrew, Aramaic, Greek and Arabic traditions, as the tyrant who
destroyed Jerusalem. Nevertheless, at home, he was traditionally the
king who rebuilt Babylon as the dynastic capital and enriched it by the
taxes and tribute he brought in from every quarter and by the skill of the
labourers he directed there.

IV. THE REBUILDING OF BABYLON

Building inscriptions from this reign are abundant but can rarely be
assigned chronologically. They give an overall view of intense activity in
Babylon and in twelve other major cities. In Babylon they supplement
the *Topography of Babylon*, a composition from the time of Nebuchadrezzar I later recopied to list the names of the city quarters, temples and cult
places, 180 wayside shrines, streets, walls and gates – all part of the plan
to make the city glorious.[50] Nebuchadrezzar first repaired the Euphrates
river wall and quay to receive building supplies and to protect the low-

---

[46] A 941, 39.   [47] A 903, 238; A 932, 94–5.   [48] A 889, 78–9.
[49] A 762, 282–94; A 941, 75.   [50] A 835; A 836; A 840.

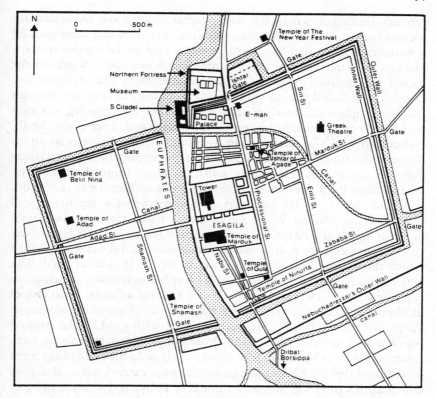

Fig. 11. Plan of Babylon in the time of Nebuchadrezzar II. (After A 694, 148, fig. 100.)

lying areas from the annual inundation. This enabled work to be resumed on the ziggurat and the southern citadel, where he resided in the east wing of the palace used by his father while his own residence to the west was built, for he had no royal residence elsewhere and designed this to become 'a building for the admiration of my people, a place of union for the land, and the seat of my royal authority'.[51] This was elaborately roofed using cedars from Lebanon, adorned with enamelled brickwork and with doors and gates of cedar as well as furnishings decorated with gold, silver, bronze and ivory. His predecessors, he claimed, had had their palaces where they pleased and 'only for the New Year festival came to Babylon to please Marduk'.[52] Since his aim was to use the capital to unite the tribes, he built law courts and central administrative buildings. To the west of his palace he built up a massive bund on the riverside; its stepped platform supported a pavilion and private quarters. On its steep

[51] A 856, 136–7 no. 15 vii 36–9.   [52] A 856, 114–15 no. 14 i 44–9.

terraces leading down to the river, rather than at the more easterly
location of the so-called 'Vaulted Building' as commonly supposed, he
constructed his royal ('hanging') gardens, said to be for his queen's
pleasure to remind her of her mountainous homeland.[53] Work on the
sacred Processional Street – Ay-ibur-shabu, 'May the arrogant not
flourish' – included paving with breccia from the *Akitu* house through
the Ishtar gateway, south to the Etemenanki and making a raised
highway to cross the refurbished Libil-hegalla canal. Like Sennacherib,
Nebuchadrezzar was interested in hydraulics; he paid particular attention to water supplies and drainage within the city and the use of canals as
defences outside the double city walls, the outer Imgur-Enlil and the
inner Nemet-Enlil. He was later conscious of the threat from the Medes
and Elam to the north and east, and constructed a defensive wall
(Xenophon's 'Median Wall') between the Euphrates and the Tigris
north of Sippar and near Opis, now traced at Ḥabl aṣ-Ṣaḥr.[54] East of the
city an outer defence wall formed an enclosure with the city walls, into
which the surrounding population could retreat in time of need. The
new retaining wall on the banks of the Euphrates enabled the ziggurat
reconstruction to be completed, together with the adjacent Ekua chapel
in Marduk's Esagila temple, now strengthened. This and the shrines of
Zarpanitu and Nabu (Ezida) were overlaid with gold.[55] The painted
Nabû-ša-harē temple west of the Processional Street appears to have
functioned also as a training school for priests and scribes, to judge from
texts found there.[56] Similar public works were carried out in Borsippa
which at this time was almost a suburb of Babylon. Its outer and city
walls, great gate, Processional Street, Ezida temple (on two façades) and
surrounding cloisters, and the ziggurat (Euriminanki) were renovated,
as was the Etilla shrine of Gula in thankfulness for restoration after
illness. Sippar was given a clean water supply and the temples of
Shamash (Ebarra) and Ninkarrak (Eulla) repaired. In Ur, Sin's temple
(Egishshirgal) was rebuilt, as was Eanna of Ishtar in Uruk, both always a
concern of the ruling house, which had estates there. Due attention was
paid also to the needs of Cutha, Dilbat, Marad, Kish, and Baṣ, and all
their temples were supplied with regular offerings. At the major cult
centres the temple administration was changed to include a royal
representative as trustee alongside the traditional governing councils.
Records show that the royal family paid their annual dues in gold, silver,
livestock, and other commodities. Rich and elaborate garments for the
statues of deities were in part paid for from the tithe or tax on temple
income collected by a state financial agent allocated to the temple.[57]

[53] A 812; A 940, 139–41.   [54] A 850; cf. A 794.   [55] A 856, 90–1 no. 9 i 29–40.
[56] A 807, 124.   [57] A 815, 56–7.

Although the Babylonians could have seen the first coinage, if it was minted in Lydia *c.* 640 B.C. (see *CAH* IV² 435), any imports on an extensive scale were, like internal transactions, currently paid for in silver as bars, rods or wire, weighed out.

The extent and impact of this public construction work is seen from the estimate of 164 million bricks made for the outer northern defence wall alone and at least as many for work in the city itself. This involved not merely the full effort of prisoners of war but also local labour brought in from outside Babylon throughout the reign, and this would have added to growing dissent during a long reign. Tax and call-up corvée service in Babylon and Borsippa excluded notables and state officials, but this privilege (*kidinnu*) appears to have been limited to those associated with the palaces and temples. Thus the specialist foreign labour attested in texts at this time was especially valuable. Among them were shipwrights from Tyre, woodworkers from Byblos and Arvad, and Egyptians working at a boat-house; this may support the tradition that a new harbour was established by Nebuchadrezzar at Teredon on the Persian Gulf, perhaps to counter Necho II's Red Sea navy.[58] Ionian Greek and other workers employed in the decoration of the royal palaces have left little or no evidence that the designs they executed were other than local styles. When not at work on royal projects the foreign workers were settled in their own ethnic communities around Nippur and Uruk.[59]

V. NEBUCHADREZZAR'S CHARACTER

The Babylonian texts present the king uniformly as an efficient military leader and firm administrator. The Daniel tradition stresses his interest in the Babylonian scribal and priestly arts, susceptible to religious influences yet dominant over his court officials. The antiquities in the 'museum' assembled in his northern palace can be attributed in the main to him.[60] His royal inscriptions are, moreover, marked by an absence of military stance despite the use of traditional epithets, and they emphasize moral qualities. Nebuchadrezzar includes some unusual phrases to describe his devotion to the god Marduk.[61] The portrayal of the king in a unique propaganda document[62] as 'king of justice' shows him to have been also a reformer on the classical lines familiar from the days of Urukagina and the better Hebrew kings. He claims to have taken the side of the weak, poor, crippled, and widowed against oppressors, enabling them to win a just hearing of their cases. He suppressed bribery and 'ceaselessly worked to please the great lord god Marduk and for the

---

[58] A 845, 271f; A 923, 927–32.   [59] A 941, 76–8; A 946.   [60] A 838; A 941, 65.
[61] A 856, 122–5 no. 15 i 23–32 and 55 ii 1.   [62] A 854.

betterment of all peoples and the settling of the land of Babylonia . . .'
Improved city regulations were enforced in the new law courts. The
citation of samples of the cases he judged was a traditional way, as in the
laws of Hammurabi, of enhancing his position as 'wise' in response to his
divine calling to office.[63] The document gives a true glimpse of 'the
spiritual revival which accompanied the final burst of Babylonian
glory'.[64] In contrast, a fragmentary epic-historical text shows an intros-
pective side to his nature in that he considered his life to be of no value,
could be angry and even sick enough to leave Babylonia for a time.[65]
This too may have been reflected in the Daniel narratives of his illness.
Yet, despite constant pressures, he held firmly all the territories he had
inherited and subsequently gained and was able to pass these on intact,
leaving Babylonian prestige at its highest point after a forty-year reign.

VI. INTERNAL RIVALRIES

It has been assumed that, since the last contract dated by Nebuchadrezzar's forty-third regnal year was written at Uruk (8 October 562) and the
first to be dated by his son and successor Amel-Marduk was written that
same day, Nebuchadrezzar died early in October.[66] However, two
contracts dated to the previous August–September by Amel-Marduk
could reflect a period of co-regency,[67] while another dated 15/v/43 (29
August 562) but with an unusual formula, 'the goddess of Uruk, king of
Babylon', if not a scribal error, might mean that Nebuchadrezzar died
somewhat earlier, and that a cautious scribe in a time of disturbance
following the king's death waited to see who his successor would be.[68]
Later tradition supposed that Amel-Marduk acted as regent during his
father's illness and that there was confusion at the time of a handover to a
successor.[69] Any hiatus was of short duration, for the same contract
datings show that Amel-Marduk was acknowledged as king in all the
major Babylonian cities by mid-October.[70] He may be identified with the
unnamed royal prince conducting business affairs in 570 B.C. It seems
likely that Nebuchadrezzar would have acted to continue the process of
hereditary succession, and his son is listed in the Uruk king list as
reigning for two years.[71] Berossus considered Amel-Marduk to have
'managed affairs in a lawless and outrageous fashion', and for this he was
assassinated. A fragmentary historical epic attributed to his reign
mentions a Babylonian (king) who gave arbitrary orders and refused to
listen to the words of a counsellor, whose attention was not devoted
towards promoting the welfare of Esagila and Babylon, who showed no

[63] A 937, 9–10.   [64] A 854, 4.   [65] A 26, 87–92; A 941, 102.   [66] A 877, 12.
[67] A 887, 3, 90, 106.   [68] A 926, xix, no. 9: 16–18.   [69] A 887, 26.
[70] A 941, 113 n. 182; cf. A 887, 3.   [71] A 44, 566; A 887, 3.

love to son and daughter and in the end undertook an act of penance before Marduk. Though this appears to describe Amel-Marduk, of whom a daughter Indu, but no son, is named, it could apply to Nebuchadrezzar in a time of decline.[72]

Building inscriptions indicate limited repair work in Babylon during this short reign, with continuing dedications to the Marduk cult. There is no evidence yet of any incipient religious schisms which would spill over into civil strife.[73] No military operations are recorded and the king's attention was upon internal affairs.[74] In his first year Amel-Marduk celebrated the New Year festival in Babylon, and this was possibly the occasion when

in the thirty-seventh year of the exile of Jehoiachin king of Judah, in the year Evil-Merodach became king of Babylon, he released Jehoiachin from prison on the twenty-fifth day of the twelfth month. He spoke kindly to him and gave him a seat of honour higher than those of the other kings who were with him in Babylon (Jer. 52: 31-2).

Later tradition, in contrast to the anti-Nebuchadrezzar feelings engendered by the sack of Jerusalem, viewed this act as a deliberate reversal by Amel-Marduk of his father's policy, though such deeds of clemency on accession are known. The royal house of Judah was not yet restored to its own land.

The economic situation now begins to show signs of strain after the years of heavy state expenditure on building enterprises, yet throughout this reign some leading individuals consolidated their acquisition of land and other property. Neriglissar (Nergal-sharra-uṣur, Biblical Nergal-sharezer), a leading official under Nebuchadrezzar and his *rab māg* during his western campaigns, was an increasingly active land-owner and business man from 598 onwards. He now bought up property of the bankrupt Nabu-apla-iddin of the Nur-Sin family through the agency of Nabu-ahhe-iddina of the Egibi business house and of one Iddina-Marduk, a wealthy banker related to the same firm in Babylon.[75] Neriglissar, the son of Bel-shum-ishkun, 'a wise noble' and governor of the Puqudu tribe, and grandson of Nabu-epir-laʾa, is listed as governor of (Bit) Sin-magir in Nebuchadrezzar's time.[76] As a trustee of Ebarra in Sippar his presence there, as at Opis in 565-564, may show some responsibility for work on the neighbouring northern ('Median Wall') defences which lay in his area. His influence was enhanced by his marriage to Nebuchadrezzar's daughter Kashshaya, through whom he became known to Berossus as 'the husband of a sister of Amel-

[72] A 7, 28; A 26, 87–92; cf. A 941, 102–3.   [73] A 857, 77; A 876, 42–3.
[74] A 922, 154 n. 8; cf. A 44, 309. A 119, 31; for building inscriptions see A 851, 78–9 fig. 50, 159 fig. 99.   [75] A 878, 41–2; A 887, 36–9.
[76] A 762, 285 iv 22, 24; A 856, 210–11 no. 1 i 14, 214–15 no. 2 i 11–14.

Marduk'.[77] If Berossus can be trusted, Neriglissar led the conspiracy which ended Amel-Marduk's life and reign. This seems to have been a case of inter-tribal or inter-family discord rather than simply the opposition of northern to southern tribes.

The latest contract dated to Amel-Marduk in Babylon was written on 7 August 560, and within four days other texts recognized Neriglissar as king there, at Uruk, and elsewhere.[78] To judge by his increased economic activity, Neriglissar was in the capital at the time, and his hold on local affairs was soon strengthened by his giving his daughter Gigitum to Nabu-shuma-ukin, the influential administrator of the Ezida temple in Borsippa. Nothing is yet known of political activity during his first two years, when he repaired the royal palace and the east bank of the Euphrates after its annual flooding, and continued work in Esagila and the 'Chapel of Destiny' in the inner city shrine of the New Year festival.[79] A small tablet bearing an extract from the Babylonian Chronicle details a military expedition in his third year. The details, reminiscent of the Assyrian annals, imply that it was composed close to the event.[80] In 557, in response to a raid planned by Appuwashu of Piriddu into Syria (*eber nāri*), Neriglissar called his army to march to Humē (east Cilicia), which the Babylonians had inherited after the fall of Assyria. Appuwashu's territory lay to the west, where he prepared ambushes of regular and local forces to hold the Babylonian advance. Despite this he was defeated and was pursued by the Babylonians over 25 km of mountainous terrain along the coast to his royal residence and capital at Ura[c], which was sacked. This is to be located in the Calycadnus delta near the place later called Seleucia. The port had been a noted centre for sea and caravan trade in the fourteenth–thirteenth centuries B.C. according to texts from Boğazköy and Ugarit. Neriglissar then carried his pursuit a further 65 km up the valley to the north to burn Kirshu (Mut, later Claudiopolis). Later, in a rare amphibious assault two miles offshore, he captured 6,000 combat troops stationed on Pitusu island (Pityussa, Manavat). Finally, he laid waste by fire the passes leading to Sallune and the Lydian border. Although Appuwashu himself escaped, this firm action reasserted Babylonian control over Piriddu and enhanced its prestige as a buffer state between Lydia and the encroaching forces of the Medes. In February 556, Neriglissar turned for home, a journey of some fifty days to judge from Xenophon's later experience.[81] Such action so far from home at this time might imply either co-ordination with the Medes or an attempt to forestall their advance. Activity on 'the borders' is referred to in the Dynastic Prophecy, which selects the highlights of this reign.[82]

[77] Quoted in Jos. *Contra Apionem* 1.146–7 (A 7, 28; A 626, 392 §146–7); cf. A 844.
[78] A 877, 12; A 888, 132.   [79] For his building inscriptions see A 856, 208–19.
[80] A 25, 103–4; A 932, 74–7.   [81] A 922, 158 n. 37.   [82] A 26, 32–3 ii 7'.

The theory that Neriglissar died on the return journey and that news of his death reached Babylon as the New Year began[83] can be questioned since the latest documents dated by him were written on April 12 (556) at Babylon and April 16 at Uruk. If he died later that month, that would accord with the Uruk King List ascription of a reign of three years and eight months.[84] Xenophon's statement that a predecessor of Nabonidus died in action against the Medes cannot be corroborated (*Cyropaedia* iv.i.8).

Neriglissar's chosen heir was Labashi-Marduk, his son. It is not certain that he was only a child, as Berossus says of Laborosoarchodos, for a commercial text suggests he was in control of his own affairs two years earlier.[85] The Uruk King List assigns him a period of three months and this agrees with the dated texts of his reign (earliest 23/1 accession year at Uruk and latest 12/III accession year probably at Sippar), rather than with the nine (possibly read two) months in Berossus' manuscript.[86] The Dynastic Prophecy, perhaps reflecting the religious party view, may suggest that he failed to control the land, and his successor put it about that he lacked intelligence and had come to the throne against the divine will: both prejudiced views.[87] The latter statement comes from Nabonidus, who headed the band of conspirators who slew Labashi-Marduk and unanimously chose Nabonidus to succeed.

VII. NABONIDUS

The faction which had hoped to take power on the death of Nebuchadrezzar and was thwarted by the subsequent succession within his family of Amel-Marduk now supported another candidate. If Nabonidus (Nabu-na'id) was indeed the Labynetus of Babylon who mediated between Lydia and the Medes in 585, then he was a good choice to counter the rising power of Cyrus, who, following his defeat of Astyages, now ruled Media, Anshan, Parsua, and Elam, according to his royal titulary. Nabonidus himself claimed to have been the popular choice, and refers to Nebuchadrezzar and Neriglissar favourably as his royal predecessors with whom he had been closely associated, guarding them day and night.[88] By the end of June 556 scribes throughout Babylonia dated their documents by the new monarch. Nabonidus refers repeatedly to his father as Nabu-balatsu-iqbi 'a learned counsellor',[89] and it is assumed therefore that he was not a close member of the royal

[83] A 922, 149, 235–7.   [84] A 44, 566; A 767, 53.
[85] A 7, 28; A 871 (Neriglissar no. 39).
[86] Quoted in Jos. *Contra Apionem* I.148 (A 7, 28; A 626, 393 §148); A 877, 13; A 922, 150.
[87] A 26, 32 ii 9–10 (restored); A 856, 276–7 no. 8 iv 38–9; cf. *CAD* 16 (S), 182.
[88] A 362, 50–1 ii 45–7.
[89] A 856, 218–19 no. 1 i 6, 230–1 no. 2 i 13, 234–5 no. 3 i 29–30, 252–3 no. 6 i 9.

'Chaldaean' family. His mother, Adad-guppi, in her biography, claims influence with Nabopolassar, Nebuchadrezzar and Neriglissar but not Amel-Marduk or Labashi-Marduk. There is no support for the idea that she was a member of the royal harem or was the official palace housekeeper.[90] It is not impossible that from such a position of intimacy in the palace and its affairs Nabonidus was himself married to a daughter of Nebuchadrezzar, as Neriglissar had been, and that this lies behind the tradition that his own son Bel-šarra-uṣur (Belshazzar) was Nebuchadrezzar's (grand) son (Daniel 5: 2).[91] Berossus designates Nabonidus a 'priest of Bel' which may explain the absence of his name in earlier business transactions and, with few exceptions, during his reign, of which he spent only about six years in Babylon. One text refers to him as city-governor ('in charge of the city').[92]

Nabonidus could not have been a young man on accession, since his mother died aged 101 or more in his ninth regnal year. On gaining the throne he led the army back to Humē to complete the operations undertaken by Neriglissar earlier, implying perhaps that Syria was once again threatened.[93] The army appears to have supported him throughout his reign and may therefore have played some part in his election. Booty, gifts and prisoners were taken to Babylon for the New Year festival, some 2,850 captives being dispersed as temple slaves on this or a similar occasion. The labour force was put to work on restoring the quay wall at Babylon, but apart from the traditional royal donations to all the temples in the capital itself the major effort was planning the restoration of Ekhulkhul, the temple of the moon-god Sin at Harran, of which his mother was a devoted supporter. Since Nabonidus is considered to have attempted a religious reform, demoting Marduk in favour of Sin, it is notable that his building inscriptions show that he both restored and contributed to the main temples of the principal cities, including the temples of Sin, Shamash, Bunene, and Anunit at Larsa, Sippar, and Nippur. Though they make frequent reference during this work to the recovery of building inscriptions by earlier kings outlining previous work, the 'antiquarian' interest of Nabonidus was not unusual. He did not seek to create any exclusive role for Sin in Babylon.[94] His mother's close association with Harran would explain his special interest there, and the dedication of his daughter Ennigaldi-Nanna as *entum*-priestess in her renovated cloister and temple at Ur follows a long Babylonian tradition. Of his other daughter, Ina-Esagila-remat, little is known. Like Nebuchadrezzar before him, Nabonidus made no structural changes in rebuilding Ur which might be interpreted as marking a modified ritual.[95]

[90] A 362, 50–1 ii 40–4; cf. A 922, 224.   [91] A 819, 79; A 941, 11.

[92] A 819, 31; but see now A 815A, 142.   [93] A 25, 105 6–7.

[94] A 800, 343–88; A 856, 218–97.

[95] A 943; cf. A 900, 56–8. On the office of *entum* see J. Renger, *ZA* 58 (1967), 134–44.

Though he granted the temple and its officials *kidinnu* privileges (freedom from tax and corvée), this did not extend to the city as a whole.[96] The visits by Nabonidus to other city temples were in the royal tradition of maintaining local and tribal unity. Such occasions included the presentation of special donations or the dedication of valuable votive offerings. At Uruk he was petitioned for, and granted, continued supplies for Eanna similar to those Nebuchadrezzar had made to the shrines of Marduk and Nabu in Babylon on an earlier occasion. The arrangements for rents for large tracts of land to be made payable to the Uruk temple must have hastened the centralization of much land-ownership under single management. Nabonidus' hold over temple administration was confirmed by the replacement of one local by two royal commissioners responsible for Eanna; one of them was an older official of Neriglissar's time and the other, Zeriya, a close associate of the king, took over as *šatammu*-official.[97] This has been taken to be part of a wide attempt by the Nabonidus circle to establish control over temple affairs here and elsewhere, but similar action had already been taken by Nebuchadrezzar.

In his second year Nabonidus was again in Syria at Hamath, where it was said to be very cold.[98] In this year his daughter was dedicated in Ur and the Ebabbar temple in Sippar was embellished. The next year Nabonidus led a campaign to Ammananu, during which some people were decapitated and their bodies hung up.[99] It was during this march in the Amanus range that the king collected plants and fruits to be taken to Babylon for the royal gardens and table. Someone, either the king or his aged mother, was taken ill, a matter of sufficiently serious concern to be noted in the chronicle, but the person recovered. Action was next taken against the Arabs; the king's forces marched to the west (Amurru) to meet with Bel-dan and besiege a city in Edom (Udummu). Further operations involved large military groupings and ended in the death or defeat of an unnamed individual and an attack against the gate of the otherwise unknown town of Rukdini.[100] The break in the chronicle for the fourth and fifth years has given rise to speculation whether it was during this time that Nabonidus set to work to fulfil the dream-revelation of his accession that he was to restore Ekhulkhul in Harran, which had been destroyed when the god 'was angry with his city and temple and went up to heaven', leaving it in ruins following the

---

[96] A 560, 74 (no. 45 ii 31).   [97] A 892.   [98] A 25, 105 9.

[99] A 25, 105–6 11–22; A 855, 7 57–64.

[100] See A 25, 282 for the critical reading of the place name as [Ú]dummu, Edom. For the earlier incorrect reading [A]dummu, see A 600, 111, 115 i 11–22; S. Smith, *Isaiah chapters XL–LV* (London, 1944), 37f, 137f nn. 79–80; A 787 (identifying Adummu with the area of modern el-Jawf); A 911, 352 n. 6.

combined attack by Medes and Babylonians in 609 B.C.[101] The Harran stela is against such a chronology, since it says that this work was not substantially completed or the images of Sin restored there from their temporary resting-place in Egishnugal in Babylon until after Nabonidus' later return from Arabia.[102] Such work must have taken some years to complete, for it involved the mobilization of labour from Gaza, Egypt, Syria, and Babylon;[103] this would not have been feasible while the Medes were in the area in force, before Cyrus had seized Astyages and robbed Ecbatana during Nabonidus' sixth year. By that time Nabonidus had left for Tema in Arabia, perhaps going there directly after his Edomite operations. It has been suggested that the chronology of the chronicle at this point may have been edited for a specific purpose, or rearranged to justify Nabonidus' absence in Tema.[104]

While the king was absent in Tema a thousand kilometres from Babylon, affairs of state were delegated to the crown prince Belshazzar, according to the chronicle for Nabonidus' seventh to eleventh years (after which that source is lost until the sixteenth year). The annual New Year festival was not celebrated, yet the services of Esagila and Ezida and offerings to the deities of Babylon and Borsippa continued as in normal times.[105] For ten years Nabonidus controlled a group of oasis towns from Tema, including Dadanu (Dedan, al-ʿUla), Padakku (Fadak), Hibrâ (Khaybar), and Yadihu (Yadiʿ, al-Hawait) as far as Yatribu (Yathrib, Medina), an area extending about 400 km in length by 160 km wide. This was won over by force of arms and garrisoned by troops who had marched there with the king and by settlers who stayed among the local Arab population. The Harran stelae which record the event give as the reason for this odd semi-abdication of power in Babylon and the subsequent exile a rebellion by the citizens and priests of Babylon, Borsippa, Nippur, Ur, Erech, and Larsa. They refused to rebuild the Ekhulkhul temple of Sin in Harran. 'They devoured each other and caused fever and famine among them and so minished the people of the land. But I hied myself afar from my city of Babylon . . . for ten years I did not go there.'[106]

It is not clear what caused the rebellion: whether despite adverse economic conditions Nabonidus tried to force through this particular Sin temple project or whether it was a symptom of general discontent, following years of harsh demands on the populace. It is generally assumed to be a priest-led protest at Nabonidus' emphasis on the cult of Sin. Various explanations have been sought for Nabonidus' withdrawal, other than personal pique. First, the king's health may have been affected

[101] A 362, 46–7 i 6–9; A 856, 284–5 no. 8 x 12–21.
[102] A 362, 75; A 911, 356; cf. A 132, 76–7, 106–7.   [103] A 856, 220–1 no. 1 i 38–43.
[104] A 869; A 911.   [105] A 25, 106–8.   [106] A 362, 56–9 i 14–27.

in some way. The Nabonidus prayer found at Qumran, dated to the first century A.D., refers to a Jew among the Babylonian exiles who gave him advice when he was suffering from malignant boils. This has usually been taken as misapplied to Nebuchadrezzar's madness by the book of Daniel as part of the vilification of that monarch. There are, however, significant differences between the two stories.[107] A medical, perhaps psychological, basis alone seems insufficient reason for a prolonged absence, which even precluded his return to take part in the lavish funeral of his cherished old mother in his ninth year (7 April 547), when she was buried at Dur-karashu near Sippar. Harran was not available, and Babylon seems to have been antagonistic to her, for official mourning there was delayed for two months, although this may have been due to fear of action by the Medes south of Erbil at the time. Secondly, Nabonidus may have gone to Tema to control the important trade routes running through it, north to Syria and from Babylon to Egypt. Along the latter track supplies of 'royal food' are known to have been sent by camel from Uruk to the king in Tema.[108] If the aim was to benefit from the lucrative spice and incense trade, or even the movement of gold – a rare commodity in Babylon at this time[109] – a good local force under strong Babylonian command would have been needed to enforce this. Others argue that it was part of a political move to extend the Babylonian empire westwards. Thirdly, any purely religious motivation for the self-imposed exile is not proven. Finds from Tema indicate structures of the period without affording specific evidence of 'the palace like that in Babylon' or any associated shrine for the moon-god Sin there.[110] Nabonidus, like many Babylonian kings, was deeply religious, and supported the national god Marduk,[111] though Cyrus in the so-called 'Persian Verse Account' of Nabonidus charged him with irreverence towards that deity. The hostility could have been the result of a combination of factors, including his continued administrative reforms whereby temple property was limited and a special royal cash box was introduced in the sanctuaries, to which a fixed portion of the temple income was allotted under the supervision of the king's own officials.[112]

Meanwhile increasing pressure on Babylonia's eastern borders enabled Cyrus, without any apparent special agreement or opposition, to cross the Tigris south of Erbil and march for a successful campaign against Croesus of Lydia as far as Sardis (Hdt. 1.75–84). In the following year Elamites entered Babylonia itself and action was taken by or against the district governor of Uruk; if by him, this may mark an attempt by the Elamites, not for the first time, to win over an opposition party to resist the ruling regime. When the Babylonian Chronicle resumes in his

[107] A 831; A 865.   [108] A 819, 114–17.   [109] Cf. A 856, 282–3 no. 8 ix 11–13.
[110] A 885; A 810.   [111] A 911, 359 n. 42.   [112] A 815, 58.

seventeenth year, Nabonidus is already back in Babylon, having returned following the diviner's advice based on favourable astronomical omens, today variously interpreted as indicating September/October 543 or 542, indicating that 'the appointed time had come'. Nabonidus claims that there had been reconciliation with the people and that nearby vassal kings renewed their oaths of loyalty. Those returning included men from distant parts who came back prosperous, though since the statement is in general terms, Babylonians from Tema are not mentioned, but may be included. The return had been made possible also by an agreement between Nabonidus and the king of Egypt (Amasis II), the king 'of the city of the Medes' (Cyrus II), and the land of the Arabs who sent messengers to promote good relations.[113] The Arabs may have moved under pressure from Cyrus who, according to Berossus and Xenophon, gained control over them and 'all Asia' before his ultimate advance on Babylon.[114]

The Harran inscription tells of abundant rainfall and fruitfulness in Babylonia and Syria; this brought famine to an end after great hardship and would have been taken as an additional favourable sign. The gap in the Babylonian Chronicle for Years 12–16 deprives us of a corroborative precise date from that source for the return. Changes among the top officials in Eanna at Uruk in his thirteenth year may mark the resumption of authority by Nabonidus, though Belshazzar as 'royal prince' had been active in all aspects of home rule during his absence. He was also aware of the threat from Persia, to judge by the special attention he paid as regent to Sippar and the nearby defences.[115]

In 539 the New Year festival was celebrated in Babylon as of old by the king, who had earlier been the major participant at other religious celebrations elsewhere.[116] His undoubted triumph had been the restoration of Sin to his temple in Harran following his own return to Babylonia. During the summer the war clouds increased to the extent that the gods of Marad, Kish, and Khursagkalamma were brought into Babylon for safety, always the first defensive step taken in anticipation of an attack from the north east. In Eanna yet another change in the hierarchy introduced a person bearing a Persian name, a token of the growing pro-Persian group there.[117] The gods of Borsippa, Cutha, and Sippar close to Babylon itself were not withdrawn, since Cyrus, having marched down the Diyala, paused opposite Opis. He then mounted a

---

[113] A 362, 58–9 i 42–5.
[114] Berossus quoted in Jos. Contra Apionem 1.150 (A 7, 28 and A 626, 393 §150); Xenophon, Cyropaedia VII.4.16; cf. Hdt. 1.190).   [115] On Belshazzar's administration see A 819, 105–37.
[116] The events of this year are described in the Nabonidus Chronicle (A 25, 109–11).
[117] A 817, 17 (Bagiazu); A 893, 12–21.

full-scale attack on the Babylonian defenders of Opis, first crossing the Tigris, forcing them to retreat with heavy casualties and loss of equipment behind the 'Median Wall'. On the fourteenth of Tashritu Sippar fell without a battle and Nabonidus fled.

Two days later (13 October) the Persian army under Ugbaru, governor of Guti, entered Babylon without a battle. His shield-bearing troops without any weapons protected Esagila and the holy places for the first two weeks, while the services within continued without interruption. Belshazzar was slain at the initial capture of the city, and Nabonidus surrendered soon thereafter in Babylon.[118] The swift and seemingly unexpected nature of the final fall of Babylon, reflected in the traditions of both Daniel and Herodotus, can best be explained by the presence of collaborators or dissident elements who assisted the invaders. According to Herodotus the deflection of the river near Opis reduced the effectiveness of the water defences and enabled a commando-type group to enter through the dried-up river bed or canals flowing through the city beneath the walls, giving both the element of surprise and an unexpected route of approach and thus a rapid take-over of key points (Hdt. 1.190–1). The later tradition that the city was so vast that it took three days for the news to spread to all its inhabitants may refer to the time taken for the news to reach the more distant cities of Babylonia.[119] The Dynastic Prophecy that 'a king of Elam will arise . . . and remove him [Nabonidus] from his throne . . . and will settle him in another land' supports Berossus' statement that Cyrus spared Nabonidus, settling him in Carmania, where he died.[120] On 30 October Cyrus himself entered Babylon, proclaiming peace to all the citizens and receiving all the rulers of the former 'Chaldaean' empire there. The people received him with acclamation, though whether only as befits a conqueror or as a deliverer from oppression, as Cyrus claimed, it is hard to tell.

Cyrus attributed his success to the permissive will of Marduk in punishment of a regime which had opposed his will. In the decree recorded in the Cyrus Cylinder he reiterated his peaceful and friendly intentions in taking the land over, reaffirmed the special *kidinnu*-privileges for the city of Babylon, and ordered the return of deities exiled there to their temples in cities to the north and east of Babylon.[121] This is noted also in the Babylonian Chronicle, and it may be assumed that by this, or a similar, decree the exiled Jews were allowed to return to

[118] A 25, 110 iii 16; Daniel 5: 30; Xenophon, *Cyropaedia* VII.5.26–30.

[119] Aristotle, *Politica* III.1 (12).

[120] A 26, 25, 32–3 ii 17–21; Berossus quoted in Jos. *Contra Apionem* 1.153 (A 7, 28; A 626, 394 §153); Eusebius, *Praep. Evang.* 9.41.   [121] A 44, 315–16; A 929, 2–9.

Jerusalem after a seventy-year exile, though their actual rehabilitation took some time to arrange and many stayed in the land. Cyrus contributed to the restoration and upkeep of the once-abandoned shrines. The defeat of Nabonidus was put down to Marduk by the Babylonians and to Yahweh by the Jews, while Cyrus stressed the weak and irreligious rule of Nabonidus who had introduced abominable deities alien to the Marduk cult. His version of events sought to justify to outsiders the fall of the city in terms reminiscent of the priestly accounts of the much earlier fall of Ur or Nippur.[122]

Cyrus set about repair work in Babylon immediately and in this he was joined by his son Cambyses. He had appointed Gubaru as senior administrator and left him to appoint district governors. The chronicle records the death of Ugbaru on 11/VIII. The Daniel version of these events has been interpreted as requiring another king of Babylon, there named as 'Darius the Mede', between Nabonidus and Cyrus, though this has been said to be a confusion between the fall of Babylon in 539 and that of 520 in the time of Darius Hystaspes. However, the tradition is detailed and ranks him as a son of Ahasuerus; he was aged sixty-two on taking over the kingdom, and an identification with Gubaru (to be distinguished from Gobryas of the Behistun inscription) has been proposed. That individual was the governor of the trans-Euphrates province (Eber nāri) and is nowhere connected with the royal line or given a royal title, nor are any documents dated by him as king. If Gubaru were to be equated with Ugbaru, the identification with 'Darius' would be ruled out by the notice of his death in the chronicle, if it is recording events in chronological order.[123] Cambyses, while working in Babylon on behalf of his father, was only styled prince ('son of the king'). The proposal that 'Darius the Mede' in Daniel was an alternative, if cryptic, description of Cyrus the Persian who also styled himself 'King of the Medes' may be a reasonable solution.[124] There is no convincing evidence that there was any gap in the dating of texts in his reign, for he was acknowledged in his accession year as king in a dated text, probably from Sippar, as early as 15 October.[125] In the Babylonian King List Cyrus is made the direct successor to Nabonidus.

The citizens of Babylon were allowed much freedom, which they used to proclaim official mourning for the dead 'wife of the king'. If it were the wife of Nabonidus[126] who was possibly a daughter of Nebuchadrezzar, or even the long-lived widow of Nebuchadrezzar, it would reflect the high esteem in which the ruling Chaldaean family was still held. The

---

[122] A 44, 312–15; A 900, 83–91. Cf. Is. 44:28; 45: 1–7.   [123] Cf. A 895, (10) 109.
[124] A 933; cf. A 895.
[125] A 87, 14 (add BM 56154 (CT 57, 157), dated 19.vii.acc. Cyrus).
[126] Xenophon, *Cyropaedia* VII.5.30, suggests that Nabonidus had been killed.

change to Achaemenid rule seems to have had little effect on the traditional way of life which had dominated Babylonia throughout its long, often hard won, years of independence. The suddenness of the decline from the splendours of Nebuchadrezzar's day to the final denouement stands as a testimony to the debilitating effects of division among the political and economic leaders who followed him.

CHAPTER 28a

NEO-BABYLONIAN SOCIETY AND ECONOMY

M. A. DANDAMAEV

With the establishment of the Neo-Babylonian kingdom there starts a rich flow of documentary sources. The period of less than ninety years between the reign of Nabopolassar and the occupation of Mesopotamia by the Persians is documented by tens of thousands of texts concerning household and administrative economy and private law, over ten thousand of which have been published so far.[1] Their content is varied: promissory notes, contracts for the sale, lease or gift of land, houses or other property, for the hiring of slaves and freemen, documents connected with international and internal trade, records of lawsuits, correspondence concerning official business, letters with family news, and so on. All these texts come from temple and private archives. We have no state archives of Neo-Babylonian times at our disposal apart from a few stray texts. The rich material in the Neo-Babylonian sources has unfortunately still been insufficiently investigated. It is therefore impossible as yet to give a complete description of Neo-Babylonian society.

I. THE SOCIAL STRUCTURE OF NEO-BABYLONIAN SOCIETY

At the time when the Neo-Babylonian state came into being the inhabitants of some large Babylonian cities enjoyed special privileges. Only the fear of losing their civic privileges can explain why citizens of some cities (such as Nippur) remained faithful, in spite of great suffering and privation, to the Assyrian rulers under whom they had won these privileges, and fought the armies of Nabopolassar, the founder of the Neo-Babylonian kingdom. As we have seen, the citizens of Babylonian cities were exempt from military conscription and corvée. A characteristic feature of these cities was self-rule by free and legally equal members of society united in a popular assembly (*puḫru*) around the principal temple of the city. The texts mention 'the assembly of the country' (probably consisting of the managers of temple estates in various cities),

---

[1] See for a brief survey of these sources A 815, 6–12.

'the assembly of the people' (or possibly of the army), assemblies of Babylon, Uruk, Nippur, Sippar and other cities.[2]

Despite this, after the establishment of the Neo-Babylonian kingdom, the centuries-long struggle between royal power and the people's assemblies had gradually resulted in the defeat of the latter; by that time their jurisdiction extended only to private disputes among their citizens and crimes of local importance. What is remarkable, however, is that the numerous inscriptions of the Neo-Babylonian kings tell only of the erection of new temples and repairs to old ones, and of pious gifts to various sanctuaries, while the many successful military campaigns are hardly ever mentioned. This points to the fact that the rulers were obliged to take account above all of the clergy, who played an important part in the people's assemblies and represented their interests.

As can be seen from the inscriptions of Nabonidus, the last king of the Neo-Babylonian dynasty, conflicts continued between the central power and the citizens of Babylon, Borsippa, Nippur, Uruk, and Larsa. Relations with them had been sufficiently strained from the very beginning of his reign, when Nabonidus started to give pride of place to the cult of Sin, the moon-god, naming him 'divine king over all gods'. In fact the moon-god whom Nabonidus worshipped was not the traditional god Sin of Ur, but according to his symbols and forms of worship, an Aramaean god. It is possible that by bringing about his religious reforms, Nabonidus strove to unite around himself the numerous Aramaean tribes of the Near East which worshipped Sin.[3]

However, the opponents of Nabonidus were not united among themselves and each city endeavoured to give pride of place to the cult of its own god. According to Nabonidus the people had wandered off the true path, had told lies, had sinned against the gods and had even begun to 'devour one another like dogs'. One Neo-Babylonian inscription says that judges took bribes and did not defend the poor, that the strong robbed the weak, usurers exacted high interest, the mighty victimized the disabled and widows, many broke into other people's homes and seized their fields. The text goes on to say that the new king had put an end to this lawlessness and had established a just order. The name of the king does not occur in the preserved part of the inscription, but in all probability he was Nabonidus.[4]

Even Nabonidus, however, was to a certain extent forced to take the traditional rights of the citizens into account. Thus he declares in one of his inscriptions that he had 'gathered the elders of the city, citizens of Babylon', in order to take counsel with them about temple-building.[5] In

[2] A 980, 45–9; A 981, 38–41.
[3] For sources and literature on the religious activity of Nabonidus see A 889.
[4] For the publication of the text see A 854; see also A 902.   [5] See A 856, 254–6.

connexion with the consecration of his daughter to the temple of Egishnugal in Ur, Nabonidus exempted this temple of the god Sin from state services and granted it special privileges;[6] however, this decree, like all similar royal decrees, did not affect all the inhabitants of Ur, but only the narrow group of priests and temple staff.

Some of the decisions of the 'people's assembly' concerned thefts of temple cattle and of other property, the collection of tithes and payments for the lease of temple fields. Other decisions related to litigation and the family disputes of individual citizens. Let us dwell briefly on the functions of the 'people's assembly'.

In the year 545 B.C. in Uruk, a woman declared in the assembly that her husband had died, famine reigned in the country, and she was unable to feed her two small sons, so she was handing them over to the temple of Eanna as slaves of the temple (*širku*).[7] In 540 B.C., also in Uruk, a certain Ibni-Ishtar, in the presence of several people near the temple of Eanna, threw himself dagger in hand at the royal commissioner (*rēš šarri*) of that temple. The assembly examined the case and 'tied up and sealed the iron dagger which he had pulled out of his belt'.[8] The document does not give the assembly's decision, because in this case the passing of the sentence came under the jurisdiction of the king's tribunal, while the assembly's role was limited to preliminary investigations; but it does represent a record of the depositions of witnesses and of the attaching of material evidence. In the same town of Uruk the king's commissioner at the temple of Eanna informed the assembly of an important deficiency in the amount of barley due as rent repayment for 553 B.C. The assembly had to establish who was responsible.[9]

In 591 'the assembly of the elders' of Sippar examined a case of the theft of property of the temple of Ebabbar by a certain man and came to the decision that, if the accusation was proved against him, he would have to make good thirty-fold the loss occasioned to the temple.[10]

When in Babylon in 555 litigation arose between three brothers about the inheritance of a field which was part of their mother's dowry, the verdict was given by the 'elders of the city'.[11] Similarly in 590 the 'elders of Nippur' examined a suit between two persons over a slave girl.[12] In 594 in Borsippa 'at the assembly of the people' (or possibly of the army, *puḫur ummāni*), Nebuchadrezzar denounced one of his generals for plotting against him. The criminal was executed and all his property confiscated. The document concerning the execution was composed in the presence of numerous people, including the civil governor of the city of Borsippa.[13]

    6 See A 801A.   7 A 1010, 33.   8 See A 565, no. 117.   9 A 817, no. 78.
    10 A 907, no. 104.   11 See for reference A 981, 38.   12 A 981, 38–9.
    13 A 924, 1–5.

Thus the assembly functioned as an organ of local self-government and justice. Its sessions were often presided over by the royal governor of the city concerned and the temple administrator.

Documents from Uruk contain frequent mentions of the 'assembly of the citizens of Babylon and Uruk'. Here the term 'Babylonians' designates state employees (scribes and other representatives of the central authority), who had been sent from Babylon by the royal administration for service in Uruk.

The members of the popular assembly were citizens (*mār banī*) who were free and in the eyes of the law equal among themselves. But they differed noticeably among themselves in economic and social standing. Among them were governors of cities, judges, high-ranking state and temple officials, merchants, businessmen, scribes, lesser officials, shepherds, lessees of fields, and artisans (who included the poorest strata of the free population). The status of the citizens was inheritable and passed on from father to sons. Naturally an active role in the work of the assembly was taken only by the wealthy:[14]

Quite often when decisions were to be taken in a case, only the elders (*šībūtu*) gathered together, as being the most influential citizens. In a number of cases their decisions were taken jointly with the senior temple officials and governors of cities. Sometimes documents containing orders from high state officials were drawn up in the presence of elders. The elders also represented the citizens of their cities before the king.[15]

The citizens took part in the cult at the local temple, as well as in the temple festivals and repasts, and were entitled to receive specific parts of the temple's revenue. All these people lived in the city and owned land in the city or in the rural district over which the power of the people's assembly extended.

Not all freemen, however, were citizens. Manumitted slaves, for instance, although free, could not obtain the status of full citizenship, as they were not allowed to occupy posts linked to the reception of the temple prebends. Aliens too were deprived of the rights of full citizenship.

At the time under study the population of Babylonia was ethnically mixed. The country was abundantly populated by Chaldaean and Aramaean tribes living side by side with the old local inhabitants, whom they gradually assimilated. Many aliens also lived in Babylonia. These were often settled in considerable groups in specified regions. Thus in the environs of Nippur and in the city itself each ethnic group was assigned a particular territory. Among aliens there were also the king's mercenaries, voluntary immigrants, and people who for various reasons

[14] A 980, 45–8.   [15] A 981, 39–40.

lived permanently or temporarily in Babylonia (merchants, political refugees, seasonal hired workers from Elam, and so on). Thus Babylonian texts mention numerous aliens living at the court of Nebuchadrezzar. Among them were Elamites, Persians, Cilicians, Jews, various emigrants from Asia Minor ('Ionians'), 'fugitives from Media', and others. It can be noted incidentally that a letter of the early sixth century B.C. mentions the arrest of several Babylonians whose father and brother had fled to Media. As can be seen from the same letter, several other Babylonians had fled to Media, and the king's order for them to return remained unanswered.[16]

Particularly numerous were people of Egyptian extraction, whose ethnic origin is often mentioned in the texts. In other cases it is easily established from proper names, which are frequently theophoric and have reference to such gods as Amun, Isis, Horus and Hapi. The Babylonian scribes knew about the theophoric character of these names, and usually set before them the divine determinative. A considerable number of Egyptians are mentioned as contracting parties and witnesses to a variety of contracts made in Babylon, Ur, Uruk, Sippar, Borsippa, and other cities. Thus Egyptians were scattered all over the country. The majority of Egyptian settlers, as a result of mixed marriages and in an attempt to adjust themselves to the surrounding ethnic milieu, gradually began to give their children Babylonian names and to assimilate themselves with the local population. In such cases the ethnic term 'Egyptian' (*miṣirāja*) was retained by their descendants as a family name. It is a curious fact that among the considerable number of aliens living at that time in Babylonia, only persons of Egyptian origin are frequently mentioned as scribes of cuneiform tablets. Assyrian texts of the times immediately preceding the establishing of the Neo-Babylonian kingdom mention Egyptian healers, farriers, interpreters of dreams, singers, jewellers, smiths, brewers, bakers, and so on. It is obvious that after the Neo-Babylonian kingdom was established, the majority of these people did not return to their homeland but remained to live in Mesopotamia.[17]

Private law documents show that representatives of different nations lived side by side, formed business relationships, and concluded mixed marriages. It is essential to keep in mind that in ancient times there were no conflicts on ethnological grounds, no racial hostility or feeling of superiority of one nation over another, and no one country was interested in imposing its language and culture on other nations. For this reason there was no disparaging of the beliefs of aliens by the local population. The aliens for their part worshipped not only their own gods but also the gods of the people among whom they lived, believing as they

[16] A 999, 134–5.   [17] A 997.

did in the power of these gods. Aliens took part in the economic and social life of the country, and became owners of houses and estates, while some of them served in administrative positions. They gradually became assimilated with the local population and spoke Akkadian and Aramaic (since Aramaic spread swiftly as the colloquial language in Mesopotamia), and in their turn exercised a definite cultural influence on the Babylonians.[18]

Aliens enjoyed no civic rights since they did not possess land within the city's common fund and therefore could not become members of the people's assembly. But in cases where they were compactly settled in distinct regions such people could create their own organization of local self-government – a people's assembly under the guidance of their own elders. We know in early Achaemenid times of the 'assembly of Egyptian elders' which functioned in Babylon. But such self-governing organs of ethnic minorities had probably already existed during the period of the Neo-Babylonian kingdom. It is known from the Bible that the Jews driven into captivity in Babylonia under Nebuchadrezzar had their own elders, who took decisions on problems of the internal self-government of the Jewish colonies, which preserved their own ethnic consciousness and traditional culture.[19]

Finally, besides citizens and freemen without civic rights, there existed several groups of dependent populations in which slaves formed a particular intermediate category. All these people naturally had no civic rights.

II. THE LAW

Justice was administered not only by the people's assembly, but also by the king's judges. The king's tribunal consisted usually of a council of five or six professional judges. Sometimes the composition of the tribunal was mixed and consisted of king's judges and elders selected from among the citizens. In Sippar the king's tribunal was presided over by the high priest of the temple of Ebabbar, who enjoyed full judicial power. In making decisions on important matters the people's assembly was subordinated to the king's judges, from whom they received various instructions, and to whom they were obliged to convey all necessary information. The king's tribunals took the decisions on the most important cases, in particular those of murder, plots, and revolts.[20]

The king appears to have been regarded as the highest judicial authority; but he did not possess absolute power and could not arbitrarily seize the property of his subjects or deprive them of life. In his

[18] See for references A 999, 139–40. [19] See for references A 999, 143–5.
[20] See A 893, 37.

private life the individual was left to himself, and as in former times the central authority did not interfere in his family life. He could move freely within the limits of the kingdom, undertaking business and commercial trips, or travel in search of earnings.

Marriage was generally monogamous, and a man who took a second wife was usually obliged to pay high compensation to the first wife, unless she was childless. A woman enjoyed a comparative independence; she could hold her own property and deal freely with it (give it away, sell, exchange or lease it), as long as it did not cause loss to her children and husband. On the husband's death the widow, even if she had no children, was allotted a part of the husband's property. Although women often acted as contracting parties, they are nevertheless very rarely mentioned as witnesses in contracts.[21]

Neo-Babylonian law apparently encouraged a written formulation of contracts except for the sale of perishable goods. Contracts were drawn up by professional scribes in the presence of witnesses (usually from three to ten or more) in two copies, each of the two parties receiving one. From the beginning of Neo-Babylonian times it is stressed in documents that the parties are concluding the deal of their own good will. The contracts enumerate the conditions of the business agreement, the place and date where and when the document was drawn up, and a penalty is defined (usually a fine) for a breach of conditions. Seals of witnesses and of the contracting parties are added (the latter usually leaving the impression of their thumbnails, especially if they are debtors).

In the period under study objects given in pledge were fields, houses, slaves, children of freemen, cattle, money, and other movable property. There were two kinds of pledge. According to the first kind, property was declared to be a pledge as security for a loan either with the creditor having right of ownership of that property ('hand pledge') or else without that right, when the property remained at the debtor's disposal (*hypotheke*). But the second kind of pledge was most common, in which the property became subject to *antichresis*, that is, the creditor was given the right to exploit the pledge in his own interest.

Slaves and houses were frequently (fields and other property less often) handed over in *antichresis* as pledges for debts. In such cases the revenue from the pledged property or from the labour of slaves or other pledged persons went to cover the interest on the loan. Documents note that the creditor shall not pay wages for the labour of slaves or members of the debtor's family (nor, for example, pay rent for houses), while the debtor remains exempt from paying interest during the time that the creditor makes use of the pledged person or of the immovable property. The debtor could take back his slave, the member of his family, or any

---

[21] See A 977.

other property pledged in *antichresis*, only after the creditor had been repaid his loan in full. If a pledged individual ran away, fell ill, or for some other reason did not fulfil his task, the debtor was obliged to refund the creditor with the equivalent of the labour services of the person pledged in *antichresis* throughout the whole time for which the latter did not work – usually to the amount of six litres of barley a day, which in terms of money amounted to twelve shekels of silver a year. In addition the debtor fed and clothed the labourer given over in *antichresis* throughout the time that the latter remained with the creditor.

Usually in the case of *antichresis* no date for the repayment of the debt was specified, and more often than not the pledged person worked for the creditor for several years until the debt was paid in full. When property was pledged without the creditor's right to make use of it, the date of redemption was always indicated. If the debtor did not redeem his debt on the agreed date and the creditor did not grant him more time, the pledge became the creditor's property. But if the value of the pledged property exceeded the sum of the loan, the creditor, on the tribunal's decision, received only a part of the pledge; and contrariwise, if the pledge was judged to be of lesser value than the loan the debtor was obliged to pay up in full.

In Neo-Babylonian times loans were usually made at 20 per cent yearly interest (1 shekel of silver per mina per month), although now, by contrast with the Old Babylonian period, the law did not regulate the amount of interest. Loans were mostly made in money, less often in grain or dates. But during this period wide use began to be made of so-called abstract promissory notes, usually for a loan but in many cases for credit for opening trade workshops, sale of commodities on credit, and so on.[22]

Towards Neo-Babylonian times debt bondage underwent considerable changes. A creditor could arrest an insolvent debtor and hold him in a debtors' prison. However he could not sell his debtor into slavery, and the latter would redeem his debt by unpaid labour for the creditor. Contrary to the practice of earlier periods a husband could not pledge his wife as security. Freemen had the right to pledge their children but such pledges, after the debt and interest had been paid in full by their labour, recovered complete freedom from the creditor. In the case of a debtor's insolvency his children could be taken into slavery. Moreover by this date the time limit on slavery, established by Hammurabi's laws in the second millennium B.C., was no longer in force. The explanation may be that during that period, owing to a comparatively high standard of living and to the possibility of earning money as hired labour, there was no longer any threat of a mass enslaving of the free.

The practice of self-pledging and self-selling had completely disap-

[22] A 878, 52ff and 111ff.

peared at the time under study. Freemen only very seldom had recourse to the sale of their children and that only in cases of catastrophic famine, devastating wars, or prolonged sieges. For instance in the year 626 B.C., while the army of Nabopolassar was besieging Nippur, which remained faithful to the Assyrians, and while barley cost almost thirty times more than its usual price, some of the population sold their children to money-lenders. It is stated in the contracts that the children had been sold to save them from starvation.[23]

In Neo-Babylonian times Hammurabi's laws were still copied and studied, as witnessed by the great number of copies made in the first millennium B.C. At least one of the articles of these laws, decreeing a thirty-fold repayment of stolen temple and palace property, was still in force.[24]

Three columns of laws have been preserved which, judging by the writing, grammatical forms, vocabulary, and matters discussed, belong to Neo-Babylonian times. In the text that survives, the beginning and end are destroyed. We can infer from its careless script and numerous clerical errors that this is a part of the text of the laws copied for teaching purposes. The laws are not set out in full but selected according to different subjects. The preserved articles concern mostly marriage and property laws. They contain various juridical conclusions with regard to disputable cases of day-to-day life. One law states that if a man builds a cistern to store water but does not sufficiently reinforce its walls and as a result his neighbour's field is flooded, the culprit must pay his neighbour compensation, calculated by reference to the harvest gathered from the adjacent fields. According to another law, if someone sells a girl-slave and she turns out to belong to someone else and her legal owner reclaims her, the seller is obliged to return to the buyer her price plus half a shekel of silver for the child she may have borne in the meantime, in order to compensate her owner for loss during her temporary inability to work.

If a man takes a second wife and has sons by both wives, after his death the sons of the first wife should receive two-thirds and the sons of the second one-third of the deceased's property. If a father gives a dowry to his daughter and she dies childless, this property must be returned to her father's house. After the death of the husband his widow, if she has had no children, receives her dowry and her husband's wedding gift. If a widow who has children wishes to marry again she can take with her her dowry and the gift received from her husband at her first marriage. If she bears children from her new marriage, her dowry must be equally divided between the sons of both marriages, while the gifts received from each husband must be given to their respective children.[25]

[23] See A 815, 157–80.   [24] A 994.   [25] A 822; A 989; A 995.

III. THE PALACE AND THE TEMPLES

In Neo-Babylonian times the royal economy weighed less in the general economy of the country; the leading role belonged to the temples and private households. There seems however to have been no clear-cut distinction between palace and state property; therefore all state revenue as well as that from royal estates, in the narrow sense, was regarded as belonging to the king. What was actually in his possession was only a comparatively negligible land fund, the management of which was based on the principles of a private household. Royal property is seldom mentioned in documents. For instance, according to a contract of the time of Nebuchadrezzar II a royal field was let on lease 'for ever' (for planting with date palms) to Shula, head of the business house of Egibi in Babylon. During the reign of Neriglissar a private citizen's house was sold to the palace. A text dated from the reign of Nabonidus mentions ducks as 'royal property'.[26]

Although we have no information on the workshops of the Neo-Babylonian kings, texts frequently mention royal carpenters, stonemasons, fishermen and shepherds, all of whom were probably freemen permanently employed by the palace. The building and upkeep of canals, palaces and temples, and the making of roads were tasks carried out by freemen as community and state services. It is worthy of mention that their patronymics are regularly recorded in documents, by contrast with slaves, whose fathers' names are not recorded.

The major part of the state revenues came from taxes, of the character and size of which we know nothing. Apparently all freemen were bound to give a tithe of their income in state tax. These taxes were usually paid in kind (cattle, grain, wool, and so on), but official experts established their value in silver. Besides this, certain groups of the population (such as merchants engaged in international trade) paid their taxes in silver. In addition to taxes the king received various tolls and dues (including port dues, city gate toll, canal dues from ships and boats, toll for the use of certain bridges) in silver or in kind. Out of the taxes the king maintained the official staff and the army. The country was divided into administrative districts governed by governors (bēl pīḫāti). Cities were administered by special governors (bēl ṭēmi). There were also overseers of royal canals and moorings and other lesser functionaries. The palace management was headed by the 'palace administrator' and included a large number of court employees and messengers.

Naturally the administrative service, branching out over the territory of an enormous realm, could not function without a large number of

---

[26] See for references A 815, 558–60.

scribes. Apparently already the state chancellery was carrying on its correspondence, at least in part, in Aramaic; this undoubtedly explains why the archives of the Neo-Babylonian kings have not come down to us, as documents written on leather and papyrus easily deteriorated in the climatic conditions of Mesopotamia. But an important role in the administrative services continued to be played by cuneiform scribes, some of whom bore the title of 'royal' or 'palace scribes'. Texts also mention 'scribes whom the king appointed to the city', 'port scribes' and so forth. A considerable number of scribes worked for governors in provincial administration. Of great importance among the administrative staff were the scribe-interpreters (*sepīru*), as in building works and in the army craftsmen and soldiers from foreign countries were employed. The entire staff of the state administration received their salaries from the king in kind, the higher ranks also partly in silver.

The mainstay of the king's power was the army, about the recruiting of which we scarcely know anything. Besides Babylonians there were also mercenaries serving in it as evidenced by Antimenidas, the brother of the Aeolian poet Alcaeus, who served in the army of Nebuchadrezzar. The soldiers were armed with spears, iron daggers, shields, bows and arrows. As can be seen from documents of the times of Nebuchadrezzar and Nabonidus, Scythian archers' tactics exerted a considerable influence on the arming of Babylonian warriors, who preferred Scythian to Akkadian bows and arrows because of their high ballistic qualities.[27]

Close links existed between the palace and the temples: some high temple officials were related to the king. Thus the administrator (*šatammu*) of the temple of Ezida in Borsippa was married to the daughter of Neriglissar. The temples of Esagila in Babylon, Eanna in Uruk, Ebabbar in Sippar, Ezida in Borsippa, E-imbi-Anu in Dilbat, Ekur in Nippur, Egishnugal in Ur, and Emeslam in Cutha were the most important temples of the time, and they also advanced loans and transacted commercial business. Thus Eanna owned some 5 to 7 thousand head of large horned cattle and 100 to 150 thousand sheep. According to one document this temple obtained during one year, 5,000 kg of wool from its sheep.[28]

An important source of temple revenue was the tithe. It was collected from all the representatives of the free population: agricultural labourers, shepherds, gardeners, artisans, priests and officials of all ranks, including governors. The king also paid the tithe to all important temples in the country at the same time. Everybody else paid the tithe to the temple near which they possessed land or other sources of income. It was paid on gardens and fields, on the increase of cattle, on the yield of

[27] See for references A 998, 99–106.   [28] See for references A 979.

wool, and so on. In most cases it was paid in the form of barley and dates, but quite often in silver, sesame, wool, clothing, cattle, fish, or artefacts. The king paid partly in gold. The tithe represented more or less a tenth part of the payer's income, though the king's tithe was relatively smaller. Special officials were engaged in collecting the tithe. Some people, unable to pay, had to borrow money from usurers pledging their houses and fields and sometimes even giving their children to the temple as slaves (*širku*).[29]

The structure of temple management is best known from data contained in the archive of Eanna. The senior administration of this sanctuary consisted of the king's governor (*bēl tēmi*) in Uruk, the estate manager of the temple (*qēpu*), the head of the temple's administrative council (*šatammu*), and 'Eanna's scribe'. The last three managed the temple's estates, supervised the temple slaves, and organized the allocation of the temple revenues to various purposes. Thus their functions were of an administrative, not religious, character. All the higher temple functionaries, except the governor of the city who was appointed by the king, were elected from among the citizens, apparently at a session of the people's assembly at the Eanna temple. A more or less similar system prevailed in other important temples in the country.

As the business correspondence of the temples was conducted for the greater part (if not entirely) on clay tablets, cuneiform scribes were indispensable. Thus in Eanna there worked simultaneously no less than twenty scribes, and a similar number would have been employed in other important temples. But not all of them were permanently occupied in writing; a temple scribe was primarily an employee of the administrative and economic system and his duties included establishing the amount of land rent, arranging the provision of cattle and other produce for sacrifices, issuing rations to the temple slaves, supervising all kinds of labour, and recovering debts from temple debtors. Many scribes fulfilled the functions of accountants. Besides this scribes were sent out to various regions subjected to the temples. Thus a letter from the archive of Eanna says that in case of an insufficiency of scribes in some particular place others would be sent there. Many scribes of Eanna made business trips to Babylon, Larsa, and other cities, including even the Phoenician city of Tyre. The majority of scribes worked in the temples for long periods (some for thirty to forty years or more) and this service was their main source of income. They received their pay in barley and dates (usually from 180 to 270 litres a month, sometimes up to 540 litres). Senior temple officials were often chosen from their number.[30]

Under Nabonidus the influence of the state over the temples gained in

[29] See A 1007.   [30] See A 982, 85–96.

strength. In particular, in 558 Nabonidus created in the Eanna temple the post of royal commissioner, whose functions to some extent had previously been carried out by 'Eanna's scribe'. The latter title now lost its importance and was held by all scribes of the temple.[31] The royal commissioner was independent of the temple, and one of his main duties was to hand over to the palace part of the temple's revenues. For this purpose a special 'king's chest' was created which received a specified part of the revenue in kind. In addition the temples had to contribute to state services by sending their slaves as farmers, shepherds, gardeners, or carpenters to work in the king's household.

The king and his staff began to interfere actively in temple matters, establishing rations for the temple slaves, the size of the temple prebend for various groups of the population, and rates of rental for temple fields.[32]

IV. BASIC BRANCHES OF THE ECONOMY

All cultivated land was exactly surveyed, as witness a large number of cadastre texts. A considerable part of it belonged to the temples, to members of the royal family, to important business houses, or to officials of the royal and temple administration. Small land-holders (especially in large cities) owned holdings from half a hectare to several hectares. Land was highly priced, making it more profitable to use it for gardens (mainly for date-palm plantations) than for cereal cultivation.

Barley was the most widely cultivated cereal but spelt, wheat, sesame, peas, and flax were also sown. The density of barley sowing averaged 133.3 litres per hectare; the yield varied from 935 to 4,050 litres per hectare, but averaged 1,890 litres. The crop was harvested from the end of April until the end of June. Dates equalled barley as a main food item and the average yield of dates from a hectare of garden was 8,820 litres. Young palm trees began to bear fruit in the sixth year after planting.[33]

Rainfall was scarce, and irrigation continued to play an important part in the country's economy; new canals were dug and old ones maintained in exemplary order. These canals belonged to the state, to temples and in some cases to private individuals, but all land-owners and leaseholders could make use of their water for a fee. Silt from the canals was used as a fertilizer together with manure.

Smallholders cultivated their fields themselves with the help of members of the family, and sometimes also with the help of labourers usually hired for the harvesting period. Owners of large estates let out their land on lease. The rent was usually either established in advance

---

[31] A 988, 108–10.   [32] A 979.   [33] A 1005.

when the contract was made and depended on the presumed fertility of
the land, the rent being paid in kind, or much less frequently in cash
(*sūtu*); or else it was assessed in arrears on the estimate of the standing
crops (*imittu*). Usually the owner of the land received one-third of the
crop and the lessee two-thirds. In most cases the contract was drawn up
for one year, but if the land had been lying fallow it lasted for three years.
For such land the lessee paid the owner nothing during the first year, in
the second year only part of the usual rental, and in the third year the
share of the crop normal for that province. Quite often extensive tracts
of land were leased to head-lessees, who in their turn parcelled them out
among sub-lessees. It also happened that two or more lessees rented land
in common.[34]

If Babylonian texts composed after the occupation of Mesopotamia by
the Persians are to be trusted, during the reign of Nabonidus famine
decimated the population. But these texts, being composed to please the
Persian king Cyrus, demand critical evaluation. Nabonidus in his own
inscriptions asserts that during his reign Babylonia flourished. Some
3,000 economic and private legal documents in his time testify to the
country's continuing economic prosperity, and the version of later
Babylonian texts is obviously tendentious in representing him as having
ruined his people. It is true that a document survives showing that in the
year 544 famine reigned in the country. This information agrees with an
official inscription of Nabonidus which says that after a drought and
famine rains had come bringing plenty, and 234 *qû* (about 230 litres) of
barley or 270 *qû* (about 270 litres) of dates cost one shekel, which is
approximately one-third less than the normal price.[35]

Side by side with agriculture the most important branch of production
was handicraft. Neo-Babylonian texts mention weavers, smiths,
jewellers, house-builders, coppersmiths, carpenters, launderers, bakers,
brewers, and other craftsmen. A craft was usually passed on within
families from father to son. However no law required a man to inherit his
father's profession. Rather it was a tradition which was often broken.

There existed in Babylonia no independent craft organization because
the economic premises necessitating its creation did not yet exist, namely
a market economy and the possibility for craftsmen to dispose freely of
raw materials in any considerable quantity. To judge by documents of
the archive of the temple of Eanna, craftsmen in Uruk, although in most
cases freemen, worked for that temple and received from it their raw
materials. They worked for the temple by voluntary agreement, and
were remunerated in cash and in kind. Besides this some craftsmen (such
as bakers and brewers) worked for the temple for a stipulated period each

---

[34] A 1022, 8ff.   [35] A 886, 247–8.

year in return for the revenue paid to persons entitled to a temple prebend.

According to documents from Babylon, Nippur, and some other cities, craftsmen often contracted with clients for the manufacture of furniture, household utensils, or clothing, using either their own or the client's materials. Some craftsmen may have worked for the open market, but on this we do not possess sufficient information.

Some people sent their slaves to learn a craft because a qualified craftsman brought his master a much larger revenue than would an unskilled slave. Contracts have survived for teaching slaves such crafts as leather-dressing, shoe-making, weaving, dyeing, carpentry, and house-building. All these contracts concern male slaves sent for training. Their age is not stated but it may be confidently assumed that they were youngsters. The craft masters too were often slaves. The training lasted from 15 months to 6–8 years, according to the complexity of the craft, and during all that time the apprentice remained with the craft master. His owner was responsible for his keep, providing him with about a litre of barley a day and with clothing, so long as he remained with the craft master. The latter was remunerated by the slave's labour and, in addition, at the end of successful training, received a present from the slave's owner. But if the craft master did not fulfil his undertaking and had not taught the slave the full measure of his craft, he was required to pay back to the slave's owner the value of the slave's labour for the entire period of training, usually about 6 litres of barley a day, which for one year represented in cash terms 12 shekels of silver.

After the completion of his training the slave either worked for his owner or remained with the craft master, who paid his hire. Sometimes such a slave opened his own workshop paying his master quit-rent.

In practice, however, only the wealthy could send their slaves for training, because during apprenticeship the owner not only had no profit from the slave but also had to provide for his keep. Therefore those who owned only a few slaves could not afford to have them trained in a craft with the prospect of drawing advantage from it only in several years' time.[36]

V. COMPULSORY AND FREE LABOUR

The greater part of the dependent population belonged to the estate of farm labourers (*ikkaru*). They owned no land of their own and laboured from one generation to the next on land belonging to the state, the temples, and private land-owners. Such labourers lived in rural districts

[36] A 1021.

which did not possess the characteristic structure of urban self-government. In the eyes of the law *ikkaru* were not considered as slaves; they lived with their families and could not be sold. Nevertheless, they were attached to the land and could not leave their place of residence without the permission of the owner. If they ran away, they were caught, shackled and brought back. These labourers worked all the year round under the supervision of their masters or the latters' agents. Lists have survived in temple archives with detailed enumerations of dozens, and sometimes several hundreds, of labourers in each separate document. In these enumerations they are split into small groups of three or four, mostly representing separate families, each consisting of a father and his sons.

The *ikkaru* received from the temple administration oxen, ploughs, shovels, seed for sowing, and quite frequently supplies of food for themselves and fodder for the cattle. When agricultural labour was over, the *ikkaru* returned the cattle to the temple. Temple officials made periodical inspections of the livestock and tools and of the seed-corn held by the *ikkaru*.[37]

The temples of Eanna and Ebabbar in Uruk and Sippar farmed out considerable tracts of land to rent collectors, the amount being established at the conclusion of the contract. The collector did not himself cultivate the land but passed it on to sub-lessees and was responsible to the temple administration for the yearly supply of a pre-determined quantity of farm produce. At the same time the temples quite often lent their *ikkaru* for hire to rent collectors together with the leased land, farming implements, and draught animals, passing on to them the *ikkaru*'s rations. The rent collectors were held responsible for the good state of the livestock and tools, and for the *ikkaru*. The latter were in their turn responsible to the rent collectors for the crops of that part of the land which they themselves cultivated. Customarily the temple supplied a quantity of draught animals and *ikkaru* corresponding to the area of land leased. Thus, according to a contract drawn up in the year 555 B.C. in Larsa, the Eanna temple leased to two men 7,410 hectares of land. In the first year of the lease the rent collectors received from the temple 3,000 *kur* (540,000 litres) of barley for sowing and 10 talents (300 kg) of iron for ploughshares. Besides this they received 400 *ikkaru*, 400 oxen, and 100 'large' cows to replace oxen that were worn out. As rent they were required to supply the temple yearly with 25,000 *kur* (4.5 m litres) of best quality barley and 10,000 *kur* (1.8 m litres) of choice dates.[38] Thus for each 18.5 hectares of land the rent collectors had at their disposal one *ikkaru* and one ox. But according to the conditions of the contract the

[37] A 815, 590–625.   [38] A 1005, 90–104.

leased land was to be cultivated in alternate years, half of it remaining fallow in each year. As only half of the land was cultivated at one time, on average some 9 hectares was the *ikkaru*'s share; but so much land could hardly be cultivated by one man. Obviously the rent collectors were obliged to hire sub-leaseholders (calculating approximately 4 hectares for each man) and also add the necessary number of oxen and quantity of seed-corn. In other words, in this particular case the rent-collectors probably had recourse to the labour of some 500 free leaseholders in addition to the 400 *ikkaru*.

According to another contract drawn up in Uruk in 545 B.C., a rent collector received 812 hectares of ploughland belonging to the temple of Eanna. A thousand *ikkaru* were put at his disposal, 100 oxen, 50 'large' cows, and for the first year of the lease also 625 *kur* (112,500 litres) of barley for sowing and 5 talents 20 minas (160 kg) of iron for plough-shares. The full amount of the lease rent was 5,000 *kur* (900,000 litres) of barley a year. Of particular interest is the statement that 30 out of the 100 *ikkaru* put at the disposal of the lessor by the temple would receive from the temple's stocks by way of provisions for the first year of the lease 120 *kur* (21,600 litres) of barley – 720 litres for each man or approximately 2 litres a day.[39]

According to a contract concluded by the temple of Ebabbar in Sippar, a man who rented 79 hectares of land also had put at his disposal 12 oxen, 8 *ikkaru*, keep for the latter and fodder for the cattle, grain for sowing and agricultural implements.[40]

The *ikkaru* put at the disposal of rent collectors were obliged to surrender a pre-determined part of the crop from the land allotted to them according to the size and fertility of the field. The rent collector having collected from all the *ikkaru* the crops due from them settled his accounts with the temple. One can cite as an example that one rent collector had during 553 B.C. collected from the *ikkaru* under his control and delivered to the temple of Eanna 10,136 *kur* (1,824,480 litres) of barley.[41]

In conquering new territories, or in suppressing rebellions in pre-viously conquered provinces, the Babylonian kings seized the local inhabitants (particularly qualified craftsmen) and enslaved them. Already at the time of Nabopolassar, the founder of the Neo-Babylonian dynasty, intensive building was in progress in Babylonia; this reached impressive proportions under Nebuchadrezzar. The labour of prisoners of war was widely used on such works as canal-digging, road-building and the construction of palaces; the text of Nabonidus' stela found at Harran in upper Mesopotamia says that the gods Marduk and Nergal

[39] A 1005, 38–40.   [40] A 815, 606.   [41] A 1005, 74–6.

granted to him 2,850 prisoners from Humē (Cilicia) to carry bricks during the building of the temple of Sin at Harran. Among the ruins of the royal quarters in Babylon texts were found enumerating the rations of prisoners of war. In these documents, dating from 595 to 570, after the wars with Egypt and the Phoenicians and the capture of Jerusalem, there are mentioned in particular 46 Egyptians and 90 ship-builders from the Phoenician city of Tyre, as well as other qualified craftsmen and Jewish prisoners.[42]

The kings handed over to temples some of the prisoners of war as slaves. Nabonidus made a simultaneous gift to several temples of 2,850 men deported from other countries. He also handed over many slaves to the temple of Sin in Ur, together with fields, gardens, large horned cattle, and sheep.[43] In this connexion one may note that a significant source for the increasing contingents of temple slaves was the consecration to the temples of privately owned slaves by their pious masters.[44]

Nebuchadrezzar brought to the building of Babylonian temples craftsmen 'from the Upper to the Lower sea' – from the Mediterranean to the Persian Gulf – but apparently the majority of these people were able to return home after the completion of their service. As a rule only an insignificant part of the prisoners of war were turned into slaves, distributed among palace, temple, and private households. The majority were settled on state land which they farmed independently, paying state taxes and carrying out services, often including service in the army. At the same time some of these prisoners of war owned their own slaves. Thus in the year 597 B.C. almost ten thousand persons, not counting women and children, mainly belonging to the nobility, warriors, and craftsmen, were taken from Jerusalem to Babylonia. Biblical sources represent this captivity as the bondage of slavery. In reality, however, the captives were not enslaved but settled in specially designated regions, in particular near Nippur, on land that had become neglected.

The question arises why the Babylonian kings did not turn the whole mass of prisoners of war into slaves. Slavery was after all the most effective form of dependence, and there was hardly ever a lack of prisoners of war, nor were there any legal or moral bars to such bondage. However the slave sector in Babylonia, as elsewhere in the ancient Orient, was unable to absorb all the prisoners of war. The reason is to be found in the comparatively low level of economic development and goods–money relations, and in the lack of intensive production methods in which slave labour could be utilized on a large scale. It was the labour of free agriculturists and leaseholders that formed the basis of the rural economy, and in crafts the labour of free craftsmen and relatively few

[42] A 923.   [43] For references see A 815, 472.   [44] See A 815, 472–82.

privileged slaves. Slave labour was less effective and needed constant supervision. An average slave sought in every way to avoid the task assigned to him, showed no initiative, and was not interested in the results of his labour or in its quality. It was difficult to establish effective control over slaves, as the basic type of economy was the smallholder's and peasant's household, and there were no large workshops employing slave labour.

The labour of slaves was thus utilized mainly for work which did not demand high qualifications or expensive supervision, work in which slaves could be occupied throughout the year, not seasonally; therefore the more complex processes of production were carried out by freemen. The documents contain hardly any data on the utilization of the labour of privately owned slaves in agriculture, with the exception of cases in which the slaves appear as leaseholders. Major land-owners preferred to deal with free leaseholders, leasing to them small plots of land, because slave labour demanded constant supervising and correspondingly heavy expense. Therefore there were in Babylonia no true *latifundia* except those of the temples, and such large land-ownership as existed relied on small-scale exploitation. When large land-owners had recourse to the help of their own slaves, they either allotted land for independent exploitation on *peculium* rights or more often rented it out to them.[45]

On the fields belonging to the temples there laboured a comparatively large number of slaves, but they cultivated only part of the temple lands, the rest being cultivated partly by *ikkaru* and partly by free leaseholders. Temple administrations also suffered from runaway slaves. It sometimes happened that when slaves took cattle to pasture they would run away and take the cattle with them. The temple management therefore sought mainly to hire free shepherds. The advantage of such economic management was that in cases of theft, outbreak of disease, and other kinds of loss, the shepherds were obliged to make the loss good to the temple out of their own property.

Although the temples and large business houses owned dozens and sometimes hundreds of slaves, and wealthy citizens had from two to five each, they were on the whole far fewer than the population of freemen.

When owners were unable to use slave labour in their household economy or thought it disadvantageous, the slaves were often left to fend for themselves, with the payment of a pre-determined quit-rent from the property (*peculium*) occupied by them. The amount of the quit-rent varied according to the slave's property, but on average it amounted in money terms to 12 shekels of silver a year. The slave himself cost at that time on average about one mina of silver, and a female slave about 50 shekels.[46]

[45] A 815, 252–78.   [46] A 815, 181–206.

There were at that time in Babylonia a comparatively large number of slaves living with their families and owning considerable property, which they were free to pledge, lease, or sell. Slaves could also have their own seals, and appear as witnesses at the conclusion of various business deals by freemen or by other slaves. They could go to law among themselves and sue freemen, with the natural exception of their masters. Such slaves could buy other slaves for work in their households as well as hire slaves and freemen. Nevertheless, such slaves could not buy their freedom, because the right to enfranchise belonged in all cases to their masters, and the wealthier the slave the less advantageous it was for his master to give him his freedom.[47]

Although from the legal point of view the freeing of slaves was admissible, documentary data on manumission are extremely rare. The freeing of slaves was limited to cases in which a slave owner in his old age, having no children or not wishing to become dependent on them, sought to interest a slave in the prospect of future freedom and ensure his loyal service to the end of his days. In such cases the freed slave was obliged to supply his late master with food and clothing, and acquired full freedom only after his death. But if a former slave neglected his duty to provide for his master, he could again be reduced to slavery by the destruction of the document of manumission. But for temple slaves, all ways to freedom were closed.[48]

As has been noted above, in Neo-Babylonian times debt bondage was of little importance: and the less debt bondage is developed the greater is the role played by free hired labour in the general structure of the economy. The amount of pay of hired freemen fluctuated from 3 to 12 shekels of silver a year, and in some cases rose to 30 shekels and more, but on the average it was 12 shekels. Boatmen and men employed on earthworks were particularly highly paid, and a large number of texts tell us about the money paid to hired workers who dug or cleared irrigation canals belonging to temples. Several documents mention the issuing of money and provisions (including ale) to hired workers in the household of the Eanna temple occupied in making, baking, and colouring bricks and bringing them to building sites. Shipwrights and shipmasters also worked as hired hands in Eanna while others were occupied in hauling boats, guarding temple property, and other comparable tasks.

By comparison the hiring of slaves was temporary and infrequent. The pay for a slave's labour was equal to that of a free hired hand, but it was received not by him but by his master. Besides, when at times a hired worker found himself in economic difficulties, the hirer was able to dictate his conditions to him. It was therefore more advantageous to hire freemen.

[47] A 815, 384–97.   [48] A 815, 438–55.

Although the temples had at their disposal a certain number of slaves trained as craftsmen, there were not enough to satisfy even to a minimal extent the needs of the temple economy. The temple administration was obliged throughout the year to turn to free jewellers, brewers, bakers, tanners, smiths, copper-smiths, carpenters, weavers, launderers and potters. Quite often the temples sought the help of craftsmen from other towns, evidently because their number in the local town was insufficient. Thus a number of documents from the archive of the temple of Ebabbar in Sippar certify the payment to 'craftsmen who have come from Babylon'.

The temple administration was also obliged to have recourse to hired labour to cultivate the land and harvest the crops, attracting men even from the neighbouring country of Elam. Private land-owners were also forced to make wide use of the labour of free hired workers. Where such labour was in short supply, pay would be correspondingly high. Particularly characteristic in this respect are letters from temple officials to their supervisors in which they ask first for money to pay hired labourers who might otherwise abandon their jobs, and secondly for iron fetters to be sent for temple slaves who run away. Hired labourers were interested in the work when they were paid punctually, while the slaves (especially when it was a case of heavy labour such as the construction of irrigation works) did all they could to escape from work.

Parties of hired labourers numbering up to several hundreds were not infrequent. They occasionally refused to work in protest against unpunctual payment of their wages, irregular issuing of victuals, or low pay. The correspondence of temple officials shows that the temple administration understood the necessity of satisfying the demands of hired labourers, for if they refused to work it would be impossible to replace them by temple slaves.[49]

VI. TRADE

Under the Chaldaean kings Babylonia enjoyed economic prosperity. Within the country there was a busy trade between the different cities, carried on mainly by boats along the rivers. In both internal and external trade a prominent role was played by a few powerful business houses. The oldest of these was the Egibi house, which had already begun its activity by the end of the eighth century and continued till the beginning of the fifth century, buying and selling fields, houses, and slaves. The Egibi also carried on banking operations, accepting deposits, issuing and receiving promissory notes, paying the debts of their clients,

[49] A 982A.

financing and founding commercial enterprises. The Egibi house, like the other Babylonian business houses, did not for the most part finance their operations from credit deposits entrusted to them but worked from their own assets. The depositors of the Egibi house were usually persons already connected with it by common business interests. Some members were also in the king's service (for example, as judges).[50]

Considerable specialization in trade is demonstrated by the fact that the texts mention not only plain *tamkāru* (merchants) but also *tamkāru* of the king and of governors, as well as *tamkāru* engaged in buying and selling cattle and dates. Temples also often had recourse to the services of the *tamkāru*. The king's *tamkāru* dealt in selling goods belonging to the king and carried on usury in the king's interest. Thus, according to a document of the time of Nebuchadrezzar, a king's merchant paid in Babylon a certain quantity of silver out of the 'king's property' for gold. It is noteworthy that the 'chief *tamkāru*' at the court of Nebuchadrezzar was Hanunu, who, judging by his name, was a Phoenician.

However, in Neo-Babylonian times trade could be carried on not only by professional merchants and their agents but also by any private person. Texts frequently mention town merchants who dealt in salt, imported wine, beer, confectionery, crockery, and so on. These vendors carried on a retail trade in the streets and took their wares to the houses of the wealthy. Concerning regularly functioning urban markets we do not possess yet any definite information.[51]

Some of the professional traders specialized in international commerce. Babylonia continued to serve as a link in the trade between the Phoenician and Palestinian world to the west and the countries to the south and east of Mesopotamia. Especially lively was the trade with Egypt, Syria, Phoenicia, Elam, Cyprus, and Asia Minor. From Egypt there came to Babylonia large quantities of alum used for bleaching wool and clothing and for medical purposes, and of linen, which was much in demand because of its high quality. From Syria and Phoenicia there came honey, aromatic substances, blue-purple wool, and timber for building. These goods were taken overland to the Euphrates and carried downstream by boat to Babylon, the largest centre of international trade of the times, and from there distributed to the various towns in the countryside. The importing of such wares was carried out by commercial companies specially created to finance trade on a large scale. Each shareholder received in proportion to the sum previously invested by him a share of the profits subsequently realized. From Syria came various substances for dyeing textiles, the production of which flourished at the time in Babylonian towns, which had become important centres for

[50] A 1028, 39–47.   [51] A 1008, 69–71.

producing woollen clothing. The clothing was exported to neighbouring countries, in particular to Elam. Grain and other agricultural products were also exported from Babylonia. Trade with Greece is attested by quantities of Greek pottery (almost all from Athens) found at Babylon. Iron from the western coast of Asia Minor and copper from Cyprus were imported in large quantities. Documents dating from the years 551–550 prove the delivery of several hundreds of kilos of iron and copper from Yaman ('Ionia', here the Greek sea-coast of Asia Minor, in other contexts Greece in general) for the temple of Eanna in Uruk. These texts tell of the import from Syria and Lebanon of various dyes, blue-purple wool, spices, honey, twenty jars of white wine, and some 130 kg of Egyptian alum. Iron was also brought from Cilicia; a document of the time of Nabonidus tells us of the acquisition there of over 900 kg of this metal. Another text from the year 601 B.C. records the delivery to weavers of over 2 kg of 'Ionian' blue-purple wool for producing garments for statues of the goddesses of the temple of Eanna.[52] In maritime trade in the time of Nebuchadrezzar the leading role was taken by Ur, which was well placed on the route from the Indian Ocean to the Mediterranean.

Prices for basic commodities were as follows: one *kur* (approximately 180 litres) of barley or dates cost one shekel (8.42 gr) of silver, one *kur* of sesame seed ten shekels, four litres of honey one shekel, one talent (30 kg) of salt one shekel, one mina (505 gr) of wool half a shekel (but one mina of imported blue-purple wool cost about 15 shekels). Outer garments could be bought for 2 shekels. An ox cost about 20 shekels, a cow a few shekels less, a sheep 2 shekels. A jug of barley or date beer cost less than one shekel. A boat cost one mina or more, a house from 1 to 5 minas. Burnt bricks cost from 50 to 100 per shekel. For the same amount of silver one could buy 25 kg of asphalt, used as building cement. Donkeys, which served as a basic means of transport for supplying heavy material, had a high price – up to 30 shekels. A field of one hectare cost 2 to 3 minas or more, a date-palm grove or a garden of the same size was one and a half or two times as expensive.

Metal, although it was exclusively imported, was comparatively low priced. Thus 303 kg of copper from 'Ionia' was sold in Uruk for 3 minas 20 shekels of silver, 18.5 kg of tin for 55.5 shekels, about 65.5 kg of iron from Lebanon for 42.6 shekels. One paid 1 mina 17.3 shekels for 217.5 kg of Egyptian alum, and 36.6 shekels of silver for 28 kg of lapis lazuli.[53]

In internal trade, payments were made by means of silver ingots in various forms, squared, circular, or star-shaped. Minted coin was not used at all in the country. There was a detailed technical terminology for

[52] A 697.   [53] A 1011.

determining the purity of the silver in common use to safeguard traders
and buyers from fraud. Silver ingots contained various proportions of
alloy (most frequently an eighth part, more rarely a fifth, tenth, or
twelfth), and carried a stamp designating the standard. Apparently
private persons as well as temples had the right to produce silver ingots,
giving them a definite shape, weight, and purity similar to those which
were already current. Frequent selling and buying wore the ingots
slightly away, but this was unimportant as they were weighed in each
transaction. Texts often mention 'refined silver' freed of alloy by melting
down. So-called 'white silver', having a high percentage of alloy, had less
value.

The palace and the temples had devised a standard technique for the
monetary realization of large sums of taxes, voluntary gifts, and other
income. As the taxes were paid in silver of lower value, to achieve
uniformity this silver was sent to palace and temple workshops for
purifying and remoulding into ingots of standard weight and quality,
after which the ingots were stored in the treasuries.[54]

Gold was regarded as merchandise and was not used as money. The
relation of gold to silver was approximately 1 to 13.6. For instance in 696
B.C. the temple Eanna bought various quantities of gold from different
individuals, among them 6 minas from one *tamkāru* on the basis of 1
talent 1 mina 3 shekels (30 kg 530 gr) of silver for 4 minas 25 shekels (2 kg
230 gr) of gold.[55]

---

[54] A 1019.   [55] A 1011, 23.

BABYLONIAN MATHEMATICS, ASTROLOGY, AND ASTRONOMY

ASGER AABOE

In no domain has the influence of ancient Mesopotamia on Western civilization been more profound and decisive than in theoretical astronomy and, principally through it, mathematics. Indeed, in the course of the last few decades it has become increasingly clear that all Western efforts in the exact sciences are descendants in direct line from the work of the Late Babylonian astronomers.

The anonymous creators of Babylonian theoretical astronomy – probably of the fourth or fifth century B.C. – drew their essential ingredients from several branches of learning and literature, chief among them mathematics and, for observations, the astronomical diaries, closely linked to the celestial omen texts.

I. BABYLONIAN MATHEMATICS

Babylonian mathematical texts are plentiful and well edited.[1] In respect of time they fall in two distinct groups: one Old Babylonian from the centuries about 1600 B.C., the other mainly Seleucid from the last three or four centuries B.C. In respect of content there is scarcely any difference between the two groups of texts. Thus Babylonian mathematics remained constant, in character and content, for nearly two millennia. Its nascent phase escapes us entirely.

The backbone of Babylonian mathematics is the sexagesimal number system. It is a place-value system, like our decimal system, but of base 60 rather than 10. It was used to write both whole numbers and certain fractions (the equivalents of our decimal fractions) and was without doubt the most efficient way of writing numbers in antiquity. It alone reduced the standard four operations of arithmetic to matters of mere routine, particularly with the aid of the multiplication and reciprocal tables that we find in great numbers. (The sexagesimal system was adopted by the Hellenistic astronomers Hipparchus (*c.* 150 B.C.) and Ptolemy (*c.* A.D. 150) for writing the fractional parts of numbers, and so we still subdivide our hours and degrees in the Babylonian manner.)

---

[1] See A 1031; A 1036; A 1037; A 1048.

The mathematical texts fall largely into two classes: table texts, in which are tabulated functions of various complexity, and problem texts, in which problems are posed and solved. A large problem text contains many examples, often ringing changes in pedagogical order on a central theme.

From the multitude of texts Babylonian mathematics emerges as a creation with well-defined features. Since the sexagesimal number system made numerate Mesopotamians sovereign computers, it is hardly surprising that Babylonian mathematics shows a strong preference for what we today would call algebra and number theory. Though we encounter a considerable amount of geometrical knowledge, geometry often serves merely as a guise for essentially algebraic problems, as when in the statement of a quadratic equation you are asked to add an area and a length in violation of geometrical sense. Further, the geometrical problems all aim at computing some numerical quantity, be it length, area, or volume.

More specifically, we find solutions of first and second degree equations (the latter according to the still current 'formula') and some of these require the reduction of expressions of great complexity. In the geometrical vein the Babylonians computed correctly areas and volumes of simple polygons and solids and, most surprisingly, they freely used the so-called Pythagorean theorem over a millennium before Pythagoras' birth. We even have a text (Plimpton 322)[2] which implies fifteen solutions in whole numbers of some magnitude of the Pythagorean equation

$$x^2 + y^2 = z^2$$

However, nowhere do we find a theorem stated in general terms, nor anything like a proof, though sometimes a solution is so detailed that the underlying general procedure becomes quite obvious.

II. BABYLONIAN ASTRONOMY

The mathematical texts of known provenance come from a number of sites scattered over ancient Mesopotamia. In contrast, the bulk of the astronomical texts derives from only three locations.

From Ashurbanipal's library in Nineveh (Kouyunjik) we have most of the texts centred on the series of celestial omens, *Enūma Anu Enlil*.

Secondly, we have a group of some 1,600 astronomical texts obtained from dealers during the last decades of the last century; they were the product of unscientific excavations of what must have been an extensive astronomical archive somewhere in the city of Babylon. About 1,200 of

[2] A 1037, 38.

these are non-mathematical astronomical texts, classified by A. Sachs as Diaries, Almanacs and Goal-Year texts.[3] The rest are concerned with mathematical astronomy, and we shall refer to them as being of the *ACT* type after the standard abbreviation of O. Neugebauer's *Astronomical Cuneiform Texts*,[4] where most of them were published.

Thirdly, there is a smaller group of texts, mostly of the *ACT* type, that come from Uruk, most likely from the domain of the Reš sanctuary.

In respect of content we have, then, three principal classes of astronomical texts. First there are those which in one way or another are concerned with astronomical omens. At the core of this class is the series of about 70 tablets now, as in antiquity, known by its opening phrase '*Enūma Anu Enlil*' (When [the gods] Anu and Ellil). The contents of this collection of omens are presumably very old, but only a few Old Babylonian fragments of some of the tablets are known. The two-tablet series *Mul Apin* is more astronomical in character and very likely younger than *Enūma Anu Enlil*. Finally there are the Royal Reports written by specialists in astronomical omens from various cities of the kingdom to the Assyrian king.[5] Such a report may contain an observation and an interpretation of its significance according to the canonical texts, mostly *Enūma Anu Enlil*. These reports date from about 700 B.C.

The second class, that of the Astronomical Diaries and related texts, contains or is based on a high proportion of observations. They come from the astronomical archive in Babylon and span in time the interval from about 750 B.C. to A.D. 75, the text from this last year being the latest datable text written in cuneiform.[6]

Thirdly, the mathematical astronomical texts, those of the *ACT* type, come from the astronomical archive in Babylon and from Uruk. They are, in respect of date, from the last three or four centuries B.C. (the Uruk texts stop before *c.* 150 B.C.), so they represent one of the last, as well as one of the finest contributions of Mesopotamian culture.

The three groups of texts are intimately connected. Indeed, all three categories were kept in the archive in Babylon; the scribes who wrote even the elaborate theoretically computed ephemerides[7] of *ACT* called themselves by the title *ṭupšar Enūma Anu Enlil* (scribe of [the series] *Enūma Anu Enlil*). The Diaries can be viewed as collections of raw material for omens, and they provided in the process the observational basis for constructing the theories behind the *ACT* texts; and, finally, the *ACT* texts predict precisely the core of the celestial phenomena recorded in the Diaries.

Lastly, a few remarks about the astronomical archive in Babylon.

³ A 1044.   ⁴ A 1039.   ⁵ A 1032.   ⁶ A 1047.
⁷ An ephemeris lists dates and corresponding astronomical information, not necessarily day by day.

Colophons, names of scribes, scribal families, runs of the British Museum's accession numbers, and many other features assure its existence, but we do not know its precise location within the vast ruins of Babylon, for all the texts from it were excavated without records being kept. The earliest Diary is dated by A. Sachs to −651 (=652 B.C.),[8] and recently he published six texts from A.D. 31 to 75.[9] These late texts throw a particularly interesting light on the activities around the archive. By 275 B.C. the government had moved from Babylon to Seleucia and Antiochus ended Babylon's civil existence. The once great and glamorous metropolis fell rapidly into decay, and some three centuries later Strabo, who died *c.* A.D. 20, writes that the greater part of Babylon is deserted and quotes the comic poet who said 'The Great City is a great desert'. Yet these six texts show that even after Strabo's time there were still people living in the ruins of Babylon who not only knew, and taught others, the difficult art of reading and writing technical Akkadian in cuneiform, but who also had access to the astronomical archive and the desire and competence to use and increase it. Here one may well recall that Pliny (d. A.D. 79) in *Natural History* VI.30.121/2 remarks about Babylon, 'The temple of Jupiter Belus still remains – it was here the creator of the science of astronomy was – the rest has reverted to desert.' Indeed, many of the astronomical texts from Babylon carry the invocation *ina amat Bel u Beltia lišlim* (at the command of [the deities] Bel and Beltia, may it go well).

III. CELESTIAL OMEN TEXTS, ASTROLOGY

Of the seventy tablets of the series *Enūma Anu Enlil* of celestial omens, the first twenty-three concern the Moon and the next twenty the Sun. Then follow a few tablets of meteorological omens, and the last twenty deal with planets and fixed stars.

Most of the astronomical protases are vague and qualitative in the extreme ('If Jupiter remains in the sky in the morning...'). Thus we find much concern about the physical appearance of the Moon, for example, on the important evening of its first appearance or during eclipses, whether it is light or dark, which way its horns point, or whether it is surrounded by a halo.

Tablet 63, the famous, if not notorious, Venus Tablet of Ammiṣaduqa, offers a sharp contrast to this vagueness. The protases of its total of fifty-nine omens give month and dates of first and last visibility of Venus as a morning or evening star, and the length in days of its periods of invisibility, for twenty-one consecutive years. The link to Ammiṣ-

---

[8] There is a difference between the astronomical and historical reckoning of early dates thus: year 0 = 1 B.C., year −1 = 2 B.C., etc.   [9] A 1047.

aduqa is provided by the tenth omen: instead of the expected apodosis it gives what Kugler brilliantly read as 'The Year of the Golden Throne', the name of the eighth of his twenty-one regnal years. It is very natural to assume that the protases constitute an observational record of the appearances and disappearances of Venus for the reign of Ammiṣaduqa, and this assumption has underlain the role this text has played in modern attempts at establishing an absolute Old Babylonian chronology.

The text's information about Venus, Sun, and Moon (this last because the calendar is strictly lunar) was used by Langdon, Fotheringham and Schoch in their edition of the text,[10] and they were able to restrict, on astronomical grounds, the beginning of Ammiṣaduqa's reign to a limited number of possibilities in the early second millennium. Most historians chose to use one of the middle chronologies, but for no strongly compelling reason.

In a lunar calendar, where a new month begins with the first appearance of the new crescent Moon, a month is either hollow (it has twenty-nine days) or full (thirty days), at least for Mediterranean latitudes. On the average there are slightly more full than hollow months, but the sequence of full and hollow months is highly irregular, and so contains much information. Langdon, Fotheringham and Schoch had tried to check their various chronologies against what they knew of full and hollow months, but their data were bad, and their results inconclusive.

In 1982 Peter Huber published the results of a long and deep investigation of these matters.[11] He had at his disposal the new edition of the Venus Tablet by Reiner and Pingree,[12] a fuller record of Old Babylonian full and hollow months provided by several Assyriologists, as well as some eclipse records and a few data from the Ur III period. He subjected this material to a highly sophisticated statistical analysis (made possible, not only by his great expertise, but also by the availability of modern computers) and reached the firm conclusion that the 'Long Chronology' made eminent sense, while the others made no sense at all. Thus we have Ammiṣaduqa $1 = -1701$ (1702 B.C.), so Hammurabi began his reign in 1848 B.C. There seems, then, to remain but two reasonable choices: one must either reject the Venus Tablet as chronological evidence, or accept the 'Long Chronology'.

The imperfectly understood seventy tablets of *Enūma Anu Enlil* are at the centre of what at present seems a morass of related texts: extracts, commentaries, and reports. Once all of this material is brought under control we shall very likely have a firm grasp of the state of astrology in Mesopotamia, and the role of 'diviners', near the end of the Assyrian

---

[10] A 1035.   [11] A 1033.   [12] A 1042.

empire, and we may also be afforded some notion of the tradition of some of the texts. The first step must, however, be to edit the relevant texts. An edition of the planetary omens by Reiner and Pingree is in progress,[13] but otherwise we have only excerpts and surveys at our disposal.

The same situation obtains for *Mul Apin*, a series of two tablets. Though it contains some omens, it is principally a compendium of astronomical lore. One could call the presentation theoretical, but the treatment of various astronomical phenomena, like length of daylight, is always schematic in the extreme. The dates of the various parts of the series *Mul Apin*, its intended use, and the tradition of the texts cannot be determined at present.

The type of astrology we find in *Enūma Anu Enlil* is called judicial: the apodoses are concerned with events and conditions that affect king or country, such as war and peace, quality of harvest, and weather ('springs will open, Adad will bring his rain, Ea his floods; king will send messages of reconciliation to king').[14]

In contrast to judicial astrology we have personal astrology with its horoscopes for important events in the life of an individual, particularly birth. There is nothing astrological in the horoscope itself: it is simply a statement of the positions of Sun, Moon, and planets, perhaps also the rising point of the ecliptic (*horoscopus*), and other astronomical matters of interest, not observed, but somehow calculated for the horizon of a given locality at a certain moment. All this is purely astronomical, in the modern sense of the word. Astrology enters only in the interpretation of the horoscope's information.

Virtually all the evidence for horoscopy is from Hellenistic and Roman times when personal astrology gained great popularity. Though there are many, but usually very vague, references to Chaldaeans and Babylonians in the Greek and Latin astrological literature, the cuneiform evidence for personal astrology was scant and published in scattered places with varying competence. Until 1952 it was, in fact, possible to build a persuasive case for a Hellenistic origin of personal astrology. However, in that year A. Sachs gathered all the published cuneiform horoscopes, added several unpublished ones as well as related texts, and subjected them to a uniform and highly competent treatment.[15] He managed to date, on astronomical grounds, the horoscopes whose dates were broken off, and the earliest was from 410 B.C. In addition he had four horoscopes from the third century B.C., so there is no doubt about the Babylonian priority in horoscopic astrology. At the moment it seems likely, but not certain, that Hellenistic and Roman personal astrology was derived from its Babylonian predecessor.

[13] A 1042; A 1043. See also A 1040.   [14] A 1042, 29.   [15] A 1044a.

IV. ASTRONOMICAL DIARIES AND RELATED TEXTS

When A. Sachs published his classification of non-mathematical astronomical texts[16] he had at his disposal a dozen of them. Half a decade later his survey of part of the holdings of the British Museum increased his material a hundred-fold, and he spent the rest of his life working on these texts. Miraculously his original classification of them as Diaries, Almanacs, Goal-Year texts, and Excerpts survived this violent expansion.

In time, the texts cover, though not uniformly, the interval from c. 750 B.C. to A.D. 75, and nearly all of them come from the astronomical archive in Babylon, as we have already said. At the centre of this group of texts are the Astronomical Diaries; all the others are derived from them in one way or another.[17]

The unit in a Diary is one month, beginning with a statement about the new crescent, whether it was high or low, and the time from sunset to moonset in time degrees (one day is 360 time degrees, so one time degree is four of our minutes). We are told if this interval was measured or estimated, and whether the previous month turned out to be hollow or full (the first sighting of the new Moon marks the beginning of a new month). The Diary then follows the progress of the Moon throughout the month, noting when it passes one of the thirty-one Normal Stars as well as the visible planets, whether above or below, and often by how much. Finally we learn when the Moon last could be seen, and how long it then was, again in time degrees, from moonrise to sunrise, and so ends the main part of the Diary unit, unless there happens to be a solar eclipse at the subsequent conjunction of Sun and Moon. At mid-month we find four time intervals between the four combinations of horizon crossings of Sun and Moon near full Moon (the full Moon rises near sunset and sets near sunrise), as well as remarks about a lunar eclipse whenever one occurs.

Interspersed in this account of the Moon's monthly behaviour, and in proper chronological order, is information about the planets, about unfavourable weather conditions and uncommon meteorological phenomena such as rainbows and haloes.

After this day-by-day account of astronomical and meteorological events we find several terse statements that concern the month as a whole, first about the state of the commodities market in the form of how much one shekel of silver would buy of certain staples, viz. barley, dates, pepper(?), cress(?), sesame, and wool (always in this order). It is noted if the prices changed in the course of the month (in one extreme case we are given quotations for morning, midday, and afternoon of a single day).

---

[16] A 1044.

[17] A 1029, in which the only English translation (by A. Sachs) to date of a Diary is published.

Next we find mentioned the zodiacal signs in which the planets resided during the month, followed by a report on the monthly change in the level of the Euphrates. Concluding the monthly unit of a Diary we often find a terse historical statement. It may concern an event of little interest to a modern scholar – an outbreak of fire in some quarter of Babylon or a theft from the temple. However, then again we can read about the enthusiasm with which the cities of Babylonia greeted Alexander's troops as liberators after Arba'il, and later about Alexander's death in Babylon.[18]

The importance of the Diaries, once they are published,[19] lies not only in the kind of information they contain – astronomical, meteorological, economic, and historical – and in the long time interval they span, but also in the fact that because of the ever-presence of the swiftly moving Moon we can date them to the very day, if we can date them at all.

Among the related texts the Goal-Year texts ought to be mentioned. Such a text predicts the behaviour of Moon and planets for a given year – the goal year – by presenting information extracted from Diaries that antedate the goal year by astronomically significant periods (71 or 83 years for Jupiter, 8 years for Venus, 46 years for Mercury, and so on). This happens to be a quite efficient way of predicting phenomena of the sort considered, and it is based on a recognition of the periodic character of planetary and lunar behaviour, a notion that is fundamental in Babylonian theoretical astronomy.

Finally a remark about the kind and quality of planetary observations in the Diaries: two sorts of phenomena are recorded, planetary phases (for an outer planet they are first and last visibility, stationary points, and opposition) with a note of the zodiacal sign in which the planet is when phase occurs, and a planet's passage past a Normal Star, whether above or below and by how much. The observations are probably made with the naked eye unaided by any sort of instrument; indeed, as far as we can see, the only instrument used to gather the information given in the Diaries was a water-clock for determining the fairly short time intervals between horizon crossings of Sun and Moon.

Babylonian arithmetical astronomy

We have 400 to 500 texts, many of them small fragments, that in one way or another deal with arithmetical astronomy. Some 300 of them were published in *ACT* in 1955, the rest subsequently in various journals. They can be roughly divided into four classes: lunar or planetary

---

[18] A 1046.
[19] A. Sachs worked on the Diaries for the last thirty years of his life. After his death in 1983, and according to his wish, the task of bringing them to publication has been taken over by H. Hunger.

ephemerides or procedure texts. The procedure texts, or precepts, tell us how to calculate ephemerides (texts that present dates and corresponding astronomical information, the ultimate aim of the theory), and ideally a set of procedure texts and a knowledge of the rules for finding initial values (these rules still escape us) should enable us to compute any ephemeris. In fact, the path to our present control of Babylonian mathematical astronomy has meandered between ephemerides and procedure texts, for it was often easier to uncover the rules underlying the ephemerides' computation than to penetrate the precepts' terse, technical terminology.

We have as yet no texts setting forth the very consistent theories that underlie the instructions of the procedure texts – and it seems unlikely that we shall find any – so these theories have had to be reconstructed by modern scholars. There emerges a theory – or rather two families of theories, Systems A and B, as they are now commonly called – with well-defined, regular features. It is alas, not possible to do justice to the beauty and elegance of these constructs in a brief, descriptive account, for their qualities reside precisely in the subtle, cunningly designed interplay of mathematically simple technical details.

We cannot decide whether there was an oral tradition of handing down the inner structures of the theories, and justifications of them, from generation to generation, but it is not completely excluded. Indeed, we find displayed in the procedure texts many basic parameters that normally lie buried well within the theories and are of no direct use to someone calculating an ephemeris.

As to the dates of the texts, there are two that are of concern when we are dealing with an ephemeris: the date it was written, and the intended date or time span of its contents. The latter is always given in an ephemeris, but usually near the left edge and thus particularly vulnerable; but even if the dates are broken off we can very often restore them securely on astronomical and structural grounds. As to the former, we can only be sure of the date of composition or writing if the scribe himself gives it in a colophon, and even completely preserved texts most often carry none. We have less than twenty texts for which we are sure of both dates, and in all instances it turns out that the date of writing is near the beginning of the time interval covered by the contents. The year numbers are given in the continuing count of the Seleucid Era (began 311 B.C.) in all but a very few texts. The exceptions with preserved dates employ regnal years in the usual fashion. The earliest of these is a text dealing with solar eclipse possibilities (we have it in duplicate).[20] The dates run from VIII/II Xerxes to IV/8 Artaxerxes I (5 December 475 to 21 July 457 B.C.). It is tempting to view this text as evidence for an early date

---

[20] Texts B, C, and D in A 1030.

for the invention of lunar System A, to which its methods belong. However, all we can be sure of is that it was written after the events it describes: first, the calculated eclipse possibilities are paired with observational remarks from Diaries and, secondly, it dates correctly in two reigns. (Incidentally, we do not know of a single text that employs a regnal year in excess of the king's natural reign until, of course, we reach the Seleucid era.) Thus the text clearly represents a calculation backwards in time for the purpose of testing theory against past observations. At the moment it seems likely that Babylonian theoretical astronomy was created sometime in the fourth century B.C.

Two features of Babylonian theoretical astronomy seem particularly peculiar to a modern eye: first, the total absence of any underlying geometrical models or 'orbits' and, secondly, its choice of independent variable. Indeed, the planetary and lunar models, as we still call them, are entirely arithmetical in character; the mathematical skills required for the computation of an ephemeris are limited to the four basic operations of arithmetic: addition, subtraction, multiplication, and division. The approach resembles curiously that of modern electronic computers, and the procedure texts often want only direct translation into computer language to become effective programs.

The other point is that since the time of Ptolemy the astronomer (*c.* A.D. 150) we have been accustomed to consider time the independent variable in astronomical theories; in other words, the principal question we have wanted our theories to answer has been: given any moment of time, past, present, or future, where among the fixed stars was, is, or will be, a certain planet, Sun, or Moon? It is far otherwise in Babylonian astronomy. To take an outer planet (Mars, Jupiter, or Saturn) as an example, all interest is focused, at least at first, on one of its five phases (first or last visibility, first or last stationary point, or opposition), and a typical question the Babylonian theory is prepared to answer is: if Jupiter is at a first stationary point on a certain date and at a certain celestial longitude, when and where will it next be at a first stationary point? The other phases are treated analogously, and the question of finding daily positions, that is, that of constructing an ephemeris in the literal sense of the word, is solved by interpolation between dates and positions of adjacent phases, if it is addressed at all.

To be more specific, we have excerpted in Table 2, columns I–IV, the first 25 of in all 56 lines of the text *ACT* No. 600, an ephemeris for Jupiter at first stationary point, Φ, for the years S.E. 113 to 173 (− 198 to − 138).[21] According to its colophon the text was written in Uruk S.E. 118, 12/VII (5 October 194 B.C.), so it is mostly a forecast.

---

[21] S.E. = Seleucid Era. See p. 279 n. 8 and p. 284 above.

Table 2

l.	I y. SE	II Δτ	III mo. & date	IV λ	V _ιλ	VI Jul. date	VII λ	VIII date
1	113**	48; 5,10	I 28:41,40 ♌	♏ 8;6 Φ		−198 Apr 22	♏ 3	II 4
	114	48; 5,10	II 16;46,50 ♌	≈14;6 Φ	36	−197 May29	≈ 8	II 21
	115*	48; 5,10	IV 4;52	♓20;6 Φ	36	−196 Jul 3	♓ 14	IV 12
	116	48; 5,10	IV 22;57,10	♈26;6	36	−195 Aug 9	♈ 21	IV 29
5	117	48; 5,10	VI 11; 2,20	♊ 2;6	36	−194 Sep 15	♉ 26	VI 15
	118*	45;54,10	VII 26;56,30	♋ 5;55	33;49	−193 Oct 19	♊ 29	VII 28
	119	42; 5,10	VIII 9; 1,40	♌ 5;55	30	−192 Nov18	♌ 0	VIII12
	120	42; 5,10	IX 21; 6,50	♍ 5;55	30	−191 Dec 20	♍ 1	IX 24
	121*	42; 5,10	XI 3;12	♎ 5;55	30	−189 Jan 18	♎ 1	XI 7
10	122	42; 5,10	XI 15;17,10	♏ 5;55	30	−188 Feb 18	♏ 2	XI 18
	123*	43;16,10	XII 28;33,20	♐ 7;6	31;11	−187 Mar21	♐ 4	XII₂ 4
	125	48; 5,10	I 16;38,30	♑13;6	36	−186 Apr 28	♑ 8	I 22
	126*	48; 5,10	III 4;43,40	≈19;6	36	−185 Jun 3	≈ 13	III 10
	127	48; 5,10	III 22;48,50	♓25;6	36	−184 Jul 9	♓ 19	III 30
15	128	48; 5,10	V 10;54	♉ 1;6	36	−183 Aug15	♈ 26	V 17
	129*	48; 5,10	VI 28;59,10	♊ 7;6	36	−182 Sep 21	♊ 0	VII 3
	130	45; 4,10	VII 14; 3,20	♋10;5	32;59	−181 Oct 24	♋ 3	VII 15
	131	42; 5,10	VIII26; 8,30	♌10;5	30	−180 Nov23	♌ 5	VIII28
	132**	42; 5,10	IX 8;13,40	♍10;5	30	−179 Dec 23	♍ 5	IX 11
20	133	42; 5,10	X 20;18,50	♎10;5	30	−177 Jan 23	♎ 5	X 22
	134*	42; 5,10	XII 2;24	♏10;5	30	−176 Feb 22	♏ 6	XII 6
	135	44; 6,10	XII 16;30,10	♐12;6	32;1	−175 Mar26	♐ 9	XII 21
	137*	48; 5,10	II 4;35,20	♑18;6	36	−174 May 3	♑ 13	II 10
	138	48; 5,10	II 22;40,30	≈24;6	36	−173 Jun 8	≈ 18	II 28
25	139	48; 5,10	IV 10;45,40	♓30;6	36	−172 Jul 14	♓ 25	IV 18

In columns I and III we find year, month, and date. The year number (S.E.) is written, for example, 1-me 13 (1 hundred 13), but all other numbers are sexagesimals.[22] The dates are in *tithis* ($\frac{1}{30}$ synodic month) and fractions thereof – the fractions are solely of computational interest (the *tithi* is so called because it was first encountered, in modern times, in Hindu astronomy; Babylonian terminology draws no distinction between *tithi* and day). The use of the *tithi* frees us from concern about which months in the future will be full or hollow; the date in *tithis* is, of course, always close to the date in days. The years with a single asterisk (the text has 'a') contain a month XII₂, those with a double asterisk ('kin a') a month VI₂. The fixed 19-year pattern of intercalations of the late period can readily be established from this short excerpt.

Column II contains the difference in *tithis* (Δτ) of the dates less 12 months. The convention of the text is that the difference between the date in line *n* and that in line *n*-1 is 12 months plus the Δτ listed in line *n*.

Column IV gives the longitude, λ, of Jupiter at its first stationary

---

[22] The sexagesimal numbers are transcribed so that, e.g., 48;5,10 = 48 + 5/60 + 10/3600. There is no equivalent of the semicolon in cuneiform writing.

point in terms of degrees of a zodiacal sign. In column V, which is not in the text, we have presented the differences, $\Delta\lambda$, of these longitudes. We note that columns II and V run parallel so that in each line

$$\Delta\tau - \Delta\lambda = 12;5,10$$

Thus we need bring but one of these columns under control to uncover the structure of the text and there are, as we shall see, good reasons to begin with $\Delta\lambda$.

Column V, the total progress of Jupiter from one first stationary point to the next, falls conspicuously into constant stretches of either 36° or 30° separated by intermediate values. The key to the structure of this column is the realization that the scheme is tied to the ecliptic. As a procedure text would have it (e.g. *ACT* No. 821):

From Gemini 25° to Scorpio 30° add 30°. Whatever exceeds Scorpio 30°, multiply it by 1;12 and add it to Scorpio 30°.
From Scorpio 30° to Gemini 25° add 36°. Whatever exceeds Gemini 25°, multiply it by 0;50 and add it to Gemini 25°.

Thus the ecliptic is divided into two parts – the fast and the slow arc – inside which the phenomenon progresses in steps of 36° and 30° respectively. If such a step crosses a boundary of the arcs, the amount that reaches into the new zone is modified by one of the factors 0;50 and 1;12. It is significant that these two factors – 5/6 and 6/5 in fractional form – are precisely the ratios 30:36 and 36:30.

With these simple rules we may now continue the text as long as we please: first we compute the column of longitudes and form their differences $\Delta\lambda$. From these we obtain $\Delta\tau$ from

$$\Delta\tau = \Delta\lambda + 12;5,10$$

and so the date columns.

In column VI we have translated the dates in columns I and III into Julian dates; in column VII we have given the longitude of Jupiter corresponding to these dates according to modern tables; and in column VIII are the Babylonian dates of Jupiter's first stationary point, again from modern tables.

From these last columns can be judged the text's quality, which is surprising for a scheme of such simplicity, particularly when we allow for the systematic difference between modern and Babylonian conventions in counting longitudes (*c.* 5° at this time).

One of the reasons for this excellence and for the quality not deteriorating even in the course of a long text is that built into these seemingly simple schemes are certain period relations. In the present instance, if we continue the longitude column of our text for $\Pi = 391$

Table 3

No. 620	I	II	III		IV	V
l.	year	$\Delta\tau$	month & date		$\Delta\lambda$	λ
0	2,7	49;42	V	27;36	37;37	✗ 24;31
1	2,8	47;54	VII	15;30	35;49	♈ 30;20
2	2,9*	46;6	IX	1;36	34;1	♊ 4;21
3	2,10	44;18	IX	15;54	32;13	♋ 6;34
4	2,11	42;30	X	28;24	30;25	♌ 6;59
5	2,12**	40;42	XI	9;6	28;37	♍ 5;36
6	2,13	41;47,30	XII	20;53,30	29;42	♎ 5;18
7	2,15	43;35,30	I	4;29	31;30	♏ 6;48
8	2,16	45;23,30	II	19;52,30	33;18	♐ 10;6
9	2,17*	47;11,30	IV	7;4	35;6	♑ 15;12
10	2,18	48;59,30	IV	26; 3,30	36;54	♒ 22;6
11	2,19	49;27	VI	15;30,30	37;22	✗ 29;28
12	2,20*	47;39	VIII	3; 9,30	35;34	♉ 5;2
13	2,21	45;51	VIII	19; 0,30	33;46	♊ 8;48
14	2,22*	44;3	X	3; 3,30	31;58	♋ 10;46
15	2,23	42;15	X	15;18,30	30;10	♌ 10;56
16	2,24	40;27	XI	25;45,30	28;22	♍ 9;18
17	2,25*	42; 2,30	XII₂	7;48	29;57	♎ 9;15
18	2,27	43;50,30	I	21;38,30	31;45	♏ 11
19	2,28*	45;38,30	III	7;17	33;33	♐ 14;33
20	2,29	47;26,30	III	24;43,30	35;21	♑ 19;54
21	2,30	49;14,30	V	13;58	37;9	♒ 27;3
22	2,31**	49;12	VI₂	3;10	37;7	♈ 4;10

lines we shall reach precisely the longitude we began with and the longitudes will have skipped $Z = 36$ times around the ecliptic in the process. Jupiter does in fact travel 36 times around in the course of 391 synodic phenomena and it takes $391 + 36 = 427$ years.

The constant stretches of $\Delta\lambda$ marks our text as belonging to System A, for $\Delta\lambda$ is treated as a step function of longitude. An example of planetary System B follows.

Table 3 gives the first 22 of at least 62 lines of *ACT* No. 620, an ephemeris for Jupiter at opposition for at least the years S.E. 127 to 194. It is arranged much like the previous text except that here both difference columns are included, and we shall first examine column IV, $\Delta\lambda$.

The entries in column IV decrease regularly by the amount $d = 1;48°$ per line until a minimum is passed between lines 5 and 6. From line 6 the values increase, again by $1;48°$, until a maximum is passed between lines 10 and 11, whence they begin to decrease, and so on. If we plot $\Delta\lambda$ as a function of line number we get a piece-wise linear graph like the one in Fig. 12. One gets from an ascending to a descending branch of such a zigzag function, as we call it, by following a simple reflexion rule (often

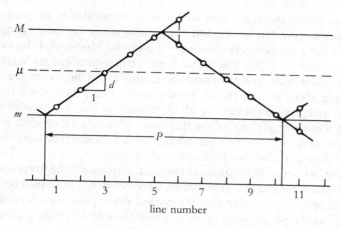

line number

Fig. 12.

stated in procedure texts); if the application of the line by line difference d (here $1;48°$) leads to a value larger than a certain fixed maximum M (here $38;2°$), then the excess over M is subtracted from M to yield the next value of the function, and symmetrically about the minimum m (here $28;15,30°$).

The zigzag function, sometimes refined in various ingenious ways, is one of the two basic modes of describing a simply periodic component of a more complex astronomical phenomenon – the other is the step function of System A. It is easy to compute, and it has a simply controlled period

$$P = \frac{2(M-m)}{d}$$

With the parameters of the present text, $M = 38;2°$ and $m = 28;15,30°$, $d = 1;48°$, we obtain

$$P = 10;51,40 = \frac{391}{36}$$

We recognize these numbers as precisely those that underlay the System A scheme for Jupiter. There they implied that $\Pi = 391$ applications of the synodic arc lead to precisely $Z = 36$ revolutions in the ecliptic. Here the period relation is that Π lines will lead to precise return in $\Delta\lambda$ and will embrace Z 'waves' of the zigzag function.

Here we can only mention the complexity of the lunar theories of Systems A and B – a lunar ephemeris may have 14 to 15 columns, each fairly simple, but all intricately interrelated. The principal anomalies of Sun and Moon were recognized and used in their proper places. As in the planetary texts, the main aim of lunar ephemerides is to predict the phenomena recorded in the Diaries: eclipses, the six interesting time intervals between horizon crossings of Sun and Moon, and the evening of first visibility. While the texts' lunar eclipse predictions were solid enough, their solar counterparts were, and could be, mere warnings, separating those conjunctions or new moons at which a solar eclipse might happen from those – nearly five times as many – at which solar eclipses were entirely out of the question. (Predictions of solar eclipses for given localities involve a knowledge of the shape of the Earth and the relative sizes and distance of Earth and Moon.)

In sum, we see in Babylonian theoretical astronomy the first successful attempt at addressing the problem that ever since has remained central in the exact sciences: to give a mathematical description of a well-defined class of natural phenomena, a description capable of yielding numerical predictions that can be tested against observations.

Transmission of Babylonian astronomy

The tradition of the reigns of the Late Babylonian and Achaemenid kings has been unbroken since Ptolemy composed his king list *c.* A.D. 150 as a useful appendix to his *Almagest* or his later *Handy Tables*. He gives the length of each reign in Egyptian years (of 365 days each) and keeps a running total from the beginning of the reign of Nabonassar (747 B.C.), 'for', as he says (*Almagest* III.7), 'that is the era beginning from which the ancient observations are, on the whole, preserved down to our own time'.[23] Ptolemy's chronology has, by and large, been confirmed by cuneiform evidence, and there is no doubt that he is referring to the Astronomical Diaries in the passage quoted above. There is, however, much more evidence for Ptolemy's knowledge of Babylonian astronomy: his use of the sexagesimal system for writing fractions, of degrees, and of several well-established Babylonian parameters like the value

$$1 \text{ month} = 29;31,50,8,20 \text{ days}$$

for the mean synodic month, taken directly from lunar System B. Further, Ptolemy's complaints about the ancient planetary observations (*Almagest* IX.2) clearly describe the kind of phenomena contained in the Diaries. It is not impossible that Ptolemy had direct access to cuneiform material – after all, the astronomical archive in Babylon was certainly still active 75 years before he wrote – but it is more likely that he used Hipparchus' compilation and convenient rearrangement of Babylonian observations (*Almagest* IX.2).

[23] A 1049, 166.

Hipparchus (c. 150 B.C.) seems the pivotal figure in the transmission of Babylonian astronomy to the West. All his works are lost save a commentary on Aratus' astrological poem, but Ptolemy is generous with references to his highly esteemed predecessor. It is clear that Hipparchus borrowed Babylonian parameters such as the length of the month cited above, and that he used Babylonian observations which would have been useless to him without control of Babylonian chronology.

Thus Ptolemy in all likelihood also acquired the substance of his king list from Hipparchus. Where Hipparchus in turn obtained his chronological knowledge is much less certain, but we can suggest two possibilities among the types of texts we have in hand: chronicles and extracts from the Diaries of a particular sort of information, e.g. about eclipses, some of which cover considerable time intervals. Finally, we must not forget that the Babylonian astronomers themselves needed a command of chronology to make proper use of their archive.

Several candidates have been mentioned in the literature as the transmitters of Babylonian astronomy, among them Aristotle. Though it is not excluded that some of these carried Babylonian lore to the West, there is no evidence at all that the sophisticated theoretical astronomy was accessible to them. Furthermore, Greek astronomy was not ready for the Babylonian lesson until after the work of Apollonius of Perge (c. 200 B.C.) on epicyclic models. Greek astronomy had hitherto been concerned with building geometrical devices that in a qualitative manner could simulate planetary behaviour.

We begin to see more clearly what Hipparchus achieved. Not only did he obtain observations, parameters, and number system from the Babylonians in addition, perhaps, to some methods,[24] but more fundamentally the idea that it is possible and desirable to have astronomical theories produce numerical predictions. He set out to adapt and modify epicyclic models to that purpose and succeeded for Sun and new and full Moon, but passed the planetary problem on to his successors. We know few of them, and most of these only by name, until we reach Ptolemy. As he sets forth in the *Almagest*, it was he who completed Hipparchus' task by devising a lunar model that works also in quadrature, and by constructing satisfactory planetary models.

The *Almagest* remained the model and foundation of treatises on theoretical astronomy to the time of Kepler, and theoretical astronomy in turn remained the exemplar of all other exact sciences until at least the eighteenth century, teaching that their aim should be to give a mathematical description of a sensibly defined class of natural phenomena, a description capable of producing numerical predictions that can be

[24] A 1034; A 1041; A 1049, 224 n. 14; for the entire subject of astronomy in antiquity see A 1038, which has very full references.

tested against observations. It is in this sense that we claim Babylonian mathematical astronomy as the common ancestor of modern efforts in the exact sciences.

In 1988, O. Neugebauer read and understood a Greek papyrus from Roman Egypt, now in private hands.[25] It turned out to give 32 lines of Column G of Babylonian lunar System B, the very column whose mean value led F. X. Kugler to recognize it as Ptolemy's for the mean synodic month.[26] This discovery completely changed our estimate of the level of understanding of Babylonian methods in Hellenism.[27]

[25] A 1039A.   [26] A 1034A.

[27] To the basic bibliography for this section, A 1029–49, should now be added A. J. Sachs and H. Hunger, *Astronomical Diaries and Related Texts from Babylonia*: I, *Diaries from 652 B.C. to 262 B.C.*: II, *Diaries from 261 B.C. to 165 B.C.* (Vienna, 1988–9); and H. Hunger and D. Pingree, *MUL.APIN: an Astronomical Compendium in Cuneiform* (AfO Bh 24, 1989).

CHAPTER 28c

FIRST-MILLENNIUM BABYLONIAN LITERATURE

ERICA REINER

I. DEFINITION AND TRADITION

We do not know what literature was composed in first-millennium Babylonia; we know only what literary works were kept in royal and private libraries of that period. Some works may merely have found a repository there; others were very much in use, on religious occasions, to be recited or to serve as guides for ritual and magic performances. Still others were copied again and again, and the scholarly literature was extensively commented upon.

At the outset it has to be stated that the word 'literature' is here used in a broad sense, to include not only *belles-lettres* but also the standardized works of various experts – in divination, magic, ritual, and linguistic scholarship. That is to say, we will be considering that body of texts that has been termed by Oppenheim the 'stream of tradition'.[1]

The material to be considered is that kept at the royal library of Ashurbanipal at Nineveh, to which may be added such provincial libraries as Sultantepe, and, at the very end of the era of cuneiform writing altogether, the libraries of scholars in southern Babylonia, mostly from Uruk, dating to the Seleucid period, which to a large measure duplicate the texts from Nineveh and thus can serve to illustrate the literature of the period in question, 747–539 B.C.

The classification of these works here will follow traditional lines, even though the categories under which we classify them are those of the West, inherited from the classical world. The customary categories used in the classification of Babylonian literature, that is, epics, hymns, wisdom texts, and so on, probably would have had little meaning for the ancients, who characterized some poetry as 'songs' – sometimes with an additional specification – or 'incantations', or who simply called a longer, usually epic, poem a 'series' or 'set' named after its hero or its author, or even referred to it by its *incipit* only. Yet it is not entirely incorrect to label some texts 'epics', or 'hymns', or 'fables', even though these terms are only approximations. There are enough similarities

[1] A 43, 249.

between Babylonian works and comparable genres of classical literatures, which determine our categories, to warrant a gross classification of
Babylonian works into these categories familiar to the modern Western
reader. By retaining this traditional classification we establish some kind
of common ground with the reader familiar with similarly named genres
in classical or later Western literature. Moreover, in view of the fact that
Mesopotamian literature is part of the entire tradition of Western
literature and can and should be integrated into it through the Judaeo-
Christian tradition on the one hand and the classical on the other, the
genres defined for Western literature should be valid for Mesopotamian
literature as well. This classification seems unavoidable at any rate, since
the Babylonians themselves never developed – or at least did not write
down – an *Ars Poetica*; nor do the occasionally indicated titles of literary
works give us a clue to a native classification. These titles sometimes
identify their function, sometimes their mode of recitation, and sometimes simply reflect a librarian's interest in their proper shelving.

Excluded from our presentation is, on the one hand, literature that is
datable to and historically belongs to earlier periods, such as the royal
inscriptions from the third and the second millennia, and certain polemic
or propaganda literature that also precedes the period under consideration, and on the other hand a certain number of poems that have not
found their way into the libraries. The reason why these poems were not
accepted into the literary 'canon' – probably established around 1200
B.C.[2] – is not clear, since the surviving material is often very similar to
comparable texts that were included.[3] Certain literary texts from the Old
Babylonian period, surviving only in a single copy, may have been
school exercises in composition and never entered the mainstream of
literature. Others, such as second-millennium versions of various epics,
were recast in a 'canonical form' and the early versions discarded, as
witness the various episodes of Gilgamesh that did not find their way
into the twelve-tablet recension known to us from Ashurbanipal's
library. Whether any of the literature was excluded on ideological
grounds, or because it reflected a religious sensibility no longer current,
cannot yet be established.

Although our purpose here is to give an overview of first-millennium
literature, we cannot escape the problem of literary periodization that
plagues interpreters of Babylonian literature.[4] It is generally assumed
that there is a single Standard Babylonian corpus, represented by late

---

[2] A 1169.
[3] For example, the Old Babylonian humorous poem At the Cleaner's (A 1080) exists in a single
copy only, while the Tale of the Poor Man of Nippur is known from copies from Sultantepe,
Ashurbanipal's library (A 1088), and on a Neo-Babylonian school tablet from Nippur (A 1074).
[4] A 1144.

copies, mainly those from royal or scribal libraries, but possibly, and in some cases almost certainly, going back to second-millennium originals. Excluded from this corpus are only those Old Babylonian or some later second-millennium texts that survive only in their original, early exemplar; these, for some reason, were not included in what is sometimes called the 'canon' but might perhaps better be called the 'scribal curriculum'.

While in this process of transmission there must have been historical developments from an earlier to a later and eventually a final version, it is only in the rarest of instances that these can be traced, unlike similar cases in Western literatures, where scholars of literary history or comparative literature often have sufficient data to study textual development or to follow transformations of a theme or poetic form within one culture, or across more than one.

A further consequence of this lack of historical perspective is our inability to date literary compositions on the grounds of style and language, and thereby to make any firm statement concerning the literary taste of a particular period.

All the libraries contain a mass of technical or scientific material, collected by the Mesopotamian scholars for their own use or copied in the course of their scribal training. These survive in several copies – usually up to six – in almost identical wording and even spelling; they may be regarded as the Babylonians' scholarly literature. This material includes not only the more narrowly scientific material, such as mathematics, astronomy, and technical manuals on glass making or wool dyeing, and such scholarly texts as sign lists and vocabularies (none of which will be considered here), but also texts used by the experts in divination or exorcism, that is, omen and magic literature, among which latter prayers, charms, and poems are sometimes also included.

Compared to the mass of such scholarly and technical literature, the number of compositions that are literary in a more narrow sense is very small (according to Oppenheim's estimate[5] about one-third of an estimated 1,500 tablets), but their visibility is that much greater, as they have been studied and translated over and over since their decipherment in the nineteenth century. To this group belong epics, myths, religious poems (hymns and prayers), philosophical or didactic literature (known as 'wisdom literature'), and an occasional political or propaganda text, usually in verse or, rarely, in prose. To the last group should be assigned the inscriptions of Babylonian and Assyrian kings which are, on the one hand, written in an elevated and, in Neo-Babylonian times, stilted and archaizing language and, on the other, exist in several copies. Only the royal inscriptions can be dated to the period under consideration; the

5 A 43, 13–18.

library texts, whether literary or scholarly, may and often do go back to second-millennium originals.

Oppenheim's estimates were based on the size of Ashurbanipal's library in Nineveh, assuming that the royal library contained at least a representative selection of the 'stream of tradition' texts. Indeed, we know from a letter of Ashurbanipal addressed to Shadunu, the temple administrator of Borsippa, that he asked for texts to be collected all over the realm and sent to Nineveh. The texts requested ('writings that are proper for royalty' – *malṭaru ša ana šarrūti ṭābu*) are, however, rituals and magical texts whose performance was required for the proper conduct of affairs, and thus illustrate only the scholarly and not the belletristic literature known or available in this period. A list recently published,[6] moreover, suggests that various scholars and experts were forced to donate tablets in their collections to the royal library. In this list, comprising a minimum of 1,441 clay tablets and 69 wax-covered polyptychs, or an estimated 2,000 tablets and 300 writing boards, only 10 tablets are inscribed with *belles-lettres*, the rest are professional works.

We will follow here the customary classification of literary texts into epics, hymns, fables, etc., although other, perhaps more promising ways of dividing the corpus could also be applied. One such division would separate literature centred around the king from literature centred around the gods and their cult. Another would be based on the difference between literary texts well established within the stream of tradition, as witnessed by many copies, and others that are extant in a single copy only and may have been composed for a specific occasion or a particular person. More difficult would be to separate the literature of the educated or upper classes, presumably centred around the court, from that of the common people, since the latter is not likely to have been committed to writing, and its existence can be inferred from scattered quotations only. Nor can the secular be sharply divorced from the religious, probably as much for the reason that it was matters concerning king, state, and cult that found their place in the stream of tradition as for the fact that the world view of Mesopotamia was closely interwoven with the ideas of religion.[7]

The relation of literary texts to their cultural context is still little known. Many of them were no doubt composed for the praise and entertainment of the king, and used on cultic occasions in which the king participated. Cultic performance was probably the *raison d'être* of various texts of religious content too, since prayers for the use of individuals other than the king are few and presumably secondarily adapted. Of the numerous narrative poems, several seem to imply that they were associated with apotropaic or prophylactic rituals, and thus to suggest that even such 'pure literature' was written down only when a practical occasion required it.[8]

These texts, which thus often represent a tradition of a thousand years or longer, remained in use even after Aramaic had replaced Akkadian as the spoken language and Aramaic writing on parchment had become the medium of everyday communication, for religious, scholarly, and display purposes; we need mention only the Akkadian versions of the trilingual Achaemenid inscriptions and certain rituals from the Seleucid period for which no earlier versions are known.

The libraries at Nineveh, Sultantepe, Babylon, and Uruk also contained a number of Sumerian–Akkadian bilingual texts. These are partly incantations against evil spirits and diseases or for some magic or apotropaic purpose, and partly lamentations and prayers. Rare are bilingual omens and hemerologies.[9] These bilingual texts are only in part older Sumerian compositions provided with an Akkadian translation; a number of them seem to have been composed in the first millennium in both languages, with the Akkadian as primary language and the Sumerian version secondary and often reflecting Akkadian syntax and poetic conventions. The interpretation of the bilingual texts therefore depends on the Akkadian version.

The reasons for the creation of these bilingual compositions elude us. It is possible that the exigencies of ritual and magic, in which certain prayers were traditionally recited in Sumerian (by the liturgist) while others were recited in Akkadian (by the patient), necessitated both composing unilingual Sumerian prayers and providing Akkadian ones with a Sumerian version;[10] in the case of laments and the like,[11] the reason may have been a revival of some genres from the period of the 'Sumerian renaissance' (c. 1800 B.C.) for a public to whom Sumerian was no longer easily intelligible.

The form of literary texts is normally verse, even though in defining it metre plays an insignificant role compared to other features. The question of the metre of Akkadian poetry has not yet been satisfactorily solved,[12] apart from the prosodic constraint of a trochaic verse-ending (long + short) which is sometimes achieved by apocopating a suffix or resorting to a grammatical form not common in prose. Yet a verse – a line of poetry – has its own characteristics which set it apart from prose.

---

[8] A 1161, 256f.

[9] See n. 124. Also known are bilingual addresses of praise to royal insignia (see A 1135, 57, and A 1131, 40ff), which formed part of the ceremony of 'mouth-washing' of the king.

[10] For example, in the ritual *bīt rimki*; see A 1113, 32.

[11] Bilingual texts found at Babylon are published in A 1162. See also A 1065.

[12] A 1084; A 1085; A 1093; A 1175.

These characteristics are reflected both in the way the line is written on the tablet and in the line's content and relation to surrounding lines.

While we are accustomed to recognizing a printed or written poem by the lines of uneven length aligned on the paper, often centred on the page, in the Mesopotamian scribal tradition all writing, whether prose or poetry, always extends to the right margin. Thus a blank space is often left in the middle or toward the end of a line to accommodate the varying numbers and sizes of the units of writing, the cuneiform signs. Conversely, no words are divided from one line to the next.[13] In poetic texts and even in high-style prose (as opposed, for instance, to private letters), not even larger units, such as phrases or clauses, are broken up, so that each line of writing is to a large extent self-contained. This practice also has the consequence that enjambement – an unexpected lack of coincidence between a syntactic unit and the (metrically defined) line – does not occur as a poetic device in Babylonian poetry.

Often several lines are united into groups set off by horizontal rulings. The smallest unit is a distich; there are other units, which may be considered stanzas, of four or more lines, a commonly used length being the ten-line stanza. While some stanzas indeed correspond to a division of the poem into sub-units, it is often the case that the rulings are for visual orientation only, and represent simple counters, such as often appear in the margin of every tenth line in longer and not exclusively literary compositions, and do not necessarily bear any relation to the articulation of the poem.

A similar visual divider is a blank space in the middle of a line, which should not be regarded as equivalent to a caesura in the classical sense. There is often, however, though not necessarily at the place of the blank, a break in the line, dividing it into two halves – two cola – with a parallel or chiastic syntactic structure.

It is in fact the building up of semantic units larger than one line or verse that is the most characteristic feature of Akkadian poetry, as it is also of other Semitic poetry such as Hebrew or Ugaritic. However, the characteristic is not necessarily of common Semitic origin; Sumerian poems too are characterized by parallelism between two lines that form a semantic unit, the extreme case being that the second line is the literal repetition of the first, with a proper name replacing, in the second line, the pronoun 'he' or 'she' of the first.[14]

---

13 Exceptionally words straddling two lines occur in the late Uruk copy of a diagnostic omen text (A 1110, Tablet XVI); see A 1184, no. 44.

14 Such parallelism of course also characterizes non-Near Eastern poetry; see J. J. Fox, 'Roman Jakobson and the comparative study of parallelism', in D. Armstrong and C. H. van Schoonereld (eds.) *Roman Jakobson: Echoes of His Scholarship* (Lisse, 1977) 59–90.

Of the formal trappings that we associate with poetry, rhyme is unknown to Mesopotamian poetry. An infrequently but cleverly used feature is the acrostic, which applies to the first sign – the first syllable – of the line. The acrostics are of two types: the initial sign is repeated at the beginning of each line of a stanza (cf. Psalm 119) (even when the sign does not have the same reading in each line, so that the acrostic is mainly for the eye, not the ear), or the initial sign occurs only once; in either case, the first sign of each successive line or stanza is to be read down from top to bottom to yield a phrase or sentence, usually containing the name of the writer, often accompanied by a pious phrase or blessing.

Acrostics may apply not only to the first sign of the line but equally to the last (whence the name telestich); as the line on a tablet is laid out much like a line in a printed book, with a justified right margin, the signs constituting the telestich also stand in a vertical row. The seven known acrostic poems are listed by R. F. G. Sweet,[15] who also established the fact that the seventh contains a telestich as well.

Midway between poetry and prose is the diction of royal inscriptions. Most of the time these do not exhibit any division into line units, and therefore may be considered simply elevated prose. Other royal inscriptions are written as if they were poems, for example Sargon's Eighth Campaign with each line a self-contained clause.

It is especially in the first millennium that royal inscriptions take a literary form. (The annals of Tukulti-Ninurta II, Ashurnasirpal, etc., recount the events of the king's campaign in a pared-down, repetitive form.) Beginning with Sargon II of Assyria the narrative expands to include descriptions of landscapes, foreign customs, and often vivid scenes of confrontation and dialogues. (A forerunner of this type of narrative is the account of the Elamite campaign of Nebuchadrezzar I on a boundary-stone.)[16]

Even the syntax and vocabulary of these narratives indicate their *recherché* character. New words appear, usually borrowed from Sumerian, and are especially frequent in Sargon and Sennacherib (*kirimāhu* and other compounds with Sumerian *mah*, *aladlammû*, *piriggallu*, etc.). Rare words that otherwise only occur in learned hymns abound.[17] The king recounts his inmost thoughts and feelings (couched in such terms as 'I said to myself').

The scribes study previous royal inscriptions (from Old Babylonian times) and often quote verbatim from them, especially in the period of antiquarianism in the Neo-Babylonian era, when the royal scribes imitate the sign-forms, the orthographic conventions, and the language of

---

[15] A 1177A.   [16] A 633, no. 6.   [17] A 1172.

illustrious royal predecessors from the Old Akkadian or Old Babylonian period,[18] and they compile lists of archaic cuneiform signs, even pictograms.[19]

II. NARRATIVE POETRY

1. *Myths and epics*

Among the narrative poems customarily classified as myths and epics,[20] the library of Ashurbanipal has preserved substantial parts or fragments of the major compositions. One group of these poems has divine protagonists, and essentially relates their rivalries; the story often culminates in special honour or status attained by some god, and so these poems often serve as aetiologies of the rise of a particular city god – and thus of his city – or purport to give a rationale for some calamity that has befallen men. For example, the myth of Anzu,[21] attested at Ashur, Nineveh, and Sultantepe, relates how Ninurta defeated the bat-like bird-monster Anzu and recaptured from him the 'Tablet of Destinies' that Anzu had stolen from Ellil, and thus reflects the added significance of the cult of Ninurta, whereas in the second-millennium version of the story the hero was Ningirsu. The Descent of Ishtar,[22] known from Ashur and Nineveh, and the story of Nergal and Ereshkigal, known from Nineveh, Sultantepe, and Uruk[23] (and in an early and much less elaborate version from El-Amarna), both deal with gods descending to the netherworld, the domain of one of their number, Queen Ereshkigal. The first is a reworking of the Sumerian poem of Inanna's Descent, possibly to accompany the rites of Dumuzi's yearly death and return from the netherworld to restore fertility to earth; the second ends with Nergal becoming Ereshkigal's husband and king of the netherworld, thus explaining how Nergal became associated with the netherworld.

As a counterpart to the descent of gods to the netherworld are the stories of mortals who ascend to heaven, whose heroes are Adapa,[24] the first of the Seven Sages, and Etana,[25] a legendary shepherd king of Kish. Both these poems, although usually classified as epics, have a humorous tinge, and may be the equivalent of the Middle French genre of fabliaux.[26] Their interpretation as myths has baffled scholars who have

---

[18] For bibliography see A 1163.   [19] For example, CT 5, pls. 7–16.

[20] For bibliography see A 1093, 26ff. For translations into English see A 44; in French substantial excerpts appear in A 1111. More recent editions with translations are cited under the individual works. See also A 1122 for fragments of Atrahasis, Irra and Anzu.

[21] A 1092.   [22] Edition with bibliography A 4 1, 95–111; philological commentary, *ibid.*, 143f.

[23] A 1089. A fragment from Uruk is published in A 1096, no. 1. See A 1183, 48ff.

[24] Latest edition A 1152.   [25] A 1126. Additional texts A 1071; A 1099; A 1110.

[26] A 1143.

sought, possibly unnecessarily, to attribute mythological significance to
a story that could find its place among Chaucer's tales. Adapa, through
his behaviour before the king of heaven, Anu, or following Ea's
mischievous advice, misses the opportunity of immortality, and with
him so does mankind. Whether this explanation of why men are mortal
was the main motif of the story is not certain, since its end is lost.
Similarly undecided is the outcome of Etana's flight, on the back of an
eagle, to heaven in quest of the plant of birth-giving. This story's parallel
in the Alexander romances was noticed long ago.[27] Apart from the main
motif, the childless Etana's journey heavenward to obtain the herb of
birth-giving, the Etana story contains an animal fable of the eagle and the
serpent; the tale of Adapa begins with Adapa breaking the wings of the
south wind, another fable-like motif. For both these fables there are
earlier versions: for Etana from Susa, for Adapa from El-Amarna, but
their relation to the first-millennium version is not clear. However, the
beginning of the Etana story seems to deal with a rivalry between the
supernal gods (Anunnaki) residing in heaven and the gods of lower rank
(Igigi) who built the city of Kish, where, according to the Sumerian king
list, kingship first descended from heaven.

This is the rivalry that forms the background of the Atrahasis epic, an
Old Babylonian composition that is also attested in several fragmentary
tablets in the Nineveh library in a recension close to its Old Babylonian
original.[28] When the Igigi gods, having been made subservient, cast
aside their tools and rebel, the god Ea, always ready with stratagems,
finds the solution: let the gods create Man, so that Man can take over the
burden of labour from the gods. Man is then created by the mother
goddess from clay mixed with the flesh and blood of a slain god.
However, as mankind multiplies and raises much clamour, the noise
becomes irksome to the gods. The gods decide to decimate mankind, by
sending first a plague, then a drought, and finally the flood, from which
Atrahasis alone, warned by Ea, escapes.

This is the earliest known version of the Flood story: it so closely
resembles the one told in the Bible that, when it was discovered in 1872
as part of the Gilgamesh epic, it made Mesopotamian literature famous
outside the small circle of Assyriologists. Gilgamesh is still the most
appealing work of ancient Near Eastern literature, as it deals with the
deepest human concerns: not only the longing for immortality which can
only be achieved by enduring fame (as not even Gilgamesh, although
two-thirds of divine lineage, can escape death), but also the friendship
between Gilgamesh and the semi-savage Enkidu who becomes his

[27] M. Lidzbarski, 'Zu den arabischen Alexandergeschichten', *ZA* 8 (1893) 266. See C. Settis-
Frugoni, *Historia Alexandri elevati per griphos ad aerem* (Studi Storici 80–2) (Rome, 1973) 48 n. 119.
[28] A 1124. For the first tablet see A 1174. See also A 1122.

companion in his exploits and whose death makes Gilgamesh face the fate that awaits him too. Thus this poem is a rare example of ancient literature that depicts the personal and emotional development – an *éducation sentimentale* – of a hero, with whom the reader can identify, because even this hero, like all humans, loses at the end to fate. The poem ends, as it began, not with the death of a hero but with the description of the ramparts of Uruk built by Gilgamesh; these will be his lasting achievements. In this respect, it singularly resembles the *Iliad*.[29] The Gilgamesh epic is also replete with intriguing episodes, many of which are still in a fragmentary state.

Unlike Atrahasis, the Epic of Gilgamesh has undergone standardization and revision so that its library exemplars greatly differ in content and form from the Old Babylonian versions, where these are known.[30] A promising area of research in literary history is the study of the changes through which these narrative poems have gone between their early versions (usually Old Babylonian) and their first-millennium versions.

The only well-known narrative poem for which no second-millennium antecedents exist is the Epic of Irra, which seems to have been composed to confront a particular historical situation[31] and which seeks to give an aetiological explanation for the troubles and epidemics of plague that had befallen Babylon in 765 B.C. Its explanation, attributing the misfortune to the absence of Marduk, Babylon's tutelary god, from his city, is a common motif in royal inscriptions and omen texts, but in them Marduk leaves the city because he is angry with its inhabitants, while here he is provoked by a ruse of the god of the plague, Irra. After having ravaged the city Irra, assuaged by his vizier Ishum, repents and pronounces blessings on Babylonia.

While other stories about the gods hardly ever deal with contemporary concerns, and even when the outcomes of the gods' victories affect mankind they do so in existential terms only, the poem about the Rage of Irra is uniquely and squarely set in the aftermath of a calamity that befell Babylon. A real sense of immediacy thus fills the fourth tablet of the Epic of Irra, a tablet that could be subtitled 'The Destruction of Babylon'. Descriptions of a destroyed city and temple are a common theme of Sumerian lamentations, but they present a static picture of houses in ruin and families decimated. The Irra epic presents the same theme in a dramatic mode, so far without parallel in Babylonian literature.

This composition shows the skill of a poet whose name, exceptionally, appears in the poem, in a unique epilogue describing how the poem was

---

[29] A 1149.
[30] Since the edition of R. Campbell Thompson (A 1060), a number of fragments, both Old Babylonian and later, have been identified. All the material known in 1982 has been incorporated in the German translation of A. Schott, revised by W. von Soden, A 1165.　　[31] A 901.

revealed to him in a dream, and how he neither added to nor withheld one line from what was dictated to him. The fiction of divine dictation aside,[32] the poet used, it seems, a cycle of texts concerned with the raging of the plague, i.e. Irra, in which the comradeship of Irra and Ishum was celebrated, and created an epic whose central theme was the contrast between the benevolence of Marduk and the wrath of Irra.

The Poem of Creation (enūma eliš)[33] is known equally only from first-millennium copies, though internal criteria indicate that it is somewhat older. It too has the common mythological theme of a theomachy – a threat to the gods by a rebellious creature, neither god nor man (thus remaining outside the world order as conceived in the mythology). The poem describes the times before creation and several succeeding generations of gods before the moment of crisis arrives: Tiamat, a salt-water monster, with her husband Kingu and the eleven monsters she has created, threatens the supernal gods, and the gods must find a champion to defeat her. This champion, in the standard version of the poem, is Marduk, who accepts the task on condition that he be made supreme god. Presumably an earlier version had as protagonist the god Ellil, just as later Assyrian versions replace Marduk with the god Ashur. After Marduk kills Tiamat and creates the universe from parts of her body, he is exalted in the divine assembly and given fifty names that are descriptive of his functions and powers. Thus the poem is a mythological tale, a theological justification of Marduk's rise to precedence, and a – somewhat cursory – account of the creation of the world (and mankind) at the same time. It is noteworthy that the creation of heaven and earth, of mountains and rivers, are dealt with in a few (22) lines only, while the creation of the heavenly bodies and their appointment to regulate the calendar is given in much greater detail (in about 44 lines), which attests the Babylonians' preoccupation with the calendar. The final quarter of the poem, that dealing with the fifty names of Marduk and their etymological explanation, is a famous and often-quoted example of Babylonian learning; it moreover received further learned commentaries.

Only in Tablet IV, at the centre of the seven-tablet poem, does the description of the battle between Marduk and Tiamat evoke other

---

[32] A device common in later antiquity, for example in the book of Thessalus of Tralles, who relates how Asclepius appeared to him in his temple of Diospolis (Thebes) and instructed him in iatromathematics, i.e. when and where medicinal plants must be gathered to be efficacious; see H.-V. Friedrich, *Thessalos von Tralles* (Meissenheim am Glan, 1968), and F. Cumont, 'Écrits hermétiques, II: Le médecin Thessalus et les plantes astrales d'Hermès Trismégiste', *Revue de Philologie* 42 (1918) 85–108.

[33] While the forthcoming edition by W. G. Lambert is in preparation the only text edition with translation is A 1109. New translation in A 1111, 36ff. English translation in A 44, 60ff and 501ff.

mythological epics, especially the battle between Ninurta and Anzu in the poem of Anzu.

At some point in history, the longer narrative poems were divided into a number of 'tablets' or 'books' consisting of around 150 lines. This may have happened about the turn of the first millennium, though this is merely a convenient chronological point to which no major historical or cultural events are attached; in fact, the possible dates are either of the two periods of Babylonian history which are characterized in the indigenous or in the Hellenistic tradition as major and eventful reigns, namely that of Nebuchadrezzar I (1125–1104 B.C.)[34] or that of Nabonassar (747–734). Later copyists mostly followed these divisions (although for special purposes other divisions may have existed, as with the use of the Erra epic on plague amulets).

The longest narrative poem, the Gilgamesh epic, is divided into twelve 'books'; Anzu into three or four; Irra into five, though the last is barely fifty lines long. Atrahasis is known to have had three tablets in the Old Babylonian version; the first-millennium copies do not preserve colophons. Other, shorter compositions are not known to have been divided into 'books'; these are the Descent of Ishtar, Nergal and Ereshkigal, and most likely Adapa and Etana. There exist other shorter stories, both mythological (Labbu, the Theology of Dunnu, etc.) and secular, the most famous being the recently discovered Tale of the Poor Man of Nippur. It is the first Mesopotamian story whose afterlife can be followed through the Thousand and One Nights and European folklore,[35] that is, whose literary connexions have not been solely the Old Testament, as is the case with the Flood story in Gilgamesh (and now also in Atrahasis). To be sure, identity of motifs with other narrative poems has been pointed out, such as the above-mentioned ascent of both Alexander and Etana, each on the back of an eagle; most comparisons between Mesopotamian and classical mythological themes[36] fit into categories so universal that direct influence cannot be adduced.

2. *Other narratives*

While most of the narrative texts discussed so far were composed with some theological purpose in mind – to exalt a particular god, to give an aetiological explanation for the rise of the city, a temple, or a cult – the theological propaganda that lies behind them seems to have meant little to their readers. Influencing the public politically could be more directly achieved through propagandistic literary works, clad in the form of narratives, the allusions of which must have been intelligible to their

[34] A 1118.   [35] A 1090.

[36] J. Fontenrose, *Python: A Study of Delphic Myth and Its Origins* (Berkeley and Los Angeles, 1959).

audience. To this group of texts probably belong some of the historical epics, though it is not possible to tell whether the propaganda they contain originated in the corridors of power – as a legitimation of the ruler's policies – or was directed against them.

Narrative poems with kings as protagonists also exist, though most of them are preserved in fragments only. They are of two types. One has recently been characterized as 'poetic autobiographies' or 'pseudo-autobiographies'.[37] What we have is less an 'autobiographical' account of an early king (Shulgi, Sargon) than a poem couched as a first-person narrative that could be styled *res gestae*. If we approach these poems as a genre defined by the fiction of a first-person narrator rather than as defined by that narrator's identity, such as a king or a god, they exhibit a particular structure that justifies uniting them as a genre. To this genre belong, in the first millennium, the so-called Birth Legend of Sargon[38] and the Marduk Prophecy,[39] both in poetic form, and the prose narrative of the mother of King Nabonidus,[40] whose service as priestess of the god Sin in Harran bespeaks a West Semitic connexion and links her autobiography to that of Idrimi, king of Alalakh, almost a thousand years earlier.[41]

The common formal characteristic of these texts is that they begin with the statement 'I am so-and-so', as opposed to royal inscriptions which begin with a direct address to the god or with a long circumstantial clause introduced by 'When . . .'. After some autobiographical material a central episode is developed; the end is a message to a future king. In the 'Birth Legend of Sargon' the central episode is fragmentary, but seems to deal with the king's accomplishments as favourite of Ishtar; in the autobiography of the mother of Nabonidus, the emphasis is on the reconciliation of the god Sin with Babylon and his choice of Nabonidus to be its ruler, and thus on the legitimation of Nabonidus.

The second type of texts also dealing with an episode of history with a famous king of the past as protagonist, but not necessarily couched in the first person or beginning with 'I am . . .' has been named '*narû* literature'.[42] The texts also end with a lesson to a future ruler. Their heroes are the kings of the Akkad dynasty, Sargon and Naram-Sin,[43] and their composition dates back to the second millennium, although some episodes are preserved in later versions.[44]

Some of these narratives, especially those with a lesson to be drawn for

---

[37] A 1083; the term 'poetic autobiographies' is proposed on p. 8. Grayson proposed the term 'pseudo-autobiography' in A 26 and A 1082, 187.   [38] Latest edition A 1128.
[39] A 1056.
[40] Translation, with bibliography, by A. L. Oppenheim in A 44, 560ff. For bibliography concerning the historical implications see A 5 II, 72ff.
[41] A 1166. Recent reinterpretation: A 1067.   [42] A 1091, 19.   [43] A 1094, 25f.
[44] A 1079; A 1087; A 1091, 65ff; A 1116; A 1138; A 1180, 48.

the ruler, no doubt had political propaganda purposes. While in many cases it is impossible to tell what the situation was that occasioned the composition of such pieces, since the tendentiousness is necessarily disguised, it could be suggested of a few works only that they contain veiled allusions against the misuse of power. Only one of these, the Babylonian Advice to a Prince,[45] exists in two exemplars; its timeliness is illustrated by a letter written from Babylonia to the king to warn him of the consequences of abolishing the exemptions of the three free cities Sippar, Nippur, and Babylon. The other two, the Vision of the Netherworld and the Verse Account of Nabonidus, have each survived in one exemplar only;[46] they spell out, just as does Advice to a Prince, a lesson for the king, and in that resemble the *narû* literature, but they are not composed according to the formal constraints prevailing in that genre. These works were composed for the king and the court, in order to influence them, as their 'library' copies and the allusions to them show, and were not, for example, subversive or clandestine literature. They also differ from the propaganda texts emanating from the king's entourage, since the royal inscriptions which could be so classified, and which moreover purport to be factual accounts, are written in prose.

Similarly for the king were composed his own – and not some ancestor's – *res gestae*, which take different forms in Assyria[47] and in Babylonia.

No doubt for the king's entertainment were composed humorous poems, such as the Tale of the Poor Man of Nippur, as the inclusion of the episode of borrowing a chariot from the king shows.[48]

III. OTHER POETRY

Poetic works without a narrative plot may be classified as hymns, prayers, and magic incantations. Only the last preserve some of the flavour of folk poetry; hymns and prayers are predominantly learned.

Hymnic poetry of the first millennium differs greatly in its formal structure from Old Babylonian hymns. In essence religious, hymns are addressed to gods and goddesses. The genre of temple hymns and hymns to kings, much cultivated in the early second millennium, mostly written in Sumerian,[49] is hardly represented, with the exception of a hymn to

---

[45] The title formerly given to it, 'Fürstenspiegel', makes the connexion between this work and the medieval and oriental genre of *Speculum principis*.

[46] Advice to a Prince: A 1115, 110–15; see also A 1160. 'A Vision of the Netherworld': translation by E. A. Speiser in A 44, 109–10. A Verse Account of Nabonidus: translation by A. L. Oppenheim in A 44, 312–15. See A 422, 198f; A 1057; A 1173.   [47] See pp. 209 and 305.

[48] A 1088. See also A 1066 and A 1090.

[49] An Old Babylonian hymn to King Gungunum in Akkadian is published as A 1180, 41.

Arbaᵓil and a hymn to the city and temple of Borsippa;[50] hymns to kings of Assyria, with the exception of a hymn to Ashurbanipal,[51] seem to cluster in the late second millennium.

As opposed to the shorter and more terse Old Babylonian hymns, these later hymns (although their exact date of composition is not known) tend to be long; especially favoured is the hymn of two hundred lines.[52] Their length immediately suggests that they were not intended for oral performance. The most famous of these is the hymn to Shamash; there is a hymn to Ishtar consisting of 237 lines, and to Nabu of 226 to 232 lines. The 200-verse hymn to Gula is a composition in which the goddess speaks her self-praise, and through this fiction it is related rather to the self-praise of Ishtar and the self-praise of Marduk (for which see below). The two hundred lines of the Shamash hymn can be broken down neither into twenty ten-line stanzas, nor into one hundred distichs; nor can similar divisions be made in the over two hundred lines of the hymns to Nabu, Ishtar, and the queen of Nippur in spite of the rulings in the Ishtar hymn after every tenth line or in the Shamash, Marduk, and Nabu hymns after every second line on the tablet, since these rulings, as mentioned above, are for visual orientation. Nevertheless, the formal device of repetition and parallelism is evident in them, and it is rather these groups of parallel verses that articulate the poems.

The central topic of a hymn is the praise of the god to whom it is addressed; this praise is spoken in the first person by the worshipper, who was no doubt the king for whom the poet composed the work. While it is true that standard and often stereotyped phrases recur in the description of the god's power and mercy, the emphasis on the god's concern toward man as much as the description of his hierarchical position among the gods gives us an insight into the way man's relation to god was conceived.

Nowhere does this appear with more poignancy than in the hymn to Shamash, the sun-god and god of justice *par excellence*. Its message is that justice and fairness are pleasing to Shamash, and dishonesty is abhorrent to him. This ethical message is expounded in a series of vignettes about persons from all walks of life who exemplify just and honest behaviour and are rewarded by Shamash or, conversely, act dishonestly and are punished. This central topic is elaborated in antithetical distichs (or occasionally, longer units); the frame of the poem, an address to Shamash describing his omniscience – as the luminary who sees all – also shows a sophisticated arrangement, as the preamble speaks of Shamash as the sun

[50] A 1072; A 1104. [51] A 1181.
[52] A 1114; also the Shamash hymn A 1115, 121–38; the Ishtar hymn, A 1161; the Nabu hymn, A 1172; the Gula hymn, A 1119; the hymn to the queen of Nippur, A 1123.

which rises ever higher over the land in its daily course, and the end of the poem returns to this cosmic topic, but depicts the functions of the sun-god as regulating the calendar and the seasons. The poem thus deals both with the sun's course over the day and with its course over the year.

The elaborations that such hymns underwent in the first millennium can be observed in the hymn to Ishtar, for which earlier versions are known.[53] The late texts retain the articulation of the hymn by a series of refrains (such as 'look on me with favour!' and 'how long yet') and strophes composed of lines all beginning with 'mercy!', but expand both the praise of the goddess and the entreaties of the supplicant by inserting at such places further strophes or lines which conform to the pattern. Characteristic of these hymns is a certain artificial diction, a vocabulary of rare and *recherché* terms, a striving to avoid ordinary or everyday words and phrases.

Similar in style but employing a different poetic fiction are those hymns in which the god or goddess speaks in self-praise. The theme of self-praise (or, as it is sometimes called, self-predication) is a common one in historical texts, in which the king boasts of his achievements and the favour bestowed on him by the gods. It is, however, only in the first millennium that self-praise by the deity enters Akkadian literature – possibly as a sort of revival of earlier Sumerian poetry in which such self-praises are more frequent. The longest and most completely preserved is the self-praise of Gula.[54] It is, as has been mentioned, one of the 200-verse hymns (divided by rulings which do not follow the internal structure of the poem) in which strophes of Gula's self-presentation as the goddess of a particular city alternate with ones in praise of the god who is her spouse in each of her many manifestations. An unusual feature of the self-praise of the goddess Nanâ is the fact that the first line of each strophe is in Sumerian.[55] In the rest of the strophe she describes herself under the names by which she is known in various cities of Babylonia.[56] That other hymns of such self-praise existed can be inferred from the *incipit* cited in the catalogue of songs from Ashur, 'I am the most venerable goddess of all.'[57] In contrast, the self-praise of the king with which some royal inscriptions begin – as opposed to a hymn to the god to whom the king's pious work is dedicated – although couched in elevated language, is in prose. In prose also are the two self-presentations of Marduk and of Shulgi.[58] Their depiction of the god Marduk's or the deified king Shulgi's impact on the events of the world is closely related

[53] For bibliography and both an Akkadian and a Hittite version from Boğazköy see A 1161.

[54] Edited in A 1119; a duplicate to lines 101ff is Sm. 1036. A self-praise of Ishtar, incompletely preserved, is A 322, no. 306 + 331. [55] A 1156.

[56] A bilingual 'self-predication' of Inanna-Ishtar begins, similarly, with the goddess enumerating the cities and temples in which she is queen; see A 1076, no. 46, and a duplicate to the first forty lines in A 184, no. 27. [57] A 322, no. 158 vi 8 and 10. [58] A 1056.

in content and form to the category of texts termed prophecies or oracles, and these in turn have a close affinity to omen texts, as they depict, sometimes in alternation, evil times and blessed times that befall the land. Such texts may in fact have drawn their imagery from omen apodoses, for which see below.

IV. PRAYERS

Prayers have many affinities with hymns, so that often it is a subjective matter in which category to classify a religious poem. Prayers are characterized by greater space and emphasis devoted to the petition, although such a petition for the welfare of the worshipper often appears at the ends of hymns too, and by a certain penitential tone that evokes the psalms of the Bible. They are usually preceded by the Sumerian word *én* (Akkadian *šiptu*), conventionally translated 'incantation', as a sort of title; indeed, many of them functioned in a variety of magic and apotropaic rituals. The purpose or setting of these prayers is usually stated in the subscript, which specifies that it is a 'recitation [*ka.inim.ma*] on the occasion of . . .' Certain motifs are typical of these prayers: the self-presentation of the supplicant; the description of the calamity that distresses him; the appeal to the deity for help; the promise of praise or sacrifice for all future time.[59] Many such prayers exist in a standard form, with the name of the supplicant left open, so that it can be supplied from case to case. Of those in which the name is filled in, it is often the king's name that appears (from Sargon to Sin-sharra-ishkun).[60] So it is likely that they were composed for the king, perhaps for a particular occasion, but were also available to private persons seeking the god's mercy and help. While many such prayers consist of stereotyped phrases – partly because such phrases were required by the accompanying ritual – and thus for the modern reader seem repetitious and hackneyed, the form could not have evolved without a basis in personal religiosity and deep emotion such as is reflected in the imagery and diction, as we have learned to appreciate in the penitential psalms of the Old Testament.

It is now known that Sumerian parallels to these prayers exist, although there is no evidence that the Sumerian versions were actually earlier than the Akkadian;[61] they may have been secondarily composed as a counterpart to those Sumerian prayers that were to be recited in the course of various rituals.

Prayers are addressed not only to deities but, in the course of magic operations, to the substances that are used in the performance, such as salt or tamarisk, and to the fire that is used in burning these substances or

---

[59] A 1129.   [60] See A 1129, 54f.   [61] A 1120.

in fumigation. Prayers are also addressed to stars and planets. While some address the astral manifestation of the deity, the main purpose of others is to draw down the celestial power inherent in the celestial body to make the magic operation or its ingredients more efficacious, and similarly to infuse with its power a medication prepared in a certain prescribed way.

The stars – the gods of the night – are also addressed before the performance of an extispicy to ask that a reliable answer be shown through the *exta* of the lamb that will be slaughtered at dawn. Most such late prayers address the gods of divination, Shamash and Adad; there are, however, first-millennium versions of the earlier, Old Babylonian, addresses to the gods of the night. The diviner in solitary vigil while city and countryside around him are in deep sleep is a *topos* that, in spite of the prayer's standard phraseology, lends itself to a lyric tone rare in other prayers.[62] Comparison of the earlier and later prayers shows that later poets had a predilection for greater elaboration and repetitions, while the Old Babylonian versions show greater restraint.

In some rituals, during the performance of which both the magical expert and the person on whose behalf the ritual is performed recited certain prayers, the professional expert – the exorcist, the lamentation priest, etc. – often has to recite a prayer in Sumerian (which may or may not be provided with an interlinear Akkadian translation), but the lay participant, even if he is the king, recites prayers only in Akkadian. This practice does not tell us much about the survival of Sumerian language, culture, and religion, since most such Sumerian prayers seem to be secondary, that is, translated from the Akkadian, and thus the fact that they are recited in Sumerian may only indicate the preference for a traditional language in a liturgical setting, as is still the case for Latin or Syriac in many Churches today.

V. WISDOM LITERATURE

A special group of learned poetry is known as 'wisdom literature', by analogy with the 'wisdom' books of the Bible. Under this name, however, a variety of types needs to be distinguished. One group, labelled 'precepts and admonitions',[63] continues an old Sumerian tradition, whether these admonitions are words of practical wisdom affecting everyday man or warnings given to the king if he does not rule wisely and fairly.[64] Another group, fables, includes disputations between inanimate things (trees or cereals) or between animals; still another comprises collections of proverbs, usually very difficult to understand

---

[62] A 1146.   [63] A 1115, 92ff.   [64] See p. 306.

because of their terse formulation and sometimes riddle-like nature.[65] All these have Sumerian and Old Babylonian forerunners. While the 'fables' – or rather, disputations between animals and inanimate objects – continue a Sumerian tradition, some rare shorter pieces are closer to the fables known from classical and Oriental literature.[66]

Newly composed, or at least without known earlier material, are the three compositions known as the Poem of the Righteous Sufferer, the Theodicy, and the Dialogue of Pessimism. The first of these is a monologue and the other two are dialogues. Some of the themes of these poems are also found in second-millennium texts, both from Babylonia and from Ras Shamra (Ugarit),[67] the Old Babylonian in a dialogue form, the Ras Shamra poem in the preserved part containing a monologue only, but possibly containing in the now lost ending an answer to the speaker.

All three poems treat the question of the sufferings that befall a man who believes he does not deserve such a divine punishment, and thus broach the question of the moral problem of the just suffering while the sinner prospers.[68]

The philosophical content – some aspects of which also infuse prayers, especially those which are comparable to the penitential psalms – makes these poems the earliest examples of reflective literature, which in Babylonia manifests itself only as poetry, never as prose, and moreover takes the typical form of 'dramatic monologue' (Nougayrol's term)[69] or dialogue, since thoughts and deliberations are normally expressed by speaking to oneself and conflicting arguments are usually couched in dialogue form.

Self-expression, then, could naturally take the pattern of this accepted way of communication, direct speech; only instead of addressing an interlocutor or messenger, the speaker addresses himself, introducing his monologue with 'I said to my heart' or the like, or creates a fancied interlocutor, simply designated as 'friend', to express his thoughts and feelings. This friend's role is hardly ever more than to utter a few comforting words. Only the 'Dialogue of Pessimism'[70] contains a verbal exchange between the servant and his master; for this reason it has been characterized not only as a humorous dialogue[71] but also as the most ancient mime.[72]

What distinguishes these 'wisdom texts' from other inner monologues or non-fictive dialogues is the artful language and abstruse vocabulary, which makes them difficult of access not only to us but obviously also to the reader they addressed. Both the Righteous Sufferer

---

[65] A 1115, chapters. 7–9, pp. 150–279. [66] A 1115, 216ff iii 50–4; see A 1054, and A 1177.
[67] A 1139; A 1142. [68] A 1171. [69] A 1143. [70] A 1115, chapter 6, pp. 139–49.
[71] A 1176. [72] A 1095.

and the Theodicy were commented on by Babylonian scholars, thus putting them on a par with other such learned texts as scientific literature (especially omens) and the Poem of Creation.

VI. SECULAR POETRY

Purely lyrical and secular poetry – love songs, awe or pleasure *vis-à-vis* nature, or work songs that according to some are at the origin of poetry – are not found in cuneiform sources. That does not mean that such poems did not exist: there is even a special term for the work song of the ploughman (*alala*); songs like these, however, were not expected to be written down. Descriptions of nature, rare as they are, appear in relations of royal campaigns or in some conjurations.[73]

As for love poems, we would surmise their existence from catalogues which list the first lines of these poems, for example, 'Darling, I spend the night awake for you'; 'Young man, ever since I beheld you'; 'Away, sleep! I want to embrace my lover'. However, as a recently found complete poem which is listed in this catalogue shows,[74] this love poetry – possibly all of the poems known to us only from their first lines cited in the catalogue – had its framework, at least as a fiction, in the domain of divine lovers, especially Ishtar and Dumuzi. Whether these songs were reserved for cultic occasions or were attributed to the religious sphere only secondarily (much like the 'Song of Songs') is not known.[75] Similarly, elegiac poems about the death of a beloved place these emotions in relation to the death of Dumuzi, with the single exception of an Assyrian poem. This elegy, preserved in a single Neo-Assyrian copy, may go back to somewhat earlier, Middle Assyrian times, as some of its linguistic features suggest.[76] It is a plaint of a dead woman, a woman who died in childbirth, who mourns how death has separated her from the husband she loved, in answer to a question by an unnamed speaker who asks why she drifts about like a boat cast loose. It is the principal metaphor of a ship cast adrift, a *topos* of Sumerian origin but also encountered in Akkadian incantations,[77] which touches our Western sensibility conditioned by such images in poetry. While a close analysis of the structure of the poem can illuminate its poetic qualities, still there is no poem comparable in Assyrian or Babylonian literature that would help us place this elegy among poetry of its time. Other poetic genres are

---

[73] Personification of nature, expressed in the *topos* of vegetation and watercourses bewailing the death of a friend or family member, is found in the lament of Gilgamesh over Enkidu and in a funerary inscription of an Assyrian king (A 1070, no. 12, and A 1168; see A 1134).

[74] A 1053.   [75] A 1121.   [76] A 1158, 85–93.

[77] E.g., 'The boat is held fast at the quay of death, the barge is held fast at the quay of suffering'; seeking to bring 'the rope of the boat to the safe mooring place, the rope of the barge to the quay of life'. Cuneiform text in A 1105 III, no. 248 ii 51–2 and ii 58ff.

preserved only embedded in the narrative literature. A lament over the dead is exemplified by Gilgamesh's lament over the dead Enkidu.[78]

The only poetry that may represent a purely secular or folk poetry, that is, poetry in no way dependent on the official cult or the royal court for inspiration, model, or tone, is possibly found embedded in magical and medical texts, as incantations or charms addressing the evil to be exorcised, or tracing the emergence of a certain evil as the end product of the creation of earth and its plants. They are characterized by repetition or concatenation, devices that also characterize folk poetry of other cultures,[79] though recorded much later. They have been preserved because they became a part of the technical or scientific literature which had its place in royal or scholarly libraries, and thus give us a glimpse of the style of songs that may have been current in the oral literature.

VII. RITUALS

It was also the first millennium that developed, if not the cultic import of long and elaborate rituals that often extend over several days, at least the scrupulous and detailed description of the happenings; the liturgical actions and the pertinent prayers or exorcisms to be recited are enumerated, although these latter may only be cited by their *incipit*. The majority of them, just like the earlier ones, involve the king, again suggesting that those that are not explicitly directed to the king may also have originated in court surroundings and eventually have been made available, or adapted, to private persons.[80]

The most famous is the New Year's ritual,[81] a series of events that took ten days, during which Marduk re-entered his temple in Babylon in a procession, and his son Nabu journeyed there from Borsippa. The ritual reaffirmed the king's mandate to rule. During its celebration the Poem of Creation (*enūma eliš*) was recited, and probably a re-enactment of Marduk's victory over Tiamat described in that poem was performed.[82]

Rituals also preceded the king's setting out on a campaign – an annual event in Assyria throughout most of its history – or other expedition; a ritual before setting out to cross the desert (*edin.na.dib.bi.da*) may have been available to any traveller.[83]

Rituals accompanied the digging of the foundations and building of a house, the digging of a well, and other secular activities. The borderline

---

[78] A 1134.

[79] R. Austerlitz, *Ob-Ugric Metrics: The Metrical Structure of Ostyak and Vogul Folk-Poetry* (Helsinki, 1958).

[80] From second-millennium Babylonia there is only one such ritual text, from Mari; from Assyria, a royal ritual; and from the Hittite empire a number of elaborate rituals, in Hittite.

[81] F. Thureau-Dangin, 'Le rituel des fêtes du nouvel an à Babylone', in A 1178, 127–54.

[82] A 1117.   [83] A 1073; A 1132; A 1179, for which see also A 1061.

between rituals designed to make the undertaking successful and those performed to avert an evil portended by an ominous event, such as an uncommon happening in the household (listed in the omen series *šumma ālu* and *šumma izbu*), is often difficult to draw, since among the *namburbi* rituals (apotropaic rituals designed to ward off such portended evil) may be found some designed to accompany the digging of wells or to secure brisk trade for a tavern.[84]

There are also elaborate rituals specifically related to the cult. Only one ritual is known for building temples,[85] apart from the narratives in royal inscriptions of the ceremonies accompanying the laying of the first brick (often carried by the king himself or the crown prince) or the preparation of the mortar, which is ceremonially made into an admixture of aromatic herbs and precious stones. A group of rituals deals with consecrating the divine statue. The image of the god has to undergo the 'opening of the mouth' ceremony (preceded by the washing of the statue's mouth), for, so the texts tell us, without it 'the god cannot smell incense, cannot eat bread, or drink water'.[86]

This variety of rituals designed to protect the king against ills portended by signs, or to make the outcome of his enterprise successful (whether campaigns against the enemy or conquests), or to propitiate the gods by dedicating to them sanctuaries, statues, and paraphernalia – this variety, combined with the rise in popularity of such omen categories (astrology, divination from the *exta*) as predominantly deal with portents of public significance, suggest that in the first millennium the royal courts were the *locus* of scholars whose activities centred around the king and his entourage. Their role at the court of Esarhaddon has been elucidated by Parpola,[87] their internal rivalries by Oppenheim.[88] The distribution of the evidence does not permit us to decide whether these activities began only under the Sargonids, or whether they can be projected back to Nabonassar and to Babylonia as well as Assyria, and it may of course also distort the picture emerging from the extant textual material, much of which obviously survived in royal or scholarly libraries. Other, non-court-centred activities may never have been recorded in writing, or if so are not so far recovered.

Especially numerous from Seleucid Uruk are texts designed as instructions for rituals. The most important one – the New Year's ritual – was mentioned above; there are also rituals for a particular undertaking: to prepare the *lilissu* drum,[89] or to avert the consequences of a

---

[84] A 1062.

[85] For bibliography and edition of some of these texts, see A 1055 and A 1184, no. 16.

[86] A 1070, 120:2 and parallels. An edition of the mouth-washing rituals is being prepared by C. B. F. Walker.   [87] A 77 *passim*, esp. pp. xiv–xxi and 448ff.   [88] A 1040.

[89] A 1178.

lunar eclipse[90] and to purify the king after such an event.[91] All these rituals are instructions for a particular behaviour, offerings to the gods or spirits; often they not only prescribe prayers to be recited, but also include these prayers among the instructions. They are, therefore, an additional source for our knowledge of prayers and incantations that are otherwise known from prayer collections outside rituals.

The exorcist and the diviner also recite prayers before they set about the performance of their duties; most famous is the 'prayer to the gods of the night'.[92]

Besides prophylactic rituals, there exist apotropaic rituals against the evil power of demons and sorcerers.[93] An array of evil demons – often referred to as the seven evil demons – and malevolent spirits of the dead, who must roam about because they lie unburied or have received no funerary offering, are exorcised with elaborate prayers and incantations. These texts are usually bilingual, Sumerian–Akkadian; they have been serialized in a composition known in Sumerian as *udug.hul* (Akkadian *utukkū lemnūtu*).[94]

Those against sorcerers and sorceresses are collected in a series called *maqlû*, 'Burning',[95] and involve a nocturnal ceremony in which effigies of the sorcerers are burned or melted in fire. Another collection with a similar name, *šurpu*, 'Burning',[96] is not directed against any particular external evil power but is conceived as a purification ritual for a man's sins. Whether its duration was one night, like that of *maqlû*, or according to some other disposition, is not certain since the tablet which gives the summary of the directions – the so-called ritual tablet – is not preserved in full, unlike that for *maqlû*. This ritual, after long series of enumerations of the man's possible infractions of divine or moral laws, and of the various evils that in consequence befell him, also ends with the burning of substances that sympathetically represent the man's sins. *Šurpu* ends with a series of prayers in Sumerian addressing the paraphernalia used in the ritual, such as the fire and the date palm branch.

The list of transgressions of *šurpu*, a list that has been dubbed the 'confession of sins', and the prayers that these various exorcistic and magical texts contain make them a source for understanding Babylonian religion as much as prayers and hymns outside such magic settings. The

---

[90] BRM 4, no. 6; edited A 1070, no. 24.

[91] See A 1113 and the latest duplicate from Uruk in A 1184, no. 12.   [92] See p. 310.

[93] An edition of the three-tablet series of incantations and rituals against the female demon Lamashtu is being prepared by W. Farber to replace the old edition, A 1136.

[94] Only parts of the series are available in modern editions, e.g., A 1081; previous edition of the then known pieces, A 1059. For bibliography see A 5 III, 88f. Some of the bilingual incantations have Sumerian forerunners from the Old Babylonian period; see A 1075.

[95] Edited, with German translation, A 1130. For analysis of its content and structure see A 1050.

[96] A 1154.

difference between them seems to be the occasion; apotropaic rituals fall under the competence of the exorcist – and are listed among the handbooks that he is to know in order to exercise his craft[97] – while the temple singer and other temple personnel propitiate the divinity with cultic acts and recitations that are prescribed in other manuals and collections.

VIII. MEDICINE

Similarly blurred are the distinctions between magic and medicine. While scientific medicine was practised by the same class of experts as various magic rituals, it was couched in that most rigorously scientific form envisaged by the ancients, the omen collection. Omens may be considered scientific because, first, they are based on observation of facts, whether these are changes in the human *milieu* or among the stars in heaven, and more important, because they rigorously exhaust, in the best casuistic manner, all possibilities and variations according to the position and the characteristic, such as colour, direction, and the like, of the phenomenon observed. One such class of phenomena, the appearance and behaviour of a sick person, fell under the competence of the *āšipu*, and his diagnosis was couched in the form of omens, with the description of the symptom constituting the protasis, and the prognosis the apodosis. These are the diagnostic omens, of which we have one small piece from the Middle Babylonian period.[98] They differ from the medical texts proper in that they do not prescribe, but only diagnose the disease and predict its outcome or, in the case of pregnant women, the viability and sex of the child. These texts served the *āšipu* who observed the patient and also derived his prognosis from ominous events encountered on the way to the patient's house; these were of the nature enumerated in the *šumma ālu* series, to which it may have been an appendix.

The *āšipu* was not the expert who treated the sick person; that task fell to the medical practitioner, the *asû*, who had at his disposal a set of therapeutic handbooks whose chapters dealt with diseases affecting a particular part of the body.[99]

Just as the diagnostic omens are arranged in a sequence from 'top to toe', *lit.* 'the crown of the head to the nails [of the feet]' (*ultu muḫḫi adi*

---

[97] This is the 'exorcist's handbook', A 322 no. 44; see A 1058.

[98] PBS 2/2 104. The canonical series was edited by R. Labat, A 1110. Of the new material excavated or identified subsequently, note especially the catalogue published in A 1098 and the commentaries from Uruk published in A 1096, nos. 27–42.

[99] An overview, with bibliographical notes, is found in A 1148, 645f. See also A 1052.

ṣupri),[100] so the therapeutic books also seem to have been arranged in a similar sequence.[101]

These medical handbooks are structured much as the Greek ones are, comprising the description of the symptoms of the illness (the indication) and the prescription of the appropriate remedy, describing both the substances to be used and the manner of preparing and administering them to the patient.[102] They would provide invaluable information about the history of medicine, were it not for the fact that many of the plants and other substances entering into the medication cannot be identified with certainty, and even the terms describing the ailment are often imperfectly understood.

The medical practitioner was, however, not only physician and, most likely, his own pharmacist or herbalist as well, but also knowledgeable in such religious and ritual matters as were necessary to make his cure efficacious. Indeed, these therapeutic texts are interspersed with prayers and invocations to the gods[103] and, even more strikingly, with prayers and rituals (including the confection of amulets) involving the celestial bodies, thus indicating that Hellenistic iatromathematics, that is, the use of astrology in medical treatment, had its precursor in Mesopotamia.[104]

A special subsection of both the diagnostic and the therapeutic handbooks was devoted to gynaecology, the former predicting the outcome of pregnancy as well as dealing with the diagnosis of infants, the latter concerned not only with obstetrics but also with treating sterility, and including tests for pregnancy.[105]

To this corpus of medical lore belong also the pharmaceutical handbooks: the series *uruanna*,[106] a two-column list of therapeutic herbs, minerals, and even fats and other substances that can enter a prescription, giving either their equivalents in Akkadian if the name of the substance is foreign – Sumerian, or from another foreign language such as 'Subarian' (probably Hurrian) and Elamite – or the equivalent substances that may be substituted for them. Other handbooks, *šammu*

---

[100] Not from 'head to toe', just as the Hippocratic books also deal with remedies for diseases starting with the 'crown of the head'; see Paulus Aegineta, *Preface*, translated by Francis Adams (1844) I, p. xix.

[101] Several medical texts have been edited by R. Campbell Thompson in *Proceedings of the Royal Society of Medicine* 17 (1924) and 19 (1926), *JRAS* (1937), *AJSL* 47 (1930), etc.; a new edition to replace the incomplete and partially outdated previous editions is expected from F. Köcher in the series *Die babylonische-assyrische Medezin*. For a brief overview, with bibliography, see A 1101.

[102] D. Goltz, *Studien zur altorientalischen und griechischen Heilkunde: Therapie – Arzneibereitung – Rezeptstruktur* (Sudhoffs Archiv Beiheft 16) (Wiesbaden, 1974).

[103] In certain medical texts the disease itself, or the evil power thought to be at its root, is addressed.   [104] A 1159.   [105] A 1077; A 1157.

[106] An edition is being prepared by F. Köcher.

šikinšu and *abnu šikinšu*, give more detailed descriptions of the vegetable or mineral substance,[107] often in terms of other plants and stones just like the Hellenistic and medieval alchemical handbooks, and also indicate the ailment for which they are suitable.

IX. SCHOLARLY LITERATURE

Scholarly and scientific activity, to which the above-mentioned lists of plants, and other descriptions of plants and animals, belong, is also manifested in a large number of scholia, commenting both on scientific texts and on difficult literary texts. Among literary texts, commentaries are made on texts of religious or theological complexity, such as the Poem of Creation, and on texts which are written in an erudite language, replete with rare words, such as the 'Righteous Sufferer' and the 'Theodicy'. The scholarly texts commented on are the omens, *maqlû*, *šurpu*, and medical texts. No commentaries exist on narrative texts (such as epics), nor on hymns and prayers. Lexical lists that originated in the second millennium to provide equations of Sumerian and Akkadian words – either to provide glosses for the no-longer intelligible Sumerian literature and vocabulary, or to teach Sumerian to the Akkadian-speaking scribes – continued to be copied and expanded in the first millennium,[108] and additional types of lexical lists were created: a type called group vocabularies[109] that list words in groups of homonyms or synonyms, and the so-called synonym lists[110] that give common equivalents to rare or foreign, mostly West Semitic, words. Moreover, the old lexical lists were provided with commentaries; the two major types of commentaries are those adding a third column with more recent or more common Akkadian words to the existing two-column Sumerian–Akkadian word list (HAR-gud),[111] and more elaborate scholia that not only add further Akkadian equivalents to the Sumerian–Akkadian lists, but also explain them in terms of etymology, real or fancied, or provide a set of terms that furnish the link, again correct or fictitious, between two terms that figure as equivalents in the original list.[112]

Similar scholia – arranged as either a simple list of equations or, more elaborate, adducing an explanation for the equation – were compiled for other scientific texts, such as medical texts[113] and above all omens (liver

---

[107] No complete edition of the various fragments is available. Excerpts from *šammu šikinšu* are quoted in A 1102 and A 1153; from *abnu šikinšu* in A 1125, 152ff.

[108] See, for example, the remarks of M. Civil in *MSL* 14, 160ff.

[109] See I. L. Finkel, *MSL* 16, 4f and 23ff; A. Cavigneaux, *MSL* 17, 1f; and M. T. Roth, *MSL* 17, 127ff. [110] Parts of synonym lists are edited in A 1097 and A 1167.

[111] They are edited, along with the Sumerian–Akkadian HAR-ra vocabularies, in *MSL* vols. 4–12. [112] For example, the commentaries to Aa, see M. Civil, *MSL* 14, 158–60.

[113] A good example is the commentary 11N-T3, edited in A 1064.

omens, diagnostic omens, *šumma ālu*, and *šumma izbu*).[114] Commentaries to celestial omens often go beyond lexical equations and explain phenomena listed in the omen's protasis in terms of other phenomena; for example, a protasis referring to a certain star is repeated with one of the planets replacing the star.[115] Such commentaries may contain the comment only, or both the citation of the passage commented on and its explanation; in the latter case they help to reconstruct such scholarly texts, if the original uncommented version does not happen to be preserved, and in the former they at least establish the sequence of the original version.

X. OMENS

Omens, observable on earth and in the sky, as the texts state,[116] may occur spontaneously or may be provoked. Among the spontaneously occurring signs are those that appear in a house, in a field, or in the behaviour of animals or humans, which are collected in *šumma ālu* (over one hundred tablets);[117] signs which derive from monstrous births of animals or humans (*šumma izbu*, twenty-four tablets);[118] characteristics of moles and similar marks on a person (the physiognomic omen series *šumma alamdimmû*);[119] dreams;[120] and the symptoms and behaviour of a sick man (the diagnostic omen series *enūma ana bīt marṣi*, forty(?) tablets).[121] Especially developed in the first millennium are omens from signs observed in the sky: eclipses of sun or moon, the conjunctions of heavenly bodies, and the like (*Enūma Anu Enlil*, seventy tablets).[122] Celestial omens in Old Babylonian are rare, and seem to deal with lunar eclipses only. A few *šumma ālu* type omens are also attested in the Old Babylonian period.[123] Even though omens are not known in Sumerian, a

---

[114] The commentary to *šumma izbu* is edited following the text of the same series in A 1127; a duplicate to lines 284–392 (Tablets VIII–XII) is A 1184, no. 37. No systematic edition is available for other types of omens; the commentaries published in autograph copy in CT 41 have been edited, along with five other texts published elsewhere, by R. Labat, A 1108. A commentary on the first tablet of the diagnostic omens is published in A 1068 (see also the remarks of A. Cavigneaux in A 1063), and several commentaries to this series are published in A 1096, nos. 27–33, 36, 38–42. Commentaries to various medical texts are published *ibid.*, nos. 47, 49–55; to various omen texts *ibid.*, nos. 72, 77–8, 81, 83–4, and 90. A commentary to *šumma ālu* is published in A 1184, no. 36. Other commentaries are scattered in various journals.

[115] See D. Pingree, A 1043, 20 §2.2.8.2.

[116] 'The signs in the sky just as those on the earth give us signals.' A 1147, 203:24.

[117] The partial edition A 1137, is expected to be replaced by a complete new edition; see A 1133.

[118] A 1127.   [119] Cuneiform texts, with introduction and glossary, A 1107; see also A 1106.

[120] A 1145.   [121] A 1110; new material in A 1096, nos. 27–42.

[122] For the time being, see the texts edited in A 1042 and A 1043; A 1164. The texts pertaining to the first fifty tablets of the series were organized, but not edited, by E. F. Weidner, A 1182. For a brief description of the organization and content of this compendium see A 1148, 643f.   [123] A 1103.

few late tablets contain bilingual (Sumerian–Akkadian) omens,[124] both
of the *šumma ālu* type, and celestial omens.

Of the provoked omens, those based on the configurations of oil
poured on water (lecanomancy),[125] or the smoke from a censer (libanomancy),[126] while still occasionally copied in the first millennium, have
largely gone out of fashion and practice. In their stead some novel
practices may have been introduced, of which only a few testimonies
survive, such as psephomancy (throwing dice), incubation dreams,
sprinkling an ox with water and observing its movements, and waiting,
after the appropriate ritual, for a shooting star, so as to derive a
prediction from its direction.[127] In continuous favour, in fact as far as we
know the only divination that had its origin in Sumer, is extispicy,
divination from the entrails (mostly the liver and gall bladder, but also
the lungs) of a lamb slaughtered for that purpose. The huge collection of
liver omens with the pertinent commentaries has not yet been organized
and edited in full; it must have been as large as or larger than *šumma ālu*.
Not only are its omens provoked, but the diviner expressly beseeches the
gods of divination, Shamash and Adad, to put a favourable sign in the
entrails of the lamb. Both the liver omen and the celestial omen
collections seem to have been in a continuous state of expansion up to the
end of cuneiform literacy, which is perhaps the reason why it is often
impossible to assign a particular text to its proper place in the compendium, and both kept being commented upon and excerpted so that
perhaps there never was a canonical version, such as we have for, e.g.,
šumma izbu or the diagnostic series.

There is also a manual for the use of the diviner, which gives the
rationale for the interconnexions between observable phenomena (on
the earth and in the sky) and the interpretations to be derived from
them.[128]

XI. HEMEROLOGIES

Hemerologies list the favourable and unfavourable days and the permitted or forbidden activities. Several types are known: listing each
consecutive day of the month, with either a short indication 'favourable'

---

[124] A 1096, no. 85 (*šumma ālu*). Bilingual celestial omens are cited in excerpt in A 1043: from
K 2241 + p. 40 note to III 6c, III 11b, xv 5, xvi 11, xvii 8; from K 8634, p. 36 ad II 3; from 82–3–23,
120, p. 77 ad xvii 8. Other unpublished bilingual omen texts are K 2286, K 8261, K 11573,
K 14036 + Sm. 154. For a bilingual hemerology see A 1086, no. 28, and B. Landsberger, *MSL* 9,
107ff.   [125] A 1150.

[126] A 1151; A 1078. See also R. D. Biggs, *RA* 63 (1969) 73–4. Another omen text deriving
prognoses from incense is published in A 1140.   [127] A 1155.   [128] A 1147.

or 'unfavourable'; listing each consecutive day and the prescriptions and proscriptions for it; listing only the favourable days with prescriptions; under each month, listing the favourable days; listing the same in tabular form.[129]

---

[129] A typology and a list of the hemerological texts with bibliography is given by A 1112.

CHAPTER 29

ISRAEL AND JUDAH FROM THE COMING OF ASSYRIAN DOMINATION UNTIL THE FALL OF SAMARIA, AND THE STRUGGLE FOR INDEPENDENCE IN JUDAH (*c.* 750–700 B.C.)

T. C. MITCHELL

I. TIGLATH-PILESER III AND THE ASSYRIAN THREAT

In the first half of the eighth century B.C. the independent kingdoms of Israel and Judah enjoyed a period of prosperity which had not been known since the time of Solomon in the tenth century. A new situation began to develop, however, with the accession of Tiglath-pileser III to the throne of Assyria in 744 B.C. At that time Uzziah (767–740) was still in power in Judah, while Menahem (752–742),[1] the founder of the fifth dynasty of Israelite kings since the death of Solomon, was ruling in Samaria. Very little is said about Menahem in the Old Testament.[2] He seems to have been violent and ruthless (II Ki. 15:16); when there was a threat from the power of Assyria he was quick to collect treasure from the wealthy men of Israel in order to pay substantial tribute in silver (II Ki. 15:19–20). This passage names 'Pul, King of Assyria' as the recipient of the tribute, Pul being another name for Tiglath-pileser III,[3] as stated in I Chron. 5:26,[4] and indeed in his annals the latter boasts that he received tribute from 'Menahem the Samarian'. The date at which Menahem paid this tribute is uncertain.

During the eighteen years of his reign Tiglath-pileser established the power of Assyria in the west, but while his own inscriptions supply a considerable amount of information about his conquests, they have been preserved in such a form as to make it very difficult to assign the military activities narrated in them to exact years in his reign. The Eponym Chronicle provides a chronological skeleton of the doings of his reign,[5] but since each entry names only one campaign target it can give only a

---

[1] The chronology adopted in Chapters 29–31 of this volume is that of Thiele (B 306). This can be no more than a working hypothesis; see *CAH* III².1, 445–6. Many argue that Menahem's dates should be set later, though there is no agreement in detail: see B 303, 261. If this trend is correct many consequential adjustments would be necessary in Thiele's system, but since the evidence is still uncertain (see discussion on p. 326 below), this has not been attempted here.

[2] The name *mnḥm* is known on a number of private seals (B 321, 373, 376, 378, 379, nos. 133, 166, 182, 195, 197), and on an ostracon from Nimrud listing men with West Semitic names (see pp. 341 and 368–9 and n. 322 below). [3] See A 535, 61–2, 240–1 n. 1544; B 225, 7, 10.

[4] Cf. B 132, 484 n. 1(b); B 333. [5] A 763, 430–1; cf. A 210, 252–3.

summary indication of the trend of his military operations in any single year, and may well ignore operations of secondary importance altogether. It is possible, for instance, that in his campaign of 733, which the Eponym Chronicle gives as against Damascus, Tiglath-pileser extended his operations as far as Israel and Philistia.[6] According to the chronicle, Tiglath-pileser became king in the spring (Ayyaru) of 745, and was already marching towards the west ('between the rivers') in the autumn (Tashritu) of the same year. The following year he campaigned in Iran (Namri), and in 743 he inflicted a defeat on Urartu 'in Arpad', that is to say, presumably, in the territory of Arpad, though 'Arpad' is preceded by the 'city' determinative URU.[7] Arpad is mentioned as the destination of the campaigns in each of the three following years, 742–740, and in the entry for 741 there is a supplementary statement to the effect that it was conquered 'within three years'. Taken at its face value[8] this would mean that Arpad was conquered in 739, in which year the chronicle records action against Ulluba in Urartu. The chronicle entry for 738 records the conquest of Kullani, which was situated in the west, but in 737 the target was the Medes in western Iran, and in the two following years it was Urartu once more. Finally, according to the Eponym Chronicle, the thrust returned to the west with campaigns against Philistia (734) and Damascus (733–732), after which Tiglath-pileser's attentions were engaged in Babylonia and at home.

The annals of Tiglath-pileser are known from the bas-relief slabs which had adorned his palace, the Central Palace, at Nimrud[9] (ancient Calah), where inscriptions ran across the reliefs, sometimes in a middle band between an upper and lower register of sculptured scenes, and sometimes across the carved part of large sculptured reliefs. In each case they were in columns continuing from one slab to the next and sometimes with a column spanning more than one slab. The slabs were, however, reused in antiquity, and were found in a poor state of preservation. The original sequence of the slabs bearing the annal inscriptions can only be reconstructed by juxtaposing appropriate scenes and passages of text.[10] The text thus reconstructed preserves references to only two chronological fixed points, Tiglath-pileser's second (744 B.C.; line 26) and ninth (737 B.C.; line 157) years,[11] so the only datable events in the Annals are those which fall on the same slabs as these dates, or possibly those which occur on slabs which may be associated with them by links supplied by overlapping duplicate passages.[12] Such

---

[6] See pp. 323–6 below.   [7] A 210, 252–4; and on the alternation of URU and KUR, B 82, 36–8.
[8] Cf. A 210, 254.   [9] A 116, 1–19.
[10] Tiglath-pileser's annals: A 35 I, 269–80 §§761–79; A 204, 1–41; and see p. 71 above.
[11] The reference to the third year in A 35 I, 272 is a speculative restoration.
[12] See A 68, 128–31; A 212.

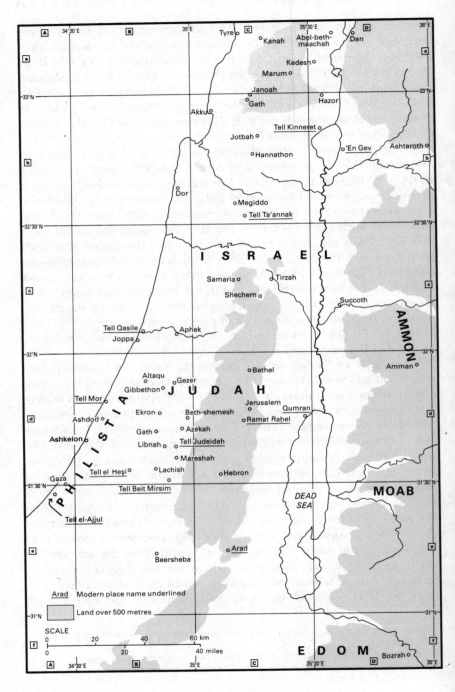

Map 4. Palestine.

overlapping passages are sometimes found because what appears to be the same text was originally inscribed in different versions. The information supplied in the Eponym Chronicle and the annals may sometimes be augmented by other texts of the Display Inscription type, when the information in these matches that in a given part of the Annals, but what appear to be parallel lists of tributaries do not necessarily stem from the same year, since successive campaigns to an area in different years may have produced similar lists.

Campaigns against, and tributaries from, the west, sometimes associated with Urartu, are dealt with in lines 59–73, 82–101, 123–33, 143–57, and 205–40 of the Annals, according to the traditional line numbering. It has been argued that since the account of Tiglath-pileser's ninth year (737 B.C.) begins in line 157, the immediately preceding passage, lines 150–7, which includes the reference to Menahem (line 150),[13] must appertain to the year 738, and therefore that Menahem's reign must have continued as least as late as that year. This is a strong argument, but the surviving form of the Annals does not make it absolutely certain.

The names of the western states which with Israel occur as tributaries (lines 150–7), namely Melid, Kummukhu, Gurgum, Que, Samʾal, Carchemish, Hamath, Byblos, Damascus, Tyre, and the Arabs, are repeated with variations and omissions elsewhere in the Annals (lines 59–73, 82–101) as well as in Display Inscriptions, some of which, at least, probably relate to different years. In lines 59–73 of the Annals, which are securely dated to Tiglath-pileser's third year (743), the rulers of Melid, Kummukhu, Gurgum and Arpad are mentioned as enemies,[14] and lines 82–101 name the rulers of Kummukhu, Gurgum, Que, Carchemish, Unqi, Damascus, and Tyre as tributaries.[15] An important Display Inscription on a stone stela from Iran gives a list of western tributaries closely similar to that in the Annals, lines 150–7, including also Menahem of Israel, but differing in omitting Hamath, and in naming Tubail (Itto-baʿal) as king of Tyre, while the Annals name him as Hiram.[16] Another Display Inscription, preserved on a tablet which, from the fact that it concludes its list of western tributaries with Judah, Ammon, Moab, Edom, Ashkelon, and Gaza,[17] may be judged to relate to the same period, 734–732 B.C., also lists many of the same city states as

---

[13] Convenient transliteration and translation of lines 150–4 in A 225, 34; translation in A 35 I, 276 §772; A 44, 283; cf. A 68, 129–30 (5).   [14] A 35 I, 272–3 §769; see also A 68, 128–9 (3).

[15] A 35 I, 273–4 §769; A 225, 35. Restored from two separate sources representing lines 82–9 and 90–101 respectively; see A 68, 129 (4). The immediately following passage, lines 103–19, has now been shown to belong to a tablet of later date (see *CAH* III².1, 503 n. 123, and see p. 331 n. 53 below).

[16] Levine Stela (A 68, 133, d(5); A 163, 96–9; A 183, 11–24, 64–7; A 225, 28–32; B 204). On the spelling *tu-ba-ilu* see A 225, 47 and nn. 85–6. For the problem of sequence see A 68, 135 (2) on ND 4301 + 4305.

[17] Tablet K.3751 (A 68, 133–5 e(1)); convenient translation of reverse lines 7–12 in A 225, 52; also A 35 I, 287–8 §801; A 44 §§, 282.

tributaries, namely Melid, Kummukhu, Gurgum, Que, Sam°al, Hamath, Arvad, Byblos, and possibly originally in passages now missing, Carchemish, Damascus, Tyre, Israel, and the Arabs.[18]

There are thus several similar surviving lists of western tributaries, stemming from different years of Tiglath-pileser's reign, and, according to the Eponym Chronicle, various possible western campaigns with which to associate them, and indeed perhaps other possible campaigns not actually named in the Eponym Chronicle. Since it cannot be positively excluded that the year (or years, if the two lists which mention him are taken to be from separate years, rather than earlier and later within a single year) in which Menahem paid tribute was 743 and perhaps 742, the present chronology can be tentatively retained, if we bear in mind that firmer evidence may necessitate its modification.[19] The passage in Kings which refers to this event says of Pul that 'he came against the land' (II Ki. 15:19), and though this phrase normally indicates a physical attack it is plausible in this context to understand it as referring to a distant threat apprehended from the presence of Tiglath-pileser in north Syria.[20] This passage affords a clue to the population of the land at this time, because it sets the tribute paid by Menahem at 1,000 talents of silver, which he is said to have raised at fifty shekels per head[21] from the men of substance in his kingdom. If the talent is taken at 3,000 shekels, this gives a figure of 60,000 for the men of substance, which, together with their families and the lower classes, foreigners, and slaves, might suggest a total population of about 800,000 for Israel, and perhaps a further 200,000 for Judah, giving about a million for the land as a whole.[22]

Archaeologically little can be connected with Menahem. The excavations at Tirzah, the old capital, have uncovered remains showing a prosperous period (level II) in the time of Jeroboam II, with a large public building, possibly the governor's residence, and since Menahem is described as coming from Tirzah when he assassinated Shallum (II Ki. 15:14) it is possible that this was his residence before he became king.[23] At Hazor certain building changes were made in stratum VB, probably in response to a northern threat, possibly in the time of Menahem.[24]

Menahem was succeeded by his son Pekahiah (II Ki. 15:22–3),[25] who,

---

[18] A 225, 53.

[19] Many scholars favour 738 B.C. as the year in which Menahem paid tribute (e.g. *CAH* III².1, 411; A 210, 251–66; B 158, 245; B 256, 257); B 306, 94–115 favours 743 as the year in question. A 80, 144–7 suggests that Menahem's tribute could have been paid some time in the years 742–40, and favours 741. See also A 62, 47–9 (= B 128, 169–72).   [20] Cf. A 210, 251–2.

[21] On which see A 108, 153.   [22] B 109, 65–6, 70; and cf. A 11, 97–8 and nn. 4–5.

[23] B 49 II, 397, 403–4, and plan p. 398; B 340, 381.   [24] B 349, 187, 200, and fig. 51.

[25] The spelling of his name *pqḥyh* in the Hebrew text may represent a revision by post-Exilic Judaean scribes, from an expected Israelite *pqḥyw*. See *CAH* III².1, 472–3.

though he is said to have continued in the heterodox religious tradition initiated by Jeroboam, has nothing recorded of his reign in Samaria, which ended after two years with his assassination by an aide-de-camp (*šališ*),[26] Pekah ben-Remaliah (II Ki. 15:25) in 740 B.C.[27] Pekah is said to have ruled for twenty years (II Ki. 15:27), but since he does not appear to have held power in Samaria for so long a period, it has been suggested that when Menahem assassinated Shallum in 752, Pekah seized that opportunity to establish himself as a rival ruler in Gilead, in Transjordan, making terms with Pekahiah on Menahem's death, when he received the honorary title *šališ*, but murdered Pekehiah at the earliest opportunity. Pekah is said to have been assisted in his coup by fifty Gileadites.[28] This must remain speculative, but at all events he brought Menahem's short-lived dynasty to an end, and, since he did not pass on the kingship to anyone of his own family, he cannot be said to have established a dynasty.

In the same year as the usurpation by Pekah in Israel, the long reign of the ailing Uzziah came to an end in Judah. During the last decade of his life he had suffered from leprosy and his son Jotham had acted as co-regent (II Ki. 15:5). Uzziah was remembered long afterwards, in the late sixth century, as the king in whose reign there had been a severe earthquake (Zech. 14:5), an event of some interest archaeologically, since it is likely that traces of it have been found at Hazor, helping to date the end of level VI at that site to Uzziah's time.[29] Jotham now succeeded him as king in his own right.

It was in this same year also that one of the greatest prophets of Judah began his public ministry. This is said to have taken place in the year that Uzziah died (Is. 6:1), and when this phrase is compared with the opening statement of the book which bears his name, 'The Vision of Isaiah ben Amoz which he saw concerning Judah and Jerusalem in the days of Uzziah, Jotham, Ahaz, and Hezekiah' (Is. 1:1), it appears that the most natural meaning is that Isaiah's ministry began shortly before Uzziah's death. That Isaiah was of age for part, at least, of Uzziah's reign is suggested by the statement in Chronicles that he made a written record of the events which took place in it (II Chron. 26:22).[30] Chronicles also records the detail, not mentioned in Kings, that because Uzziah had been a leper he was buried slightly apart from the other kings in Jerusalem (II Chron. 26:23; cf. II Ki. 15:7). The book which has survived under Isaiah's name[31] extends to sixty-six chapters and falls, in general, into

[26] See B 109 I, 188.

[27] See B 306, 121–5, table x (p. 129), but cf. discussion of Menahem above, pp. 325–6, and nn. 1 and 19.   [28] B 306, 124–6 and (on the chronology of Pekah) 120–32.   [29] B 349, 113, 181.

[30] See B 38, 57–8.

[31] The name, spelt *yšʿyhw* as in the Old Testament, is known from private seals (B 321, 366, 381, nos. 52, 211).

two main sections, divided by chapters 36–9, which, with minor variations, duplicate the historical account in II Ki. 18–20 of the dealings of Hezekiah with Sennacherib and Merodach-baladan II.[32] Chapters 1–35 deal in the main with the world of Isaiah's own lifetime in the eighth century, while chapters 40–66 refer forward to the sixth century. Opinions differ about the dating of the two parts of the book, the most common view holding that the portions which refer to the sixth century were not predictive prophecy spoken or written by Isaiah in the eighth century, but the work of anonymous authors in the time to which they refer.[33] In the chapters directed to his own time Isaiah condemned social injustice and formal worship without religious commitment, and he named the Assyrians as the agents of Yahweh's punishment on Judah, as well as on Ammon, Edom, Moab, Philistia, Damascus, Tyre, Egypt, and Babylon.[34] An element in these chapters which became important in Judaism, and indeed later in Christianity, was the foretelling of the coming of an ideal ruler (Is. 7: 13–16; 9: 2–7) to whom was applied later, though not in these passages, the title Messiah, 'anointed one', a designation which had been used in the Old Testament particularly of Saul and David.[35]

The Messianic element is found also in the words of a younger contemporary of Isaiah, Micah, who is said to have come from Judah, though he included Samaria in the message which he communicated.[36] The situation presupposed by his message was one of great prosperity enjoyed by a rich minority and of oppression of the poor, together with religious indifference which was connived at by priests and even prophets. There were also heterodox religious practices involving sorcery and soothsaying (Mi. 5:12).[37] Micah held that the consequence would be the destruction of the whole land including Jerusalem, but eventual restoration.

Jotham had played a dominant part in national affairs when he was co-regent with his sick father Uzziah (II Ki. 15:5), and it was perhaps during this time that he engaged in building activities, both in Jerusalem and in the sparsely settled areas of the kingdom. In Jerusalem he is said to have extended the wall of Ophel and to have built the 'Upper Gate' of the Temple (II Ki. 15:35; II Chron. 27:3). What part of the wall of Ophel

---

[32] See B 88, 69–103, 137–40; B 169; B 171, 367–97; B 229, 513–18.

[33] For this view see, e.g., B 120, 303–46; B 126, 364–88; B 127, 251–7, 322–7, 363; B 275, 9, 269–75, 287–94, 331. For the view that the book is in the main of eighth-century date see B 147, 764–800; B 263; B 353, 9–101; B 354, 215–42. See also pp. 327–8, 424 below.

[34] Many commentators take part of these prophecies also as dating later than the time of Isaiah; cf. B 120, 317–28.

[35] B 274, especially pp. 25–33; and (in general) B 127, 347–53; B 182 IX, 496–520.

[36] B 29, 238–404; B 120, 406–13; B 126, 443–7; B 127, 257–8; B 147, 919–25; B 274, 34–5; B 275, 275–6.   [37] B 116, 244 (*mᶜwnn*), 255 (*mkšp*); B 219, 118 n. 115.

might have been extended by him is uncertain, but it is possible that he and his father were together, or successively, responsible for a north-eastern extension of the fortified area of Ophel to the south of the Temple, which has been uncovered in excavations.[38] His work on the 'Upper Gate' of the Temple must have been simply a matter of rebuilding or repair, for this gate, which connected the Temple with the royal palace, is already mentioned as the way by which, nearly a century earlier, Jehoiada had brought Joash in triumph to the palace after the overthrow of Athaliah (II Ki. 11:19). The building operations outside Jerusalem were very likely also done in Uzziah's lifetime or, at any rate, in continuation of projects initiated by him, of which possible archaeological evidence has been found.[39]

The account in Chronicles goes on to state that Jotham exacted tribute by force of arms from Ammon for three years (II Chron. 27:5),[40] and though this citation of years may simply be intended to refer back to the military victory, it is perhaps more probable that it refers to his years of sole reign, and to his restoration of the Judaean dominance which might have lapsed on the death of Uzziah.[41]

Near the end of Jotham's reign, it seems that his northern contemporary Pekah invaded Judah with the aid of the Aramaean king Rezin, and that this precipitated the usurpation of power by his son Ahaz (II Ki. 15:37, and 16:5), probably in 735 B.C., though Jotham lived for a further two years, ostensibly as co-regent with Ahaz, until 732 or 731.[42] Rezin[43] is mentioned several times in the inscriptions of Tiglath-pileser. In the Display Inscription on the stone stela mentioned above[44] he is named immediately before Menahem; and in the passage in the annals,[45] perhaps dealing with the campaign of 743 or 742, he is again mentioned immediately before Menahem. This suggests that he had succeeded Khadianu as king of Damascus sometime around 750 B.C.

The motive for this assault on Judah, the beginning of the 'Syro-Ephraimite War', is uncertain, but it may have been the desire on the part of the Israelites and Aramaeans to regain control of the northern end of the incense route which ran up from southern Arabia by way of the Hijaz, and which could be tapped by the power commanding Transjordan. In the days of Jeroboam II and Uzziah the two kingdoms had controlled much of Transjordan, but it seems that in the unsettled period which immediately followed the death of Jeroboam in 753 B.C.,[46] Uzziah, before he was handicapped by leprosy, may well have been able to extend

---

[38] See *CAH* III².1, 505.   [39] See *CAH* III².1, 504.   [40] See B 259.
[41] Cf. B 306, 126–7.   [42] B 306, 126–30.
[43] This name (*rēṣîn*) is distinct from that of his tenth-century predecessor Rezon (*rēzôn*), mentioned in I Ki. 11:23.   [44] Levine Stela (n. 16 above), ii 4 (*ra-qi-a-nu*).
[45] Annals (n. 10 above), line 150 (*ra-ḥi-a-nu*).   [46] See *CAH* III².1, 508–9.

his control to the erstwhile Israelite sphere in northern Transjordan, for he is described in Chronicles as having received tribute from the Ammonites (II Chron. 26:8).[47] Such a move would not have been improbable in the light of long-standing connexions between the area of Gilead and the Tribe of Benjamin, which had remained within the kingdom of Judah, and the attempt by Rezin and Pekah to regain control of Transjordan may well explain their aggression against Judah in the time of Jotham.[48]

This Syro-Israelite (or Syro-Ephraimite) action against Judah is said to have been renewed in the time of Ahaz, when Jerusalem was threatened and Ahaz besieged within it (II Ki. 16:5), and though the city did not fall (II Ki. 16:5; Is. 7:1), Chronicles states that Judah suffered heavy casualties, and that a large number of prisoners were deported to Samaria and Damascus (II Chron. 28:5–8). The chronology and sequence of events at this time are uncertain. According to the Assyrian Eponym Chronicle, Tiglath-pileser, who had been engaged in military action on the eastern and northern margins of Assyria during the years 737–735, turned his operations to the west once more in 734 with a campaign against *pi-liš-ta*, presumably Philistia (rather than Palestine).[49] It is possible that this campaign is referred to in a fragmentary tablet from Nimrud which preserves details of parts of the king's advance through Phoenicia to Gaza, which he sacked. According to this text Khanunu (Hanno), Gaza's king, escaped to Egypt, but was induced to return and to act as a vassal ruler. Tiglath-pileser then continued to the 'City of the Brook of Egypt',[50] probably near modern El-ʿArish, where he set up a stela.[51] The motive behind this was presumably to gain control of that part of the south Arabian incense trade which passed through Gaza, an interpretation possibly born out by the latter part of this same inscription which speaks of booty taken from the land of the *mu-ʾu-na-a-a*, Muʾunites, perhaps to be identified with the *mēʿûnîm*, 'Meunites' of the Old Testament, a north Arabian people, and both possibly to be identified with the Minaeans (Epigraphic South Arabian *mʿn*) of south Arabia,[52] who had northern trading outposts and would most certainly have been engaged in this trade.

It is possible that a fragmentary cuneiform tablet which refers to the campaign of an unnamed Assyrian king against '. . .iah' king of Judah is

---

[47] The Septuagint reads μιναιοι, taking up the name from the end of the previous verse, where the Hebrew has *mēʿûnîm*, 'Meunites' (see below).   [48] B 259.

[49] See e.g. B 257, 8.

[50] *ālu naḫal muṣur*, with which compare *naḫal miṣrayim*, 'the Brook of Egypt', the southern limit of Solomon's kingdom (I Ki. 8: 65).

[51] Tablet ND.400 (A 68, 137 e(4); B 131, 56, no. 25) on which see A 11, 98–9 n. 9, and A 70, 88–9.

[52] A 70, 89; B 234, 243–7. For cuneiform ʾ as reflecting West Semitic ʿ, cf. *ga-al-ʾa-[a-da]* (p. 335 n. 82 below) with *glʿd*.

relevant to this time.[53] It speaks of the capture of Azekah and of an unnamed Philistine city in the hands of '. . .iah'. While there are difficulties, one possibility is that '. . .iah' was Uzziah (cf. II Chron. 26: 6).[54]

How the Philistian campaign of Tiglath-pileser fits in with the Syro-Israelite attack on Ahaz in Jerusalem is uncertain, but if the aim of the latter venture was to secure trade routes through Transjordan it is possible that it was projected partly in reaction to the loss of the coast and maritime routes to the Assyrians. In that case it might have taken place in 734 following, or even possibly partly contemporaneously with, the Assyrian campaign. According to Kings, the Syro-Israelite attack on his territory led Ahaz to appeal for help to Tiglath-pileser (II Ki. 16:7), and Chronicles, having referred to this appeal, goes on to say, 'and the Edomites had again come and attacked Judah and taken captives, and the Philistines had raided the cities of the Shephelah and the Negeb, and had taken Beth-shemesh', mentioning also a number of other cities in that area (II Chron. 28:17–18).[55] This might imply that Judah had suffered these attacks before the major Syro-Israelite invasion, and that they weighed with Ahaz in his decision to appeal to Tiglath-pileser, and might indeed have encouraged Rezin and Pekah to make their attack. If this was the correct sequence of events it is possible that a passage in Kings referring also to the Edomites relates to a separate occasion arising out of the Syro-Israelite action (II Ki. 16:6).

There are some difficulties in this passage but a possible rendering runs, 'At that time Rezin, king of Aram, restored Elath to Aram and drove out the Jews from Elath, and the Edomites came to Elath and they have lived there until today.' The Hebrew consonantal text gives $w^{\circ}rmym$, 'and the Aramaeans' in place of $w^{\circ}dmym$, 'and the Edomites'. Many commentators would take the whole passage as referring solely to Edom, but this requires the assumption that the reference to Rezin is a later addition, for which view there is no manuscript justification. As it stands, this verse not only states that the Aramaeans campaigned as far south as Elath, but also appears to imply that this had previously been part of Aramaean territory. In the present state of evidence it can only be said that this, though apparently improbable, is not impossible.[56] Assuming, therefore, that there existed some sort of agreement between Aram and Edom, the Aramaeans may be seen tentatively as the conquerors of Elath, and as then having handed it over to their allies the

[53] K.6205 (formerly attributed to Tiglath-pileser) + 82-3-23, 131 (formerly attributed to Sargon); see p. 325 n. 15 above, and A 4, 134–5; A 274, 25–39.

[54] Cf., however, pp. 369–70 below.   [55] In verse 17, cf. AV, RV and RSV, 'For again . . .'.

[56] The implication of previous Aramaean control in this area depends on the form *hēšîb*, 'he restored'.

Edomites, with whom they could well have been co-operating in the southern trade.

In the account of Solomon's activities at Eziongeber, that city is said to have been 'with' or 'beside Elath' (I Ki. 9:26), so, in view of the fact that Tell el-Kheleifeh is the only site which has so far been found at the head of the Gulf of ᶜAqaba, it seems reasonable to take it as representing both Eziongeber and Elath. The destruction of the period III city there may tentatively be seen as the work of the Aramaeans, and the establishment of new buildings (period IV) as the work of the Edomites. The statement in Kings quoted above, that the Edomites occupied Elath 'until today', presumably until the effective completion of the Book of Kings in the sixth century, is borne out by the discovery in the period IV levels of pottery jar-handles stamped with the impression of a late seventh- to early sixth-century seal inscribed, 'Belonging to Qausᶜanal, servant of the king'.[57] This is identifiable as an Edomite seal from the element Qaus (*qws*), the name of the principal god of the Edomites.[58] Another seal from Tell el-Kheleifeh, a scaraboid, set in an elaborate copper attachment and cut with a figure of a ram and the inscription 'Belonging to *ytm*', has usually been interpreted as the seal of Jotham, the eighth-century king of Judah.[59] There are difficulties in this interpretation, however, because the form of the script probably points to a seventh-century Edomite origin:[60] the name of Jotham the king is regularly spelt *ywtm* in the Old Testament, presumably a post-Exilic revision spelling from original *yhwtm*,[61] so it may well be that the name *ytm* on the seal should be taken as *yatôm*, 'orphan', rather than *yôtām*, 'yhwh is perfect'.[62] The excavator states that the seal was found 'in the disturbed debris of the Period III city',[63] and it may therefore actually belong to the later, period IV, levels, in which case it would simply be the private seal of a seventh-century Edomite, when the site was no longer part of Judaean territory. Level IX of the southern Judaean site of Arad, which had flourished since the time of Uzziah, and which included one phase of the unorthodox temple, seems to have been destroyed about this time, perhaps by the Edomites.[64] Among the legible ostraca from this site, a brief message concerning allocation of rations and three lists of personal names probably belong to level IX.[65] These are all in poor condition, and are of interest mainly for the examples of personal names

[57] B 136, 132–4 fig. 68; B 157, 164–5 no. 4; B 321, 372 no. 119.
[58] B 323A; and cf. B 342, 245–6.
[59] B 39; B 136, 126 and fig. 61; B 321, 373 no. 131 (cf. also p. 375 no. 158).
[60] B 157, 163 figs. 78 and 80 no. 2.   [61] See *CAH* III².1, 472.
[62] B 133, 61, 63 no. 4.   [63] B 136, 126.   [64] B 49 I, 84.
[65] Arad Ostraca nos. 60 and 59, 72, 74 respectively (B 17, 90, 89, 96, 97; B 199, 216–17 and 215–16, 219–20 and see also 224).

which they give, several of them compounded with the divine element -*yhw*.

According to Kings, Ahaz appealed to Tiglath-pileser for help with the words, 'I am your servant and your son' (II Ki. 16:7), perhaps thereby committing himself to vassal status,[66] which, to judge from surviving examples of vassal treaties, would have involved among its conditions his tacit acceptance of the existence of the Assyrian pantheon of gods.[67] It is not surprising therefore that the prophet Isaiah is said to have personally transmitted to Ahaz a message from Yahweh warning him not to become involved with Assyria, and assuring him that the attack would not ultimately succeed (Is. 7). This must have been a dramatic encounter, for it seems to have taken place outside the city walls, at a place described as 'the end of the conduit of the upper pool, in the highway of the fuller's field' (Is. 7:3), probably in the presence of a number of witnesses. The location of the place described in this clause is uncertain, but there is some reason for thinking that it was in the Kidron valley, to the east of the city, where a water channel conducted the surplus outflow from the ancient natural spring Gihon southwards along the foot of the eastern wall.[68]

In this passage there is reference to a further element in the plan of Rezin and Pekah, not mentioned in Kings or Chronicles. This concerned a man named Ben-Tabeel,[69] whom they intended to establish on the throne of Judah in place of Ahaz. The form of his name suggests a connexion with the areas which lay in the Aramaean sphere of influence, and it is possible that it is to be associated with the place name Tabilu which is mentioned in a letter from Nimrud,[70] in a context which might point to a location in the area of Ammon in Transjordan. It has indeed been suggested that Ben-Tabeel might have been an early representative of the Tobiads, a noble family which owned extensive territories in Ammon, and in whose genealogy the recurring name might have been changed from *ṭbʾl* to *ṭbyh(w)* at a time of Yahwistic reform.[71]

It seems however that Isaiah was right in claiming that the Syro-Israelite plan to replace Ahaz by Ben-Tabeel would not succeed, and though Tiglath-pileser campaigned against Damascus in the next two years Judah derived only very dubious benefits from this. The surviving passages of the annals of Tiglath-pileser, which probably relate to the Damascus campaigns of 733 and 732, appear in lines 191–240 of the

[66] Cf. A 11, 66 n. 4; B 326, 368–9 n. 6; B 215A.

[67] See e.g. the seventh-century Vassal Treaties of Esarhaddon, lines 13–40 (A 44, 534–5; A 307, 29–32).   [68] See pp. 361–5 below.

[69] Spelt *ṭābeʾal* ('good for nothing'), presumably reflecting scribal contempt (see B 311, 9 and n. 82), but ταβεηλ in the Septuagint and, of a different individual, *ṭābeʾēl* ('God is good') in Ezra 4: 7.

[70] Tablet ND.2773; A 80, 131–3.

[71] B 212, 236–8; B 227, 16–18. For a different interpretation see B 23A.

standard edition,[72] which derive from paper squeezes made by Layard. Lines 191–210 and 229–37 are based on the text running across 'three Colossal Figures of Eunuchs' found in the South-West Palace at Nimrud where they had been badly damaged by fire,[73] and of them lines 229–37 are duplicated by the inscription from another slab which continues the text to line 240. It has been suggested that the passage given in these two sections, which includes an account of the destruction of a number of the Aramaean cities of Rezin and the deportation of prisoners, may describe the campaign of 733.[74] It also mentions the Arabian queen Samsi, presumably the successor of Zabibe who had been encountered by Tiglath-pileser in 738, and it goes on to list prisoners taken from Khinatuna, Qana, Aruma, Marum, and other cities of which the names are only partially preserved. These are plausibly to be identified with Biblical Hahhathon, Kanah, Rumah, Merom, and perhaps others in the area to the north and west of the Sea of Galilee.[75] The list ends with a reference to the deposition of Metinti, king of Ashkelon, and his replacement by Rukibti, and mentions the Arabian tribe of Idibiʾilu.[76]

If this does describe the campaign of 733, it suggests that Tiglath-pileser dealt with the western margins of the territory of Damascus on this expedition, moving on through northern Israel to settle trouble which had arisen at Ashkelon since his expedition of the previous year, when he had presumably imposed vassal status on Metinti. It may have been during that campaign that he thought it necessary to take Gezer, which stood in a commanding position some fifteen miles from the coast in south-west Israel, an event depicted on a relief from the South-West Palace at Nimrud, which shows a city labelled URU *ga-az-ru* succumbing to an attack by the Assyrians who are breaching the wall with a siege engine.[77] Excavations at Gezer have shown evidence of this attack in the destruction of level VI, after which even the great gate built in Solomon's time went out of use,[78] and an Assyrian administrative building was erected there.[79] According to Kings, Tiglath-pileser attacked Damascus, deporting its population and putting Rezin to death (II Ki. 16:9),[80] and it is reasonable to associate this event with the latest entry of his reign in the Eponym Chronicle, that for 732, which reads 'against Damascus'. Another non-annalistic text, which probably contains material relevant to this campaign, presupposes the end of

---

[72] A 35 1, 278–80 §776–9; A 44, 283 (lines 205–40 only); A 204, 34–41.

[73] A 116, 30; A 267, pls. 72b–73a.   [74] A 212, 179–80, 185–6; and see A 68, 130–1 c(7).

[75] B 16, 371–6 and map 30. For the identification of Biblical places with archaeological sites see B 16, 429–43.   [76] A 70, 89–90.

[77] A 11, 65 n. 2; A 45 no. 369; A 70, 89 n. 15; A 116, 24 and pl. LXIII; A 212, 181–2; B 191, 43–4; and cf. B 16, 329 n. 11.   [78] B 49 II, 442.   [79] B 273A.

[80] Removing the deportees to *qîr*, which B 140, 633 takes as 'the city', i.e. Nineveh; cf., however, B 139, 368–9.

Damascus as an independent state. It aso refers to some of the Arab groups mentioned in the Annals, and to the establishment by Tiglath-pileser of the Idibiʾilu as guardians of the desert zone between Palestine and Egypt.[81] This text begins by listing areas conquered by Tiglath-pileser in the north west and goes on to describe the conquest of Gilead (URU ga-al-[. . .]), Abel-beth-maachah, and the whole of the Aramaean territory of Damascus (the 'Land of Hazael').[82] Gilead and Abel-beth-maachah are defined as adjacent to Israel, the continued independence of part of which is thereby implied. This account is partially paralleled by the statement in Kings that Tiglath-pileser took Ijon, Abel-beth-maachah, Janoah, Kedesh, Hazor, Gilead, and Galilee, all of which were in northern Israel.[83] There is reference in this same text to further action against Khanunu (Hanno) of Gaza who had already caused trouble in 734 B.C., and to an attack on Israel leading to the deportation of population and receipt of tribute, and to the appointment of Hoshea to the kingship in place of Pekah, who had been deposed by the people.[84] In Kings, Hoshea ben-Elah is said to have conspired against, and killed, Pekah (II Ki. 15:30). This, perhaps, gives a more precise description of the change, the credit for which was assumed by Tiglath-pileser. Hosea's tribute was paid at Sarrabanu in southern Babylonia in 731, and the deposition of Pekah therefore took place before that date.[85]

There is archaeological witness at a number of sites to the invasions by Tiglath-pileser in 733–732,[86] and, though it is uncertain to precisely which year the destruction levels belong, it is likely that in 733 his route skirted the territory of Damascus, and then continued to Philistia, so it seems probable that the remains belong to that year. At Dan in the far north of the kingdom, the destruction of level II is probably to be assigned to this time,[87] and at Hazor, not much further south, the fortified Israelite city of level V was violently destroyed.[88] In the debris was found a stone jar on which was scratched an inscription probably reading lpqh smdr, 'For Pekah, vine-blossom [wine?]', where Pekah, though he may have been the king, is perhaps more likely, in view of Hazor's distance from Samaria, and the frequency of the personal name, to have been simply a private individual.[89]

[81] CIWA III, 10 no. 2 (A 68, 132 d(3)); A 35 I, 292–4 §§815–19; A 44, 283–4; B 131, 58–9, no. 27. Cf. A 211, 114–19; A 70, 89–90.
[82] Damaged here but restored from ND.4301 + 4305 (A 227; B 131, 57–8, no. 26; cf. A 68, 135–6). The fragmentary tablet K.2649 (CT 35, 39; A 211, 116–17), which probably joins ND.4301 + 4305 (A 5 I, 639), gives ga-al-ʾ-[. . .], perhaps to be restored as ga-al-ʾa-a-da or the like (see B 326A, 154–5). 'Hazael' here supersedes the previous restoration 'Naphtali' (e.g. A 44, 283).
[83] A 211, 114–19; B 16, 372–4.
[84] There is no evidence for the restoration of the name 'Menahem' (so A 35 I, 239 §815; A 44, 283) in line 12 (CIWA III, 10 no. 2 line '23'); cf. B 131, 58–9, no. 27.   [85] B 76, 244–9.
[86] B 299, 31.   [87] B 299, 31.   [88] B 349, 113, 115, 190.
[89] B 121, no. 109; B 133, 18–19 no. 5C; B 134, 192 fig. 20; B 346, 73–4 no. 7, pls. CLXXI–CLXXII; B 349, 190 n. 4, pl. xxxvd.

On the Sea of Galilee occupation ended, probably at this time, at TelᶜKinneret and ᶜEn Gev,[90] and in central Israel there are signs of destruction at Megiddo at the end of level IV, at Dothan at the end of level 2, and probably at Beth-shan at the end of level IV.[91] On the line of an advance along the coast route towards Philistia, the site of Tell Qasile was destroyed at the end of level VII, and on the estuary of the River Yarkon, not far away, a fortress at Tell Kudadi was probably destroyed at the same time.[92]

A probable illustration of an event in the final campaign of 732 is to be found on a bas relief from the South-West Palace at Nimrud, which shows Assyrian soldiers driving out prisoners with booty from a walled town on a mound above which is inscribed the name *as-tar-tu*,[93] probably the Biblical city of Ashtaroth in Aramaean territory in Transjordan. In order to secure these conquests, Tiglath-pileser set up a system of provincial administration under Assyrian governors in the conquered areas. Israel lost a substantial part of its territory, being confined to an area centring on Samaria, with the new provinces, already established, perhaps, in 733,[94] of Dor, Megiddo, and Gilead on its west, north, and east, while the territory of Damascus was divided, presumably in 732, into the provinces, from north to south, of Damascus, Karnaim and Hauran.[95] This left Judah, Philistia, and a reduced Israel on the west of the Jordan, and Edom, Moab, and a reduced Ammon to the east of the river, all still with a measure of independence, though Ahaz of Judah, Metinti and Khanunu of Ashkelon and Gaza in Philistia, Qaush-malaku of Edom, Salamanu of Moab and Sanibu of Ammon had all been obliged, according to one of the Display Inscriptions,[96] to pay tribute to Tiglath-pileser. The name of the king of Ammon, *šnb*, is preserved on a statue, probably representing the king, which was found near Jebel el-Qalᶜa, the citadel of Rabbah, modern Amman, the ancient capital of Ammon. This statue bears a damaged inscription on its base, of which the major part may plausibly be restored to read *yrḥᶜzr [br z] kr br šnb*, 'Yerah-ᶜazar [son of Za]kkur son of Shanib', thus giving the names of the son and grandson of Shanib (Sanibu).[97]

Ahaz, who was at this time still co-regent with Jotham, is named *ia-ú-ḥa-zi* in the inscription of Tiglath-pileser just mentioned, and though his name is always given as *ʾāḥāz* in the Old Testament, and even possibly on

[90] B 49 II, 385 and III, 719.
[91] B 49 III, 855; B 49 I, 339 and B 101, 267, 270, 273–4; B 175, 289.
[92] B 49 III, 720 and IV, 967.
[93] BM 118908; A 45, no. 366; A 116, 30, and pls. LXVIII–LXIX; B 5 no. 13.
[94] A 420, 59–61; B 16, 371–4 and maps 30–1; and see A 211.
[95] A 420, 62–3, 69; B 16 map 31.
[96] Tablet K.3751 (see n. 17 above); and cf. A 11, 66 n. 5.
[97] B 356; see also pp. 359, 452 below, and cf. B 97, 14.

the seal of an official which is inscribed,[98] 'belonging to Ashnaᵓ official of Ahaz', it is clear that this is a shortened form of Jehoahaz (*yhwᵓḥz*).[99] According to II Ki. 16:10 he went to meet Tiglath-pileser in Damascus, presumably in 732, and therefore on a different occasion from that of the tribute mentioned in the Display Inscription, unless the tributes there referred to were not all paid in the same year. He is characterized in both Kings and Chronicles as unfaithful to true Yahwism, and one symptom of this is described in his reaction to an altar which he saw while paying court to Tiglath-pileser in Damascus. He sent its specifications home with orders that a replica be made in Jerusalem. This was done, and Ahaz is said on his return to have offered the 'burnt-(whole) offering', 'grain-offering', 'peace-offering', and 'libation' on it (II Ki. 16:10–13), all of which were normally at this period the prerogative of the temple priesthood. He was so pleased with the new altar that he had the bronze altar of burnt offerings, the main altar which had stood opposite the entrance of the Temple since Solomon's time, moved a little to the north and its place taken by the new one, which appears then to have continued in use until the fall of Jerusalem, a century and a half later (II Ki. 16:14–16).[100]

These innovations were symptomatic of Ahaz's religious policy. At various times he is said to have closed the Temple and set up altars all over Jerusalem (II Chron. 28:24), built cultic platforms[101] in all the cities of Judah (II Chron. 28:25), sacrificed on them (II Ki. 16:4; II Chron. 28:4), cast images for pagan gods (*bĕᶜālîm*; II Chron, 28:2),[102] burnt incense to pagan gods (II Chron. 28:25), and sacrificed to the gods of Damascus (II Chron. 28:23). For the first time, reference is made to the Valley of the Sons of Hinnom, *gēᵓ ben-hinnōm*,[103] which ran round the west and south sides of Jerusalem, and which is described by Jeremiah some decades later as the site of 'the cultic platforms of Tophet' (Jer. 7:31), probably cultic fire-pits, or incinerators, at which children were sacrificed, a Phoenician practice attested at Carthage and elsewhere in the west Mediterranean.[104] In some contexts these sacrifices are defined by the term *lamōlek*, taken in many versions as 'to Molech', but more probably to be understood as 'namely the *mlk* (-sacrifice)'.[105] Ahaz is said

---

[98] B 133, 62–3 no. 12; B 157, 83 fig. 54 no. 2; B 321, 374 no. 141. See also B 321, 365 no. 44. On ᶜ*bd*, 'official', see *CAH* III².1, 501 and n. 110, and cf. below, pp. 346, 381, and 411.

[99] B 186 I, 31; B 255, 22, 62, 179.

[100] See B 109, 410–11; B 236 II, 22 on Solomon's altar; but cf. B 275A, 485–9 for a different interpretation.   [101] Cf. *CAH* III².1, 460 and n. 137.

[102] See, however, B 236 II, 97–8, holding that *bĕᶜālîm* refers to a single Baᶜal.

[103] Later contracted to Gehenna, Greek γεεννα. See B 182 I, 657–8.

[104] B 110, 79–87; B 141, 182–3; C 5, 86–9, 95; C 6, 49, 141–3, 150–1, 202, 214–18. See also A 11, 77–83; B 28, 235–44, 275 n. ee; B 68, 266–7; B 219, 39–40, 105 n. 91.

[105] A 44, 658; B 28, 235–7; B 68, 234–5; B 186, 560; B 310,, 182; B 141, 179–87.

to have sacrificed his son (II Ki. 16:3) or sons (II Chron. 28:3)[106] in this way, so when the author of Kings says of him that 'he did not do what was right in the sight of Yahweh his God' (II Ki. 16:2; also II Chron. 28:1), he was only summarizing the situation in very moderate terms. These religious aberrations would seem to have been in the tradition of earlier rulers, particularly those of Israel, who drew upon surviving Canaanite practices and current Phoenician influences. The altar in Damascus was presumably of Syrian workmanship, for it can hardly have been Assyrian in view of the very short time that had elapsed since the Assyrian conquest.[107] The contacts between Damascus and Phoenicia[108] and the known skill of Phoenician craftsmen, suggest that there may well have been Phoenician workmanship in it.

In Israel, Tiglath-pileser's nominee, Hoshea (732/31–723/22), continued a faithful Assyrian vassal during the remaining five years of Tiglath-pileser's reign, paying annual tribute, but when Shalmaneser V came to power in Assyria in 727 it seemed that he relaxed his loyalty. According to Kings, 'Shalmaneser[109] king of Assyria came up against him, and Hoshea became his servant and brought him tribute. And the king of Assyria found conspiracy in Hoshea, because he sent messengers to sôʾ king of Egypt and did not offer tribute to the king of Assyria as in previous years' (II Ki. 17:3–4). The most natural sense of this statement would appear to be that at the beginning of Shalmaneser's reign Hoshea ceased to pay tribute, resuming this duty under the threat of an advancing Assyrian army, but that he then sought what may have seemed to him a less costly alliance with one of the rulers then in power in Egypt.

The question of the identity of 'sôʾ king of Egypt' has given rise to much debate. A suggested identification with Sibʾu, apparently mentioned by Sargon as commander of the Egyptian army in 720, cannot be maintained, since this name should be read Reʾe.[110] Of other suggestions[111] the most plausible is that Sôʾ was Osorkon IV.

II. THE FALL OF SAMARIA

Shalmaneser V ruled for only five years, 727–722 B.C., and no annals or substantial historical inscriptions have survived from his reign.[112] The Eponym Chronicle is damaged at this point,[113] but the Babylonian

---

[106] Cf. B 336, 114–18.   [107] See also A 11, 73–7; B 219, 5–12.

[108] A 845, 136–9, 180–1, 184–5; Ezek. 27: 18.

[109] For the Hebrew spelling of the name (šlmnʾsr) see B 225, 7–8.

[110] A 6 no. 295m; A 160, 49–53; B 131, 62, no. 32; and cf. A 309, 38 n. 144; also pp. 340–1.

[111] A 11, 99–100 n. 14; A 30, 373–5 and chart p. 472 and map p. 367; B 137. See CAH III².1, 575–6.

[112] A 25, 242, 292; A 68, 140; A 531, 102 no. 43.

[113] See A 763, 432 no. cb3. A 35 11, 437 follows B 259A in restoring 'Damascus' for 727 and 'Samaria' for 725, 724 and 723 B.C., but without evidence (see n. 119 below).

Chronicle mentions him briefly,[114] and it is likely that there is reference to him under the name Selampsas in a passage quoted by Josephus from a book of annals compiled by Menander of Ephesus, who made use, according to Josephus, of the Tyrian archives. In this passage it is stated that during the reign of Elulaios (Luli), king of Tyre (c. 727–701), Selampsas king of Assyria invaded Phoenicia, concluded treaties with cities which had previously been subject to Tyre, and withdrew. The defection of its subject cities led Tyre to refuse submission, and this resulted in the return of the Assyrians to attack Tyre, with the help of the other cities. Since this was unsuccessful, they set up a siege which lasted for five years. At the end of his quotation from Menander, Josephus states that this is what is written in the Tyrian archives about Salmanassēs, king of Assyria.[115]

This pattern of two campaigns, or possibly two phases of one campaign, has some similarities with what is said of Israel in Kings, and the siege of Tyre to some extent matches the statement in Kings that Shalmaneser invaded Israel and besieged Samaria for three years (II Ki. 17:5; 18:9–10). Kings appears to state that this siege was preceded by the capture and imprisonment of Hoshea (II Ki. 17:4). It is possible that the sequence of narration is not intended to be chronological; but if we assume that it is, such an imprisonment would not be intrinsically improbable, though no information is given about other leaders in Samaria during the siege.[116] The statement that Samaria finally fell to the king of Assyria in the ninth year of Hoshea (II Ki. 17:6; 18:10) need not militate against such an interpretation, since years could still be reckoned in terms of the reign of an exiled king, just as was later done in the case of Jehoiachin.[117] At all events Kings states that the siege of Samaria began in Hoshea's seventh year (II Ki. 18:9),[118] that is between spring 725 and spring 724 B.C., and since the summer months would have been the most likely time for the start of such a siege, this points to the year 725. The city is said to have fallen in Hoshea's ninth year (II Ki. 17:6; 18:10), which would have been in 723 or early 722. The portion of the Assyrian Eponym Chronicle which covers the years 725–722 is badly damaged, but for the years 725–723 the word *ana*, 'against', is partially or wholly preserved, indicating foreign campaigns, and it has been suggested that 'Samaria' be restored as the target for each of these three years.[119]

According to the Babylonian Chronicle, Shalmaneser V died in the

---

[114] See below.

[115] *Ant. Jud.* IX.283–7; see A 845, 224–9. Cf. for the dates of Luli, A 163, 98–99.

[116] See A 209, 37.   [117] On the spelling Jehoiachin see p. 392, n. 164.

[118] On the references to Hezekiah in II Ki. 18: 9–10 see B 306, 147–52, 118–40, 182–91.

[119] A 35 II, 437 follows a suggestion in B 259A citing WVDOG 35, no. 21 viii (the left column on the reverse, wrongly labelled vi), which, however, gives only the names of the eponyms (see A 763, 414 no. 17). See also A 209, 33 no. 100.

month Tebetu of his fifth year,[120] that is to say, at the end of 722 B.C., in which case the fall of Samaria is likely to have taken place before the end of his reign. This view appears to be supported by the Babylonian Chronicle, which gives as the principal event of his reign the destruction of the city *šá-ma-ra-ʾi-in*.[121] This chronicle tablet is dated to the early Persian period (500/499 B.C.),[122] so this spelling reasonably reflects the Aramaic form current at that time, which is found as *šmryn* in the Elephantine papyri, and as *šămĕrayin* in Biblical Aramaic, rather than the Assyrian *sa-mì-ri-na*, *sa-mir-i-na* or *sa-mar-na*, 'Samaria'.[123]

Sargon, who succeeded Shalmaneser as king at the beginning of 721 B.C., appears to claim, in a damaged passage in his annals, that he conquered Samaria at the beginning of his reign,[124] and a similar statement is made on a prism fragment from Nimrud.[125] These two texts help partially to restore one another, but it has been plausibly suggested that in the compilation of this passage both texts made use of another document of the Display Inscription type, now lost, which gave its information in a geographical rather than a chronological sequence, and which like two other texts from Khorsabad[126] associated the fall of Samaria with operations against the Arabs and Egypt. Since Sargon did not campaign against Egypt until 720, doubt is thus cast on the veracity of his claim to have been the conqueror of Samaria.[127] It may well be that after the death of Shalmaneser, when the siege forces had returned to Assyria, Samaria attempted to break away from Assyrian domination, and such a reconstruction is possibly borne out by the so-called 'Ashur Charter',[128] which, though damaged at the significant portion, appears to say that Samaria joined with Arpad and Hamath in rebellion in 720.[129] This is also the sense of Sargon's annals which, in addition to Hamath and Arpad, mention that Khanunu of Gaza was also party to the rebellion. The annals state that Khanunu obtained aid from Egypt, where one of the pharaohs, possibly Osorkon IV of the Twenty-second Dynasty in the eastern Delta, sent his army commander Reʾe[130] with a military contingent, but that Sargon put down this rebellion, campaign-

---

120 Babylonian Chronicle I i 29 (A 25, 14–17, 69–87). Here and subsequently the Babylonian Chronicles are quoted by their number in A 25.

121 Babylonian Chronicle I i 28 (A 25, 73; B 130 no. 29). Formerly read as *šá-ba-ra-ʾi-in*; see now A 702, 302.   122 Babylonian Chronicle I iv 23 (A 25, 87).   123 See A 209, 39–40.

124 Sargon's Annals lines 11–14 (A 35 II, 2 §4; A 44, 284; A 185, 4–5; A 209, 34; A 226, 4–5); Sargon's Annals, on which see p. 87 above, are here quoted according to the line numbering of A 185. For a line concordance with the earlier edition of A 226, see A 5 I, 630–1.

125 Nimrud Prism (A 170, 179–80; A 209, 34; B 131, 60–1, no. 30), fragment D iv 25–30.

126 Cylinder Inscription, lines 19–20 (A 35 II, 61 §118; A 170, 199–200 (lines 16–18); A 663, 32–3). Display Inscription lines 23–7 (A 35 II, 26–7 §55; A 44, 284–7; A 226, 100–1).

127 See A 209, 33–6; B 306, 145–6.   128 See pp. 87–8 above.

129 Ashur Charter (A 206), lines 16–28; and see A 209, 94.

130 See p. 338 and n. 110 above. See *CAH* III².1, 575–6.

ing as far as Gaza, where he took Khanunu prisoner, destroyed Rapikhu
(Raphia) on the border of Egypt, and put Re²e to flight.[131] It thus appears
that Sargon brought his army against Samaria during this south-western
campaign of 720, probably in the course of his victorious return from
Rapikhu. It is stated in Kings that the 'king of Assyria took Samaria and
deported Israel to Assyria and settled them in *ḥălaḥ* and *ḥābôr*, the river of
gôzān, and cities of *mādāy*' (II Ki. 17:6). '*Ḥābôr*, the river of *Gôzān*', is a
clear reference to the region of the upper River Habur (modern Khabur)
on which stood the city of Guzanu (modern Tell Halaf) in north Syria.
Mādāy is Media, and though the remaining place, *ḥălaḥ*, is less clearly
known, it may well have been the *Halaḥḥu* of the Assyrian inscriptions,
which was situated to the east of the Tigris in the general area of Erbil
and Kirkuk.[132] The most natural sense of this passage would make
Shalmaneser V the 'king of Assyria' responsible for this deportation, and
pending evidence to the contrary this may be taken to have been the case.

It is relevant here to cite the post-Biblical book of Tobit, because it
purports to describe the adventures of a Jew deported from Israel by
Shalmaneser (*᾿Ενεμεσσάρου*, Syriac *ᶜšlmnᶜsr*), to Nineveh where he had
trading relations with other Jews in Media. This book may well preserve
genuine historical traditions, and the discovery of fragments of an
Aramaic version at Qumran which exhibits linguistic features associated
with imperial Aramaic of the fifth or fourth century B.C.[133] supports this
view. In it Sennacherib and Esarhaddon are mentioned, as well as the
sage Ahiqar (*᾿Αχιάχαρος*). Ahiqar is now known not only from the
composition bearing his name, which is partially preserved in a fifth-
century B.C. Aramaic version on papyri from Elephantine (and in several
later versions),[134] but also from a cuneiform literary list of the second
century B.C. which explains that 'Ahuqar' was the name given by the
Aramaeans to Aba-Enlil-dari, a wise man in the time of Esarhaddon.[135]
The presence of Jews in Assyria is attested by the occurrence of Hebrew
names in Assyrian sources, the name Hoshea being found on a document
from Nineveh,[136] the name Halbishu, or Haldu,[137] designated 'man of
Samaria' in a letter written from Guzana and found at Nineveh,[138] and
possibly such other names as Menahem ben Elisha on an ostracon
inscribed in Aramaic script from Nimrud.[139] Other evidence for the

[131] Sargon's Annals (see n. 124 above), lines 23–57 (A 35 II, 3 §5; A 44, 285; A 185, 6–9; A 226, 6–7).
See A 70, 91; A 209, 38.   [132] See A 702, 142.   [133] B 27, 74, 107 n. 147.
[134] A 44, 427–30; B 86 II, 715–84; B 92, 204–48; B 339, 270–5.
[135] A 767, 45, 51–2, lines 19–20.
[136] A 97, no. 64 = *CIS* II no. 17; cf. A 62, 52 (= B 128, 176).
[137] If *bi-šú* is taken as a badly written *du* (B 25, 36 n. 25), the name is perhaps comparable, e.g., with
Hebrew Ḥuldâ (II Ki. 22: 14); and cf. A 948, 116 n. 112.
[138] K.1366 (A 72 no. 633; A 88 I, 440–3, II, 208–21, no. 633), on which see B 25, 36 (and nn. 22 and
27 there for other possibilities).   [139] See pp. 368–9 and n. 322 below.

presence of Israelites, or possibly only of booty from Israel, in Assyria is found in a group of bronze bowls, probably of the eighth century B.C., from Nimrud, several of which bear their owners' names in alphabetic script.[140] While most of these are West Semitic, but not specifically Hebrew, one, 'Ahio' (*ḥyw*), with the distinctive Israelite, as opposed to Judaean, spelling of the divine element, would appear to be connected with the northern kingdom.[141]

The Jews thus deported are referred to as 'ten tribes' by Josephus, who states that the majority of them elected to stay 'beyond the Euphrates' when, in the fifth century, Ezra made known to them Artaxerxes' decree encouraging their return to Jerusalem.[142] In the apocryphal book II Esdras they are said to have moved to a remote region,[143] and in later literature the fate of these 'ten tribes' became the subject of extensive speculation.[144] In reality there is no reason to think that the majority of Jews who remained in the regions to the east of the Euphrates did other than gradually assimilate to the local populations.

It seems likely that a further statement (II Ki. 17:24), to the effect that the 'king of Assyria' settled deportees from Babylonia and Syria in Samaria and other cities of Israel, refers to the activities of Sargon, possibly in 720, after he had had an indecisive encounter with Merodach-baladan and the Elamite Khumban-nikash in Babylonia,[145] and in the course of his punitive campaign in Syria and the west.[146] It seems that at this time the territory of Israel was united with Dor on the coast, which was already, probably since 733, an Assyrian province, to form the new Assyrian province of Samirina.[147]

Though the Biblical account appears to attribute the main deportation to Shalmaneser rather than Sargon, and it seems reasonable to see Sargon as the king responsible for bringing foreign settlers into Israel,[148] it is highly probable that Sargon was responsible also for deportations, and the statement in his annals that he removed 27,280 Israelites to Assyria in 722 probably describes what he did in 720.[149] Sargon goes on to say that he rebuilt and enlarged Samaria, bringing in people from conquered territories, and installing his own *bēl piḫati*,[150] 'provincial governor' or

---

[140] B 54; B 156.

[141] B 54, 4*, 5*, 7*, pl. III; B 55, 62 figs. 42–3; but cf. B 81, 26; B 255, 222. Cf. also pp. 343 and 457 below.   [142] *Anti. Jud.* XI.131–3, but wrongly naming Xerxes instead of Artaxerxes.

[143] II Esdras (= Vulgate IV Esdras) 13: 40–7; see B 238, 311–12.   [144] See B 250.

[145] See pp. 88–9 above.

[146] See however A 11, 101 n. 23, 109 n. 75. The frequently repeated identification (e.g. B 140, 652) of Sepharvaim (*sĕparwayim*) in this passage with Shabara'in in the Babylonian Chronicle will not stand if the latter is read Shamara'in and is correctly identified with Samaria (see p. 340 and n. 121).

[147] B 16, 333–4; and cf. A 420, 63.   [148] See above.

[149] Sargon's Annals (see n. 124), line 15; Nimrud Prism (see n. 125), D iv 31; Khorsabad Display Inscription (see n. 126) 24 (A 11, 50; A 209, 34). The number of deportees is damaged in the annals but appears as 27,280 in the Nimrud Prism and as 27,290 in the Khorsabad Display Inscription.

[150] Written as LÚ.EN.NAM, on which see A 105, 181–2. Taken by A 11, 50 and n. 42 as *šaknu*.

'administrator'. The excavations at Samaria showed clear signs of the Assyrian destruction, with a thick layer of ashes in all the excavated areas, and destruction levels in all the buildings on the summit.[151] No Assyrian buildings have, however, survived, presumably having been levelled from the site in the Hellenistic period. Among the destruction debris were found the ivories (Pls. Vol., pls. 148–50), carved in the Phoenician style, which had probably been used to adorn the furniture, and perhaps the internal walls of the buildings, in the earlier part of the century.[152] Other finds at Samaria included a number of fragmentary inscribed ostraca dating from the period shortly before the Assyrian conquest.[153] These relate to the issue of rations or simply list personal names, and are of interest in including a number of Yahweh-names in which the divine element is spelt -yw.

Further evidence of the punitive activities of Shalmaneser has been found at the Old Israelite capital, Tirzah, where the buildings of level II were destroyed by fire,[154] and only about six miles south east of Samaria at Shechem, where again there is evidence of destruction by burning at the end of level III.[155] Tirzah and Shechem presumably fell to the Assyrians before Samaria, which held out for a considerable period. At each of these three sites the Assyrian presence is demonstrated by the discovery of pottery bowls of Mesopotamian manufacture in the levels following the destruction.[156] These are supplemented at Samaria by a fragment of a limestone cuneiform stela, a clay cuneiform docket, a clay bulla impressed with the Assyrian royal seal, and an Assyrian cylinder seal; and at Megiddo by a cylinder seal.[157] Further north at Hazor the destruction of level V is probably to be attributed to Shalmaneser, and the level (IV) immediately following this destruction is characterized by the erection of inferior buildings on the ruins, an activity probably to be attributed to the surviving Israelites. In the next level (III), a substantial fortress measuring 30 m × 25 m was built on the western end of the citadel mound.[158] Though archaeologically it can only be dated to some time between about 700 and 400 B.C., it is probable that it was the work of the Assyrians, as they consolidated their position in northern Palestine.

The new settlers introduced into Israel by the Assyrians are said to have set up images of their own gods in the heterodox cult areas which had previously been established by the Israelites (II Ki. 17:30–1), and this activity was no doubt tolerated by the Assyrian governor.[159] That

[151] B 105, 107–8; B 177, 133–4.   [152] CAH III².1, 471, 506–7.
[153] B 133, 14–15 no. 3; B 199, 245–50; B 232, 37–9; B 300.   [154] B 49 II, 404; B 175, 289.
[155] B 344, 160–2.   [156] B 36, 291 and pl. 99; B 344, 163–4. See also B 299, 42–4.
[157] B 131, 61, no. 31.   [158] B 349, 190–4.
[159] See in general A 11, 9–61, 111–13, and in particular 101–3 and 104–7.

the Israelites had, against the teaching of strict Yahwism, installed statues of various alien gods in Samaria is suggested by the fact that Sargon counts 'the gods in whom they trusted' among the spoil which he took from the defeated city.[160] The imported gods are said to have included Nergal, 'the city god of Cutha in Babylonia', known mainly for his associations with plagues and the underworld; while the other deities named in this passage are uncertain or unknown,[161] there seems to be no reason to doubt the introduction of foreign cults at this time.

A possible glimpse of polytheism among Israel's eastern neighbours under Assyrian occupation at about this time or within the next few decades is afforded by an Aramaic inscription in red and black ink on plaster discovered at Tell Deir ʿAlla in Transjordan.[162] The plaster was discovered in fragments, having fallen, perhaps from a stela, and the reconstruction presents many difficulties; but the text appears to report a message from the gods delivered by a man described in the first line as 'Balaam son of Beor, the man who was seer of the gods'.[163] The surviving text preserves the names of a few of these gods, ʾEl, ʿAshtar, Sheger, and two groups of male and female deities, the Shadayan and Shadayat. To the extent that these gods are known from other sources, their associations are with the West Semitic area, and this is to be expected since there is no indication that foreign populations were settled in Transjordan.

In Samaria, the presence of settlers from Cutha led the Jews in later times to refer to the Samaritans as Χουθαῖοι[164] and *Kûtîm*.[165] Other elements with quite different religious traditions were also soon brought in, when Sargon in his campaign of 716, settled the Arabs of defeated desert tribes in Samaria.[166] The religious pollution of Israel symbolizes, perhaps more than anything else, its final fall. It also manifested a material threat to neighbouring Judah.

III. AHAZ AND HEZEKIAH

After the fall of Samaria, Judah, still under Ahaz, remained largely untouched by the Assyrian operations,[167] but territory administered by the Assyrians now lay across its northern approaches, only a few miles from Jerusalem, and Ahaz must have been perpetually conscious of the

---

[160] Nimrud Prism (see n. 125), D iv 32–3. Cf. A 170, 179–81 and pl. XLVI; B 131, 60, no. 30 n. 1; B 339, 60, 62; see also A 11, 104–5.

[161] For attempted identifications see, e.g. B 229, 473–5; B 268, 171–3.

[162] B 162. For a later dating of this inscription see B 99, 12.

[163] *Blʿm br bʿr ʾš ḥzh ʾlhm* (line i 1 restored with the aid of i 2, i 5 and viii d. 2). On *ḥzh*, 'seer', see *CAH* III².1, 454–5.   [164] Jos. *Anti. Jud.* XI.88.

[165] For Rabbinic references see B 270, 89 n. 2, 119–20.   [166] See pp. 345–6 below.

[167] Cf. A 274, 32, who adopts a chronology which makes Hezekiah king at this time.

dominating presence of so powerful a neighbour. The Assyrians evidently regarded the area as important, for the governors of Samaria were counted as high officials of the empire. This is known from the fact that two of them, Nabu-kittu-uṣur and Nabu-shar-ahheshu held the office of eponym in 690 and 646 B.C. respectively,[168] as, indeed, did Itti-Adad-aninnu, the governor of Megiddo province in 679.[169]

Sargon's attention was diverted from the area of Palestine by military campaigns on his east and north for much of his reign, but when the circumstances were right in 716 and 712 he did bring his armies to the south west again. According to a fragmentary prism inscription from Ashur he campaigned near the Egyptian border in 716, where he reached Nakhal Muṣri, probably el-ʿArish, and received tribute from Shilkanni, king of Egypt.[170] It is probable that this name referred to Osorkon IV (730–715) of Bubastis,[171] with whom Hoshea had sought an alliance in 727, and with whose field commander, Reʾe, Sargon had had an earlier encounter in 720. In his Annals for the following year, 715, Sargon states that he again received tribute from Egypt, this time from Pirʾu (pharaoh), king of Egypt.[172] There is reason for thinking, however, that the scribe responsible for compiling the annals misplaced this and the adjacent material from its proper place, and that it in fact also describes events in the campaign of 716.[173] The pharaoh in question was presumably again Osorkon IV. In this probably displaced material there is reference also to tribute from the Arabian queen Samsi, and from Itʾamra the Sabaean. Samsi, who, like her probable predecessor Zabibe had already encountered Tiglath-pileser, may plausibly be seen as queen by virtue of some religious role, of loosely knit tribal groups whose seasonal movements brought them in the summer months as far north as the area to the east of Damascus. In the same passage of Sargon's annals, and still relating to this year, reference is made to the defeat of four desert Arab tribes, the Tamudi, Ibadidi, Marsimanu, and Haiapa, the first bearing a name, Thamud, well known in later sources, classical and Islamic, which suggest a location in the Hijaz centring perhaps on Medaʾin Salih, ancient Hegra, near Dedan.[174]

The other three tribes mentioned in Sargon's inscription were also very likely located in the area of the Hijaz[175] thriving, like the northern Sabaeans and the Thamud, on the incense trade from South Arabia. The

[168] A 763, 427, 451 ('Nabû-kêna-uṣur') = A 250, 96; A 763, 452 = A 161, 36.
[169] A 763, 427 (18); A 234, 6.
[170] Prism Fragment VA 8424. A 44, 286 (text wrongly cited as VA 8412); A 209, 77–8 and cf. p. 95; A 224; B 131, 62, no. 33.   [171] A 30, 143, 376; B 24, 23–5. See *CAH* III². 1, 576.
[172] Annals, lines 123–5 (A 35 II, 7–8 §18; A 44, 286; A 185, 22–3; A 226, 20–1).
[173] A 209, 77–8, 95.
[174] B 320; B 338, 37, 42–54, 130–1; W. Montgomery Watt, *Bell's Introduction to the Qurʾān*. Revised edn (Islamic Surveys 8) (Edinburgh, 1970), 128.   [175] B 234, 289, 291–2; B 235, 479.

latter probably survived by exacting passage payments from caravans, and were therefore likely to have come up against the Assyrians who now controlled the northern end of this trade. According to the account in his annals, Sargon was able to master them to the extent of forcibly settling the survivors of his action in Samaria.[176]

The power of Assyria in the south west at about this time is illustrated by a tablet from Nimrud which lists Judah together with Ammon, Moab, Edom, Ekron, Ashdod, Gaza, and Egypt as sending emissaries to Calah (Nimrud) with tribute.[177] That faithful vassals were favourably treated by the Assyrians is shown by another document from Nineveh (also possibly to be dated to about this time), which lists gold and silver rings issued to emissaries of states who had brought tribute to Assyria.[178] These included Ammon and Ekron, as well as tribal Arabia. Another document possibly to be dated to this time is a letter found at Nineveh and probably directed to Sargon from Sennacherib the crown prince. It lists tribute, chiefly silver, textiles, and fish from *a-zu-r[i]*, very likely Azuri king of Ashdod.[179]

These Assyrian campaigns took place around Judah without directly affecting Ahaz in his last years, and according to both Kings and Chronicles he died a natural death and was buried in Jerusalem, though not, according to Chronicles, in the normal royal tombs (II Ki. 16:20; II Chron. 28:27).[180] He died between autumn 716 and autumn 715, and was succeeded by his son Hezekiah.[181] In the Old Testament Hezekiah's name is spelt both *ḥzqyh(w)* (vocalized *ḥizqîyāh[û]*), and *yḥzqyh(w)* (vocalized *yĕḥizqîyā[û]*), and both forms, representing presumably the perfect and imperfect of the verb, 'Yahweh has strengthened' and 'Yahweh strengthens' respectively, are perhaps attested on not very legible monuments, *ḥzqyhw*, referring possibly to the king himself, on the private seal of Jehozarah ben Hilkiah, who is designated *ᶜbd*, 'servant' or 'official' of Hezekiah,[182] and *yḥzqyhw* on an early sixth-century ostracon from Jerusalem.[183]

Both Kings and Chronicles devote a considerable amount of space to the reign of Hezekiah and in particular to measures which he took to

[176] Annals, lines 120–3 (A 35 II, 7 §17; A 44, 286; A 185, 20–3; A 226, 20–1). See also Cylinder Inscription, line 20 (n. 126 above).

[177] Tablet ND.2765 (A 11, 66, 118; A 80, 134–5 no. 16; A 464, 117–18 and 123–5; B 131, 64–5, no. 36A). See also A 70, 92–3.

[178] Tablet K.8787+ (A 93, nos. 1110+; A 464, 113–14, 124, 337–42).

[179] Tablet K.956 (A 72, no. 568; A 78, no. 99; A 88, no. 568; A 457, 40–9; A 464, 111, 283–4). See also A 70, 93.

[180] See B 180, 203, and on the use of the name Israel in the Chronicles passage see B 336, 102–3, 106–10, 117–18.   [181] B 306, 135–6, 139, 149, 184; cf. n. 118 above.

[182] B 157, 83–4 and fig. 54 no. 3; B 160. On *ᶜbd* see n. 98 above.

[183] A 15, no. 190; B 121, no. 138; B 133, 25–6 no. 9; B 199, 239–44 (reading *ḥzqyhw* without the initial *y*-).

reverse the religious aberrations introduced by Ahaz. In this he met the approval of the author of Chronicles, who says of him, in summing up these activities, that 'he did the good (*ṭôb*), the *yāšār* and the true (*ʾemet*) before Yahweh his God. Every work which he undertook, whether in the service of the house of God or in the law or in the commandments, he carried out with utter devotion in the worship of his God' (II Chron. 31:20–1)'.[184] The first part of this statement represents an unusual expansion of a standard phrase 'he did the *yāšār* in the eyes of Yahweh' which is employed by both Kings and Chronicles at the beginning of their accounts of the reigns of a number of Hezekiah's predecessors as kings of Judah: Asa, Jehoshaphat, Joash, Amaziah, Uzziah and Jotham;[185] and this same briefer phrase is applied elsewhere to him (II Ki. 18:3; II Chron. 29:2). It has been suggested that *yāšār*, which is usually translated 'that which was right', may have had reference to the institution of reforms and re-establishment of just law at the beginning of a king's reign, an institution known particularly from Babylonia.[186] The fuller formula referring to Hezekiah is otherwise paralleled partially only by the statement about Asa, nearly two centuries earlier, that 'he did the good and the *yāšār* in the eyes of Yahweh' (II Chron. 14:1). It is conceivable that the use of the word *ṭôb* ('good') in both these formulae had some reference to the renewal of the covenant, or agreement, between the people and Yahweh which is specifically mentioned as having taken place in the reign of Asa,[187] and seems in effect also to have taken place under Hezekiah; 'doing the *ṭôb* before [or in the eyes of] Yahweh' has perhaps, in the context, something of the connotation 'establishing good [relations by covenant] with Yahweh'.[188]

Hezekiah is said to have been twenty-five years old when he became king (II Ki. 18:2; II Chron. 29:1), which would mean, assuming the system of chronology adopted here to be correct, that he was nine when Ahaz came to power, so that he would have observed, presumably with increasing dismay, what was going on in the kingdom during the whole of his father's reign. It seems that he must have disapproved of what he saw, for he is described as losing no time in reversing the trend. During his first month in power he opened up the Temple (II Chron. 29:3) which had been closed by his father (II Chron. 28:24; 25:7) and which had presumably remained sealed and out of use ever since. The Temple seems even to have suffered dilapidation, since, in order to reopen it, it was apparently necessary to repair the doors. According to Chronicles, Hezekiah's next step was to summon the religious officials ('the priests

---

[184] See B 236 II, 182 and II Ki. 18: 5–6.   [185] See references in B 81, 449, *yāšār* 2a.
[186] D. J. Wiseman in *Journal of Semitic Studies* 7 (1962) 167–8; and see *CAH* III².1, 453.
[187] See *CAH* III².1, 463.   [188] Cf. *CAH* III².1, 453.

and the Levites')[189] of the Temple to the open space to the east of the Temple where he called upon them to sanctify, or make holy, both themselves and the Temple (II Chron. 29:4–5), because he intended to make an agreement or covenant (*bĕrît*) with Yahweh (II Chron. 29:10). The officials are said to have readily obeyed the king's injunction and, indeed, it is probable that there were others in the kingdom who longed for reform, and who may have helped to form the ideas of the young king.

Among these significant figures were of course the prophet Isaiah, and his younger contemporary Micah.[190] Micah is said to have been a Morashtite (Mic. 1:1) presumably a native of Moresheth-Gath (Mic. 1:14) near Lachish. Though he was preaching in the time of Jotham and Ahaz (Mic. 1:1), and speaking indeed against Samaria before its fall (Mic. 1:2–9), his main ministry appears to have been in the time of Hezekiah. This is shown by a reference to him, and a quotation from his prophecy, by Jeremiah about a century later (Jer. 26:17–19; Mic. 3:12). In the consonantal text of Jeremiah his name is spelt *mykyh*, but *mykh* in the book of Micah itself. These spellings, both of which are found in the Elephantine papyri,[191] probably represent respectively a scribal revision from, and an abbreviation of, *mykyhw*, a spelling which is found elsewhere in the Old Testament and on an eighth-century seal,[192] and, in the form *mkyhw*, in a seventh-century vase inscription from Jerusalem and in the Lachish ostraca.[193] Micah conveyed Yahweh's condemnation of unjust rulers, oppressive rich men, and corrupt priests and prophets, and his impending judgement involving invasion and destruction in Israel and Judah, including Jerusalem itself. He spoke also, however, of a time of restoration, and he referred, as did Isaiah, to the ideal ruler who would come in the future.[194] This was one of the influences on the young king Hezekiah. The priests thoroughly cleansed the interior of the Temple, bringing all equipment which was foreign to the true worship of Yahweh into the court, which had already been cleared up, to be thrown by the Levites into the Kidron valley (II Chron. 29:12;17). The Temple was then ceremonially rededicated and the system of offerings and worship reinstituted (II Chron. 29:18;36).

According to the sequence of events outlined in Chronicles, Hezekiah then issued an invitation to the entire nation, as well as to the Jews in what had been Israel (now under Assyrian occupation) to assemble at Jerusalem and celebrate the Passover, which, according to the normal

---

[189] On priesthood and the relationship of priests and Levites see B 109, 358–71 (especially 364–6); B 145, 58–83; B 275, 210–12; B 280, 95–101; B 294A, 11–14.

[190] See pp. 327–8 and n. 36 above.   [191] B 92, 296; B 143, 479; B 268, 137 and n. 88.

[192] B 186, 546; B 157, 133 and fig. 61 no. 119; B 255, 107, 144, 249.

[193] B 43, 195; Lachish Ostracon 11:3 (B 199, 128–9).   [194] See p. 328 above.

religious calendar, was about a month overdue (Ex. 12:1–27; II Chron. 30:13). It has been suggested that in the north the Passover was celebrated about one month later than in the south and that Hezekiah deliberately delayed his celebration to encourage the participation of the northerners,[195] but this must remain a speculation. There is no further specific mention of covenant renewal, but the solemn celebration of the Passover ceremony, which commemorated the deliverance of the Israelites from Egypt by Yahweh, in some sense the preliminary to the forming of the covenant between Yahweh and the people at Sinai (Ex. 19:1–24:18), may have been regarded by Hezekiah and his sympathizers as, in effect, a covenant renewal ceremony. Chronicles states that a large number of people, including many from Israel (II Chron. 20:18),[196] responded to Hezekiah's invitation, and that before performing the ceremonies they collected the pagan altars and incense-burners from the city and hurled them into the Kidron valley (II Chron. 30:13–14). The lengthy description of the Passover celebration in Chronicles (II Chron. 30:1–27) is not paralleled in Kings, but, though this is taken by some as an indication that there was no such event and that the account was invented by the author,[197] this is not necessarily so,[198] and the desirability of some ceremony which could symbolize covenant renewal argues in its favour.

Kings makes brief mention of religious reforms, involving the destruction of every cultic platform, cult pillar,[199] and standing cult pillar in Judah (II Ki. 18:4), and Chronicles repeats this with the modification that cultic platforms and altars were also destroyed in the territories of the northern kingdom (II Chron. 31:1), presumably by those from Assyrian occupied territory who had returned home after attending the Passover ceremony in Jerusalem. A possible manifestation of this reform is the destruction at Beersheba of a horned altar of dressed stone which stood over 1.5 m high and measured at least 1.5 m wide. The dimensions are uncertain because the blocks which made up the altar had been reused as building stones, and only a selection of them were recovered, built into the repaired wall of a storehouse area in level II, which went out of use with the destruction of the city by the Assyrians in 701.[200] Such an altar of dressed stone would have been liable for demolition in a reform such as that instituted by Hezekiah, in view of the prohibition on using worked stone in an orthodox altar (Ex. 20:25; Deut. 27:5; Josh. 8:30–1). A further objection to this altar would have been what appears to be an engraved representation of a snake on one of the blocks.[201] Another

[195] B 155, 444.   [196] Cf. A 11, 107 n. 64; B 236 II, 178.
[197] B 106, 470–1; B 280, 89–90 n. 4; B 287, 18–19.
[198] Cf. B 78, 281; B 236 II, 176–7; B 336, 119f. On II Ki. 23: 22–3 and II Chron. 35: 18, see below, pp. 389–90.   [199] See CAH III².1, 470.   [200] B 14; B 14A, 154–6; B 291A.   [201] B 14, 4 fig. 2.

manifestation of the reforming zeal of Hezekiah and his supporters was, according to Kings, the destruction of a bronze serpent, Nehushtan, which dated from the time of Moses (Num. 21:4–9) but which had come to be treated simply as an idol (II Ki. 18:4).[202] This action could be said to symbolize the seriousness of Hezekiah's intentions, for the destruction of an object which had associations with the almost legendary figure of Moses must have been likely to arouse resentful opposition in some quarters. There is no mention of such opposition at this point, but it may be deduced from the rapidity of the reversion to pagan practices which followed Hezekiah's death. That there was no special rejection of the past in these reforms is suggested by the statements that in re-establishing the Temple worship Hezekiah arranged for musicians to take part in the same way as they had done in David's time (II Chron. 29:25–30), and that certain proverbs of Solomon were transcribed in Hezekiah's time (Prov. 25–29).[203] Implicit in all these reforms was evidently an attempt by Hezekiah to concentrate all worship in Jerusalem,[204] an aim which was abandoned by his immediate successors, but readopted by his great-grandson Josiah.[205]

Hezekiah's early years appear to have been largely undisturbed by foreign intervention, in spite of the fact that Sargon again mounted a campaign to the west in 712.[206] The occasion for this was a revolt in Ashdod against Ahimetu its king, who had been installed in that position by the Assyrians in place of his brother Azuri after the latter had defaulted on his payment of tribute. This affair is described in Sargon's annals in the account of his eleventh year (*palû*) 711,[207] but it has been plausibly argued that its date is more reliably indicated by the text on a broken prism from Nineveh which places it in 712.[208] According to both these sources, and a Display Inscription at Khorsabad,[209] Ahimetu was deposed by a usurper named Yamani, often read as 'the Greek', but he was more probably, on the basis of Common Semitic *ymn*, 'right [hand], lucky, happy', simply a Semitic-speaking native of Palestine.[210] According to the Nineveh prism,[211] a number of others, including the rulers of *pi-liš-te*, presumably the other Philistine cities, as well as Judah, Edom, and Moab, were induced to side with Yamani, who also endeavoured,

[202] Cf. B 219, 13–14, 85–6 nn. 7–10; for a different interpretation see B 275, 165; B 280, 87; cf. also B 14, 4.   [203] See B 181, 99–100, 102.   [204] See B 331A, 109.   [205] See pp. 383–4 below.

[206] On the document 82–3–23, 131, formerly thought to give evidence of an Assyrian attack on Azekah and therefore of Hezekiah's involvement with Yamani's rebellion in 712 B.C. (A 11, 66; A 209, 80–4), see now A 274, 25–6; also p. 331 and n. 53 above and p. 369 below.

[207] Annals (n. 124 above), lines 249–62 (A 35 II, 13–14 no. 30; A 44, 286; A 185, 38–41; A 226, 36–9).

[208] Fragmentary Prism (A 209, 87–92); A 35 II, 105–6 §§193–5; A 44, 287a (2).

[209] Wall Slabs, lines 90–112 (A 35 II, 31–2 §62; A 44, 286; A 226, 114–17).

[210] See A 209, 80 n. 217; B 114, 192 n. 3; and cf. A 84, 77–8; B 186 II, 384 (*ywn*), 396–7 (*ymn*); B 255, 224.

[211] Fragmentary Prism (see n. 208) vii 26–8 (K.1668b + DT.6; A 35 II, 105 §195); and see A 274, 32.

unsuccessfully, to enlist the support of 'Pirʾu king of Egypt', very likely Shabako (716–702 B.C.), second pharaoh of the Twenty-fifth (Nubian) Dynasty.[212] This same text refers in a damaged passage to defensive works, presumably undertaken by Yamani. They involved digging a trench to the water table at a depth of over twenty cubits, or ten metres.[213] The location of this work is not supplied by the text. It has been suggested that this passage might refer to the site of Minet el-Qalʿah, probably Ashdod-yam, which lies only about fifty metres from the sea shore, and where a ten-metre trench would easily strike the water table. Excavations at the site have revealed substantial fortifications of the eighth century B.C., but no traces of a defensive trench or moat. The possibility remains open, however, since only a limited part of the fortification was uncovered in the excavations, and a trench in an unexcavated sector cannot be ruled out.[214]

Sargon's campaign to deal with this trouble in the south west is described in his annals (for 711 B.C.) and also in the Display Inscription, in both of which he claims that he besieged and conquered Ashdod, Gath, and as-du-di-im-mu, clearly Ashdod-yam. There is probably archaeological attestation of this campaign at Ashdod, where level VIII was destroyed, and where skeletal remains representing some three thousand individuals, many with traces of wounds, buried collectively in a number of locations, may represent those who perished at the hands of the Assyrians.[215] It seems that the victorious Assyrians set up a basalt stela on the site to commemorate the event. Three fragments of this stela, inscribed in cuneiform, have been found; they are too fragmentary to show more than that they come from a standard type of victory stela, and can be assigned to Sargon on the grounds of palaeography and of parallel passages in his other inscriptions.[216]

There are signs of destruction, probably to be attributed to this campaign of Sargon, at the mound of Tell Mor, in the territory of Ashdod.[217] It is probable that the sieges of two walled cities, and possibly also a third, depicted in reliefs from Sargon's palace at Khorsabad, are to be assigned to this campaign of 712.[218] Two of these cities are labelled respectively ʾa-am-qa-ru-na, Ekron, and gab-bu-tú-nu, Biblical Gibbethon, described in the ninth century as belonging to the Philistines (I Ki. 15:27; 16:15).[219] The third walled city is shown under siege between the other two in this same series of reliefs,[220] and though it is not labelled presumably represents some other important site in the general area of

[212] A 30, 143, 155, 380.   [213] Cf. CAD 6 (Ḥ), 198, ḫirīsu A. 'moat, ditch'.
[214] B 49 I, 119–20; B 172.   [215] B 49 I, 155; B 114, 21, 92–4.   [216] B 114, 192–7.
[217] B 49 III, 890.
[218] A 70, 94 and figs. 9–10; A 118 II, pls. 89, 93 (and cf. pl. 85), V, 138, 141; A 166, 36–40 and plan, fig. 2; A 209, 83 n. 243; B 316, 111 and pls. 78b, c.
[219] B 16, 377; for the reading ʾa-am-qa-ru-na see A 109a, 110.   [220] A 118 II, pl. 90, V, 138–9.

the other two, possibly Ashdod.[221] At the important site of Ashkelon there is no sign of destruction at this time,[222] because it seems to have taken no part in Yamani's rebellion. A damaged tablet from Nimrud, which is probably to be dated to about this year, mentions Ashkelon and Gaza as payers of tribute.[223]

Though Sargon's annals give the impression that he conducted this campaign in person, the Eponym Chronicle states that he spent that year 'in the land',[224] that is to say, in Assyria. In this context, the true situation is probably described in the Book of Isaiah, where a message from Yahweh to the prophet is dated to the year in which Sargon sent *tartān* to Ashdod, which he captured (Is. 20:1). The *turtānu* was the military officer ranking next below the king,[225] and he is quite likely to have been given such a military assignment, the accomplishment of which would have been attributed in the royal annals to the king himself. It is possible indeed, in this instance (if we assume that the officer who held the rank of *turtānu* had held it already four years before), that he had some personal involvement with Ashdod, since the Nimrud tablet which mentions the bearers of tribute to Calah in about 716 B.C. speaks of the emissary from Ashdod making a special expedition outside Calah in the company of an officer of the *turtānu*.[226] The relief depicting the siege of Ekron appears to show Sargon inspecting the prisoners, but since this might have taken place in Assyria after the return of the *turtānu* with the victorious army, it need not rule out the association of the sculptures with the campaign of 712.[227] It is possible to interpret some of the defenders shown in the relief of the siege of Gibbethon as negroes, so it may be that though Shabako would not involve himself in the war, Nubian mercenaries were present at the action.[228]

The passing reference to Sargon in Isaiah cited above is the sole passage in the Old Testament in which he is mentioned.[229] Ashdod and its surrounding territory were annexed by Sargon and made into an Assyrian province,[230] but Judah continued independent and saw no more of the Assyrians in the lifetime of Sargon. His attentions were engaged in Babylonia and the east and north. In fact, while campaigning to the north east in 705 he was killed in action, and was succeeded by his son Sennacherib. It was usually at the beginning of the reign of a new Assyrian king that subservient and tributary nations sought to break away to independence, and Hezekiah became involved in such moves in

[221] A 166 (1), 40, argues for Gaza because he takes the whole series (Room V) as illustrating the campaign of 720 B.C. Cf. also, arguing for 720 B.C., A 202, 99–102.

[222] B 49 I, 122.   [223] Tablet ND.2672 (A 100, 42; A 464, 147, 387–9; cf. A 70, 94).

[224] A 763, 413; A 209, 85.   [225] A 43, 102; A 429, 60–3.

[226] Tablet ND.2765 (see n. 177 above).   [227] Cf. A 202, 100–1.   [228] Cf. A 202, 100–1.

[229] Spelt *sargôn*, on which see B 225, 8.   [230] A 420, 63.

the early years of Sennacherib's reign (II Ki. 18:7). According to Kings and a virtually duplicate account in Isaiah, Hezekiah received an embassy from Merodach-baladan, king of Babylon (II Ki. 20:12–19; Is. 39:1–8), which may have been connected with attempts by the latter to break free from Assyrian domination, perhaps by encouraging the opening of a 'second front' to distract Sennacherib in the west. Merodach-baladan was king in Babylon in 721–710 and again for a period of nine months in 703, and it is possible that this embassy, whose intention was perhaps to assess Hezekiah's worth as a potential ally, took place in 703 when Merodach-baladan mounted a military rebellion in Babylonia.[231] The description of this embassy is placed in Kings after an account of events which probably took place later, but the phrase 'at that time' which introduced it may be no more than a literary device for introducing a new topic, the account of Hezekiah's reign not necessarily being given in chronological sequence.

Merodach-baladan's father is not named in the cuneiform sources, but both Kings and Isaiah identify him as Baladan, *bl'dn*, and it has been plausibly suggested that this might represent Babylonian Bêl-iddina, an equation supported by the occurrence of this name referring to a private individual on a fifth-century cuneiform tablet from Nippur, on which the Aramaic endorsement gives its alphabetic spelling as *bl'dn*.[232] If this is correct, it would be a rare instance of the Old Testament supplying the name of a Babylonian historical figure not known in the native sources.

According to the accounts in Kings and Isaiah, Hezekiah showed the Babylonian delegates treasures of gold, silver, balsam oil, aromatic oil, and arms, in his storehouses (II Ki. 20:13; Is. 39:2), and this catalogue may be amplified by a list of his riches, not specifically connected with the Babylonian embassy, in Chronicles, which includes mention of grain, wine, and olive oil, the three staples which were derived from the land (II Chron. 32:28). The words used for these three products, *dāgān*, 'unground grain', *tîrôš*, 'new (partially fermented) wine' and *yiṣhār*, 'raw olive oil',[233] suggest that Hezekiah's storehouses contained the collected dues, or taxes, of the kingdom in their natural state. It is possible that the administrative machinery by which these dues were collected finds archaeological expression in the markings on large storage vessels which have been found in a number of excavated sites.[234] These vessels were marked by seal impressions stamped on the handles before baking (Pls. Vol., pls. 162 *a–b*). The impressions fall into two major groups: royal, with a winged symbol accompanied by the inscription *lmlk*, 'belonging

[231] See A 532, 31–3.
[232] B 108 no. 76; B 223, citing BE 10 no. 60 and p. 44; J. Kohler and A. Ungnad, *Hundert ausgewählte Rechtsurkunden* (Leipzig, 1911), no. 4.   [233] See B 116, 103 on Deut. 7: 13.
[234] B 36, 242 and pl. 82.1.

to the king', and a place name;[235] and private, with a two-line inscription giving a personal name. If illegible examples are included, over eight hundred handles with royal seal impressions have been found at over twenty sites,[236] which, with minor exceptions, are situated in the limited territory to which the kingdom of Judah was reduced in the late eighth and early seventh centuries B.C. The place names Hebron, Ziph, Socoh, and *mmšt* (possibly Emmaus)[237] are plausible administrative centres, and the distribution of the stamped handles suggests that the jars, which had capacities of nine to ten gallons, contained products which were collected at the four centres, passed to Jerusalem, and were then redistributed throughout the kingdom.[238]

The date of these stamped jars is not certain. A very large number, over three hundred, of *lmlk* jar handles were excavated at Lachish,[239] with few exceptions deriving from level III.[240] This level was destroyed by fire, and though the date of its destruction has been a matter of debate, there is good reason to attribute it to Sennacherib in 701, and therefore to assign the stamped jar handles to Hezekiah or one of his predecessors.[241] The evidence from other sites is limited, since most excavators have not distinguished a stratigraphical division which can be dated to Sennacherib's invasion. At Ramat Rahel, the site at which, next to Lachish, the largest number of stamped handles (147) were found,[242] it is only possible to say that they were in use some time in the eighth or seventh century since, though some were found in level VA, over half came from the rubble fill of the earlier, eighth to seventh century, level VB, which was razed and cut into during the building of level VA.[243] At Arad in the south, however, the end of level VIII is possibly to be dated to this time,[244] and though two of the five *lmlk* stamped jar handles from that site were found in the later level VII, and the three others were unstratified, several of the complete jars were found in level VIII.[245] Close examination of the impressions of the *lmlk* seals suggests that they were made from fewer than thirty actual seals;[246] the form of the script used on them argues for a date in the eighth century, and shows sufficient uniformity to suggest a relatively short period of use.[247]

No indication of date is to be derived from the personal names which occur on the associated private seals. At one time it was thought that the

[235] B 330, 4–30.
[236] B 194, 16–17 and n. 33; B 330, 57–92, 175–88 (23 sites).   [237] B 197.
[238] B 16, 420 n. 24.   [239] B 330, 183–4, to which add B 318, 76–81.
[240] B 314, 315, 340; B 317, 54–6.
[241] A 896; B 7; B 15, 47–51; B 317, 31–57. For a different view see B 192; B 315, 49–53.
[242] B 330, 184–6. Large numbers are now reported from Jerusalem.
[243] B 49 IV, 1001–3, 1006.   [244] B 7, 78–9 fig. 3; B 49 I, 85.
[245] B 18, 138; see however B 245, 35 and chart 4.   [246] B 330, 36–44, distinguishes 28.
[247] B 198, 679–80.

seal of Eliakim, steward of Jehoiachin, should be associated with Jehoiachin, king of Judah in 598–597 B.C.,[248] but the probability that this seal was used on a jar also marked with the *lmlk* Hebron seal, and the fact, now clear from more recent seal discoveries, that the term *n^{c}r*, formerly thought to designate a royal official, usually referred only to the servant or steward of a private citizen,[249] suggests that this Jehoiachin was simply a local official in eighth-century Hebron. One of Hezekiah's high officials, his royal steward, was named Eliakim, but there is no way of knowing whether the man mentioned in so humble a capacity on this seal would have risen to that position. Another high official in the service of Hezekiah, a scribe, was named Shebna, but there is again no way of knowing whether 'Nera son of Shebna' named on the seal impressions was his son, serving in a more junior capacity in Hebron.

There is insufficient evidence to connect the administrative system implied by the stamped jar handles with any particular king; though the question should remain open, Hezekiah must be considered one of the main possibilities. The distribution of *lmlk* jar stamps, according to which the sites yielding the most substantial numbers are largely spaced in a defensive arc round the north and west of Jerusalem, suggests that one of the main purposes to which the rations contained in the jars were put was the provisioning of defensive garrisons.

These preparations may have been connected with Hezekiah's involvement in moves to break away from Assyrian domination. The statement in Kings that he revolted against Assyria is immediately followed by reference to substantial territorial conquests on his part in Philistia (II Ki. 18:7–8), and indeed Sennacherib in his annals states that the people of Ekron overthrew Padi their ruler, and handed him over to Hezekiah for internment in Jerusalem.[250] Two ostraca from Tell Qasile, incised with a record of 30 shekels of gold and 1,100 measures (possibly jars) of oil, the latter *lmlk*, 'belonging to the king',[251] may date from this period, and they may possibly reflect the placing by Hezekiah of administrative agents in outposts outside his territory. Though the site of Tell Qasile lies to the north of Joppa in what had probably been Israelite territory, the spelling of a personal name *ḥyhw*, Hiyahu (or possibly Ahiyahu) on one of these ostraca suggests, by the termination *-yhw*, that the scribe was from Judah.[252] The gold ('Ophir gold' (*zhb.'pr*) – probably a designation of quality rather than origin) is consigned on the other ostracon 'to Beth-horon',[253] on the direct route from Tell Qasile to Jerusalem. The gold, which amounted to a fairly modest

[248] B 20; B 22, 50 (= 107).   [249] B 101, 294–300.
[250] Annals ii 73–7 (A 35 II, 119 §240; A 44, 287; A 270, 31; B 339, 66); see p. 359 and n. 269 below.
[251] B 133, 15–17 no. 4; B 134, 192 fig. 18; B 199, 251–5.   [252] See *CAH* III².1, 472.
[253] Spelt *byṭhrn*, on which see B 102, 48 no. 6; B 199, 253–4.

quantity (about 345 grammes)[254] seems to have been on its way to Jerusalem, but it is quite probable that the oil, which was in its finished state, *šemen*, rather than raw, *yiṣhār*,[255] was being exported, perhaps to Phoenicia, and it has been pointed out that 1,100 jars, if jars are the unspecified measures in question, would have constituted a reasonable boat load.[256] The king of Tyre at this time, with whom trade is likely, was Elulaios (Assyrian Luli), who had been king since the time of Shalmaneser V.[257] He had been a loyal vassal and ally of Sargon,[258] and his consequent freedom to trade without material interference no doubt brought prosperity. He must have found his subservience to Assyria irksome, however, for he was one of the leaders in the western rebellion against Sennacherib. Those taking part in this rebellion understood the risks involved in confronting the power of Assyria, and the Ekronites, and perhaps others, seem therefore to have sought to enlist the aid of Egypt, now under the Twenty-fifth Dynasty, and probably under a new king, Shebitku (702–690), who was more willing to co-operate with his Palestinian neighbours than his predecessor Shabako had been.[259]

Hezekiah's rebellious preparations were not confined to his outer defences. According to Chronicles (II Chron. 32:5), he rebuilt, or repaired, all the damaged parts of the existing wall of Jerusalem, probably 'raised up towers (or bastions) on it',[260] and reinforced the Millo, a reference to the terraces built out on the eastern slope of the old city.[261] There can be little doubt that the digging of the Siloam tunnel was associated with these works. This was a major engineering project which brought water from the natural spring, modern ʿAin Sitti Maryam, almost certainly the Gihon of the Old Testament, on the north east slope of Ophel (the south-eastern hill of Jerusalem) a distance of about 533 m to the south-west corner of the hill. The tunnel was hewn out of the solid rock by two gangs of workmen who started at opposite ends, and met near what is now the middle point. The meeting and completion was commemorated by an inscription cut on the wall about 6.5 m from the present debouchment.[262] It states that, as the two parties of workmen neared one another, a man's voice could be heard calling, and that the labourers eventually met, striking 'pick against pick', and the water flowed from the 'outlet' (*mwṣ³*) to the 'pool' (*brkh*), a distance of

---

[254] Taking the shekel at 11.5 grammes.

[255] See p. 353 and n. 233 above.   [256] B 199, 253.

[257] 727–701 B.C. A 163, 98; A 845, 349, proposes 729–694 B.C.   [258] A 845, 229–45.

[259] Taylor Prism (p. 359 and n. 269 below ii 78–81 (A 35 II, 119–20 §240; A 44, 287; A 270, 31; B 339, 66); see A 30, 154–5, 385. Cf. *CAH* III².3, 694.

[260] Reading, with RSV and NEB, *wayyaʿal ʿāle<y> hā migdālôt*, in place of *wayyaʿal ʿal-hammigdālôt*, 'and he raised [or went] up on the towers'.   [261] See B 178, 100–3.

[262] A 15 no. 189; A 44, 321; B 57 I, fig. 87 (situated at A); B 131, 66–7, no. 38; B 133, 21–3 no. 7; B 339, 209–11.

1,200 cubits. Simple inspection of the tunnel associated with this inscription shows that the complex of spring and subterranean pool on the north-east side of the city must have been the 'outlet', and that the new destination of the waters on the south west would have been the 'pool'. The outlet or spring is referred to in Chronicles, where it is stated that 'Hezekiah stopped up the upper outlet [*mwṣ*] of the waters of Gihon, and brought them down on the west side of the city of David' (II Chron. 32:30); the lower pool is mentioned in Kings, where Hezekiah is said to have 'made the pool [*brkh*] and the conduit, and brought water into the city' (II Ki. 20:20).

Before the Israelite conquest of Jerusalem in the early tenth century, the main water supply of the city was obtained from the natural spring on the north-eastern slope of Ophel, accessible from inside the wall by way of a twisting passage leading to the top of a vertical shaft some 15 m deep. This gave on to a water channel connected with the spring.[263] Originally the waters of the spring must have run down the eastern slope into the Kidron valley, but the outer opening had subsequently been built up sufficiently to back up the waters along the channel to the foot of the vertical shaft. This water system had been inherited by the Israelites; but at some point during the monarchy the water, which must continually have run away down the eastern slope – for the water had no other exit, and is unlikely to have been completely consumed inside the city – was channelled southwards in an aqueduct along the west slope of the Kidron valley, just outside the eastern wall of the city, to a pool at the southern end of the hill, located in the area of the modern Birket el-Hamra.[264] It is probably this channel to which reference is made in Chronicles, where it is said that Hezekiah assembled a large work force, and blocked all the springs outside the city, as well as the water course (*naḥal*) which flowed through the middle of the land. The passage specifically states that this was done in order to deny water to the Assyrians (II Chron. 32:3–4).[265] The blocking of this conduit would have caused surplus water once again to flow away down the eastern slope of the city hill, showing attackers where the water supply was located. This may have been one of the main motives for the cutting of the tunnel, for once the water had been made to debouch at the southern end of the city, it would not have been difficult to disperse it on down the valley, where tangled vegetation would have obscured it.[266] The precise location and form of the lower pool into which the waters flowed is unknown, since much of the rock at the south-western tip of the Ophel hill has been quarried and otherwise eroded away, and the evidence thus

---

[263] See B 178 figs. 16–17.
[264] B 288, 110; B 292, 176–8, fig. 23, canal II; B 335, 36 and fig. 2.   [265] Cf. B 335, 37–8.
[266] B 288, 110; B 335, 37–8.

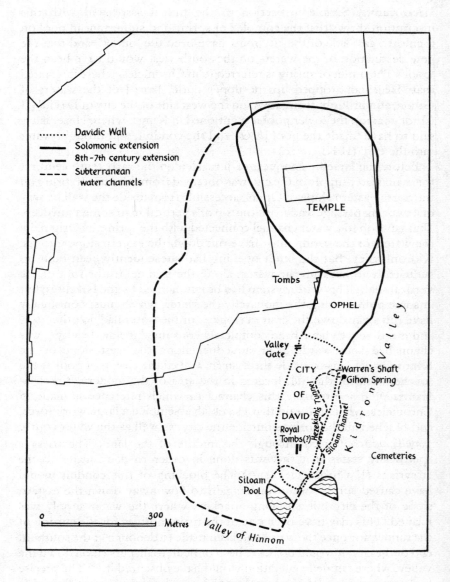

Fig. 13. Plan of Jerusalem. (After B 350, pl. on p. 5.)

destroyed. At present, the waters flow from Hezekiah's tunnel into the Pool of Siloam. It is possible that this lay in a subterranean chamber outside the city wall in Hezekiah's time, but recent work can be interpreted to suggest that Hezekiah's wall extended far enough west to enclose the pool.[267]

In addition to these structural measures, Hezekiah is said to have equipped the defenders with small shields and hand-weapons of some kind, perhaps a type that could be thrown or projected from the walls of the city (II Chron, 32:5).[268] The Assyrian threat was now sufficiently serious for Hezekiah to introduce martial law in the city and to deliver an encouraging address to the assembled people (II Chron. 32:6–8).

It is not clear how these activities corresponded in time with the rumours of the Assyrian military preparations and advance. The annals of Sennacherib survive in a number of editions, but are best known from that of 691–689 B.C., represented by several exemplars, including the Taylor and the Chicago Prisms, which describe eight campaigns (Pls. Vol., pl. 163).[269] It is clear from these that in his third campaign, which took place in 701, he marched to the west, dealing first of all with the cities in Phoenicia, including Sidon and Tyre, where Luli, who had just managed to escape to Cyprus, was replaced by Sennacherib's nominee, Ethbaᶜal. Sennacherib then moved southwards where Pudu-ilu of Ammon, Kammusu-nadbi of Moab and Aiarammu of Edom, all in Transjordan, as well as Metinti of Ashdod, all hastily submitted with tribute.[270] The probable predecessors of Pudu-ilu are known from the statue inscription of Yerah-ᶜazar, which names the latter's father Zakkur, and grandfather Shanib,[271] and Pudu-ilu is himself probably mentioned on an Ammonite seal inscribed 'Belonging to Bayadʾel retainer of Peda-ʾel'.[272] The annals then narrate Sennacherib's replacement of Ṣidqa, the rebellious ruler of Ashkelon, with Sharru-lu-dari, and the conquest of Joppa and a group of neighbouring towns, which are described as 'towns of Ṣidqa'.[273] Since Sennacherib would have reached these towns, which were some 50 km to the north of Ashkelon, before Ashkelon itself, and there is no specific mention of a siege of the latter, it may be that when the fate of these northern dependencies became known, Ṣidqa was overthrown by a pro-Assyrian party in the city, so, Sennacherib would have been spared the trouble of conquering the city.[274] Ṣidqa's

---

[267] B 79; B 350, 41–51.   [268] *magen* and *šelaḥ*, on which see B 109, 243–5.

[269] See A 4 II, 60, 67–9, for a convenient transliteration of the account of the third campaign (Chicago and Taylor Prisms). See also A 285, 193–4 for the edition of 691–689 B.C.

[270] Annals ii 37–60 (A 35 II, 118–19 §239; A 44, 287; A 270, 29–30; B 339, 66). The name Aiarammu was formerly read Malik-rammu (see B 285, 467–8).   [271] See p. 336 and n. 97 above.

[272] CIS I no. 76; B 99, 13 and n. 9; B 157, 59–60 no. 3; and cf. the Biblical name *Pĕdaḫʾel* (Num. 34: 28).   [273] Annals ii 61–72 (A 35 II, 119 §239; A 44, 287; A 270, 30–1; B 339, 66).

[274] Cf. the translation in A 44, 287.

successor, Sharru-lu-dari, was the son of Rukibti, who had been installed as king of Ashkelon over thirty years before by Tiglath-pileser, and whose sympathies were reflected by the purely Assyrian name which he had given to his son.[275]

According to the annals, Sennacherib was now confronted by the Egyptian army, whose assistance had been solicited by the rebels. This seems to have consisted of a combined force from Egypt and Nubia (Meluhha),[276] reflecting the fact that the whole of Egypt was ruled at this time by the Nubian dynasty under Shebitku. This army, together with a contingent from Ekron, met Sennacherib near Altaqu, Biblical Eltekeh (II Ki. 19:8–9; Is. 37:9),[277] a little over 15 km south of Joppa, suffering a defeat which was followed by the Assyrian conquest of Ekron and the neighbouring Timnah.[278] According to virtually duplicate accounts in Kings and Isaiah (II Ki. 19:9; Is. 37:9), both possibly derived from the source described in Chronicles as the 'Vision of Isaiah' (II Chron. 32:32),[279] the commander of the Egypto-Nubian army, who is not named in the Assyrian text, was Taharqa (Hebrew *tirhâqâ*), here described as 'king of Nubia (*kûš*)'. While Taharqa, a younger brother of Shebitku, did not become king until 690, it has been plausibly argued that he was about twenty years old at the time of Sennacherib's invasion, and could have been placed by Shebitku in titular command of the expeditionary force to Palestine.[280]

While Ekron was a Philistine city, it is probable that Timnah was within the territory of Judah. Hezekiah had taken Padi, the deposed pro-Assyrian king of Ekron, into custody at the request of his Philistine allies, and, though the details of the transaction are not stated, Sennacherib's annals claim that he 'caused Padi . . . to come out of Jerusalem', and reinstated him as ruler of Ekron.[281] It may be that Hezekiah, learning of the fall of Timnah, only about 30 km to the west of Jerusalem, hoped to placate Sennacherib by releasing Padi.[282] If so, the gesture did not achieve its object; and the fact that Hezekiah did not personally submit to 'the yoke' of Sennacherib, led the latter, according to his annals, to besiege forty-six fortified Judaean cities, as well as numerous small towns, deporting 200,150 people, and investing Hezekiah himself in

---

[275] Cf. A 70, 96–7; J. J. Stamm, *Die akkadische Namengebung* (Leipzig, 1939) 316.

[276] Annals ii 79–80 (A 35 II, 119–20 §240; A 44, 287; A 270, 31; B 339, 55). On Meluhha see A 344, 797, and 794–5 s.v. Makan; I. J. Gelb in *RA* 64 (1970) 7.

[277] B 16, 376; B 213, 72–7. See below, p. 693.

[278] Annals ii 80–iii 12 (A 35 II, 119–20 §240; A 44, 287–8; A 270, 31–2; B 339, 66–7).

[279] See B 293, 382–3, and see in general p. 361 and n. 286 below.

[280] A 30, 157–66, and especially 159–60, 386 n. 823 on the proleptic use of the designation 'king'. For the view that Taharqa could not have been in command in 701 B.C. and that Sennacherib must have made a second invasion of Palestine some time after 690 B.C., see B 78, 296–308.

[281] Annals iii 15 (A 270, 32).   [282] For an alternative explanation see B 210, 183–4.

Jerusalem.[283] His annals do not state by what route Sennacherib's forces approached Jerusalem, but this information may be deduced from the series of sculptured reliefs from room XXXVI of his palace at Nineveh, which depict the siege of a fortified city (Fig. 14, Pls. Vol., pl. 164), and the reception of its surrender by Sennacherib seated on his throne.[284] The event depicted in this series is identified by an epigraph above the enthroned figure as the capitulation of Lachish to Sennacherib.[285] Chronicles states that Sennacherib was 'in front of Lachish' with all his forces, and that from there he sent his servants to Jerusalem (II Chron. 32:9), an action more fully described in the parallel accounts in Kings and Isaiah.[286] In Kings, Sennacherib is described as sending his senior military officer, the *tartānu*,[287] together with the *rab-sārîs* and *rab-šāqēh*, two senior officials (Assyrian *rab ša rēši* and *rab šaqê*),[288] and a large army (II Ki. 18:17). Only the *rab-šāqēh* is mentioned in Isaiah (36:2), possibly because he may have seemed to the Jews the most prominent of the three on account of his role as spokesman. It seems likely that the Assyrians established a camp on high ground to the north west of the city, a site, according to Josephus, chosen by Titus for his camp some 770 years later, and still known at that time as 'the camp of the Assyrians'.[289] According to the Biblical account, the *rab-šāqēh*, whose title is treated as a personal name, and his fellow officers then came and stood in or 'by the conduit of the upper pool which is by the highway of the fuller's field' (II Ki. 18:17; Is. 36:2). This location, near to the place at which Isaiah had delivered Yahweh's message to Ahaz some thirty years before,[290] cannot be certainly identified, but the implied combination of a water conduit and a fuller's field, that is to say, a field in which cloth was cleaned by treading or beating, almost certainly with the aid of water,[291] suggests the area at the foot of the eastern wall of the ancient city which, until the cutting of Hezekiah's tunnel, could have been watered from the aqueduct running southwards from the Gihon spring.[292] In this case the pool at the Gihon spring would have been the 'upper pool'. Though the terminology would not correspond to that implied by Chronicles, according to which this aqueduct or conduit was called *naḥal* (II Chron. 32:4) rather than *tĕʿālâ*, as here, it is not to be supposed that such vocabulary was rigidly used. If this is the correct interpretation, the

[283] Annals iii 18–30 (A 35 II, 120 §240; A 44, 288; A 270, 32–3; B 339, 67). On the number 200,150 see A 480, 1, 18–19, and n. 2; and cf. A 4, 136.

[284] BM 124904–15. A 45 nos. 371–4 (partial illustration); A 126, 174; A 133 pls. 20–4; A 147 pls. 68–76; B 317, 28–30.   [285] A 44, 288; A 155, 43; A 270, 156 no. xxv; B 339, 69–70.

[286] For the view that the account in Kings and Isaiah reflects three separate and mutually inconsistent sources see, e.g., B 88, 69–103; B 126, 234–5.   [287] See p. 352 and n. 225 above.

[288] See A 6, 91 and 112; A 52, 974 and 1182 respectively; and on *rab ša rēši*, A 431A; A 535, 309–11.

[289] *Jewish War* v.303, 504–7; on which see B 319.   [290] See p. 333 above.

[291] Cf. for Egypt, A. Erman, *Life in Ancient Egypt* (London, 1894; reprint Toronto, 1971) 217–18.

[292] See pp. 356–9 above.

Fig. 14. Series of bas-reliefs which decorated the walls of room XXXVI in the Palace of Sennacherib at Kouyunjik, the citadel mound of ancient Nineveh. The reliefs depict the siege and capture of the city of Lachish by Sennacherib in 701 B.C. The sequence of the action proceeds from left to right: Assyrian troops, including bowmen and slingers, advance on the city; the city is attacked up ramps by infantry following siege engines which are protected with water from large scoops against burning brands thrown down by the defenders; booty and captives are driven out of the city; Sennacherib on his throne in front of his tent receives the capitulation of the city; Sennacherib's chariot stands by, and behind him other troops wait in front of his fortified camp. A cuneiform inscription beside the king identifies him and names the city. (Drawing by Ann Searight.)

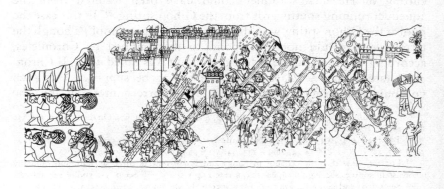

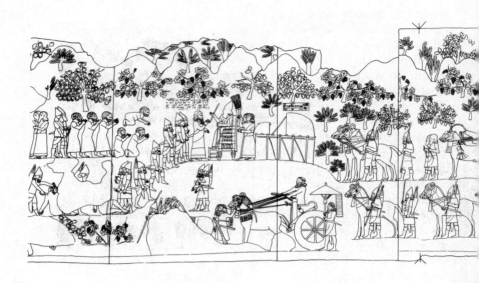

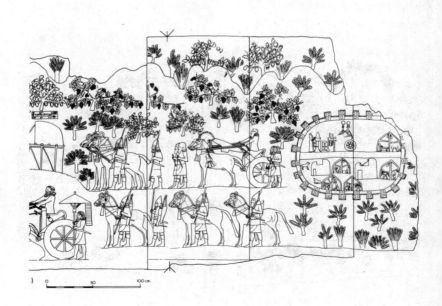

| | 0 | 50 | 100 cm. |

phrase 'upper pool' (*habbĕrēkâ hāᶜelyônâ*) would refer to one part only of the spring and pool which are together designated the 'source' (*môṣāʾ*) in Kings and the Siloam inscription.

It is a plausible interpretation that the Assyrians stood below the wall on the west slope of the Kidron valley,[293] and that from there the *rab-šāqēh* addressed the inhabitants. According to Kings, he called for Hezekiah, but was met by three high Judaean officials, Eliakim, Shebna, and Joah (II Ki. 18:18; cf. Is. 36:3), who presumably stood looking down from the wall. It appears that a considerable number of people also watched from inside the city, and if this encounter took place at the eastern wall many of them could have done so from the built-out terraces, Millo, which rose up the hill above it. The *rab-šāqēh* delivered his message in Hebrew (II Ki. 18:26; Is. 36:11), and when Eliakim asked him to speak Aramaic, already the language of diplomacy, so that the exchanges should be confidential, the *rab-šāqēh* continued in Hebrew, raising his voice so that all could hear (II Ki. 18:27–28; Is. 36:12–13; II Chron. 32:18). The *rab šāqēh*'s message was the simple one that Hezekiah should surrender the city because the Jews stood no chance of withstanding the power of Assyrian arms. He received no answer, but Eliakim and his colleagues took the message to Hezekiah, who received it in a despondent frame of mind, adopting the signs of mourning and withdrawing to the Temple, at the same time sending Eliakim and Shebna to Isaiah for advice.

Eliakim ben Hilkiah, on whom so much fell at this time, occupied the position of chamberlain,[294] Shebna, a man of pride and extravagance, now his junior, having been demoted from that office and that also of royal steward (*sōkēn*),[295] possibly through the influence of Isaiah, who had condemned him for these failings and for preparing a tomb for himself in a conspicuous situation (Is. 22:15–23). Though Shebna's name is here usually spelt *šebnāʾ*, or occasionally *šebnāh*, it is possible that these were abbreviated forms of the name *šebanyāhû* (*šbnyhw*)[296] attested in the Old Testament of other individuals, and that a rock-hewn tomb which has been discovered in a prominent position on the east side of the Kidron valley, facing towards the city, and identified by a damaged lintel inscription as that of . . . *yhw ʾšr ᶜl hbyt*, '. . . iah, the Chamberlain' (Pls. Vol., pl. 161)[297] was the tomb of Shebna of which Isaiah spoke. While Eliakim is himself unknown outside the Old Testament, it is possible that the seal impression, already mentioned, of 'Jehozarah ben Hilkiah

---

[293] See B 83A, which proposes, however, the lower end of the Kidron valley, not knowing, in 1958, of the location of the eastern city wall.

[294] On this title see *CAH* III².1, 465 and n. 174.   [295] See B 109, 131.

[296] B 255, 258 no. 1302.

[297] A 15 no. 191; B 131, 65–6, no. 37; B 133, 23–4 no. 8; cf. however B 173, suggesting that Hilkiah (*ḥlqyhw*), father of Eliaqim, was the owner of the tomb.

servant of Hezekiah',[298] is that of his brother, who was in that case also in the royal service.

According to the Biblical narrative, Isaiah assured Hezekiah's delegation that the message from Yahweh promised that there was no occasion for uneasiness, and that the Assyrians would withdraw from Judah without the need for any military action on the part of Hezekiah (II Ki. 19:5–7; Is. 37:5–7). The *rab-šāqēh* is then described as returning, perhaps to report an unsatisfactory response to Sennacherib, who was now besieging Libnah, having moved camp from Lachish (II Ki. 19:8; Is. 37:8). He may have been summoned to report to Sennacherib in view of rumours of the remustering of the Egyptian forces. Though the fate of Lachish is not described either in Sennacherib's annals or in the Biblical account, it is vividly depicted in the series of bas-reliefs already referred to (Fig. 14).

The evidence of these scenes is augmented by the discovery in the ruins of the level III gateway at Lachish of an Assyrian bronze helmet-crest together with numerous iron arrowheads, and some of bone, made perhaps by the defenders to replace scarce metal ones, as well as a number of sling stones.[299] These objects were associated with signs of violent destruction with burning which were found in different parts of the site.[300] A sloping mass of boulders covered by a layer of stones cemented together with a mortar of lime plaster and sand at the south-west angle of the city wall has been plausibly interpreted as the remains of the Assyrian siege ramp, which is clearly depicted in the bas-reliefs, and it appears from the reliefs that causeways of wooden beams were laid over the stones of this ramp to give smooth passage for the siege engines.[301] It is not clear why Sennacherib should have moved to Libnah after his success at Lachish, but it may be that this action simply formed part of a strategy of taking the towns and cities in the Shephelah, the lower western slopes of the Judaean hills, in order to secure the coastal plain. A number of towns in this region are named as under threat in a message proclaimed as from Yahweh, probably some time between 720 and 714, by Micah (Mic. 1:10–15),[302] and it is probable that the majority of the forty-six fortified cities claimed among his conquests by Sennacherib were in this zone (cf. II Ki. 18:13). They certainly seem to have been within the orbit of Philistia, since Sennacherib states in his annals that he handed over a number of Hezekiah's towns to Metinti of Ashdod, Padi of Ekron, and Ṣilli-Bel of Gaza.[303]

[298] See p. 346 and n. 182 above.
[299] B 314, 55–6, 90, 385, 387, 396, 398, pls. 39, 40, 60, 63. See (in general) B 55 no. 17.
[300] B 314, 45, 48, 55–6; B 317, 31–2, 43–4, 46–7, 50–2.
[301] B 53; B 318, 71–4 and figs. 1 and 19.   [302] See B 29, 241–2, 276–83; and cf. B 16, 339.
[303] Annals iii 31–4 (A 35 II, 120 §240; A 44, 288; A 270, 33; B 339, 67).

It appears that at this time Taharqa was once again threatening the Assyrian army, having presumably recovered from his defeat at Eltekeh, and having remustered his forces (II Ki. 19:9; Is. 37:9).[304] Sennacherib may, in the light of this, have felt that with a substantial part of his army away in the east besieging Jerusalem his position was unduly exposed. At all events he is said to have again sent messengers to Hezekiah (II Ki. 19:9)[305] carrying a written message, which they also delivered orally, once more calling upon him to surrender. Hezekiah is said to have taken the document into the Temple where he prayed to Yahweh for help, and in consequence received a message through Isaiah that Yahweh would ensure that the Assyrian attack would not succeed (II Ki. 19:9–34; Is. 37:9–35). This is followed by a much debated statement that during the night the messenger, or angel, of Yahweh struck down 185,000 in the Assyrian camp; they were found in the morning to be dead. Following this Sennacherib withdrew and returned to Nineveh (II Ki. 19:35–6; Is. 27:36–7). Since the time of Josephus[306] this has commonly been taken to be a reference to sickness of some kind in the Assyrian camp, and it has been further suggested that a garbled reflection of it is to be found in an Egyptian tradition, quoted by Herodotus,[307] according to which the army of Sennacherib which was besieging Pelusium was forced to retreat as a result of the destruction of their equipment by a swarm of field mice. It has been pointed out that in both the Old Testament (I Sam. 6:4–5) and Greek literature[308] the mouse is a symbol of plague.[309] The apparently very large number of those who perished is given in the form 'hundred eighty and five ʾālep', and one possibility worth considering is that ʾālep (ʾelep), 'thousand', here was originally ʾalûp, 'commander of a thousand', or 'picked man', subsequently misunderstood and wrongly vocalized, and that the passage is stating that 185 picked men died.[310] An element of speculation must at present remain in the interpretation of this passage, but that the Assyrians did indeed withdraw without taking Jerusalem is tacitly admitted in Sennacherib's annals, where no claim is made that Jerusalem capitulated.

Some reflection of part of the reason for Sennacherib's withdrawal is possibly to be seen in the predictive statement of Yahweh transmitted by Isaiah, that the Assyrian king would hear a rumour, in this case perhaps news of trouble in Babylonia, and return to his own land (II Ki. 19:7; Is.

---

[304] A 30, 385 n. 822. See below, pp. 696 and 698–9.
[305] Literally 'and he returned (wyšb) and sent', while the parallel in Isaiah reads 'and he heard (wyšmʿ) and sent'. [306] Anti. Jud. x.21. [307] Histories II.141. [308] Homer, Iliad I. 39.
[309] See, e.g., A. D. Godley, Herodotus I (1920) 447 n. 2; W. W. How and J. Wells, A Commentary on Herodotus I (Oxford, 1912) 236.
[310] For possible instances in other passages, in which the form is ʾelep rather than ʾalûpîm, see B 332, 24–7.

37:7).[311] The annals say that Hezekiah was shut up in Jerusalem and that fortifications were established around it to intercept any who might seek to get out,[312] and they claim that there were desertions from Hezekiah's forces, including even some of his elite troops.[313] In speaking of tribute from Hezekiah, however, it is only stated that it was sent later ('after me').[314] This tribute is presumably that referred to earlier in the sequence of the Biblical account (II Ki. 18:13–16), since the latter passage appears to encapsulate the entire war, while episodes within it are given more expanded treatment in subsequent passages. The two accounts agree in listing 30 talents of gold among the tribute, but differ over the quantity of silver, the Assyrian claiming 800 talents as against the Hebrew 300. It has been suggested that this discrepancy is to be explained by reference to a 'light' and a 'heavy' talent,[315] but in that case it is not clear why the figures for the gold should not differ by the same proportion. It appears more likely that an error has arisen in the transmission of the figure in one of the sources.

According to the Biblical account, Hezekiah stripped parts of the Temple in order to obtain the gold and silver,[316] and he probably had to resort to similar measures to obtain the remainder of the tribute, not named in the Old Testament, but given in the Assyrian annals as including precious stones, valuable woods, furniture decorated with ivory, iron daggers and raw iron,[317] and male and female musicians.[318] This illustrates the fact that, in addition to repeated exactions of tribute, the Assyrians, particularly since the time of Tiglath-pileser III, imposed deportations of population, the example of Samaria being only the best known of many. According to the surviving Assyrian texts, Tiglath-pileser had deported over 360,000 individuals throughout the areas of his wars, Sargon claims over 200,000, Sennacherib over 400,000, and while Esarhaddon and Ashurbanipal give no figures, they each mention over ten mass deportations, in which comparable numbers of people were no doubt moved.[319] To the extent that deportations from the south west are specifically mentioned in the documents, it can be seen that their destination was most often the Assyrian homeland, or the areas adjacent to it,[320] and it is in this context that the Aramaic ostracon from Nimrud mentioned above, which may be dated palaeographically approximately

---

[311] For the suggestion that mice attacking the camp might have been taken as an omen of disaster see B 178A, 363 n. 81.   [312] Annals iii 27–30 (A 35 II, 120 §240; A 44, 288; A 270, 33; B 339, 67).

[313] Annals iii 37–41 (A 35 II, 120–1 §240; A 44, 288 and n. 4; A 270, 33–4; B 339, 67); on which see A 41, 136; *CAD* 2 (B), 176, s.v. *baṭiltu.*

[314] Annals iii 41–9 (A 35 II, 121 §240; A 44, 288; A 270, 34).

[315] B 229, 485.   [316] See B 145, 284–5.

[317] Rassam Cylinder C i 57 (A 4, 75; A 270, 60); see A 463, 286, 293.

[318] On *nâru*, 'musician', and *nârtu*, 'female musician', see *CAD* 11 (N) I, 363–4, 376–9.

[319] A 480, 19–22.

[320] A 480, 116–35 (from area 20 in column 2 to areas 31 or 33–5 in column 4).

to the late eighth century B.C.,[321] or the reign of Sargon or Sennacherib, should be considered.[322] This ostracon is inscribed in ink on both sides, probably by two different but contemporary scribes, each side simply giving a list of personal names, mostly in the form X *bn* Y, 'X son of Y'. Altogether fifteen individuals are named including what may have been two pairs of brothers, and three instances of more than one man with the same first name, so only twenty-two fully legible names are attested. Of these, half are known either from the Old Testament or from inscriptions to have been the names of Hebrews. There are none compounded with the divine element *yhwh*, so all that can be said of the ethnic affinities of the men mentioned on this ostracon is that they were Western Semites from conquered populations in Aram, Phoenicia, Ammon, Edom, Israel, or Judah, and that while such a man as Menahem ben Elisha may have been a Hebrew, it seems most likely that the group was a mixed one.[323]

Pictorial evidence that Judaeans were among those taken to Assyria is afforded by the sculptures from the Palace of Sennacherib at Nineveh. In Fig. 14 the defenders of Lachish are depicted wearing a distinctive head-dress formed by a wide band of cloth wound round and over the head, with the end hanging down at the side. Men with this same head-dress appear among the labourers shown moving the colossal winged bulls which were incorporated in Sennacherib's Palace, while another appears elsewhere in the more favoured role of a royal bodyguard.[324] One isolated relief, not part of the main Lachish series, which depicts three lyre players, two wearing this head-dress without the hanging end, escorted by an Assyrian soldier in mountain scenery, may show some of the musicians mentioned as part of the tribute taken by Sennacherib being assembled in Palestine for deportation.[325]

The fragmentary text tentatively cited above,[326] which describes the conquests of a Philistine city and of Azekah in western Judah by an unnamed Assyrian king, cannot be absolutely separated from the time of Hezekiah, for though the traces of signs and the space at the crucial lacuna do not agree with the restoration of his name,[327] the name Uzziah, the other likely candidate, itself remains uncertain. An abnormal writing of *ḫa-za-qi-a-u* should not be ruled out, for he like Uzziah had made conquests in Philistia, and an Assyrian conquest of Azekah, lying as it

---

[321] B 246, 14, fig. 2 nos. 3–4.

[322] Ostracon ND.6321; A 400; B 25; B 75; B 247; and p. 322 n. 2 and p. 341 above.

[323] B 247 argues that the group was entirely Ammonite.

[324] BM 124822 and 124901. A 155, 57–63, figs. 14–16, 19–21, pls. 2:2–3, 3:1–2; B 53, 163–4, pl. 32B; B 55, 65 and figs. 41, 46.   [325] BM 124947 (A 126, 176); A 155, 61–2, fig. 18, pl. 3:3.

[326] P. 331 and n. 53 above.

[327] It is possible to read *ḫa-x-y-a-a-u*, but while *az* (rather than *za*) is acceptable at x, there is insufficient space at y for *qi* or *qí*.

does about 10 km east of Libnah on the way to Jerusalem, would have been plausible. The attribution of this tablet must therefore remain an open question.

At some unspecified time, evidently during the Assyrian threat, Hezekiah is said to have been seriously ill (II Ki. 20:1–6; Is. 38:1–6), and this episode affords an interesting glimpse of the medical practice of the time. It is reported that Isaiah directed that the inflammation associated with his ailment be treated by the application of a fig cake (II Ki. 20:7; Is. 38:7) as a poultice, a treatment known for horses at Ugarit some centuries earlier.[328]

Hezekiah survived both the Assyrian invasion and his illness, and the kingdom of Judah was to survive in independence, though sometimes with vassal status, for a further century.

[328] See B 125, 406–7 no. 38; B 140, 698; B 229, 512, 597. The interpretation of II Ki. 20: 9–11 and Isaiah 38: 8 as referring to some kind of sun-clock (B 229, 508–9; B 345A) is improbable; see B 109, 183.

CHAPTER 30

JUDAH UNTIL THE FALL OF JERUSALEM

(*c.* 700–586 B.C.)

T. C. MITCHELL

I. HEZEKIAH'S LATER YEARS

Sennacherib failed to take Jerusalem in 701 B.C., and Judah remained an independent state, but the kingdom had been weakened, Sennacherib having laid waste, as he put it in monumental inscriptions on a bull colossus and a stone slab, 'the wide district of Judah'.[1] Pudu-ilu of Ammon, Kammusu-nadbi of Moab and Aiarammu of Edom had all escaped such devastation by paying tribute to Sennacherib without delay, and it seems likely that they now saw an opportunity to take advantage of the weakness of Judah. Levels II at Beersheba and VIII at Arad were destroyed at about this time,[2] and though this might have been part of Sennacherib's operation, both cities lie rather far south of the area in which the Assyrians seem mainly to have conducted their campaign. It might well be that they mark an incursion of the Edomites, who indeed seem to have suffered an encroachment on the part of Judah earlier in Hezekiah's reign (I Chron. 4:41–3). That the Edomites were a threat in this area at about this time is suggested by a letter found in level VIII at Arad.[3] This appears to have been sent by two officers, Gemariah and Nehemiah, in a military outpost to their superior Malkiah, presumably in Arad, and it states that the king should know that, thanks to trouble from the Edomites, they have been unable to send something (the text at that point is damaged). If the destruction of level VIII was the result of Edomite action this could have been a presage of the coming threat to the weakened state.

The unorthodox temple at Arad, which had been founded in the tenth century, had continued in use in level VIII, though the built altar had gone out of use, perhaps as a result of Hezekiah's reforms. If this is so, however, the effectiveness of the reform would seem to have been only partial at the site, for it appears that the sanctuary was served by a body of, presumably unorthodox, functionaries. This is suggested by a group

---

[1] Bull Inscription (A 4, 66–7), 20–2; Nebi Yunus Slab (A 4, 6), 15; for both texts see A 4, 76, and A 44, 288.   [2] B 13, 5–6, 107; B 49 I, 167, and 85 respectively.
[3] Arad Ostracon 40 (B 17, 70–4; B 121, no. 62; B 199, 207–9, 234; B 262, 323–5; B 327, 202–3 no. 1).

of ostraca from the temple, each inscribed with a single name, including two, Meremoth and Pashhur, known from the Bible as recurring in priestly families.[4] It is possible that these ostraca had served as lots to determine the periods of duty at the temple of the men whose names they bore, in the same way as is recorded of the cultic musicians in the time of David (I Chron. 25:8). Also in the temple were found the remains of a pottery bowl inscribed in ink on both the inside and the outside with marked-off columns giving lists of individuals and groups followed by numerals, indicating perhaps the participants in an offering ritual.[5]

The destruction level at Beersheba has also yielded fragmentary inscribed ostraca, probably records of the issue of rations, perhaps to members of the local garrison.[6] There is evidence of sporadic occupation during the eighth and seventh centuries B.C. at Khirbet Qumran at the north-west corner of the Dead Sea and also in caves in the Wadi Murabbaᶜat, some 18 km to the south. It is possible that these caves served as temporary refuges and perhaps military outposts at this time, when Judah had been weakened by Assyria and was now threatened from Transjordan. This may explain the discovery in Cave 2 at Murabbaᶜat of a fragmentary Hebrew letter on papyrus which may be dated palaeographically to about this time.[7] This document is too fragmentary to convey any historical information, but it is of special significance as representing the only pre-Hellenistic inscribed papyrus known from Palestine. Papyrus was, however, widely used in Egypt and the Levant and may be presumed to have been the principal writing material in Israel and Judah during the period of the monarchy, as is shown by Biblical references to inscribed scrolls (Ps. 40:8; Jer. 36:2–4; Ezek. 2:9), which suggest papyrus rather than leather,[8] and seal impressions with backs showing the imprint of the papyrus documents which they sealed.[9]

Little can be said about the activities of Hezekiah after the removal of the Assyrian threat. Since there seems to be reason for associating the *lmlk* jar-handle stamps with the period preceding Sennacherib's invasion, their virtual disappearance from the archaeological record after this event suggests the collapse of Hezekiah's administrative system, and a failure to restore it. It seems likely that both Isaiah and Micah died, or certainly became too old to work, in the early seventh century, since they both name Hezekiah as the last king under whom they prophesied. It has been suggested that Hezekiah, his energies

4 Arad Ostraca 50–7 (B 17, 85–7; B 121, nos. 65–72; B 199, 211–15).
5 Arad Ostracon 49 (B 17, 80–4; B 121, no. 72; B 199, 209–11).   6 B 199, 271–3.
7 B 61, 93–100, pl. XXVIII; B 133, 31–2 no. 11. See B 49 III, 692 fig.; B 94.
8 See B 5, 30–2; B 115, B 1–4, 240–1; N. Lewis, *Papyrus in Classical Antiquity* (Oxford, 1974) 6–9, 84–5.   9 E.g. B 11, 164–8; B 41, 193–4; B 45; B 161 nos. 4, 26.

having been sapped by the worries of the Assyrian invasion and by the ill-health which he suffered at that time, decided to associate his young son Manasseh on the throne with him, in order to begin the process of passing the burdens of rule to him, and to prepare him for kingship. There is no specific evidence for this, the suggestion depending upon chronological deductions, which, it is argued, favour the commencement of such a co-regency in 697 or 696 B.C., when Manasseh was twelve years old and Hezekiah forty-four.[10] This must remain purely hypothetical. In the account of his death in Chronicles, Hezekiah is said to have been buried in the upper section of the royal cemetery, and to have been honoured on the occasion by the people (II Chron. 32:33).[11]

II. THE REIGNS OF MANASSEH AND AMON

Manasseh succeeded his father Hezekiah in 687/686 B.C.,[12] beginning a reign of forty-five years (II Ki. 21:1; II Chron. 33:1).[13] Both Kings and Chronicles begin their accounts of his reign by stating that 'he did evil in the sight of Yahweh', and that he allowed, or indeed fostered, the kind of pagan practices which had characterized the religion of the Canaanites at the time of the conquest (II Ki. 21:2–7; II Chron. 33:2–7).[14] They then catalogue a remarkable series of aberrations from true Yahwism. The old cultic platforms and cult pillars were reintroduced, as well as altars to foreign gods (bĕʿālîm) and to 'the whole host of heaven', the latter referring to the worship of the sun, moon, and stars, probably in anthropomorphic form, an observance dating back to Canaanite times, but perhaps with some Babylonian elements brought in via Assyria through the agency of Aramaean contact.[15] Pagan altars were brought into the Temple, as also was a cult pillar described as an 'image' (pesel), perhaps bearing the rudimentary attributes of the female figure.[16] This introduction of pagan objects into the actual Temple established a new extreme of apostasy, because, while several earlier rulers had introduced foreign images and altars into the land, these had always been outside the Temple precincts. The Holy of Holies was the site of the Ark of the Covenant, which had been placed there by Solomon and had presumably remained there ever since, and it has been plausibly suggested that Manasseh now had it removed and replaced by the cult pillar.[17] What was done at that time with the Ark is unknown, but it may well have been

---

[10] B 306, 157–61.

[11] On 'upper section' (maʿăleh) and other possible interpretations see B 106, 493–4, and p. 381 below. Cf. also B 292, 203.   [12] B 306, 157–61.

[13] Fifty-five from the beginning of his co-regency. See n. 10.   [14] B 219, 20–7.

[15] A 11, 84–8; B 219, 45–59. See also B 275, 99, and in general A 845, 115–52.

[16] B 77 I, 441–4; B 219, 22–3.   [17] B 144; B 145, 276–82.

deposited in one of the Temple treasuries.[18] Further activities included the practice of sorcery, necromancy, and divination by cloud movements and snake behaviour,[19] and a return to the strange practices of the time of Ahaz in the Valley of the Sons of Hinnom, where Manasseh is said to have made his sons[20] 'pass through the fire'.[21]

The presence in Jerusalem of these pagan practices is possibly reflected by two caves cut into the eastern slope of the old city, one associated with two standing stone pillars (possibly *maṣṣēbôt*) and what may have been a rectangular stone altar, and the other opening off a small cobbled room. Both of these caves contained large deposits of pottery, the second associated also with an incense-burner, terracotta female figurines, models of furniture, and animal figurines, among the last a horse with what could be a sun disk on its head.[22] It is very probable that these caves were depositories for objects which had been used for some cultic purpose and could therefore not be returned to daily use.

It is possible that one influence in the introduction of some of these pagan elements was Manasseh's wife Meshullemeth, who came from Jotbah in Assyrian-occupied Israel (II Ki. 21:19), and had therefore presumably been exposed to foreign influences.[23] Manasseh's relations with Assyria seem to have been peaceful in the earlier part of his reign, which coincided with the last years of Sennacherib, who was assassinated in 681, and was succeeded by his son Esarhaddon. In the account of Manasseh's reign in Chronicles, however, there is brief mention of an episode in which he is said to have been captured by an army of the 'king of Assyria' and taken in chains to Babylon, but allowed to return to Jerusalem as a result of the providential activity of Yahweh (II Chron. 33:11–13). There is no reference to such an episode in Kings or in extra-Biblical documents, and doubts have been expressed about the authenticity of the account. It is not intrinsically impossible, however, and there is indeed no reason why a recalcitrant vassal should not have been brought to Babylon rather than Nineveh, for Esarhaddon and Ashurbanipal, the two kings mainly contemporary with Manasseh, are both likely to have visited Babylon. Though the city had been sacked by Sennacherib, and the interruption of observance of the *Akitu* festival which began at that time continued through the reign of Esarhaddon,[24] the latter practised a policy of civil and military restoration towards

---

[18] For the suggestion that it was destroyed by Manasseh see B 145, 276–88. See also pp. 390, 408–9 below.   [19] B 219, 128 n. 115.

[20] Kings gives 'son' as well as 'Baʿal' and 'cultic pillar', where Chronicles has the plural. See the remarks of B 336, 114–18, which equally apply here.   [21] See p. 337 above.

[22] B 178, 135–43; and on the horse (B 178, pl. 61) see A 11, 86–7; B 219, 32–4 fig. 5.

[23] See A 11, 91.

[24] Chronicle 14 (Esarhaddon Chronicle): 31–3; Chronicle 16 (Akitu Chronicle): 1–4 (A 25, 127, 131).

Babylon,[25] which is likely to have given occasion for personal visits. Although during Ashurbanipal's reign Babylon was ruled by his brother Shamash-shuma-ukin and then his nominee Kandalanu, he was very much the senior ruler, and, apart from his known presence there when he put down Shamash-shuma-ukin's rebellion of 652–648, he may well have visited on other occasions. The Biblical text does not name the Assyrian king in whose time Manasseh was taken to Babylon, but it has been suggested that a likely occasion might have been the revolt of Shamash-shuma-ukin. It seems more likely, however, that such an episode might have been connected with the western campaign of Esarhaddon in 671.[26] According to the Babylonian Chronicle he had conducted an unsuccessful campaign against Egypt in 674,[27] which might well have encouraged some of the kingdoms in the area to throw off their vassal status. The Vassal Treaties of Esarhaddon which were discovered at Nimrud, and which specify the obligations of some of his eastern vassals, illustrate his likely response to rebellion, typical, of course, of all Assyrian kings, and the Babylonian Chronicle entry for 671 states that he was able to take Memphis and put the Egyptian king to flight.[28] The king of Egypt had been, since 690, the Nubian Taharqa, and a rock inscription cut by Esarhaddon at the Nahr el-Kelb, presumably during his return from this conquest, refers to the seizure of Memphis and flight of Taharqa, and in a badly damaged passage at the end probably names Ashkelon, Tyre, and twenty-two kings,[29] who may be presumed to have been restored tributaries. The reference to Tyre is further elucidated by a stone inscription from Ashur which describes the defeat of Baʿal king of Tyre immediately before the conquest of Taharqa in Egypt,[30] and perhaps by two stelae erected by Esarhaddon at Samʾal (Zincirli) and Til-Barsib (Tell Ahmar), both showing him receiving the submission of two prisoners, a Nubian and a Caucasian.[31] The inscription on the former refers to the Egyptian campaign, mentioning both Taharqa and his son Nes-Anhuret (ú-šá-na-ḫu-ru),[32] but the surviving inscription on the latter, which is much damaged, does not mention Egypt, and refers only to Abdi-milkutti king of Sidon in Phoenicia,[33] so the identification of these two figures remains uncertain.

The humiliation of Baʿal presumably following this defeat, is plain

---

[25] See pp. 41–2, 134–5, 340 above. [26] See A 11, 67–70.

[27] Babylonian Chronicle 1 (p. 340 n. 120 above), iv 16–18 (Year 7) (A 25, 84). For the Esarhaddon Chronicle (Chronicle 14), which mentions no defeat, see A 25, 126 (Chronicle 14: 20), and 219.

[28] Babylonian Chronicle 1 iv 23–7 (Year 10) (A 25, 85).

[29] A 35 II, 228–9 §§582–5; A 44, 293; A 60A, 139–41, 287–9, 298; A 234, 101–2; B 329, 27–30.

[30] A 35 II, 273–6 §§709–12; A 44, 290; A 65 no. 75; A 234, 78, 86–9, nos. 52, 57.

[31] A 45 no. 447; A 144, fig. 136; B 206, 11–29, pl. 1; F. Thureau-Dangin and M. Dunand, *Til Barsip* II (Paris, 1936) pl. XII.

[32] A 35 II, 224–7 §§573–81; A 44, 293 (in part); A 60A, 136–8, 285–6, 298; A 234, 96–100.

[33] A 60A, 142–3, 280–91, 298; A 234, 100–1.

from the treaty concluded with him by Esarhaddon,[34] and the general effectiveness of the latter's military success is illustrated by an undated claim in his annals that he received substantial tribute in the form of building materials, including timber beams and planks and stone slabs, from a number of western rulers including several Cypriot kings, and the ruler of Byblos, as well as Ba'al of Tyre, Pudu-ilu of Ammon, Musurri of Moab, Qaush-gabri of Edom, and in Philistia Ikausu of Ekron, Ahimilki of Ashdod, Metinti of Ashkelon and Ṣilli-Bel of Gaza, and also from Manasseh of Judah.[35] Though this occasion is undated, Esarhaddon lived for only two years after his campaign of 671, so it is probable that the tribute of building materials by Manasseh and the other kings was paid between 671 and 669, perhaps in 670.

Manasseh's name is written *me-na-si-i* in the principal edition of Esarhaddon's annals, but appears as *mi-in-si-e* in two other versions,[36] and the name is also known in alphabetic spelling on a scarab seal inscribed 'Property of Manasseh, son of the king',[37] which it has been tempting to connect with this king. However, though of seventh century date, it is almost certainly to be identified on palaeographic grounds as Moabite rather than Hebrew,[38] and the designation *bn hmlk* 'son of the king' appears, both in the Old Testament and on the known seals which bear it,[39] to have been applied to men who, though they were of royal descent, were only of middle rank in the kingdom. This particular seal is decorated with a star and a crescent, symbols common on Assyrian and Babylonian seals of the period, and also, under Assyrian influence, on Phoenician, Ammonite, and Moabite seals.

It is possible that two others among Esarhaddon's tributaries are mentioned in inscriptions respectively on a clay-seal impression, and on a scaraboid seal. The former, from Umm el-Biyara (Petra), is in a damaged condition but may plausibly be restored to read '[Belonging to] Qaus-g[abri], king of E[dom]'. The second, a private seal, is described in the inscription as the property of a certain 'Abd'eli'ab ben Shib'at, who designates himself 'bd mtt bn ṣdq', perhaps 'servant of Metinti son of Ṣidqa'.[40] If this does indeed refer to Metinti the king of Ashkelon, not to be confused with his namesake, the king of Ashdod in Sennacherib's time, it shows that Ṣidqa, who had been removed by Sennacherib in

---

[34] A 35 II, 229–31 §§586–91; A 44, 533–4; A 234, 107–9 no. 69.

[35] Annals (Nineveh A) v 55–71 (A 234, 60; and cf. A 4, 93); A 44, 291 ('Prism B'); B 131, 70, no. 41; B 339, 74.   [36] A 234, 60.

[37] B 40; B 321, 381 no. 209; B 133, 62, 64 no. 16; B 134, 192 fig. 25; B 157, 131 no. 114.

[38] B 245, 29 n. 24; B 282, 280, 283 n. 19, 289, 294 nn. 37 and 52.

[39] B 40; B 200. On the seal *yhw'ḥẓ bn hmlk*, see p. 392 below.

[40] BM 48502; A 70, 99 fig. 12; B 66A; B 111, 233–4 no. 73, pl. XXI. 10; B 321, 368 no. 73. The seal was found in Ireland, probably having travelled there in the eighteenth or nineteenth century, or even perhaps in Roman times, not by Phoenician trade (cf. B 273).

favour of Sharru-lu-dari, an Assyrian puppet, was succeeded in due time by his own son Metinti.

In 672, Esarhaddon had organized a ceremonial gathering of his vassals at Calah to ensure their loyalty to his heir Ashurbanipal, the surviving evidence for which is the Vassal Treaties, already referred to, which laid down the conditions imposed by Esarhaddon as their overlord.[41] Each subject kingdom was allotted its own copy of the treaty, and though, of the surviving fragments, the identifiable rulers were from the east and south east only, it has been suggested that the attending delegations would also have included the city states of Syria–Palestine, with Manasseh of Judah among them.[42] If it is correct, however, that there was a breaking away from Assyrian control by the western states following Esarhaddon's unsuccessful Egyptian campaign in 674, and that this was only effectively quelled in 671, it is unlikely that Manasseh or his neighbours would have been present in Calah in 672.

Esarhaddon is mentioned in the Old Testament only in connexion with the assassination of Sennacherib (II Ki. 19:37 = Is. 37:38), probably at the hands of Esarhaddon's older brother Arda-Mulissi, written ʾadrammelek in the Old Testament for a probable ʾardammeles,[43] and in a post-Exilic statement that he had brought fresh settlers to Samaria (Ezra 4:2),[44] implying recalcitrance perhaps on the part not of the Samaritans but of the people settled, whose place of origin is not given.

A passage in Chronicles, again not reflected in Kings, states that after Manasseh had been allowed to return from Babylon to Jerusalem he 'built an outer wall for the City of David, on the west side of Gihon, in the wadi [naḥal], and for the entrance into the Fish Gate, and it went around Ophel, and he made it very high' (II Chron. 33:14). While this presents some ambiguities, it can plausibly be taken to mean that he built an extra wall, either immediately adjacent to, or a short distance outside, the existing defences at the two points named, with the result that Ophel was fully enclosed.[45] The designation naḥal in this passage probably refers not to the conduit mentioned in connexion with Hezekiah's works, but to the Wadi Kidron, the location referred to being therefore, presumably, the west slope of the Kidron valley, above the original Gihon spring. The excavations at Jerusalem have revealed that for a time the eastern defences of the city had included a re-entrant angle at the north-eastern corner of Ophel, where Solomon's northern extension had joined the defences higher up the slope than the eastern wall of Ophel.[46] A short portion of wall discovered at the south-eastern corner of the re-entrant angle suggests that at some time in the eighth or seventh century

[41] A 44, 534–41; A 307.   [42] A 307, 4.   [43] See A 704.
[44] See A 11, 69, 101 n. 23; and on the spelling ʾsr-ḥdn see B 225, 9–10.   [45] Cf. B 83, 852.
[46] See CAH III².1, 505.

this angle was walled in,[47] and while an earlier date cannot be ruled out it remains a possibility that it represents the work of Manasseh. The Fish Gate, which is mentioned later in the account of Nehemiah's building operations (Neh. 3:3; 12:39), was located, in all probability, somewhere near the north-west corner of the northern part of the city in an area now inaccessible.

This same passage goes on to say that Manasseh placed army officers in all the fortified cities of Judah,[48] a measure of his freedom of action within the kingdom now that he had fully submitted to Assyrian domination. There is also reference to what must have been only a partial and short-lived religious reform, with the removal of idols from the Temple (II Chron. 33:12–13, 15–17).

In Egypt there were stirrings of rebellion against Assyria, but when, in 669, Esarhaddon set out on a fresh punitive campaign, and fell ill and died on the way, he was succeeded by his son Ashurbanipal,[49] who continued his father's imperialistic policy. The military campaigns of Ashurbanipal cannot be precisely dated because his historical inscriptions, though several of them are set out in apparent annalistic form, disagree among themselves as to the campaigns in which particular events took place.[50] All open with the account of an invasion of Egypt, a fulfilment, in fact, of Esarhaddon's intention, and it is reasonable to place this event in 667 or 666.[51] According to the most accessibly published, though not the most reliable, edition, Prism A ('Rassam Cylinder'), probably compiled c. 643/2, Taharqa was at that time once again in effective control of Egypt, but Ashurbanipal was able to penetrate as far south as Thebes,[52] when Taharqa presumably escaped further to the south. Ashurbanipal claims to have received submission and gifts from twenty-two kings on his line of march, and indeed to have augmented his army with contingents pressed into service from the forces of these kings. An earlier version of the text gives the names of these kings, who included the ruler of Byblos, as well as Baᶜal of Tyre, Amminadab of Ammon, Musurri of Moab, Qaus-gabri of Edom, Ikausu of Ekron, Ahimilki of Ashdod, Metinti of Ashkelon, Ṣilli-Bel of Gaza, and Manasseh of Judah.[53] These same kings, with the exception of Amminadab who had apparently succeeded Pudu-ilu as ruler of Ammon, had been listed half a decade before as tributaries by Esarhaddon.[54]

Since this list of kings agrees so closely with that given by Esarhad-

---

[47] B 178, 144–7.   [48] See B 109. 231.
[49] Babylonian Chronicle 1 (p. 340 n. 120 above) iv 30–3 (A 25, 86).
[50] See p. 142 above.   [51] See A 326, 244 (667 B.C.).
[52] Prism A (A 344 I, xvii–xxi, II, 2–91; and cf. A 317, 65, 85) i 52–89 (A 4, 89–90; A 35 II, 292–3 §§770–1; A 44, 294; A 344 II, 6–11).
[53] Prism C (A 344 I, xxvii–xxx, II, 138–53; and cf. A 317, 65 n. 1) i 24–47 (A 4, 93; A 35 II, 340–1 §876; A 44, 294; A 344 II, 138–41).   [54] See p. 376 above, and cf. A 4, 93.

don, it has been argued that it was taken over from that source by Ashurbanipal's scribe and cannot be treated as reliable evidence for the identities of the kings involved.[55] This is certainly a possibility in view of the flexible fashion in which Ashurbanipal's scribes are known to have handled their sources, but the fact that the two lists are not identical, different kings of Ammon and Arvad being cited,[56] suggests that it should not be totally ruled out as genuinely applicable to the time of Ashurbanipal. If this is a reasonable assumption, it may be noted that the gifts received by Ashurbanipal on this occasion are described as *tāmartu*,[57] and that another probable instance of this kind of payment is found on a small cuneiform tablet from Nineveh, listing tribute of gold and silver from Byblos, Ammon, Moab, and Edom, as well as Judah.[58] No names of rulers are given on this tablet, so it cannot be precisely dated. The quantities, as far as they survive, are relatively small, 10 manas (about 5 kg) of silver from Judah, 2 manas of gold from Ammon and 1 mana of gold from Moab; so this may merely record part-consignments of larger totals. The new king of Ammon, Amminadab, is known also from two Ammonite seals inscribed 'Belonging to Adoni-pelet retainer of Amminadab' and 'Belonging to Adoninur retainer of Amminadab',[59] and probably from a late seventh-century Ammonite inscription on a bronze bottle from Tell Siran near Amman. This inscription also names his son Hiṣṣalᵓel and grandson Amminadab, the author of the inscription, all three being designated 'King of the Ammonites'.[60] It has been assumed that the two Amminadabs mentioned in this inscription were respectively the grandson and great-great-grandson of Ashurbanipal's contemporary, rather than simply himself and his grandson.[61] Though this is a reasonable possibility in view of the length of time, nearly seventy years, involved, there is no evidence for it, and the example of Joash–Amaziah–Uzziah (121 years) and Ahaz–Hezekiah–Manasseh (100 years) of Judah, show that successions of rulers can sometimes, though unusually, rule for long periods. Pending further evidence, two rather than three Amminadabs may be assumed.

In most of the editions of Ashurbanipal's historical texts which supply a framework of campaigns, the second is given to another expedition against Egypt. This account suggests that Taharqa had been succeeded by his nephew Tantamani (664–656), who had been able to reclaim the territory lost by his uncle. Ashurbanipal sent a punitive force, probably

[55] A 234, 60; and see p. 144 above.   [56] A 4, 93.
[57] On which, and its equivalent *nāmurtu*, see A 464, 154–5.
[58] Tablet K.1295 (A 44, 301; A 72 no. 632; A 78 no. 96; A 88 no. 632; A 457, 60; A 464, 152–3; B 55, 60 fig. 40; B 131, 64–5, no. 36B).
[59] B 99, 12–13; B 157, 59 nos. 2, 1; B 321, 370, 376, nos. 98, 164.
[60] B 97; B 188; B 205; B 291; B 308; B 309; B 357.   [61] B 97, 15.

in 664 or 663,[62] to deal with this new trouble,[63] and though there is no specific mention of the matter in the Old Testament it is probable that the news of the passage along the coast route of a large Assyrian force encouraged Manasseh to continue his loyalty.

It is possible that the prudence of this loyalty was again shown not long after, because it seems that at some time in the next decade and a half Ashurbanipal again came to the west in a campaign or campaigns directed largely against the Arabs.[64] This is described at some length in Prism A under the heading 'ninth campaign',[65] but since an account of the major part of it appears already in an earlier edition of the historical inscriptions, Prism B,[66] probably to be dated to about 650/649,[67] the operations must have taken place before that time. The account, which appears to combine events of more than one expedition, suggests that the initial thrust was directed mainly against Uaite' (sometimes written Yauta', both perhaps reflecting epigraphic ywt^c)[68] bin[69] Hazael, here called 'king of Arabia' but elsewhere 'king of Qedar',[70] who probably controlled the tribes to the east of the settled states of Transjordan, and moved within the area between Damascus and Adummatu (al-Jawf),[71] which lay in the territory of Qedar.[72] Uaite' had already caused trouble to both Sennacherib and Esarhaddon, but he seems to have been bound to Ashurbanipal early in the latter's reign by a Vassal Treaty.[73] This had now been violated, and Uaite', with other north Arabian leaders, notably Ammuladi and Adia, was raiding in territory controlled by the Assyrians.

The operations against Uaite' and his allies involved savage fighting in the eastern marches of Ammon, Moab, and Edom,[74] where, indeed, the account in Prism B mentions the involvement on the Assyrian side of Kamas-khaltu, the king of Moab,[75] who had evidently succeeded Musurri since Ashurbanipal's earlier campaign against Egypt. In Kamas-khaltu's name, as in that of his predecessor Kammusu-nadbi, the first element represents the principal Moabite god Kamosh, Biblical Chemosh.[76] The fact that Ashurbanipal was able to fight on the borders

---

[62] Cf. A 326, 232 (666–663 B.C.). See below, p. 702.

[63] Prism A ii 28–48 (A 4, 92; A 35 II, 295–6 §§776–8; A 44, 295; A 344 II, 14–17). Cf. A 30, 148–9 (and n. 276), 394–5.   [64] See in general A 777, 39–73, whose reconstruction is largely followed here.

[65] Prism A vii 82 – x 5 (A 35 II, 313–20 §§817–31; A 44, 297–300; A 344 II, 64–83; A 777, 39–48).

[66] Prism B (A 337, 19–93) vii 93 – viii 63 (A 35 II, 337–9 §§869–70; A 337, 80–7; A 344 II, 130–7 (vii 87 – viii 57); convenient conspectus in A 777, 53–4; and see A 326, 230, 'Arabs 1').

[67] A 317, 78 n. 25; A 337, 19–20.   [68] A 777, 30 n. 6.

[69] Written TUR, read *māru* in Assyrian, but presumably representing Epigraphic North Arabian *bn*, perhaps to be vocalized *bin*.   [70] A 777, 66–7.

[71] B 1, 4–5; B 235, 477, 480–1; B 338, 71–2.   [72] B 338, 71, 95.

[73] A 777, 41 n. 8, 51–2, 53 no. 2h.

[74] Prism A vii 107–24 (A 35 II, 314 §818; A 344 II, 64–7).

[75] Prism B viii 43 (A 35 II, 338 §870; A 337, 84–5; A 344 II, 134–5 (viii 37); A 777, 53 no. 4c).

[76] See B 151, 292; B 285, 472.

of Ammon and Edom suggests that they, like Moab, remained docile vassals. The Assyrian campaign was a success; Ammuladi and Adia were taken captive to Nineveh, and Uaite², having fled to the Nabayatu, possibly the area of Ha²il in northern Najd,[77] was replaced by a more promising nominee, Abiyate² bin Te²ri. All these events, which are included in the account in Prism B, must have taken place before the Babylonian rebellion of Shamash-shuma-ukin, which occupied Ashur-banipal during the years 652 to 648,[78] and are unlikely to have escaped the attention of Manasseh, perhaps acting as an encouragement to him to remain subservient to Assyria. The wisdom of the choice of Abiyate² as the replacement of Uaite² as king of the Arabs was not vindicated by events, for he apparently joined Shamash-shuma-ukin in his rebellion,[79] bringing further Assyrian military action upon himself. Though the Arabians had been involved with Babylonia, it seems that the Assyrian punitive expedition came by way of the north west, passing through Palmyra,[80] and successfully capturing Abiyate² and Uaite², who must have returned from his distant refuge, both of them being brought back to Nineveh. According to Prism A, Ashurbanipal had occasion, on his return route, to put down rebellious movements at Akku (Acre) and Ushu (the mainland settlement of Tyre),[81] episodes which must again have demonstrated to Judah that Assyria was not to be trifled with.

When Manasseh died in 643/642,[82] he is said to have been buried in the garden of his Palace (II Ki. 21:18; II Chron. 33:20).[83] No explanation is given of this change of practice, but in view of the cryptic statement that his predecessor Hezekiah had been buried in the upper section of the royal cemetery it might be that the traditional royal cemetery was now becoming crowded, and a sepulchre in the palace grounds was con-sidered the next best thing.[84] He was succeeded by his son Amon, of whom little is said in the Old Testament except that he continued the false religious practices of his father (II Ki. 21:20–2; II Chron. 33:22–3), a situation for which the influence of his mother Meshullemeth may have been partly responsible.[85] His reign was of only short duration, and he is said to have been killed by a group of his own retainers (II Ki. 21:23; II Chron. 33:24).[86] It may be that most of these retainers were in fact those who had served Manasseh, and who had perhaps transferred their

[77] B 338, 99–100.   [78] See A 326, 229–30, 233, 235, 239–40; and see pp. 53–60 above.
[79] Prism A viii 30–4 (A 35 II, 315 §821; A 44, 298; A 326, 231; A 344 II, 68–9; A 777, 42).
[80] Cf. A 777, 63–6; B 235, 487.
[81] Prism A ix 115–28 (A 35 II, 319 §830; A 44, 300; A 344 II, 80–3; A 777, 48; on Ushu, cf. A 845, 14–15, 293–4.   [82] B 306, 161.
[83] Chronicles should probably read 'and they buried him in [the garden of] his palace' to agree with the Hebrew of Kings, and the Septuagint text of both Kings and Chronicles (see B 106, 500), and cf. B 292, 303.   [84] See B 140, 710–11.   [85] See p. 374 above.
[86] On ²bd, 'servant' or 'official', see p. 337 n. 98 above.

allegiance only unwillingly to Amon, planning to replace him by one of their own number. If this is so, the fact that they had served Manasseh without protest would suggest that it was the person of Amon and not his religious policy to which they objected. This must remain a matter of speculation; for, according to both Kings and Chronicles, the conspirators were almost immediately exterminated in what may fairly be seen as a popular uprising of the people, who installed Amon's son Josiah in his place (II Ki. 21:24; II Chron. 33:25). The active agents in this revolt are designated ʿam-hāʾāreṣ, 'the people of the land', a term which has been taken by some to be a technical term designating a select body of influential citizens who played a special role in the state, albeit one that changed with the passage of time.[87] It seems more probable, however, that this term had no special meaning of this kind, and that in this context it simply referred to the population in general, who took the law into their own hands in order to right a grievous wrong. The common population had been involved in a comparable way on the occasion of the assassination of Athaliah and installation of Joash, when, indeed, the designation ʿam-hāʾāreṣ is also applied to them.[88]

It has been suggested that the assassination of Amon was perpetrated by an anti-Assyrian group in Judah associated with the leaders of the rebellions in Tyre, Akku, and Arabia described in Ashurbanipal's Prism A.[89] They chose a time when Ashurbanipal was heavily involved with troubles in Elam in 642–640,[90] and it was the approach of Ashurbanipal that prompted the counter-coup. In the light of the probability that the Assyrian campaign in question is to be dated some years earlier, however, this hypothesis will not stand.[91]

A possible repercussion on the Assyrian province of Samaria is indicated by the much later statement relating to the Achaemenian period in the Book of Ezra, that Ashurbanipal (ʾsnpr from ʾs < rb > npr from ʾsrbnpl) had settled deportees in 'the cities of Samaria' as well as in the rest of eber nāri, the province to the west of the Euphrates (Ezra 4:9–10). The localities from which these deportees are said to have come (in this Aramaic passage) are a matter of debate. The text gives eight nouns with the plural gentilic ending -āyēʾ, some of which have been variously interpreted as ethnic names or as official titles.[92] Even when the list is reduced by the elimination of all possible putative titles, however, there remain Babylonians (including possible Urukites), Elamites ('Susians, that is Elamites'),[93] and possibly, though uncertainly, Persians (ʾăpār-

---

87 B 109, 70–2, 524; B 267; B 345.   88 B 252.   89 B 207; A 62, 60–1 (= B 128, 186).
90 See however A 326, 231, 235, campaigns 'Elam 7' and '8' dated in about 645 and 643 B.C.
91 See pp. 379–80 above, and cf. A 11, 70 and n. 31.
92 B 60, 165–6, 169–72; B 130A; B 237, 33.
93 Reading dēhû, 'that is', in place of dehāwēʾ, 'Dehavites'.

sāyēʾ). If it be assumed that these deportees were all moved on one occasion, the most likely time would appear to have been following the suppression in 648 of the revolt of Shamash-shuma-ukin in Babylonia, which had Elamite support. Whether Persians might have formed part of such a deportation is uncertain. Their presence is attested in the Assyrian inscriptions from the mid-ninth century B.C. onwards, under the names Parsua, Parsuash and Parsumash, at first near Lake Urmia, but probably already by the late ninth century in the area to the north east of Elam,[94] and a letter from the time of Ashurbanipal suggests the possibility of Persian aid for the Babylonians or Elamites.[95]

When Amon's murderers had been dealt with, his body, like that of his father, was buried in the garden of the royal palace (II Ki. 21:26),[96] a location which perhaps gave rise to a critical allusion to its proximity to the Temple in the account by Ezekiel of his vision of the future ideal temple (Ezek. 43:7–9).

III. THE REIGN OF JOSIAH

Josiah ben Amon was made king of Judah in 641/640 when he was only eight years old. He reigned for thirty-one years (II Ki. 22:1; II Chron. 34:1),[97] and both Kings and Chronicles say of him that 'he did that which was right before Yahweh' (II Ki. 22:2; II Chron. 34:2), the standard phrase applied to those kings who by and large remained faithful to true Yahwism.[98] Little is said of his early years, except that when he was sixteen years old he began to 'seek the god of David his father' (II Chron. 34:3), an indication, presumably, that he grew up within the influence of faithful Yahwists; and indeed it may be that among his relatives there were those who preserved this faith, for his younger contemporary, Zephaniah, who began a challenging prophetic ministry only a few years later, was probably a kinsman, being described as a great-great-grandson of Hezekiah (Zeph. 1:1),[99] of whom Josiah was the great-grandson. This seeking for God may be seen as the precursor of major religious reforms in Judah, the details of which occupy most of the space devoted to the rest of his reign in both Kings and Chronicles. The two accounts do not run precisely parallel to each other, Kings not mentioning Josiah's teenage religious aspirations, nor, apparently, certain religious reforms which, according to Chronicles, were instituted in his twelfth year, 629/628, when he would have been twenty years old (II Chron. 34:36–7). The first event which is specifically mentioned by both sources is placed in Josiah's eighteenth year, 623/622 when he was twenty-six, at which time

[94] A 8, 179–80; A 702, 274–5.   [95] A 8, 192; A 72 no. 1309; A 88 II, no. 1309.
[96] Cf. B 292, 204.   [97] B 306, 161.   [98] See p. 347 above.
[99] See B 269A, 182–3.

an important document referred to as 'The Book of the Law' is said to have been discovered in the Temple (II Ki. 22:8; II Chron. 34:14). The finding of this book is said to have led to a number of reforms, but, according to the passage in Chronicles (II Chron. 34:3–7), these were not the first to be instituted during his reign. According to that passage, in his twelfth year Josiah had begun a purge of the cultic platforms and cultic pillars, as well as of the altars of Baal, incense altars,[100] and moulded (probably bronze) idols[101] in Jerusalem and Judah. A passage in Kings, which follows the account in that book of the discovery of the Book of the Law, appears in some respects to parallel this description of events six years earlier. It mentions Josiah's elimination of cultic platforms and their pagan priests (kĕmārîm),[102] specifying three particular installations dedicated to the gods Ashtoreth of Sidon, Chemosh of Moab, and Milkom of Ammon, which had been established to the east of Jerusalem by Solomon (II Ki. 23:5, 8, 13), of cultic pillars, specifying one in the Temple (II Ki. 23:14 and 6), and of at least two altars in the Temple (II Ki. 23:12). In view of this parallelism it has been suggested that the passage II Ki. 23:5–20 has been displaced in the text to follow the account of the consequences of the discovery of the Book of the Law (II Ki. 23:4), but should rather follow the initial characterization of Josiah's reign in II Ki. 22:2.[103] Such displacement of passages of text is known from contemporary Assyrian sources,[104] and though this can only remain a hypothesis in relation to this passage, it will be convenient to assume it here. The passage describes the elimination of heterodox installations and equipment not mentioned in Chronicles. In addition to standing cult stones (II Ki. 23:14), Josiah removed sun-horses from the Temple entrance, and a sun-chariot, probably from the Temple precincts (II Ki. 23:11).[105] He demolished in that same area buildings which housed sacred prostitutes (II Ki. 23:7), and defiled the cultic fire-pits which had been set up by Ahaz in the Valley of Hinnom, where mlk-sacrifices were made (II Ki. 23:10; and cf. Jer. 7:31).[106]

One material manifestation of religious change possibly to be assigned to this phase of Josiah's reforms is the effective elimination of the sanctuary at Arad in southern Judah, where in level VI a defensive casemate wall passed directly through the site previously occupied by the sanctuary.[107] In a more general way Josiah's reforms may well be reflected in the fact that in the personal names found on the ostraca at Arad there was a steady increase in the proportion of those compounded with the divine element 'Yahweh', until in levels VII (the latter part of which coincided with about the first thirty years of Josiah's reign) and VI

[100] See B 109, 286–7.   [101] Literally 'poured out', or 'molten' idols.   [102] B 219, 36–7.

[103] B 276, 5–15.   [104] A 317, 82–3, 85 table 1.   [105] See B 219, 32–6; B 220, 167–9.

[106] See pp. 337–8 above.   [107] B 49 I, 84, 86; B 340, 397.

they came to constitute over 50 per cent.[108] The ostraca discovered in
level VII at Arad, the level probably ended by Josiah, included
administrative texts in the form of lists of personal names and records of
the issue of wheat to named individuals.[109] Two of these were found in a
small room together with three inscribed seals, two inscribed shekel
weights, a hieratic ostracon,[110] a decorated tridacna-shell bowl, and some
fine pottery.[111] The three seals each bear the inscription '[Belonging] to
Eliashib ben Eshiah',[112] and suggest that this Eliashib held an important,
possibly the principal, administrative position in the town, the three
duplicate seals no doubt enabling him to delegate some of his official
functions. A small archive of letters found in the next level at Arad, and
probably to be dated at least thirty years later, are directed to an official
named Eliashib ben Eshiah,[113] in whom it is difficult to see other than the
same man. While it is theoretically possible that the later man was the
grandson of the earlier, this is unlikely since the practice of papponymy,
which it would be necessary to assume is otherwise unattested among the
Hebrews until the fifth century B.C.[114]

    The wall cutting across the sanctuary at Arad formed part of a fortress
with projecting towers, a construction illustrating another side of
Josiah's activity. Accepting still the passage II Ki. 23:5–20 as describing
events contemporary with those narrated in II Chron. 34:3–7, it is found
that both accounts speak of religious reforms carried out by Josiah in
what had been the northern kingdom. Chronicles speaks of the destruction of cultic pillars, altars, incense altars, and idols in the northern cities
(II Chron. 34:6–7), and Kings of the suppression of cultic platforms and
the killing of their priests in the 'cities of Samaria', and in particular of
the destruction of the cultic platform, altar, and cultic pillar which had
been established by Jeroboam I at Bethel over three centuries before (II
Ki. 23:19 and 15). While similar religious reforms seem to have been
carried out by residents of the Assyrian-occupied northern kingdom in
Hezekiah's time, those of Josiah are described as though he was in
personal control of the territory. The final decades of the Assyrian
empire saw the weakening of its hold on subject and vassal states. There
are gaps in the documentary record, and the dates of Ashurbanipal's four
successors are uncertain.[115] The latest surviving economic document of
Ashurbanipal's reign is dated to 631,[116] but according to the inscription
of Adad-guppi, the mother of Nabonidus, found at Harran, Ashurbanipal reigned for forty-two years, and therefore died in 627/626.[117]

[108] B 17, 141; B 199, 227.   [109] Arad Ostraca 31–9 (see B 17, 56–9; B 199, 199–207).
[110] See p. 393 below.   [111] B 10, 2–18; B 340, 399–400.
[112] B 157, 83–5 nos. 5–7; B 161 nos. 11–13.   [113] See p. 399 below.
[114] Cf. B 255, 56–60.   [115] A 353; A 390; and see pp. 162–84 above.
[116] A 353, 62; A 390, 135; A 932, 92 and n. 2; B 301, 229 n. 20.
[117] Harran Inscription I.B, i 30 (A 44, 561; A 362, 46–7, and 69–72).

His successor Ashur-etel-ilani had a struggle to secure the throne and was soon confronted with the breaking away of Babylonia under Nabopolassar, the founder of the Chaldaean dynasty. If we assume that the dates are correct, this breakdown of Assyrian authority began in the year following the commencement of Josiah's reforms. These reforms are probably to be seen as continuing over a period, and it may well be that the loosening of Assyrian power in the north came at about the time when Josiah was seeing success before him in Judah, and that, desiring to bring religious reform to the land which had once formed part of the kingdom of David and Solomon, he took advantage of the situation to annex the provinces of Samaria, Megiddo, and Gilead (Manasseh, Ephraim, and Simeon as far as Naphtali; II Chron. 34:6).[118] Archaeological evidence for such an annexation is only limited. At Megiddo the walled city of level III, which had been the Assyrian provincial capital, was succeeded in level II by an unwalled settlement with a substantial newly built fortress, possibly the work of Josiah,[119] and at Shechem it is possible that one or other of two minor destructions in level VI is to be associated with him.[120]

Evidence for Judaean control and administration in the south west of the former Assyrian province of Samaria is afforded by an ostracon from Meṣad Ḥashavyahu (Pls. Vol., pl. 171), on the coast about a mile to the south of Yabneh-Yam. This bears the text of an appeal by a farm labourer to a local official against the confiscation of his garment as punishment for an offence of which he declares himself innocent.[121] The official is addressed as 'my lord the *śr*', the *śar* being a man of some importance.[122] The word is often used in the Old Testament of military officers, so it is possible that the official was military governor of the district. The letter is written in an accomplished, if somewhat careless, cursive hand, unlikely to have been that of the labourer, and judging from the spelling by a Judaean, perhaps a scribe or benevolent man of education from Josiah's administration. The name of the man against whom the appeal is made, Hoshaiah ben Shobai,[123] exhibits the characteristic Judaean spelling of the divine element -*yhw* (-iah).[124] The fact that a man in so humble and penurious a condition as the petitioner should

---

[118] On the inclusion here of Simeon, normally given as south of Judah, see B 336, 104 and n. 2; and on such annexation (with different dates) see B 103.

[119] B 49 III, 856; cf. B 208, 267–74, assigning level II to Psammetichus I.

[120] B 344, 165–6.

[121] A 15 no. 200; A 44, 568; B 131, 70–1, no. 42; B 133, 26–30 no. 10; B 199, 259–68; B 241, 129–39.

[122] B 109, 69–70. Whereas Biblical Hebrew distinguishes *š* and *ś* by the position of a dot over a single character, this character shows no such distinguishing feature in the archaic script and is consequently always transliterated here as *š*.

[123] Reading *hwšʿyhw* (A 15, 200; B 199, 264) in place of *hšbyhw* (B 133, 28 (but cf. p. 30); B 241, 133), the form on which the modern Hebrew name of the site is based, 'Fortress of Hashabyahu'.

[124] See *CAH* III².1, 470.

have been able to have such a letter written on his behalf suggests a high level of literacy at this time.[125]

This ostracon was discovered in a small fortress dated by the local pottery to the late seventh century, but among this pottery was a considerable quantity of East Greek ware, including household types, suggesting the presence there of Greeks.[126] It was a long-standing practice in Judah to employ Aegean mercenary troops, David and Solomon having had a bodyguard of Philistines and Cretans, and in the time of Joash there is mention of a similar guard of Carians,[127] so it is possible that the garrison at Meṣad Ḥashavyahu was reinforced by a contingent of Greek mercenaries in the employment of Josiah. The Egyptian pharaohs were using such troops at this time,[128] and there is evidence in inscriptions found at Arad that Mediterranean troops were being used at the end of the seventh century to help in guarding the south-eastern approaches of the Judaean kingdom.[129]

During the period of religious reform instituted in Josiah's twelfth year, he received prophetic support in his endeavours. His probable kinsman Zephaniah condemned idolatry and warned of coming judgement 'in the days of Josiah' (Zeph. 1:1);[130] Jeremiah, a man of priestly family 'to whom the word of Yahweh came in the days of Josiah ben-Amon, King of Judah, in the thirteenth year of his reign' (Jer. 1:2), that is in the second or third year of his reform,[131] continued active until the end of the kingdom;[132] and Huldah, a prophetess, the wife of the 'keeper of the wardrobe' and therefore permanently resident in Jerusalem, was evidently active at this time (II Ki. 22:14; II Chron. 34:22). Jeremiah's message was one of condemnation of false prophets and corrupt priests and of idolatry and immorality throughout the nation, and of consequent judgement. He spoke also, however, of the future ideal king (Jer. 23:5–6; 33:15–16)[133] and a time of restoration.

It is in this context of continuing and active reform that the discovery of the Book of the Law may reasonably be set. According to both Kings and Chronicles, in his eighteenth year (623/622), Josiah turned his attention to the repair of the Temple which had fallen into a dilapidated state, and it was in the early stages of this programme that Hilkiah the high priest found the book (II Ki. 22:3–8; II Chron. 34:8–15). This is

---

[125] See in general B 224.

[126] B 49 III, 862–3; B 241; B 242; B 243; B 244; J. Boardman, *The Greeks Overseas* (2nd edn, Harmondsworth, 1973) 51.   [127] B 340, 414, 424 nn. 146–8; *CAH* III².1, 491.

[128] J. Boardman, *The Greeks Overseas*, 114–17. See below, p. 713.   [129] See p. 399 below.

[130] On the Book of Zephaniah see B 120, 423–5; B 126, 456–8; B 147, 939–43.

[131] Assuming Jeremiah's dating to be based on the spring (Nisan) New Year, as against the Judaean autumn (Tishri) New Year (see B 306, 161, and 162 table; see *CAH* III².1, 446).

[132] On the Book of Jeremiah see B 77A; B 120, 346–65; B 126, 388–402; B 147, 801–21.

[133] See B 77A, 143–4; B 274, 35–6.

described as *sēper hattôrâ*, 'The Book of the Law' (II Ki. 22:8; II Chron. 34:14),[134] and since the time of Jerome and Chrysostom in the fourth century A.D. it has commonly been identified with some form of the Biblical book of Deuteronomy,[135] which indeed refers to itself as a copy of the *tôrâ* (*mišnēh hattôrâ*; Deut. 17:18). Opinions have differed concerning what proportion of the existing Deuteronomy constituted the Book of the Law in Josiah's time: whether only parts,[136] or substantially the whole.[137] This question is associated also with that of the origin and authorship of Deuteronomy, concerning which views range from the time of Moses in the thirteenth century B.C. to the post-Exilic period in the fifth or fourth century B.C.[138] Suffice it to say that the description of its discovery and use suggests that at that time it had the appearance of age, being immediately accepted as authoritative, and that those who discovered it, who made it known to the king, and who participated in the actions to which it led, were presumably honest men. It is unlikely, therefore, to have been a recent compilation expressly placed in order to be found, pseudo-accidentally, soon after its deposit. It was evidently of such a length that it could be read through twice, and possibly three times, in one day, and therefore could well have constituted the major part of the Biblical Book of Deuteronomy, which can be read through in under an hour and a half.[139]

The book was taken to Josiah by the scribe Shaphan. When the contents were read out, the king was deeply concerned, and sent a delegation to consult the prophetess Huldah, who pronounced, in the name of Yahweh, a condemnation of apostasy and heterodoxy and a prophecy of coming judgement on Jerusalem and Judah, which, however, in consideration of Josiah's faithfulness, would be deferred until after his death (II Ki. 22:9–20; II Chron. 34:16–28). When this was reported to the king, he is said to have summoned all citizens, both religious and secular, to the Temple where he read out the text of the newly discovered book (II Ki. 22:20–3:2; II Chron. 34:29–30). In this passage the book is referred to as *sēper habběrît*, 'The Book of the Covenant [or Treaty]', and indeed the surviving Book of Deuteronomy contains the same elements and takes the same general form as a number of Near Eastern treaties of the latter part of the second millennium B.C.[140] Secular treaties dealt with the relations between nations, while Deuteronomy was concerned with those between Yahweh and the Hebrews, and the reading of the text presumably showed to Josiah that not only was

134 On *tôrâ* see *CAH* III².1, 475.
135 B 78, 318; B 116, xliv–xlv; B 126, 167–9; B 127, 293–4; B 158, 267; B 253, 1–17.
136 B 120, 212–19; B 127, 169–70.   137 B 92A, 46–9.   138 B 253, 1 n. 4, 37 n. 1.
139 The English translation can be read in about eighty-five minutes, and the Hebrew version is considerably shorter.   140 B 92A, 22–3; B 180, 90–102; B 215; B 216; B 264, 3–4.

Judah violating the terms of the ancient agreement (or covenant) with Yahweh but that, through ignorance of these terms, the nation had allowed it to lapse. The next logical step was therefore the renewal of the covenant, and Josiah is said to have done this, standing in the same position as his ancestor Joash when he renewed the agreement with Yahweh two centuries before (II Ki. 23:3 and 11:14; II Chron. 34:31 and 23:13),[141] all the people present joining in the same commitment.

According to the sequence of narration in Kings (assuming, however, the displacement of II Ki. 23:5–20[142]) Josiah's renewal of the covenant was followed by a purge of all the pagan cultic equipment[143] from the Temple (II Ki. 23:4). Chronicles at this point states that he put an end to all cultic violations and moral lapses[144] throughout Israelite territory, this designation no doubt including the former northern kingdom (II Chron. 34:33).[145]

Both Kings and Chronicles describe what seems to have been the culmination of Josiah's reforming activities in the celebration of the Passover ceremony on a major scale (II Ki. 23:21–3; II Chron. 35:1–19).[146] Josiah is quoted as saying that it should be observed in the manner prescribed in 'this Book of the Covenant' (II Ki. 23:21). Such a prescription does indeed occur in the Book of Deuteronomy (16:1–8), according to which an animal was to be sacrificed and eaten communally (*pesaḥ*), and unleavened bread was to be eaten for six days and an assembly held on the seventh day, the festival of unleavened bread. According to the Pentateuch the need to depart immediately after the *pesaḥ* meant that the festival was not observed on the first occasion in Egypt (Num. 33:3), but the normal association of the two elements is otherwise assumed.[147]

According to both Kings and Chronicles, Josiah's Passover was celebrated in a manner different from all celebrations since before the beginning of the monarchy (II Ki. 23:22; II Chron. 35:18), but no indication is given of the nature of the innovation. The Passover was a festival of outstanding importance to the compilers of both Kings and Chronicles, and probably also to many of the scribes who recorded the events of the two kingdoms over the centuries, so it may be significant that these sources refer to the observance of the Passover under only three kings during the whole period of the monarchy: Solomon, by implication (I Ki. 9:25; II Chron. 8:12–13),[148] Hezekiah, and Josiah. In view of Solomon's acceptance in Jerusalem of pagan deities (I Ki. 11:1–8), it may be that his observance of Yahwistic festivals such as the

---

[141] See *CAH* III².1, 491–2; and on covenant making *CAH* III².1, 453 n. 72.
[142] See p. 384 above.   [143] See B 186, 456, *kĕlî*.   [144] See B 81, 1072–3, *tôʿēbâ*.
[145] Cf. B 336, 100. 126–7.   [146] See B 287, 5–6, 12–16.   [147] B 287, 55–65.
[148] B 287, 4–5.

Passover was only perfunctory and improper; and it is said of Hezekiah's celebration that there were certain irregularities (II Chron. 30:17–20), so possibly it is in some such sense as this, that is to say in being completely acceptable in religious terms, that Josiah's Passover differed from those which had preceded it.

It appears from the reforming activities of his reign that one of Josiah's aims was the concentration of all official worship of Yahweh in the Temple at Jerusalem. This ideal is also set out in the Book of Deuteronomy, but it is unnecessary to assume from this that Deuteronomy was written in his own time in order to promote this aim, and that there had been no move in this direction until it was 'discovered'. According to the Biblical text, Hezekiah seems to have attempted such a reform over half a century before, and Josiah's own reforms had already achieved much in this direction before the discovery of the book.[149]

The account in Chronicles of this Passover celebration contains a somewhat obscure instruction from Josiah to the Levites, which makes one of the rare references in the later historical books to the ark. A fairly literal rendering of the significant section runs, 'put the holy ark in the house which Solomon . . . built; not for you a burden on the shoulder; now serve Yahweh your God' (II Chron. 35:3; I Esdras 1:3–4). The passage is sometimes condemned as historically unreliable,[150] but this judgement stems from a similar view of the whole book, whereas it is equally plausible to treat it as essentially accurate.[151]

The Biblical accounts say no more of Josiah's reign until his last year (609), when both Kings and Chronicles describe his involvement with the Egyptian king Necho and the king of Assyria at Megiddo (II Ki. 23:29; II Chron. 35:20–3). As has been mentioned, there had been a rapid and marked decline in the cohesion and power of Assyria since the latter part of the reign of Ashurbanipal, and particularly under his ephemeral successors.[152] One reflection of this is the dearth of Assyrian written sources, the Babylonian Chronicle now becoming of special importance, the more so as it records the rising power of Babylon.[153] Nineveh fell to the Babylonians under Nabopolassar, together with his allies, in 612, and Ashur-uballiṭ II, the last Assyrian king, retreated with a remnant of his army to Harran where he sought to hold out until he could receive assistance from the Egyptians, who saw Babylonia as a threat. It is clear from the Babylonian Chronicle that the Assyrians and Egyptians were allies at this time,[154] and the Biblical statement that 'Necho came up to

---

[149] See B 331; and see p. 350 above.   [150] E.g. B 145, 282–3.

[151] E.g. B 236 II, xxxi–ii. See also pp. 408–9 below.

[152] See pp. 66, 164 above.   [153] See pp. 160–84 above.

[154] Tablet BM 21901, Fall of Nineveh Chronicle (Chronicle 3; A 25, 18–19, 90–6), 61–2 (A 25, 95; A 932, 62–3). Cf. also Jos. *Ant. Jud.* x.74.

the King of Assyria, to the River Euphrates' (II Ki. 23:29) is to be understood in this light.[155] No explanation of Josiah's motive is given, but such a military enterprise would be understandable if he viewed Necho's expedition to meet and support the Assyrians as an undesirable attempt to prop up the hated Assyrians, now in eagerly awaited decline.

Necho's predecessor, Psammetichus I, is said by Herodotus (II.157) to have taken Ashdod in Philistia,[156] and a fragmentary Egyptian inscription from Sidon suggests that Necho controlled the Phoenician coast.[157] Thus Josiah must have been alert to the Egyptian presence, and since Necho, in making for the Euphrates to join the Assyrians, may have passed across his regained northern territories, as is indeed specifically claimed by Josephus,[158] it is entirely natural that Josiah should have attempted to intercept him at the strategic pass of Megiddo. According to Chronicles, Necho had sent a message to Josiah denying any hostile intentions against Judah, but this was disregarded by Josiah who came determined to fight. At the encounter he was mortally wounded by a bowshot, and had himself transferred from his war chariot to 'the second chariot', perhaps a larger supply vehicle, in which he was carried back to Jerusalem, a distance of something like 100 km. The text concludes 'and he died' (II Chron. 35:21–4), presumably in Jerusalem, though possibly on the road. Kings states more briefly that Necho (presumably in the sense of 'the Egyptians') 'killed him at Megiddo' and that Josiah's retainers drove him dying[159] from Megiddo to Jerusalem, where he was buried in his tomb (II Ki. 23:29–30), which, according to Chronicles, was in the cemetery of his fathers (II Chron. 35:24).[160] This appears to have been a reversal of the innovation introduced at the death of Manasseh, and followed after Amon's death, of burying the king in the palace grounds. If this practice had indeed been adopted because of crowding in the royal cemetery,[161] it may be that the religious authorities made a particular point of fitting Josiah into the traditional cemetery, out of deference to his memory as a reformer, and the feeling that he should not be put with the obnoxious Manasseh and Amon. His loss was evidently regretted by faithful Yahwists, because Jeremiah is said to have lamented over his death, his lamentation being taken up by the professional singers and preserved in writing with other such lamentations (II Chron. 35:25). Josephus claimed, some centuries later, that Jeremiah's lament was still extant in his own time.[162] There is no reason to connect it with the Biblical Book of Lamentations.

---

[155] Taking the ʿal... ʿal in this verse as 'to ... to ...' (with RSV and NEB) rather than as 'against ... to ...' (with AV and RV).   [156] See B 286 II, 108–9.   [157] F 133 VII, 384; F 44, 358.
[158] Ant. Jud. x.75.   [159] Rather than 'dead' (cf. B 140, 748).   [160] Cf. B 292, 204.
[161] See p. 381 above.   [162] Ant. Jud. x.78.

IV. THE LAST KINGS OF JUDAH

After what must have been an emotional ceremony at the burial of Josiah, it seems reasonable to take the statement of both Kings and Chronicles that 'the people of the land' made his son Jehoahaz king in his place, as an indication of his elevation to this position by popular acclaim (II Ki. 23:30).[163] Kings records the names and ages of three sons of Josiah – Eliakim (Jehoiakim,[164] twenty-five years old) by his wife Zebidah (II Ki. 23:36); Jehoahaz (Shallum (Jer. 22:11),[165] twenty-three years old); and Mattaniah (Zedekiah, nine years old) by Hamutal (II Ki. 23:31; 24:18) – and it may be surmised from the manner of Jehoahaz's enthronement, and the fact that he was not the eldest son, that Hamutal was, if not the senior wife, at least the one most in sympathy with Josiah's reforms. According to Chronicles there had been a fourth son, Johanan, Josiah's first-born (I Chron. 3:15), but nothing more is known of him, and he may not have survived to manhood.

The name Jehoahaz is known from a red jasper scaraboid seal inscribed lyhwᵓhz bn hmlk, 'Belonging to Jehoahaz, son of the king', above a fighting cock,[166] but this is unlikely to have been the seal of the king himself since the quality of the intaglio cutting is inferior. The designation bn hmlk is usually applied to men of middle rank,[167] and indeed the device of a fighting cock is known on the seal of an official, Jaazaniah, who occupied a position of this kind only a few years later;[168] moreover, if it is correct that Jehoahaz bore the name Shallum until his accession to the throne, this could not have been his seal. A fragmentary ostracon from Arad reading 'I myself have become king in a[ll] . . . strengthen the arm! and . . . the king of Egypt t[o] . . .' may represent a message sent by Jehoahaz, on his accession, to the various outposts of the kingdom.[169] Whether or not Jehoahaz instituted any action against the Egyptians, or whether Josiah's opposition to Necho had drawn the latter's critical attention to Judah is not clear, but it appears that Necho was not satisfied with the people's choice of king, and he is said to have deported Jehoahaz after only three months' rule, first of all to Riblah and then to Egypt, setting on the throne in his place, Eliakim, Jehoahaz's half brother (II Ki. 23:33–4; II Chron. 36:2–4). Eliakim's name was changed to Jehoiakim, involving a substitution of the divine name Yahweh for the more general element ᵓel, 'God'. The change of name

---

[163] See B 252, 62; and see p. 382 above.
[164] Jehoiakim, Hebrew yehôyāqîm, to be distinguished from Jehoiachin, Hebrew yehôyākîn.
[165] See B 77A, 141, and cf. B 106, 100.
[166] B 121, no. 20; B 157, 124–5 no. 97; B 160, 21 no. 6; B 321, 385 no. 252.
[167] See p. 376 above.   [168] See p. 411 below.
[169] Arad Ostracon 88 (B 17, 103–4; B 199, 220–1). Cf. B 89; B 351.

was presumably aimed at establishing his legitimacy in the eyes of the people, in spite of his subservient position as a vassal of Necho.[170]

The dominance of Egypt in the latter part of the seventh century is illustrated by the discovery at Arad of an ostracon inscribed in the hieratic script,[171] and another in Hebrew script, but with what are probably hieratic numerals and the symbol for the Egyptian grain-measure *ḥqᵗt*.[172] Though there are no precise data bearing on the extent of the territory controlled by Judah at this time, the dominance of Egypt suggests that the larger area embraced by Josiah had been once more reduced to what it had been before his time.[173]

It is probable that Jehoahaz had become king in the summer of 609, and Jehoiakim succeeded him in the autumn of the same year,[174] beginning a reign of eleven years which ended with the fall of Jerusalem to Nebuchadrezzar. Nothing is recorded of the first few years of his reign, though a passage in Jeremiah suggests that he may have indulged himself by building a new palace with conscripted labour (Jer. 22:13:1).[175] It has been suggested that the palace in question is to be identified with a substantial building probably constructed at about this time by the completion of a destroyed, or unfinished, structure of the ninth century B.C. at Ramat Raḥel, possibly ancient Beth-hakkerem (Neh. 3:14). This structure, which was carefully built and appears to have been occupied for a relatively short time, incorporated window balustrades in the form of short voluted palm-columns (Pls. Vol., pl. 168), probably reused from the ninth-century building, and may match the description contained in Jeremiah.[176] A discovery of particular interest in the building was a potsherd bearing a depiction in black and red paint of a bearded man in an ornamental robe seated on a chair or throne (Pls. Vol., pl. 169), possibly a depiction of Jehoiakim himself, though perhaps more probably one of his officials.[177] A stamped jar handle found in this complex, with the inscription 'Eliakim steward of Jehoiachin' belongs with the royal jar stamps of a century earlier,[178] and is no guide to the dating of this structure. An indication of the religious situation at this time is given by an episode, dated to the accession year, when Jeremiah narrowly escaped death for proclaiming the destruction of Jerusalem and the Temple if the nation failed to observe the law of Yahweh (Jer. 26:1–24). The account cites the case of another prophet, Uriah, who fled to Egypt after delivering a similar message, only to be

[170] Cf. also B 6, 70, 73–4.   [171] Arad Ostracon 34 (B 17, 62–4); see B 199, 221, 235.

[172] Arad Ostracon 25 (B 17, 50–1; B 199, 195–6).   [173] Cf. B 16, 403.

[174] B 306, 163–5.   [175] See B 16, 405; B 77A, 145.

[176] B 8, 10–15, 35–40, 60; B 9, 23–9, 49–58, 122–4, fig. 6 (plan); B 49 IV, 1001–6, 1009; B 340, 178–83. For a different dating see B 230, 128–35; B 209 IV/2, 211–13. See also p. 448 below.

[177] A 45 no. 771; B 8, 42–3, pl. 28; B 9, 85–94; B 49 IV, 1003; B 340, 180, pl. VIA.

[178] See pp. 354–5 above.

extradited and executed. Jeremiah was spared, thanks to the intervention of Ahikam ben Shaphan, son of one of the high officials who had been sent by Josiah to consult Huldah after the discovery of the Law Book a decade before. This attitude to the prophets of Yahweh was now typical of the closing years of the monarchy (II Ki. 23:37, II Chron. 36:5).

The Egyptians remained in Palestine, receiving tribute from Judah (II Ki. 23:35), and also in Syria, and the Babylonian Chronicle states that in 606 Nabopolassar had an encounter with them on the Euphrates, and that at the beginning (month of Shabatu) of 605 they defeated the Babylonian garrison at Quramati, probably on the great bend of the Euphrates.[179] This action seems to have prompted the energetic crown prince, Nebuchadrezzar, to muster the Babylonian army and, leaving his father in Babylon, to lead a punitive campaign to the west, where he defeated the Egyptians at Carchemish, and the fleeing remnant at Hamath.[180] Though Josephus implies that Necho was himself present at Carchemish,[181] he is not mentioned in the Babylonian Chronicle nor in an extract from Berossus quoted by Josephus which, anachronistically, speaks of the 'satrap' of Egypt,[182] and the Old Testament refers only to 'the army of pharaoh Necho' (Jer. 46:2), so it may well be that Nebuchadrezzar had only to defeat garrison troops.[183] Nebuchadrezzar's military operations were interrupted by the death of Nabopolassar,[184] but after he had assumed the throne in Babylon he returned in the autumn and 'marched about victoriously in Khatti', finally returning with booty to Babylon in early 604.[185] 'Khatti' was not a precise term, referring in the first millennium mainly to north Syria, but the fact that later in this document it is treated as including Judah[186] suggests that Nebuchadrezzar's victorious march may have extended into Palestine.

The passage of Berossus quoted by Josephus goes on to speak of the transportation of Jewish, Phoenician, Syrian, and Egyptian prisoners to Babylonia at this time,[187] and the Biblical Book of Daniel, if it is taken to be following the Judaean (autumn–autumn) dating system,[188] assigns to this year a siege of Jerusalem by Nebuchadrezzar followed by the deportation to Babylon of a number of young men of royal and noble birth, including Daniel himself (Dan. 1:1–4). Josephus elsewhere states that, following the battle of Carchemish, Nebuchadrezzar 'took' Syria as

[179] Babylonian Chronicle 4 (A 25, 19, 97–8), 16–23 (A 25, 98; A 932, 66–7; B 131, 72–3 no. 44A). See A 25, 261; A 932, 22 map 2. See below, p. 716.

[180] Babylonian Chronicle 5 (A 25, 19–20, 99–102), obv. 1–8 (A 25, 99; A 932, 66–9; B 131, 72–4 no. 44B), reading 'Hamath' (A 25, 99) rather than 'Hattu' (A 932, 68). See also above, p. 320, and below, pp. 716–17.   [181] *Ant. Jud.* x.84–6.   [182] *Contra Apionem* 1.135–6; A 7, 26; A 626, 389.

[183] Cf. A 932, 24–5.   [184] See pp. 230–1 above.

[185] Babylonian Chronicle 1 obv. 12–14 (A 25, 100; A 932, 68–9; B 131, 74, no. 44B).

[186] Babylonian Chronicle 5 rev 11–12 (A 25, 102; A 932, 72–3 and cf. p. 25; B 131, 74, no. 44B).

[187] *Contra Apionem* 1.137; see A 7, 37 n. 104.   [188] B 306, 165–6.

far as Pelusium (in the north-east Delta), but he goes on specifically to exclude Judah from this conquest.[189] Thus, though Josephus cannot be regarded as a particularly significant witness for this period, the occurrence of a Babylonian siege of Jerusalem in 605 remains to be demonstrated.[190] The majority of scholars consider the Book of Daniel to be a historically unreliable compilation of the second century B.C.,[191] though this is not a universally held view,[192] but even assuming it to be correct there is no reason to deny that a historical nucleus lies behind it, some details of the text possibly having suffered in the course of scribal transmission and revision.[193] To the year 605, in which the evidence of Nebuchadrezzar's military power must have been compellingly obvious to those in Palestine, Jeremiah assigns an injunction from Yahweh for him to record in a book-scroll, probably of papyrus,[194] all the condemnatory messages which he had delivered since the time of Josiah (Jer. 36). He is described in the same year as delivering stinging condemnation of Judah and Jerusalem with a forecast of an invasion by northern people, notably the Babylonians under Nebuchadrezzar, and a period of subservience to Babylon (Jer. 25: 1–14). Jeremiah engaged his friend Baruch ben Neriah to write out his prophecies, a process which seems to have occupied at least nine months, for it was not until the ninth month of Jehoiakim's fifth year, November–December in 604, that the scroll was completed and ready for public reading (Jer. 36:9–10). Baruch, who was a scribe (Jer. 36:26, 32), a role of some importance in the ancient world, is known in the Old Testament only as the amanuensis of Jeremiah, and as a truly faithful and self-denying friend to the prophet. According to Josephus he came from a distinguished family,[195] and a clay sealing bearing what could be his name may throw further light on his status.[196] The name *brk* is known from two Samaria ostraca and a number of seals;[197] they have been taken as defectively written examples of the Biblical name *brwk, bārūk*, 'blessed one', but comparison of the inscription on the sealing mentioned above, which reads *lbrkyhw bn nryhw hspr*, 'belonging to Berechiah ben Neriah, the scribe', with the Biblical descripton *brwk bn nryhw hspr*, 'Baruch ben Neriah, the scribe' (Jer. 36:32), raises the strong possibility that *brkyhw* and *brwk* were one and the same man, the Biblical form being an abbreviation of that found on the seal, and that the sealing bears the impression of Baruch's personal seal. This sealing, which shows the marks of a papyrus document on its

---

[189] *Ant. Jud.* x.84–6.
[190] On Daniel 1: 1 see B 341, 16–18; and on the date (and Jer. 25: 1 and 46: 2) see B 306, 162 table, 163, 165–6. [191] E.g. B 120, 520–2; B 126, 477–8; B 148, 16; B 184; B 195.
[192] E.g. A 819, 200; B 50, 29; B 147, 1110–27; B 352, 19–20.
[193] For discussion of all details see B 226. [194] See p. 372 and nn. 8–9 above.
[195] *Ant. Jud.* x.158. [196] B 45.
[197] A 15, no. 188; B 133, 14–15 no. 3; B 199, 246–8, 250; B 321, 369 no. 97, 382 no. 225, 383 no. 229.

underside, was one of a group among which was also the impression of
the seal of 'Jerahmeel, son of the king', probably to be equated with the
man of that name who is also designated 'son of the king' in Jeremiah
(36:26).[198] This title, while it probably indicates that Jerahmeel was of
royal descent, need not suggest that he was of more than middle rank,
but if the *brkyhw* sealing was indeed that of the Biblical Baruch, it
suggests that he had served in the official administration and occupied a
respectable position in the kingdom. In this case it would be a significant
mark of his devotion to Jeremiah that he should have been willing to
give this up in order to court public obloquy by helping his friend. When
he read the scroll out publicly, word of this was taken to a group of
officials (*śārîm*) who seem to have been seated in council at the time (Jer.
36:11–13). They called for the scroll, which was then read out to them,
and being disturbed by it they reported the matter to Jehoiakim, first
warning Jeremiah and Baruch to go into hiding in case the king should
react strongly (Jer. 36:14–20). Their forecast of Jehoiakim's reaction
was accurate. He had the scroll read out in his presence and showed his
unconcern and contempt for it by cutting off sections of three or four
columns (*dělātôt*) as they were read, and feeding them into the brazier by
which he was warming himself because of the winter weather. Some of
the officials tried unsuccessfully to dissuade him from this, one of them
being Gemariah ben Shaphan, very likely a brother of Ahikam who had
intervened on Jeremiah's behalf on a previous occasion. When the entire
scroll had been burnt, Jehoiakim called for the arrest of Jeremiah and
Baruch, but the advice to them to hide themselves proved good, for they
could not be found (Jer. 36:21–6).

The immediate threat from Jehoiakim seems to have died down,
because Jeremiah is said to have re-dictated the whole contents of the
scroll to Baruch (Jer. 36:27–32). During the preparation of the first
scroll, which must have occupied much of the year 604, the Babylonian
Chronicle states that Nebuchadrezzar was again in the west. He
mustered his army in the late spring and remained there until the
beginning of 603, and during that time he 'marched about victoriously',
received tribute from 'all the kings of Khatti', and in particular attacked
and captured a city the damaged name of which is possibly to be read *iš-
qi-il-lu-nu*, Ashkelon.[199] The Babylonian Chronicle entry for 603 is badly
damaged, several lines being absent altogether, but it may well have
described another successful campaign in the west,[200] during which
Nebuchadrezzar laid siege to a city, the name of which is lost.[201] If this

---

[198] B 45.

[199] Babylonian Chronicle 5 obv. 15–20 (A 25, 100; A 932, 68–9; B 131, 74 no. 33B). On *[iš-qi]-il-lu-nu* see A 25, 100; A 932, 85; B 271.   [200] A 25, 200; A 932, 28–9, 70–1; see also n. 215 below.

[201] Babylonian Chronicle 5 obv. 21–3 (A 25, 100; A 932, 70–2).

was a western campaign, a possible identification of this city is to be found in an Aramaic papyrus from Saqqara. This papyrus, which is probably to be dated on palaeographic grounds to the end of the seventh century B.C.[202] and of which something like half is broken away, is a letter from one ʾAdon, king of a city of which the name is lost, to an unspecified king of Egypt. He reports that the forces of the king of Babylon had reached Aphek,[203] and begs for assistance against them.[204] The reference to Aphek comes near the lost portion of the document, so a siege of Aphek is not necessarily involved, and excavations at the site have so far revealed only very limited remains from the seventh and sixth centuries B.C.[205] Nevertheless, since the Babylonian Chronicle mentions the siege of a city, of which the name is lost, during Nebuchadrezzar's campaign to Khatti in 603, it is a plausible suggestion that Aphek was this besieged city, and that ʾAdon's letter was therefore written in that year.[206] Aphek lay in the south-western part of the former kingdom of Israel, by this time probably lost to Judah, in the foothills between the coastal plain and the central highlands, and therefore on the probable route of an army advancing southwards. On the reverse of the papyrus, in a position which would have been on the outside when the document was rolled up, a line of demotic (Egyptian) may be read plausibly, though not certainly, to include the name Ekron (ʿqrn), which could thus well be the city of ʾAdon.[207] The location of Ekron is not certainly fixed, but there are arguments for placing it at Khirbet al-Muqannaʿ,[208] also in the western foothills of the hill country, and some twenty-five miles south of Aphek. It is thus a site which could well have felt itself under threat if Nebuchadrezzar was only twenty-five miles away, and from which an appeal for help to Egypt would have been a logical expedient. There is no surviving evidence of an immediate response on the part of Necho II to this request, and the fate of ʾAdon is unknown.

Nebuchadrezzar is said in the Babylonian Chronicle to have campaigned successfully in the west (Khatti) in 602[209] and again in 601, meeting the Egyptians in an indecisive battle on the latter occasion.[210] The perhaps somewhat garbled statement of Herodotus that Necho defeated the 'Syrians' at Magdolus and took the city of Kadytis[211] is possibly to be connected with this encounter, if the 'Syrians' are understood as the Assyrians,[212] a mistake for Babylonians. The identifi-

---

[202] B 246, 16 and fig. 3:1.   [203] B 185.
[204] A 15 no. 266; B 125A; B 125B, 231–42; B 131, 71–2, no. 43; B 134, 110–16 no. 21; B 269; B 339, 251–5.   [205] B 185, 83.   [206] B 290.   [207] B 269, 42–5.   [208] B 240; B 16, 376.
[209] Babylonian Chronicle 5 rev. 2–4 (A 25, 101; A 932, 70–1).
[210] Babylonian Chronicle 5 rev. 5–7 (A 25, 101; A 44, 564; A 932, 70–1; B 131, 74, no. 44B).
[211] Hdt. II.159.
[212] Cf. Hdt. VII.63, speaking, however, of Achaemenian times, and distinguishing the Chaldaeans.

cation of the two place names is uncertain, but Kadytis could be Gaza,[213] and Magdolus is most simply interpreted as West Semitic *mgdl*, 'tower', frequently used in place names, and could designate some fortified settlement in the area of the Egyptian border, such as there seems to have been in the time of Esarhaddon.[214] If this is so it suggests an Egyptian incursion into only the very south-westernmost region of Palestine, and a dominating presence of Nebuchadrezzar's forces.

The situation of Jehoiakim and Judah at the time of these events is uncertain. According to Kings, at some unspecified point in his reign he was the vassal of Nebuchadrezzar for three years, at the end of which period he rebelled (II Ki. 24:1). One possibility, and it can be no more than this, is that he became a vassal of Nebuchadrezzar during the latter's campaign of 603, much of the account of which is missing from the Babylonian Chronicle,[215] avoiding deportation by paying tribute in the form of Temple treasure (II Chron. 36:6–7), and submitting to the taking of young men as hostages.[216] It could be that in 601, three years later (counting by the inclusive system), knowledge of a Babylonian set-back at the hands of the Egyptians encouraged him to rebel. If this is a correct reconstruction Jehoiakim then enjoyed a respite from the Babylonians lasting more than a year, for Nebuchadrezzar's encounter with the Egyptians took place in the winter of 601–600; he spent the year 600/599 rearming in Babylonia, and did not come again to the west until November–December 599. On this latter expedition he deployed his forces into the desert, concentrating on the neutralization of Arab tribes, from whom plunder, including divine images, was taken.[217] It may be that these activities set up a chain of disturbances which resulted in raiding parties moving against those areas not in a position to claim Babylonian protection.

Kings states that Judah suffered raids from 'Chaldaeans, Aramaeans, Moabites and Ammonites' (II Ki. 24:2),[218] the Chaldaean and Aramaean elements perhaps stemming from Babylonian garrison troops together with local contingents raised in the former area of Aram. The disturbance caused by these Babylonian and Aramaean raiding parties seems to have been sufficiently severe in the rural areas to have forced the

---

[213] B 286 II, 98–9; B 298, 5; see, however, F 43 I, 191 and F 75, 22 n. 1.

[214] A 234, 113 *Frt.* F, rev. 12. On *mgdl* see B 186 II, 516; F 43, II, 214*. Cf. also Ex. 14:2; and for Migdal Thauatha many centuries later near to Gaza see B 47, 151; B 48, 80, 110. Many scholars take Magdalus as Megiddo (A 70, 102 n. 60; B 298, 4–5; F 75, 22 n. 1).

[215] About four lines missing (A 932. 70); and see p. 396 above.

[216] See Jos., *Ant. Jud.* x.88; and see p. 394 above for the possibility of deportations.

[217] Babylonian Chronicle 5 rev. 6–10 (A 25, 101; A 44, 564; A 932, 70–1; B 131, 74, no. 448), and cf. Jer. 49: 28–33. For the Egyptian encounter see above, p. 232, and below, p. 717.

[218] The Syriac (Peshitta) and Arabic versions read *ʾdm*, 'Edom', in place of *ʾrm*, 'Aram', which is a reasonable alternative, but one best rejected pending better manuscript evidence.

Rechabites,[219] whose rigid vows normally restricted them to living in tents, to come into Jerusalem for protection (Jer. 35:1–11). The Moabites and Ammonites might have suffered raids from the roused bedouin Arabs and have been seeking gains in Judah to compensate for losses on their eastern margins. This is again a largely speculative reconstruction, but the fact of eastern incursions is illustrated by a reference in an ostracon from Arad of about this date[220] to the threat of an Edomite attack on Ramat-Negeb, probably modern Khirbet el-Gharra, a little over 24 km to the south west of Arad, on what was presumably the southern border of Judah.[221] This ostracon, of which the obverse is largely effaced, is a letter addressed to someone named Eliashib, very likely the official of this name who held an administrative position in the town at least thirty years before.[222] He is known also in this later period from a small archive, consisting of eighteen ostraca, which were found in one of the chambers of the casemate wall which cut across the sanctuary after its destruction at the end of level VII.[223] These ostraca are mainly letters directed to him as 'Eliashib', though once he is named 'Eliashib ben Eshiah',[224] and they give brief instructions for the issuing of specified rations, either to named individuals, or in several cases to the 'Kittim' or Kittiyim (*ktym*).[225] The meaning of this term changed over the centuries. Starting as the designation of inhabitants of the city of Citium in Cyprus, which was from about the ninth or eighth century B.C. a Phoenician outpost, it came to refer to the Greeks who settled there in large numbers, and by extension to Greeks and Graecized peoples throughout the Mediterranean, and eventually, by the time of the Qumran texts, to their successors, the Romans.[226] A roughly contemporary reference in Jeremiah to the 'isles of the Kittiyim' (Jer. 2:10) suggests that the meaning had shifted by this time to the Mediterranean in general, and since the employment of Aegean mercenaries was a long-standing practice in Judah, and the Egyptians were using Greek and related troops at this time, it is reasonable to see these Kittim as mercenaries of this type engaged by Jehoiaqim to help to guard his borders.[227]

One of the other recipients bears the name . . . *sᶜnl*, very likely to be

---

[219] See *CAH* III².1, 492–3.

[220] Arad Ostracon 24 (B 17, 46–9; B 121, no. 63; B 199, 188–95; B 262, 319–32 no. 19; B 299, 30 and fig. 3; B 327, 205 no. 11). [221] B 199, 191–2 and 152 (map). [222] See p. 385 above.

[223] Arad Ostracon 1–18 (A 44, 568–9 (nos. 1, 17–18); B 17, 12–38; B 121, nos. 49–55 (= nos. 1–5, 16–17); B 133, 49–54 nos. 13, B–D (= nos. 1, 17–18); B 199, 155–84, 231–2; B 262, 291–318 nos. 1–17 (= nos. 1–14, 16–18).

[224] This full form is given in Arad Ostracon 17: 2–3 (B 17, 32–4; B 121, no. 54; B 133, 53–4; B 199, 174; B 262, 312). [225] Mentioned in Ostraca 1, 2, 4, 7, 8, 10, 11, 14, and 17.

[226] A 845, 85–6; B 142; B 146, 113; B 186, 380; B 199, 56; B 262, 293; E. Oberhummer, 'Kition', in P–W 21 (1921), 535–45. Cf. J. Boardman, *The Greeks Overseas* 44. [227] See p. 387 above.

restored as *qws^nl*, Qaus-ʿanal, marking him as an Edomite, but most of the others have typical Hebrew names, all but two being compounded with the orthodox element *-yhw*. One of these other two has the gentilic form 'the Kerosite' (*qrsy*),[228] perhaps connecting him with a family of temple slaves (*nĕtînîm*), probably of foreign origin, but fully integrated into Israelite religious life.[229] The name of Eliashib himself had been borne by a priest in the time of David (II Chron. 24:12), and was subsequently that of one of the high priests in Nehemiah's time,[230] so he may have had cultic connexions, and indeed the letter to him in which the Kerosite is mentioned concludes with a reference to an unnamed individual who is described as living in the 'house of Yahweh', probably the Temple at Jerusalem. This suggests that this particular letter came from a superior in Jerusalem, and, though it opens with the rather elaborate address: 'To my lord Eliashib. May Yahweh desire your peace. And now . . .', while the majority of the others begin more bluntly 'To Eliashib. And now . . .',[231] it is reasonable to see them all as instructions from the capital to an official in a southern outpost, authorizing him to issue rations, apparently to both military and religious personnel. If the Eliashib of this archive was indeed the same man as the one who already occupied an official position at Arad at the time of Josiah's great reforms, he should perhaps be seen as a man who adapted to each change in religious policy; a type, to judge from the statements of the prophets, not uncommon in ancient Israel.

It seems that Jehoiakim did not himself have to contend with the results of his defection from Babylonian control, for he died, probably in December 598,[232] before Nebuchadrezzar could bring retribution upon him. It was at about this time in fact that, according to the Babylonian Chronicle, Nebuchadrezzar mustered his army and set out for Khatti, where he laid siege to 'the city of Judah' (*āl ia-a-ḫu-du*),[233] that is to say, Jerusalem. The defender was now Jehoiakim's son Jehoiachin,[234] who surrendered to Nebuchadrezzar on 16 March 597 (2 Adar), only a little over three months after becoming king. Since the Babylonian army is unlikely to have reached Jerusalem before about mid-January, the siege must have been relatively short, a fact which accords with the comparatively mild treatment meted out to Jehoiachin and his court. Apparently no great damage was done to the city, but according to Kings Jehoiachin was deported to Babylon together with his family and several thousand

---

[228] Arad Ostracon 18: 5 (B 17, 35–6; B 133, 53; B 199, 180; B 262, 315).
[229] See B 109, 89–90, 364, 382–3; B 202; B 203; B 237, 19; B 262, 317.
[230] B 237, 197   [231] On *w^t*, 'and now', see *CAH* III².1, 486.   [232] B 306, 168.
[233] Babylonian Chronicle·5 rev. 11–12 (A 25, 102; A 44, 564; A 932, 72–3; B 131, 74, no. 44B; B 339, 80).   [234] See n. 164 above, and p. 418 and n. 34 below on the spellings of his name.

men ranging from the leaders, both secular and religious, of the kingdom to skilled craftsmen, and a substantial amount of loot was taken from the Temple and the royal palace (II Ki. 23:12–16).[235] Among the deportees was a priest named Ezekiel, whose prophetic messages to his fellow deportees are known from the book bearing his name. Nebuchadrezzar replaced Jehoiachin with his uncle Mattaniah, a half brother of his father, whose name was changed to Zedekiah (II Ki. 24:17; II Chron. 36:10).[236] The Babylonian Chronicle says more briefly that Nebuchadrezzar seized the king, appointed a substitute of his own choice, and took heavy tribute.[237]

Little is known of the earlier years of Zedekiah's reign. Kings states that he was twenty-one years old when he became king, and that he reigned eleven years (597–586),[238] during which time he merely continued in the heterodox policies of his nephew (II Ki. 24:18–20 = Jer. 52:1–3), which were, in the international circumstances, foolish and even hazardous. At some point during his reign he was, according to Jeremiah, visited by emissaries from Edom, Moab, Ammon, Tyre, and Sidon (Jer. 27:3), whose aim seems to have been to enlist his participation in a rebellion against Nebuchadrezzar. The year by year record provided by the Babylonian Chronicle reports that in his campaign of 597/596 Nebuchadrezzar came only as far west as Carchemish, that he was engaged at home and in the east in 596/595, that he had to suppress a revolt at home in late 595, but that he came to Khatti in 594, where he received tribute from unnamed kings, and that at the end of the same year he mustered his army and marched again to Khatti.[239] This concludes the material supplied by the Babylonian Chronicle tablet which covers the ten years 605–595, and since the following tablet has not been recovered, and there is indeed no other extant tablet of the series until the year 556, this valuable source of evidence now fails.

The indications in the surviving Hebrew text of Jeremiah concerning the date of the visit from the neighbouring emissaries are contradictory. Chapter 27 assigns this embassy to the 'beginning of the reign of Jehoiakim ben Josiah' (27:1), while the next chapter refers to 'the same year at the beginning of the reign of Zedekiah king of Judah, in the fourth year' (28:1). Since, in the course of chapter 27, reference is made both to Zedekiah (Jer. 27:3, 12), and to the exile of Jehoiachin[240] (Jer. 27:16–22), the reference to Jehoiakim at the beginning must be pre-

---

[235] The discrepancy between 10,000 deportees in v. 14 and 7,000 in v. 16 is presumably to be explained as the result of an error in transmission (cf. *CAH* III².1, 450 n. 55). The figure of 3,023 given in Jer. 52: 28 represents adult males only (see B 77A, 369).   [236] Cf. B 6, 70, 73, 74.
[237] Babylonian Chronicle 5 rev. 12–13 (A 25, 102; A 44, 564; A 932, 72–3; B 131, 74, no. 448; B 339, 80).   [238] B 306, 167–9.
[239] Babylonian Chronicle 5 rev. 14–26 (A 25, 102; A 44, 564 (lines 14–15); A 932, 72–5).
[240] Written Jeconiah (*yĕkonyāh*), on which see B 283, 92*; and see p. 418 n. 34 below.

sumed to be an error. The Septuagint omits the entire reference but the Syriac version, more logically, names Zedekiah,[241] also of course a son of Josiah, and this may represent the original text, the name 'Jehoiakim' possibly having been substituted by a later copyist by inadvertent repetition of the heading of chapter 26. If this is correct, the embassy would appear to have come to Zedekiah almost immediately after his patron, Nebuchadrezzar, had left him in office and returned to Babylon. While there is no evidence that the visit of the foreign embassies led to any rebellion in the west, it is not impossible that the emissaries were somehow in communication with the instigators of the revolt which Nebuchadrezzar had to suppress in Babylon in 595,[242] and indeed reference is made in this passage to the claim of the false prophet Hananiah that the exile would last for only two years (Jer. 28:1–4), which, if made in 597, would refer to 595.

That there was contact between Jerusalem and the exiles in Babylon is shown by a letter addressed by Jeremiah to the Jewish elders, priests, prophets, and people there, urging them to resign themselves to a long exile, and to make the best of it (Jer. 29). Though there is thus no indication of overt dissident activity on the part of Zedekiah at the beginning of his reign, and he is indeed said to have visited Nebuchad-rezzar in Babylon in 594 (Jer. 51:59), he did, according to Kings, eventually rebel against the king of Babylon, presumably a few years later, for the narrative goes on to say that on the tenth day of the tenth month of Zedekiah's ninth year Nebuchadrezzar brought his entire army to Jerusalem, which he besieged with the aid of a surrounding siege wall (II Ki. 25:1; Jer. 52:3–4 and 39:1).[243] If this date is reckoned according to the Tishri-Elul year, which was normally used for Judah in Kings, the day referred to would have been 11 July 588;[244] but if, as is perhaps more likely in view of the recent subservience to Babylon, the Babylonian Nisan-Adar year is assumed, the day would have been 5 July 587.[245] This would also accord with the timing of Nebuchadrezzar's later recorded campaigns to the west, for which, according to the Babylonian Chron-icle, he mustered his troops in the months of Kislimu (6th, 7th, and 11th campaigns), and Tebetu (8th campaign). The siege is said to have lasted for one and a half years (Jer. 39:2; 52:5–6; II Ki. 25:2–3).[246]

A store jar fragment found in the destruction levels at Lachish, inscribed 'in the ninth, Beyt . . . iah, Hekalia[h ben A]zn[y]' may refer to the successful gathering of part of the harvest in Zedekiah's ninth year,

[241] B 77A, 195, 199.   [242] B 283, 95*.   [243] Cf. A 42, 3 (D), 27, dāiqu.
[244] 10 Tammuz 588. assuming Thiele's assignment of years (B 306, 164), 1 Tammuz being 2 July 588 (A 877, 28). See chronological table, pp. 748–9.
[245] 10 Tebet 587, 1 Tebet being 27 December 588 (A 877, 28). B 306, 164, 168, places the event one year earlier on 15 January 588, as does B 124, 205–6; B 301, 230, proposes 26 January 587.
[246] 10th month of 9th year to 4th month of 11th year = 18 months.

Beyt . . . iah being perhaps the point of collection, and Hekalia(h) being the official collector.[247] The main elements of the harvest were normally gathered in April–June (barley and wheat), August–September (grapes), and September–November (olives),[248] so assuming that this inscription does refer to Zedekiah's ninth year, and that the Babylonian calendar had been adopted in Judah, the entire harvest of 588 would have been in before the tenth month when the siege began, so this jar could have contained grain, wine, or oil. In spite of such provisioning, however, Jeremiah is said, in response to the inquiry of Zedekiah, to have forecast famine in Jerusalem and its eventual destruction by Nebuchadrezzar (Jer. 21:1–7; 34:1–7), and even to have advised the people to give themselves up to the Babylonians (Jer. 21:8–10). It seems that under pressure of the siege wealthy citizens released slaves from their servitude, as indeed according to the Torah they should have done automatically every seventh year (Deut. 15:1, 12–18), but a little later, when the severity of the siege was relaxed, they went back on their action, taking the men and women into slavery once again (Jer. 34:8–22).[249] The respite seems to have been occasioned by the entry of an Egyptian army into Palestine. This episode is unknown in extra-Biblical sources, and Jeremiah who records it (Jer. 37:5–11; and cf. Ezek. 17:11–21) refers to the king responsible for it only as 'pharaoh', but he must have been Apries (589–570), who is referred to in a later passage in Jeremiah as Hophra (Jer. 44:30), and who is known to have adopted a more aggressive foreign policy than his predecessors.[250]

The relaxation of the Babylonian siege was evidently such that the inhabitants were able to travel some distance away from the city, for Jeremiah is said to have planned to go to his home at Anathoth in Benjamin to deal with family business (Jer. 37:12).[251] He was presumably, however, a marked man in view of his condemnation of armed resistance to the Babylonians, for he was arrested as he was leaving the city, beaten and imprisoned on the charge of deserting to the Babylonians (Jer. 37:13–16). He was confined in the vaults of the cistern house, but brought out for a secret meeting with Zedekiah to whom he gave an uncompromising assurance of Babylonian victory. Zedekiah, nevertheless, perhaps now seeing that his message should be heeded, had him moved to milder confinement near the palace, with regular rations (Jer. 37:12–21). According to the sequence of the narrative in the Book of Jeremiah, Zedekiah then handed Jeremiah over to a group of high officials who demanded his execution, and who lowered him into a partially dried-out cistern, where an unpleasant death awaited him as he

---

[247] B 199, 134–5.   [248] B 343, 183–5.   [249] See B 77A, 223–4; and cf. also B 51, 54–8.
[250] A 30, 407; F 44, 360.   [251] For this interpretation see B 77A, 224, 229.

sank into the damp mud at the bottom. From this plight he was rescued by an official who, though he had evidently adopted the Hebrew name Ebed-melek, was of foreign origin, being identified as a native of Kush, the area to the south of Egypt. This man is described as obtaining Zedekiah's permission to haul Jeremiah out of the cistern, following which the king sought another interview with him at which he received the same message of impending Babylonian conquest, and the desirability of making terms with the Babylonians. Zedekiah swore him to secrecy and had him returned to his place of confinement near the palace (Jer. 38:1–28). There is, of course, an element of repetition in the way Jeremiah was apparently twice confined in cisterns and twice brought out for interviews with the king, and it cannot be ruled out that the two accounts describe a single sequence of events.[252] Nevertheless, there are sufficient differences between the two to justify the tentative view that Jeremiah suffered similar treatment on two separate occasions. Whichever view is taken, however, the episode or episodes demonstrate the typical scapegoat-seeking of a nation in dire straits, and also the vacillating character of the king.

It may have been during this time of relaxation in the siege that Jeremiah performed an action which looked forward to a time when life would return to normal in Judah. He was visited by Hanamel, a cousin from Anathoth, a man who had fallen on hard times no doubt on account of the unsettled state of the country, and who came to call upon Jeremiah to discharge his Levitical duty and right of purchasing a plot of land in Anathoth, which he, Hanamel, could no longer maintain (Jer. 32:6–8; Lev. 25:25). Jeremiah, though still in detention, is said to have purchased the land, and the text gives an illuminating account of the transaction, in which he weighed out seventeen silver shekels on a balance, wrote the deed, sealed it, having it signed by witnesses before whom he handed it to Baruch with instructions that it be placed in a pottery vessel for safe keeping (Jer. 32:9–15).[253] Such storage of documents in jars is now well known from the later example of Qumran, and a detail of the deed, which is described as having an open and a sealed part, is illustrated by parchment documents, again of later date (c. first century B.C.) from Avroman in western Iran. These take the form of scrolls on which the text is twice repeated, the two versions being separated by a row of holes so that the upper part could be rolled up and tied with cords passing through the holes and secured with sealed clay lumps, the lower version being left open for consultation without danger of alteration, since the

---

[252] See B 77A, 232–4, for mild advocacy of this view.
[253] See B 77A, 237–9; B 187, 50–1.

original closed text could always be unsealed for inspection and verification.[254]

When the Egyptian diversion was ended, the Babylonians once more tightened the siege of Jerusalem, at the same time presumably moving to occupy the strategic points of the kingdom. It seems that, apart from Jerusalem, the best defended cities in Judah were Azekah, about 30 km to the south west, and Lachish, some 20 km further off. This is suggested by the statement of Jeremiah that toward the end of Zedekiah's resistance only these two cities remained untaken among the strongholds of the kingdom (Jer. 34:6–7). This situation is partially illustrated by a group of inscribed ostraca (Pls. Vol., pl. 173), found in or near a side chamber of the main gate at Lachish,[255] in a burnt layer associated with the final destruction of level II in 586. Several of these ostraca are only partially legible, but that they are closely related is shown not only by similarities in the form of the script, though more than one scribe is clearly represented,[256] but also by the fact that five of them are written on sherds from the same broken jar.[257] Two of these five, and one other, are sufficiently preserved to show that they were addressed to an officer named Ya'osh, who seems to have been in a position of authority at Lachish,[258] having had access even to the king.[259] The writers of these three letters address him as 'my lord ['dny] Ya'osh' and it is likely that some of the other letters which address the recipient as 'my lord' without naming him[260] were likewise intended for Ya'osh. In spite of the disastrous situation which must now have been confronting the nation, these letters are couched in the language of polite formality. After the opening address most of them proceed with some such phrase as 'May Yahweh let my lord hear news of peace even today',[261] and in three of them the writers continue with the phrase, 'who is your servant but a dog that . . . ?' followed by a reference to some condescending action on the part of the recipient,[262] a phrase paralleled in the Old Testament (e.g. II Ki. 8:13).

---

[254] E. H. Minns, 'Parchments of the Parthian period from Avroman in Kurdistan', *JHS* 35 (1915) 22–65; P. Gignoux, *Glossaire des inscriptions pehlevies et parthes* (London, 1972) 43–4. For papyrus examples of the second century A.D., tied but without seals, from the Dead Sea caves, see B 347, 236–8, pl. 488; B 348, 229–31 and figs. on pp. 238, 240, 242–3.

[255] Lachish Ostraca 1–15, and 18 in the chamber, 16–17 associated with the road of the Persian period leading to the gate. A 15 nos. 192–9 (nos. 2–6, 9, 13, 19); A 44, 321–2 (nos. 2–6, 8–9, 13); B 112, 331–9; B 131, 75–8, no. 45 (rios. 2–6); B 133, 32–49 no. 12 (nos. 1–6, 9, 13, 18); B 199, 83–143 (nos. 1–9, 11–12, 16–18); B 311; B 339, 212–17 (nos. 1, 3–4).

[256] B 311, 43, 87, 99, 119, and alphabet chart.   [257] Lachish Ostraca 2, 6–8, and 18.

[258] Lachish Ostraca 2, 3, and 6.   [259] Lachish Ostracon 6: 4.

[260] Lachish Ostracon 4, 5, 17, and probably 8, 9, 12, and 18, the other examples being too illegible to permit identification.   [261] See B 199, 98.

[262] Lachish Ostraca 2: 3–5; 5: 3–5; 6: 2–3. Cf. B 199, 99.

The letters seem to have been written by the commanders of military outposts, one of them, Hoshaiah, evidently situated on the route between Jerusalem and Egypt, possibly at Eglon,[263] and another, un-named, on the road from Jerusalem to Lachish, perhaps at Mareshah.[264] Both Lachish and the fort at Azekah[265] were within sight or nearly so of the latter post, for the sender of the letter refers to a system of signals, probably depending on smoke, the word *mś't* 'signal', having something of the sense of 'uprising' (from *nś'*, 'to lift'). There may have been prearranged times for such signals to be sent, because the writer reports that no signal from Azekah was to be seen, as though one was expected. This is perhaps an indication that Azekah had already fallen to the Babylonians, a serious loss if this is so because it was near enough to the route between Jerusalem and Lachish to threaten this vital communication.[266] The fall of Azekah is perhaps further indicated by the statement in the same letter that there was no one at another post named Beth-Harapid, between Lachish and Azekah, suggesting perhaps that the close approach of the Babylonians had led to its abandonment. That it was still possible for a messenger to reach Jerusalem from Mareshah, perhaps by following a south-eastward detour before making north for the capital, is suggested by a reference in the same letter to a messenger going up to 'the city', presumably Jerusalem, and the expectation that he would go again the following morning. One letter concludes with a reference to a message from 'the prophet', the identity of whom is uncertain.[267]

Among the other letters there is a probable reference to the Babylonians by the same name, *kśdm*, as is found in the Old Testament (*kaśdîm*, in II Ki. 25, Jer. 38 etc.),[268] and also possibly to the name of the then king of Moab, otherwise unknown, Chemosh, the latter part of the letter being missing.[269] The dating of these ostraca is uncertain, but a possible clue is to be found in a reference to the movement of royal grain by an official named Tobiah, following the phrase 'May Yahweh cause you to see the harvest'.[270] This suggests composition in the early spring following the successful collection of the harvest in Zedekiah's ninth year, namely in early 587. It is possible that the letter of Hoshaiah, which also mentions Tobiah, is to be dated to about the same time.[271]

---

[263] Lachish Ostracon 3; see B 199, 106–7.
[264] Lachish Ostracon 4; see B 199, 114–15. Mareshah is modern Tell Sandahanna.
[265] See B 199, 114 n. 79.
[266] For an alternative interpretation of the letter see B 199, 113, 116–17.
[267] Lachish Ostracon 3: 19–21; see B 199, 105–6.
[268] Lachish Ostracon 6: 6, following the reading of B 199, 123. For Biblical *kaśdîm* see B 186, 477–8. On š/ś see n. 122 above.   [269] Lachish Ostracon 8: 3–4, following B 199, 125.
[270] Lachish Ostracon 5: 7–8, reading 'the harvest' (B 199, 118) rather than 'the conspiracy' (B 133, 43–4).   [271] Lachish Ostracon 3: 19, and see B 199, 143 (suggesting, however, spring 589 B.C.).

In spite of the respite during the siege of Jerusalem its long duration eventually told on the defenders. The food supplies ran out causing famine in the city (II Ki. 25:3) and, probably largely as a result of the weakness and lack of vigilance caused by this, the Babylonians were able to penetrate the defences (II Ki. 25:4) on the ninth day of the fourth month of Zedekiah's eleventh year (II Ki. 25:2–3; Jer. 39:2). This, according to the Babylonian calendar, and assuming Zedekiah's first full year to have begun in Nisan 596, would have been on 18 July 586.[272] Lachish and Azekah had presumably fallen to the Babylonians well before this, perhaps during 587; but Jerusalem had a fine defensive system, weak only on the north side where it ran on to higher ground, and it may have been in this sector that the Babylonians finally made their entry.[273] When he saw that the city was lost, Zedekiah, according to the Biblical account, escaped with his troops by way of 'the gate between the two walls', possibly though by no means certainly at the southern tip of the city, where a later wall surrounding the west hill and the Siloam pool may have met the western wall of Ophel,[274] This sector was likely, if the Babylonians had entered in the north. The Babylonians are said to have overtaken and dispersed this force near Jericho, where they captured Zedekiah together, apparently, with some of his sons. They were taken to Riblah, nearly 320 km north of Jerusalem in Syria, where Nebuchadrezzar had his military headquarters. Zedekiah, having been Nebuchadrezzar's own nominee, was dealt with severely. His sons were executed in his presence, and he was blinded and taken captive to Babylon (II Ki. 25:4–7; Jer. 39:4–7).

The Book of Jeremiah reports, in a slightly confused passage, that when the Babylonians had gained possession of Jerusalem a group of senior officers, including Nergal-sharezer, *samgar*, Nebu-sarsekim, *rab-sārîs*, and Nergal-sharezer, *rab-māg*, sat in the Middle Gate, presumably thus establishing themselves as a military government (Jer. 39:3). The three titles are those attaching to senior positions in the Babylonian hierarchy: *simmagir*, something like 'royal commissioner',[275] the *rab ša rēši*,[276] and *rab mugi*, another official of uncertain responsibility.[277] It is not clear, however, whether there were two Nergal-sharezers or whether one man of that name occupied both the offices of *simmagir* and *rab mugi*; and the identity of the *rab ša rēši* is uncertain, because, according to the account in Jeremiah, only a little over one month later, when it is hardly likely that a new man had assumed the office, he is named Nebushazban (Jer. 39:13). There is at present no satisfactory explanation for this. The

---

[272] 9 Tammuz 586; 1 Duʾuzu being 10 July 586 (A 877, 28). B 306, 164, 169, also arrives at this date. Views vary regarding the year concerned, 587 being favoured by some and 586 by others; see B 301, 230; B 303, 261.   [273] B 178, 167–9.   [274] See p. 359 above.   [275] A 52, 1045; A 743.
[276] See above, p. 361, and A 356, 37–8.   [277] A 52, 667, *mugu* 1; A 743, 86.

name *Nērgal šar'eṣer* presents no difficulty since it clearly represents Babylonian *Nergal-šar-uṣur*, and there is a strong possibility that the man in question was the son-in-law of Nebuchadrezzar, the Neriglissar of the Greeks, who twenty-seven years later became king of Babylon (559–556). The administration established by these officers was only an interim one, set up to deal with immediate issues until further instructions were received from Nebuchadrezzar, who had evidently remained in Riblah. About a month later Nebuchadrezzar sent one of his senior officers, Nebuzaradan (Babylonian Nabu-zer-iddin), to Jerusalem to complete the neutralization of the city. This officer, who is designated *rab-ṭabbāḥîm* ('chief cook') in the Old Testament (II Ki. 25:8, 11; Jer. 39:9–10), is known from a passage in a building inscription on a clay prism of Nebuchadrezzar listing court officials, among whom he is named first, with his office, *rab nuḫatimmu* ('chief cook'), or, perhaps, 'master of the royal kitchen', clearly the designation of a man of rank and importance.[278]

This officer is said to have burned down the Temple, the royal palace, and 'all the houses' of Jerusalem, and to have broken down the walls round the city (II Ki. 25:8–12; Jer. 39:8–10; 52:12–14; II Chron. 36:19–21). To ensure that the destruction of the Temple was fully effective, Nebuzaradan is said also to have removed the cultic equipment to Babylon, some of it in the form of scrap metal, including the enormous bronze water container from the forecourt, the two bronze pillars which flanked the entrance door, and a quantity of gold and silver (II Ki. 25:13–17; Jer. 52:17–23). He is said moreover to have arranged further deportations, amounting to 832 souls (Jer. 52:29), this time of those who had remained in the city, and, apparently, also of those who had deserted to him (II Ki. 25:11; Jer. 39:9; 52:15),[279] and also of the remaining skilled workers or artisans.[280] However, following instructions from Nebuchadrezzar, he had Jeremiah released from detention, given protection, and subsequently committed to the care of the new governor (Jer. 39:11–14). It is possible that Jeremiah was mistakenly seized for deportation during the confused period following his release, because he is said to have been taken in chains as far as Ramah (about 8 km to the north of Jerusalem) before being again set free, having perhaps been recognized by Nebuzaradan (Jer. 40:1–6).[281]

---

[278] Istanbul Prism 7834 (A 800, 313), iii 36 (A 44, 307; A 762, 284, 289 and n. 2); see A 42, 11 (N/2), 316.

[279] *nōpĕlîm*, 'the deserters' ('the fallen'), could alternatively be 'the wounded', but it is hardly likely that he would have committed himself to the burden of deporting wounded (cf. A 480, 37–8).

[280] Preferring the reading *'amôn* here against *hāmôn*, 'crowd' (II Ki. 25: 11), and the redundant *hā'ām hanniš'ārîm* 'the people who remained' (Jer. 39: 9), and taking *'āmôn* as a loanword from Akkadian *ummānu/ummiānu*, 'artisan' (see A 52, 1415–16; B 186, 60).

[281] On this see B 77A, 245–6.

A puzzling feature of the accounts of booty is the absence of any reference to the Ark of the Covenant, one of the most important items of the Temple equipment.[282] The much later apocryphal Second Book of Maccabees contains a passage stating that Jeremiah had rescued it together with the tabernacle and the incense altar, and sealed them up in a cave in the mountain from which Moses had viewed the land (II Macc. 2:4–8).[283] This passage occurs in the second of two letters (1:1–10 and 1:10–2:18) which are prefixed to the body of the book. The first is dated to c. 124 B.C. (1:10), and the second, by referring to the cleansing of the Temple which followed the death of Antiochus IV (Epiphanes), implies a date soon after 164 B.C.[284] Inaccuracies in this account, however, cast doubt on its reliability,[285] and the passage referring to Jeremiah (2:1–15), which forms part of a longer inclusion (1:18–2:15), is said to have been derived from the 'records'; (2:1, 13) and from the 'commentaries of Nehemiah' (2:13), documents unknown to the Old Testament and probably belonging to the numerous class of Jewish literature of the Hellenistic period known as Pseudepigrapha.[286] The extreme disfavour in which Jeremiah stood in Judah at the time of the Babylonian invasion, as well as his evident belief in the transient nature of the Temple and its cultus,[287] condemns this already improbable story as legendary. In the absence of better evidence, the most likely reconstruction remains that Manasseh removed the ark from the Temple, Josiah replaced it, and that it stayed there until it was removed by the Babylonians in 586, and was perhaps broken up for the sake of the gold with which it was overlaid and decorated.

Life continued in the defeated land, but only under Babylonian domination, administered by a new puppet, Gedaliah, who came from a family of position in the kingdom.

---

[282] It was not in the temple at the time of the invasion of Titus (Jos., *Jewish War* v, 219).

[283] On the mountain see B 281, 1–16; and see B 334, 103–8, 218–20, for a fourth-century A.D. traveller's account of the area, with commentary.

[284] For the argument that the date in II Macc. 1: 10 appertains to the second letter, see B 312, 122, 124–6.   [285] B 228, 81–4; B 286 I, 151 n. 61.

[286] See, e.g., B 87. Other references to this story about Jeremiah are found in *The Lives of the Prophets* II, 11–18, and Eusebius, *Praeparatio Evangelica* 9, 30–5 (quoting Eupolemus), for bibliography on which see B 87, 107–8 and 118–77.

[287] See, e.g., B 77A, cxv–cxvi.

CHAPTER 31

THE BABYLONIAN EXILE AND THE
RESTORATION OF THE JEWS IN PALESTINE
(586–c. 500 B.C.)

T. C. MITCHELL

I. PALESTINE DURING THE EXILE

When Nebuchadrezzar returned to Babylon in the autumn of 586 B.C., he took with him a substantial part of the remaining population of Jerusalem, including the skilled craftsmen, who may well at that time have been concentrated in the city. Gedaliah ben Ahikam ben Shaphan (II Ki. 25:22), the puppet ruler left in command by Nebuchadrezzar, was not, as the previous nominee, Zedekiah, had been, in the royal Davidic succession, but he did come from a line of distinguished state officials, his grandfather having played a part in the promulgation of the Book of the Law in Josiah's time, and his father having on one occasion intervened with Jehoiakim to preserve the life of the prophet Jeremiah.[1] A clay seal impression from Lachish suggests that he himself may well at an earlier date have held the position of royal chamberlain.[2] This impression, which is probably to be dated to the latter part in the seventh century, reads 'Belonging to Gedaliah the chamberlain',[3] and if it does indeed come from his own seal it shows that he held this office in the time of Jehoiakim, Jehoiachin, or Zedekiah, probably the last, since his father was still active in the time of Jehoiachin and he would not have reached years of seniority until later. It is possible, though by no means certain, that another clay seal impression of unknown provenance, but palaeographically of the early sixth century B.C., inscribed 'Belonging to Hananiah ben Gedaliah', might refer to an otherwise unknown son.[4]

Jerusalem had been largely destroyed by the Babylonians, so Gedaliah moved his residence to Mizpah (II Ki. 25:23, Jer. 40:8), about 13 km to the north. According to Kings the military commanders[5] and their men came to Gedaliah at Mizpah when they heard of his appointment. It is not clear where these forces had been during the recent war, but it is

---

[1] See pp. 388 and 394 above.
[2] On this title see *CAH* III².1, 465 and n. 174, 509 and n. 163.
[3] B 133, 62, 64 no. 18; B 157, 91 no. 18; B 232, 61–2 no. 30; B 314, 347–8; B 321, 375 no. 149; B 339, 223–4, pl. 13.   [4] B 41, 193–4; B 157, 123 no. 92; B 305, 168–9; B 321, 382 no. 218.
[5] On *śar haḥayal* see B 186, 298–9.

possible that they had evaded the Babylonian troops, who in fact can hardly have visited every area of the kingdom, and that they had emerged from their refuges when the Babylonians had left. Four of the commanders are named, Ishmael, Johanan, Seraiah, and Jaazaniah (II Ki. 25:23; Jer. 40:7–8), and it may be that a fine scaraboid seal of black and white banded onyx decorated with a fighting cock in intaglio below the inscription 'Belonging to Jaazaniah, servant of the king', which was found in a tomb at Mizpah,[6] was the personal seal of the last named of these men. The tomb in which this was found had been cleared and reused in the Byzantine period, but, though the seal can thus not be dated by provenance, the form of the script suggests a date in the late seventh century B.C. The title 'servant of the king'[7] probably referred to a civilian official, a fact which need not rule this man out, because the seal presumably related to an earlier period of his career, and it is not unknown for a civilian administrator to become a successful military commander in times of national emergency.

Gedaliah is said to have pledged himself to these men and their followers, and to have urged them to accept the Babylonian domination and settle down in the land (II Ki. 25:24; Jer. 40:9). Both Kings and Jeremiah describe this episode, but Jeremiah goes on to quote Gedaliah as saying that he would remain in Mizpah to undertake the necessary dealings with the Babylonians and urging his hearers to resume the cultivation of the land (Jer. 40:10). Though a certain number of Babylonian garrison troops evidently remained in Mizpah (Jer. 41:3), Gedaliah seems to have restored some sense of normality and stability to the territory, because a number of Jews who had taken refuge from the Babylonians in Ammon, Moab, and Edom are said now to have returned, bringing agricultural produce with them (Jer. 40:11–12). It seems that the breakdown of order which must have accompanied the Babylonian conquest could not be entirely mended by a man of moderation and conciliation such as Gedaliah seems to have been. It may be that he was seen by some as a weak ruler, because Ishmael ben Nethaniah, one of the commanders who had acknowledged him as leader after the departure of the Babylonian army, appears now to have allied himself to Baalis, king of Ammon,[8] and to have plotted to kill him, presumably seeing this as an opportunity to seize power for himself, being, it is stated, of royal descent. An Ammonite ostracon from Heshbon, datable palaeographically to the late seventh or early sixth century B.C., may give a brief glimpse of the condition of the court of

---

[6] A 45 no. 277; B 111, 229 no. 69, pl. xxi.6; B 133, 62, 64 no. 14; B 157, 104 no. 46; B 161, 20 no. 5; B 217 I, 163; B 321, 368 no. 69; B 339, 221, pl. 13.

[7] See bibliography in B 161, 15, and add B 109, 120, and B 199, 105; and on ʿbd see p. 337 n. 98 above. [8] On whom see B 97, 15 and n. 23; B 356, 136.

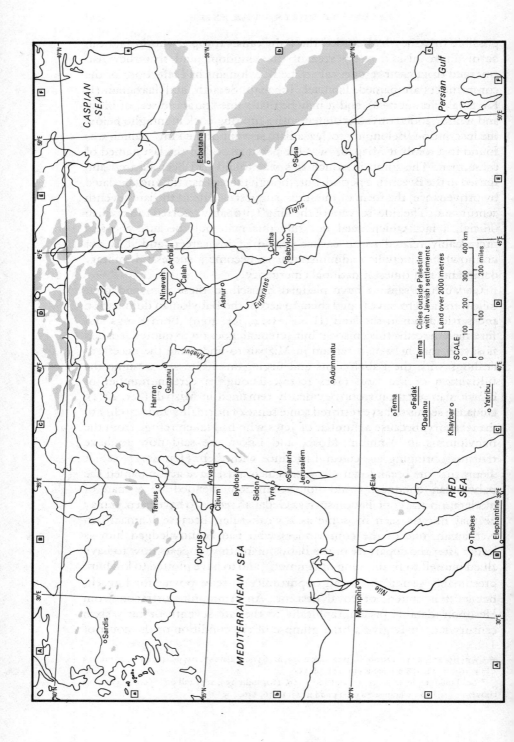

CASPIAN SEA

Ecbatana

Susa

Tigris

Cutha
Babylon

Arbā'il
Calah
Nineveh
Ashur

Khabur

Euphrates

Adummatu

Harran

Guzanu

Fadak
Tema

Dadanu

Khaybar

Yatribu

Tarsus

Arvad
Citium
Byblos
Sidon
Samaria
Tyre
Jerusalem

Elat

Cyprus

RED SEA

MEDITERRANEAN SEA

Sardis

Thebes

Memphis

Nile

Elephantine

Persian Gulf

Tema   Cities outside Palestine
with Jewish settlements

Land over 2000 metres

SCALE

0 100 200 300 400 km

0 100 200 miles

Baalis. This text, which seems to be a record of the distribution of rations from the royal stores, begins with the assignment of a considerable quantity of grain and eight cattle to 'the king', and mentions a courtier 'from Elat', thereby showing friendly relations with Edom in the south.[9] Gedaliah did not believe the account of Ishmael's treachery when it was reported to him by Johanan ben Kareah, another of the returned military leaders, but he was proved to have misjudged the situation when he and his court, as well as some Babylonians attached to it, were murdered by Ishmael and his supporters while they were all dining together (Jer. 40:13–31:3; II Ki. 25:25). Ishmael compounded this action by gratuitously slaughtering a large number of men from the northern kingdom who were travelling to Jerusalem to make offerings at the site of the Temple. He then seized those of Gedaliah's court who had survived, including the king's (probably Zedekiah's) daughters who had been confided by the Babylonians to Gedaliah's care, and probably also Jeremiah, and, recognizing perhaps at this late stage that the Babylonians were unlikely to let his actions pass without some response, he began to travel with his captives towards Ammon, where Baalis would presumably have been prepared to give him refuge (Jer. 41:4–10). He may have been following a circuitous route for tactical reasons because he is said to have been intercepted at Gibeon, actually south west of Tell-en-Naṣbeh, and therefore not on a direct route to Ammon. Johanan, Gedaliah's faithful supporter who intercepted the column, released the captives, leaving Ishmael to escape to Ammon with a small group of supporters (Jer. 41:11–15). Johanan evidently now felt himself to be in a threatened position also, because he feared that Nebuchadrezzar would misunderstand the assassination of Gedaliah and execute vengeance on the innocent; so, going against a firm message from Yahweh which Jeremiah had conveyed to him at his own request, he took all the survivors of Gedaliah's court, including, against their will, both Jeremiah and Baruch, to Egypt, where he settled them in Daphnae (Hebrew *taḥpanḥēs*) in the north-east Delta (Jer. 41:16–43:7; II Ki. 25:26).[10]

No information survives concerning the response of Nebuchadrezzar to the assassination of his governor in Judah, but according to the Book of Jeremiah there does seem to have been some sort of reprisal albeit after a lapse of five years, because there is brief mention of the deportation of 745 further exiles in Nebuchadrezzar's twenty-third year, 582/581 (Jer. 52:30).[11] Apart from a brief appendix concerning Jehoiachin in Babylon, the Book of Kings ends with the account of the flight of Ishmael and his party to Egypt, the Book of Chronicles having concluded with the destruction of Jerusalem, so no information survives

---

[9] Heshbon Ostracon IV; B 99. [10] See p. 429 below. [11] See B 124, 308.

concerning the decades following 586. It is probable that Nebuchadrezzar installed a new governor, very likely a Babylonian this time, whose
regime would no doubt have been considerably harsher. A century and a
half later, Nehemiah refers to the oppression of former governors of
Judah (Neh. 5:15). The version of events given by Josephus is that
Nebuchadrezzar mounted a campaign to the west in his twenty-third
year (582/581), in the course of which he conquered Coele-Syria,
Ammon, and Moab, following which he invaded Egypt, killed the king
and replaced him with another man, and deported to Babylon the Jews
resident there.[12] Though this account, which may have been based on
data contained in the Chaldaean History of Berossus,[13] is clearly
unreliable, it is highly probable that Nebuchadrezzar would have
campaigned in the west during these years. A fragmentary cuneiform
text preserving part of a prayer in his name suggests that he may even
have succeeded in reaching Egypt. The prayer requests divine assistance
for a campaign in Nebuchadrezzar's thirty-seventh year (568/567)
against Egypt and its king . . .-a(?)-su, probably Amasis (570–526).[14] That
at some time, possibly on this same expedition, Nebuchadrezzar conducted a campaign to Lebanon to assure the supply of timber from that
area, which seems to have been threatened by local unrest, is shown by an
undated inscription in his name in a contemporary and an archaizing
version, on the rock face of the Wadi Brissa near Hermel at the northern
end of the Lebanon range.[15] There may therefore be some core of truth in
Josephus' account (cf. also Jer. 43:8–13), though Nebuchadrezzar
obviously did not kill Amasis, who outlived him by well over thirty
years, and Apries his predecessor (589–570) is said by Herodotus
(IV.159) to have been overthrown by a domestic revolt.[16] It is thus
probable that Judah and the neighbouring areas were kept in effective
subjection by the Babylonians, with a display of military force when
necessary. Josephus states that Nebuchadrezzar did not resettle Judah
with deportees from elsewhere and that the area remained deserted for
the period of the exile.[17] It is probably correct that no new deportees
were brought in, but the extent to which the area remained depopulated
is a matter of debate.[18] The fact that Gedaliah was installed as governor,
and that military bands assembled round him at Mizpah, suggests that

[12] *Ant. Jud.* x.181–2.   [13] Cf. *Ant. Jud.* x.219–26.

[14] Tablet BM 33041 (A 44, 308; A 800, 68–9, 321; A 856, 206–7 n. 48; A 932, 94–5; and cf. A 30, 307;
F 44, 362; cf. B 277, 367, with incorrect reading of the royal name). The additional fragment BM
33053 (A 932, 94–5) is irrelevant (A 800, 321).

[15] A 44, 307; A 800, 316–18; A 856, 150–77 no. 19.

[16] Three cuneiform inscriptions of Nebuchadrezzar in the Boulaq Museum, Cairo, said to have
been found at Suez (B 284, 490; W. M. F. Petrie, *History of Egypt* III (London, 1905) 353), are now
known to be casts taken from a standard cylinder type of Nebuchadrezzar (B 337; B 800, 228–35 NbK
Zyl II.1, text no. 11).   [17] *Ant. Jud.* x.184.   [18] See B 4, 21–5.

some people were left. The dearth of archaeological material from the period following the final Babylonian conquest in excavated town sites in Judah indicates, however, that this remnant population must have been sparse, many of the people perhaps following a semi-nomadic way of life.

The administrative divisions of the Neo-Babylonian empire are not well known, because though a large number of royal inscriptions have survived from the period the majority of them deal with building works in Babylonia but few with foreign activities. A possible indication is to be found in Ezekiel's vision of the restored future Jerusalem, dated to 573 (Ezek. 40:1), in which reference is made to the north-eastern territories of Hamath, Damascus, Hauran, and Gilead (Ezek. 47:15–19). These had been Assyrian provinces, but Ezekiel, though he was writing in Babylonia, had lived in Palestine under Neo-Babylonian rule. Therefore it is reasonable to assume that in these areas, and by extension in most others, the Babylonians had taken over the Assyrian provincial administrative system largely as they had found it. The province of Samaria, lying in the territory of the former northern kingdom, but now resettled with deportees from the east, bounded the northern border. The coastal territories to the west may have been allowed by the Babylonians to retain a large measure of autonomy, as they had for much of the time under the Assyrians, in the interests of lucrative sea trade from which Babylonia could benefit. Possible support for this view is found in a somewhat damaged section at the end of the list of court officials of Nebuchadrezzar mentioned above. It lists the kings of Arvad, Sidon, Tyre, Ashdod, Gaza, and others (the names being damaged or completely destroyed).[19] Since the original text might have included the king of Judah, it could be argued that these kings were detainees, and indeed men from Arvad and Tyre are listed in the Babylonian ration texts among those receiving provisions. This conclusion does not necessarily follow, however, since detainees could be held to ensure the good behaviour of semi-independent rulers, and those names which do survive on this list were all coastal sites, three of which at least, Sidon, Tyre, and Gaza, had usually contrived to retain their independence. A prophecy of Ezekiel dated to 571 refers to a siege of Tyre by Nebuchadrezzar, one which, according to Josephus, lasted thirteen years.[20] This might appear to militate against a theory of the continuing independence of Tyre, but the same passage states that he gained nothing from it (Ezek. 29:17–18), and Josephus makes no mention of an actual fall of the city.[21] It is possible therefore that these cities retained their independence, that their kings were in Babylon for diplomatic reasons and not as detainees,

---

[19] Istanbul Prism 7834 (p. 408 n. 278), v 23–7 (A 44, 308; A 762, 282–94).
[20] *Contra Apionem* 1.156.   [21] Cf. A 915.

and that in this role they played some part in the ceremonial of the court.

To the east, the two kingdoms of Ammon and Moab may have lost their independence in 582/581, if the account of Josephus is accepted. Edom, being furthest south, may have escaped conquest at that time, and indeed in the apocryphal book I Esdras it is stated that the Edomites set fire to the Jerusalem Temple when the Chaldaeans devastated Judah (I Esdr. 4:45).[22] Possible support for this is found in the book of Obadiah, though uncertainty concerning the dating of this book and the interpretation of the text makes this a debatable witness. This very short book gives no obvious clues to the date of its composition, and views have ranged from the ninth to the fifth century. A reasonable case can be made for a post-Exilic date,[23] perhaps in the late sixth or the early fifth century B.C., in which case the substantial part of it which consists of a condemnation of Edom may give some historical information concerning the time of the Babylonian invasion, then in the not too distant past. One verse which may refer to the destruction of Jerusalem in 586 speaks of Edom as standing, literally 'from opposite', taken by some commentators to mean 'aloof', possibly indicating a failure to lend aid, and after referring to looting and occupation concludes 'also you like one of them', which could presumably indicate participation in the destruction (Obad. 11).[24] A clearer indication of the attitude of the Edomites is given in the famous Exilic Psalm which begins 'By the rivers of Babylon we sat down and wept when we remembered Zion', and goes on to recall that at the time of the fall of Jerusalem the Edomites had said 'Down with it, down with it, down to its very foundations!' (Ps. 137:7). Whether the statement in Jeremiah referred to above, that there were Jewish refugees in Edom, would militate against this interpretation is not clear. The passage merely states that the Jews were 'in' Ammon,[25] Moab, and Edom (Jer. 40:11–12), so they might have been making the best of what refuge they could find without regard to the stance of the rulers. At all events the Edomites were ready to take advantage of Judah if the opportunity arose, and another statement in Esdras to the effect that at the end of the sixth century Darius gave orders that the Edomites should give up the villages which they had taken over from the Jews (I Esdras 4:50) may well reflect the beginning of Edomite encroachment into southern Judah, an area later called Idumaea because of their presence there. This western movement was occasioned, to a considerable extent,

[22] Cf. B 238, 15, 56–7; and see below.
[23] B 29, 129–33; see also B 120, 401–3; B 126, 438–40; B 147, 893–903.
[24] Cf. B 342, 241; and see B 29, 154–6.
[25] The distinction of *běnê-ʿammôn* as against plain *moʾab* and *ʾĕdôm* in Jer. 40:11 has no significance because Ammon is always mentioned in this form in the O.T.; cf. the Assyrian use of Bīt-Ammān as against Māʾab and Udūmu.

by the infiltration into Edom proper of the Arab groups who were later known as Nabataeans.[26]

It has been argued that the apocryphal book I Esdras, which sets out to narrate the history of Judah from about 620 to 450 (Josiah to Ezra), has value as a historical source.[27] That it includes fictional material is clear from the so-called 'Story of the Bodyguards [or Pages]' (3:1–4:63), the account of a Wisdom Contest from which Zerubbabel emerges as the victor and is rewarded with permission to return to Judah.[28] Thus it can only be used selectively, but it is nevertheless necessary to take it into account alongside the traditional text of Ezra-Nehemiah.

For the latter part of the Neo-Babylonian period information once again becomes available from the Babylonian Chronicle, the previous surviving part of which had ended with the year 595. This source suggests that Nabonidus had begun campaigning to the west in his first year, and that in his third year, that is in early 552, he 'encamped against' ... *du-um-mu* in the west (Amurru).[29] It is reasonable to restore this place name as 'Edom',[30] probably preceded by the city determinative, signifying that Nabonidus laid siege to the principal city of the kingdom. It is not clear what was the capital of Edom at that period, but excavations at Buseirah, the site of Bozrah, one of the major Edomite centres, show signs of destruction and burning which might date from this time,[31] and the destruction of level IV at Tell el-Kheleifeh[32] on the Gulf of ʿAqaba may also have resulted from this campaign. The Babylonian Chronicle goes on to name another city which was apparently taken, but none of the possible readings of the name can be identified with any existing site. Whether this campaign had any effect on the hill country of Judah is unknown, but it is doubtful, because Nabonidus would have had no need to divert his troops in that direction. There follows a lacuna in the Babylonian Chronicle until Nabonidus' sixth year (550/549), during which Cyrus' conquest of Ecbatana is described as having taken place. In the following year (549/548), Nabonidus is said to have been in Tema. According to the implication of another text, one probably composed in the time of Cyrus to criticize the conduct of Nabonidus, he led an army from Harran in north Syria to Tema where many of the inhabitants, including the local king, were killed and the city completely taken over.[33] It was presumably during this expedition, when Nabonidus had to pass

---

[26] B 58, 33–5; B 59, 62–6. See however B 107 for a different interpretation.

[27] B 98, 7–9; B 101, 373; B 182A; B 183. See also B 167, 290–4; B 238, 5–7, 15–16.

[28] See B 238, 53 and nn. 1–2.

[29] Nabonidus Chronicle (Chronicle 7; A 25, 21–2, 104–11; A 44, 305–7; A 900, 98–123), i 14–17.

[30] A 25, 282.   [31] B 62; and see B 59, 54–5.   [32] B 49 III, 717; B 340, 442.

[33] Persian Verse Account of Nabonidus (A 900, 27–97), ii 2–32. The text reflects the Persian point of view, but is in Akkadian. On Nabonidus in Tema see pp. 246–8 above and pp. 425–6 below.

through Edomite territory, that the Edomite city was besieged. No evidence has survived concerning events during the last decade of Neo-Babylonian rule in Palestine.

II. THE JEWISH EXILE IN BABYLONIA

With forcible transportation of the leading figures of Judah to Babylon in 597 and 586, and of further population in 582/581, a considerable settlement was formed in this place of exile, many members of which remained there permanently. Those who had come in 597 seem to have been comparatively well treated, and Jehoiachin himself is known from Babylonian documents to have received regular provisions. Jehoiachin's name appears also in the Old Testament as Jeconiah and Coniah,[34] and it is found variously spelt on four cuneiform tablets from an extensive, largely unpublished, archive found at Babylon, which gives details of rations issued to foreigners, presumably internees, during the period from Nebuchadrezzar's tenth to thirty-fifth years (595–570). The four tablets in question designate Jehoiachin 'king'[35] of Judah (*ia-a-ḫu-du/ia-ku-du*), and refer also to rations issued to 'five sons of the king of Judah, in the hands of Qenaiah [*qa-na-a-ma/qa-na-ʾa-a-ma*]'.[36] These tablets appear to belong to the earlier part of the period of the archive, one of them giving the year as Nebuchadrezzar's thirteenth, 592, and though on this tablet the number of sons is damaged, it cannot be restored as less than '5',[37] and on one of the others the numeral '5' is twice preserved complete.[38] This shows that Jehoiachin already had five of his seven sons (I Chron. 3:17–18)[39] by 592, when he must have been only twenty-three or twenty-four years old,[40] a situation not abnormal in days of early marriage, but a further indication of the easy conditions of the detention, in which man and wife were evidently permitted to remain together. Thirty years later he is described by Kings as confined in a place of detention, and as wearing prison clothing (II Ki. 25:27–9), so it may be that the commodious internment implied by these ration tablets was ended by Nebuchadrezzar in 586, when he was obliged to deal much more severely with Judah, and Jehoiachin may have suffered from the

[34] Basically *y(h)w-ykn* and *(y)kn-yh(w)*. For references see B 81, 220; and in general B 255, 202 and n. 1.

[35] Once, presumably by mistake, 'son of the king of Judah' (A 923, 925–7, Babylon 28186 rev. ii 17).

[36] A 44, 308; A 923, 925–7; B 131, 78–9, no. 46; B 339, 84–6. Cf. A 948, 38–9; B 22. On Babylonian -*(iaʾa)-a-ma* for Hebrew -*yaw*, the late form of -*yahū*, '-iah', see A 948, 8; *CAH* III².1, 461 n. 149.

[37] A 923, 925 (Babylon 28178 ii 39).   [38] A 923, 926 (Babylon 28186 ii 11, 18).

[39] For a convenient list see B 236 I, 22.

[40] He was eighteen at the time of his accession (II Ki. 24: 18) in December 598, so he would have been twenty-four by December 592. The 'eight years old' in II Chron. 36: 9 is presumably a scribal error.

imprudence of his fellow countrymen in Palestine. In one instance where Jehoiachin and his five sons are mentioned in the ration lists a reference follows to the issue of grain to '8 men, Jews [ia-a-ḫu-da-a-a]',[41] possibly members of his court who were permitted to be with him.

At this point it has been convenient, quite arbitrarily, to introduce the term 'Jew', which derives ultimately from Aramaic yĕhûdāy 'Judaean', by way of Greek Ἰουδαῖος, Latin Iudaeus, and Old French giu, gyu etc., to distinguish the expatriate Judaean from the man still resident in Judah. Another individual, Ur-milki, is designated Jew on one of the tablets,[42] and the same tablet lists two others, Shelemiah, a gardener, and Semakiah, whose names identify them as Jews, and who are listed in the same part of the tablet as Jehoiachin.[43] Other West Semites accounted for in these ration lists included 90 sailors and 126 men of unspecified trade from Tyre, all unnamed, 8 carpenters from Byblos, likewise unnamed, 3 from Arvad,[44] and a man named Gadi-ilu whose country of origin is largely broken away. Outside this archive there is further limited evidence for West Semites in Babylonia in the seventh and sixth centuries. The seventh-century scaraboid seal of a Phoenician named Shebak ben Elisha was found, without context, at Ur.[45] A small number of seventh-century seals suggest the presence in Babylonia of men from the kingdoms of Transjordan:[46] two Moabite seals from Ur and Telloh inscribed, respectively, Kamoshnathan and Baalnathan,[47] and an Edomite seal from Babylon itself, inscribed 'Belonging to Qaus-gabri', a name already known as that of the king of Edom in the time of Ashurbanipal.[48] These may have been the seals of merchants but, in view of the repeated westward military operations of the Assyrians and Babylonians, forced service as mercenaries, or plain deportation, cannot be ruled out as the origin of their presence there. The woman owner of a late seventh-century scaraboid seal of unknown provenance may have been the descendant of a Judaean who came to Mesopotamia in the earlier part of the century. This seal, inscribed 'Belonging to Yehoyishma, daughter of Shamash-shar-usur'[49] displays the Judaean

[41] A 923, 925 (Babylon 28178 ii 40).

[42] A 923, 927 (Babylon 28122 rev. 13 and probably obv. 11).

[43] A 923, 927–8 (Babylon 28122 obv. 28, 31, and rev. 22); see also A 948, 39.

[44] A 923, 928–9.

[45] A 943, 122, pl. 30 (U.16805); A 866, 136; A 948, 45–6; L. Legrain, Seal Cylinders (UE x; London and Philadelphia, 1951), no. 576. For other Phoenicians in Babylonia see A 945, 59–61.

[46] The acquisition of an Ammonite seal (A 948, 45; B 129; B 157, 64 no. 15) in Baghdad cannot be taken as evidence of Babylonian provenance. For the seal of a possible Assyrianized Ammonite see B 42, 222–8, pl. 40B–D; B 157, 62 no. 9; B 302; B 321 no. 225.

[47] A 943, 32, 109 (U. 520, wrongly quoted as U. 526); B 157, 156 no. 3; B 282, pl. 30. Also B 135, 42; B 157, 158 no. 8; B 321, 368 nos. 81–2. See also A 945, 62.

[48] B 166, 44 no. 186, pl. 9. See p. 332 and n. 38 above.

[49] A 948, 40; B 42, 229–30, pl. 40E; B 157, 125 no. 98; B 321, 383 no. 226. B 42 favours the later date, about 540 B.C.

spelling *yhw*-[50] in the name of the owner, while her father's name was Assyrian, possibly implying that he was born of a Hebrew father who was in Assyrian service.[51] That such Judaeans were brought back to Assyria following Sennacherib's invasion in 701 is shown by the Assyrian reliefs,[52] and it may be that other Judaeans were made to come to Assyria following Ashurbanipal's western campaign of 667/666.[53] Whether there was contact between these Jews in Assyria and the new arrivals in Babylonia is unknown.

According to the Book of Daniel, selected Jews among the exiles were favoured by the Babylonians and given Babylonian names, and though, as has been said, many scholars would reject the book as a historical source, it has been argued that the new names given to Daniel, Hananiah, and Mishael, namely Belteshazzar, Shadrach, and Meshach, represent the plausible though not actually attested Neo-Babylonian names Bēlet-šarra-uṣur, Šādurāku, and Mēšāku, while that of Azariah, namely Abednego, might be the result of Aramaizing word play on Arad-Nabu.[54] These individuals have not been traced in the cuneiform sources, and others renamed in the same way would, of course, be unrecognizable as Jews.

The Babylonian ration tablets show that among Jehoiachin's fellow detainees were a number of other westerners, including Egyptians,[55] and, from nearer home, Philistines from Ashkelon.[56] Among these Philistines were two sons of a king named Aga, presumably the second or third successor of Metinti,[57] and rations are recorded for eight foremen (LÚ.SAG) of the Ashkelonites, implying a considerable contingent, as well as a number (damaged) of head musicians, and three sailors.

The journey of the Jews to Babylonia in 597, and the problems of adjustment which confronted them there, exacerbated by the rebellion in the heart of Babylonia in late 595 to early 594 which Nebuchadrezzar only put down with much loss of life,[58] evidently left them a ready prey to assurances from some among their number that they would soon be able to return home, and that it was therefore unnecessary for them to make any effort to establish themselves. It seems that news of this unrest reached Judah, for Jeremiah is said to have felt impelled to send a letter by the hand of two envoys who were travelling to Babylon, probably in 594, on a mission from Zedekiah to Nebuchadrezzar (Jer. 29:1–3). In

---

[50] See *CAH* III².1, 472.
[51] For instances of fathers with Phoenician names having sons with Assyrian names see A 945, 59.
[52] See pp. 360–1 above.
[53] See p. 378 above, and for another possible Jew in seventh-century Babylonia see A 948, 34–5.
[54] B 66.   [55] A 923, 930–2. See also A 1003, 172–3.
[56] A 923, 928. See also A 945, 61.   [57] See pp. 376, 378 above.
[58] See p. 233 above, and A 932, 36–7.

this letter he transmitted a message from Yahweh, urging the exiles to reconcile themselves to a long stay, to build houses, plant gardens and settle down to family life, paying no attention to lying prophets and diviners (Jer. 29:4–20). This message seems to have elicited a response in the form of a letter from one of the criticized prophets in Babylon, calling on the Jerusalem authorities to silence Jeremiah (Jer. 29:24–9). This remonstrance was evidently ignored, because later in 594 when Zedekiah himself went to Babylon[59] Jeremiah was able to entrust another document to Saraiah ben Neriah, who was to accompany the king on his journey (Jer. 51:59). This man, who was very possibly the brother of Jeremiah's faithful friend Baruch, is described as the *śar-mĕnûḥâ*, 'ruler of the resting-place' or 'bivouac commander' of the king,[60] an appropriate officer for the journey. It may be that a seal of unknown provenance which has come to light, inscribed 'Belonging to Saraiah [ben] Neriah',[61] was his own personal seal. Jeremiah's written message predicted the fall of Babylon, and he requested Saraiah to weight it with a stone after reading it aloud, and to let it sink in the Euphrates as a symbol of the end of Babylon (Jer. 51:60–4). The message was therefore that the exile in Babylon would eventually end, and this element also appears in the teaching of Jeremiah's younger contemporary, Ezekiel, who had been taken to Babylon with the great deportation of 597.[62] According to the book which bears his name, he began seeing divine visions in the fifth year of Jehoiachin's exile, 593 (Ezek. 1:1,3),[63] the year following the reading of Jeremiah's second message. This passage gives an indication of the area in which the exiles had been settled for it states that Ezekiel was among the *gôlâ*, the deportees, by the *nĕhar kebār*, probably the Kabaru canal, which is known from the Murashu archives of the fifth century to have been within the commercial orbit of Nippur,[64] and indeed, though the Murashu family were themselves Babylonians, a number of Jews were involved in the business transactions recorded in these documents. Twenty-four distinct names, probably representing a considerably larger number of individuals, are identified as certainly Jewish by the elements Jeho- or -iah,[65] and among the large number of other individuals with West Semitic names there were no doubt many other Jews.

The area of Jewish dispersal in Babylonia is unknown from contemporary sources, but a possible clue to the distribution of Jewish

---

[59] See p. 402 above.   [60] See B 77A, 210.   [61] B 45, 56, pl. 15D; B 46, pl. 1: 3.
[62] B 127, 316–21; B 275, 284–7. Also on the Book of Ezekiel see B 120, 365–82; B 127, 403–17; B 147, 822–55.   [63] See B 306, 163. On 'thirtieth year' in Ezek. 1: 1, see B 91, 6–7.
[64] BE 9, nos. 4: 9 and 84: 2 and see pp. 28, 76; G. Cardascia, *Les archives des Muraŝû* (Paris, 1951) 108–9. For suggestions on the location of the Kabaru canal see B 258, 327–8.
[65] B 90, 49–53. See also p. 418 n. 36 above.

settlement is to be found in the situation existing in the early centuries of the Christian era, as deduced from the Talmudic sources. According to this evidence the Jews were situated in an area extending roughly from Hit and Baᶜquba in the north to about Kifl and Kut al-Amara in the south, with concentrations in a number of towns, notably Pumbaditha, Nehardea, Hagronia, Mata-Mahasia, Sura, Neresh, and Kaphri on or near the Euphrates.[66] While there was no doubt some movement in the area of settlement during the half millennium since the sixth century B.C., and indeed only one of these towns, Nehardea, is mentioned in earlier sources and then only of the first century A.D.,[67] it is reasonable to assume that the main distribution was similar. If this is accepted, this later evidence would seem to suggest that the majority of the Jews were located to the north of Babylon, with smaller numbers to the south.

A possible indication of the conditions of settlement of the deportees is found in some of the names of Jewish settlements. A Jewish settlement on the Kabaru canal, *tēl ʾābîb*, meaning literally 'mound of ears [of grain]', and the scene of some of Ezekiel's activities (Ezek. 3:15), may have been an ironical Hebraized version of the Akkadian designation *til abūbi*, 'mound of the deluge', applied to settlement mounds abandoned because of destruction, as the Babylonians thought, by the great mythological deluge,[68] implying that the Jews were obliged to settle on such inferior sites. Other, less subtle, instances are *tēl melaḥ*, 'mound of salt' and *tēl ḥarśaʾ*, possibly 'mound of the potsherd' (Ezra 2:59; I Esdras 5:36), which imply a site abandoned because of over-salinization, and one strewn with the sherds of early settlement.[69] It is probable that for some time after their arrival in Babylonia, the Jews were mainly engaged in agriculture with the necessary ancillary crafts, and though, as the Murashu archives show, they were involved in commerce by the next century, they appear still to have been only producers, the town life of the Talmudic period being probably a later development.

In the period before the final destruction of Jerusalem in 586, Ezekiel pressed upon his fellow exiles the same message as that sent by Jeremiah, that there was no prospect of an early return to Palestine, and that Jerusalem was due to suffer destruction (Ezek. 1:1–23:49). The book then states that on 15 January 588,[70] the word of Yahweh came to Ezekiel instructing him to record the date in writing as that on which the king of Babylon had laid siege to Jerusalem (Ezek. 24:1, 2). Three years later, in January 585, almost five months after the fall of the city, a fugitive from Jerusalem reached the exiles in Babylonia with the news

---

[66] B 251, 6–7, and map at front; B 258, 215–318, and map at end.
[67] Jos. *Ant. Jud.* XVIII.311, etc.
[68] A 42, I (A/I), 78; B 91, 42; G. R. Driver and J. C. Miles, *The Babylonian Laws* I (Oxford, 1952) 299 n. I.   [69] B 63, 162.   [70] B 306, 168.

(Ezek. 33:21).[71] If this lapse of time is accurately recorded, it suggests that there was little regular contact at this time between Babylon, where Jehoiachin and his circle were detained, and the Jewish settlements further south. The news must have reached Babylon before Ezekiel heard it, and this may support the suggestion that, with the eruption of further trouble in Jerusalem, Nebuchadrezzar is likely to have placed Jehoiachin in much closer and harsher confinement, effectively cutting him and the others interned with him in Babylon off from contact with the rural exiles. In the years following the second fall of Jerusalem, Ezekiel's message turned more to the future restoration of Israel (Ezek. 33:1–48:35), most vividly depicted in the image of a valley of dry bones, representing the present state of the people, which could be clothed with flesh by the power of Yahweh, and, as the final act of regeneration, filled with his spirit (Ezek. 37:1–14). The final part of this latter section of the book contains the account of a vision, dated by the prophet to 573, in which he was conveyed to Palestine to see an ideal Temple which figuratively represented the people of God restored to his favour (Ezek. 40:1–48:35).

The forty-three years' reign of Nebuchadrezzar, for the last thirty-two of which the Babylonian Chronicle is lacking, ended with his death in late 562, when he was succeeded by his son Amel-Marduk.[72] The Book of Kings makes brief mention of this year when, in an appendix, it states that at the beginning of his reign, ʾĕwîl mĕrōdak, the Evil-Merodach of the English versions, released Jehoiachin from prison, recognized his royal status, and changed his prison clothing, perhaps from plain dress to the type of elaborately decorated garments which are known from bas-reliefs and frescoes to have been worn by the Assyrian king and his court, and which may reasonably be assumed in Babylon. Jehoiachin was once again given regular provisions, as at the beginning of his detention, and was evidently admitted to the king's banqueting chamber (II Ki. 25:27–30).

This appendix to Kings closes the book and gives some indication of the date of its compilation. Apart from this appendix the material concludes with the fall of Jerusalem in 586, and since there is no mention of, or even allusion to, the Persian conquest of Babylon in 539 it is reasonable to conclude that the compilation took place between 586 and 539. The main aim of the compilers appears to have been to demonstrate what had led up to the fall of the kingdom, and not merely to make a continuous record of events without regard to the spiritual or moral lessons conveyed. If this is correct, the silence of the narrative concern-

---

[71] B 306, 169.   [72] See A 877, 12; B 306, 172; and cf. A 887, 28–31.

ing events after the final fall of Jerusalem does not necessarily mean that the compilation was done in the years immediately following 586.

It is nevertheless arguable that, allowing for a time for recovery from the shock, the period of perhaps twenty years following 586, when the bitter memory was still green, is the most plausible time of compilation, the appendix concerning 561 having been added when news of that event became known.

Whether the compilation was done in Babylonia, where so many of the elite were detained, or in Palestine, where the numbers of those capable of such a task had been severely depleted, is unknown. While it might appear, *prima facie*, more probable that the work would have been done in Babylonia, it may be questioned whether the exiles are likely to have been able, or indeed to have been permitted, to transport to Babylonia the documents which the compilers, by their own account, used in preparing the text.[73] According to the Biblical documents, Jeremiah, who had consistently urged submission to the Babylonians, had been permitted to remain in Palestine, and it may be that others who took this view were also allowed to stay. The compiler of Kings certainly took the same clear-sighted and critical view of the failings of the rulers and people during the period of the monarchy as that found in the prophetic literature, and this might support the suggestion that the final composition of Kings was the work of prophetic writers.[74] The evidence is not sufficient to settle the matter, and it remains a subject for speculation.[75]

It is in the period of the exile in Babylon that some of the events narrated in the Book of Daniel are set, but since the authenticity of the material found in it is widely questioned, it will not be used here as a historical source. The latter part of the Book of Isaiah will equally be left aside as a source for this period, since there is disagreement concerning its date of composition. It is worth noting, however, that in this part of the book Cyrus is mentioned by name (*kôreš*) as the agent of Yahweh's purpose, and is indeed designated *māšîaḥ*, 'anointed one' and *rōᶜeh*, 'shepherd' (Is. 44:28; 45:1).

One possible new religious development in this period was the synagogue. This institution, familiar in later Judaism as a meeting place for public scripture reading and prayer, was well established by New Testament times, but there is no specific evidence concerning its origin. The name συναγωγή for the building in which meetings were held is not attested in this sense until the New Testament, and its Hebrew counterpart, *bêt hakkĕnēset*, is not found before the Mishnaic period. Archaeological remains of actual synagogue buildings do not go back

---

[73] See *CAH* III².1, 442.   [74] See *CAH* III²1, 443.   [75] See B 4, 64–8.

before the first century B.C., and inscriptions only carry the evidence back to the third century.[76] Moreover, a general consideration against the probability of pre-Exilic synagogues in Palestine is the fact that the Jewish colony at Elephantine in Egypt, the foundation of which post-dated the fall of Jerusalem, had established an unorthodox temple to Yahweh there, and evidently knew nothing of synagogues.[77] In the Septuagint the word συναγωγή, which occurs over 200 times, almost always refers to a group of people, in the sense 'assembly', 'congregation' or the like, most commonly translating Hebrew ʿēdâ and qāhāl, and practically never refers to a building.[78] This usage, which goes back to the third century B.C., indicates that the synagogue institution was, at the beginning of its history, simply a gathering of people, either in a private residence, or even in the open air, and that the construction of a building for the purpose was a later development. It can only be speculation that this beginning took place in the Babylonia of the Exile.[79]

The sources give no further direct information about the history of the Jewish exiles in Babylonia during the twenty-two years between the release of Jehoiachin and the Persian conquest in 539. A possible indication of an extension of Jewish settlement in a new quarter is found, however, in the documents of Nabonidus. Having taken Tema in the Hijaz of Arabia, he spent about a decade there during the years 552–540[80] and, in an inscription from Harran found duplicated on two stone stelae, he claims to have moved around among a number of cities in the area, implying some sort of military dominance, involving perhaps the establishment of garrison troops in them.[81] With the exception of Iadiḫu, the location of which is uncertain, these cities may be identified, respectively, with the Arabic Taymāʾ, al-ʿUlā (Biblical Dĕdān), Fadak, Khaybar, and Yathrib (later renamed Medina).[82] It is clear from early Islamic sources that Taymāʾ, al-ʿUlā, Fadak, Khaybar, and Yathrib were all centres of Jewish settlement in the sixth and seventh centuries A.D.,[83] and it has been plausibly argued that this coincidence of the existence of later Jewish colonies at the very sites earlier controlled by Nabonidus may be evidence that he had made use of Jewish contingents recruited from among the exiles in Babylonia to help to garrison outposts at these sites in the Hijaz.[84] This hypothesis leaves, of course, an unfilled gap of over a millennium, but very tenuous support is perhaps to be found in a

---

[76] B 280, 218–21; B 286 II, 425; B 289, 18–30.

[77] On the origin of the synagogue in general see B 4, 32–5; B 109, 343–4; B 182 VII, 810–12; B 280, 213–29; B 286 II, 423–7. [78] B 150 II, 1309–10; B 182 VII, 802–5.

[79] For arguments for a later date see B 123, 96–8. [80] See conveniently B 190.

[81] A 44, 562; A 362, 58–9; A 886, 220–4; B 131, 79–81, no. 47. [82] A 362, 80–4; B 338, 91.

[83] See in M. T. Houtsma et al. (eds.) The Encyclopaedia of Islam (Leiden and London, 1931–4) IV, 622; II, 35; II, 870; and III, 83–5 respectively; and in general see A 362, 79–89; H. Lammens, Islām: Beliefs and Institutions (London, 1929) 4–5, 21–2.

[84] A 362, 83–8. See B 64; B 64A; B 338, 91 n. 23.

fragment of an Aramaic papyrus from Qumran, dating from about the early first century A.D., possibly a copy of an earlier text, which purports to record the words of a prayer of Nabonidus (*nbny*) concerning the curing of an inflammation which he suffered in Tema (*tymn*) by the skill of an exorcist (*gzr*), presumably resident there, who is described as a Jew (*yhwdy*).[85]

Nabonidus, the last king of the Neo-Babylonian dynasty, was overthrown in 539 by Cyrus, who instituted more liberal measures towards the peoples who formed part of the Babylonian empire. According to his own account in a cylinder inscription from Babylon,[86] Cyrus brought material relief to the inhabitants of Babylon itself, and in the general area of Babylonia, Assyria and western Iran he returned to their proper temples the divine images (*ilāni*) which Nabonidus had collected in the city, arranging at the same time for the restoration of these temples, and also organizing the return of the people to their homelands.[87] Though this text refers only to Mesopotamia and Iran, it is reasonable to assume that similar provision was made throughout the empire. It is in this light that an Aramaic document, transcribed in the Old Testament and described as a 'scroll' (*mĕgillâ*; Ezra 6:3–5; I Esdras 6:23–5) is to be understood. The Books of Ezra and Nehemiah, which cover the period from the conquest of Cyrus to the latter part of the fifth century B.C., now become significant for the history of the Jewish people. These books, treated as one in Rabbinic tradition,[88] consist essentially of the personal memoirs of the fifth-century Jewish leaders Ezra and Nehemiah, together with material dealing with the fairly recent past,[89] all this having been brought together in more or less its present form by about the end of the fifth century.[90]

The scroll transcribed in Ezra 6 is said to have been found in Ecbatana not long after 512, during the reign of Darius I (Ezra 6:1–2; I Esdras 6:22). It was labelled 'Memorandum', and stated that in his first year (538/537) Cyrus issued an order that the 'House of God' in Jerusalem be rebuilt, following the lines of its original foundations (Ezra 6:3).[91] Overall dimensions and certain details of construction were specified, and an official subsidy and the return to Jerusalem of the gold and silver vessels which Nebuchadrezzar had removed half a century before were authorized. When he had entered Babylon in 539, Cyrus had

[85] B 119, 321–5; B 148, 178–9; B 322, 229; B 323, 72–3; B. Jongeling *et al. Aramaic Texts from Qumran with Translations and Annotations* (Semitic Study Series 4) (Leiden, 1976), 123–31.

[86] BM 90920, Cyrus Cylinder (A 44, 315–16; A 929, xi, 2–9; B 55 no. 21; B 66; B 131, 82–4, no. 50; B 339, 92–4).   [87] Cyrus Cylinder, 30–4. On 'homeland' see A 42, 3 (D), 19, *dadmū*.

[88] Baba Bathra 14b and 15a (I. Epstein, *The Babylonian Talmud. Seder Nezikim*, III: *Baba Bathra* I (London, 1935) 71–2; B 196, 51–3).   [89] See B 237, xlviii–l.

[90] B 237, lxviii–lxx. See also in general B 120, 541–57; B 147, 1135–51.

[91] The base form *ʾōš, 'foundations', being an Akkadian loanword *uššu*; see A 52, 1442; B 174, 110.

adopted the city as his second capital and had shown great respect for its ancient civilization and religion. His order that the rebuilt Temple in Jerusalem should follow the original foundations may well have been a reflection of this, for this was a long-standing aspiration in Babylonian temple building. Cyrus retained Ecbatana as his summer capital, so it is likely that a separate archive would have been maintained there, and, though the official archives in Babylon and Susa, and later in Persepolis, were kept in cuneiform on clay tablets, it is plausible that a copy of an order issued in Babylon, which was to be carried over 500 km to Ecbatana, should have been made in Aramaic (the well established *lingua franca* of the Near East) on papyrus, which, though probably not grown in Babylonia at that time, was certainly known as an import.[92]

The form of Aramaic preserved in the putative transcription of this document of Cyrus exhibits, as do the other passages of Aramaic in the Book of Ezra, certain characteristics which appear to point to a date later than the fifth century B.C. The spelling *dikrôn* (memorandum), for instance, matches *dkrn* found in Nabatean, Palmyrene and Hatrean, rather than the *zkrn* of Old and Imperial Aramaic. These characteristics may, however, be simply the result of later scribal revision or modernization of the spelling, of a kind commonly introduced in written texts which are copied and recopied over a long period. Though dissentient opinions remain, it is a tenable view, therefore, that the Aramaic of the Old Testament could have originated in the late sixth or fifth century B.C.[93] It is thus reasonable to take Ezra 6:3–5 as a reliable transcription of an ancient document issued by Cyrus.

The Hebrew part of the Book of Ezra begins with an account of what is described as a proclamation made by Cyrus throughout his kingdom, which gives substantially the same command but in language perhaps more suited to a verbal proclamation, literally 'causing a voice to pass' than to a written archive. In the proclamation Cyrus is quoted as declaring that Yahweh, God of the heavens, had given him all the kingdoms of the earth and had appointed him to build a house for him in Jerusalem in Judah. He called upon the Jews to go to Jerusalem in order to undertake this rebuilding, and those who chose not to go he invited to contribute towards the needs of the work (Ezra 1:1–4; I Esdras 2:1–6).[94] The claim that this was done by the favour and under the direction of Yahweh is paralleled by the statements in his cylinder inscription that he conquered Babylonia and introduced his reforms under similar guidance from Marduk, the king of the gods and great lord.[95]

---

[92] On papyrus see A 37 II, 343–4; A 52, 748 *niāru*; N. Lewis, *Papyrus in Classical Antiquity* (Oxford, 1974) 10–11, 84–5.
[93] See B 279, 60–71 (63–5 on Ezra); B 341, 31–79 (on Daniel); B 188A, 399–403.
[94] For a discussion of Ezra 1: 1–4 see B 68A; and cf. B 238, 36–7.
[95] Cyrus Cylinder (n. 86 above), 7, 14, 23, 26, 33.

The response to this proclamation was, according to the Book of Ezra, good. It states that heads of families and priests and Levites took steps to travel to Jerusalem to rebuild the Temple, and others who did not choose to go donated treasure in kind, including gold and silver vessels as well as livestock (Ezra 1:5–6; I Esdras 2:7–8). Cyrus had the Temple equipment, which had been taken to Babylon by Nebuchadrezzar,[96] counted out by the treasurer[97] Mithredath[98] to Sheshbazzar, who is called the *nāśî'* of Judah. The term *nāśî'* is used in the Pentateuch and Joshua in something of the sense of an elected chieftain, and then after a virtual break in usage in texts dealing with the period of the monarchy it is again found in the Book of Ezekiel, but in the modified sense of the ruler of a small state – as opposed to the *melek*, 'king', of a major state – and also of the ideal future ruler of Judah.[99] It would appear from this that Sheshbazzar may have been the acknowledged leader of the Jewish exiles, but on the grounds of merit rather than heredity, and that the designation *nāśî'* was a reflection of his status among the Jews rather than an official title. According to a statement of the Jewish elders in Palestine in the time of Darius I, and reported to him by Tattenai, the governor (*peḥâ*) of the province *eber nāri*,[100] Cyrus had appointed Sheshbazzar governor (*peḥâ*), presumably of Judaea, though this must have been a loose, rather than a precise use of the term[101] (Ezra 5:6–17; I Esdras 6:1–21). It has been argued that he is to be identified with Shenazzar, who is listed as the fourth son of Jehoiachin (I Chron. 3:17–18),[102] and who must have been in his mid-fifties by this time, but this is unlikely.[103] It is probable that Jehoiachin, who would have been about seventy-eight years old,[104] was too infirm (if he were not indeed already dead) to take an active part in any arrangements to return to Palestine, and that none of his sons, who must have been well into middle age, was man enough for the task. There was, however, a representative of the Judaean royal line among those who returned to Palestine in the person of Zerubbabel, who is described as the son of Shealtiel (Ezra 3:2, 8; 5:2; I Esdras 5:47, 54; 6:2; Neh. 12:1; Hagg. 1:12, 14; 2:2, 23), who was, according to Chronicles, one of the sons of Jehoiachin (I Chron. 3:17). This passage in Chronicles goes on to describe Zerubbabel as the son of Pedaiah (I Chron. 3:19) rather than Shealtiel, but since according to the sequence of names Shealtiel was the eldest and Pedaiah the third son, it

---

[96] See p. 408 above, and cf. B 238, 37–8.

[97] *Gizbar*, Old Persian *ganza-bara-. A 358, 77 n. 2; B 122, 55; B 324, 42; W. Brandenstein and M. Mayrhofer, *Handbuch des Altpersischen* (Wiesbaden, 1964) 120.

[98] Cf. the name Mitrada (a diminutive of Mithra-data) in the cuneiform archives from Persepolis: M. Mayrhofer, *Onomastica Persepolitana* (Vienna, 1973) 207, 282.   [99] B 295.

[100] See p. 434 below.   [101] On which see p. 342 n. 150 above.

[102] B 19, 108–10; B 27, 86.   [103] B 65.

[104] He was eighteen in December 598 (II Ki. 24: 8 and B 306, 168), so seventy-eight in 538.

could be that Zerubbabel was the physical son of Pedaiah, born to him by a widow of Shealtiel, but raised up in the name of the latter, according to the provisions of levirate marriage (cf. Deut. 25:5–10).[105] Zerubbabel, like many other Jews in Babylonia, particularly those born in exile and including some others among those who returned to Palestine, bore a Babylonian name.[106] According to I Esdras the Temple treasure was handed over to 'Zorobabel and Sanabassarus' (6:18). This may reflect an accurate record of the event and show that Zerubbabel, though junior to Sheshbazzar, was playing a significant part before the departure from Babylon.[107]

III. THE BEGINNING OF THE JEWISH DIASPORA IN EGYPT

When Johanan ben Kareah took the survivors of Gedaliah's court, including Jeremiah and Baruch, to Egypt in or soon after 586 B.C.,[108] this influx of Jews was no new thing. Apart from such single refugees as Rehoboam and the prophet Uriah,[109] and the remote possibility that Sargon took Israelite troops with him in 716 when he campaigned to Nakhal Muṣri on the border of Egypt,[110] it seems that a certain number of Hebrew troops had been pressed into service by Ashurbanipal, together with contingents from neighbouring states, on his invasion of Egypt in 667 or 666,[111] though it is not known whether any of them remained. When Psammetichus II mounted an expedition to Nubia in 591 he made use of Ionian, Rhodian, and Carian as well as Phoenician mercenaries, as is shown by graffiti left by them on one of the colossi of Ramesses II at Abu Simbel,[112] and it is possible that the claim in the late pseudepigraphic work, the Letter of Aristeas, that Jews had been sent to Egypt to help Psammetichus in his campaign against the Nubians might contain a kernel of historical truth and refer to this campaign.[113]

In the latter part of the sixth century a demotic papyrus from Elephantine records that a number of Palestinians and Syrians, among whom there may have been Jews, formed part of an expedition sent by Amasis to Nubia in 529.[114] The presence of Jews at Elephantine in upper Egypt during most of the fifth century is very clearly demonstrated by the archives of Aramaic papyri found there, the earliest dating back to 495.[115] A letter from this archive, written in 407, appealing to Bagoas the

---

[105] B 237, 21; but cf. B 238, 10.
[106] Zerubbabel: A 912, 218; B 255, 63 no. 441; for other names, B 237, 12–14.
[107] See B 238, 15, 76, 78.   [108] See p. 413 above.
[109] CAH III².1, 451–2; and see pp. 393–4 above.
[110] Cf. A 362, 86–7 n. 4; and see p. 345 above. See also below, p. 728.
[111] See p. 376 above.   [112] B 268, 9 and n. 28; B 304, 269–70; F 75, 41–2; and see M–L no. 7.
[113] Letter of Aristeas, 13 (B 86 II, 96). See B 268, 8; H. I. Bell, *Cults and Creeds in Graeco-Roman Egypt* (Liverpool, 1957) 27.   [114] B 268, 15–16 and n. 57.   [115] B 92 no. 1.

governor of Judah for help in obtaining permission to rebuild the (unorthodox) Yahweh temple on Elephantine island, which had been destroyed by the Egyptians in 410, implicitly claims that it had been in existence before 525[116] by mentioning that this temple had been spared during the campaign of Cambyses in that year. The apparent benevolence on the part of Cambyses implied by this claim would accord with a statement in the Letter of Aristeas that there were Jewish immigrants in Egypt in the wake of 'the Persian conquest', probably that of Cambyses.[117]

The settlements of Jews in Babylonia, Egypt, and probably northwest Arabia, were early outposts of what has come to be known as the 'Diaspora', from the Greek counterpart of the Hebrew word *gôlâ*. In the Septuagint, which shows the Jewish usage in the last pre-Christian centuries, this term is not used to translate *gôlâ*, nor indeed any single Hebrew word, but its sense is clearly the 'dispersion of the Jews among the Gentiles', or simply the 'Jews among the Gentiles'.[118] By the beginning of the Christian era the Diaspora had, in addition, extended to Syria, Asia Minor, Greece, Italy, and North Africa (see Map 5).[119]

IV. THE RESTORATION OF THE JEWS IN PALESTINE

The remnant population in the Judaean hills in the later part of the sixth century B.C. seem to have received a considerable augmentation to its numbers between 538, when Cyrus issued the order permitting the Jews to return to Palestine, and 520, when Darius I had Cyrus' order traced, and the permission renewed.[120] The Book of Ezra gives a list of the names of those who are said to have been among the captives in exile (*gôlâ*) in Babylon and who returned to Judah (Ezra 2). Virtually the same list appears in the Book of Nehemiah (Neh. 7) but with certain differences in the numbers of individuals. These differences can be explained for the most part by the assumption of an original text in which the numbers were recorded in figures rather than words (as they now stand in the Massoretic text), and by the accidental omission of certain of these figures.[121] Since the figures in the Nehemiah version are, with few exceptions, greater than those in the Ezra version, by amounts which could have been represented by relatively few numerical symbols and therefore were vulnerable to accidental omission, it is reasonable to see

---

[116] B 92 no. 30: 13–14 (A 44, 491–2; B 131, 84–7, no. 51; B 339, 260–5). The date, Darius 17, Marheshwan, is not 408 (as B 92) but 407 (A 877, 33).

[117] Letter of Aristeas, 13 (B 86 II, 96). For a survey of the evidence of early Jewish settlement in Egypt see B 268, 3–19.   [118] B 150 I, 311; B 182 II, 98–101.

[119] Old but still useful summary in B 149 V, 91–9; see also B 294, 120–2; B 304, 269–95.

[120] See below.   [121] See B 30.

the Ezra version as deriving from that in Nehemiah, or alternatively to postulate an original list from which both surviving versions were copied, that in Nehemiah with more care than that in Ezra. A third version of the list in I Esdras 5 differs from each of the others in both their Hebrew and Greek versions.[122]

All five versions agree in setting the total of full citizens (members of the qāhāl), the assembly or congregation,[123] at 42,360, together with 7,337 slaves and 245 (200) singers, making a total of 49,942 (49,897), or virtually 50,000 souls (Neh. 7:66–67; Ezra 2:64–65; I Esdras 5:41). This figure differs from the mathematical total of the listed component contingents, which amounts to only 31,089 full citizens (according to the figures in Nehemiah), and 38,671 including slaves and singers, so it might be that the component figures represent the numbers of returnees in 538, and the total, those who had returned by 520.[124] If this is correct, it would indicate the return of a substantial number of people in 538 followed by a further 10,000 either spread out over the next two decades or in a second major wave at the time of the renewal of official backing in 520. The list is in each version headed by the statement that these people came with Zerubbabel and a number of other leaders (Neh. 7:7; Ezra 2:2; I Esdras 5:8), but no mention is made of Sheshbazzar, though I Esdras names 'Zerubbabel and Sheshbazzar the governor' as together receiving the Temple treasure from Cyrus (I Esdras 6:17), and according to the Jewish elders in the time of Darius I, 'Sheshbazzar laid the foundations of the house of God at Jerusalem' (Ezra 5:16; I Esdras 6:19). This latter account would appear to conflict with the statement in the Book of Zechariah that 'the hands of Zerubbabel have laid the foundation of this house' (Zech. 4:9). A possible explanation is to be found in the hypothesis that soon after the arrival of the large contingent of returnees in 538 Sheshbazzar laid the foundations for the Temple, but that after the initial enthusiasm the work lapsed while the people sought to re-establish their own interests, and that at some later time a fresh start was made by Zerubbabel with a symbolic foundation-laying ceremony.[125] According to the census list in the Book of Nehemiah, those who returned were able to contribute 41,000 gold darics, that is some 345 kg[126] of gold and 4,700 manas, that is about 2,355 kg,[127] well over two tons, of silver, as well as other things for the Temple (Neh. 7:69–70).[128] These contributions would appear to have been distinct from those

---

[122] For comparison of the lists see B 30, 22; B 237, 223–32; B 238, 68; cf. also B 183.
[123] B 80 I, 292–3.   [124] See B 237, 20–1.
[125] On this question see B 237, xxvii n. 20; B 238, 10–12.
[126] Taking the daric as 8.424 g = 130 grains (B. V. Head, *Historia Numorum: a Manual of Greek Numismatics* (London, 1977) 827, 966).   [127] Taking the mana as 500 g (A 6, 142).
[128] See in general, and for differences in the sources, B 60, 101–3; B 237, 21, 147–8, 227.

raised in Babylonia (Ezra 1:6; I Esdras 2:8), and imply considerable affluence on the part of many of those who returned.

It is a reasonable hypothesis, therefore, that work was begun on the Temple site under the direction of Sheshbazzar as soon as the returning exiles reached Jerusalem, probably in 538 since, though Cyrus' first year ran from spring 538 to spring 537, he had taken Babylon in October 539, and it is unlikely that he would have allowed any great time to elapse before he issued the decree. According to the Book of Ezra, Zerubbabel, Joshua the high priest, and others assembled in Jerusalem in the seventh month. There they built an altar and re-established the giving of burnt-offerings on it, celebrating in particular the observances of the festival of Succoth (Booths or Tabernacles) (Ezra 3:1–6; I Esdras 5:46–52). In the Jewish calendar, Succoth was kept in the seventh month, Tishri, to mark the time of harvest (Lev. 23:33–6; Deut. 16:13–15). This strongly suggests that the 'seventh month' in which Zerubbabel built the altar was Tishri in 538, rather than simply the seventh month after the return, and that the end of the summer, when the people had been able to collect some kind of harvest from the untended plants of many decades and perhaps from those inadequately tended by those who had remained in the land, was a time when the distractions of self-interest relaxed and thoughts could turn again to religious matters. It seems that the people also now made financial contributions towards the bringing of cedar wood from Lebanon (Ezra 3:7; I Esdras 5:53). This transaction presumably took several months, for Zerubbabel is said to have begun organizing the building operations in the spring of the following year (second month of the second year of the return), at which time the foundation of the Temple was laid to the sound of music and song (Ezra 3:8–11; I Esdras 5:54–9). This reconstruction would therefore see an initial symbolic foundation-laying by Sheshbazzar in the spring or early summer of 538, followed by a failure on his part to inspire the people to continue; then a renewal of the operation under Zerubbabel some four or five months later, with the building of the altar in the autumn; and, finally, the laying of the foundations in the spring of the following year, 537, after a winter during which arrangements were made for the supply of building materials.[129] This event would have taken place almost fifty years after the destruction of the Temple by Nebuchadrezzar, and it is recorded that many of those present wept because they had seen the first Temple (Ezra 3:12–13; I Esdras 5:60–2), a strong indication that the 'second year' in question (Ezra 3:8; I Esdras 5:54) was the second year after the return in 538, and not after a second return in 520 by which time it is unlikely that 'many' would have remembered the first Temple.

---

[129] For other reconstructions see B 3.

This promising second start appears to have encountered opposition from neighbouring people, probably particularly the inhabitants of Samaria, who had at first offered to join in the work, and when they were rejected made every effort to obstruct it throughout the lifetime of Cyrus and until the reign of Darius (Ezra 4:1–5; I Esdras 5:63–70).[130]

When Cyrus took over the former Babylonian possessions it is probable that to a large extent he adopted the existing administrative system, with the geographical divisions which went with it. The documents do not supply full details of the system in his time, but accounts of an administrative reorganization carried out by Darius later in the century may give some indication of the main outlines of that under Cyrus.[131] The empire was divided into satrapies or governorates, more or less corresponding to the component countries, each ruled by a satrap. In the inscriptions of Darius the section in which Palestine must have fallen consists of Babirush (Babylonia), Athura (Assyria), and Arabaya (Arabia), though the precise extent of these satrapies is not clear, nor how, and to what extent, they match probable equivalents listed by Herodotus, which are numbered but not precisely named. In his enumeration,[132] the Fifth Satrapy included Phoenicia, Palestine, and Syria, the Ninth comprised Babylonia and 'the rest of Assyria', while Arabia was not included; so it may be reasonable to conclude that Babirush consisted of Babylonia together with some part of northern Mesopotamia, perhaps the ancient Assyrian homeland, making up Herodotus' Ninth Satrapy, while Athura embraced the western part of the former Assyrian empire where the last kings of Assyria had made their final stand, together with Phoenicia and Palestine, making up Herodotus' Fifth Satrapy. The omission of Arabia by Herodotus may merely reflect his use of a later source which recognized that this area could not form a practical satrapy.[133]

Possible support for this conclusion about the extent of Athura is to be found in a building inscription of Darius from Susa. This is known in an Old Persian, an Elamite, and a Babylonian version, all preserved in fragments found in the ruins of the palace of Darius on the northern, or Apadana, mound at Susa, as well as elsewhere on the site.[134] It gives details of the building of the palace, including some of the materials used, and the people who assisted. An important element was cedar wood

---

[130] The passage Ezra 4: 6–24 (and cf. I Esdras 2: 15–25) which deals with the later time of Xerxes I (Ahasuerus) is here assumed to have been displaced (see B 237, 34, 36–9; and cf. B 238, 41–3).

[131] In general B 159, 288–97; B 201, 43–144; and for Palestine, B 16, 356–8; B 47, 11–13.

[132] Hdt. III.89–94.   [133] See B 201, 6–7, 145; Hdt. III.88.

[134] E. Herzfeld, 'Die Magna Charta von Susa, I: Text und Commentar', AMI 3 (1930–1) 29–81, pls. v–vii; E. Herzfeld, Altpersische Inschriften (Berlin, 1938) 13–17 no. 5; Old Persian text in R. G. Kent, Old Persian: Grammar, Texts, Lexicon (New Haven, 1950) 110, 142–4 no. DSF; W. Brandenstein and M. Mayrhofer, Handbuch des Altpersischen (Wiesbaden, 1964) 86–7 no. 5. See also B 261, 167–8.

from Lebanon, which is said in the Old Persian version to have been transported as far as Babylon by the Assyrian (*athuriya*) people, being carried the rest of the way to Susa by Carians and Ionians. In the Babylonian version of the text the transportation to Babylon is credited to the people of *eber nāri*, showing that to the scribe or scribes of these inscriptions the Babylonian equivalent of Old Persian Athura was *eber nāri*.[135] The designation *eber nāri*, 'across the river', or, from the Mesopotamian point of view, 'west of the river [Euphrates]' is found in the Assyrian royal inscriptions from the time of Sargon as a general term for the west,[136] but according to the Books of Ezra and Nehemiah it later became the name of the administrative district in which Palestine lay (Ezra 4–7; 8:36; Neh. 2:7–9; 3:7).[137]

Eber-nāri does not seem to have constituted a complete satrapy, however, because soon after the conquest by Cyrus a senior officer, Gubaru, is shown by the inscriptions to have been governor of the much larger area 'Babylon and *eber-nāri*'. He is mentioned several times in legal texts between the fourth year of Cyrus (535) and the fifth year of Cambyses (525).[138] The Babylonian Chronicle mentions an officer of this name who was involved in the administration of Babylon immediately after its conquest by Cyrus,[139] and the same passage records the death of one Ugbaru, formerly governor of the Guti.[140] There is a strong possibility, though it cannot be a certainty, that the Gubaru and Ugbaru of this passage were variants of the name of a single man, presumably the Gobryas known from the *Cyropaedia* of Xenophon.[141] He is indeed there described as an elderly man before Cyrus' Babylonian campaign.[142] He can hardly have been the same as Cyrus' governor of Babylon and *eber nāri*, and it is highly probable that a follower of Darius I, also named Gubaru,[143] possibly to be identified with the Gobryas of Herodotus,[144] was a third and distinct individual.[145] Gubaru held the position of governor of Babylon and *eber nāri* for at least the ten years attested by the legal texts mentioned above, and possibly for a longer period. The documents show that by the first year of Darius (520)[146] his successor Ushtanu was in office, but the evidence is lacking to indicate when the transition took place, or indeed whether there might have been another

---

[135] Old Persian, line 32, Babylonian, line 23 (E. Herzfeld, *AMI* 3, 36, 58–9, pls. v–vi; E. Herzfeld, *Altpersische Inschriften* 14–15; for Babylonian text, MDP 14, 8–9, pl. ii fragment 1). See in general B 159, 304–8.   [136] See A 702, 116.

[137] This designation is not used in I Esdras (see B 238, 12). Its use in I Ki. 5: 4 (English versions 4: 24) in relation to Solomon's empire may reflect an updating of the text in Palestine in the Persian period.   [138] Cyrus year 4, month 8, to Cambyses year 5, month 6 (A 893, 56 n. 1; B 278).

[139] Nabonidus Chronicle (Chronicle 7; see n. 29 above) iii 20.

[140] Nabonidus Chronicle (Chronicle 7) ii 15, 22.   [141] *Cyropaedia* vii.5 and elsewhere.

[142] *Cyropaedia* iv.6.1.   [143] Behistun and Naqš-i Rustam inscriptions; B 278.

[144] Hdt. vii.2.

[145] See B 278; B 893, 54–6.   [146] Darius year 1, month 12 (B 201, 36; B 893, 57 and n. 3).

holder of the office in the blank period. Ushtanu is known from two other documents, the latest dated to the sixth year of Darius (516/515).[147] It is possible, though unverifiable on present evidence, that he was installed by Darius when he came to power. At all events, the fact that Ushtanu was still in office well after Darius had suppressed the rebellions and unrest which confronted him at the beginning of his reign shows that he held Darius' confidence, and may well have continued for some years after 516/515.

The area of Babylon and *eber nāri* continued to be governed as a unit until a reorganization carried out by Xerxes in the next century,[148] but until that time *eber nāri* evidently had its own sub-governor. This is the situation presented by the Book of Ezra, in which there is mention (in Aramaic) of 'Tattenai, governor of *eber nāri*' (Ezra 5:3, 6; 6:6, 13; cf. I Esdras, 6:3, 7, 26; 7:1), at the time of resumed work on the Temple in 520, and, though this man is not otherwise mentioned in the Old Testament, he is known almost certainly to have been still in office in 502, when he is mentioned in a slightly damaged passage in a Babylonian legal document.[149] Whether Tattenai had held this governorship before the time of Darius, or indeed, whether there was a governor of *eber nāri* alone before his time is unknown.

The area of *eber nāri* seems to have been subdivided, in Palestine at least, into provinces, of which Judah was one. In the Books of Ezra and Nehemiah the term *mĕdînâ*, 'province',[150] is used either directly or by implication of Judah (Ezra 2:1; 5:8; Neh. 1:3; 7:6; 11:3), and in the later Book of Esther it is stated that in the time of Xerxes I (Ahasuerus) the empire comprised over 127 of these 'provinces'. The Book of Ezra actually describes Babylon and Media as 'provinces' (Ezra 7:16; 6:2), but these may in each case have referred only to the capital cities of Babylon and Ecbatana and their immediate environs, rather than to the full satrapies of Babirush and Mada. The governor of Judah is designated, like his two superiors and fellow governors in *eber nāri* (Ezra 8:36; Neh. 2:7, 9), by the title *peḥâ* (Neh. 5:14; Hagg. 1:1, 14; 2:2, 21). This title, a loan word from Akkadian,[151] was thus clearly not used in any precise technical sense. The province of Judah occupied only a very limited area in the Judaean hills. To the north, in the territory of the former state of Israel, lay the provinces of Galilee and Samaria, the latter, now dominated by the alien populations brought in by the Assyrians and Babylonians, having a common border with Judah, only about 25 km to the north of Jerusalem. Some 25 km to the south of Jerusalem lay the northern border of Idumaea, a large area, formerly the southern half of

---

[147] A 893, 57 and n. 3; A 951 no. 101; B 201, 36–7.   [148] B 201, 89–91; B 265, 86 n. 81.
[149] A 966 IV, no. 152: 25; B 260; B 316A.   [150] B 324, 72 no. 152.
[151] See pp. 342 and 428 above; B 174, 82; B 201, 38–9.

Judah, now occupied by Edomites who may have been displaced from their own territory in Transjordan by encroaching Arabs.[152] To the east, the restricted province of Judah came down to the northern end of the Dead Sea and the southern part of the Jordan valley, on the other side of which lay the province of Ammon, ruled in the fifth century B.C., and perhaps already in the sixth, by the descendants of the powerful Tobiad family.[153] Finally, the old Philistine coastal area formed the western neighbour. It was ruled from Ashdod, but had Phoenician dominated enclaves at Ashkelon (under Tyre) and Joppa (under Sidon).

Judah was thus well encircled, and any activity at Jerusalem must have been well known to its neighbours. After the initial rebuff in 537, the people of Samaria were very ready to seek to obstruct the rebuilding of the Temple. Cyrus had been succeeded in 529 by his son Cambyses and, following the death of the latter in 522 while he was hurrying back from Egypt to deal with a rebellion in Persia, there was a struggle for the leadership, which ended in late 521[154] with the establishment of Darius in power. At the beginning of his reign two prophets, Haggai and Zechariah, began to speak in Judah. Their messages are precisely dated to times in the second and fourth years of Darius, Haggai in the autumn and winter of 520, and Zechariah in the spring of 519 and the winter of 518 (Hagg. 1:1, 15; 2:1, 10, 20; Zech. 1:7; 7:1).[155] A significant element in their message, particularly that of Haggai, was the need to complete the rebuilding of the Jerusalem Temple. Reference is made in the Book of Ezra to their activity, and, according to the text, 'then' Zerubbabel and Jeshua (the high priest) began to build the Temple (Ezra 5:1–2; cf. I Esdras 6:1–2). This clearly connects the effective resumption of work on the Temple with the prophesying of Haggai and Zechariah in 520 and the period immediately following (see also Ezra 6:14; I Esdras 7:3). This elicited the attention of Tattenai the governor, no doubt prompted by the neighbours of Judah. He required explanation of their activity, and an account of the authority by which they were undertaking such major work (Ezra 5:3–5; I Esdras 6:3–6). They referred to the original permission issued by Cyrus nearly twenty years before, so Tattenai wrote a letter to Darius setting out the situation and asking the king to have the royal archives in Babylon searched for the order of Cyrus which would verify this claim (Ezra 5:6–17; I Esdras 6:7–21). It was as a result of this search, according to the Book of Ezra, that the document of Cyrus discussed above was found in the archives at Ecbatana (Ezra 6:1–5; I Esdras 6:22–5). Darius is then reported to have issued very firm instructions to Tattenai not only to permit the work to

---

[152] See pp. 416–17 above. B 107, 56–63, argues that Idumaea was not established as a Persian province until the fourth century B.C.   [153] See p. 333 above.   [154] A 877, 16.

[155] See B 3, 13–22; B 49A, 29.

proceed but also to assist it from the official revenues of *eber nāri*, and to supply to the Jews the animals and other commodities needed for the maintenance of the sacrifices and other religious observances of the Temple (Ezra 6:6–12; I Esdras 6:26–33). Tattenai complied with these orders. It is briefly stated that the 'house' was completed on the third day of Adar in the sixth year of Darius (Ezra 6:13–15), 12 March 515 B.C.[156] It has been calculated that this date fell on a Sabbath day, unlikely for the completion of such a project, in which case the alternative date given in I Esdras (7:5), the twenty-third day of Adar, namely 1 April, a Friday, is perhaps to be preferred. The discrepancy between the two versions is possibly to be explained by an inadvertent omission of '20' from the text of Ezra.[157] This event was celebrated with offerings, and twenty days later, on the fourteenth day of Nisan, 21 April 515,[158] there was a great celebration of the Passover (Ezra 6:19–22; I Esdras 7:10–15).

The form of the Temple thus completed in 515, sometimes called the Second Temple, is unknown, though clues to some of its characteristics are to be found in the literature. In the letter from Tattenai to Darius it is said that the temple is 'being built of dressed stone and timber is being placed in the walls' (Ezra 5:8). The actual surviving remains of the Jerusalem Temple and its surroundings are confined to the platform known today as the Haram as-Sharif. This platform is supported on the west, south, and east sides by a retaining wall, the lower courses of which are composed for most of its extent of massive dressed stone blocks identifiable as Herodian, the upper courses being mainly medieval. In 1966, however, an operation to clear a bank of rubble from against the eastern face revealed, at a point 32.72 m to the north of the corner, a vertical division at which the Herodian masonry to the south abutted on masonry of a different character to the north,[159] which, since the Herodian masonry is clearly an extension of it, must be earlier in date. Both types of masonry are composed of massive blocks of varying widths laid in horizontal courses. In each case the blocks have narrow dressed margins and projecting central portions, but while on the Herodian blocks this central portion is shallow and smoothed flat, in the older section the central portions stand out much more prominently and amount to projecting bosses. It has been argued that this earlier masonry may be identified as the work of Solomon;[160] but the case is not convincing, and there is more force in the observation that masonry closely comparable to it has been found at Sidon and Byblos in Phoenicia.[161] At Sidon this masonry forms part of the podium of the

[156] Cf. B 237, 50; B 238, 15, 77, 79–80.   [157] Adar 1 = March 10, 515 B.C. (A 877, 30).
[158] Nisan 1 = April 8, 515 B.C. (A 877, 30).
[159] B 176, 104–5, pl. xxxvii; B 178, 111–12, pls. 35–6; B 193, 355–9.   [160] B 193, 378–92.
[161] B 118.

temple of Eshmun, identified by Phoenician inscriptions on the stone blocks as the work of Bodᶜashtart, king of Sidon.[162] His date is uncertain[163] but it is unlikely to have been earlier than about 500 because his predecessor next but one as king of Sidon in the likely sequence Tabnit–Eshmun ᶜazor–Bodᶜashtart was buried in a reused Egyptian sarcophagus probably only removed to Sidon on or after the Persian conquest of Egypt in 525.[164] Moreover, the number of kings known from classical sources, coins, and inscriptions to have ruled between his time and the conquest by Alexander in 333 suggests that he could have ruled considerably later.[165] The published evidence concerning the comparable masonry at Byblos does not allow of any more precise dating. According to the excavator, the section of wall in question was associated with Attic red-figure pottery,[166] which would indicate a date sometime between about 530 (at the earliest) and 400.[167] It is likely that the Jerusalem stonework owes its inspiration to Phoenicia. The parts of the text of Ezra and Nehemiah which refer to events in the fifth century, and the various subsequent literary references to the Temple, give little indication of any further building work on it between the sixth century and the major rebuilding by Herod the Great in the first century B.C.[168] The evidence from Sidon and Byblos would not rule out the possibility that the early terrace stonework at Jerusalem was the work of Zerubbabel in 520–515, but since its general trend indicates a somewhat later date, probably in the fifth century, it may be more realistic to assume that Zerubbabel's work was confined to the actual Temple building, a reasonable five years' task for him with his resources, and that the very major project of erecting the retaining wall of the Temple terrace or platform was a later accomplishment. If so, it is natural to consider whether this construction might have been the work of Nehemiah. It is outside the scope of these chapters to enter into the much debated question of the chronology of Ezra and Nehemiah.[169] The Book of Nehemiah dates the period of Nehemiah's governorship of Judah to the years 445–433 (Neh. 5:4),[170] which may be taken as a reasonable indication of the period during which the defensive perimeter wall around the ancient south-eastern hill and the Temple area was completed (Neh. 3).[171] While the work described in this account was confined to the outer defences, it may be that a passing reference concerns the Temple terrace within the perimeter wall. In the account of Nehemiah's initial

162 RES, nos. 287–96, 765–7, 1200; A 15, nos. 15–16; B 168, 58, fig. 184.
163 For discussion see B 265, 75–87.   164 B 265, 86, n. 79; F 44, 364.
165 B 117; B 233; B 265, 72–6.   166 B 118, 66.
167 R. M. Cook, *Greek Painted Pottery* (London, 1960) 165–85, 268.
168 Convenient summary in B 84 IV, 547–50.
169 On which see B 101, 370–2; B 237, xli–xlviii.
170 Artaxerxes 20–32 (A 877, 32); see B 98, 7, 16–18.   171 See B 237, 116–19.

request to the Persian king it is recorded that he asked for documents which he could present to the governors in *eber nāri* so that they would give him safe conduct through their territories, and also an order to the guardian of the royal forest to supply him with timber 'for the beams of the gates of the *bîrâ* of the *bayit*, and for the wall of the city, and for the *bayit* where I will live' (Neh. 2:7–8). Though the '*bayit* where I will live' is clearly here simply the governor's residence, the probability is that the first, unqualified, *bayit* is the Temple, with which the *bîrâ* was closely associated. *Bîrâ*, a loan word from Akkadian *birtu*, 'fortress, citadel',[172] appears to have borne much the same meaning in Hebrew, and in this context could well have referred to the Temple terrace or platform, the 'great court' of Solomon's time (I Ki. 7:12). The retaining wall of this platform would presumably have had gates, just as does the Haram platform today, allowing access by flights of steps to the terrace level. It is thus a reasonable speculation, backed by this possible allusion, that among Nehemiah's operations was the rebuilding of the Temple platform, and that this small area of exposed masonry was part of his work.

Of the latter part of the sixth century in Palestine little is known. No information is given by the Old Testament about the governors of Judah during the period of nearly three-quarters of a century which separated Zerubbabel from Nehemiah. The name of one of these governors has been supplied, however, by an archive of clay *bullae* and seals said to have been found in a jar, now lost, 'in the Jerusalem region'. These *bullae* bear the impressions of seals of the Persian period, and among them was one inscribed 'belonging to Elnathan the Governor' (*pḥwʾ*), giving him the same title as that borne by Zerubbabel (Hagg. 1:1) and Nehemiah (Neh. 5:14).[173] One of the actual seals found with the *bullae*, inscribed 'belonging to Shelomith, maidservant of Elnathan the Gov[ernor]' gives the name of one of his household.[174] That this man was probably governor in the late sixth century, being very likely Zerubbabel's immediate successor, is suggested by the occurrence of the names of two other governors of Judah, Yehoʿezer and Ahzai, on stamped jar handles which may be dated on palaeographic grounds after Elnathan, but before the middle of the fifth century.[175] A list of the descendants of Zerubbabel given in Chronicles does not mention any of these three men, though the line of descent which it appears to indicate, somewhat obscurely in parts, runs well into the second half of the fifth century (I Chron. 3:19–24).[176] This shows that the Persian overlords by whom

---

[172] A 52, 129; B 56, 252; B 174, 44; B 324, 34–5.   [173] B 44, 5–7 (no. 5).
[174] B 44, 11–13 (no. 14).   [175] B 44, 22 (nos. 7–8), 32–6.
[176] See B 236 I, 20–2; and cf. B 98, 17, following a slightly different line and omitting one generation.

the governors were presumably appointed made no particular attempt to follow the hereditary principle in the succession of their subject rulers, though there is no reason to think that the governors of Judah were not Jews.

V. ASPECTS OF HEBREW CULTURE

1. *Ancient Hebrew literature*

The Hebrew people have been particularly known to later history for their literature, a representative portion of which has been preserved in the Old Testament. It is clear from the Old Testament itself that other compositions existed which have not survived,[177] and it may be deduced from the content of the literature of the surrounding nations, from the unorthodox nature of the sectarian documents found at Qumran, and from the Jewish literature known as Old Testament Apocrypha and Pseudepigrapha, that the Old Testament documents represent only that part of the literature which was deemed religiously acceptable, and that some body of material which did not pass this standard has been eliminated in the process of transmission. The sort of peculiar combination that would certainly have condemned any such literature is that found at the site of Kuntillet Ajrud in southern Judah on the edge of the Sinai desert. Here was found an invocation which more than once associated the name of Yahweh with 'his Ashera' (*'šrth*),[178] and in one instance this appears in an inscription on a pottery vessel which also bears the painted representation of two Bes-like figures and a seated lyre player.[179] This site is probably to be dated between about 850 and 750, a time when Phoenician influence was strong, and when indeed, as is clear from the statements of the prophet Amos, heterodoxy was rife. This is merely one example of this element in Israelite life, which was presumably represented by written literature in the Canaanite and Phoenician tradition, all of it now lost except when it happens to be found in an exceptional form such as that at Kuntillet Ajrud.

The portion of ancient Hebrew literature which survives in the Old Testament contains a considerable variety of literary types in both prose and verse,[180] and most modern Bible translations make the distinction clear typographically by setting the text out in prose or verse form.

A limited number of the literary types found in the Old Testament are found also in the surviving inscriptions. The earliest Hebrew inscription at present known, the Gezer Calendar,[181] which lists the typical agricul-

---

[177] See *CAH* III².1, 442–3. Cf. B 126, 49–50; B 196, 17–19.   [178] B 222.
[179] B 222 fig. 12. On the Ashera see B 159A; B 199A.   [180] See B 138, xxv–xxvi.
[181] A 44, 320; B 124, 33–4; B 133, 1–4 no. 1; B 339, 201–3.

tural activities of the year in terms of unnamed month divisions, does not have a clear equivalent in the Old Testament. Three different calendrical systems are known from the Old Testament, but in each case only from scattered references and not from systematic expositions. The unnamed months of the Gezer Calendar probably match the earliest of these three systems, presumably adopted from the Canaanites, of which only four month names, Abib, Ziw, Ethanim, and Bul survive.[182] This system was superseded by reference to the months by number only, and, after the Babylonian Exile, by the use of the Babylonian month names in Hebrew garb.[183] On a pedestrian level from the literary point of view, a number of ostraca merely give lists, sometimes of men's names, for the purpose of civil or military registration,[184] and sometimes of commodities, with or without the names of those to whom they were to be issued.[185] Such lists are, of course, only ephemeral records, and no examples are found in the Old Testament, which does however contain a number of more elaborate compilations such as lists of Solomon's administrative officers (I Ki. 4:1–19), and in the post-Exilic period lists of those who returned from Babylonia to Palestine (Ezra 2; Neh. 7), and of the population in Judah soon after (Neh. 11:3–36). Other lists detail cities, towns, and fortresses (Josh. 15–19), temple offerings (Ex. 35:21–9; Ezra 2:68–9) and captured cattle and slaves (Num. 31:32–47). Such lists were probably compiled from more ephemeral written records noted down on the spot, but there are reflections in the Old Testament of the drawing up of much more academic scholarly lists of a kind well known in Mesopotamia and Egypt. Solomon is said to have known all the trees, animals, birds, and fish (I Ki. 4:33), perhaps indicating a knowledge of such scholarly lists, and their existence is perhaps implied by some poetic compositions (Ps. 104; 108; Prov. 24; Job. 38:28, 36–41).[186]

Another type of composition of which a considerable number of ancient Hebrew examples are known, is the letter.[187] A number of transcriptions of parts of what may reasonably be taken to have been contemporary letters of the period under consideration are preserved in the Old Testament (I Ki. 21:9–10; II Ki. 5:6; 10:2–3, 6; 19:10–13 (= Is. 37:10–13); II Chron. 21:12–15; Neh. 6:6–7).[188] Some of the letters, in particular those written in time of war, contain reports of events,[189] and

---

[182] B 109, 183–4; B 124, 34–7. On a fifth possible month name, ṣaḥ, read by some on Arad Ostracon 20, see B 17, 40–1; B 124, 34 n. 7; B 133, 51; and cf. B 19, 185.   [183] B 109, 184–6; B 124, 37–44.
[184] Ostraca: Ophel (B 199, 239–43), Lachish nos. 1, 11, 19 (B 199, 93–7, 128–9, 132–4), Arad (B 199, 224 section 1). Murabbaʿat palimpsest, top text, B 133, 31–2 no. 11B.
[185] Samaria (B 199, 29–38, 71–3); Arad nos. 25, 33–4 (B 199, 25–7, 204, 226 section 6).
[186] See B 126, 96–7, 314–15; and on Solomon see B 31.
[187] Ostraca: many from Arad (B 199, 224–6 sections 3–5); most from Lachish (B 199, 97f); Yabneh-Yam (B 199, 259–69). Papyrus: Murabbaʿat palimpsest, underwriting (B 133, 31–2 no. 11A).
[188] See B 120, 22–4; B 126, 84–5; *CAH* III².1, 486–7.   [189] E.g. Lachish nos. 3–4.

in this respect approach the type of record exemplified by the Siloam Inscription, which describes a particular event, the cutting of the water tunnel under Jerusalem.[190] There is reference to the preservation of an account of what was almost certainly this event in the 'Book of the Chronicles of the Kings of Judah' (II Ki. 20:20), and this and other such narratives were undoubtedly used in the compilation of the Books of Kings,[191] the descriptions of individual events perhaps sometimes following the wording of the original sources.

A more elaborate historical document is found in the Moabite Stone (Pls. Vol., pl. 146),[192] which, while it principally describes the events of a war which only occupied one year, refers also to previous episodes. It has some similarity to the literary form frequently used by the Assyrian kings which has been termed the 'Boast Inscription' (German *Prunkinschrift*), in which the author may refer to the events of several years to demonstrate his achievements. A related type, well known in both Mesopotamia and Egypt, is the Annals of a king, in which his activities are set out year by year, or for military matters campaign by campaign. Both of these types were evidently compilations from yearly records, and it may be that a document such as the 'Book of the Acts of Solomon' referred to in I Ki. 11:41 was an annalistic text of this kind, such passages as I Ki. 9:15–23 and I Ki. 11:7 being possible extracts; and in the same way the account of the invasion of Shoshenq in I Ki. 14:25–8 may have been taken from the annals of Rehoboam.[193] A related literary form is what may be called the Autobiography, well known in Egypt and from Syrian and Hittite examples, and in Israel in certain passages in the prophetical books (e.g. Amos 7:10–17; Hosea 3) and, outside the periods covered by this volume, in the books of Ezra and Nehemiah.[194] Also autobiographical are the accounts of dreams and visions, examples of which are described in I Ki. 3:5–15, Zechariah 1:7–6:8, and elsewhere.[195]

In Babylonia and Assyria the type of document known as the Chronicle was a compilation by scribes from pre-existing sources such as yearly records and annals, and it set out the main events of the kingdom over a period of several years through the reigns of several monarchs.[196] The Books of Kings have a framework which, while the form is different, has the function of an expanded chronicle, giving the ancestry, age at accession, date of accession in terms of the years of the monarch of the other kingdom, and other such information for each king of Judah and Israel. A similar synchronous chronicle is found in the so-called

---

[190] B 133, 21–3 no. 7; and pp. 356–9 above.   [191] See B 120, 48–50; B 126, 98–9.
[192] *CAH* III².1, 482–3. See also p. 450 below.   [193] See B 127, 97.
[194] See B 120, 52–3, 55–6; B 126, 99.   [195] See A 1145, 345–6; B 120, 53–5; B 126, 99.
[196] Collected in A 25.

Synchronous History, in which the rulers of Assyria and Babylonia and their chronological links are set out, in that case from a rather tendentious Assyrian point of view.[197] The synchronous history provided by Kings incorporates a considerable amount of varied material within the basic framework, drawn from other sources, some of which are named.[198] Another type of composition, examples of which were sometimes used by the compiler or compilers of Kings, or which occur elsewhere in the Old Testament, are formal public speeches (e.g. II Ki. 18:17–35), possibly recorded soon after the events at which they were delivered, or from later reminiscences.[199]

The forms of literature mentioned so far consist of the records of events or situations. Another important category of composition, well known from Babylonian, Assyrian, and Hittite examples, but not from ancient Hebrew inscriptions, was the Law Code. The Old Testament, however, contains a number of passages which may be described as Law Codes, comprising collections of laws, the content often mixing secular and religious matters. The Decalogue (Ex. 20:1–17; Deut. 5:6–21),[200] referred to in Deut. 4:13 and 10:4 as the 'Ten Words', is described as having been written originally on both sides of two stone tablets (Ex. 34:1; cf. 31:18),[201] a form not implausible in the context of the known ancient Near Eastern codes inscribed on stone stelae and clay tablets.[202] A subsequent instruction to Moses is reported in Deut. 27:2–3, according to which he was to set up large stones, plaster them, and transcribe the law on to them, as soon as he entered western Palestine. According to Josh. 8:32, Joshua actually carried this out, the resulting monument perhaps having been similar to that inscribed in Aramaic, fragments of which were discovered at Deir ʿAlla.[203] The collection of laws given in Ex. 20:22–3, 33 is conventionally, and probably rightly, identified as the 'Book of the Covenant' (*sēper habbĕrît*) referred to in Ex. 24:7.[204] The same designation used in II Ki. 22:2 of the book found in the Temple in Josiah's time refers to a different composition, elsewhere described as the 'Book of the Law' (II Ki. 22:8). It was probably the major part of the Biblical Book of Deuteronomy, a Covenant document[205] which, however, incorporated a collection of detailed treaty stipulations (Deut. 12–26), and it has been referred to by some modern scholars as the Deuteronomic Code.[206] The use of the word *sēper* to refer to the Book of the Covenant gives no indication of its form or of the material on which

---

[197] A 25, 51–6, 157–70 (Chronicle 21).   [198] See n. 177 above.

[199] See B 120, 12–15; B 126, 82–3.   [200] See B 254; B 297.

[201] The qualifier 'stone' does not occur in Ex. 32: 15. On *lûăḥ* see B 5, 34–5; B 115, 79, 230.

[202] Convenient summaries in B 221, 49–53; R. Haase, *Einführung in das Studium keilschriftlicher Rechtsquellen* (Wiesbaden, 1965), 15–35.   [203] See p. 344 above.

[204] See B 69, 135–75; B 120, 212–13; B 126, 133–7.   [205] See pp. 383–4, 387–9 above.

[206] E.g. B 120, 143.

it was written,[207] but in view of its length, and the fact that the Moabite Stone, for instance, a typical monumental inscription, only contains about 250 words, the likelihood is that it would have been on papyrus.[208] Other collections of laws are found in Leviticus (17–26), commonly referred to, on the basis of Lev. 19:2 and other such passages, as the 'Law of Holiness', or 'Holiness Code';[209] the instructions for sacrificing in Lev. 1–7, which is identified as a unit by what amounts to a colophon in Lev. 7:37–8,[210] including such shorter sections as Lev. 6:2–6, 7–11, and 18–21 which have been described as Cultic Ordinances, as have the passages 19:10–13, and 14–22;[211] as well as other less clearly defined groups of legal material.[212]

No inscriptions giving examples of Hebrew case law, that is to say, records of court proceedings, have survived, though the letter from a farm worker to a senior official found at Yabneh-Yam[213] in seeking to establish the injustice of his treatment uses vocabulary which, though in the Old Testament it occurs in largely religious contexts, would be appropriate in a legal setting, 'bear witness', 'be innocent'.[214] Equally, the Old Testament contains no full accounts of, and few references to, actual legal proceedings in the period of the monarchy (cf. I Ki. 21:11–13; and, perhaps, Ruth 4:1–12), the descriptions of breaches of the law being introduced by 'when . . .' or 'if . . .' and being typical rather than actual.[215]

A particular type of legal text, the Contract, while not known in the Hebrew inscriptions, is clearly referred to, in the form of a contract of sale for a field, with a sealed and an open copy, in Jer. 32:6–14. This was a form of contract concluded between individuals, and was really a simpler form of the document recording a treaty between groups or nations. A number of ancient treaties have been discovered,[216] and reference is made in the Old Testament to one in the period of the monarchy between Solomon and the king of Tyre (I Ki. 5:2–12 [Heb. 5:16–26]). In ancient Israel what amounted to treaties ('covenants' in Authorized Version English) were concluded between kings newly come to office and their people (e.g. Jehoash, II Ki. 11; Josiah, II Ki. 23),[217] and between God and his people (Asa, II Chron. 15:1–15; Hezekiah, II Chron. 29; Josiah, II Ki. 22–3; Zedekiah, Jer. 34:8–22), and though these are known only

---

[207] See B 115, 83, 230; and for an example of *spr* as an inscribed stone monument, Kilamuwa 1.13 and 14 (A 15 no. 14; B 134A, 30–9 no. 13).   [208] See B 115, 84.

[209] B 69, 186–9; B 120, 233–9; B 126, 137–42.   [210] B 120, 145; B 126, 142; B 275, 167.

[211] See B 120, 29–32.   [212] B 126, 143; and on the codes in general, B 120, 26–9, 143–5.

[213] See pp. 386–7 above.

[214] Yabneh-Yam letter, 11–12 (A 15, no. 200; B 133, 26–30 no. 10; and cf. p. 386 above).

[215] See B 33, 79–132; B 120, 26–9, 69–70, 143–5; B 126, 67–70; B 221, 72–3, on the distinction between casuistic and apodictic law.   [216] B 120, 19–21; B 126, 71–3; B 215.

[217] *CAH* III².1, 491–2; see pp. 388–9 above.

from references to the circumstances of their ratification, the Book of Deuteronomy can itself be reasonably regarded as an example of such a document. Two of the elements which appear in the Covenant document, the blessing and the curse, are also found as separate elements.[218]

A quite different category of text, well represented in Hebrew literature as well as in the literature of the ancient Near East, is that of instruction, typically the result of human experience rather than divine revelation, of which the Wisdom Saying (*māšal*) is the most familiar, as known particularly in the Books of Proverbs, Ecclesiastes, and Job, as well as in shorter sections in other compositions (e.g. I Ki. 20:11, Jer. 23:28; Ezek. 18:2; Zeph. 1:12; Ps. 37; 49; 73; 91).[219] Such sayings, in addition to proverbs proper, took the form of riddles (Jdg. 14:10–18), fables (Jdg. 9:8–15), allegories (Prov. 5:15–23), dialogues (Job), autobiographical confessions (Prov. 4:3–9; 24:30–4), and didactic poems (Ps. 37; 49; 73; 139) and narratives (Prov. 7:6–23).[220] A literary form or device which has something of the spirit of wisdom, or worldly cleverness, is the acrostic, found for instance in Proverbs 31:10–31, a description of the ideal wife, in which these twenty-two verses begin with words whose initial letters follow in sequence the complete Hebrew alphabet. Other full or partial acrostics are to be found in Psalms 25, 34, 37, 111, 112, 119, 145; Nahum 1:2–8; and Lamentations 1–5.[221]

Another literary form, the song, either accompanied by musical instruments (Is. 5:11–12; Amos 6:4–6) or unaccompanied (Is. 16:10; Jer. 25:30), is represented by many examples in the Old Testament. Secular types include the love song (Song of Solomon), drinking song (Is. 22:13; 56:12), war song (I Sam. 18:7) and funeral song (II Sam. 1:19–27; 3:33–4), but religious examples are more fully represented, notably hymns, or songs of praise to God (e.g. Ps. 8, 19, 29, 33; Job 5:9–16; 9:5–12; 12:13–25; 26:5–14; 28), songs of thanksgiving (e.g. Ps. 9, 10, 18. 30), Lamentations (e.g. Ps. 3–7; Jer 14:7–10; Lamentations) and pilgrimage songs (Amos 4:4–6; Ps. 15, 24).[222] Religious songs of this kind represent communal worship, but the literature contains examples of prayers, most commonly as spoken by individuals in penitence (Ps. 6, 32, 38, 51, 102, 130, 143; I Sam. 12:10), petition (I Ki. 3:6–9) and thanksgiving (II Sam. 7:18–29).[223] The best known religious figures in the Old Testament are the prophets[224] who, in addition to preaching what may be called sermons (e.g. Jer. 7:1–8:3; Ezek. 20),[225] delivered what they believed to be messages from God to men, most commonly as poetry, and taking

[218] See B 126, 75–6; B 328, 42–3.　　[219] See B 126, 304–41; B 218; B 231; B 328, 40–2.
[220] B 153, 225–64; B 154, 151–2.　　[221] See B 126, 270–1; B 138, xxxvii–ix, 187–9, 243–95.
[222] See B 126, 263–76, 285–93 (classification of psalm types); B 328, 25–39.
[223] See B 120, 17–18; B 126, 83–4.　　[224] See *CAH* III².1, 454–5.
[225] See B 120, 15–17; cf. B 126, 83.

one of the main forms: warning (or threat) of coming disaster (Is. 3:25–
4:1; Amos 7:11; 8:11–14), condemnation (or invective) of those who do
not reform (Hos. 7:1–7), exhortation to a change of behaviour (Is. 1:18–
20; Amos 5:4–5, 14–15; Zeph. 2:3), and words of salvation, comprising
promises (Is. 43:1–4), announcements (I Ki. 22:11–12; Is. 41:17–20; Jer.
28:2–4) and descriptions (Is. 2:2–4; 11:1–9; Mic. 4:1–3; Zech. 8:4–5) of
God's blessings on those who please him.[226] The two passages Isaiah
2:2–4 and Micah 4:1–3 are significant since they virtually duplicate one
another, and could represent an oracle already existing in written form
which was reused by each of these prophets on an appropriate occasion,
for, though prophetic messages are most commonly described as oral
communications, there are a number of references to their being written
down (Is. 30:8; Jer. 30:2–3; 36; 51:59–64; Ezek. 2:9–3:3; 43:11; Hab.
2:2).[227] Their surviving form probably results from the collection of
messages written down at various times by the prophets themselves or
by their disciples.

This survey has not exhausted all the possible types of documents and
compositions which go to make up the contents of the Old Testament.
Among the most discussed, for instance, are the accounts of the creation,
the flood, and, somewhat less disputed, the Tower of Babel, all in the
first section of Genesis.[228] The processes by which the many elements in
Hebrew literature were written down, in some cases probably from oral
sources, and combined to result in the twenty-four books making up the
Hebrew scriptures[229] (thirty-nine in modern versions) and the dates at
which these took place, is very largely a matter of speculation.

A hypothesis, tentatively accepted above as reasonable, suggests that
the Book of Kings was compiled by prophetic schools in the sixth
century B.C.[230] The existence of such schools is suggested by references
to groups of prophets in the time of Saul (I Sam. 10:5, 10; 19:20) and
particularly in the time of Elisha (II Ki. 2:3 etc.), and later evidently
associated with the Jerusalem Temple (Jer. 23:11; 26:7). In general, in
view of the existence of writing throughout the period of the Hebrew
monarchy, there is no reason to doubt that descriptions of events, or
records of utterances, could have been written down more or less
contemporaneously.[231] It is reasonable to view theories of literary
history in this light.[232]

---

[226] See B 170, 292–5.   [227] See B 170, 298–30.

[228] See for standard critical views B 120, 32–7; B 126, 85–8; for an assessment of the relationship
with Babylonian literature, B 189; and for a conservative view, B 147, 542–51.

[229] See conveniently B 154, 17.   [230] *CAH* III².1, 443.

[231] See, e.g. B 147, 201–10.   [232] As is done by B 147. Cf. B 120; B 126.

2. *Society and religion*

Other aspects of Hebrew culture have been mentioned in their historical setting in the preceding pages, and they are usefully discussed in more detail elsewhere.[233]

3. *Art and architecture*

If an account of the arts of Israel and Judah is confined to strict chronological limits and restricted to the archaeological remains actually recovered from Palestine, the material available for consideration is very limited. The accounts of the building and adornment of the Temple in the time of the united monarchy present a picture of sumptuous art, largely in the Phoenician tradition, but while a great many buildings have been found in excavations, they are only preserved to the extent of the lower parts of their walls. Thus, while plans can be restored, it is difficult to obtain an idea of their overall appearance. The royal quarter, built largely in the ninth century at Samaria, shows masonry of a very high quality,[234] which argues that the complete palace buildings must have offered an imposing and well-finished appearance, indicative to some extent of the look of the public buildings in Jerusalem. The evidence of the Assyrian bas-reliefs, which affect to show the city of Lachish at the end of the eighth century, has to be used with caution since the artists were inclined to use a standard convention of walls and towers to represent all foreign cities without regard to the particular features of any individual one.[235]

Prominent among the elements of architectural decoration which have survived are the so-called proto-Aeolic column and pilaster capitals[236] of the tenth and ninth centuries. These mainly range in height from about 40–50 cm and in breadth from 90–115 cm.[237] Four examples from Megiddo and probably one from Jerusalem are of Solomonic date, while other examples from Megiddo, Samaria, and Hazor in Israel, and from Ramat Raḥel in Judah (Pls. Vol., pl. 152), all probably of the ninth century, show that the design continued to be used in both parts of the divided kingdom, and indeed also in Moab, where one has been found at Medeibiyeh.[238] Though it has been suggested that this decorative element originated in Palestine,[239] a Phoenician origin, or at least inspiration, is more likely,[240] and this would explain the fact that, though

[233] B 109; B 275; B 280.   [234] *CAH* III².1, 467–8.
[235] See, e.g., A 129, 60–4, 123–4, 175.   [236] See *CAH* III².1, 469.
[237] B 291B, 14, 15.   [238] B 67, 27–44; B 291B, 1–11.   [239] B 291B, 88–91.
[240] See *CAH* III².1, 469.

at Megiddo and probably at Samaria and Ramat Raḥel the already existing examples continued in use and were visible until the Assyrian and Babylonian destructions respectively, no new examples seem to have been made after the end of the period of strong Phoenician influence.

A comparable architectural element is a short column with palmette capital above a collar of pendant leaves, 36.4 cm in total height, fragments of four examples of which were found at Ramat Raḥel (Pls. Vol., pl. 168).[241] These, when restored, were found closely to resemble balustrades shown in the lower parts of window apertures in carved Phoenician ivories, and are therefore plausibly interpreted in this way. These Ramat Raḥel examples appear to have been used in threes,[242] but the number presumably varied according to the size of the aperture, because some carved ivories show windows with four,[243] and a bas-relief from the palace of Sennacherib at Nineveh shows two.[244] The fragments bore traces of iron-based red paint, suggesting a brightly coloured appearance, such as is known from surviving traces on other monuments from the ancient Near East.[245] If this building is indeed that of Jehoiakim condemned by Jeremiah,[246] this evidence would confirm the traditional interpretation as 'red'[247] of the Hebrew word šāšar used by him to describe the paint on it (Jer. 22:14), and by Ezekiel of Babylonian wall decorations (Ezek. 23:14). Though these balustrades were associated with a late phase of the building (late seventh to early sixth century B.C.), they probably originally formed part of a structure of about the ninth century, one also decorated with proto-Aeolic capitals,[248] and are yet another manifestation of Phoenician influence on early Hebrew art.

Another example of architectural decoration is a small column base, three examples of which out of a probable original four were found at Dan in the far north of Israel, near Lake Huleh.[249] In this instance the function of these appears to have been to receive the bases of four pillars, perhaps of wood, which supported a canopy over a throne or something of the kind. Their well-seated positions on the ground, when found, argued against an alternative explanation of them as capitals. This type had the form of a circular cushion or a partially flattened flower bud with six petals enclosing it, separated by vertical divisions. These examples come from a level dated by the excavator to the late tenth century B.C. They belong in the same tradition as eighth-century examples from the

---

[241] B 9, 56–8, pls. 44–8; B 67, 42–3.   [242] B 67, 42.

[243] A 114, 145–51, 172–3, pl. IV; B 67, 142–4.

[244] A 114, 146 fig. 53; A 133, pl. 40; B 67, 43 fig. 11.   [245] A 125, 28; A 140, 15–17.

[246] See p. 393 above.   [247] Septuagint μίλτος; Vulgate sinopis.   [248] B 209 IV/2, 211–13.

[249] B 49 I, 320.

Aramaean and Neo-Hittite cities of Zincirli, Arslan Tash,[250] and Car-chemish,[251] which differ in having a rather more complex petal pattern, and in being carved in one with a square plinth. The north Syrian examples perhaps represent a later stage in the sequence, but the fact that the examples from Dan are earlier and simpler does not necessarily mean that the design originated in Israel. Indeed the probability is that it represents an Aramaean tradition, present in northern Israel as a result of the close contacts with Aram in the period of the early monarchy.[252]

An idea of the kind of architectural decoration used in important buildings by Israel's near neighbours in the earlier centuries of the Hebrew monarchy is given by the carved stone orthostat slab showing a winged sphinx of the ninth or eighth century B.C. found at Damascus.[253] This sculpture is in the Phoenician tradition and shows accomplished and elegant workmanship. Two basalt orthostat slabs, one showing a crudely carved palm tree and the other simple vertical lines, from ʿEn Gev on the east shore of the Sea of Galilee,[254] in what was probably Hebrew territory, show a very marked contrast with this Damascus relief. These slabs are not precisely dated, the settlement itself having been occupied from the tenth to the second century B.C., so that they could represent a crude local tradition, or a late decline from the sophisticated foreign standards of the earlier centuries.

In the category of religious furnishings made of stone is a type of horned altar or offering stand in the form of a squared block with a slightly depressed top and 'horns' at the four upper corners, the whole tapering towards the base. The best known examples of this type, averaging 54–5 cm in height, were found with other religious cult equipment, mainly pottery, in a late Canaanite, perhaps eleventh or tenth century, context at Megiddo,[255] but an example from a ninth to eighth century context at Tell Abu Qudeis in northern Israel,[256] probably the Kedesh mentioned in Judges 4:11, shows that such altars were used by the Hebrews. The same 'horns', mentioned in references to altars in the Old Testament (Ex. 29:12; Lev. 4:7), were also present on the larger eighth-century altar built of several blocks which was found at Arad.[257] An incense altar of different design, two cone shapes tapering to a disk at their junction, was found in a tenth-century context at Beersheba.[258]

While the carved slabs from ʿEn Gev and that from Damascus were

---

[250] B 239, 130, figs. 123–6.

[251] A 942 II, 155, figs. 60–1; E. Akurgal, *The Birth of Greek Art: The Mediterranean and the Near East* (London, 1968) 83–5 and figs. 30–1.   [252] *CAH* II³.2, 533–4; *CAH* III².1², 451, 462.

[253] *CAH* III².1, 494 and n. 47.   [254] B 49 II, 385, fig. on p. 382; B 214, 18–19, pls. 7A, B.

[255] A 45, no. 575; B 211, pl. 12; B 49 III, fig. on p. 846.   [256] B 49 III, fig. on p. 702.

[257] *CAH* III².1, 481. Pls. Vol., pl. 159.   [258] B 12; B 13; B 49 IV, fig. on p. 168.

presumably elements of architectural decoration, another type of monument familiar from the Near East in the time of the Hebrew monarchy
was the stela, either with carvings in relief, or with monumental
inscriptions. Such stelae were erected to commemorate victories, to
record the completion of building projects or the fulfilment of vows, or
sometimes the burial of important men. None has been found in
Palestine proper, but the Moabite Stone (Pls. Vol., pl. 146), a well-
executed black basalt stela in the form of a smoothed slab tapering
upwards to a rounded top and surrounded by a projecting rim, the face
bearing a thirty-four line inscription in a very elegantly cut alphabetic
script, is typical of what might have been set up in Israel or Judah. This
ninth-century monument is a building inscription, recording the construction by Mesha of a cultic platform, though it also gives much other
historical information.[259] The inscription in the Siloam tunnel, while not
free-standing, falls into this same category.[260] It was executed on a
specially dressed surface about 50 cm high, which left sufficient space
above the inscription for some other form of carving. Though the
Hebrews violated the religious ideal of the faithful Yahwists in many
ways, they may have been exceptional in the world of their time in not
setting up stelae. The official, Shebna, was condemned by Isaiah for
building himself an elaborate tomb, but if this tomb is that which has
survived in Siloam[261] it bore only a funerary inscription (Pls. Vol., pl.
161), and no other form of decoration. Two funerary stelae of the early
sixth century B.C. from Nerab near Aleppo show the type of monument
which might have been used by the unorthodox in Israel or Judah. These
two stelae are inscribed in Aramaic with funerary inscriptions of two
priests, Sin-zer-ibni and Siʾ-gabbari, and bear sculptures in low relief
representing the two dead men.[262] From Shihan in Transjordan, a basalt
slab carved in fairly high relief showing a kilted male figure holding a
spear, of uncertain date but possibly of the early first millennium B.C.,
may again show the kind of palace or temple decoration known to the
Hebrews by way of their near neighbours.[263]

In the category of stone sculpture in the round, a number of statues
and heads from the kingdom of Ammon give a good idea of the art of the
period. This sort of representation was of course forbidden to the
Hebrews by the Decalogue, but the fact that no comparable examples
have yet been found in Hebrew territory does not mean that they were
not made in the many periods of religious deviation. Over twenty

---

[259] See p. 442 above. *CAH* III².1, 466 n. 185, 482–3; B 68, 237–40.
[260] See pp. 356–7 and 442 above.   [261] See p. 365 above.
[262] *šnzrbn* (A 15, no. 225; A 45, no. 280; B 134, 93–7 no. 18); *šᵍgbr* (A 15, no. 226; A 45, no. 635; B 134, 93–8 no. 19).   [263] A 45, no. 177; B 34, 238, dated earlier by some (e.g. B 26, 79, pl. 11).

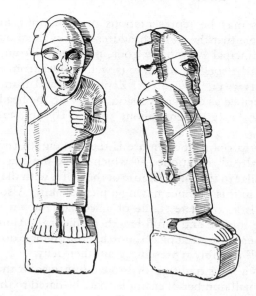

Fig. 15. Stone statuette from Amman. (After B 52, pl. 10.)

examples, including seven statues and seventeen heads, have been found, several on the citadel at Amman (cf. Fig. 15) and others at neighbouring sites.[264] On the basis of stylistic variations these have been classified into five chronological groups, covering the period from about 800 B.C. to the Babylonian conquest in the early sixth century B.C.,[265] the inscribed statue of Yeraḥ-ᶜazar, which dates from the late eighth century,[266] falling in the third group, and thus helping to date the sequence. Several of these sculptures, including two from the earliest group, all four pieces making up the second group (from about the third quarter of the eighth century), and three heads from the final group (late seventh to early sixth century), are shown bearded and wearing a stylized version of the Egyptian *atef* crown. This head-dress, which consisted of the white crown of Upper Egypt with plumes on either side, was part of the characteristic dress of the god Osiris.[267] The better preserved of the full-length figures is shown dressed in an ankle-length garment with a band of cloth draped diagonally from the left shoulder downwards across the chest.[268] The other figure is too damaged for the details of the garment to be clear.

---

[264] See conveniently B 2.   [265] B 2, 70–6.
[266] See p. 336 n. 97, and p. 359 above.   [267] B 2, 34–6.
[268] B 49 IV, 991; B 52, pl. X; B 164, pl. 1–2; B 296, 421–4, nn. 317, 326, pl. 273.

These figures may be representations of Ammonite kings, but it is equally possible that the exotic headdress marks them out as images of one of the principal Ammonite gods, perhaps Milkom, whose name, sometimes in the spelling *malkām*, is well known from the Old Testament (I Ki. 11:5–33; Jer. 49:1–3; Zeph. 1:5), and from whose image David is described as on one occasion removing the head-dress of solid gold, weighing a full talent (about 30 kg) (II Sam. 12:30 = I Chron. 20:2).[269]

A similarly proportioned figure is the late eighth-century statue of Yeraḥ-ʿazar, already mentioned,[270] which shows the king in a full-length garment, similar to that of the figure of the deity, with the diagonal band of cloth, but in this instance having a pleated skirt. Also clearly of this same group is a complete statue of a woman, shown with long hair parted in the middle and a full-length garment.[271] Amman is also the source of other sculptured pieces, notably four female double, or Janus-type, heads,[272] possibly representing another deity.

There was a long tradition of bronze figurines in the ancient Near East, and a small number of examples may be dated to the period of the monarchy in Palestine. From near Tel Dan comes a figurine, probably of Egyptian inspiration, of a pacing woman in a long close-fitting garment, probably dating from the eighth or seventh century (Fig. 16).[273]

In the field of animal sculpture in stone all that can be cited from Palestine is a couchant lion of about the ninth or eighth century from Tell Beit Mirsim;[274] but a well-executed bronze lion was found in the level of about the eighth century at Arad (Fig. 17).[275] In decorative bronze working an idea of outside influences is given by a bronze horned 'standard' possibly of Assyrian manufacture, found in a seventh/sixth-century context (level VI) at Tell esh-Shariʿa,[276] and a number of furniture fittings of the Achaemenian period from Samaria[277] and Tell el-Farʿah (south).[278] Associated with the fittings from Tell el-Farʿah were a fine silver fluted bowl, and a silver ladle with its handle in the form of a nude female holding the scoop.[279]

A flask-shaped bronze jug found inside two simple bronze buckets from a ninth- to eighth-century context at Jerusalem[280] is an example of earlier accomplishments in this field, and the inscribed seventh-century

---

[269] Taking ʿaṭeret-malkām in this sense rather than 'crown of their king' of the English Versions.

[270] See p. 336 n. 97, and p. 359 above. A 45, no. 64; B 2, 25–7 no. IX; B 52, pls. 11, 13; B 296, 421–4 and n. 317, pl. 274; B 192A, 79–80, fig. 1 (= B 128, 82–3, pl. 7).   [271] B 164, 93–4, pls. 1, 3.

[272] B 355, 33–5, pls. XXI–XXIII.   [273] B 249, 270, pl. 56A–B; B 296, 427.

[274] B 21, 67–8, pl. 23; B 37, pls. 1–3; B 296, 438–9, n. 416.

[275] *CAH* III².1, 504; A 45 no. 806; B 49 I, 84.   [276] B 49 IV, 1069.   [277] B 49 IV, 1040.

[278] A 45 no. 140; B 165; B 266 I, 14. pl. XLV–XLVI; B 325, fig. 44.

[279] A 45, no. 137; B 49 IV, 1080; B 57 I, 389, fig. 142.   [280] B 178, 132–5, pls. 49–51.

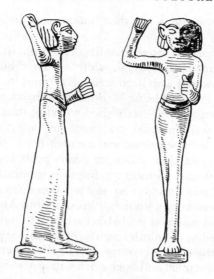

Fig. 16. Bronze figurine of a woman from Tel Dan. (After B 249, pl. 56a.)

Fig. 17. Bronze lion from Arad. (After B 49 1, 84.)

bronze bottle from Tell Siran mentioned above[281] is the production of a near neighbour. Another indication of the type of outside artistic influence that was probably coming to Judah is given by a bronze bowl, among a large cache of western booty or tribute of the ninth or eighth century, found in the North Palace at Nimrud. This was decorated with a chased and engraved central rosette within a looped chain of stylized marsh reeds, and identified as the actual or intended property of Ahiah

[281] See p. 379 and n. 60 above.

(^{c}hyw), a Hebrew name with the Judaean spelling of the divine element.[282]

A carefully decorated bone handle (Pls. Vol., pl. 156), perhaps originally from a bronze mirror, showing a winged human figure with hands extended towards a stylized tree, was found in the early eighth-century B.C. level (VI) at Hazor.[283] Bone was the cheap equivalent of ivory, a material with a well-established working tradition in the Near East. The most accomplished craftsmen in ivory during the first millennium were the Phoenicians, and the majority of the carved ivories so far found in Iron Age Palestine were probably of Phoenician manufacture. A substantial group was found in the ninth/eighth-century palace at Samaria, and though they did not come from a closely dated context, stylistic similarity with major groups from Arslan Tash, Khorsabad, and Nimrud makes it probable that, apart from some examples possibly to be dated in the ninth century,[284] the major part of the group was imported in the eighth century. These show very skilful carving executed both in low relief and openwork with provision for decoration of glass and paste inlays. The main decorative motifs are winged sphinxes, winged goddesses, the child Horus seated on a lotus, and lotus and palmette patterns (Pls. Vol., pls. 148–50).[285] That this style of carving was imitated locally is shown not only by the bone mirror handle from Hazor mentioned above but also by an ivory cosmetic spoon from the same eighth-century level (VI) at Hazor, crudely carved with a palmette pattern (Pls. Vol, pl. 155).[286]

A fragment of shell, perhaps from a bowl, decorated on the outside with an incised band of alternating looped flowers and buds around a stylized rosette, found in a late seventh-century B.C. context at Arad,[287] shows the continuing use of Phoenician motifs at this date, though this piece may have been an import. Phoenician inspiration is also evident in the decoration of some examples of a group of stone bowls with tubular spouts, variously described as 'censers', 'incense spoons', or 'incense pipes', and widely known in the Levant.[288] An example, probably of the ninth century, from Tell Beit Mirsim takes the form of a shallow bowl with a lion's head at the rim and a tube entering the bowl through his gaping jaws, and projecting as a pipe outside. The back is decorated with a pattern of palmettes and volutes (Fig. 18a).[289] Other examples include one of about the ninth century from ^{c}En Gev,[290] and two of the eighth or

---

[282] B 54, 4–5 (fig. 3, N. 75), 7 (no. 4), pl. III; B 55, 62, figs. 42–3; B 156.

[283] A 45, no. 854; B 349, pl. XXXVIA.   [284] B 104, pls. X.1–2, XI.1, XXII.1.

[285] *CAH* III².1, 471, 506–7; A 45, no. 649; B 49 IV, 1039; B 104; C. D. de Mertzenfeldt, *Inventaire commenté des ivoires phéniciens* (Paris, 1954) 62–75, pls. VIII–XXII.   [286] B 349, pl. XXXVIb.

[287] B 49 I, 88.   [288] B 57 II, 387–8.

[289] A 45, no. 592; B 21 III, 70–3, pls. 28: 1–3, 59 a–b; B 26, 132 fig. 37.   [290] B 49 II, 382.

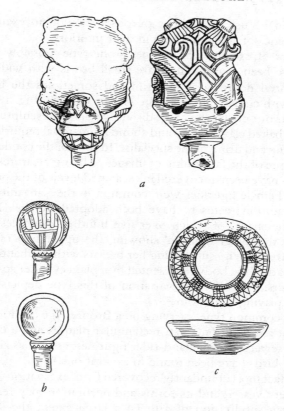

Fig. 18. Stone 'incense spoons' (*a*, *b*) and saucer (*c*), from Tell Beit Mirsim (*a*), Megiddo (*b*), and Shechem (*c*). (After (*a*) A 45, no. 592; (*b*) B 211, pl. 17; (*c*) B 307, pl. 16*a*, *b*.)

seventh century from Megiddo.[291] These are cruder and more simply decorated. One of the Megiddo examples and that from ʿEn Gev, like others found outside Palestine, are decorated on the outside with the representation of a human hand, the wrist coinciding with the tube or pipe, and the fingers reaching to the further rim (Fig. 18*b*). This feature has led to a plausible connexion with the item of Hebrew Temple furniture referred to as a *kap*, literally 'hand' (Ex. 25:29; 37:16; Num. 17:14 + etc.), variously translated 'spoon', 'dish' or the like. The Old Testament references show that the Temple *kappôt* were made of gold (or bronze; Jer. 52:18) and suggest that they were used both for libation (Ex. 25:29; 37:16) and for incense (Num. 17:14), and this type of object

[291] B 57 II, 386 fig. 335; B 211, 18–19, pl. XVII.

could indeed be used for either purpose, though no examples have shown evidence of actual burning in their interiors.

A number of examples of another stone type, possibly a cosmetic palette, have been found. These are small bowls with wide rims and shallow central depressions, the rim and sometimes the bowl being decorated with circles and simple geometric designs (Fig. 18c).[292]

A popular or vulgar type of art distantly related to sculpture was that executed in baked clay, a cheap and abundant material requiring only the skill in mixing and firing of the specialist. In spite of the condemnation in the Decalogue of the fashioning of images of living creatures, a number of examples have been uncovered in excavated levels of the period of the monarchy. Female figurines were common in the Canaanite period,[293] and this tradition seems to have been adopted by the Hebrews. A characteristic shape, of which over five hundred examples have been found, was the 'pillar figurine' showing the upper part of a woman, usually wearing a wig, supporting her breasts with her hands, and with the lower part of the body represented by a plain cylinder spreading to a trumpet-shaped base.[294] One variation of this type depicts the female holding or playing a tambour.[295]

Another common type, carrying on a Bronze Age tradition, shows a female figure in relief on a flat, rectangular plaque; and a considerable number of terracotta horse-and-rider figurines, as well as simple quadrupeds and birds have been found in excavations.[296]

The artefact most abundantly recovered from excavations in Palestine is the pottery vessel, and its forms and decoration may reasonably be counted as a subdivision of art. To a large extent the shapes were developments of those already in use in the Canaanite period of the second millennium, while the surface decoration consisted most commonly of a plain slip, usually red, with very little use of decorative painting other than in the form of lines and circles.[297] The shapes comprised bowls, chalices, goblets, kraters, amphoriskoi, jugs, juglets, pilgrim bottles, and pyxides, as well as cooking pots, storage jars, and lamps.[298] A number of imported Phoenician, Cypriot, and Assyrian types were also in use,[299] and the very fine pottery with highly burnished red slip recognized first at Samaria and therefore often referred to as 'Samaria ware' is most probably to be seen as a Phoenician import, or

---

[292] B 307.   [293] A 45, no. 469 (nos. 1, 5, 10, 11, and probably nos. 2–4, 6).
[294] A 45 no. 469 (no. 8); B 23, 69–70, pls. 31, 54, 56–7; B 26, fig. 38; B 55, fig. 21; B 163, 121–2, 124–5 (Type A); B 313, 9, 13, pls. 3, 8; B 343, 118 and fig. 72.
[295] A 45, no. 469 (nos. 9, 12); B 49 IV, 1103.
[296] B 163, 122–7, Types C–H.   [297] See B 35, 205–6; B 36, 191–2.
[298] B 36, 195–265, 276–85, 291–3.
[299] B 36, 270–5, 286–91; on bichrome ware as Phoenician, see B 85, 177, 194.

perhaps as made locally by Phoenician potters.[300] There are occasional instances of decorative painting of pottery going beyond the simple lines and circles mentioned above, and the sherd preserving part of the painting of a bearded figure seated on a throne from Ramat Raḥel (Pls. Vol., pl. 169)[301] shows a good mastery of line by the artist. Whether this was simply a trial sketch on a broken sherd, or part of a large scene on a complete pot is not clear. That some pots were decorated is shown by the finds from Kuntillet Ajrud,[302] but these are by comparison extremely crude, as are incised representations of birds on sherds from Gibeon, both of the seventh century B.C.[303] The skill of the artist of the Ramat Raḥel sherd suggests that he was a specialist, and it raises the possibility of the existence of fresco paintings in Israel and Judah like those known in Egypt, Mesopotamia, and Syria in the first millennium.

Throughout the ancient Near East a minor art form of great importance which reflected the artistic styles of different areas and periods was the seal. Over three hundred seals, usually in the form of stamps rather than cylinders, have either been found in Palestine, or may be associated with the ancient Hebrews by the personal names which they bear. This latter line of evidence is not entirely straightforward, however, since, while those which incorporate the divine element 'Yahweh' are clearly Hebrew, others are marked by their find spots and from their usage in the Old Testament are likely to be Hebrew, but this cannot be fully relied upon. They include Shema from Megiddo, Hosea from Lachish and Tell Judeideh, Shebna from Tell en-Naṣbeh and Ramat Raḥel, Eliakim from Tell Beit Mirsim and Ramat Raḥel, Menahem from Jerusalem, Ramat Raḥel, Beth Shemesh, and Tell Judeideh, and Haggai from Jerusalem, Nablus, and Tel Aviv. Probably more reliable is the evidence of palaeography. Proposed identifications of Hebrew, as against Phoenician, Ammonite, Moabite, Edomite, and Aramaic, seals have been made, with a tentative relative chronology based on typological development and occasional absolute dates, such as that provided by a seal reasonably associated with Jeroboam.[304] On the basis of this framework, and making use of the spellings of the divine element with $-yhw$, and $-yw$ as dialect indicators between Judah and Israel,[305] a tentative idea of the artistic elements on Hebrew seals may be obtained. It appears first of all that no clearly datable examples belong to the ninth century,[306] but by the middle of the eighth century a sufficient number were in use, and survivals give an idea of the kind of decoration favoured at the time.

---

[300] See *CAH* III².1, 472 and n. 224. [301] See p. 393 and n. 177 above.

[302] B 222. [303] A 45, nos. 792–3.

[304] B 157, 79–151 (and cf. B 248); B 161, 18–120. [305] *CAH* III².1, 470.

[306] The Phoenicianizing seal of *yzbl* tentatively connected with Jezebel, the ninth-century queen (*CAH* III².1, 470), is dated palaeographically to the late eighth or early seventh century (B 157, 175–6 no. 6).

Israel ceased to exist as an independent state before the end of the eighth century, so that the Israelite seals are confined to this short period.

One of the finest seals recorded, almost certainly Israelite, of the time of Jeroboam II (782–753),[307] though lost and known only from casts (Pls. Vol., pl. 147), can be seen to show fine and skilful modelling in the intaglio representation of a lion. The lion was used as an artistic motif in all of the cultures of the Near East including that of the Hebrews (I Ki. 7:29, 36; 10:19–20), and this example cannot be said to be particularly Mesopotamian, Egyptian, or Phoenician in style or stance, and indeed other inscribed seals decorated with comparable lions are probably mainly Aramaic or Ammonite;[308] so it may be a largely local product with possible influences from the east and north east. A clear Phoenician device showing a winged, kilted, human figure is shown on the seal of Joab, probably of the first half of the eighth century,[309] and at about the same date a scaraboid of Shebnaiah shows a human figure in a long robe, holding a staff, and two winged discs framing the inscription on the reverse.[310] The figure is not specifically Phoenician in style, but the upper, drooping winged disk is found frequently on Phoenician seals.[311] Another version of the drooping winged disc is found on the slightly later, probably mid-eighth-century, scarab seal of Qeniah,[312] which bears the Egyptianizing *udjat* eye, a device not commonly used in Phoenician art; and another seal of about the same date, that of Abiah, shows similar Egyptianizing elements typical of Phoenician art in the *ankh* ('life') sign above, and a winged *uraeus* (cobra) below the inscription (Fig. 19a).[313] Another popular Phoenician motif, the child sun-god squatting over a lotus bud, is found on the seals of Abiah and Asaiah,[314] probably of the first and second halves of the eighth century respectively. These seals, chosen from a greater number identified as Israelite by the *-yw* ending, show clearly the strong Phoenician influence on the northern kingdom in the last century of its existence.

It has to be noted that the seals of Shebnaiah and Abiah designate the owners 'servant of Uzziah'. This Uzziah has been identified with Uzziah, king of Judah (767–740), and if this is correct these seal inscriptions would have to be identified as Judaean rather than Israelite, and the validity of *-yhw* and *-yw* as dialect indicators would fall into doubt. The title 'servant' is very commonly used in association with 'the king' or a known king's name, but there are examples giving names not known

307 *CAH* III².1, 501 and n. 110; B 160, no. 3.   308 B 130, 175–6, pl. 5, nos. 18–24.
309 B 111, pl. XIX.9; B 321, 361 no. 9.
310 B 111, pl. XXI.4; B 157, 84 no. 4; B 321, 367–8 no. 67.
311 Cf. B 130, 8 (nos. 101, 102, 125), 12 (no. 175), pls. 6 (no. 55), 7 (nos. 69, 98).
312 B 111, pl. XIX.13; B 157, 110 no. 60; B 321, 361 no. 13.
313 B 157, 115 no. 72; B 160, no. 36; B 232, pl. XII.3; B 321, 372 no. 123.
314 B 111, pls. XXI.2, XX.8; B 321, 367 (no. 65), 364 (no. 38).

Fig. 19. Palestinian seals from the mid-eighth and seventh centuries B.C. (After (*a-b*) B 111, pls. 19.13, 21.6; (*c*) B 160, no. 44; (*d*) B 232, pl. 12.4; (*e*) B 111, pl. 20.20.)

from other sources as those of kings,[315] though they may nevertheless be so: the matter must remain open. The relations between Israel and Judah were probably peaceful at this time in any case,[316] so that manufacture of these Uzziah seals in Israel for use in Judah cannot be ruled out. The division of seals by these criteria, however, shows no marked difference between the two kingdoms. While some mid-eighth-century examples such as the seals of Jeremiah and Nathaniah[317] are decorated with not particularly Phoenician gazelles, and the later seal of Jaazaniah (Fig. 19*b*)[318] of the second half of the seventh century has a cleverly stylized cock, again without clear Phoenician influence, the Phoenician element is nevertheless clearly evident in Judaean seals. The late eighth-century scarab of Ashna[319] has an Egyptianizing device of *uraei* and lotus buds round a disk; the scaraboid of Jekamiah (Fig. 19*c*)[320] of about 700 B.C. shows a kilted man with an Egyptian wig spearing a griffin; the mid-seventh century scaraboid of Shephatiah (Fig. 19*d*)[321] is decorated with a crudely stylized winged *uraeus* facing an *ankh* sign; and typically Phoenician stylized voluted palmettes are used to decorate the mid-seventh-century seal of Hananiah[322] and the scaraboid of the second half of the seventh century of Shebnaiah.[323]

It seems that besides owners who accepted this sort of decoration others held to another, more orthodox, tradition which favoured only very simple motifs. Examples of this are a seal of the second half of the eighth century of Nehemiah[324] which has two lines of script separated by a simple quasi-floral device; the mid-seventh-century scaraboid of Hananiah (Fig. 19*e*),[325] with an even simpler linear divider; and the late seventh-century seal of another Hananiah,[326] dating from the last years

---

[315] Edomite: *ybᶜl* (B 157, 166–7 no. 7); Aramaic: *ᵓtršmn* (B 157, 40 no. 78) and possibly *ḥrbᶜd* (B 157, 16 no. 12). The seal inscription *lykl ᶜbd ᵓbrm* (B 157, 41 no. 82) is probably spurious (B 248).

[316] *CAH* III².1, 505.   [317] B 111, pl. XX.2; B 161 no. 45.

[318] B 111, pl. XXI.6; B 161 no. 5.   [319] B 157, 83 no. 2; B 232, pl. XII.9.

[320] B 157, 128 no. 105; B 160 no. 44.   [321] B 157, 91 no. 19; B 160 no. 50; B 232, pl. XII.4.

[322] B 111, pl. XIX.25; B 157, 123–4 no. 94; B 232, pl. XV.5.

[323] B 111, pl. XIX.15; B 157, 112 no. 64.   [324] B 111, pl. XIX.30; B 157, 133 no. 119.

[325] B 111, pl. XX.20; B 157, 103 no. 44.   [326] B 111, pl. XIX.24; B 157, 123 no. 93.

of the southern kingdom, has a simple linear frame for the inscription, encircled, however, by a more elaborate border of linked pomegranates. The simple inscribed form of seal predominates in the -*yhw* seals dated palaeographically to the end of the seventh and the early sixth century,[327] as in those showing the late -*yh* spelling,[328] and this form is found also in the post-Exilic Hebrew seals inscribed in Aramaic script of which the impressions on clay *bullae* were found in a cache in the Jerusalem region.[329] While further study may necessitate revision of the datings and national ascriptions of these seals, the Yahweh names ensure that they were the property of Hebrews, and therefore that they give a reasonable idea of the types of decoration in use during the eighth and seventh centuries.

The backs of scaraboid seals were sometimes decorated, and two examples, both carved with what appear to be negroid heads, were found at two sites, both near to the Mediterranean, Tell Qasile and Azor.[330]

---

[327] B 157, figs. 58–60 nos. 78, 92, 96(?), 99 (= B 321, nos. 239, 218, 241, 26 respectively).
[328] B 157, figs. 60–1 nos. 111, 126 (= B 321, nos. 153, 175 respectively).
[329] B 44, pls. 1, 5, 6, 8, 10, 12. See also p. 439 above.   [330] B 49 I, 147, IV, 966.

CHAPTER 32

PHOENICIA AND PHOENICIAN
COLONIZATION

W. CULICAN

I. SETTING AND HISTORY

'Phoenicia' in the widest sense was the name given by the Greeks to the coasts of what is now Syria, Lebanon, and Israel. (For the name 'Phoenicia' see *CAH* II³.2, 520.) In a narrower sense it was interpreted as the coast from about Dor in the south, northwards to about present-day Tripoli (an area referred to as Metropolitan Phoenicia in this chapter). It consisted of a chain of towns situated in a narrow coastal strip of land seldom more than 3 km in width backed by the Lebanon mountains and the Carmel range. Of these Tyre, Sidon, and Byblos, all flourishing towns in the Late Bronze Age, remained important throughout most of the first millennium B.C.; they were the Phoenician towns best known to ancient writers and have provided the bulk of Phoenician inscriptions of any historical importance. Together with Arados (modern Arvad or Ruad), the island town off the Syrian coast (Pls. Vol., pl. 129), these three issued the main Phoenician coinages during the fifth century. From these inscriptions and coins certain broad historical and cultural information may be gleaned. All other direct sources of Phoenician history have been lost; even the Phoenician inscriptions are not noted for the historical information they contain. Tyre at least kept historical records, written down probably in annalistic form. We gather from the Wen-Amun story that Byblos also had chronicles. Josephus, the Jewish historian of the first century A.D., made use of the Hellenistic historian Menander of Ephesus (*Contra Apionem*, 116ff; *Ant. Jud.* VIII.144; IX.283), who had derived from Tyrian chronicles a list of the kings of Tyre together with their individual lengths of reign and other details, some of which Josephus reproduced. It is not known whether the work of Dius, a Greek historian otherwise unknown who composed a 'History of the Phoenicians' to which Josephus briefly referred, was based on original sources or not. The Christian historian Eusebius quotes Philo of Byblos who had transmitted in Greek dress details of Phoenician religion from Sanchuniathon, the oldest (about 700 B.C.?) Phoenician writer whose

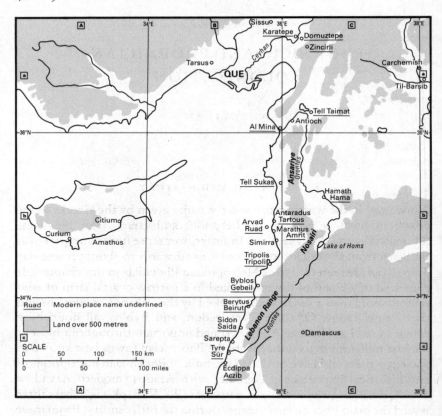

Map 6. Phoenicia.

name has been preserved.[1] The Bible is the only other source, but of course is indirect: Kings and Chronicles give accounts of the dealings of Hebrew royalty with Phoenician rulers, whilst the prophecies of Isaiah and Ezekiel gloat over the downfall of Sidon and Tyre. Papyrus was certainly the material used for Phoenician records and communications, and, except for a few personal letters which have been preserved in the dry conditions of Egypt, has generally perished. The clay *bullae* carrying seal impressions and the imprints of the papyrus documents which they once sealed have been found in both Phoenicia and the western colonies.[2] Inscriptions on stone, pottery ostraca and clay, some seventy of which have been found in the Phoenician homeland, are mostly funerary and dedicatory, but they remain important sources for the

[1] C 9, 195, 212.   [2] C 60, 57–60.

existence of individual rulers and of supplementary information, especially concerning religious practices and personal names.

Since Phoenicia was thought of by the Greeks as a group of individual city states rather than as a 'nation' or 'race' we gain nothing from them about either its ethnic composition or its territorial extent. Basically the population was descended from the coastal Canaanites of the Bronze Age; their language was descended from Canaanite; but the population may well have included more northerly Semitic groups, particularly Amorites and men of Ugarit who had moved southwards. A small admixture of Cypriots, Aegeans, and Sea Peoples is only to be expected from the facts of geography and commerce.

Byblos is the first city to provide primary evidence of the revival of the traditional Egyptian links which it had maintained in the second millennium. Statues of members of the Twenty-second dynasty (945–715), Shoshenq I (945–924), Osorkon I (924–889) and Osorkon II (874–850), found in the ruins of Byblos, were gifts from the pharaohs. Two of them are superinscribed in Phoenician by the local kings Abibaᶜal and Elibaᶜal.[3] There is also, on a separate slab, an inscription of a further king Shipit-baᶜal.[4] These three appear to have belonged to a dynasty headed by king Ahiram, whose sarcophagus, made for him by his son Ittobaᶜal, has provided the earliest substantial inscription in Phoenician script, usually dated to the early part of the tenth century B.C. (Pls. Vol., pl. 136B). It is slightly predated perhaps by an inscribed bronze spatula from Byblos,[5] naming Azar-baᶜal, the earliest Phoenician known to us, and possibly royal. The decoration of Ahiram's sarcophagus itself dates from about three centuries earlier, and the inscription is written in the place of the erasure of an earlier inscription in Proto-Byblian[6] of which traces remain. Whilst this casts doubt on the claim of Ittobaᶜal to have had the coffin made for his father, it does not alter the date of the inscription itself, whose epigraphy is firmly placed in about 1000 B.C.[7]

Sidon was the 'first-born of Canaan' (Gen. 10:15) and according to classical tradition was the founder of both Arvad and Tyre.[8] Admirably situated for the conduct of coastal trade, with harbours to north and south, Sidon was in a small plain of high fertility much noted by Arab geographers.[9] Its dominion at one stage extended into the Valley of Lebanon (Biqaᶜ) and to Galilee (Jdg. 18:7, 28). There has been much debate about both the primacy and territorial control of Sidon, especially because in both Homeric and Biblical terms 'Sidonians' appears synonymous, if not with Phoenicians as a whole, then certainly with more than the inhabitants of that city. This presupposes that at one period, perhaps

[3] A 15, nos. 5–6.   [4] C 5, 108, fig. 34.   [5] A 15 no. 3; C 26.   [6] C 26.
[7] A 15, no. 1.   [8] C 21, 130.   [9] C 17.

from the reign of Ittobaʿal in the ninth century to Luli in the late eighth, Tyre and Sidon comprised a united kingdom, with the king of Sidon at the head.[10] Ittobaʿal (Ethbaʿal) himself, for instance, whom I Kings 16: 31 designates the 'King of the Sidonians', appears as king of Tyre in Menander (Jos. *Ant. Jud.* VIII.324). Likewise Hirummu, named as king of Tyre in the inscriptions of Tiglath-pileser III (744–727), can scarcely be other than Hiram, king of the Sidonians, to whom one of the Mouti Sinoas bronze bowls was dedicated.[11] Luli (Elulaios), according to Menander, ruled both Sidon and Akku, but is named by Sennacherib as ruling Tyre and Akku.[12] On the other hand, there is no doubt that in the time of Esarhaddon the kings of these two cities were different men.[13] We have too little information about the roles of these two cities to postulate their political relationship, but it seems likely that at some period they formed a joint state and acted in concert and without the implication of Byblos, Arvad, and others; that Sidon had either some kind of historical or formal precedence; and that Tyre dominated politically and commercially from about 800 to 500 B.C. If there is any truth in the notion that Sidon founded both Tyre and Arvad, both of which were flourishing in the Late Bronze Age, then it is a question of 'refoundation' only, perhaps after the depredations of the Sea Peoples; but it must be noted that it is a late tradition, born perhaps of inter-city rivalry. Nor is the commercial pre-eminence of Tyre necessarily to be deduced from the famous 'burden of Tyre' in Isaiah 23. Indications are that the original, the date of which is slightly later than that of the prophet himself who lived in the late eighth century, was composed about the destruction of Sidon probably in Esarhaddon's campaign, and later adapted to lament the fall of Tyre to Nebuchadrezzar.[14] It is also to this event that the prophecies of Ezekiel 27, with their fulsome profile of Tyre's trading network, essentially relate, though the dates of their original composition and interpolation, like that of the prophet himself, cause great difficulty.[15]

1. *Commerce*

The location of Tyre had many advantages; the island on which the old city was situated had natural defences and in time of siege could draw water from deep wells (Pls. Vol., pl. 130*a*).[16] There was abundance of water on the mainland opposite, and in addition there were fresh-water springs under the sea at many points, similar to those in the Bay of Shakka and off Arvad.[17] In fact these springs might well have given rise

[10] C 21, 133–4.   [11] A 35 II, §§ 309, 326, 347.   [12] C 52, 252, 261.
[13] C 52, 252, 261.   [14] C 25.   [15] C 3, 79–91.   [16] C 14, 56–9.   [17] C 3, 59.

to Tyre's conceit of itself as a seat of cosmic creation obliquely referred to by Ezekiel.

The Biblical evidence (I Ki. 7:13–47; II Chron. 2:3–16) makes clear that Tyrians were expert bronze workers, and in Homer (*Od.* xv.425) Sidon is *polychalkos*, rich in bronze. We have no knowledge of where these ores were obtained, but the coast of Syria and Palestine had an abundant metal supply in the Late Bronze Age and presumably it continued into the Iron Age together with, in the case of Phoenicia, the control of Cypriot resources.[18] Two Babylonian cuneiform documents from Uruk show that in about 550 B.C. iron from Lebanon and both bronze and iron from Yaman (Cyprus or beyond) were imported to Babylonia together with valuable blue-dyed wool and cheaper red and purple dyes. Tin of unspecified origin is also listed in these documents of Iddina-ahu, who was importing from Phoenicia and Egypt.[19] The joint trading expeditions of Hiram and Solomon to Ophir and Tarshish have already been discussed.[20]

From Mediterranean ports the Tyrians made shorter journeys to the ports on the coast of Cilicia, the land of Que. Since in later times both Tyre and Sidon are said in Assyrian inscriptions to have had alliances with kings of Que, Solomon's horse-trading connexions with it (I Ki. 10:28) were probably made within the framework of Phoenician enterprise in this area. Tyre, according to Ezekiel (27:14), obtained horses from Togarmah in Cilicia. One Cilician ruler, Kilamuwa of Zincirli (Sam'al), writing in Phoenician about 825 B.C., gives the names of four earlier kings, all with Phoenician names. About a century later at Karatepe in the Taurus hills the local Hittite king Azatiwatas saw fit to have a full Phoenician translation set up of his monumental inscription[21] in Hittite hieroglyphs. Some of the accompanying iconography is also Phoenician in character, as are the sculptured slabs of nearby Domuz-tepe. Both these sites lie above the Ceyhan river valley which gives access to the Meyemicil Pass of the Anti-Taurus. These and a few other minor Phoenician texts can only be explained by the existence of Phoenician entrepreneurs, if not colonists, in Cilicia.[22] Some of the pottery and trinkets from Zincirli have an unmistakably Phoenician cast. Pottery from Tarsus of about 1000 B.C. has many aspects of Cypro-Phoenician ware. Taken together with the fact that the inscriptions of the Cilician rulers after 730 B.C. are written in either Hittite or the Aramaic of north Syria, it is clear that the Phoenicianizing tendencies of the first quarter of the first millennium were due to Phoenician presence. Xenophon alone (*Anab.* 1.4.6) speaks of Phoenician colonies, on the eastern Cilician coast.

---

[18] C 29. [19] C 14, 100.
[20] For Ophir see *CAH* II³.2, 526, 587, 594 and III².1, 479–80; for Tarshish see *CAH* II³.2, 525–6, 768, and III².1, 479–80. [21] A 15, no. 26; C 36, 134–5. [22] C 36, 138–40.

Phoenicia's own chief natural resource was timber.[23] The cedars and junipers which clothed the Lebanon and the *beroŝim* of Senir (Antilebanon) were as sought after by the Assyrians in the first millennium B.C. (Pls. Vol. pl. 131*a*) as they had been imported by the Egyptians in the second. It was this timber which determined much of Phoenicia's history, gave her a fleet, involved her in international politics, trade, and colonization.

The centrepoint of this trade was probably Byblos, but the Babylonian Talmud (*Bekoroth* 576) names 'Arqath-Libna' as an important lumbering centre, and this is probably the Arkē of earlier documents, whose location is unknown. Although the forest reserve set up by the emperor Hadrian was in the northern Lebanon, it must not be assumed that in antiquity significant timber resources were not available further south. In the poetic imagination of Ezekiel (27:5–6), Tyre itself is likened to a ship made of timbers, not only of Lebanon and Senir but also of oaks of Bashan and *te'aŝŝurim* from Kittiyyim (Cyprus). However poetic, the prophet correctly emphasizes, like Theophrastus,[24] the highly specialized selection of various timbers for a single ship, a factor which would have involved Tyre, once her shipyards were established, in the timber trade itself, perhaps importing from both the deciduous woods of northern Syria and the coniferous forests of the Amanus and eastern Cilicia.

2. *Relations with Israel*

Subsequent Phoenician history was much involved with that of its Hebrew neighbours. With the division of the monarchy after Solomon into the rival states of Israel and Judah, its access to wide-ranging caravan routes was much curtailed and control of the Galilean cities offered by Solomon to Hiram was probably lost. The period of Ittoba'al (887–856) in Tyre and the establishment of a triple alliance with Omri of Israel (or his son/co-regent Ahab) in 873 saw a return to better conditions. Jehoshaphat of Judah in partnership with Ahaziah of Israel, son of Ahab, reopened trade with Ophir from Eziongeber (I Ki. 22:48; II Chron. 20:35–6) and no doubt this created markets for Tyre. Phoenician influence inland soon reached its peak not only in the architecture of Samaria in Ahab's time but also at Ramat Raḥel in Judah, and elsewhere.[25] The marriage of Ahab to Jezebel, Ittoba'al's daughter, brought with it the royal patronage of Phoenician cults in Samaria, and temples to Ba'al and Asherah were built in Jerusalem (I Ki. 16:32; II Ki. 10:21; 11:18). Despite the reported abhorrence of the Hebrews for these

---

[23] C 14, 140–208.   [24] C 14, 157–8.   [25] C 100.

cults and what appears to be a very ill-defined territorial border between Israel and Phoenicia, we are not informed of any hostility or friction until the revolt of Jehoash in Israel and Jehoiada in Jerusalem.[26] Significant though they are in themselves, these religious clashes were coloured by a shift in international politics.

The alliance of Tyre with Hazael of Aram–Damascus, who made war on Israel, was seen as traitorous (Amos 1:4). But Tyre was not slow to retain the security of the inland route to Arabia and the Red Sea which now passed east of the Jordan through territory annexed by Hazael from Israel. Moreover, Tyre became an important port for Damascus' trade (Ezek. 27:18). But the break in the relations between Phoenicia and Israel was only temporary; their mutual political interests resumed in the reigns of subsequent kings, Jeroboam, Menahem, Pekah, and Hoshea, either in joint opposition to Assyrian dominance or in support for Aram, as in the Syro-Ephraimite war, waged by Pekah and Rezin of Damascus against Judah.[27]

3. Assyrian domination

Although there had been some earlier contact between the Phoenician cities and the Assyrian kings, it was not until the time of Tiglath-pileser III (744–727) that Assyria asserted direct control. The earlier inscriptions of Tiglath-pileser I (1114–1076) and Ashurnasirpal II (883–859) indicate that certain seaboard cities, especially the more northerly ones, had acknowledged, and paid tribute to, the hegemony of Assyria. Among them Arvad, Byblos, Sidon, and Tyre paid tribute to Ashurnasirpal and emissaries of both Tyre and Sidon were invited to the dedication of his new royal palace at Calah (Nimrud) in 879 B.C.[28] Later, when Shalmaneser III mounted his campaign against the Syrian coalition led by Irkhuleni of Hamath and Adad-Idri of Damascus, some northern Phoenician cities – Byblos, Irqata, Arvad, Usanat, and Siannu – are expressly mentioned among the 'twelve kings of Hatti and the sea coast' allied with Irkhuleni who fought Shalmaneser at the Battle of Qarqar (853 B.C.).[29] Though the Sidonian king Ittoba'al (Ethba'al) was at this time in alliance with Ahab, it is uncertain whether Sidon or Tyre was involved. As the thrust of Assyrian aggression was towards northern Syria it probably concerned the 'Hattic' coastal towns within the political sphere of Hama. Already in his first campaign in the west in 858 Shalmaneser had received tribute 'from the ships' of Tyre and Sidon, which are shown on the Balawat gates as leaving an island, probably Tyre (Pls. Vol., pl. 130b) and sailing to meet Shalmaneser's army on the coast.[30] It may be assumed that both Tyre and Sidon continued to pay

[26] C 21, 181.   [27] C 21, 212–13.   [28] C 37, 32.   [29] See CAH III².1, 261, 393.
[30] C 21, 133–4.

this tribute to Shalmaneser, for he claims to 'spread the splendour of his lordship' over them for some years;[31] but he himself did not march on Tyre or Sidon until after his campaign against Hazael of Damascus in 841, to take tribute from Ba°ali-ma-an-zeri of Tyre (Ba°alazor I), Ittoba°al's successor. The Assyrian record of this campaign provides a valuable synchronism between Shalmaneser's eighteenth year (841) and the Ba°alezorus of Josephus.[32] A significant aspect of Shalmaneser's campaigns is the attention he paid to Arvad. Like Tiglath-pileser I he made short voyages to visit the island; his relations with its king, Matinu-ba°alu, were particularly close.

The following century saw little Assyrian activity against Phoenicia, but the usurpation of Tiglath-pileser III ushered in a new aggressive policy against the west, aiming to establish Assyrian administration and military presence to the borders of Egypt. In 738 B.C. Tiglath-pileser broke through to Hama and marched to the coast in order to punish the cities on the 'coast of the western sea'. Ushnu and Siannu, both cities situated within the political sphere of Ugarit some centuries earlier, as well as Simirra and Kashpuna, are mentioned, but there is no complete list. Thousands of inhabitants were exiled and replaced by Mesopotamians and probably at this point the cities of the north Syrian coast were organized into an Assyrian province centred on Simirra, which begins to be mentioned a number of times in documents of Tiglath-pileser and later. By 734 B.C. this province extended southwards to include Kashpuna, situated somewhere to the south of the mount *Sa-ú-a* (Gebel-ez-Zawiyé) east of Tripoli.

Tiglath-pileser's later campaigns in the west (734–732) were principally aimed at Philistia and Damascus, and particularly against a new anti-Assyrian coalition led by Rezin of Damascus and joined by Ashkelon. A fragmentary inscription found at Nimrud makes it quite clear that Hiram II of Tyre (c. 739 B.C.) was part of this coalition. Tiglath-pileser claims the destruction of great towns in Phoenicia, of which only the name of Mahalib (Ahlab) north of Tyre survives, and to have taken garments and personnel as booty. But Hiram's acknowledgement of Assyrian overlordship appears to have saved his kingdom. A further Nimrud text, probably relating the same campaign against Philistia, describes the surrender of a town 'in the midst of the sea', which was later entrusted to the town governor of Simirra (whom Tiglath-pileser describes as 'my official'). Thus the island town was probably nearby Arvad, whose king Matan-ba°al had joined the kings of North Syria against Tiglath-pileser, though he, like Hiram, had paid tribute and rendered formal submission.

31 C 30, 39–40.   32 C 3, 294, 322–3.

The Assyrians do not appear to have set up the southern Phoenician cities into a province at this point. Sidon is not mentioned at all, probably because it was incorporated into the Tyrian kingdom; but towards both Tyre and Sidon the Assyrians conducted themselves with leniency, though they placed Assyrian officials in both cities, imposed a tax on the felling of cedar trees in Lebanon, and placed restrictions on their overseas timber trade. Hiram II is no longer mentioned amongst the Phoenician vassal kings paying tribute to Assyria drawn up in Tiglath-pileser's seventeenth year. Sibitti-bel of Byblos (Shipit-baʿal II) and Matan-baʿal of Arvad are listed, but after a special messenger had been sent to Tyre a tribute of 150 talents of gold was paid by Metenna of Tyre (Matan II, c. 730 B.C.). This massive tribute has been taken to indicate that the new king owed his elevation to Assyrian intervention. Indeed the terms of Nimrud letter XIII, in which Qurdi-Ashur-lamur,[33] the governor of Simirra, informs the king, 'In the palace of Tyre verily all is well, in the palace which is in Ushshe', suggest perhaps Assyrian interference in the dynastic succession; this is the first naming of the mainland part of Tyre (as distinct from the Palaetyrus, the island city) which in later Assyrian documents is called Ushu.

Important information repeated by Josephus (*Ant. Jud.* IX.283–7) deals with the war against Tyre in the reign of Elulaios, who appears to have ascended the throne in about 728 B.C., a year or so before Tiglath-pileser's death.[34] He is the Luli of Assyrian records, who, after a turbulent history which covered the reigns of Shalmaneser V and Sargon (721–705), was finally forced by Sennacherib to flee Phoenicia and seek refuge in Citium, though before this Luli's relationship with Assyria seems to have improved. Sargon must have lifted the siege of Tyre begun by Shalmaneser V in 724 B.C.[35] Sargon's only mention of Tyre is one in which he claims to have pleased both Tyre and Que by reducing Ionian piracy. It gives an important counterpoint to theories that present Assyrians as hindering Phoenician trade. The scene of Luli's departure, in which he is lowered from the quay at Tyre into the last ship of the departing Phoenician fleet, is recorded in the reliefs of the palace of Sennacherib at Nineveh (Pls. Vol., pl. 131b).[36] Having taken Sidon and Bit-zitti (ʿAin ez-Zeitun?), Sarepta, Mahalib, Ushu, Ecdippa (Akhziv), and Akku, Sennacherib placed Tabalu on the throne in Sidon and later accepted rich gifts in tribute from him. Some time before the death of Sennacherib, Abdi-milkutti succeeded Tabalu and remained loyal to his overlord, though not to his successor. Abdi-milkutti's revolt from Esarhaddon brought about severe retribution. He was executed in 677 and Sidon was destroyed. The treasures of his palaces were carried off to

Assyria and a 'Fortress of Esarhaddon', probably with a garrison and small population transported from Assyria, was established in the vicinity of the city. In a second campaign against Phoenicia in 671, Esarhaddon celebrated his victory over Ba'alu of Tyre (Ba'al I) by erecting commemorative stelae at the Nahr-el-Kelb, north of Beirut, Zincirli, and Til-Barsib in north-west Syria. In these he celebrated also his victory over Taharqa of Egypt,[37] for the Egyptians had attempted to counter the Assyrian advance onto the coast by forming alliances with Phoenician rulers. Clearly also Esarhaddon intended to break once and for all the alliance between Abdi-milkutti and Sanduarri, king of Kundi and Sissu, places in Cilicia. For good measure limits on trade north of Byblos were imposed by his later treaty with Ba'alu of Tyre.

Ashurbanipal continued to claim the vassalage of Tyre, Byblos, and Arvad. His inscriptions mention a further campaign against Egypt as well as against Ba'alu, though in a doubtful chronological framework.[38] Again Tyre appears to have come out of it fairly well, and the Assyrian king returned to Ba'alu his son Iaki-milki, whom he had taken hostage. With the Babylonians taking over the role of Assyrian aggression, the cities of Phoenicia once more were caught in the rivalry between Egypt and Mesopotamia. Against the visitations of Nebuchadrezzar to Palestine and Phoenicia in 597 B.C. and the long campaign of 588–573 which included the siege of Tyre in 587, the pharaohs Psammetichus II and Apries brought down retaliatory raids in 591 and 588 respectively on the Babylonian garrisons and their Phoenician vassals. Whereas the Babylonians held the upper hand on land, it is certain that they could not counter the offensive of the Egyptian navy. According to Diodorus (1.68.1), Apries sent large land and sea forces against Cyprus and Phoenicia, took Sidon and induced the other Phoenician cities to side with him. Herodotus (II.161.2) merely records that the pharaoh led his army against Sidon and fought Tyre at sea.

4. Relations with Egypt

The weakness of Egypt during the Twenty-first Dynasty allowed both Hiram I and Solomon unparalleled freedom in building their commercial empire, even in Egypt's traditional Red Sea preserves. A brief attempt to reassert control came under Shoshenq I (945–924), founder of the Twenty-second Dynasty, who invaded Palestine and Syria during the reign of Balbazer of Tyre, son of Hiram (955–919). Although Shoshenq portrays himself in the reliefs of his Karnak temple as 'smiting the princes of all the lands of Fnḫ-w', his invasion made no lasting changes except perhaps at Byblos, where his statue and that of his son

[37] A 44, 302b; C 21, 277–8. See below, pp. 699–700 and 724–6.   [38] A 44, 295–6; C 21, 288–94.

Osorkon I were erected. However, it is difficult to interpret the inscriptions of Abibaᶜal and Elibaᶜal written on these statues in any detailed political sense[39] or to assume that Shoshenq renewed political and commercial ties with Byblos to counter the Phoenician leadership assumed by Tyre.[40] During the three centuries following this feeble 'revival' of interest in Phoenicia, Egypt remained unable to counter the Assyrian advance into Philistia and to the 'Brook of Egypt' (Wadi el-Arish).

The campaigns of Necho in 609–605 B.C. briefly restored Egyptian suzerainty over Palestine and Phoenicia but his final defeat by Nebuchadrezzar at Carchemish and the rise of the Persian empire ushered in a new era for the West. Meanwhile Egypt under Necho (610–595) and his successors Psammetichus II (595–589), Apries (589–570) and Amasis (570–526) had turned some of her trading interests towards other Mediterranean lands and seems to have fostered the growth of communities of foreigners in her own towns. Already during the Eighteenth Dynasty Canaanite shipwrights from the Phoenician coast had been settled in a district of Memphis called *Prw-nfr*, where the cults of Baᶜal and Astarte were maintained by priests from the homeland.[41] Phoenicians probably continued to work the Memphis shipyards in the Late Kingdom, when 'Baᶜal of Memphis' is mentioned in Twenty-fifth Dynasty documents.[42] Herodotus (II.112) encountered a 'Tyrian camp' there. Its temple of 'Proteus' is most likely that of Baᶜal himself and in its precinct stood a temple of 'foreign Aphrodite' – certainly Astarte. Herodotus does not state whether the resident Tyrians were engaged in ship-building, but the fact that pharaoh Necho invited the Phoenicians to circumnavigate Africa (Hdt. IV.42) must surely mean that they had an arsenal to hand in Egypt.[43] The triremes which Necho had built before his expedition to Syria in 609 B.C. (Hdt. II.159) may also be attributed to Phoenician shipyards. It seems that Clement of Alexandria (*Strom.* I.16.76) was correct in regarding the trireme as a Phoenician invention,[44] though certainly the Greeks improved it in lightness and speed. Warships equipped with rams and two banks of oars are already shown in Sennacherib's relief from Nineveh depicting the flight of Luli, and in a wall-painting from Til-Barsib of about 730 B.C. Although there is no firm evidence that Phoenicians added the third bank of oars, the historical circumstances and terracotta models from Egypt strongly suggest it.[45]

The cultural impact of the Egyptians on the Canaanites and Phoenicians had always been formative, especially in art and religion. Astarte,

---

[39] C 23, 12–13.   [40] C 21, 121.
[41] C 19; C 21, 372–3.   [42] C 21, 485–90. See below, pp. 720f.
[43] C 379, 7–16. See below, p. 723.   [44] C 11.   [45] C 12.

for instance, often appears in the dress of Isis in Phoenician and Punic art. One of the few Phoenician inscriptions from Egypt is a dedication to Ashtart on a statuette of Isis. In the early fourth century the stela of Yehwmilk depicts the 'Mistress of Byblos' as Hathor[46] and in the late third century a shrine from Memphis itself depicts Isis-Astarte enthroned with Phoenician priests in attendance.[47] The cult of Astarte at Byblos was already Egyptianized as a Hathor cult in the second millennium,[48] but it was probably not until after 600 B.C. that major developments of cult syncretisms took place. The locating of part of the Osiris legend at Byblos and its fusion with the local cult of Tammuz-Adonis, about whom we know nothing at all from Phoenician sources (since neither is mentioned), appear as part of this 'developed' theology. Theophoric personal names incorporating Isis, Osiris, Horus and Bastet also entered Phoenician–Punic usage no earlier than the fifth century.[49] But in another aspect Egyptian influence begins somewhat earlier. Tubular amulet cases containing pseudo-Egyptian magical texts[50] as well as medallions, scarabs, and other Egyptian-like talismans[51] were used by Phoenicians before 700 B.C., with their popularity at its maximum in the fifth–fourth centuries.[52] Significant too is their adoption at varying times of the Egyptian *naos* shrine,[53] the Egyptian altar, the *cavetto* cornice (in architecture), and the anthropoid sarcophagus.[54] By contrast to this latterday Egyptianism, such fragments of Phoenician cosmology as have been preserved by Philo of Byblos from the works of Sanchuniathon of Tyre and Mochus of Sidon, though much transformed by Greek dress, are greatly influenced by the cosmologies of Memphis and Hermopolis, in terms which appear characteristic of the Middle Kingdom and therefore must preserve Egyptian ideas about creation current in the intellectual circles of Phoenicia in Canaanite times.[55]

II. ARCHAEOLOGY, ARTS, AND CRAFTS

It is only recently that an outline of the development of pottery in Phoenicia has been recognized.[56] This is largely based on material from a deep stratigraphic sounding at Tyre,[57] excavations at Sarepta (modern Sarafand on the coast south of Sidon),[58] the partial publication of pottery from a large necropolis at Akhziv (Phoenician Ecdippa, between Tyre and Akku), and of material from some of the tombs excavated at Khaldeh (Phoenician Haldua) immediately south of Beirut.[59] There is, in addition, a considerable amount of pottery, catalogued but not scientifi-

---

[46] C 23, 19; C 34, 64.   [47] C 8.   [48] C 34, 63–6.   [49] C 34, 78.   [50] C 32.
[51] C 15; C 24.   [52] C 15.   [53] C 12; C 34, 76–7.   [54] C 23, 19.   [55] C 1, 195–6.
[56] C 41, 617–20; C 44, table 8A.   [57] C 44.   [58] C 41; C 65; C 93.
[59] C 63, 58–63, figs. A, B; C 92; C 98.

cally excavated from tombs and burial caves at Qrayeh and Tambourit[60] in the vicinity of Sidon, from Qasmieh, Joya, Khirbet Selim[61] near Tyre, and at Tell er-Reshidiyeh, south of Tyre.[62] There is a little Iron Age material from Tell Abu Hawam and Athlit, north and south respectively of Haifa, and tomb groups from Mt Carmel itself.[63] Much less is known from the northern coast of metropolitan Phoenicia: unpublished Iron Age tombs from Byblos, pottery from Sheikh Zenad 40 km north of Tripoli, and in Syria some Iron Age material from Tell cArqa,[64] and Amrit itself.[65]

Thus it may rightly be claimed that the main Phoenician towns are archaeologically unknown to us, apart from a few early soundings in Sidon and recent limited research at Tyre. Excavations at Tell el-Fukhar, ancient Akku,[66] have so far not yielded rich Iron Age strata though there is some typical Phoenician ware of the later Iron Age. Material from the tell at Akhziv remains unpublished. Botrys, modern Batrun, founded by Ittobacal (Jos. *Jud. Ant.* VIII.324), Berytus (Beirut) and several sites equated with towns listed in the Assyrian annals remain unexplored. But what is at present known of Phoenician culture from discoveries in metropolitan Phoenicia gives a definite pottery profile, whose impact we can detect with confidence upon neighbouring Palestine and Cyprus.[67] The bulk of it, though, dates from the middle period of the Iron Age (*c.* 850–600 B.C.). The pottery of Iron Age I (1050–850 B.C.) is little known and that of the later Iron Age (Persian period) scarcely known at all north of Shiqmona on the Haifa coast.[68] An even greater problem surrounds the sequence from the Late Bronze Age to Iron I, for although there is plenty of Mycenaean ware from the Lebanon, especially from Sidon, the local ceramics of the late second millennium are poorly known and the stratigraphy at Tyre, Sarafand, and Akku (the only stratified sites) does not disclose any destruction levels such as may be equated with the coming of the Sea Peoples or the 'Dark Age' elsewhere on the coast.

Clearly the beginning of the Iron Age saw the introduction of a very simple bichrome painted style of pottery in Phoenicia, using two colours on a plain ground or pale slip. The three chief forms are globular flasks with round mouths, small 'pilgrim flasks' and tall-necked jugs with strainer side-spouts, not unlike the well-known Philistine 'beer jugs' from further south.[69] These are widely represented in Phoenicia and Palestine.[70] The tradition of these round-mouth flasks, with many variables, was long-lasting, and their occurrence, albeit in a developed

[60] C 54; C 99.   [61] C 54.   [62] C 87.   [63] C 78.   [64] C 105.
[65] Unpublished.   [66] C 67, 23–6.   [67] C 39, 271.   [68] C 71.
[69] C 39, figs. 280, 282; C 65, 47–50.
[70] At Khaldeh; at Tyre (C 48, pl. 29, 3; C 54, 148–50; C 98, nos. 49, 57; C 111, figs. 24, 25, 27, 28); at Dor (C 72, 42); at Beth-shan (C 39, 304, no. 11; C 90, 107, fig. 476, 24; C 101, 60–2); at Tell Qasile (C 101, 61); at Lapethos, Salamis, and Kaloriziki in Cyprus (C 478, pl. 28; C 48A, 37).

form, alongside Greek pottery in tomb 7 at Amathus in Cyprus shows that they continued until about 750 B.C. The round-mouth flasks in the earliest Akhziv tombs can be placed mid-way in their development, about 900 B.C. But the upper date for the beginning of the typical shapes of Phoenician Iron I pottery is confirmed by their cross-referencing with Philistine wares in the cist graves and stratum XI at Tel Zeror,[71] inland from Haifa, where a date in the early tenth century is the very latest which could be assigned. It is interesting to note also that here, as at Akhziv and Khaldeh, the earliest tombs were stone-built cists with individual burials, a tradition perhaps carried over from the Late Bronze Age tombs at Tell Abu Hawam.[72] Almost all of the homeland Phoenician tombs are dug chamber tombs of the later Iron Age (Iron II), used for collective burials, often containing cremations as well as burials 'laid out'. For instance at Tell er-Reshidiyeh, about 7 km south of Tyre, three chamber tombs were found, two of which were provided with rock-cut benches around the walls. In one of these bodies had been laid out with offerings, but in the other and in the third tomb, which had no benches, the burials consisted of jars containing bones, some merely rotted, others superficially incinerated. All the urns in question belonged to Cypriot White Painted IV or Black-on-Red IV or were local copies, which would date all three chambers to about 650 B.C. Since cremation appears already in the Late Bronze Age at Kaloriziki (Curium) in Cyprus,[73] it cannot be claimed as a 'Phoenician' rite exclusively, but the use of cremation and inhumation together, often in the same tomb, is characteristic of Phoenician practice. Simpler burials at Azor[74] and at southern Palestinian coastal sites[75] consisted of 'crater' urns of cremated bones buried in shallow graves under small 'dolmens' of loose stones. It must be pointed out that the crater shape (in bichrome as well as other fabrics), like the strainer-spouted jug, stem from an Aegean rather than a Syro-Palestinian pottery tradition.

The tenth century saw the beginning of a new pottery in the Levant, whose origins can now fairly safely be placed in Phoenicia. This is 'Black-on-Red' ware of the Swedish Cyprus Expedition classification,[76] long believed to be Cypriot (and indeed it must also have been made in Cyprus), but equally common in Phoenicia and Palestine. Its main features are its bright orange-red slip, polished or (more rarely) burnished, on which groups of closely set concentric circles and encircling lines are painted in matt black. Certain stratigraphic contexts in Palestine show that bowls of this ware became current in the tenth century B.C.[77]

[71] C 89.   [72] C 40, 93–4.   [73] C 47B, 21.   [74] C 68.
[75] W. Culican, 'The graves at Tell er-Reqeish', *Australian Journal of Biblical Archaeology* II.2 (1973) 66–105.   [76] C 48A, 32–6; C 74A, 68–73.
[77] Hazor Xa, Tell Abu Hawam III, and Tell Mevorakh VII (C 101, 52–61).

The small neck-ridge juglets, a popular and widespread shape initiated in this ware, also began at this same time and are common on northern sites in Palestine and in Phoenicia.[78] They remain current to the middle of the eighth century, a few reaching Egypt, Hama on the Orontes, Al Mina in Syria, and the island of Rhodes.[79] At present neither the clay nor pigments of Black-on-Red ware from Cyprus help to separate it from that of Palestine–Phoenicia;[80] in both areas there is a range of minor variables in clay and treatment. It is not only of course because a significant number of examples are known there that Phoenicia must be considered the homeland; the shapes of Black-on-Red vessels relate predominantly to those of other types of contemporary Phoenician pottery rather than to any other group. Shapes taken from Cypro-Geometric pottery are relatively few. A closely related Black-on-Red style appears at Tarsus in Cilicia about 1000 B.C.[81]

Even more distinctively Phoenician is the ware classified by the Swedish Cyprus Expedition as 'Red-Slip' ware, Red-Slip I (III) and II (IV)[82] being part of the later phase of the Cypriot Iron Age. This is a tradition of jugs, craters, and bowls of pinkish orange clay with a crimson-red slip, burnished on the wheel or by hand with vertical or horizontal strokes. Only very rarely is it painted. Quantities of it have been found at Akhziv, Sarepta, and Byblos, Khirbet Selim,[83] and other sites in south Lebanon. Since by far the finest examples come from clandestine finds in the Sidon region (now in private collections), there can be no doubt about the definition of the 'metropolitan' Red-Slip ware and its separation from other contemporary tradition of red-slipped ware in the early Iron Age of the Levant. In inland Palestine, at Ashdod in the south and at Hama and the Turkish Hatay sites in the north, as well as at Tarsus, the red-slipped and burnished pottery of the Iron I–II periods is manifest in different styles: none contains the jug shapes, the flask with disc-top and the piriform jug with narrow trefoil mouth characteristic of the metropolitan Red-Slip repertoire. At Hama red-slipped wares made their appearance in the ninth century and continued down to the destruction of the town by Sargon in 720 B.C., and indeed Hama-type red-slip extends as far southwards as Tell Kazel (Iron II).[84] But it must not be connected with the Red-Slip of Al Mina, for here, at the mouth of the Orontes, an enclave from the central Phoenician towns was established along with Cypriots and Greeks, a mixed emporium in a foreign environment.[85]

[78] In tomb 32 at Tell en-Naṣbeh. Beth-shan, Tell ʿAmal, Megiddo (c 101, 59–60), Akhziv (c 63, fig. Aj–l; c 92, pl. 38, nos. 16, 17), Khaldeh (unpublished), and other sites (c 54, 142–5).

[79] C 74A, 240–69.   [80] C 48, 88; C 101, 52–7.   [81] C 76, 50, 93–4.

[82] C 65, 55, figs. 7–10; C 74A, 80–1, figs. 37, 43.

[83] C 39, nos. 292–3; C 41, 577–83, pls. 34–7; C 53, 132–6; C 178.

[84] C 70; C 97, 84–5.   [85] C 51, 39–44; C 104.

The Phoenician craft fullest attested by ancient sources is the making of purple dye.[86] Though there is no purple compound as such in the glands of the *murex* and *thaisidae* sea-snails, careful extraction of the hypobranchial glands, oxidization and exposure to light produced from a virtually colourless glandular fluid a whole range of dyes from light green to blue, purplish red, and deep purple.[87] The process the Phoenicians employed, as well as the precise colour of 'Tyrian purple', are both open to question, but precise control of colour as well as techniques of double-dyeing were the main Phoenician speciality. Pliny (*HN* ix.62.135) rather obscurely described the best type of Tyrian purple as 'the colour of clotted blood, dark by reflected light and brilliant by transmitted light'. It is not known if they could make these dyes mordant. The dyeworks demanded intense labour: the extraction of glands best taken from live snails was painstaking, and the dye when ready had to be used immediately: it could not be stored. It was expensive, used a lot of salt and other materials and although the more useful *murex trunculus* prefers a shallow water habitat, the *murex brandaris*, which was also used, prefers depths from 10–15 m. Both shells were commonly available, and mounds of them have been reported in the vicinity of Sidon and Tyre. In the west Mediterranean and Atlantic the superior *purpura haemastoma* was used.[88] The art of extracting dye from these shells was known to other ancient peoples. The Phoenicians, apart from their willingness to organize a tedious and malodorous industry, had perhaps discovered simple chemical means of stabilizing the various shades and seem to have invented, according to Pliny, a technique for double-dyeing the wool. After dyeing, the wool was made up into cloth and garments, both much in demand and mentioned in the lists of tribute taken from Phoenicia by the Assyrian monarchs. Dyed linen was amongst the commodities traded by Idinna-aḫu.[89] Whether Phoenicia grew flax or acted as middleman for Egyptian linen garments is not known.

The Phoenician craft best represented by archaeological discoveries is that of carving ivory for the making of toilet articles, furniture panels, and even harness fittings (Pls. Vol., pl. 132). Here, as in other luxury arts, it is difficult to sort out homeland Phoenician work from that of 'Syrian' workshops and products which may have been produced by Phoenicians resident in other Levantine centres. By style they may be divided fairly distinctly into an earlier 'Syrian' group, which draws its inspiration from Hurrian and Aramaean motifs, and a later group which includes many Egyptian-derived and Canaanite themes and specializes in decorating the

---

[86] C 14, 98–103; C 82.   [87] C 43.   [88] C 43.   [89] C 14, 99, 101.

ivories with coloured inlay.[90] This group is certainly Phoenician; whilst it overlaps the work of the 'Syrian' schools, it has a more southerly distribution and includes a small number from Tyre, Sarepta, and Byblos,[91] the only early carved ivories found in Phoenicia itself. In many respects the ivories of the Phoenician school are the descendants of Canaanite ivory work of the Late Bronze Age, such as the 'Megiddo ivories'. In fact a seventh-century ivory exported to Samos has had the same treatment as a thirteenth-century Canaanite ivory from Megiddo.[92] Since the 'Syrian' school has no such clear antecedents, and since at Nimrud and Gordium products of both schools occur together, and since furthermore the distribution in Syria of both schools overlaps,[93] it is possible that Phoenicians were the originators of both groups. On the whole, however, the 'Syrian' products have an earlier and more northerly distribution in the Near East. The firmest date for them is from Hasanlu in north-west Iran, where ivories were found in a citadel burnt down by the Urartians in the late ninth century.[94] Most relevant comparisons with other forms of north Syrian and Neo-Hittite art suggest that the floruit of the 'Syrian' workshops was from the mid-ninth to the late eighth century. By contrast 'Phoenician' ivories occur in contexts dated later than the last quarter of the eighth century,[95] though regrettably the largest group, found at Samaria[96] and once attributed to Ahab's 'ivory house' there, cannot be stratigraphically dated. The wealth of 'Phoenician' ivories from Salamis Tomb 79 is to be dated to about 700 B.C., and includes items like ivory fittings for furniture[97] and ivory 'candelabra',[98] which are uniquely Phoenician (cf. Pls. Vol., pls. 204–5). Apart from these two major groups, other contemporary carved ivories from Near Eastern sites are Assyrian and occasionally even Iranian and Urartian in style. To what degree these are the products of either 'Syrian' or 'Phoenician' workshops or itinerant craftsmen must remain doubtful, especially in view of the difficulty of attributing even the main groups to any one individual centre, though some of the 'Syrian' group seem to have come from the region of Zincirli in eastern Cilicia.[99] Whilst artistically the majority of the Phoenician pieces are stiff and 'hieratic', often symmetrical in composition after the Egyptian manner, their technical quality and decorative effect seem superior to Syrian work, especially in the highly sophisticated ajouré fretwork as seen on a panel from Gordium, and the effective use of inlay as instanced in the lion-and-negro-in-a-thicket panel from Nimrud,[100] itself a remarkable naturalistic departure from the often dull schematization of the Phoenician school.

[90] A 137; C 45; C 109.   [91] C 110.   [92] C 73, 92–4, fig. 26.   [93] C 110.
[94] C 110.   [95] C 110.   [96] C 59.   [97] C 85A III, pl. 77.
[98] C 85A III, 41, 49, pl. 54–5.   [99] C 109.   [100] A 137, 140–1; C 113.

Though we have but few surviving examples, the art of ivory carving certainly continued in Phoenicia down to the Persian period, with branches appearing in Carthage, producing a group of ivory caryatid figures[101] and some carved ornaments at Tharros.[102] South Spain seems to have had a somewhat distinctive ivory carving workshop and to have shared with Carthage a tradition of ivory engraving (mainly on combs) very different from anything yet known in the east.[103]

Metalwork poses a problem very similar to that of ivories. The tradition of late Canaanite work, as instanced in the cauldrons of Zarethan (Tell es-Saʿidiyeh)[104] and the four-sided wheeled cauldron-stands from Cyprus, is likely to have continued into the Iron Age; cauldrons were found together with 'Phoenician' decorated bronze bowls in the palace of Ashurnasirpal at Nimrud by Layard in 1849 (Pls. Vol., pl. 133a–b),[105] and the wheeled cauldron-stands in Phoenician style survived in Crete well into the first millennium.[106] Tripod stands (for cauldrons) made of iron rods with bronze fittings seem to have been made in both Phoenicia and Cyprus in the Iron Age, and one from Nimrud carries an Aramaic inscription.[107] The decorated bowls from Nimrud also carry letters in Phoenician and Aramaic,[108] probably representing the names of their owners before they were carried off as booty or tribute to Assyria. A silver Phoenician bowl from the Bernardini tomb in Praeneste is inscribed with the owner's name in Phoenician: Eshmunazer ben Asto.[109] Thus there can be no doubt that some of these bowls circulated amongst Phoenicians, and there is much artistic evidence that they manufactured some of them. But the problem of their involvement in the making and distributing of a whole group of bronzes stylistically aligned with the sculptures of Aramaean and Neo-Hittite states such as Tell Halaf, Zincirli, and Sakçegözü (and hence usually called 'North Syrian'), remains obscure.[110] Bronzework attributed to these workshops comes mainly from Nimrud, the Mount Ida cave in Crete (Pls. Vol., pls. 277–8), the sanctuary of Hera on Samos, Delphi and Olympia in Greece, the tombs of Praeneste and Vulci in Etruria, and the shrine at Satricum in Latium.[111] Though it is not homogeneous it has features in common, particularly the high repoussé, and certain links with Assyrian and Urartian metal styles: it also presents some similarities to the 'Syrian' group of ivories. Only one piece has been found in Syria, a harness head-piece from Tell Tainat near Antioch.[112] None of it is inscribed. Amongst the bronze bowls found at Nimrud there is a group in a quite different style, with rather flat

---

[101] C 4 II, pls. 73–5; C 49.   [102] C 107.   [103] C 279; C 300.   [104] A 133.
[105] C 88.   [106] C 51, 64–6.   [107] C 45, 48; C 46.   [108] C 46.   [109] C 5, 107–8.
[110] C 51.   [111] C 112, 151.   [112] C 112, 29; cf. C 45, 101.

engraved designs, often minuscule and widely spaced and incorporating Egyptian religious motifs. Similar bowls come from the Idaean cave,[113] from Athens,[114] and from Iran.[115] These are Phoenician products and although in general the Syrian-type metalwork has an earlier diffusion in the Aegean than most 'Phoenician' types of bowl, there is at present no reason why the Nimrud type of the latter cannot be contemporary with it. In fact a bowl from Calabria, because of its Egyptianisms certainly to be classed as Phoenician, is of early to mid-eighth century date,[116] and little 'Syrian'-type metalwork in Crete, Greece, or Italy is demonstrably earlier. Phoenician bowls elsewhere appear to span the late ninth- to mid-seventh-century period: the two main finds at Nimrud and at Idalium in Cyprus[117] probably represent 'collections' of bowls representative of much of this time span. Further west, some of the bowls found in Italy form a distinctive group, connected with two in Cyprus but not represented elsewhere:[118] both their context and style tie them down to the mid-seventh century, and there are points to suggest that some of them may have been made in Italy by a workshop established there. So complex are the inter-relationships of Oriental metalwork in the Levant and Mediterranean during this period that the problem of attributions may never be solved. There is, after all, the likelihood that tinkers of varied schools and origins sat down in the same bazaar and hammered out themes ancient and modern side by side. We have the same problem with the ivories. However, there is certainly an earlier 'Syrian' polarity and a later 'Phoenician' one, and the shift to the Phoenician south of ivory and metalwork export might be because of Sargon's devastation of the north Syrian cities compared with the more lenient Assyrian attitude to Phoenicia;[119] but this argument does not warrant putting the *origins* of Phoenician style at so late a date. Here, though it is in fact of later date (about 700 B.C.), the bronzework from Tomb 79 at Salamis plays a crucial, though not decisive, part, for it has the main elements of 'Syrian' style and technique and yet incorporates many Egyptian details[120] (Pls. Vol., pl. 203), which Syrian work does not. Does it represent a late version of the Tyrian equivalent to Syrian work, a more southerly style which was not exported until after the market for the latter had declined – and then only in small amounts – to Cyprus and Rhodes?[121]

No such variety of doubts surrounds another class. Bronze and silver piriform jugs with palmette-shaped lower handle-attachments are certainly Phoenician and provide the prototypes for this shape in Red-Slip

---

[113] C 80, pls. 6, 7.   [114] C 74, 18.   [115] C 62.   [116] C 51, fig. 218.
[117] A 133; C 74; C 87A; cf. Pls. Vol., pl. 210.
[118] L. Pareti, *La tomba Regolini-Galassi*, nos. 321–4 (Rome, 1947); I. Ström, *Problems Concerning the Origins and Development of Etruscan Orientalizing Style* (Odense, 1971) 123–7.
[119] C 110.   [120] C 85A III, pls. 267–79.   [121] C 110.

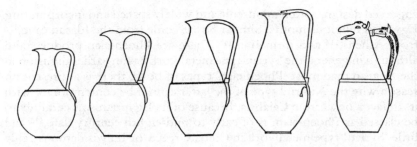

Fig. 20. Types of Phoenician piriform jugs. (After C 77, 163, figs. 1–5.)

II (IV) pottery (Fig. 20). Even though there are only two examples in the east (Sidon and Tamassus) eked out by pottery versions covered with tin-foil to simulate the originals (Salamis and Trikomo, Cyprus), their contexts in Etruria, and especially in Spain, leave no doubts about their origin: the palmettes which form the lower handle-attachments are specifically Phoenician, and in the rich Orientalizing tombs at Praeneste, Caere, and Pontecagnano they were found together with Phoenician bowls or other imported objects. At Nimrud, Samos, and Carthage, copies in ivory have been found, in mid-seventh century contexts at the two latter places. These jugs provided an important stimulus for Italian metal jugs and were widely imitated in Etruscan *bucchero*. Bronze dishes with lotus-topped handles were another Phoenician type which gave rise to copies in both bronze and pottery in Crete, Greece, and Cyprus, but more especially in Etruria. Important, though less closely demonstrable, is the influence of Phoenician metal prototypes on incense stands and lamp stands in Italy, which was a natural consequence of the Phoenician oil and incense export.[122]

There is little to point to in other sumptuary arts. Only an eleventh-century sceptre head from Curium (Pls. Vol., pl. 196) and a pair of gold crowns in Baltimore[123] give a glimpse of Phoenician goldwork before the Persian period (Fig. 21). A set of fine jewels from a woman's grave at ᶜAin el-Hilwy near Sidon[124] shows a blend of Phoenician, Greek, and Achaemenian motifs, though the workmanship is clearly Phoenician. With the exception of Tartessian work, much of which is unique, Phoenician jewellery east and west, though sometimes technically excellent[125] is mostly stereotyped and dull, much of it amuletic. It was in the spreading of techniques and their adaptation to local style that Phoenician jewellers excelled, and although there are some sporadic

[122] C 77; C 13, 95–8 pl. 27 (ivory); C 51, 68 fig. 52.   [123] C 51B, nos. 317, 774; C 64.
[124] C 7, 107–8, pl. 108.   [125] C 94.

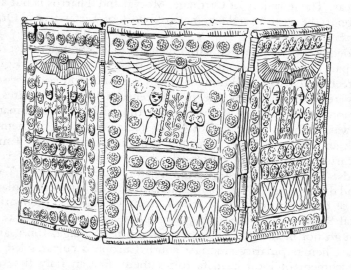

Fig. 21. The Baurat–Schiller gold crowns. The fertility themes link them to the jointed crowns worn by women shown on carved ivories. Tenth century B.C.? Diameters 21.6 and 22.5 cm. (Baltimore, Walters Art Gallery 57.968–9; after C 64, figs. 1–4.)

imports to Greece and Italy, especially of seal-mounts, it is remarkable what little influence the known forms of Phoenician jewellery had overseas. The jewellery of Carthage, Motya, and Tharros is but a poor relation to the wealthy and original goldwork of Tartessus and Orientalizing Etruria.

Phoenicians were credited with inventing glass, though in fact for the most part they revived, some time in the seventh century, the Egyptian Eighteenth-Dynasty tradition of making small sand-core vessels of variegated colours.[126] By the fourth century these miniatures were common throughout the Mediterranean, though by then their manufacture was probably shared with Greek factories: many of them copy Greek amphorae and jugs in shape. Older is the minor art of making polychrome beads with impressed white or multicoloured eyes and strands. These are earliest attested in Iron Age Cyprus and Twenty-second dynasty Egypt, but their establishment in inland Palestinian contexts of the eighth century (Lachish, Samaria) suggests their origin in coastal Phoenicia, for there they are well attested in the fifth century, although not in the great numbers found in Carthage, Ibiza, and the West. Their popularity amongst south European cultures led to the establishment of local bead factories there, first in Italy (late eighth century), later in Istria and south France. Beads and pendants in the shape of comic human masks (Fig. 22)[127] and animals, made of molten glass strands worked on a pontil-stick, were appealing trinkets which appear first to have been invented in the sixth century. Much rarer is evidence of moulded and cold-cut glass working: the Aliseda glass jug[128] is the prime example of it, but there are bowls from Nimrud[129] and green glass bottles from Atlit and Cyprus. There is also evidence from Nimrud and Cyprus of Phoenician work in rock-crystal and a surprising number of minor objects in this material have been found in Carthage tombs.[130]

The making of fancy cosmetic palettes out of carved and engraved shells of the *tridacna squamosa*[131] scallop has also been attributed to the Phoenicians (Pls. Vol., pl. 134). Their distribution is a wide one and includes Delphi, Samos, Cyrene, and Etruria as well as inland sites in the Near East (Tel Arad, Bethlehem, Nimrud) and Egypt. A few alabaster palettes come from the same workshops as the carved shells and make up a corpus of highly distinctive designs in which Phoenician motifs predominate. But in fact their style is difficult to pin down. It is quite possible that since the shells themselves belong to the Red Sea they are the work of a group of Phoenician craftsmen settled at Elath. The Delphi 'shell' is of alabaster and adds a technical link to the stylistic links between tridacna carving and a group of alabaster and terracotta

---

[126] C 3, 66–112; C 5, 114–16.   [127] C 79.   [128] C 302, 107–20.   [129] C 86.
[130] C 15; C 152, 19.   [131] C 103.

Fig. 22. Glass face beads from Carthage (*a-d*) and no provenance (*e*). (After C 79, figs. 1–5, nos. 5, 17, 86, 470, 577.)

alabastra shaped like female votaries.[132] Some of these are certainly Rhodian, but their prototypes are either Phoenician or Syrian.

Many of the ivories and bronzes are fittings for harness, especially blinkers and headpieces. The fine leatherwork which accompanied them and which in itself must have constituted an important export industry has perished. Warriors are represented in Cypriot sculpture wearing short tunics decorated in a Phoenician panelled style[133] suggesting tooled and dyed leather. Indeed the importance to Phoenician trade of crafts dependent on humbler materials must not be overlooked. Carpentry and upholstery are well attested Carthaginian trades (Cicero, *Pro Murena* 36; Varro, I.52.1 and III.7.3), using the varied timbers from the Maghreb forests and feathers from migratory birds on the Tunisian marshes. According to surviving terracotta models, it was serviceable rather than stylish furniture. Cedar coffins from Tunisian sites,[134] some from Carthage and Kerkouane with their lids carved to represent the dead, attest in the West skills which must derive from homeland craftsmanship. Among the many natural resources which must have given Phoenician enterprise a host of new directions in North Africa is the ostrich: it is well represented in archaic Etruscan art, and the export of live birds and feathers was probably a profitable side-line for Carthage. The painting and etching of ostrich eggs, the former going back to Neolithic times in North Africa, are of exceptional interest in that they preserve in many cases the earliest motifs of Libyan–Berber folk-art, quite different from Phoenician.[135] There is a good example from Tarquinia.[136] Painted ostrich eggs were placed in many west Phoenician graves – at Carthage, Ibiza, Gouraya, Villaricos, and Tangiers[137] – some with Phoenician decoration, others parts of shell painted

[132] C 96.   [133] C 51B, nos. 69, 70.   [134] C 4 II, pl. 68.   [135] C 42.
[136] C 106.   [137] C 390, 130–40.

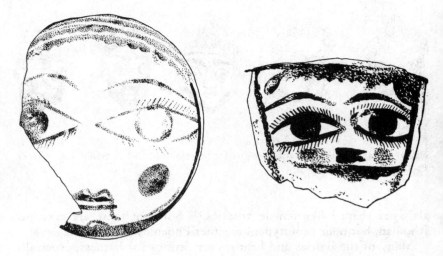

Fig. 23. Painted ostrich eggs from Carthage. (After C 42, pls. 2.2, 5.)

with humpty-dumpty faces, wide-eyed in anticipation of the life-from-death the eggs themselves symbolized (Fig. 23). Decorated eggs are not, of course, a major art form, but they are an important illustration of an independent western cultural development resulting from new ethnic contacts.

Although they have not contained the international exotica of the shrines of the Aegean world, the votive deposits from the small temples of Phoenicia and Palestine are important in another respect. Votive terracotta models from shrines at Sarepta,[138] at Kharayeb,[139] and the Eshmun temple (both near Sidon), and country chapels at Makmish, Tell es-Safi, and Tell Sippor in Palestine throw light on the much-neglected Phoenician coroplastic art and religious iconography, making it possible to distinguish the Phoenician cult images from the better studied series of Cypriot terracottas. There has also come to light a small group of Phoenician pottery vessels with appliqué modelled panels.[140] On examples from Cyprus and Nimrud the plaques take the shape of four-winged seraphs. Though little is known about the origins of a distinctively Phoenician glyptic, smothered as almost all seals are with Egyptian iconography, it is nevertheless possible to distinguish a definite Phoenician pseudo-Egyptian style of scarab seal in the ninth century[141] and to find, especially on scarabs of the Persian period, religious images of purely Phoenician form, in part reviving an imagery unattested since the thirteenth century B.C.[142] Here, as in all Phoenician art, there is a profound conservatism which prized the talismanic above the aesthetic

[138] C 93, 22–6.   [139] C 85.   [140] C 102.   [141] C 108.   [142] C 61.

virtues of images, but which nevertheless merged with Greek styles of gem-cutting. The strong influence of Greek art on Phoenician is nowhere better seen than in the purely Greek forms of some of the terracottas of sixth-/fourth-century deposits and in the emergence of a joint style of gem-cutting called 'Greco-Phoenician'. At the end of the fifth century and during the fourth the influence of Egypt on Phoenician and Punic art somewhat receded, but conversely this was the period of maximum interest in Egyptian scarabs and amulets in the West. Many of these are not canonical Egyptian objects and it is difficult to establish whether they were made in the colonies or by some Phoenician enterprise in Egypt.

III. PHOENICIANS IN THE WEST

Phoenician contacts with Greece, Cyprus and Italy are discussed in *CAH* III².3, Chapters 36*a*, 36*c* and 38, and in *CAH* IV², Chapter 13. The remainder of this chapter is concerned with the evidence for Phoenician trade and colonies in the west Mediterranean.

1. *Colonial problems*

The idea is now fashionable that, in contrast to Greek colonists, the Phoenicians sought to establish a regular but flimsy commercial network of 'comptoirs', 'échelles', and other ports of call. This certainly was an important aspect, but we have no grounds to suppose that Phoenicians might not also have sought space, food, and freedom. Carthage itself commanded a large agricultural and arboricultural basis, as probably did Cagliari, Malta, and Ibiza and some of the towns in Morocco and Spain.[143] Furthermore, use of the large tracks of forest along the Maghreb coast and perhaps access to the iron deposits there must have made some inland control necessary, and whilst the Greek colonies certainly relied heavily upon the acquisition of a fertile *chora*[144] even ignoring excellent harbours such as Brindisi which did not have them, the Phoenicians normally and initially selected sites for security and sea access. But obviously the necessity for wood, charcoal, and pasturage alone must soon have led to substantial acquisitions of land.[145]

Near Eastern experience did not include colonization on the Greek model of founding new *poleis*. Some of the network of international trade in the Orient was maintained by establishing trading colonies in foreign cities and it appears most likely that the Phoenicians did this in some of the inland cities of Syria, Mesopotamia, and the Aegean at least, maintaining not merely trade missions but also workshops for the local

[143] C 4 II, 52.   [144] C 130, 15.   [145] C 136, 72.

manufacture of 'Phoenician goods'. The only hint of this in literature is in Judges (18:7, 27–8), which refers to a colony of Sidonians living at Laish, east of the Jordan, not said to be in trade, but certainly well placed for it. This policy certainly began earlier than the turn to colonies overseas. What brought the change is unknown. Assyrian oppression is a factor often suggested, and indeed it cannot be denied that the great expansion of colonial activity in the first half of the seventh century might be a result of Esarhaddon's policies towards Phoenicia.[146] At the same time, Assyrian control of the inland markets might have driven the merchants to seek alternative overseas outlets. Population explosions, bad harvests, and political unrest are amongst the many factors we cannot ignore or yet measure. A rise rather than a fall in the standard of living at home might have sent the first pioneers overseas to satisfy the market for metals and other raw materials, and in fact, contrary to what has been suggested above, the growth of Assyrian interest in Phoenicia might have stimulated that market. But it seems quite evident that, apart from Cyprus, Phoenicia had no substantial colonial interests overseas before 700 B.C. Diodorus speaks of pre-colonial trading contacts[147] and Thucydides of the contraction of Phoenician interest in Sicily when the Greeks 'began to arrive in number'.[148] But we do not know what presuppositions ancient authors had about Phoenician precedence. A bronze figure of Ba^cal, dredged from the sea off Sciacca in southern Sicily, alters nothing; though it compares generally with Bronze Age Canaanite figurines,[149] it has substantial differences and even if early – which is highly doubtful – could well have come by the same, presumably Mycenaean, channels which brought Cypriot vases to Bronze Age graves in eastern Sicily. A second-millennium Near Eastern cylinder seal from Vélez Málaga,[150] found in unknown circumstances, is too isolated (and too early) to enter into the picture of pre-colonial contact, for which generally there is a remarkable lack of evidence. The earliest direct evidence is provided by the Nora Stone from southern Sardinia, certainly the earliest Phoenician inscription in the West.[151] All that can be said about this inscription with certainty is that it was inscribed on local stone, refers to events in Sardinia concerning a certain Pumai, and is in a script which is eighth century at the latest.[152] That it is complete, mentions Tarshish, and relates historical events which show Sardinia was Tarshish (or that it was not), and that it was written in the ninth or even tenth centuries are all uncertain.[153] It does not, however, necessarily imply Phoenician colonization.

The type of site which appealed to the settlers was unfortunately in

---

[146] C 289.   [147] C 3, 153–4.   [148] C 3, 381.   [149] C 121.   [150] C 273, 23.
[151] C 3, 30–43; C 117; C 122; C 131.   [152] See p. 507.   [153] C 136, 425–6.

itself not ideal for preservation. Tips of promontories and small islands at little distance from the coast, especially where good anchorage in a nearby delta or lagoon was available, were preferred:[154] nowhere do the Phoenicians appear to have aimed initially to settle large tracts of land. Many of these small toe-holds probably saw very brief settlement before abandonment. Erosion, changes in sea-levels, and silting of deltas must have obliterated many of them. But it was not only their sea-links and harbour requirements which dictated such sites, nor yet only that they could be easily defended or quickly evacuated. They were easy to trade from and to fish from: for the first settlers the shallow waters were the surest source of protein. In the course of settlement it must soon have been realized that this necessity could be turned to commercial advantage and from it grew the salted and dried-fish industry of the Phoenicians in the West, celebrated by ancient writers.[155] Many settlements have lagoons in their vicinity, suitable for the set-net fishing which the Phoenicians are said to have introduced. It is remarkable also how many settlements were placed near natural salt-pans, some of which, as at Motya and Isla Plana (Ibiza), are still worked today. Salt, of course, was the basic necessity in the preserved fish industry, but it may also have been a trading commodity in itself. Osiers and reeds, too, for the making of ropes, traps, and panniers were available in the deltas and marshes.

A major insoluble problem besets the history of Phoenician colonization – the part played by Carthage itself. Were other colonies founded from Carthage, or as a result of its prospection of suitable sites, and did Carthaginians aim from soon after its foundation to cast a network of colonies over the West and build a commercial 'empire'? Alternatively, did colonies come independently from the motherland or, in Spain, from Cadiz? If so at what stage did they fall under Carthaginian domination, and what kind of domination was it? The ethnic and ideological hegemony of Carthage is only to be expected. About 550 B.C. the Carthaginian general Malchus mounted a campaign to consolidate the Phoenician hold on Sardinia, but it was not until the rise of the Magon family in the late sixth century that Carthage seems to have been in a position to exercise political and military control in the West. The terms of the first treaty with Rome (509 B.C.) given by Polybius (III.22) make clear that Carthage could lay down conditions about trade in Sardinia and that part of Sicily which was under Phoenician control.[156] In the later treaty with Rome (348 B.C.), Carthage was able to delimit Roman navigation on the eastern coast of Spain as well. It is interesting that Polybius expressly includes the 'Tyrians' on the side of the Carthaginians in this treaty, meaning probably the Tyrians of the West, other than

---

[154] C 4 II, 53–64; C 184, 137. [155] C 276, 413. [156] C 5, 154–5.

those of Carthage.[157] But it was essentially Carthage's superiority at sea which made its treaties with Rome operable and gave it some *de facto* control of all the western colonies. According to Strabo (XVII.1.19), its ships were able to intercept all foreign vessels sailing its shores in the directions of Sardinia or the Pillars of Hercules.

Inscriptions and coins throw little light on either Carthage's internal or external affairs. We do not know what type of government existed at Carthage in its first centuries; by the fifth century, when we have our first inscription evidence,[158] the Magonids appear as *rbm*, but by about 450 B.C. the civil magistrate of the suffetes (*sōfim*) had been instituted as some form of republican control. The Magonids themselves, though designated *rb* in Punic inscriptions (probably meaning 'general'), were elected suffetes, and certainly not 'kings' as classical sources imply. The West Phoenician colonies had no coins before the end of the fifth century: the first were struck in Sicily on both Phoenician and Attic standards, with the mint at Carthage following late in the fourth century. Punic coinages in Sardinia, Ibiza, Pantelleria, and Malta cannot be shown to begin before Roman times and those of the southern towns of Spain not before 250 B.C. Except for the coins of Pantelleria and Malta, which have Phoenician motifs, all coins are frankly Greek in design. Their legends are useful sources of information on place names (though not on the Sardinian–Punic issues). *Ann* on coins of Malta, and *Ziz*[159] ('The Splendid') on those of Palermo alone preserve what are probably the names of these important West Phoenician centres.

No account of Phoenician colonization can ignore the religious dimension. Melqart of Tyre, himself a sea god, was probably conceived, like Heracles in Greek legend, to have preceded the pioneers into the far West. In a bilingual inscription from Malta he is named 'archegetes', founder. The peopling of the new lands with the Semitic gods, the sanctification of capes and promontories with dedications and shrines, the conversion of ancient shrines such as Tas Silg in Malta and Mt Eryx in Sicily, the hallowing of caves and grottoes such as Es Cuyram in Ibiza and Grotta Regina near Palermo[160] – all these represent a vital process in assimilation. Large and ancient temples were a phenomenon of the West Phoenician world – at Lixus, Cadiz, Utica, the temples of Juno and Melqart in Malta and Juno at Carthage. They had probably more than a purely religious role in Phoenician society by acting as places of asylum, centres for the ratifying of commercial contracts, the taking of oaths – and even perhaps as suppliers of capital.[161] Soon a distinctive Western emphasis emerged in Phoenician religion, with the overwhelming emphasis on the cults of the Tyrian Ba'al Hammon (called *melek*, king)

157 C 5, 154–5.   158 C 129.   159 C 127, 141–9; C 202.   160 C 132.
161 C 3, 282–5.

and Tanit (Astarte) as well as composite versions of homeland deities, such as Milk-Ashtart. The cult of Tanit, now attested both in name and symbol in the homeland,[162] completely eclipsed (or subsumed) that of Phoenician Astarte. Another western emphasis was on child sacrifice, called *molk*, evidenced in the 'tophets' established during the earliest stages of certain Western colonies.[163] These were open-air walled enclosures in which the remains of incinerated children were deposited as public evidence of piety. Though no tophets have been found there, literary evidence shows that this was a custom practised in Phoenicia,[164] though probably not on the west Phoenician scale. In Punic inscriptions associated with urn deposits, especially those from El-Hofra near Constantine in Algeria,[165] distinction is made between a *mlk ʾmr* and a *mlk ʾdm*, the sacrifice of a lamb and of a human. Although it has been thought that the sacrifice of an animal substitute became prevalent,[166] new evidence from the Tanit Precinct at Carthage shows that child sacrifice did in fact predominate down to the time of the Punic Wars.[167] Quite possibly the insecurity and vulnerability of the colonists led to the revival of a practice deemed to assure community safety. Diodorus (xx.13–14) describes how the Carthaginians resorted to child sacrifice at a time of national crisis, when Agathocles of Syracuse invaded North Africa in 310. It is also possible that native Libyan practices had contributed to the popularity of human sacrifice amongst the colonists.

In the tophet urns, as also in normal incineration burials, birds, rodents, and small reptiles were placed, dead or alive.[168] Cockerels were also sometimes buried with the dead. These are, perhaps, the symbols of the resurrection of the soul; for intangible though such matters are in the context of our ignorance, it would be foolish to deny the Phoenicians an advanced eschatology,[169] or to imagine that by sacrificing their children, for whatever cause, they were not thereby advancing their souls to a higher state of existence. Scores of gravestones erected over the tophet urns or other urn burials are sculptured with a clearly defined set of abstract symbols, amongst them the 'twin pillars' which appear to have symbolized both in Tyre and the western colonies the supports of the sky at the approach of the abode of God.[170] The colonial process duplicated the essential iconography of Tyre's Melqart temple – the pillars, the perpetual flame, the tomb of Melqart, and probably also his empty throne – to the tip of Cadiz. Thereby the ultimate cosmic realities were incorporated into the new geography, for all records are ambiguous about what exactly the 'Pillars of Hercules' were. And it is probably their ambiguity which is the true answer. On the physical level they were the

[162] C 93; C 123. [163] C 184, 140. [164] C 9, 207; C 126, 39–40; C 134, 156; C 135, 16–20.
[165] C 119. [166] C 134, 161. [167] C 134, 162. [168] C 133, 83.
[169] C 124; C 138, 17–19. [170] C 141, pls. 98–104.

rocks of Gibraltar and Abila (Jebel Tarifa) flanking the entry to the ocean; in cult, they were the pillars set up in the Melqart temple at Cadiz; to human knowledge they represented the separation of the Mediterranean known from the oceanic unknown; in the graveyard they surely symbolized the ultimate abode of the supreme god to which the dead had now been called. Beginning in the sixth century, this intense use of funerary religious symbols, obscure as their iconography is, seems to betoken specifically West Phoenician theological developments. They are an important factor indicating a corpus of beliefs common to the important central colonies (Carthage, Sousse, Motya, Sulcis, Nora, Tharros), where tophets and accompanying grave stelae have been found. Does this indicate the cultural domination of Carthage in these centres? Though not exclusive to tophets, it is remarkable that this iconography is not instanced in Malta, Palermo, Ibiza, or the far West. Is this because their tophets, if they had them, have not been found? Or is it because they were poorer, provincial, and untouched by Carthaginian theology – or just different?

2. *Carthage and North Africa*

Carthage (*Qartihadasht* in Phoenician, meaning 'New Town'), Tyre's most famous colony, was founded according to legend by Elissa (called Dido by the Libyans), sister of King Pygmalion of Tyre. This version goes back to the Greek historian Timaeus of Syracuse writing at the end of the fourth century.[171] An earlier fourth-century fragment of Philistos of Syracuse names the Tyrian founders as Azoros and Karchedōn, the former either a Phoenician personal name or taken from the name of Tyre (Tşor), the latter from the rather inexplicable Greek form of the name 'Carthage'. Late tradition (Stephanus of Byzantium and Eustathius[172]) preserves this name and records 'Kakkabe' and 'Kambe' as other names for the city. Both names are found on late coins of Sidon, who calls herself mother of *kkb* and *kmb*,[173] but are not understood and might be Libyan in origin.

Both literary evidence (Polybius 1.73.4; 75.4) and landscape study confirm that the site of Carthage was a sea-girt peninsula inside a deep gulf (Pls. Vol., pl. 138). Aggradation of the land surface and the deposition of silt from the Medjerda and other rivers have removed the lagoons which formerly separated it from the land on the northern side; the Lake of Tunis lies to the south.[174] The hills of Djebel Amar and Djebel Nahli lay in the neck of the peninsula, providing natural defences on the landward side. The headland of Sidi Bou Said in the centre is the

[171] C 3, 318; C 172, 139–235.   [172] C 3, 260.   [173] C 160, 106.   [174] C 4 II, 59–69.

peninsula's most prominent point. To the north are other heights at Gamart and La Marsa; to the south the eminence of the Byrsa (Hill of St Louis), which became the traditional acropolis of the city. It is on this hill and the nearby graveyards of Douïmès, Dermech (Pls. Vol., pl. 138b) and the 'Hill of Juno' (Junon) that the earliest graves have been found. But there is no certainty that this is where the Tyrian pioneers first established themselves: the heights of Sidi Bou Said are more easily defensible and the inlets of the northern lagoon probably provided better shelter than the exposed shore east of the Byrsa, where eventually artificial harbours had to be dug out.

The foundation date of Carthage has been preserved in two ways.[175] First, the absolute date given by the Sicilian Greek historian Timaeus (second half of the fourth century B.C.) is forty-eight years before the first Olympiad, thus in 814/13 B.C. This date cannot be satisfactorily explained as 'artificial', made by Greek genealogical or other computations, but may be argued to be the date known to Sicilian writers from the Carthaginians themselves, who are most likely to have had at least dedicatory inscriptions concerning the foundation of the first temple in their city. Secondly, the early Tyrian king list summarized by Josephus from Menander (Contra Apionem, 1.121–5) records how Carthage was founded in the seventh year of King Pygmalion by his sister. The most satisfactory calculation that can be made at present is that Pygmalion's seventh year was 814/813 B.C. Basic to this calculation is the synchronism between Baʿalazor (Baʿalezorus) and Shalmaneser III.[176] The former's reign was followed by the short reign of Matan I (829–821); then came Pygmalion (820–774).[177]

Classical historical tradition certainly placed other Phoenician foundations earlier. Aristotle placed the foundation of Utica 287 years before that of Carthage (De mirab. auscult. 134), and Pliny (N.H. XVI.79.216), writing in A.D. 77, states that the cedar beams in the temple of Apollo at Utica had lasted 1,178 years. This gives a date of 1101 B.C. A Tyrian source also records (Jos. Ant. Jud. VIII.324) the founding of Auza in Libya about 875 B.C. by Ittobaʿal, the predecessor of Baʿalazor. Nothing is known from either historical or archaeological sources to support these high dates for Phoenician arrival in North Africa, nor is the site of Auza known. A Greek historical tradition which placed colonists from Naxos and elsewhere on the Tunisian coast before the foundation of the Naxian colonies in Sicily and Italy (i.e., late eighth century B.C.), a tradition itself of doubtful accuracy, says nothing of Phoenicians there.[178] Modern scholarship has therefore doubted the likelihood of Phoenician settlements in Africa older than Carthage. The high date for

[175] C 41, 106–52.   [176] C 3, 322; C 21.   [177] C 21, 117–28.   [178] C 140, 25–6.

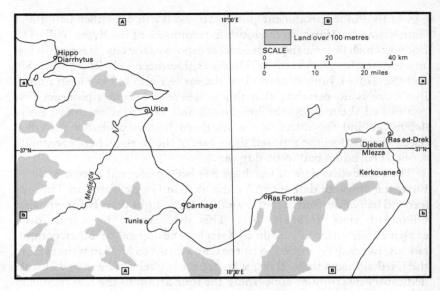

Map 7. North Africa.

Utica has been scarcely accepted by modern scholars and seems too uncomfortably close to the calculated date of the Trojan War.[179]

The record of quite extensive excavated material at Carthage gives no grounds to believe that anything yet found there can be dated before 750–720 B.C. P. Cintas, the chief protagonist of the traditional foundation date, has used quite questionable methods in trying to ratify it from archaeology. For instance, bone rectangular plaques[180] from diadems or caskets of a type known at Megiddo in Palestine and Villaricos, Carmona, and Rachgoun in the West in contexts no earlier than 650 B.C. were found at Carthage in a tomb containing a scarab of Pedubast, which he ascribes to Pedubast I (818–793). Not only can it be shown that Pedubast scarabs were used in Naucratis, Carthage, and elsewhere down to the fifth century,[181] but no mention is made of a set of exactly similar plaques found in 1918 by A. Merlin[182] in a grave at Carthage containing two Proto-Corinthian cups and an Etruscan *bucchero* amphora of about 650 B.C. Nor do a few Proto-Corinthian globular aryballoi[183] from unrecorded graves at Carthage push back the date beyond 730 B.C. More significant is the Cycladic 'chevron cup',[184] a type which began to be imported to Italy shortly before 760 B.C., though they appear to have lasted over a long period and continued to reach Italy much later.[185]

[179] C 3, 199–211.   [180] C 4 I, 298–302.   [181] C I, 445; C 302.   [182] C 164, 298–9.
[183] C 4 I, pl. 18 fig. 86.   [184] C 4 I, pl. 18 fig. 87.   [185] C 169.

One of the mainstays of Punic chronology, since its discovery in 1927, has been the stratified deposit of burial urns in the Precinct of Tanit in the harbour area of Carthage (Pls. Vol., pl. 139a).[186] This was a tophet in which sacrificed children and animals were buried. It appeared to have 'phases', based both on a loose stratigraphy and on differences in urn types ('Tanit I–III'). With the middle phase (Tanit II) was associated (though precisely how is unclear) a single Proto-Corinthian kotyle of a type current about 670 B.C.[187] But this by no means allows one to assume that Tanit I goes back to the foundation in 814 B.C., since the speed and means by which the deposit was built up is unknown. In any case recent and sophisticated re-excavation of the Tanit Precinct[188] has cast great doubt upon the precision of the Tanit I–III sequence and turned up no Greek pottery associated with Tanit II earlier than 400 B.C. The only control on Tanit I types is therefore still the tomb groups in which they occur, which in turn depend for date on their Proto-Corinthian imports.[189] It must also be stressed that the Punic pottery found at Carthage provides nothing demonstrably typologically earlier than Tanit I shapes, and that no tomb groups can be recognized more archaic in style than those with the earliest Greek imports. Homeland Phoenician pottery provides no comparisons before about 750 B.C. It is also remarkable that the pottery at Motya and Malta begins at the same stage. Urn shapes typical of Tanit I cover the first half of the sixth century at Motya, except for 'crater-urns' (i.e., with handles to rim)[190] which are peculiar to Tanit I and certainly indicate a slightly more archaic aspect of West Phoenician pottery than is known elsewhere in the West.

Thus, if the traditional date for the foundation of Carthage is to be accepted, there is a gap of about a century before the first archaeological record of it. Proto-Corinthian pottery is plentiful in the earliest recorded tombs and a group of pots from a bedrock 'chapel' below level I at the Tanit Precinct is vaguely Late Greek Geometric in style.[191] The group includes a jar, a bottle-like carafe, a bird-shaped 'feeder' and some cups. With them was found a plain crater of Akhziv type and some Phoenician plates. Dating this pottery before 750 B.C. is not possible: much of it appears to be a local (or possibly south Italian) version of Late Corinthian Geometric.[192] The bird-shaped feeder or askos, whatever its derivation, was part of the West Phoenician repertoire as shown by a similar (though red-slipped) example from Sulcis. At least one vessel, a small narrow olpe with upswung handle, has its best parallel in graves at Pontecagnano and Suessula[193] in Campania, dated to the late eighth and

[186] C 159.   [187] C 159, 86, fig. 8.   [188] C 171, 33.
[189] C 141, 12–8, pls. 2–3, 18–20.   [190] C 159, fig. 3j, l.
[191] C 41, 316–22, pls. 10–11; C 55, 386.   [192] Compare C 41, pl. 36; C 151, 604, fig. 14.
[193] C 2, pl. 9 h; C 41, pl. 9 fig. 43; C 150, 101–3, figs. 18, 33, 59; C 157, pl. 49, 1; C 166, 663.

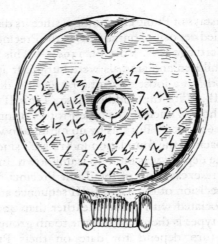

Fig. 24. Inscribed gold medallion from Carthage. (After C 156, 47, pl. 1.)

early seventh centuries. There are others from Tarquinia, Cumae, and Capua. Nor are the twisted handle of the amphora or the cups from this 'chapel' difficult to parallel there.[194] The carafe too is of a shape at home in the Italian Late Geometric and foreign to Greece.[195] Although the deposit might not be an archaeologically 'closed group' as was originally thought, all datable parallels impose a late eighth-century date; no single item can be put back in the ninth.

The oldest tombs of Carthage, at Douïmès,[196] Dermech,[197] and the 'Hill of Juno',[198] excavated late in the last century and earlier this century, were all published very sketchily. One of the most important is a tomb in the Douïmès area[199] which contained a small gold medallion inscribed with a dedication to Ashtart by one Iadamelek (Fig. 24).[200] This is the oldest inscription from North Africa, and since the same tomb contained a Proto-Corinthian kotyle it cannot be dated before about 700 B.C., though it is argued that the script is more archaic. The rest of the tomb furniture was typical of that of the oldest Phoenician tombs in the West: trefoil-mouth jug, disc-topped jug, cup, and cooking pots. The cemetery of Ard-et-Touibi[201] appears to have been in part contemporary with those of Douïmès and Dermech. One of the trefoil-mouth jugs is described as having a brilliant red slip[202] and other ceramic forms and

194 C 4 1, pl. 10, 32; C 150, figs. 16–17.   195 C 4 1, pl. 9, 37; C 168, pl. xv, 12; C 163.
196 C 4 II, 302–5; C 152.   197 C 4 1, pls. 21–2, II, 226–81; C 158, 1–139.
198 C 4 II, 286–93, pls. 93–4; C 155; C 164.   199 C 152, 13–15.
200 C 156.   201 C 4 II, 322.   202 C 164.

jewellery are of seventh-century types. Corinthian cups and Etruscan *bucchero* feature prominently in the graves here as well as in the Dermech graves.[203] The clearest import is a bichrome flask with red slipped body, close to Citium pottery, but found here in a group with late Proto-Corinthian material.[204]

Next to Carthage in importance was Utica, originally a port at the mouth of the River Bagradas (Medjerda), which since antiquity has changed its course, leaving the site now 12 km inland.[205] Its position alone on the most direct route from Tyre to Cadiz suggests its importance, though in fact Utica's history is scarcely mentioned in ancient sources. Its Phoenician name and coinage are unknown.[206] The site is little explored because of the high water table. Pottery from tombs certainly includes some archaic pieces, but nothing for which even an eighth-century date can be clearly claimed; the earliest published imports are Late Corinthian, though some Proto-Corinthian has been mentioned.[207] All early pottery forms fall within the types known in Motya and Malta in dated contexts of the early seventh century. The island of Pachès, though too far offshore to be a likely first settlement point, has apparently provided evidence of West Phoenician occupation.

Though neither major nor necessarily early, other Phoenician sites are claimed for the coast of present-day Tunisia and Libya (Tripolitania). Sallust (*Jugurtha*, 19.1) claimed a Phoenician migrant origin for Hippo (but does not specify which of the two Roman Hippos, whether Regius (Bone) or Diarrhytus (Bizerta)); and also for Leptis, where again there were two, Leptis Minor, near Sousse, and Leptis Magna in Tripolitania. Silius Italicus (III. 256–8) gives Sabratha in Tripolitania a Tyrian origin. In the case of these last two cities excavation has confirmed their pre-Roman foundation, the fifth century for Sabratha[208] and mid-seventh for Leptis Magna, though so far the West Phoenician material from neither of them is impressive.[209] The date for Leptis Magna is based on some Corinthian pottery found in soundings there.

In Tunisia[210] Punic remains, often from later Roman sites, have been found on the north coast at Tabarca (Thabraca) and Bizerta (Hippou Akra); on the Cap Bon peninsula at Kerkouane, Djebel Mlezza, Ras ed-Drek, Ras Fortas, Ras Sidi Ali el-Mekki, Nabeul (Neapolis), and Siagu; south of Cap Bon towards the Gulf of Gabes at Sousse (Hadrumetum), Lemta (Leptis Minor), Ras ed-Dimas (Thapsus), Gummi (Mahdia), Ras Botria (Acholla), and Thana (Thaenae). There is also an important tomb at La Rabta, within Tunis itself.[211] The Punic population inland is less well represented archaeologically, but Dougga (Thugga), Maktar, and

---

[203] C 4 II, 234; C 141, 35. [204] C 4 I, fig. 87.
[205] C 4 I, 283–308, pl. 3; C 147, 8–13; C 148. [206] C 4 I, 294. [207] C 147, 62.
[208] C 145, 7. [209] C 145, 125–6. [210] C 7, 151–3. [211] C 154.

Le Kef (Sicca) were important centres. Material from none of these sites is as early as that from Carthage and Utica. Many indeed are very late, but most bear evidence of expansion in the fourth century, when Carthage was at her most powerful. Only the material from the tophet at Sousse approaches a sixth-century B.C. date.[212] Noteworthy are Kerkouane and Ras ed-Drek for the light they shed on architecture. Kerkouane was a flourishing well-planned town in the fourth century and was founded already in the sixth.[213] Next to the fortress of Ras ed-Drek on the tip of Cap Bon was a small rectangular temple, unique in North Africa: both temple and fortress were probably founded in the fifth century.

The Mediterranean shores of Algeria and Morocco are not covered by any literary source with regard to Phoenician colonies. A relay of coastal sites east and west of Algiers present suitable harbour and settlement conditions, beginning with Bone in the east and stretching to Rachgoun off the Oran coast. Of these sites, Tipasa, originally an island site west of Algiers, is known from recent archaeological work to have been founded a little before 600 B.C.[214] Chullu (Collo), Djidjelli (Igilgili), Cherchel (Iol), Gouraya (Gunngu), Les Andalouses, and Mersa Madakh have all produced later Punic material (fourth to second centuries), whilst Algiers itself (originally an island) is known from its coins to have had a Phoenician name (ʾykšm – Ikosim). Other headlands whose Phoenician names have been preserved in Latin inscriptions are Rusicade (Skikda), Rusubbicari (Mers el-Hedjedj), Rusuccuru (Dellys), Rusippisir (Taksebt), Rusazus (Azeffoun) and Rusguniae (Bordj el-Bahri).[215] The tiny island of Rachgoun,[216] lying about 2 km off the coast opposite the Wadi Tafna, is an exceptionally important site, probably the Acra of Pseudo-Scylax.[217] Infertile, without anchorage except for a small artificial *cothon* (a small rectangular rock-cut basin), and with poor water supply, the island cannot have been intended for permanent settlement and indeed the pottery from the dwellings and incineration necropolis is concentrated in the second half of the seventh century. Whereas the early pottery of Tipasa derives from that of Carthage, perhaps confirming the statement of Pseudo-Scylax[218] that the cities of the central Maghreb were under Carthaginian control, that of Rachgoun has a distinctly Tartessian cast. Between Rachgoun and Oran two coastal sites seem to have shared in the trade ambience of Rachgoun. The small 'comptoir' of Mesa Madakh, predominantly native, was visited by Phoenicians who left a little archaic pottery; and Les Andalouses, a substantial Numidian town in the second century, was previously occupied along a short coastal strip by Phoenicians in the seventh century.

[212] C 6, 122.   [213] C 165.   [214] C 137, 123–31, figs. 80–2.   [215] C 170.
[216] C 173, 55–130.   [217] C 152, 38.   [218] C 379, 107–8.

The native 'Libyan' or 'proto-Berber' population of North Africa at the time of Phoenician contact seems to have been one of scattered pastoralists, practising a little agriculture here and there. Their remains come entirely from tombs, dolmens, or rock-cut chambers (*haouanet*), heavily concentrated in Tunisia and around Constantine (Algeria). Although of considerable antiquity and for some time familiar with the use of bronze, the relics of their culture are difficult to date: it is not certain, for instance, whether their concentration in Tunisia predates the Phoenician colonies to any degree, or whether it is the result of the organized employment which Phoenician agriculture provided. Their part-contemporaneity with the early stages of colonization is evident from finds of archaic West Phoenician pottery and jewellery in native graves at Djebel Lindlès[219] on the Oran coast and in the Tangiers region. Considerable amounts of their hand-made pottery, in a tradition deriving in part from that of the Sicilian Bronze Age (Castellucio and Serraferlichio), have been found in Punic sites, particularly at Djebel Mlezza,[220] and in the early sites of Mersa Madakh[221] and Rachgoun.[222] But it is remarkable how resistant their own ceramic traditions were to Punic influences.

Their late survival and admixture with the colonists is shown particularly in burial practices, especially at Henchir el-Alia[223] and on other sites on the Tunisian littoral. Here, in contrast to the normal native dolmen burial, crouched burials together with burials of a different sort showing signs of partial cremation were found in Punic-type chamber tombs. These mixed rites, together with the use of ochre and ochre-stained coffins (these latter not normally used in native burials) associated with the crouched burials, suggest a mixed population. Nor is evidence confined to the outskirts: ochre burials are reported from Utica.[224]

The role of the native Libyans in the growth of Phoenician power in North Africa must not be underestimated.[225] They probably provided the work force which the Carthaginians organized into the massive tillage of the Tunisian plains, or used as mercenary troops. The archaeological evidence suggests a symbiosis rather than an enslavement, and most certainly does not suggest that the Libyans were exploited as a vital market for Phoenician goods, for apart from a few earrings from the dolmens of Beni Messous and Tayadirt,[226] no oriental luxuries have been found in inland Tunisia and Algeria. It is disputed whether the term *Libyphoenices*, used by Strabo[227] to denote non-Carthaginian inhabitants of North Africa, refers to a racial or legal status,

[219] C 173, 259–82.   [220] C 143, 67–8; C 146, 182–4.   [221] C 173, 145–6.
[222] C 173, 77–80.   [223] C 164.   [224] C 137, 70.   [225] C 144.
[226] C 161.   [227] C 4 II, 52.

that is whether people of mixed blood or Phoenicians living outside the
official boundaries of Carthage; but mixed marriages must have been
frequent, especially in the smaller towns like Sousse. Much in Carthaginian
life may have been Libyan from the start: face-amulets, the 'bottle-
idol' which appears on many of the earliest Punic tombstones, the
placing of rats, mice, birds, and snail-shells in the burial jars, the amuletic
use of pieces of ostrich eggs and tortoise-shell, as well as one or two
shapes in pottery. Though it was certainly Syro-Palestinian in origin,[228]
the curious Punic architecture with its megalithic stanchions might also
have some Libyan contribution. It would, of course, be presumptuous to
ascribe to Africa all that we cannot explain as Oriental; nevertheless there
is increasing reason to believe that the Phoenician colonial process
involved a degree of assimilation to local cultures, and that this is a
contributory reason for the marked regional differences in West Phoenician culture, as important as the varied homeland backgrounds of the
colonists themselves.

3. Sicily

Thucydides (VI. 2,6) informs us that the Phoenicians had established
themselves on islands and promontories all round Sicily for the sake of
trade and withdrew to western Sicily on the arrival of Greek colonists.
He was right about their withdrawal to Panormus (Palermo), Soloeis
(Solus), and Motya (Mozia), for archaeology has shown these three alone
to have been early Phoenician settlements. But there is not a trace of early
settlement elsewhere even though the island sites of Thapsus and
Plemmyrium (Syracuse) were ideal for it. A few scarabs reached Siculan
III sites in the east (800–650 B.C.), though these may have been brought
by Greeks. The only other clue to Phoenician presence is in the early
Greek graveyards themselves, where Phoenician commercial amphorae
of types well dated in Malta were used for the interment of children,
especially at Megara and Mylae (Milazzo).[229] In later times Selinus
(Selinunte) and Heraclea Minoa on the south-western coast fell under
Punic cultural and political domination. At Selinus Phoenician elements
in cult practices have been detected even before 409 B.C. after which the
city fell under a century of Punic rule.[230] Lilybaeum (Marsala) was a late
foundation from Motya, though Phoenicians were probably interested
in the headland of Lilybaeum at an earlier date. A Sicilian–Punic coinage
with the legend 'Ras-Melkart' has been ascribed to either Cephaloedeum
(Cefalù) or Heraclea Minoa. Inland from Trapani on Mt Eryx the
Phoenicians established a shrine dedicated to Astarte (Venus Ericina).

228 C 7, 153.   229 C 177, pls. 51–2.   230 C 180; C 192.

Attached to it was a settlement which dates back to at least the fifth century B.C.

Panormus was certainly a flourishing city in the late sixth and early fifth centuries B.C., and a great deal of the grave material dates from that time. This may be attributed to the consolidation of Phoenician power in the west of the island following the establishment of the westernmost Greek colonies at Selinus and Himera in the second half of the seventh century. A few tombs with archaic jewellery and Corinthian vases can be dated to that time. The settlement itself was placed on the south-western side of a forked harbour with inlets from two streams,[231] and the nucleus of the old city was between these on high ground. Parts of the archaic walls remain. The information supplied by excavations in the necropolis[232] is important in indicating the differences between Panormus and other West Phoenician centres. The burials were mostly made in rectangular rock-cut chamber tombs containing monolithic sarcophagi or slab-cists, often closed by roofing tiles. Although there are a few cremations in small stone-built 'loculi', cremation is rare and late. Corinthian pottery indicates that the use of this graveyard dates back to about 630 B.C.,[233] but there is very little archaic West Phoenician pottery.[234] In the bulk of the tombs, which date to the second half of the sixth and the first half of the fifth centuries, the main types are of Sicilian Greek derivation with a great deal of Greek imported pottery.[235] Many of the amphorae come from Marseilles. Though there is a little Phoenician jewellery from the earlier tombs,[236] the Oriental amulets and terracottas which are so characteristic of Punic burials of the sixth/fourth centuries were not fashionable at Panormus.

Motya is the 120-acre island of San Pantaleo (Mozia) in a shallow bay to the north of Lilybaeum (Marsala)[237] (*CAH* IV², 744, Fig. 72). Both Pausanias (v.25.6) and Diodorus (XIV.47.4) regarded the inhabitants as having come from Carthage, rather than from earlier Sicilian sites. The island is protected from the open sea by the much larger Isola Grande on the eastward side and the 2.5 km circumference was itself in the sixth century surrounded by substantial fortifications. Though there are traces of occupation on the Isola Grande, there was no significant spread on to the mainland except for the secondary cemetery on the shore at Birgi to the north, to reach which a causeway was built. Apart from the fortified towers and gates (Pls. Vol., pl. 137), which finally fell to Dionysius of Syracuse in 398, the island's main features are an artificial *cothon* harbour in the south, a large shrine building (called Cappiddazzu) on the north, a

[231] C 174, 223–48; C 188, 354–9.   [232] C 181; C 185; C 188, 271–7; C 189; C 190; C 191.
[233] C 186, item 2940, figs. 66–8.
[234] C 181; C 185, fig. 7; C 190, 258, fig. 19; C 191, 281, fig. 11.   [235] C 281, 289–301.
[236] C 185, 486, fig. 5; C 186, item 2940.   [237] C 184; C 187; C 188, 259–61.

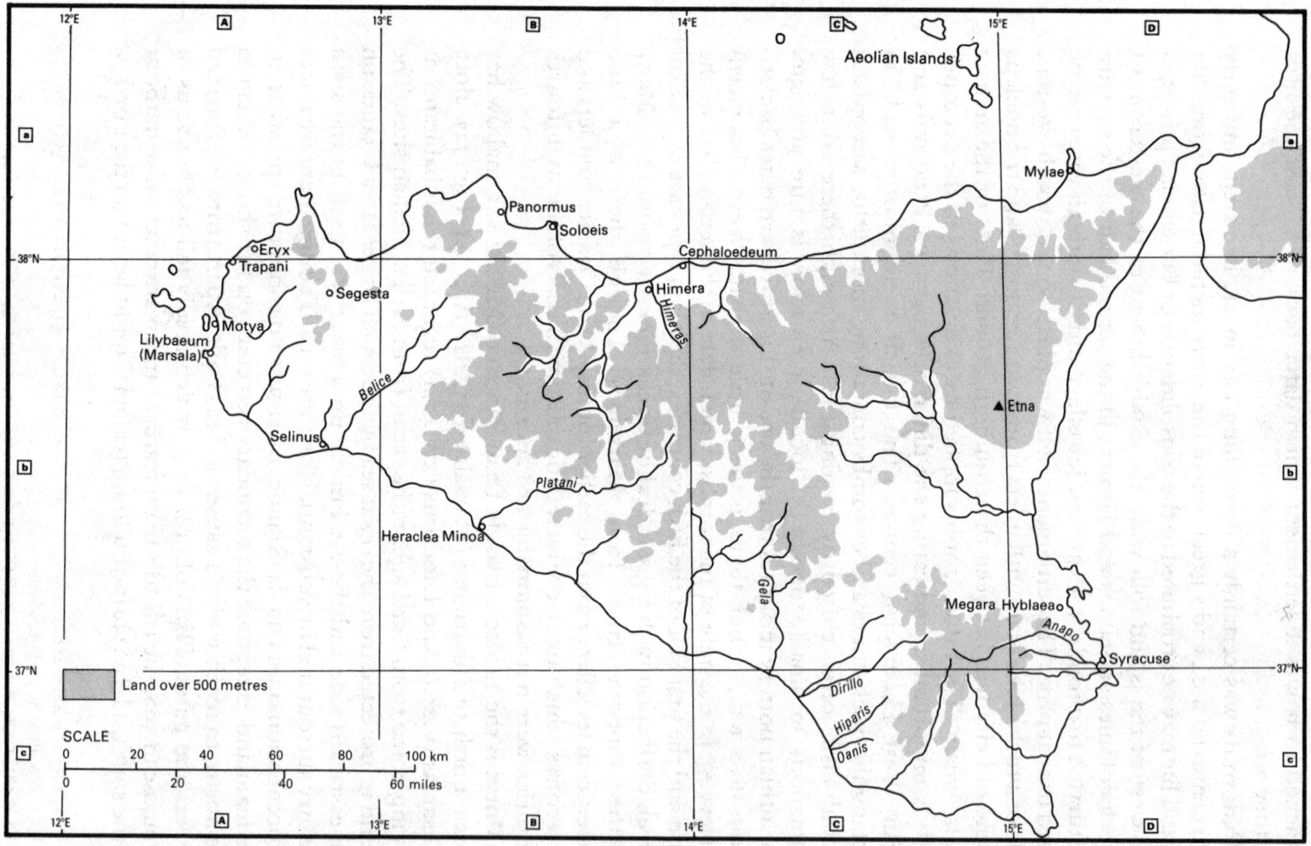

Map 8. Phoenician sites in Sicily

Places labeled on map: Mylae, Aeolian Islands, Etna, Megara Hyblaea, Anapo, Syracuse, Dirillo, Hipparis, Oanis, Gela, Cephaloedeum, Himera, Himeras, Soloeis, Panormus, Platani, Heraclea Minoa, Segesta, Selinus, Belice, Eryx, Trapani, Motya, Lilybaeum (Marsala)

SCALE

0   20   40   60   80   100 km
0   20   40   60 miles

Land over 500 metres

tophet and a cremation cemetery outside and under the northern walls. The *cothon* is puzzling; certainly in its present form it is too small (51 × 35 m) to have been an effective harbour, but it could have been a dry dock for ship-building. The Cappiddazzu[238] appears to have been a tri-cella temple with an open temenos in which votive deposits were made, and stelae were erected from archaic times. The most archaic Motyan material comes from the extensive incineration graveyard on the northern margin of the island, its pottery partly comparable to that of Tanit I and containing a great deal of imported Proto-Corinthian pottery and its imitations. These include a form of Corinthian cup identical to one found at Taranto, which according to Eusebius was founded in 706 B.C.[239] Globular aryballoi are similar to those in tombs from Phalerum (Attica) dated to the last two decades of the eighth century.[240] A stratified fragment of a Late Geometric vessel from near the monumental north gate confirms that Motya was founded in the late eighth century,[241] though the bulk of imports are between 700 and 675. Though prehistoric pottery has been found on the island, it mostly dates to well before the first millennium.[242] Hand-made cooking pots are found together with West Phoenician remains here as at Panormus,[243] but there is no indication that they are a continuum from earlier times on the island itself.[244]

Soloeis lies 20 km west of Palermo at Pizzo Cannita and was a large Hellenistic town, partly Punic in culture. A third-century B.C. coinage with the Punic legend *kphr* – Kephara, the Village – has been ascribed to it. But this was not the original foundation. Considerable remains of early Phoenician settlement appear in a graveyard at Punta di Solanto and to the south at settlement sites inland at La Cannita and Monte Porcara near the town of S. Flavia in a fertile valley; they are certainly archaic and are accompanied by Corinthian material of the seventh century.[245]

There can be little doubt that a close friendship existed between the Phoenician settlers and the indigenous Elymians of western Sicily. It was in Elymian alliance that in 415–413 B.C. the Carthaginians first made war against the Greeks, and Elymians would surely welcome the presence of an ally against the gradual Greek aggression in Sicily. The grey-slipped pottery typical of Elymian culture and characteristic of Elymian Segesta is found at Motya and at Eryx (Erice), itself an Elymian town. The large cyclopean walls at Eryx and Segesta have been thought to be Elymian in

[238] C 187 II, 7–24, IV, 7–47, VIII, 5–33; C 193, 202–5.   [239] C 187 VIII, 68, pl. 50, 2.
[240] C 1, pl. 17, 66–7; C 179, 112, fig. 6.   [241] C 184, 73.   [242] C 187 IX, 84–6.
[243] C 187 VII, pl. 58, 2; C 187 IX, figs. 3, 6, 10, pl. 7.   [244] C 184, 73.
[245] C 178, 135; C 182; C 183.

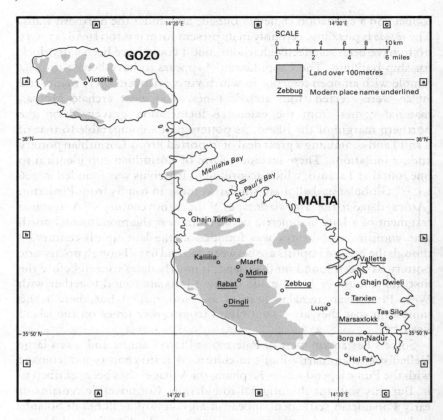

Map 9. Phoenician sites on Malta and Gozo.

origin,[246] though the later walls and gates of Eryx are more Phoenician in construction.

4. *Malta and Pantelleria*

According to Diodorus (v.12.4) Malta was colonized as part of the Phoenician trading drive towards southern Spain because of its position on the high seas. The Grand Harbour of Valletta may, however, have been unsuitable for ancient merchant ships. The main Phoenician site of the island, Tas Silg, undoubtedly on or near the renowned temple of Astarte[247] (and later of Juno), dominates the shallower Marsaxlokk Bay on the south-east corner of the island, which probably gave easier access. In the north east St Paul's Bay may have played a similar role. But the

[246] C 175; C 176.   [247] C 196.

extensive remains of Malta's Phoenician past do not suggest that it was an important Mediterranean entrepot. The carved ivory pieces and Greek imports from the sacred site of Tas Silg[248] are unusual for Phoenician Malta, which generally seems to have been out of the mainstream. After the early tomb groups, dated by a little Proto-Corinthian material and some pottery of archaic West Phoenician type, Malta's pottery follows its own pattern, diverges considerably from that of Carthage, and is scarcely touched by influences from Punic Sicily.

Few townscapes in the Mediterranean have been altered as much as Valletta: the knights and their fortifications may have removed its Phoenician past entirely, for there are no archaic tombs in its vicinity or at Msida inlet. Graveyards at Pawla, Ghajn Dwieli, Tal Liedna, Tar-xien,[249] Luqa, and Qormi[250] (within modern Valletta's outer urban fringe) begin in the late sixth century and last through to the early third. By contrast almost all earlier material is concentrated inland on the limestone ridges of Mdina and Rabat and it is here that the earliest (sixth-century) Phoenician inscription was found. The likely conclusion is that the early Phoenician urban centre was on what is the natural capital of the entire island (at Mdina-Notabile) – and indeed at one of the farthest points from any harbour, since there is none whatever on the south-west coast. There are other reasons. The structural fault which runs across the island virtually from north to south, and which uplifts the eastern part, has caused fresh-water springs there on the harder limestone, which provide some relief from Malta's notoriously bad water. Off the harder limestone ridges in the west-centre runs a network of streams such as the Wied il-Hemsija and the Wied Qlejgha, which produce a terrain of gardens. Indeed the bulk of Romano-Punic tombs are concentrated in this, as well as the earliest Phoenician tombs known in the island.[251] Besides Proto-Corinthian pottery from tombs, a little Corinthian has been found in Rabat itself.[252] After this imports drop off abruptly. Further west there are a few archaic tombs at Ghajn Tuffieha and Zebbieh, but those in the Mellieha Bay area in the furthest north west are fourth-century.[253] In fact the distribution of Phoenician tombs (of all periods) throughout both Malta and Gozo suggests a concentration of population in Rabat and a rural scatter of smallholdings and hamlets through the rest of the islands, as in Ibiza. No early habitation sites are known, but the cemeteries suggest such a large population that there is perhaps some truth in the statement of Stephanus of Byzantium that Acholla in Tunisia was a colony of Malta.[254]

[248] C 196 (1972), 77–95. [249] C 194. [250] C 197 (1964), 6.
[251] Ghajn Qajjied (C 195), Ghien Is-Sultan (C 197, 1916–17, 4; 1926, 7; 1937, 3–4; 1946, 4), Mtarfa, Ghajn Klieb, Ghien Iz-Zghir, Is-Sandar Lands (C 65, 77–8, figs. 13–4, etc.).
[252] C 198, 493–4; C 201. [253] C 203. [254] C 3, 380.

Certainly the prehistoric population was still alive, but a pale remnant of the Borg en-Nadur phase (1300–1200 B.C.). Though the shrine at Tas Silg was built into the ruins of a long abandoned megalithic temple, there is no evidence that Phoenicians took any interest in the rest of the ruined megalithic shrines in the land. But Late Bronze Age pottery from caves at Ghar Mirdum in Dingli cliffs[255] seems to represent a very late prehistoric population and finds of local pottery in the same tradition have come from Punic tombs in the Rabat area. In fact a prehistoric burial ground was in use on the small plateau of Kallilia overlooking the Wied Qlejgha in the period of Phoenician establishment in the area in the seventh/sixth centuries.

There is no archaic Phoenician ware from Gozo. It too had, in later times, an island capitol at the citadel (Il Castell) of Victoria (Rabat) in the centre of the island. Around it a lot of fourth-century pottery has been found. Gozo had a few distinctive pottery forms, rare even on Malta.

Presumably the Greeks called the island 'Melita' ('Honeyed'), first mentioned by Pseudo-Scylax in the late sixth century,[256] after Malta's Phoenician name. This is unknown, though the Punic legend *Ann* on coins of Malta issued after the Roman occupation in 218 B.C. is perhaps an alternative Phoenician or native name for the island.[257] Gozo's name, *Gaulos*, is the Greek form of the Phoenician *gûl*, a small boat, but has not been preserved in Punic inscriptions.

Malta's western neighbour Pantelleria, 200 km distant, did not enter history until the Romans captured it in the Second Punic War (in 217 B.C.), after which it issued a remarkably widespread coinage with the legend *ʾIranim*. The Romans called it Cossura. Pantelleria might have been a more important anchorage than Malta, and is more directly on the route between Carthage and the west Sicilian colonies. There are shelters for small craft on both north and south sides (Cala Scauri and Cala Cinque Denti), but the only decent port is Pantelleria harbour. The ancient acropolis (some walls still stand) was on the southern side of Pantelleria town on the hills of S. Marco and S. Teresa, 1.5 km from the harbour. Almost all the archaic material from it comes from a shrine beside the Bagno dell'Acqua,[258] a thermal pool in the north of the island. It consists mostly of figurines of female votaries, but there is a Corinthian vase. A Middle Corinthian amphoriskos in Palermo museum came from Cavallari's excavations in the Polviera cemetery on the island.[259] But the rest of the material, from various graveyards, is Maltese–Punic,[260] even though the island is closer to both Sicily and Cap Bon.

[255] C 197 (1965), 3.   [256] C 379, 94, 102.   [257] C 202.   [258] C 200, 527–33.
[259] C 200, 523–4, figs. 56, 59.   [260] C 198; C 204.

5. Sardinia

In the colonization of Sardinia the Phoenicians met a unique situation. The Bronze Age dwellers in the megalithic fortified farms called 'nuraghi' had attained a high degree of technology and wealth, were in trading relationship with Etruria, and had perhaps already in the eighth century B.C. begun to form urban clusters round nuraghic nuclei. Bronze figurines represent these early Sards as a fierce people, dour and long-faced, and equipped with metal arms and armour (see CAH II³.2, 736–42).

Ever since the discovery of bronze Cypriot-type 'bull's-hide' ingots at Serra Ilixi in south-eastern Sardinia,[261] pre-settlement contact with the Orient has been suggested; also on the grounds that the sophisticated nuraghic bronze figurines of warriors, and especially the armour they sport, derive from the Near East, or are connected with the 'Sea Peoples'.[262] There are no strict grounds for this. Though at least two 'smiting god' Canaanite-type figurines have been found in Sardinia, they are not necessarily pre-colonial, nor is the nuraghic weaponry oriental.[263] Bronze figures from Nurra and Olmeda (both Sassari district) certainly show Phoenician influence, but are not necessarily early; and claims to see Assyrian influence in the armour of figures of the Sardara group are not convincing. These proposals of a Near Eastern derivation take too little account of local west Mediterranean development of weapons, especially as shown by the Corsican menhirs. Some technical exchange in the late second millennium B.C. remains possible. Especially impressive is a bronze from Pani Loriga,[264] a metalliferous area in the south west of the island, which copies a Cypriot Late Bronze Age tripod of the type known at Tiryns in the tenth century B.C. Phoenician bronze objects, such as the thymiateria from S. Vero Milis and S. Vittoria di Serri, as well as architectural elements from inland nuraghic sites, must be discounted as evidence of pre-colonization contact, since in no case do they demonstrably predate the colonies themselves and are mostly late.[265] Nuraghic copies of Phoenician bronzes found at Santa Cristina near Paulilatino and Fluminilongu (Alghero) cannot be dated; the latter, a copy of an Egyptian sekhmet figure, could be quite late. On the other hand, two sixth-century bronze figures from Monte Sirai (see below) might show a fusion of Phoenician and nuraghic ideas.[266] Copper, lead, and probably silver were all available in ancient Sardinia and must all have been worked in proto-historic times even though actual evidence of mining is no earlier than that of the Romans.[267]

[261] C 214, 915.   [262] C 207, 17.   [263] C 214, 918.   [264] C 224.   [265] C 223, 335.
[266] C 214, 927–30, figs. 11–13.   [267] C 219.

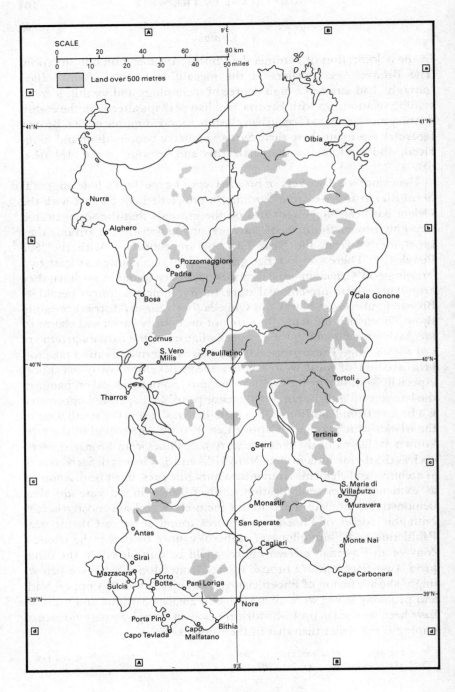

Map 10. Phoenician and Punic sites in Sardinia.

All the classical sources on Sardinia's early history are of the first century B.C. and later; and all appear to be part of a rather belated and muddled attempt to put Sardinia on the Greek mythological map. The pretence that the Greeks had founded colonies there (at Olbia and Ogryle) is no more than a Greek guess based on place names. Most attempted to people it in pre-Carthaginian times with one or more of Trojans, Libyans, Iberians, Cadmeians, Lokrians, Heracles, his companion Iolaus and Aristaeus – for example Silius Italicus XII.355–69; Pausanias x.17.1–7, 9; Solinus 1.61; IV.1. The two latter preserve the information that Nora, the oldest city, was founded by Iberians led by a certain Norax, a Tartessian. The finding of two Iberian inscriptions in Sardinia,[268] a similarity in tribal names, and likenesses between Iberian and Sard bronze weapons and figurines have been taken to support some connexion with Spain. It has also been supposed that the Norax story preserves an authentic piece of West Phoenician history. If true, the best that can be deduced is that some Tartessians may have been amongst Nora's founding fathers, for the name itself is local – *nur* is a common toponymic in Sardinia – and there is no need to bring in an eponymous founder. Apart from this episode, what classical authors preserve, including the Ionian-type name for the island, Ikhnoussa, 'The Footprint', probably results from Ionian and Athenian fifth-century commercial interest in Sardinia,[269] Tharros having provided to the local antiquarians the richest crop of Greek vases of any West Phoenician site.

The archaic inscription of the Nora stone is by far the earliest on the island (above, p. 486). Situated on a small promontory in the south-western corner of the Gulf of Cagliari, Nora is the most extensively explored town site in Sardinia. Most surviving remains are fourth-century Hellenistic.[270] The earliest tombs excavated alongside the shore at Nora by P. Nissardi (1871) contained more archaic material than the better-known graveyard excavated by Patroni,[271] but they did not provide pottery older than the late sixth century and have been compared with the Tanit II types at Carthage.

In the south, a settlement was also made before 600 B.C. at Bithia[272] on the eastern side of Cape Spartivento. Ptolemy (III.3.3) knew it as a Roman town and harbour, and although no ancient author mentions its Phoenician origin its name *Bitan* is preserved in a late Punic inscription from the Bes temple.[273] The site suits Phoenician requirements admirably.[274] The main town lay between a small inlet and the Rio di Chia, whilst Su Cardulinu, a small island in the river mouth, was chosen as the site for a tophet. There was a small walled acropolis on the headland of

[268] C 304, 651. [269] C 215, 62–6. [270] C 213. [271] C 230.
[272] C 188, 139–40; C 228 II, 142–7; C 238; C 231, 354–5. [273] C 216.
[274] C 231, 26, 231–4.

Torre di Chia, and between it and the town a temple, excavated in the 1950s, was found to contain a large number of terracotta figurines of the primitive 'snowman' type found on Motya and Ibiza,[275] and a gigantic statue of the Egyptian god Bes. The temple was certainly a late construction and the Bes statue itself, like others found in Sardinia, is of Hellenistic date; but even though nothing is known of earlier buildings, the tophet and burials beneath the Bes temple contained archaic pottery and Etruscan *bucchero* of sixth-century date. Stratum D, the lowest stratum of the necropolis[276] included cremation urns laid in dolmen-like cists; its pottery of the late seventh to mid-sixth centuries again included Etruscan ware and a local copy of an Italo-Geometric jug.[277] The iron weapons frequently buried with the urns suggest a hostile environment. In the upper levels (C–A), continuous to the first century B.C., sarcophagus burial was practised.

Much of the early colonial activity was centred round Sardinia's south west, where the richest mineral deposits occur and where also the nuraghic population was thickest. Here the main colony was Sulcis[278] (an old Sard name; Sulkoi in Pausanias (x.17.9) and *Slk* in an inscription from Antas),[279] on an island connected to the mainland by a long causeway, probably constructed in antiquity. A large bay, the Gulf of Palmas, provides safe anchorage to the north of the causeway and is itself sheltered on the north by the small island of San Pietro. On this at Carloforte was built a sanctuary of Baᶜalshamem; an inscription[280] from Cagliari preserves its name – ᵓynṣm, 'hawk island', the *hierakōn nēsos* recorded by Ptolemy (III.3.8). A smaller and even more sheltered harbour lay to the south, accessible from the northern harbour by a canal through the causeway. In fact no harbour installations have been preserved at Sulcis. Traces of an archaic city wall indicate that the Phoenician town was placed on the high ridge of Cresia hill and the Fortino to the north of the modern town of Sant'Antioco. Large graveyards of chamber tombs flank the Cresia hill and have been found in the modern Via Belvedere.[281] In the rocky area of Guardia'e in Pingiadas (the 'guardian of the urns'), about a kilometre to the north of Cresia, lies the large tophet of votive incineration graves.[282] An inscription on gold leaf from one of these is in seventh-century style,[283] and is the earliest Phoenician inscription found in context in Sardinia. Two 'Greek' ollas,[284] apparently Euboean-inspired Italian copies (*CAH* Pls. to Vol. IV, pl. 271), and a faience flask of 'Camirus' type provide further evidence that this tophet was in use early in the seventh century B.C.[285] Sulcis pottery alone in Sardinia preserves the archaic shapes and the red

---

[275] C 7, 219–23, figs. 238–41; C 240.   [276] C 220.   [277] C 212.
[278] C 188, 239–44; C 216, 93–8; C 234.   [279] C 209, 23.   [280] A 15, no. 64.
[281] C 223, 106–15.   [282] C 212.   [283] C 208.   [284] C 51, 212, fig. 521.   [285] C 237.

slip and burnish of homeland Phoenician pottery, though almost all the important pieces come from unrecorded tombs. No archaic buildings are known, but there is important evidence for later sanctuaries in the Fortino area,[286] itself probably the 'high place' of sacrifice for the early Phoenician colony, built upon nuraghic foundations. To judge from its masonry, the Carloforte temple is also archaic.

Phoenician control of the Sulcis hinterland is shown by two important sites, both policing routes from Sulcis to the plain of Cagliari. Monte Sirai,[287] a hill 4 km north west of the modern town of Carbonia, was occupied in the sixth century B.C. and became a shrine and tophet with country houses and rock-cut tombs in the neighbourhood. About 20 km to the south west, on the plain of Pani Loriga near Santadi,[288] a considerable community must have flourished, for here a rich tophet contained scores of cremation burials, some with archaic jewellery and a little late Corinthian pottery.[289] The earliest West Phoenician pottery from both these sites bears a close relation to that of Sulcis itself. In this general area, possibly at Mazzacara, was the town of Poupoulon (Ptolemy III.3.3),[290] Phoenician perhaps.

The entire stretch of the south-western coast, from Sulcis round to Bithia, seems to have invited settlement.[291] The natural harbour at Porto di Malfatano (probably Portus Herculis of the Peutinger Table) bears strong evidence of having been a Phoenician port, and the small Isola di Tuerreda offshore has yielded fourth-century Punic sherds. Inland from Porto di Teulada, at Sant'Isidoro, a definite Punic layer underlies the Roman remains. As yet, the initial date of none of these settlements is known. The fertility of the area is evident from the heavy nuraghic settlement and it appears to have been the part of Sardinia where Phoenicians existed in closest relationship with natives. The only site for which an early date is claimed lies between Porto Pino and Porto Botte on the slopes of Guardia sa Perda Fitta, where sherds of the seventh/sixth centuries B.C. have been noted in association with the type of quadrangular building characteristic of Phoenician 'keeps' throughout Sardinia. There are a number of signs of early port installations in this entire area, all of which await investigation.

The largest settlement in Sardinia was certainly that at Cagliari (Greek Karalis), at least to judge from the wide area of the modern town and its vicinity over which West Phoenician remains have been found.[292] Apart from an urban nub under the acropolis, the Castello of the modern town, much of Phoenician Cagliari was probably made up of hamlets strung around the extensive surrounding salt-water lagoons. Nothing dating before the sixth century has come from either of the two large graveyards

[286] C 225.   [287] C 2, 134; C 228.   [288] C 228 II, 142–7; III, 162–5.
[289] Unpublished.   [290] C 217, 184–6.   [291] C 228 II; C 237.   [292] C 188, 231–5.

of chamber tombs. S. Avendrace and Tuvixeddu (and especially tombs at Predio Ibba in the former)[293] have provided almost all the earlier material: the tombs at Bonaria are mostly fourth century and later. Certainly some of the Tuvixeddu tombs were wealthy; one at least had frescoes, a rare item in the West,[294] but the contents of these tombs have little of pre-fourth-century date to show for that international ambience expected of a port so admirably placed.[295] In contrast to the prevailing custom of inhumation in the chamber tombs of these graveyards, cremation urns placed in the soil in rows have been found at S. Paolo, between Tuvixeddu and the western lagoon.[296] The precise location of the port (or ports) at Cagliari remains uncertain.[297] Various sites of temples of the Late Punic period are known, for instance in the Piazza del Carmine,[298] but there is little to show of the ordinary town at any stage.

Cagliari took early steps to control her boundaries and food supply by occupying key points in the plain of the 'campidano', which stretches to the north.[299] For the peopling of this plain colonists were imported from Libya, according to Cicero (*Pro Scauro* 19.42) and Diodorus (IV.82.4). These are important references: they tell how colonization opened a better life to some.

Sardinia's western coast was dominated by the important city of Tharros,[300] one of the wealthiest cities in the entire Phoenician West. Set on a narrow basalt appendix to the marshy alluvial plain of the Sinis peninsula, between the Sardinian sea to the north and the Gulf of Oristano to the south, it was perfectly situated for controlling coastal traffic. Inland traffic went up the valleys of the Tirso and Andio rivers. Across the Campidano of Oristano the city had excellent communication with the metalliferous Iglesias region and Phoenician Sulcis. The peninsula itself was occupied by two nuraghic villages at Muru Mannu and Capo San Marco, where stood the nuraghe of Baboe Cabizzu. Initially the Phoenicians occupied only the southern end of Capo San Marco and constructed a 'rialto' and port, of which underwater installations remain on the eastern side of the cape, south and north of modern Torre Vecchia. Soon the settlement spread onto the eastern and northern slopes of the cape and the adjoining isthmus, where the graveyards and urban remains have been excavated, with the tip of the cape itself providing a natural rocky acropolis for the siting of the temple of Ashtart.[301]

[293] C 2, 128–30; C 236.   [294] Unpublished.   [295] C 2, 128.   [296] C 233, 13.
[297] C 231, 331–4.   [298] C 225.
[299] San Sperate (C 209, 29; C 216, 87), Monastir (C 209, 29; C 228, 127–43), Narbolia, and the Cuccuru Nuraxi nuraghe (C 216, 31).   [300] C 205; C 216, 102–8; C 219, 250–1; C 232.
[301] C 207.

The most archaic material, from chamber tombs dug into the rocky flanks of the Capo San Marco itself, includes jewellery of almost all known Phoenician types[302] as well as a range of terracotta figures rare in Sardinia (Pls. Vol., pls. 140a, 141b, 142a). The wealth of Tharros is chiefly shown by the rich goldwork found in its tombs, by ivories, and an abundance of amulets and gems. Etruscan *bucchero* pottery, a little Corinthian and some Italo-Corinthian wares, pieces of Etruscan armour and, at a later date, wine amphorae from Rhodes and Marseilles all amply demonstrate Tharros' commercial importance.[303] But there are no earlier imports, and West Phoenician pottery which can reasonably be dated before 600 B.C. is rare. No inscriptions are earlier than the fifth century; thus we would be left in doubt about the date of the city's origin except for material lately come from the lowest level of the tophet. This shrine lay outside the urban area proper and covered about 1,000 m². Here the cremation urns were buried partly inside the abandoned nuraghic structures of the Muru Mannu. Though this tophet has been much disturbed by later reconstructions of the fourth century, there is abundant seventh-century West Phoenician pottery in the lowest stratum.[304]

About 20 km up the coast from Tharros lay the Roman regional capital of Cornus at S. Caterina di Pitinnuri.[305] There are old records of the finding of some Punic tombs nearby at Fanne Massa and Furrighesus[306] and a few archaic pieces in museum collections are said to come from the site. But there is nothing definite about its Phoenician past and indeed there are no significant port facilities. From Bosa, further up the coast, comes a fragment of a Phoenician inscription in the archaic script of the Nora stone, giving the name as Bsˀn.[307] The site would theoretically attract settlement, for a small island, the Isola Rossa, sits in what was once the much wider estuary of the Temo river.[308] But there are no signs of Phoenician remains.

In the rest of north Sardinia Punic influence is limited and late. Olbia in the north east was the natural port for commerce with Italy.[309] Extensive graveyards in the vicinity[310] show its importance in the third/ second centuries B.C., with a few burials dating back to the fourth. There is only a handful of earlier pottery (from unknown context)[311] but enough to suggest that Olbia may have had an important place in the scheme of colonization. South of Olbia, Sardinia's eastern coast is virtually harbourless and inhospitable, but at a late stage the Carthaginians garrisoned it, building a chain of forts at Pranu de Monte Nai, S.

---

[302] C 5, figs. 104–6, 108; C 7, fig. 267.   [303] C 221.   [304] C 209, 137.
[305] C 216, 84; C 219, 251–4.   [306] C 227.   [307] C 117, 20.   [308] C 188, 254–6.
[309] C 188, 256–7.   [310] Fontana Noa, Abba Ona, Joanne Canu: C 222.
[311] C 229, 56, fig. 5.

Maria di Villaputzu, Tertinia, Tortoli, S. Giovanni di Sarala, Dorgali, and others, finishing with one near Cape Carbonara itself, on the south-eastern tip of the island.[312] None of these appears to have been built before the fourth century, and even the evidence for so high a date remains slender. However, 'archaic' Punic sherds are mentioned from the fort built into nuraghic remains at Cala Gonone (Dorgali). A watch against Rome is the obvious explanation; and this is unlikely to have been required on this coast before the Punic wars. The system was not entirely coastal, for a second line of 'forts' further inland is claimed to have stretched from Padria Possomaggiore in the north to Muravera in the south east.

We have no solution to the problem of how Sardinia was colonized, whether from Carthage or the homeland. Sardinia's main Phoenician settlements kept names derived from the pre-Latin Mediterranean sub-stratum;[313] none is demonstrably Semitic. From such evidence as there is, the Phoenicians in Sardinia were a fringe: forts certainly point to a control of the inland, but the cultural impact, though it existed, was not great. Punic cults had a late effect on nuraghic centres like Paulilatino and Terresen di Narcao, the latter particularly impressive with its Punic terracottas and urns of burnt sacrifices;[314] but we can say nothing of how the Phoenician settlements in their sixth/fifth-century heyday affected the native Sards; nothing of how and why their nuraghic culture declined.

6. The Spanish peninsula

It was most likely the quest for metals which brought the Phoenicians to Spain. The Greeks had been greatly impressed by the cargo of silver brought back by a Samian explorer, Colaeus, from the kingdom of Arganthonius of Tartessus in about 630 B.C.[315] Strabo (III.2.14) and Pliny amongst others inform us of the later Phoenician monopoly of the Spanish mines. The pyrite lodes which lie in the slates south of the Sierra Morena and north of the Andalusian plain have been an important source of copper in modern times. Besides copper they provide silver, lead, tin, and mercury.[316] Many of the metalliferous sites can be approached through the watershed of the Guadalquivir, or further west by the less hospitable Guadiana. Between these two rivers lie two minor ones, the Odiel and Río Tinto, which converge and flow into the sea in a large estuary at Huelva, the Onuba Aestuaria of Roman times. Both rivers rise in the pyrite deposits themselves and give closest access to

---

312 C 209, 24; C 228 IV, 105–21.   313 C 218.   314 C 209, 128.
315 C 3, 387; C 271; *CAH* III².3, 20, 139, 214.   316 C 29, 112; C 241; C 285.

them: their waters are in fact discoloured by dissolved iron salts and oxides. The Phoenician interest in Iberia's metals was certainly encouraged by the navigability of these rivers. Boats today can still ascend the Guadalquivir some 85 km to Seville, and the Tagus is navigable some 190 km from its mouth; even the Guadiana, the least important of the rivers of the Atlantic shore, is navigable to 50 km inland. Indeed the distribution map of Phoenician bronze and silver jugs[317] and other metal objects found in Spain and Portugal strongly suggests a major thrust of Phoenician interests by way of the Atlantic rivers. Lodes at the head of the Guadalquivir, especially those at Linares,[318] were more economically reached by an overland route from the south-eastern coast of Spain, and it was in this region that in 1906 L. Siret first discovered evidence for the Phoenician mining of a silver lode at Herrerias, 20 km up the Río Almanzora and near the modern lead mines of the Sierra Almagrera.[319] But the finds from the nearby settlement at Villaricos[320] do not predate the sixth century B.C., and although there is now much important evidence for Phoenician settlement about 700 B.C. in the Málaga region, it is only from the Huelva mines that precise evidence of Phoenician mining at the earlier date has come.

Of silver the Phoenicians in Spain appear to have had a plentiful supply for making silver jugs and other luxury objects, such as an omphalos bowl from Cástulo (Jaén).[321] Furthermore, the early graves at Carthage, Motya, and Tharros have produced small silver ornaments in impressive numbers when compared with grave-goods in contemporary Greece or Palestine; and not only small items, for a silver patera and bowl are recorded from Carthage tombs.[322] In Etruria some of the more impressive silver objects are Phoenician imports or have a Phoenician style about them – all of which leaves no doubt of Phoenician access to a Western source of silver.

But there is a further and most important index of Spain's wealth. Large numbers of stelae (Fig. 25),[323] either carved or engraved with representations of metal objects, have been found in the south and south-western part of the peninsula, the carved ones concentrated in the Algarve province of southern Portugal (exactly the area which has yielded a crop of inscriptions in 'Tartessian' script), the engraved ones concentrated in Cácares and adjoining provinces, together with outliers in the Castelo Branco region of Portugal, and Algarve. There is also a scatter in the Guadalquivir valley.

The importance of this second type lies in the objects depicted – carts and chariots, swords, helmets, spears, combs, mirrors, and, more significantly, fibulae and shields of types known in East Mediterranean

[317] C 273, map 1.   [318] C 347.   [319] C 347.   [320] C 260.
[321] C 268, 58–60, fig. 18.   [322] C 142, 444.   [323] C 244; C 276, map 323; C 341, 168–71.

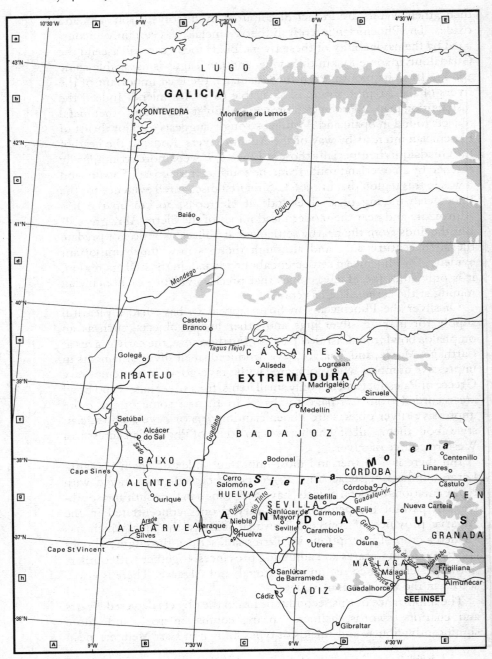

Map 11. Phoenician and Punic sites in Spain.

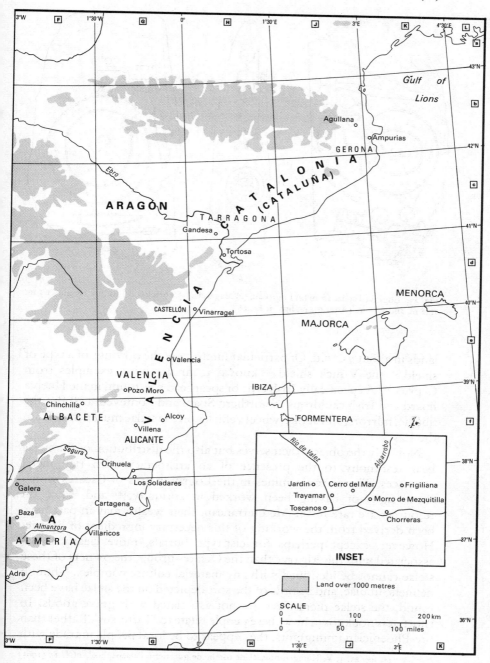

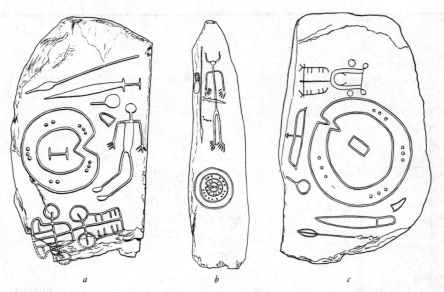

Fig. 25. Engraved stelae from (*a*) Logrosan, (*b*) Magacela, (*c*) Torrejón del Rubio. Heights 1.3 m, 1.42 m, and 1.17 m. (After C 244, figs. 2, 24, 26.)

lands in about 750 B.C. Of particular interest are the carvings of a type of shield – the V-nick shield – known from surviving examples from Cyprus.[324] A specifically Irish type of spearhead was found in the Huelva hoard and Irish cauldrons in northern Spain and Pontevedra.[325] But the fibulae, mirrors, and spoke-wheel vehicles on the stelae must derive from the East.

Not only the objects themselves but also the distribution of the stelae bear testimony to the presence of an aristocracy with rich metal resources. There are tin mines in the Logrosan area of Cácares which show signs of having been worked in antiquity,[326] and, since tin resources are rare in the Mediterranean, their wealth may in part have been derived from the working of this necessary ingredient of bronze. However, except perhaps for cist-type burials, more clearly to be associated with the Algarve than the Cácares group, the owners of these stelae cannot be identified with any material culture complex. Though helmets, fibulae, and swords of the sort depicted on the stelae have been found, the stelae themselves are not associated with grave-goods. In short, it is not known how these people relate to 'Tartessus'. Rather than pre-Phoenician immigrants, they appear to be local people in trade with

[324] C 74A, fig. 23, 3; V. Karageorghis, 'Une tombe de guerrier à Palaepaphos', *BCH* 87 (1963) 265–300.   [325] C 247; C 276, 294; C 292.   [326] C 243, 206; C 273, 49, 393.

the east Mediterranean, perhaps with both Phoenicians and Ionian Greeks. Equally they had contacts with north-west Europe. Quite likely they were the ethnic basis of the Tartessians themselves.

That foreign merchants or metalsmiths were active in southern Spain about 800 B.C. is demonstrated by a hoard of bronze swords and fibulae dredged from the estuary of Huelva.[327] In it was the Irish spearhead mentioned above. Slightly earlier than this hoard is the spectacular treasure discovered at Villena (Alicante province),[328] consisting of gold and silver copies of Late Bronze Age bowls and flasks of the post-Argar cultures of the south-western peninsula. Some iron pieces in the treasure suggest that it was precious and still rare, preceding its use for weapons in Spain in the eighth century B.C. The total absence of Phoenician influence, together with the fact that the gold itself contains tin and is therefore of Galician origin, whilst the techniques are a mixture taken both from northern and south-eastern regions, is ample testimony to the sophistication of local metallurgy. Phoenician influence is also absent from a whole group of goldwork such as the treasure of Bodonal (Badajoz), which links Spain with Ireland through the trade routes of the 'Atlantic Bronze Age'.[329] But the metal trade between Spain and the north, which may have included Cornish tin, was over before Phoenicians demonstrably became actively involved in manufacturing metal objects in Spain, though there remains the possibility that the legendary voyages of Phoenicians to the 'tin islands' (Oestrymnides)[330] in the Atlantic were prospections of the resources used by this established exchange system in about 750 B.C.

Direct Phoenician contact with places in the north Atlantic rests primarily on the text of Festus Avienus' *Ora Maritima*, a romantic geographic work in verse composed in the fourth century A.D. but acknowledgedly based upon a logbook of the Carthaginian Himilco, probably a near contemporary of Hanno[331] in the sixth century B.C. Himilco had visited a promontory or islands called Oestrymnides, perhaps Brittany or Cornwall or islands adjacent, probably as part of a Carthaginian exploration of import routes already well known to the merchants of Tartessus, who may also have obtained tin from the river valleys of Galicia. Strabo (III.5.11) places 'tin islands' (Cassiterides) north west of the Galician coast, at a little distance, but it is likely that in the time of their exploration in the first century B.C. to which he refers, the true location of the areas from which the Tartessians obtained tin was no longer strictly known. Meanwhile Pytheas of Marseilles (in Diodorus v.22), exploring in the fourth century B.C., expressly mentions the mining of tin in Cornwall (Belerium), though in his day it was shipped across to Gaul and passed overland to Marseilles.

---

[327] C 274. [328] C 345. [329] C 247. [330] C 310, 83. [331] C 312, 95–107.

The discovery of the Spanish peninsula as a source of metals probably came about through contact with local metal-using cultures and not through original prospecting on the part of the Phoenicians. Quite possibly a period of trading in metals preceded direct Phoenician involvement in mining, in turn leading to more extensive settlement. The Cácares stelae as well as the Huelva hoard imply a pre-Phoenician wealth in metals, but more importantly recent archaeology has shown that in the Huelva region and much of the Guadalquivir basin Phoenician wheel-made pottery is stratigraphically preceded by a new upsurge in hand-made ceramics, producing a new style called 'cerámica a reticula bruñida',[332] 'pattern-burnished' or 'stroke-burnished' ware, in which network patterns are made, sometimes well indented and differing in colour from the surface of the pot. Whatever its origin – and there is nothing to suggest that it is intrusive – it certainly implies a dramatic rise in the local standard of living before the proper establishment of the Phoenicians.

This pattern-burnished pottery has two main areas of concentration, one centring on the Guadalquivir, the other on the lower Tagus, though stylistic differences exist between the two regions.[333] Its distribution indicates a population more orientated to the coast than the locally evolved Late Bronze Age population moving southwards from the Meseta. Its date is stratigraphically controlled to the period of the tenth–seventh centuries B.C. Both its shape and pattern-burnish technique were evolved in Spain, though not demonstrably in the areas of its later concentration. The burnishing technique possibly derives from pottery of the El Argar culture, though indeed burnishing has recently been shown to have been used in about 2000 B.C. on the little known Early Bronze Age pottery of Andalusia.[334]

An association between pattern-burnished ware and the engraved stelae has not been demonstrated, though there are some suggestive juxtapositions. For instance, a stela engraved with a U-nick shield at Sanlúcar de Mayor (Seville prov.) stands near the pattern-burnished ware site of Torres Alcoaz.[335] The stelae are most common in Extremadura, between the Tagus and the Guadiana, less numerous south of the Guadiana and uncommon in the Guadalquivir basin.

Besides metals there were undoubtedly many perishable resources which drew the Phoenicians to the Spanish peninsula: among these timber deserves special consideration.[336] Not only was timber abundant, but it was accessible for river and sea floatage. Certainly in Roman times the Turdetanian ports were well known for their large ships and naval timbers.[337] Esparto grass, the kinds of which grew on the Alicante coast,

[332] C 274, 13–17, pls. 22–7; C 282, 99; C 281, 599–607; C 337, 8–9; C 341, 168–77; C 349, 104–6.
[333] C 337, 8–9.   [334] C 336, 86.   [335] C 328.   [336] C 314.   [337] C 314, 75.

was not an inconsiderable resource for an economy involving much
package, wrapping, and ships' dunnage (Livy XXVI.47.9; Pliny XIX.
7–8.26–30).

Tartessus and Tartessian culture The problem as to whether the southern
Iberian kingdom of Tartessus was the Biblical Tarshish is much
debated.[338] The equation of the name with Tarsus is often suggested.[339]
Phoenicians were certainly established in this area in some way, as the
Phoenician translation on the Hittite hieroglyphic inscription of Azatiwatas at Karatepe bears witness.[340] But the only extra-Biblical literary
reference is in a text of Esarhaddon, who boasts that 'the kings of the
middle of the sea, the land of Yaman and the land of Tarsisi' had
submitted at his feet.[341] This would certainly have little point if only
Tarsus were intended, since the Syro-Cilician region had long been
subject to the Assyrians; the 'kings of the middle of the sea', Yaman –
and Tarsisi – had not.

In the Bible Tarshish and Tyre have an especially close link. Isaiah
(23:1) describes the ships of Tarshish learning of the fall of Tyre as they
put into Kittim (Citium) on their return journey.[342] This situation
suggests rather ships returning from the west Mediterranean than from
Tarsus. However, the name Tarshish, if, as is suggested, it is derived
from a function (from *rashashu*, Akkadian 'to be smelted', meaning
therefore smelting plant),[343] may well have moved about the map as
Phoenician trade explored ever further westwards; at one stage nearby
ports like Tarsus may well have been designated, but by the time of
Isaiah and Ezekiel something further west is implied. Equally 'ships of
Tarshish', meaning simply 'refinery ships', plied many waters, but the
text of II Chron. 20:36 in which ships leave ʿAqaba for Tarshish (in the
direction therefore of the Arabian Gulf and India) is corrupt and should
be corrected by the parallel text in I Kings 22:48.

The reading of *tršš* for Tarshish on the Nora stone from Sardinia, the
earliest Phoenician inscription in the West Mediterranean, is not at all
certain[344] though widely accepted, mostly as referring to some general
region of the West. Basically the problem of Tarshish is not one of
locality, but rather of understanding of the geographical notions of the
Semites. In the Bible tin and silver feature largely in cargoes from
Tarshish, making clear that metal was an important item in its trade. The
philological equation of Tarshish and Tartessus is difficult to make,
especially if at the root of the Greek word lies the Iberian 'Turta' from

---

338 C 350. See *CAH* III².3, 20–1.   339 C 3, 335–6, 339–40; C 21, 286.
340 C 36, 137–9.   341 A 234, 86 §57, 10f.   342 C 21, 250.   343 C 117, 21–2.
344 A 15, no. 46.

which the later Greek geographers took the term 'Turdetania' to refer to south-eastern Spain.[345]

Festus Avienus is again our main source for the early history of the kingdom of Tartessus[346] (*Ora* 85; 267–70; *Desc.* 610–17). Unfortunately, like many other Roman authors, he confused Tartessus with Cadiz, though his source, Himilco the Carthaginian explorer, certainly cannot be held responsible for this equation. The earliest reference to it by a historian other than Avienus' source is that of Ephorus (405–340 B.C., in Scymnus 162–8), who places Tartessus two days' sail beyond the Pillars of Hercules and calls it a city and an emporium exporting river-borne tin from 'Celtic parts'. The poet Stesichorus (frag. 4 in Strabo III.2.11) refers to the silver-rooted springs of the river Tartessus, and Pausanias too (VI.19.3), probably using Ephorus, speaks of a Tartessus river debouching into the sea, having two mouths with the city of Tartessus in between them. Avienus' source also knew of an island of Tartessus as well as a bay, a river, and mountain of that name, and although he thought it was Cádiz, and Pausanias identified the Tartessus river with the Betis (Guadalquivir), the largest and best known Spanish river in his time, all in all the conditions described fit the site of Huelva better than any other region, and modern scholarship has relied heavily upon Ephorus' statement about its distance past Cádiz in arguing for this identification.[347] Huelva is situated between the Odiel and Río Tinto, and although not an island, its promontory-like situation might well have been confused for one. Also the island of Saltés in the bay itself, or at least a former island of which the present is a remnant, might also have added to the concept that the Tartessus river had an island in its mouth. No comparable site can be located at the mouth of the Guadalquivir or in the Coto de Doñana where the site of Tartessus has long been sought.[348]

Working the term 'Tartessus' into the present archaeological context in the Spanish peninsula is problematical. Is the term to be equated with the local Late Bronze Age, in which some scholars would see some Oriental inspiration anyway, either in the stelae or pattern-burnished ware or both, though essentially they are autochthonous developments?[349] Or should Tartessus be equated with the mixed material culture engendered from that local base by Phoenician and probably some Ionian influence, and developing eventually a style and dynamic of its own at a time when it first became known to our written sources of information? It seems preferable to adopt the latter sense, especially since present evidence shows that the combination of elements typical of the latter period belonged to a very expansive culture established and

[345] C 3, 190.   [346] C 271, 31.   [347] C 271, 93; C 304, 252–3.
[348] C 273, 226–32; C 304, 296.   [349] C 283, 181–4.

growing in the Guadalquivir valley and Jaen, whereas in Huelva and the Ourique and Tagus regions the Late Bronze Age complex had little posterior development. Furthermore, though standard West Phoenician pottery was both imported and made in the trading colonies Phoenicians established, it soon developed a far-west Mediterranean style, for which the most suitable term is 'Tartessian'.

The local hand-made wares can be sharply distinguished from West Phoenician wheel-made wares and their Tartessian derivatives. A whole group of the former is in the tradition of red-slip ware of the Phoenician homeland, which developed a distinct facies in Spain (*cerámica a barniz rojo*)[350] and which was maintained until about 400 B.C. But especially characteristic of Tartessian style is the use of reserved bands in the slip, often edged with painted black lines and closely set, a style known in Phoenicia and Carthage[351] but rare there. Other Phoenician-derived pottery in Spain is decorated with 'polychrome' horizontal painted bands in red, black, and various purplish browns.[352] This 'Tartessian' Phoenician pottery group has close connexions with that of Rachgoun,[353] Mogador,[354] and nearer sites in Morocco, which may be expected to have had close trade links with Tartessus.

Two further pottery types characterize the Tartessian repertoire – both of unknown inspiration. One is of a light brown fabric with a fussy 'geometric' decoration in brown or dark red paint, finely executed with patterns closely set, often in metopes.[355] It has been found in the Huelva region and in the Late Bronze Age tholos at Nora Vehla in Ourique, but the finest specimens come from El Carambolo[356] and Alcores in the Guadalquivir valley with some from Mesas de Asta (Jerez). The second ware is a grey or black burnished ware (sometimes brown), hard-fired, mostly wheel-made, and largely contemporary with the earliest Phoenician imports.[357] The excavations at Medellín (Badajoz)[358] have shown it to have a heavy concentration there and in Extremadura. Overall the repertoire is distinctive and dull, consisting almost entirely of shallow dishes and plates without decoration; and although this 'grey ware', like *cerámica a barniz rojo*, spread northwards into the Iberian and Greek regions of the north-east peninsula, it has no demonstrable relationship with the 'Phocaean grey ware' of southern colonial France and lacks both its enclosed forms and wavy-line and ribbed decorations.[359]

Quite different and truly Oriental is a polychrome painted ware with

[350] C 242, 207–8; C 273, 286–97, figs. 14–18; C 282, 101; C 281, 553–9; C 327, 122 pls. 49–53.
[351] C 41, figs. 103, 106; C 48, pl. 7, 3; C 93, fig. 48, 6.
[352] C 261, pl. 3; C 264, 174–9; C 278, figs. 111, 193; C 282, 385, figs. 543–4; C 326, 72–3, pls. 1–6.
[353] C 173, 64–5, figs. 20, 22.   [354] C 378, fig. 89b.
[355] C 273, 298–305, figs. 28–32, 53.   [356] C 283; C 341, 60.   [357] C 266; C 282, 96.
[358] C 245, 95–102.   [359] C 266; C 359, 153–7.

figurative designs in panels: lotuses, palmettes, and griffins on Andalusian pieces, all straight from Phoenician art. At Medellín, from which most of the pieces come, the style is more local and primitive, though the layout and colours, sometimes faintly reminiscent of Cypriot Bichrome IV–V pottery, are equally of Oriental inspiration, perhaps taken from embroidered fabrics. Its distribution is as yet restricted but gives a new insight into Orientalism in Spain.[360]

To Tartessian culture we can also ascribe certain groups of tumulus burials in which both inhumation and cremation were practised and which are all associated with one or more of the pottery types described above. Whilst these tumuli all have clear trade and cultural connexions with the Phoenician settlements on the coast and belong to a culture heavily influenced by this contact, the mixed burial rite is perhaps as much due to influences coming from Hallstatt Europe as from Phoenicia; and the dead may be Indo-Europeans, not Semites. Although in fact the introduction of iron-working itself may have been due to Phoenician stimuli, the tools and weapons found with the burials are either European or local types. These include socketed spear-heads and pikes of bronze, prong-and-hook belt-clasps,[361] hooked knives, and fibulae of double-spring and annular types.[362] While certainly the double-spring fibulae follow Oriental or Aegean prototypes – one has been found at Ischia –[363] their precise type is local to Spain and southern France, and like the belt-clasps which have no foreign equivalent, must be taken for Tartessian developments.

The Huelva region On the one site where we have direct evidence for Phoenician involvement in silver mining, the bulk of the work appears to have been in native hands. Most of the pottery found in the Cerro Salomón village[364] in the western Sierra Morena is rough hand-made ware of the Late Bronze Age of central Spain, but lamps, tripod bowls, and other vessels of distinctive Phoenician type as well as West Phoenician storage jars suggest that the management was in Phoenician hands. The evidence for smelting[365] comes from the tuyères used for the nozzles of the bellows and from the stone hammers used in working the mine trenches.

Other evidence for silver mining comes from the lower levels of the well stratified site of Cabezo de San Pedro, which dominates the confluence of the rivers Tinto and Odiel within modern Huelva.[366] The sequence established by the most recent excavations is: Phase I, eighth/

---

[360] C 245; C 250, 42–69; C 335.

[361] C 278, 151–2, figs. 9–13, 269, fig. 69, 278–9, figs. 91–101; C 304, fig. 411. Much remains unpublished.   [362] C 278, fig. 96; C 304, fig. 411.   [363] C 322, 297.

[364] C 269, nos. 10, 46, 47, 114, 366, pls. 17, 21.   [365] C 269, 14.   [366] C 274; C 276.

ninth-seventh centuries with pattern-burnished wares predominant: Phase II, 700–625 B.C. with red-slip wares appearing: Phase III, 650–550 B.C. with Tartessian reserve slip and polychrome band prominent.[367] From this site, but unfortunately unstratified, comes a fragment of an Attic Late Geometric I amphora dating from the first half of the eighth century and at present the earliest known Greek object in Spain.[368] Crucibles and slags show that here a local populace using pattern-burnished wares and established in about 900 B.C. was working silver from nearby mines for well over a century before the arrival of the Phoenicians, whose characteristic pottery appears in later levels dating to the seventh and sixth centuries B.C. Similar evidence has been provided by a sounding made at Cerro de Esperanza,[369] again within Huelva, though here most of the scoriae come from levels containing a considerable amount of West Phoenician pottery, but pattern-burnished and other local wares are present in the lowest levels. A Phoenician graffito on a jar is in letters of the seventh century.[370] But again there is no doubt that the settlement was pre-Phoenician, and much the same pattern emerges from excavations at Aljaraque and La Rabida south west of the city,[371] and on the Río Tinto.[372] At El Palmarón, 2 km north east of Niebla, was found a rich tomb containing a silver brazier and a bronze piriform jug together with iron weapons.[373]

The El Palmarón tomb was the foretaste of the chief evidence for the Oriental impact in Huelva: the twenty tombs explored in the La Joya[374] park area of the city itself. They possibly belonged to the settlement on Cabezo de San Pedro. At La Joya rectangular tombs contained both inhumation and cremation burials (sometimes together), accompanied by jewellery and other exotic luxury items of Phoenician origin or inspiration. These included an incense stand, engraved ivory, a gold mounted amber pendant,[375] a comb, and a flat metal brazier decorated with lotuses and Egyptianizing Hathor heads.[376] Tomb 17 contained fittings for a chariot or cart, including two bronze lion heads which were probably originally attached to the chariot body.[377] In contrast to this finery, a large amount of pottery from the La Joya tombs (apart from a few West Phoenician amphorae) is hand-made and poor, including much late pattern-burnished ware. A few items which can be dated, such as the Rhodian bronze jug from Tomb 5,[378] suggest a date of about 500 B.C. for some of the tombs, but individual burials, including one with a scarab of Psammetichus II, may be almost a century earlier. The foetal position of some of the skeletons as well as the local pottery suggest that the dead

[367] C 275, 156–77.   [368] C 295, 55–6.   [369] C 276, 330–1.   [370] C 297.
[371] C 27.   [372] C 292.   [373] C 332.   [374] C 305; C 306; C 307.   [375] C 242, 254.
[376] C 306, 28–30, pls. 16–17.   [377] C 273, pl. 149.   [378] C 306, 23–8, pls. 13–15.

belonged to the indigenous population, or people of mixed blood, rather than of pure Phoenician stock.

The Málaga coast It is from the coast of the Málaga region that the archaeological evidence for the earliest Phoenician settlement has come. The main sites are the settlements of Toscanos and Alarcón[379] on the west bank of the Río de Velez together with the graveyards of Cerro del Mar at nearby Casa de la Viña on the east bank (early)[380] and Jardín[381] on the west (later); settlements at Morro de Mezquitilla[382] and Chorreras on the eastern side of the Río Algarrobo estuary,[383] together with the necropolis of Trayamar on its west.[384] Since antiquity these two rivers have cut down their beds and no longer have the spreading estuaries on whose bluffs the Phoenicians settled. Morro de Mezquitilla BI/II, the short-lived site of Chorreras and Toscanos I/II were probably founded before 700 B.C., and quite possibly nearer to 800 B.C. At least this is a stratigraphic possibility, the hard evidence of imported datable Greek pottery not extending earlier than 720 B.C.[385]

To this clutch of sites must be linked a somewhat later (seventh-century) one on the western side of Málaga at the mouth of the Rio Guadalhorce,[386] and eastwards some tombs on the shore at Almuñécar in the province of Granada.[387] Also eastwards, at Frigiliana, inland from Nerja, a yard of incineration graves has been explored at Cortijo de las Sombras,[388] belonging to an unknown settlement. Its pottery is of the greatest importance for its external links with Carmona, Rachgoun, and Mogador and fibulae and belt-clasps found with the burials date it quite firmly to the seventh century.

All these sites are characterized by Phoenician red-slip band-painted and plain wares, mostly dishes and plates in large numbers but with a few lamps and 'oil-bottles'[389] of forms current before 600 B.C. Though red-slip jugs and mushroom-mouth flasks are rare, excellent specimens of East Phoenician type were found in one of the four carefully built chamber tombs at Trayamar.[390] From Cerro del Mar at Casa de la Viña, between the mouths of the Velez and Algarrobo rivers, two very archaic vessels[391] of Phoenician red-slip ware are known. Archaic red-slip is also a feature of the well-like tombs in the Cerro de San Cristóbal area of Almuñécar (Granada), whose discovery in 1955 marked a renaissance of study on Phoenician Spain.[392] Though neither well constructed nor wealthy, two Proto-Corinthian cups from Tomb 7 establish a date for them in the first quarter of the seventh century B.C. In this and neighbouring tombs the ashes of the dead were buried in

[379] C 326; C 327.   [380] C 344.   [381] C 342.   [382] C 343.
[383] C 263; C 265; C 323.   [384] C 327.   [385] C 295, 57; C 325, 91, pl. 24.
[386] C 255; C 256.   [387] C 273, pls. 76–85; C 289; C 329.   [388] C 257.   [389] C 327.
[390] C 327, 122, pls. 48, 49, 51, 53.   [391] C 246.   [392] C 273, pls. 64–5.

alabaster vessels bearing Egyptian hieroglyphic inscriptions of pharaohs of the Twenty-second Dynasty, the latest being Takeloth II, who reigned in the mid-ninth century B.C.[393] Certainly the burials are not as early as these pharaohs and in fact no really satisfactory explanation has been given of the occurrence of these and other inscribed alabaster jars in Spain. Similar uninscribed alabaster jars have been found in Carthage tombs, at Motya,[394] and one at Tyre.[395] A further alabaster jar from Almuñécar, not from one of the excavated tombs, bears the name of the Hyksos ruler Apophis,[396] which supports the suggestion that these jars are ancient fake antiques.

The purpose of these closely sited settlements is far from clear.[397] A large building in drafted ashlar masonry at Toscanos appears to have been a storehouse and contained a large proportion of imported ware, as distinct from ware made in local clays from elsewhere on the site. Certainly they may be regarded as distribution and export centres of some kind: the names 'emporia' and 'Faktorei' are applied to them by the excavators. Direct evidence of metal smelting is lacking and their main involvement might thus have been in agricultural produce. It is an old suggestion that either Cerro del Mar or Almuñécar was the Greek Maenace, and the evidence for the participation of Greek traders in this Phoenician venture – plus the subsequent vagueness of Greek geographers as to where Maenace was – may contribute to this suggestion.[398]

At Guadalhorce are the remains of a large rectangular building like that at Toscanos and an abundance of polychrome and red ware, but from the surface from level IV, which dates well after the construction of the major building, come sherds of Attic or East Greek cups which can be plausibly dated to 580–540 B.C. The site has also yielded part of an unstratified SOS amphora, which would place Greek contact back in the seventh century, and fragments of Etruscan *bucchero*, the earliest in Spain. A Phoenician inscription on a dish and an Egyptian scarab of the Saite period also confirm that Guadalhorce was occupied in the seventh century B.C.[399]

The necropolis at Jardín[400] belongs to the sixth-to-fourth centuries B.C., according to carbon-14 dates. Extended burials in cist graves, a scarab of Pedubast and pottery[401] that more resembles that of Tharros and Utica make these tomb groups important, representing a poorly known period of Phoenician activity on the coast. Quite clearly the heyday of the Phoenician Málaga settlements was over by 600 B.C. and only two foundations in the area lived long enough to issue Punic coinages, when the remnants of Phoenician populations were revived by later Carthaginian settlers and by the Carthaginian conquest of Spain under the Barcids in 230 B.C. One of these towns was Sexi, at Almuñécar, the other Adra.[402]

Quite possibly Villaricos at the mouth of the Almanzora river (Almeria) was the easternmost and latest of an important group of sites on the southern coast of Spain centred on Málaga. Close by at Baria and Herrerias the settlers operated silver mines. The excavations there produced abundant material of the fifth century.[403] Further east a group of graves at the site of Sierra del Molar at the mouth of the Segura river in the province of Alicante contained Iberian pottery and some Punic,[404] but the earliest burial urns are difficult to date; a globular aryballos of faience is of a type current in the sixth century and two Attic bell craters are of late fifth-century style, but it would be reasonable to suppose the existence of a Phoenician factory somewhere in this area as a source of supply for the late seventh-century West Phoenician ware reaching Los Soladares further up the Segura.[405] In any case the material from Sierra del Molar appears earlier than the date of the Barcid foundations on this part of the coast, including Carthagena in 230 B.C. Certainly earlier than this is the evidence from the other direction. From Gorham's Cave high in the Rock of Gibraltar come sherds and scarabs left by local residents or chance visitors over a long period.[406] Some of the scarabs appear to be seventh-century types.[407]

The Guadalquivir basin   By contrast with the slender agricultural basis of the sites around Huelva, whose economy appears to have been dependent to a large extent on hunting and gathering, the wide valley drained by the Guadalquivir offered opportunities for olive and cereal cultivation.[408] At the same time the river gave access to important mineral deposits in the upper valley of the Guadalimar, at Linares, La Carolina, Viches, and Centenillo in the province of Jaén.

Although nothing is known of it archaeologically, Seville itself had a Tartessian past. Sherds from the Cuesta del Rosario site within the old city certainly show this; but at Carambolo by the Guadalquivir just outside Seville, excavation subsequent to the finding of a treasure of gold jewellery in 1958 has uncovered a *poblado*, whose lowest levels have provided some of the best red-slip Phoenician pottery in Spain, together with much pattern-burnished and polychrome linear wares.[409] Carambolo proves that Phoenicians were plying the Guadal-

---

[402] C 294.   [403] C 260; C 347.   [404] C 311, 7–20.   [405] C 259.
[406] C 302, 66–73.   [407] C 302, 69.   [408] C 333.   [409] C 281, 330–1.

quivir by 700 B.C., and even before if we accept the eighth-century date for a Phoenician inscription on a bronze figure of Astarte said to come from Carambolo or elsewhere around Seville.[410]

Sixty-five tumulus burials in the region of the Roman town of Carmona near Seville have, since their excavation in the late nineteenth century, been a much-debated source for our knowledge of Phoenician Spain.[411] They are situated on an escarpment overlooking the Guadalquivir river flats. Both inhumations and cremations, single or multiple, were buried under these tumuli, placed either in simple rock-cut trenches or rough stone cists. The cremated bones were often deposited in urns, but it seems likely that some of the mounds had been heaped over the cremation pyres. The pottery recovered represents the full Tartessian range, including grey ware. A silver fibula from Acebuchal tumulus G[412] has analogies in early graves at Carthage[413] and is typologically earlier than a double-spring fibula from Los Alcores. The general dating of the tumuli therefore must lie in the seventh and early sixth centuries. There are pre-Roman strata in Carmona itself[414] which have produced pottery from level IV of the four main types represented in the tumuli – red-slipped, pattern-burnished, polychrome-banded and grey wares.

Bone combs and ivory articles with incised decorations from these tumuli (Pls. Vol., pl. 143)[415] as well as from others at Osuna and Setefilla[416] can be paralleled by pieces in the seventh-century well deposit on the Greek island of Samos,[417] and indeed there is a similar comb from a contemporary tomb at Carthage.[418] These, together with a few other ivories from Carthage and Tharros, are enough to establish the existence of ivory workshops in the West, for similar pieces are unknown in the Levant. But parts of two very large carved open-work ivory cosmetic trays from Carmona tumuli,[419] though typologically derived from Phoenician ivories, have no parallel in style and open the possibility (since ivory is rare at Carthage and combs common in Spain)[420] that the 'West Phoenician' ivory-carving tradition was in fact Tartessian. It is quite clear that the Carmona ivories represent an individual Western tradition. Ivory hand-shaped amulets found with the rest at Carmona are purely West Phoenician,[421] and the decorative dark blue staining on some of the items is unknown in the East.

A further set of tumuli comparable to those at Carmona has been excavated at Setefilla (Seville province).[422] They were erected over either simple earth graves or built rectangular tombs containing both

[410] C 334.   [411] C 278.   [412] C 278.   [413] C 346.   [414] C 282, 96–103.   [415] C 279.
[416] C 261; C 262.   [417] C 300.   [418] C 4 II, 281, figs. 32–7, pl. 74, 3, 5.   [419] C 309.
[420] C 299.   [421] C 279.   [422] C 262; C 264.

inhumations and cremation urns. One of the built tombs (Tomb H) was truly monumental, a chamber over 3 m high in a mound 29 m in diameter, and had been constructed on top of a graveyard of earlier, mostly cremation, graves belonging to local Tartessians in the eighth and seventh centuries. The same kind of burial continued to be placed in the tumulus itself, the whole monument thus providing an important insight into local custom in a period contemporary with Phoenician settlement.[423] There is indeed, in the later burials, a good deal of Tartessian pottery with tall biconical pot-stands in reserve-band ware imitating those found in black-burnished ware at Carambolo, but a round-based 'Palestinian' dipper juglet and some 'thistle-head' vases are in authentic West Phoenician tradition.[424] The culture represented in tumuli A and B has also been found at the nearby site of Mesa de Setefilla.[425] In addition there is pottery with painted floral and figured design (of Medellín–Andalusian type) and thistle-head vases of West Phoenician derivation as at Carmona. The Carmona phenomenon was certainly not an isolated one: two rock-cut tombs at Osuna (south-east Seville province) on the route from Seville to Málaga provided a further ivory comb of Carmona type and an alabaster flask.[426]

It is perfectly clear from these finds that there was intensive Phoenician trade and influence. How precisely it operated and what the proportion of local to intrusive Phoenician settlement was are unknown to us. But much suggests a unified and expansive Tartessian culture. Possibly because the Guadalquivir basin was a semi-detached economic unit it became necessary to defend its major trade routes. Rectangular forts with corner towers at Herrera near Ecija (Seville province),[427] and at Al-Honoz in the valley of the Genil, were built to protect an important route via this river to the upland of Penafler.

There are, of course, other important aspects of Phoenician presence besides mining. At most of the early sites sherds of a certain type of oblique-shouldered baggy amphora, suitable for storage and transport, appear, sometimes slightly before the arrival of other Phoenician artefacts. At Cerro Macareno, for instance, a *Bastetani* site with little evidence of direct Phoenician presence, they occur in quantity.[428] Wheel-made storage jars of this size cannot have been evolved locally but are clearly foreign. We do not know what they contained (they seem more suitable for dried and salted goods than for liquids), but Aristotle (*De mir. ausc.* 135) records that oil was introduced to Iberia by the Phoenicians. The number of Attic SOS amphorae from Phoenician sites in Spain – though again not necessarily for transporting oil –

[423] C 276, 349–54.   [424] C 264.   [425] C 336, 168.   [426] C 261, 113, 119–24, pl. 1.
[427] C 321.   [428] C 276, 138.

remind us of the important export market the Phoenicians and Greeks had found in the burgeoning centres of the Spanish Late Bronze Age.

Cádiz The long thin island of Cádiz (Phoenician 'Gadir', The Redoubt), lying opposite the mainland and Guadalete estuary, had two temples at its extremities.[429] The famous temple of Melqart was at the eastern end, where the island was nearest to the mainland. Here fresh water was available in springs later incorporated in the temple itself; and it seems likely that the Phoenician colonists would have initially erected the kind of inscription found at Nora or set up a dedication to Melqart of Tyre. Of the temple itself nothing is known. Representations of it which appear on the Hadrianic coins of Cádiz show a standard classical temple facade, which reveals nothing of the Phoenician building. Late accounts of it show that it duplicated some of the iconography of the temple of Melqart at Tyre.[430] At the western end of the isle was the temple of Cronus (the Latin equivalent of Punic Moloch) and, according to Pomponius Mela (III.6.46), the city itself, now under the modern town.[431]

Of old Phoenician Cádiz nothing is known from archaeology. Two items, a Ptah-like bronze statue with a gold-plated face from under the Cádiz Post Office[432] and an inscribed agate seal of Naʿamʾel from the Puerta di Tierra cemetery[433] may be early, but cannot be precisely dated. A Proto-Attic jug, an old and chance find in Cádiz and now in Copenhagen, seems to have a good enough history for acceptance as the oldest datable find in Cádiz.[434] Another interesting item, though not early in itself, is an inscribed gold finger ring in Madrid[435] which is dedicated to archaic cults: 'Molech and Ashtart of Agadir'.

Graveyards have been explored along a ridge in an oblique line south of the present city from Punta de la Vaca in the north through Puerta di Tierra to Los Corales beach and Asterillo in the south east of the island.[436] Most of these are rock-cut chamber tombs, though one or two were built and paved. But the Punta de la Vaca tombs are unusual *columbaria*, multiple adjoining slab-built sarcophagi, unknown elsewhere except at Lixus. There are other unusual elements in the Cádiz graveyards: cremation is virtually absent, almost all tombs contained single burials, pottery is scarce, but jewellery is plentiful. Without much pottery dating is difficult, but none of these graveyards came into use before the fifth century B.C.

Textual evidence is quite conclusive on the Gadiran role.[437] The Cádizans were intrepid sailors and explorers according to Strabo

[429] C 276, 451–61; C 304, figs. 216–58.   [430] C 303, 100–31.   [431] C 4 1, 262–7; C 276, 452.

[432] C 118, 262–7.   [433] C 273, 28.   [434] C 295, 57.   [435] C 273, 26, pl. 1.

[436] C 276, 455–8.   [437] C 276, 453.

(III.1–8), and it was with their help that Eudoxus of Cyzicus set out to circumnavigate Africa in the days of Ptolemy II of Egypt (146–117 B.C.). Even in their small 'horses' (oval boats with horse-head prows), according to Posidonius (in Strabo II.3.4), they fished the coasts of Mauretania as far as the Lixus river; and in Alexandria their ships were known.

Tartessian gold Some important treasures, all chance finds, illustrate Tartessian goldwork: all have a mixture of Phoenician and local Spanish elements.[438] The goldwork from Aliseda (Cáceres) was found together with a jug of thick dark green glass imitating the pear-shaped jugs in metal and bearing a meaningless inscription in Egyptian hieroglyphs.[439] The glass is lathe-turned and is similar in technique to glassware from Nimrud. In shape it closely resembles two alabaster jugs from tombs in Nubia which can be dated to the mid-seventh century.[440] This date would also suit the iron sword and grey ware dish found with the treasure. Chief amongst the goldwork are a belt (Pls. Vol., pl. 142b) and a hinged diadem, this latter of a type frequently seen on Iberian sculptures of a later date, but, as with the belt, the techniques and motifs used are purely Phoenician and most clearly comparable to early Etruscan work. Another gold joint diadem is the main item found at Sanlúcar de Barrameda at the mouth of the Guadalquivir.[441] Excavations at the site suggest a date no later than 500 B.C. for its original context. The site from which the gold treasure of Carambolo (Seville province) came has been excavated with important results.[442] From level IV, to which the treasure probably belonged, comes a whole series of flaring-mouth jars of the geometric-painted group, which are unlikely to descend beyond 600 B.C. The treasure itself consists of curiously shaped plaques which were strung together to make a collar or belt, certainly in local Iberian fashion, but a pendant with hanging seal-stones is of purely Phoenician type. Other goldwork from Spain, especially from Extremadura, shows a strong Orientalizing current, but spreading northwards with an ever-increasing qualification of southern influence. Important earrings from Madrigalejo[443] (Cáceres), from Golegã (Ribatejo), and Utrera (Seville province) show essentially peninsular adaptations of Asiatic types' technological links between Galicia and the south. An important pair from Baião in eastern Portugal[444] are decorated with granulated Phoenician dish-palmettes. Even some of the Galician jewellery, though

---

[438] C 270; C 290; C 324.
[439] C 7, 254–5, figs. 275, 292–5; C 276, 369–75; C 304, 479–81, figs. 393–406.   [440] C 302, 119.
[441] C 242, 128.   [442] C 281.   [443] C 267, 273.   [444] C 273, pl. 104B.

generally held to be no earlier than the fourth century B.C., shows the impact of southern styles on goldwork of an essentially Hallstatt tradition. Most important here are granulated earrings from Buiela (Lugo) and Monsato da Beira.[445]

Phoenicians and Iberians Throughout southern and south-eastern Spain the formation of Tartessian material culture gave an impetus to the Iberians themselves, who built upon it their own distinctive style of pottery and bronzes. In western Andalusia it is difficult to draw the line between the Tartessian and earliest Iberian, or 'Turdetanian' culture, to use the name given by classical authors to the Iberian Turdetani who inhabited this area.[446] At Cabezo de San Pedro, Los Quemados, Cerro Macareno, Carambolo, and Setefilla the change occurs about 600 B.C., and in upper Andalusia at Galera. But in Jaén at Cástulo and elsewhere the Iberian culture seems to grow straight out of a retarded Late Bronze Age with only minor Tartessian influence. In Valencia and Castellón,[447] on the contrary, the Iberian appears suddenly grafted upon local cultures by spreading from Andalusia itself. But even in the extra-Tartessian regions there appear secondary direct Phoenician impulses in the formative 600–550 B.C. period. Possibly the population of the south and south-east coastal regions from Cádiz to Almería, where neither Iberian nor northern urnfield cultures appear to have been strongly established, remained partly of Phoenician extraction, as is implied by the names *bastuloi poenoi* (Ptolemy II.4.9), the Latin *Bastetani*, and the *Libiopoeni* of Avienus (*Ora.* 419–23) and Scymnus (195–98, based on Ephorus).

The impact of Tartessian material on the formation of Iberian culture is clearly seen in southern and eastern Spain. The distinctive Iberian pottery style of the fifth-to-third centuries B.C. seems now to have grown initially out of Tartessian wares.[448] The best stratified sites are Los Quemados (Córdoba) and Los Soladares, near Orihuela (Alicante province), 30 km up the Segura river, where there is an unbroken sequence from Late Bronze Age to a full Iberian horizon, with Tartessian imports in the pre-Iberian level IA–B and copies in the Early Iberian level II.[449] Also important is the 'tell' of Vinarragel, near Castellón at the mouth of the Río de la Vinda in Valencia province.[450] Here the successive levels of Tartessian and Iberian wares are much richer, but it is especially the urn forms with double-cordon handle which make up the continuity. Incineration burials with similar

---

[445] C 267.   [446] C 276, 151–2.
[447] At Los Soladares, Crevillente, and Vinarragel: C 259; C 283, 187; C 319, 20–4; C 330.
[448] C 330.   [449] C 259.   [450] C 330.

urns placed under small 'dolmens' have been found at Collado de la Cova del Cavall and El Puntalet near Valencia and are the only 'Tartessian' burials in this region.[451]

Although after the middle of the sixth century few exotic objects of Oriental origin are to be found in the later tombs, a type of flat dish with swing-handles, the so called *braserillo*, found in seventh-century tombs in the south (La Joya, Carmona) was still produced, whether by Phoenicians or Iberians.[452] The rim decorations on some of the early examples, as well as the handle attachments in the shape of human hands, show clearly that these were originally Phoenician-made, the handle-bars inspired by Egyptian prototypes; but since nothing similar has been found in the Near East or the Mediterranean, they must be taken for original Tartessian products. Their late survival is assured by the late fifth/early fourth-century Attic vases found with them in graves at Gigarralejo (Alicante) and Mirador de Rolanda (Granada).[453]

It was in sculpture more than in pottery painting that the Iberian native genius drew most from the Phoenicians. Greek influences were certainly present too, for Phoenician domination in south Spain did not close it to Greek influence, as is shown by the number of fine Greek imports, especially the fine black cup from Medellín (Badajoz)[454] and good pieces from Cástulo.[455] The resultant sculptural style was an original creation. At its beginning in the sixth century B.C., the carved slabs from Pozo Moro near Chinchilla (Albacete province) show themes taken straight from Near Eastern art and rather weirdly transcribed.[456] Some archaic lions (particularly that from Nueva Carteia, Córdoba)[457] and the partly preserved figure of a griffin from Redovan[458] illustrate the sixth-century interest in Oriental animals which the Iberians subsequently lost. But it is most clearly in architectural elements that the specific Phoenician theme of 'tied-volutes' survived in Iberian art, giving some late and oblique idea of what Tartessian architecture may have looked like (Fig. 26).[459] The same scroll-like designs are also to be found on the late group of Iberian belt plaques[460] dating from the fourth century. This late 'baroque' Orientalism is best seen in the sculptured reliefs and painted amphorae from the Iberian-built tombs at Tútugi (Toya) near Galera[461] and recently discovered at Baza[462] (both Granada province). Attic bell craters from the built Galera tomb show that this important if localized artistic efflorescence took place in the fourth century B.C., though a statue in alabaster representing a goddess enthroned between

---

451 C 298, 16–17, fig. 10.   452 C 287.   453 C 254; C 301.   454 C 258, 160–79.
455 C 258, 160–79.   456 C 248; C 251.   457 C 272, 90–103.   458 C 276, 263, 425.
459 C 312.   460 C 312, 198–9.   461 C 280.   462 C 276, 251–2.

Fig. 26. Stone capital from Cerro de las Vírgenes (Córdoba). (After C 312, figs. 1–4.)

sphinxes is one of the most archaic Phoenician-looking objects from the West, an antique perhaps (Pls. Vol., pl. 144*a*).[463]

Another important Iberian development contemporary with Phoenician contact was writing.[464] Graffiti on pottery from Carambolo, Córdoba and Setefilla in Andalusia, from Cabezo de San Pedro in Huelva and Medellín in Jaén show that the Tartessian (or 'Bastulo-Turdetan') script was already developing in the early seventh century.[465] Inscribed stelae from Abóbada and sites mentioned above in the Ourique region of Portugal also affirm the use of script by the Tartessians, the first also making an important link between script and the representation of the defunct and his armour. Linked with these are stelae with long inscriptions, often written boustrophedon or in spirals, from Algarve and from Siruela and Almoroqui in Badajoz. The regional differences in the script are relatively minor. If we read into it the consonantal values of later Iberian script (concentrated in the east of the peninsula), its general debt to the Phoenician script is obvious; but it is not direct, for Tartessian is not purely alphabetic but has some syllabic non-Semitic signs. Although it cannot be read with certainty,[466] there are some indications that it belongs to an Indo-European language. Use of writing was probably as much a product of trade and urbanization as it was of contact with literate cultures.

The Atlantic shore Two reasons may be suggested for Phoenician interest in Portugal. Algarve in the south was heavily wooded and the river mouths of the Atlantic coast, particularly that of the Rio Arade at Silves and the Río Sado at Alcácer do Sal were noted for their

---

[463] C 273, pl. 75.   [464] C 249; C 276, 138–40, 216–20.   [465] C 351.   [466] C 351.

access to excellent timber down to medieval times.[467] The rivers Tagus, Mondego, and Douro were gateways to sources of tin and gold. The Galicians especially were noted goldsmiths in late prehistoric times.

The only direct evidence of Phoenician presence is a fragment of a third-century B.C. Punic inscription said to come from Monforte de Lemos, near Lugo[468] in the north. Late prehistoric tombs in the Algarve region have provided glass beads and gold earrings of Punic type,[469] and beyond Cape St Vincent a cist grave at Gaio (Cape Sines region) contained an important group of jewellery including a collar of gold-embossed plaques in Orientalizing style, large gold earrings of Tartessian–Galician type, and beads of gold, amber, tin, and turquoise.[470] A glass flask from the grave is of fifth- or fourth-century B.C. date. Though an isolated find, the Sines treasure is a valuable demonstration of the coastal movement of Phoenician trade: both its decorative motifs and use of gold granulation are intermediaries between the goldwork of Tartessos and the goldwork of the northern provinces of Portugal.

Further north Phoenicians certainly frequented the Bay of Setubal and the Tagus estuary. At Alcácer do Sal on the Sado a few incineration burials in the Senhor dos Martires graveyard contained archaic Phoenician pottery and a scarab of Psammetichus II.[471] A large but poorly explored necropolis at Cezimbra, a commanding coastal site east of Setúbal, has also yielded West Phoenician pottery.[472] A built tholos tomb at Casal do Meio assigned to the seventh century B.C. contained an ivory comb, bronze tweezers, and a fibula, not Phoenician but certainly exotic.[473] Other evidence of contact comes from two graveyards of small tumulus graves with incinerations in Baixo Alentejo, at Monte de A-Do-Mealha-Nova, and Herdade do Pego,[474] which together with some glass and metal beads contained an Egyptian scarab of Pedubast. Scarabs of Pedubast are also known from Carthage and Jardín (grave 30) and are thought to belong to Pedubast III (about 520 B.C.).[475] Apart from a West Phoenician commercial amphora, the pottery from these graves is local and hand-made. A stone connected with one of the graves bore an inscription, one of the earliest known in Tartessian characters.[476] Here as in Algarve the Phoenician contact appears to have been slight.

To the north important evidence of Phoenician contact has come early this century from Crasto and Santa Olaya, two fortified sites deep in the estuary of the Mondego river.[477] Here the cultural intru-

---

[467] C 314, 75.   [468] C 348.   [469] C 293.   [470] C 290.   [471] C 284; C 286.
[472] C 320.   [473] C 349.   [474] C 252.   [475] C 302, 107.   [476] C 252, 191–3.
[477] C 308; C 339.

sion of the refined Phoenician wheel-made pottery upon the local hand-made ceramics is quite clear; and there is much evidence from the well-built rectangular houses for extensive back-yard smelting of copper and iron. Much of the exotic pottery has a relationship to West Phoenician pottery in southern Spain,[478] which would suggest a date as early as the sixth century B.C. for Phoenician contact with this region. A few late Punic pots from Guifoẽs and a hoard of Cádizan and Ibizan coins from Bares, though no earlier than the second century B.C., perhaps follow the route of earlier commerce.[479]

Glass beads with fancy incrustations have been found in great numbers and variety in the castra of Galicia;[480] they have often been given a Phoenician or Carthaginian origin, but until they are studied in detail their dating significance is doubtful. Certainly on present archaeological indications, elaboration of the bead-making industry comes no earlier than the fourth century B.C. at Carthage.

It was, according to Avienus (Ora 113–15), the Tartessians who traded for tin with the Oestrymnides by way of the Atlantic. The Oestrymnides cannot be placed, but it is clear that one of the richest metalliferous regions to be reached by Atlantic voyages was Galicia, and clearly also Galician–Tartessian contacts in goldwork are more demonstrable overland by way of Jaén and Extremadura than they are by Andalusia and Granada, which indicates, but does not, of course, prove, that the cultural dispersion came from the south east and not the south west.

7. The Balearic Islands and the north-west Mediterranean coast

The extent and nature of Phoenician intercourse with peoples of the shores of the north-west Mediterranean and the Gulf of Lions are matters of controversy. Although two isolated stelae carved with V-nick shields have been found in Aragón and at Montpellier in the south of France,[481] no Phoenician settlements are known north of Villaricos and the few Punic remains from the regions of Valencia and Alicante either date later than the Carthaginian occupation of Spain or are the result of trading stations established in the fourth century B.C. from either Carthage or Ibiza. North of this region, Phoenician presence may chiefly be argued either from the impact of Punic vase shapes on those of local Iron Age Urnfield cultures[482] or from the presence of Phoenician commercial amphorae. In addition there is a scatter of Egyptian scarabs of Naucratite type,[483] and a handful of faience

---

[478] C 339, 334–44, 508–9, pls. 22–4, 35.   [479] C 317, 29–34.   [480] C 288, 177–9, 219.
[481] C 362.   [482] C 366, 36–56.   [483] C 302, 195–203; C 377.

amulets and beads found at sites stretching from Mas de Mussols at the mouth of the Ebro to Montlaurès in Narbonne. Some of these are of types current in the early sixth century B.C. and could just as well have been distributed by Greeks as by Phoenicians. A whole range of ovoid commercial amphorae of Phoenician shape and of a type found in the earliest graves at Ampurias[484] have been found in the lowest levels of many oppida in Languédoc and Provence.[485] Their association with imported Greek and Etruscan ceramics at Mailhac, Bessan, and Mont Garou shows that they were reaching southern France from the first quarter of the sixth century, and continued well into the fifth. At Ampurias their occurrence in the lowest stratum is not necessarily earlier than 550 B.C.[486] Similar (but fewer) such amphorae have been found on the Spanish side, as far south as Saladares, where they are tied to an early-Iberian pottery type evolved from the more southerly proto-Iberian sites such as Cástulo and Quemados. From this, the beginning of this 'Phoenician' trade in the Gulf of Lions has been pushed back to the last quarter of the seventh century and its floruit placed between 625 and 575 B.C.[487] But most of the amphorae are certainly later than this and, although they clearly belong to Phoenician ceramic tradition, their origin is obscure. Even if they are Phoenician, there is no certainty that they indicate direct Phoenician trade, since they occur at most sites together with Greek and Etruscan amphorae, whose numbers are considerably greater.[488] As study of wrecked cargoes of later ships has shown, Punic amphorae were sometimes distributed by Greek and Italian export houses. There is little else in southern France to support a Phoenician presence. A few sherds with linear bichrome decoration from Montlaurès,[489] Bessan, and Pech Maho are again perhaps Tartessian, as are the red-slipped and polychrome-band vases from Coll de Moro (Gandesa)[490] and Maçalió. A small oil bottle from the graveyard of Mas de Mussols (Tortosa)[491] is certainly Phoenician, but probably travelled north from the Málaga coast settlements, where these bottles were well known. Otherwise all that the sites of the lower Ebro have to show for Phoenician contact is a few amphora parts and sherds of polychrome ware.[492]

The origin of certain 'Punic' shapes and fabrics amongst the pottery of the Catalonian urnfields, like that in the necropolis of Agullana, Gerona, is equally elusive. Certainly ollas, jars, and handleless 'thistle'

---

[484] C 352, 41.

[485] Pech Maho, Mailhac, Montlaurès, Ensérune: C 354, 131–2; C 359, 56–7, 64–6.

[486] C 352, 41–2.   [487] C 354, 131–2.   [488] C 373, 130–2.   [489] C 366, 88, figs. 66–7.

[490] C 372, 162–5.   [491] C 368, 248, fig. 1, pl. 1; C 372, fig. 2.   [492] C 372, 162–3.

vases are close to West Phoenician shapes,[493] but it is an open question whether they come from direct contact with Punic trade pottery or from migrant West Phoenician potters; or whether by way of the internal selective evolution of the Tartessian shapes taken over by proto-Iberian pottery in south-eastern Spain. Another item which has been associated with the Phoenicians in Catalonia and southern France is the bronze double-spring fibula,[494] whose earliest datable contexts are in the Phoenician or Tartessian centres of southern Spain. Fibulae of this type certainly appear to be later in reaching Catalonia and France, but they cannot be shown to have been invented by Phoenicians or distributed by them.

Ibiza According to Diodorus (v.16.2–3), Ibiza was founded by the Carthaginians 160 years after the foundation of Carthage itself – that is, in 654 B.C. Except for one small group of urns of perhaps slightly earlier date, nothing from the large number of tombs on Ibiza predates 500 B.C.[495] There is no imported archaic Greek pottery, but later Greek wares become abundant in the fifth and through the fourth centuries. It is in this period that the Carthaginian hold on Ibiza was greatly extended and it is doubtful whether Ibiza played a significant colonial role before that time. Quite possibly the Carthaginians established a small colony of traders there in the seventh century, whose remains are entirely lost under the modern town of Ibiza. A suggestion that Ibiza had independent Phoenician connexions is based entirely on the evidence of scarabs (Pls. Vol., pl. 141c).[496] It cannot be denied that the range of genuine Egyptian scarabs found there predates that of Carthage and elsewhere and that the range of Egyptianizing items from Ibizan tombs is somewhat different. For some reason, Ibiza had an advanced Egyptomania, but this in itself is not a valuable chronological criterion. Also suggestions that the name itself (Phoenician *ʾybsm*, Greek *Eβουσος*) derives from the name of the Egyptian god Bes (who features on its later coinage) have little foundation.[497] The Greek name was Pityoussa, 'island of Pines', and this is probably the doublet of the Phoenician name.

What is most unusual is the evidence from the distribution of the many graveyards in the island for a rural Punic population.[498] In addition to the large scatter of graveyards in the south-west coastal region, of which that of Cala d'Hort is the most important, there are others at Sa Barda in the west and Can Guasch in the very centre of the island. These are not perhaps so wealthy as the graveyards of Tala-

---

[493] C 366, 47–56, figs. 22–9. [494] C 346. [495] C 374. [496] C 302, 174–5; C 358.
[497] C 302, 127–9. [498] C 276, 472–9.

manca, Puig d'es Molíns, and Puig d'en Valls on the outskirts of the city, but are nevertheless typically Punic. There were also two important sanctuaries: Isla Plana, on a small peninsula east of the town of Ibiza, and the cave sanctuary at Es Cuyram in the north east of the island, which has yielded an ex voto inscription to Astarte and a large number of terracotta representations of her (or her devotees).[499]

The material culture of Ibiza is wholly Punic: absent are the red-slipped and polychrome wares of Tartessian tradition[500] and likewise the later developments of the proto-Iberian wares, which were certainly in part contemporary with Ibiza's growth. Equally rare are the grey wares of the Phocaean Greeks, though some links with the later pottery of Ampurias do exist.[501] Ibiza was a colony in the true sense, a transplanted part of the Carthaginian metropolis, with the Punic cult apparatus of masks, bronze razors, kernoi, the cult of Tanit, and the intense Carthaginian interest in terracotta figurines.[502] In this art the Ibizans excelled and seem to have combined a basically Phoenician art of mould-made terracotta figures with influences from south Italy and Sicily (Fig. 27).[503] What precise purpose these terracotta models served, especially the *grandi busti* in the funerary contexts in which most have been found, is obscure, but some of the figures of women illustrate from the rich ornamentation of their dresses what might have been an important textile industry. Diodorus (v.16) especially noted the quality of wool. Scarcely anything can be said about the rural settlements themselves, since remains of the many well-built houses, also mentioned by Diodorus, have not been recorded. Amongst the graveyards, all of which consist of underground chamber tombs, that of Puig d'es Molíns is the earliest, largest, and richest, but even so, contains nothing earlier than 500 B.C.

Ibiza's early role in the trade of the Mediterranean north west cannot be estimated. Certainly there was a little traffic which seems Ibizan with Phocaean Ampurias on the Catalonian coast[504] and even with Ensérune in the Rhône valley, bringing a few polychrome glass bottles and terracottas.[505] A little Corinthian pottery and two Cypriot Iron Age juglets from Ampurias' earliest graveyard at Purtitxol[506] precede the strengthening of the Phocaean hold on Ampuritan trade[507] but cannot with certainty be attributed to Ibizan traders; nor can a Cypriot commercial amphora found in Menorca,[508] nor the Naucratite scarabs from Can Canyis and Mas de Mussols, nor the Naucratite aryballoi from Ampurias and Ibiza itself.[509] Late in the fifth–fourth

499 C 357; C 358.   500 C 36.   501 C 364.   502 C 36, 234; C 304, 294–351.
503 C 360.   504 C 352, 81–2, 242–3, pls. 5, 14; C 364.   505 C 357, 65.
506 C 365, 201–10.   507 C 368, 251.   508 C 369 I, 31, no. 14, pl. 46.
509 C 302, 239–40; C 303, 570.

Fig. 27. Terracotta figurine from Ibiza. Height 13 cm. (Ibiza Museum 6.525; after c 360, 42, fig. 2.)

centuries grey monochrome ware of a type apparently evolved from the grey-ware sub-stratum of Iron-Age I in Valencia reached both Ibiza and Majorca.[510] Conversely, a few Ibizan Punic items reached the sites of La Serreta (Alcoy), Alcudia de Elche and El Molar, Alicante.[511]

Brief mention must be made of Formentera (Greek Ophioussa, for it was infested with snakes), the small flat island on Ibiza's south. It had valuable sea-salt deposits and probably for this reason it was visited by Bronze Age people and important to the Arabs. Punic and Massilian pottery has been found at a few minor Formentera sites.[512]

Majorca and Menorca Unlike Ibiza, Majorca, and Menorca were heavily settled by native peoples, who developed in the course of the second millennium their distinctive megalithic culture. Possibly Ibiza was too heavily wooded for the implantation of these agricultural communities, for no trace of their 'talyots', 'taulas' and other megalithic structures has been found on Ibiza, though a little Talyotic pottery has been found there.[513] Certainly these neighbouring prehistoric cultures were

[510] C 252, 279–81.   [511] C 367.   [512] C 370; C 371, 124–5.   [513] C 363.

flourishing at the time of Phoenician colonization.[514] A remarkable Egyptian bronze statuette of Imhotep, the god of healing, has been found in the Talyotic village of D'En Gaumés in southern Menorca.[515] It dates to the sixth–fifth century B.C. and provides both valuable dating evidence and proof that Oriental traders were around. West Phoenician imports to Majorca and Menorca do not antedate 400 B.C., and mostly consist of glass bottles and beads.[516] Whilst these islands had mineral resources of their own, ironwork might have come from Ibiza, which, like Majorca, used double-axes of iron[517] (found in Ibizan tombs). A little Phocaean grey ware reached both islands,[518] as well as some late Iberian painted wares,[519] but neither Greeks nor Iberians seem to have bothered about the Balearics. Italian Campanian pottery is found there in the third century onwards and a considerable amount of late Punic pottery from Trapucó[520] in Menorca dates to the third–second century B.C. In this same period, at Turó de Ses Beies near Calviá in western Majorca, the Carthaginians established a small trading station (to judge from pottery found)[521] – but this was not before Mago the Carthaginian general took possession of the Balearics in the course of the first Punic War in 206 B.C.

8. *Morocco and the Atlantic coast*

West of Oran, nothing significant is known of the early Phoenicians until we reach the Straits. Rusaddir, modern Melilla on the Tres Forcas peninsula, certainly had a Phoenician name and was a neo-Punic station,[522] and a site at Sidi Abdselam del Behar,[523] a little to the east of Tetuan at the mouth of the Rio Martin, may have been a small settlement made in the sixth century from Tartessus. On the Atlantic coast of Morocco only the valleys of the Loukkos and Sebou rivers permitted the Phoenicians that type of penetration and commercial exchange enjoyed in Spain. The Sebou especially gave access to the important fertile inland valley region of the Gharb, where local sedentary tribes practised agriculture.

Early settlement certainly took place in the Tangiers region. Two monumentally built tombs between Cape Spartel and Ras Achakar containing Punic pottery and jewellery[524] are constructed in precise Phoenician style and probably belonged to an early Phoenician settlement. Cultural influence is also amply demonstrated in the megalithic

[514] C 371, for chronology, pp. 40–1.   [515] C 302, 175–7.
[516] C 359, 69–71; C 368, fig. 6⅓; C 369 I, 40–2.   [517] C 353, fig. 20.   [518] C 369 I, 29.
[519] C 369 I, 3204, pls. 47–50.   [520] C 369 I, pl. 44; C 369 II, 22–4, pl. 26.   [521] C 361.
[522] C 2, 99–100.   [523] C 395; C 396, 88–9; C 399, 437.   [524] C 384.

cist graves inland and south from the Cape at Ain Dalhia Kebira, Djebila, and Dar Shiro.[525] Pottery in these graves was mostly hand-made, but it selectively copied West Phoenician shapes. The Phoenician jewellery and amulets buried with the dead[526] are archaic and suggest a date in the sixth or late seventh century. To date they furnish the most cogent evidence we possess of the impact of Phoenician civilization on native culture, including the introduction of iron for the making of jewellery and tools.[527]

At the mouth of the river Loukkos the Phoenicians, according to Pliny (XIX.22.63), founded their oldest western city, Lixus (Phoenician Ligs, Greek Loukkos). Its temple, he claims, was founded before that of Cádiz. The ancient site is supposedly beneath modern Larache,[528] on the south bank of the marshy estuary. Sondages beneath the ruins of Roman Lixus on the north bank have produced both polychrome-band and red-slipped wares, together with Attic black-figure pottery, a combination which would place it at least in the early fifth century.[529] Larache itself has provided at least one pre-sixth-century Phoenician pot, a disk-top jug with bright red burnished slip, now in Tetuan museum, but there is certainly no indication to justify the view that Cádiz and Lixus were early 'twin' foundations to guard the Straits.[530] It is, however, interesting to note that a group of *hypogeum* tombs at Lixus exactly parallel the unusual rows of contiguous slab tombs used at Cádiz.[531] That a native Libyan town existed close by on the south bank of the river is stated by Pseudo-Scylax. This is perhaps the Tingis of Strabo (XVII.3.2), the Libyan name from which Ligs was derived.[532]

North of Lixus on a plateau at the mouth of the Wadi Garifa stands an important Punico-Berber settlement at Kouass. Though it dates far later than the earliest Phoenician penetration of these parts, its pottery provides an important reminder of the late date to which Tartessian painted pottery styles survived in north-west Africa. South of Lixus stretches an inhospitable shore, with the mouth of the Sebou river providing the next shelter for ships. Twenty-five kilometres up it the Romans built Thamusida (Sidi Ali ben Ahmed). This was quite possibly the West Phoenician colony of Thymiaterion of Pseudo-Scylax and Hanno (see below). Excavations have uncovered deep levels of Phoenician pottery[533] going back to the seventh century. Another port at Banasa[534] further upstream has levels containing much Tartessian-style polychrome-band pottery as well as some jewellery and graffiti of the sixth century.

[525] C 390, 66–168.   [526] C 390, 140–58.   [527] C 390, 157.   [528] C 41, 246–8.
[529] C 396, 63–73.   [530] C 376, 50–1.   [531] C 394.   [532] C 379, 113.
[533] C 376, 78–9, pl. 39.   [534] C 386.

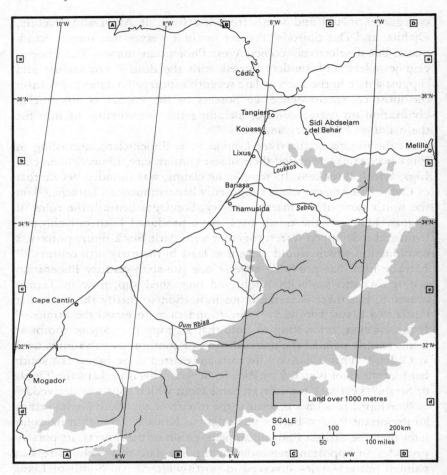

Map 12. Phoenician sites in Morocco.

Two sites further south appear eminently suited for naval stations: Cape Fedala (Fedala-Mohammedia), formerly an island and now built up, and Mogador island a few kilometres off Essaouira.[535] Here excavations have brought up an abundance of Phoenician pottery of both Carthaginian and Tartessian types together with parts of Archaic Ionian (of probably Chiote or Phocaean origin) and Attic SOS amphorae.[536] Phoenician graffiti on pottery fragments give epigraphic

[535] C 383.
[536] C 397, 6–8. For the links with Tartessian pottery see C 2, 104–5; C 302, 31.

confirmation that Mogador was occupied by the Phoenicians in the seventh century B.C. The abrupt cessation of the pottery record shows that it was abandoned in the course of the sixth century.

Whether the Phoenician presence at Mogador island was due to the exploitation of local sea produce (as is perhaps suggested by the establishment of a purple dye industry on the island in later times by the Numidian king Juba II),[537] or whether it was a staging post for trade either inland or further down the African coast cannot be decided. No graveyard has been found there, such as might indicate a permanent settlement, and indeed there are no further certain Phoenician tombs on the rest of the African coast, though claims have been made for many empty *hypogea*, especially those at Tit.[538] The only tomb which is Phoenician in shape is an isolated example at El Hafire, north east of Cape Cantin.

For the rest we must turn to history, although the eighteen-section text of the *Periplus* of 'king' Hanno of Carthage down the west coast of Africa is of highly doubtful value.[539] Even if it stems from an original account written in Punic, the vicissitudes of its transmission to the Greek text of the tenth century A.D. preserved in Heidelberg have much obscured its place names and distances. So unsuccessful have been attempts to reconstruct Hanno's voyage that it has been considered a piece of Greek fiction,[540] or a piece of pseudo-intelligence of West Africa extrapolated from exploration of the Nile and East African regions.[541] Whilst strong arguments can be advanced against both these propositions,[542] there seems little doubt that the Heidelberg manuscript is a combination of two stylistically different documents joined together by material (section 7) taken from Herodotus.[543]

Hanno's voyage beyond the Pillars of Hercules was aimed at colonization as well as exploration: he took 30,000 settlers and some livestock. Colonies were founded at Thymiaterion, Karikon Teichos (the 'Carian fort'), Gutta, Akra, Melitte, and Arambus, with the furthest colony at Cerne. The positioning of all these unidentified places depends upon whether the text has preserved the geographic sequence in its original order, for the main group is claimed to have been founded between the Pillars of Hercules and the Lixus river, a distance so short as to appear unlikely if the Lixus is the Loukkos (at Larache) on which the Phoenician town of Lixus stood. Consequently many scholars would identify the Lixus with the Wadi Draa further south, also on the grounds that after Thymiaterion Hanno reached Cape Soloeis, which is claimed to be Cape Cantin (rather than Cape Spartel). These equations accommodate a more southerly voyage, even as far, it

---

[537] C 378, 88. [538] C 378, 25. [539] C 5, 162–9; C 379, 39–85. [540] C 380.
[541] C 379, 32–85. [542] C 389, 231. [543] C 389, 234.

is claimed, as the Senegal river,[544] the large river Chretes which was the farthest point reached and from the banks of whose estuarine lake Hanno's party was driven by hostile natives (section 9). It is, on the other hand, unlikely that the Lixus is anything but the Loukkos, situated in a region well known in antiquity, remarkable though it is that the city of Lixus itself is not mentioned in the surviving text. Furthermore, the identification of Cerne with Herne island opposite Villa Cisneros on the coast of the Spanish Sahara rests solely on a quite misleading similarity of names.[545] The settlement at Thymiaterion, the Poseidon temple at Cape Soloeis, and particularly Cerne were all known to Scylax 112 (GGM ed. C. Müller). To him Cerne was an island reached by the Phoenician merchants in their round boats, twelve days (600–700 km?) past the Pillars of Hercules. No permanent settlement is implied, since the Phoenicians erected tents for their merchandise, which they ferried by lighters to the opposite coast. The sources of Pseudo-Scylax are difficult to determine but are quite independent of Hanno's *Periplus* and appear to incorporate some sixth-century Greek source material.[546] In Avienus (*Desc.* 328) Cerne rates a brief mention as the furthest known point.

There are also two points of natural history involved. If the 'gorillas' which Hanno captured (section 18) were indeed gorillas, then Hanno must have reached tropical Africa, and the same may be indicated by the odoriferous and diversified forest (tropical rain forest? section 12) which the voyagers encountered. Although neither of these points can plausibly be taken to have come from a Greek source (and especially not one which elaborated the gorilla episode from the story of Perseus and the *gorgades*),[547] they are too imprecise to be clinching evidence.

Despite its drawbacks, we may take Hanno's *Periplus* to reflect a genuine Punic reconnaissance of the West African coast, perhaps about 600 B.C. under the early Magonids, preserved in a text exhibited beside the 'gorilla' skins in the temple of Saturn at Carthage. The foundation of a temple of Poseidon (Melqart) on the wooded headland of Cape Soloeis and the emphasis on prospecting island sites, and even the interest in hostile hairy beasts (as depicted on gems and the Huntsman's Day bowl from Praeneste)[548] are all typical Phoenician concerns.

Of course, the difficulties of reconstructing Hanno's voyage entail more than the difficulties of the text. Many geomorphological changes have taken place on the Atlantic coast since antiquity. Islands, head-

---

[544] C 5, 169; C 310, 94; C 388, 223.   [545] C 379, 20.   [546] C 379, 87–120.
[547] C 379, 64.   [548] C 5, 180, fig. 55.

lands, and inland lakes, such as Lake Cephesias (between Ras Achakar and Ras el-Kouass),[549] reported on by Polybius on his voyage in about 147 B.C. (Pliny, *N.H.* v.19–10), have either disappeared entirely or been modified; and although these factors render reconstruction futile, since Mogador was reached repeatedly, there is great likelihood that Phoenicians had prospected, but not settled, southwards beyond it. It has been suggested that it was impossible for ancient mariners to sail along the west Saharan coast, and especially to cope with the return journey against prevailing northerly winds and offshore currents.[550] But there is little doubt that the Romans could solve this navigational problem, and, to judge from ships on Punic gravestones, Carthaginians used similar sails.[551] A hoard of fourth-century A.D. Roman coins found at San Pedro (330 km west of Abijan) on the Ivory Coast,[552] though far removed from Hanno's time, demonstrates the attainment of the shores of tropical West Africa. A hoard of Punic coins from Corvo island in the Azores[553] and some Roman amphorae from the Canaries[554] may prove occasional ventures far into Oceanic waters.

In fact no Phoenician settlement is known south of Mogador and, apart from one amphora from Cape Bojador,[555] no evidence of contact has turned up in surveys from Mogador to the Wadi Draa,[556] nor from the Seguiet el-Hamra and Rio de Oro.[557] Herne island itself has nothing but a few miserable remains of native settlement,[558] and the shores of Senegal have no traces of Phoenicians. Thus we remain with the possibility that Mogador was the furthest settled point, and was in fact Cerne,[559] the amphorae being part of the wine trade specifically mentioned in Pseudo-Scylax. In exchange for wine, ivory, and lion and leopard skins the Phoenicians traded perfumed oil and Attic pottery, all specifically mentioned by Pseudo-Scylax, who, furthermore, gives important details of the handsome 'Ethiopians' who took part in this exchange. They were tall horsemen, skilled in use of bow and spear. Easily accessible from Mogador through the Wadi Ksob is the western end of the High Atlas, where numerous rock engravings attributed to the Late Bronze III period attest the existence of chariotry, cavalry, lances, halberds, and bows in the first half of the first millennium.[560] Presumably these engravings (of which there are important examples at Yagour and Azibs N'Ikkis)[561] belonged to pastoral communities (cattle are frequently depicted) who followed a transhumant nomadism. As a bronze halberd and arrowhead from dolmen graves in the Tangiers region show,[562] their metalwork only slightly preceded

---

[549] C 379, 112–13, map 3.   [550] C 387.   [551] C 385.   [552] Unpublished.
[553] C 5, 178–9; C 310, 138–52.   [554] C 375, 14–16.   [555] C 381, fig. 8.
[556] C 378, 17–34.   [557] C 381, 2.   [558] C 381.   [559] C 379, 116–19.
[560] C 382, 22–3.   [561] C 382.   [562] C 390, 50, 58, pl. 13.

Phoenician settlement or more probably overlapped it. The possibility must not be overlooked that Mogador lay opposite a caravan route which operated a trade in food, metals, and luxuries with these mountain folk, who appear to have been an offshoot of the Garamantes (Hdt. IV.183) of Libya, the Fezzan, and the eastern Atlas. It has often been suggested that chariotry and a knowledge of iron was brought to the Garamantes through contact with the Carthaginians in the Gulf of Gabes and the Tunisian Sahel.[563] A further possibility is contact through the western Atlas. Ironworking in Nigeria may have come from Carthage by one or other of these routes.

[563] C 393, 40–2.

CHAPTER 33a

THE SCYTHIANS

T. SULIMIRSKI AND T. TAYLOR*

I. PROLEGOMENA

In the first half of the first millennium B.C., new and powerful nomadic groups emerged on the Eurasian steppes to pose a military threat to more southerly urban and literate states and empires. By the sixth century B.C. a complex 'core–periphery' system had developed, in which true nomadism was only one element. The economic structure of steppe life changed and large-scale trade developed between the Greek Black Sea colonies and the vast new fortified centres of Scythian power.[1]

The nomads can be traced at first archaeologically; later some names are attached to them in ancient texts. The most famous of these groups was known to the Greeks as the Scythians, against whom, Herodotus tells us, Darius the Great of Persia launched a massive and unsuccessful punitive expedition (*CAH* IV², 235ff). This chapter concerns the Scythians' rise to fame rather than their disappearance. By 500 B.C. they constituted one of the most powerful military forces in the known world.

1. *History of research*

The name 'Scythian' is met in the classical authors and has been taken to refer to an ethnic group or people, also mentioned in Near Eastern texts, who inhabited the northern Black Sea region. They were considered to be divided into a number of tribes, mainly located between the Dniester and Don rivers, who were at heart nomadic and raided widely.

'Scythian' is a very widespread term in Soviet archaeological literature. Ilinskaya and Terenozhkin, in their major work *Scythia: VII–IV Centuries* B.C., provide the following general statement: 'Scythian culture

---

* For the division of authorial responsibility in this chapter, see Preface, p. xviii.

[1] D 170; D 113. The best general survey in English is now D 171. D 128; D 172; D 166; D 52 and D 23 are still of value, as is Minns' original chapter in *CAH* III¹, 187–205, if we bear in mind that chronologies have undergone several recent revisions (see n. 8). D 154 provides an attractive introduction to the Siberian material. Amongst Slavic-language works, D 72 and D 125A are the most comprehensive, but see also D 22; D 135; D 137; on Scythian social structure see D 79.

Map 13. Scythia.

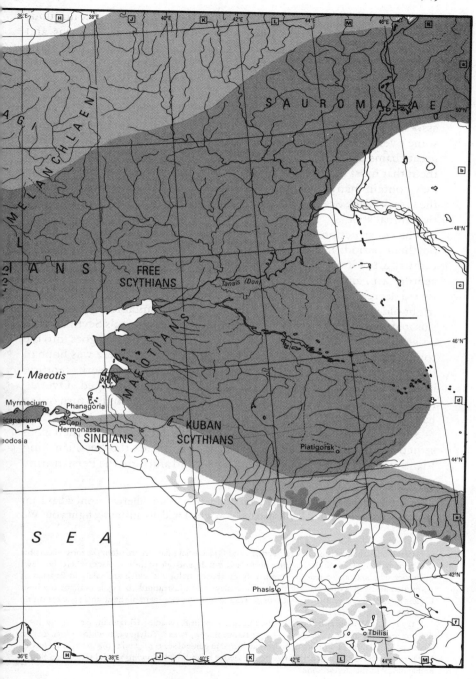

exerted a strong influence on all the tribes [occupying areas] contiguous
with Scythia, [including] those living in the northern Caucasus and
Transcaucasus, the Sindo-Maeotae in the Kuban region, the Tauri of the
Crimean hills, the Thracians of the Carpatho-Danubian basin, the north-
eastern region of the Lusatian tribes [Byelorussia and Poland], the tribes
. . . to the north of Scythia and so on.'[2]

The most obvious and impressive of the archaeological remains
associated with the Scythians are the great burial mounds (kurgans),
some over 20 m high, which dot the south Russian steppe and extend in
great chains for many kilometres along ridges and watersheds. It is from
them that most has been learnt about Scythian life and art: intact graves
may contain many precious metal artefacts, both luxury items made in
the Greek Black Sea colonies, and locally made objects in the characteristic 'animal style'.[3]

The construction of kurgans in this region was not exclusive to the
Scythian period: it is known from the Copper Age to the eighteenth
century A.D. Grave-robbing is documented from as early as the fifteenth
century A.D. and continued until recent times. In 1718, Peter the Great
issued decrees (ukazy) regarding the collection and delivery of all objects
'right old and rare' to St Petersburg in return for suitable compensation;
this material forms the basis of the Leningrad Hermitage's Scythian gold
collection. By 1764 it was claimed that, for Siberia, 'no one goes into the
tomb trade any more, because all the tombs in which there was hope of
finding treasure have been ransacked'. In the nineteenth century,
mounds in the Ukraine, Kuban, and Crimea were pillaged. Overall,
more than 85 per cent of mounds excavated by archaeologists turn out to
have been robbed.[4]

Some robbing of kurgans probably occurred soon after their construction. In a famous passage, Herodotus makes the Scythian king
Idanthyrsus answer Darius' challenge to stand and fight the Persian army
with

I am not fleeing from you. What I am doing now is no different from what I am
wont to do in peacetime. I will also tell you why I will not instantly fight you. We

---

[2] D 72, 89. See also D 153, 5.

[3] Catalogues from exhibitions of Scythian and Graeco-Scythian art are often the most accessible
source of general views on the Scythian period as a whole, and one of the few places where the views
of Soviet scholars can be read in English. Even those catalogues which are solely in Russian or
Ukrainian are well worth consulting for their maps and illustrations. D 153 is perhaps the best.
Others include D 3; D 37; D 49. For discussion of the early development of the animal style see D 174;
D 74; D 223; D 98; D 42; D 88.

[4] D 127, 14. Monographs on individual kurgans are in Russian or Ukrainian. Among the most
famous are Arzhan, D 55; Pazyryk, D 175; Krasnokutsk, D 125; Adygeya, D 76; Solokha, D 112;
Tolstaya Mogila, D 134. For Scythian kurgan burial in general see D 104 and D 168 (both in German).
For recent archaeological work in the steppe see D 120 and the following special section on Soviet
archaeology in the steppe zone.

have neither cities nor sown land among us for which we might fear – that they be captured or destroyed – and so might be quicker to join in battle against you to save them. But if you needs must come to a fight with us quickly, there *are* our fathers' graves. Find them and try to ruin them, and you will discover whether we will fight you or not – for the graves. (Hdt. IV.127)

Although these 'Royal' Scythians were prepared to attempt to protect their ancestral burial ground from spoliation by military force, the rich ostentation of Scythian burial was well known in antiquity, and, as Scythian power waned, grave-robbing almost certainly began.

The cited passage is important here for other reasons. The implication that the Scythians had no permanent settlements and no agrarian base, and that their mode of life was nomadic, has been taken as a programmatic statement.[5] The antiquarian interest and the beginnings of scientific connoisseurship that were engendered by treasure hunting remained focused on the kurgans. The only other conceivable index of Scythian activity was the razing of the settlements of others, and attempts have been made to discover such 'destruction levels' in the archaeology of certain towns in Asia Minor.[6] Large-scale regional survey, first developed during the period of the New Economic Policy (1921–9), changed the emphasis of archaeological work on the Scythians away from reconstructions based on burials alone.[7] Since the work of Yatsenko in the late 1950s, Scythian periodization and chronology have been completely revised.[8] Recent work has provided reliable regional chronologies and a wealth of new data, including the mapping of an extensive network of large fortified production centres within the forest-steppe zone[9] (e.g. Belsk: see below, p. 588), and a much fuller understanding of the development of Scythian animal style art.[10]

2. *Natural environment*

The principal geographical feature of the Scythian world is the steppe, 'a level grassland, without trees' (Hippocrates, *De Aere* 28) stretching from

[5] From the time of Herodotus and Hippocrates onward, the idea of a steppe population who lived in waggons and had no fixed abode has been pervasive in descriptions of the steppe. Ammianus describes the Hunnish way of life in terms closely similar to Herodotus on the Scythians. Although early archaeologists were aware of the 'Agricultural Scythians' (for which see below, Section III, 6) and Artamonov in 1947 (reference in D 182) conjectured on what form of land ownership pertained among them, it was not until the more widespread application of palaeobotanical techniques and excavation of settlement sites that the details of sedentary agricultural systems on the steppe began to become known: D 182 and further references in D 113; on the Scythian legend of the 'golden plough' see D 58.　　[6] D 167.　　[7] D 127, 11.

[8] Iessen and Yatsenko's chronologies were revised upwards in the 1970s (D 64; cf. no. 47; D 72). With the availability of calibrated carbon-14 date estimates and the reworking of local typological sequences a new chronology has now been established: D 88; D 126.

[9] D 183; D 184.　　[10] D 153; D 42. In Russian see particularly D 123.

the Danube plains in the west to the marches of China in the east.[11] The characteristic soil of the steppe, *chernozem* or Black Earth, is caused in part by high summer evaporation and long freezing in winter. The climate is strongly continental, with vegetation changing in line with latitude: north of the steppe belt is a zone of forest steppe, beyond which lie mixed coniferous and deciduous woodlands, followed by coniferous *taiga* and, finally, treeless tundra. This horizontal pattern is broken by the rivers, running mainly from north to south (but with many tributaries), of which the Volga, Don, and Dnieper are the largest.

Medium-term climatic changes appear to have played an important part in the cultural development of the region. The development of true nomadic pastoralism in the Central Asian and Siberian areas (where the 'animal style' also originated) occurred during the onset of cooler, drier conditions from the ninth century B.C. onwards.[12] This was probably an important causal factor in the appearance in the northern Black Sea region, from the mid-eighth century B.C., of successive waves of eastern nomads, who were in search of better pastures in the forest-steppe zone and northern foothills of the Caucasus. At the beginning of the fifth century B.C. the climate became warmer and wetter again, and these groups, along with further new arrivals from the east, were able to expand onto the south Russian steppe proper.[13]

3. *Nomads, Herodotus, and Scythia*

The Scythians were one of many groups recorded by the classical authors as living in Scythia. The use of the ethnonyms Scythae, Sauromatae, Sarmatae, Massagetae, Cimmerii, etc. in Near Eastern texts and Greek literature has been dealt with thoroughly and at length by Kretschmer and this need not be duplicated here.[14] Extant *glossae* and *onomastica* indicate that these groups were probably Iranian speakers.[15] The most important single textual source of information on Scythia and the Scythians is Herodotus' *History*.[16]

Because, archaeologically speaking, the situation in the northern Black Sea region was far from static, it is important to distinguish clearly the different epistemologies involved in correlating Herodotus' accounts with evidence from the early fifth century B.C. (his own day), the seventh and sixth centuries B.C. (for which his knowledge was

---

[11] D 120, fig. 1.

[12] For Siberia in the Scythian period see D 117; for climate, see references in D 57, 20ff.

[13] D 113. For a general perspective on steppe nomadism, see D 206; D 119; D 80; D 11.

[14] Kretschmer, P–W.

[15] Cf. D 88, 85. The linguistic material is too scanty for any serious attempt at reconstruction to be made.

[16] The best English translation is now D 54.

'historical'), and the later fifth and fourth centuries B.C. (after Herodotus, but the period to which the most spectacular archaeological material dates).

Herodotus' information on the various Scythian tribes is very detailed.[17] He reports what he himself believes and what he says he does not believe, recording mythical accounts as such. Recent scepticism concerning the value of Herodotus' account for understanding the Scythian world has been archaeologically and anthropologically ill-informed. The coincidence between Herodotus' location and description of the 'Royal Scythian' (or *Sakaurakoi*: Lucian, *Macrobius* 15) burial ground and its funerary rites and the archaeologically investigated kurgans of the Lower Dnieper region is striking.[18]

Herodotus gives two versions of a 'foundation myth' for Scythia – one Scythian and one Greek colonial – along with his own non-mythically structured account (Hdt. IV.5–12). In the first:

The Scythians say their nation is the youngest of all the nations and that it came into existence in this way: the first man to be in this country of theirs, which then was desolate, was one Targitaus by name. They say – they *do* say so, though for my part I do not believe it – that the parents of this Targitaus were Zeus and a daughter of the river Borysthenes [Dnieper]. From this breeding came Targitaus and he had three sons – Lipoxaïs, Arpoxaïs, and the youngest, Colaxaïs. (Hdt. IV.5)

Colaxaïs became king and a version of his name (perhaps a 'pet name'), Skoloti, became the name for all of them – Σκύθαι to the Greeks. In the Greek version, Heracles slept with a 'monster, half-woman, half-snake' (Hdt. IV.9) who bore three sons: Agathyrsus, Gelonus, and the youngest, Scythes, who became king. Herodotus then tells 'another story, which is strongly urged, and it is this one to which I myself incline', in which the nomad Scythians were driven out of Asia by the Massagetae and were forced to cross the Araxes (Volga) into Cimmerian-controlled territory. Under pressure to fight the Scythians, the Cimmerian 'commonality' revolted, provoking a bloodthirsty internecine war among the 'princes'. The Scythians were then able to move in and take over an 'empty land' – i.e., one devoid of an elite – pursuing the remainder of the mounted Cimmerians south of the Caucasus into Media (Hdt. IV.11–12).

[17] There are numerous Soviet works which address this body of information, including D 176 and D 96.

[18] Hartog (D 61) has characterized Herodotus' Scythians as 'imaginary' in his exegesis of Herodotus' guiding ideology. The view that Herodotus principally used objective information (albeit for a purpose) is not given much consideration; Hartog's understanding of what little relevant archaeological data he cites appears limited. For a defence of Herodotus' account in the light of archaeology, see D 106. An attempt at reconstructing aspects of indigenous Scythian ideology (or *Weltanschauung*) is made in D 165.

Herodotus adds that the Geloni – actually Budini (Hdt. iv.109) – inhabited the Graeco-Scythian town of Gelonus, while other passages have been taken to imply that, in the fifth century b.c., a Scythian group called Agathyrsi lived to the west, in the Carpathian region. The latter have sometimes been identified archaeologically with metalwork of the Mureş-Tîrnave group in Transylvania, but both the Scythian character of the Agathyrsi and the south Russian origin of the relevant metalwork are open to question.[19] Elsewhere Herodotus implies that the Agathyrsi and Budini are 'non-Scythians' (e.g. Hdt. iv.49; 104; 119); thus, it seems that the designation of the word 'Scythian' was variable, even for the same author within the same text.

The myths Herodotus records probably reflect an attempt to legitimate a relatively recent take-over of a territory by referring to a mythical ancestor and his three sons, and to provide a framework for claiming hegemony over surrounding territories and peoples. By the fifth century b.c. at least, a 'polyethnic' situation had developed in the northern Black Sea region, involving interactions between Greeks, successive waves of warlike mounted nomads, and local steppe and forest-steppe populations with their own separate ethnic identity and (probably) physical appearance (e.g. the Budini 'with very blue eyes and red hair': Hdt. iv.104).

Physical characteristics and the perception of ethnicity are often correlated. This is natural when we consider that a major channel for the transmission of ethnic awareness from one generation to the next is the family, and that it is family structures that generally govern genetic transmission too.[20] Physical anthropological attempts to detect the arrival of new groups, or the presence of two or more ethnically distinct components within a local population, cannot yet form the basis of secure generalization, but may do so after more detailed study. For present purposes it is enough to note that two major currently recognized racial types, *Caucasoids* and *Mongoloids*, are considered to have

---

[19] D 15; D 194 for the Ferigile-Bîrseşti group; D 99 for relevant chronology. There has been considerable debate over the 'ethnic allegiance' of areas west of the Dniester and north of the Danube; among Soviet scholars Mantsevich and Meliukova (D 124) have held different views. The debate has usually taken a form in which Scythian presence in a particular area is identified on the basis of diagnostic artefact types; these then turn out to be different in significant respects from 'actual Scythian' examples and Scythian presence is refuted. It seems likely, however, that often artefacts of Scythian type could have been made locally for use by a mobile 'Scythian' elite, as, indeed much Graeco-Scythian art was made in the colonies: D 195, 96 and cf. *Pls. to Vol IV*, pl. 104. For evidence of 'Scythians' further west see, for Hungary: D 43; D 144; D 145; D 32; D 9 and D 35 (on Tápioszentmárton and Zöldhalompuszta); for Poland: D 20 and D 38 (on Vettersfelde); for Austria and Czechoslovakia: D 36.

[20] D 204.

existed historically in geographical proximity on the steppe and its southern and western interfaces.[21]

Archaeologically, it is clear that the eighth- and seventh-century B.C. 'Scythians' were not the same as the fifth-century 'Scythians'.[22] Both were mounted elite war-bands originating in the more easterly regions of the steppe, and the Greeks, quite naturally, called both groups by the same name. Archaeologically, five major phases can be distinguished between 750 and 250 B.C., with a fresh nomadic component arriving in three of them: 750–650 B.C. ('Cimmerians' and 'Scythians'); 475–430 B.C. ('Scythians'); and 300–250 B.C. ('Sarmatians').[23] These unstable periods were punctuated by more peaceful ones. In the first of these the Greek colonies were founded and economic relations between them, the nomads, and local agricultural populations emerged. These were developed in the second period, when the colonies expanded and 'Graeco-Scythian' art flourished.[24]

Thus, the terms *Scythia* and *Scythian* can be seen to have had a variety of meanings in antiquity. For classical authors, the south Russian steppes are designated Scythia for many centuries after the demise of Scythian military might. It seems that the word Scythian, supposedly derived from a personal name, Scoloti, came to designate a group which claimed hegemony over other groups, by virtue of which the Greeks generalized the name further to include a large number of steppe nomad peoples who existed at various times.

II. THE CIMMERIANS

The Cimmerians were one of the earliest peoples of Eastern Europe whose name has come down to us, and whose history is interwoven with that of the Scythians. The earliest reference is found in Homer, *Odyssey* XI.14, which may refer to the ninth century B.C.

The Cimmerians are widely regarded as a people of Indo-European stock, a branch of the Thracians or at least closely related to them. Some scholars consider them an Iranian-speaking people, or a Thracian one with an Iranian ruling class; some believe in their identity with the Maeotians, who in antiquity lived along the eastern coast of 'the Maeotian Sea' (the Sea of Azov). There are also several other theories. In general, it seems that the Catacomb culture, typical of the second

[21] Although much work has been done on this, many difficulties remain, both in terms of sample biases and in controlling for the complex environmental and post-depositional factors involved. The standard prehistoric overview for the Soviet Union is D 29.
[22] D 113, 807ff.   [23] D 113.
[24] See D 153, 61ff; for material of this period in a British collection see D 209.

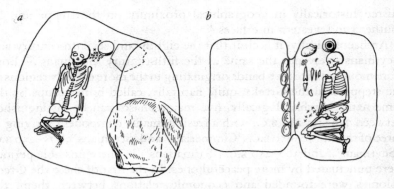

Fig. 28. Examples of Catacomb graves of the Bronze Age in the Ukraine. (*a*) 'Flat' grave at Leontiivka near Kakhivka. (*b*) 'Catacomb' of a barrow grave in the region of Izium.

millennium B.C. in the North Pontic steppes east of the Dnieper,[25] has been seen as providing all the archaeological desiderata which are needed for its identification with the Cimmerians.[26]

The Cimmerians consisted of two distinct sections 'equal in numbers': the 'kings' or the 'royal race', and the 'Cimmerian people' (Hdt. IV.11–12). There must have been some antagonism between them. In Herodotus' story of the murderous fight between them it is evident that the Cimmerian rulers and those ruled by them were originally two different peoples who had not blended into a single nation by the end of the second millennium B.C. A credible suggestion is to link the 'royal race' with the expansion of the 'Median line' of the Early Western Iranians, who in the thirteenth or twelfth century B.C. imposed themselves upon that part of the Catacomb people which yielded to them. This assumption may perhaps explain the Iranian names of Cimmerian rulers, and may clear up the cause of antagonism between the two sections of Cimmerians.

According to Herodotus (IV.11–12), the Cimmerians 'evidently appear to have fled from the Scythians into Asia and settled in the peninsula in which the Grecian city Sinope now stands'. This must have taken place around the twelfth century B.C., when the Catacomb culture retreated, at least if this culture was the archaeological equivalent of the Cimmerians.

A large section of retreating Cimmerians must have entered the Crimea in the thirteenth century B.C., if they had not lived there already before that date. A few hundred barrow-graves mostly of the Early and Late Srubnaya culture attributable to the Scythians, were excavated in

[25] D 193; D 161; D 62; D 136; D 191, 222–30 [and see now D 30 with further references].

[26] D 190, 65. [The archaeological support for this view is not clear-cut: Terenozhkin identified the Srubnaya culture with the Cimmerians (D 201); other possibilities exist.]

recent years in the Crimean steppe; but several proved to be of the Catacomb culture which implies that the Cimmerians must have lived there before the Scythian influx. In this respect the investigation of the settlement at Kirovo, in the western part of the Kerch peninsula, is of importance. Its earliest remains were of a late stage of the Catacomb culture,[27] followed by those of the Srubnaya culture. The final date of the settlement has been put at *c.* 800 B.C., but bone arrow-heads of 'Scythian type' and the bones of two camels found in the upper layer of the settlement imply that it must have been in existence up to about the late fifth century B.C.

Three princely barrow-graves may, perhaps, be connected with the Cimmerians. Two lie one on each side of the Straits of Kerch, the third in the south of the peninsula. In one, the Temir Gora barrow north east of Kerch, a Rhodian oinochoe of *c.* 640–620 B.C. was found in the primary burial. Other grave-goods were a bone plaque in the shape of a curled panther or tiger, and a bone terminal of a bow carved in the shape of an eagle-griffin head, of the same type as those found in Karmir-Blur (see below, p. 583). The two latter articles are often considered the earliest specimens of the 'Scythian animal style' found in Europe. In fact they were either brought from Western Asia, or made locally after an Asiatic model. Many scholars regard the burial as that of a Cimmerian prince, but more often it is considered Scythian. The prince, if Scythian, was definitely not of the West-Asiatic–Kuban stock. The other, the Tsukur barrow on the Tsukur Liman at the western end of the Taman peninsula, was of about the same date: a Rhodian oinochoe was also found in it together with a kylix, bronze double-edged arrow-heads and a bronze open-work belt-clasp in the shape of two confronting upright lion figures (Pls. Vol., pl. 254). It recalls the heraldic figures on pole-tops from Cappadocia and from other sites in Western Asia, and implies that the prince buried in the grave had connexions with the Cimmerians of Asia Minor. The bronze battle-axe from this grave is the earliest article of this type found in the North Pontic area.[28] The battle-axes do not represent a weapon proper to Western Asia: they were frequently found in Siberia and in burials of the Ananino culture in the Kama-Ural region, although the eastern specimens are different in their shape. The burial has been usually considered Cimmerian, which seems to be most likely. The third princely burial of the pre-Scythian period, at Zolnoe near Simferopol,[29] was the earliest of the three. Its equipment was of the Novocherkassk type and showed close connexions with the Piatigorsk group of the Koban culture in the central part of the northern Caucasus.

Another indication of the presence of Cimmerians in the Crimea are

[27] D 101; D 102.   [28] See D 172, 40.   [29] D 178, 57ff; D 201, 44ff, fig. 17.

the names of two towns, situated one on each side of the Straits of Kerch, which bore the name 'Cimmerian'; the Straits have been sometimes called the 'Cimmerian Bosporus'.[30] The Crimean Cimmerians were later assimilated by the Scythians who subsequently took the country into their possession.

Around 1200 B.C., a large group of Catacomb-Cimmerians, pressed by the Srubnaya Iranians, had retreated from the Ukrainian steppe southwards into the North Caucasus, and settled in its north-western and central parts; they survived there at least until the eighth century B.C., especially in the region of Piatigorsk, where Catacomb graves have been found in numbers.[31] They mingled with the natives and became one of the formative elements of the local group of the Koban culture, called so after a village in the centre of the Causasian highland. This group was formed in about the eleventh century on the basis of carbon-14 dates,[32] which is consistent with the remark of Eusebius that the Cimmerians invaded Western Asia three hundred years before the first Olympiad of 776 B.C., i.e. in the eleventh century B.C.

Archaeological traces of these Cimmerians are rather meagre. Among them are twenty Catacomb graves at Artik in Soviet Armenia, c. 25 km south east of Leninakan.[33] Their grave-goods have been dated to about 1200 B.C., but they seem to be of a later date, since a burial 'of the Catacomb type' was found on the slope of Mount Ararat, c. 20 km south east of the graves at Artik; its carbon-14 date is 900 ± 50 B.C.[34] Attribution of Artik graves to the Cimmerians is supported by the Urartian report of c. 774 B.C., which concerns the Urartian campaign in the region between Lakes Sevan and Childir in Transcaucasia. It has been surmised that the Cimmerians in Western Asia were there mentioned for the first time, but under the name of 'Ish-qi-Gu-lu'.[35] This surmise has been strengthened by an Urartian rock inscription of Argishti I (786–764 B.C.) at Ganlidzha near Leninakan, according to which a people called Ish-qi-Gu-lu lived then in the region of Leninakan in Armenia.

Next is a report by Sennacherib, the Assyrian crown prince who collected intelligence about Urartian affairs in the north; he informed his father, Sargon II of Assyria (721–705), of a defeat of the Urartians in Gamir, a Cimmerian territory probably in east Cappadocia. According to some authorities, the battle was fought in 707 B.C., and the defeated Urartian king was Argishti II, but others are of the opinion[36] that the

---

[30] [The view that the name Crimea derives from the name Cimmerian is no longer generally held. It probably comes from the Turko-Tatar *qyrym* – 'fortress': D 59, 17.]

[31] D 62; D 93, 77ff.   [32] D 94, 13–18.   [33] D 77.

[34] LE–818. The carbon-14 date estimate, 890 ± 60 B.C., for the 'Cyclopean fortress' at Lchashen on Lake Sevan in Armenia, is similar.

[35] D 208, 15.   [36] D 151, 233; D 208.

battle was fought before 714 B.C., i.e. before the rout of the Urartian army by Sargon II, and that the vanquished Urartian king was Rusa I, father of Argishti II. According to some scholars, the battle took place near 'Gurania', probably modern Gurunon in east Cappadocia; according to Melikishvili,[37] the site lay on the north-western border of Urartu near Lake Childir north of Kars.

A few years later, in 705 B.C., the Cimmerians tried to cross the Assyrian frontier, but were heavily defeated by the Assyrians under Sargon II, although he himself fell in this battle. The next assault took place in 679 B.C., when, according to Assyrian annals, 'the Gimmirai' under king Teushpa were defeated by the governor of Esarhaddon (680–669) at Khubushna on the north-western confines of the Assyrian empire. Religious texts of Esarhaddon subsequent to 673 B.C. certify that Rusa II recruited a large contingent of Cimmerians as mercenaries. A document of 672 B.C. mentions an inroad by Rusa II into south-west Asia, in which probably some 'allied' Cimmerians participated.

The Cimmerians were quite successful in Asia Minor. They seized Cappadocia, penetrated into Paphlagonia and captured Sinope, a Greek city on the Black Sea coast. In 696–5 B.C., allied with Rusa II, they invaded Phrygia, and in 680 they shattered the Phrygian kingdom of Midas.[38]

Although they were defeated c. 663 by King Gyges of Lydia, they finally captured Sardis, Lydia's capital city, in c. 640. They were now at the summit of their power, but their hegemony in Asia Minor did not last long. In 626 or 637 they were routed by Alyattes, king of Lydia, who killed their king Dugdamme (Lygdamis). Herodotus 1.15 says that Alyattes drove the Cimmerians out of Asia; in fact, the Cimmerians retreated to Cilicia and threatened Assyrian territory. Thus the last Cimmero-Assyrian encounter took place either shortly after 635 B.C. or about 625. The Cimmerians, under Sandakshatru, son of Dugdamme, were then defeated by Ashurbanipal. After this blow, to which also the Scythians under Madyes contributed, they disappeared from history. Some scholars[39] put the Cimmerian collapse between 604 and 560 B.C. We may, however, conjecture that despite their defeat the Cimmerians still remained in Cappadocia, since the Armenian name of that country is 'Gamirq'. They also managed to subsist for many years at Antandrus in the Troad, in the region of Edremit.

Assyrian records of the seventh century B.C. mention the Cimmerians

[37] D 122, 313.

[38] An 'incense burner' (D 177, 33, fig. 496) from the Cimmerian layer of 680 B.C. at Alishar Hüyük in Phrygia supports the identification of the bearers of the Catacomb culture with the Cimmerians. [The theory of an alliance between Urartu and the Cimmerians against Phrygia is rejected by van Loon (D 208, 20).]

[39] D 17.

in connexion with wars and unrests in Iran. After their first recorded encounter with the Urartians they probably split into two groups, of which one moved westwards and the other went south eastwards, along Lake Urmia. Assyrian religious texts of the time of Esarhaddon mention the Cimmerians in the region of Lake Urmia (see below, p. 581) and their alliance with the Medes.[40] Several scholars believe that a section of these Cimmerians proceeding further south reached Luristan, and that they were responsible for the introduction of a series of bronze articles proper to the Koban culture of the Caucasus into the Luristan bronze industry of the eighth–seventh centuries B.C.[41]

Finally, two peoples who might have been of Cimmerian derivation deserve mention. One is the bearers of the Chornoles culture,[42] in the Ukrainian forest-steppe zone west of the middle Dnieper. According to archaeological evidence the culture was formed around 800 B.C. by newcomers from the western Koban group of the Northern Caucasus, who were bearers of the Novocherkassk type of remains (see below, p. 562). The newcomers evidently conquered the country hitherto held by people of the Belogrudovka culture as suggested by the destruction of 'open' settlements of the latter culture and their replacement by the earthworks of the new one.

Archaeological relics of the same or similar type and of the same period were also found in a few countries in the eastern part of Central Europe. In some areas (Transylvania, Hungarian plain) they formed small concentrations. They have usually been called 'Thraco-Cimmerian' assemblages, and the people who brought them into Eastern Europe have been named 'Thraco-Cimmerians', perhaps the latest survivals of the ancient Cimmerians.

III. THE SCYTHIANS

1. The early Scythians

The circumstances in the Volga steppe did not alter much after the upheaval of the thirteenth century B.C. (see above, p. 558) until the ninth century B.C. when considerable changes took place. The starting point was a new invasion by steppe nomads from Asia, which forced the retreat of the Srubnaya-Khvalynsk people westwards into the Ukraine, southwards towards the north Caucasian foothills,[43] and along the Caspian coast into Transcaucasia[44] and Iran. The Srubnaya-Khvalynsk

---

[40] D 47, 32f.　　[41] D 46, 48f.
[42] D 6, 170–7; D 64, 49–110; D 65, 112–31; D 63, 119.
[43] Cf. D 72, 44ff.
[44] D 56, 132; D 211, 258–63; D 93, 186ff; D 187, 44.

culture represents the earliest archaeological remains attributable to the Scythians. In the Ukraine the name 'Late Srubnaya culture' has been given to these remains, and the name 'Early Scythians' to their bearers, to distinguish them from the 'Scythians' of the 'Scythian culture'.[45] They took over all the territory of the Catacomb culture and mingled there with its successors, the Early Iranians. Some moved southwards and settled among the natives in a few regions of the Caucasian foothills. The differences in the inventory of graves and in the burial rites of the North Caucasian cemeteries of the ninth to seventh centuries B.C. of that area (Khutor Kubanskii, Krasnoarmeyskoe)[46] imply the existence of social differences within the population which arose from the invasion by the Early Scythians.

The advance of the Early Scythians into the east Ukrainian steppe country around 800 B.C. was not a peaceful enterprise, nor were its consequent displacements of other peoples. A pathetic witness to the disturbances connected with these events are scores of settlements of the Sabatinovka culture in the valley of the Dnieper and other rivers of the area which were totally destroyed at that time. Moreover, the centre of the 'Cimmerian' bronze industry of the preceding period ceased to exist, and only meagre traces of its revival have been noted in the subsequent period.

Several articles of Siberian origin, especially those of the Karasuk culture of the eighth century B.C., were brought to the North Pontic area by eastern invaders and became a characteristic element of the Early Scythian culture. Among these were cast bronze cauldrons, daggers, swords, and in particular horse harness. In a special study of the last, A. A. Iessen[47] distinguished two types representing two different cultural and ethnic groups. The standard types were bronze bits, those of Type I being of West Asiatic origin and proper to indigenous North Caucasian peoples, and those of Type III being of Siberian origin, introduced in the North Pontic area by the invading Scythians. Those of Type I were products of Koban metallurgical workshops and were a North Caucasian adaptation of West Asiatic horse-trappings to suit local requirements. They were also adopted by the ruling class of the Chornoles culture, who were probably of Catacomb–Cimmerian derivation, and fought not only on horseback, but presumably also from chariots. They reached the Ukraine by the way northwards along the western side of the Dnieper, avoiding the area held by the Royal Scythians. Bits of Type I

[45] D 103, 90f.

[46] D 65, map on p. 128; D 64, 49–110; D 188, 77–81; D 212; D 201; and also published by many other scholars.

[47] D 64, 54, 98ff; D 65, 125ff; D 93, 143. [This typology and chronology has been superseded. See n. 8.]

usually appear in association with specific articles of the pre-Scythian period (eighth–seventh centuries B.C.), to which the name of the 'Novocherkassk type' has been given after the name of the town on the lower Don where a hoard was found.

Of Siberian derivation were bronze bits of Iessen's Type III, with stirrup-shaped terminals. They were introduced into the north Pontic area by the Early Scythians, and their gradual westward spread marked the advance of Scythian invaders. The earliest bronze bits of Type III were found in the princely barrows of the pre-Scythian period, either on the eastern periphery of the Royal Scythian territory (Kamyshevakha, Chernogorovka), or near its western limit, south of the Dnieper bend (Malaya-Tsymbalka) (see below, pp. 574f).

In the eighth and seventh centuries B.C. horse harness, bits of Types I and III, swords, daggers, and other objects of the Novocherkassk sort found their way into a few countries of Central Europe, where they were given the name of the 'Thraco-Cimmerian' assemblage.[48] They were probably brought there by North Caucasians who retreated westwards before the invading Early Scythians of the Srubnaya–Khvalynsk derivation. The Caucasian newcomers settled mainly in Transylvania and in the Hungarian plain. Mingling with the native populations they gradually lost their identity.

A large section of the Early Scythians proceeded southwards, crossed the Caucasian mountains, and advancing along the western coast of the Caspian reached Azerbaijan in Transcaucasia. They settled there among the indigenous population in the regions of Mingechaur on the Kura, of Kirovograd, and in the Muganskaya steppe.[49] The country was later known to Xenophon as the Land of the Skythenoi, and to Ptolemy as Sakasene; the people were called the Sacassani by Livy. Those near Kirovograd were called by the natives Scyzhini.[50]

Transcaucasia consequently became for a century the main Scythian abode in Asia. The newcomers adopted some local weapons. The akinakes-daggers, and the three-edged bronze socketed arrow-heads, often considered 'typically Scythian', were mostly Transcaucasian, in particular Georgian, inventions.[51] Almost the only artistic expression of the Early Scythians (Srubnaya-Khvalynsk) when they arrived in Transcaucasia was a variety of geometric decorative patterns,[52] to which not

---

[48] D 86, 111ff; D 43; D 191, 383f; D 162; D 163. [For a more recent view see D 87.]

[49] For Mingechaur see D 130 = D 131, 226ff. Of importance was the 'Small Mound' (Fig. 29). Its equipment consisted of 21 vessels, all local Transcaucasian ware, nearly 300 bone, paste, and carnelian beads, and a set of bronze articles – all Transcaucasian products except for the bridle frontlet which was probably a Urartian import. The grave has been dated to about 650–600 B.C.: D 66, 22ff; D 199, 71ff. The question of the 'Scythian kingdom' in ancient Azerbaijan has been discussed in D 78, 183–7 and D 159, 55ff.

[50] D 108.   [51] D 157, 22; D 158, 11; D 107, 25; D 205; D 93; D 189, 295.

[52] D 143, 71–81, fig. 1.

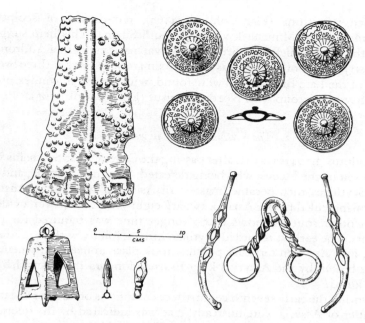

Fig. 29. Bronzes from the princely burial of the second half of the seventh century B.C., the so-called 'Small Mound' (Malyi Kurgan) in the Milskaya steppe, East Soviet Azerbaijan. (After D 66, 22ff.)

only rank-and-file Scythians but also princes remained faithful for a long time.

Important changes due to the Scythian newcomers took place in burial rites and in the social structure of the native population. The equipment of graves of the pre-Scythian time showed no marked social division among the native people. The position after the eighth century B.C. was different. The richly furnished graves of the chieftains, some accompanied by human sacrifice, were in marked contrast with the burials of ordinary people and imply a considerable degree of social differentiation. Furthermore, anthropological study of the bones has revealed that serfs were of a different racial type from their masters, on whose graves they were put to death.[53]

Further south, in the region of Lake Urmia (Iranian Azerbaijan), traces of the Early Scythians have been found at a few sites. Of interest are finds from graves under mounds at Sé Girdan near the ancient settlement of Hasanlu.[54] In a tumulus of the seventh century B.C. a crouched skeleton was found strewn with ochre in the manner proper to the Andronovo burials in Kazakhstan; near the skeleton lay a feline-

[53] D 97, 135–77.   [54] D 138, 5–25; D 139, 5–28.

headed whetstone (Pls. Vol., pl. 256a), reminiscent of sculptures common in the Minusinsk valley in south Siberia. This item suggests that the buried chief was a Srubnaya-Khvalynsk Scythian of Andronovo ancestry.[55] In another tumulus of approximately similar age three bronze axes of the Late Bronze Age were found, which point to connexions of this Scythian group with North Caucasus (Pls. Vol., pl. 256f).

2. The Scythian century in western Asia

Herodotus (1.104) says that after passing the Caucasus the Scythians were opposed by the Medes, who being defeated, 'lost their empire', and that the Scythians then became 'masters of Asia'. At iv.1 he says that the Scythians 'ruled Upper Asia for twenty-eight years'. However, evidence from other sources shows that a longer time was required for these events. The earliest recorded Scythian inroad, jointly with the Cimmerians, into Assyrian territory possibly took place in 676 B.C., when they were beaten by the Assyrian king Esarhaddon and their king Ishpaka was killed.

During the early seventh century B.C. conditions on the north-eastern frontier of Assyria were unsteady,[56] as was indicated by the queries of Esarhaddon addressed to the sun-god Shamash.[57] One mentions a great coalition of Mannaeans, Cimmerians, and Medes against Assyria headed by Kashtaritu (Khshathrita). Esarhaddon cleverly warded off the danger by contracting friendship with the Scythians; Kashtaritu was defeated in 674, and the coalition disintegrated. A Scythian irruption into Urartu resulted in a considerable curtailment of Urartian territory in the south east. Subsequently Urartu was subdued by Scythians, and soon afterwards, probably in 652, the countries of Mannaea and Media were subjugated.[58]

At the time of the reign of Esarhaddon, Bartatua (the Protothyes of Herodotus, 1.103) was king of the Scythians in Western Asia (c. 678–c. 645). He may have been the successor of Ishpaka, possibly even his son.[59] Bartatua was probably well aware of the precarious position of Esarhaddon in 674, and must have considered himself powerful enough to ask in marriage the hand of the Assyrian princess, Shern᾽a-etert, Esarhaddon's daughter.[60] Esarhaddon apparently did not resent her marriage to a barbarian, but his fear was that 'the sacrifice' might be in vain. His worries have been recorded in queries addressed to the sun-god Shamash, asking him: 'Whether Bartatua will speak with him true words

[55] D 24, 116, fig. 21; D 25, 212, fig. 2.7–11.   [56] D 44, 24ff; D 33, 208ff.
[57] D 141, 359f; D 121, 300; D 48, 105.   [58] For Urartu see D 45, 98.
[59] D 31, 258.   [60] D 216, 6.

of peace; will truly say "the peace" which acknowledges his nominal submission; will keep his oath to Esarhaddon; will he do that which is good for Esarhaddon?'[61]

From the legal point of view the queries imply that Bartatua, in marrying Esarhaddon's daughter, had to take an oath of allegiance and thus legally become an Assyrian vassal, and to hold the countries ruled by himself as a fief. Consequently, his kingdom might have been considered a nominal extension of the Assyrian kingdom. The agreement seems to have worked; for in 653–652 the Assyrians defeated Media and left the country to be ruled by the Scythians who had aided them. History does not explicitly tell us whether Bartatua actually married the Assyrian royal princess, but this seems to ensue from the firm Assyro-Scythian alliance and the loyal support of Assyria by the Scythians nearly to the end of that kingdom.

The presumed marriage of Bartatua into the Assyrian royal family, probably in 676, and his consequent legal submission to Esarhaddon were undoubtedly important events in the history of north-west Iran. Family links with the royal house evidently exposed the Scythian royal family to a strong impact of Assyrian culture, and also to influences emanating from Mannaea and Urartu, both countries then under Scythian overlordship, whose culture had developed under strong Assyrian impression.

By the mid-seventh century B.C. the Scythians, still under Bartatua, reached the summit of their might in Western Asia, and the region of Saqqez seems to have been their political centre. This was the beginning of the twenty-eight years of 'Scythian rule over Asia' which, if we trust Herodotus, began c. 645 or 650 B.C. Bartatua died probably in 645, and was succeeded by a son Madyes, supposedly by the Assyrian royal princess.[62] He was then some twenty-seven years of age.

In 1947 a very important discovery was made at Ziwiye on the top of a steep hill, some 200 m above the level of the valley. Excavations by the Iranbastan Museum in Tehran have established so far that the site was a very strongly fortified castle, probably the seat of a Scythian ruler. The most important find was a broken bronze 'bath', sarcophagus or coffin, discovered in the eroded part of the Ziwiye hill in which a 'hoard' is said to have been found. This consisted of gold articles (Pls. Vol., pls. 258 and 262) and personal ornaments, presumably belonging to the person or persons buried in the coffin. But according to recent study,[63] the articles labelled as from Ziwiye at present in many museums all over the world

---

[61] D 141.   [62] D 84; D 155, 473; and many others.
[63] D 140, 197ff. [Muscarella rightly casts doubt on the 'assemblage' as a whole, as well as on the supposed context of its discovery. It follows that any construction based on the 'Ziwiye' material must be hypothetical.]

Fig. 30. Two sections of the incised scene on the rim of the bronze coffin from Ziwiye: (a) viceroy and court officials; (b) a group of foreigners being ushered into the presence of the viceroy. (After D 215, 215, fig. 3; 216, fig. 6.)

were for the most part of other provenance and several were forgeries. But the find of the bronze coffin has not been questioned.

The coffin, almost identical with bronze coffins excavated at Ur and other sites,[64] has been variously dated, but crucial for its dating are the scenes engraved on its silver rim (Fig. 30), which represent rows of Median and Urartian tribute-bearers being marshalled into the presence of an official of exalted rank, perhaps a prince or viceroy. No person of any importance would have had a coffin after the Assyrians had suffered complete subjugation in 609 B.C.[65] The scenes on the rim must have been engraved at a time at which both nations had submitted to the Scythians or to the Assyrians. Media submitted in 652 and freed itself soon after 625 when Cyaxares II ascended the Median throne. Accordingly, the scenes on the rim must have been engraved between the two dates.

[64] D 10, 114–16.   [65] D 215, 213–20.

The personality depicted on the rim was neither an Assyrian governor nor an Urartian or Median king, nor the Mannaean king.[66] The most credible identification is Bartatua, 'the Great Scythian king',[67] who died about 645. By his marriage with the Assyrian royal princess he would have become an Assyrian prince. The engravings suggest that under the terms of the treaty with Esarhaddon the realm of Bartatua may have been regarded by the Assyrians as a fief of Assyria, and he himself as a viceroy in charge of Media, Mannaea and Urartu.

One of the early feats of Bartatua's son Madyes was his victory over the Cimmerians some time after 650. During his reign the Scythians undertook a great raid into the countries south of Assyria and reached the Egyptian border (Hdt. I.105);[68] their evil reputation was reflected in a few passages in the Old Testament, mainly by Jeremiah and Zephaniah. The date of this raid is disputed.

A study of Scytho-Assyrian relations during the second half of the seventh century B.C. suggests that the might of the Scythians under both Bartatua and Madyes depended in great measure on their close co-operation with Assyria. But the last great king of Assyria, Ashurbanipal, died in 627, and the young and very able Cyaxares ascended the throne of Media at about that time. Soon the ageing Madyes had to contend with young Cyaxares and managed to hold Nineveh (Hdt. I.103), probably in 617 or 616. This was the last show of force by the Scythians in Western Asia under Madyes, who died very soon afterwards at the age of some sixty years.

While the position of Assyria worsened, the decisive fact, it seems, was the Scythian change of sides. From 615 onwards Babylonian records mention the Scythians as allies of the Medes, perhaps perforce. Thus Scythian domination 'over Asia' came to an end, and the Medes annexed both Mannaea and Urartu between 609 and 585. The final struggle with the Scythians is said to have taken place shortly before the war of the Medes against the Lydians in 590. The Scythians, 'being afterwards expelled by the Medes, returned in this manner to their own country' (Hdt. IV.4).

The Scythians did not leave any good memory of their 'rule over Asia'. Herodotus (I.106) says that 'everything was overthrown by their licentiousness and neglect: for, besides the usual tribute, they exacted from each whatever they chose to impose; and in addition to the tribute, they rode round the country and plundered them of all their possessions'. Traces of the Scythian stay in Iran and in other regions of Western Asia are very scanty. They consist of Assyrian and Urartian commemorative inscriptions on rocks, mainly on the border of Transcaucasia, and

[66] D 215.   [67] As postulated by Ghirshman.
[68] 'Scythopolis' in Palestine probably owes its name to Scythian mercenaries in the pay of the Egyptians.

of mentions in Assyrian and Babylonian records. Scythian finds from ancient Urartu belong to the time of Scythian decline in Western Asia. A series of 'Scythian' bronze arrow-heads and other articles come from the top layer of the debris at Argishtikhili, the Urartian fortress near Oktemberian west of Erevan, and from the fortress of Karmir-Blur (Teishebaini) in the same region of Soviet Armenia, both destroyed presumably by the Median army between 609 and 585,[69] during the conquest of Urartu. A Scythian splinter group may have joined the Median army and taken part in this act of destruction.

3. The development of Scythian culture

Almost nothing is known of the forced retreat of the Scythians to 'their own country' (Hdt. IV.1.3). Herodotus says that before entering 'their own country the Scythians found an army of no inconsiderable force ready to oppose them', namely the sons of their slaves and of their wives who had not accompanied them in their expedition into Iran. In fact the opponents were a larger Scythian tribe of the Srubnaya-Khvalynsk stock, descendants of those who had not followed their kindred in the southward drive into Western Asia but had settled in the Ukraine (see above, p. 558).

Herodotus placed the decisive battle in the Crimea without any mention of the Caucasus or the steppe on the river Kuban, although before reaching the Crimea the Scythians must have crossed these. The arrival of the Scythians in the north-west Caucasus at the end of the seventh or the beginning of the sixth century B.C. initiated a new period in Scythian and North Caucasian history. Not being numerous enough to spread over all north Caucasus they seized the steppe south of the middle course of the river Kuban. Finds east of the river may be attributed to the descendants of those Scythians who in the early eighth century had settled among the natives and had not proceeded southwards into western Asia. Now, in the early sixth century, they may have been joined by some splinter groups of the Transcaucasian Scythians who had retreated northwards independently of the West Asiatic Scythians.[70]

Well over a hundred settlements, cemeteries and barrow-grave groups have been recorded in the area of the native Late Koban population which was engaged mainly in agricultural activities.[71] In several settlements, however, pottery of the 'early Scythian ware' was found and Scythian elements have also been distinguished in the cemeteries of the Late Koban culture. Evidently in these settlements the Scythians lived side by side with the local population. In later graves, for

[69] D 118; D 148; D 149; D 150.　　[70] D 221.　　[71] D 92; D 93.

example at Goyty,[72] the impact of the Sauromatian culture is distinguishable throughout the whole area, and in the fourth century the country was already in the possession of the Sauromatians.

The arrival of the West Asiatic Scythians in the Kuban steppe *c.* 600 B.C. brought about a marked change. The Novocherkassk type of remains was replaced by the new 'Scythian' culture, to which belong barrow-graves in the steppe and settlements and earthworks, situated mainly in the Kuban valley where the indigenous Maeotians lived. The latter buried their dead in 'flat' cemeteries, whereas members of the Scythian ruling class were buried under mounds. The earliest relics found in Scythian graves have close links with the Ziwiye complex and were mostly of Oriental provenance.[73]

No other Scythian group so clearly reflects the non-Iranian features of its burial rites. Burials with several human sacrifices and with hecatombs of immolated horses were alien to the Srubnaya and Andronovo nomads and the Sarmatians and Sacians (Sakas) east of the Urals, but such funerals of members of the ruling class have been met in Western Asia (Ur), in Transcaucasia in the Bronze Age (Trialeti) and in Armenia in the tenth–ninth centuries B.C. Their practices seem to have been adopted by the Scythians during their stay in Transcaucasia. The idea of the divine origin of the royal power possibly stood at the roots of such usages. In their disregard for the life of their subordinates and in their waste of resources the Kuban Scythians surpassed all royal burials of the period under review.

The earliest Scythian barrow-graves in the Kuban country were excavated at Kelermes. Like most princely burials, they had been generally plundered. Nevertheless, the few intact burials yielded many fine examples of 'Scythian' and Greek toreutic art and other articles of Greek provenance, and also a variety of objects decorated in the Scythian animal style. The finest and most valuable inventory was found in barrow 1/1903 of Kelermes, consisting mainly of items of Assyrian and Urartian origin, presumably brought by the buried king during his retreat from Iran. In barrow 4/1903 a rectangular gold plaque was found divided into regular squares, each containing a stamped figure of a recumbent stag (Pls. Vol., pl. 259). It was evidently modelled on an Urartian prototype and on that of Ziwiye (Pls. Vol., pl. 258).[74] Another remarkable find from this barrow is the Greek silver mirror overlaid by thin decorated gold sheet; it dated from 580–570.[75] In barrow-graves of the sixth century B.C. skeletons of immolated horses usually numbered 16 to 24. But the extreme example of waste of resources and of disregard for human life was afforded by the 15 m high Ulskii barrow 1/1898, of

[72] D 115; D 116.   [73] D 173, 297–305; D 129, 22ff.
[74] D 45, 110, fig. 143.   [75] D 109; D 172, pl. VI; D 8, 26.

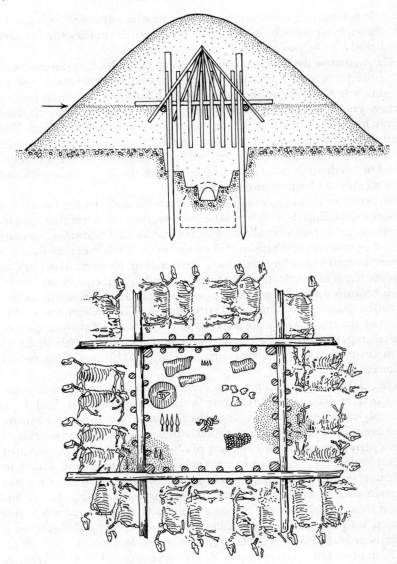

Fig. 31. The Kostromskaya barrow, fifth century B.C. The main burial was in the lowest pit, with other human burials (sacrifices) in the earth above. Over all was a raised wooden platform covered by a pyramidal roof where the weapons and offerings were laid out, and at this level (arrow), outside, were the sacrificed horses. (After D 49, 44–5.)

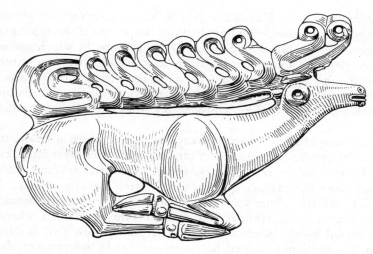

Fig. 32. Gold stag from the iron shield in the Kostromskaya barrow (Fig. 31). (Leningrad, Hermitage Museum 2498/1.)

about 500 B.C., which contained the skeletons of several attendants and over 400 horses and 10 oxen. The layout of the sepulchral construction under the mound corresponded well with Herodotus' description (IV.71–2) of the funeral of a Scythian king.

The Ulskii funeral must have been famous among all Scythians in the North Pontic lands, and its fame must have reached Olbia. During his stay in the city in the mid-fifth century B.C., Herodotus was probably considerably impressed to hear of it, and he recorded it as typical of Scythian rulers. In fact it is unique among Scythians in its grandiosity, and it was more lavish than the Sindian Elisavetinskaya barrow of about 400 B.C., in which several human skeletons were found and skeletons of 'only' 200 horses (see below, p. 573). The Ulskii barrow was plundered in antiquity, and only a few items from its very rich inventory were left. The large number of horses sacrificed in this and other Kuban barrow-graves suggest that horses were the main animal reared by the Kuban Scythians. A barrow-grave of the fifth century at Kostromskaya (Fig. 31) contained skeletons of 13 attendants and 22 horses as well as the famous golden plaque in the shape of a recumbent stag (Fig. 32), a masterpiece which is regarded by many as a perfection of the Scythian animal style.

The burial rites of the Scythian royal and princely burials in the Kuban area and the decorative patterns of the articles found in the earliest graves of this group were alien cultural elements which had been introduced from the south. Furthermore, the relevant articles were for the most part simply products of Assyrian or Urartian workshops which had been acquired by members of the Scythian upper class when still in Iran.

However, once in the Kuban country, no Near-Eastern master-artisans were available to provide their products for the princes. Their role had to be taken over by Greek and Bosporan workshops in which ancient Oriental elements and motifs began to be so blended with those used locally that they applied to the taste and met the wishes of their patrons. In consequence, the art of the Late Scythian period from the fifth century B.C. onwards began to differ considerably from that of the preceding period.

In the second half of the fifth century, the Kuban group lost more and more of its eastern territories: first the area east of the river Laba, and then, by the end of that century, the Kuban territory came under pressure from the advancing Sarmatian Siraces. Thus by 400 B.C. the splendid Scythian culture was extinct there; it survived only in Sindica, the country west of Krasnodar, including the Taman peninsula, where it was adopted by the Sindian ruling class, possibly itself of Scythian origin. The Sindians remained, however, only briefly independent, their country being soon incorporated into the Bosporan kingdom.

At the end of the fifth century, almost suddenly a fully formed Scythian culture appeared in the steppe on the lower Dnieper that had no local antecedents. A study of its remains, in particular of its human and horse sacrifices and of the articles found in its graves, showed that close parallels were to be found only in the Scythian Kuban culture of the preceding period. The Ukrainian group evidently succeeded the Kuban group, being its continuation; it was formed by the Kuban Scythians who by the end of the fifth century were forced to abandon their Caucasian abodes. They were distinct from the Royal Scythians, and have never been so called by Herodotus. Their arrival was not a peaceful affair:[76] they were one of the nomad groups responsible for the destruction at that time of a large number of settlements in valleys of the Ukrainian steppe rivers.

In the area west of Krasnodar, including the Taman peninsula, and also along the middle Kuban river, the indigenous Maeotians lived in earthworks and settlements, being engaged in agricultural activities and fishing. The Maeotians were not of Iranian stock, to judge from the toponomy of the country. Many scholars maintain that they were of Cimmerian ancestry, akin to the Thracians, but some consider them to have been Caucasian aborigines under Iranian overlordship.[77] The upper class in this area were the Sindians, a people probably of Scythian origin, possibly of West Asiatic stock, who imposed themselves upon the natives.

Another racial element in this region were the Greeks who in the sixth and fifth centuries founded many colonies, mainly on the southern and

[76] D 83, 27–35.   [77] E.g. D 179, 102–23.

western coasts of the Taman peninsula. Among the most important of these were Phanagoria and Hermonassa, which later formed part of the Bosporan state. The state was at first organized as a union of Greek colonies which aimed to protect itself against the native tribes; later, it grew into a powerful kingdom with its capital city Panticapaeum on the western side of the Straits. This Bosporan kingdom stopped the westwards advance of the Sarmatian Siraces.

The kingdom was an important outpost of Hellenic culture, which influenced the neighbouring peoples on both sides of the Straits. Its cities became centres of production for customers in the steppes. They greatly contributed to the development of 'Scythian' art and style, and eventually brought about a marked Hellenization, not only of the Sindian princes, but also of their subjects of lesser rank.[78]

The richly furnished princely barrow-graves of the Sindian country west of Krasnodar, including the Taman peninsula, and the poorly equipped burials in the 'flat' cemeteries of the same area reflect the considerable gap which separated the subdued native population from the Sindian ruling class. A similar gap separated the Maeotians from their Scythian rulers, before they were ousted by the Sarmatians. This is particularly well reflected in the archaeological material from the Scythian earthworks built in the sixth century along the river Kuban on its right bank, and their 'flat' cemeteries. The earthworks were abandoned in the fourth century B.C. on the Sarmatian conquest of the country. But at that time a series of earthworks was constructed along the eastern border of the Sindian territory, evidently to protect the country against a further advance of the Siraces. At about the same time the Elisavetinskaya earthwork was constructed near modern Krasnodar, to which a group of barrow-graves belonged, one, as we have seen, containing 200 skeletons of sacrificed horses.

4. *The Royal Scythians*

According to Herodotus (IV.20), the most valiant and numerous of the Scythian tribes were the Royal Scythians, 'who deem all other Scythians to be their slaves'. They lived 'beyond the river Gerrhus', in the steppe east of the Dnieper up to the Donets, but 'some of them reach the river Tanais' (the lower Don). The Crimean steppe also belonged to them. Only a few burials attributable to these Royal Scythians, whose equipment was proper to the sixth and fifth centuries, have been found in this huge area, *c.* 500 km wide, and they had mostly been plundered in antiquity. Their meagre number contrasts with the large number of lavishly equipped Scythian burials of the fourth and third centuries in the

[78] D 75, 257–95; D 40; D 156, 244 n. 19; D 210, 74–9.

same area; and with the very large number of graves of the rank-and-file Scythians of that period, unknown in the Early Scythian period. This leads us to infer that another group of archaeological remains, although not recognized as such, must be considered to represent the Scythians of the Early Scythian period, namely relics of the Late Srubnaya culture. This culture cannot have ceased to exist at the end of the seventh century: it undoubtedly survived to the late fifth century. The remarks of Herodotus are decisive in this matter; for he says (IV.76) that the Scythians studiously avoided the use of foreign customs, and in particular that they avoided 'all Grecian usages' (IV.81). The extreme conservatism of the Scythians of lesser ranks has always to be taken into consideration when estimating the date of relevant archaeological remains.

The bearers of the Late Srubnaya culture were among those who still kept to their ancient ways. The continuity of settlement from the Srubnaya stage to the Scythian stage in ancient Scythia has been emphasized by most scholars,[79] although they rarely mention that the actual transition did not take place in the early sixth century but later. The Scythian common people began to adopt the 'Scythian culture' and the 'Scythian animal style' not before the late fifth century B.C., and this is true also of the Royal Scythian upper class. Out of sixteen princely barrow-graves of the sixth and fifth centuries, as listed by M. Artamonov,[80] found within the territory of the Royal Scythians, none was of the sixth century; five were of the advanced stage of the fifth century, and the latest of this group, the very richly equipped royal barrow-grave of Solokha, many times described and published, was of the turn of the fifth to the fourth century. Three barrows of this list were in the Crimea. All others were of the fourth and third centuries B.C.

The earliest princely burials in this area which may be attributed to the Royal Scythians are three secondary burials, two in old mounds excavated at Chernogorovka and Kamyshevakha, both in the region of the middle Donets, and a third, called Malaya Tsimbalka, at Bolshaya Belozerka south of the Dnieper bend. Their grave-goods were of the Novocherkassk type, and the bronze bits with stirrup-shaped terminals imply that the princes buried there were Scythians. The early graves of the 'Scythian' type investigated within the territory of the Royal Scythians were also nearly all secondary burials in mounds of the Srubnaya culture of the preceding period. Timber constructions found in many Scythian graves exhibit a marked similarity to those found in Srubnaya graves; Scythian sepulchral pottery also shows many features in common with those of the Srubnaya ware. Furthermore, in several graves with a genuine Srubnaya inventory, especially in the region of

[79] E.g. Grakov, Terenozhkin, and Yatsenko.   [80] D 8.

Izium and Kramatorsk, 'Scythian' three-edged bronze arrow-heads were found: they indicate the proper date of the graves in question. These convergencies imply a continuity of settlement within the territory of the Royal Scythians between the Srubnaya and Scythian stages, and they indicate that the actual transition did not take place everywhere in the early sixth century but later.

The territory of the Royal Scythians extended eastwards to Port of Remni on the Sea of Azov according to Herodotus (IV.20 and 110), which already belonged to the 'Free Scythians'. The country beyond the port likewise belonged to this people, although Herodotus mentions that 'Part of their country . . . stretches to the Tanais' (the Don). But probably the Donets was meant here, the large tributary of the lower Don, sometimes mistaken for the main river. Accordingly, Scythian burials of the sixth century B.C. found on the lower Don, for example at Kostantinovsk,[81] should be attributed to the 'Free Scythians', a tribe probably of mixed Scytho-Sarmatian origin. So too the Liventsovka earthwork in the town of Rostov-on-Don, which must have been an important harbour in antiquity, was not a Royal Scythian possession. Its upper occupation layer was of the sixth–fifth centuries, i.e. of the Early Scythian period. It was undoubtedly used by Greek merchants for bringing Ionian pottery, which is found in barrow-graves of the wide hinterland. The earthwork was destroyed at the end of the fifth century B.C., presumably by the Sarmatians. A small mound of stones was excavated at Alekseevka (Krivorozhe) on the junction of the Kalitva with the Donets, about 120 km north east of the Liventsovka earthwork. It contained a princely cremation-burial of *c.* 600 B.C.[82] Objects of Oriental provenance which formed part of its equipment, included an electrum wreath which probably adorned a bronze helmet, an East Greek zoomorphic beaker, and a silver terminal of an Assyrian stool in the shape of a calf's head (Pls. Vol., pl. 260); they imply that the buried prince was connected with the West Asiatic Scythians and came from the same cultural and tribal circle to which these belonged, and who were buried in the Kuban country in the Kelermes type of interment. He was definitely not a Royal Scythian prince.

A few Early Scythian graves have been found along the coast of the Sea of Azov in the regions of Zhdanov (formerly Mariupol), Berdiansk, and Nogaisk. For the most part they were burials of the local Scythian chiefs of the fifth century. More burials of this period have been investigated in the regions of Izium, Slaviansk, and Kramatorsk, at about twenty sites situated along the north-eastern confines of the Royal Scythian territory, south of the Donets. The earliest was a barrow-grave at Shpakovka, of the fifth century B.C. Other burials were mostly poorly

[81] D 81; D 82, 170–7.   [82] D 111; D 110, 197ff; D 18, 243; D 1, 63–8.

furnished interments in ancient Srubnaya mounds; occasionally a bronze ornament was found in them but no weapons apart from a few bronze arrow-heads. In this respect these burials differed markedly from graves of the same period in the region further north, in the forest-steppe zone on the Vorskla and Sula (p. 586ff). In the vicinity of Kramatorsk, at Shcheglova, a burial of a local chief was found in a barrow, accompanied by his attendant and his horse; the grave had been rifled, as had almost all better equipped burials in this region. Traces of several short-lived encampments but not of any permanent settlement were recorded.

More burials were investigated in the steppe south of the Dnieper bend, in the region on the river Molochne, in the area east of Skadovsk and in the steppe north of the Shivash, near the Crimean border.[83] Here again, they were mostly secondary burials in earlier mounds of the Srubnaya culture, and were poorly equipped.

The steppe country of the Crimea was also in the Scythian domain. The Royal Scythians seem to have been in possession of the whole eastern part of the Crimea up to the Straits in the seventh and early sixth centuries.

Several barrow-graves, flat cemeteries, and settlements have been recorded in the Crimean steppe, including the Kerch peninsula. The camels whose bones were discovered in the upper level of the late Srubnaya settlement at Kirovo were evidently brought there by Scythians.[84] A few hundred burials have been excavated.[85] They were mainly of the Srubnaya culture but many were of the Late Scythian period. This applies not only to the burials of the rank-and-file Scythians, but also to the princely burials. Only a few were of the late fifth century B.C.

Crimean Scythians were a sedentary population;[86] they were in some degree engaged in farming as well as in pastoral activities. Their settlements were usually situated close to small rivers now dried up. Investigations have revealed that the Crimea was relatively densely populated in the Scythian period, although no settlements but only traces of temporary encampments were found. It has also been established that the Crimean Scythians had a considerable admixture of Taurians,[87] the native population of the Crimea. The impact of Greek culture from the Crimean colonies is well reflected in the culture of the Scythian nobility in the Crimea, and also in that of the Crimean Scythians of lesser ranks.

Over thirty burials, all almost entirely robbed, of a considerably Hellenized Scythian nobility were found in the vicinity of the Greek colony of Nymphaeum. The earliest interments were of the first half of the fifth century, the latest of the early fourth century B.C.[88]

---

[83] See the various articles in D 198.   [84] D 16; D 101, 34.
[85] D 218; D 217; D 103; D 101; D 207.   [86] D 100; D 28.   [87] D 85.   [88] D 185.

Noteworthy is the fact that in Scythian rank-and-file burials of the fifth century in this area no articles were found decorated in the Scythian animal style, no golden objects, no parts of horse-harness, although these often appeared in burials of local Scythian nobility. Of importance is also the survival into the Late Scythian period of some burial customs and practices proper to the Late Srubnaya culture. This implies a continuity of settlement in the country and the adoption by the Srubnaya Early Scythians (see above, p. 568) of the 'Scythian' culture brought there by the immigrants.

Scythian graves in the central and western parts of the Crimea were almost exclusively of the Late Scythian period. An exception is formed by two princely barrow-graves in the region of Simferopol, and a third one on the western coast of the Crimea.[89] In one of these, the Zolotoy Kurgan or 'Golden Barrow', a prince was buried around 500 B.C. The other barrow-grave, called 'Kulakovskii' after its excavator, was of about the mid-fifth century B.C. The third Crimean princely burial, called Karamerkit barrow, lay at Ak-Mechet on the western coast, and apparently was also of the mid-fifth century. Three gold plaques, each with a representation of a recumbent stag, which formed part of the sepulchral equipment, seem to link the buried prince with the West Asiatic Scythians.

5. *Other nomad Scythians*

In the steppe west and north of the lower Dnieper up to the Ingul ('Panticapes') lived the Nomadic Scythians according to Herodotus (IV.54–7). But Herodotus' description of the Dnieper and other rivers of the area is misleading. His mistake is to regard a large section of the lower Dnieper (Borysthenes) from the beginning of its bend in the north to the junction of the Ingulets ('Hypacyris') in the south as a distinct river, to which he gives the name of 'the Gerrhus'. His assertion (IV.56) that the supposed Gerrhus, 'flowing towards the sea divides the territory of the Nomadic and the Royal Scythians and discharges itself into the Hypacyris', clearly indicates that 'the Gerrhus' was only a name given to a section of the Dnieper-Borysthenes, and that no such distinct river existed.

Climatic conditions in ancient Scythia were evidently very favourable for settlement during the first millennium B.C. This was the period of the sub-Atlantic climate, more wet and damp than today; no wonder therefore, that the Greeks looked upon Scythia as damp and foggy. The border between the steppe and forest-steppe undoubtedly lay south of the present one, in the Ukraine, and the steppe with its luxuriance of

[89] D 178; D 8.

grass enabled the nomads to keep large herds of horse and cattle. The wooded country of Hylaea, extending along the lower course of the Dnieper, and the valleys further up the river, were well watered and offered good conditions for agriculture. There lived the Scythian Agriculturalists (Georgoi), whose country extended northwards 'for a ten days' journey' (Hdt. IV.18).

East of the Ingul lived the Nomadic Scythians who were the western neighbours of the Royal Scythians. The dividing line between the territories of these two tribes was formed by the lower Dnieper. The area of the Nomadic Scythians reached up to the Ingul, in the valley of which already lived the Scythian Agriculturalists. Herodotus says that all this country, 'except Hylaea', was destitute of trees, and he also emphasizes (IV.19) that the Nomadic Scythians 'neither sow at all, nor plough'. Recent excavations of a number of almost entire barrow-grave cemeteries mainly in the various regions of the steppes on the lower Dnieper have revealed that burials of the rank-and-file Scythians were chiefly secondary interments in these mounds and that only a few mounds contained Scythian primary graves.[90] The bulk of Scythian burials were of the Late Scythian period, and only a few were Early Scythian. Within the territory of the Nomadic Scythians only a few princely graves of the Early Scythian period were recorded. The earliest was the barrow-grave from Boltyshka near Shchorsk,[91] in the steppe *c.* 70 km west of Dnepropetrovsk; in it was found the upper part of a fine painted East Greek vase. Further west, at Annovka on the upper Ingulets, near the northern limit of the territory of the Nomadic Scythians, a fine Ionian bronze mirror was the only article saved from the contents of a princely barrow of *c.* 500 B.C.[92] Both graves evidently were those of the local ruling class which maintained close commercial connexions with Olbia.

The secondary princely cremation-burial uncovered in a big mound of the Bronze Age called the 'Pointed barrow', at Tomakovka west of Zaporozhe,[93] is definitely attributable to the Nomadic Scythians. The removal of large boulders from the mound has ruined the grave, usually dated to the late sixth century B.C. Among the articles found there were a gold torque, a gold crescent-shaped plaque decorated with rows of twisted animals, a gold chape, and 200 bronze arrow-heads. The decoration on the gold articles consists of rows of lion-heads, triangles, spirals, some enamelled, executed in the Oriental style adopted by the Scythians in Western Asia. A scabbard has its parallels in the princely barrows of the same period in the Crimean region of Simferopol (see above, p. 577), and the Shumeyko barrow in the country on the Sula east of the Dnieper.[94] It has been emphasized by some scholars that the grave-

[90] D 12; D 13; D 51; D 53.　　[91] D 142, no. 1; D 1, 63f.　　[92] D 128, 377f; D 142, no. 26.
[93] D 142, nos. 30, 33, 34, 37; D 8, 32, 292.　　[94] D 172, 51; D 142, no. 248.

goods of this burial represent a new strange element in the culture of the country. The prince must have been an alien newcomer in the area, who had some connexions with the West Asiatic Scythians; he must have passed through the Tiasmin territory and the country east of the Dnieper.

Of special significance are two princely burials in the neighbourhood of Mikhailovo-Apostolovo.[95] Both had an underground chamber or 'catacomb' dug down to a depth of over 5 m. Unfortunately both had been ransacked, and little remained from their originally rich inventory. Objects worthy of note were in the Baby grave, a gold plaque decorated with the figure of a recumbent stag, the first example in this area, and in the Raskopana mound a fine decorated semi-oval bronze cauldron on a hollow stand. In the latter mound two skeletons and seven skulls of horses were found, a phenomenon hitherto unknown in the Ukrainian steppe and in particular among the Nomadic Scythians, but common already in the sixth century B.C. in the Caucasian Kuban country. This practice was brought into the Ukraine by the Kuban Scythians as they retreated before the Sarmatian Siraces. The graves have usually been dated c. 450 B.C., but if we take into account the time of the Scythian migration from the Kuban country, their graves in the new country should be dated to the end of the fifth century.

The westernmost Scythian tribe of the steppe were the Alazones, who lived in the area where the Dniester and the Southern Bug flow closest to each other (Hdt. IV.52). Eastwards their country seems to have extended up to the Ingul and to have covered the territory of the Sabatinovka culture of the preceding period (tenth to eighth centuries). Their northern neighbours were the 'Scythian-Husbandmen'. The Alazones 'fed on wheat, onions, garlic, lentils and millet' according to Herodotus (IV.17). This may have been true of those who lived in the valleys of the Southern Bug and other rivers but the economy of those who lived in the steppe must have been based chiefly on nomad pastoralism. These 'Husbandmen' seem to have been descendants of the indigenous people of the Late Bronze Age Sabatinovka culture, of Thracian or Cimmerian origin, who in the late second millennium were subdued first by the Srubnaya Iranian intruders with whom they subsequently mingled, and then, in the early sixth century, by the Scythians. According to V. Tomaschek,[96] the name of the Alazones derived from Aryan 'Ara-Zana', which means 'heterogeneous'. The non-Iranian, indigenous Thracian element must have considerably prevailed among the Alazones for them to have been given that name.[97]

The country of the Alazones has been insufficiently investigated.

---

[95] D 8, 33, 290, 292; D 142, nos. 10, 15, 18, 20-4, 29, 32, 35, 38.
[96] Tomaschek, 'Alazones' in P-W.   [97] D 186.

Around 800 B.C. most settlements of the pre-Scythian Sabatinovka culture, situated mainly in the river valleys, were destroyed by the conquering Early Scythians. Many were subsequently rebuilt and survived at least to the sixth century B.C. The economy of the inhabitants was based, as before, on agriculture and animal husbandry. Archaeological remains of this period compared with those of the preceding one reflect the impoverishment of the population.

6. *Scythian-Husbandmen*

To the north of the Alazones were the Scythian-Husbandmen (Aroteres) of Herodotus, occupying the fertile black-earth region of the forest-steppe zone which stretches along 250 km of the middle course of the Dnieper and is about 100 km wide in the south and up to 250 km in the region west of Kanev. Archaeological remains from the fifth to the third century B.C. have been listed by V. G. Petrenko.[98] Some fifty burials in about twenty sites, known as the Middle Dnieper group, were of the Early Scythian period. Within it two somewhat differing groups have been distinguished, namely the Tiasmin or Cherkassy branch in the south, and the Kiev branch north of it.

The common people of both groups were agriculturalists who 'did not sow wheat for food but for sale' (Hdt. IV.17). They were not genuine Iranians but a people of Thracian stock, descendants of the people of the Chornoles culture, now governed by a Scythian ruling class. The earliest Scythian remains, found on the border of the steppe and the forest-steppe zones, show unmistakable Oriental and Transcaucasian features and links. They were presumably the archaeological traces of the West Asiatic newcomers who subdued the native agricultural population, and initiated the formation there of a coherent group of the Scythian culture called the Tiasmin group; it soon extended further north to form the Kiev group of the local Scythian culture. Remains of both groups reflect the organization of its warlike people into a series of smaller territorial units.

The population of both groups lived in open undefended settlements, one of the earliest of which was that at Tarasova Gora near Zhabotin, founded *c.* 600 B.C. There were also large earthworks. That at Sharpivka near Zlatopol, built in the second half of the sixth century and abandoned in the fourth century B.C., was over 16 ha in area. It had a large industrial quarter, where remains of metallurgical workshops were found in which small implements and utensils were manufactured. In the debris a gold plaque with a stamped bull-head was found, and also a large

---

[98] D 146. For the Greek imports see D 142.

number of sherds of imported Greek and Olbian pottery, which implied close contact with Olbia. The earthwork at Pastyrske near Zlatopol, called Galushchino, had a kind of citadel-acropolis protected by a triple rampart; it must have been the seat of a chief or governor of the district. The huts of the Early Scythian period were mainly pit-dwellings, whereas those of the fourth and third centuries were built on the surface. The largest earthwork, covering 52 ha, was at Matronin. The ramparts of these earthworks had a core of hard-baked clay upon which earth was mounded up, and the whole was strengthened by vertical timber posts. The Matronin earthwork was one of several forts built along the southern confines of the country of the Tiasmin group. They were evidently built to protect the country from the assaults of the steppe nomads.

Each earthwork had one or more barrow-grave cemeteries with up to 400 mounds each, evidently burial grounds of inhabitants of the sites. They dated from the sixth to the third centuries. Their number points to a relatively dense population and attests the continuity of settlement during the whole Scythian period. Skeletons lay supine, seldom crouched; cremations also occurred. Graves in these cemeteries were of two distinct types. The more common were simple shafts covered with beams, modestly equipped and without any Greek or Oriental imports. The others were large, nearly square burial chambers dug in the ground, with posts in the corners and one in the centre supporting the roof; some were provided with a corridor and steps cut in the earth. Buried in these structures were members of the Scythian ruling class. Many graves had evidently been plundered soon after the funeral. The difference of types indicates a difference within the society. Another proof of the complexity of the Tiasmin society is seen in the well-fortified strongholds. Presumably they were inhabited by the Iranian Scythians who were descendants of the West Asiatic Scythians.

The origin of the Scythian conquerors is suggested by the large number of parts of equipment, personal ornaments, weapons and so on of West Asiatic provenance found in the earliest 'Scythian' graves and settlements of the Tiasmin and Kiev groups. A large number of West Transcaucasian (Georgian) articles were also found:[99] they were manufactured not later than the end of the seventh century B.C., and were most likely brought by the Transcaucasian Scythians who joined their West Asiatic kinsmen in their retreat into Europe (see above, p. 560). One of the West Asiatic inventions was scale armour which, once introduced into the Ukraine, came into general use among the Scythian aristocracy.[100]

---

[99] D 95; D 93, fig. 10; D 193.   [100] D 21.

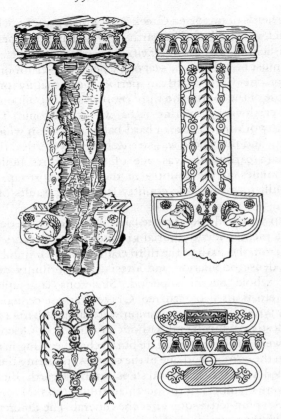

Fig. 33. Gold casing of a sword hilt from the Litoi (Melgunov) barrow-grave, with a reconstruction drawing and details of the decoration. About 600 B.C.

To this West Asiatic group belongs the earliest and most important find of the area, the Litoi barrow-grave, or Melgunov barrow.[101] It lay near the sources of the Ingulets, at Kutcherovka near Znamenka, about 25 km north east of Kirovograd, on the southern limit of the Tiasmin group of the Scythian-Husbandmen, some 8 km from the Chornoles earthwork. This was a richly endowed royal cremation-burial of a ruler of West Asiatic extraction. All authorities concerned with this find emphasize its predominantly Oriental aspect, although they also admit the presence of Greek elements in the decoration of some articles. The sword (Fig. 33) and its scabbard were Oriental made not later than 600 B.C.

Of interest is the barrow-grave of the mid-sixth century excavated at Mala Ofirna near Fastov,[102] south west of Kiev, one of a group of four

101 D 128, 171–3; D 8, 22, 291f; D 142, no. 226.   102 D 147, 164ff.

mounds. It is the northernmost of all barrows of the middle Dnieper branch of the Scythian culture. A warrior, presumably a local chief, was buried there with his wife and two serfs; the skeletons of the serfs lay outside the main burial chamber. The timber construction of the grave was set on fire after the funeral, and the mound was raised over the cinders. The grave was furnished with weapons, horse-gear, personal ornaments of bronze, and several clay vessels. Horse cheek-pieces found there were of iron and their type was characteristic of the Early Scythian period in the north-west Caucasus; similar ones were found in the Karmir-Blur Urartian fortress destroyed by the Scythians (see above, p. 557).[103] They suggest that the buried warrior might have belonged to the Western Scythian newcomers into the Ukraine.

The area of the Tiasmin group of the Scythian culture, and possibly also that of the Kiev group, was undoubtedly identical with the country of Gerrhus which Herodotus described. We may guess that the names Gerrhus and Gerrhi were pre-Scythian, possibly of the Chornoles people, which were still in use in the time of the Early Scythian successors.

Greek imported articles found in graves and earthworks were probably obtained in exchange for cereals and other agricultural products exacted as tribute from the subject population. Another important source of wealth for the Scythian rulers was their favourable position on the main commercial route that connected Olbia with the hinterland. It ran northwards from Olbia into the centre of the Tiasmin group; then, after crossing the Dnieper, it turned eastwards and followed the age-old gold trade route to the Urals and even the Altai mountains in eastern Kazakhstan.[104] 'Some Scythians frequently go there,' wrote Herodotus (IV.24), 'and the Scythians who go to them transact business by means of seven interpreters and seven languages.' It is evident that Olbia was a most important commercial and cultural centre in the north Pontic area for at least two centuries and maintained very friendly relations with the surrounding peoples.

A number of earthworks, a few scores of settlements and some flat cemeteries of the Scythian age have been recorded in the relatively wide strip of land along the northern coast of the Black Sea between the Southern Bug/Dnieper and the Dniester limans.[105] They are attributable to the Callipidae or 'Greek-Scythians' (Hdt. IV.17), whom some authors called Mixhellenes. These were considerably Hellenized 'Scythians', or rather Thracians.[106] Remains attributable to this people have been found

---

[103] D 65, 114, figs. 1 and 3; D 148.
[104] The relevant literature is given in articles of Sulimirski in *BIA* 7 (1968), 47–9; 8/9 (1970), 122; 12 (1975), 151f; and 13 (1976), 225.
[105] D 186, 13ff.   [106] D 186, 23ff. See also a collection of articles in D 4.

also in the valley of the Southern Bug as far northwards as Voznesensk, and as far westwards as the Dniester. On the west side of the Dniester, in Bessarabia, lived the Thracian Getae, and to the north east of the coastal strip the 'Scythians', who were Thracian people under Scythian overlordship.

Investigations have revealed that the Callipidae were a settled population who lived in open settlements and earthworks, several of which have been excavated. They were engaged in cultivating wheat, millet, and other crops. Animal husbandry was also of importance, and maritime fishing was well developed. Houses were mostly of pisé on stone foundations, and graves, mostly flat, were grouped in small cemeteries. Barrow-graves have also been recorded in small groups, for example at Solonchaki,[107] in which presumably the Scythian overlords were buried. The graves were richly furnished with Greek pottery and bronze objects; in an early barrow scale armour was found with daggers, bronze arrow-heads, and other weapons. The country around Olbia seems to have been under direct Olbian rule; for the settlements and cemeteries were purely Greek and the graves contained many Greek articles.[108]

During the Early Scythian period Olbian connexions with the Tiasmin group of the Scythian culture were very close. Members of the Scythian royal family seem often to have visited the city; some even settled in the city or in its vicinity according to Herodotus, who has also described the reaction of the rank-and-file Scythians to such behaviour by their superiors (IV.76–80). The period ended in the late fifth century B.C. when a large number of settlements in the area were destroyed.

The region on the lowest course of the Dnieper around modern Kherson seems to have been the country of Hylaea, 'full of trees of all kinds' (Hdt. IV.54, 76). A richly endowed princely burial of c. 500 B.C. at Kherson-Rozhnovka was ruined by treasure-seekers; it was later investigated by V. I. Goshkevich.[109] This was a secondary burial in an ancient mound. Unfortunately, not much of its inventory has been saved: thirteen arrow-heads and an iron blade of a knife imply that a man must have been buried there, but other articles must have belonged to the equipment of a princess or queen: four gold earrings, a necklace of gold, carnelian and clay beads, and a very fine Ionian bronze mirror-handle in the shape of a goddess. We may conjecture that a chief and his wife of the local branch of the Scythian Agriculturalists were buried there. Sherds of Ionian pottery were also found.

The Scythian Agriculturalists seem to have lived mainly in the valley of the lower Dnieper. Attributable to them are settlements of the Early

[107] D 34.   [108] D 213; D 214.
[109] D 220, 51f; D 128, 375–7; D 142, nos. 17, 25, 31; D 8, 32, 291.

Scythian period such as Khortitsa and Nizhniy Rogatchik.[110] Presumably to the same group belonged a series of settlements of the Early Scythian period along the north-western coast of the Sea of Azov, from Kirilovka on Lake Molochne eastwards up to about Mariupol (Zhdanov). These settlements of the 'Obitochnaya 12 type' are considered to be a further development of the Late Bronze Age culture of the region.[111] The identity of the people of these coastal settlements remains unknown. They were not mentioned by Herodotus.

The territory of the Scythian-Husbandmen probably extended westwards nearly to the region of Vinnitsa. North of it lay the territory of the Milograd culture attributable to the Neuri (Hdt. IV.17.100, 105), presumably a Baltic-speaking people. Herodotus says that 'they observe Scythian customs', 'they seem to be magicians', and 'once every year each Neurian becomes a wolf for a few days and then is restored again to his original state'.[112] The southern neighbours of the Scythian-Husbandmen, chiefly in the steppe, were the Alazones.

The western confines of the Scythian-Husbandmen have not been sufficiently investigated, and only a small number of relics of the Early Scythian period have been recorded. The most important relic, although possibly already outside the Scythian confines, is the earthwork at Nemirov south east of Vinnitsa, the largest earthwork in the Ukraine west of the Dnieper. It is about 1,000 ha in area, encircled by a rampart 6–9 m high and up to 32 m wide at the base, which ran for a distance of some 5.5 km. A stream flows through it. It was once ruined by enemy action and was then reconstructed on a larger scale; the date of its destruction has not been established. The tentative suggestion is that the earthwork was constructed in the pre-Scythian period by the native population of the Holihrady culture, presumably of Thracian stock. Its first destruction might have been due to the conquering Scythians, and the second destruction, after which the site was abandoned, was probably connected with the advance c. 400 B.C. of eastern racial elements, possibly the Sauromatians. This is the date at which the 'citadel', surrounded by an additional rampart, was destroyed. The earthwork probably served as a refuge for the people of the surrounding country.

Important articles found in the earthwork were sherds of East Greek vases of the late seventh or early sixth century B.C., and a fragment of an Olbian bronze mirror of the sixth century B.C. Zoomorphic figurines of horses and dogs, and a large number of animal bones were found in the kitchen refuse.[113]

---

[110] D 14.   [111] D 91.

[112] The belief in the existence of werewolves is still current among the Byelorussian people in the same area.

[113] D 132, 201f; D 41, 84–9; and, for the Greek imports, D 142, nos. 2, 5, 6, 106, 117, 131, 154.

Another Early Scythian earthwork was investigated at Severinovka near Zhmerinka, about 60 km west of Nemirov.[114] Two occupation layers have been distinguished, one of the pre-Scythian Late Bronze Age, and the other of the Archaic Scythian period. When the defensive constructions were built, the settlement was already in existence. Several graves with crouched skeletons lay within the earthwork, but no barrow-graves of the Early Scythian period were found in the vicinity. The remains found in the earthwork show close parallels with those of the Scythian West Podolian group. No Greek imported pottery was present, and barrow-graves in the area were almost exclusively of the Late Scythian period.

7. *The country east of the middle Dnieper*

Hundreds of barrow-graves and over 150 settlements of the Scythian age have been recorded and investigated in the Ukrainian forest-steppe zone east of the middle Dnieper. The archaeological material bears a decisive 'Scythian' character. Settlements, earthworks, and burials were concentrated in the valleys of the few main rivers of the country and have been called after the rivers, the Sula group in the west, the Vorskla group in the centre, and the Donets group in the east. A smaller concentration appears further east, near Voronezh. These remains have recently been treated in a series of special monographs.[115] Some authors consider that all these groups formed an entity, which they call the 'Zolnichnaya culture' (the Ash-Mounds culture).[116] The presence of kitchen and other refuse in these mounds, usually close to dwellings, has not been explained. The Sula and Donets groups differ somewhat from each other; the Vorskla group shows marked deviations.

Many earthworks of the Sula group have been recorded. Built by the mid-sixth century B.C., they were abandoned in the fourth century. The largest, at Basovka on the upper Sula,[117] is nearly 2 km long and 500 m wide. It had moats up to 2 m wide, and its ramparts were 8 m wide and about 3 m high. The core was of baked clay, as in the Tiasmin group west of the Dnieper. Sherds of Greek pottery and other imported articles of the late sixth century indicate the beginning of commercial relations with Greek colonies.

Human and horse sacrifices were the exception. Instead, horse-harness was deposited in the grave, and in a few cases as many as eighteen or twenty. Cheek-pieces of bone or antler, with carved terminals,

114 D 160.
115 The Sula group: D 69. The Vorskla group: D 90. The Donets group: D 180; D 181; D 105. Other, smaller groups: D 2, 134ff; D 222; D 164.
116 E.g. D 105.
117 D 68. For Greek imports see D 142, nos. 43, 64, 72, 140, 156, 181, 253, etc.

represent one of the most characteristic items of the Scythian horse-harness,[118] more than 120 pairs having been found in the graves of the Sula group alone. At the earliest stage they were frequently made of iron. Animal bones were identified mainly as those of domestic species, only 10 per cent being of wild animals. The population was evidently engaged in agriculture and animal husbandry, hunting playing a subordinate role.

The most striking discoveries at the Basovka earthwork were the bones of seventeen individuals at several parts of the site and in various levels of the occupation layer, mixed with bones of animals and kitchen refuse. These human bones were intact and unbroken. Human bones were also found in similar circumstances in at least seven earthworks within the Sula and Vorskla groups.[119] This leads us to the description by Herodotus of a people that lived somewhere in the region during the sixth and fifth centuries. He says (IV.106) 'of these nations they are the only people that eat human flesh'. He calls them 'the Androphagi' (man-eaters). We may identify the Sula group as the Androphagi. We shall return to this theme later.

Princely barrow-graves were mostly large in size, some being over 20 m high and up to 90 m in diameter. Remarkable features are the abundance of weapons and the large number of articles of North Caucasian provenance, found mostly in the earliest graves of the group. This implies that they were brought into the country by conquering Scythians coming from the Caucasian area, partly no doubt from the Kuban group but mainly from the central North Caucasian branch.

One of the largest barrow-graves of the Sula group and one of the earliest was the huge barrow 'Starshaya Mogila' at Aksiutintsy. Its grave-shaft measured 8.5 m by 5.7 m and it was 4 m deep. Partly plundered, it had no gold articles or Greek pottery, but there remained a profusion of weapons, two bronze 'standards' or 'pole tops', and many parts of horse harness, including 15 pairs of bits and bone or antler cheek-pieces. Several objects were decorated in the Scythian animal style. Another richly equipped princely burial was the Shumeyko barrow-grave of the early sixth century. The people of the group were probably descended from the Early Scythians who had settled in the North Caucasus c. 800 B.C. Around 600 they had been forced by the advance of the West Asiatic Scythians to move again and so entered the Ukrainian forest-steppe zone east of the Dnieper. They were evidently different from the Royal Scythians; their earliest grave-goods bore a marked North Caucasian character. Herodotus (IV.18) considered them a distinct people, not in any respect Scythian (IV.106), and called them the Androphagi, evidently a descriptive name, not their tribal name, which remains unknown.

[118] D 69, 106; D 67, 38ff.   [119] D 70, 29, 35.

The Donets group is thought by some to be closely related to the Sula group. About 80 settlements, 20 earthworks and 25 barrow-grave cemeteries of the Early Scythian period have been recorded in the forest-steppe zone on the middle Donets, chiefly in the region of Kharkov and Izium. They are very similar but inferior to those of the Sula group. Burials were almost exclusively secondary ones in ancient mounds. Graves were at the bottom of quadrangular shafts and were usually covered with timber. No cremations were found. Many graves had been plundered in antiquity, and in a few cases human sacrifice immolations were noted. Graves were better furnished than contemporary ones in the steppe further south and contained small quantities of weapons. Life was evidently insecure, as we see also from the earthworks. Only a few graves had Greek pottery or jewellery of bronze or occasionally gold or silver. The burial rites show connexions with the Bondarykha[120] and other local cultures of the Late Bronze Age, which formed the substratum for the Scythian culture of the whole region. The group may be attributed to the Melanchlaeni.

The Vorskla group, formed first in the late seventh century, is of special interest. It was created by invaders of the Chornoles culture from the Ukrainian forest-steppe country west of the Dnieper, who were probably descended from the North Caucasian Cimmerians. The flat cremation-burial at Butenki,[121] the southernmost point of finds of the Vorskla group, may be that of their leader.

The settlements of the group were mostly 'open' and lay chiefly in the southern part of the area, whereas the earthworks were typical of the northern part. Huts were built at ground level, and all settlements had zolniks (ashy mounds) of kitchen refuse of animal bones and potsherds.

The largest earthwork of the group was at Belsk on the Vorskla and may be identified with the 'wooden town of Gelonus' (Hdt. IV. 108),[122] which consisted of three distinct earthworks and an encircling rampart 30 km long. Two earthworks of the mid- and late-seventh century lie within the enclosed area of 4,020 ha but are 5 km distant from each other. The third, the Kuzeminskoe earthwork, was built in the fourth century to defend the adjoining river port. The earlier earthworks were inhabited by different peoples, the indigenous Budini and the Geloni.

The eastern earthwork was a political and industrial centre. Traces of many workshops were found, and copper and iron were smelted from ores brought from outside. Potsherds in the lower strata were of the same type and kind as those of the Chornoles culture of the forest-steppe west of the Dnieper. The western earthwork, on the other hand, had pottery deriving from a local ware of the Bondarykha culture of the pre-Scythian period, and kindred to that of the Sula and Donets groups.

[120] D 67, 26ff.   [121] D 89, 66ff.   [122] D 184, 96, fig. 1.

Noteworthy was the find in the western earthwork of a bronze flange-hilted sword of Naue IIa type[123] of Central European provenance. The large amount of Greek pottery found in both earthworks implies that the site was an important commercial emporium on the Olbian eastern trade route in the fifth century B.C. (Hdt. IV.24).

Barrow-graves formed larger cemeteries which were mostly attached to a settlement or earthwork. That at Machukhy consisted of over 150 mounds. Burials were for the most part poorly furnished. Two richly furnished graves *c.* 500 B.C. deserve mention, both at Lukhachevka, not far from the Belsk earthwork. A rare object for this area was a decorated wooden bow-case at Opishlanka and a quiver at Vitova Mogila. The decoration consisted of rows of small figures pressed from below on thin gold plates, representing undefined animals in the one case, and rows of panthers, ibexes, and griffins in the other. All the figures were typical of West Asiatic decorative art.

Finally, the isolated Scythian group south of Voronezh should be mentioned. Its settlements, earthworks, and best known cemeteries, at Mastiugino and 'Chastye Kurgany',[124] do not differ from those of the Sula and Donets groups. What is striking is the relatively large amount of Greek pottery and of other imports, which were probably due to the position of the Voronezh group on the Olbian trade route. Connexions with Olbia were very lively from late in the sixth until the end of the fifth century, when they ceased altogether. They were replaced by Bosporan connexions, which were consequent on the rise of the Sarmatians who supplanted the Scythians.

8. *Conclusion*

In this short account of the origins and the distribution of the Scythian tribes it has not been possible to discuss in detail the culture, the way of life and the internal organization of the various peoples. The written sources tell us little of the tribal rulers, their names and their sequence, and the narrative which Herodotus has given of the invasion of Scythia by Darius is reserved for Volume IV. However, the study of the funeral rites and of the equipment which has been found in the graves reveals that in the early stages the social differences within each tribe were not very marked. Later the differences became greater, especially in those tribes or groups of tribes which subdued alien peoples.

Considerable transformations in the cultural and political scenery of ancient Scythia and the adjacent countries took place during the late fifth and early fourth century. These were a consequence of the advance from the east of the Sarmatian tribes, who ultimately mingled with the

---

[123] See D 27; D 71; D 183; D 184; D 133.   [124] D 50.

Scythians and were absorbed. Thereby the Early Scythian period came to an end. The Late Scythian period, which followed, had a hybrid culture, to which several factors made their contribution, but principally the traditions of the Early Scythian period and the culture of the Sarmatian invaders. The history of that period lies beyond the scope of this chapter.

THRACE BEFORE THE PERSIAN ENTRY INTO EUROPE

G. MIHAILOV

I. SOURCES

The sources for this period are neither rich nor of a consistent value. Of contemporary literary sources we have first the evidence of the Homeric poems,[1] then some very scanty passages in Hesiod, a few fragments of lyric poets such as Archilochus and Alcaeus, to which may be added some data, fragmentary and imprecise, in the logographers, especially Hecataeus. The historians Herodotus and Thucydides provide valuable, if limited, information. In later Greek and Latin literature can be found statements directly bearing on our period, for example in Aristotle or Strabo, or in the scholia of Homer or of Apollonius Rhodius. There are in addition indirect literary references; they are concerned with later events, but show a process of evolution from earlier times. To this first category of sources should be added the material evidence provided by archaeologists, which is, however, in itself not very rich.

II. A GEOGRAPHICAL SUMMARY

After the migrations during the second half of the second millennium and the first centuries of the first millennium, the Thracians were settled in an extensive area stretching from the Euxine (Black) Sea to the neighbourhood of the Axius (Vardar), and from the Aegean Sea to the Transdanubian lands (below, Section IV). They straddled the Propontis (the Sea of Marmora), and had a foothold also in the Troad and in Bithynia.

Geographically, their country offers a varied picture of mountains and plains watered by many wide rivers and their tributaries. To the north,

[1] It has to be borne in mind that there are great difficulties in extracting historical facts from the world of the Homeric poems. Containing many layers of traditions, they often interpret 'the past' in contemporary terms, and treat the 'present' in a manner archaic and traditional for the purposes of epic. Similarly, the 'present' does not lend itself to a precise chronology; it stretches over a span of several centuries, from the ninth or eighth centuries to the time of Pisistratus, in whose court it seems the poems reached their final literary form. This all naturally affects those passages which concern the Thracians. See D 246A.

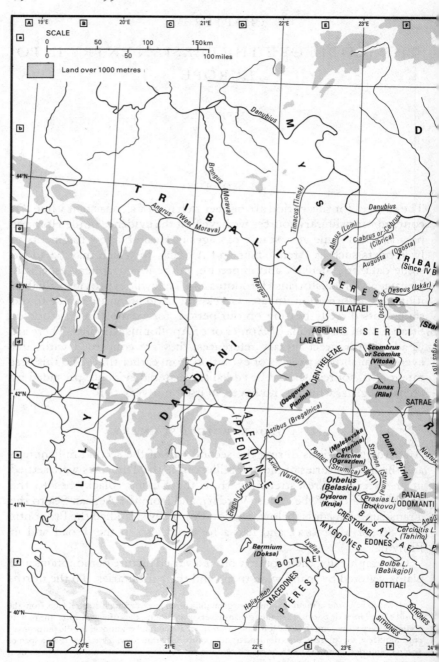

Map 14. Thrace.

Thrace is divided into two parts by the Stara Planina or Balkan range (the ancient Haemus), 550 km in length with an average width of 50 km and an average height of 735 m (highest peak 2,376 m). It is pierced by passes in several places. In the south, there is the Sredna Gora range, 285 km long and no more than 50 km wide, and fairly low (highest summit 1,604 m), whose ancient name we do not know (if it had one), as it might not have been considered an independent feature. Further to the south rises the impressive bulk of the mountains of Rhodope, 240 km long and 100 km wide, with an average height of 785 m (highest peak 2,191 m). Like the Stara Planina and the Sredna Gora, this area provides fairly good living conditions. Adjoining this range is Rila, the highest mountain in the Balkan peninsula, with an average height of 1,487 m (highest peak 2,925 m), a wild and desolate mountain, with more than 150 glacial lakes at a height of 2,100–2,400 m. Its ancient name was apparently Dunax or Donuca.[2] Close alongside Rila is Pirin Planina, which extends into inhospitable rocky escarpments between the valleys of the Mesta (Nestus) and the Struma (Strymon) and harbours more than 120 lakes at a height of nearly 2,000 m (highest peak 2,015 m). Its ancient name is unknown, but as it represents a natural extension of Rila, it is reasonable to suppose that the whole range of Rila and Pirin bore the name of Dunax. Between Stara Planina and Rila is Mt Vitoša, the ancient Scombrus (or Scomius or Scopius),[3] which does not cover a very large area – 20 km long and about 19 km wide – but is relatively high (2,290 m). To the west rises a long range of mountains which separates the valley of the Strymon from that of the Axius, Osogovska Planina, about 110 km long and 49 km wide (highest peak 2,252 m), Vlahina Planina (Pastuša; highest peak 1,924 m) and Maleševska Planina (highest peak 1,744 m), the last apparently identifiable as the ancient Cercine.[4] To the extreme south rises Belasica, the ancient Orbelus (highest peak 2,029 m). If the Orbelus of Herodotus (v.16) is Belasica, it is not always so for some later writers: the name was used to include other mountains in the vicinity. For lack of accurate information, Orbelus was for Arrian (*Anab.* 1.1.4–6.) merely the southern ramifications of Pirin.[5] Not far from Belasica is Kruša Planina, the ancient Dysoron (1,179 m). One should mention also Pârnar-dag or Kušnica, the ancient Pangaeum (1,872 m). Finally, along the length of the Euxine Sea stretches the Strandža Planina which is 260 km in length and as wide as 80–90 km in places, not high (highest peak 1,031 m) but fairly difficult to surmount. Its early name is unknown, for the 'mons Asticus' of the Peutinger Table is not Thracian, the name being taken from the tribe of the Astae.

---

[2] The sources are in D 228, 153. The description of the Donuca mountain in Livy XL.58 suits it well; see D 237 I, 242–3.

[3] D 228, 459.   [4] D 237 I, 167.   [5] D 237 I, 167f; D 240, 198f.

To the north flows the Danube, the ancient Istros or Danuvius, which irrigates a large area of Thrace, and whose tributaries are the great rivers Morava (the ancient Margus-Brongus), Timok (Timacus), Lom (Almus), Cibrica (Ciabrus), Ogosta (Augusta?), Iskâr (Oscius, Oescus), Vit (Utus), Osâm (Asamus), Jantra (Athrys, Ieterus), and Rusenski Lom (Almus? Artanes?). The Kamčija (Panysus) discharges its waters into the Black Sea. In antiquity, there were yet other rivers since dried out, such as the Noës (Hdt. iv.49), which apparently flowed near the township of Novae (Svištov).[6] The rivers which flow south are the great Marica river (Hebrus), with its three main tributaries, the Tundža (Tonzus), Arda (Ardescus, Artescus), and Ekrene (Agrianes, Erginus), and to the west, the Mesta (Nestus) and the Struma (Strymon). The Vardar (Axius), whose tributaries are the Bregalnica (Astibus), the Cerna (Erigon) and lesser rivers, drains a large area which was inhabited in antiquity by several tribes of differing ethnic origins.

The area had relatively few lakes, some of which have been drained recently. They were mainly in the southern regions: Derkos (Delcus), Ismaris, Tahino (Cercenitis), Butkovo (Prasias), Burugjol (Bistonis), Bešikgjol (Bolbe), and, near the Danube delta, the Raselm lagoon (Halmyris, Salmyris).

Thrace possessed some very large fertile plains: the Danubian plain, the plain of Marica, and the coastal sector facing the Aegean up to the Vardar, as well as the plain of Serdica and the valleys of the Mesta, Struma, Bregalnica, and Morava.

The country contained many forests, whose timber was much valued by the Greeks for ship-building. It was rich in fish and game; special mention should be made of buffalo and bison in Maedica and Paeonia, and even panther and lion in Aegean Thrace, which later all vanished. In addition, some parts of Thrace were fairly rich in precious metals and in iron and copper ores, and in particular gold and silver were mined in Aegean Thrace: on Mt Pangaeum, in Thasos, on Mt Dysoron, and Mt Bermium. Some rivers had gold-bearing sand.

III. MIGRATORY MOVEMENTS AND THE CIMMERIAN PROBLEM

After the confused period of the great migrations, late in the second millennium and early in the first millennium, Thrace experienced a relatively calm period. The movements of tribes – which hardly ceased before the Roman epoch – were more or less partial, and were not reflected in the general physiognomy of the country ethnically speaking;

---

[6] D 228, 332. V. Georgiev correctly explains the rivers Atlas, Auras, Tibisis, Noës, and Artanes as southern tributaries of the Danube, but his identifications are hypothetical; cf. for the identification of Artanes, D 256.

this was the period of consolidation for the Thracian people. A more considerable change took place in the region to the east of the lower Axius, where the Thracian tribes had to endure Macedonian conquest (below, Section IV). The Cimmerian problem merits special attention.

Between the years 700 and 650 B.C., the Cimmerians, under pressure from the Scythians, overran Asia Minor (Hdt. IV.11–12; VII.20). Some sources give them as allies the Treres and the Edones (Strab. 1.3.21; XIV.4.8; St. Byz. 97.16), which indicates that a wave must have passed through the Balkans and the Propontid area.[7] Thucydides (II.96.4) speaks of the Treres in Thrace in the Serdica region, while a rather ·obscure text of Strabo (1.3.18) places them 'with the Thracians' near Lake Bistonis, evidence which probably means that they were new-comers amongst the original inhabitants of the region.[8] This tradition is somewhat confused, especially as Strabo treats the Treres of Asia Minor sometimes as Cimmerians (1.3.18, cf. XIV.1.10), and sometimes as Thracians (XIII.1.8, cf. also St. Byz. 634.3), which leads one to conclude that the European Treres had nothing in common with the Treres from Asia Minor who were allies of the Cimmerians.[9] As for the Edoni or Edones[10] – whose principal tribes were the Edones, the Mygdones, and the Sithones (Strab. VII fr. 11), to whom one might add the Odones, the Panaei, and, with reservations, the Bistones[11] – one imagines that, profiting from their alliance with the Cimmerians, they occupied Mygdonia and advanced their realm as far as the Axius, where were already established the Sinti and the Paeonian tribe of the Siriopaeones. To support the hypothesis that the Cimmerians crossed all that wide area as far as the Axius basin and penetrated even into Epirus, an apparently decisive argument has been put forward, namely the presence of objects, especially horse-trappings, of a 'Cimmerian' type, even at Dodona.

However, recently the existence of objects of this type in all the areas where they are found has been accounted for in another way. It has been maintained that they are due to the influence of Near Eastern art which made its way to the north by two independent routes: in Scythia through the Caucasus region, and in Thrace by crossing the Dardanelles.[12] Given then that the literary sources are scanty in the extreme and unreliable, and that the archaeological evidence is open to differing interpretations, one cannot be at all sure whether the changes in these areas were due to a Cimmerian invasion. For a second possibility exists: that the changes

---

[7] D 261, 75–8; D 240, 427–9; and D 233, V. See above, pp. 555f.   [8] D 237 II, 18.

[9] D 262.   [10] The forms in D 228, 197f.

[11] If one can give credit to the evidence that the mythical ancestors Edonos, Mygdon, Biston, and Odomas were brothers, St. Byz. 171.8, Parthen. *narr.* 6; see D 240, 428.

[12] D 260, 125.

were instigated by the migration of the Phrygians in Asia Minor around 800 B.C.[13] It is probably with this migration that one should relate the movement in Asia Minor of certain Thracian tribes or groups of tribes, such as the Edones (St. Byz. 97.16) and the Mygdones,[14] as previously the Bithyni who left the area of the lower Strymon at the time of the migration of the Mysi.[15]

IV. THE THRACIAN TRIBES

A formal enumeration of all the Thracian tribes which were known to the sources, without consideration of chronology, would provide a more or less unbalanced picture of the elements of the Thracian people and their role in the history of the country. Each historical period has concerned itself with those tribes which were involved in the events of that period, and thus one can arrive at a chronological stratification. In spite of the correctness of this principle, a description, however short, of the main tribes can provide, on the one hand, an idea of the great tribal variety which is seen in the historical aspect of these people, and, on the other, the great transformations which have taken place through the ages. At the same time, one must remember that the irregular and inadequate nature of the evidence prevents us from reaching exact conclusions in most cases. If one glances even casually at Map 14, one will come to the conclusion that the areas north of the Haemus were occupied by very widespread but not at all numerous tribes, and the further south one goes, the more numerous and the smaller the tribes become. This unbalanced picture is due to the fact that our information for the southern areas is fuller and more detailed, because these tribes had closer links with the Greek world.

We have no way of knowing what the 'Thracians' called themselves, if indeed they had a common name. The name occurred in Homer and Hesiod in the eighth and seventh centuries, before there was any idea of a national Thracian identity. Thus the name Thracians and that of their country, Thracia, were given by the Greeks to a group of tribes occupying the territory described above (Section II). The origins of the name are not clear;[16] but it is probable that at first the names applied only to a very restricted area and group of people, and that later they covered a whole region occupied by tribes of the same ethnic origin.

Leaving to one side the Dacians and their ethnic relationship with the 'Thracians', the first Thracians who lived south east of them were the

---

[13] Cf. D 240, 410f; D 238, 12f, 16f.   [14] The sources: D 228, 306f.
[15] The sources: D 228, 306f.   [16] D 245.

Getae, who formed a large group consisting of several tribes.[17] The
Getae occupied a vast territory on both banks of the Danube; on the left
bank approximately to the east of the Alutas, and on the right bank in the
Dobrudža area, into which other tribes, both Thracian and non-
Thracian, penetrated in their turn: Crobyzi, Scythae, and Sarmatae, after
which the Dobrudža was called Scythia Minor. But it seems that at a
period before the fifth century the Getae bordered upon the Moesi, if we
are to give credit to Dio Cassius (LI.27: 'in former times, the Moesi and
the Getae occupied all the region between the Haemus and the Istros'). It
is very likely that the situation was the same on the left bank. The sources
do not tell us which tribes comprised the Getic group. However, a text of
Hellanicus (*FGrH* 4 F 73), associates the Crobyzi as well as the Terizi
(from the Tirizian promontory) with the Getae, who 'immortalize' (Hdt.
IV.94), that is, 'render immortal' by ritual. The Crobyzi were a sub-
group of the Getae tribes. Already known to Hecataeus (*FGrH* 1 F 170),
they are grouped by Herodotus (IV.49) with the Thracians. He knew of
them to the east of the Asamus, in the basin of the rivers Athrys, Noës,
and Artanes. Later, one sees them much more to the east, in the
hinterland of Odessus and Callatis (Ptol. III.10.4. cf. Strab. VII.5.12,
Scymn. 145, 750, 756); it is probable that the Crobyzi were displaced by
pressures from the Triballi, and their drift continued during the period
of domination by the latter. Getic tribes were probably the Aedi, the
Scaugdae and the Clariae (Pliny *N.H.* IV.41).[18] The cultural level of some
Getic tribes was so low that they lived in 'houses' dug into the earth
(such underground villages are known among Phrygians and Arme-
nians). The Greeks called them Troglodytae (Strab. VII.5.12).

As stated above, to the west of the Getic tribes lived the Moesi (Dio
Cass. LI.27), whose territory also stretched along the left bank of the
Danube (Strab. VII.3.2). According to tradition, a large number of them
had emigrated to Asia Minor (Strab. VII.3.2) before the Trojan War
(Strab. XII.8.4.). Herodotus' statement (VII.20: cf. VII.75 and V.12) that
the Mysi and the Teucri passed, before the Trojan War, from Asia into
Europe by the Bosporus, subjugated the Thracians and reached the

[17] Principal sources: D 228, 103f. They were known in antiquity as Getae, and almost never as
Thracians, which caused them to be called by some scholars 'Thraco-Getae'. This term is incorrect.
Our primary source, Hdt. IV.93, tells us that 'the Getae are the bravest and the most just amongst the
Thracians'. The evidence is categorical and leaves no doubt as to their Thracian origins. It is
supported by Strabo VII.3.2 ('The Greeks considered the Getae as Thracians'). In another passage in
Strabo VII.3.12, the Getae are connected with the Dacians, which allows some scholars to talk of
'Daco-Getae'. But the logic of the evidence is more to the effect that the Dacians belonged also to the
Thracian group without having been called Thracians, owing to their position remote from the rest
of the group, and their separate historical development. But given that the Getae were Thracian, and
thus spoke a Thracian dialect, the evidence of Strabo VII.3.13, that 'the Dacians speak the same
language as the Getae', links the Dacians with the group who spoke the Thracian language.
[18] The three last-named tribes Detschew (D 228 s.vv.) identifies as 'Sonderstämme des getischen
Inlandes'.

river Peneus in Thessaly and the Ionian (Adriatic) Sea, is enigmatic because it is not verifiable. Still, an invasion or migration from the east to the west is not in principle impossible. The first reference to the Moesi as Mysi, which is the traditional form for them in Asia Minor, is in Homer (*Il.* XIII.1–7), and it remains almost the only one up to the first century B.C. with the exception of a brief fragment of Hellanicus (*FGrH* 2 F 74 = St. Byz. 427) which is a problem; the evidence reappears with the entry of the Romans into the Balkans.[19] Even after the migration of the Asiatic Mysi, the Moesi remained sufficiently numerous, consisting of several tribes, for the Romans to call the province Moesia. Pliny speaks of the 'Moesic tribes' (*N.H.* IV.3 'Moesiacae gentes'), but their names remain almost unknown; in the Roman period, the tribes of the Artakioi (Dio Cass. LI.27.1) or Artakai (St. Byz. 127.23)[20] were known.

South of the Moesi were the Triballi. Most of the ancient authors designate them as Thracians (Strab. VII.3.8; VII.5.6; VII.5.11),[21] and those names which have been preserved, both human and geographical, suggest that their origin is Thracian rather than Illyrian.[22] It is true that writers refer to them quite often as a separate entity from the Thracians,[23] but this is owing to their reputation as an important tribe, paralleled for example by the Getae being referred to as a separate unit. They could not possibly have been Illyrians. The fact that St. Byz. (634.8) designates them as of Illyrian ethnic origin is due to his mistaken interpretation of a passage of Aristophanes (*Av.* 1520–2), which was his source. The mythical genealogy in Appian (*Ill.*2) which links in kinship the Triballi, the Illyrians, and the Paeones is a later speculation and has no more validity than the Thracian genealogy in Antoninus Liberalis (21). Appian, it is true (*Ill.*3), formally describes them as Illyrians, but in the same passage he describes the Scordisci also as Illyrians. This opinion can be accounted for by the fact that at first they lived in the borderland between Thrace and Illyria.[24] According to the evidence of Herodotus (IV.49), and of Thucydides (II.96; IV.101.5), we can place, in the fifth century, the large group of Triballi in the vast region of middle Morava, including the plain of Niš (Naissus) and the Nišava valley; to the east, their neighbours were the Treres and the Tilataei. It is likely that they had occupied these territories from the earliest times. In the fourth century, in the time of Philip and Alexander, they are found in the region

---

[19] Papazoglu (D 250, 434–6) suggests that this long silence could be explained by the fact that the Moesi should be understood to be included under the name of the Getae; this is naturally in the nature of a hypothesis only.

[20] Cf. D 250, 433 n. 141.   [21] See D 237 II, 20 with n. 1.

[22] D 237 II, 20 n. 2.   [23] D 237 II, 20 n. 1, and the texts in D 250, 573–86.

[24] Amongst those recently concerned with the Triballi, B. Gerov (D 237 II, 20 (bibl.)) has asserted, in my opinion correctly, their Thracian origin, while F. Papazoglu (D 250, 67–81) considers them to be a separate ethnic group with an inter-mixture of Thracian and Illyrian elements.

between Ciabrus and Utus, which had previously belonged to the eastern Moesian tribes; naturally, some Triballi remained in their original territory, but they are no longer mentioned.[25]

Before they moved eastwards in the fourth century, the Triballi were the western neighbours of the Treres and the Tilataei who occupied in general the region of Serdica: to the north of the mountain of Scombrus (Vitoša) and to the east as far as the river Oescus (Iskâr), according to Thucydides' description (II.96). We have referred to the Treres above (Section III); the Tilataei are known only through the evidence of Thucydides. These two tribes were probably assimilated by the Triballi during their advance eastwards, and have disappeared from the sources.[26]

In place of the vanished Treres and Tilataei, we later find the Serdi for whom there is no evidence before the end of the first century B.C. It has for long been supposed on convincing linguistic and archaeological grounds that this tribe was of Celtic origin; it established itself during the period of the Celtic invasions at the end of the fourth century and the beginning of the third century, and was gradually 'Thracianized' over the centuries while still preserving some of its national traditions up to a relatively late date.[27]

There is no doubt that the Agrianes and the Laeaei who occupied the land on the uppermost reaches of the river Strymon were Paeones; the evidence of Thucydides and of other later authors is conclusive (Thuc. II.96, Appian, *Ill*. 41, cf. St. Byz. 21.13, Hesych. 67). The only writer who describes the Agrianes (under the form Agrii) as Thracians, is Theopompus (F 257(a)), but his evidence, isolated as it is, carries less weight.[28]

To the south of these two tribes lived the Dentheletae,[29] in the neighbourhood of the towns of Stanke Dimitrov and of Kjustendil (Pautalia), as well as in the mountains to the west towards the valleys of the Morava and the Vardar. Probably the Agrianes and the Laeaei were

---

[25] See B. Gerov (D 237 II, 20–4 and 55–62 (bibl.)), according to whom the migrating Celts had set the Illyrian tribes in motion, and the Autariatae (together with other tribes) had chased out the Triballi and occupied their land. Against the opinion of A. Mócsy (D 247, 89 n. 5, 103ff) that the central area of the Triballi was always sited (even in the fifth century) to the east, that is towards the Oescus, see the objection of B. Gerov (D 237 IV, 35f). F. Papazoglu (D 250, 46–52) does not share Gerov's view, and supports, without success, the early view that the Triballi had always lived between Morava and Iskâr (Oescus). Latterly A. Fol (D 232, 9–25) sees in the movements of the Triballi eastwards the expansion of a state similar to that of the Odrysae in the fifth century and rivalling them.

[26] D 237 II, 17; D 232, 23. There exists however some evidence in Pliny, *N.H.* IV.35, which speaks of the Treres to the west in Illyria: *mox in ora Ichnae, fluvius Axius. Ad hunc finem Dardani, Treres, Pieres Macedoniam accolunt.* For possible explanation of this information see Gerov (D 237 II, 19), who is inclined to accept that it reports a former situation; it stems probably from Varro, whose sources were no earlier than the time of Philip and Alexander. On Pliny's sources, see also D 237 II, 60 and 67.

[27] D 237 II, (30-), 41–5, IV, 37–8, addenda.   [28] D 237 I, 231 n. 7.

[29] The forms of the name: D 228, 115f.

overwhelmed by them. The first reference to them is found in Theopompus (*FGrH* 115 F 221 = St. Byz. 217.21), in connexion with certain events around the year 340; they continued to occupy this area throughout the Roman era.[30]

Their southern neighbours were the Maedi.[31] Their territory extended along the valley of the central Strymon between the Kresna Pass and the Rupel Pass, but probably included also the plain of Blagoevgrad (Scaptopara). The Pirin mountain separated them to the east from the Digerri and from some Bessi tribes. To the west, the area of the upper and middle Astibus (Bregalnica) formed part of their territory. Beyond the Rupel Pass, they bordered upon the Sinti who also occupied the upper reaches of the Pontus (Strumica), whose lower course flowed through the Maedica. From the time of their first mention for the year 429 (Thuc. 11.98), they continued to live in this area up to the late Roman period.[32] Earlier, certain tribes of the Maedi emigrated to Asia Minor, where they were known under the name of the Maedobithyni.[33] One can only surmise the reasons for their migration: was it perhaps connected with the Phrygian migration and the Illyrian expansion, and had it some connexion with the migration of the Bithyni? As for the Sinti, they never occupied the Strymon valley north of the Rupel Pass where certain scholars place them.[34] Whether there was any relationship between the Sinti and the Homeric Sinties at Lemnos (*Il.* 1.593–4), it is not possible to say with any confidence. Strabo (VII fr. 46) identifies the Sinti with the Sinties, but in another passage (XII.3.20) he writes that the Sinties later called themselves Sinti, then Sai and Sapaei: it is evident that the tradition is utterly confused, for the Sai and Sapaei are associated with one another because they occupied the same territory, but they have nothing in common with the Sinti and the Sinties.

To the west of the Strymon as far as the basin of the lower Axius, extensive territories belonged to the Thracians, who in the course of the seventh and sixth centuries contracted eastwards under pressure from the Macedonians. We learn of this process from Thucydides (11.99), who describes the situation in Lower Macedonia in 429 under Perdiccas. From this text we see that before the Macedonian conquest, from west to east, the Thracian tribes lived as follows: the Pieres to the south of the Haliacmon; the Bottiaei between the Haliacmon and the Axius, in the Lydias basin; to the east of the Axius, the Edones, who had been driven out of Mygdonia, where only Mygdones remained; to the north of the Mygdones, the Crestonaei, who occupied the upper reaches of the

---

[30] D 237 1, 226–30.

[31] Undue importance is attached to Maedus figuring in the genealogy of Illyrius by Hammond (D 240, 422, 427), who believes the Maedi were Illyrians.

[32] D 237 1, 159–65, bibl.   [33] D 237 1, 159.   [34] D 250 A, 366–8; D 240, 197.

Echedorus, whose lower course ran through Mygdonia; and to the east of these last two tribes, the Bisaltae. After the Macedonian conquest, the situation was as follows: the Mygdones in Mygdonia; the Crestonaei in Crestonia, and to the east, up to the Strymon, the Bisaltae; in Chalcidice, the Crousi in the Crousis, the Bottiaei in Bottice, and the Sithones in the two little peninsulas of Sithone and Pallene.[35]

The Mygdones were an Edonian tribe, Strabo (VII fr. 11): 'Of the Edones some call themselves Mygdones, some Edones (''Ηδωνες, app. cr. ''Ωδονες?), some Sithones.' We cannot say if the form Odones (''Ωδονες), is preferable here, but such a form did exist, and it is difficult to dissociate it from the Edones (''Ηδωνες). St. Byz. (706. 8) has listed a Thracian tribe ''Ωδονες adjoining the Maedi, and Athenaeus (xv.683 a-b) cites the toponym 'Ωδονίη, quoting Nicander. On the other hand, Hesychius tells us that the ancient name of Thasos, before its Greek colonization, was Odonis ('Οδωνίς), which ought to indicate that an Edonian tribe had occupied this island too. These Odones (''Ωδονες), who were neighbours of the Maedi, could not have been very far removed from the Odomanti or Odomantes, whose name undoubtedly relates to the Odo-group ('Ωδο- or 'Οδω-). The Odomanti occupied part of the region between the Strymon and Nestus to the north of the Angites, and are mentioned in connexion with the campaigns of Megabazus in 512 B.C. and of Sitalces in 429 B.C. (Hdt. v.16; VII.112; Thuc. II.101.3; v.6.1; cf. Aristoph. *Acharn.* 157). In the time of Strabo, they were still in that area. South of the Angites and the Odomanti were the Edones and the Pieres, who had found their new home here. To the north of the Odomanti, also east of the Strymon, lived the Panaei (Thuc. II.101.3), who also belonged to the Edonian group (St. Byz. 499.3); it was an unimportant tribe, and after Thucydides it is not mentioned again in the sources.

To the east of the Edonian group, towards the right bank of the Nestus, are found the Dröi, who are mentioned only once by Thucydides (II.101.3; for the year 429 B.C.), their neighbours the Dersaei, known to Herodotus (VII.110; for the year 480 B.C.) and Thucydides (II.101.3),[36] and the Saei. It is reasonable to site the last mentioned opposite Thasos. The fragment 6 (Diehl) of Archilochus, where the poet describes how he had his shield stolen by a Saean, does not justify us in concluding that the Saei lived in the island of Thasos, for before the arrival of the Greeks on the island it was known as Odonis (see above). It is less likely that the Saei came to attack the colonists than that the latter gave battle to these

---

[35] D 240, 123–62, 176–91, 430–9; the sources: D 228, s.vv.

[36] It is not known for certain whether they are the same as the Darsii (St. Byz. 220.6, after Hecataeus), as Detschew (D 228, 120) believes. On the possibility of a connexion of the name of the Dersaei (Δερσαῖοι) with that of the 'strategia' Dresapaïke (Δρησαπαϊκή), see D 242, 40–1.

Thracians on the mainland in order to conquer the coastal strip.[37] But it is possible to accept the evidence that in archaic times the Saei also lived on the island of Samothrace (Strab. x.2.17, etc.).[38] According to Strabo they occupied the mainland opposite also and were the same as the Homeric Sinties or the historical Sapaei, or 'others', but these statements are not plausible and maybe arise from later learned speculations (see also above). According to Hesychius, the Saei were in former times the Cicones, but in fact the Saei and the Cicones were contemporaneous[39] and are here confused on account of the proximity of their territories.

To the east of the Nestus lies the country of the Bistones with the lake Bistonis. After Herodotus (VII.110), who mentions them in connexion with Xerxes' march, they figure mainly in the legendary tradition.[40] North east of them lived the Trausi, whom Livy (XXXVIII.41.5) places in 188 B.C. to the east of the Hebrus, in the hinterland of Maronea and Aenus,[41] and with their name one must associate the name of the river Trauus which flows into Lake Bistonis (Hdt. VII.109; today Karadžasu). Their disappearance from the sources can be accounted for by their subjugation by the Sapaei. These latter were known from the time of Herodotus until the Roman epoch with the Sapaean dynasty (Hdt. VII.109; Appian, B.C. IV.368; etc.).[42] East of the Bistones lie the Cicones, in whose land Maronea is situated. According to Pliny (N.H. IV.43; cf. Mela II.28, Solin. x.7), they occupied all the maritime zone as far as the Hebrus. They were known from the time of Homer, and Herodotus mentions them in connexion with Xerxes' expedition; but later they mostly figure in the mythological tradition.[43] It ought to be accepted that they were subdued by the Sapaei, and perhaps, to the east, in the hinterland of the Aenus, by the Corpili. The description in Livy (XXXVIII.40–1) of the march of Cn. Manlius Vulso through Aegean Thrace in 188 B.C.[44] and of the march of Brutus and Cassius in Appian (B.C. IV.368–73 and 426–38) by the same route, allows us to site this tribe in the hinterland of Aenus. Apart from Livy (loc. cit.),[45] the Corpili are

---

[37] D 251, 16, 32–4. [38] See D 228, 41of.

[39] The sources: D 228, s.vv. [40] Evidence in D 228, 72.

[41] The passage in Herodotus v.3–4, where their name is first mentioned, does not indicate the location of their territory. [42] Some sources: D 228, 421.

[43] Sources: D 228, 245. The Homeric text (Il. 11.846) gives no justification for seeing the Cicones as non-Thracian, 'perhaps related to the Thracians', as is the opinion of V. Velkov (D 257, 289f). See the objections of G. Mihailov and V. Georgiev, ibid., 324 and 329.

[44] The Corelli in the passage quoted from Livy are without doubt a corruption of Corpili (D 228, 254 s. Κορπίλοι). Relying on the passage in Livy, I. Venedikov (D 258A, 51–88) places, correctly, the 'Passes of the Corpili' not to the west of the Hebrus as has been done up to now, but to the east of the river. That this tribe extended to the east of the Hebrus he concluded also from the evidence of Demosthenes (XII.3): Διοπείθης ἐμβαλὼν εἰς τὴν χώραν Κρωβύλην μὲν καὶ τὴν Τιρίστασιν (on the coast of the Propontis) ἐξηνδραποδίσατο where Κρωβύλη could only be the land of the Κορπῖλοι, and the text of Strabo (VII fr. 58) quoted below: 'Apsynthis, actually the Corpilike', ἡ μὲν γὰρ Αἶνος κεῖται κατὰ τὴν πρότερον Ἀψυνθίδα, νῦν δὲ Κορπιλικὴν λεγομένην. [45] See above, n. 44.

mentioned rather late, about the first century B.C., but at that time this tribe was the most important in the region in having given its name to the Strategia Corpilike which comprised ancient Apsynthis and Aenus (Strab. VII fr. 58).[46] To the north of the Corpili, Strabo (VII fr. 48), the only source, places the Brenae, who played no part in the history of the country.

To the east of the Cicones were the Paeti, one of the tribes enumerated by Herodotus (VII.110) who were connected with the march of Xerxes. According to Arrian (*Anab.* 1.11.4), in 334 B.C. the Paetice was situated on the left bank of the Hebrus. This is the last reference to this tribe. Their neighbours were the Apsinthii or Apsynthii, mentioned first by Herodotus (VI.34) for about the year 555 B.C. as neighbours of the Dolonci.[47] The river Melas is also known as the Apsinthus (Dion. Perieg. 575). The frontier between them, the Paeti and the Cicones, and in general the frontiers between the tribes of this region would doubtless be variable, for with Strabo (VII fr. 58) Aenus was not in the territory of the Cicones where Pliny placed it (*N.H.* IV.43), but in the former Apsynthis, 'actually the Corpilike'. The Thracian Chersonese belonged to the Dolonci, whom mythology made kin to the Bithyni (St. Byz. 169.19), but the origin of that genealogy is unknown. Their history dies out with the activities of the Philaïds during the second half of the sixth century (Section V, below), and their name is not mentioned until several centuries later in the geographical descriptions of Thrace by Pliny (*N.H.* IV.41) and by Solinus (LXVIII.3). The length of the Propontis was inhabited by the Caeni, the Caenici of Pliny,[48] known from the first century B.C. They were probably a considerable tribe, for it was after them that the strategia was named Kainike.

The Astae appeared only from the late Hellenistic era, second–first century B.C. (the first evidence in a decree of Mesambria Pontica, second century B.C., honouring an Ἀστάς: *IG Bulg.* I² 312).[49] They inhabited a very extended area to the north of Byzantium (Strab. VII.6.12); Strabo (VII.6.1) knew of them too in the Pontic Salmydessus, and in the Tab. Peut. Strandža Planina is marked as 'mons Asticus'. In the Roman 'Strategia Astice' which lay between Perinthus and Apollonia, the Astae formed the principal tribe. But at an earlier period other tribes existed in this territory, some only mentioned incidentally. Amongst them, the Thyni should first be noted.

The Thyni occupied the land north of Perinthus and Selymbria. They also occupied part of the Strandža Planina and touched the Black Sea in the region known as Salmydessus (above), which stretched as far as Apollonia and which included Cape Thynias. These Thyni, very well

[46] Some of the sources: D 228, 254.   [47] The sources: D 228, 39.
[48] The sources: D 228, 221.   [49] The other sources: D 228, 32.

described by Xenophon (*Anab.* VII.2.32–4), were a large tribe, a part of which had moved to Asia Minor, probably at the time of the migration of the Mysi, along with the Bithyni, to whom they were related, as their ethnic names suggest.[50] The former were later subdued by Croesus (Hdt. I.28). According to tradition, the Bithyni were formerly called Strymonii (Hdt. VII.75), because their original homeland was near the Strymon. This evidence places them a long way from the territory of the Thyni whom we know from the outset as living only between the Propontis and the Black Sea. A section of the Thyni tribe who lived near Salmydessus, bore the name Melinophagi (Xen. *Anab.* VII.5.12, cf. St. Byz. 442). To the north of the Thyni, in the plain and on the slopes west of the Strandža Planina lived the Tranipsae (Xen. *Anab.* VII.2.32), whom Theopompus (*FGrH* 115 F 16 = St. Byz. 406.1) describes as a tribe of the Thyni (ἔϑνος Θυνῶν) and whose name is associated with that of the Nipsaei (below). Generally, one would place in this area also the Melanditae, but if there is an etymological connexion between their name and that of the river Melas,[51] and if one considers the order in which Xenophon (*Anab.* VII.2.32) enumerates the tribes in rebellion against Seuthes II (Malanditae, Thyni, and Tranipsae), one would expect to find their territory not to the north but to the south, near the river Melas and neighbouring the Apsynthii (note that according to Dion. Perieg. 575 Melas was also known as Apsinthus).

At the time of Darius' campaign against the Scythians, there lived in the region of Salmydessus and in the hinterland of Apollonia and Mesambria the Scyrmiadae (Hdt. IV.93); in the forms Σκυρμιάδαι and Κυρμιάναι (codd. ABCP) and Σκυμνιάδαι (St. Byz. 579.12);[52] and the Nipsaei (Hdt. IV.93), of whom we hear nothing later. Probably the Nipsaei were connected with the tribal group of the Thyni (above), which may be true also of the Scyrmiadae, which would help to reconcile the evidence that both these two tribes and the Thyni were situated in the region of Salmydessus.

The fact that the river Artescus (the Arda)[53] 'runs through the country of the Odrysae' (Hdt. IV.92) fixes their territory firmly. Archaeological monuments, and in particular the monumental tomb at Mezek (although dated in the fourth century), confirm that the Odrysae, who were in effect a tribal group, inhabited the area of the lower and doubtless the middle Arda, and occupied the region of the Hebrus towards the town of Harmanli.[54] To look for the Odrysae in the area of the Strandža Planina[55] is without justification. The homeland of the Odrysae should not be

---

[50] Sources: D 228, 53f, 211f.
[51] This is the opinion of I. Venedikov (D 258A, 48).   [52] See D 244, 5.
[53] D 256.   [54] D 242, 42; D 258, 29–32; cf. D 236.
[55] As does, for example, Danov, D 227, 121f, 265 n. 118.

confused with their realm which extended, in the fifth century, over a vast area (Thuc. II.96–7).

Westward of the Odrysae, on the upper reaches of the Arda, in the neighbourhood of the present-day towns of Zlatograd and Kârdžali and on the northern slopes of the Rhodope mountain facing the town of Haskovo dwelt the Coelaletae minores. The other branch of this tribe, the Coelaletae maiores, lived in the region of the High Tonzos between Stara Planina and Sredna Gora. Pliny's evidence on which these conclusions are based (N.H. IV.41) is not very clear.[56] The sources for the Coelaletae are late (Pliny, Tacitus);[57] and give us no clue to their original territory nor the date of the split into the two branches, between which other tribes established themselves.

In the middle Hebrus valley, to the north east of the Odrysae and the Coelaletae minores, are the Ben(n)i, as we can conclude from the position of the Roman strategia Bennike.[58] Their name appears only in Pliny, Ptolemy, and St. Byz.,[59] and then very late, but the fact that this tribe gave its name to the strategia indicates that it had been important and had been eclipsed by the powerful Odrysae.

West of the Odrysae lived the tribes known under the names of Satrae, Dii, and Diobessi. Their relationship presents a difficult problem. Having been mentioned by Hecataeus (FGrH I F 157 = St. Byz. 557.24) and Herodotus (VII.110–12), the Satrae disappear from the sources, if one discounts the proper name Satres (Σάτρης) registered six centuries later in a catalogue of Thracian families in the Roman period (IG Bulg. III 1, 1516.29, Cillae). Herodotus' account leads to the conclusion that they were a large tribe which one must place in the western Rhodope area. The text, somewhat obscure, associates the Satrae and the Bessi: οὗτοι (= Σάτραι) οἱ τοῦ Διονύσου τὸ μαντήιόν εἰσι ἐκτημένοι [. . .] Βησσοὶ δὲ τῶν Σατρέων εἰσὶ οἱ προφητεύοντες τοῦ ἱροῦ which should mean: 'Bessi who are part of the Satrae carry out the functions of prophets in the temple', or 'Bessi amongst the Satrae are those who carry out . . . [etc.]'. After Herodotus, the early authors speak of the Bessi as being a large group of tribes.[60] They occupied a large area west of the plain of Plovdiv, that is to say the valley of the Hebrus up to the region of the Succi Pass, to

---

[56] *Coelaletae maiores Haemo, minores Rhodopae subducti.* The Coelaletae minores were neighbours of the Dii, 'who mostly lived in the Rhodope' (Thuc. II.96). This proximity enabled the Coelaletae to take part, together with the Odrysae and the Dii, in the rising of A.D. 21, the 'Coelaletican War' mentioned by Tacitus (*Ann.* III.38). So one cannot interpret Pliny's evidence to mean that the Coelaletae minores lived on the northern slopes of Rhodope near to Pazardžik facing the Coelaletae maiores on the opposite mountains, because the Bessi (with their Bessapara) lived in that area (see D 242, 42).   [57] D 228, 248f.

[58] D 242, 44. In spite of the evidence of St. Byz. 162.17, s. Βέννα, that there is a Βεννικὸς κόλπος, identified by Detschew (D 228, 51) with the Gulf of Melas, there is no way by which one can descend to the sea coast from the territories of the Cicones, Paeti, and Apsynthii.

[59] D 228, 51.   [60] The sources: D 228, 57–9.

the north a corresponding area of the Haemus (Strab. VII.5.12), to the
south a section of the Rhodope mountains from the side opposite the
Haemus as far as the river Nestus (Plin. *N.H.* IV.40). The existence of a
tribe called Diobessi (Plin. *loc. cit.*) links together ethnically the Bessi and
the Dii, who in the main, according to Thucydides (II.96.2), lived in the
Rhodope mountains.[61]

V. POLITICAL HISTORY

The political history of this period is almost unknown. What one can be
certain of are the migratory movements of the tribes, which are naturally
accompanied by inter-tribal conflicts. Of these interminable struggles,
which never ceased to plague Thrace, the best known are those between
the Apsynthii and the Dolonci in the sixth century (Hdt. VI.34–40), which
can serve us as an example. They resulted in the establishment of the
Philaïds in the Thracian Chersonese *c.* 555 and up to 493 B.C. with the
arrival of the first Miltiades, rival of Pisistratus in Athens but his partner
in the Chersonese.[62] On the one hand Sigeum, whose possession had
been an object of litigation between Lesbos and Athens, and on the other
the Chersonese would assure to Athens the control of the Hellespont;
from this time on, the Chersonese was always to be of vital importance to
Athens. The activity of Pisistratus at Rhaecelus on the Thermaic Gulf,
and in the mining area of Mt Pangaeum, whence especially came the
wealth which enabled him to become tyrant, and the activity of the
Philaïds in the Chersonese mark the beginning of Athenian expansion in
Thrace. This policy became part of the general framework of Greek
colonization in this region, where Athens had been anticipated by other
Greek cities, particularly by Chalcis, Megara, and Miletus. Their
colonies, established partly in the eighth century but mainly in the course
of the seventh and sixth, and extending along the coast from the
peninsula of Chalcidice to as far as the mouth of the Danube, facilitated
the contacts of Thrace with Asia Minor and the Greek world. Thrace
was rich in natural resources and received Greek manufactured goods in
exchange. But the rare finds of imported objects, whose small number is
not due only to chance or limited excavations or other similar factors, do
not indicate very intensive relations at the outset. Literary sources show
that the settlement of the newcomers was not always welcome, and was
usually accompanied by fighting, sometimes prolonged and ending in
disaster for the colonists. The poems of Archilochus (Diehl 6, 19, 51) are
eloquent, and the instance of Abdera which was founded only at the
second attempt (the first being in 654 or 652 B.C. and the second *c.* 546

[61] Complete bibliography on the Satrae, Bessi, Diobessi, D 253, largely hypothetical; see D 245A.
[62] D 239; D 243, 30–1; D 231, 82–6 bibl. See *CAH* III².404f.

B.C.) is instructive. For in most cases the colonies were established in the Thracian area whose Thracian name they preserved (Tomi, Bizone, Mesambria, Salmydessus, Selymbria, Byzantium, Maronea, Abdera, etc.).

VI. THRACIAN SOCIETY AND CIVILIZATION

The poverty of evidence at our disposal, either from written or archaeological sources, prevents us from having anything more than a nebulous idea of Thracian society in the eighth to the sixth centuries B.C.

The Thracians did not emerge from a patriarchal system, since they continued to preserve their tribal organization, but they evolved towards the formation of a state of the pre-classical type. This process was evidently long and slow and took place in stages, one of which can be found in the setting-up of tribal unions. It seems that this progressed more intensively in the southern areas, where the proximity of the Greek world in the form of the Greek colonies and of Asia Minor was a favouring factor.[63] The appearance of coinage amongst the Thracians of the southern zone towards the end of the sixth and beginning of the fifth centuries indicates some political activity, which originated evidently in the preceding period.

The first state we hear of is that of the Odrysae. Their first powerful king, according to Thucydides (II.92), was Teres, but it was not necessarily he who founded the Odrysian state. He died towards the middle of the fifth century at the age of 92 years (Lucian, *Macr.* 10), and would have been already king at the time of Darius' expedition (dated variously between 519 and 512 B.C.). Thus the Odrysian kingdom must have been in existence at least in the sixth century, and its origins can no doubt be sought at an even earlier date. Herodotus' account (IV.89–93) of Darius' invasion of Thrace makes it clear that the Great King conquered the Thyni, the Odrysae, and the Getae; for the last he states the fact in so many words (αἱρέει Γέτας IV.93). Later, Teres had the greatest difficulty in subduing these Thyni, who succeeded in liberating themselves towards the end of the fifth century. Thus one must assume that there existed alongside the Odrysae a political organization of the Thyni,[64] which was more developed than a single tribal unit and should be termed a 'state'. This is equally valid in the case of the Getae, amongst whom one can suppose the existence of several 'states'.

In the heart of Thrace, in the neighbourhood of Plovdiv, near the village of Duvanlij, there is a large complex of several dozen tumuli, the earliest dating from the end of the sixth century and from the beginning of the fifth century, the 'cemetery's life' continuing up to the fourth

---

[63] D 231, 69–114. See *CAH* III²3.113–22.   [64] D 258, 25–9.

century. Some of these tombs are most impressively equipped with large numbers of gold ornaments, wrought with artistic skill, and with an abundance of other funerary furniture consisting of handsome containers in silver or bronze and other objects either local or imported. The golden jewels in the earliest tomb in the Mušovica tumulus, from the end of the sixth century, weigh 436 grams (Pls. Vol., pl. 249), those from the tomb in the Kukova mogila tumulus, dating from the first decade of the fifth century, weigh 1,266 grams, and together with them were found two receptacles in silver (1,766 grams) and others in bronze, glass, and alabaster. Such richly furnished tombs continued during the following period,[65] indicating that at this place persons of high rank were buried and that the richest funerary material belonged to those of royal stock. This argues a long tradition which can be attributed to the kings of the Bessi, whose kingdom was overwhelmed by the Odrysae in the fifth century.

The Thracian states which we assume were an established fact in the sixth century were of an archaic type similar in spirit to the Lydian and Persian kingdoms. The king, his court, and the nobility held a privileged position. The principle of royalty explains several cultural phenomena. From mythological evidence it seems that at the beginning power in Thrace was in the hands of priest-kings. This is how one should interpret for example the legend of the family of Orpheus in Diodorus (XII.65. 4–5): when the Thracian king Lycurgus betrayed and attacked Dionysus, the latter destroyed him and transferred his power to Charops, teaching him secret rites and mysteries; in his turn, Charops transmitted them to his son Oeagrus, and he to *his* son Orpheus. Although this is a late version, it still conveys a certain historic reality. We know that at a later period the chiefs of the Cebrenii and Sycaeboae tribes were priests of Hera (Polyaen. VII.22). For the period of the eighth to the sixth centuries proof is provided in the existence of bronze cult-axes (Pls. Vol., pl. 246), which used to symbolize supreme power, and have parallels and prototypes in Iran.[66] However, in spite of this evidence, one cannot generalize so far as to assume that from Mycenaean times to the sixth century Thracian kings without exception were all 'priest-kings'. Given that the cult-axes do not extend beyond the sixth century, it is clear that the nature of royal power developed and that what one finds at a later date amongst the Cebrenii and the Sycaeboae was a survival. In the tenth book of the *Iliad*, which belongs to the sixth century (or more precisely to the era of Pisistratus), the king Rhesus is represented like other great Achaean chiefs, and this description, even though anachronistic and much idealized, shows, in contrast to the description of other Thracian and Paeonian leaders, that in Thrace there already existed chieftains who

[65] D 230. [66] D 260, 23–4.

were no longer the simple tribal leaders of a more archaic time.

At this period of social disruption, the privileged position of the kings and nobles enabled them to acquire riches in the form of objects in bronze, whose value was also great, and in silver and gold and no doubt in precious fabrics, as one may judge retrospectively from the practice of the fifth century (Thuc. II.97, Xen. *Anab.* VII.3.16–18). Harness pieces in bronze or bronze bracelets and other objects (e.g. Pls. Vol., pl. 248) and the gold cup of Sofia (Pls. Vol., pl. 251) of the eighth–seventh century and the tombs rich in gold jewellery of the end of the sixth century (e.g. Pls. Vol., pl. 249 *a–d*) bear witness to the ease and luxury of the ruling class.[67] We do not know precisely the status of the 'slaves' and the 'servants', *dmoës* and *amphipoloi*, or of the 'housekeeper', *tamie*, of the priest Maron (*Od.* IX.206), unique evidence for our period. It is uncertain whether these terms corresponded exactly to reality in Thrace, and therefore the nature of slavery at this period cannot be determined.

With social and political life, particularly with the process of the formation of statehood, is linked the problem of military institutions. Our information is inadequate. Homer, our sole written source in this area for this period, does not, because of the specific nature of the material, furnish us with information which is chronologically precise. Nor does his information correspond faithfully to the reality which emerges from the meagre findings of archaeology. In the Homeric poems the weapons, both offensive and defensive, of the Thracian (and Paeonian) leaders do not differ from those of the Achaean chiefs; the descriptions give the impression that they are more concerned with poetic conventions than factual reality in Thrace.[68]

There is no reason to suppose that the shield worn by the nobles was different from the light shield, the *pelta*, known in the sixth century, and that there was any question of a large shield of Achaean type. But there is no doubt that a helmet was sometimes used, not necessarily of an Achaean type ('a helmet with horse-hair crest', *Il.* VI.9), and that the javelin and javelot as well as the sword and dagger were commonly used. Homer speaks of the 'long javelin' (δολίχ᾽ ἔγχεα *Il.* IV.533), of the 'pike',

---

[67] It is not impossible that the celebrated Vâlčitrân treasure belongs to precisely this period (for varying opinions, D 260, 27–9 and D 258B). The objects, at least the greater part of them, had a ritual function, but it is unknown whether they belonged to a sanctuary or to a king.

[68] *Il.* IV.527–32; VI.5–11; X.434–41; XI.246–7; cf. for the Paeonians *Il.* XXI.161–83; XXIII.560–2. The poet manipulates his military material to suit his own purposes. In his combat with Achilles, Asteropaeus the Paeonian wears a cuirass and carries two javelins, but appears not to have a sword (*Il.* XXI.161–83), while later (*Il.* XXIII.806–7) one reads that Achilles has removed from him his 'fine Thracian dagger with silver studs': it seems that the poet has conjured up the dagger to fit the occasion. One cannot draw the conclusion from the phrase 'he (the Achaean) cannot take away from him (the Thracian) his weapons' (IV.532) that the Thracian customarily carried all the weapons usual in Homer (τεύχεα), for this is a Homeric formula. The Thracian chief Peirōs, who was fully equipped (τεύχεα, IV.532) does not throw a javelin but a large stone (IV.518–22).

(δόρυ Il. IV.525, which corresponds to the earlier term ἔγχος), of the Ciconian 'spearmen' (rather than 'warriors', αἰχμηταί Il. II.846) who fought with javelins (χαλκήρεσιν ἐγχείῃσιν Od. IX.55), of 'the mighty Thracian sword' (ξίφος Θρηίκιον μέγα Il. XIII.576–7), of the 'fine Thracian dagger with silver studs' (φάσγανον, Il. XXIII.807–8). The description of the Mysi 'fighting hand-to-hand' (ἀγχέμαχοι Il. XIII.5) implies that they fought with a stabbing spear or a sword. Archaeology has provided two funerary monuments and some weapons which are isolated finds. The stones, the first of which is a slab (0.87 × 0.28 / 44 × 0.25 m, Kalište, dep. of Pernik), and the second a column 'statue' (2.10 × 0.38 / 32 × 0.18 m, Belogradec, dep. of Varna), show Thracian princes or noblemen and in all probability belong to the seventh or sixth centuries. The figures wear helmets. On the slab are engraved the hands, the soles of the feet, and the weapons attached to a baldric: a sword in a leather scabbard (the fringe is shown), and an axe, and on the 'statue' are carved a shell collar and arms attached to a baldric: in the front a knife, on the right side a sword in a decorated scabbard, on the left a bow, and behind probably a leather bag.[69] The other archaeological finds have produced a bronze helmet of Corinthian type of the sixth century (Čelopečene, dep. of Sofia), undoubtedly an import (similar ones are found in north Greece, in Macedonia, and in Illyria),[70] an iron javelin-head (43 cm), bronze arrow-heads, and an iron dagger (40.5 cm), all from a tomb of the seventh century (Endže, now Carevbrod, dep. of Šumen),[71] another iron dagger of the type known as 'Cimmerian', with scabbard (42 cm) of the seventh century (Belogradec, dep. of Varna),[72] but not yet any breast-plates or shields.

There are some Attic black-figure vases of the middle sixth century which portray Thracian peltasts: light foot-soldiers protected by hats of animal-skin (fox), but without any cuirass, shod in boots high or low, wearing a chiton and a cloak (zeira), and armed with a light shield of crescent shape (pelta), and one or two spears which they would throw one at a time, and a sword.[73] (The two spears are characteristic of the Thracian people and of certain of their neighbours, such as the Paeonians in the Iliad and during the ensuing epoch also.) The vases date from the period of Pisistratus who had seized power with the help of Thracian mercenaries, consisting of peltasts, archers, and cavalry. This shows that the Thracian peltasts, who played a special role in the art of war both in the classical and Hellenistic periods, are not a creation of the sixth century, but date back to a very much earlier time. This is confirmed too by the fact that this type of warrior was characteristic of the Thracians not only of Europe, but also of Asia Minor (Hdt. VII.75).[74] The

---

[69] D 254. [70] D 225. [71] D 252, 98–113; date D 226, 87–9. [72] D 255.
[73] D 224, 5–7; D 243, 153–4. [74] D 224, 11–13; D 243, 154–8.

peculiarities of different tribes should be borne in mind; for those who lived in the plains could be foot-soldiers without necessarily being peltasts. Thucydides, for example, referring to the army of Sitalces in 429 B.C. gives an idea of these peculiarities and local traditions (II.96, 98): the Getae are cavalrymen armed with the bow, the Dii 'who for the most part live in Rhodope' are armed with a dagger known as *makhaira*, and most of the horsemen come from the Odrysae and the Getae. There is no doubt that some tribes were equestrian by tradition. In connexion with this, we may ask if the Homeric term ἀφ' ἵππων,[75] when it was applied to the Cicones who 'knew how to fight from chariots and when to fight on foot' (*Od.* IX.49–50), does not mean rather that they fought as cavalry.[76] If not, we must assume that Homer was describing a battle in his traditional manner without any relation to the reality of Thracian methods.

Thracian civilization was not an urban one. The fact that Homer referred to Ismarus of the Cicones as a 'city' (*polis, Od.* IX.40) does not prove that there were veritable towns in Thrace at that time. Fragments of Hecataeus record the names of several 'cities' (*poleis*) in Thrace, but those of which we know something – such as Abdera, Maronea, Drys, or Zone – lead to the conclusion that these were Greek towns set up on earlier Thracian sites. There is only one of these Hecataean 'cities', Cabassus, which is situated north of Mt Haemus (*FGrH* I F 169) and remained a Thracian area. But was it in fact a city? According to Strabo (VII.6.1, cf. St. Byz. 446.15), the Thracian word *bria* meant *polis*, but it is an inaccurate translation, and Mesambria, Selymbria, or Poltymbria were not cities in the real sense of the word. As shown by the Thracian walls at Pontic Mesambria (Pls. Vol., pl. 252 *a, b*), dating from before the foundation of the Greek colony at the end of the sixth century,[77] Thrace possessed only fortified areas, and 'cities' such as Cabassus would have been no more than large villages. In general the population lived in villages and hamlets. Herodotus (V.16) tells of pile dwellings in Lake Prasias, referring evidently to very early traditions. Apart from Greek coastal cities, and even several of these were no more than small settlements (cf. e.g. the synoikismos of Olynthus), towns in Thrace only appeared, sporadically, from the time of Philip II, the urbanization of the country not being accomplished until Roman times.[78] In a country of this sort, economic life was naturally at a very low level. The single fact that the archaeological finds are neither numerous nor rich up to the end of the sixth century proves this. It is not until after this century that the

---

[75] Translated as 'chariot with equipment' in L–S–J s.v., Chantraine, *Dict. ét.* s.v.
[76] Cf. D 224, 11.
[77] On other fortresses of the first half of the first millennium: D 259, 128–77.
[78] D 246.

archaeological material improves in quantity and quality. Thrace was and remained for many centuries longer a rural country. Its fertile soil, already praised by Homer (*Il.* XI.222), provided wheat and other crops of which we have evidence in succeeding periods, but which doubtless also existed at this time; for example, barley, with which they made a sort of beer, *bryton* (Archilochus),[79] millet or hemp (for cloth). Viticulture flourished and Thracian wine was renowned (*Il.* IX.71–2, *Od.* IX.196, 204–11). In animal breeding, horses and sheep (*Il.* XI.222) were raised, and Homer particularly characterized the Thracians with the epithet 'herders of horses' (ἱπποπόλοι *Il.* XIII.4; XIV.227; cf. *Od.* IX.49). Nor must we forget the role of hunting and fishing in the life of a country abounding in game and fish.

As yet the Thracians did not know the use of coinage. Their coins do not appear until towards the end of the sixth century, mainly at the beginning of the fifth century. Precious metals found their way into the coffers of the princes and nobles in the form of ingots or as receptacles or ornaments (cf. *Od.* IX.211–13, *Il.* XXIV.234–5). Even the bronze 'coins' in the form of an arrow minted during the period from the end of the seventh century to the end of the sixth century at the latest, discovered in the Pontic zone in the territories of Apollonia, Istrus, Tyras and Olbia, represented a Greek innovation used solely for commercial purposes with the indigenous hinterland.[80] The circulation of real coinage in the country is rare, and finds like that near Serdica, including coins from the area of Mount Pangaeum, the oldest ones dating from 550 B.C. onwards, are exceptional.[81] Everything goes to show that the flowering of Thrace began towards the end of the sixth century, and coincided with the political interest of Persia in Europe, whose first manifestation was Darius' expedition against the Scythians.

From the meagre information at our disposal, we can learn very little of the Thracian customs and rituals of this period. Given the conservatism of the area – some folk-lore traditions continuing to exist even to our own day – we should be able to reconstruct a wider picture by relying on the sources for the succeeding eras. However, such a study must be reserved for a later volume, and here we are limited to some remarks called forth by the original evidence for the period. There existed at all times individual tribal characteristics, a fact emphasized by Herodotus (V.3–8). If we can believe Homer (*Od.* IX.199), the priest Maron had only one wife. But that does not exclude the existence of concubines, for from the statements of authors of the fifth and succeeding centuries one must conclude that polygamy and concubinage rested on an ancient tradition, without however being able to assert that it was a general practice; this would depend upon social conditions as much as

[79] See all the texts in D 228, 93.   [80] D 229.   [81] D 235.

upon tribal traditions. Upon these conditions and traditions depended also such customs as hair-styles and tattooing. Even though Homer (*Il.* IV.553) and Archilochus (Diehl 79a) call the Thracians *akrokomoi*, 'with hair on crown', the expression allows of more than one interpretation,[82] and doubtless that was not the only way of wearing the hair. Again, the Attic vases of the period which show that a beard was fashionable do not imply that it was universal.

We have no direct evidence about the practice of tattooing from the eighth to the sixth century – the first evidence is in Herodotus v.6 – though on account of its primitive nature there can be no doubt that its origins spring from an even earlier period; but we need not assume on that account that it was a universal or common practice.[83] For male dress – for women no evidence at all exists – we rely on the Attic black-figure vases which depict Thracian warriors of the sixth and fifth centuries (above, p. 611); the primitive 'statues' of Kalište and Belogradec (above, p. 611) give little clear indication on the subject. The mythical figures of Orpheus and Thamyris (as well as the invention of the *syrinx* with a single reed or pipe attributed by Athenaeus (IV.184a) to the Maedi Seuthes and Rhonaces, and of the *magadis* to Thracian Magadis by Athenaeus (XIV.636f after Douris)) bear witness to the part played by music and the dance amongst the Thracians.

There is relatively more information concerning funeral rites. During this period both inhumation and incineration were practised. In different areas kings and nobles were interred in different fashions. In the region of Strandža Planina and Sakar Planina and very rarely in the eastern area adjoining the Haemus, the dolmen tradition persisted from the twelfth century up to the seventh (Pls. Vol., pl. 244) (Fig. 34). They were in fact tumulus-tombs. In eastern Rhodope they cut beehive-shaped tombs in the rock. These two types of tomb form the link between the beehive tombs of Mycenae and similar Thracian tombs of the fifth and fourth century. In eastern Rhodope an unusual burial arrangement has been found. A rock cut in pyramidal form contains two burials; steps give access to a burial niche; and then on a higher platform there is cut a tomb open to the sky (Pls. Vol., pl. 245).[84] But the most typical for Thrace are the tumuli. Herodotus (v.5) reports that among the Thracians 'who live above the Crestonaei' they sacrificed the favourite wife and buried her with the husband, but so far this practice has not been confirmed by archaeological evidence. On the other hand, chance finds of scraps of horse-trappings of the eighth to the sixth century (Pls. Vol., pl. 248) (Fig. 35) show that the burial of a horse beside the tomb – which excavations have frequently shown for the period from the fifth century – was in fact

---

[82] D 241, 109; D 243, 97.   [83] D 241, 67–70; D 243, 105.
[84] D 259, 31–127, summary 215–18.

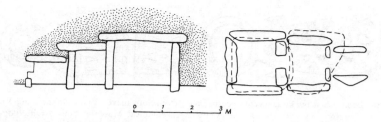

Fig. 34. Early Iron Age dolmens in the Strandža Mountains and in the village of Bâlgarska Poljana (Topolovgrad District). (After D 260, figs. 1, 2.)

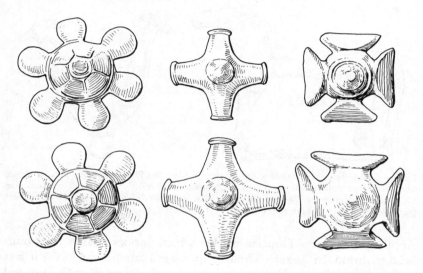

Fig. 35. Bronze horse-trappings (harness pieces and decorative plaques) from the village of Sofronievo (Vraca District), Gevgeli, and Bjala Slatina. Seventh century B.C. Width 5–9 cm. (Vraca Archaeological Museum; Sofia Archaeological Museum 795, 1593/4; after D 260, pls. 11–13.)

an earlier custom too.[85] Within the tombs was sometimes placed a funerary inventory, usually quite small, of precious objects alongside the noble person.[86] The two stone funerary monuments (above, p. 611) are exceptional.

Of religion little is known, but the Thracian pantheon evidently became a fairly complex one. There is general evidence in Xenophanes (F 14 Diehl = F 16 Diehls *Vorsokratiker* 6) to show that the Thracians represented their gods as having russet-red hair and blue eyes like themselves. Homer speaks of the priest of Apollo, Maron, who dwelt in a sacred wood at Ismarus (*Od.* IX.198–201). This is not poetic invention. In neighbouring Abdera, Pindar (*Paean* II.5) mentions the sanctuary of

[85] D 260, 20–1.   [86] Seventh century: D 252; D 255; sixth century: D 230.

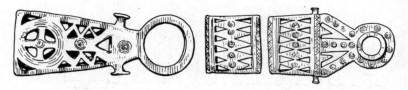

Fig. 36. Bronze belt buckles, seventh century B.C., from Sofronievo (Vraca District) and Vidin District. Lengths 10.5 and 9 + 5.1 cm. (Vraca Archaeological Museum; Sofia Archaeological Museum 124/5; after D 260, pls. 19, 20.)

a　　　　　　　　　　　　　　　　　　　　　　　　　*b*

Fig. 37. (*a*) A bronze horse of the seventh century B.C. from near Philippi (Aegean Thrace). Height 6 cm. (Sofia Archaeological Museum 1578.) (*b*) A bronze 'axe-amulet' of the seventh–sixth centuries B.C. from Rila Monastery. The two-headed bird has an axe-blade instead of feet. Height 9.4 cm. (Sofia Ecclesiastical Museum; after D 260, pls. 5, 8.)

Apollo Deraenus, a Thracian epithet which implies a fairly important local tradition. In Aegean Thrace, Apollo is a familiar deity, for it was not by chance that the Dolonci went to consult the oracle at Delphi, and on its instruction chose Miltiades as their leader (above, Section V). From contemporary sources another divinity is known: this was Bendis, mentioned by Hipponax:[87] 'the daughters of Zeus, Cybebe and Thracian Bendis' (Θρηϊκίην Βενδῖν). Later she was associated with and was absorbed into the person of Artemis. This evidence indicates that polytheism existed amongst the Thracians.

In Thracian art painted decoration was at no time a feature of Thracian pottery, in spite of the proximity of the Greek world and of an ever increasing number of imported Greek ceramic articles. During this period the decoration took the form of engraved geometric patterns (Pls. Vol., pl. 250) (Fig. 36). Sometimes some elements of the technique and decoration of metal receptacles were imitated, as for example fluting, which is a reminiscence of Bronze Age metal bowls. Metal objects were nearly always of bronze; small figurines of animals (horse (Fig. 37*a*), stag

[87] D 228, 50.

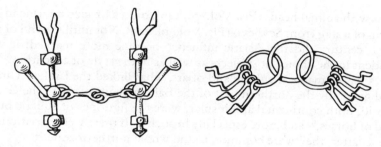

Fig. 38. A bronze bit and bronze horse-trappings of the ninth–sixth centuries B.C. from the village of Gigen (Nikopol District). (After D 260, figs. 7, 9.)

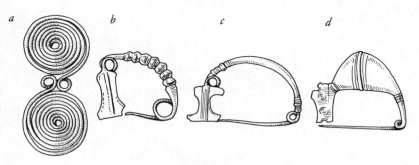

Fig. 39. (*a*) Bronze spiral fibula from Dâržanica near Vidin. Length 11 cm. (*b–d*) Bronze fibulae from the same site, from the Vidin area and from Panagjurište. Lengths 5.4, 5.6, 7.4 cm. Seventh century B.C. (Sofia Archaeological Museum 3089, 1803, 1942, 2790; after D 260, pls. 23–6.)

(Pls. Vol., pl. 247) and birds), small cult-axes decorated with animal heads (bull, ram, goat (Pls. Vol., pl. 246); or in the form of a bird (Fig. 37*b*)),[88] portions of harness (Pls. Vol., pl. 248; Fig. 38), hair-pins, bracelets, fibulae (Fig. 39), and rings. Gold objects were as yet rare, such as the Sofia cup (Pls. Vol., pl. 251), the Carevbrod crown (Endže)[89] or the sword sheath of Belogradec,[90] apart from the Vâlčitrân treasure, whose date is in dispute (see above, n. 67); they become more common towards the end of the sixth century.[91]

The geometric style which is the principal characteristic of the whole of Thracian art of the period not only continues the tradition of the preceding period, but reveals the dominant aesthetic attitude at all social levels; it was a truly national art. This traditional local style is seen in its purest form in the ornaments made in bronze, such as bracelets and rings. The influence, however, of the art of Asia Minor was beginning to be felt, though as yet slight, and the figures created by the Thracian artists had none of the fantasy of the oriental animals: they were real creatures, however inadequately executed. This is clearly seen in the cult-

[88] D 260, ill. 8.　　[89] D 252, 100.　　[90] D 255.　　[91] D 230, 229–30.

axes with animal heads (Pls. Vol., pl. 246), or in a bronze figurine in the form of a stag from Sevlievo (Pls. Vol., pl. 247). Not until the end of the sixth century did the Asiatic influence become more marked; it was evident in the choice of subjects as well as in the style of execution.[92] In the areas of material culture and of art, what linked the land of Thrace and generally the northern part of the Balkan peninsula with the Greek world, both continental and insular, were the figurines of aquatic birds and of horses,[93] and more especially brooches. If there were variations in these latter, they were common to the whole northern zone.[94]

[92] D 260, 26, 110–12.   [93] D 260, 26f, figs. 16, 17 and ills. 5 and 8.
[94] D 260, 22.

THE NATIVE KINGDOMS OF ANATOLIA

M. MELLINK

Western Anatolia in the pre-Persian era was basically a land of native peoples, survivors from the Bronze Age or acclimatized intruders of the Early Iron Age. Along the west coast, Greek contacts and settlements existed as they did in the Late Bronze Age (*CAH* III².1, ch. 18*a*; III².3, ch. 39 *a*). The western plateau and the river valleys beyond the estuaries were free of Greek intrusions. We can identify the native peoples and tribes chiefly with the aid of Greek sources and a tenacious nomenclature which in Roman times still aided in establishing provincial entities and boundaries. The peoples emerge classicized as Phrygians, Lydians, Carians, Lycians, also Mysians, Bithynians, Paphlagonians, Pisidians, Isaurians, Lycaonians, to name the most prominent groups. The Pamphylians by their name indicate their Greek and conglomerate origin.

To the east, the neighbours of the West Anatolians were the conquerors and survivors of the Hittite empire and the founders of neo-Hittite kingdoms, their variety reflected in the large number of royal centres. The boundaries of the individual realms are being reconstructed with the aid of Luwian historical inscriptions (*CAH* III².1, ch. 9). The neo-Hittite kingdoms experienced the advantage and the menace of being neighbours to the north Mesopotamians, who in the past had often forcefully encroached upon Anatolia through economic and military undertakings. In the Iron Age, proximity to Assyria led to vassalage and ultimate annexation. The west of Anatolia was spared this fate, being traditionally outside the Mesopotamian orbit, but this salvation means a loss of information to the historian – the conflicts and subjugation are recorded in Assyrian annals with names, dates, and selective detail about the victims. Only in exceptional cases (Midas and Gyges) do we have direct evidence from contemporary cuneiform sources.

Unlike their neo-Hittite neighbours, therefore, the West Anatolian native kingdoms did not inherit a tradition of historical interaction with the Mesopotamian and Syrian Near East. The western plateau, its mountainous buffer zones, and the coastal plains had seen their share of Hittite campaigns in the Late Bronze Age. The Hittite conflicts were not wars with old established powers but with uncompromising West

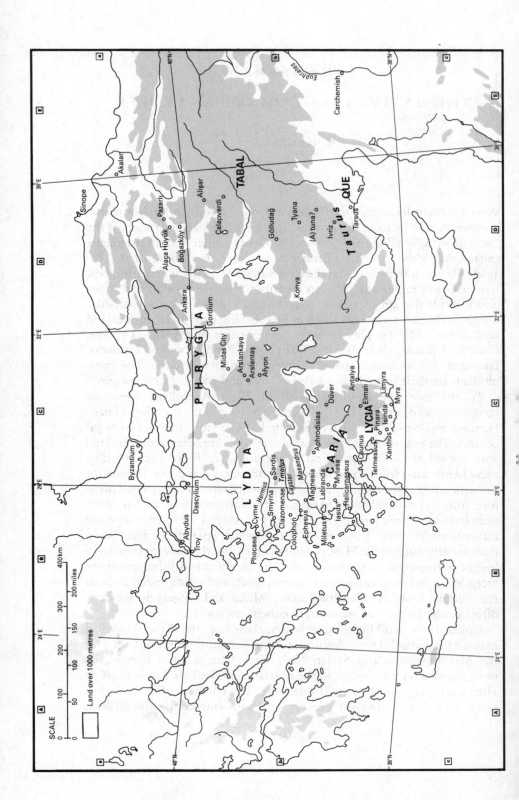

Anatolian chieftains who were beginning to carve out small realms and economic power bases of their own, or with newcomers from outside: islanders, Achaeans who ventured raids into Anatolian territory. Firm Hittite administrative rule may have extended at least as far west as Gordium and Afyon on the plateau.[1] The coastal towns, from Troy to Ephesus and Miletus, were apparently never annexed by kings from the capital of Hattusha.

Western Anatolia had a period of respite after the fall of the Hittite empire and after the Trojan War, upheavals which affected the coastal areas as well as the districts once under Hittite rule. The West Anatolians were not put under Near Eastern rule until the conquest by Cyrus in 546 B.C., and thus had some 600 years of relative independence, being left to their own internal ambitions and rivalries, with minor skirmishes against the coastal Greeks.

The tribes or peoples listed above remain obscure, historically, with the exception of those whose languages are known to us from the pre-Persian and Persian periods: the Phrygians, Lydians, Carians, and Lycians. Their languages and some incidentally preserved minor idioms are discussed in the second part of this chapter. The Lydians and Lycians are survivors of Bronze Age Anatolians of Hittite and Luwian linguistic parentage; as such, they continue their West Anatolian heritage through the Iron Age. The Carians, although of different linguistic stock, have other credentials attesting their Bronze Age presence in Anatolia, if indeed they are to be identified with the people and land of Karkiša of Egyptian and Hittite sources.[2] The Phrygians are different: linguistically their affinities are with Greek or Thracian; as Greek tradition claims, they were newcomers to West Anatolia, having crossed from south-eastern Europe during or after the turmoil of the early twelfth century B.C. (Hdt. VII.73; Strab. XIV.5.29; Xanthus FGrH 765 F 14.).

All four of these peoples, Phrygians, Lydians, Carians, and Lycians, borrowed the alphabet to record their language, confirming their independence of the neo-Hittite hieroglyphic and the Assyrian cunei-form traditions. The dates and routes of introduction differ, but the cultural pattern is coherent; it must be compared with the Greek development and denotes a new start of literacy in the Iron Age, regardless of whatever scripts may have been used by Bronze Age West Anatolian ancestors. As in Greece, we have a Dark Age in Western Anatolia, a recordless, scriptless era lasting some three or four centuries after the end of the Late Bronze Age.

From this darkness, native kingdoms emerge: first the Phrygians, next the Lydians, and somewhat belatedly (to our present knowledge) the

---

[1] E 139 (1966), 276–7, pl. 74, figs. 24–5.
[2] CAH II³.2, 253, 349–50, 360–1; E 52, 107–8.

Lycians; for the Carians, in spite of their literacy and the presence of graffiti of their mercenaries in Egypt, we do not detect a dynasty until the later Persian period, when it is too late for West Anatolian ambitions of grandeur.

I. THE PHRYGIAN KINGDOM

The Phrygian kingdom as such is largely a historical and archaeological reconstruction. Historical information centres on the figure of king Midas, who in the mythologized tradition of the Greeks is barely recognizable as a ruler of stature. Yet he was an ambitious king known from Assyrian records, Mita of Mushki (Mushku), the first West Anatolian to have attempted to build up a kingdom including the core of the former Hittite empire. His land and people are designated by the Assyrians as Mushki, probably in recognition of his factual rule over a tribe known to them as belonging in North and East Anatolia. According to the Assyrian records, Mita was approached for joint anti-Assyrian action by Pisiri of Carchemish (717 B.C.), had captured towns belonging to Que in the north Cilician–Taurus region, which were retaken by the Assyrians (715), was appealed to for help against Assyria by Ambaris, king of Tabal and temporarily was an ally of Kurti (Matti) of Atuna (713), was the target of an Assyrian defensive system of fortresses to seal off Mushki (712), and was repeatedly attacked by the Assyrian governor of Que, resulting in devastation of several Mushki towns. Finally Mita sent an envoy for peace and offered tribute to Sargon (709) (See *CAH* III^2.1, 416–20).

This shows Mita as an aggressor in the region of the Taurus mountains, encroaching upon Que by capturing fortresses along the northern edge of the Taurus. He was considered a desirable ally by neo-Hittite kings of Shinukhtu, Carchemish, Tabal, and Atuna on the basis of military strength, which is only indirectly reflected in Sargon's records.

A Nimrud letter discovered in 1952 refers to a pro-Assyrian move by Mita.[3] He had intercepted fourteen men of Que, sent by Urik(ki) to Urartu, and had delivered them to the Assyrian governor of Que. This action of Mita has been interpreted as belonging in the framework of the events of 710–709, perhaps as a conciliatory move after military losses against the Assyrian governor of Que.[4] It has also been suggested that the events of the Nimrud letter took place under Tiglath-pileser III's rule, *c.* 735–732,[5] but the governor of Que, Ashur-sharru-uṣur, is referred to in other letters of the Sargon period. Both Urik(ki) of Que, who in this instance was betrayed by Mita, and Urballa-Warpalawas, whose mes-

---

[3] A 82, 182–7; E 113; A 77A, 4–7.   [4] E 113, 32–4.   [5] E 76, 122; A 10, 22.

senger came to the Assyrian governor along with the Mushki messenger, sent tribute to Tiglath-pileser III in his third year, as did Pisiri of Carchemish. Mita's associations attested for the years 717–709 certainly will have been preceded by alliances and actions north of the Taurus in the 720s and perhaps the 730s.

Mita's neo-Hittite liaison is not yet directly attested in hieroglyphic inscriptions, but the 'Mushka' appear in Yariris' inscriptions at Carchemish in the first half of the eighth century B.C.;[6] this is about the time when the Assyrian general Shamshi-ilu had his gate lions in Til-Barsib, on the Euphrates below Carchemish, inscribed with hostile references to Mushki and Urartu.[7] Urartian interests were involved in the case of the Que messengers intercepted by Mita, and also in the 713 appeals to Mita by Ambaris of Tabal. From Urartu itself only one late reference to Mushki is known, in a seventh-century text of Rusa II.[8]

The historical gain from the Near Eastern references is in the chronological precision for the career of Mita, in the scope of his activities in neo-Hittite, Urartian, and Assyrian context, and in the evidence for Mita's rule over Mushki. His strength must have been partly based on control of the land and military resources of the Mushki, a tribe whose activities are first referred to in Assyrian records of the late twelfth century B.C., when Tiglath-pileser I defeated a large army of them south of the upper Tigris valley, in the land of Kutmuhi (*CAH* II[3].2, 457). The Mushki paid tribute to Ashurnasirpal II, along with Kutmuhi, in the first year of his rule.[9] Mushki elements therefore continued to live in the East Anatolian region across the Euphrates until the ninth century; this eastern group, however, cannot have been the source of support for Mita, whose activities were largely concentrated on the plateau and in the Cilician Taurus. Mushki had a reputation of strength in the eighth century before Mita's rise, as is evident from the inscriptions at Til-Barsib and Carchemish. There must have been Mushki also on the Anatolian plateau who became allies and subjects of Mita. The available area is the no man's land between western Phrygia and the Luwian–Urartian kingdoms. This includes the former Hittite coreland in the bend of the Halys river. The possibility of an affiliation of Kaska, the traditional northern enemies of the Hittites, and Mushki is strong.[10] Although the association with Greek Moschoi and Biblical Meshech is probable, we have no indication of the linguistic identity of the Mushki.

The Assyrians and neo-Hittites are familiar with Mita as the man of Mushki, not as the man of Phrygia. Phrygia and Phrygians are names unknown in the cuneiform and Hittite hieroglyphic tradition. Our

[6] E 75, 152; A 6, 2–3.   [7] E 132, 149.   [8] A 63A, 128.
[9] A 35 II, 442.   [10] E 56, 179; E 123, 66–9.

traditional view of the kingdom of Midas is based on Greek sources, which associate him exclusively with the Phrygian people and Western Anatolia. The explanation of this dual aspect of Midas' kingdom must be the separate and different experiences of his western and eastern neighbours, and the consequent bias of information.

To the Greeks, Midas belonged in the area of the Sangarius valley, with Gordium as his capital, although the sources for the site are later than those for the people and the king.[11] Herodotus reports the dedication of a throne of Midas in Delphi (1.14) and has a somewhat romanticized notion of a later dynastic sequence with the names of Gordias, Midas, and Adrastus (1.35). There is no clear Greek record of the successors of Midas. Nor does the father of Midas, Gordios or Gordias, have a historical status in the Greek tradition; he owes his fame to his son and to the story of the chariot he dedicated at Gordium, binding the yoke to the pole with the Gordian knot (Arrian II.3).

Midas was supposed to have been married to Demodice or Hermodice, daughter of Agamemnon of Cyme (Pollux IX.83; Aristotle fr. 611, 37). The Greeks therefore put him in a perspective of friendship with Delphi and alliance with rulers of Aeolic Greece. Midas is the first West Anatolian Iron Age king to have crossed their horizon (cf. Hdt. 1.14) as he is the first to enter the historical horizon of the Assyrians.

All of the preserved Greek sources concerning Midas are several centuries later than his rule. Dates for Midas given in Eusebius' chronicle include the years 738 and 696/5 B.C., the latter the date of his suicide in distress over the Cimmerian invasion (cf. Strab. 1.3.21). The alleged method of suicide is the drinking of bulls' blood. Eusebius bases his chronicles on Assyro-Babylonian tradition and confirms the chronology derived from Assyrian records contemporary with Tiglath-pileser III, Sargon, and Mita. The date of 676, given by Julius Africanus for Midas' suicide, agrees less well.

The modern historical exploration of the Phrygian kingdom can only make progress through linguistic–epigraphic analysis and through archaeological exploration. The distribution of Old Phrygian alphabetic inscriptions and graffiti gives us the geographical boundaries of the Phrygian kingdom and its expansion.[12] The new excavations at Gordium have nearly tripled the number of known Phrygian inscriptions.[13] A long rock-cut inscription has recently been discovered at Germanus south of Göynük, on the west bank of a northern tributary of the Sangarius river.[14] The other major western group has long been known; it comprises inscriptions in Midas City–Yazılıkaya and other sites of the Phrygian highlands between Eskişehir and Afyon. The core-land of the

---

[11] E 83, chapter 2; E 50, 882–91.   [12] E 154, 123–8; E 145, 65–74; E 157; E 151.
[13] E 165; E 160; E 151, 73–214.   [14] E 164, 230–41; E 151, 62–8.

old Phrygian inscriptions is indeed in and near the upper and middle Sangarius valley, in the highlands, at Gordium and Germanus. A second important group clusters around the former Hittite capital in the Halys bend at Boğazköy, Alaca Hüyük, Kalehisar, and Pazarlı. The third location is at Tyana, just north of the Taurus mountains.[15] A fourth has recently come to light in the plain of Elmalı in northern Lycia, in the form of Phrygian graffiti on silver ware found in a tumulus burial near Bayındır.[16]

The excavations at Gordium have made it clear that Phrygian alphabetic writing was in use well before 700 B.C. and therefore at least as early as Midas' rule. The western group of Phrygian inscriptions represents the authentic records of the Phrygian-speaking tribe(s) in the native centres of the eighth-century Phrygian kingdom. The Boğazköy inscriptions in the Halys bend indicate an extension of the Western Phrygians eastward into formerly Hittite, at this time perhaps largely Mushki–Kaska, territory, a first stage of expansion also toward the neo-Hittite realm. Hittite hieroglyphic inscriptions of the Iron Age occur not far to the south east at Alishar and Çalapverdi; the boundary of the Luwian inscriptions runs obliquely through the territory of the Halys bend.

The black stone of Tyana with its Phrygian alphabetic inscriptions, published by Garstang and Myres as evidence for 'Midas beyond the Halys',[17] indeed is best understood as a document dating to the rule of the king whose interest in the region of Tyana and the Cilician Taurus is amply demonstrated by the Assyrian records. We know from the Nimrud letter cited above that the contemporary ruler of Tyana, Warpalawas, sent his messenger along with the representative of Mita to the Assyrian governor of Que. At Tyana, Midas–Mita penetrated into neo-Hittite territory where Luwian was spoken and written, and set up a monument in a city of a Luwian friend and ally. In doing so, he did not borrow the language and script of the Luwians but instead displayed his Phrygian language and alphabet. The name Mida appears in the text. The king, through his alphabetic Phrygian writing, declares himself not a Luwian East Anatolian imposing his rule on Mushki and Phrygians, nor even a Mushki ruler of North Anatolian affinity, but a genuine king of those Phrygians who brought their language into Anatolia from the west and who developed their alphabetic writing in western tradition. In spite of his name, which is not new in Anatolia, Mita–Midas must have spoken Phrygian as his native language and must have had his roots in Phrygia.

The black stone of the inscription (at present unfindable) surely is a local basalt. The cylindrical shape with the lines of inscription on both

---

[15] E 151, 253–68. [16] E 48, 32–49, 187–95. [17] E 53; E 93.

flat sides and along the curved edge might have been the top of a stela. The Tyana inscription may indeed have been a historical monument of the type paralleled in the regional Luwian tradition, a Phrygian counterpart of, for example, the stela of Warpalawas from Bor-Kemerhisar.[18] A second Phrygian inscription on a similar grey stone was found in Tyana recently.[19] The son of Warpalawas is now known also to have had a bilingual inscription on a stela at Ivriz in Hittite hieroglyphic and Phoenician.[20] The cosmopolitan situation of Tyana in culture and writing is becoming more and more evident.

Most of the known Old Phrygian inscriptions are votive in character and are associated with rock-cut façades, niches, altars, cut blocks, and small votive objects. Graffiti on pots may be of secular relevance. The potential administrative importance of Old Phrygian writing is suggested by the use of wax as a medium for writing on three bronze bowls in the large royal tomb chamber at Gordium (Pls. Vol., pl. 232).[21] Writing on wax-coated wooden tablets may have been the normal vehicle for Phrygian scribes, perhaps the same scribes who put the special writing on the bowls for the king's tomb. The odds against survival of Phrygian archives are heavy. Historical inscriptions on stone may still be expected to come to light in Midas' greater Phrygia.

Archaeology by now is contributing considerable material evidence for the reconstruction of Phrygian history and culture. Through the results of the 1950–73 campaigns at Gordium, a stratified sequence of Phrygian citadels has become known and co-ordinated with the findings from a number of Phrygian tumuli in the outlying cemetery areas.[22] The mound of Gordium, Yassıhüyük, has yielded no references to its own Phrygian name, nor to that of king Midas, yet the results of the excavations present convincing confirmation that the site was the major West Anatolian centre of Phrygian dynastic rule. The identification had been correctly inferred by the Koerte brothers.[23] Its position on the Sangarius river where a major east–west road crosses, its size, and the large number of important tumuli identify it as the ancient capital whose memory survived to the era of Alexander and the Romans.

The Phrygian levels of the large mound (c. 500 × 350 m; Fig. 40) overlie a site of the third and second millennia B.C., with an apparently uneventful transition from the Hittite empire strata to those of recognizable Phrygian character. The difference is mainly visible in pottery: whereas the Hittite empire levels are characterized by the wheel-made buff pottery repertoire we know from Boğazköy, Alaca Hüyük, and

[18] E 23, 288–9.   [19] E 43; E 136.   [20] E 120.
[21] E 165; Brixhe in E 143, 273–7.
[22] R. S. Young, *University Museum Bulletin* 16.1 (1951) 3–20; 17.4 (1953) 3–30; E 139 (1955–66); E 141.   [23] E 83, 28–35.

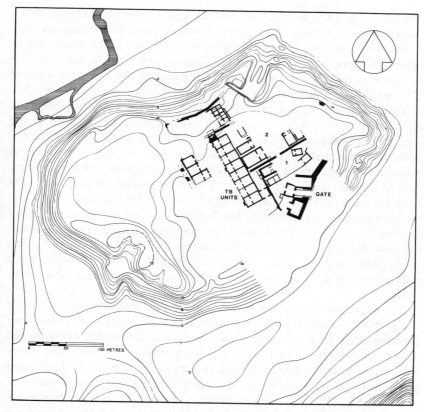

Fig. 40. Plan of Gordium, Phrygian period at destruction level. Drawing by W. W. Cummer. (Gordion Publications, University Museum, Philadelphia.)

Tarsus, the Iron Age levels, after a minor intrusion of hand-made black wares, exclusively yield black and grey wheel-made wares. We cannot yet tell if there was a lacuna at the site, or a period of peaceful co-existence of the old and new pots, potters, and their communities. Nor can we confidently date the last Hittite pottery or the earliest Phrygian wares at Gordium in terms of absolute chronology. The transition still lies in the Dark Ages. The top of the Early Bronze Age citadel was razed by Phrygian building operations. A new sounding in 1988 suggests that the latest Hittite levels were also truncated by Phrygian builders.

The series of Phrygian fortification systems at Gordium shows a basic continuity of forms with improvement of technique. In the oldest known Phrygian stage a 7-metre thick rampart, built with masonry faces but filled with a packing of clay and beams, ran along the outer edges of the mound as an embankment and retaining wall. Its superstructure is lost. It had an early gate at the north-east side, later transformed into a roofed postern-tunnel. This set of fortifications may be estimated to date to the ninth century. Monochrome pottery of the black–grey variety belongs to this stage, as yet without signs of alphabetic graffiti. We do not know if there were earlier Phrygian citadel walls, nor what kind of Hittite fortifications existed at Gordium.

The oldest known system was replaced in what must have been the eighth century B.C. Clay terraces were added along the outside of the original embankment and a new, more capacious circuit wall was built with its own retaining system. Both inner and outer faces were built of improved limestone masonry of roughly rectangular blocks; the core was of rubble with anchor beams. The outer face of this wall was battered and stepped with ledges in its lower part (Pls. Vol., pl. 225). The rampart stands to 9 m in height and is pierced by an oblique east gateway of 9 m (*Pls. to Vols. I–II*, pl. 160). An inner gate chamber gives access to the citadel; large storage rooms flanked the gate on the north and south sides. This east entrance system still stands as one of the major monuments of ancient Anatolian architecture. It belongs to the era of Midas.

The citadel of Gordium was subdivided internally by major enclosure walls which created privileged and controlled areas. A cross wall running NW–SE set the north-eastern part of the mound off from the lower south-western area. The buildings within the inner enclosures were basically of the megaron plan, rectangular structures with a roofed porch in front, with doorways set axially. They were oriented NE–SW and NW–SE. Two such megara stood in the first east court of the Midas period. Their walls were heavily timbered; round hearths lay in the main rooms. The floor of megaron 2, perhaps a temple, was decorated with a pebble mosaic of irregular geometric patterns. The elevation of these eighth-century megara can be reconstructed with the aid of a fallen stone acroterium and also through small sketches incised on the outer walls of megaron 2, showing a gabled building with central doorway, the gable crowned by a voluted acroterium (Fig. 41). In the main inner court of the citadel stood megaron 3, perhaps the palatial mansion of the eighth-century kings of Phrygia and hence also of Midas himself. The building measured over 18 m by 30 m; its interior width is about 15 m; an elaborate system of wooden posts supported galleries and the roof. The megaron had two hearths and was lavishly furnished.

Other megara stood to the east and north. Behind the main series of megara 1–4, in the final stages of the Midas citadel, a large terrace was erected, burying the semi-demolished remnants of superseded megara. The terrace supported two enormous service buildings of multiple megaron plan, facing each other across a wide street. The complex was

Fig. 41. Graffiti showing gabled buildings from megaron 2, Gordium. Drawing by J. S. Last. (Gordion Publications, University Museum, Philadelphia.)

largely devoted to the provision and preparation of food, supplies, and clothing, and also to the storage of more special and precious equipment. The large megara and the terrace complex had been the principal targets of looting and destruction by the Cimmerians.

The organization reflected in the citadel plan is one of a privileged society prepared for war and siege, with storage for its supplies and treasures, with strict protection of hierarchy, to judge by the control points in the internal citadel courts, and with a tribal orientation toward the west, whether Anatolia or Europe. This capital of Midas does not resemble an oriental palatial establishment with multiple interior courtyards, nor the so-called *hilani* buildings of the South-east Anatolians, but it maintains the old system of large open courts in front of parallel freestanding megara, individual buildings which may be monumentalized and decorated but not subordinated in an intricate layout of rooms, vestibules and corridors. One cannot escape the conclusion that a Bronze Age style of living manifests itself at Gordium, and that the Phrygians show themselves heirs to a long tradition, to which the Trojans of Troy II and VI belonged and to a branch of which, on the other side of the Aegean, the Mycenaeans were also indebted.

The fortifications of the Midas citadel were about to be remodelled and new terracing was in progress when the citadel was attacked by Cimmerian raiders and part of its monumental buildings looted and burnt down. After the catastrophe of 696/5, the citadel proper was not immediately rebuilt, but an outer fortification circuit of mud-brick with rectangular towers was erected along the east and south sides of the citadel, creating a protected lower city (Pls. Vol., pl. 226). Reconstruction of the main citadel was completed in the early sixth century B.C. if not in the seventh; the available area of the main mound was again enlarged by the building of terraces of clay and rubble, which now filled the ancient gate and were held back by stepped stone retaining walls on the east side, on top of which the new walls, towers, and gate rose. The new structures thus stood on the stumps of the old system, raising the level of the entire citadel by four to seven metres; analogous fills were laid over the entire built-up area of the main citadel. The new East Gate had a more regular plan than its oblique predecessor, again with flanking chambers; the walls were vertical with horizontal beams set at intervals in the regular masonry.

If we can confidently associate the burnt and looted citadel with the final stages of Midas' rule, we are at a loss for the historical identification of the kings who rebuilt the town. The reconstruction, thoroughly Phrygian in type, must have taken place during the rise of Gyges and the Mermnad dynasty of Lydia, to be discussed as the second major native kingdom of Anatolia. Yet, Gordium and other West Phrygian sites continue to be dominated archaeologically by the series of Phrygian traits noticed for the Midas era. In form and organization, the seventh/sixth-century citadel at Gordium is a rebuilt version of its predecessor.

We have no other good examples of this type of West Phrygian citadel. The old buildings on top of the rocky Midas City (Pls. Vol., pl. 228*a*) in the Phrygian highlands[24] were lost through erosion, although rock-cut tunnels and cisterns belong to the fortification system of the early period. We do not know the Phrygian citadel of Ankara. The new excavations at Hacıtuğrul-Yenidoğan some 35 km to the east of Gordium[25] have begun to yield fortifications and inner enclosure systems of the eighth and seventh centuries B.C.; terracing and artificial embankments are also in evidence; the buildings within have not yet been exposed.

In the area of Phrygian expansion to the east, we have one extensively excavated citadel, the Iron Age version of Büyükkale, former citadel of the Hittite capital of Hattusha (Boğazköy).[26] The first reoccupation of the citadel (level II) is apparently not provided with fortifications, but small megaron houses are of typically Phrygian construction and plan. In level I, the citadel is equipped with ramparts and towers, partly reusing the remnants of the massive Hittite circuit, and with a stone-paved glacis along the south side. On the west slope, outside of the rampart, a staircase was sunk in the embankment, winding its way down to a well-shaft, a strategic device which has its counterparts in the rock-cut tunnels and shafts of Midas City.

The upper city of the Phrygian era at Hattusha, with a fortification of the south citadel east of Nişantepe, is still being studied, but the differences in monumentality of the Büyükkale buildings as compared to Gordium are evident, as are the Phrygian characteristics of its inventory, including Phrygian alphabetic graffiti.

[24] E 74, 37ff.   [25] E 130 (1975), 210; (1976), 272.   [26] E 22, 132ff; E 101; E 102; E 103.

The chronology and historical analysis of the West Phrygian citadels and of Büyükkale II–I will have to be based principally on the relative ceramic sequence now becoming known from Gordium. There, as we now know, wheel-made monochrome pottery of grey and black finish predominates through all of the Phrygian levels, with gradual and diagnostic changes of shapes. Alphabetic graffiti on grey ware are stratified in the pre-Cimmerian level. No imported Greek pottery has been found in this level, nor other objects of Greek origin; the alphabet may be the first sign of Greek contact. This absence of Greek material contrasts with the Greek legends of Midas' interest in Delphi and his alleged marriage to a Cymaean princess. The first stratified Greek ceramic imports turn up in post-conflagration levels in the form of Rhodian bird bowl fragments and related pieces.[27] Oriental imports do occur in the burnt debris of the pre-Cimmerian citadel, as in the terrace building; a number of ivory horse-bridle attachments betray their close affinity to blinders and frontlets from Nimrud; precious pieces of equestrian equipment, but not precisely datable.[28]

Parallel with this early sequence on the citadel of Gordium is the series of burials of Phrygian noblemen in the tumulus cemetery to the north east. Some eighty tumuli, varying in size, can be counted. The majority of these contain individual burials in flat-roofed wooden chambers, covered with rock-piles and earth mounds. These chambers, usually set in a bedrock cutting, have no doorways or dromoi, but were roofed over permanently after installation of burial and tomb gifts. The most elaborate chamber was found in the colossal tumulus which dominates the necropolis and the landscape at Gordium with its preserved height of 53 m (Pls. Vol., pl. 229). The tomb chamber, reached through tunnelling in the excavations of 1957, was a gabled cabin measuring 6.20 × 5.15 m with a height of 3.25 m on the inside, with an added interior central gable support under its pitched ceiling. This was a traditional sample of Phrygian timber architecture adjusted to the purposes of the burial complex. An additional wooden casing enveloped the tomb in the rock-pile which covered it; the rock-pile itself was retained by an ashlar wall of limestone blocks; over the rock-pile a mass of clay had been piled up so solidly that it had acquired dome-like strength; additional earth fills brought the tumulus to its enormous original height, well over the preserved 53 m.[29]

We have here a royal and monumental version of a burial custom which is new to Anatolia. Door-less timber graves crowned by tumuli

[27] E 139 (1959), 264, pl. 65, 1. K. DeVries, who is studying the Greek ceramic material from Gordium, has discovered some unstratified Late Geometric Corinthian and East Greek sherds in post-Cimmerian deposits from the city mound. This raises the possibility that Greek ceramic imports will turn up in pre-Cimmerian context.

[28] E 139 (1962), 166–7, pls. 46–7; E 108, pls. 20–1, 28–32.   [29] E 143.

are known from prehistoric Europe: in south Russia (middle and lower Volga basin) they occur in the second millennium B.C., but the exact chronological and geographical connexion between south Russian and Scythian tumuli and the Phrygian series is not yet clear.[30]

The earliest excavated tumuli at Gordium by contents and comparative cross-dating cannot much antedate the eighth century B.C.; the most important tumuli (the large tumulus, and tumuli P, W, and Koerte III) belong in the pre-Cimmerian period of the second half or the last quarter of the eighth century B.C.; several seventh-century tumuli with wooden chambers have also been excavated. As a Phrygian cultural characteristic, tumuli are as important as the forms of buildings and citadel layout which are exemplified at Gordium. It is at present as impossible to determine the chronological start of the Gordium tumulus series as it is to date the arrival of the Phrygians at Gordium; the custom of tumulus burial in timber graves was most likely brought in by the first tribal leaders of the Phrygians who settled in Anatolia. It has been recognized in other Phrygian sites, notably in the excavated series of Phrygian tumuli of Ankara.[31] Unexcavated tumuli lie near the large citadel of Hacıtuğrul-Yenidoğan, other tumuli can be seen in the Dinar–Afyon area and in 'Mushki' territory, at Kerkenes Dağ 23 km north west of Alishar and at Çalapverdi about 50 km to the south east, perhaps a semi-Luwian site.[32] Phrygian tumuli also appear as far to the south west as the plain of Elmalı in north Lycia. A tumulus built of stones without earth filling or cover contained a wooden chamber with typical Phrygian paraphernalia for the deceased; graffiti are Phrygian, and the use of silver for some of the fibulae, omphalos bowls, small cauldrons, belts, horse trappings and furniture appliqués indicates wealth not attested at Gordium.[33] Expansion of Phrygian tumuli is now also attested in the region of Tyana (Niğde–Bor).[34]

The Phrygian timber grave differs from the built stone chambers in Lydian tumuli which have doorways and dromoi; hybrids occur in the later West Anatolian development. The pedigree of the Phrygian tumulus is independent of the Mycenaean tholos tomb, which, although covered by a tumulus, is always provided with doorway and dromos.

In the Gordium cemetery some of the smaller and later tumuli contain cremations in shallow unlined pits; cremation also occurs for many of the simple graves of the commoners. Cremation as a burial custom was not new to Western and Central Anatolia; both in Troy and in the central Hittite area cremation was practised in the second millennium B.C.; at Boğazköy, cremations are characteristic of the earlier Phrygian levels.

[30] E 19, 88–95; E 54; E 55, 528–84.   [31] E 109; E 49; E 36.   [32] E 19, 54–8; E 20.
[33] E 48, 32–3, figs. 32–40, 45–6, 48–55.   [34] E 3.

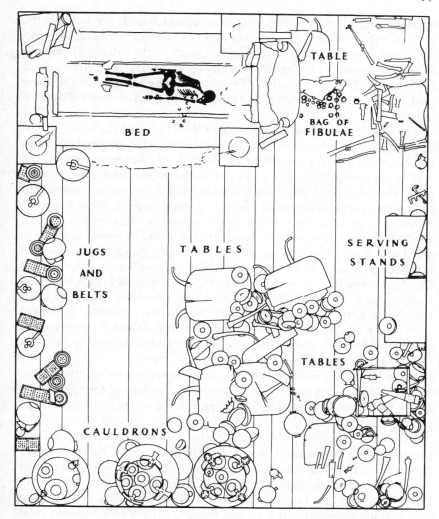

Fig. 42. Plan of the tomb chamber (the Midas tomb) in tumulus MM, Gordium. (After E 143, fig. 66.)

The dominant position of the large tumulus at Gordium and its unusually rich contents have to be interpreted historically as the burial monument of the most important king of the citadel. The chamber (Fig. 42) contained the body of a man in his mid-sixties, laid in an open coffin with elaborate textile covers. His age allows for a long career as a king and warrior (Pls. Vol., pl. 230). The material in the tomb chamber corresponds in type and date to that in the burnt level of the citadel. Again, alphabetic graffiti occur in this context, both incised on wax strips applied to bronze bowls (Pls. Vol., pl. 232) and directly scratched in the clay of some vessels. Greek imports are absent, oriental bronzes (cauldron attachments, lion and ram's head situlae) denoted imports from the lands with which the historical Midas–Mita maintained connexions. The identification of the buried king as Midas is the more probable because the fame and historicity of the dynasty rests solely with him.[35]

The sequence of events at the time of the Cimmerian raids on Midas' kingdom and Gordium will have to be hypothetically restored. So far as can be read from the record of the burnt and plundered citadel, the raiders came and went. They did not settle at Gordium, nor did they demolish the stronghold. They must have killed, looted, and continued their expedition carrying with them the portable wealth of the Phrygian capital, the precious metal, the useful weapons, some captives, and, surely, large numbers of horses and other animals. Phrygian manpower was hurt, the strength of the army and cavalry gone, and Midas was killed after a long and famous rule. We do not know if he was at Gordium when the raid took place, and we do not know how he died, the story of the bulls' blood being a Greek dramatization. His tomb must have been partially prepared during his lifetime, so that the burial ceremonies could be completed soon after the death of the king; the tomb would then be roofed, covered with the additional timber and with rubble, and the tumulus could be erected in stages.

Since Midas was active on the Assyrian scene from 730 or 717 to 709, he would have been born by 755 or 760. By the date of the Cimmerian attack he would have been in his sixties, the age of the king in the large tumulus.

The paraphernalia with which Midas was buried do not include precious metal, nor are weapons part of the equipment. This is however true of most Phrygian tomb chambers excavated. The tomb gifts consist of wooden furniture, including some of the finest inlaid wooden serving stands (Pls. Vol., pl. 231), large numbers of bronze vessels, to a total of 170, textiles, personal garments and fibulae (175), studded leather belts (10), and some pottery.

Midas' anonymous successors were buried with less pomp in smaller tumuli at Gordium. The seventh-century tumuli of Gordium and Ankara, datable by Greek imports, continue the burial customs of the timber graves in mounds. Eclipsed by their Lydian neighbours, these local kings are not known to us by name, although some of them have been respectfully disinterred by the excavators.

---

[35] E 141, 50–1; here and in previous reports Young dates the tomb 725–720 B.C. and attributes it to the father of Midas; E 143, 271–2.

Phrygian Crafts, Industries and Monuments

From the remnants of the inventory of the burnt citadel at Gordium and from the furnishings of the eighth-century tumuli we can form a general impression of the originality of Phrygian art and its relationship to east and west.

The most remarkable discoveries are the elaborately carved and inlaid pieces of wooden furniture, the best samples of which came to light in the tomb of Midas and in tumulus P, the grave of a young child.[36] The inlay work of juniper in boxwood is done in a precise, miniaturist fashion. The designs are variants of rectangular geometric motifs (swastika, extended swastika and cross, simple running meander, stacked and chained hooks); many of these are set in small square panels against an openwork background or a solid background with tiny triangular and rhomboid inlays. Curvilinear, knotted versions of the swastika occur, also incurved squares with semicircular filling motifs, and closed or openwork roundels with looped designs (Fig. 43). Both the forms and the decoration of some of these pieces denote a long Phrygian tradition. The serving stands, two of which stood against the east wall of the Midas tomb chamber (Pls. Vol., pl. 231), and one in the grave of tumulus P, are at present unparalleled in their form. They were meant to be set up vertically, supported by a single leg in the rear, attached to an ornamented ledge which projected backward from the top. This ledge had two or three circular openings in which small cauldrons were set, some provided with ladles. In front of the two serving stands in the Midas tomb, but at some distance, stood a large number of tables, one highly decorated, with bronze vessels (Fig. 42).

The geometric repertoire of the wooden furniture betrays no foreign influence; we must consider it of authentic Phrygian derivation. The Phrygians also carved wood in the round and in relief. Among the burnt furniture of megaron 3 are panels with horsemen (Fig. 44), and with a file of horned animals preceded by a horseman. The slanting stance of the animals is similar to that of stags painted on pottery of Alişar IV type, specimens of which are represented in the burnt level at Gordium.[37] Ivory inlay plaques from furniture in megaron 3 are carved in a native style but use an imported oriental medium. One of these small plaques gives us a good rendering of a Phrygian horseman with helmet, spear, and round shield (Pls. Vol., pl. 233). Wooden figurines carved in the round come from tumulus P. They are of an animal style which betrays 'nomadic' affinities and as such belongs neither to the traditions of the

---

[36] E 140; E 125; E 126.

[37] E 139 (1960), pl. 61, figs. 23–4, charred plaque; 240, pl. 58, fig. 15, painted sherd.

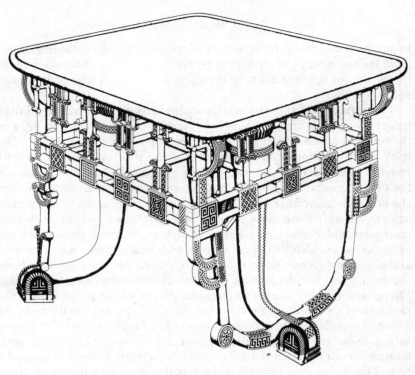

Fig. 43. Reconstruction of a table from the Midas tomb, Gordium, by Elizabeth Simpson.

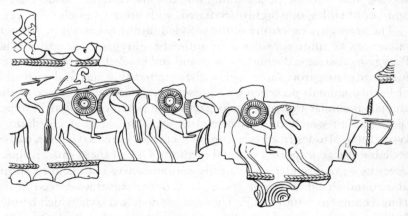

Fig. 44. Wooden relief panel with horsemen, from megaron 3, Gordium. Length 29 cm. (After *From Athens to Gordion* (R. S. Young Memorial Papers, ed. K. DeVries (Philadelphia 1980), 47, fig. 8.)

Fig. 45. Bone bridle crossings from building R, Gordium. Drawn by A. Seuffert. (Gordion Publications, University Museum, Philadelphia; cf. E 139 (1964), pl. 84, fig. 14.)

Near East nor to those of Greece. Near Eastern motifs and groupings are used, however, such as a winged griffin and a lion-versus-bull fight; both of the latter have their inspiration in the Near Eastern *koine*.[38]

The same Phrygian independence can be noted for the textiles, fragments of which came from the tumuli, many from the Midas tomb, and from megaron 3. *Kilim*-like weaves are apparent; the patterns, so far as analysed, are rectangular stepped motifs, crosses and blocks, half-swastikas, rhomboids, in a remarkable anticipation of later Anatolian *kilim* designs. The walls of tumulus P's tomb chamber were probably covered with fabric.[39]

The unusual preservation of the wood and textile material at Gordium strengthens the evidence for Phrygian native traditions. Both media were amply available in Western Anatolia. Wooden architecture and carpentry, cabinet-making and joinery thrived; many containers were still made of wood. Weaving was a major industry, with evidence for looms in the service buildings at Gordium, in a land where sheep were the great providers of wool, milk, and meat. The Sangarius valley had large open grazing fields, although the ancient forests were nearer to Gordium than they are today. The juniper and cedar logs in the Midas tomb are enormous trees, with tree-rings recording life-spans of up to 700 years for some of the trees.[40]

A major industry of the Phrygians was metallurgy, but in this they were indebted both to the West Anatolian tradition of their predecessors and to the East Anatolian, Urartian, and Mesopotamian schools of metallurgy. Phialae, cauldrons, ladles, pitchers are largely of a *koine* type belonging to prosperous courts in the Near East and listed as tribute to the Assyrian king. Two of the cauldrons in the Midas tomb have Urartian attachments and thus emphasize the royal connexions with the Urartian court.[41] The two situlae from the Midas tomb are luxury

[38] Ivory plaques from furniture, E 139 (1960), 240, pl. 60, fig. 25; wooden figurines (1957), 326, pls. 91–2, figs. 17–21; E 81; Kohler in E 143, 51–6; E 81.

[39] L. Bellinger, 'Textiles from Gordion', *Bulletin of the Needle and Bobbin Club* 46.1–2 (1962) 5–33; E 139 (1957), 326; Ellis in E 143, 294–310.   [40] E 86.

[41] E 139 (1958), 151, pls. 25–6, figs. 15–7; E 7, 39–48, pls. I, II, IV; E 139 (1958), 152, frontispiece.

imports, whether of Assyrian or related origin; they are lion's and ram's head vessels with bucket handles, used as dippers also at the Assyrian court in Sargon's days.

Apart from these orientalizing items, typical Phrygian metalwork also can be recognized. Among the vessels, bowls with ring-handles set in bolster attachments and with encircling metal bands are characteristic of Phrygian tumuli (Gordium and Ankara; *Pls. to Vols. I–II*, pl. 158c); in tumulus P a wooden bowl of this form was found. This kind of bowl makes its way from Phrygia to the West.[42] Typical Phrygian personal adornments are bronze belts with engraved geometric decoration and adjustable hook-and-loop attachments; the end with the hook was pulled tight with the aid of a half-loop which was shaped like a fibula-bow. The belts from tumulus P had very fine engraving on the surface; the designs are set in panels and have combinations of meander, swastika, and rhomboid patterns. The belts were backed with leather. Such Phrygian belts were exported to the West and imitated by the Greeks (*CAH* III². 3, 449, Fig. 59).[43] Silver Phrygian belts were found in the Elmalı plain tumulus near Bayındır.[44] Other Phrygian belts had patterns of metal studs set in leather, such as the ten wide belts found in the tomb of Midas. The studs on the belt in tumulus W are even finer, bead-like, and form interlaced loop patterns. A studded belt is worn by Midas' ally Warpalawas (*Pls. to Vols. I–II*, pl. 159a) in the rock relief at Ivriz, conceivably as a Phrygian gift. Warpalawas also wears a fibula of Phrygian type to fasten the upper edges of his cloak together. Even his costume may be of Phrygian derivation.[45]

The fibula as a basic ingredient of costuming is not a Phrygian invention, but there are distinctive types of Phrygian fibulae and within Anatolia Phrygia sets the fashion.[46] The finest collection was found in Midas' tomb (*Pls. to Vols. I–II*, pl. 158b). The most elaborate Phrygian fibulae were so well cast and decorated that even in bronze they could count as works of minor art and personal adornment. In the terrace building on the city mound at Gordium three fibulae of precious metal were found, overlooked by the plunderers. Phrygian fibulae are clear indicators of trade and cultural exchange, both in Anatolia, where, as in Boğazköy, the presence of numerous typically Phrygian fibulae reinforces the conclusion of Phrygian presence based on many other traits; and in the west, where fibulae occur especially in sanctuaries, perhaps as part of votive garment offerings.[47] Whatever the origin of fibulae in general, the Phrygian fibula is evidently a necessary adjunct of the Phrygian costume, and it must be a piece of authentic Phrygian

[42] E 5, 81–3; E 18, 189–90; E 28, 89–90.
[43] E 139 (1957), 327, pl. 92, fig. 23, tumulus P; E 28, 90–1; E 26; E 27, 214–22.
[44] E 48, no. 48.   [45] E 8, pls. 140, XXIV; E 23, 291–2, figs. 327–8; E 31.
[46] E 99; E 30, 46–7; E 41.   [47] E 99, 59–63; E 18, 186–9; E 28, 88.

equipment, perhaps of European origin, improved and shaped into its characteristic forms in the period when Phrygian metallurgy was reaching its acme.

The more modest medium of pottery demonstrates again that the roots of Phrygian arts and crafts were West Anatolian (even if adjusted from a European tradition); this leads to a basically monochrome grey ware tradition. The relatively rare painted variants betray affinities to three different repertoires. The first is the Alişar IV style, already mentioned above as occasionally represented in local imitations at Gordium. This style, best known from the abundant examples of craters with stag friezes against a background filled with small concentric circles, has been discussed by Ekrem Akurgal as the early Phrygian style of pottery.[48] Geographically the distribution of the style is weighted towards the Alişar area and East rather than West Anatolia, but the examples and imitations in eighth-century Gordium, as well as the affinity of the carved wooden furniture panel from megaron 3 to this style make a link with Phrygia clear: are we looking at Mushki rather than West Phrygian motifs? The second painted style is more at home in Phrygia proper; it has a rather simpler geometric repertoire than the carved woodwork and the engraved metal; the pots are of buff or reddish fabric and have friezes of triangles, rhomboids, checkerboards, hatched panels, with a preference for wavy lines set between simple bands; groups of large compass-drawn concentric circles betray an affinity to the Cypriot repertoire (or to its Cilician equivalent). In tumulus P a small black-on-red Cypro-geometric juglet was found along with an imitation in blue paste. The paint of the simple Phrygian geometric ware is put directly on the smoothed clay; a variant develops before the end of the eighth century introducing a white ground panel in a red-polished background; the panels contain geometric motifs in the early stages of this technique; in the seventh century, animals and other representational motifs occur. The third painted style is best exemplified in the tombs; tumuli III Koerte, P (*Pls. to Vols. I–II*, pl. 158a), and W. On a well levigated light buff clay, designs are painted with a fine brush in a reddish-brown paint; the surface is burnished all over after painting into a fine glossy finish. The designs are networks of continuous decoration: checkerboard, rhomboid net, hatching, dotting, striping, with an occasional simple or double-hooked meander, and small panels opened for animal decoration: hawks, ibexes, lions, sphinxes. The bodies of the animals are textured in linear patterns, quite unlike the silhouetted stags of the Alişar IV style.[49] This kind of Phrygian pottery is rare and precious at Gordium. The shapes are often strainer-spouted jugs of exaggerated proportions. The ware is known in several fragments from

[48] E 5, 1–8.   [49] E 122.

the site of Alaeddin Tepe in the heart of Konya.[50] This suggests that Konya rather than Gordium may be the centre of production and innovation in this instance; the occurrence of rather less disciplined but related painted wares at the site of Göllüdağ north of Niğde[51] suggests that we may be looking here at a South Phrygian variant of painted pottery.

All three painted styles borrow motifs back and forth. It is important to note that running meanders appear in the painted repertoire before 700 B.C., with no trace of Greek affinity otherwise. Although many of the painted vessels in the tumulus groups may have been imported from special workshops in the Phrygian kingdom, no Greek pottery appears in the pre-Cimmerian burials or citadel strata, as noted above. On the other hand, Phrygian and part-Phrygian painted pottery of eighth-century style is widely represented in East Anatolia, especially in its Alişar IV variant. A painted jug from Carchemish is surely to be labelled Phrygian.[52]

The references to Carchemish, Göllüdağ and Ivriz in connexion with Phrygian minor arts underline the existence of historical contacts in the Midas era. The reverse current has been noted in connexion with metal imports in the tomb of Midas and ivories in his citadel. Whether Midas intended to give his citadel some embellishment in neo-Hittite style in the form of a sculptured gateway we cannot state with certainty, but broken fragments of sculpted orthostats have been found in the vicinity of the inner gate between the courts of megaron 1–2 and that of 3. The pieces are partly unfinished, but they betray neo-Hittite inspiration both as orthostats and in their iconography. One slab with a lion's head rising as a three-dimensional frontal sculpture out of the relief is of a Phrygian linear execution, as are two lion protomes which must have projected from a façade, perhaps of megaron 2.[53]

Sculpted orthostats did ornament Phrygian buildings in the vicinity of Ankara, where a series of andesite slabs carved with lion, bull, horse, sphinx, and griffin designs has been found.[54] The Ankara orthostats are much more proficient works of art than the Gordium pieces, and evidently closer to neo-Hittite art. They may have belonged to ceremonial entrances of hitherto unexcavated official or sacred buildings. Phrygian sculptural experiments are also known from the area of Emirdağ–Afyon and from Mihallıççık, combining neo-Hittite technique and inspiration with local adaptation.[55] The date of this hybrid

[50] E 5, 14, pls. 21b, 22.   [51] E 128 (Türk AD), figs. 22–3.
[52] E 5, pl. 13 for a related, although somewhat different piece; E 139 (1960), pl. 58, fig. 21, from megaron 3, Gordium.
[53] E 139 (1956), 262, pl. 92, figs. 42–3; orthostats: E 139 (1958), pl. 21, fig. 4; (1964), 288.
[54] E 5, 67–8; E 23, 292–4; AJA 68 (1964), 159, 74; (1970), 167; E 63; E 37.
[55] E 134; AJA 70 (1966), 153 (Mihallıççık).

Phrygian sculpture must be pre-Cimmerian, late eighth century; although some of it may continue into the seventh and sixth, we cannot move far beyond the neo-Hittite frame of reference.

The most original monumental stone carvings of the Phrygians are the famous rock façades of Midas City and other sites in the highlands. They form a regional concentration unparalleled in the Gordium area, but the natural environment of Midas City is rupestrian, as opposed to the river valleys near Gordium.

The carved façades, of which the Midas monument is the principal one (Pls. Vol., pl. 228),[56] probably owe their first impetus to the Hittite rock carvings of central and also Western Anatolia, the nearest of which would have been at Gavurkalesi between Ankara and Gordium, the farthest at Karabel and Sipylus near the west coast. The form of the rock-cut façade is completely Phrygian. The Midas monument in its height of 16 m and width of 16.40 m renders the front of an old Phrygian megaron of about the size of Gordium megaron 3, the 'palace' of Midas, complete with pediment and acroterium. Its decoration is in geometric patterns of Phrygian, non-Greek derivation. The upright frame has continuous motifs, presumably rendering wood carving and inlays of the prototype. Plaques rather than tiles are rendered on the tie beam. The wall surface with the repetitive meandroid cross-pattern could represent wooden carved panelling, all of this burnt and lost at Gordium. The large inscription on the side and over the pediment will ultimately reveal the relationship of this monument to Midas, whose name and old-fashioned titles appear in the dative. The proper understanding of the inscription may also settle the disputed matter of chronology. The monument has no features which are unparalleled in pre-Cimmerian Gordium, and may date to the Midas period or the next generation.

This type of monument with a clearly rendered doorway and niche is thought to represent a shrine rather than a palace. A dowel-hole preserved in the top rear of the niche may have served to keep a statue or relief in place. Other façades confirm this arrangement, most explicitly the façade of Arslankaya to the west of the mountain range, which has a niche with carved opened doors revealing the Phrygian goddess Kubile with two rampant lions. Here the religious symbolism is evident: the rock formation has been given the shape of a Phrygian building in front, but remains part of the natural mountain setting; the tall rock has a lion carved on one rough side and a griffin-like animal on the other. Arslankaya is inscribed on the horizontal cornice of the pediment, in which sphinxes flank the king-post. Here Phrygian sculpture enlivens and explains the severe basics of the Midas monument; again the date is disputed.

[56] E 74, 73ff.

In the highlands, Phrygian rock-cut monuments continue to be made from the Midas period into the Lydian era; the same development can be traced for the monumental tombs of the area, which start with an awe-inspiring Phrygian chamber tomb flanked by rampant and reclining lions at Arslantaş; continuing with large chamber tombs decorated with appropriate reliefs, including warriors, a Gorgo, and gigantic lions; and develop in the direction of increasing Hellenization during the seventh and sixth centuries B.C.[57]

All of this art is rock cut and as such typically Anatolian. The Phrygians in the highlands set an example which was in turn influential in the art of their Anatolian Iron Age neighbours, who began to copy their own architectural forms in rock-cut replicas.

Sculpture in the service of cult and religion also thrived in the central Phrygian cities. In the eighth century, the cult of the goddess Kubaba of Carchemish was conflated with a local worship of a Phrygian goddess Matar Kubile. Kubile's image now became a cult-relief, borrowing essential features from the neo-Hittite goddess. The long robe, the *polos*, the veil covering head and shoulders, and the pose, a frontal relief rather than a statue facing the worshipper, are traits common to an eighth-century cult-relief of Kubaba from Carchemish and Kubile *naiskoi* from Ankara (*Pls. to Vols. I–II*, pl. 159d) and Gordium. These *naiskoi* are replicas of a Phrygian shrine, often with tell-tale architectural features such as acroteria and geometric decoration, indicating that temples indeed may have existed as prototypes both of the *naiskoi* and of the giant rock-cut version of a Kubile shrine at Arslankaya.[58] The most elaborate variant was found all but *in situ* in a built niche of the outer south-east gate of the Phrygian citadel at Boğazköy (*Pls. to Vols. I–II*, pl. 159c). Here the goddess is accompanied by two musicians; the other reliefs mostly render her as holding a vase and a bird.[59] Lions are not associated with this central Phrygian version of Kubile, but appear prominently in the highlands at Arslankaya. As such, Matar Kubile(ia) and *oreia*, the Phrygian goddess migrated to many peripheral districts in Anatolia and ultimately to Greece.

It may finally be noted that Phrygian art rarely shows us the appearance of the Phrygians themselves. As warriors and horsemen we see them in the minor arts of the Midas level at Gordium, in ivory plaques from megaron 3 (Pls. Vol., pl. 233) and megaron 4. Equestrian equipment (snaffle-bits, frontlets, blinders) lay stored in the terrace-building. At Boğazköy, a simple miniature votive stela has a Phrygian archer on horseback, a hunter, carved among animals on the side. A mounted warrior appears on the orthostat from Mihallıççık, the latter perhaps of sixth-century date.[60]

[57] E 74, 112ff.   [58] E 94.   [59] E 22, 150ff; E 21.
[60] E 24, 21–33; *AJA* 70 (1966), 153 (Mihallıççık).

More explicit renderings of Phrygian soldiers, hunters, and horsemen make their appearance on sixth-century terracotta revetments from Düver in Pisidia to Gordium, and to Pazarli near Alaca (Pls. Vol., pl. 234).[61] At the same time, bichrome painted pottery becomes more prolific in renderings of the human figure. The largest sculptured warriors appear on the sixth-century(?) Yılan Taş, a rock-cut tomb chamber in the highlands. The colossal reliefs show warriors with crested helmets, spears, and round shields.[62]

In the days of Midas, military action seems to have preoccupied the Phrygians rather than the depiction of their deeds and appearance. They must have taken pride in their colourful equipment, which included ornaments of geometric or animal style. Among the finest pieces of Phrygian minor art are four bone carvings decorating bridle crossings, with figures of hawks seizing hares, an Anatolian motif carved now in firm Phrygian style (Fig. 45).[63]

The original forms of the first Phrygian buildings and artefacts have come to light through the excavations of recent decades; the world of Midas is being recovered from Phrygian soil. It looks a bit different from the Hellenized and Romanized images of Phrygian culture and people.

II. THE LYDIAN KINGDOM

Unlike the Phrygian kingdom, the Lydian kingdom boasts a dynastic sequence, as we gather from the Greek tradition and first of all from Herodotus. It emerges from a mythologized past in the Dark Ages and rises to historicity with a ruler who closely follows Midas in time and fate: Gyges, who became king of Lydia, was threatened by the Cimmerians raiding Western Anatolia, and who appealed to faraway Ashurbanipal of Assyria for an alliance and for help. He was given support, but went under in one of the Cimmerian attacks, as did his predecessor in Phrygia.

Gyges ruled in Sardis and is a much better known historical figure than Midas, principally because his connexions with the Greeks were so close. His original land was the middle and upper Hermus valley and the realm to the north and south as far as Lydian was spoken; he, like Midas, undertook conquests outside his territory and tried to establish a kingship of international rank. In his cosmopolitan outlook he reached as far as Egypt, where he established contact and an alliance with Psammetichus I.

The origin of the Lydians, as the linguists have established, is Bronze Age Anatolian. Their land, if we go by the range of Lydian inscriptions and tradition, bordered on the Mysians to the north, the Phrygians to the east, the Carians to the south, and the Greeks to the west. Boundaries

---

[61] E 2; E 45. [62] E 74, figs. 154–6. [63] E 139 (1964), 283, pl. 84, fig. 14.

were imprecise, but the Lydians evidently did not inherit a Bronze Age tradition of seafaring.

The land was wealthy agriculturally, given the plains of the Hermus and the Cayster; sheep, cattle, and horses were plentiful. Prehistoric and Late Bronze Age sites are attested for the area, which attracted the military attention of Hittite kings as early as the fifteenth century B.C. (Tuthaliya's Assuwa campaign). Sardis, at the northern slope of the Tmolus mountain, became the main city in the Iron Age. It is an acropolis town (Pls. Vol., pl. 236 a, b) with a natural stronghold dominating a lower city and the plain; it was not founded on a compact prehistoric mound of the type seen at Gordium or at Old Smyrna–Bayraklı. Deep soundings in the lower town at Sardis have reached Early Iron Age levels, below which are indications of Late Bronze Age occupation.[64] Of the earliest strata, pottery is the main indication; from the beginning of the Iron Age it is mixed with local Protogeometric and Geometric wares.[65] In the course of its development Lydian pottery, although establishing a repertoire of its own, betrays its affinity to contemporary Greek wares. This is the result of the vicinity of the Aeolic and Ionian settlers; on the other hand, Phrygian resemblances and exchanges may also be noted, and there is some Egyptian influence.

A combination of archaeological and pseudo-historical data is as yet premature, but the tradition reported by Herodotus (1.7) of a Heraclid dynasty may refer to a new start at Sardis after the wars of the Sea Peoples, with Greek participation.[66] The names of the rulers of this dynasty are, however, an unreliable mixture, ending with Kandaules–Myrsilus, whose names are Lydian–Hittite. The dynasty, if originally Greek and Heraclid (rather than Tylonid) must have been Lydianized by the generation of Kandaules whose hapless end is related by Herodotus (1.8–12).

Gyges, the new ruler and founder of the Mermnad dynasty, was the son of Dascylus, a name belonging with Dascylium and perhaps pointing to Mysian and Phrygian affiliation. Gyges' actions, as indicated above, somewhat resemble those of Midas, whose death may have preceded Gyges' accession by about ten years. Gyges' first embassy to Nineveh took place some time between 668 and 665 B.C., and was sent under the threat of a Cimmerian invasion.[67] According to the fragmentary texts of Ashurbanipal, Gyges was apparently inspired by a dream to seek his aid. He sent his messenger on horseback, presumably by the road through Phrygia and Tabal, but when the rider arrived in Nineveh

---

[64] E 73 (1963), 7–9; (1966), 8; (1967), 36–7; E 72, 308–9; E 69, 20–3.

[65] E 69, 23–4, 26–7.   [66] E 73 (1967), 38; E 72, 309; E 67, 15ff.

[67] A 344 I, ccclii, II, 20–3, 156–7, 167–9; A 35 II, * 784–5, 849, 893; E 112, nos. 292–5; E 107, 202, 249; A 327; A 342; A 343; E 44.

his land and language were initially a mystery to the Assyrian king. 'But of all the languages of East and of West, over which the god Ashur has given me control, there was no interpreter of his tongue. His language was foreign, so that his words were not understood.'[68] The precise effect of Gyges' request for aid is not known, but some form of Assyrian assistance was probably made available. In a later embassy Gyges sent two captive Cimmerian chieftains in iron fetters along with rich gifts to Ashurbanipal. Then, however, his loyalty to the Assyrian waned, and he was accused by Ashurbanipal of having sent his forces to the aid of Tushamilki–Pishamilki, Psammetichus, king of Egypt, to support the latter's rebellion against Assyria. Ashurbanipal cursed his disloyal ally and the Cimmerians indeed overcame Gyges and his land. The chronology of these events is not strictly clear from Ashurbanipal's records. An Assyrian astrological text records the Cimmerian threat for 657 B.C.[69] The war of Psammetichus, whether directed against Ashurbanipal or against his Egyptian rivals, was successful by 655 B.C.; the auxiliary forces allegedly sent by Gyges are generally interpreted to have been the Carian and Ionian 'bronze men from the sea' (Hdt. II.152) who helped Psammetichus gain the upper hand in Egypt. The sending of troops overseas could only have taken place in Ionian or Carian ships.

The end of Gyges' reign and the catastrophic attack under the chieftain Lygdamis occurred several years after this demonstration of Lydia's strength and disrespect vis-à-vis the weakening Assyrian king. Gyges' dates have been variously calculated as c. 685–645.[70] In the Greek chronology, Herodotus gives Gyges a reign of 38 years. A synchronism with Archilochus (fr. 19 West) fits right in the span of c. 685–645 proposed on Assyrian and Egyptian evidence. Of the Egyptian diplomatic connexions of Gyges we do not know the beginning nor the entire cultural scope.

Gyges' relationship to the Greeks in Ionia is recorded as an aggressive policy against Magnesia (Nic. Damasc. FGrH 90 F 62), Miletus, Smyrna, and Colophon (Hdt. 1.14; Paus. IV.21.5; IX.29.4). The support of the Delphic oracle for his claim to the Lydian throne (Hdt. 1.13–14) was rewarded by Gyges with sumptuous dedications at Delphi, much silver ware and six gold craters of thirty talents each, set up in the Corinthian treasury next to the throne of Midas. The friendship with Delphi was based on diplomatic considerations evidently combined with superstition, as later Lydian embassies to various oracles confirm.

In the Anatolian districts, Gyges must have had some influence in the Mysian region, if indeed he controlled the road and allowed the Milesians to found Abydus (Strab. XIII.590). Dascylium and Dascylus, Gyges' father, would theoretically fit into this sphere of influence. The

[68] E 44, 68.   [69] A 327, 25.   [70] E 79; A 343.

relationship to the Phrygians is likely to have been friendly. Even if we do not know the names of Midas' successors, we know from the buildings at Gordium and Midas City, and from the tumuli at Gordium and Ankara, that local princes continued to rule Phrygia and lived in the same cultural tradition as Midas, although in less cosmopolitan style. Striking Near Eastern imports begin to fade from the tomb groups as East Greek and Lydian objects made their appearance. Among the pottery in both Lydia and Phrygia are Protocorinthian wares, Rhodian bird bowls, and regional imitations; these would belong in the period of Gyges' rule and attest the increasing infiltration of Greek trade and contacts via Lydia into Phrygian territory.[71]

The wealth mythologically attributed to Midas is factually attested for Gyges. His 'Gygadas' (Hdt. 1.14) in Delphi must have made a dazzling display of gold and silver vessels and implements; by comparison Midas' bronze inventory in Gordium is sturdy but modest, and remarkable more for its admixture of genuine Oriental items than for its intrinsic wealth or artistry. In Delphi, Phrygian wooden furniture stood alongside Lydian precious metal. Gyges had begun the exploitation of Lydian gold from the Pactolus and had access to silver mines in Anatolia.[72] We do not have Gyges' tomb furnishings to test the comparison with Midas in detail. The excavations at Sardis may have identified the tumulus of Gyges in Karnıyarık Tepe,[73] one of the large tumuli in the spectacular necropolis of Sardis on the north bank of the Hermus river, nicknamed Bintepe, a thousand mounds. Here indeed is a royal tumulus cemetery rivalling that of Gordium, and attesting a similar tradition of monumental mound-building over noblemen's graves. Karnıyarık Tepe was investigated by tunnelling; a stone *krepis* was found inside the mound, enclosing a preliminary tumulus some 90 m in diameter; it was built of two courses of ashlar blocks crowned with a round moulding (Pls. Vol., pl. 237*a*, *b*). On the upper ashlar course large monograms were carved, some of which were tentatively read as *Gugu*. The identification of the mound as that of Gyges depends, however, on its size and prominence at Bintepe. The chamber has not yet been found.

Whether this tumulus indeed contains the chamber of Gyges or not, the tradition of tumulus burial was surely honoured by the Mermnad dynasty. All excavated tumuli at Bintepe contain stone chambers with doors and *dromoi* or antechambers and are as such technically more developed and formally different from the doorless timber graves of Phrygian tumuli. The earliest Gordium tumuli antedate the oldest excavated Lydian tumuli by at least a century. In view of the geographi-

71 R. S. Young, *University Museum Bulletin* 17.4 (1953) 33; E 82; E 5, pl. H3; E 73 (1966), 11, fig. 6.
72 E 72, 313; E 118, 54–5; E 69, 37–41.
73 E 73 (1964), 53–5; (1965), 27–35; (1966), 27–30; (1967), 43–7; E 105, 84–5; E 69, 57–8.

cal and chronological proximity of the Phrygian and Lydian dynasties, the similarity in burial customs is as important as the structural variant in chamber-building. It seems that tumulus graves were introduced by the Phrygians in Western Anatolia, and adapted by their neighbours the Lydians in a hybrid type, which borrows features from the built or rock-cut chamber tomb; Egyptian architectural stimuli are perhaps to be considered.

In the habitation levels at Sardis, material contemporary with Gyges has been reached; signs of destruction may indeed be due to Cimmerian raids in Gyges' time, but in the outer north-western sector a violent attack is attested at an earlier date, perhaps as early as 725 or 740 B.C.[74] The strata sealed in by a later destruction contain Lydian ware associated with Middle or Late Protocorinthian, Rhodian, and Ephesian wares. Here, as in most Iron Age strata of Sardis, the admixture of Greek pottery is constant. The association is chronologically valuable and will potentially extend Lydian correlative chronology back into the Dark Ages; it also emphasizes the difference between the Lydians and Phrygians in accessibility to Greek contacts.

The immediate successors of Gyges, less famous and colourful, still suffered Cimmerian raids until Alyattes drove the predators out for good. Ardys, the son of Gyges (c. 645?-615?), restored friendship with Ashurbanipal as we infer from the Assyrian record. During his rule, the lower city of Sardis was captured and presumably looted by Cimmerians (Hdt. 1.15), perhaps in conjunction with attacks by Treres and Lycians (Strabo XIII.4.8; Kallisthenes, Kallinos FGrH 124 F 29). Ardys continued hostilities against some Ionian cities; Herodotus records action against Priene and Miletus (1.15).

Sadyattes, his son (c. 615-610), started a protracted series of raids to destroy the crops in the Milesian countryside which he ruined for six consecutive years (Hdt. 1.18); Alyattes continued this strategy for five more years until he was overcome by illness, which struck him in revenge for the burning of the temple of Athena at Assessus. With sage advice from Delphi and a stratagem suggested by Periander of Corinth to Thrasybulus of Miletus, a general reconciliation came about (Hdt. 1.18–22). Gifts to Delphi on this occasion were a large silver crater with a welded iron stand made by Glaucus of Chios (Hdt. 1.25); the merging of Lydian and Ionian artistic interests is evident in this choice of offering.

Alyattes had a long and eventful career (c. 610–560). Under him Lydia prospered, new connexions were established, and electrum coinage started its spectacular role in the ancient economy. Alyattes' exploits against his Ionian and Carian neighbours included the capture of Smyrna (Hdt. 1.16, Nic. Damasc. FGrH 90 F 64), which has been recognized in

---

[74] E 73 (1961), 12, 22; (1966), 10; E 69, 21, 26–8; E 116, 6–15 (and pers. comm. A. Ramage).

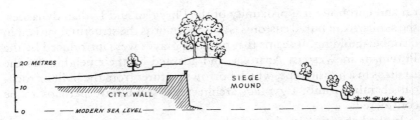

Fig. 46. Section through the siege-mound and walls at Old Smyrna (Bayraklı). (After E 28, 97, fig. 110.)

the archaeological remains at the site of Old Smyrna–Bayraklı.[75] A siege-mound still rises at the north-west corner of the site, piled up of miscellaneous debris and datable to *c.* 600 B.C. on ceramic grounds (Fig. 46). From the height of this ramp the battle was fought principally by archers and slingers. Many arrow-heads were found in the debris, some still stuck in the mud-brick of houses. The precision in the archaeological dating of the siege-mound helps in establishing the chronological order of Alyattes' undertakings; his Milesian wars came first according to Herodotus (1.17); his attack on Smyrna followed (*c.* 600); a subsequent attempt to take Clazomenae met with failure (Hdt. 1.16). There is no indication that Alyattes remodelled or rebuilt Smyrna; the capture must have been in the nature of a destructive raid. Other military activities were directed against Caria, with troops brought in by (among others) Croesus, who was governor of the Adramyttium area (Nic. Damasc. *FGrH* 90 F 65).

Alyattes' moves in the direction of Ionia and Caria, like the Ionian wars of his predecessors, were perhaps disciplinary actions in his attempt to maintain access to Aegean harbours while securing a larger West Anatolian realm beyond the Hermus and Cayster valleys and Mysia, increasingly putting Phrygia under Lydian auspices. We do not know the nature of the controls Alyattes imposed upon his eastern neighbours, but the traditionally friendly relations with the Phrygians may have allowed him to put reinforcements in the main Phrygian citadels (e.g., Midas City, Gordium, Hacıtuğrul, perhaps also in the cities of the Afyon and Konya area), and to enjoy safe access to the produce and roads of Phrygia. This would have given him economic and military advantages; the grazing grounds and wheatfields of Phrygia could supplement the resources of Lydia proper; metallurgy continued to be a major enterprise in the Phrygian centres; horses, horsemen, and soldiers could be found in large numbers; weapons, tools, bronze vessels and utensils, and chariots were surely available in quantity after the Cimmerian raids stopped endangering the Phrygian centres.

[75] J. M. Cook, *BSA* 53/4 (1958/9), 23–8, 88–91, 128–34; *CAH* III².3, 197, 202–3.

Gordium by this time was rebuilt to its former glory; the citadel again had its fortifications and its subdivision in outer and inner courts; the storage buildings replacing the terrace units were again broken up into individual megara; the entire plan, fortifications as well as monumental buildings, was a detailed modernized replica of the plan in Midas' time.[76] Lydian pottery makes its appearance in burials at Gordium of the early sixth century B.C., both in simple graves and tumuli (now mostly containing cremations): in the houses of the walled suburb of the Küçük Hüyük, East Greek wares mingle with Lydian imports and local wares; along with this material, Phrygian monochrome dark pottery continues to appear as the predominant ware in coarse and fine versions.

Proof of contact with the Alyattes era is found in the hoard of forty-five electrum coins from one of the storage buildings at Gordium.[77] These are coins from the Lydian mint at Sardis. Coinage originated in Lydia during the rule of Alyattes or earlier, in interaction with the East Greek communities.[78] The Gordium hoard shows that Alyattes' practical use of coinage in trade and payment of stipends had reached the citadel of Gordium, as it must have reached other inland areas of formerly Phrygian, now predominantly Lydian organization. We have no documents concerning Alyattes' control of the lands beyond the west coast. A system of control and protection had existed under Midas, and expanded into central and Eastern Anatolia. Alyattes seems to have been the first Lydian king to have aimed towards a similarly firm expansion. This brought him into clashes with the Medes, whose analogous interests pushed them into Anatolia from the east. The war was not an all-out military confrontation but a series of conflicts and vicissitudes.

Herodotus (1.73–4) describes how one conflict started over a group of Scythian refugees who were first accepted by the Median king Cyaxares but later fled to Alyattes in Sardis. Remnants of Scythians and Cimmerians may still have caused disruption and local wars. The Lydo–Median war went on spasmodically for five years until the battle on the fateful day of the total eclipse predicted by Thales of Miletus. Interrupted by this cosmic omen on 28 May 585, the war was brought to an end through the good offices of two other kings, Syennesis of Cilicia, a successor of the Que kings of the Midas era, and, according to Herodotus, Labynetus of Babylon (this name is unclear, Nebuchadrezzar II being king of Babylon at this time, but Nabonidus may have acted as a representative). The reconciliation was sealed by the dynastic marriage of Aryenis, Alyattes' daughter, to Astyages, son of Cyaxares.

The peace achieved by this agreement must have lasted for a prosperous period, which benefited greater Lydia as much as Phrygia

---

[76] E 139 (1964), 281–2; E 141, 4–5.   [77] E 139 (1964), 283; E 17.
[78] E 131; E 10; E 85, 24–8.

and allowed increasing cultural interaction from the Ionian coast to the Anatolian plateau. As one symptom of this, we may note that both at Sardis and at Gordium Greek iconographic motifs were introduced in architectural decoration. Theseus and the Minotaur, for instance, appear, on a small scale, in a Lydian sima frieze, and in bold format on revetment plaques at Gordium (Pls. Vol., pl. 235),[79] where a new meaning surely must have been read into the triumphant theme of 'hero vanquishing monster': the king as conqueror and protector, similar to the later Achaemenid reliefs at Persepolis. In Gordium, figural themes replace the old Phrygian diamond patterns in a new inspiration from the Greek world. Perhaps we may see more direct Lydian reference in the revetment plaques with a lion and bull opposed decoratively.[80] Hellenization moves into Phrygia and continues via the old channels into Phrygianized Mushki territory. At Pazarlı, a stronghold 29 km north east of Alaca Hüyük, Phrygian warriors are shown on architectural terracottas (Pls. Vol., pl. 234) in a manner more articulate than in Phrygian times; battle motifs occur, centaurs appear, old-fashioned Phrygian diamond patterns continue.[81] There is a blend of old and new; designs are rather barbaric, but polychromy adds vivid detail to the representations and allows the painters to bring variety into the renderings.

In the lands closer to the Lydian centres, the timber grave tradition continues in the Afyon–Dinar (Celaenae) area. A tumulus excavated in 1969 proved to contain a chamber built of juniper beams painted with friezes in Phrygian–Lydian style. Among the designs are warriors related to the Pazarlı figures, with shields, spears, and crested helmets; chariots, sphinxes, and winged bulls.[82] Thus the possibility looms of a Phrygo-Lydian tradition of tomb painting in the early sixth century B.C., with strong elements antedating the Greek infiltration. To confirm this, we note in minor arts the development of fine Lydianizing pottery with polychrome animal friezes in the Burdur area. The site of Düver, south west of Burdur, has yielded specimens different from the East Greek, orientalizing pottery painted at Sardis; the local elements are evident in the Lydian provinces.[83]

At the end of his spectacular career, Alyattes was probably buried in the largest mound of Bintepe at Sardis, a tumulus over 60 m high and some 250 m in diameter, situated at the eastern end of the necropolis.[84] Hipponax and Herodotus (1.93) give grounds for the identification. The tumulus was investigated by Spiegelthal in 1853 and again by the

[79] E 2, pls. 37 (Sardis), 76–9 (Gordium); E 66.   [80] E 2, pl. 86.
[81] E 2, pls. 90–6; E 5, pls. 45–50.   [82] E 135; *AJA* 76 (1972), 178.
[83] E 57; E 58.
[84] E 106; E 73 (1963), 52–9; E 105, 66; E 69, 56–7; E 59 (26–7, Alyattes' tomb); E 60 (20–2, Alyattes' tomb).

American excavators in 1962 and the 1980s. It had a tall *krepis* of ashlar masonry, now lost. As is the case for most tumuli at Bintepe, the interior had been tunnelled and the tomb chamber plundered. The chamber was constructed of large marble blocks well fitted and clamped, and finely finished on the interior. Workmanship and technique show great experience. The chamber (3.325 × 2.37 m in plan, 2.25 to 2.33 m in height) had a door and anteroom; there apparently was no *dromos*. On top was a charred mass of wood, but detailed observations are not available.

The splendours of this tomb and tumulus have survived only in structural aspects; from loot of recently plundered Lydian tombs and from the lists of Lydian donations to sanctuaries we can infer that the burial gifts would have included wood and ivory furniture, textiles, jewellery, and above all extensive sets of silver and gold bowls, pitchers, craters, and ladles. Alabastra and ceramic *lydia* were among the robbers' leavings. Even in its damaged and stripped form, the marble burial chamber of Alyattes is the first clear example of a built royal Lydian tomb chamber, since the Gyges chamber remains undiscovered. The architects of the Lydians were familiar with stone and especially marble; the techniques represented in the Alyattes chamber must have been developed by the builders of large public monuments and temples close to East Greek architecture and informed by Egyptian contacts.

The reign of Croesus (560–547), the son of Alyattes, is closely linked with Greek history. The intensity of his interests in Greece and Greek culture is such that it becomes difficult to see Croesus as a truly Anatolian king, in spite of his Lydian father and Carian mother. Yet his rule meant the culmination and defeat of West Anatolian ambition.

The struggles with individual cities in Ionia now became a series of actions aimed at subjugation and tribute (Hdt. 1.26–7); even Ephesus was not immune. The story of Croesus' ambition to build ships and attack the islands serves mainly to emphasize his real power, the Lydian cavalry (Hdt. 1.27). For Croesus, hegemony over Western Anatolia, including Phrygia as far as the Halys, is explicitly stated, with a list of other Anatolian subjects, from which only the Cilicians and Lycians (who had their own kingdoms, although Cilicia had become the target of interest to the neo-Babylonian kings)[85] remained exempt. The result was the fulfilment of Alyattes' policies in western Asia Minor, increased organization and communication for the main centres in this part of the country, commercial and military routes functioning well, and messengers travelling back and forth.

Croesus' clash with Cyrus and the Persians was a more serious conflict with more determined opponents than the six-year war of Alyattes and the Medes. Now both kings had conquerors' ambitions, and the Lydian empire had become a desirable prize for Cyrus. It is in characteristic Lydian dynastic tradition that in preparation for the war Croesus concluded alliances with Amasis of Egypt and Nabonidus of Babylon, and consulted a series of Greek oracles, adding the oracle of Ammon in Libya. Lavish gifts were bestowed upon Delphi, gold bricks supporting a gold lion of 10 talents, and large gold and silver craters, originally set up in the temple of Apollo. In addition there were silver *pithoi*, silver and gold *perirrhanteria*, silver bowls, a gold statue of a woman, jewellery and belts of Croesus' queen. We can again reconstruct the splendours to some extent with the aid of incidental archaeological discoveries such as the inventory of the somewhat later tombs at Ikiztepe near Güre–Uşak.[86] The fabulous opulence of the Croesus regime exceeded all previously known forms of material glory.

Croesus in the course of his rule changed Lydian coinage from electrum to gold and silver to facilitate trade and exchange with non-Anatolian lands.[87] His search for allies among the mainland Greeks led to his special friendship with the Spartans, who intended a giant crater as a gift for Croesus (Hdt. 1.70) and who earlier had been given gold by Croesus to adorn their statue of Apollo on Mount Thornax, in good diplomatic exchange of favours.

The great encounter of Croesus and Cyrus was fought with large armies and Anatolian auxiliaries. Croesus marched to Cappadocia, crossing the Halys, which had become the boundary between the Lydians and the Medes. He came to Pteria, the strongest place in this area (Hdt. 1.76), captured it and the surrounding villages, and ransacked the countryside. After some uncertainty, it is again thought probable that Pteria was the sixth-century name for the rebuilt site of the former Hittite capital Hattusha.[88] Croesus would have followed the Phrygian track to the Halys and the Mushki land, where Midas once had taken over the old sites, including Hattusha and Alaca Hüyük, and where numbers of Phrygians may still have resided in the sixth century.

The battle between Croesus and Cyrus was thus fought in historical territory. The indecisive outcome, Croesus' retreat to Sardis, his reliance upon future reinforcement by his allies in a strong spring campaign, and Cyrus' decisive move against the unsuspecting Lydian king, are related by Herodotus (1.76–81). The great cavalry of the Lydians was frustrated by Cyrus' strategic use of camels, and a siege of the walled city and acropolis of Sardis followed. After a fortnight the citadel was captured, allegedly via a weak spot in the otherwise impregnable defences. Cyrus had reached the aim of his conquest.

In striking to the west, Cyrus also must have followed the main

---

[86] *AJA* 71 (1967), 172, pl. 59; E 129.
[87] E 85, 29–31; Hdt. 1.14; *CAH* IV², chapter 7d; *Pls. to Vol. IV*, chapter 15.   [88] E 22, 156.

Phrygian road via Ankara and Gordium. The excavations at Gordium have shown that the large mud-brick rampart around the south-eastern suburb, built in the seventh century and repeatedly repaired in the sixth, was attacked in the mid-sixth century by large numbers of archers, especially in the strategic section opposite the East Gate of the main citadel, where a mud-brick fortress defended the outer rampart (Pls. Vol., pl. 226).[89] In the outcome the defenders lost the battle and the mud-brick rampart was demolished, with the exception of a truncated part of the mud-brick east fortress which became part and parcel of a tumulus erected opposite the main sixth-century citadel, perhaps the grave of the local prince who fell in the battle against Cyrus' army. By the economical decision of the tumulus builders, and with the sanction of the Persian commander, a fragment of the mud-brick citadel was left standing on its base of 120 courses of mud-brick for the rampart (a height of 12 m); the rooms of the fortress itself had an additional height of 6–8 m. The barracks had gone up in flames, the fire fed by ceiling beams, floors, window-frames, embrasures, and also by the overhanging outer balconies. The outer face of the rampart and towers was full of arrow-heads (Pls. Vol., pl. 227), predominantly of the triangular barbed type.

Gordium after this attack became the citadel of a Persian governor. The entire suburb on the east side was abandoned, but the main citadel with its stone walls and gates was kept in good repair at least until the fifth century. Some new buildings were added in the course of the Persian period.

The fate of Sardis, captured but not destroyed, was to become the residence of Persian satraps. The palace of Croesus, or at least one of his buildings, survived into Roman times. Pliny (*N.H.* xxxv.172) and Vitruvius (II.8.9–10) refer to the mud-brick building. On the acropolis and its northern spurs (Pls. Vol., pl. 236b) remnants of elegant terraces, stairs, and walls of ashlar masonry go back to the Lydian era.[90] They must have supported buildings of stone, perhaps matching in splendour the workmanship of the tomb chamber of Alyattes. The buildings of Sardis impressed the Persian conquerors; Cyrus borrowed ideas and craftsmen from Sardis and Ionia to work for him at Pasargadae. To what extent he used Croesus' advice and friendship is uncertain. Herodotus' account of Croesus' activities after his rescue from the pyre (1.86) is contradicted by the Babylonian record, which seems to claim that the Lydian king was killed, but the reading of the name of the land is uncertain.[91]

[89] R. S. Young, *University Museum Bulletin* 17.4 (1952), 26–9; *Archaeology* 6 (1953), 159ff; *AJA* 61 (1957), 324.

[90] E 73 (1961), 37–9; C. H. Greenewalt, *BASOR* 206 (1972), 15–20; E 72, 316–17; E 105, 85; E 116, 6–15.

[91] A 44, 306, Nabonidus Chronicle; E 112, no. 296; A 25, 107, 282.

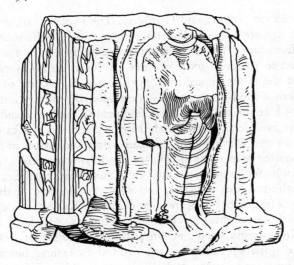

Fig. 47. Marble relief *naiskos* of Cybebe from Sardis. (After E 70, no. 7, fig. 27.)

Among the architectural remnants of the Croesus era are his contributions to the building of the Artemisium at Ephesus, where inscriptions on the column bases attest to his munificence.[92] The archaic temple of Cybebe at Sardis, burnt down in 499 B.C. (Hdt. V.102), has not yet been located, but a marble model of a Cybebe shrine, a decorated *naiskos*, was found reused in a pier of the synagogue (Fig. 47). The figure of the goddess, the Lydian counterpart of the Phrygian Matar Kubile, stands frontally in the door-frame; the sides of the monument are decorated in friezes behind the columns. The Ionicizing transformation of the Phrygian goddess is evident.[93]

A beginning has been made to explore the Sardians' gold-working establishments. An area on the east bank of the Pactolus has traces of gold refineries and jewellery workshops. The splendid products of Sardian jewellers have become known through excavated burials of the Persian period, and also through the robbers' loot purchased by various museums.[94]

The question of the relationship of Lydian and Persian art has been clarified through recent excavations and studies of architecture. What is not yet clear is whether Lydian art in its formative period was independent of Greek (Ionic and Aeolic) influence. Our first indications of Lydian minor arts belong to the seventh century, when the Ionic milieu is already clearly noticeable. We cannot yet study the earlier stages

[92] E 68, 11; E 114, figs. 31, 69.
[93] E 73 (1964), 39–43; E 68, 12, figs. 23–6; E 71; E 70, 43–51, no. 7, figs. 20–50.
[94] E 68, 6; E 73 (1970), 18–28; E 72, 311–15; E 69, 34–6; E 61.

of Lydian culture, which ought to have existed in the cities of the Hermus valley, and for which the Sardis excavations have given us promise. Nor do we know the native art of the Late Bronze Age ancestors of the Lydians, whose cities lay in Assuwa and who had a similar marginal position *vis-à-vis* the Anatolian hinterland and the Aegean peoples. We may see in the Ephesus ivories (Pls. Vol., pls. 286–7) a glimpse of a surviving Asiatic world, non-Greek in appearance and fashion, in beliefs and culture. This world also appears in a group of ivories found in the Phrygian tumulus at Bayındır near Elmalı, which has one direct parallel to the Ephesus series.[95] An original West Anatolian artistic idiom is thus coming to light as an Anatolian component in the formation of East Greek art. We can only speculate about its roots and affinities in the Dark Ages.

Lydia and Phrygia shared authentic Anatolian traits in the seventh century B.C., but we do not yet have an image of the Lydians as a cultural entity in the ninth or eighth centuries. It is clear that through the Lydians Phrygia was exposed to interaction with Greek culture, which lasted into the Roman period with all its repercussions in the classical world.

III. LYCIA

The Lycians are now known to be descendants of a Luwian-speaking group of West Anatolians of the Bronze Age. Their name in the Bronze Age was probably Lukka, although the geographical distribution of the Lukka is disputed. The Lukka were seafarers and participated aggressively in the raids and wars of the fourteenth–thirteenth centuries, including raids on Cyprus–Alashiya in the mid-fourteenth century, aid to the Hittites at Qadesh, and a conspiracy with the Libyans and Sea Peoples against Merneptah. At the end of the Bronze Age, some of the final naval battles against the Sea Peoples were fought off the Lukka coasts.[96]

The Lycians known to the Greeks and to Homer as vigorous allies of the Trojans lived mainly in the mountainous coastal district between Caria and Pamphylia (between Telmessus–Fethiye and Attaleia–Antalya), a rugged land with good harbours, mountains rising to 3,000 m, large forests, and few river valleys, several of them seasonal mountain torrents. The most fertile river plain is that of the Xanthus river, on the east bank of which the Lycian capital of Xanthus (Arñna) was located, with its harbour town at Patara. Coastal plains also favoured the foundation of the cities of Limyra and Myra and other smaller harbour towns. Inland towns, such as Tlos and Pinara, were mountain citadels with natural strongholds. Smaller communities existed in the upland

[95] E 48, 190, nos. 41–2.   [96] E 104, 87–9, R. S. 20.238.

valleys and along the natural passes to the plateau of Pisidia and south Phrygia. The resources of the land are the forests which provide timber for architecture and ship-building; fertile coastal plains, vineyards and orchards; abundant water; sufficient grazing land for sheep, goats, cattle, and horses; bee-keeping; good hunting. Communications between the cool upland sites and the coastal plains must through the ages have been active, especially for the migration upland of people and animals during the hot summer season.

The Iron Age land of Lycia qualifies as part of the Bronze Age Lukka lands by nature and location. Herodotus (1.173) indicates some of the complications of the ethnic and geographical nomenclature. He relates that the Lycians originally came from Crete. After a dispute, Minos would have driven out his brother Sarpedon and his partisans; Sarpedon would have settled in Lycia, which at the time was called Milyas, with the Solymi occupying the land later held by the Milyans. The Lycians at the time of Sarpedon, and indeed in classical times in their own inscriptions, called themselves Termilai. The name Lycians, Herodotus adds, was introduced after the Athenian Lycus joined the Termilai and Sarpedon as a fellow refugee.

The shifts in nomenclature are typical of the semi-mythological history of the Bronze Age and Dark Ages. The modern rediscovery of the Lukka discredits the Athenian Lycus considerably. The classical Greek usage of the names Lykia, Lykioi for land and people in spite of the native use of Termilai can be better explained as the survival of a Bronze Age, Achaean usage of the name of Lukka-Lukioi for the land and its inhabitants. Lukka may possibly be a by-form of the 'Luwian' designation.[97]

The Homeric Lycians are the carriers of the Bronze Age name and tradition. They came to Troy from the Xanthus valley (*Il.* 11.877), where the dynasty of Bellerophon ruled. The *Iliad* speaks of Bronze Age dynastic ties between Corinth–Ephyre, Argos, and Lycia. Proetus exiled Bellerophon to the Lycian king, who was Proetus' father-in-law and who made Bellerophon also his son-in-law after the latter's heroic exploits in killing the Chimaera, and battling the Solymi and Amazons (*Il.* VI.155ff). The only Homeric reference to writing occurs in the Bellerophon story; Bellerophon carries a folded (wooden) tablet to the Lycian king. It is an ironical coincidence that the first Late Bronze Age wooden folding tablet from Anatolia turned up in the fourteenth-century shipwreck east of Kaş–Antiphellus on the Lycian coast.[98] The Bellerophon story is detailed enough to contain elements of historical contact between Peloponnesian and Lycian rulers (cf. the visit of Bellerophon to Oineus, *Il.* VI.216), even including the use of written

---

[97] E 88; E 76, 3ff.   [98] E 14 (tablet, 730–1).

messages. This would have been Achaean contact with Lycia remembered by epic poetry, and perhaps also by Greeks who survived the Dark Ages as Greeks, for example in Pamphylia, where the classical dialect is proof of the lasting presence of Achaean elements.[99]

The Luwian descent of the Lycians–Termilai is linguistically clear, and confirms the Anatolian character of the Lycians as a Bronze Age group. What both the *Iliad*, with its story of Bellerophon, and Herodotus, with his reference to the exile of Sarpedon, suggest is dynastic relationships with Minoans and Mycenaeans rather than large-scale Aegean immigration. The Lycians were allies and friends also of the Trojan dynasty (*Il.* XVII.150).

To the *Iliad*, Lycia is a land of rulers who live in the Xanthus valley with fertile domains. Bellerophon receives a special *temenos* (VI.193–5), while his grandsons Glaucus and Sarpedon have inherited those lands and enjoy near-divine respect (XII.310–14). Sarpedon ruled Lycia with justice and vigour (XVI.542). Glaucus' wealth is evident in his precious armour (VI.236). The semi-divine status of Sarpedon, the son of Zeus, the compassionate rescue of his body by Apollo, the conveying of the dead king to his homeland by Death and Sleep, impressed the Greek poet and vase-painter; we may in Homer's description of the transference of the dead king and his burial rites (XVI.667ff) see allusions to Lycian beliefs and practices. The kind of rule the *Iliad* suggests for Lycia seems to have continued into the Early Iron Age, the leading chieftains and land-owners residing in the Xanthus valley with their residence at Xanthus–Arñna.

Excavations in Lycia have not yet revealed traces of Late Bronze Age settlement in the coastal zone, nor have the French excavators of the classical acropolis at Xanthus found evidence of occupation antedating the eighth century B.C.[100] The coastal plain and the harbour site of Patara are heavily silted and sanded up, so that only deep soundings below the present water table could yield prehistoric material.[101] The occupation of the site of Xanthus may have started in the plain rather than on the archaic acropolis, as the excavators hint.[102] An additional problem of the recovery of Lycian habitation sites is the local use of timber as the preferred building material, occasionally combined with large rough stone foundations, but not extensively covered or filled in with clay mortar and mud-brick. We can still see the indigenous building methods and materials in the villages of the Lycian area as they have survived through the ages into present times; they are threatened by the technical progress of concrete and roof-tiles and will disappear in another generation. Travellers in Lycia have commented on the resemblances of the timber storage sheds of the nineteenth and early twentieth century to

[99] E 35.   [100] E 95; E 97, 187–8; E 47, 1381–2.   [101] E 38.   [102] E 47, 1382.

the rock-cut tombs of the classical era; several modern studies have been devoted to this relationship. When the carving and cutting of stone and rock begins in archaic Lycia, the models for the funeral monuments are age-old building-types of the local timber tradition. Just as the Phrygians in Midas City carved replicas of Phrygian megara in the cliffs of their citadel, the Lycians copied their own native architectural types. Here, however, the originals do not survive because they were made of perishable materials, unlike the Gordium megara which contained abundant timber but had well-fitted stone foundations and socles, mud-brick superstructures and even carved stone acroteria.

Without mud-brick, mud mortar and mud plaster, prehistoric mound formation does not occur in Anatolia. The problem affects the archaeological exploration of many areas in Western (and Northern) Anatolia, typical instances being Lycia, Pamphylia, and parts of Caria. Entire successions of habitation complexes on one and the same site may archaeologically be barely noticeable or retrievable, given the additional hardship of erosion on rocky sites and the wear and tear on any surviving pottery fragments not safely embedded in pockets and crevices. The best preserved remnants of the prehistoric era will be cemeteries, if embedded in the lower plains and provided with jars and tomb gifts. So far, the only Lycian area which has yielded both architectural evidence and burial sites of the third and second millennia B.C. is the upland plain of Elmalı, where a mixed building tradition of timber, wattle-and-daub, pisé, and mud-brick helped in the preservation of prehistoric houses and fortifications. Elmalı is in the region which may have been labelled the Milyad by the fifth century B.C., but it is directly connected with the Lycian coastal sites of Limyra and modern Finike; it shared many cultural characteristics, including probably the late Luwian idiom, with coastal Lycia.[103]

If we may reconstruct the physical appearance of early Lycian buildings and citadels with the aid of later replicas in their rock-cut cemeteries, and rely on the mythological and Homeric tradition to give the lower Xanthus valley the status of the principal royal and dynastic Lycian domains, we still know very little about the actual rulers and inhabitants of Iron Age Lycia. No historical names have survived for the kings in the Lydian era, although we know the Lycians maintained their independence even under Croesus (Hdt. 1.28). A strong trend to independence and recalcitrance to foreign rule existed in Lycia, as shown in the famous and heroic defence of the plain and citadel of Xanthus against the Persian general Harpagus in c. 545 B.C., when the inhabitants resisted to the last desperate suicidal stand, having set fire to their women, children, slaves, and possessions in the citadel. This catastrophe has been identified by the excavations, but not as a total destruction of

[103] E 90 (1964–70); E 92.

the citadel.[104] Eighty Xanthian families survived the war because they happened to be away, probably in upland summer villages, when disaster struck (Hdt. 1.176).

From the fifth century on, Lycian rulers become known to us through their coinage, issued in individual cities.[105] Lycian alphabetic inscriptions, mostly funeral, become available for this period also. The development of several Lycian cities to the north and east of Xanthus, culturally homogeneous, but of regional independence and prosperity, is clear from the record of the classical period. The Persians required tribute and military aid. A Lycian commander, Kybernis(kos), served under Xerxes in 480 B.C. with fifty ships. His men wore cuirasses and greaves, felt caps with feathers, and goat-skin capes. They were archers and hoplites, carrying javelins, daggers, and curved swords (Hdt. 1.92, 98). The tradition of seamanship is clearly ancient; the weapons and accoutrements may be traditional also. We do not know how much of the dynastic organization of fifth-century Lycia may be projected back into the pre-Persian era.

Archaeology provides a sequence of material evidence, first of all in the form of a ceramic record from the Xanthus excavations. From the eighth century B.C. on, traces of occupation survive. A local geometric ware with painted bichrome patterns is characteristic of the Lycian as well as the general South-west Anatolian area. It is related to pottery of contemporary Cilicia and Cyprus, and also to Lydian and Phrygian painted wares. Its chronological development has not yet been worked out in detail, because stratified sequences are as yet meagre, but potentially the bichrome wares will provide an index of Lycian settlement from the eighth to sixth centuries. At Xanthus these wares are accompanied by imported Greek pottery of Cycladic, Rhodian, Samian, and generally East Greek origin, with very little Corinthian import.[106]

Through ceramic chronology, building A on the acropolis at Xanthus (Pls. Vol., pl. 238), perhaps the rulers' palace, can be attributed to the seventh century. Its stone foundations preserve a rectangular plan with subdivisions which would allow a reconstruction with porch, corridor, and storage rooms. Remnants of magazines were found along the south slope, and archaic material also remained in the favissa of the later temple, but the pre-Persian form of the citadel and the fortifications remain inadequately known. In the rebuilding after the destruction of 545 B.C., a larger building, perhaps the palace, rose over the ruins of building A. Only the basements are preserved; as in the previous period, the building must have consisted of several halls and corridors, unlike the Phrygian megaron plans. An enclosure wall formed a court around this south-east sector of the acropolis. To the north west, a temple with a

---

[104] E 47, 1381.   [105] E 98; E 85, 269–73.   [106] E 97, 61–8, pls. 21–4.

triple cella has been recognized in a structure facing west, with a favissa in the rear of the central cella. Thick orthostats form the rear wall. The contents of the earliest Persian level were found in the debris of a second destruction which dates to *c.* 470. Black-figure Attic vases were imported in quantity in Xanthus from 540 on.[107]

The natural rock which forms the base of the Xanthian acropolis is not conducive to the preservation of more than the outlines of the archaic buildings, the superstructure of which must have been continued in timber on the stone basements. The forms of Lycian indigenous architecture become known at Xanthus in the 'heroa' or tombs F, G, and H built on the west side of the acropolis in the early fifth century, also in the archaic and classical pillar tombs to the north, and in various other combinations of rock-cut socles, freestanding house-tombs, and sarcophagi belonging to the cemetery on the north and east slopes of the main acropolis as well as on the heights of the later north-east acropolis. The Lycian architectural imprint is unmistakable also in the funeral monuments of Myra, Limyra, Pinara, Tlos, and other Lycian cities. The stone replicas of Lycian timber architecture are as a rule of reduced format, given the nature of the funeral requirements, but dimensions and units are flexible. Behind this display of local building traditions is the rather sudden rise of the trend to carve funeral monuments out of solid rock instead of constructing them out of the ordinary native building materials. As noted above, the Phrygians may have been the first to revive the art of rock carving in the Anatolian Iron Age and to create rock-cut replicas of architectural façades. Whatever the impetus, by the mid-sixth century rock carving becomes the preferred medium for the making of prominent Lycian tombs, and sculptural decoration appears.

At Xanthus and elsewhere, the earliest funeral monuments are pillar tombs (Pls. Vol., pl. 239).[108] The Lion Tomb is perhaps still pre-Persian, with bold lion sculptures and scenes of real or heroic combat: other pillar reliefs depict scenes of sport and wrestling accompanied by music; the early fifth-century Harpy Tomb with its quiet dynastic(?) scenes alludes to the conveying of the dead by friendly winged beings to the other world, perhaps remotely connected with Homer's allusion to Sarpedon's voyage after death. The pillar tombs are funeral towers, the prototypes of which may be local protective towers still in use in parts of Lycia as pedestals of beehives, with hollow chambers in the top and overhanging flat roofs.[109] Pillar tombs at Isinda, Pinara, and elsewhere show a development parallel to the dynastic monuments at Xanthus. Such tombs continue to be made in the fifth century, along with replicas of timber houses, sarcophagi on pedestals, and rock-cut façades. Lycian alphabetic inscriptions begin to appear in conjunction with the funeral monuments.

[107] E 95, 16–19, 20–3, 29–32, 44–7.   [108] E 46; E 4; E 114.   [109] E 80; E 92.

Soundings in the lower city of Limyra have reached levels of the sixth and seventh century B.C.[110] The continuing excavations of the Letoum on the west bank of the Xanthus river, the later sanctuary of the Lycian League, have come upon archaic strata under the northern stoa area.[111]

As for the area of the Elmalı plain, some Iron Age habitation and a number of simple Iron Age burials have been excavated on the western fringes of the site of Karataş.[112] The tombs are of conservative type, individual burials in large banded *pithoi*. Burial gifts consist of bichrome local pottery also known from eighth- to sixth-century levels on the acropolis at Xanthus. Similar burials have been noted in a disturbed cemetery near the village of Yalnızdam west of Elmalı. In such simple graves we see the burial customs of Lycian or Milyan commoners. In the Elmalı area prominent graves were either rock-cut Lycian tombs with timber-style façades, or built stone chambers covered by tumuli. The tumulus tradition reached from the Phrygian–Pisidian plateau into Lycia, maintaining Phrygian features in the Elmalı district, and blending with Carian forms in the mountain zones.[113] Many of the seventh-century tumuli in the Elmalı-Bayındır area contain cremations.[114] The Kızılbel tumulus near Elmalı contains a small chamber built in character-istic Lycian polygonal masonry. It had a portcullis door but no *dromos*. Its interior walls are decorated with multiple painted friezes rendering scenes characteristic of the lifestyle of a North Lycian nobleman as well as appropriate mythological motifs. Over the *kline* is the main frieze depicting the warrior's departure by chariot. The iconography is indebted to the long series of Greek (and evidently also East Greek) representations of the theme and to its mythological variant of Amphiar-aos' departure; yet the Lycian version, the first to be preserved in wall painting, has local detail such as a winged demon over the chariot, which belongs with related winged beings in Lycian funeral art. The other Kızılbel tomb scenes are concerned with warriors, horsemen, chario-teers, court life, dignitaries; with sport and hunting; and with travel by sea. The style is closely connected with East Greek art and its offshoots, yet the iconography betrays Anatolian traditions as well. The most clearly Greek mythological theme at Kızılbel, the Gorgons, Medusa, and the birth of Pegasus and Chrysaor, has its topical relevance in Lycia as well as an implication of rebirth, being painted in prominent position at the foot of the *kline*.

Prominent noblemen and regional rulers lived in the individual mountain sites of inner Lycia and on the mounds of the northern plain of Elmalı. Their life-style was partly Hellenized in the sixth century B.C., as we can infer from the funeral art. Perhaps an old affinity to the Greeks,

---

[110] E 32.   [111] E 96, 317–21.   [112] E 90 (1969), 330; (1970) 250–1.

[113] E 90 (1970), 251–3; (1971), 246–9; (1973), 301–3; (1976), 377–82; J. Zahle, *Acta Archaeologica* 46 (1975) 77–94.

[114] E 48, 187–95, nos. 29–34, 43–4, 47, 60–2, tumulus C; E 90 (1972), 261–3, figs. 7–12.

and shared traditions of the Bronze Age past, stimulated the new cultural and artistic interaction, in spite of the tenacious persistence of the Lycian language and alphabet. What is evident in Iron Age and archaic Lycian history, as opposed to events in Phrygia and Lydia, is the lack of an expansionist drive. Lycians clung to their territory and traditions with pride and independence, but they did not resume the activities of their Bronze Age predecessors the Lukka, nor rally around a dynasty which could have met the Near Eastern powers as a potential ally or rival. Limited naval contacts are to be presumed in interaction with the Greek islanders, especially with the Rhodians who founded Phaselis on the Lycian east coast in the seventh century B.C., and who controlled the island of Megiste off Antiphellus.[115] The Lycian internal development will still emerge more clearly from Lycian inscriptions and monuments of the classical period, but Lycia was not a country which aimed at leadership in Western Anatolia.

IV. CARIA

The main historical problems concerning the Carians have been dealt with in the context of East Greece in this volume and the previous one (*CAH* II³.2, Chapter 38; III².1, Chapter 18a).

The basic identification of the Iron Age Carians will have to be made through their language, since historical continuity is lacking. Anatolian continuity has been proved for Lydians and Lycians. The case of the Carians is not yet clear. This puts the burden on the analysis of Dark Age history, which has been tried since the days of Homer, Herodotus, and Thucydides, and on archaeology, which may ultimately yield clues at least by enriching the epigraphical record.

The Carians were a maritime people by general consensus of the ancient sources. In historical times they lived in south-west Anatolia from Miletus to Caunus along the coast and inland up the Maeander valley and its southern tributaries as far east as Aphrodisias. They were neighbours of the Lydians, Phrygians, and Lycians on the land side, and were mingled with Ionian and Doric Greeks along the coast. Not all Carians could have been concerned with navigation, although linguistically the inland Carians, whose pursuits were agricultural, may have been one with the coastal population. Also resident in Caria was a population referred to as Lelegians, but the ethnic and linguistic stratification is not clear. The Carians are likely to have been the descendants of the Late Bronze Age mercenaries known as Karkiša who fought against the Egyptians with Muwattalli at the battle of Qadesh (*CAH* II³.2, 253, 360–1).

[115] E 15, 151–64.

In the *Iliad* the Carians are the allies of the Trojans, listed in the catalogue just before the Lycians (II.867–75), but not nearly so prominent in the war. Herodotus discusses the problem of their origins, the Carians claiming that they were autochthonous, whereas the Cretans maintained that the Carians originally came from the islands, once having been called Lelegians (cf. Strab. XIV.2.27); they would have manned the navy of Minos. Driven off their islands by Ionians and Dorians, they would have settled in their later homeland (Hdt. I.171). The Cretan version makes the coastal Carians descendants of Cycladic sailors of the second millennium B.C., allies and subjects of Minos. There are elements of truth in both the Carian and Cretan stories. The Karkiša must have lived at least partly on Anatolian soil, with maritime interests developed by their coastal population. To what extent the islanders were also Carians in the second millennium we cannot at present determine. The conflation of Carians with Middle and Late Cycladic sailors may be too exclusive in some Greek accounts (Thuc. 1.4), but we can assume that the islanders were neither Minoans nor Achaeans, and the story of island crews for Minos rings true.

In the Iron Age, Carian soldiers and sailors were active as mercenaries (Archilochos fr. 216 West). They would sail to their destination in Carian ships. The Carian nicknames of improved equipment, helmet crests, emblems and hand grips for shields, reflect Carian military efficiency and pride.[116] The Lydians began to use Carians early in their ventures. Gyges was helped by Arselis of Mylasa in his accession (Plutarch, *Quaest. Gr.* 45); he later apparently sent Carians and Ionians as supporting forces to Psammetichus I in *c.* 660 B.C. This was the beginning of the Iron Age service of Carians in Egyptian wars and settlements of Carians in the Delta on the Pelusian branch of the Nile, opposite the camp of the Ionians (Hdt. II.154). Gyges must have made use of the experience and knowledge of Carian sailors, since the initiative in East Mediterranean navigation was never with the Lydians. Carians and Ionians are jointly involved in the mercenary support for Egyptian kings; the Carians and Ionians maintain good relations as equivalent forces in Egypt. Both appear as auxiliaries of Psammetichus II in his Nubian expedition of 591 B.C., as recorded in graffiti at Abu Simbel. Ionian and Carian mercenaries again appear as supporting forces in the battle of Apries against Amasis in 570 B.C. (Hdt. II.163). Amasis then moved the Carians and Ionians from their original camps on the Nile to Memphis to be his special guards (Hdt. II.154). Notable Carian records from the Memphis area are stelae with Carian inscriptions and engravings, some of them illustrating Carian ships.[117] Recently more stelae have been discovered at Saqqara,

---

[116] A. M. Snodgrass, *Early Greek Armour* (Edinburgh, 1964), 185.
[117] E 235, 20–7, pl. 2.

with inscriptions and representations of Carian men and women (Pls. Vol., pl. 240).[118]

What history does not report is organization and some form of hierarchy of the Carians in their homeland during the Iron Age and the archaic period. The Carians evidently came to some form of symbiosis with the Greek settlers in the coastal cities. The inland cities apparently had prominent families of land-owners who became some kind of aristocracy, but who did not produce an ambitious dynasty, nor were the circumstances and logistics conducive to such developments. By the time of Croesus the region of Caria, Greeks included, was under Lydian domination. When the Persians took over Lydia, Harpagus campaigned in Caria without encountering resistance except in Pedasa, a 'Lelegian' town north of Halicarnassus (Hdt. 1.174–5). Under Persian rule the leading Carian families continued their regional responsibilities.[119] When during the Ionian revolt the Carians congregated at a place called Leukai Stelai near the Marsyas river, a leading Carian nobleman was Pixodarus of Cindya, son of Mausolus and son-in-law of the Cilician king Syennesis, showing a certain interdependence of the ruling families in coastal Anatolian districts (Hdt. v.117–18). A more famous or notorious Carian aristocrat was queen Artemisia, daughter of Lygdamis of Halicarnassus and a Cretan mother (Hdt. vII.99), who became Xerxes' adviser and naval ally at Salamis. The Carians provided a contingent of seventy ships to Xerxes, twenty more than the Lycians.

Among the unifying traditions of the Carians were their sanctuaries, hitherto insufficiently known. An old sanctuary of Zeus Carius in Mylasa was an Anatolian shrine also sacred to the Mysians and Lydians (Hdt. 1.171). At Labranda was the shrine of Zeus Stratius or Labraundeus, a grove of plane trees (Hdt. v.119), later embellished architecturally.[120] We do not know the antiquity of the sanctuary of Zeus Chrysaoreus near Stratonicea, but a Carian Chrysaoric league may have been in existence before the Persian period, united in the cult of perhaps the most authentic Carian god (Strab. xIV.2.25).[121]

Archaeologically, the study of Caria confronts the same kind of problem as encountered in Lydia, that of separating Carian from Greek material. The Carians forcibly intermingled with Greek newcomers in the Bronze Age and Iron Age, and may indeed have begun their Aegean inter-relations with Minoans in the early second millennium B.C. Miletus and Iasus are now known to have had Middle Minoan and Late Minoan contacts before Late Helladic influences became prevalent. In the Iron Age at Iasus, the levels and cemeteries of the Protogeometric and Geometric periods show such strong Greek traits that the native

---

[118] F 39, 6, pl. 10.   [119] E 29.   [120] E 87; E 16, 58ff.   [121] E 121.

elements remain obscure.[122] Even inland sites such as Lagina[123] and Beçin near Mylasa[124] show this Hellenized aspect. Native sites are the 'Lelegian' protected farmsteads investigated in the Bodrum peninsula[125] and similar buildings near Iasus,[126] but these are rural establishments, not the residences of the leading Carian families.

The Carians of the Iron Age were not politically ambitious or expansionist on their own behalf. Their foreign ventures were far flung but subservient to outside interests. Within their country, the most Carian of traditions will have to be sought through more excavation, especially of the original Carian sanctuaries. The maritime aspect will become clearer not only through the continuing excavations of such prominent coastal sites as Iasus and Miletus, but also, as Thucydides suggested, through the study of the Cycladic islands in the Bronze Age, which may contribute archaeological as well as written records to reconstruct the background of the most prominent West Anatolian sailors of the Iron Age.

---

[122] D. Levi, *Annuario* NS 30/1 (1969/70), 461–81.   [123] E 33, 63–93.
[124] E 1; E 16, 50–3.   [125] E 115; E 42, 193–205.   [126] Levi, *Annuario*, 514–17.

ANATOLIAN LANGUAGES

O. MASSON

I. THE PHRYGIAN LANGUAGE

The Greeks had undoubtedly known of the Phrygians for an extremely long time. Certain writers, such as Herodotus and Hipponax, have left us some indication of the nature of their language, and Hesychius' Lexicon has provided us with glosses of unequal value.[1] It is, however, largely from epigraphic sources that our knowledge of Phrygian is derived. These texts may be divided into two groups, separated in time by several centuries and originating from relatively different geographical regions.[2] There can, however, be no doubt that we are dealing with two successive stages – separated by (for us) a long interruption – in the development of one and the same language.

The ancient, or Palaeo-Phrygian, texts are distributed over a vast area:[3] Phrygia proper, including in particular Midas City (1 F etc.; Pls. Vol., pl. 241); Bithynia, where we have the longest extant text, that of Germanos;[4] central Galatia, with Gordium,[5] and eastern Galatia, with Boğazköy,[6] Kalehisar, etc.; and Cappadocia, with the black stone of Tyana (19 F).[7] For the most part, these are texts carved on some rock-cut façades of cult-places (in the west) and various graffiti on vases, the latter being particularly interesting on account of the script used (Fig. 48). There are, in all, close on 50 inscriptions on stone and over 170 graffiti. It is mainly for the graffiti that it has been possible to establish a chronological sequence. Many of the Gordium texts date from the fifth and fourth centuries, some even from the third; one of them, however, can be dated as far back as 750 B.C. (or even before), and the specimens from the Great Tumulus around 720.[8]

The Palaeo-Phrygian script is basically dextroverse, although sinistroverse and boustrophedon script is by no means rare. The alphabet is similar to the archaic Greek alphabets, comprising a stock of seventeen

---

[1] E 155, 868ff; E 157.   [2] E 154; E 145 with figs. 11–12.
[3] E 151, X, 1–29 for the 'City of Midas'.   [4] E 164; E 151, 57–68.
[5] E 160; E 165; E 151, 73–214.   [6] E 162; E 151, 223–51 ('Ptérie').
[7] E 151, 253–68 ('Tyanide'); E 93.   [8] E 165, no. 29, nos. 25, 30–3; E 151, 8off.

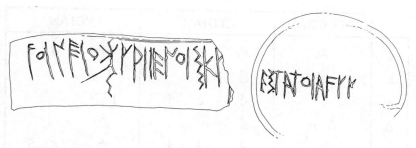

Fig. 48. Phrygian graffiti on vase fragments from Gordium. Fifth century B.C. (E 151, G 144–5.)

letters which correspond to the Greek letters: *A, B, Γ, Δ, E, F, I, K, Λ, M, N, O, Π, P, Σ, T, Y*.[9] In addition to these letters there are ⟨ or *y*, which is encountered on the western sites,[10] and the rare signs ↑ and Ψ of uncertain origin.[11] Since the oldest extant texts date from the same time as the oldest Greek texts it has been conjectured that the two alphabets might have developed independently from a Semitic proto-type, but the most plausible solution would still appear to be that Phrygian writing was dependent on a Greek model.[12]

It is puzzling that the Phrygians should have remained silent for over half a millennium and yet have re-emerged in the Roman period, in the second and third centuries A.D., as is shown by at least a hundred so-called Neo-Phrygian texts that are extant today (1–88 F).[13] They are written in the customary Greek alphabet of the period, but are distri-buted over a far less extensive region than the Palaeo-Phrygian docu-ments.[14] These texts are exclusively funerary inscriptions, of which somewhat more than half are accompanied by epitaphs in standard Greek.[15] The passages that can be understood consist mainly of curses against possible tomb-robbers: 'may whoever harms this tomb be . . .'. The formula follows a strict stereotype, but the language itself does not appear to be very remote from that of the Palaeo-Phrygian texts.

The paucity of documents (for the first period), the over-monotonous formulae (of the second) and the brevity (of the graffiti), are additional barriers to our understanding of Phrygian, which, particularly with regard to vocabulary, remains a poorly-known language. Nevertheless, modern linguistic research has provided us with more conclusive results than those reached in the last century.[16]

The classification of Phrygian within the Indo-European language

[9] E 159; E 160; E 151, 4, 34, 60, 79 etc. (local repertories), 279–82.
[10] E 159, 30–8 etc.; E 151, 281.   [11] E 159, 42–6; E 160, 62–3; E 151, 281–2.
[12] E 159, 40f; E 160, 64.   [13] E 154; E 153; E 157.   [14] E 145, fig. 12.
[15] E 153; E 157; E 158.
[16] E 154, 124 for bibliography; also E 158, E 144–6; E 159; E 160; E 151, bibliography to 1983, xiv–xvii.

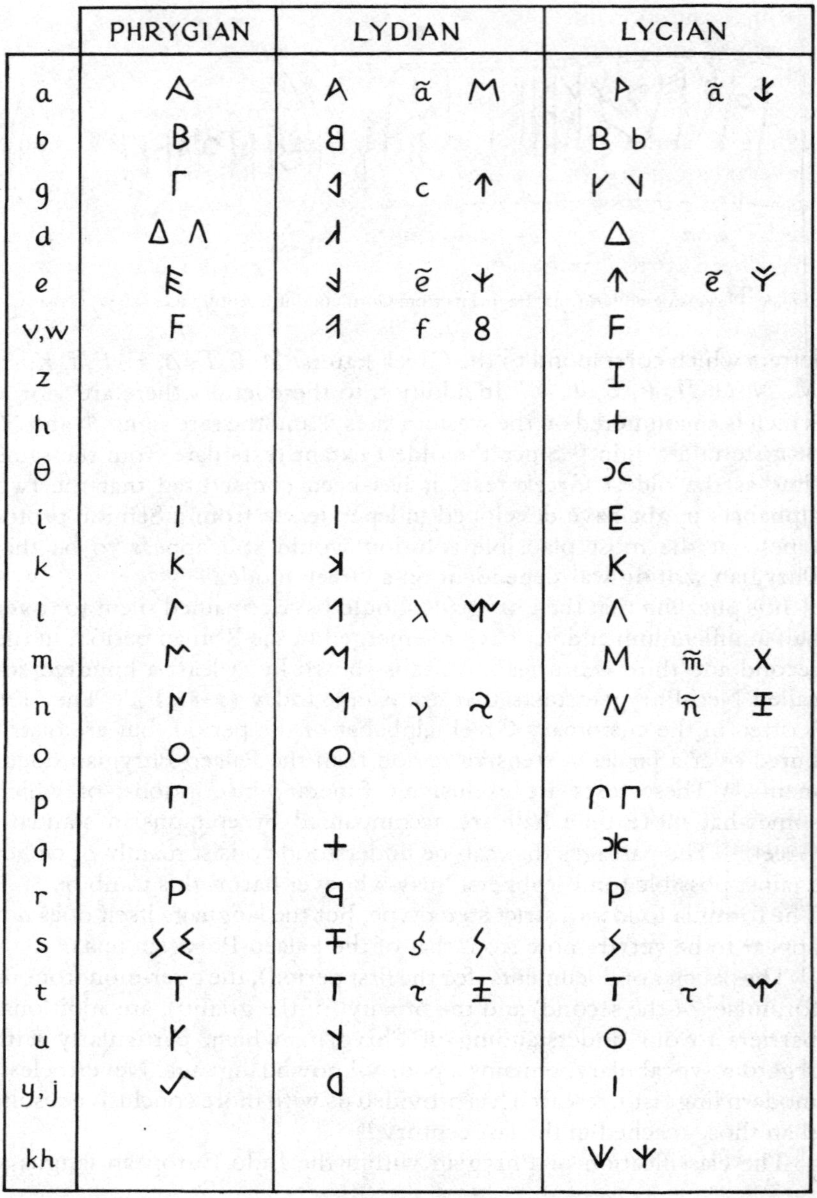

	PHRYGIAN	LYDIAN			LYCIAN		
a	ᴧ	ᴧ	ã	M	Ρ	ã	↙
b	B	Ꞓ			B	b	
g	Γ	⅃	c	↑	Ⅴ	Ⅴ	
d	Δ Λ	⋏			Δ		
e	Ɛ̧	⅃	ẽ	Ψ	↑	ẽ	Ɏ
v,w	F	⅂	f	8	F		
z					I		
h					+		
θ					)C		
i	I	I			E		
k	K	⋊			K		
l	Λ	↑	λ	ⵣ	Λ		
m	Ϻ	Ϻ			M	m̃	X
n	Ν	Ⴤ	ν	⟩	Ν	ñ	Ⱶ
o	O	O					
p	Γ				∩ Γ		
q		+			*		
r	Ρ	ꟼ			Ρ		
s	⧘ Ξ	Ŧ	š	⟩	Ϟ		
t	T	T	τ	Ⱶ	T	τ	Ψ
u	Ⴤ	Ⴤ			O		
y, j	⌄	Ꝺ			I		
kh					Ⱶ Ɏ		

Fig. 49. The Phrygian, Lydian, and Lycian alphabets.

group is questionable. One can no longer speak, as before, of a 'Thraco-Phrygian' group; moreover, there is still little known about Thracian. Phrygian does share certain isoglosses with Hittite, but these are relatively uncharacteristic.[17] The shared elements between Greek and Phrygian are of greater interest: these include isoglosses common to several languages, such as the use of the relative *yos* and of the augment, as well as isoglosses peculiar to these languages, such as the participial suffix -*meno*-, the pronoun *auto*-, and the stem *kako*- 'bad' (which cannot have been borrowed from Greek, as it forms a verb in Palaeo-Phrygian), etc. These features reveal close prehistoric links between the two languages: do they arise from mere geographical proximity or from the fact that Greek and Phrygian belong to the same Indo-European branch? It is by no means impossible that we shall one day be able to speak of 'Greco-Phrygian'. We may also, however, conceive of connexions reaching even further back in time, to the Proto-Latins. There are certain striking similarities that incline us towards this conjecture: the use of the preverb *ad*- in *addaket*, *abberet*; the extension of the infix -*k*- to the present stem – *addaket* being probably equivalent to *afficiat*; -*tor*, the ending of the third person singular in the medio-passive, Latin -*tur*, etc.[18] Many problems, nevertheless, still remain to be solved, and we must hope for fresh discoveries.

II. THE LYDIAN LANGUAGE

The language of ancient Lydia, which had long been almost completely unknown, was first revealed to us early this century after the discovery of a series of epichoric inscriptions found at Sardis before 1914; very little material was yielded by the other sites.[19]

The most important documents are the great funerary stelae, especially the Lydian–Aramaic bilingual (1 F, Lydian above, Aramaic below), the discovery of which stimulated work on decipherment of the language. Some of the stelae carry fairly long texts (2–9 F, 22–24 F; Pls. Vol., pl. 242), others bear inscriptions in verse (10–15 F, etc.) characterized by vocalic assonance at the ends of lines.[20] In addition to the Sardis texts, we should also mention a short Lydian–Greek bilingual from Pergamum (40 F) and a Lydian–Aramaic bilingual from Falaka (41 F), etc. One Lydian graffito, short but extremely old (49 F, from the region known as Silsile) was found in Egypt. Finally, the American excavations at Sardis, resumed in 1958, led to the discovery of other inscriptions and fragments, the most outstanding of which was the stone known as the

[17] E 144, 316–17. [18] E 144, 318–19; E 145, 70–4.
[19] E 168, nos. 1–53F; E 171, suppl. 3. [20] E 190.

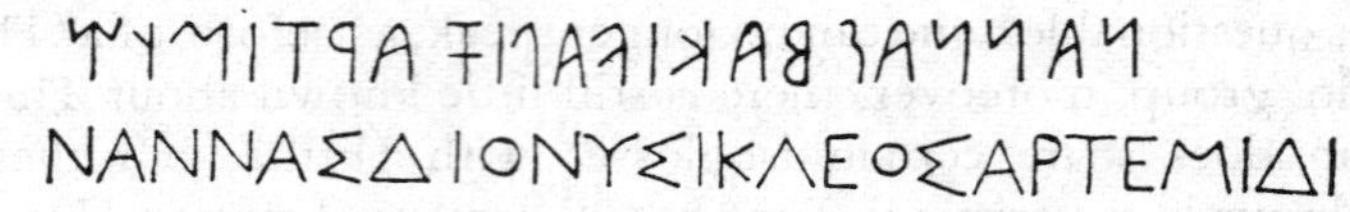

ᵀᵞᴹ́ᵀ⁹ᴀ ⱻ́ᴫ⟨ᴀⰅↃᴀ⟩ᴫ⟨ᴀᵞᵞᴀᵞ
NANNAΣΔIONYΣIKΛEOΣAPTEMIΔI

Fig. 50. Lydian–Greek bilingual inscription from Sardis. Fourth century B.C. A dedication to Artemis (Lydian *artimuś*) by Nannas, son of Dionysikles. (E 168, no. 20.)

Synagogue Stela, which is written in an alphabet somewhat different from Lydian, and may well be in a different language.[21]

Chronologically, the Lydian documents belong to the period between the early sixth century (49 F?) and the beginning of Alexander's reign (50 F, dated 323/322), with the majority of the texts dating from the fifth century;[22] a later bilingual from Sardis is shown in Fig. 50.

The Lydian alphabet proper is fairly restricted, containing only twenty-six letters, most of which have now been transcribed with certainty by the linguists.[23] The script is normally sinistroverse. The alphabet is comparable to that of Lycian, but with certain important differences. The vowels afford no difficulties: A = *a*, ↓ = *e*, I = *i*, O = *o*, ↑ = *u*; there are in addition two signs which probably indicate nasalized vowels, M = *ã* and Y = *ẽ* (Greek forms used with a new value), and ◑, at present transcribed as *y*, a rare letter (which may be related to a Carian letter). The consonantal stops include T = *t*, ⟩ = *k*, ᚷ = *b* (but equivalent to /*p*/), ⟨ = *d*, ⟨ = *g*, and two further letters of unclear origins, ↑ = *c* and Ŧ = *τ*. There is likewise uncertainty as to the origin of +, currently transcribed as *q*, which may represent the result of an old labiovelar stop in view of the accepted equivalences + *is* = qis and + *aλmλuś*, 'king' (rendered in Greek as πάλμυς). There is no uncertainty about the nasals and liquids: ⟨ = *l*, ⟨ = *m*, ⟨ = *n*, ⟨ = *r*; but there is still doubt about the origin of the variants of complex shape transcribed as λ and ν. Besides the ⟨ = *v* there is a fricative 8 = *f* (which, as it also occurs in Etruscan, has given rise to various speculations). No problem is posed by the sibilants, since Lydian *s* is the equivalent of Greek *zeta* and Lydian *ś* of *shin*. Altogether, there is a majority of Greek letter-forms, with certain shifts in function; there are also certain forms for which the background is more or less obscure.[24]

Research into the language passed through a fairly long initial stage of tentative speculation during which Lydian was linked even with Caucasian, or Etruscan.[25] Since 1935, the Indo-European character of Lydian has gradually emerged and we now assume that Lydian belongs to the group of Anatolian languages which originate from the Hittite–Luwian branch.[26] Nevertheless, the phonetics of Lydian still present

---

[21] E 174, 113–32.   [22] E 176, chronology 268–74.
[23] E 171, 29 (table); E 174, 50; E 182, 399–401; for the formation of the alphabet E 177 and E 183.
[24] E 183.   [25] E 182, 401–3 for a brief history.   [26] E 186; E 187; E 182, 419ff.

difficulties and little is known of the vocabulary, with the result that it is impossible to make coherent translations or to provide a detailed table of correspondences.[27]

The animate gender has the following endings: in the nominative, -*ś* (nouns) and -*s* or *ś* (adjectives), and in the accusative, -*v* and -*n*; the neuter ends in -*d* (an ending derived from the pronominal inflexion), e.g. *mrud*, 'stela'. The genitive is replaced by a possessive adjective in -*li*, for instance, *vãnaś manelis*, 'Mane-ian tomb / tomb of Manes', which also serves as a patronymic, as in *Karoś Katovalis*, 'Karos the Katova-ian / son of Katovas'; this -*li*- form may be compared to similar morphemes in Hittite.

Among the pronouns, we may mention *amu*, 'me', and *ēmis*, 'my', *bis*, 'he', and *bilis*, 'his', the relative *qis*, *qid*, and the indefinite *aλaś*, 'other'.

The verb in Lydian is complex, and preverbs are a frequent characteristic, e.g. *kat-sarloki-*, 'destroy(?), curse(?)'.

Among the indeclinable forms, it is not surprising to find the negative *ni* and the enclitic copula -*k*, 'and'.

The vocabulary still remains very obscure.[28] The correspondences with Hittite and Luwian are of particular interest; similarities have long been observed between, for instance, the Hittite *pir*, gen. *parnas*, 'house', and the Lydian *bira-*, of the same meaning; similarly, between the Hittite *arha-*, 'boundary', and the Lydian *aara-*, 'estate', etc. The word for 'god' probably has a root *civ-* which must be compared to the Hittite *siun(i)-*, 'god', though the position is different in Lycian, where *mahãi*, 'god', corresponds to the Luwian *massani-*.

The study of Lydian, which is certainly now moving along the right lines, still has much progress to make; just how imperfect our knowledge remains was shown by the appearance in 1963 of the inscription known as the Synagogue Stela, which may be written in a different language (that of the Maeonians or the Torrhebians having been suggested).[29]

III. THE LYCIAN LANGUAGE

Of the languages studied here, Lycian is the one that has the longest history in modern scholarship, since Lycian monuments had already begun to attract attention in the early nineteenth century. Today, it is also the best understood of all these languages.

Numerous inscriptions have been discovered, some of considerable length and importance, and there is also a great variety of legend-bearing coins. Friedrich's corpus already contained 150 inscriptions and almost

---

[27] E 171, 30–48; E 182, 403–19 for summary of grammar.
[28] E 171, a practical alphabetical repertory, 49–228, with supplements.
[29] Apparently 'Maeonian' was a separate language (Hipponax fr. 3a West).

50 inscribed coins;[30] in recent years, this basic repertory has been enlarged by some remarkable discoveries.[31]

From west to east, the principal sites are Telmessus (1–5 F), Karmylessus (6–8 F), Pinara (10–21 F), Kadyanda, and Tlos (22–34 F), and in particular Xanthus (36–51 F), with the celebrated 'Stela of Xanthus' (44 F), with its four inscribed faces (one of which is in 'Lycian B', see below); in addition, important discoveries have now been made at the Letoum of Xanthus (4 km south west), one of the most outstanding of these being the great trilingual stela with complete texts in Greek, Lycian, and Aramaic (Pls. Vol., pl. 243). This discovery, dating from the year 1 of an Artaxerxes (either 358 or 337) has given fresh impetus to research into Lycian.[32] Other significant sites include Antiphellus (55–60 F), Isinda (62–65 F), Myra (85–97 F),[33] Limyra (98–148 F), and Rhodiapolis (149–150 F).

The majority of the texts consists of funerary inscriptions, with the fortunate exception of several important historical or religious documents: the Stela of Xanthus (44 F), the inscriptions from the Letoum, particularly the trilingual stela, the sacred law of Tlos (26 F), and the bilingual text of Isinda (65 F).

The Lycian alphabet, which is not attested before the sixth century, is now well known. It contains a maximum of 29 letters, and corresponds basically to a Greek alphabet of the Doric type. The script is generally dextroverse, and makes use of separation marks.[34]

There are four basic vowels, which, however, are indicated by letters with somewhat different values from Greek: although *A* is still equivalent to *a*, *E* is used for *i* and O has a *u* value (Lycian having no *o*); there is also a sign of different origin ↑, which is equivalent to *e*. In addition, there are two letters for nasal vowels, 𐊙 (etc.) for *ã*, and 𐊚 (etc.) for *ẽ*. For the semi-consonants we have I, transcribed *j* or *y*, F which stands for *w*. Many of the consonant signs correspond to Greek letters. Among the stops, ß indicates *b*, *Δ* = *d*, 𐊄 = *g*, 𐊓 = *p*, *T* = *t*, *K* = *k* (long transcribed as *c*). Likewise, Ѱ stands for *χ* (long transcribed as *k*), ͻ|ͼ for *q*,)(for θ, ϒ for *τ*. For the liquids and nasals we have *Λ* = *l*, *M* = *m*, *P* = *r*, *N* = *n*, *X* = *m̃*, and Ɨ = ñ. Sibilants, etc.: ⟆ = s, I = *z*, + = *h*. We are still unsure of the value and origin of the rare signs ◇ and /ʍ.

For a long time, modern scholars have been exploring the language,[35] looking for extremely different linguistic connexions, such as Greek, Iranian, Albanian, Slavic, Etruscan, 'Pelasgian' or 'Asianic', Caucasian, etc. At the end of the nineteenth century, however, the Scandinavian school pressed strongly in favour of a possible Indo-European origin.

[30] E 195. [31] E 215, retrospect from 1901; E 207, the trilingual; E 211 coins.
[32] E 198; E 204; E 207. [33] E 214 with new texts.
[34] E 213, 371ff, 374 (table); E 211, 32–3 (coins). [35] E 213, 361–71.

After the appearance and decipherment of Hittite, the Indo-European connexion was gradually substantiated, largely through the works of Meriggi and Pedersen.[36] A direct relation was then established between Lycian and Luwian, the Anatolian language of the second millennium,[37] a connexion which has been confirmed by the most recent discoveries.[38] Obscurity, however, still surrounds the related language, known as 'Lycian B' or 'Milyan' (44 F, end; 55 F), which appears to be an archaic form of regular Lycian.[39]

The noun declension is clarified by comparison with Luwian. In the nominative singular, there is generally a bare stem for roots which end in a vowel: e.g. *tideimi*, 'child', *lada*, 'woman', etc.; there are also consonantal stems, such as *tuhes*, 'nephew'. The accusative singular ends in -*ã*, -*u*, or -*ñ*: *ladã, ladu, tuhesñ*. Several possibilities exist for the genitive singular: either the terminations -*he*, -*h*, or 'zero' (old endings?) or an adjectival form in -*ahi*, -*ehi*, e.g.: *mahan-ahi*, 'divine, of God (godly), of the Gods'.

The suffix -*ahi*, -*ehi*, just mentioned, was used in the formation of adjectives. Ethnics, which occur frequently in the inscriptions, had various suffixes, in a nasal as in *Pilleñni*, 'from Pinara'; in -*ẕi*, as in *Atãna-ẕi*, 'Athenian', *Spparta-ẕi*, 'Spartan', *Pttara-ẕi*, 'Patarean', etc.; in -*ili*, as in *Trm̃mili*, 'Termilian, Lycian' (from Trm̃mis, the local name of the country).[40]

Among the pronominal forms we note *amu*, 'I', the demonstrative *ebe*, gen. *ebehi*, etc. (compare the Hittite and Luwian stem *apa*-), with *ehbi*, 'his'; the relative *ti* (from *$k^w i$-s*, Luwian *kuis*), and the indefinite *tike*.

Less is known of the detailed morphology of the verbs. We mention *prñnawati*, 'he builds', *pijeti, pibijeti* (with reduplication), 'he gives', contrasted with *prñnawate*, 'he has built', *pijetẽ*, 'he has given', *pijẽtẽ*, 'they have given', etc. For the verb 'to be', we note *esi*, 'is', *hãti*, 'are'.[41] There was also a participle in -*mi*, as in Luwian: *tideimi*, 'child', to compare with the Luwian *titai(m)mi*, 'nursling'.

Invariable words: *se*, 'and', e.g. *hrppi ladi se tideime*, 'for (his) wife and (his) children'; *me*, used particularly as a conjunction; the negatives *ne* and *ni*, the latter being the prohibitive negative; the preposition or preverb *hrppi*, 'for'.

In addition to the words mentioned above, the following vocabulary items may be mentioned: *mahani*, 'God', Luwian *massani*-; *uha*-, 'year', Luwian *ussa*-; *χñtawata*, 'lord, king', Luwian *hantawat*-; *arawa*, 'free'; *kuma*-, 'concept of the holy', Luwian *kummai*-, 'holy/sacred', with *kumaẕa*, 'priest' and *kumeẕi*-, 'to sacrifice'.[42]

Lycian was already the best known of the epichoric languages of

---

[36] E 208; E 217.   [37] E 203; E 212; E 213; E 220.   [38] E 204; E 207; E 216.
[39] E 213; cf. E 209 and 197.   [40] E 206.   [41] E 204, 123; E 207, 87.
[42] E 204, 122–4 with new results from the trilingual.

western Asia Minor; the discovery of the trilingual inscription from the Letoum at Xanthus and the elaboration of the results obtained will further improve this already favourable situation.

IV. THE CARIAN LANGUAGE

Already in the time of Homer there is evidence for the existence of Carian speech, in an allusion to the *Kares barbarophónoi* in the *Iliad*.[43] The first extant documentary evidence, however, belongs to the seventh and, especially, the sixth century B.C. And this comes not so much from Caria itself as from Egypt and Lydia. In Lydia, archaic fragments have been discovered at Sardis;[44] but it is mainly to pharaonic Egypt that we owe our knowledge of the Carians and their language.[45] It was Psammetichus I who began engaging foreign mercenaries, particularly Ionians and Carians, and these soldiers left numerous traces of their passage through the land and of their temporary settlements. During the campaign of Psammetichus II against the Nubians in 591 B.C., Carian soldiers carved their names at Abu Simbel (beside those of Greeks and Phoenicians),[46] and these same soldiers may have left their marks still further afield, at Buhen.[47] After settling with their families in the Nile Delta, and in a quarter in Memphis, they raised children and became known as the 'Caromemphites'.[48] They lived for some time in an autonomous community and left monuments which were most probably part of a Carian cemetery and were later reused in the necropolis of North Saqqara (Pls. Vol., pl. 240 and here, Fig. 51; stelae and fragmentary inscriptions, mid-sixth century).[49] In due course, the Carians became absorbed into the cosmopolitan population of Hellenistic Egypt, and lost their script and language.

In the territory of Caria proper, the discoveries thus far have been less rich.[50] The three inscribed bronzes, recently published, are the oldest available records (sixth century) of the motherland.[51] Later, in addition to some rare coins to which an exact locality has not yet been assigned there are also some stone inscriptions dating from around the fourth or third century, as well as funerary inscriptions and religious or political documents (Tralles, Hyllarima, Sinuri–Mylasa, etc.). At a still uncertain date Carian was to give way to Greek. There is, however, one site where a special situation has emerged; this is Caunus, near Lycia, where a distinctly different alphabet was found;[52] variants of the alphabet were also discovered at smaller sites, such as Chalketor.[53]

---

[43] E 229, 187; E 231, 407.　　[44] E 225, 79–111.　　[45] E 233–5; E 237; E 242.

[46] E 224, nos. 31–7; new edition, O. Masson, 'Les graffites cariens d'Abou-Simbel', *Hommages à la mémoire de S. Sauneron* II (Cairo, 1979), 243–7.　　[47] E 234, nos. 50–5.

[48] E 231, 408, 412–13; E 234, 6.　　[49] E 234, nos. 1–49.

[50] E 223; E 230; E 240; E 245; E 246.　　[51] E 226–7.　　[52] E 230.　　[53] E 240.

Fig. 51. Carian false door with inscription, from Saqqara. Two lines in Carian script, dextroverse, with three words, the meaning obscure but funerary in content. (E 234, no. 16.)

It seems clear now that there never was a single Carian script, but rather that there were at least four groups.[54] (1) Of these, the oldest on record and the best known is the Carian of Egypt (seventh to fifth century), comprising about 35 signs. (2) The Carian of the great sites of Caria, with the exception of Caunus (sixth to fourth or third century), which is almost identical and contains 36 or 37 signs. (3) The Carian of Caunus (which is difficult to date), with approximately 30 signs. (4) A residual group, which is made up from various finds in Caria (Chalketor, etc.) and is still little known.

In spite of many attempts to understand the Carian scripts, and the discovery of a number of new documents over the past twenty years, they have still not been completely deciphered.[55] It is evident that there is a series of alphabets which, while containing a majority of letters identical to those of the Greek alphabet – with values that are probably matching, or at least fairly close (such as for the letters A, C, Δ, E, F, Λ, N, O, P, M (the *san*), T, Y) – also include letters of unknown origin, often used with great frequency, to which no definitive value can be assigned

[54] E 233; E 234, introduction, 8–16.
[55] E 229 (to 1972). More optimistic views in the work of V. Ševoroškin (E 248–50), and J. Ray (E 241–4).

(e.g. ⏀ and ☐), with one fortunate exception (ϑ for *ĕ*, possibly related to the Lydian Ɒ). It is chiefly here that the difficulties in reading arise. The only progress that has been made thus far has been in abandoning the theory – so long dominant – that this was a script that might have been half-alphabetic, half-syllabic, and that there was a relationship between the signs believed to be syllabic and either an 'Asianic' syllabary, as suggested by A. H. Sayce,[56] or even the Cypriot syllabary.[57]

Since the script has not yet been completely deciphered, the Carian language itself remains an enigma. In theory there are two possible solutions: either Carian, unlike Lydian and Lycian, is truly an 'Asianic' language, relatively autochthonous and not Indo-European, or else it is an ancient Anatolian language of Indo-European origin, like the languages mentioned earlier, by which it was surrounded. But, in spite of the recent intensive efforts, the key has not yet been discovered.[58] It must also be added that the far from numerous glosses preserved by ancient writers are of no help. The Carian anthroponyms, of which numerous examples have reached us through Greek sources, such as *Arliomos*, *Bruassis*, *Kasbollis*, *Kbodes*, *Luxes*, *Mausollos*, *Panyassis*, *Sidulemis*, and *Tymnes*,[59] have a curious structure which would at first sight incline one towards the first solution, although this impression may be deceptive. Recent attempts to explain such names as good Anatolian could now be taken into consideration.[60]

The solution could ultimately come from the discovery of a clear bilingual text, with a satisfying structure. The bilingual material at present available is either incomplete or very difficult to analyse; it includes: (a) a short, partly mutilated, Greek–Carian bilingual (Athens, fifth century);[61] (b) several apparently bilingual inscriptions from Egypt in which the two parts are not easy to relate to each other;[62] (c) two bilingual texts from Caria, seriously damaged (from Hyllarima, a short Carian text, and the beginning of a Greek text; from Sinuri, the end of a Greek text and the beginning of a Carian text).[63]

It is still possible that light may be shed by new documents, either through chance discovery or as the result of systematic search, which will enable us finally to solve this perplexing enigma of western Anatolia.[64]

[56] E 224, 156, with Sayce and Bork.   [57] E 222.

[58] Numerous works by V. Ševoroškin (E 247–50), and more recent suggestions by J. Ray (E 241–4).   [59] E 246.

[60] See, for instance, for the name *Cheramyes*, the interpretation in the light of Hittite and Luwian comparisons by G. Neumann, *Würzburger Jahrbuch für die Altertumswissenschaft* 10 (1984) 41–3.

[61] E 229, 198–205; E 232, 94.

[62] E 234, introduction, * 9, etc. The results obtained by Zauzich (E 251) were not conclusive; Ray's approach is more promising (E 241–4).

[63] E 223, 315, 317, etc.   [64] The Bibliography does not go beyond 1987.

CHAPTER 35

EGYPT: THE TWENTY-FIFTH AND TWENTY-SIXTH DYNASTIES

T. G. H. JAMES

I. THE ORIGINS OF THE TWENTY-FIFTH DYNASTY

The historical tradition preserved in the pages of Manetho's history allows three kings to the Twenty-fifth Dynasty, Sabacon, Sebichos, and Tarcos, to be identified with Shabako, Shebitku, and Taharqa. These three are the middle monarchs of the five now generally included together to make the historical Twenty-fifth Dynasty of the monuments. Historians have expressed surprise that Manetho made no mention of Py (Piankhy), who established the fortunes of his line in Egypt,[1] but his absence from the chronicler's list may be due more to a desire for chronological tidiness than to ignorance or malicious omission. For the greater part of his reign Py was absent from Egypt, and, as an earlier chapter of this history made clear,[2] much of Egypt during this period was controlled by princes and chieftains, some of whom form, in Manetho's tradition, the lines of the Twenty-third and Twenty-fourth Dynasties. The overlap of dynastic lines presents problems to the annalistically-minded historian. To start the Twenty-fifth Dynasty with Shabako, who earned the royal title 'King of Upper and Lower Egypt' by extending Nubian rule over the whole land in about 713 B.C., was altogether neater.[3]

Unfortunately, neatness is not customarily to be observed in the sequences of historical events. The narrative of a country's history is like a river which, from time to time along its course, is joined by tributaries. Each tributary represents a new stream which, to be fully understood, needs retracing back along its separate course. In a consideration of the Twenty-fifth Dynasty, set firmly in the main line of Egyptian history, some attention must be given to the origins of the Nubian royal line, the Kushite rulers whose centre of power, Napata, lay in the region between the Fourth and Third Cataracts of the Nile. Unfortunately this Nubian

---

[1] F 44, 335.   [2] *CAH* III².1, 571ff.
[3] F 77, 153f; on p. 472 he gives 715 B.C. as the date from which Shabako was king of all Egypt; so too in his 2nd edn, 557, 593, *contra* F 185, 221, who accepts 713 B.C.

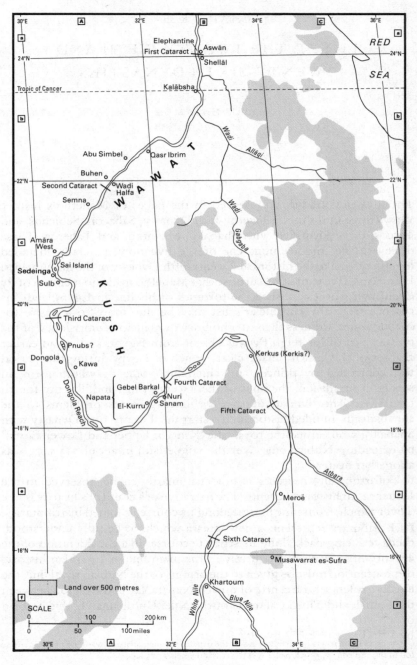

Map 16. Nubia.

tributary may be traced back with only limited success, and its origins lie lost, as it were, in the sands of Kush.

Napata, named clearly as a town in Egyptian texts of the New Kingdom, marked the southern limit of pharaonic penetration into Nubia.[4] Whether it may be identified with Gebel Barkal, where temples dedicated to the Theban god Amun were built in the Eighteenth and Nineteenth Dynasties, remains debatable;[5] but it seems possible that the district which contained Gebel Barkal and the separately identifiable sites of El-Kurru, Nuri, and Sanam, may in a collective sense have subsequently been known as Napata. A loose parallel may be drawn with Thebes itself, a name which in its Greek form was (and still is) applied to the districts on the west and east banks of the Nile, and included the separately identifiable temple districts of Karnak and Luxor and the various necropolis areas. Yet in origin Thebes may owe its name to a corruption of the ancient name of Luxor.[6]

A complete absence of evidence prevents any reconstruction of the history of Napata, or indeed of Nubia in general, from the late Twentieth Dynasty.[7] The conventional view, based both on the lack of textual evidence and on the sparse surviving archaeological record in those centres settled by Egyptians until the New Kingdom, maintains that Nubia was gradually abandoned as internal events in Egypt led to the political division of the country which marked the Twenty-first Dynasty. At Buhen in Lower Nubia, for example, it is suggested that at the end of the Twentieth Dynasty Egyptian resources were concentrated solely on servicing the temples and their domains.[8]

It has equally been the conventional view that at Napata the only surviving tie with metropolitan Egypt resided in the continued maintenance of the cult of Amun, the Theban god.[9] The basis for this particular contention lies in the belief that devotion to the cult of Amun brought about the Nubian intervention in Egyptian affairs, which led ultimately to the establishment of the pharaonic line known as the Twenty-fifth Dynasty. Much is made by Py of his desire to promote the interests of the Theban god, and the supporting evidence provided by Taharqa's wide-ranging building campaign on behalf of Amun establishes beyond doubt that the kings of the Twenty-fifth Dynasty devoted themselves with energy to the cult of Amun. 'You know that Amun is the god who has dispatched us,'[10] declared Py as he sent off his army in swift reaction to events in Egypt during his twentieth regnal year. By this time, however, the political advantages of declaring unequivocal support for Amun, and of accepting it as the spring for action, had no doubt been fully accepted by Py. Throughout Egyptian history religious reasons were used to

---

[4] *CAH* II³.1, 347.   [5] F 1, 254.   [6] F 43 II, 25*.   [7] *CAH* II³.2, 656.
[8] F 152 II, 217.   [9] The view taken in F 1, 257f.   [10] F 197, 8 (text l.12).

justify political actions; the primacy of a deity, or the apparent insult to a deity, was sufficient cause for political intervention. The use by the Nubian rulers of the interests of Amun as cause and justification for their first involvement in Egyptian affairs would be more acceptable as the mainspring of their action if it could be shown that the cult of Amun was truly an active force at Napata during the dark age following the Twentieth Dynasty. Unfortunately, it cannot be shown.

There appears to be a long hiatus in the sequence of archaeological evidence from the Twentieth Dynasty until about 850 B.C.[11] Then the first burials were made at El-Kurru (a short way downstream from Gebel Barkal), the site of the royal cemetery which was to form the last resting place of most of the kings of the Twenty-fifth Dynasty. Among the scanty remains of the funerary equipments placed in the earliest burials only one object, a gold nugget, bored and strung as a pendant, bears an inscription naming Amun,[12] and this may not have been made locally but imported.[13] A fragment of faience inscribed with Kashta's name, and also that of Amun,[14] is even less satisfactory as evidence in favour of the persistence of a cult of Amun in the early reigns of the Napatan or Kushite kingdom. The burial from which it was recovered is dated by Reisner and Dunham to the mid-fourth century B.C.[15] Neither at Napata nor anywhere else in Nubia is there a shred of evidence to support the belief that a cult of Amun survived the end of the Twentieth Dynasty.

Historians of Nubia are generally agreed that the emergence of a Kushite kingdom in the neighbourhood of Napata took place in the ninth century B.C. and that the first local ruler who can be identified by name is Alara, an older brother of Kashta, of whom unfortunately no contemporary records have survived.[16] Doubt has already been thrown on the belief that the worship of Amun persisted at Napata at this time. Equal doubt, therefore, must be thrown on the view that the rise of the Kushite monarchy depended on an alliance between the priesthood of Amun at Napata and the local Nubian chieftains.[17] There is, in reality, no evidence at present available which provides any clue to the political and social movements which led to the establishment of the Kushite monarchy.[18] The bald facts are that a monarchy was founded, that after Alara the next ruler, Kashta, is found making some possible move against metropolitan Egypt, and that under Py, his son and successor, a strong Nubian presence was established in much of Egypt.

In spite of the paucity of evidence there is, nevertheless, a strong compulsion to speculate on the reasons for Nubian involvement in

[11] F 168, 140.   [12] F 34, 16; F 32, 125, fig. 2.   [13] F 168, 142.
[14] F 34, 24, fig.7c.   [15] F 34, 3 (burial Ku.1).   [16] F 104 I, 121ff; F 137, 21ff.
[17] E.g. F 1, 258; and *contra*, F 168, 144.
[18] F 32, 121ff, argues strongly against the old view that the Napatan house was Libyan in origin.

Egyptian affairs, and to ponder why the Nubians appear to have been so readily acceptable, at least to the Thebans, as rulers worthy to carry the ancient royal designation 'King of Upper and Lower Egypt'. Some intrusion of Egyptian culture, perhaps not particularly in the religious sense, resulted from the continuous contacts between Nubia and Egypt on the levels of trade and military involvement. For many centuries Nubia had formed the reservoir of manpower from which Egypt's rulers had drawn the professional element of their fighting forces and police. Through Nubia passed the commercial routes along which Egyptian traders travelled to bring back to Egypt both the products of the mines and quarries of Nubia, and the exotic commodities of equatorial Africa, insofar as they might still be required, and available, after the political withdrawal of the Egyptians from Nubia at the end of the New Kingdom. Such contacts, with or without the religious bond of the worship of Amun, provided the necessary basis for mutual interest. On the part of the Nubian ruling house, the desire to extend and deepen contacts with a country so infinitely more advanced in all respects, except military strength, surely gave sufficient stimulus for intervention. But the impression provided by the subsequent behaviour of the Nubians in Egypt is that respect and a nostalgia for the past greatness of Egypt – still probably aroused by the imposing remains of temples, cities and fortresses throughout Nubia – inspired this intervention, rather than a desire for conquest.

The Nubian rulers themselves had initially little to offer Egypt except the promise of stability, made palatable by their evident respect for Egyptian institutions, both political and religious. Furthermore, Nubians were no strangers in Egypt, particularly in Upper Egypt, and their native ruler could be seen not only as a source of stability, but also as a power greatly preferable to the Libyan chieftains who had brought such division and misery to the lands of the Delta and Middle Egypt.[19] But the Nubian ruling house, in spite of this respect for things Egyptian (assumed here as probable, but not established with reasonable certainty), did not ape Egyptian ways in religious beliefs and funerary practices until after their intervention in Egyptian affairs.[20] Py introduced a pyramidal superstructure for his tomb at El-Kurru, but his burial was executed in a traditional Nubian manner, his body being placed on a low bed. Sarcophagi in the Egyptian manner were not introduced until the burial of Taharqa, who opened the new royal cemetery at Nuri. The fact that the Nubian rulers chose to be buried near their native capital sufficiently confirms their attachment to their own Nubian traditions – an attachment equally to be observed in their devotion to horses,[21] in their peculiar methods of succession,[22] and in the

[19] *CAH* III².1, 571ff.   [20] F I, 278ff.   [21] F I, 282ff.   [22] F 104 I, 119ff; F I, 259f.

special authority exercised by their queens.[23] In spite of their deep involvement in Egyptian affairs they remained steadfastly Nubian and, when in due course withdrawal from Egypt became politically prudent, it was accomplished with no apparent damage to their personal status in their Napatan homeland.

II. PY'S CONQUEST AND WITHDRAWAL

Doubt has already been cast on the commonly stated reasons for Nubian involvement in Egyptian affairs. There is no wholly acceptable evidence to show that a desire to restore the prestige and power of the Theban god Amun prompted a kind of crusade launched from Napata by Nubian chieftains, either themselves devoted to the cult of Amun in Napata, or persuaded to act, as part of some political deal, by a priesthood of Amun at Napata. There is also no good evidence earlier than the great stela of Py (dated in his twenty-first year) on which to base the faintest semblance of a historical account of the earliest moves in the Nubian intervention.

A few small pieces of evidence have been put together to prove that Kashta, Py's father, actually invaded Egypt, and penetrated as far as Thebes.[24] Unfortunately they remain less than adequate to prove anything more than that Kashta during his lifetime may have used cartouches to include his names, and perhaps even assumed the Egyptian royal title 'King of Upper and Lower Egypt'. It is not impossible that he formed an intention to invade Egypt, or even actually did lead an expedition to Thebes, but satisfactory supporting evidence is still required.[25] A fragmentary stela from Aswān bearing his name, on which so much is based, is a miserable document which may not even be contemporary with Kashta.[26]

Py is thought to have succeeded his father, Kashta, in about 747 B.C.[27] His political inheritance is quite unknown, but those who believe in Kashta's actual invasion of Upper Egypt would maintain that Py continued to control the Kushite dominion in Egypt from his capital at Napata through the agency of loyal Theban officials and Nubian forces, but without exercising any very active role in Egyptian affairs.[28] In this extraordinarily blank period, the one act which requires serious historical interpretation is the adoption of Amenirdis, Py's sister, by Shepenupet, the God's Wife of Amun, and virtual ruler in Thebes. The power and significance of the office of God's Wife of Amun, and of her adopted daughter (and, therefore, successor), the God's Adorer of Amun (often

---

[23] F 104 I, 119ff.   [24] F 88, 74ff; F 137, 17f.

[25] For a more favourable view of the possibility of Kashta's invasion, see *CAH* III².1, 570; see also F 137, 20ff.   [26] F 88, 75.

[27] On the reading of the royal name as Py or Piye (against the former Piankhy), noted in *CAH* III².1, 569, see further F 53, 10 n.2.   [28] E.g. F 1, 261.

called the Divine Adoratrice), have been discussed earlier in this work, and more will be added later in the present chapter.[29] No date can be placed on the act of adoption of Amenirdis, but it is highly probable that it had already taken place by Year 12 of Py.[30] The old supposition that the adoption was effected by Kashta has now generally been abandoned in favour of the view that it was Py who brought it about.[31] Whatever might be the truth of the matter, there can be no question that the adoption could not have been made without the exercise of considerable pressure, possibly military as well as political; it is also beyond question that the ceremony of adoption would have been performed in the presence of the ruling Kushite chieftain of the time (Kashta or Py), or of his representative. As Amenirdis appears to have been in office in Year 12 of Py, it follows that her adoption by Shepenupet took place earlier, and more probably during Py's reign than during that of his father, Kashta. That event, therefore, may well have marked Py's first intervention into Egyptian territory, an intervention which represented either a continuation of Kashta's supposed involvement in Egyptian affairs, or a new initiative of Py's own devising.

Many possible reconstructions of the course of events during the early years of the Nubian participation in Theban affairs can be propounded. The adoption of Amenirdis, a very astute political act, may have been part of Py's first intervention, or a move made subsequent to this first intervention, and designed to secure a formal tie with the highest religious authority in Thebes. It could, however, scarcely have been a move contemplated by Py without good knowledge of the political scene at Thebes and of the importance of the office of God's Adorer of Amun, or without very well-informed advice provided by agents in Thebes or advisers in Napata.[32]

Whatever may have been the movements behind the adoption, one thing is certain: when Py made the fateful move into Egypt in his twentieth regnal year, his influence in Thebes was already prime, exercised through his sister, Amenirdis, and through officers of his own forces stationed in Egypt. He was, in fact, taking steps to protect an Egyptian dominion threatened from the north. Southern Upper Egypt from at least Hermopolis seems to have been nominally under the control or protection of the Nubian king, but Py had not thought it necessary to establish a court in Thebes, any more than the Assyrian kings later were to find it politically necessary, or desirable.[33] His court

---

[29] See *CAH* III².1, 567–8, 570 and below, p. 706.   [30] *CAH* III².1, 570.

[31] F 14, 103; see also F 77, 151 and n. 289; F 168, 145. F 1, 280, retains the old view without argument. Leclant in F 61 1, 196 leaves the question open. See also *CAH* III².1, 570.

[32] F 137, 25ff, on the basis of a doubtful date on Khartoum stela 1852, suggests that Py held formal claims on Egyptian territory by his Year 3.   [33] So F 137, 20.

was at Napata, and there he was content to stay until he was obliged to go north.

An account of the events leading up to the action taken by Py's representatives in Egypt, and of Py's own actions after he himself left Napata to establish his authority in his Egyptian dominion, is set out on the great red granite stela found in the temple at Gebel Barkal and now in the Cairo Museum.[34] The text, consisting of 159 lines of well-composed narrative in a somewhat awkward form of Middle Egyptian (with some Late Egyptian usages of syntax and grammar), common in official Egyptian inscriptions of the Late New Kingdom and subsequent periods, is, in the words of Sir Alan Gardiner, 'one of the most illuminating documents that Egyptian history has to show'.[35] It is hard to believe that it was not composed, at least in the form found on the stela, by native Egyptian scribes, although the 'vivacity of mind, feeling and expression' noted by Gardiner may well reflect the drafting and inspiration of a Kushite originator.[36]

The scene which occupies the upper part of Py's stela has already been described in an earlier volume, in which the history of the contemporary rulers of the Twenty-fourth Dynasty was discussed.[37] It represents the moment of triumph which attended the successful end of Py's campaign before he withdrew southwards to Napata, probably without more than a short stay in Thebes. With Amun and Mut, the Theban deities, Py is shown receiving the submission of the Delta rulers, with the notable exception of Tefnakhte. It is indeed rare to find so explicitly illustrative a scene used to introduce and support a historical text of this kind. The stela, however, was set up not in Egypt, but in the Kushite temple at Gebel Barkal, the great southern shrine of Amun, built in the New Kingdom and restored and enlarged by Py. Visually, and in words, it clearly expressed Py's triumph.

Composed after the conclusion of the campaign, the text on this stela is dated at the start of Py's twenty-first regnal year, about 727 B.C.[38] The events described in the text, however, began at least two years earlier.[39] Receiving news of the steady annexation of lands in Middle Egypt by the great Prince of the West, Tefnakhte, Py took little action until he heard that Nimlot, prince of Hermopolis, had deserted his cause and gone over to Tefnakhte.[40] Stung to action by the reproaches of his officers in Egypt, he first instructed them to stand fast and to do what they could to hinder

[34] Cairo JE 48862; see F 133 VII, 217.   [35] F 44, 335f.
[36] For a consideration of the grammar and syntax of the text, see F 53, 194ff.
[37] CAH III².1, 571ff.   [38] F 53, 10 n. 1.
[39] For the hieroglyphic text, see F 147, 1–56; a full republication in F 53; an English translation in F 95 III, 66ff. In general, see F 42, 219ff.
[40] For an account of the matter from the point of view of the northern dynasts, see CAH III².1, 571ff; on the campaign generally, F 164, 273ff; F 74, 227ff.

Tefnakhte's advance, while he prepared and dispatched an army to support the garrison in Egypt. The retrospective text of the stela recounts that Py ordered his army to allow Tefnakhte to choose the ground for battle, while the Nubian would rely on the help of Amun, to whom they should dedicate themselves when they reached Thebes.

With the support of Amun, the Nubian army moved north and secured a crushing victory on the Nile over the confederate forces of Tefnakhte, followed by another further north in the neighbourhood of Hermopolis, which was then invested with Nimlot inside. Unfortunately, Py found little satisfaction in the success of his army, because he felt that in allowing many of the enemy to escape it had only partly fulfilled the task it had been set. Now he himself would go north to settle the matter, but only after he had celebrated the New Year's feast at Napata and the Opet festival of Amun at Thebes. Thus consecrated, 'I shall let the Delta taste the taste of my fingers.'

The news of Py's intentions stimulated his army to further success, but its capture of three towns, Oxyrhynchus, El-Hiba and Hutbenu, did not divert him from his purpose. At the beginning of his Year 20 he left Napata, celebrated the Opet festival at Thebes, and moved north to reinforce the siege force at Hermopolis. He is again described as showing great displeasure at the poor showing of his troops already deployed in Egypt: 'Does this delay in executing my commission represent the determination of your fighting?' Here and elsewhere in the text Py's impatience contrasts strikingly with what seems to be a fair degree of success on the part of his army. The exemplary behaviour required by Py allows for no weakness or indecision. But this text is very much a carefully composed account, a means of declaring in no uncertain terms the greatness of Py and of proclaiming the glory of his father Amun. Every opportunity, therefore, is taken to diminish the successes of others, even though the factual record of these successes cannot be wholly suppressed. The text is exceptionally discursive and full of picturesque detail, which the reader, accustomed to the prosaic quality of most Egyptian royal texts, can only find refreshingly unexpected and enlivening. So, as the siege continued: 'Days passed by and Hermopolis was offensive to the nose, lacking her [usual] sweet smell.' Things were so bad that the time for treating had come. First, great quantities of treasure were sent out; then Nimlot's wife interceded on behalf of Nimlot and the inhabitants of the city. In accepting the wretched Nimlot's submission, Py could not resist chiding him for his defection. The incident is incorporated in the scene in the lunette of the stela: Nimlot brings Py a horse and a sistrum of gold and lapis lazuli. After making sacrifice to Thoth, Lord of Hermopolis, Py proceeded to inspect the official buildings of the city, expressing his horror and disgust at the condition of the horses in Nimlot's stables – an incidental indication of the Nubian devotion to horses.

This capture of Hermopolis with Nimlot's surrender was the crucial act of Py's campaign. It was followed by the voluntary submission of Peftjauawybast, the ruler of Heracleopolis, who had successfully resisted the attempts of Tefnakhte's forces to secure his adherence to the cause of the Prince of the West.[41] Moving north from Hermopolis, Py next found his way obstructed by the heavily garrisoned town of Pisekhemkheperre at the entrance to the Faiyūm. A strong threatening appeal to the besieged was enough, apparently, to secure their surrender without a fight. Among those in the town was a son of Tefnakhte, but, according to the account in Py's great stela, no one was killed. It is not recorded whether captives were taken, although the contents of the treasury and granaries in the town were confiscated, those of the former for Py's treasury, and of the latter for the offerings of Amon-Re. They were the common beneficiaries of most of the booty taken by Py throughout this campaign. After taking the towns of Maidūm and El-Lisht by persuasion alone, Py and his forces approached Memphis. His usual appeal for surrender was ignored, even though he pointed out that in the southern nomes only blasphemers had been slain. In Memphis he only wished to make offerings to Ptah and the other gods of the city. The refusal of the garrison to surrender was inspired apparently by the approach of Tefnakhte himself. He reinforced the garrison with 8,000 picked troops, reminded the defenders of their strong position and wealth of supplies, and promptly returned north to rally support from the Delta chiefs. In the words of the inscription, 'He set himself on a horse, not asking for his chariot, and travelled north out of fear of His Majesty.'

When the Nubian force prepared to attack the great northern capital city they found it protected by water and by heightened walls. Offered a great deal of advice by his commanders, Py, relying on the support of Amun, decided on a frontal assault on the harbour of Memphis, using every kind of ship fit for requisitioning. The assault, no details of which are contained in the inscription, was overwhelming; many people in the city were slain, and many captives taken. The city was then ritually purified, Py was greeted with the sacred rites due to a king, and he made offerings to Ptah in his temple. The booty of the city, undoubtedly considerable, was assigned to Amun, Ptah, and the other gods of Memphis. This great victory was followed by visits to Heliopolis, and to Athribis (at the invitation of Pediese, the prince of that city), and the submission of most of the Delta rulers who had allied themselves with Tefnakhte. According to the record preserved on the great stela, the various princes and chiefs submitted to Py in groups, the majority at

41 See *CAH* III².1, 573; F 164, 284f.

Athribis.[42] Tefnakhte's submission was not made to Py in person, but to the emissaries sent by Py, presumably to Saïs, Tefnakhte's capital. With the collapse of all serious resistance, the few remaining places which had maintained support for Tefnakhte offered allegiance to Py, notably the Faiyūm and Atfih on the east of the Nile opposite the Faiyūm. The final act of submission, which may ceremonially have included most of the defeated princes and chiefs, took place before Py, probably in Memphis, although the inscription is not explicit on this point. The lunette scene at the top of the stela records in graphic terms the submission, either as it may have taken place on this last occasion, or as a conflated representation of several acts of submission.[43]

In the final sentence of the inscription Py's departure southwards is described. His ship was loaded with booty, and his progress upstream universally cheered. What the text unfortunately does not tell is whether Py travelled directly to Napata, or paused *en route* at Thebes. The commonly accepted view is that he made straight for Napata and never set foot in Egypt again.[44] Indeed this may well have been the case, but it is almost beyond belief that his victorious flotilla would have passed by Thebes without stopping for Py to give thanks to Amon-Re, offering in person a generous portion of the spoils of his victory in the temple of Karnak. Again, although there is no evidence directly to support this supposition, it should be surmised that Py spent enough time in Thebes to settle matters of future administration in Egypt. His natural instrument of control in Egypt remained his sister Amenirdis, the adoptive heiress of Shepenupet, the God's Wife of Amun. Between them Amenirdis and Shepenupet wielded great power at Thebes, supported by a body of native Egyptian officials, priestly and civil, among whom the most influential seems to have been Harwa, Amenirdis' major-domo, who may have instituted the practice of having a huge tomb constructed for himself in the area of the Theban necropolis now known as the Asāsīf.[45] The view that Harwa was Nubian, based principally on the manner in which he is represented in some of his sculptures, is quite unsupported by any specific evidence.[46] That Nubians were installed in important positions in Thebes – the natural consequence of Py's intervention in Egypt – is hard to substantiate. One Kelbasken, who was a mayor of Thebes possibly under Py and his successor, and who from his name must certainly have been Nubian, was buried in a Theban tomb;[47] but there is little to show that Py set up, or felt it necessary to set

---

[42] F 53, 242ff.
[43] For a more detailed account of the submissions, see *CAH* III².1, 573f; F 164, 287.
[44] F 77, 366; but see F 53, 301.
[45] Theban Tomb 37, see F 133 I².i, 68; D. Eigner, *Die monumentalen Grabbauten* (Vienna, 1984), 37ff. The career of Harwa remains to be studied in detail; for much material, see F 85, viii.
[46] F 85, 260 n.4.   [47] F 77, 382. For the tomb see F 133 I². i, 441 (no. 391).

up, a substantial Nubian cadre of officials in Thebes to maintain his rule. In general, his supremacy seems to have been accepted with little opposition in Thebes, and documents were readily dated by his regnal years, the numbering going back to his accession as king in Napata in about 747 B.C.[48]

However Py acted during his return from Memphis to Napata after his triumph, there can be no disputing the generally accepted view that he never subsequently returned to Egypt. Further, he seems to have been little concerned with maintaining actively his supremacy over the Delta rulers. In the north the way was left open for Tefnakhte to re-establish his authority, and, apparently, to extend his influence until he may have proclaimed himself king.[49] In northern Upper Egypt, likewise, Py's conquest led to few changes in the distribution of power locally between the rulers at Hermopolis, Heracleopolis and elsewhere.[50] In fact, this first substantial intervention by a king of Napata into Egyptian affairs had very limited results, the principal of which was the establishment of a Nubian hegemony (rather than a supremacy) in the name of Amon-Re. This god, in consequence of Py's campaign (if he did not occupy the position previously) became a dominant force in Nubian policy, and his cult was fostered before all others in Nubia. Py added considerably to the New Kingdom temple at Gebel Barkal,[51] perhaps the first of his line to do so, embellishing his constructions with granite rams previously set up by Amenophis III at Sulb.[52] Few further monuments have survived to demonstrate the extent of his activities in his Nubian realm.[53]

The length of Py's reign, and, consequently, the date of his death, have been subjects of much dispute. The highest surviving monumental date is Year 24,[54] but a linen fragment in the British Museum preserves a date which may be of Year 30 or Year 40. It is difficult wholly to justify 40, and the reading of 30 must remain uncertain. Other considerations weigh in favour of the lower figure, and a reign of at least 31 years seems to fit the known facts best, giving a date of about 716 B.C. for Py's death.[55] He prepared tombs for himself and for members of his family at El-Kurru, the earliest royal cemetery of Napata, lying about ten miles downstream from Gebel Barkal on the same side of the Nile. While the character of the burials was Nubian in the use of beds to carry the bodies, the influence of Egyptian funerary practices was already strong; mummification was employed, and the funerary equipment included characteristic Egyptian items such as canopic jars and *ushabti*-figures.[56] The most

---

[48] For papyri of Years 21 and 22, see F 127, 111ff; for a stela of Year 24, see F 64, 165ff.
[49] *CAH* III².1, 574.   [50] F 77, 371; O'Connor in F 169, 243.
[51] F 139, 263ff; F 36.   [52] F 133 VII, 216, 219.   [53] F 77, 369.
[54] F 64, 165ff; see also F 77, 152.
[55] F 77, 142, 144, 151f; 2nd edn, 559; for 40 years, see F 7, 7f.
[56] F 34, 64ff, for Py's tomb; 121ff for general considerations.

striking Egyptian element, however, was the pyramidal superstructure, inspired undoubtedly by Egyptian royal tombs. Whether the inspiration for the Nubian pyramids came from those of the Old Kingdom in the region of Memphis, or those of the Seventeenth Dynasty at Thebes, remains to be decided, although the smaller size of the latter, and their steeper sloping sides provide, in theory, better models.[57] Characteristically, horses were also buried in accompanying graves, at some distance from Py's own burial. This practice was followed by his successors.[58]

III. DYNASTIC EXPANSION AND ASIATIC ADVENTURE

Shabako, who succeeded his brother Py as Napatan king in about 716 B.C.,[59] within two years renewed active Nubian intervention in Egypt. It is possible only to surmise at his reasons for moving north, but among them may well have been the desire to match the brilliant campaign of Py ten years or so earlier, and the need to demonstrate to the apparently insurgent Bocchoris that his increasingly independent activities in the Delta and in the region of Memphis represented a threat to Nubian dominion which could not be tolerated. The activities of the Delta rulers after Py's withdrawal were, as far as can be judged from the sparse evidence, much the same as they had been before the Nubian's triumph. Humiliated by Py, they were yet treated with extraordinary moderation, and allowed to remain in control of their petty principalities.[60] But news from the Delta, whatever form it took, stimulated Shabako to action, and it seems that in a relatively short time, and with little difficulty, he succeeded in extending Nubian control over most of the Delta. His Year 2 corresponded with Bocchoris' Year 6, and it saw the downfall of that ruler.[61] So successful was his campaign that Shabako had it commemorated in a text inscribed on large scarabs, one example of which has, happily, survived. The first line, which probably included a date, is unfortunately lost, but the substantial part of the text is completely preserved; after the royal titulary, in which Shabako is described as 'more beloved of Amun than any king who has been since the creation of the land', it continues,

He has slain those who rebelled against him in the South Land and the North Land, and in all foreign lands. The Sand-dwellers languish because of him, fallen for terror of him. They come of their own accord as captives, each one of them

---

[57] Average angle of inclination for Old Kingdom pyramids was 52°; for Seventeenth Dynasty pyramids, 65°; for Nubian pyramids, 68°; see F 38, 88, 230 and 236. Adams' view (F 1, 278) that the small pyramids of Theban private tombs provided the models is unlikely.

[58] F 34, 110, 116ff.

[59] On the range of possible dates for Shabako's accession, see F 77, 2nd edn, 553, 555ff.

[60] *CAH* III².1, 574ff.   [61] *CAH* III².1, 575.

having seized his fellow, because of the beneficent acts he has performed for his father, inasmuch as he loves him.[62]

While it would be a mistake to regard this text as an exact statement of what Shabako achieved, its very existence argues in favour of some degree of verisimilitude. It represents a public announcement intended for wide circulation which would not have been believed if it had departed too far from the truth.[63] It is further of interest that the scarab was first reported in Syria, and finally purchased in Jerusalem,[64] which may indicate a dispersal of royal propaganda beyond Egypt's boundaries.

Evidence of Shabako's conquest of Lower Egypt, and his apparent acceptance by the Delta rulers as their overlord, is provided by a small number of donation stelae from Delta sites dated by years of his reign: from Pharbaithos (Year 2), from Bubastis (Year 3), from Saïs (Year 6).[65] But the measure of his acceptance may not have been total. There is no strong evidence to show that he actively exercised his dominion in Lower Egypt; there is, on the contrary, good reason to believe, as has long been suggested,[66] that the principalities of the Delta and their chiefs never wholly submitted to Nubian rule. For the time it was enough to acknowledge the overlordship of the Napatan kings, and tacitly accept their assumption of the significant title 'King of Upper and Lower Egypt', and their wearing of the double *uraeus*, indicating, possibly, their rule over Egypt and Nubia.[67] The division of rule in the Delta, of long standing, and well characterized (if only symbolically) as a rule of twelve (dodecarchy) by Herodotus (II.147), continued until the emergence of Psammetichus I, who established a single authority at the beginning of the Twenty-sixth Dynasty. Shabako's conquest and unification was, therefore, more apparent than actual, and its lack of substance, as far as the Delta was concerned, was to have important consequences in foreign affairs – a matter to which a return will be made later.

For Upper Egypt, from Memphis southwards, Shabako's authority seems to have been exercised more directly, and indeed this king, unlike his brother Py, probably spent a great part of his reign in Egypt. At least, the evidence of new constructions in Thebes and elsewhere suggests an involvement in Egyptian affairs beyond the formal expression of a fanatical devotion to the god Amun. The buildings added to the great temple complexes at Thebes were not in themselves considerable,[68] but

---

[62] The scarab is in the Royal Ontario Museum, no. 910.28.1; see F 181, 457ff; F 183, 206ff.

[63] Probably many copies were issued, as with the commemorative scarabs of Amenophis III, which possibly served as models for Shabako.

[64] F 181, 457.   [65] F 77, 379.   [66] F 184, 121.

[67] F 86, 79 n.4; F 157, 65; F 141, 35ff takes the view that the *uraei* represent Upper and Lower Egypt.   [68] Listed and described in F 89.

they represented a marked change in the policy of the Napatan house towards Egypt. Elsewhere in Upper Egypt traces of Shabako's interest and activity in connexion with the religious establishments of the land have been found at Abydos, Dendera, Esna, and Edfu.[69] But the most notable monument of his endeavours to foster and rehabilitate the religious traditions of Egypt is the so-called Shabako Stone, a black basalt slab inscribed at Shabako's order with the text of what was declared to be a very ancient dramatic composition concerned with the Memphite theological system of which Ptah was the centre (Pls. Vol., pl. 187).[70] Preserved, as it was said, only in a worm-eaten copy, it was transferred to the stone for preservation. Unfortunately the success of Shabako's solicitude has not wholly been realized; the subsequent use of the stone as a nether millstone resulted in the loss of much of the text. Shabako's sympathy towards the religious establishment at Memphis, including the cult of the Apis bull, should not, however, be over-emphasized,[71] and it would be wrong to deduce from such tenuous evidence that he made Memphis his capital for a part of his reign.[72] He would undoubtedly have used Memphis as his base if ever he travelled north, but there is no reason to believe that he spent long periods of time there.

A statue in the British Museum establishes that Shabako ruled at least into his fifteenth year,[73] about 702 B.C., and he was buried, like his brother Py, at El-Kurru.[74] The paucity of evidence for royal activities during his reign is even greater for Nubia than for Egypt. Apart from his pyramid, the only building erected for him in Nubia seems to have been a shrine or small temple at Kawa,[75] a few miles to the south of New Dongola between the Third and Fourth Cataracts, the site of important pharaonic foundations of the late Eighteenth Dynasty, and subsequently specially chosen for extensive buildings by Shabako's nephew and second successor, Taharqa. But in spite of this slender evidence there is no reason to believe that Shabako thought of himself as more an Egyptian ruler than a Napatan king. Unlike Py, however, he probably found it more politic to maintain his residence in Thebes, and this alone would account for his building activities in the Theban area and elsewhere in Upper Egypt. It was also probably during his reign that the new development of cults and the priesthood in the great sanctuaries of Thebes (very evident from the study of Twenty-fifth Dynasty private votive inscriptions)[76] took place. The office of High Priest of Amun

[69] F 77, 381.

[70] BM 498; see A 44, 4ff, for translation and bibliography. For a different view of the antiquity of this text, see F 67, 195ff; cf. F 95 III, 5, who now also considers the text a pseudepigraph.

[71] For a judicious assessment, see F 170, 76.

[72] F 44, 343. For Shabako's works at Memphis, see F 77, 2nd edn, 584.

[73] BM 24429; see F 84, 15ff.   [74] F 34, 55ff.   [75] F 104 II, 14.   [76] F 84, 103ff.

which for unknown reasons seems to have been in abeyance for many years, was almost certainly revived by Shabako. The first recorded holder of this highest priestly position after the lapse was Horemakhet, Shabako's eldest son. Although it is not known when he was appointed, it is a fair assumption that it was while his father was still alive. The position of High Priest no longer carried with it the political power which had so notably been acquired by the incumbents of the office in the Late New Kingdom.[77] This power had passed into the hands of the God's Wife of Amun, who throughout Shabako's reign was his sister Amenirdis; and she was possibly supported politically by the mayor of Thebes, and Fourth Prophet of Amun,[78] a dignitary with a conjunction of secular and religious power which made him especially influential in the Theban state, where the pre-eminence of the cult and temples of Amun was at this time undisputed. There is no direct evidence to suggest who held these offices during Shabako's reign, but it may have been the same Kelbasken who was probably installed by Py.[79] If the situation in Thebes was truly as suggested here, then Shabako's rule was well supported as far as southern Upper Egypt was concerned. When he died in about 702 and was succeeded by his nephew, Shebitku, he passed on at Thebes an established and experienced administration, which should have resulted in the further strengthening of Nubian power throughout Egypt. The expectation, however, was thwarted by external events, and the imprudence of his successor.

The trouble lay on Egypt's north-eastern frontier, where danger was threatened by the campaigns of Sargon II of Assyria in Palestine and Syria. In 720 Osorkon IV had foolishly gone to the aid of Hanun of Gaza,[80] and his forces had suffered in the subsequent battle with Sargon's army. At that time Sargon apparently had no wish to press home his advantage in Egypt itself, and his evident power no doubt made a significant impression on the various rulers in Egypt, whether Delta princes or Nubian kings, the rulers, ostensibly, of the whole land. Shabako, it would seem, maintained a prudent caution in respect of his Asiatic neighbours and, far from engaging in punitive adventures beyond his north-eastern frontier, chose, when put to the test, to adopt a more than conciliatory line. In 712, when Sargon's forces ousted Yamani from Ashdod after he had raised the banner of revolt against the Assyrians, Shabako refused to give him asylum in his flight, and turned him over to the Assyrians.[81] This seemingly treacherous act was, in the circumstances, undoubtedly a shrewd practical move, which may have

[77] F 77, 197.

[78] On the position of the vizir during the Twenty-fifth Dynasty, see F 14, 105.

[79] See above, p. 687.   [80] CAH III².1, 576f. See also above, p. 89.

[81] For sources, see F 154, 95ff. For a clearer statement of the order of events, see F 77, 380; also 2nd edn, 552. Shabako is not named directly in cuneiform records.

led to regular and friendly diplomatic exhanges between Assyria and Egypt. At least two seal-impressions bearing figures of Shabako smiting an enemy have been found at Nineveh; it would be a mistake to draw too strong a conclusion from these small objects, but it would equally be wrong to ignore them as being random finds of small significance. The impressions indicate a seal of some grandeur, which would not have been applied to insignificant documents.[82]

Neutrality did not, apparently, commend itself to Shabako's successor, although it would probably be unjust to ascribe the provocative actions he took early in his reign to simple ambition or to foolhardiness. As ever, the springs of action remain unknown, but neutrality was undoubtedly a position difficult to sustain for very long in the circumstances which generally obtained in the Near East at this time. It may also be suggested that when Shebitku succeeded Shabako in about 702 he had only recently come to Egypt from Napata, and was to a great extent a tiro in Egyptian politics, and unacquainted with the possible dangers of an active foreign policy in Asia.[83] At about this time the petty princes of Palestine developed a counter-move against Assyrian rule, and engaged the interest of the Nubian ruler of Egypt, presumably Shebitku. No adequate reason for his readiness to support the planned revolt can be advanced from the evidence at present available, but it is known that, surely in the expectation of serious military involvement in Asia, he brought up from Nubia an army and his brothers, among whom was the future king Taharqa, then aged twenty.[84] Taharqa states explicitly that he journeyed to Lower Egypt with Shebitku, but he makes no mention of a campaign, presumably because the outcome was not particularly creditable.

Assyrian and Biblical sources provide all that is known of the Egyptian participation in the abortive campaign of 701, in which Sennacherib forcefully confirmed Assyrian supremacy in Palestine.[85] At Eltekeh the confederacy forces, which included Egyptians and Nubians,[86] were defeated by Sennacherib's army, and from both the Biblical and the Assyrian sources it may be deduced that the support

---

[82] F 57, nos. 2775, 2776. Shabako is shown wearing the Lower Egyptian crown. F 185, 237f, reactivates an old suggestion of Olmstead that the impressions might have been from documents sent to Sennacherib in 701 B.C. and not to Sargon in 712 B.C. F 77, 2nd edn, 584, considers this idea 'theoretical and uncertain'. Shabako was in any case probably already dead by 701 B.C.: see F 77, 554ff.

[83] The question of a co-regency between Shabako and Shebitku remains unresolved; *contra*, see F 92, 24ff; *pro*, on the basis of chronological minutiae, F 154, 98; F 123, 189f; F 185, 221ff; F 77, 2nd edn, 555ff, finds the idea of a co-regency seductive, but is not fully convinced.

[84] Kawa stelae IV, 7–9; V, 13, 14, 17; see F 104 I, 15, 28. For Taharqa's age at the time, see F 185, 222f.   [85] For details of the whole Assyrian campaign, see above, chapter 23.

[86] F 162, 36, has two Egyptian forces, one of the Delta princes and one led by Shebitku. The evidence is slight, but his conclusion is more than reasonable; see F 185, 225ff. See above, pp. 110 and 360.

from Egypt did not contribute much to the opposition to the Assyrians. Part of the message delivered to the beleaguered Hezekiah in Jerusalem from Sennacherib included the scornful 'Egypt is a splintered cane that will run into a man's hand and pierce it if he leans on it. That is what Pharaoh king of Egypt proves to all who rely on him.'[87] The Assyrian record claims that Egyptian and Nubian charioteers were captured in the battle,[88] but it is unlikely that the force under Taharqa's command was actually involved in this engagement.[89] In the aftermath of the battle of Eltekeh the Egypto-Nubian army prepared once more to engage the Assyrians, but neither the Biblical nor the Assyrian sources confirm that any action took place. Some time subsequently a disaster struck the Assyrian army and obliged Sennacherib to withdraw to Nineveh.[90] In the meanwhile, Taharqa had presumably led his own force back to Egypt, possibly never having been engaged, and scarcely in triumph. The military adventure as a whole may not have been particularly disastrous to Egypt in the short term, but it held promise of dire consequences for the future. The sensible neutrality maintained by Shabako had been forfeited.

For the time being Egypt was spared retaliatory action from the Assyrians, but an almost complete lack of evidence from Egyptian sources renders it impossible to determine whether Shebitku in the ten or so years remaining to him pursued a policy towards Assyria which continued the hostile attitude of his early reign, or endeavoured to return to the neutrality of his predecessor. It may also be wondered to what extent Taharqa, who had been brought north from Napata and put in charge of part, if not all, of the army sent against Sennacherib, determined the course of action in foreign affairs. As had so often been the case in Egypt's relations with her Asiatic neighbours, the petty squabbles between minor states and city states in Palestine and Syria provided the opportunities for interference which were frequently attended by disastrous results. At this time, interference in the Near East, no matter how small and local, would lead inevitably to hostile involvement with Assyria. After his abortive, and possibly peripheral, participation in the Eltekeh campaign, Taharqa may well have urged caution and a period of non-involvement. It seems to have been in fact a time of peace *vis-à-vis* Asia which lasted well into Taharqa's own reign.

---

[87] II Ki. 18: 21; Is. 36: 6 (New English Bible).

[88] A 44, 287f.

[89] F 77, 386, argues for the anachronistic mention of Taharqa in the Biblical record. F 186, 26, argues for two forces, the second under Taharqa avoiding the encounter at Eltekeh. F 162, 39, would eliminate Taharqa from the whole campaign. F 185, 222ff, supports Taharqa's involvement in the campaign, but argues strongly against his presence at Eltekeh. See also F 79, 250ff.

[90] II Ki. 19: 35–6; Is. 37: 36–7. On the late tradition which would have had an abortive invasion of the Eastern Delta by Sennacherib, see F 185, 234f.

Some evidence of peaceful conditions within Egypt itself throughout Shebitku's reign may be provided by the remains of public works, including modest temple buildings and decoration carried out in his name;[91] but, in truth, there is very little that can be said of the reign. Even its length is in doubt, the one dated record (in Year 3) providing little substance for a reign now thought to have lasted about twelve years, until 690 B.C.[92]

IV. TAHARQA — THE BRIEF TRIUMPH AND DISASTER

Devotion to the Nubian homeland, so evident in the behaviour of Py, was again strongly to be found in the actions of Taharqa, who in many ways was to show himself to be the outstanding monarch of the Napatan line. Lack of evidence prevents any reliable assessment to be made of the Nubian attitudes and policies of Shabako and Shebitku, but it would probably be wrong to maintain, on the basis of this lack of evidence, that these two kings neglected their southern domain. It has already been shown that there is equally scarcely any evidence of Shebitku's activities in Egypt, and his twelve or so years cannot be thought of as a total void. Like his uncle Shabako, Shebitku was buried at El-Kurru,[93] and it could not seriously be thought that there was any significant slackening of the ties which bound the Egyptian monarchs of the Twenty-fifth Dynasty to Napata. The late tradition that Shebitku was assassinated by Taharqa, and the consequent deduction that Taharqa was not of royal blood, but a usurper,[94] can no longer be considered seriously. The texts of a series of five stelae dated to Taharqa's reign, discovered at Kawa in Nubia, have helped to resolve some of the difficulties previously faced by historians of the period,[95] although the evidence these stelae provide has not always been used with sufficient care and understanding. In the first publication of the text Kawa IV, a co-regency between Shebitku and Taharqa of five or six years was proposed,[96] but this view has not been generally accepted by Egyptologists.[97] What may now be taken as the received view is that Shebitku summoned Taharqa and his other brothers north from Napata not long after he himself had become king, in about 702. Taharqa may then have been put in command of the whole, or part, of the army sent by Shebitku into Asia, a matter discussed in the preceding section; but thereafter he played no recorded part in Egyptian political life until he was crowned king in Memphis after Shebitku's death.[98] In his Kawa inscriptions (IV.8–9; V.14), Taharqa explains that

[91] For the Theban monuments, see F 89, 340ff.
[92] For the chronology, see F 77, 154ff; also F 78, 64ff. [93] F 34, 67f.
[94] F 186, 30; F 104 I, 20. [95] Published in F 104 I. [96] F 104 I, 18f.
[97] F 92, 17ff; F 77, 164ff; F 123, 190ff. [98] F 104 I, 28 (Inscr. V, 15).

he was preferred by Shebitku over his brothers, and, by whatever means the succession was determined (by election, collateral seniority, or simple choice),[99] he achieved it in about 690.

In the best ancient tradition Taharqa was crowned in Memphis, a city which, in addition to its special position in the ceremonial of the coronation, seems to have had a particular attraction for the Nubian kings.[100] As a seat of government it was of unparalleled convenience among the cities of Egypt, strategically sited at the apex of the Delta, and relatively easily accessible to the areas of potential trouble at this time – the Delta principalities, still possessed of vestiges of their former power, and the Asiatic frontier regions. In the latter Taharqa may have been taught a severe lesson in his earliest military expedition, but it may seem that the lesson was not sufficiently salutary in the light of what was to happen later in his reign. It has been suggested that the absence of direct evidence of active involvement by Taharqa in Asia may be wholly misleading, and that indirect evidence drawn particularly from the Kawa inscriptions supports a view that he did in fact prosecute a lively and provocative policy in Asia Minor during the first half of his reign, a period of about thirteen years.[101] The presentation of Asiatic timber, metals, and other products to the Kawa temple, and the sending there of Asiatic gardeners, may surely indicate no more than the continuance of commerce between Egypt and Asia. There were few times in Egypt's long history when the trade routes were firmly closed. More significant may be a mention of the discontinuation of tribute from the land of Khor (Syria–Palestine) to the temple of Amon-Re in Karnak,[102] tribute which would have been the result of an active aggressive policy by Taharqa in the early years of his reign.[103] A more cautious interpretation would see no more than a rather extravagant reference in a religious inscription to the products of Asiatic trade described hyperbolically as tribute.[104] It may be said with some confidence that no Egyptian king could wholly ignore at this time what was happening in Asia, but the evidence at present available does not warrant the view that Asiatic products were acquired in any way other than by trade.

Even if Taharqa had engaged in potentially dangerous adventures in Asia during his early years, his surviving records recount nothing explicitly of them.[105] On the contrary, his energies were devoted, according to these same records, to the pious activities of temple-building and restoration, and other peaceable works. From the texts found at Kawa, it seems evident that as soon as he became king he was

---

[99] No single system fits the known facts. F 1, 259f, touches the subject superficially.
[100] F 87, esp. 281ff; see also F 111, 221ff.   [101] So F 162, 22ff.
[102] F 171, 26ff.   [103] F 162, esp. 41ff.   [104] Suggested in F 171, 46.
[105] Listed in F 162, 44ff.

able to fulfil vows which he had been obliged to hold in suspense, as it were, during the years of Shebitku's reign. He recounts (Kawa IV.9ff) how he passed by Gempaten (Kawa) on his way to join Shebitku when he was a young man, and the memory of the sad state of the temple there remained with him, to be recalled vividly after he himself had become King of Upper and Lower Egypt. The visible evidence of the fulfilment of Taharqa's vow rests in the restored temple of Tutankhamun, and in the great new temple he himself built at Kawa.[106] The lavish gifts with which he showered his foundation are listed in detail in the Kawa stelae. Presentations began in Year 2 (Kawa III), and continued until Year 10 (Kawa VI), when the inauguration of the new temple took place on the Egyptian New Year's Day (Kawa VII); it had taken four years to complete. The work at Kawa was carried out by gangs of workmen sent from Egypt, probably from the Memphite region where Taharqa maintained his court (Kawa IV.21–2). Memphite influence is clearly to be seen not only in the representations carved on the walls of the temple, some of which reproduce scenes known on Old Kingdom royal monuments at Saqqara and Abusir, but also in architectural design and detail, which seem in some respects to be based on Old Kingdom Memphite originals.[107] In addition to sending to Kawa Asiatic gardeners to tend the vineyards specially planted for the temple, he further assigned to temple duties there the wives of Lower Egyptian chieftains (Kawa VI.20), which may indicate successful action on Taharqa's part against the Delta dynasts who had never fully succumbed to the Nubian overlords, the self-styled Kings of Upper and Lower Egypt of the Twenty-fifth Dynasty.

The practical devotion shown to the domain of Amun at Kawa was but part of the fairly comprehensive programme of building and reconstruction undertaken by Taharqa in his Nubian homeland. He built, or added to, temples in the capital Napata,[108] and he established a new foundation at Sanam, across the Nile from Napata.[109] Traces of his work have been found at Old Merowe and Buhen, and there was a small shrine at Semna West.[110] Blocks from an unidentified building have been found at Sedeinga.[111] At Qasr Ibrim, the fortress site in Lower Nubia, where blocks bearing Taharqa's name had been observed in secondary contexts since the place was first visited in modern times,[112] excavation as recently as 1972 revealed the temple from which these blocks presumably came.[113] It is interesting to speculate on Taharqa's reasons for establishing a shrine in this lofty place at a time when it seems not to have been

---

[106] F 133 VII, 180ff.
[107] See F 104 II, 61, 63 (reliefs), 107f (architecture); also F 153, 240f.   [108] F 36.
[109] F 133 VII, 198ff.   [110] F 133 VII, 198, 136f, 149f.
[111] F 91, 1113ff; see below, n.130.   [112] E.g. F 93 V, 129, 132.
[113] F 132, 229; F 131, 19f; F 4, 24f.

the site of a garrison, as it was so often to be in later, more troubled times.

In spite of these abundant signs of official activity in Nubia during Taharqa's reign, there is little in the records to show that he himself spent much time in his southern territories. Even the account of the inauguration of the completed temple at Kawa makes no mention of the royal presence on that most auspicious occasion (Kawa VII). Memphis was his seat in Egypt, and some few traces of his sojourn there have been found.[114] Their modest nature and quantity must be considered against the inadequate and random excavation of that city site, and the paucity of standing remains there. But they cannot fail to be compared, to their disadvantage, with the very considerable surviving buildings and monuments which were erected in Thebes during his reign, of which the most striking was the great colonnade in the first court of the great temple of Amon-Re at Karnak.[115] Extensive building works tend, in Egyptian history, to be associated with peaceful conditions, and the early years of Taharqa's reign seem, from such evidence as is at present available, to have provided these conditions. The *annus mirabilis* was Year 6 (*c.* 685), when there was an exceptionally high inundation of the Nile. High Niles, like low Niles, tended to be associated with disaster, physical destruction in the case of the former, famine following the latter. The high Nile of Year 6, however, was accompanied by four 'events' which together were taken as marvels: a splendid cultivation, the extermination of rats and snakes, the prevention of destruction by locusts, and the failure of the damaging south wind[116] – all granted by Amon-Re. In consequence there was such a harvest as had never been experienced before.

Good works, pious buildings, and a just administration were the marks of Taharqa's early years, as he himself wished them to be remembered. The peace and plenty which followed such a regime were the proper returns for outstanding devotion in the service of Amon-Re. Unfortunately, however, divine favour was not to be continued beyond a certain point, and it remains uncertain whether Taharqa in these early years had other irons in the political fire which in time burnt the hand that manipulated them. While there is no direct evidence of Egyptian involvement in Asiatic affairs, the subsequent enmity displayed by the Assyrian kings, directed particularly at Taharqa personally, suggests that something more than simple imperial purposes prompted the successive Assyrian invasions of Egypt. The Assyrian sources, from which most of the positive detail for the passage of events involving

[114] F 192, 28; F 111, 221ff.

[115] For the Theban buildings, see F 84; for blocks of Taharqa formerly thought to belong to Shoshenq I, near the barque sanctuary at Karnak, see F 171, 1ff; F 77, 2nd edn, 558, 586.

[116] F 104 V gives the most complete text. For this and the parallels from Coptos, Mata'na and Tanis, see F 104 I, 23ff. For the interpretation preferred here, see F 92, 22ff.

Egypt in the international field are derived, yield a distinct picture of a far from united Kingdom of Upper and Lower Egypt.[117] The unity of the land, a condition proclaimed in the official Egyptian records, was almost certainly less real than Taharqa would have had it thought to be. In the Delta, the principalities which had flourished with varying degrees of autonomy for the preceding century and a half remained not wholly assimilated within the realm of the Napatan pharaoh.[118] His suzerainty was, it may be conjectured, tolerated, but in spite of his patent devotion to certain Egyptian deities, and generally to the religious and cultural traditions of the land, he was seen as a foreign overlord. He is so considered in the Assyrian records, and the emphasis there on his Nubian origin possibly reflects the attitude of potential (if presently powerless) Delta dynasts who, by diplomatic approaches to the Assyrian king, hoped to substitute for the objectionable overlordship of a Kushite ruler in Memphis the less objectionable control of an Assyrian king established far away in Nineveh.

The possibilities of trouble from the disloyal Delta dynasts were, however, matched by the actual inter-state rivalries which characterized the politics of the Mediterranean lands of the Near East. Trouble among the latter was of more immediate concern to the Assyrians who, possibly rightly, saw Taharqa and his representatives as prime stirrers of the pot of dissidence. Esarhaddon, who had succeeded Sennacherib in 681 B.C., took up the problem of the Levant in his fourth year, seeing in the disturbances there the hand of Taharqa.[119] He levelled his attack at Sidon and its ruler Abdi-milkutti, capturing the city, and subsequently executing its king. Both Egyptian and Assyrian records are silent about what may have been Esarhaddon's first direct move against Egypt, reported in the Babylonian Chronicle. According to that record, in Esarhaddon's seventh year the Assyrian army was defeated severely in Egypt.[120] Subsequently, in his tenth year (671) the Assyrian invasion was altogether more successful. Of this campaign the Assyrian records contain substantial information. In a lightning advance from Palestine, Esarhaddon inflicted a series of defeats on the Egyptian forces, and took and sacked Memphis.[121] It was claimed that among the prisoners taken were members of Taharqa's family, including his heir, named Ushanahuru, who may have been the Kushite depicted on the stela set up after the campaign by Esarhaddon at Zincirli in Syria.[122] The text of this stela further records that all Kushites were taken captive to Assyria, and that throughout Egypt Taharqa's officials and administrators were replaced with others, presumably native Egyptians well-inclined towards the Assyrians. In this reorganization of the local bureaucracies it may be

---

[117] A 44, 289ff; also F 156, 295ff.   [118] F 184, 136ff.   [119] A 25, 126.   [120] A 25, 84.
[121] A 44, 85, 127. See above, pp. 42, 124, 126, 375.   [122] F 156, 303f; F 90, 16.

possible to detect the use by Esarhaddon of the long-standing lack of
national cohesion already considered as a likely element in the political
struggle between Egypt (more particularly, its Napatan regime) and
Assyria.

It is unlikely that Esarhaddon's force penetrated far to the south of
Memphis after this campaign of 671. Taharqa presumably withdrew to
Thebes, if not to Napata, but soon began to stir up trouble again, if such
may be taken to have been the cause of a further excursion into Egypt by
Esarhaddon two years later. On this occasion, however, a halt was
imposed on the Assyrian force by the unexpectedly sudden death of its
king.[123] He was succeeded by Ashurbanipal.[124] Taking advantage of this
change of ruler, and seemingly misjudging the probable outcome of a
counter-strike, Taharqa reasserted his authority over the local princes of
Lower Egypt, and reoccupied Memphis. Ashurbanipal reacted with
vigorous promptitude, and in 667/6 led a second successful invasion of
Egypt. Again, as the Assyrian sources record, Taharqa's army was
soundly defeated, he deserted Memphis, fled to Thebes, and as this city
also was perhaps subsequently taken by Ashurbanipal, Taharqa presumably retired south to Napata.[125] The Assyrian king once more
established the local rulers who, he claimed, had been installed by
Esarhaddon and lately dismissed from their positions by Taharqa. He
then withdrew to Nineveh with many prisoners and substantial booty.
The list of local rulers included in the Assyrian record contains,[126]
among others, Necho, described as king of Memphis and Saïs, many
princes and governors of Delta cities, and, among the few from Upper
Egypt, Mentuemhat, prince of Thebes, whose career will be considered
in the next section. If the Assyrian account is to be believed, the
assumption then must be that the wholesale defection of local rulers
from the cause of the Napatan king was prompted either by true
dissatisfaction with the Napatan regime, or by the wish to avoid serious
trouble through simple submission. In many cases it must be supposed
that self-interest rather than loyalty determined the actions of the local
rulers, and this same self-interest was soon shown again when these same
local rulers plotted against their Assyrian overlord.[127] They undoubtedly
found the rule imposed by Ashurbanipal far more restrictive than they
had hoped, and they turned once more to Taharqa in whom they saw a
less arrogant, and probably less interfering suzerain. To their great
misfortune, however, the plot was discovered, many of the rulers were
captured and sent to Nineveh, while brutal vengeance was taken on the
inhabitants of certain Delta cities, including Saïs, Mendes, and Pelusium.

[123] A 25, 86, 127. See above, pp. 124, 378.
[124] For an analysis of the Assyrian sources, see F 155, 316ff.
[125] A 44, 294. See above, pp. 143–4.   [126] See below, p. 704.
[127] A 44, 294f; also F 155, 320f.

In the aftermath of this retributive action Ashurbanipal took a decision which was to have far-reaching effects both on Egypt and on the future of Assyrian power in Egypt. Of all the local rulers taken from the Delta cities, Necho of Saïs alone was spared, and he, for reasons unspecified in the Assyrian records,[128] was further signally honoured by Ashurbanipal and returned to Saïs as ruler. Necho's son Psammetichus, named Nabashezibanni by the Assyrians, was similarly favoured and made prince of Athribis. By these inexplicable acts of favour,[129] Ashurbanipal in effect founded the Egyptian Twenty-sixth Dynasty, which in due course truly reunited the lands of Upper and Lower Egypt, putting an end to the political disunity which had troubled the land for centuries, and provided the opportunities for foreign interference from the south and the east. As far as Taharqa himself was concerned, nothing further is recorded, and it is likely that he withdrew to Napata where he died in about 664 B.C. He was buried, unlike his immediate predecessors, at Nuri, about seven miles upstream from Gebel Barkal, and on the other side (east) of the Nile.[130] His reign, which had begun with great promise, and which had in its earlier years seen great achievements in Egypt and Nubia, sadly deteriorated in its last years, assailed from within Egypt by fickle, but essentially dissident, Delta princes, and from without by an enemy endowed with great determination, ambition, and a better organization. His legacy to his successor, his cousin Tantamani, was, at least as far as the Egyptian part of his realm was concerned, of very little worth.[131] In one sense, surely, his death marked the end of the Kushite adventure in pharaonic Egypt; although his successor, Tantamani, enjoyed ostensibly a rule of eight or nine years as pharaoh, and was recognized as such at Thebes, the first king of the Saïte Twenty-sixth Dynasty, Psammetichus, dated his reign from the time of Taharqa's demise. Thus Manetho, in the surviving epitomes, brings the Twenty-fifth Dynasty to an end with Taharqa's death.

In fact, Kushite rule in Egypt petered out somewhat ignominiously, although with one strong gesture which unfortunately prompted the most serious Assyrian incursion into Egypt. A great inscription set up by Tantamani at Gebel Barkal tells of a dream experienced by Tantamani, and of the events which brought the dream to fulfilment.[132] On his succession he travelled first to Napata, presumably to accept his Kushite

---

[128] A 44, 295.

[129] F 155, 323, considers it as the conscious acceptance by Ashurbanipal of the failure of the Assyrian attempt to control Egypt.

[130] F 35, 6ff. For the unlikely view that Taharqa was deposed by Tantamani and buried modestly at Sedeinga, see F 60, 8; F 91, 1113f, shows that blocks from an unidentified building of Taharqa have been found in more than one pyramid tomb at Sedeinga.

[131] For Tantamani as cousin and not nephew of Taharqa, see F 83, 43ff.

[132] The 'Dream Stela' (Cairo JE 48863); see F 147, 57ff; translated in F 18 IV, 469ff. The text is newly collated in F 52, 3ff.

realm after Taharqa's death.[133] He then returned to Egypt, made festival especially at Elephantine and Thebes, and proceeded in triumph to Memphis where he fought a bloody battle to occupy the town. Subsequently he attempted to engage the forces of the Delta rulers, but they avoided combat, and chose rather to submit peacefully, accepting Tantamani's overlordship. Such, briefly, is the account preserved in the 'Dream Stela'. A somewhat different version is found in Assyrian records.[134] After succeeding Taharqa, Tantamani (called Urdamane) is said to have established himself in Thebes and Heliopolis, and invested Memphis (held, according to the chronicles, by Assyrians and their Egyptian allies, although Assyrians are not mentioned in the Dream Stela). News of the fall of Memphis reached Ashurbanipal in Nineveh, and he set out to recover his Egyptian dependency. Tantamani fled first to Thebes, leaving Memphis to the Assyrian king, and then from Thebes to Kipkipi (somewhere in Nubia, presumably). Thebes fell to Ashurbanipal, was sacked, and great booty removed from there to Nineveh.

This decisive blow, although not followed by the imposition of a military administration, put an end to Tantamani's rule in Egypt. It seems he never again left Nubia, yet his sovereignty remained formally acknowledged in Thebes, and inscriptions dated to his third year, and as late as his eighth year (656) are reported from that city.[135] The continuity of civil rule under local and provincial officials secured the stability which seems to have prevailed in Upper Egypt throughout this difficult period; to recognize one ruler as legitimate King of Upper and Lower Egypt in preference to another was scarcely more than a formality, representing the need to place a label for dating on the performance or record of some act which required to be fixed in temporal, if not political, terms. The reality of the situation will be examined in the next section. It was a reality in which the Kushite king had no part; he was now a Nubian king alone, and he and his successors were to find it expedient to confine themselves principally to this role for the future. He survived only until about 653, and was buried in a tomb with pyramidal superstructure at El-Kurru, returning, as it were, to the cemetery used by all his royal predecessors before Taharqa.[136]

Nubia did not wholly cease to be a region of significance to the succeeding kings of the Saïte Dynasty; but the attentions devoted to the southern country were determined by events on the sensitive Asiatic frontier, and the policies of Assyria and, subsequently, Babylon. Apart from the major expedition of Psammetichus II, the few indications of hostility between Egypt and Nubia may be thought residual to the

---

[133] The belief that there was a short co-regency is no longer generally held; see F 77, 173; F 123, 193ff, 236.   [134] A 44, 295, 297. See above, pp. 379–80.   [135] F 89, 140f, 187.
[136] F 34, 60ff; F 45, 67ff.

Kushite intervention in Egypt, and the inimical attitude of the Delta rulers, of whom Psammetichus I was the natural heir and successor.[137]

V. THE THEBAN PRINCIPALITY

The strange phenomenon of the recognition, at Thebes at least, of the kingship of Tantamani many years after he had effectively renounced the throne of Egypt and withdrawn to Napata, draws attention to the insubstantiality of that kingship, and to the fact that civil administration (and probably political initiative) depended very little on the presence of the Kushite king in what was his Egyptian capital. Equally, it provokes consideration of the position of the king in the administration and life of Egypt generally throughout the Twenty-fifth Dynasty. The indications, extracted from a reading of the surviving royal inscriptions of the dynasty, do not support a view that the Kushite kings sought much more than to rehabilitate and foster the divine realm of Amun, and, secondarily, the cults of the other principal state gods, and to secure their formal hegemony over all Egypt. Their adventures in foreign affairs, almost invariably disastrous, were, it seems, not prompted by any consistent policy, but by misguided interest in the machinations of Palestinian and Syrian states, compounded with a misjudgement of the competence of their armies in opposition to the well-organized might of Assyria. In political matters the Nubians behaved with extraordinary naivety, failing wholly, it would seem, to grasp the reality of the exercise of power within Egypt. The title King of Upper and Lower Egypt, which represented so potently the overall dominion of the pharaoh throughout Egypt, was accepted as a supreme dignity, but its political implications were ignored. The unity of the north with the south in the understanding of the Egyptian monarchy since the First Dynasty meant the physical control of the whole of Egypt; it was not simply titular. This fact seems never to have been appreciated by the Nubians, and their acceptance from time to time of the submission and formal loyalty of the Delta rulers reveals how little they were able to justify, in the terms of long-established practice, their assumption of the supreme pharaonic designation. It is perhaps not unlikely that they were never in a sufficiently strong position to impose a true unity on the whole of Egypt. They could not have done so without radically changing the administration of the states of Lower Egypt.[138]

As far as it can be determined from surviving records, including the highly inaccurate (but yet significantly informative) historical memoir included in Herodotus' account of Egypt,[139] the practicality of political life within the Delta states during the Twenty-fifth Dynasty was little

[137] See below, Section IX. [138] F 77, 395. [139] Particularly II, 147; F 103, 119.

different from what had obtained in the preceding two centuries. An acceptance of the Kushite hegemony seems mostly to have meant very little in practical terms, and the entrenched positions of the local princes or chiefs were generally as much respected by the Assyrian king as by his pharaonic counterpart. What they had renounced, in some cases at least, was the use of royal designations; what they accepted was a hegemony involving a modest lip-service towards the Kushite king, made evident in the use of his name and regnal year for dating purposes. He was a superior power to whom appeal and submission could be made when the plotting against Assyria went wrong; but his overlordship could equally be rejected when the invading Assyrian forces showed how ineffective that overlordship was.

In 667/6, when Ashurbanipal first invaded Egypt, he reinstalled throughout Egypt, as his record claims, the local rulers who had previously been appointed by Esarhaddon, and subsequently dismissed by Taharqa. Whether or no these rulers had been appointed, dismissed, and reappointed may be doubted, but the list of their names and seats of power is of exceptional interest.[140] It illustrates, in the first place, how the old Delta divisions had survived in the exercise of practical politics. First to be named was Necho of Memphis and Saïs (the old Principality of the West), then nineteen others, including rulers of the four one-time great chieftainships of the Ma, Pekrur of Pi-Sopd (Saft el-Hina), Harsiese of Sebennytos, Buaimi of Mendes, and Shoshenq of Busiris. Other Delta chiefs of important cities were Bakennifi of Athribis, Nahki of Heracleopolis, and Petubastis of Tanis. The list ends with four Upper Egyptian rulers, Djedhor of Siut, Nimlot of Hermopolis, Nespamedu of Thinis and Mentuemhat of Thebes; from which it can clearly be deduced that for the Assyrians Upper Egypt, like the Delta, consisted of a series of small autonomous states, owing some allegiance to the Kushite king, but easily turned from this allegiance to an acceptance of Assyrian suzerainty without noticeable opposition. Here again the divisions of Upper Egypt show to some extent the same situation which faced Py when he led his conquering army to Memphis in 728. The one city with its ruler which might have been expected in the Assyrian list, in addition to those enumerated, was Upper Egyptian Heracleopolis. At the time of Ashurbanipal's campaign, the local 'ruler' was Pediese,[141] whose son, Somtutefnakht, was to become an important ally of the Saïte house in Middle Egypt. Pediese's absence from the list can scarcely be explained except as an oversight, for his history, in so far as it is known, suggests no other reason which might have qualified him for omission.

Of all the rulers named in this Assyrian list, the most notable was undoubtedly Mentuemhat, Prince of Thebes. Much is known about him

---

[140] A 44, 294; F 186, 52ff; F 180, 212ff.   [141] F 77, 234ff.

and also about the other contemporary great dignitaries of the southern capital – not enough, perhaps, to allow a substantial and detailed account of the administration and the processes of government at Thebes to be constructed for this time, but sufficient to indicate how one local administration operated under the Kushite kings. Thebes was the seat of the southern vizir, and the heart of the priestly state of Amun, the domain of the God's Wife of Amun, supported by her influential steward and the priesthood of Amun, at the head of which was the First Prophet, or High Priest, of the god.[142] And yet, the person who undoubtedly controlled the city in the later years of Taharqa's reign, and continued to do so well into the reign of Psammetichus I, the first king of the Twenty-sixth Dynasty, was Mentuemhat, who bore as his principal titles 'Fourth Prophet of Amun' and 'Prince (more precisely, mayor) of the City (i.e. Thebes)'.[143] He belonged to a family whose members had occupied high offices in Thebes for many generations: his great-grandfather and grandfather had been southern vizirs before and after Py's invasion, and two uncles had subsequently held the same office before it passed to another family (that of Nespekashuty).[144] His own father, Nesiptah, had been mayor of Thebes in the reign of Shebitku, if not earlier, and had been succeeded by a nephew, Raemmaakheru, before Mentuemhat assumed the succession.[145] From the earliest times Egyptian bureaucracy, whether in the central administration or in the provincial cities, had demonstrated dynastic tendencies. Succession of office from father to son was at all times common, and had equally at all times to be regarded with caution by the king. During the Twelfth Dynasty Sesostris III found himself obliged to strip the nomarchs (provincial governors) of their powers, which were to a great extent based on feudal practices.[146] In Egypt during the period following the Twentieth Dynasty, the lack of strong central control had resulted in the acquisition of extraordinary power by local families throughout Egypt, and fragmentation of political control in the Delta well illustrates how disastrous to the country as a whole such a reversion to feudalism could be.

In Thebes the process is strongly evident. Religious and civil power lay in the hands of a very few families, whose members and their interconnexions are well documented.[147] But Thebes, because of its metropolitan status, developed a particular and uncharacteristic local administration, which rendered it exceptional among the 'principalities' making up the notional kingdom of Upper and Lower Egypt, especially during the Twenty-fifth Dynasty. Because Thebes contained the mighty cult

---

[142] On the administrative officials of the God's Wife, see F 50 generally.
[143] F 85; F 77, 230f; F 14, 104ff; F 173, 172.   [144] F 114, 71ff.
[145] F 85, 262ff; F 77, 231.   [146] *CAH* I³.2, 505f.
[147] In general, see F 77, 195ff; F 14, 102ff; F 173, *passim*.

centre of Amon-Re, it attracted the primary attention of the Kushite kings, who demonstrated their attachment to the deity not only in building works but also by introducing Nubian princesses into the highest office serving the cult. The first evident act of intervention by the Kushites in Egyptian affairs was the adoption of Amenirdis, sister of Py, by Shepenupet, the God's Wife of Amun. This priestly potentate seemed virtually to be the head of the Theban priestly state in the years leading up to the Nubian intervention.[148] Supported by the priesthood of Amun, the God's Wife became possibly the principal agent of royal power in the Theban area during the dynasty in its early years, although there is little evidence to show in what way she exercised her power beyond the requirements of the cult. Nevertheless, with names written in cartouches, and with a position *vis-à-vis* the deity which is shown to be almost divine, the God's Wife and her adopted daughter enjoyed a status of divine royalty which put them on an equal footing with the reigning monarch. This equality is seen clearly in the way in which they were shown in association with the monarch in temple representations.[149]

Amenirdis succeeded Shepenupet perhaps about 700 B.C., in the reign of Shebitku, and she took as her adopted daughter her niece, Shepenupet II, daughter of Py. When this Shepenupet became God's Wife, perhaps not many years later, she acted with considerably greater independence than her predecessors, for example in the dedicating of monuments in the Theban area – just one indication of the growing power of the God's Wife within an increasingly autonomous Theban state.[150] Shepenupet II adopted in turn a daughter of Taharqa, Amenirdis II, sometimes known as the Younger, and together they exercised their offices of God's Wife and Adorer of the God at Thebes during the time when Mentuemhat held the position of mayor of the city. It was this strong and unusual combination, if not alliance, between the priestly and the civil powers which enabled Thebes to survive the troubles which beset the last Kushite kings, including the invasion of the Assyrians. It was also this combination into which Psammetichus I successfully inserted an influential wedge in 656, when he obtained the adoption of his daughter, Nitocris, by Amenirdis, even though Shepenupet II remained alive in office as God's Wife.[151] To this event a return will be made later. Here it needs only to be pointed out that this act of adoption properly indicates the power and influence of the God's Wife and her associate in the politics of Upper Egypt at that time. The act of adoption in fact represented the annexation of the Theban state by Psammetichus.

Where in this involved constitution did Mentuemhat's function lie? It

---

[148] See F 142, generally. F 61 II, 792, s.v. Gottesgemahlin; F 50 II, 108ff.
[149] For the best summary, F 61 II, 799f; also F 89, 374ff.
[150] F 89, 360f.　　[151] F 169, 335.

is scarcely possible to be precise in determining his role, or in establishing his political relationship with the God's Wife on the one hand, and with the vizir on the other. It is often suggested that Mentuemhat developed his office of mayor of the city into a position of virtual monarchy, although he never attempted to usurp the outward signs of royalty by putting his name in a cartouche, for example. The actuality of his power is clearly demonstrated by inscriptions in a room in the temple of Mut at Thebes, which is commonly called the Crypt of Taharqa.[152] Mentuemhat is shown in a scene with Taharqa, and with his father and son, both named Nesiptah. This scene establishes the somewhat subservient position of the mayor of Thebes, as following behind his monarch; but the inscriptions, which recount Mentuemhat's many works and benefactions for the temples and sacred buildings in his domain, show him in a role commonly occupied by the pharaoh himself. His power was exercised mostly in the Theban area, but extended, nominally at least, far to the south and the north. 'I was mayor of Thebes; all Upper Egypt was under my control, the southern boundary being at Elephantine, and the northern at Hermopolis,' he claimed in an inscription on a fine seated statue of himself.[153] It is not quite a royal claim, but it suggests the exercise of that kind of autonomy practised by provincial nobles in Egypt whenever the central control of the royal residence weakened or failed. Mentuemhat in effect ran affairs at Thebes, and it was in this respect that he was regarded by Ashurbanipal as king of Thebes.

What happened at Thebes during the Assyrian invasion is unrecorded on the Egyptian side. The Assyrian annals give some account of the booty carried back to Nineveh, including two obelisks, possibly of electrum, or electrum-plated,[154] but do not record any physical destruction in Thebes. It is unlikely that the Assyrian army would have taken the city without inflicting damage on buildings, but it is possible that, by some accommodation with the leaders of the invading army, Mentuemhat saved Thebes from the worst excesses of violent occupation. The truth remains unknown, but it is known from the Assyrian side that Ashurbanipal considered Mentuemhat as the ruler of Thebes, even an appointee of Esarhaddon; and from the Egyptian side that Mentuemhat remained securely in office after the Assyrian withdrawal, and up to at least Year 14 of Psammetichus I. Politically he seems to have steered a very successful course through some particularly nasty waters, and in doing so preserved to a great extent the integrity of the Theban state, including the hierarchy of the priesthood of Amun.[155]

---

[152] F 85, 193ff.
[153] Berlin 17271, see F 85, 58ff, pls. XII–XV; F 61 IV, 204, s.v. Monthemhet.
[154] A 44, 295; on the obelisks, F 31, 58f.
[155] F 173, generally.

Mentuemhat's career, in spite of the lack of detailed evidence about it, can be seen as providing an outstanding example of how Egypt functioned administratively, and to a great extent politically, during the Kushite dynasty. Stability lay in the separate states; within the states the administration lay secure in the hands of high officials who exercised their offices by hereditary custom. These officials were mostly native Egyptians. Mentuemhat himself was at one time thought to have been Nubian, but this view is no longer generally held.[156] The Kushite kings clearly saw no need to interfere with established practice, even at Thebes. Here what truly mattered to them was the temple and cult of Amun; by contriving the succession of Nubian princesses to the office of God's Wife of Amun they secured control in religious matters. They strengthened this control further by the appointment of Nubians to the high priesthood of Amun; from Taharqa's reign to the end of the dynasty (and later), the First Prophet was Horemakhet, a son of Shabako, succeeded by his son, Horkhebi; while the office of Second Prophet was at the same time filled by Taharqa's own son, Nesishutefnut.[157] But, in spite of the undoubted strength of Nubian influence in the religious field, the exercise of civil power by Mentuemhat does not appear to have been noticeably pro-Nubian. The débâcle which marked the end of Nubian power in Egypt seems to have left Thebes and its *de facto* ruler singularly unaffected. His power continued unabated well into the first reign of the Twenty-sixth Dynasty, and the condition of his many votive and funerary monuments suggests no deliberate posthumous programme of defacement and destruction. His vast tomb at Thebes (Pls. Vol., pl. 183),[158] which must have been begun in Kushite times, was certainly completed in the reign of Psammetichus I, and there is no reason to believe that he was not buried in it. This was a tomb on a royal scale, especially grand even in the splendid tradition of the time, which may have been initiated by Harwa, major-domo of Amenirdis I. Not even the great vizirs of the Eighteenth and Nineteenth Dynasties had tombs on this scale. In Mentuemhat's case his tomb truly expressed his status in the Theban principality.

VI. THE RISE OF PSAMMETICHUS I

An inscription recording the death of the Apis bull in Year 20 of Psammetichus I provides acceptable proof that this ruler from Saïs dated his reign from the death of Taharqa, ignoring the subsequent reign of Tantamani.[159] He may have employed some of the traditional titles of

---

[156] F 85, 260f.   [157] F 77, 390; F 85, 275.
[158] See F 133 I², i, 56f; F 85, 171ff. On its form, see Eigner, *Die Grabbauten*, 44ff.
[159] F 106, 146 (no. 192), pl. 52; F 125, 267f.

Egyptian royalty in the early years of his reign,[160] but he seems not to have assumed the emotive and significant title 'King of Upper and Lower Egypt' until, perhaps, as late as his Year 9 when he secured the adoption of his daughter, Nitocris, by Amenirdis II, already the adopted daughter and nominated successor of Shepenupet II, as God's Wife of Amun at Thebes. By this symbolic assertion of his supremacy in Thebes, Psammetichus registered the end of Nubian rule in Egypt, a rule which had been less than nominal since Tantamani's withdrawal to Napata in the face of Ashurbanipal's invasion and capture of Thebes in 664 B.C. The act of adoption is recorded on a great stela originally set up in Karnak.[161] It tells how Nitocris set off for Thebes accompanied by a large flotilla under the command of 'the General and Chief of the Harbour' Somtutefnakht, the local ruler of Upper Egyptian Heracleopolis. In this progress to Thebes he acted as 'viceroy' of Psammetichus, and his support was undoubtedly an important factor in the Saïte ruler's move against Thebes.[162] This support was, however, prompted by more than simple political interest; Somtutefnakht's mother was a princess of the Saïte ruling house,[163] and he was therefore possibly a cousin of Psammetichus.

The events and negotiations leading up to the dispatch of Nitocris are mostly lacking from the inscription but, in the preamble before the account of her journey, Psammetichus points out that he is not depriving either Shepenupet II or Amenirdis II of their inheritances, but only inserting Nitocris as the next in line. A great part of the text contains an enumeration of the endowments of land, and of food and drink, made on behalf of Nitocris by various benefactors. It is noteworthy that most of the donated land comes from Lower Egypt and the northern nomes of Upper Egypt, while most of the food endowments come from Delta temples and the great dignitaries of the Amun priesthood in Thebes.[164] This geographical distribution reveals the extent to which Psammetichus' power remained unestablished in much of Upper Egypt at this time. There can be little doubt that by the adoption Psammetichus effectively took over southern Upper Egypt, and he did so with great moderation, seeking not to upset the religious feelings of the powerful priesthood of Amun, or to diminish (formally, at least) the local jurisdiction of the civil authority in the person of Mentuemhat.[165]

The year 656 may therefore be taken as the date when Egypt was once again reunited as a single realm under the rule of a king who fully understood that titles and good religious intentions were not enough to secure lasting loyalty and peace. It was the triumph of a man who had so nearly met with utter disaster earlier in his career, and who was the latest

---

[160] F 46, 66ff.   [161] F 25, 71ff.   [162] F 169, 284.   [163] F 77, 225f, 402f.
[164] F 25, 79f.   [165] F 50 II, 111.

representative of a line whose final success depended as much on Assyrian patronage as on its own resources. The origins and ethnic identity of the Saïte line remain matters of unresolved debate. According to Manetho,[166] the Twenty-sixth Dynasty found its beginning long before the accession of Psammetichus; four royal predecessors are named, the first of whom was Ammeris, described as 'the Ethiopian' (Nubian). If this detail is correct, it may well have been the case that Ammeris was a Nubian placed in control in Saïs by Shabako after he had defeated Bocchoris in about 715.[167] Of the next three 'kings', two remain difficult to identify: Manetho calls them Stephinates and Nechepsos, assigning them seven and six regnal years respectively. The Manethonian tradition does not indicate that these two were blood descendants of Ammeris, and it has been suggested that they represented a new line, possibly related to that of the ill-fated Bocchoris, established in Saïs after Ammeris' death.[168] If this opinion is not capable of proof, neither is it possible to determine whether the re-establishment of the old line at Saïs was due to Nubian action or to the direct (or indirect) influence of Assyria. And yet there remains a strong presumption that there was a Nubian connexion,[169] even though the later policies and actions of the Saïte contemporaries of Taharqa and Tantamani do not show any special sympathy for the Nubian rulers of Egypt.

The obscurity which envelops Manetho's Stephinates (possibly a rendering of Tefnakhte, but not to be identified with the well-known predecessor of Bocchoris) and Nechepsos (probably the Nekau-ba named on one small object)[170] lightens a little when Necho is reached. With him some solid historical ground can be trod, although the tenuous thread of his career is better charted from Assyrian than Egyptian sources. As ruler of the so-called Kingdom of the West with its capital at Saïs, Necho is first mentioned in the Assyrian Chronicle when Ashurbanipal confirms him in his rule of Saïs and Memphis, a position to which he had been supposedly appointed by Esarhaddon in 671.[171] Subsequently, taken captive to Nineveh, and spared with honour and generosity by Ashurbanipal, Necho was reinstalled in Saïs, and his son, presumably Psammetichus, placed as ruler in Athribis.[172] As Psammetichus seems to have succeeded Necho in 664 B.C., it must follow that the latter died at that time, probably in the act of resisting the futile northern strike by Tantamani which marked the beginning of his reign.[173] It is not improbable that Necho, like Tefnakhte in the face of Py's northern advance, found himself in the position of being the leader of northern

---

[166] F 174, 169ff.   [167] F 77, 145.   [168] F 77, 145. See *CAH* III².1, 574.
[169] F 112, 19f; F 182, 364; F 55, 26.
[170] F 77, 146. There is insufficient evidence to allow any serious discussion on the length of the reigns of these early Saïte rulers.
[171] See above, p. 700.   [172] See above, p. 701.   [173] See above, p. 702.

opposition. But there is no evidence to show that he occupied any special position of authority over his fellow dodecarchs. That he is commonly referred to as Necho I is more a way of distinguishing him from his grandson Necho II, a fully accepted ruler of all Egypt, than a gesture of recognition of a kind of royalty in his case. It was left to his son Psammetichus to achieve, first a dominion over the other Delta rulers, and, eventually, the full pharaonic titles of an Egyptian king with his appropriate powers and authority.

How Psammetichus achieved his supreme position in the Delta is a matter of considerable speculation. Satisfactory argument is not much helped by the stories told by Herodotus and other classical writers, although more than a substratum of true fact may be detected in much of what Herodotus, in particular, writes. After Necho's death, it is not at all improbable that Psammetichus was obliged to flee to Assyria, to be installed later in his expected princedom of Saïs by Ashurbanipal after the latter's devastating invasion of Egypt in 664/3. Subsequently if Herodotus is to be believed (II.151), Psammetichus secured a spurious primacy among his fellow dodecarchs by pouring a libation in the temple of Ptah at Memphis from his bronze helmet, thereby fulfilling an oracle which foretold that he who should pour a libation from a cup of bronze would become king of all Egypt. Sent in exile to the Delta marshes, he eventually secured his triumph over the other dodecarchs with the aid of Carian and Ionian pirates. It has very reasonably been suggested that, in this employment of foreigners by Psammetichus, may be seen the use of a force sent by Gyges, king of Lydia, to help the Saïte prince in about 662 B.C.,[174] an act, perhaps, of defiant independence on the part of Gyges, but not one aimed directly at Assyria. The situation in the Delta when Psammetichus became prince of Saïs was almost certainly very unsettled. He had probably retained the favour of the Assyrian king, while his fellow dodecarchs may (all or some) have lost the trust formerly placed in them by Ashurbanipal through their temporary defection to Tantamani in 664. Nevertheless, as a young ruler Psammetichus seems to have felt uncomfortable in his relationship with the other Delta rulers, and there is nothing to suggest that there was any kind of Assyrian occupying force in Egypt on which he could call if trouble occurred. In such uncertainty Psammetichus no doubt felt it necessary to look elsewhere for the means to support his regime, and would surely have welcomed a Lydian force.

Neither Egyptian nor Assyrian sources indicate that Psammetichus was hostile towards Assyria. On the contrary, he had every reason to be grateful to Ashurbanipal, and probably enjoyed some form of favourable relationship with Assyria.[175] It was not therefore necessary for him to recruit foreign mercenaries to expel Assyrians from his domain;[176] but

---

[174] F 158, 134ff; F 161, 402f; F 103, 133.   [175] F 155, 323; F 158, 136f.   [176] F 97, 15f.

such strangers could be of use in helping him to further his plans to take over the whole of the Delta. In pursuing such a policy he clearly rejected the assistance of the Libyans, on the one hand, while at the same time he must have felt confident that his actions would not be seen as hostile by the Assyrians. The means by which Psammetichus succeeded in dominating the whole of the Delta can only be surmised. With the support of foreign mercenaries he was no doubt in a position to use force of arms, and it may be supposed that in the case of some of the independent principalities force was used. But the threat of force may have been sufficient to persuade some of the dodecarchs to accept Psammetichus' overlordship, and to renounce their grandiose titles and claims to independence.[177] The fulfilment of his policy did not, however, come quickly, and it is unlikely that the last principality fell to him before his seventh or eighth year. Here was no whirlwind campaign, but a process of skilful, and probably relentless, pressure.

With the Delta generally under his control,[178] Psammetichus was free to turn to Upper Egypt, where, in a sense, the writ of the Nubian house still ran. He had already a strong ally in the local ruler of Heracleopolis, first Pediese (up to Psammetichus' fourth year), and Somtutefnakht thereafter.[179] This Heracleopolitan house had, in all probability, ties with the Saïte ruling house through marriage, and possibly also by territorial connexions with the Delta. It is not surprising, therefore, that Psammetichus should have used Somtutefnakht to conduct Nitocris to Thebes for her adoption by Amenirdis II in his Year 9. In so doing he behaved in a singularly diplomatic way. To have taken his daughter himself to Thebes would have been excessively provocative in the circumstances of the time. Recently established in the Delta, and making a claim for the Theban principality and all Upper Egypt, he chose not to arouse active opposition by a show of direct force in Thebes. By what steps he brought about the acceptance of the proposal for the adoption is unknown. There may have been long negotiations and even threats, for there could have been no doubt at Thebes that, by accepting Nitocris, the college of Amun and the civil authorities were also accepting Psammetichus as their new ruler.

If the account given on the Adoption Stela can be trusted, Nitocris was welcomed in Thebes with enthusiasm. It may, however, be supposed that Mentuemhat and his fellow administrators at Thebes had no special reason to think that the overlordship of Psammetichus would be any more direct than that of the Nubian king (who had not been in Thebes for eight years or more), or that of the Assyrian king (who never settled in Egypt). If they were mistaken in thinking this way, they were

---

[177] Progress charted in F 77, 400f.
[178] The caution shown in F 158, 139 may be unwarranted.   [179] F 77, 402f.

in the event not to be too disturbed in the continuation of their local administration. Psammetichus had every intention of fulfilling the role of King of Upper and Lower Egypt, which he proclaimed himself to be in the text of the Adoption Stela, but he moved cautiously, it would seem, seeking to extend his control more by persuasion, and by refraining from making changes until suitable occasions presented themselves.[180] Thus Mentuemhat remained mayor of Thebes until he died, when he was succeeded by his son Nesiptah, who continued in office until almost Year 25. Again, in the new appointment of a major-domo for Nitocris, the chosen candidate, Aba, was not a northerner brought in specially to support the Saïte princess.[181]

Internal affairs engrossed the attention of Psammetichus in the first decade of his reign, and he was singularly fortunate in not having to face serious trouble from outside. The direction from which most trouble might have come was the east, but the potential threat of Assyria might not have been recognized in the Delta after the defeat and flight of Tantamani. The evidence provided by the earlier Egyptian campaigns from the time of Esarhaddon to that of Ashurbanipal suggests that the Assyrians first were hostile to the Nubian regime in Egypt, and secondly were content to allow local rulers to continue in power provided that they did not meddle in the politics of the Levant. What advantage Assyria gained from such a relationship was seemingly modest: peace on her western frontier; but in those troubled times peace in the west was not to be discounted.

Likewise, there is only slender evidence to support the belief that there was an encounter between the forces of Psammetichus and those of Nubia, perhaps even at Memphis. The vague details of such an encounter, preserved in Greek authors, are implausible and not sufficiently substantiated to carry much weight, and the tenuous Egyptian evidence does nothing to provide a solid basis for these later fictions.[182] Nubia must have been considered a source of possible armed attack, but in the absence of convincing evidence, skirmishing on the southern border of Egypt remains no more than a reasonable probability.[183]

Herodotus reports that, after the Carian and Ionian mercenaries had completed the tasks for which Psammetichus had engaged them, he settled them in two 'camps' on the Pelusiac branch of the Nile north of Bubastis, where, it has been supposed, they could best watch the routes into Egypt from Asia.[184] It is, however, possible that these 'camps' were so sited for reasons of internal security in a region recently annexed to the Saïte dominion, and possibly still unsettled. What is noticeable is that

---

[180] F 69, generally; but see F 158, 139 with n.51.   [181] F 49, 201ff; F 50 II, 110.

[182] F 77, 405; F 158, 137.

[183] F 116, 29f, argues strongly in favour of a Nubian encounter; see also F 41, 476f; also below, Section IX.   [184] E.g. F 97, 17; F 99, 137.

Psammetichus did not apparently feel that any great threat was posed by the Libyans, constant provokers of trouble in preceding periods. There is some evidence of skirmishing in the area between the Faiyūm and the Mediterranean, but the crucial texts[185] do not report hostilities of a sufficiently serious character to be described as a Libyan war.[186] Year 11, in which one of these texts is dated, may have marked the end of any immediate trouble from Libyans, and it may also be taken as the date when Psammetichus could reasonably have considered his unification of Egypt to be complete, and the borders of his realm secure.

VII. THE SAÏTE CONCERN WITH ASIA

At the outset of its dominion over Egypt, the Saïte dynasty was fortunate in being able to regard with some equanimity the power of Assyria in Western Asia. In a sense Necho I and Psammetichus I were puppet princes, owing their positions to the backing of Ashurbanipal, but the client character of Psammetichus' relationship with the Assyrian king after the first few years of his reign seems never to have been more than nominal, and possibly even less than that. It has already been suggested that the supposed Assyrian presence in Egypt was negligible; it is by no means unlikely that in the course of Psammetichus' reign Egypt became in the eyes of the Assyrians a support and buttress in the west, a potential ally in the expected trouble brewing to the east in Babylon. On the basis of Egyptian records, and in the absence of contrary evidence from Assyrian and Biblical sources, most of Psammetichus' reign represented a time of peace vis-à-vis Asia. The sole records to the contrary are contained in two passages of Herodotus, one of which (II.157) states that the Egyptian king laid siege to Ashdod, the Philistine city, which fell after twenty-nine years. The other passage (I.105) tells how Psammetichus turned an invasion of Scythians away from Egypt by presenting them with gifts and entreaties. The lack of confirmatory evidence of any kind has generally led historians to throw doubt on both of these occurrences,[187] but there is some reason to believe that there was Egyptian activity in Asia, at least towards the end of Psammetichus' reign.[188]

In the Babylonian Chronicle for 616 B.C. there is mention of an Egyptian army allied with an Assyrian army in pursuit of the Babylonian king, Nabopolassar, as far as Gablini on the Euphrates.[189] In this mention can be found the first positive evidence of the Egyptian involvement in Asiatic politics since the start of the Twenty-sixth

---

[185] F 47, 33f; F 12, 57ff.   [186] So F 158, 140.
[187] F 112, 30; F 75, 17; F 33, 576; for the contrary view, F 169, 338; F 163, 49ff.
[188] F 159, 223; F 103, 146ff.   [189] A 25, 91. See above, p. 179.

Dynasty – an involvement on the side of Assyria which would in due course develop, at times promisingly, but ultimately, disastrously. It is easy to find in the actions of the successive Egyptian rulers a foolhardy attraction towards the complicated politics of their Asiatic neighbours, but it should be remembered that for one thousand years Asia had been the source of repeated danger for Egypt. The lesson, which had never been learned, was that small-scale intervention in the affairs of the small states of Palestine and Syria provided no long-term solution for the aggressive intentions of the powerful empires which lay further east. Egyptian activity in Asia Minor attracted hostile attention; it was no effective deterrent. During the Twenty-fifth Dynasty the threat was Assyria; during the Twenty-sixth Dynasty it became Babylonia.

Although the evidence is so slight, it is difficult to avoid the conclusion that, towards the end of Psammetichus' long reign of fifty-four years, a distinct change of policy led the Egyptian king to take vigorous action in Asia Minor in alliance with the Assyrians.[190] This active policy was continued by his successor, Necho II, who became king in 610. The Babylonian Chronicle records that late in that year the Assyrian king, Ashur-uballiṭ II, together with a supporting Egyptian army, abandoned Harran before the advance of Nabopolassar's forces.[191] No doubt the Egyptian army had been sent while Psammetichus I was still alive, but its ignominious withdrawal probably took place after the new king had assumed the double crown.[192] In the following year Harran was retaken, Ashur-uballiṭ again receiving substantial Egyptian help;[193] but neither Babylonian nor Egyptian records provide any information about the immediate sequel of this action. The presence of Egyptian forces in Asia may be explained on the grounds both of possible treaty obligations towards the Assyrians, and of the defence of a recently established Egyptian hold over Phoenicia and Lebanon, the only positive evidence for which is the doubtful siege and taking of Ashdod, mentioned above, and a reference on an Apis stela of Psammetichus' fifty-second year to chieftains who pay taxes to Egypt, and who seem almost certainly to have been Levantine.[194]

Necho's own appearance in the field at this time, unmentioned in the Babylonian record, is supported by the Biblical accounts[195] of the attempt made by Josiah, king of Judah, to obstruct an Egyptian advance to the Euphrates which may possibly have formed a prelude to the successful Harran campaign of 609.[196] The opposing armies met at

[190] F 182, 374.

[191] A 25, 95; see above, chapter 25, for the general movements in Asia at this time and, in particular, p. 182. [192] F 41, 474f. [193] A 25, 96.

[194] F 133, III².2, 797; see F 41, 477; F 159, 228f.

[195] II Ki. 23: 29–30; II Chron. 35: 20–5; also Jos. *Ant. Jud.* x.74–80.

[196] For the date see F 182, 377ff. See above, pp. 182, 390.

Megiddo, the site of a famous victory by Necho's illustrious predecessor, Tuthmosis III, in 1481 B.C. Josiah was killed, his army defeated, and his son and successor, Jehoahaz, replaced after a reign of three months only, by his own brother Jehoiakim. Necho is said to have secured this change, taking Jehoahaz captive to Egypt, and extracting a substantial tribute from Judah. Attention has been drawn to the relatively generous attitude of Necho towards Judah in comparison with the subsequent severe treatment meted out by the Babylonian king.[197] Apart from the fact that the Egyptian king did not seek to establish an empire in the conventional sense in Asia Minor, he had far more to gain in his expected confrontation with Babylon by retaining an undestroyed state of Judah with a compliant king. For a few years, therefore, Necho may have been able to maintain a general, but loose, control over a large part of Asia Minor, extending from the Mediterranean as far eastwards as the Euphrates in the north at Carchemish, including Judah and possibly some of the former Assyrian tributary states lying between.[198] At Carchemish in particular there are some traces of Egyptian occupation during Necho's reign.[199]

While the nature and extent of Necho's Asiatic empire are matters wholly of speculation, it is at least possible to discern good reason for the presence of an Egyptian army in Western Asia at this time. The sudden collapse of the Assyrian domination after 609 resulted in a serious void of power which threatened to be filled by the aggressive forces of Babylon.[200] Egyptian arms had overcome a Babylonian force in 609; the opposition therefore could not have seemed invincible. Subsequent events were to some extent encouraging. In 606, to counter aggressive moves in the region of Carchemish, an Egyptian army laid siege to, and captured, the town of Kimuhu, south of Carchemish, with its Babylonian garrison, and later in the year the same, or another, Egyptian force left Carchemish, crossed the Euphrates, and defeated the Babylonian army at Quramati, forcing it to withdraw.[201] These provocative acts stimulated the Babylonians into quick and decisive action. The Babylonian Chronicle describes, in its laconic manner, the campaign in which the crown prince, Nebuchadrezzar, destroyed the Egyptian army in comprehensive manner. Early in 605 he led his force north, crossed the Euphrates, and engaged the Egyptians who were encamped at Carchemish. His victory was complete, and he followed it up by destroying a second Egyptian force at Hamath, to the south west of Carchemish.[202] The massive defeat of the Egyptian forces led to the rapid abandonment of Asia Minor by Necho, and to the occupation of the whole region by the Babylonians. It had dire effects on the history of Judah, and in

---

[197] F 159, 226f.   [198] F 182, 382.   [199] F 133 VII, 398.   [200] See above, chapter 25.
[201] A 25, 98. See above, pp. 230, 394.   [202] A 25, 99.

consequence was suitably recorded as a catastrophe by Jeremiah (44: 2–8), and later described in vivid detail by Josephus.[203]

Whether or no Necho himself led his army in this disastrous campaign, its outcome surely convinced him of the futility of trying to maintain an Egyptian imperial presence in Asia. In the aftermath of Carchemish Egypt was spared an immediate attack on its eastern frontier by the death of Nabopolassar, which brought Nebuchadrezzar back to Babylon to claim his throne. The Babylonian king, however, campaigned regularly in Western Asia in the following years, and Necho wisely seems to have refrained from engaging in ill-considered interventions. A letter from the ruler of a Phoenician city requesting help against the Babylonians, and invoking some treaty between his city and Egypt, almost certainly belongs to this time.[204] Necho in the meanwhile reserved his forces for the inevitable assault by Nebuchadrezzar, which came eventually in 601. The Babylonian record describes the encounter, presumably on Egypt's eastern border (although no exact location is given):[205] a bitter battle took place in which both sides inflicted heavy casualties on each other, and the Babylonians were obliged to withdraw to Babylon. To that extent, therefore, the encounter may be counted an Egyptian victory, for Necho had successfully preserved his kingdom from invasion with all its dread accompaniments.

The domination of Western Asia by Nebuchadrezzar was now complete, and Necho probably pursued an interest in the region only through the development of his naval policy, which is discussed later. The only possible recorded action taken by him on land in Asia after 601 would be the campaign recorded by Herodotus (II.159), in which he supposedly gained a victory at Magdolos and captured Kadytis (possibly Gaza), but there is at present no certainty about the location of the places mentioned, or of the time at which the events took place.[206] There is no reference to such a campaign in the Babylonian Chronicle, but that reliable source does record in the following years the frequent campaigns by the Babylonian king. Thus was Necho discouraged from active land intervention, and his most reliable ally, Jehoiakim was, according to Josephus,[207] disappointed that no Egyptian army was sent to encourage him to oppose Babylon. In consequence, the stand made by Jehoiakim received the expected chastisement from Nebuchadrezzar in the spring of 597. Jehoiakim himself avoided personal ignominy by dying just before the Babylonian assault, but his young son Jehoiachin was taken captive to Babylon and replaced by Zedekiah, Jehoiakim's uncle.[208] The

---

[203] *Ant. Jud.* x.86. For all sources, see A 932, 23ff. See above, pp. 182–3.
[204] F 182, 387f; F 159, 230, with useful bibliography.   [205] A 25, 101. See above, pp. 232, 398.
[206] F 182, 389f; see F 41, 475; F 103, 161ff.   [207] *Ant. Jud.* x. 88–9.
[208] See above, chapter 30; A 932, 32ff.

caution which marked Necho's policy towards Asia in the last years of his reign seems to have been accepted as reasonable and prudent by his son and successor, Psammetichus II, who succeeded in 594. His first concern in the field of foreign policy was Nubia, and the campaign of Year 3, described later in this chapter, formed the main preoccupation of this king during his short reign of six years. It is not impossible that some of the Semitic mercenaries who took part in the Nubian campaign, and who left their names in graffiti at Abu Simbel, had been specially sent to help Psammetichus II as a result of the conference held in Jerusalem by Zedekiah, perhaps just before the launching of the expedition.[209] The slender evidence certainly suggests that Judah retained some kind of treaty attachment to Egypt throughout the years when Asia Minor was dominated by Nebuchadrezzar. But when this domination weakened, the Egyptian king was not slow to encourage his Asiatic allies by making a peaceful expedition to Khor (generally, Syria–Palestine).[210] The one record of this unusual event places it in Year 4 of Psammetichus II (591/90);[211] it must, therefore, have taken place either immediately after the end of the Nubian campaign or before its end, but when its outcome was no longer in doubt.[212]

Although Psammetichus' progress through Syria–Palestine, as described in P. Rylands IX, was completely lacking in warlike demonstration, its effect could only have been one of encouragement to the king of Judah and his associates, who had already displayed a readiness to revolt from Babylon. It may be supposed that it was Psammetichus' own intention to turn against Babylon, but unfortunately for his Asiatic allies their trust in the ability of their Egyptian champion – now to be seen as the triumphant victor of Nubia – was wholly misplaced. Not long afterwards Psammetichus fell ill, and in 589 he died. Consequently Nebuchadrezzar, who no doubt had fully appreciated the significance of the renewed understanding between Judah and Egypt, was encouraged to make a move against Zedekiah. Even before Psammetichus' death he laid siege to Jerusalem in the early months of 589, and, according to Biblical sources, an Egyptian force was sent to succour the garrison.[213] It is thought that this force would have been sent by Apries, the successor of Psammetichus II, but no confirmation is to be found in Egyptian records. The Jewish account tells that Nebuchadrezzar intercepted the Egyptian force before it reached Jerusalem, inflicted a severe defeat on it, and drove the Egyptians from the whole of Syria.[214] In no way, therefore, was Apries able to prevent the ultimate fall of Jerusalem in 586. His only line of action, in maintaining an Asiatic policy, was to

209 F 41, 476; see above, chapter 30.   210 F 43 I, 180*ff.
211 F 51 II, 95f (Pap. IX, 14.16–15.9).   212 F 41, 479; F 159, 233.
213 Jer. 37: 5; see *Ant. Jud.* X.110.   214 F 41, 481. See above, p. 234.

operate by sea along the Levantine coast.[215] The maritime strategy of the
Egyptians throughout the greater part of the sixth century was based on
their inability to achieve any kind of success in Asia by conventional land
expeditions.[216] It seems to have been an alternative strategy, whereas in
earlier times land and sea operations were conducted jointly, forming
two parts of a single strategic plan.[217]

Unwilling, and very probably unable, to risk his forces in the field
against the Babylonians, Apries nevertheless seems to have sustained a
tenuous support for Judah, unappreciated though this support might
have been by those Jews like Jeremiah and Ezekiel who could think no
good of Egypt. After the fall of Jerusalem in 586, many Jews who had
escaped deportation by Nebuchadrezzar to Babylon took refuge in
Egypt,[218] adding their numbers to those who had earlier settled in that
land with, apparently, the permission, if not encouragement, of the Saïte
rulers. According to later tradition, it was to secure the extradition of
these Jews that Nebuchadrezzar invaded Egypt in 571, killing Apries
and replacing him, presumably, with Amasis.[219] Egyptian sources are
silent on this invasion, which should not probably be identified with the
encounter between Babylon and Egypt mentioned in a reliable, though
incomplete, Babylonian text dating it to 568,[220] Year 37 of Nebuchadrezzar and Year 2 of Amasis (who had in fact succeeded Apries through a
military coup in 570). With insufficient evidence available, it is impossible to determine with any precision what happened between the two
powers in these crucial years. It is unlikely that Nebuchadrezzar played a
major part in the struggle which led to the fall of Apries, but it is not
improbable that a tradition developed out of an incursion by Nebuchadrezzar into Egypt in 571, of which neither Egyptian nor Babylonian
records have preserved any mention. It would have occurred at the time
of the conflict between Apries and Amasis, and might have had some
influence on the outcome of that conflict. It has been suggested that
Amasis may have led an Egyptian army into Asia soon after his
accession, and it is the clash between this force and Nebuchadrezzar
which is recorded in the Babylonian text mentioned above.[221] If so, it
seems to have been his sole adventure by land to the east. The sea was to
provide the arena for his principal external operations, as the next section
will make clear.

Amasis spent the greater part of his reign of forty-four years involved
with affairs at home, and in the eastern Mediterranean. But during this
time there developed in the east a threat which became the common

[215] See below, p. 724, for Apries' campaign against Tyre and Sidon.   [216] F 112, 60.

[217] F 41, 482, for earlier parallels. Apries may have followed this pattern at the outset of his reign,
but after his repulse from Jerusalem he found it impossible to maintain.

[218] Jer. 43: 6.   [219] See F 159, 236f, for the sources and traditions; F 37, 13ff.

[220] A 932, 94; F 159, 236f.   [221] F 159, 243.

concern of Egypt and of Babylon, now less menacing after the death of Nebuchadrezzar in 562. Persia, under the vigorous Cyrus II (*c.* 558–529) rapidly overcame those powers which had dominated the politics of Asia for the past century or more.[222] Media was the first victim, and it became apparent to the surviving states that some form of mutual support would be necessary to meet the Persian challenge. Amasis formed a treaty of alliance with Croesus, king of Lydia,[223] and a similar treaty was formed between Lydia and Babylon. When Cyrus attacked, Croesus was disappointed in his expectations of help from his allies, and his kingdom quickly fell into Persian hands. Babylon was soon to follow, and Egypt's turn was postponed probably only by Cyrus' death. His son, Cambyses, delayed by internal problems within his empire, finally marched on Egypt in 525, only months after Psammetichus III had succeeded his father, Amasis.[224] In his march Cambyses received vital advice from Phanes of Halicarnassus, a mercenary leader of the Egyptian army, who had, for unknown reasons, deserted the Egyptian cause. At Pelusium the two armies met, the Egyptian force being strongly augmented by Greek and Carian mercenaries. The battle was fierce and bloody, the Persians won the day, and the Egyptians withdrew in disorder to Memphis. With little difficulty Memphis was taken, and along with it Psammetichus III and his family. According to Herodotus, the Egyptian king's life was spared, but he was subsequently slain when he was discovered plotting an insurrection against Cambyses. So died the last king of the Saïte dynasty, and Cambyses, now declared King of Upper and Lower Egypt, inflicted a final insult on that royal line by having Amasis' body exhumed and desecrated. It was a miserable fate for a monarch who had added so much lustre to the Egyptian tradition in the last years of pharaonic rule.

VIII. THE GROWTH OF EGYPTIAN MARITIME POLICY

Among the notable events recorded by Herodotus for the reign of Necho II, three involve the sea, or the facility of using the sea: the cutting of a canal linking the Nile with the Red Sea (II.158), the establishment of squadrons of triremes for action in the Red Sea and the Mediterranean (II.159), and the dispatch of a Phoenician sea-borne expedition to circumnavigate Africa (IV.42). The plausibility of these events has been much debated, and they will shortly be considered in more detail. They may here, however, be employed to introduce two of the most striking developments of the Saïte period, the construction of an Egyptian navy,

---

[222] See generally F 75, 32ff.

[223] Hdt. I.77. The treaty with Polycrates of Samos was also probably entered into with the Persian threat in mind; see below, p. 725.

[224] For the whole campaign and aftermath, Hdt. III.4–16. See *CAH* IV², 254ff.

and the prosecution of an active maritime policy. Some reference has already been made to the latter in the preceding section, with the suggestion that Necho first turned to the sea when he found that land action in Asia proved too costly.[225] There must, nevertheless, have been other reasons to encourage such a change of policy, and it may be found in the advice which Necho may have received from some of his senior Greek mercenaries, men who might well have had considerable experience in warfare by sea.[226] Unlike the Egyptians, the Greeks were by necessity, and probably by inclination, accomplished sailors, using the sea with confidence and skill. It would surely have been a matter of sensible policy for Greek mercenary leaders to urge their Egyptian employer to provide them with naval equipment without which they could not operate at full efficiency.

To request good fighting ships was not in itself sufficient; the ships had to be built, adequate timber obtained, and a proper complement of craftsmen and sailors recruited for the equipping and manning of the ships. It has reasonably been suggested that Necho could have found all the skilled Greeks he needed at Naucratis,[227] a city founded by Greeks for Greeks, and a centre of Greek trade, and, therefore, a hive of maritime activity. Although there remains much doubt about the date of its founding,[228] there are grounds for believing that Naucratis was well established by the last decade of the seventh century.[229] In addition, it lay only a short distance to the west of Saïs, Necho's capital. In a discussion concerning the origins of Necho's commitment to a naval arm, almost everything is open to doubt, not least the importance of Naucratis in fulfilling the requirements of the initial inspiration. It can be doubted that Naucratis played any part, if only on the grounds that the young settlement was at that time probably little more than a river station. But even if it could not have provided from its own population the craftsmen and sailors required, it could certainly have acted as a recruiting centre, a magnet drawing the many displaced Greeks ready to serve the pharaoh of Egypt.

There is agreement that what Necho set out to do was to build up an Egyptian navy, albeit one manned by Greeks. There is, however, lively debate on whether the ships he had constructed were built to a Greek or a Phoenician design. The argument is probably not yet settled; it is carried forward on points of detail of design (often hypothetical) considered to be either typically Greek or typically Phoenician, and on the determination of which people can claim priority in inventing the trireme.[230] There appears at present to be more positive evidence, and indeed more

---

[225] See generally F 112, 60ff.   [226] F 98, 55ff.   [227] F 98, 57.
[228] See *CAH* III².3, 37ff.   [229] F 97, 24ff; F 103, 222ff; F 169, 329.
[230] F 103, 160 for full bibliography.

persuasive argument, on the side of the Greek (Corinthian) design, though it is accepted that the wood for the construction of the triremes was, almost without a doubt, obtained from the Lebanon (Phoenician). It is, further, likely that Necho in his intention, and in his subsequent prosecution of policies, would have relied more on the Greeks resident in Egypt and serving in his forces (their presence and service are well attested), than on Phoenicians (for whom the evidence is less ample).[231]

With very little information about Necho's maritime involvement coming from Egyptian sources, it is difficult to do more than suggest when he undertook to construct a navy.[232] Herodotus places the cutting of the canal before the building of the triremes, and this sequence has indicated to at least one writer that the decision to build triremes was taken as a direct result of the disasters suffered by the Egyptian army on land in Asia.[233] The suggestion has already been made in the previous section that Necho concentrated on naval activities after the disaster of Carchemish and its aftermath, but there is no reason to suggest that the naval resource was not already available and in service at that time. The construction of a canal between the Nile and the Red Sea implies the development of a maritime policy which would require easy access between the Mediterranean and the Red Sea; that it was not fulfilled in Necho's reign represents failure of execution, not lack of intention. Herodotus states that the canal was abandoned by Necho after the loss of 120,000 lives, and that it was completed by Darius I, a fact that is fully confirmed by inscriptional evidence.[234] The belief that Necho actually completed the canal, which subsequently sanded up, to be re-excavated by Darius, remains unproved;[235] but there is some substance in the view that Necho may have based his canal on an existing irrigation canal leading from the Nile above Bubastis along the Wadi Tumīlāt.[236] The purpose of the canal may have been wholly military in conception, but considerations of trade would surely have entered into the scheme at an early stage. The argument that a revival of trade with Punt, inspired by the antiquarian inclinations of Saïte rulers, formed the principal reason for cutting the canal is difficult to support,[237] but such a consideration should not be ruled out. There may, in fact, have existed a more general interest in the Red Sea and the trade routes south, which can be seen in Necho's other maritime exploits, as reported by Herodotus.

The second of these exploits, the establishment of squadrons of triremes in the Red Sea and the Mediterranean, probably indicates the

---

[231] F 182, 371f.
[232] A fragmentary stela from Elephantine, dated to Necho's reign, enumerating ships, mentions warlike activity in an unspecified context; see F 68, 89f.
[233] F 182, 372; but see F 103, 160.
[234] F 135, 259ff. Necho's canal may have taken a different course; see F 61 III, 312.
[235] F 182, 369f.   [236] See, e.g. F 100, 142ff; also F 15, 138.   [237] F 100, 143ff.

maturing of his maritime policy. As far as the Mediterranean is concerned, there is no reason to doubt what Herodotus says; the history of naval activity in that sea during Necho's reign and subsequently confirms the existence of a substantial Egyptian fleet. That it was equipped with triremes of Greek or Phoenician design is debatable, but its existence is not. Equally there is no reason to doubt the setting up of a squadron in the Red Sea, although there is no independent evidence to support its existence. What may be questioned is the purpose of this second naval force. Herodotus states that both squadrons were intended for military purposes, and it is not impossible that the Red Sea force may have been conceived as part of the general defence of Egypt against Babylonian attack. But it is by no means clear how it might have been employed tactically, and it is unlikely that Necho would have been advised by his Greek counsellors to embark on the expensive construction of a squadron of triremes, the employment of which might be in doubt. The suggestion that the Red Sea force was intended to neutralize pirates and other hostile groups operating from the Gulf of ʿAqaba and from the coast of the Arabian peninsula is, on the other hand, much more acceptable, especially in view of the steps taken later by the Ptolemaic rulers of Egypt to counter pirate attacks in the third century B.C.[238]

Herodotus' report of the circumnavigation of Africa by Phoenicians commissioned by Necho is not included in the historian's general account of the achievements of Necho's reign, and the validity of the story has been much questioned. The voyage is supposed to have lasted three years, the mariners replenishing their food stores by laying up at the appropriate season to plant and harvest crops. In general, Egyptologists have been inclined more to accept the historicity of the account than to reject it.[239] The crucial detail in its favour is Herodotus' statement that the mariners in the course of their voyage unexpectedly found the sun on their right; this fact was rejected by Herodotus, and his rejection has been considered conclusive in testing the reliability of the account.[240] Weighty arguments have, however, been used to demonstrate the implausibility of what Herodotus says,[241] and it must be admitted that the manner in which the circumnavigation is introduced (in a discussion of continents) is not a little melodramatic: Necho's extraordinary achievement points up the ignominious failure of a similar Persian enterprise, the abortive voyage of Sataspes.[242]

Nevertheless, the circumnavigation of Africa, whether myth or fact, forms firmly a part of the tradition which credits Necho with the establishment of a properly organized Egyptian naval arm.[243] His forethought, or that of his advisers, was seemingly amply justified when,

---

[238] F 100, 145ff.   [239] F 112, 62f; F 182, 370; F 109, 44f. See above, p. 471.
[240] E.g. F 33, 584.   [241] F 100, 148ff.   [242] Hdt. IV.43.   [243] F 112, 60ff.

at the end of the seventh century, he ceased to be able to operate by land in Asia Minor.[244] Mobility by sea would provide him with the ability to prosecute an active foreign policy which might bring valuable advantages to Egypt. Unfortunately, there is no direct evidence of subsequent maritime operations by Necho. Herodotus' statement that Necho used his fleets wherever they were needed (II.159) is far too inexplicit to give substance to the claim that the later years of his reign were marked by naval activity (presumably against the Phoenician littoral).[245] But it is fair to make the claim that during this time and later, through the possession of a naval arm, the Saïte kings were enabled to foster important contacts with Greek maritime powers – a development of mutual interest between Egyptians and Greeks which was to be of particular value to Egypt in the future.

More substantial evidence of the importance of the navy during the Twenty-sixth Dynasty is provided by the surviving records of important Egyptian officials bearing naval titles.[246] Pa-akhrof, an 'overseer of king's ships', was a contemporary of Psammetichus I;[247] others holding the same title were Hor and Yewelhen, who served under Psammetichus II, Psamtik-meryptah, one of Amasis' captains, and Tjanenehbu and Hekaemsaef, who also served during Amasis' reign.[248] The activities of these officials are, sadly, wholly unknown. Something, however, is known of the career of Udjahorresne; in a biographical inscription on a statue in the Vatican Museum he states that he commanded the king's sea-going (probably naval) ships during the reigns of Amasis and Psammetichus III.[249] Surviving the Persian invasion, he remained in favour during the reigns of Cambyses and Darius, serving them as chief physician, not in a maritime capacity. While the career of this apparent turncoat provides no solid information about his naval duties under the last Saïte kings, it does indicate that the holding of high naval office might not be accompanied by more than nominal responsibility for the activities of the pharaoh's navy at sea. Similar nominal responsibilities may have represented the naval duties of the other high officials mentioned above; but the very need to assign naval titles to high officials must have arisen from the existence of an active navy.

The first positive record of the use of the Egyptian navy in hostile action comes in Herodotus' account of Apries (II.161).[250] He states that, in the course of his reign, Apries attacked Sidon by land and Tyre by sea. There is doubt not only about the date of this expedition, but also about whether the land attack was mounted from the sea or by a force which

[244] See above, p. 717.   [245] Implied by F 159, 232, 236.
[246] See especially F 48, 168ff; also F 112, 61f; F 159, 235f.   [247] F 129, 269ff.
[248] F 19, 19.   [249] F 134, 1ff, 164ff; F 102, 166ff.
[250] Also Diodorus 1.68. See above, p. 470.

had marched overland from Egypt.[251] After the defeat of the Egyptian army sent to relieve Jerusalem in 588, most of Asia Minor was almost certainly under the control of Nebuchadrezzar, and there would surely have been no possibility of an Egyptian force operating by land. Seaborne operations, therefore, would have been not only strategically more sensible, but also tactically more practicable. There is some reason to believe that Apries' move against the Phoenician cities was the result of an invitation from the Phoenicians themselves, in an attempt to engage the Egyptian king in the Phoenician struggle with Babylon, which had not so far been carried to a final outcome. If this were the motive behind Apries' campaign, whether by secret agreement or openly admitted, it would suitably account for the determined effort made by Nebuchadrezzar subsequently to reduce Tyre by siege – a task which is said to have taken him thirteen years.[252] It has also been suggested that Apries' purpose was principally to sustain Egyptian commercial interests in the eastern Mediterranean.[253] But at this time, with the main opposition provided by the might of Babylon, it would have been difficult to consider commerce as an activity easily to be carried on without territorial supremacy or a state of truce.

Egyptian naval activity in the mid-sixth century extended well beyond the coastal plain of Syria–Palestine. Diodorus reports a victory over Cypriot arms (1.68) in Apries' reign, and the island itself was taken by the Egyptians in the reign of Amasis;[254] this conquest is not confirmed by other evidence. There can, however, be little doubt that through maritime contacts, supported by naval activity, the last Saïte kings were able to maintain lively commercial and diplomatic relations with states which formerly lay well outside the traditional Egyptian sphere of interest. Here to the greatest extent knowledge depends on the information supplied by Herodotus. He alone reports the treaty between Amasis and Croesus of Lydia (1.77),[255] and his alliance with Polycrates of Samos (III.39ff). Herodotus makes much of Amasis' partiality for the Greeks, which led not only to the establishment of Naucratis as a monopolistic emporium for Greek trade, but also to donations and favours granted to temples in Greece and the Greek islands (II.178–82).[256] There is, on the other hand, not much evidence that his infatuation (for such it is made out to be) was reciprocated beyond the requirements of common expediency.[257] Polycrates readily switched his allegiance to Persia in 525 when Cambyses had secured the Phoenician cities and fleet, and Amasis' navy no longer appeared to offer the kind of protection which had been expected when the alliance between Samos

[251] F 41, 481ff; F 159, 234; F 33, 596. See above, p. 718.   [252] So F 90, 18; F 41, 483.
[253] F 159, 235.   [254] Hdt. 11.182; F 103, 240.   [255] See above, p. 720.
[256] F 103, 163, 221ff.   [257] On Amasis and the Greeks, see further below, p. 737.

and Egypt was concluded.[258] With former maritime allies in desertion, and the Levantine harbours denied as havens, the Egyptian navy, towards the end of Amasis' reign, lost its ability to operate freely in eastern Mediterranean waters. When, therefore, the Persians finally attacked Egypt by land, there was little that the Egyptian navy could do to help in defence, particularly as it may have been partly, or wholly, neutralized by the Phoenician navy and by defections of high-ranking officers like Phanes of Halicarnassus and Udjahorresne. Although this sad conclusion may diminish the achievement of the navy which Necho had, with such sagacity, developed at a time when Egypt's land forces were capable of little success, that navy's presence in the Mediterranean in time provided the Saïte kings with a resource which projected the attention of their essentially conservative and archaizing regime to the vigorous emerging states of the Greek world.

IX. THE NUBIAN CAMPAIGN OF PSAMMETICHUS II

When Tantamani withdrew to Napata before the invading forces of the Assyrians, he left the field in Egypt open for a comprehensive assumption of power by the prince of Saïs, Psammetichus I. It is impossible to say whether the Kushite monarch retained any hope of returning to Egypt when circumstances appeared propitious, but there is little evidence to show that either he or any of his immediate successors attempted to mount an expedition of restitution. Nevertheless, the Napatan kings continued to use Egyptian titles and insignia for centuries, and retained the use of the hieroglyphic script for royal and funerary purposes. In these respects, therefore, they demonstrated an attachment to things Egyptian which might have been construed as embodying a simple nostalgia for the years when the Nubian dynasty ruled Egypt. It could also have been interpreted as containing the desire for a revival of Nubian power in Egypt. For the Saïte rulers the latter might be thought the more likely interpretation. Tantamani had gone, but he or one of his successors might return. The relative quiet on the southern frontier during the period between 656 when Psammetichus I installed Nitocris in Thebes, and 591 when Psammetichus II dispatched his army into Nubia, no doubt did much to persuade the Saïte kings that no serious trouble would come from the south.[259] The disillusionment brought about by the movements which led to Psammetichus' attack would amply account for the violence of that attack, and the subsequent measures taken against the memorials of the Kushite kings in Egypt, mentioned below.

---

[258] F 120, 79f.
[259] For the belief in campaigns by Psammetichus against Tantamani, supported by the slenderest evidence, see F 145, 135f; F 116, 30; F 103, 133.

The southern frontier of Egypt at Elephantine was one of the places where Psammetichus I established a camp for his foreign mercenaries, and, according to Herodotus (II.30), the garrison there mutinied after having remained unrelieved for three years. He states that 240,000 mercenaries deserted and marched south, ignoring an appeal made by the Egyptian king himself. They offered themselves to the Nubian king, who in return gave them land for settlement far to the south of Meroë. This story of trouble in the frontier garrison may find a trace of support in a fragmentary text found at Edfu, dated by context to the reign of a king Psammetichus. Wawat (Lower Nubia) is mentioned, along with a slaughter by the king's army, and the bringing back of booty to the king's palace.[260] Unfortunately, this Edfu text can only be tied to the reign of Psammetichus I by a slender thread of evidence, and it may, in any case, be a record of a simple military expedition into Wawat unconnected with the mutiny.[261] A fog of uncertainty envelops this mutiny, even if the improbability of the huge number of deserters reported by Herodotus is left out of consideration. It is not impossible that a conflation should be made with the better supported mutiny which occurred in the reign of Apries, discussed below. Tradition talked of a mutiny of a garrison at Elephantine; Psammetichus established the garrison at Elephantine; therefore, the mutiny took place in the reign of Psammetichus I; so it was reported by Herodotus.[262]

Apart from this doubtful event, relations between Egypt and Nubia remained, apparently, quiet until something occurred in the south which roused Psammetichus II to make a pre-emptive strike. In the inscription celebrating the coronation of the Nubian king Aspelta (c. 593–568), mention is made of the presence of a Nubian army in the neighbourhood of Abu Simbel at the time of the death of Anlamani, Aspelta's predecessor.[263] The mustering of a force in Lower Nubia could only have been regarded as a threat by the Egyptians, and it was probably to counter any resumption of Anlamani's plans by Aspelta that Psammetichus attacked. Parts of the official record of the expedition are preserved on royal inscriptions found at Shellāl,[264] Karnak, and Tanis;[265] they provide some details of the campaign, which took place in Year 3 of Psammetichus II (591). The Tanis stela confirms that Psammetichus acted in response to a Nubian threat. He accompanied his army as far as Elephantine, and it then proceeded southwards, making for a region named Shas, which has reasonably been identified with the district containing Napata, the principal city of the kingdom of Kush at that time. The Shellāl and Karnak stelae report the arrival of the army at

---

[260] F 56, 323ff, pl. xxb.   [261] F 144, 201.

[262] F 99, 125ff, examines Herodotus' account in great detail, and favours a revolt probably by troops of Libyan extraction; cf. F 112, 41f.   [263] F 147, 86 (l.2 of text); F 52, 51; F 144, 203.
[264] F 8. 225ff.   [265] F 146, 157ff.

Pnubs, which lay in the Dongola Reach, south of the Third Cataract, and the Tanis stela records the first victorious encounter at a place, Ta-dehnet ('The Hill'), which may have been in the neighbourhood of Dongola,[266] or at Gebel Barkal itself.[267]

Further valuable details of the campaign are provided by graffiti left at Abu Simbel by foreign mercenaries, Carians, Semites,[268] and Greeks. A short Greek text names two of the leaders, Potasimto (i.e. Pedismatawy), who commanded the foreigners, and Amasis, who commanded the Egyptians; it confirms that Psammetichus came only as far as Elephan-tine, and states that a force under Psamtik, son of Theocles, penetrated Nubia to Kerkis, *as far as the river allows*. This Kerkis may have been Kurgus, well beyond the Fourth Cataract, in the region where early Eighteenth Dynasty boundary texts have been found,[269] and not so far short of Meroë, which was to become the principal city of the Nubian kings from this time, probably as a result of the success of this Egyptian expedition.[270]

The vigour with which Psammetichus launched his attack on Nubia, and the success which attended the efforts of his army, testify to the outstanding qualities of the king and to the remarkable organization of the Egyptian military forces. The foundation of the success may perhaps be distinguished in the steps taken by Psammetichus I to establish permanent garrisons in strategic parts of Egypt, the troops from which, mostly mercenary foreigners, could quickly form the core of any army needed for hostile action. Not least of the problems faced in an expedition of this kind were those of servicing the fighting troops – the logistics of the campaign. It is not even known whether the Nile was used; but ships in sufficient quantity, it may be assumed, could not easily have been provided to convey more than part of a large army. There is no evidence to suggest that Necho, as part of his ship-building programme, constructed flotillas for river use, although the Nile had always been Egypt's highway. A damaged stela of his reign found at Elephantine, and containing an enumeration of ships, has no apparent relevance to river activity or to Nubia.[271]

A lasting result of Psammetichus' expedition was a deep-rooted hostility towards the Nubian kings, which was expressed immediately in a campaign of destruction aimed at the monuments of the Kushite kings of the Twenty-fifth Dynasty. The campaign probably began in Nubia itself with the smashing of royal statues at Gebel Barkal;[272] it was extended subsequently to Egypt where the Kushite royal names on

---

[266] F 146, 183.   [267] So F 6, 93.
[268] Phoenicians, see F 146, 188; Jews, see F 41, 476; also above, pp. 428, 718.
[269] F 133 VII, 233; F 5, 36.   [270] So F 6, 94; on the idea of a 'capital' in Nubia, see F 1, 269f.
[271] F 68, 83.   [272] F 146, 203.

monuments were systematically hammered out, and one of the two *uraei*, commonly found in representations of these kings, cut away; sometimes both *uraei* were destroyed.[273] Psammetichus also followed up his Nubian campaign by what appears to have been a triumphal, but peaceful, progress into Syria–Palestine,[274] in the course of which, no doubt, the success of the Nubian expedition was suitably emphasized. This visit may well have been a prelude to a serious intervention by land into Asia Minor by the Egyptian king. He was, however, denied further military triumphs by his untimely death in 589.

There is substantial agreement now that the Nubian campaign of 591 was a much more important event than it was formerly thought to be.[275] As far as Egypt was concerned, it served particularly as a reviver of confidence; for Nubia it represented a defeat of the greatest magnitude. Thereafter, in the south, the focus of official life apparently drifted to Meroë – whether that city can be described as a 'capital' or not – and there were no further suggestions of hostile action against Egypt. It is, however, undoubtedly a misjudgement to claim that Nubia and Egypt after 591 'had few interests in common. Both were now second-rate powers, preoccupied with local affairs.'[276] In matters of trade alone the southern country remained of vital importance to Egypt. Rock inscriptions in the region of Elephantine and the First Cataract, containing the names of Psammetichus II, Apries, and Amasis, testify to an abiding Saïte interest in this border area, and it has very plausibly been suggested that this interest must be linked with the important routes passing south from there.[277] Furthermore, Nubia may have been defeated, but it had not been destroyed, and a proper vigilance had to be maintained by the Egyptians.

The biographical inscription of Nesuhor relates how he was appointed by Apries to a position equivalent to that of viceroy of Kush during the New Kingdom.[278] His commission was to put down rebellious countries, and he reports that he broadcast the terror of Apries in the southern lands. This last claim may be taken as a conventional, but meaningless, boast; but more significant is Nesuhor's account of the mercenary revolt mentioned above. The rebels, consisting of Greeks, Asiatics, and other foreigners, declared an intention of defecting to Shasheret (possibly 'distant' Shas, or 'upper' Shas), by which they probably meant Napata, or the residence of the Kushite king. Nesuhor states that he managed to talk them out of their defection, and delivered them over to Apries, presumably for punishment. This unsettling episode, possibly a repetition of the suspected revolt under Psammetichus I, emphasizes

[273] F 146, 192f; F 179, 215ff.   [274] See above, p. 718.
[275] For a more cautious assessment, see F 160, 23.   [276] F 1, 268.
[277] F 56, 317ff.   [278] F 18 IV, 507f; on Nesuhor, see F 124, 162; F 117, 14.

the danger inherent in maintaining large forces of professional soldiers, probably insufficiently employed, on the outposts of Egypt. The revolt under Apries, however, may not have been specifically concerned with conditions on the southern frontier; it may have indicated a more general malaise in the country, a dissatisfaction with Apries which led eventually to his downfall. But, as far as the southern garrison was concerned, there were surely particular reasons for disgruntlement, not least of which were the heat and the distance from the settled foreign communities of Memphis and the Delta. Yet, to defect to the south, to the even more inhospitable region of Nubia, postulates exceptional dissatisfaction. It is known that Nesuhor continued his career under Amasis,[279] but there are no further indications of activities carried out by him on the southern frontier. The lack of evidence suggests that there was no more trouble in the south, either with rebellious mercenaries or with Nubia, during Amasis' reign. Nevertheless, a substantial indication of the continuing importance of Elephantine at that time – an importance which could scarcely, in any case, have been open to question – is provided by the great granite stela set up there, in which the events accompanying Amasis' assumption of the throne are described.[280] The Cataract region formed the southern gateway to Egypt; it was a suitable place for the public display of important inscriptions, especially if they carried texts, like the Amasis text, charged so distinctly with royal propaganda. Here visitors from Nubia could read of his triumph, and carry back to Napata or Meroë the implied message: keep away from Egypt; Amasis will not fail to meet an attack with strength and fury.

X. DOMESTIC POLICIES AND INTERNAL AFFAIRS OF THE SAÏTE KINGS

With the reunification of the whole of Egypt in the early years of Psammetichus I, the political situation within the country presented many problems requiring the attention and skill of the new King of Upper and Lower Egypt. The anarchy which had prevailed for centuries in Egypt, scarcely dispelled by the indeterminate rule of the Kushite kings of the Twenty-fifth Dynasty, had been an anarchy of a not wholly destructive kind. It was a political rather than a cultural anarchy; it manifested itself in the fragmentation of the country, especially in the north. Not only administration, but to a great extent sovereignty also, was exercised locally; but so well established was the general administrative system of Egypt that the practice of government in the small principalities and semi-autonomous states showed, as far as can be judged, an extraordinary adherence to ancient forms and procedures.

[279] F 117, 14.   [280] See below, p. 736.

Egypt did not necessarily fall apart when central government failed because it was not a confederacy of states, diverse in customs, language, and religion, but a nation with strong regional characteristics, the regions to a great extent being identifiable with the old nomes, or with groups of nomes. The lack of central government, however, led inevitably to a breakdown in common services, the maintenance of water-ways, the administration of justice over the whole land, the organization of agriculture and taxes, and, above all, the prosecution of national policies in the field of foreign affairs. When Psammetichus I reunified the country, his principal task was to bring the parts together again, to take up in his own grasp the threads of administration which had remained in the hands of provincial rulers for so long.[281]

The first requirements for the re-establishment of a central administration were a firm hand and determination. Reconstruction, in the simplest sense, represented the diminution of locally based political power, and the enforcement of the writ of the pharaoh. The need for firmness was greater undoubtedly in Lower Egypt than in the south. The Delta dynasts, the dodecarchs, had become accustomed to a high degree of independence, even though, throughout the Twenty-fifth Dynasty, they had owed their very existence on the one hand to the interference of the Assyrians, and on the other to the lack of resolve of the Kushite kings. Upper Egypt had remained very much within the ambit of royal power, although, again locally, there existed much independence. But Egypt was not a congeries of warring states, and there was evidently the greatest freedom of movement throughout the country. Land could be held by temples, for example, in many parts of the country, and the same seems to have been the case for individuals, even officials highly placed in their local administrations, as the text of the Nitocris Adoption Stela reveals.[282]

The difficulty of discovering how Psammetichus established first his supremacy, then his authority, over the Delta states has already been mentioned.[283] It has also been suggested that the camps for mercenaries set up in the eastern Delta were intended as much to impress Egyptians and keep them in order as to protect the eastern frontier.[284] In the south, the means by which he established his authority in Thebes have equally been described in the account of the adoption of Nitocris by Amenirdis II in 656.[285] This act, accompanied no doubt by various diplomatic moves, marked Psammetichus' acceptance at Thebes. It was apparently an acceptance without opposition, and already in the following year the Nile-level inscription on the quay at Karnak was dated in Year 10 of the Saïte king.[286] In return, the administration of Thebes was left, virtually

---

[281] F 55, 75f; F 69, 96ff. [282] F 25, 75f, 99f. [283] See above, p. 711.
[284] See above, p. 713. [285] See above, p. 709. [286] F 13, 54, no. 39.

unaffected, in the hands of the mayor of the city, Mentuemhat. Psammetichus' seeming forbearance may have represented an act of reciprocity,
but it may more probably have been characteristic of his general policy
throughout Egypt. He did not tamper with good administration unless
it was made necessary for reasons of prudence. It has frequently been said
that he and his successors introduced northerners into senior positions in
Upper Egypt,[287] and while some clear cases can be identified, the process
should not be overstressed.[288] In particular, there is no reason to think
that Psammetichus I looked with special favour on the northerner as
such; it was in the Delta that he surely had found the greatest opposition
to his rule. Furthermore, it was in the Delta that pretensions to the
reacquisition of divested power and past glory might be expected to be
detected in the behaviour of the nomarchs in the recently re-established
nomes. Possible examples of such behaviour have, however, almost
certainly been incorrectly identified.[289]

Nevertheless, it would be wrong to maintain that Psammetichus and
the later Saïte kings did not practise favouritism and nepotism in making
appointments. The arranged adoption of Nitocris is a prime example of
the latter. On the other hand, the commissioning of an officer of
Memphite origin, Djedptahiufankh, to command a force including
mercenaries of foreign origin in Thebes,[290] probably represents simply a
sensible choice of a man with the right kind of experience. Equally, in the
preferment of Nesenwiau, who was made governor of eight cities in
Upper and Lower Egypt and 'observer' (whatever that may signify) in
Thebes,[291] a very special appointment must be recognized. By such
commissions, and by relying on the support of old allies like Somtutefnakht, the harbour chief of Heracleopolis (also, probably, a relative),[292]
order was slowly restored to the fragmented administration of Egypt.

In the subsequent history of Thebes, similar steps were taken by the
Saïte kings to perpetuate the administration of the old southern capital,
the political power of which had long waned, even though it remained
important as a religious centre. There is not much indication, however,
that the control of southern Upper Egypt was seen as needing the close
attention of the king.[293] A papyrus from Thebes, dated in Year 14 of
Psammetichus I, reveals not only the weight and grandeur of the Theban
priesthood and officialdom at the time, but also the extent to which
offices remained in the old Theban families.[294] Other papyrus evidence
shows that by Year 17 Nesiptah had succeeded his father Mentuemhat as
Fourth Prophet of Amun and Overseer of Upper Egypt; and Nesiptah
himself seems to have died before Year 25.[295] At the same time the

---

[287] F 77, 405.   [288] See the judicious remarks in F 116, 31.
[289] F 55, 65.   [290] F 116, 21ff.   [291] F 138, 42ff; F 69, 97.   [292] See above, p. 709.
[293] F 116, 31.   [294] F 126, 14ff.   [295] F 126, 24.

southern vizirate remained in the family which had held the office over three generations, the last incumbent being Nespekashuty.[296] In the relatively uneventful environment of Thebes, and apparently in other major centres which had lost their former political function, the business of local and, particularly, temple administration, with the attendant perquisites of property and wealth, became matters of principal concern to the holders of office.[297] The enjoyment of official and temple revenues, becoming an end in itself, led not unexpectedly to abuse, and there is some evidence to show that among the initial problems dealt with by Amasis later in the dynasty was administrative and temple corruption.[298]

The highest priestly office at Thebes, that of the God's Wife of Amun, had been occupied by Nitocris for an unknown number of years when, in his first regnal year (595) Psammetichus II arranged for her to adopt his daughter, Ankhnesneferibre.[299] In this way royal control in the great priestly college of Amun was perpetuated for the remaining years of the dynasty. Ankhnesneferibre succeeded Nitocris in Year 4 of Apries (584), and remained in office until the arrival of the Persians. By assuming the title First Prophet of Amun probably at this same time she further strengthened her authority at Thebes, and she took steps to see that the position would not regress after her death by passing the pontifical title on to her own adopted daughter, Nitocris II, a daughter of Amasis. There is little to suggest that the Saïte kings found much to worry about in Theban affairs,[300] but the concentration of power and wealth in the hands of their female representatives provided a temptation for unscrupulous local advisers. It is not surprising, therefore, to find that the successive major-domos who managed the affairs of Ankhnesneferibre were all from families of Saïte origin, appointed no doubt with clear political intent. Successively they were Shoshenq, son of Harsiese, Pedineith, and Shoshenq, son of Pedineith.[301]

Although records and monuments from Thebes provide a large part of the surviving documentation of the Twenty-sixth Dynasty,[302] there can be no doubt that the focus of Egyptian life, both culturally and politically, lay in the north of the country. Saïs remained the city which held the affections and loyalty of the royal house, and it was to Saïs that the dead kings were brought for burial.[303] Unfortunately, no substantial remains of the period have as yet been discovered at Saïs,[304] where the modern town of Sā el-Hagar covers much of the ancient city; while the standing remains, and results of excavation at Memphis, the administra-

---

[296] F 113, 195f; F 114, 71ff. [297] F 69, 97f; F 55, 64f. [298] F 66, 277f.
[299] For text, see F 142, Textanhang 4; also F 61 I, 264f; II, 805; F 50 II, 111. For Ankhnesneferibre, see Pls. Vol., pl. 188.
[300] F 119, 187. [301] F 27, 83ff; F 50 I, 74ff, 149–50, 151ff.
[302] See further, next section. [303] Hdt. II.169.
[304] F 133 IV, 46ff; F 146, generally.

tive capital throughout the Twenty-sixth Dynasty, are almost equally disappointing.

Memphis was closely linked with Saïs in the original domain of Psammetichus I, and it was both natural and sensible that the old northern capital of Egypt should achieve the status of administrative capital during the Twenty-sixth Dynasty. The importance of Memphis had indeed never been greatly diminished, but now there was a striking increase in its fortunes, marked by extensive royal buildings[305] (now for the most part comprehensively ruined), but also by the large number of substantial burials of high officials in the Saqqara necropolis, the most notable of which is the tomb of Bakenrenef, northern vizir under Psammetichus I.[306] Court officials of all kinds chose to be buried at Saqqara in tombs which show a striking revival of funerary architecture and decoration. Nothing like them had been constructed at Saqqara since the prosperous days of the New Kingdom.[307] The evidence of a vigorous administrative society in Memphis during this time is to be found not only in this expansion of funerary practice, but also in the development of the various religious complexes connected with the ancient funerary cults established at Saqqara. The results of excavation, particularly in the northern sector of the Saqqara necropolis, have provided many indications of the Memphite society which supported these cults.[308] A picture of a flourishing capital city is slowly being retrieved from the tattered documents of the period somewhat later than the sixth century; but it is quite evident that the importance of Memphis throughout the last centuries of pharaonic Egypt sprang from the revitalization which had taken place in the Saïte period.

One of the most significant developments during the Twenty-sixth Dynasty was the steady increase in the numbers of foreigners who came to Egypt, not only to serve as mercenaries, but also to engage in trade, and to settle permanently in the country.[309] The important part played by foreign mercenaries has already been discussed in earlier sections of this chapter, and the special contribution of the Greeks is dealt with later in this volume.[310] Substantial evidence of foreign settlements in the Memphite region comes from both literary and archaeological sources.[311] Quarters of the city were given over to Greeks, Carians, Phoenicians, and, possibly a little later, Jews. Excavation in the city area proper has not as yet produced much tangible evidence of these foreign enclaves; but gravestones from the Carian cemetery have been found in quantity at Saqqara, reused, no doubt after the wilful plundering of burials during

[305] F 133 III². 2, 830ff; Kemp, *MDAIK* 33, 101ff; *idem.*, *GM* 29, 61. For a comprehensive review, see F 65.   [306] F 133 III², 2, 588ff.   [307] F 71, 181.   [308] F 151, 13ff.
[309] F 168, 316ff.   [310] *CAH* III².3, chapter 36a.   [311] F 151, 12.

the Persian period.[312] There were other Carian settlements elsewhere in Egypt,[313] but the Memphite *Karikon* was undoubtedly the most important. It is not clear, however, whether this foreign quarter should be identified with the camp to which Amasis is said to have transferred the Carians when he moved the Ionian and Carian mercenaries from the Delta to Memphis, to protect himself, as Herodotus says (II.154), probably erroneously, from the Egyptians. It is likely that the funerary remains at Saqqara represent the burials of members of a civilian community of Carians.

There are similar problems over the establishment of Jewish communities at Memphis and other places in Egypt. In the troubled times of the seventh and sixth centuries there were many occasions when Jews would have found it expedient to flee to Egypt. Jeremiah (44: 1) specifies colonies of Jews at Migdōl (Pelusium), Tahpanhes (Daphnae), Noph (Memphis), and Pathros (in Upper Egypt), all seemingly civil settlements. Jews were also found among the mercenary troops employed by the Saïte kings, particularly in the army used by Psammetichus II against the Nubians in 591.[314] Large numbers of fragmentary papyri written in Aramaic have been found at Saqqara, but they, for the most part, belong to the period after the Persian invasion;[315] the community which generated these documents probably dated back to the sixth century or earlier, like the parallel and better documented Jewish colony at Elephantine.[316] It has recently been suggested, on the basis of somewhat subjective evidence, that the latter colony may have been founded by survivors of those Jews left behind in Egypt after the Exodus, more than five hundred years earlier.[317]

Much of the improved condition of Egypt during the Saïte period was due to the influx of these foreign settlers, in respect both of the security of the country and of its commercial performance. Substantial credit for allowing, and indeed encouraging, the immigration of foreigners must be granted to Psammetichus I. If one may judge from his reported actions, however, he was not blind to the dangers inherent in such a policy, and the steps taken later in the dynasty by Amasis to confine Greek commercial activities to Naucratis surely indicate that the situation had become in some respects difficult to control. It may be wondered to what extent there was sufficient direct contact between Egyptians and foreigners in the dealings of daily life. Psammetichus I had, according to Herodotus (II.154), established a corps of interpreters

---

[312] F 107, esp. 6f.   [313] F 61 III, 333ff; also F 108, 2.
[314] The reference in the Letter of Aristeas, 13, to the Jews sent to help Psammetichus against the Ethiopians probably concerns the campaign of 591 B.C.; see F 128, 108.
[315] F 149, 7f.   [316] B 187, 41f.   [317] F 105, 89ff.

to facilitate mutual understanding between Egyptians and Greeks, and similar steps were probably taken for other foreign groups. All may not have been well, however, and a mutiny (or mutinies) of mercenaries at Elephantine may have shown up only one aspect of a general dissatisfaction which eventually led to the downfall of Apries.

According to Herodotus (II.161; IV.159), the event which brought the trouble to a head in Egypt was the sending by Apries of an army of Egyptians against the Greeks of Cyrene in Libya, at the request of the Libyans.[318] The Egyptian army was conclusively beaten, and its survivors revolted from Apries on their return from Libya. Amasis, a member of Apries' entourage, and a native of Siouph in the Saïte nome,[319] was sent to quell the mutineers, but was persuaded by them to become king. Herodotus further reports that Apries mustered an army of Greek and Carian mercenaries, and a battle was fought near Momemphis in the western Delta. Defeated by Amasis' force, Apries was captured and taken to Saïs, where he was at first treated with great kindness. When Amasis found the extent to which his predecessor was loathed, he handed him over to the populace, who strangled him. He was then properly buried, with the honours of a king, in Saïs. A much-damaged stela in red granite from Aswān tells a somewhat different story.[320] It is dated in Year 3 of Amasis, and it contains an account of the battle which took place at Sekhetmefkat, a place near Terenuthis on the Canopic branch of the Nile. As far as can be determined from the fragmentary text, Amasis encouraged his troops by reminding them of the ruin brought to Egypt by the Greeks; in the battle Apries was slain, and subsequently buried with honour, as Herodotus reported.

Without further evidence it is impossible to determine with greater precision the circumstances by which Amasis became king. It would seem, however, that for three years after his usurpation of the throne he reigned in parallel with Apries. There can scarcely be any suggestion of a co-regency,[321] in the usual Egyptian sense, for Amasis had no blood-relationship with the main line of Saïte royalty. The evidence of stelae dated to Year 1 of Amasis strongly suggests that from the beginning of his reign his rule was widely recognized. Apries, presumably, had withdrawn to Delta retreats with his Greek supporters, awaiting the opportunity to depose Amasis. In the meanwhile Amasis had begun the task of rehabilitation, which seems to have been necessary throughout Egypt.

The impression gained from the classical accounts of Amasis' reign is of the rule of an efficient legislator who brought great prosperity to

---

[318] F 103, 169ff, 178f.   [319] See F 119, 183.   [320] See F 28, 1ff.
[321] F 66, 263f.

Egypt.[322] The extent to which Amasis himself should receive the credit for the well-organized administration of the last decades of the Saïte period is open to question. It has been suggested that his role was not so much that of an innovator as of a disciplinarian who tightened up a good system which had been allowed to become slack.[323] From the time of the Twenty-sixth Dynasty numbers of private business documents have survived, revealing a freedom in the conduct of private affairs far beyond anything enjoyed by ordinary Egyptians in earlier periods.[324] The increase in private land-holdings led to new independence for local officials, and this development posed something of a threat to the state. One measure by which the Saïte kings endeavoured to curb excessive wealth was the encouragement of the donation of land by influential private persons to temples,[325] a practice which had existed in earlier times, but was now exploited systematically, so it seems, as a matter of deliberate policy.[326] Among the problems Amasis found it necessary to solve after his assumption of power was corruption in the exercise of temple administration in some parts of Egypt.[327] He was also obliged to reorganize the administration of customs at the principal ports of entry into Egypt, and in this matter again there is evidence suggesting that affairs had fallen into disarray, either during Apries' reign, or as a result of the struggle between Apries and Amasis.[328] The tightening up of commercial practices undoubtedly lay behind the restriction he placed on the Greeks to operate through Naucratis alone. Herodotus reports the act as one of signal favour (II.178); it may indeed have appeared so at the time he visited Egypt, because through the restriction Naucratis itself flourished.[329] In origin, however, it must surely be seen as a curbing measure.

The long periods of peace with which Egypt was blessed internally throughout the Twenty-sixth Dynasty provided ideal conditions for the establishment and maintenance of good administration, and a climate of confidence in which agriculture and commerce could flourish. The evidence for the prosperity of the land, which undoubtedly reached a high point in the reign of Amasis, lies as much in the manifestation of culture and art, to be discussed in the next section, as in the direct documentation of private transactions. The Greeks had already appreciated the opportunities offered in this recently opened country. Others,

---

[322] Hdt. II.173–7; Diodorus I.68.95. Herodotus' picture of Amasis as a slightly disreputable *bon vivant* is probably based on a posthumous tradition also found in a story preserved on the reverse of the Demotic Chronicle, of fourth-century date; see F 165, 26ff.

[323] F 66, 252ff.   [324] F 33, 587; F 150, 45ff.

[325] On donation stelae, see F 148, 33ff; F 143, 2, 141; F 110, 605ff; F 82, 77ff.

[326] F 69, 97f; F 33, 585f.   [327] See above, p. 733.   [328] F 136, 117ff.

[329] F 103, 222ff.

with more violent intentions, were to follow, and they were sadly to destroy the substantial edifice of Saïte success.

XI. ART AND CULTURE DURING THE NUBIAN AND SAÏTE DYNASTIES

From the visible manifestations of life and culture which have survived from the seventh and sixth centuries B.C., in particular the sculptures of royal and private persons, and the design and decoration of temple buildings and tombs, a strong impression has been obtained that 'archaism' was the cultural keynote of the times.[330] Yet, while it is undoubtedly true that, in matters of art and religion in particular, the inspiration of much that is characteristic of the period may be found in the works and beliefs of earlier times, it is equally possible to discern a general upsurge of purpose and enthusiasm in many fields of activity which owes very little to a backward-looking attitude to life. The paradox of Egyptian culture in the Saïte period is that the Egyptians, who had been quite suddenly exposed to the harsh realities of power politics, and been obliged to adapt their ways in life to accommodate the progressive ideas of the foreigners in their midst, nevertheless chose to express themselves in art and religion by an eclectic attention to the products of much earlier times. It was not the action of a people trying to revive a glorious past to escape the decadence and misery of their present. It may be seen rather as an attempt, in a period of true renaissance, to express the prevailing enthusiasm in forms which represented the best of the past, or which at least were thought to do so. Exemplars were consciously sought and copied – copied not slavishly, but with the subtle adaptation employed by skilled artists and craftsmen seeking their inspiration in ancient models.

The archaizing tendencies of the period, which cannot be discounted, are, however, on examination confined almost exclusively to the sphere of religion, both in its daily practice and in its funerary aspect. It is not surprising, consequently, that 'archaistic' has become the principal epithet applied to Saïte culture, for the majority of surviving monuments and objects are religious. To adjust the picture, the inadequate evidence of secular documents needs to be considered. Can a collection of papyri, scarcely more in bulk than would fill a few moderately sized files,[331] be set in the balance opposite a wealth of sculpture and funerary monuments, and yield a significant result? In this matter bulk is not the criterion. Through the content and variety of private papers, which lack the

---

[330] Hall in *CAH* III¹, 316ff; F 33, 588ff; F 3, 132ff.
[331] For the range and number of documents, see F 143, 3, 93ff.

tendentiousness of royal propaganda and the bland platitudes of religious texts, a more reliable picture can be built up of the life of the times. It was long ago pointed out that, dating from about the reign of Shabako, legal texts begin to survive in ever-increasing numbers, a phenomenon to be explained by some significant legal or commercial change.[332] These texts deal with transactions of all kinds, resulting from private activities in business and daily life: contracts for sales of buildings, lands, and general commodities; wills, commercial accounts, legal proceedings, mostly of a civil nature. Greek tradition credited Bocchoris of Saïs, the ephemeral king of the Twenty-fourth Dynasty, with reforms of Egyptian law, in particular that he 'brought more precision into the matter of contracts'.[333] His short reign straddled the last years of Py and the first of Shabako. Reform was in the air, brought about probably by the need to regulate transactions between Egyptians and the foreign traders who found Egypt to be an increasingly attractive sphere for exploitation in business.[334]

Trading in itself, carried on between willing parties, requires few rules; but trading, like all activities in which personal interests are involved, generates problems requiring careful solution. Solutions to be acceptable need the backing of rules – legal rules, the judgements arising from which can be written down on documents and suitably witnessed. The steps by which trade with non-Egyptians within Egypt developed cannot be accurately charted, but strong indications can be obtained from the business documents surviving from this period of rapid development. Though in bulk the number of documents is not great, it is distinctly greater than for earlier periods. The survival of documents is a haphazard matter, especially from the remains of Delta cities, notably wetter than those of Upper Egypt. It is not surprising, therefore, that not many have survived from Lower Egypt, which first experienced the great developments of trade between Egyptians, Greeks, and Asiatics, and the consequent generation of documents during the second half of the seventh century B.C.[335] There was, however, another development in the preparation of documents at this time which requires no substantial number of texts to determine its significance. It was the emergence of the demotic script.

Since the beginning of writing in Egypt there had existed, in parallel to the formal hieroglyphic script, a cursive form for use in circumstances where it would be difficult to produce the detailed signs of the formal script, as, for example, on papyrus using a rush brush. This cursive form, the hieratic script, developed over the centuries its own characteristics of

---

[332] F 51 III, 10.   [333] Diodorus 1.94.5; see *CAH* III².1, 575.   [334] F 59, 319.
[335] F 51 III, 10.

writing, spelling, and even, in a sense, of grammar. Thus the language in which the very cursive hieratic documents of the Late New Kingdom are written is close to the spoken Egyptian of the time, a form of Egyptian not found in contemporary monumental texts written in hieroglyphs.[336] The gap between formal hieroglyphic texts and cursive documentary texts continued to widen as time went by, and by the Twenty-fifth Dynasty cursive hieratic in southern Egypt had diverged so far from the parent hieroglyphic script that it is now called abnormal hieratic. Its special characteristics can be traced back to documents of the Twenty-first and Twenty-second Dynasties, but as an identifiable stage in the development of Egyptian cursive hands it achieved its full flowering between the reigns of Taharqa and Amasis (c. 702–526).[337]

Even more distinctive, however, was the script developed in Lower Egypt, undoubtedly in answer to the demands made for a rapidly written medium for use in business and legal documents. It was truly independent of hieroglyphs, an efficient, flexible script which demonstrated its usefulness by surviving in common practice throughout Egypt until the fifth century A.D. The need for a practical script, better than any form of hieratic formerly used, clearly indicates that the businessmen and scribes of Lower and Middle Egypt, who first used demotic in the reign of Psammetichus I, were faced with producing a volume of written documentation unparalleled in earlier times. The demotic script, as much as anything, signals the cultural advance of Egypt in the Saïte period. And in the forms and formulae of the documents written in the new script, developments of terminology can be distinguished which set them distinctly apart from earlier documents. It has justly been said that there is a greater similarity between demotic legal texts of Ptolemaic times and those of the sixth century B.C., than between the latter and those in abnormal hieratic of the reign of Taharqa.[338] In effect, abnormal hieratic documents belong to the tradition leading back to the New Kingdom and earlier;[339] the demotic documents of the sixth century are of a new tradition. From the time of Amasis demotic prevailed throughout Egypt.

The new spirit which showed itself in many departments of Egyptian life during the stirring times of the seventh and sixth centuries B.C. should properly also have found an outlet in literary compositions. Unfortunately, no papyri containing literary texts clearly dating from this period have survived.[340] A famous cycle of stories, the principal characters of which, Pedubastis, Inaros, and Pimay, lived during the

---

[336] So Černý; see F 26 iiiff.   [337] F 143 I, 31f; F 51 III, 12ff.   [338] F 51 III, 12.
[339] Cf. the 50 witness texts in P. Brooklyn 47.218.3, a Theban text of Year 14 of Psammetichus I: 17 are written in hieratic, 27 in abnormal hieratic, 6 in mixed script; see F 126, 15.
[340] F 143, 2, 142.

anarchic times of Delta disunity and later, may have been composed during the Saïte period, but no copies earlier than the fourth century are known.[341] The various stories, some of which are named 'The Struggle for the Benefice of Amun', 'The Struggle for the Breastplate of Inaros', and 'Egyptians and Amazons', are imaginative romances which show a marked advance, in a literary sense, over the stilted and stylistically repetitive tales of earlier times. It has been shown, however, that it would be wrong to find, in the changes of form and style exhibited by these and other stories written in demotic, valid evidence of the influence of Greek literary models.[342]

While the new scripts were developed for the writing of secular texts on papyrus, two traditional scripts continued to be used for religious texts, one a stereotyped hieratic based on the regular book hand of the Nineteenth Dynasty, the other a strictly hieroglyphic script in which the signs, detailed to a varying degree, reproduce recognizable hieroglyphs. Religious papyri, dating from the later dynasties, have survived in large numbers from the Theban area, but few can as yet be accurately assigned even to the nearest century. The principal funerary text of the New Kingdom, *The Book of the Dead*, remained a very popular composition, undergoing a revision, termed the Saïte Recension, in the early years of the Twenty-sixth Dynasty.[343] In addition, many of the compositions formerly reserved for use in royal tombs, had now lost their exclusivity, and were commonly used in private funerary compilations for the officials and priests of Thebes. The same, no doubt, happened elsewhere in the country, but funerary papyri from Lower Egypt have not survived. What texts were thought suitable for royal tombs is not known. The Kushite royal tombs at El-Kurru and Nuri are all so robbed and destroyed that little can be determined from the surviving remains.[344] The Saïte royal tombs, all of which were at Saïs,[345] have not been discovered, but there is good reason to believe that they would have been elaborate structures, well decorated with religious scenes and inscriptions. Private tombs of the period provide the evidence by implication.

Mention has already been made of the great tombs built for senior officials at Thebes and Memphis during the Twenty-sixth Dynasty. The revival of private tomb construction had already started at Thebes in the time of the Kushite kings, the earliest large tomb at present known being that of Harwa, major-domo of Amenirdis I.[346] Vast underground complexes of chambers, sometimes on more than one level, great open courtyards, enclosure walls and pylon entrances of mud-brick (but on a

[341] F 143, 3, 87, 89f; F 77, 455ff.   [342] F 10, 29ff.   [343] F 23, 235ff; F 9, 12f; F 40 I, xv.
[344] F 34, 64ff (Py); 55ff (Shabako); 67ff (Shebitku); 60ff (Tantamani); F 35, 7ff (Taharqa).
[345] Hdt. II.169; F 103, 203.   [346] F 133 I², i, 68; Eigner, *Die Grabbauten*, 37ff.

huge scale), characterize these tombs at Thebes.[347] Those at Saqqara, for reasons of space, were not as great, but, in the context of the Memphite necropolis, still very considerable structures,[348] in particular the tomb of Bakenrenef, vizir of Psammetichus I. Lavish use was made of the great religious texts in the tombs of both cemeteries, most extensively by Pedamenope, a lector priest probably of the reign of Psammetichus I, whose tomb is by far the largest at Thebes.[349] Among the texts revived for use at Saqqara especially were the Pyramid Texts, copied from the burial chambers of the pyramids of the kings of the Fifth and Sixth Dynasties in the same necropolis.

The interest in things ancient – the archaistic tendency of the period – revealed itself in many ways. It involved, among other things, a kind of pious archaeology, inspired no doubt by a respect for the past which, as far as the Kushite kings were concerned, formed part of their general desire to be seen as acceptable rulers of Egypt. At royal level it can be seen in Shabako's solicitude for the supposedly ancient text of the Memphite Theology, transferred at his instruction from worm-eaten papyrus to enduring stone.[350] At Kawa, in Taharqa's temple, there are scenes copied from the valley temples of the pyramids of Fifth- and Sixth-Dynasty kings at Abusir and Saqqara (Pls. Vol., pl. 186).[351] From the Twenty-sixth Dynasty there is good evidence that responsible agents entered pyramids and carried out repairs and other works. In the pyramid of Mycerinus at Giza, a new coffin was provided for the body, presumably robbed and desecrated, of that Fourth Dynasty king.[352] At Saqqara, the Step Pyramid of Djoser was entered, and the fine reliefs of the king on panels in the eastern subterranean gallery were marked with grids, undoubtedly for copying by artists. The grid used here is based on a revised canon of proportions introduced into Egyptian art during the Twenty-sixth Dynasty.[353] These Third Dynasty panels may have been used as models for some of the fine reliefs of *sed*-festival ceremonies on a monumental doorway in the palace of Apries at Memphis.[354]

In private tombs, further copyings can be detected. The tomb of Ibi, major-domo of Nitocris, contains a number of scenes copied from the Old Kingdom tomb of an official of the same name at Deir el-Gabrāwi, two hundred miles downstream from Thebes.[355] The artists of the tomb of Mentuemhat, on the other hand, chose many of their subjects for copying from the Theban necropolis itself; a well-known scene from the tiny Eighteenth Dynasty tomb of Menna being adapted for the great funerary complex of the influential mayor of the city.[356] The extent to

---

[347] Discussed in F 15 1, 30ff; Eigner, *Die Grabbauten*, generally; also see F 166, 111ff.

[348] F 133 III².2, 588ff.   [349] F 133 1², i, 50ff; Eigner, *Die Grabbauten*, 46ff.

[350] See above, p. 691.   [351] F 104 II, 61ff.   [352] BM 6647; see F 38, 141.

[353] F 62, 75ff.   [354] F 130, pls. ii–ix, dates them to the Twelfth Dynasty (5f); F 153, 400.

[355] F 29, 36ff; F 80, generally.   [356] F 17, 17.

which copying of specific scenes in tombs of earlier periods was practised in tombs of the Twenty-fifth and Twenty-sixth Dynasties should perhaps not be overstressed. For the first time in centuries great funerary monuments were being constructed for private persons. The repertory of scenes used in tombs from the Old Kingdom to the New Kingdom contained many common subjects. It is therefore not surprising to find the old repertory revived; and where better could models be found than in the ancient tombs which lay throughout the land, robbed and open for inspection?

There was, further, much more to the decoration of tombs and temples than simple reproduction of ancient scenes, executed according to the new canon of proportions. A remarkable revival of craftsmanship formed part of the general renaissance. In the tomb of Mentuemhat, for example, the carving of scenes in sunk and low relief is precise, detailed, and completely assured; compositions are economical, and colouring sensitive.[357] The charge that much Saïte relief work is mechanical and lacking in feeling is in no way supported by the freshness of execution, strength, and sheer style of a great deal of what has survived.[358] It was clearly not the intention of the artists of the Saïte renaissance simply to copy what was the best of the past, in their opinion, or in the opinion of their masters, the kings and high officials who ordered the building and decoration of tombs and temples. Inspiration was sought in the past, in subject matter and style, and ancient models were adapted to superlative effect.

The quality of precision which distinguishes so much of the relief work of the period is also found in miniature in the few ivory carvings which have survived – tantalizing relics of what must have been a remarkable flowering of the minor arts. Fragments have come from the Kushite royal tombs,[359] and a particularly fine series of panels from a casket is now in the Gulbenkian Museum in Lisbon.[360] An assessment of the minor arts of the two dynasties is, however, difficult to achieve on the basis of what has survived.[361] The Kushite tombs have yielded large numbers of undistinguished amulets and pieces of jewellery of faience and semi-precious stones,[362] and a few spectacular pieces such as a mirror with silver-gilt handle of Shabako, and a fine sheet-gold collar from the burial of a queen of Shebitku.[363] From the Twenty-sixth Dynasty, survivals of quality are very few, due no doubt to the comprehensive plundering of the country at the time of the Persian invasion. The great new tombs of kings and officials offered choice pickings to the invaders.

---

[357] See above, n.158.   [358] E.g. the figure of Mentuemhat in Kansas City; F 17, pl. 13.
[359] E.g. F 34, fig. 20g–j.   [360] F 21, pl. xxxi; probably of Twenty-sixth Dynasty date.
[361] F 3, 169ff, 227ff.   [362] In general, see F 176, 184ff.
[363] F 34, pls. lxii, lxiii; also F 175, 61f, 177ff.

Among pieces which can be closely dated to the period is a splendid gold seal, in the form of a ring with heavy bezel, inscribed for one of the two Shoshenqs who were major-domos of Ankhnesneferibre (Pls. Vol., pl. 195c);[364] also, probably, a striking gold dish-handle from Daphnae, now in Boston (Pls. Vol., pl. 195b).[365]

During the seventh and sixth centuries the art of bronze casting, which had achieved some spectacular successes in the preceding two centuries,[366] developed into a thriving industry, providing the vast numbers of divine figures, and reliquaries for the bones and mummies of sacred creatures, used in the cults which flourished throughout Egypt in the last centuries of the pharaonic period.[367] The wealth of small bronzes, mostly of a routine character, which crowd museum collections has obscured the fact that many are the products of high technical competence, while some are true works of art. The absence of large pieces of first quality has prompted the view that the achievement of earlier times was never reached again.[368] But there are notable examples of large-scale bronze figures of men and women in museums. These pieces are little known and suffer from imprecision in their dating.[369] There are, however, several well-dated medium-sized pieces which are both competently made and artistically very stylish, such as a figure of Khonsirdis, governor of Upper Egypt in the reign of Psammetichus I (Pls. Vol., pl. 194b),[370] and an unusual statuette of Ihat, a prophet of Amun, which is inscribed with the cartouches of Psammetichus II, probably replacing originals of Necho II.[371] The latter piece, of undoubted Egyptian, indeed Theban, origin, was found at Ephesus, surely taken there in antiquity as a prized acquisition.

From the period between the early New Kingdom and the Twenty-fifth Dynasty there has survived a small number of royal representations in bronze.[372] From the Twenty-fifth Dynasty onwards many more are known, possibly separated in most cases from ritual objects, like sacred barks, on which the ruling monarch was shown making an offering or in an attitude of worship.[373] Those representing Kushite kings are particularly distinctive, and among the few which are of high quality is a finely modelled figure of Shabako in Athens. It displays, albeit on a small scale, many of the characteristics of large royal sculpture of the Twenty-fifth Dynasty,[374] but it lacks the harsh strength and muscular emphasis which are found in sculptures on a larger scale.[375] The mingling of styles and

---

[364] BM 68868; also F 176, 195.   [365] F 153, pl. 402.   [366] CAH III².1, 578f.
[367] F 3, 190; for rich deposits of bronzes of the late period at Saqqara, see F 151, 49ff.
[368] F 17, 50.
[369] E.g. BM 43371–3 (women); see F 20, 25 (dated to the Twenty-second Dynasty); BM 22784 (parts of a fine male figure), loc. cit.   [370] F 58, 1f.
[371] F 177, 146ff. For the cutting out of Necho's cartouches, see F 182, 370f.
[372] F 2, 6.   [373] So F 167, 48ff.   [374] F 175 II, 166; F 3, 283.
[375] F 153, 399.

traditions – Kushite itself, the historical Egyptian, and the new archaizing – gives the sculpture of the Twenty-fifth Dynasty a particular interest and liveliness.[376] They are all to be found in the surviving sculptures of Taharqa, which range from the strong but idealizing head in Cairo[377] to the almost grotesque brutality of a sphinx from Kawa (Pls. Vol., pl. 189).[378]

It is, however, in the field of private sculpture that the full flowering of artistic skills in the Nubian and Saïte Dynasties can be best observed. The upsurge of cultural enthusiasm, already mentioned as being a distinguishing feature of this period, was accompanied by a number of other trends, all of which contributed to a massive output of fine sculpture. Excellent craftsmanship was encouraged; techniques were so well developed that the hardest stones were apparently worked with consummate ease. The practice of placing votive statues of living persons in temples[379] became almost commonplace for high officials, so that the demand for private sculpture greatly increased. In earlier times only a few people of non-royal station were, apparently, allowed the privilege of placing several votive statues in temple precincts. A notable example was the steward of Amun, Senenmut, who occupied to some extent a position *vis-à-vis* queen Hatshepsut similar to that of the major-domos of the God's Wife of Amun in the Nubian and Saïte periods. The parallel should not, probably, be pressed, but it is interesting to note that Harwa, the first notable major-domo of later times, who seems to have set the fashion for great tombs at Thebes, also enjoyed the privilege of having numerous votive statues (Pls. Vol., pl. 191*a*).[380] Some of these are of conventional form, if not particularly archaizing; others show an extraordinary individuality, like the squatting figure in Cairo,[381] in which the subject is portrayed with cruel frankness. The equally numerous statues of Harwa's successor, Akhamenru, who served Shepenupet II, show in their variety distinct signs of the archaizing trends which influenced sculpture in the first half of the seventh century in particular.[382] A standing figure of Akhamenru, now in the Louvre,[383] is clearly based on Middle Kingdom originals, although it is no slavish copy. Of about the same period, and of outstanding quality, is a head found in the temple of Mut at Karnak, which was inspired by Old Kingdom models.[384] But in the delineation of the features of the subject one may detect an attempt at naturalism, approaching portraiture – a marked feature of Egyptian sculpture of the period of transition between the Twenty-fifth and Twenty-sixth Dynasties. Again, however, too much should not be claimed for the intentions of the artists of the period,

---

[376] An excellent general account in F 175 II, 49ff. For the iconography of the Kushite kings, see F 141.   [377] CG 560; see F 153, pls. 396, 397.   [378] BM 1770, see F 175 II, 50.
[379] F 17, xxxiii.   [380] F 54, 791ff.   [381] See F 175 II, 53.   [382] F 94, 163ff.
[383] E.13106; see F 94, 167, pl. xii.   [384] BM 67969; see F 140, pl. xxv; F 63, 65; F 133 II, 260.

who were still firmly controlled by conventional forms of representation.[385]

Undoubtedly the masterpiece of this naturalistic school, the products of which demonstrate 'likeness' rather than 'portraiture',[386] is the bust of a man, also found in the temple of Mut at Karnak, and usually identified as Mentuemhat.[387] It is a remarkable study of mature old age, so convincing in its individuality as to persuade that it is a true portrait. It has, unfortunately, been pointed out with justice that there are ten surviving heads of Mentuemhat, no two of which are very alike.[388] Of the many statues, and fragments of statues, of Mentuemhat which are known,[389] two others warrant special mention. The first, a noble standing representation in the Cairo Museum,[390] exhibits features which suggest a remarkable range of putative sources: the attitude and the kilt are of the Old Kingdom, the modelling of the abdomen derives from Middle Kingdom royal statuary, the wig is an adaptation of a late Eighteenth Dynasty form.[391] Yet the statue as a whole presents a coherent and completely satisfactory appearance – a triumph of eclectic artistry. The other, a statue in Berlin,[392] shows Mentuemhat seated on a simple block seat and wearing an enveloping cloak, a careful reinterpretation of a standard Middle Kingdom type of private sculpture.

Identifiable sculptures of the kings of the Twenty-sixth Dynasty are few, although there exists a number of fine heads which may plausibly be assigned to specific monarchs,[393] helping thereby to swell a disappointingly small tally. Such is the imposing quartzite head in Philadelphia (Pls. Vol., pl. 190), identified as Amasis, an idealized portrait of exceptional technical finish, showing clearly the strength and weakness of much Saïte sculpture, after the early exciting years of artistic drive under Psammetichus I. Technical mastery, already emphasized, combined with a wide repertoire of standard sculptural forms, ensured that the majority of statues were at least competently conceived and carved. Most were produced as vehicles for votive texts, and consequently the block-statue with its splendid broad surfaces inviting inscription was especially popular. Large-scale production unfortunately could not sustain artistic quality beyond the superficial level of high competence. Most Saïte sculptures, therefore, are good studio pieces, exceedingly well finished, with crisp detail, carried out in the hardest of Egyptian stones, particularly schist and basalt, and completed with a high polish (Pls. Vol., pl. 193). The artist of a stylish asymmetrical squatting figure of Bes, a piece in hard limestone, and a product of Lower Egypt,[394] not Thebes,

---

[385] F 17, xxxviii.   [386] F 17, xxxviii.
[387] Cairo CG 647; see F 153, pl. 408; F 3, 142.   [388] F 17, 15.
[389] Fully published in F 85, docs. 1–16.   [390] Cairo CG 42236 = F 85, doc.1.
[391] So F 153, pl. 407.   [392] Berlin 17271 = F 85, doc.9.   [393] See F 122, 181ff; F 121, 46ff.
[394] In the Gulbenkian Museum, Lisbon (no. 158); see F 81, pl. 261.

has, however, succeeded in achieving something beyond the common-place. The type is that of the unusual statue of Harwa, mentioned above, but here it is completely refined. And yet it is redeemed from being ordinary by a felicitous simplicity. Of the type of figure holding a divine effigy, which became particularly common in the Saïte period, an excellent example is the statue of Harbes in New York, dated by inscription to the reign of Psammetichus II.[395] He is shown standing, holding a large figure of Osiris between his hands. The modelling of the body is unusually subtle, while the head, slightly downturned, is exceptionally sensitive. Here is a piece of the greatest technical finish which wholly avoids the brittle coldness characteristic of so much Saïte sculpture.

The great officials who placed their statues in the courts of temples in Thebes and the Delta cities, in particular, inflated their dignity by reviving the multifarious official and priestly titles of the Old Kingdom. The inscriptions with which their statues are richly furnished are, by a similar principle, carved after the best ancient models, exhibiting archaizing writings and formulae. The inspiration of the texts is again eclectic, the models being for the most part the monumental texts of the Middle and New Kingdoms.[396] But the expectations which lay behind the production of these statues and their being placed in the temples, built or renewed by the Saïte monarchs, were relatively shortlived. The splendid foundations described by Herodotus (e.g. 11.169, 175) have not survived; they were undoubtedly the first buildings to suffer from the assaults of the Persians and the predatory quarrying of later times. Nevertheless, while the visible memorials of the Saïte kings are even fewer than those of their accursed predecessors the Kushites, there remains, through the literary tradition of Egypt itself, and the work of the great Greek historian, a noble reputation for cultural and political achievement, which is strongly supported by the monuments of the great officials who served them.

[395] MMA 19.2.2; see F 17, pls. 44, 45.   [396] F 95, 178f.

CHRONOLOGICAL TABLE

	ASSYRIA	BABYLONIA	EGYPT	ISRAEL	JUDAH	TYRE	ELAM
750		Nabonassar 747–734	Osorkon IV (= So?) 747–740	Menahem 752–742	Uzziah 767–740	Ethbaal II	Khumban-tahrah 760?–744
	Tiglath-pileser III 744–727	Nabu-nadin-zeri 733–732	Py c.747–716	Pekahiah 742–740	Jotham 740–735	Hiram II	Khumban-nikash I 743–717
		Nabu-shuma-ukin II 732		Pekah 740–732	Ahaz 735–715	Matan II	Shutur-nahhunte 717–699
		Nabu-mukin-zeri 731–729		Hoshea 732–722		Elulaios	
		Tiglath-pileser III 728–727		FALL OF SAMARIA 722			
	Shalmaneser V 726–722	Shalmaneser V 726–722					
	Sargon II 721–705	Merodach-baladan II 721–710	Shabako c.716–702		Hezekiah 715–687		
		Sargon II 709–705	Shebitku c.702–690				
	Sennacherib 704–681	Sennacherib 704–703					Khallushu-Inshushinak 699–693
		Marduk-zakir-shumi II 703					Kudur-nahhunte 693–692
		Merodach-baladan II 703					Khumban-nimena 692–689
		Bel-ibni 702–700	Taharqa 690–664		Manasseh 687–642	Ba'al I	Khumban-khaltash I 689–681
700		Ashur-nadin-shumi 699–694	Tantamani 664–616				
		Nergal-ushezib 693	DYNASTY XXVI				
		Mushezib-Marduk 692–689					
		Sennacherib 688–681					

Year	Assyria	Babylonia	Egypt	Judah	Tyre	Elam
	Ashurbanipal 668–627	Ashurbanipal 668 Shamash-shuma-ukin 667–648	Psammetichus I 664–610			Urtak 675–664 Teumman 664–653 Khumban-nikash II 653–652 Tammaritu I 652–649 Indabibi 649–648 Khumban-khaltash III 648–647 Tammaritu II 647 Khumban-khaltash III 646 FALL OF SUSA 646
650		Kandalanu 647–627		Amon 642–640 Josiah 640–609		
626–612	Ashur-etel-ilani Sin-shumu-lishir Sin-sharra-ishkun FALL OF NINEVEH 612 Ashur-uballit II 611–609	interregnum 626 Nabopolassar 625–605	Necho II 610–595	Jehoahaz 609 Jehoiakim 609–598		
600		Nebuchadrezzar II 604–562	Psammetichus II 595–589 Apries 589–570 Amasis 570–526	Jehoiachin 598 Zedekiah 597–587 FALL OF JERUSALEM 587	Ethba'al III Ba'al II Iakin-ba'al Chelbes Abbar Matan III Baal-eser III Mahar-ba'al Hiram III	
550		Amel-Marduk 561–560 Neriglissar 559–556 Labashi-Marduk 556 Nabonidus 555–539 FALL OF BABYLON 539	Psammetichus III 526–525			

Note: For Urartu, see vol. III.1, 891. Dates of kings of Israel, Judah and Elam are subject to revision. For the pharaohs of the mid-eighth century see *CAH* III².1, 890.

NOTE ON THE CALENDAR

In Assyria, Babylonia, Israel, and Judah a lunar calendar was used, each month beginning with the first sighting of the crescent of the new moon in the evening. Since a lunar year of 12 months amounts to 354 days, the lunar year is about 11 days shorter than the solar year of 365.25 days. In order to keep the lunar calendar approximately in line with the solar calendar extra months had to be added at intervals; thus a total of seven months was needed in each cycle of nineteen years. In Assyria and Babylonia the additional months were 'second Ululu' or 'second Addaru'. During the period covered by this volume the addition of these 'intercalary' months does not seem to be governed by any defined principle. It is not known how the problem was dealt with in Israel and Judah.

The traditional Jewish month names were taken over from the Babylonians during the Exile. These month names were used in the Old Testament even to date events occurring during the pre-exilic period.

In Assyria and Babylonia the year started around the time of the spring equinox, beginning with the month Nisannu and ending with Addaru. In Israel and Judah it started around the time of the autumn equinox, beginning with Tishri and ending with Elul. Since each Assyrian or Babylonian year overlaps two years in the Julian calendar, it is given the number of the earlier Julian year. Thus the first full year of the reign of Nebuchadrezzar II ran from 2 April 604 B.C. to 21 March 603 B.C. In terms of the Babylonian calendar the latter date would be given as 29/XII/604, i.e. the 29th day of Addaru in the year which began in the spring of 604 B.C.

Month names

	Assyria/Babylonia	Israel/Judah	Approximate equivalent
I	Nisannu	Nīsān	March/April
II	Ayyaru	Iyyār	April/May
III	Simānu	Sīwān	May/June
IV	Duʾūzu	Tammūz	June/July
V	Abu	Āb	July/August
VI	Ulūlu	Elūl	August/September
VIa	Ulūlu šanû		
VII	Tašrītu	Tišrī	September/October
VIII	Araḫsamna	Marḫešwān	October/November
IX	Kislīmu	Kislēw	November/December
X	Ṭebētu	Ṭēbēt	December/January
XI	Šabāṭu	Šebāṭ	January/February
XII	Addaru	Adār	February/March
XIIa	Addaru šanû		

BIBLIOGRAPHY

Abbreviations

AAAS   *Annales archéologiques arabes syriennes*
AASF   Annales Academiae Scientiarum Fennicae
AASOR   Annual of the American Schools of Oriental Research
Acta ant. Hung.   *Acta antiqua Academiae scientiarum Hungaricae*
Acta arch. Hung.   *Acta archaeologica Academiae scientiarum Hungaricae*
ADAJ   *Annual of the Department of Antiquities of Jordan*
AEA   *Archivo Español de Arqueología*
AfK   *Archiv für Keilschriftforschung*
AfO (Bh.)   *Archiv für Orientforschung* (Beiheft)
AIU   *Arkheologicheskie Issledovaniya na Ukraine* (Kiev)
AION   *Annali dell' Istituto Universitario Orientale di Napoli*
AJA   *American Journal of Archaeology*
AJSL   *American Journal of Semitic Languages and Literatures*
AK   *Arkheologiya, Kiev*
AMI   *Archäologische Mitteilungen aus Iran*
Anat. Stud.   *Anatolian Studies*
Ann. Serv.   *Annales du Service des Antiquités de l' Egypte*
An. Or.   Analecta Orientalia
AO   *Arkheologicheskie Otkritiya*
AOAT (S)   Alter Orient und Altes Testament (Sonderreihe)
AOF   *Altorientalische Forschungen*
AOS   American Oriental Series
AP   *Arkheologichni Pamiatky, Kiev*
Arch. Anz.   *Archäologischer Anzeiger*
Ar. Or.   *Archiv Orientální*
AS   Assyriological Studies (Chicago)
ASOR   American Schools of Oriental Research
AUM   Andrews University Monographs
AUSS   *Andrews University Seminary Studies*
AV   Authorized Version of the Bible
Bagh. Mitt.   *Baghdader Mitteilungen*
BAM   *Bulletin d' archéologie marocaine*
BAR   *Biblical Archaeologist Reader*
BASOR   *Bulletin of the American Schools of Oriental Research*

BCH *Bulletin de correspondance hellénique*

BE Babylonian Expedition of the University of Pennsylvania, Series A:
    Cuneiform Texts

BIA *Bulletin of the Institute of Archaeology*, University of London

Bi. Ar. *The Biblical Archaeologist*

BIFAO *Bulletin de l'Institut français d'archéologie orientale*

Bi. Mes. Bibliotheca Mesopotamica

Bi. Or. *Bibliotheca Orientalis*

BMFA *Bulletin of the Museum of Fine Arts, Boston*

BM Quart. *British Museum Quarterly*

Boll. d'Arte *Bollettino d'Arte*

BRM Babylonian records in the library of J. Pierpont Morgan

BSA *Annual of the British School of Archaeology at Athens*

BSOAS *Bulletin of the School of Oriental and African Studies*

BSR *Papers of the British School at Rome*

Bull. Inst. Arch. Bulg. *Bulletin d'Institut archéologique, Académie bulgare des
    sciences*

Bull. Inst. fr. Caire *Bulletin de l'institut français d'archéologie orientale, Le Caire*

Bull. MB *Bulletin du Musée de Beyrouth*

Bull. Soc. Ling. *Bulletin de la Société de linguistique de Paris*

CAD *Chicago Assyrian Dictionary*

CAH *The Cambridge Ancient History*

CBQ *Catholic Bible Quarterly*

CG *Catalogue général des antiquités Egyptiennes du Musée du Caire*

Chron. d'Eg. *Chronique d'Egypte*

CIS *Corpus Inscriptionum Semiticarum*

CIWA Rawlinson, H. C. *The Cuneiform Inscriptions of Western Asia* i-v.
    London, 1861–84

CRAI *Comptes-rendus de l'Académie des inscriptions et belles-lettres*

CRRA Compte-rendu de la . . . rencontre assyriologique internationale

CSCA *California Studies in Classical Antiquity*

CT Cuneiform Texts from Babylonian Tablets in the British Museum

CTN Cuneiform Texts from Nimrud

EI *Eretz Israel*

Eos *Commentarii Societatis philologae Polonorum*

ESA *Eurasia Septentrionalis Antiqua*

FGrH *Fragmenta der griechischen Historiker*, F. Jacoby, Berlin, 1922–

GM *Göttinger Miszellen, Beiträge zur ägyptologischen Diskussion, Göttingen*

HSS Harvard Semitic Series

HTR *Harvard Theological Review*

HUCA *Hebrew Union College Annual*

ICC International Critical Commentary

IEJ *Israel Exploration Journal*

IFAO Institut français d'archéologie orientale

Ir. Ant. *Iranica Antiqua*

JA *Journal asiatique*

JANES *Journal of the Ancient Near Eastern Society*

JAOS   *Journal of the American Oriental Society*
JARCE   *Journal of the American Research Center in Egypt*
JBL   *Journal of Biblical Literature*
JCS   *Journal of Cuneiform Studies*
JDAI   *Jahrbuch des deutschen archäologischen Instituts*
JEA   *Journal of Egyptian Archaeology*
JEOL   *Jaarbericht van het Voorasiatisch-Egyptisch Genootschap 'Ex Oriente Lux'*
JESHO   *Journal of Economic and Social History of the Orient*
JHS   *Journal of Hellenic Studies*
JKF   *Jahrbuch für kleinasiatische Forschung*
JNES   *Journal of Near Eastern Studies*
JPEK   *Jahrbuch für prähistorische und ethnographische Kunst*
JRAS   *Journal of the Royal Asiatic Society*
JRGZM   *Jahrbuch des Römisch-Germanischen Zentralmuseums, Mainz*
JSS   *Journal of Semitic Studies*
JSSEA   *Journal of the Society for the Study of Egyptian Antiquities*, Toronto
JTS   *Journal of Theological Studies*
JTVI   *Journal of the Transactions of the Victoria Institute*
KB   Keilschriftliche Bibliothek
KSIAK   *Kratkie Soobshcheniya Instituta Arkheologii, Kiev*
KSIAM   *Kratkie Soobshcheniya Instituta Arkheologii AN SSSR*, Moscow
KSIIMK   *Kratkie Soobshcheniya Instituta Istorii Materialnoy Kultury*, Moscow
LAAA   *Liverpool Annals of Archaeology and Anthropology*
LAPO   Littératures anciennes du Proche-Orient
Ling. Balk.   *Linguistique balkanique*
L–S–J   *Greek–English Lexicon*, H. G. Liddell and R. Scott, rev. H. S. Jones, with Supplement, Oxford, 1968
MAOG   *Mitteilungen der altorientalischen Gesellschaft*
MAPP   *Materialy z Arkheologii Pivnichnoho Prichornomoria*, Odessa
MDAIK   *Mitteilungen des deutschen archäologischen Instituts für ägyptische Altertumskunde in Kairo*
MDOG   *Mitteilungen der Deutschen Orient-Gesellschaft*
MDP   Mémoires de la Délégation en Perse
MEFR   *Mélanges d'archéologie et d'histoire de l'Ecole française de Rome*
Mém. inst. fr. Caire   Mémoires publiés par les membres de l'Institut français d'archéologie orientale du Caire
MIA   *Materialy i Issledovaniya po Arkheologii SSSR*
MIO   *Mitteilungen des Instituts für Orientforschung*
M–L   Meiggs, R. and Lewis, D. M. *A Selection of Greek Historical Inscriptions to the End of the Fifth Century B.C.* Oxford, 1969
MM   *Madrider Mitteilungen*
MMJ   *Metropolitan Museum Journal*
Mon. Ant.   *Monumenti Antichi*
MSL   *Materialien zum Sumerischen Lexicon*
MVAG   *Mitteilungen der Vorderasiatisch-Aegyptischen Gesellschaft*
Nachr. Göttingen   *Nachrichten von der Akademie der Wissenschaften in Göttingen*
NEB   New English Bible

NICOT   The New International Commentary on the Old Testament
Not. Scav.   *Notizie degli Scavi di Antichità,* annexe to Atti della Accademia
   Nazionale dei Lincei, Rome
Num. Chron.   *Numismatic Chronicle*
OECT   Oxford Editions of Cuneiform Texts
OIC   Oriental Institute Communications
OIP   Oriental Institute Publications
OLZ   *Orientalistische Literaturzeitung*
Or.   *Orientalia*
Or. Ant.   *Oriens Antiquus*
PAPS   *Proceedings of the American Philosophical Society, Philadelphia*
PBS   The University Museum Publications of the Babylonian Section
PCPhS   *Proceedings of the Cambridge Philological Society*
PEF   *Quarterly Statement of the Palestine Exploration Fund*
PEQ   *Palestine Exploration Quarterly*
PPS   *Proceedings of the Prehistoric Society*
PSBA   *Proceedings of the Society of Biblical Archaeology*
P–W   Pauly–Wissowa–Kroll–Mittelhaus, *Real-Encyclopädie der klassischen
   Altertumswissenschaft,* Stuttgart, 1893–
QDAP   *Quarterly of the Department of Antiquities of Palestine*
RA   *Revue d'assyriologie et d'archéologie orientale*
Rec. Trav.   *Recueil de travaux relatifs à la philologie et l'archéologie égyptiennes et
   assyriennes*
Rendic. Acc. Lincei   *Rendiconti della Accademia nazionale dei Lincei*
Rend. Ist. Lombardo   *Rendiconti del r. Istituto Lombardo di scienze e lettere*
RES   Répertoire d'Epigraphie Sémitique
Rev. Arch.   *Revue archéologique*
Rev. Arch. Bib. Mus.   *Revista de archivos, bibliothecas y museos*
Rev. Bibl.   *Revue biblique*
Rev. d'égyptol.   *Revue d'égyptologie*
Rev. de Philol.   *Revue de philologie, de littérature et d'histoire anciennes*
RHA   *Revue hittite et asianique*
RIDA   *Revue internationale des droits de l'Antiquité*
Rom. Mitt.   *Römische Mitteilungen. Mitteilungen des deutschen archäologischen
   Instituts, römische Abteilung*
RSF   *Rivista di Studi Fenici*
RSO   *Rivista degli Studi orientali*
RSV   Revised Standard Version of the Bible
RV   Revised Version of the Bible
SA   *Sovetskaya Arkheologiya*
SAI   *Arkheologiya SSSR. Svod Arkheologicheskikh Istochnikov*
SAK   *Studien zur altägyptischen Kultur*
SANE   Sources from the Ancient Near East
Stud. Etr.   *Studi Etruschi*
TAM   Tituli Asiae Minoris
TB   *Tyndale Bulletin*
TCL   Textes cunéiformes du Louvre

TCS   Texts from Cuneiform Sources
TIM   Texts in the Iraq Museum
UE(T)   Ur Excavations (Texts)
UF   Ugarit-Forschungen
UVB   Vorläufiger Bericht über die . . . *Ausgrabungen in Uruk-Warka*
VAB   Vorderasiatische Bibliothek
VAS   Vorderasiatische Schriftdenkmäler
VDI   Vestnik drevnei istorii
VSSA   Voprosy Skifo-Sarmatskoy Arkheologii, ed. D. B. Shelov, Moscow, 1954
VT (Supp.)   *Vetus Testamentum* (Supplements)
We. Or.   Die Welt des Orients
WHJP   World History of the Jewish People
WTJ   Westminster Theological Journal
WVDOG   Wissenschaftliche Veröffentlichungen der Deutschen Orient-Gesellschaft
WZKM   Wiener Zeitschrift für die Kunde des Morgenlandes
YNER   Yale Near Eastern Researches
YOS (R)   Yale Oriental Series (Researches)
ZA   Zeitschrift für Assyriologie
ZÄS   Zeitschrift für ägyptische Sprache und Altertumskunde
ZAW (Bh.)   *Zeitschrift für die alttestamentliche Wissenschaft* (Beiheft)
ZDMG   Zeitschrift der deutschen morgenländischen Gesellschaft
ZDPV   Zeitschrift des deutschen Palästina-Vereins
ZPE   Zeitschrift für Papyrologie und Epigraphik

A. ASSYRIA AND BABYLONIA

I. GENERAL

1. Alster, B. (ed.) *Death in Mesopotamia* (Mesopotamia 8). Copenhagen, 1980
2. Biggs, R. D. and Brinkman, J. A. (eds.) *Studies Presented to A. Leo Oppenheim.* Chicago, 1964
3. Böhl, F. M. Th. de L. *Opera Minora.* Groningen and Jakarta, 1953
4. Borger, R. *Babylonisch-assyrische Lesestücke.* Rome, 1963. 2nd edn 1979
5. Borger, R. *Handbuch der Keilschriftliteratur* 1–3. Berlin, 1967–75
6. Borger, R. *Assyrisch-babylonische Zeichenliste* (AOAT 33). Kevelaer and Neukirchen-Vluyn, 1978
7. Burstein, S. *The Babyloniaca of Berossus* (SANE 1/5). Malibu, 1978
8. Cameron, G. G. *History of Early Iran.* Chicago, 1936
9. Cassin, E. *La splendeur divine: introduction à l'étude de la mentalité mésopotamienne.* Paris, 1968
10. Cassin, E. *et al.* (eds.) *Die altorientalischen Reiche,* III: *Die erste Hälfte des 1. Jahrtausends* (Fischer Weltgeschichte 4). Frankfurt, 1968
11. Cogan, M. *Imperialism and Religion: Assyria, Judah and Israel in the Eighth*

and Seventh Centuries B.C.E. (Society of Biblical Literature Monograph Series 19). Montana, 1974

12. Contenau, G. Everyday Life in Babylon and Assyria. London, 1954

13. Dandamayev, M. A. et al. (eds.) Societies and Languages of the Ancient Near East: Studies in Honour of I. M. Diakonoff. Warminster, 1982

14. Diakonoff, I. M. (ed.) Ancient Mesopotamia. Moscow, 1969

15. Donner, H. and Röllig, W. Kanaanäische und aramäische Inschriften I–III. 2nd-3rd edns. Wiesbaden, 1969–73

16. Ebeling, E. et al. (eds.) Reallexikon der Assyriologie. Berlin and Leipzig, 1928–

17. Edzard, D. O. (ed.) Gesellschaftsklassen im Alten Zweistromland (Bayerische Akademie der Wissenschaften, Phil.-Hist. Klasse, Abhandlungen NF 75). Munich, 1972

18. Eichler, B. L. et al. Kramer Anniversary Volume (AOAT 25). Kevelaer and Neukirchen-Vluyn, 1976

19. Eph῾al, I. The Ancient Arabs: Nomads on the Borders of the Fertile Crescent, 9th–5th Centuries B.C. Jerusalem and Leiden, 1982

20. Fales, F. M. (ed.) Assyrian Royal Inscriptions: New Horizons in Literary, Ideological, and Historical Analysis. Rome, 1981

21. Finet, A. (ed.) La Voix de l'Opposition en Mésopotamie. Brussels, 1973

22. Garelli, P. (ed.) Le palais et la royauté. Paris, 1974

23. Garelli, P. and Nikiprowetzky, V. Le proche-orient asiatique: les empires mésopotamiennes, Israël. Paris, 1974

24. Goedicke, H. and Roberts, J. J. M. (eds.) Unity and Diversity: Essays in the History, Literature, and Religion of the Ancient Near East. Baltimore, 1975

25. Grayson, A. K. Assyrian and Babylonian Chronicles (TCS 5). Locust Valley, 1975

26. Grayson, A. K. Babylonian Historical–Literary Texts. Toronto, 1975

27. Grayson, A. K. 'Histories and historians of the Ancient Near East: Assyria and Babylonia', Or, 49 (1980) 140–94

28. Güterbock, H. G. and Jacobsen, Th. (eds.) Studies in Honor of Benno Landsberger on his Seventy-fifth Birthday, April 21, 1965 (AS 16). Chicago, 1965

29. Hallo, W. W., and Simpson, W. K. The Ancient Near East: A History. New York, 1971

30. Kitchen, K. A. The Third Intermediate Period in Egypt. Warminster, 1973

31. Klengel, H. (ed.) Gesellschaft und Kultur im alten Vorderasien (Schriften zur Geschichte und Kultur des Alten Orients 15). Berlin, 1982

32. Larsen, M. T. (ed.) Power and Propaganda: A Symposium on Ancient Empires (Mesopotamia 7). Copenhagen, 1979

33. Levine, L. D. Geographical Studies in the Neo-Assyrian Zagros (reprint of articles in Iran 11 (1973) 1–27 and Iran 12 (1974) 99–124). Toronto and London, 1974

34. Lipiński, E. (ed.) State and Temple Economy in the Ancient Near East II. Louvain, 1979

35. Luckenbill, D. Ancient Records of Assyria and Babylonia I–II. Chicago, 1926–7

36. McCullough, W. S. (ed.) *The Seed of Wisdom: Essays in Honour of T. J. Meek*. Toronto, 1964
37. Meissner, B. *Babylonien und Assyrien* I–II. Heidelberg, 1920
38. Nissen, H. J. and Renger, R. (eds.) *Mesopotamien und seine Nachbarn* 1–2 (Berliner Beiträge zum Vorderen Orient 1). Berlin, 1982
39. Olmstead, A. T. E. *Western Asia in the Days of Sargon of Assyria*. Lancaster, Pennsylvania, 1906
40. Olmstead, A. T. E. 'Western Asia in the reign of Sennacherib of Assyria', *Proceedings of the American Historical Association* (1909), 91–139
41. Olmstead, A. T. E. *History of Assyria*. Chicago and London, 1923
42. Oppenheim, A. L. *et al.* (eds.) *The Assyrian Dictionary of the Oriental Institute of the University of Chicago*. Chicago and Glückstadt, 1956–
43. Oppenheim, A. L. *Ancient Mesopotamia*. 2nd edn. Chicago, 1977
44. Pritchard, J. B. *Ancient Near Eastern Texts Relating to the Old Testament*. 3rd edn with supplement. Princeton, 1969
45. Pritchard, J. B. *The Ancient Near East in Pictures Relating to the Old Testament*. 2nd edn. Princeton, 1969
46. Rogers, R. W. *A History of Babylonia and Assyria* I–II. 6th edn. New York and Cincinnati, 1915
47. Roux, G. *Ancient Iraq*. London, 1964
48. Saggs, H. W. F. *The Greatness that was Babylon*. London, 1962
49. Saggs, H. W. F. *Everyday Life in Babylonia and Assyria*. London and New York, 1965
50. Schmökel, H. *Geschichte des alten Vorderasiens* (Handbuch der Orientalistik). Leiden, 1957
51. Seux, M.-J. *Epithètes royales akkadiennes et sumériennes*. Paris, 1967
52. Soden, W. von. *Akkadisches Handwörterbuch* I–III. Wiesbaden, 1958–81
53. Tadmor, H. and Weinfeld, M. (eds.) *History, Historiography and Interpretation: Studies in Biblical and Cuneiform Literatures*. Jerusalem, 1983
54. van Driel, G. *et al.* (eds.) *Zikir šumim: Assyriological Studies Presented to F. R. Kraus on the Occasion of his Seventieth Birthday*. Leiden, 1982
55. Wevers, J. W. and Redford, D. B. (eds.) *Essays on the Ancient Semitic World* (Toronto Semitic Texts and Studies 1). Toronto, 1970
56. Winton Thomas, D. (ed.) *Documents from Old Testament Times*. London, 1958

II. ASSYRIA

I. GENERAL HISTORY

57. Böhl, F. M. Th. de Liagre. 'Das Zeitalter der Sargoniden nach Briefen aus dem Königlichen Archiv zu Nineve', in A 3, 384–422 (1953)
58. Böhl, F. M. Th. de Liagre. 'Blüte und Untergang des Assyrerreiches als historisches Problem', in *Studia Biblica et Semitica Theodoro Christiano Vriezen dedicata*, 204–20. Wageningen, 1966
59. Cavaignac, E. 'A propos du début de l'histoire des Mèdes', *JA* 1961, 153–62

60. Forrer, E. 'Assyrien', in A 16, 1 (1929–30) 299–303
60A. Genge, H. *Stelen neuassyrischer Könige*, 1: *Die Keilinschriften*. Berlin, 1965
61. Goosens, G. 'Asie occidentale ancienne', in Grousset, R. and Léonard, É. G. (eds.) *Histoire Universelle* 1, 289–495. Bruges, 1956
62. Hallo, W. W. 'From Qarqar to Carchemish', *Bi. Ar.* 23 (1960) 34–61; reprinted in Freedman, D. N. and Campbell, E. F. Jr (eds.) *BAR* 11, 152–88. New York, 1964
63. Johns, C. H. W. *Ancient Assyria*. Cambridge, 1912
63A. König, F. W. *Handbuch der chaldischen Inschriften* (*AfO* Bh. 8). Graz, 1955–7
64. Melikišvili, G. A. 'Nekotorye voprosy istorii Maneiskogo tsartsva' [Some questions on the history of the kingdom of Manna], *VDI* 27 (1949/1) 57–72
65. Messerschmidt, L. *Keilschrifttexte aus Assur historischen Inhalts* 1 (WVDOG 16). Leipzig, 1911
66. Oates, D. *Studies in the Ancient History of Northern Iraq*. London, 1968
67. Piotrovskii, B. B. 'Skify i Drevnii Vostok' [Scythians and the ancient East], *SA* 19 (1954) 141–58
68. Schramm, W. *Einleitung in die assyrischen Königsinschriften*, 11: *934–722 v. Chr.* Leiden, 1973
69. Smith, S. Chapters 2–5 in *CAH* III¹, 32–131. London, 1925
70. Tadmor, H. 'Philistia under Assyrian rule', *Bi. Ar.* 29 (1966) 86–102
71. Young, T. C., Jr. 'The Iranian migration into the Zagros', *Iran* 5 (1967) 11–34

2. LETTERS

72. Harper, R. F. *Assyrian and Babylonian Letters Belonging to the Kouyunjik Collection of the British Museum* 1–XIV. Chicago, 1892–1914
73. Parpola, S. *Letters from Assyrian Scholars to the Kings Esarhaddon and Assurbanipal*. Part I: *Texts* (AOAT 5/1). Kevelaer and Neukirchen-Vluyn, 1970
74. Parpola, S. *Letters from Assyrian Scholars to the Kings Esarhaddon and Assurbanipal*. Part II A: *Introduction and Appendices*. Kevelaer and Neukirchen-Vluyn, 1971
75. Parpola, S. *Neo-Assyrian Letters from the Kuyunjik Collection* (CT 53). London, 1979
76. Parpola, S. 'Assyrian royal inscriptions and Neo-Assyrian letters', in A 20, 117–142 (1981)
77. Parpola, S. *Letters from Assyrian Scholars to the Kings Esarhaddon and Assurbanipal*. Part II: *Commentary and Appendices* (AOAT 5/2). Kevelaer and Neukirchen-Vluyn, 1983
77A. Parpola, S. *The Correspondence of Sargon II, Part I. Letters from Assyria and the West*. Helsinki, 1987
78. Pfeiffer, R. *State Letters of Assyria* (AOS 6). New Haven, 1935
79. Saggs, H. W. F. 'The Nimrud letters, 1952. Part I: The Ukin-zer rebellion and related texts', *Iraq* 17 (1955) 21–50

80. Saggs, H. W. F. 'The Nimrud letters, 1952. Part II: Relations with the West', *Iraq* 17 (1955) 126–54

81. Saggs, H. W. F. 'The Nimrud letters, 1952. Part III: Miscellaneous letters', *Iraq* 18 (1956) 40–56

82. Saggs, H. W. F. 'The Nimrud letters, 1952. Part IV: The Urartian frontier', *Iraq* 20 (1958) 182–212

83. Saggs, H. W. F. 'The Nimrud letters, 1952. Part V: Administration', *Iraq* 21 (1959) 158–79

84. Saggs, H. W. F. 'The Nimrud letters, 1952. Part VI: The death of Ukinzer; and other letters', *Iraq* 25 (1963) 70–80

85. Saggs, H. W. F. 'The Nimrud letters, 1952. Part VII: Apologies; a theft; and other matters', *Iraq* 27 (1965) 17–32

86. Saggs, H. W. F. 'The Nimrud letters, 1952. Part VIII: Imperial administration', *Iraq* 28 (1966) 177–91

87. Saggs, H. W. F. 'The Nimrud letters, 1952. Part IX: Assyrian bureaucracy', *Iraq* 36 (1974) 199–221

88. Waterman, L. *Royal Correspondence of the Assyrian Empire* I-IV. (University of Michigan Studies, Humanistic Series 17–20). Ann Arbor, 1930–6

3. LEGAL AND ADMINISTRATIVE DOCUMENTS

89. Ebeling, E. *Keilschrifttexte aus Assur juristischen Inhalts* (WVDOG 50). Leipzig, 1927

90. Ebeling, E. *Stiftungen und Vorschriften für assyrische Tempel* (Deutsche Akademie für Wissenschaften zu Berlin, Institut für Orientforschung, Veröffentlichung 23). Berlin, 1954

91. Fales, F. M. *Censimenti e Catastati di Epoca Neo-assira* (Studi economici e tecnologici 2). Rome, 1973

92. Friedrich, J., Meyer, G. R., Ungnad, E. and Weidner, E. F. *Die Inschriften von Tell Halaf, Keilschrifttexte und aramäische Urkunden aus einer assyrischen Provinzhauptstadt* (*AfO* Bh. 6). Berlin, 1940

93. Johns, C. H. W. *Assyrian Deeds and Documents . . . , Chiefly of the Seventh Century B.C.* I–IV. Cambridge, 1898–1923

94. Johns, C. H. W. *An Assyrian Doomsday Book or Liber Censualis of the District round Harran in the Seventh Century B.C.* (Assyriologische Bibliothek 17). Leipzig, 1901

95. Johns, C. H. W. 'Assyrian deeds and documents', *AJSL* 42 (1925–6) 170–204, 228–75

96. Kinnier Wilson, J. V. *The Nimrud Wine Lists* (CTN 1). London, 1972

97. Kohler, J. and Ungnad, A. *Assyrische Rechtsurkunden*. Leipzig, 1913

98. Parker, B. 'The Nimrud tablets, 1952 – business documents', *Iraq* 16 (1954) 29–58

99. Parker, B. 'The Nimrud tablets, 1956 – economic and legal texts from the Nabu Temple', *Iraq* 19 (1957) 125–38

100. Parker, B. 'Administrative tablets from the North-West Palace, Nimrud', *Iraq* 23 (1961) 15–67

101. Parker, B. 'Economic tablets from the Temple of Mamu at Balawat', *Iraq* 25 (1963) 86–103
102. Postgate, J. N. *Neo-Assyrian Royal Grants and Decrees* (Studia Pohl: Series Major 1). Rome, 1969
103. Postgate, J. N. 'More "Assyrian deeds and documents"', *Iran* 32 (1970) 129–64
104. Postgate, J. N. *The Governor's Palace Archive* (CTN 2). London, 1973
105. Postgate, J. N. *Fifty Neo-Assyrian Legal Documents.* Warminster, 1976
106. Wiseman, D. J. 'The Nimrud tablets, 1949', *Iraq* 12 (1950) 184–200
107. Wiseman, D. J. 'The Nimrud tablets, 1951', *Iraq* 14 (1952) 61–71
108. Wiseman, D. J. 'The Nimrud tablets, 1953', *Iraq* 15 (1953) 135–60
109. Wiseman, D. J. and Kinnier Wilson, J. V. 'The Nimrud tablets, 1950', *Iraq* 13 (1951) 102–22

4. ART AND ARCHAEOLOGY

109A. Albenda, P., *The Palace of Sargon King of Assyria.* Paris, 1986
110. Andrae, W. *Die Festungswerke von Assur* (WVDOG 23). Leipzig, 1913
111. Andrae, W. *Die Stelenreihen in Assur* (WVDOG 24). Leipzig, 1913
112. Andrae, W. *Das Wiedererstandene Assur.* 2nd edn. Munich, 1977
113. Barnett, R. D. 'Hamath and Nimrud, shell fragments from Hamath and the provenance of the Nimrud ivories', *Iraq* 25 (1963) 81–5
114. Barnett, R. D. *A Catalogue of the Nimrud Ivories . . . in the British Museum.* 2nd edn. London, 1975
115. Barnett, R. D. *Sculptures from the North Palace of Ashurbanipal at Nineveh (668–627 B.C.).* London, 1976
116. Barnett, R. D. and Falkner, M. *The Sculptures of Aššur-naṣir-apli II (883–859 B.C.), Tiglath-pileser III (745–727 B.C.), Esarhaddon (681–669 B.C.) from the Central and South-West Palaces at Nimrud.* London, 1962
117. Barnett, R. D. and Lorenzini, A. *Assyrian Sculpture in the British Museum.* Toronto, 1975
118. Botta, P. E. *Monument de Ninive, découvert et décrit par M. P. É. Botta; mesuré et dessiné par M. E. Flandin* i–v. Paris, 1849–50
119. Budge, E. A. W. *The rise and progress of Assyriology.* London, 1925
120. Campbell Thompson, R. 'The British Museum excavations at Nineveh, 1931–32', *LAAA* 20 (1933) 71–127
121. Campbell Thompson, R. 'The buildings on Quyunjiq, the larger mound of Nineveh', *Iraq* 1 (1934) 95–104
122. Campbell Thompson, R. and Hamilton, R. W. 'The excavations on the Temple of Nabû at Nineveh', *Archaeologia* 79 (1929) 103–48
123. Campbell Thompson, R. and Hamilton, R.W. 'The British Museum excavations on the Temple of Ishtar at Nineveh, 1930–31', *LAAA* 19 (1932) 55–116
124. Campbell Thompson, R. and Hutchinson, R. W. *A Century of Exploration at Nineveh.* London, 1929
125. Gadd, C. J. *The Assyrian Sculptures.* London, 1934

126. Gadd, C. J. *The Stones of Assyria*. London, 1936
127. Hall, H. R. *Babylonian and Assyrian Sculpture in the British Museum*. Paris and Brussels, 1928
128. Haller, A. *Die Heiligtümer des Gottes Assur und der Sin-Šamaš-Tempel in Assur* (WVDOG 67). Berlin, 1955
129. Hrouda, B. *Die Kulturgeschichte des assyrischen Flachbildes*. Bonn, 1965
130. Jacobsen, T. and Lloyd, S. *Sennacherib's Aqueduct at Jerwan* (OIP 24). Chicago, 1935
131. Layard, A. H. *Discoveries in the Ruins of Nineveh and Babylon*. London, 1853
132. Layard, A. H. *The Monuments of Nineveh*. London, 1853
133. Layard, A. H. *A Second Series of the Monuments of Nineveh*. London, 1853
134. Loud, G. *Khorsabad* I (OIP 38). Chicago, 1936
135. Loud, G. and Altman, C. *Khorsabad* II (OIP 40). Chicago, 1938
136. Madhloom, T. *The Chronology of Neo-Assyrian Art*. London, 1970
137. Mallowan, M. E. L. *Nimrud and its Remains* I–II. London, 1966
138. Mallowan, M. E. L. and Davies, L. G. *Ivories in Assyrian Style* (Ivories from Nimrud II). London, 1970
139. Mallowan, M. E. L. and Herrmann, G. *Furniture from SW.7 Fort Shalmaneser* (Ivories from Nimrud III). London, 1974
140. Moortgat, A. *Alt-Vorderasiatische Malerei*. Berlin, 1959
141. Orchard, J. J. *Equestrian Bridle-Harness Ornaments* (Ivories from Nimrud I/2). London, 1967
142. Parker, B. 'Excavations at Nimrud 1949–1953: seals and seal impressions', *Iraq* 17 (1955) 93–125
143. Parker, B. 'Seals and seal impressions from the Nimrud excavations, 1955–58', *Iraq* 24 (1962) 26–40
144. Parrot, A. *Archéologie mésopotamienne*, I. *Les étapes*. Paris, 1946
145. Parrot, A. *The Arts of Assyria*. Trans. by S. Gilbert and J. Emmons. New York, 1961
146. Parrot, A. *Nineveh and Babylon*. London, 1961
147. Paterson, A. *Assyrian Sculptures: Palace of Sinacherib*. The Hague, 1915
148. Place, V. *Ninive et l'Assyrie* I–III. Paris, 1867–70
149. Pleiner, R. and Bjorkman, J. K. 'The Assyrian Iron Age: the history of iron in the Assyrian civilization', *PAPS* 118 (1974) 283–313
150. Postgate, J. N. and Reade, J. E. 'Kalḫu' in A 16, 5 (1977–80) 303–23
151. Preusser, C. *Die Paläste in Assur* (WVDOG 66). Berlin, 1955
152. Sachs, A. 'The Late Assyrian royal seal type', *Iraq* 15 (1953) 167–70
153. Smith, S. *Assyrian Sculptures in the British Museum from Shalmaneser III to Sennacherib*. London, 1938
154. Turner, G. 'Tell Nebi Yūnus: the Ekal Māšarti of Nineveh', *Iraq* 32 (1970) 68–85
155. Wäfler, M. *Nicht-Assyrer neuassyrischer Darstellungen* (AOAT 26). Kevelaer and Neukirchen-Vluyn, 1975

5. REIGNS OF TIGLATH-PILESER III AND SARGON

156. Anspacher, A. S. *Tiglath Pileser III* (Contributions to Oriental History and Philology 5). New York, 1912

157. Astour, M. 'The arena of Tiglath-pileser III's campaign against Sarduri II (743 B.C.)', *Assur* 2/3 (1979) 69–91

158. Boehmer, R. M. 'Volkstum und Städte der Mannäer', *Bagh. Mitt.* 3 (1964) 11–24

159. Boehmer, R. M. 'Zur Lage von Muṣaṣir', *Bahg. Mitt.* 6 (1973) 31–40

160. Borger, R. 'Das Ende des ägyptischen Feldherrn Sib'e', *JNES* 19 (1960) 49–53

161. Campbell Thompson, R. *The Prisms of Esarhaddon and Ashurbanipal Found at Nineveh, 1927–8.* London, 1931

162. Campbell Thompson, R. 'A selection from the cuneiform historical texts from Nineveh (1927–32)', *Iraq* 7 (1940) 85–131

163. Cogan, M. 'Tyre and Tiglath-pileser III', *JCS* 25 (1973) 96–9

164. Diakonoff [D'iakonov], I. M. 'Assiro-vavilonskie istochniki po istorii Urartu' [Assyro-Babylonian sources for Urartian history], *VDI* 36 (1951/II) 255–356; 37 (1951/III) 205–52; 38 (1951/IV) 283–305

165. Donner, H. 'Neue Quellen zur Geschichte des Staates Moab in der zweiten Hälfte des 8. Jahrh. v. Chr.', *MIO* 5 (1957) 155–84

166. El-Amin, M. 'Die Reliefs mit Beischriften von Sargon II. in Dûr-Sharrukîn', 1: *Sumer* 9 (1953) 35–59, 214–28; 2: *Sumer* 10 (1954) 23–42

167. Farber, W. and Kessler, K. 'Eine Inschrift Sargons II. aus Til Barsip', *RA* 67 (1973) 163–4

168. Follet, R. '"Deuxième Bureau" et information diplomatique dans l'Assyrie des Sargonides, quelques notes', *RSO* 32 (1957) 61–81

169. Ford, M. 'The contradictory records of Sargon II of Assyria and the meaning of palû', *JCS* 22 (1968–9) 83–4

170. Gadd, C. J. 'Inscribed prisms of Sargon II from Nimrud', *Iraq* 16 (1954) 173–201

171. Garelli, P. 'Nouveau coup d'oeil sur Muṣur', in Caquot, A. and Philonenko, M. (eds.) *Hommages à André Dupont-Sommer*, 37–48. Paris, 1971

172. Garelli, P. 'Problèmes archéologiques à Karatepe: les données assyriennes', *RA* 75 (1981) 54–60

173. Ghirshman, R. 'Un Mède sur les bas-reliefs de Nimrud', *Iraq* 36 (1974) 37–8

174. Goedicke, H. 'The end of "So, King of Egypt"', *BASOR* 171 (1963) 64–6

175. Grayson, A. K. 'The empire of Sargon of Akkad', *AfO* 25 (1974–7) 56–64

176. Guralnick, E. 'Composition of some narrative reliefs from Khorsabad', *Assur* 1/5 (1976) 1–23

177. Hawkins, J. D. 'Assyrians and Hittites', *Iraq* 36 (1974) 67–83

178. Hawkins, J. D. 'Some historical problems of the Hieroglyphic Luwian inscriptions', *Anat. Stud.* 29 (1979) 153–67

179. Herrero, P. 'Un fragment de stele neo-assyrien provenant d'Iran', *Cahiers de la Délégation Archéologique en Iran* 3 (1973) 105–13
180. Kapera, Z. J. 'Was Ya-ma-ni a Cypriote?', *Folia Orientalia* 14 (1972–3) 207–18
181. Kapera, Z. J. 'The Ashdod stele of Sargon II', *Folia Orientalia* 17 (1976) 87–99
182. Kessler, K. 'Die Anzahl der assyrischen Provinzen des Jahres 738 v. Chr. in Nordsyrien', *We. Or.* 8 (1976) 49–63
183. Levine, L. C. *Two Neo-Assyrian Stelae from Iran.* Toronto, 1972
184. Levine, L. C. 'Sargon's eighth campaign', in Levine, L. C. and Cuyler Young, T. *Mountains and Lowlands* (Bi. Mes. 7) 135–51. Malibu, 1977
185. Lie, A. G. *The Inscriptions of Sargon II King of Assyria* Part I. *The Annals. Transliterated and Translated with Notes.* Paris, 1929
186. Melikishvili, G. A. *Urartskie klinoobraznye nadpisi* [Urartian cuneiform inscriptions]. Moscow, 1960
187. Na'aman, N. 'Looking for KTK', *We. Or.* 9 (1978) 220–39
188. Na'aman, N. 'The Brook of Egypt and Assyrian policy on the border of Egypt', *Tel Aviv* 6 (1979) 68–90
189. Nassouhi, E. 'Les autels trépieds assyriens', *RA* 22 (1925) 85–90
190. Nassouhi, E. 'Textes divers relatifs à l'histoire de l'Assyrie', *MAOG* 3/ 1–2 (1927) 1–38
191. Nougayrol, J. 'Un fragment méconnu du "Pillage de Muṣaṣir"', *RA* 54 (1960) 203–6; 55 (1961) 100
192. Oates, D. 'Excavations at Tell al Rimah, a summary report', *Sumer* 19 (1963) 69–77
193. Oded, B. 'Observations on methods of Assyrian rule in Transjordania after the Palestinian campaign of Tiglath-pileser III', *JNES* 29 (1970) 177–86
194. Oganesian, K. L. 'Assiro-Urartskoe srazhenie na gore uaush' [The Assyro-Urartian battle at Mount Uaush], in *Istoriko-filologicheskii Zhurnal* 3 (1966) 107–18
195. Oppenheim, A. L. 'The city of Assur in 714 B.C.', *JNES* 19 (1960) 133–47
196. Piotrovskii, B. B. *Vanskoe tsarstvo (Urartu)* [The kingdom of Van (Urartu)]. Moscow, 1959
197. Piotrovskii, B. B. *Il Regno di Van, Urartu* (Transl. of A 196 by M. Salvini). Rome, 1966
198. Postgate, J. N. 'Assyrian texts and fragments', *Iraq* 35 (1973) 13–36
199. Postgate, J. N. 'The inscription of Tiglath-pileser III at Mila Mergi', *Sumer* 29 (1973) 47–59
200. Postgate, J. N. 'Excavations in Iraq, 1976', *Iraq* 39 (1977) 301–20
201. Reade, J. E. 'The palace of Tiglath-pileser III', *Iraq* 30 (1968) 69–73
202. Reade, J. E. 'Sargon's campaigns of 720, 716, and 715 B.C.: evidence from the sculptures', *JNES* 35 (1976) 95–104
203. Rebuffat, R. 'Une bataille navale au VIIIe siècle', *Semitica* 26 (1976) 71–9
204. Rost, P. *Die Keilschrifttexte Tiglat-Pilesers III. nach den Papierabklatschen und Originalen Britischen Museums* I–11. Leipzig, 1893

205. Safar, F. 'The Temple of Sibitti at Khorsabad', *Sumer* 13 (1957) 219–21
206. Saggs, H. W. F. 'Historical texts and fragments of Sargon II of Assyria.
      1. The "Aššur Charter"', *Iraq* 37 (1975) 11–20
207. Schmitt, R. 'Deiokes', *Anzeiger der österreichischen Akademie der
      Wissenschaften* 110 (1973) 136–47
208. Shea, W. H. 'Menahem and Tiglath-pileser III', *JNES* 37 (1978) 43–9
209. Tadmor, H. 'The campaigns of Sargon II of Assur: a chronological–
      historical study', *JCS* 12 (1958) 22–40 and 77–100
210. Tadmor, H. 'Azriyau of Yaudi', *Scripta Hierosolymitana* 8 (1961) 232–71
211. Tadmor, H. 'The southern border of Aram', *IEJ* 12 (1962) 114–22
212. Tadmor, H. 'Introductory remarks to a new edition of the Annals of
      Tiglath-Pileser III', *Proceedings of the Israel Academy of Sciences and
      Humanities* 2/9 (1967) 168–87
213. Tadmor, H. 'Fragments of an Assyrian stele of Sargon II', in Dothan,
      M. *Ashdod* II–III (ᶜAtiqot English Series 9–10), 192–7, Jerusalem. 1971
214. Tadmor, H. and Cogan, M. 'Ahaz and Tiglath-pileser in the Book of
      Kings: historiographic considerations', *Biblica* 60 (1979) 491–508
215. Thureau-Dangin, F. *Une relation de la huitième campagne de Sargon* (TCL
      3). Paris, 1912
216. Thureau-Dangin, F. 'La stèle d'Asharné', *RA* 30 (1933) 53–6
217. Thureau-Dangin, F. *et al. Arslan Tash*. Paris, 1931
218. Turner, G. 'The Palace and Bâtiment aux Ivoires at Arslan Tash: a
      reappraisal', *Iraq* 30 (1968) 62–8
219. Unger, E. *Die Reliefs Tiglatpilesers* III. *aus Arslan Tash* (Publications des
      Musées d'Antiquités de Stamboul 7). Constantinople, 1925
220. Unger, E. *Tiglatpileser* III-*ün Oglu Asur Kirali Sargon II* [Sargon II of
      Assyria, son of Tiglath-pileser III] (Istanbul Asariatika Müzeleri
      Neşriyati 9). Istanbul, 1933
221. de Vogüé, M. *Corpus Inscriptionum Semiticarum, Pars Secunda,
      Inscriptiones Aramaicas Continens* I. Paris, 1889
222. Weidner, E. F. 'Assyrische Emailgemälde vom achten Feldzuge
      Sargons II', *AfO* 3 (1926) 1–6
223. Weidner, E. F. 'Neue Bruchstücke des Berichtes über Sargons achten
      Feldzug', *AfO* 12 (1937–9) 144–8
224. Weidner, E. F. 'Šilkan(he)ni, König von Muṣri, ein Zeitgenosse
      Sargons II.' *AfO* 14 (1941–4) 40–53
225. Weipert, M. 'Menahem von Israel und seine Zeitgenossen in einer
      Steleninschrift des assyrischens Königs Tiglathpileser III. aus dem
      Iran', *ZDPV* 89 (1973) 26–53
226. Winckler, H. *Die Keilschrifttexte Sargons nach den Papierabklatschen und
      Originalen neu herausgegeben* I–II. Leipzig, 1889
227. Wiseman, D. J. 'A fragmentary inscription of Tiglath-Pileser from
      Nimrud', *Iraq* 18 (1956) 117–29
228. Woolley, C. L. and Barnett, R. D. *Carchemish, Report on the Excavations
      at Jerablus on Behalf of the British Museum* III. London, 1952

6. REIGNS OF SENNACHERIB AND ESARHADDON

229. Andrae, W. 'Aus den Berichten Dr. W. Andraes aus Assur. April bis Oktober 1910', *MDOG* 44 (1910) 28–48
230. Aro, J. 'Remarks on the practice of extispicy in the time of Esarhaddon and Assurbanipal', in A 1141, 109–17 (1966)
231. Bauer, T. Review of three books on Sennacherib, *ZA* 42 (1934) 170–84
232. Baumgartner, W. 'Herodots babylonische und assyrische Nachrichten', *Ar. Or.* 18 (1950) 69–106
233. Bing, J. D. 'A further note on Cyinda/Kundi', *Historia* 22 (1973) 346–50
234. Borger, R. *Die Inschriften Asarhaddons Königs von Assyrien (AfO* Bh. 9). Graz, 1956
235. Borger, R. 'Die Inschriften Asarhaddons, Nachträge und Verbesserungen', *AfO* 18 (1957–8) 113–18
236. Borger, R. 'Assyriologische und altarabistische Miszellen', *Or.* 26 (1957) 1–11
237. Borger, R. 'Zu den Asarhaddon – Texten aus Babel', *Bi. Or.* 21 (1964) 143–8
238. Bottéro, J. 'Le substitut royal et son sort en Mésopotamie ancienne', *Akkadica* 9 (1978) 2–24
239. Campbell Thompson, R. 'The site of the palace of Ashurnasirpal at Nineveh, excavated in 1929–30 on behalf of the British Museum', *LAAA* 18 (1931) 79–112
240. Childs, S. *Isaiah and the Assyrian Crisis*. London, 1967
241. Cooper, J. S. 'A new Sennacherib prism fragment', *JCS* 26 (1974) 59–62
242. Deller, 'Neuassyrisches aus Sultantepe', *Or.* 34 (1965) 457–77
243. Diakonoff, I. M. *Istoria Midii ot drevneishikh vremen do kontsa IV veka do n.e.* [History of Media from the most ancient times to the end of the 4th century B.C.]. Moscow and Leningrad, 1956
244. Diakonoff, I. M. 'The Cimmerians', in *Monumentum Georg Morgenstierne* I, 103–40. Leiden, 1981
245. Elat, M. 'The political status of the Kingdom of Judah within the Assyrian Empire in the 7th Century B.C.E.', in Aharoni, V. *Investigations at Lachish: The Sanctuary and the Residency* (Lachish v), 61–70. Tel Aviv, 1975
246. Furlani, G. 'Un iscrizione di Sennacheribbo d'Assiria trovata a Kakzu', *Rendiconti della R. Accademia Nazionale dei Lincei, Classe di Scienze morali, storiche e filologiche* VI/10 (1934) 475–8
247. Furlani, G. 'Kakzu – Qaṣr Šemāmok', *RSO* 15 (1935) 119–42
248. Galter, H. 'Die Bautätigkeit Sanheribs am Assurtempel', *Or.* 53 (1984) 433–41
249. Geyer, B. '2 Kings XVIII 14–16 and the Annals of Sennacherib', *VT* 21 (1971), 604–6
250. Grayson, A. K. 'The Walters Art Gallery Sennacherib inscription', *AfO* 20 (1963) 83–96 and pls. I–IV
251. Heidel, A. 'The octagonal Sennacherib prism in the Iraq Museum', *Sumer* 9 (1953) 117–88

252. Heidel, A. 'A new hexagonal prism of Esarhaddon', *Sumer* 12 (1956) 9–37

253. Hirsch, H. Review of A 96, *WZKM* 70 (1978) 214–16

254. Horn, S. H. 'Did Sennacherib campaign once or twice against Hezekiah?', *AUSS* 4 (1966) 1–28

255. Hulin, P. 'Another Esarhaddon cylinder from Nimrud', *Iraq* 24 (1962) 116–18

256. Hulin, P. 'The inscriptions on the carved throne-base of Shalmaneser III', *Iraq* 25 (1963) 48–69

257. Johns, C. H. W. 'Sennacherib's letters to his father Sargon', *PSBA* 17 (1895) 220–39

258. Knudsen, E. E. 'Fragments of historical texts from Nimrud, II', *Iraq* 29 (1967) 49–69

259. Kümmel, H. M. *Ersatzrituale für den hethitischen König* (Studien zu den Bogazköy-Texten 3). Wiesbaden, 1967

260. Labat, R. 'Asarhaddon et la ville de Zaqqap', *RA* 53 (1959) 113–18

261. Labat, R. 'Kaštariti, Phraorte et les débuts de l'histoire Mède', *JA* 1961, 1–12

262. Laessøe, J. 'The irrigation system at Ulḫu, 8th Century B.C.', *JCS* 5 (1951) 21–32

263. Lambert, W. G. 'A part of the ritual for the substitute king', *AfO* 18 (1957–8) 109–12; 19 (1959–60) 119

264. Lambert, W. G. 'An eye-stone of Esarhaddon's queen and other similar gems', *RA* 63 (1969) 65–71

265. Landsberger, B. and Bauer, T. 'Zu neuveröffentlichten Geschichtsquellen der Zeit von Asarhaddon bis Nabonid', *ZA* 37 (1927) 61–98, 215–22

266. Larsen, M. 'Unusual eponymy-datings from Mari and Assyria', *RA* 68 (1974) 15–24

267. Layard, A. H. *Inscriptions in the Cuneiform Character from Assyrian Monuments*. London, 1851

268. Lewy, H. 'Nitokris-Naqî'a', *JNES* 11 (1952) 264–86

269. Lewy, J. 'The chronology of Sennacherib's accession', in *Miscellanea orientalia dedicata Antonio Deimel annos LXX complenti* (An. Or. 12) 225–31. Rome, 1935

270. Luckenbill, D. *The Annals of Sennacherib* (OIP 2). Chicago, 1924

271. Mallowan, M. E. L. 'The excavations at Nimrud (Kalḫu), 1951', *Iraq* 14 (1952) 1–23

272. Meissner, B. 'Naki'a', *MVAG* 8/3 (1903) 96–101

273. Millard, A. R. 'Esarhaddon cylinder fragments from Fort Shalmaneser, Nimrud', *Iraq* 23 (161) 176–8

274. Na'aman, N. 'Sennacherib's "Letter to God" on his campaign to Judah', *BASOR* 214 (1974) 25–39

275. Na'aman, N. 'The Brook of Egypt and Assyrian policy on the border of Egypt', *Tel Aviv* 6 (1979) 68–90

276. Na'aman, N. 'Sennacherib's campaign to Judah and the date of the LMLK stamps', *VT* 29 (1979) 61–86

277. Nougayrol, J. 'Nouveau fragment de prisme d'Asarhadon relatant la restauration de Babylone', *AfO* 18 (1957–8) 314–18
278. Nougayrol, J. and Parrot, A. 'Asarhaddon et Naqi'a sur un bronze du Louvre', *Syria* 33 (1956) 147–60
279. Olmstead, A. T. E. 'The Assyrians in Asia Minor', in Buckler, W. H. and Calder, W. M. (eds.) *Anatolian Studies presented to Sir William Ramsay*, 283–96. Manchester, 1923
280. Oppenheim, A. L. 'On royal gardens in Mesopotamia', *JNES* 24 (1965) 328–33
281. Parpola, S. Review of A 96, *JSS* 21 (1976) 165–74
282. Parpola, S. 'The murderer of Sennacherib', *Mesopotamia* 8 (1980) 171–82
283. Postgate, J. N. 'Two Marduk ordeal fragments', *ZA* 60 (1969) 124–7
284. Postgate, J. N. 'Excavations in Iraq 1973–74', *Iraq* 37 (1975) 57–74
285. Reade, J. E. 'Sources for Sennacherib: the prisms', *JCS* 27 (1975) 189–96
286. Reade, J. E., 'Elam and Elamites in Assyrian sculpture', *AMI* N.F. 9 (1976) 97–106
287. Reade, J. E. 'Studies in Assyrian geography', *RA* 72 (1978) 47–72, 157–80.
288. Roberts, J. J. M. 'Myth *versus* history', *CBQ* 38 (1976) 1–13
289. Röllig, W. 'Nitokris von Babylon', *Beiträge zur Alten Geschichte und deren Nachleben* 1 (1969) 127–35
290. Safar, F. and Basmaji, F. 'Sennacherib's project for supplying Arbil with water', *Sumer* 2 (1946) 50–2
291. Sarkisian, D. N. 'On the causes of Esarhaddon's Šubrian campaign', *Drevneii Vostok* 3 (1978) 168–78, 273
292. Scheil, V. 'Une brique de Sennachérib avec mention probable du nom du meurtrier de ce roi', *ZA* 11 (1896) 425–7
293. Scheil, V. 'Notes d'épigraphie et d'archéologie assyriennes', *Rec. Trav.* 20 (1898) 200–10; 22 (1900) 27–39; 26 (1904) 22–9
294. Schott, A. and Schaumberger, J. 'Vier Briefe Mâr Ištars an Asarhaddon über Himmelserscheinungen der Jahre – 670/668', *ZA* 47 (1941) 89–130
295. Smith, G. *Assyrian Discoveries.* New York, 1875
296. Smith, S. *The First Campaign of Sennacherib, King of Assyria, B.C. 705–681.* London, 1921
297. Soden, W. von. 'Beiträge zum Verständnis der neuassyrischen Briefe über die Ersatzkönigsriten', in Schubert, K. (ed.) *Festschrift für Prof. Dr. Viktor Christian*, 100–7. Vienna, 1956
298. Spalinger, A. 'Esarhaddon and Egypt: an analysis of the first invasion of Egypt', *Or.* 43 (1974) 295–326
299. Spalinger, A. 'The foreign policy of Egypt preceding the Assyrian conquest', *Chron. d'Eg.* 53/105 (1978) 22–47
300. Speiser, E. A. 'University of Pennsylvania Museum – Baghdad school expedition at Billah', *BASOR* 40 (1930) 11–14
301. Suleiman, A. 'Mosul University excavations at Tarbişu', *Adab al-Rafidain* 2 (1971) 41–93 [In Arabic]
302. van Leeuwen, C. 'Sanchérib devant Jérusalem', *Oudtestamentische Studiën* 14 (1965) 245–72

303. Vieyra, M. 'Notes d'histoire', *RA* 54 (1960) 41–4
304. Weidner, E. F. 'Hochverrat gegen Asarhaddon', *AfO* 17 (1954–6) 5–9
305. Weinfeld, M. 'The loyalty oath in the Ancient Near East', *UF* 8 (1976) 379–414
306. Winckler, H. *Sammlung von Keilschrifttexten* i–iii. Leipzig, 1893–5
306A. Winter, I. 'On the problems of Karatepe: the reliefs and their content', *Anat. Stud.* 29 (1979) 115–51
307. Wiseman, D. J. 'The vassal-treaties of Esarhaddon', *Iraq* 20 (1958) 1–99
308. Wiseman, D. J. 'Fragments of historical texts from Nimrud', *Iraq* 26 (1964) 118–24
309. Young, T. C. 'The Iranian migration into the Zagros', *Iran* 5 (1967) 11–34
310. Zeissl, G. von. *Äthiopen und Assyrer in Ägypten* (Ägyptologische Forschungen Heft 14). 2nd edn. Glückstadt, 1955

7. REIGN OF ASHURBANIPAL

311. Arnaud, D. 'Assurbanipal et le dieu Nabû: un nouveau témoignage', in *Mélanges d'Histoire des Religions offerts à Henri-Charles Puech*, 27–32. Paris, 1974
312. Aynard, J.-M. *Le prisme du Louvre AO 19.939* (Bibliothèque de l'Ecole des Hautes Études 309). Paris, 1957
313. Bauer, T. *Das Inschriftenwerk Assurbanipals* i–ii. Leipzig, 1933
314. Borger, R. 'Reliefbeischriften Assurbanipals', *AfO* 23 (1970) 90
315. Buis, P. 'Un traité d'Assurbanipal', *VT* 28 (1978) 469–72
316. Campbell, A. F. 'An historical prologue in a seventh-century treaty', *Biblica* 50 (1969) 534–5
317. Cogan, M. and Tadmor, H. 'Gyges and Ashurbanipal: a study in literary transmission', *Or.* 46 (1977) 65–85
318. Craig, J. A. *Assyrian and Babylonian Religious Texts* i–ii. Leipzig, 1895–7
319. Deller, K. 'The ruling class of Nimrud c. 640 B.C.', *Or.* 35 (1966) 190–2
320. Deller, K. 'Die Briefe des Adad-šumu-uṣur', *AOAT* 1 (1969) 45–64
321. Deller, K. and Parpola, S. 'Ein Vertrag Assurbanipals mit dem arabischen Stamm Qedar', *Or.* 37 (1968) 464–6
322. Ebeling, E. *Keilschrifttexte aus Assur, Religiösen Inhalts* (WVDOG 28 and 34). Leipzig, 1915–23
323. Ebeling, E. and Köcher, F. *Literarische Keilschrifttexte aus Assur*. Berlin, 1953
324. Fales, M. 'A literary code in Assyrian royal inscriptions: the case of Ashurbanipal's Egyptian campaigns', in A 20, 169–202 (1981)
325. Gelio, R. 'La délégation envoyée par Gygès, roi de Lydie. Un cas de propaganda idéologique', in A 20, 203–24 (1981)
326. Grayson, A. K. 'The chronology of the reign of Ashurbanipal', *ZA* 70 (1980) 227–45
327. Hartman, L. F. 'The date of the Cimmerian threat against Ashurbanipal according to ABL 1391' *JNES* 21 (1962) 25–37
328. Hinz, W. *The Lost World of Elam*. London, 1972

329. Labat, R. 'Un prince éclairé: Assurbanipal', *CRAI* 1972, 670–6
330. Lambert, W. G. 'Two texts from the early part of the reign of Ashurbanipal', *AfO* 18 (1957–8) 382–7
331. Langdon, S. *Babylonian Penitential Psalms* (OECT 6). Paris, 1927
332. Macmillan, K. D. 'Some cuneiform tablets bearing on the religion of Babylonia and Assyria', *Beiträge zur Assyriologie* 5/v, 531–712. Leipzig, 1906
333. Meissner, B. 'Die Gemahlin Assurbanipals', *OLZ* 18 (1915) 37–8
334. Meissner, B. and Opitz, D. *Studien zum Bît Hilâni im Nordpalast Assurbanaplis zu Ninive* (Abhandlungen der Preussischen Akademie der Wissenschaften 1939/xvii). Berlin, 1940
335. Millard, A. R. 'Fragments of historical texts from Nineveh: Ashurbanipal', *Iraq* 30 (1968) 98–111
336. Perry, G. *Hymnen und Gebete an Sin* (Leipziger semitistische Studien 2/iv). Leipzig, 1907
337. Piepkorn, A. C. *Historical Prism Inscriptions of Ashurbanipal I: Editions E, B₁₋₅, D, & K* (AS 5). Chicago, 1933
338. Schawe, J. 'Das Land Ḫu(Pak)-di(ki)-mi-ri', *AfO* 8 (1931–2) 52–3
339. Solovéva, S. S. 'Lidii pri Gigese i ee vzaimootnosheniia s Assiriei' [Lydia in the time of Gyges and its relations with Assyria], *Drevnii Vostok*, Sbornik 1, 246–61. Moscow, 1975
340. Spalinger, A. 'Assurbanipal and Egypt: a source study', *JAOS* 94 (1974) 316–28
341. Spalinger, A. 'An Egyptian motif in an Assyrian text', *BASOR* 223 (1976) 64–7
342. Spalinger, A. 'Psammetichus, king of Egypt: 1', *JARCE* 13 (1976) 133–47
343. Spalinger, A. 'The date of the death of Gyges and its historical implications', *JAOS* 98 (1978) 400–9
344. Streck, M. *Assurbanipal und die letzten assyrischen Könige bis zum Untergange Ninivehs* I–III (VAB 7). Leipzig, 1916
345. Thapar, R. 'A possible identification of Meluḫḫa, Dilmun and Makan', *JESHO* 18 (1975) 1–42
346. Weidner, E. F. 'Assyrische Beschreibungen der Kriegs-Reliefs Aššurbânaplis', *AfO* 8 (1932–3) 175–203
347. Weidner, E. F. 'Assurbânipal in Assur', *AfO* 13 (1939–41) 204–18 and plates
348. Zimmern, H. 'Gilgameš-Omina und Gilgameš-Orakel', *ZA* 24 (1910) 168–71

8. THE FALL OF ASSYRIA

349. Andrae, W. and Lenzen, H. *Die Partherstadt Assur* (WVDOG 57). Leipzig, 1933
350. Baatz, D. 'The Hatra Ballista', *Sumer* 33 (1977) 141–52
351. Bellinger, A. R. *The Excavations at Dura-Europos*, VI: *The Coins*. New Haven, 1949

352. Borger, R. 'Mesopotamien in den Jahren 629–621 v. Chr.', *WZKM* 55 (1959) 62–76

353. Borger, R. 'Der Aufstieg des neubabylonischen Reiches', *JCS* 19 (1965) 59–78

354. Cooper, J. S. 'A Sumerian šu-íl-la from Nimrud with a prayer for Sin-šar-iškun', *Iraq* 32 (1970) 51–67

355. Curtis, J. E. and Grayson, A. K. 'Some inscribed objects from Sherif Khan in the British Museum', *Iraq* 44 (1982) 87–94

356. Dalley, S. and Postgate, J. N. *The Tablets from Fort Shalmaneser* (CTN 3). London, 1984

357. Donbaz, V. and Grayson, A. K. *Royal Inscriptions on Clay Cones from Ashur now in Istanbul* (The Royal Inscriptions of Mesopotamia, Supplements 1). Toronto, 1984

358. Driver, G. R. *Aramaic Documents of the Fifth Century B.C.* Oxford, 1954

359. Edzard, D. O. 'Eine Inschrift Aššuretillilānis aus Nippur', *AfO* 19 (1959–60) 143

360. Falkner, M. 'Neue Inschriften aus der Zeit Sin-šarru-iškuns', *AfO* 16 (1952–3) 305–10

361. Falkner, M. 'Die Eponymen der spätassyrischen Zeit', *AfO* 17 (1954–6) 100–20

362. Gadd, C. J. 'The Harran inscriptions of Nabonidus', *Anat. Stud.* 8 (1958) 35–92

363. Grayson, A. K. 'Cylinder C of Sîn-šarra-iškun, a new text from Baghdad', in Wevers, J. W. and Redford, D. B. (eds.) *Studies on the Ancient Palestinian World* (Toronto Semitic Texts and Studies 2) 157–68. Toronto, 1972

364. Gurney, O. R. 'The Sultantepe tablets', *Anat. Stud.* 2 (1952) 25–35, 3 (1953) 15–25

365. Heidel, A. 'A new hexagonal prism of Esarhaddon (676 B.C.)', *Sumer* 12 (1956) 9–37

366. Jacob-Rost, L, 'Die Tonnagel-Inschriften aus Assur', *Forschungen und Berichte* 22 (1982) 137–77

367. Kennedy, D. A. 'Documentary evidence for the economic base of early Neo-Babylonian society: Part II: a survey of Babylonian economic texts, 626–605 B.C.', *JCS* 38 (1986) 172–244

368. Killick, R. G. and Black, J. A. 'Excavations in Iraq, 1983–84', *Iraq* 47 (1985) 215–39

369. Kinnier Wilson, J. V. 'The Kurba'il statue of Shalmaneser III', *Iraq* 24 (1962) 90–115

370. Leichty, E. 'An inscription of Aššur-etel-ilani', *JAOS* 103 (1983) 217–20

371. Lidzbarski, M. *Altaramäische Urkunden aus Assur* (WVDOG 38). Leipzig, 1921

372. Madhloum, T. 'Nineveh: the 1967–1968 campaign', *Sumer* 24 (1968) 45–51

373. Maricq, A. 'Classica et Orientalia 2. Les dernières années de Hatra: l'alliance romaine', *Syria* 34 (1957) 288–96

374. Millard, A. R. 'Some Aramaic epigraphs', *Iraq* 34 (1972) 131–7
375. Millard, A. R. 'Assyrians and Arameans', *Iraq* 45 (1983) 101–8
376. Mustafa, M. A. 'The discovery of a statue of Hermes at Nineveh', *Sumer* 10 (1954) 280–3 [In Arabic]
377. Oates, D. 'A note on three Latin inscriptions from Hatra', *Sumer* 11 (1955) 39–43
378. Oates, D. 'The Roman frontier in northern Iraq', *Geographical Journal* 122 (1956) 190–9
379. Oates, D. 'Ezida: the Temple of Nabu', *Iraq* 19 (1957) 26–39
380. Oates, D. 'The Assyrian building south of the Nabu Temple', *Iraq* 20 (1958) 109–13
381. Oates, D. 'Fort Shalmaneser – an interim report', *Iraq* 21 (1959) 98–129
382. Oates, D. 'The excavations at Nimrud (Kalḫu), 1960', *Iraq* 23 (1961) 1–14
383. Oates, D. 'The excavations at Nimrud (Kalḫu), 1961', *Iraq* 24 (1962) 1–25
384. Oates, D. 'The excavations at Nimrud (Kalḫu), 1962', *Iraq* 25 (1963) 6–37
385. Oates, D. 'Dilmun and the Late Assyrian Empire', in Al Khalifa, Shaikha, H. A. and Rice, M. (eds.) *Bahrain Through the Ages: The Archaeology*, 428–34. London, 1986
386. Oates, D. and Oates, J. 'Nimrud 1957: the Hellenistic village', *Iraq* 20 (1958) 114–57
387. Oates, D. and Oates, J. 'Ain Sinu: a Roman frontier post in northern Iraq', *Iraq* 21 (1959) 207–42
388. Oates, D. and Reid, J. H. 'The Burnt Palace and the Nabu Temple: Nimrud excavations, 1955', *Iraq* 18 (1956) 22–39
389. Oates, J. 'Late Assyrian pottery from Fort Shalmaneser', *Iraq* 21 (1959) 130–46
390. Oates, J. 'Assyrian chronology, 631–612 B.C.', *Iraq* 27 (1965) 135–59
391. Oppenheim, A. L. '"Siege documents" from Nippur', *Iraq* 17 (1955) 69–89
392. Postgate, J. N. 'An Assyrian altar from Nineveh', *Sumer* 26 (1970) 133–6
393. Reade, J. E. 'The accession of Sinsharishkun', *JCS* 23 (1970–1) 1–9
394. Reade, J. E. 'Narrative composition in Assyrian sculpture', *Bagh. Mitt.* 10 (1979) 52–110
395. Safar, F. and Mustafa, M. A. *Hatra, the City of the Sun-God.* Baghdad, 1974 [In Arabic]
396. al-Salihi, W. *Hatra.* Baghdad, 1973
397. al-Salihi, W. 'New light on the identity of the Triad of Hatra', *Sumer* 31 (1975) 75–80
398. Scheil, V. 'Sin-šar-iškun fils d'Aššurbanipal', *ZA* 11 (1896) 47–9
399. Schramm, W. 'Assyrische Königsinschriften'. *We. Or.* 8 (1975) 37–48
400. Segal, J. B. 'An Aramaic ostracon from Nimrud', *Iraq* 19 (1957) 139–45
401. Soden, W. von. 'Aššuretellilāni, Sînsarriškun, Sînšum(u)līšer und die Ereignisse im Assyrerreich nach 635 v. Chr.', *ZA* 58 (1967) 241–55

402. Toynbee, J. M. C. 'Two male portrait-heads of Romans from Hatra', *Sumer* 26 (1970) 231–5
403. Vattioni, F. 'Epigrafia aramaica', *Augustinianum* 10 (1970) 493–532

9. ASSYRIAN LIFE

(a) The monarchy

404. Frankfort, H. *Kingship and the Gods*. Chicago, 1948
405. Gadd, C. J. *Ideas of Divine Rule in the Ancient East* (The Schweich Lectures of the British Academy, 1945). London, 1948
406. Garelli, P. 'Les temples et le pouvoir royal en Assyrie du XIVe au VIIIe siècle', in *Le Temple et le Culte* (CRRA 20) 116–24. Leiden, 1975
407. Garelli, P. 'Hofstaat B. Assyrisch', A 16, 4 (1975) 446–52
408. Garelli, P. 'L'Etat et la légitimité royale sous l'empire assyrien', in A 32, 319–28 (1979)
409. Garelli, P. 'Les empires mésopotamiens', in Duverger, M. (ed.) *Le concept d'empire*, 25–47. Paris, 1980
410. Garelli, P. 'La conception de la royauté en Assyrie', in A 20, 1–11 (1981)
411. Garelli, P. 'La propagande royale assyrienne', *Akkadica* 27 (1982) 16–29
412. Grayson, A. K. 'The early development of Assyrian monarchy', *UF* 3 (1971) 311–19
413. Labat, R. *Le charactère religieux de la royauté assyro-babylonienne*. Paris, 1939
414. Labat, R. Review of A 404, *JCS* 2 (1948) 157–60
415. Reade, J. E. and Renger, J. 'Kronprinz' in A 16, 6 (1981) 248–50
416. Soden, W. von. 'Religiöse Unsicherheit: Säkularisierungstendenzen und Aberglaube zur Zeit der Sargoniden', *Analecta Biblica* 12 (1959) 356–67
417. Tadmor, H. 'History and ideology in the Assyrian royal inscriptions', in A 20, 13–33 (1981)
418. Zablocka, J. 'Bemerkungen zum Problem der neuassyrischen Königsideologie', *Zeszyty Naukowe Uniwersytetu Jagiellonskiego* DXXXVI, *Prace Historyczne*, z. 63 (1980) 17–28

(b) The bureaucracy

419. Follet, R. '"Deuxième bureau" et information diplomatique dans l'Assyrie des Sargonides, quelques notes', *RSO* 32 (1957) 61–81
420. Forrer, E. *Die Provinzeinteilung des assyrischen Reiches*. Leipzig, 1920
421. Garelli, P. 'Problèmes de stratification sociale dans l'empire assyrien', in A 17, 73–9 (1972)
422. Garelli, P. 'Les sujets du roi d'Assyrie', in A 21, 189–213 (1973)
423. Garelli, P. 'L'organisation de l'Empire Assyrien', in A 23, 128–39 (1974)
424. Garelli, P. 'Remarques sur l'administration de l'Empire Assyrien', *RA* 68 (1974) 129–40
425. Garelli, P. 'Les pouvoirs locaux en Assyrie', in Finet, A. (ed.) *Les*

pouvoirs locaux en Mésopotamie et dans les régions adjacentes, 76–91. Brussels, 1981

426. Grayson, A. K. 'Studies in Neo-Assyrian history: the ninth century B.C.', *Bi. Or.* 33 (1976) 134–40

427. Henshaw, R. A. 'The office of Šaknu in Neo-Assyrian times', *JAOS* 87 (1967) 517–25; 88 (1968) 461–83

428. Jakobsen, V. A. 'The social structure of the Neo-Assyrian empire', in A 14, 277–95 (1969)

429. Klauber, E. *Assyrisches Beamtentum nach Briefen aus der Sargonidenzeit* (Leipziger Semitistische Studien v/3). Leipzig, 1910

430. Olmstead, A. T. E. 'Assyrian government of dependencies', *The American Political Science Review* 12 (1918) 63–77

431. Opitz, D. 'Beamter: Assyrische Zeit', in A 16, 1 (1932) 457–66

431A. Oppenheim, A. L. 'A note on ša rēši', *JANES* 5 (1973) 325–34

432. Page, S. 'A stela of Adad-nirari III and Nergal-ereš from Tell al Rimah', *Iraq* 30 (1968) 139–53

433. Pecírková, J. 'The administrative organization of the Neo-Assyrian Empire', *Ar. Or.* 45 (1977) 211–28

434. Postgate, J. N. '"Princeps Index" in Assyria', *RA* 74 (1980) 180–2

435. Reade, J. E. 'The Neo-Assyrian court and army: evidence from the sculptures', *Iraq* 34 (1972) 87–112

436. Reade, J. E. 'Neo-Assyrian monuments in their historical context: novi homines', in A 20, 156–60 (1981)

437. Smith, S. 'The Assyrian state', in *CAH* III¹, 92–5. Cambridge, 1925

438. Tadmor, H. 'Assyria and the west: the ninth century and its aftermath', in A 24, 36–48 (1975)

439. Unger, E. 'Two seals of the ninth century B.C. from Shadikanni on the Habur', *BASOR* 130 (1930) 15–21

(c) Social structure

440. Diaknonoff, I. M. *Razvitie zemel'nikh otnoshenii v Assirii* [The development of agrarian conditions in Assyria]. Leningrad, 1949

441. Diakonoff, I. M. 'K voprosu o sud'be plennykh v Assirii i Urartu' [On the question of the fate of prisoners of war in Assyria and Urartu], *VDI* 39 (1952/1) 90–100

442. Fales, F. M. 'Populazione servile e programmazione padronale in tarda età Neo-Assira', *Or. Ant.* 14 (1975) 325–60

443. Postgate, J. N. 'Some remarks on conditions in the Assyrian countryside', *JESHO* 17 (1974) 225–43

443A. Tallquist, K. L. *Assyrian Personal Names*. Helsinki, 1914

444. van Driel, G. 'Land and people in Assyria', *Bi. Or.* 27 (1970) 168–75

445. Zablocka, J. 'Landarbeiter im Reich der Sargoniden', in A 17, 209–15 (1972)

446. Zablocka, J. 'Zum Problem der Neuassyrischen Dorfgemeinde', in *Studia Historiae Oeconomicae* 13 (1978) 61–72

(d) Law

447. Deller, K. H. 'Die Rolle des Richters in neuassyrischen Prozessrecht', in *Studi in Onore di Edoardo Volterra* VI, 639–53. Milan, 1972
448. Iakobson, V. A. 'Poruchitel'stvo v novoassiriiskoi prave' [On guaranty in Neo-Assyrian law], in *Palestinskii Sbornik* 25 (1974) 45–52
449. Iakobson, V. A. 'Studies in Neo-Assyrian law', *AOF* 1 (1974) 115–21
450. Postgate, J. N. 'Royal exercise of justice under the Assyrian Empire', in A 22, 417–26 (1974)

(e) The economy

451. Elat, M. 'The economic relations of the Neo-Assyrian Empire with Egypt', *JAOS* 98 (1978) 20–34
452. Fales, F. M. 'Il villaggio assiro Bit Abu-Ila'a', *Dialoghi di Archeologia* NS 3 (1981) 66–84
453. Garelli, P. 'Le système fiscal de l'empire assyrien', in van Effenterre, H. (ed.) *Points de vue sur la fiscalité antique* (Publications de la Sorbonne, Série 'Etudes' 14), 7–18. Paris, 1979
454. al-Jadir, Walid. 'Le statut social des Tisserands à l'époque des Sargonides', *Sumer* 27 (1971) 63–75
455. Jankowska, N. B. 'Some problems of the economy of the Assyrian Empire' in A 14, 253–76 (1969)
456. Levine, L. D. 'East–west trade in the late Iron Age', in *Colloques Internationaux du Centre National de la Recherche Scientifique* No. 567, 171–86. Paris, 1976
457. Martin, W. J. *Tribut und Tributleistungen bei den Assyrern* (Studia Orientalia 8/1). Helsinki, 1936
458. Maxwell-Hyslop, K. R. 'Assyrian sources of iron', *Iraq* 36 (1974) 139–54
459. Oppenheim, A. L. 'Essay on overland trade in the first millennium B.C.', *JCS* 21 (1967) 236–54
460. Oppenheim, A. L. 'Trade in the Ancient Near East', in *Fifth International Congress of Economic History*, 1–37. Moscow, 1970
461. Pecírková, J. 'On land tenure in Assyria', in Hruška, B. and Komoroczy, G. (eds.) *Festschrift Lubor Matouš* II, 187–200. Budapest, 1978
462. Pecírková, J. 'Social and economic aspects of Mesopotamian history in the work of Soviet historians (Mesopotamia in the first millennium B.C.)', *Ar. Or.* 47 (1979) 111–22
463. Pleiner, R. and Bjorkman, J. K. 'The Assyrian Iron Age: the history of iron in the Assyrian civilization', *PAPS* 118 (1974) 283–313
464. Postgate, J. N. *Taxation and Conscription in the Assyrian Empire* (Studia Pohl, Series Major 3). Rome, 1974
465. Postgate, J. N. 'The economic structure of the Assyrian Empire', in A 32, 193–221 (1979)
466. Salonen, A. *Agricultura Mesopotamica* (AASF B/149). Helsinki, 1968

467. Salonen, A. *Die Ziegeleien im Alten Mesopotamien* (AASF B/171). Helsinki, 1972
468. Salonen, E. *Über das Erwerbsleben im Alten Mesopotamien. Untersuchungen zu den akkadischen Berufsnamen* (Studia Orientalia 41). Helsinki, 1970
469. Zablocka, J. *Stosunki Agrarne w panstwie Sargoniden* (Universytet im. Adama Michiewicza w Poznaniu, Wyzdial filozoficzno, historyczny, Seria historica, 47). Poznan, 1971
470. Zablocka, J. 'Palast und König: ein Beitrag zu den neuassyrischen Eigentumsverhältnissen', *AOF* 1 (1974) 91–113
471. Zawadski, S. *Podstawy Gospodarcze Nowasyryjskiej Çwiatyni* [The economic foundations of the Neo-Assyrian temple]. Poznan, 1981

(f) Warfare

472. Farber, W., Littauer, M. A. and Crouwel, J. H. 'Kampfwagen', in A 16, 5 (1980) 336–51
473. Grayson, A. K. 'Ambush and animal pit in Akkadian', in A 2, 90–4 (1964)
474. Hroude, B. 'Der Assyrische Streitwagen', *Iraq* 25 (1963) 115–18
475. Hunger, H. 'Heerwesen und Kriegführung der Assyrer', *Der Alte Orient* 12/4 (1911)
476. Madhloum, T. 'Assyrian siege-engines', *Sumer* 21 (1965) 9–16
477. Manitius, W. 'Das stehende Heer der Assyrerkönige und seine Organisation', *ZA* 24 (1910) 97–149, 185–224
478. Nagel, W. *Der mesopotamische Streitwagen und seine Entwicklung im ostmediterranien Bereich* (Berliner Beiträge zur Vor- und Frühgeschichte 10). Berlin, 1966
479. Oakeshott, R. E. *The Archaeology of Weapons, Arms and Armour from Prehistory to the Age of Chivalry*. London, 1963
480. Oded, B. *Mass Deportation and Deportees in the Neo-Assyrian Empire*. Wiesbaden, 1979
481. Saggs, H. W. F. 'Assyrian warfare in the Sargonid period', *Iraq* 25 (1963) 145–54
482. Salonen, A. *Die Landfahrzeuge des Alten Mesopotamien* (AASF B/72/3). Helsinki, 1951
483. Salonen, A. *Hippologica Accadica* (AASF B/100). Helsinki, 1955
484. Salonen, E. *Die Waffen der Alten Mesopotamien* (Studia Orientalia 33). Helsinki, 1965
485. Smith, S. 'The army', in *CAH* III[1], 99–101. Cambridge, 1925
486. Soden, W. von. 'Die Assyrer und die Krieg', *Iraq* 25 (1963) 131–44
487. Weippert, M. '"Heiliger Krieg" in Israel und Assyrien', *ZAW* 84 (1972) 460–93
488. Wiesner, J. 'Zum Stand des Streitwagenforschung', *Acta Praehistorica et Archaeologica* 1 (1970) 191–4
489. Yadin, Y. *The Art of Warfare in Biblical Lands*. New York, 1963

(g) The hunt

490. Grayson, A. K. 'New evidence on an Asssyrian hunting practice', in A 55, 3–5 (1970)
491. Meissner, B. 'Assyrische Jagd', *Der Alte Orient* 13/2 (1911)

(h) Religion

492. Bottéro, J. 'Symptôme, signes, écritures', in Vernant, J. P. *et al.* (eds.) *Divination et rationalité*. Paris, 1974
493. Contenau, G. *La divination chez les Assyriens et les Babyloniens*. Paris, 1940
494. Dhorme, E. 'Les religions de Babylonie et d'Assyrie', in *Les anciennes religions orientales* II, 1–330. Paris, 1949
495. Frankena, R. *Tākultu: de sacrale maaltijd in het Assyrische ritueel*. Leiden, 1954
496. Frankena, R. 'New materials for the Tākultu ritual: additions and corrections', *Bi. Or.* 18 (1961) 199–207
497. Klauber, E. G. *Politisch-religiöse Texte aus der Sargonidenzeit*. Leipzig, 1913
498. Knudtzon, J. A. *Assyrische Gebete an den Sonnengott für Staat und königliches Haus aus der Zeit Asarhaddons und Asurbanipals* I–II. Leipzig, 1893
499. McKay, J. W. 'The Assyrian religio-political ideal', in *Religion in Judah under the Assyrians*, 60–6. Naperville, Illinois, 1973
500. Menzel, B. *Assyrische Tempel* I–II (Studia Pohl: Series Major 10/1–2). Rome, 1981
501. Pecírková, J. 'The administrative organization of the Neo-Assyrian Empire: 3. Administration of the temples', *Ar. Or.* 45 (1977) 217–20
502. Postgate, J. N. 'The role of the temple in the Mesopotamian secular community', in Ucko, P. J. *et al.* (eds.) *Man, Settlement and Urbanism*, 811–25. London, 1972
503. Postgate, J. N. 'The Bit Akiti in Assyrian Nabu temples', *Sumer* 30 (1974) 51–74
504. Schwenzer, W. 'Das national Heiligtum des assyrischen Reiches: die Baugeschichte des Aššur-Tempels Ehursagkurkurra', *AfO* 7 (1931–2) 239–51; 8 (1932–3) 34–45, 113–23; 9 (1933–4) 41–8
505. Soden, W. von. 'Religiöse Unsicherheit: Säkularisierungstendenzen und Aberglaube zur Zeit der Sargoniden', *Analecta Biblica* 12 (1959) 356–67
506. Tallquist, K. L. *Der Assyrische Gott* (Studia Orientalia 4/III). Helsinki, 1932
507. van Driel, G. *The Cult of Aššur*. Assen, 1969

(i) Libraries

508. Parpola, S. 'Assyrian library records', *JNES* 42 (1983) 1–29
509. Weidner, E. F. 'Die Bibliothek Tiglathpilesers I.', *AfO* 16 (1952–3) 197–215

510. Weitemeyer, M. 'Archive and library technique in Ancient Mesopotamia', *Libri (International Library Review)* 56/3 (1956) 217–38

III. BABYLONIA

I. HISTORICAL EVENTS, 747–626 B.C.

511. Adams, R. *Land behind Baghdad: A History of Settlement on the Diyala Plains.* Chicago, 1965

512. Adams, R. 'Settlement and irrigation patterns in ancient Akkad', in Gibson, McG. *The City and Area of Kish*, 182–208. Coconut Grove, 1972

513. Adams, R. *Heartland of Cities: Surveys of Ancient Settlement and Land Use on the Central Floodplain of the Euphrates.* Chicago, 1981

514. Adams, R. and Nissen, H. *The Uruk Countryside: The Natural Setting of Urban Societies.* Chicago, 1972

515. Ahmed, S. 'Ashurbanipal and Shamash-shum-ukin during Esarhaddon's reign', *Abr-Nahrain* 6 (1965–6) 53–62

516. Ahmed, S. 'Causes of Shamash-shum-ukin's uprising, 652–651 B.C.', *ZAW* 79 (1967) 1–13

517. Ahmed, S. *Southern Mesopotamia in the Time of Ashurbanipal.* The Hague, 1968

518. Barrelet, M.-T. *Figurines et reliefs en terre cuite de la Mésopotamie antique*, I: *Potiers, termes de métier, procédés de fabrication et production.* Paris, 1968

519. Bayliss, M. 'The cult of dead kin in Assyria and Babylonia', *Iraq* 35 (1973) 115–25

520. Becking, B. 'The two Neo-Assyrian documents from Gezer in their historical context', *JEOL* 27 (1981–2) 76–89

521. Bezold, C. 'Inschriften Sanheribs', in Schrader, E. (ed.) *Keilinschriftliche Bibliothek* II, 80–119. Berlin, 1890

522. Biggs, R. D. 'A Chaldaean inscription from Nippur', *BASOR* 179 (1965) 36–8

523. Böhl, F. M. Th. *Assyrische en nieuw-babylonische oorkonden (1100–91 v. Chr.).* Amsterdam, 1936

524. Böhl, F. M. Th. 'Eine Tauschurkunde aus dem fünften Regierungsjahr des Aššur-nādin-šumi (694 v. Chr.)', in *Orientalia neerlandica*, 116–37. Leiden, 1948

525. Borger, R. 'Zur Datierung des assyrischen Königs Sinšumulišir', *Or.* 38 (1969) 237–9

526. Borger, R. Review of A 644, *Bi. Or.* 29 (1972) 33–7

527. Borger, R. 'Zur Königsliste aus Uruk', *AfO* 25 (1974–7) 165–6

528. Boserup, E. *Population and Technological Change.* Chicago, 1981

529. Bottéro, J. 'Le substitut royal et son sort en Mésopotamie ancienne', *Akkadica* 9 (1978) 2–24

530. Brice, W. C. (ed.) *The Environmental History of the Near and Middle East since the Last Ice Age.* London, New York, and San Francisco, 1978

531. Brinkman, J. A. 'A preliminary catalogue of written sources for a political history of Babylonia: 1160–722 B.C.', *JCS* 16 (1962) 83–109

532. Brinkman, J. A. 'Merodach-Baladan II', in A 2, 6–53 (1964)

533. Brinkman, J. A. 'Elamite military aid to Merodach-Baladan', *JNES* 24 (1965) 161–6

534. Brinkman, J. A. 'Ur: 721–605 B.C.', *Or.* 34 (1965) 241–58

535. Brinkman, J. A. *A Political History of Post-Kassite Babylonia, 1158–722 B.C.* (An. Or. 43). Rome, 1968

536. Brinkman, J. A. 'The Akītu inscription of Bēl-ibni and Nabû-zēra-ušabši', *We. Or.* 5/1 (1969) 39–50

537. Brinkman, J. A. 'Ur: "The Kassite period and the period of the Assyrian kings"', *Or.* 38 (1969) 310–48

538. Brinkman, J. A. 'Documents relating to the reign of Aššur-nādin-šumi', *Or.* 41 (1972) 245–8

539. Brinkman, J. A. 'Foreign relations of Babylonia from 1600 to 625 B.C.: the documentary evidence', *AJA* 76 (1972) 271–81

540. Brinkman, J. A. 'Sennacherib's Babylonian problem: an interpretation', *JCS* 25 (1973) 89–95

541. Brinkman, J. A. 'The early Neo-Babylonian monarchy', in A 22, 409–15 (1974)

542. Brinkman, J. A. *Materials and Studies for Kassite History*, I: *A Catalogue of Cuneiform Sources Pertaining to Specific Monarchs of the Kassite Dynasty.* Chicago, 1976

543. Brinkman, J. A. 'Mesopotamian chronology of the historical period', in A 43, 335–48 (1977)

544. Brinkman, J. A. 'Notes on Arameans and Chaldeans in southern Babylonia in the early seventh century', *Or.* 46 (1977) 304–25

545. Brinkman, J. A. 'Babylonia under the Assyrian Empire, 745–627 B.C.', in A 32, 223–50 (1979)

546. Brinkman, J. A. 'Kandalānu', in A 16, 5 (1980) 368–9

547. Brinkman, J. A. 'Kudurru, A. Philologisch', in A 16, 6 (1981) 267–74

548. Brinkman, J. A. 'Babylonia c. 1000–748 B.C.' in *CAH* III².1, 282–313 (1982)

549. Brinkman, J. A. 'Bel-ibni's letters in the time of Sargon and Sennacherib', *RA* 77 (1983) 175–6

550. Brinkman, J. A. 'Through a glass darkly: Esarhaddon's retrospects on the downfall of Babylon', *JAOS* 103 (1983) 35–42

551. Brinkman, J. A. *Prelude to Empire: Babylonian Society and Politics, 747–626 B.C.* Philadelphia, 1984

552. Brinkman, J. A. 'Settlement surveys and documentary evidence: regional variation and secular trend in Mesopotamian demography', *JNES* 43 (1984) 169–80

552A. Brinkman, J. A. 'The Elamite-Babylonian frontier in the Neo-Elamite period, 750–625 B.C.,' in L. De Meyer *et al.*, eds. *Fragmenta historiae elamicae: mélanges offerts à M.-J. Steve* 199–207. Paris, 1986

552B. Brinkman, J. A. 'Textual evidence for bronze in Babylonia in the Early Iron Age,' in J. Curtis, ed. *Bronze-Working Centres in Western Asia, 1000–539 B.C.*, 135–68. London, 1988

552C. Brinkman, J. A. 'The Babylonian Chronicle revisited,' in *Festschrift for William L. Moran* (Harvard Semitic Series), 73–104

553. Brinkman, J. A. and Kennedy, D. A. 'Documentary evidence for the economic base of early Neo-Babylonian society: a survey of dated Babylonian economic texts, 721–626 B.C.', *JCS* 35 (1983) 1–90

553A. Brinkman, J. A. and Kennedy, D. A. 'Supplement to the survey of dated Babylonian economic texts, 721–626 B.C. (*JCS* 35 (1983) 1–90)', *JCS* 38 (1986) 99–106

553B. Brinkman, J. A. and Dalley, S. 'A royal kudurru from the reign of Aššur-nādin-šumi', *ZA* 78 (1988) 76–98

554. Buccellati, G. and Biggs, R. D. *Cuneiform Texts from Nippur: The Eighth and Ninth Seasons* (AS 17). Chicago, 1969

555. Buchanan, B. *Catalogue of Ancient Near Eastern Seals in the Ashmolean Museum*, 1: *Cylinder Seals*. Oxford, 1966

556. Calmeyer, P. Review of Jantzen, U. *Ägyptische und orientalische Bronzen aus dem Heraion von Samos*, *ZA* 63 (1973) 123–33

557. Caquot, A. 'Une inscription araméenne d'époque assyrienne', in *Hommages à André Dupont-Sommer*, 9–16. Paris, 1971

558. Civil, M. 'Note sur les inscriptions d'Asarhaddon à Nippur', *RA* 68 (1974) 94

559. Clay, A. T. *Legal and Commercial Transactions Dated in the Assyrian, Neo-Babylonian and Persian Periods Chiefly from Nippur* (BE VIII/1). Philadelphia, 1908

560. Clay, A. T. *Miscellaneous Inscriptions in the Yale Babylonian Collection* (YOS 1). New Haven- 1915

561. Cogan, M. 'Ashurbanipal prism F: notes on scribal techniques and editorial procedures', *JCS* 29 (1977) 97–107

562. Cogan, M. 'Omens and ideology in the Babylon inscription of Esarhaddon', in A 53, 76–87 (1983)

563. Cogan, M. and Tadmor, H. 'Ashurbanipal's conquest of Babylon: the first official report – Prism K', *Or.* 50 (1981) 229–40

563A. Collon, D. *First Impressions: Cylinder Seals in the Ancient Near East*. London, 1987.

564. Combe, E. *Histoire du culte de Sin en Babylonie et en Assyrie*. Paris, 1908

565. Contenau, G. *Contrats néo-babyloniens*, 1: *De Téglath-phalasar III à Nabonide* (TCL 12). Paris, 1927

566. Crawford, V. E. 'Nippur, the holy city', *Archaeology* 12 (1959) 74–83

567. Dalley, S. 'The nār-*d*banītu canal at Kish', *RA* 74 (1980) 189–90

568. De Meyer, L. *Tell ed-Der III*. Louvain, 1980

569. Diakonoff, I. M. 'A Babylonian political pamphlet from about 700 B.C.', in A 28, 343–9 (1965)

570. Dietrich, M. 'Neue Quellen zur Geschichte Babyloniens (I)', *We. Or.* 4 (1967–8) 61–103

571. Dietrich, M. 'Neue Quellen zur Geschichte Babyloniens (II)', *We. Or.* 4 (1967–8) 183–251; 5 (1969–70) 51–6

572. Dietrich, M. 'Neue Quellen zur Geschichte Babyloniens (III)', *We. Or.* 5 (1969–70) 176–90

573. Dietrich, M. 'Neue Quellen zur Geschichte Babyloniens (IV)', *We. Or.* 6 (1970–1) 157–62

574. Dietrich, M. *Die Aramäer Südbabyloniens in der Sargonidenzeit (700–648)*

(AOAT 7). Kevelaer and Neukirchen-Vluyn, 1970

575.   Dietrich, M. *Neo-Babylonian Letters from the Kuyunjik Collection* (CT 54). London, 1979

576.   Driver, G. R. 'The sale of a priesthood', *JRAS* Centenary Supplement (1924) 41–8

577.   Dubberstein, W. H. 'Assyrian-Babylonian chronology (669–612 B.C.)', *JNES* 3 (1944) 38–42

578.   Durand, J.-M. 'Les "slaves documents" de Merodach-Baladan', *JA* 267 (1979) 245–60

579.   Durand, J.-M. 'Note à propos de la date d'ABL 290', *RA* 75 (1981) 181–5

580.   Durand, J.-M. *Textes babyloniennes d'époque récente.* Paris, 1981

581.   Durand, J.-M. *Documents cunéiformes de la IVe section de l'École Pratique des Hautes Études, I: Catalogue et copies cunéiformes.* Geneva and Paris, 1982

582.   Edzard, D. O. 'Kaldu', in A 16, 5 (1977) 291–7

582A.   Ellis, M. 'Neo-Babylonian texts in the Yale Babylonian Collection,' *JCS* 36 (1984) 1–63.

583.   Eph'al, I. '"Arabs" in Babylonia in the 8th century B.C.', *JAOS* 94 (1974) 108–15

584.   Eph'al, I. 'On warfare and military control in the Ancient Near Eastern empires: a research outline', in A 53, 88–106 (1983)

585.   Fales, F. 'Il taglio e il trasporto di legname nelle lettere a Sargon II', in Carruba, O., Liverani, M. and Zaccagnini, C. (eds.) *Studi orientalistici in ricordo di Franco Pintore*, 49–92. Pavia, 1983

586.   Fecht, G. 'Zu den Namen ägyptischer Fürsten und Städte in den Annalen des Assurbanipal und der Chronik des Asarhaddon', *Mitt. deutsch. Inst. Kairo* 16 (1958) 112–19

587.   Follet, R. 'Une nouvelle inscription de Merodach-Baladan II', *Biblica* 35 (1954) 413–28

588.   Frame, G. 'Babylonia 689–627 B.C.: a political history.' Unpublished Ph.D. dissertation, University of Chicago, 1981.

589.   Frame, G. 'Another Babylonian eponym', *RA* 76 (1982) 157–66

590.   Frame, G. 'The "First Families" of Borsippa during the early Neo-Babylonian period', *JCS* 36 (1984) 67–80

591.   Fried, M. H. *The Notion of Tribe.* Menlo Park, California, 1975

592.   Frymer-Kensky, T. 'The tribulations of Marduk: the so-called "Marduk ordeal text"', *JAOS* 103 (1983) 131–41

593.   Gadd, C. J. *Royal Inscriptions* (UET 1). London, 1928

594.   Gadd, C. J. 'Babylonian antiquities from the Alnwick Castle collection', *BM Quart.* 16 (1951–2) 43–5

595.   Gadd, C. J. 'Inscribed barrel cylinder of Marduk-apla-iddina II', *Iraq* 15 (1953) 123–34

596.   de Genouillac, H. 'Texte de Sargon le jeune provenant des fouilles d'el-Aḥymer', *RA* 10 (1913) 83–7

597.   Gibson, McG. *The City and Area of Kish.* Coconut Grove, 1972

598.   Gibson, McG. *et al. Excavations at Nippur: Twelfth Season* (OIC 23). Chicago, 1978

599. Gibson, McG. (ed) *Uch Tepe* I: *Tell Razuk, Tell Ahmed al-Mughir, Tell Ajamat.* Chicago and Copenhagen, 1981

600. Gibson, McG. 'Current Oriental Institute excavations in Iraq', *Bulletin of the Society for Mesopotamian Studies* 3 (1982) 16–32

601. Gibson, McG. 'Nippur under Assyrian domination: 15th season of excavation, 1981–82', *The Oriental Institute 1981–82 Annual Report,* 40–8. Chicago, 1982

602. Gibson, McG., Zettler, R. and Armstrong, J. 'The southern corner of Nippur: summary of excavations during the 14th and 15th seasons', *Sumer* 39 (1983) 170–90

603. de Goeje, M. J. 'Zur historischen Geographie Babyloniens', *ZDMG* 39 (1885) 1–16

604. Goetze, A. 'Additions to Parker and Dubberstein's Babylonian chronology', *JNES* 3 (1944) 43–6

605. Goetze, A. 'Esarhaddon's inscription from the Inanna Temple in Nippur', *JCS* 17 (1963) 119–31

606. Grayson, A. K. 'Problematical battles in Mesopotamian history', in A 28, 337–42 (1965)

607. Grayson, A. K. 'Königslisten und Chroniken, Akkadisch', in A 16, 6 (1980) 86–135

608. Greenfield, J. C. 'Babylonian–Aramaic relationship', in A 38, 471–82 (1982)

609. Gurney, O. R. 'Three contracts from Babylon', in A 13, 120–8 (1982)

610. Hallo, W. 'Dating the Mesopotamian past: the concept of eras from Sargon to Nabonasser', *Bulletin of the Society for Mesopotamian Studies* 6 (1983) 7–18

611. Hannoun, N. 'Recent excavations in the Himrin Basin: Tell al-Seeb and Tell Haddad', *Bulletin of the Society for Mesopotamian Studies* 2 (1982) 5–6

612. Hansen, D. and Dales, G. 'The Temple of Inanna *Queen of Heaven* at Nippur', *Archaeology* 15 (1962) 75–84

613. Hansman, J. F. 'The Mesopotamian delta in the first millennium B.C.', *Geographical Journal* 144 (1978) 49–61

614. Harper, P. O. 'Five clay sculptures of the Neo-Babylonian period', *Ir. Ant.* 17 (1982) 65–84

615. Heltzer, M. *The Suteans.* Naples, 1981

616. Hilprecht, H. *Explorations in Bible Lands during the 19th Century.* Philadelphia, 1903

617. Höffken, P. 'Heilszeitherrschererwartung im babylonischen Raum', *We. Or.* 9 (1977–8) 57–71

618. Hrouda, B. 'Zusammenfassender Vorbericht über die Ergebnisse der 1. Kampagne in Ishan Bahriyat/Isin', *Sumer* 29 (1973) 37–45

619. Hrouda, B. (ed.) *Isin-Išān Baḥrīyāt*, I: *Die Ergebnisse der Ausgrabungen 1973–1974* Munich, 1977

620. Hrouda, B. (ed.) *Isin-Išān Baḥrīyāt*, II: *Die Ergebnisse der Ausgrabungen 1975–1978.* Munich, 1981

621. Hunger, H. *Babylonische und assyrische Kolophone* (AOAT 2). Kevelaer and Neukirchen-Vluyn, 1968

622. Hunger, H. and Hirsch, H. *Vorträge gehalten auf der 28. Rencontre Assyriologique Internationale in Wien 6.–10. Juli 1981* (*AfO* Bh. 19). Horn, Austria, 1982

623. Hunger, H. and Kaufman, S. 'A new Akkadian prophecy text', *JAOS* 95 (1975) 371–5

624. Jacobsen, T. 'The waters of Ur', *Iraq* 22 (1960) 174–85

625. Jacobsen, T. *Salinity and Irrigation Agriculture in Antiquity* (Bi. Mes. 14). Malibu, 1982

626. Jacoby, F. *Die Fragmente der griechischen Historiker* III c 1. *Aegypten-Geten Nr. 608a–708*. Leiden, 1958

627. Jakob-Rost, L. 'Urkunden des 7. Jahrhundert v. u. Z. aus Babylon', *Forschungen und Berichte* 12 (1970) 49–60

628. Jantzen, U. *Ägyptische und orientalische Bronzen aus dem Heraion von Samos* (Samos 8). Bonn, 1972

629. Joannès, F. 'La localisation de Şurru à l'époque néo-babylonienne', *Semitica* 32 (1982) 35–43

630. Jordan, J. *UVB* 1 (1930)

631. Kienast, B. 'Mitteilung von einer Tontafel mit altsüdarabischer Beschriftung', *UVB* 14 (1958) 43–4

632. King, L. W. CT 22 and 26. London, 1906–9

633. King, L. W. *Babylonian Boundary-Stones and Memorial-Tablets in the British Museum* I–II. London, 1912

634. Koldewey, R. *Die Pflastersteine von Aiburschabu in Babylon* (WVDOG 2). Leipzig, 1901

635. Koldewey, R. *Die Tempel von Babylon und Borsippa* (WVDOG 15). Leipzig, 1911

636. Koldewey, R. *Das wieder erstehende Babylon*. 4th edn. Leipzig, 1925

637. König, F. W. *Die elamische Königsinschriften* (*AfO* Bh. 16). Graz, 1965

638. Krückmann, O. *Neubabylonische Rechts- und Verwaltungstexte* (Texte und Materialien der Frau Professor Hilprecht Collection II/III). Leipzig, 1933

639. Kyrieleis, H. 'Babylonische Bronzen im Heraion von Samos', *JDAI* 94 (1979) 32–48

640. Labat, R. 'Assyrien und seine Nachbarländer (Babylonien, Elam, Iran) von 1000 bis 617 v. Chr.: das neubabylonische Reich bis 539 v Chr.', in A 10, 9–111 (1968)

641. Lambert, W. G. 'The seed of kingship', in A 22, 427–40 (1974)

642. Lambert, W. G. *The Background of Jewish Apocalyptic*. London, 1978

643. Lambert, W. G. 'A Neo-Babylonian Tammuz lament', *JAOS* 103 (1983) 211–15

644. Landsberger, B. *Brief des Bischofs von Esagila an König Asarhaddon*. Amsterdam, 1965

645. Langdon, S. 'The religious interpretation of Babylonian seals and a new prayer of Shamsh-shum-ukin (BM.78219)', *RA* 16 (1919) 49–68

646. Langdon, S. 'Kandalanu and Ašurbanipal', *JRAS* 1928, 321–5

647. Larsen, C. E. 'The Mesopotamian delta region: a reconsideration of Lees and Falcon', *JAOS* 95 (1975) 43–57

648. Larsen, C. E. and Evans, G. 'The holocene geological history of the

Tigris–Euphrates–Karun delta', in A 530, 227–44 (1978)

649. Leemans, W. F. 'Marduk-apal-iddina II, zijn tijd en zijn geslacht', *JEOL* 10 (1945–8) 432–55

650. Leemans, W. F. '*Kidinnu*: un symbole de droit divin babylonien', in David, M. *et al.* (eds.) *Symbolae ad jus et historiam antiquitatis pertinentes Julio Christiano van Oven dedicatae*, 36–61. Leiden, 1946

651. Lehmann, C. F. *Šamaššumukîn, König von Babylonien 668–648 v. Chr.: Inschriftliches Material über den Beginn seiner Regierung* (Assyriologische Bibliothek 8). Leipzig, 1892

652. Leichty, E. 'Bel-epuš and Tammaritu', *Anat. Stud.* 33 (1983) 153–5

653. Lenzen, H. 'The Ningišzida temple built by Marduk-apla-iddina II at Uruk (Warka)', *Iraq* 19 (1957) 146–50

654. Lenzen, H. *et al. UVB* 12/13 (1956)

655. Lenzen, H. *et al. UVB* 14 (1958)

656. Lenzen, H. *et al. UVB* 18 (1962)

657. Levine, L. D. 'Manuscripts, texts and the study of the Neo-Assyrian royal inscriptions', in A 20, 49–70 (1981)

658. Levine, L. D. 'Sennacherib's southern front: 704–689 B.C.', *JCS* 34 (1982) 28–58

659. Lipiński, E. *Studies in Aramaic Inscriptions and Onomastics* I. Louvain, 1975

660. Liverani, M. 'Critique of variants and the titulary of Sennacherib', in A 20, 225–57 (1981)

661. Lutz, H. F. *Selected Sumerian and Babylonian Texts* (PBS 1/2). Philadelphia, 1919

662. Lutz, H. F. 'The Warka cylinder of Ashurbanipal', *University of California Publications in Semitic Philology* 9 (1927–31) 385–90

663. Lyon, D. G. *Keilschrifttexte Sargon's Königs von Assyrien* (722–705 v. Chr.). Leipzig, 1883

664. McCown, D. E. and Haines, R. C. *Nippur* I: *Temple of Enlil, Scribal Quarter, and Soundings* (OIP 78). Chicago, 1967

665. McCown, D. E., Haines, R. C. and Biggs, R. D. *Nippur*, II: *The North Temple and Sounding E* (OIP 97). Chicago, 1978

666. McEwan, G. 'Agade after the Gutian destruction: the afterlife of a Mesopotamian city', in A 622, 8–15 (1982)

667. McEwan, G. 'Late Babylonian Kish', *Iraq* 45 (1983) 117–23

667A. McEwan, G. *Late Babylonian Texts in the Ashmolean Museum* (Oxford Editions of Cuneiform Texts, 10). Oxford, 1984

668. McFadyen, W. A. and Vita-Finzi, C. 'Mesopotamia: the Tigris–Euphrates delta and its holocene Hammar Fauna', with an appendix by J. E. Robinson, *Geological Magazine* 115 (1978) 287–300

669. Maddin, R., Muhly, J. D. and Wheeler, T. S. 'How the Iron Age began', *Scientific American* 237/4 (October 1977) 122–31

670. Malbran-Labat, F. 'La Babylonie du sud, du XIIe au VIIe siècle avant notre ère d'après deux ouvrages récents', *JA* 260 (1972) 15–38

671. Malbran-Labat, F. 'Nabû-bêl-šumâte, prince du Pays-de-la-Mer', *JA* 263 (1975) 7–37

672. Malbran-Labat, F. 'Eléments pour une recherche sur le nomadisme en

Mésopotamie au premier millénaire av. J.-C., I: "L'image du nomade"',
JA 268 (1980) 11–33

673.   Malbran-Labat, F. 'Le nomadisme à l'époque néo-assyrienne', in Silva
Castillo, J. (ed.) *Nomads and Sedentary Peoples*, 57–76. Mexico City, 1981

674.   Malbran-Labat, F. *L'armée et l'organisation militaire de l'Assyrie d'après les
lettres des Sargonides trouvés à Ninive*. Geneva and Paris, 1982

675.   Manitius, K. (translator) *Ptolemäus, Handbuch der Astronomie* I–II.
Reissue. Leipzig, 1963

676.   Messerschmidt, L. and Ungnad, A. VAS I. Leipzig, 1907

677.   Millard, A. R. 'Another Babylonian Chronicle text', *Iraq* 26 (1964) 14–
35 and plates VI–VII

678.   Millard, A. R. 'Some Esarhaddon fragments relating to the restoration
of Babylon', *AfO* 24 (1973) 117–19

679.   de Miroschedji, P. 'Prospections archéologiques au Khuzistan en 1977',
Cahiers de la Délégation Archéologique Française en Iran 12 (1981) 169–92

680.   de Miroschedji, P. 'Notes sur la glyptique de la fin de l'Elam', *RA* 76
(1982) 51–63

681.   Moorey, P. R. S. *Ancient Iraq (Assyria and Babylonia)*. Oxford, 1976

682.   Moorey, P. R. S. *Kish Excavations 1923–1933 with a Microfiche Catalogue of
the Objects in Oxford Excavated by Oxford – Field Museum, Chicago
Expedition to Kish in Iraq, 1923–1933*. Oxford, 1978

683.   Moritz, B. 'Die Nationalität der Arumu-Stämme in Südost-Babylonien',
in Adler, C. and Ember, A. (eds.) *Oriental Studies published in
commemoration of . . . Paul Haupt*, 184–211. Baltimore and Leipzig, 1926

684.   Mullo-Weir, C. J. 'The return of Marduk to Babylon with
Shamashshumukin', *JRAS* 1929, 553–5

685.   Myrhman, D. *Babylonian Hymns and Prayers* (PBS I/I). Philadelphia, 1911

686.   Nashef, K. 'Der Ṭaban-Fluss', *Bagh. Mitt.* 13 (1982) 117–39

687.   Nashef, K. *Die Orts- und Gewässernamen der mittelbabylonischen und
mittelassyrischen Zeit* (Répertoire Géographique des Textes Cunéiformes
5). Wiesbaden, 1982

688.   Nassouhi, E. 'Prisme d'Assurbânipal daté de sa trentième année,
provenant du temple de Gula à Babylone', *AfK* 2 (1924–5) 97–106

689.   Nies, J. B. and Keiser, C. E. *Historical, Religious and Economic Texts and
Antiquiti-s* (Babylonian Inscriptions in the Collection of James B. Nies
2). New Haven, 1920

690.   Nöldeke, A. *et al. UVB* 8 (1937)

691.   Nöldeke, A. and Lenzen, H. *UVB* 11 (1940)

692.   North, R. 'Status of the Warka excavation', *Or.* 26 (1957) 185–256

693.   Nougayrol, J. 'Parallèles, duplicata, etc.', *RA* 36 (1939) 29–40

694.   Oates, J. *Babylon*. London, 1979

695.   Olmstead, A. T. 'Babylonia as an Assyrian dependency', *AJSL* 37
(1920–1) 212–29

696.   Olmstead, A. T. 'The fall and rise of Babylon', *AJSL* 38 (1921–2) 73–96

697.   Oppenheim, A. L. 'Essay on overland trade in the first millennium B.C.',
JCS 21 (1967) 236–54

698.   Oppenheim, A. L. *Letters from Mesopotamia: Official, Business, and Private*

Letters on Clay Tablets from Two Millennia. Chicago, 1967

699. Oppenheim, A. L. 'Babylonian and Assyrian historical texts', in A 44, 265–317, 556–67 (1969)

700. Oppenheim, A. L. 'Neo-Assyrian and Neo-Babylonian empires', in Laswell, H. D., Lerner, D. and Speier, H. (eds.) *Propaganda and Communication in World History*, I: *The Symbolic Instrument in Early Times*, 111–44. Honolulu, 1979

701. Owen, D. and Watanabe, K. 'Eine neubabylonische Gartenkaufurkunde mit Flüchen aus dem Akzessionsjahr Asarhaddons', *Or. Ant.* 22 (1983) 37–48

702. Parpola, S. *Neo-Assyrian Toponyms* (AOAT 6). Kevelaer and Neukirchen-Vluyn, 1970

703. Parpola, S. 'A letter from Šamaš-šumu-ukīn to Esarhaddon', *Iraq* 34 (1972) 21–34

704. Parpola, S. 'The murderer of Sennacherib', in A 1, 171–82 (1980)

705. Parr, P. J. 'Settlement patterns and urban planning in the ancient Levant: the nature of the evidence', in Ucko, P. J., Tringham, R. and Dimbleby, G. W. (eds.) *Man, Settlement and Urbanism*, 803–10. London, 1972

706. Peat, J. A. '*Hanšû* land and the *rab hanšî*', *Iraq* 45 (1983) 124–7

707. Petschow, H. 'Zur Forderungsabtretung im neubabylonischen Recht', *Eos* 48/2 (1957) 21–7

708. Pinches, T. 'Notes upon some of the recent discoveries in the realm of Assyriology, with special reference to the private life of the Babylonians', *JTVI* 26 (1893) 123–71

709. Pinches, T. 'The fragment of an Assyrian tablet found at Gezer', *PEF* (1904) 229–36

710. Pinches, T. *The Babylonian Tablets of the Berens Collection* (Asiatic Society Monographs 16). London, 1915

711. Pinches, T. 'Ein babylonischer Eponym', *AfO* 13 (1939–41) 51–4

712. Pinckert, J. *Hymnen und Gebete an Nebo.* Leipzig, 1907

713. Porada, E. 'Suggestions for the classification of Neo-Babylonian cylinder seals', *Or.* 16 (1947) 145–65

714. Postgate, J. N. 'Royal exercise of justice under the Assyrian Empire', in A 22, 417–26 (1974)

715. Powell, M. A. 'Merodach-Baladan at Dur-Jakin', *JCS* 34 (1982) 59–61

716. Prince, J. D. 'A new Šamaš-šum-ukîn series', *AJSL* 31 (1914–15) 256–70

717. Ravn, O. E. 'Sankerib af Assur's babylonske Politik', in Jacobsen, J. (ed.) *Studier tilegnede Professor Dr. Phil. & Theol. Frants Buhl i anledning af hans 75 aars fidselsdag den 6 September 1925*, 217–30. Copenhagen, 1925

718. Rashid, F. 'A royal text from Tell Haddad', *Sumer* 37 (1981) 72–80 [Arabic section]

719. Reade, J. 'Assyrian campaigns, 840–811 B.C., and the Babylonian frontier', *ZA* 68 (1978) 251–60

720. Reade, J. 'Kassites and Assyrians in Iran', *Iran* 16 (1978) 137–43

721. Reade, J. 'Neo-Assyrian monuments in their historical context', in A 20, 143–67 (1981)

722. Reiner, E. 'Inscription from a royal Elamite tomb', *AfO* 24 (1973) 87–102

723. Reiner, E. 'The Babylonian Fürstenspiegel in practice', in A 13, 320–6 (with an appendix by M. Civil) (1982)

724. Reuther, O. *Die Innenstadt von Babylon (Merkes)* (WVDOG 47). Leipzig, 1926

725. Röllig, W. 'Kisiga, Kissik', in A 16, 5 (1980) 620–2

726. Roux, G. 'Recently discovered ancient sites in the Hammar Lake district (Southern Iraq)', *Sumer* 16 (1960) 20–31

727. Safar, F. 'Soundings at Tell Al-Laham', *Sumer* 5 (1949) 154–72

728. Saggs, H. W. F. 'A cylinder from Tell al Laham', *Sumer* 13 (1957) 190–5

729. San Nicolò, M. *Babylonische Rechtsurkunden des ausgehenden 8. und des 7. Jahrhunderts v. Chr.* Munich, 1951

730. Scheil, V. 'Notes d'épigraphie et d'archéologie assyriennes', *Rec. Trav.* 16 (1894) 90–2

731. Scheil, V. *Une saison de fouilles à Sippar.* Cairo, 1902

732. Scheil, V. 'Nouvelles notes d'épigraphie et d'archéologie assyriennes', *Rec. Trav.* 36 (1914) 179–92

733. Schiffer, S. *Die Aramäer: Historisch-geographische Untersuchungen.* Leipzig, 1911

734. Schmidt, J. *UVB* 26/27. Berlin, 1972

735. Schnabel, P. *Berossos und die babylonisch-hellenistische Literatur.* Leipzig, 1923

736. Schollmeyer, A. *Sumerisch-babylonische Hymnen und Gebete an Šamaš.* Paderborn, 1912

737. Seidl, U. 'Die babylonischen Kudurru-Reliefs', *Bagh. Mitt.* 4 (1968) 7–220

738. Seux, M.-J. 'L'auteur de BBSt no xxxv', *RA* 54 (1960) 206–8

739. Soden, W. von. 'Gibt es ein Zeugnis dafür, dass die Babylonier an die Wiederaufstehung Marduks geglaubt haben?', *ZA* 51 (1955) 130–66

740. Soden, W. von. Review of A 932, *WZKM* 53 (1956–7) 316–21

741. Soden W. von. 'Ein neues Bruchstück des assyrischen Kommentars zum Marduk-Ordal', *ZA* 52 (1957) 224–34

742. Soden, W. von. 'Aramäische Wörter in neuassyrischen und neu- und spätbabylonischen Texten. Ein Vorbericht', *Or.* 35 (1966) 1–20; 37 (1968) 261–71; 46 (1977) 183–97

743. Soden, W. von. 'Der neubabylonische Funktionär *simmagir* und der Feuertod des Šamaš-šum-ukīn', *ZA* 62 (1972) 84–90

744. Sollberger, E. *Royal Inscriptions*: Part II (UET 8). London, 1965

745. Spalinger, A. 'Assurbanipal and Egypt: a source study', *JAOS* 94 (1974) 316–28

745A. Steiner, R. C. and Nims, C. F. 'Ashurbanipal and Shamash-Shum-Ukin: A Tale of Two Brothers from the Aramaic text in demotic script', *Rev. Bibl.* 92 (1985) 60–81

746. Steinmetzer, F. X. *Die babylonischen Kudurru (Grenzsteine) als*

Urkundenform (Studien zur Geschichte und Kultur des Altertums 11/4–5). Paderborn, 1922

747. Steinmetzer, F. X. 'Die Bestallungsurkunde des Königs Šamaš-šum-ukîn von Babylon', in *Miscellanea orientalia dedicata Antonio Deimel annos LXX complenti* (An. Or. 12), 302–6. Rome, 1935

748. Steinmetzer, F. X. 'Die Bestallungsurkunde Königs Šamaš-šum-ukîn von Babylon', *An. Or.* 7 (1935) 314–18

749. Stephens, F. J. *Votive and Historical Texts from Babylonia and Assyria* (YOS 9). New Haven, 1937

750. Stigers, H. G. 'A Neo-Babylonian quit-claim deed', *Jewish Quarterly Review* 63 (1972–3) 171–4

751. Stolper, M. W. 'Political history', in Carter, E. and Stolper, M. *Elam: Surveys of Political History and Archaeology*, 3–100. Berkeley, 1984

752. Stolper, M. W. 'šarnuppu', *ZA* 68 (1978) 261–9

753. Strassmaier, J. 'Einige kleinere babylonische Keilschrifttexte aus dem Britischen Museum', in *Actes du Huitième Congrès International des Orientalistes tenu en 1889 à Stockholm et à Christiana* 11/1B, 279–83 and plates 1–35. Leiden, 1893

754. Streck, M. *Die alte Landschaft Babylonien nach den arabischen Geographen.* Leiden, 1900–1

755. Streck, M. 'Die nomadischen Völkerschaften Babyloniens und des angrenzenden Elams', *MVAG* 11 (1906) 203–46

756. Tadmor, H. 'The "Sin of Sargon" and the problem of Sargon's and Sennacherib's attitude toward Babylon and her culture', *Eretz-Israel* 5 (1958) 150–62, 93*. [In Hebrew]

757. Tadmor, H. 'Tri poslednikh desiatiletiia Assirii', *Trudy dvadtsat' piatogo Mezhdunarodnogo Kongressa Vostokovedov* 1, 240–1. Moscow, 1962

758. Tadmor, H. and Cogan, M. 'Ahaz and Tiglath-Pileser in the Book of Kings: historiographic considerations', *Biblica* 60 (1979) 491–508

759. Tadmor, H. 'An ancient scribal error and its modern consequences: the date of the Nimrud slab inscription No. 1', *Anat. Stud.* 33 (1983) 199–203

760. Tadmor, H. 'Autobiographical apology in the royal Assyrian literature', in A 53, 36–57 (1983)

761. Ucko, P. J., Tringham, R. and Dimbleby, G. W. (eds.) *Man, Settlement and Urbanism.* London, 1972

762. Unger, E. *Babylon: die heilige Stadt nach der Beschreibung der Babylonier.* Berlin and Leipzig, 1931

763. Ungnad, A. 'Eponymen', in A 16, 2 (1938) 412–57

764. Ungnad, A. 'Figurenzauber für den kranken König Šamaš-šumu-ukîn', *Or.* 12 (1943) 293–310

765. Vallat, F. *Suse et l'Elam* (Recherche sur les grandes civilisations, Mémoire no. 1). Paris, 1980

766. van der Spek, R. 'The struggle of King Sargon II of Assyria against the Chaldaean Merodach-Baladan (710–707 B.C.)', *JEOL* 25 (1977–8) 56–66

767. van Dijk, J. 'Die Inschriftenfunde', *UVB* 18 (1962) 39–62

768. van Driel, G. Review of A 517, *Bi. Or.* 26 (1969) 367–8

769. Vita-Finzi, C. 'Recent alluvial history in the catchment of the Arabo-Persian Gulf', in A 530, 255–61 (1978)
770. Wachsmuth, C. *Einleitung in das Studium der alten Geschichte.* Leipzig, 1895
771. Walker, C. B. F. *Cuneiform Brick Inscriptions in the British Museum, the Ashmolean Museum, Oxford, the City of Birmingham Museums and Art Gallery, the City of Bristol Museum and Art Gallery.* London, 1981
772. Walker, C. B. F. 'Episodes in the history of Babylonian astronomy', *Bulletin of the Society for Mesopotamian Studies* 5 (1983) 10–26
773. Walker, C. B. F. and Kramer, S. N. 'Cuneiform tablets in the collection of Lord Binning', *Iraq* 44 (1982) 70–86
773A. Watanabe, K. *Die adê-Vereidigung anlässlich der Thronfolgeregelung Asarhaddons (Bagh. Mitt.,* Beiheft 3). Berlin, 1987
774. Watelin, L. C. *Excavations at Kish* III. Paris, 1930
775. Weidner, E. F. 'Die älteste Nachricht über das persische Königshaus: Kyros I. ein Zeitgenosse Aššurbânaplis', *AfO* 7 (1931–2) 1–7
776. Weidner, E. F. 'Keilschrifttexte nach Kopien von T. G. Pinches. Aus dem Nachlass veröffentlicht und bearbeitet. 1. Babylonische Privaturkunden aus dem 7. Jahrhundert v. Chr', *AfO* 16 (1952–3) 35–46 and plates III–VI
777. Weippert, M. 'Die Kämpfe des assyrischen Königs Assurbanipal gegen die Araber', *We. Or.* 7 (1973–4) 39–85
778. Weissbach, F. 'Zu den Inschriften der Säle im Palaste Sargon's II. von Assyrien', *ZDMG* 72 (1918) 161–85
779. Wetzel, F. *Die Stadtmauern von Babylon* (WVDOG 48). Leipzig, 1930
780. Wetzel, F. and Weissbach, F. *Das Hauptheiligtum des Marduk in Babylon, Esagila und Etemenanki* (WVDOG 59). Leipzig, 1938
781. Woolley, L. *The Kassite Period and the Period of the Assyrian Kings* (UE VIII). London, 1965
782. Woolley, L. *Ur 'of the Chaldees'.* Revised by P. R. S. Moorey. London, 1982
783. Wright, H. 'The southern margins of Sumer: archaeological survey of the area of Eridu and Ur', in A 513, 295–345 (1981)
784. Zadok, R. 'Arabians in Mesopotamia during the Late-Assyrian, Chaldean, Achaemenian and Hellenistic periods chiefly according to the cuneiform sources', *ZDMG* 131 (1981) 42–84
785. Zadok, R. 'The toponymy of the Nippur region during the 1st millennium B.C. within the general framework of the Mesopotamian toponymy', *We. Or.* 12 (1981) 39–69
786. Zawadski, S. 'The economic crisis in Uruk during the last years of Assyrian rule in the light of the so-called Nabu-ušallim archives', *Folia Orientalia* 20 (1979) 175–84

2. HISTORICAL EVENTS, 605–539 B.C.

787. Albright, W.F. 'The conquests of Nabonidus in Arabia', *JRAS* (1925) 293–5
788. Albright, W. F. 'Cilicia and Babylon under the Chaldean kings', *BASOR* 120 (1950) 22–5

789. Albright, W. F. 'The Nebuchadnezzar and Neriglissar chronicles', *BASOR* 143 (1956) 28–33

790. Ali, S. M. 'The Southern Palace', *Sumer* 35 (1979) 92–3

791. Amusin, J. D. and Heltzer, M. L. 'The inscription from Meṣad Hashavyahu: complaint of a reaper of the seventh century B.C.', *IEJ* 14 (1964) 148–57

792. Artzi, P. 'A barrel cylinder of Nebuchadnezzar II King of Babylon', *Israel Museum News* 10 (1973) 49–51

793. Avigad, N. 'Jerahmeel and Baruch', *Bi. Ar.* 42 (1979) 114–18

794. Barnett, R. D. 'Xenophon and the Wall of Media', *JHS* 83 (1963) 1–26

795. Bartlett, J. R. 'Edom and the fall of Jerusalem', *PEQ* 114 (1982) 13–24

796. Beljawski, V. A. 'Der politische Kampf in Babylon in den Jahren 562–556 v. Chr.', in Lurkner, M. (ed.) *In Memoriam Eckhard Unger. Beiträge zur Geschichte, Kultur und Religion des Alten Orients*. Baden-Baden, 1971

797. Ben-Barak, Z. 'The coronation ceremonies of Joash and Nabopolassar in comparison', in Oded, B. (ed.) *Studies in the History of the Jewish People and the Land of Israel* 5, 43–56. Haifa, 1980

798. Ben-Barak, Z. 'The coronation ceremony in Ancient Mesopotamia', *Orientalia Lovaniensia Periodica* 11 (1980) 55–67

799. Bergamini, G. 'Levels of Babylon reconsidered', *Mesopotamia* 12 (1977) 111–52

800. Berger, P. R. *Die neubabylonischen Königsinschriften: Königsinschriften des ausgehenden babylonischen Reiches (626–539 a. Chr.)* (AOAT 4/1). Kevelaer and Neuchirchen Vluyn, 1973

801. Biggs, R. D. 'More Babylonian "Prophecies"', *Iraq* 29 (1967) 117–32

801A. Böhl, F. M. Th. de L. 'Die Tochter des Königs Nabonid', in Friedrich, J., Lautner, J. G. and Miles, J. (eds.) *Symbolae ad iura Orientis Antiqui pertinentes Paulo Koschaker dedicatae* 2, 151–78. Leiden, 1939

802. Braun, T. F. B. G. 'The Neo-Babylonian Empire and the Greeks', *CAH* III².3 (1982) 21–4

803. Brewer, J. A. 'Nergalsharezer Shamgar in Jer. 39:3', *AJSL* 42 (1925–6) 130

804. Brinkman, J. A. 'Cuneiform texts in the St Louis Public Library', in A 18, 49–50 (1976)

805. Brinkman, J. A. 'Neo-Babylonian texts in the Archaeological Museum at Florence', *JNES* 25 (1966) 202–9

806. Cavigneaux, A. 'Les textes cunéiformes sur Babylone', *Histoire et Archéologie* 51 (1981) 35–7

807. Cavigneaux, A. 'Le temple de Nabû ša ḫarê: rapport préliminaire sur les textes cunéiformes', *Sumer* 37 (1981) 118–26

808. Clines, D. J. A. 'Regnal year reckoning in the last years of the Kingdom of Judah', *Australian Journal of Biblical Archaeology* (Sydney, 1972) 9–34

809. Crown, A. D. 'Tidings and instructions: how news travelled in the Ancient Near East', *JESHO* 17 (1974) 244–71

810. Damerji, M. S. 'A new portrait of Nabû-Naʾid, King of Babylon', *Sumer* 37 (1981) 67–71

811. Damerji, M. S. 'Babylone; les fouilles nouvelles et les travaux de restauration', *Histoire et Archéologie* 51 (1981) 26–34

812.   Damerji, M. S. 'Where are the Hanging Gardens in Babylon?' *Sumer* 37 (1981) 56–61 [In Arabic]

813.   Dandamayev, M. A. 'About life expectancy in Babylonia in the first millennium B.C.', in A 1, 183–6 (1980)

814.   Dandamayev, M. A. 'The social position of Neo-Babylonian scribes', in A 31, 35–9 (1982)

815.   Dandamayev, M. A. *Slavery in Babylonia from Nabopolassar to Alexander the Great (626–331 B.C.)*. DeKalb, 1984

815A. Dandamayev, M. A. Review of A 941, *ZA* 76 (1986) 141–3.

816.   Dossin, G. 'Marduk, dieu poliade de Babylone', *Akkadica* 22 (1981) 1–2

817.   Dougherty, R. P. *Records from Erech, Time of Nabonidus (555–538 B.C.)* (YOS 6). New Haven, 1920

818.   Dougherty, R. P. *Archives from Erech, Time of Nebuchadnezzar and Nabonidus* (Goucher College Cuneiform Inscriptions 1). New Haven, 1923

819.   Dougherty, R. P. *Nabonidus and Belshazzar: A Study of the Closing Events of the Neo-Babylonian Empire* (YOS 15). New Haven, 1929

820.   Dougherty, R. P. *The Sealand of Arabia* (YOSR 19). New Haven, 1932

821.   Dougherty, R. P. *Archives from Erech, Neo-Babylonian and Persian Periods* (Goucher College Cuneiform Inscriptions 2). New Haven, 1933

822.   Driver, G. R. 'Neo-Babylonian laws', *The Babylonian Laws* II, 324–47. Oxford, 1955

823.   Dupont-Sommer, A. 'Un papyrus araméen d'époque saïte découvert à Saqqara', *Semitica* 1 (1948) 43–68

824.   Eissfeldt, O. 'Das Datum der Belagerung von Tyrus durch Nebukadnezzar', *Forschungen und Fortschritte* 9 (1933) 421–2

825.   Eph'al, I. 'Israel: fall and exile', in Malamat, A. (ed.) *WHJP* IV/I (Jerusalem, 1979) 276–89

826.   Evetts, B. T. A. *Inscriptions of the Reigns of Evil-Merodach, Neriglissar and Laborosoarchod* (Babylonische Texte VI/B). Leipzig, 1892

827.   Fensham, F. C. 'Nebukadrezzar in the Book of Jeremiah', *Journal of Northwest Semitic Languages* 10 (Leiden, 1982) 53–65

828.   Ferrara, A. J. 'An inscribed stone slab of Nebuchadnezzar', *JCS* 27 (1975) 231–2

829.   Figulla, H. H. *Business Documents of the New-Babylonian Period* (UE(T) IV). London, 1949

830.   Foster, B. R. 'Nabonidus at Kesh', *RA* 77 (1983) 92–3

831.   Freedman, D. N. 'The prayer of Nabonidus', *BASOR* 145 (1957) 31–2

832.   Freedy, K. S., and Redford, D. B. 'The dates in Ezekiel in relation to Biblical, Babylonian and Egyptian sources', *JAOS* 90 (1970) 426–85

833.   Friedrich, J. 'Ein kilikischer Mannesname', *AfO* 18 (1957) 61

834.   Funck, B. 'Studien zur sozialökonomischen Situation Babyloniens im 7. und 6. Jahrhundert v.u.Z.', in A 31, 47–67 (1982)

835.   George, A. R. 'The cuneiform text tin.tir.ki = Ba-bi-lu and the Topography of Babylon', *Sumer* 35 (1979) 226–32

836.   George, A. R. 'The series Tintir = Bābilu and the Topography of Babylon.' Unpublished Ph.D. dissertation, University of Birmingham, 1984

837. Goetze, A. 'A cylinder of Nebuchadrezzar of Babylon', *Crozier Quarterly* 33 (1946) 65–78

838. Goosens, G. 'Les recherches historiques à l'époque néobabylonienne', *RA* 42 (1948) 149–59

839. Greenberg, M. 'Ezekiel 17 and the policy of Psammetichus II', *JBL* 76 (1957) 304–9

840. Gurney, O. R. 'The fifth tablet of "The Topography of Babylon"', *Iraq* 36 (1974) 39–52

841. Hallo, W. W. 'Nebukadnezzar comes to Jerusalem', in *Through the Sound of Many Waters: Writings Contributed on the Occasion of the 70th Birthday of W. Gunther Plaut*, 40–56. Toronto, 1982

842. Horn, S. H. 'The Babylonian Chronicle and the ancient calendar of the Kingdom of Judah', *AUSS* 3 (Berrien Springs, 1967) 12–27

843. Ismail, B. K. 'Structures of the Babylonian King Nabopolassar', *Sumer* 35 (1979) 167–8

844. Joannès, F. 'Kaššaia, fille de Nabuchodonosor II', *RA* 74 (1980) 183–4

845. Katzenstein, H. J. *The History of Tyre: From the Beginning of the Second Millennium B.C.E. until the Fall of the Neo-Babylonian Empire in 538 B.C.E.* Jerusalem, 1973

846. Katzenstein, H. J. 'Before Pharaoh conquered Gaza', *VT* 33 (1983) 249–51

847. Kenyon, K. M. 'Jerusalem', in Avi-Yonah, M. (ed.) *Encyclopedia of Archaeological Excavations in the Holy Land* II, 591–7. Oxford, 1976

848. Khalil, B. and Cavigneaux, A. 'Les textes cunéiformes sur Babylone', *Histoire et archéologie* 51 (1981) 35–7

849. Kienitz, F. K. 'Die Säitische Renaissance', in A 10, 256–82 (1968)

850. Killick, R. G. 'Northern Akkad project: excavations at Ḥabl Aṣ-Ṣahr', *Iraq* 46 (1984) 125–9

851. Koldewey, R. *The Excavations at Babylon*. London, 1914

852. Koldewey, R. *Die Königsburgen von Babylon* I–II (WVDOG 54–5). Leipzig, 1932

853. Krischen, F. *Weltwunder der Baukunst in Babylonien und Jonien*. Tübingen, 1956

854. Lambert, W. G. 'Nebuchadnezzar King of Justice', *Iraq* 27 (1965) 1–11

855. Lambert, W. G. 'A new source for the reign of Nabonidus', *AfO* 22 (1968–9) 1–8

856. Langdon, S. *Die neubabylonischen Königsinschriften* (VAB 4). Leipzig, 1912

857. Lewy, H. 'The religious background of the Key Kâûs legend', *Ar. Or.* 17/2 (1949) 28–109

858. Lewy, J. 'The Late Assyro-Babylonian cult of the Moon and its culmination at the time of Nabonidus', *HUCA* 19 (1945–6) 405–89

859. Lipiński, E. 'The Egypto-Babylonian war of the winter of 601–600 B.C.', *Annali dell'Istituto Orientale di Napoli* 32 (1972) 235–41

860. Lutz, H. F. *Neo-Babylonian Administrative Documents from Erech* (University of California Publications in Semitic Philology 9/1). Berkeley, 1927

861. Malamat, A. 'A new record of Nebuchadrezzar's Palestinian campaigns', *IEJ* 6 (1956) 246–55

862. Malamat, A. 'The last kings of Judah and the fall of Jerusalem: an historical-chronological study', *IEJ* 18 (1968) 137–56

863. Malamat, A. 'The last years of the Kingdom of Judah', in Malamat, A. (ed.) *WHJP* IV/I (Jerusalem, 1979) 205–21

864. Mazar, A. 'The excavations at Khirbet Abu et-Twein and the system of Iron Age fortresses in Judah', *Eretz Israel* 15 (1981) 229–49

865. Milik, J. T. '"Prière de Nabonide" et autres écrits d'un cycle de Daniel', *Rev. Bibl.* 63 (1956) 407–15

866. Millard, A. R. Review of A 943, in *PEQ* 95 (1963) 134–7

867. Moore, E. W. *Neo-Babylonian Business and Administrative Documents*. Ann Arbor, 1935

868. Moore, E. W. *Neo-Babylonian Documents in the University of Michigan Collection*. Ann Arbor, 1939

869. Moran, W. L. 'Notes on the new Nabonidus inscriptions', *Or.* 28 (1959) 130–40

870. Nasir, M. 'The so-called Summer Palace (Nebuchadnezzar's Life Palace)', *Sumer* 35 (1979) 151–9

871. Nassouhi, E. 'Deux vases royaux néobabyloniens', *AfO* 3 (1926) 65–6

872. Noth, M. 'Die Einnahme von Jerusalem in Jahre 597 v. Chr.', *ZDPV* 74 (1958) 133–57

873. Nötscher, R. '"Neue" babylonische Chroniken und Altes Testament', *Biblische Zeitschrift* 1 (1957) 110–14

874. Oded, B. 'When did the kingdom of Judah become subject to Babylonian rule?' *Tarbiz* 35 (1965–6) 103–7 [In Hebrew]

875. Oded, B. 'Judah and the Exile', in *Israelite and Judean History*, 435–88. Philadelphia, 1977

876. Olmstead, A. T. 'The Chaldean dynasty', *HUCA* 2 (1925) 29–55

877. Parker, R. A. and Dubberstein, W. H. *Babylonian Chronology: 626 B.C.– A.D. 75* (Brown University Studies 19). Providence, 1956

878. Petschow, H. *Neubabylonisches Pfandrecht*. Berlin, 1956

879. Pinches, T. G. 'On a cuneiform inscription relating to the capture of Babylon by Cyrus', *Transactions of the Society of Biblical Archaeology* 7 (1882) 139–76

880. Pinches, T. G. *The Old Testament in the Light of the Historical Records of Assyria and Babylonia*. London, 1902

881. Pomponio, F. 'Considerazioni sulla cronaca neo-babilonese BM 25127', *RSO* 47 (1972) 23–35

882. Quinn, J. D. 'Alcaeus 48 (B 16) and the fall of Ascalon (604 B.C.)', *BASOR* 164 (1961) 19–20

883. Rainey, A. F. 'The fate of Lachish during the campaigns of Sennacherib and Nebuchadrezzar', in Aharoni, Y. (ed.) *Investigations at Lachish*, 47–60. Jerusalem, 1975

884. Rashid, S. A. 'Einige Denkmäler aus Tēmā und der babylonische Einfluss', *Bagh. Mitt.* 7 (1974) 155–65

885. Rashid, S. A. 'The Babylonian king Nabonidus in Tema', *Sumer* 35 (1979) 172–4

886. Röllig, W. 'Erwägungen zu neuen Stelen König Nabonids', *ZA* 56 (1964) 218–60

887. Sack, R. H. *Amēl-Marduk 562–560 B.C. A Study based on Cuneiform, Old Testament, Greek, Latin and Rabbinical Sources* (AOATS 4). Kevelaer and Neukirchen-Vluyn, 1972

888. Sack, R. H. 'Nergal-šarra-uṣur, King of Babylon as seen in the cuneiform, Greek, Latin and Hebrew sources', *ZA* 68 (1978) 129–49

889. Sack, R. H. 'Nebuchadnezzar and Nabonidus in folklore and history', *Mesopotamia* 17 (1982) 67–131

890. Sack, R. H. 'The Nabonidus legend', *RA* 77 (1983) 59–67

891. Sack, R. H. *Records from Erech: 562–556 B.C.* (YOS 16). New Haven, forthcoming

892. Saggs, H. W. F. 'Two administrative officials at Erech in the 6th century B.C.', *Sumer* 15 (1959) 29–38

893. San Nicolò, M. *Beiträge zu einer Prosopographie neubabylonischer Beamten der Zivil- und Tempelverwaltung.* Munich, 1941

894. Schmidt, H. 'Ergebnisse einer Grabung am Kernmassiv der Ziggurat in Babylon', *Bagh. Mitt.* 12 (1981) 87–137

895. Shea, W. H. 'An unrecognised vassal king of Babylon in the early Achaemenid period', *AUSS* 9 (Berrien Springs, 1971) 51–67, 99–128; 10 (1972) 88–117, 147–78

896. Shea, W. H. 'Nebuchadnezzar's Chronicle and the date of the destruction of Lachish III', *PEQ* 111 (1979) 113–16

897. Shea, W. H. 'Nabonidus, Belshazzar and the Book of Daniel', *AUSS* 20 (Berrien Springs, 1982) 133–49

898. Sherrifs, D. C. T. 'Empire and the Gods: Mesopotamian treaty theology and the sword in the first millennium B.C.' D.Litt. thesis, University of Stellenbosch, 1976

899. Shiloh, Y. *Excavations at the City of David,* I: *1978–1982 Interim Report of the First Five Seasons* (Qedem 19). Jerusalem, 1984

900. Smith, S. *Babylonian Historical Texts Relating to the Capture and Downfall of Babylon.* London, 1924

901. Soden, W. von. 'Etemenanki von Asarhaddon nach der Erzählung vom Turmbau zu Babel und dem Erra-Mythos', *UF* 3 (1971) 253–63

902. Soden, W. von. 'Kyros und Nabonid. Propaganda und Gegen-propaganda', in Koch, H. and MacKenzie, D. N. (eds.) *Kunst, Kultur und Geschichte der Achämenidenzeit und ihr Fortleben,* 61–8. Berlin, 1983

903. Spalinger, A. 'Egypt and Babylonia: a survey (c. 620 B.C. – 550 B.C.)', *Studien zur altägyptischen Kultur* 5 (1977) 221–44

904. Spar, I. 'Studies in Neo-Babylonian economic and legal texts'. Ph.D. dissertation, University of Minnesota, 1972

905. Starcky, J. 'Une tablette araméenne de l'an 34 de Nabuchodonosor (AO, 21.063)', *Syria* 37 (1960) 99–115

906. Strassmaier, J. N. 'Die babylonischen Inschriften in Museum zu Liverpool nebst andern aus der Zeit von Nebuchadnezzar bis Darius', *Sixth International Congress of Orientalists* 2/1, 571–6. Leiden, 1885

907. Strassmaier, J. N. *Inschriften von Nabonidus, König von Babylon (555–538 v. Chr.) von den Thontafeln des Britischen Museums* (Babylonische Texte I–IV). Leipzig, 1889

908. Strassmaier, J. N. 'Inschriften von Nabopolassar und Smerdis', *ZA* 4 (1889) 106–52

909. Strassmaier, J. N. *Inschriften von Nabuchodonosor, König von Babylon (604–561 v. Chr.)* (Babylonische Texte V–VI). Leipzig, 1889

910. Strassmaier, J. N. 'Inscription of Nebukadnezzar son of Nin-ab-nadin-šum', *Hebraica* 9 (1892–3) 4–5

911. Tadmor, H. 'The inscriptions of Nabunaid: historical arrangement', in A 28, 351–63 (1965)

912. Tallquist, K. L. *Neubabylonisches Namenbuch* (AASF 32/2). Helsinki, 1906

913. Thiele, E. R. 'New evidence on the chronology of the last kings of Judah', *BASOR* 143 (1956) 22–37

914. Tsevat, M. 'The Neo-Assyrian and Neo-Babylonian vassal-oaths and the prophet Ezekiel', *JBL* 78 (1959) 199–204

915. Unger, E. 'Nebukadnezar II und sein *šandabakku* (Oberkommisar) in Tyrus', *ZAW* 44 (1926) 314–17

916. Unger, E. 'Babylon', in A 16, 1 (1931) 330–69

917. Ungnad, A. *Neubabylonische Rechts- und Verwaltungsurkunden* 1 (Leipzig, 1935); Glossar (Leipzig, 1937)

918. Ussishkin, D. 'Answers at Lachish', *BAR* 5 (1979) 16–39

919. van Selms, A. 'The name Nebuchadnezzar', in Heerma van Voss, M. *et al.* (eds.) *Travels in the World of the Old Testament*, 223–9. Assen, 1974

920. Vogt, E. 'Die neu-babylonische Chronik über die Schlacht bei Karkemisch und die Einnahme von Jerusalem', *VT* (Supp.) 4 (1957) 67–96

921. Vogt, E. 'Der Nehar Kebar: Ez. 1', *Biblica* 39 (1958) 211–16

922. Voigtlander, E. N. von. 'A survey of Neo-Babylonian history'. Ph.D. dissertation, University of Michigan, 1963

923. Weidner, E. F. 'Jojachin, König von Juda, in babylonischen Keilschrifttexten', *Mélanges Syriens offerts à Monsieur René Dussaud* II, 923–35. Paris, 1939

924. Weidner, E. F. 'Hochverrat gegen Nebukadnezar II', *AfO* 17 (1954–5) 1–5

925. Weisberg, D. B. 'Royal women of the Neo-Babylonian period' in A 22, 447–54 (1974)

926. Weisberg, D. B. *Texts from the Time of Nebuchadnezzar* (YOS 17). New Haven, 1980

927. Weisberg, D. B. 'Wool and linen material in texts from the time of Nebuchadnezzar', *Eretz Israel* 16 (1982) 218–26

928. Weissbach, F. H. *Die Inschriften Nebukadnezars II im Wâdī Brîsā und am Nahr el-Kelb.* Leipzig, 1906

929. Weissbach, F. H. *Die Keilinschriften der Achämeniden* (VAB 3). Leipzig, 1911

930. Wetzel, F. *Die Stadtmauern von Babylon* (WVDOG 48). Leipzig, 1930

931. Wetzel, F. and Weissbach, F. H. *Das Hauptheiligtum des Marduk in Babylon, Esagila und Etemenanki* (WVDOG 59). Leipzig, 1938

932. Wiseman, D. J. *Chronicles of Chaldaean Kings (626–556 B.C.) in the British Museum.* London, 1956

933. Wiseman, D. J. 'Darius the Mede', in Wiseman, D. J. *et al.*, *Notes on Some Problems in the Book of Daniel*, 9–18. London, 1965

934. Wiseman, D. J. 'Some Egyptians in Babylonia', *Iraq* 28 (1966) 154–8

935. Wiseman, D. J. 'A Late Babylonian tribute list?', *BSOAS* 30 (1967) 495–504

936. Wiseman, D. J. 'A Babylonian architect?', *Anat. Stud.* 22 (1972) 141–7

937. Wiseman, D. J. 'Law and order in Old Testament times', *Vox Evangelica* 8 (London, 1973) 5–21

938. Wiseman, D. J. Review of A 25, *Bi. Or.* 34 (1977) 335–6

939. Wiseman, D. J. Review of A 926, *BSOAS* 44 (1981) 567

940. Wiseman, D. J. 'Mesopotamian gardens', *Anat. Stud.* 33 (1983) 137–44

941. Wiseman, D. J. *Nebuchadrezzar and Babylon* (The Schweich Lectures of the British Academy 1983). London, 1985

942. Woolley, C. L. *Carchemish: Report on the Excavations at Jerablus on behalf of the British Museum* I–III. London, 1921–52

943. Woolley, C. L. *The Neo-Babylonian and Persian Periods* (UE IX). London, 1962

944. Zadok, R. *On West Semites in Babylonia during the Chaldean and Achaemenian Periods. An Onomastic Study.* Jerusalem, 1977

945. Zadok, R. 'Phoenicians, Philistines and Moabites in Mesopotamia', *BASOR* 230 (1978) 57–65

946. Zadok, R. 'The Nippur region during the late Assyrian, Chaldean and Achaemenid periods chiefly according to written sources', *Israel Oriental Studies* 8 (1978) 266–332

947. Zadok, R. *Sources for the History of the Jews in Babylonia during the Chaldean and Achaemenian Periods. With an Appendix on West Semitic Names in 1st-Millennium Mesopotamia.* Jerusalem, 1979

948. Zadok, R. *The Jews in Babylonia during the Chaldean and Achaemenian Periods according to the Babylonian Sources* (Studies in the History of the Jewish People and the Land of Israel 3). Haifa, 1979

949. Zadok, R. 'Babylonian Notes: 1. The Neo/Late Babylonian pronunciation of two divine names', *Bi. Or.* 38 (1981) 547–9

3. NEO-BABYLONIAN SOCIETY AND ECONOMY

(a) Editions of texts

950. Campbell Thompson, R. (CT 22). London, 1906

951. Clay, A. T. *Babylonian Business Transactions of the First Millennium* B.C. (BRM I). New York, 1912

952. Clay, A. T. *Neo-Babylonian Letters from Erech* (YOS 3). New Haven, 1919

953. Contenau, G. *Contrats et lettres d'Assyrie et de Babylonie* (TCL 9). Paris, 1926

954. Delaunay, J. A. *Nouvelle édition de A. B. Moldenke, Cuneiform Texts in the Metropolitan Museum of Art (New York).* Paris, 1977

955. Freydank, H. Spätbabylonische Wirtschaftstexte aus Uruk. Berlin, 1971

956. Hunger, H. 'Das Archiv des Nabû-ušallim', *Bagh. Mitt.* 5 (1970), 193–304

957. Jakob-Rost, L. 'Ein neubabylonisches Tontafelarchiv aus dem 7. Jahrhundert v. u. Z.', *Forschungen und Berichte* 10 (1968) 39–62

958. Jakob-Rost, L. and Freydank, H. *Spätbabylonische Rechtsurkunden und Wirtschaftstexte aus Uruk* (VAS 20). Berlin, 1978

959. Keiser, C. E. *Letters and Contracts from Erech, Written in the Neo-Babylonian Period* (Babylonian Inscriptions in the Collection of J. B. Nies I). New Haven, 1917

960. McEwan, G. J. P. *The Late Babylonian Tablets in the Royal Ontario Museum* (Royal Ontario Museum Cuneiform Texts 2). Toronto, 1982

961. Peiser, F. E. *Babylonische Verträge des Berliner Museums*. Berlin, 1890

962. Pinches, Th. G. *Inscribed Babylonian Tablets in the Possession of Sir Henry Peek* 1–4. London, 1888–94

963. Pinches, Th. G. *Neo-Babylonian and Achaemenid Economic Texts* (CT 55–7). London, 1982

964. Pohl, A. *Neubabylonische Rechtsurkunden aus den Berliner Staatlichen Museen* 1–11 (An. Or. 8–9). Rome, 1933–4

965. Stigers, H. G. 'Neo- and Late Babylonian business documents from the John Frederick Lewis collection', *JCS* 28 (1976) 3–59

966. Ungnad, A. *Vorderasiatische Schriftdenkmäler* III–VI. Leipzig, 1907–8

(b) Translations of texts

967. Ebeling, E. *Neubabylonische Briefe aus Uruk* 1–IV. Berlin, 1930–4

968. Ebeling, E. *Neubabylonische Briefe*. Munich, 1949

969. Joannès, F. *Textes économiques de la Babylonie récente*. Paris, 1982

970. Kohler, J. and Peiser, F. E. *Aus dem Babylonischen Rechtsleben* 1–IV. Leipzig, 1890–8

971. Peiser, F. E. *Texte juristischen und geschäftlichen Inhalts* (KB 4). Berlin, 1896

972. Salonen, E. *Neubabylonische Urkunden verschiedenen Inhalts* 1–III. Helsinki, 1975–80

973. San Nicholò, M. *Babylonische Rechtsurkunden des ausgehenden 8. und des 7. Jahrhunderts v. Chr.* Munich, 1951

974. San Nicholò, M. and Petschow, H. *Babylonische Rechtsurkunden aus dem 6. Jahrhundert v. Chr.* Munich, 1960

975. San Nicholò, M. and Ungnad, A. *Neubabylonische Rechts- und Verwaltungsurkunden* 1. Leipzig, 1929–37

(c) Society

976. Cardascia, G. 'Documents Babyloniens des 8me et 7me siècles', *RIDA* (3rd series) 1 (1954) 101–24

977. Cardascia, G. 'Le statut de la femme dans les droits cunéiformes', in *Recueils de la Société Jean Bodin* 11 (Brussels, 1959), 79–94

978. Cuq, E. *Études sur le droit babylonien, les lois assyriennes et les lois hittites*. Paris, 1929.

979. Dandamayev, M. A. 'State and temple in Babylonia in the first

millennium B.C.', in A 34, 589–96 (1979)
980. Dandamayev, M. A. 'The Neo-Babylonian citizens', *Klio* 63 (1981) 45–9
981. Dandamayev, M. A. 'The Neo-Babylonian elders', in A 13, 38–41 (1982)
982. Dandamayev, M. A. *Babylonian Scribes in the First Millennium B.C.* Moscow, 1983 [In Russian with English summary]
982A. Dandamayev, M. A. 'Free hired labor in Babylonia during the sixth through fourth centuries B.C.' in Powell, M. A. (ed.) *Labor in the Ancient East*, 271–9. New Haven, 1987.
983. Dougherty, R. P. 'The Babylonian principle of suretyship as administered by temple law', *AJSL* 46 (1930) 73–103
984. Figulla, H. A. 'Lawsuit concerning a sacrilegious theft at Erech', *Iraq* 13 (1951) 95–101
985. Klíma, J. 'Beiträge zur Struktur der neubabylonischen Gesellschaft', in *Compte rendu de l'onzième Rencontre Assyriologique internationale*, 11–21. Leiden, 1964
986. Korošec, V. 'Keilschriftrecht', in *Orientalisches Recht* (Handbuch der Orientalistik) 49–219. Leiden, 1964
987. Koschaker, P. *Babylonisch-assyrisches Bürgschaftsrecht.* Leipzig, 1911
988. Kümmel, H. M. *Familie, Beruf und Amt im spätbabylonischen Uruk. Prosopographische Untersuchungen zu Berufsgruppen des 6. Jahrhunderts v. Chr. in Uruk.* (Abhandlungen der Deutschen Orient Gesellschaft 20). Berlin, 1979
989. Petschow, H. 'Das neubabylonische Gesetzesfragment', *Zeitschrift der Savigny-Stiftung für Rechtsgeschichte. Romanistische Abt.* 76 (1959), 37–96.
990. Sack, R. H. 'The scribe Nabû-bāni-ḫi, son of Ibnā, and the hierarchy of Eanna as seen in the Erech contracts', *ZA* 67 (1977) 42–52
991. Sack, R. H. 'The temple scribe in Chaldean Uruk', *Visible Language* 15/4 (1981) 409–18
992. San Nicolò, M. 'Über Adoption und die Gerichtsbarkeit der mâr-bânê im neubabylonischen Rechte', *Zeitschrift der Savigny-Stiftung für Rechtsgeschichte. Romanistische Abt.* 50 (1930) 445–55
993. San Nicolò, M. *Beiträge zur Rechtsgeschichte im Bereiche der keilschriftlichen Rechtsquellen.* Oslo, 1931
994. San Nicolò, M. 'Der §8 des Gesetzbuches Hammurapis in den neubabylonischen Urkunden', *Ar. Or.* 4 (1932) 327–44
995. Szlechter, E. 'Les lois néo-babyloniennes', *RIDA* (3rd series) 18 (1971) 43–107; 19 (1972) 43–126; 20 (1973) 43–50
996. Weisberg, D. B. *Guild Structure and Political Allegiance in Early Achaemenid Mesopotamia* (YNER 1). New Haven and London, 1967

(d) On ethnic minorities in Babylonia

997. Dandamayev, M. A. 'Egyptians in Babylonia', in *Drevnij Egipet i drevnaja Africa*, 15–26. Moscow, 1967 [In Russian]
998. Dandamayev, M. A. 'Data of the Babylonian documents from the 6th to the 5th centuries B.C. on the Sakas', in *Prolegomena to the Sources on the History of Pre-Islamic Central Asia*, 95–109. Budapest, 1979
999. Dandamayev, M. 'Aliens and the community in Babylonia in the 6th–

5th centuries B.C.', *Recueils de la Société Jean Bodin pour l'histoire comparative des institutions* 41 (1983) 133–45

1000. Eilers, W. 'Kleinasiatisches', *ZDMG* 94 (1940) 189–233

1002. Eph‘al, I. 'The western minorities in Babylonia in the 6th–5th centuries B.C.: maintenance and cohesion', *Or.* 47 (1978) 74–90

1003. Zadok, R. 'On some foreign population groups in first-millennium Babylonia', *Tel Aviv* 6 (1979) 164–81

(e) The Babylonian economy

1004. Bolla-Kotek, S. von. *Untersuchungen zur Tiermiete und Viehpacht im Altertum* (Münchener Beiträge zur Papyrusforschung und antiken Rechtsgeschichte 30). Munich, 1969

1005. Cocquerillat, D. *Palmeraies et cultures de l'Eanna d'Uruk (559–520)* (Ausgrabungen der Deutschen Forschungsgemeinschaft in Uruk-Warka 8). Berlin 1968

1006. Cocquerillat, D. 'Recherches sur le verger du temple campagnard de l'Akītu', *We. Or.* 7 (1973) 96–134

1007. Dandamayev, M. A. 'Der Tempelzehnte in Babylonien während des 6. bis 4. Jh. v. u. Z.', in *Beiträge zur Alten Geschichte und deren Nachleben: Festschrift für F. Altheim* 1, 82–90. Berlin, 1969

1008. Dandamayev, M. A. 'Die Rolle des tamkārum in Babylonien im 2. und 1. Jahrtausend v. u. Z.', in *Beiträge zur sozialen Struktur des Alten Vorderasien*, 69–78. Berlin, 1971

1009. Dandamayev, M. A. 'Die Fischerei in neubabylonischen Texten des 6. und 5. Jahrhunderts v. u. Z.', *Jahrbuch für Wirtschaftsgeschichte* 1981/IV, 67–82

1010. Dougherty, R. P. *The Shirkûtu of Babylonian Deities.* (VOSR 5/2). New Haven, 1923

1011. Dubberstein, W. H. 'Comparative prices in later Babylonia', *AJSL* 56 (1939) 20–43

1012. Ehrenkranz, M. *Beiträge zur Geschichte der Bodenpacht in neubabylonischer Zeit.* Berlin, 1936

1013. Eilers, W. 'Akkad. *kaspum* "Silber, Geld und Sinnverwandtes"', *We. Or.* 2 (1957) 322–37

1014. Krecher, J. 'Das Geschäftshaus Egibi in Babylon in neubabylonischer und achämenidischer Zeit.' Unpublished dissertation. Münster, 1970

1015. Lambert, M. 'Le destin d'Ur et les routes commerciales', *RSO* 39 (1964) 89–109

1016. Lanz, H. *Die neubabylonischen ḫarranu-Geschäftsunternehmen.* Berlin, 1976

1017. Mendelsohn, I. 'Free artisans and slaves in Mesopotamia', *BASOR* 89 (1943) 25–9

1018. Mendelsohn, I. *Slavery in the Ancient Near East.* New York, 1949

1019. Oppenheim, A. L. 'A fiscal practice of the Ancient Near East', *JNES* 6 (1947) 116–20

1020. Petschow, H. *Die neubabylonischen Kaufformulare.* Leipzig, 1939

1021. Petschow, H. 'Lehrverträge' in A 16, 6 (1983) 556–70

1022. Ries, G. *Die neubabylonischen Bodenpachtformulare*. Berlin, 1976

1023. Salonen, E. *Über das Erwerbsleben im Alten Mesopotamien, Untersuchungen zu den akkadischen Berufsnamen* 1. Helsinki, 1970

1024. Salonen, E. *Über den Zehnten im Alten Mesopotamien. Ein Beitrag zur Geschichte der Besteuerung*. Helsinki, 1972

1025. San Nicholò, M. 'Materialien zur Viehwirtschaft in den neubabylonischen Tempeln', *Or*. 17 (1948) 273–93; 18 (1949) 288–306; 20 (1951) 129–50; 23 (1954) 351–82; 25 (1956) 24–38

1026. San Nicholò, M. *Der neubabylonische Lehrvertrag in rechtsvergleichender Betrachtung*. Munich, 1950

1027. Ungnad, A. 'Das Haus Egibi', *AfO* 14 (1941) 57–64

1028. Weingort, S. *Die Haus Egibi in neubabylonischen Rechtsurkunden*. Berlin, 1939

4. BABYLONIAN MATHEMATICS, ASTROLOGY, AND ASTRONOMY

1029. Aaboe, A. 'Observation and theory in Babylonian astronomy', *Centaurus* 24 (1980) 14–35

1030. Aaboe, A. and Sachs, A. 'Two lunar texts of the Achaemenid period from Babylon', *Centaurus* 14 (1969) 1–22

1031. Bruins, E. M. and Rutten, M. *Textes mathématiques de Suse* (MMAI 34). Paris, 1961

1032. Campbell Thompson, R. *The Reports of the Magicians and Astronomers of Nineveh and Babylon in the British Museum* I–II. London, 1900

1033. Huber, P. J. *Astronomical Dating of Babylon I and Ur III* (Occasional Papers on the Near East, 1/4). Malibu, 1982

1034. Jones, A. 'The development and transmission of 248-day schemes for lunar motion in ancient astronomy', *Archive for the History of Exact Sciences* 29 (Berlin, 1983–4) 1–36

1034A. Kugler, F. X. *Die Babylonische Mondrechnung*. Freiburg im Breisgau, 1900

1035. Langdon, S., Fotheringham, J. K. and Schoch, C. *The Venus Tablets of Ammizaduqa*. London, 1928

1036. Neugebauer, O. *Mathematische Keilschrifttexte* I–III (Quellen und Studien zur Geschichte der Mathematik, Astronomie und Physik, Abt. A, 3). Berlin, 1935–7

1037. Neugebauer, O. and Sachs, A. *Mathematical Cuneiform Texts* (AOS 29). New Haven, 1945

1038. Neugebauer, O. *A History of Ancient Mathematical Astronomy* I–III (Studies in the History of Mathematics and Physical Sciences 1). New York, Heidelberg and Berlin, 1975

1039. Neugebauer, O. *Astronomical Cuneiform Texts* I–III. London, 1955 (Reprinted as Studies in the History of Mathematics and Physical Sciences 5). New York, Heidelberg and Berlin, 1983

1039A. Neugebauer, O. 'A Babylonian lunar ephemeris from Roman Egypt', in Leichty, E. *et al.* (eds.) *A Scientific Humanist: Studies in Memory of Abraham Sachs* (Occasional Publications of the Samuel Noah Kramer Fund 9), 301–4. Philadephia, 1988

1040. Oppenheim, A. L. 'Divination and celestial observation in the last Assyrian Empire', *Centaurus* 14 (1969) 97–135

1041. Pingree, D. 'The Mesopotamian origin of early Indian astronomy', *Journal for the History of Astronomy* 4 (1973) 1–12

1042. Reiner, E. and Pingree, D. *Babylonian Planetary Omens*, 1: *Enūma Anu Enlil Tablet 63: The Venus Tablet of Ammiṣaduqa* (Bibliotheca Mesopotamica 2/1). Malibu, 1975

1043. Reiner, E. and Pingree, D. *Babylonian Planetary Omens*, 2: *Enūma Anu Enlil Tablets 50–51* (Bi. Mes. 2/2). Malibu, 1981

1044. Sachs, A. 'A classification of the Babylonian astronomical tablets of the Seleucid period', *JCS* 2 (1948) 271–90

1044A. Sachs, A. J. 'Babylonian horoscopes', *JCS* 6 (1952) 49–75

1045. Sachs, A. (ed.) *Late Babylonian Astronomical and Related Texts Copied by T. G. Pinches and J. N. Strassmaier* (Brown University Studies 18). Providence, 1955

1046. Sachs, A. 'Babylonian observational astronomy', in Hodson, F. R. (ed.) *The Place of Astronomy in the Ancient World*, 43–50. London, 1974

1047. Sachs, A. 'The latest datable cuneiform texts', in A 18, 379–98 (1976)

1048. Thureau-Dangin, F. *Textes mathématiques babyloniens*. Leiden, 1938

1049. Toomer, G. J. (trans.) *Ptolemy's Almagest*. London, 1984

5. FIRST-MILLENNIUM BABYLONIAN LITERATURE

1050. Abusch, T. 'Mesopotamian anti-witchcraft literature: texts and studies: Part 1: The nature of Maqlû: its character, divisions and calendrical setting', *JNES* 33 (1974) 251–62

1051. Aro, J. 'Anzu and Sīmurgh', in A 18, 25–8 (1976)

1052. Biggs, R. D. 'Babylonien', in H. Schipperges *et al.* (eds.) *Krankheit, Heilkunst, Heilung*, 91–114. Freiburg and Munich, 1978

1053. Black, J. A. 'Babylonian ballads: a new genre', *JAOS* 103 (1983) 25–34

1054. Borger, R. 'Die Mücke und der Elephant', *Or.* NS 33 (1964) 442

1055. Burger, R. 'Das Tempelbau-Ritual K 48 +', *ZA* 61 (1971) 72–80

1056. Borger, R. 'Gott Marduk und Gott-König Šulgi als Propheten: zwei prophetische Texte', *Bi. Or.* 28 (1971) 3–24

1057. Bottéro, J. *Ecole Pratique des Hautes Etudes IVe Section. Annuaire* 1972/3, 93–103

1058. Bottéro, J. *Ecole Pratique des Hautes Etudes IVe Section. Annuaire* 1974/5, 95–142

1059. Campbell Thompson, R. *The Devils and Evil Spirits of Babylonia* 1. London, 1903

1060. Campbell Thompson, R. *The Epic of Gilgamish*. Oxford, 1930

1061. Caplice, R. I. 'Namburbi texts in the British Museum. V', *Or.* NS 40 (1971) 133–183

1062. Caplice, R. I. *The Akkadian Namburbi Texts: An Introduction* (SANE 1/1). Malibu, 1974

1063. Cavigneaux, A. 'Remarques sur les commentaires à Labat TDP 1', *JCS* 34 (1982) 231–41

1064. Civil, M. 'Medical commentaries from Nippur', *JNES* 33 (1974) 329–38

1065. Cohen, M. E. 'An analysis of the Balag compositions to the god Enlil copied in Babylon during the Seleucid period.' Ph. D. thesis, University of Pennsylvania, 1972

1066. Cooper, J. S. 'Structure, humor, and satire in the Poor Man of Nippur', *JCS* 27 (1975) 163–74

1067. Dietrich, M., Loretz, O., Klengel, H. and Mayer-Opificius, R. 'Untersuchungen zu Statue und Inschrift des Königs Idrimi von Alalaḫ', *UF* 13 (1981) 201–90

1068. Durand, J.-M. 'Un commentaire à TDP 1, AO 17661', *RA* 73 (1979) 153–70

1069. Ebeling, E. *Keilschrifttexte aus Assur religiösen Inhalts*, I–II (WVDOG 28, 34). Leipzig, 1919–23

1070. Ebeling, E. *Tod und Leben nach den Vorstellungen der Babylonier*. Berlin and Leipzig, 1931

1071. Ebeling, E. 'Ein mittelassyrisches Bruchstück des Etana-Mythus', *AfO* 14 (1941/4) 298–307

1072. Ebeling, E. 'Ein Preislied auf die Kultstadt Arba-ilu aus neuassyrischer Zeit', *JKF* 2 (1952/3) 274–82

1073. Elat, M. 'Mesopotamische Kriegsrituale', *Bi. Or.* 39 (1982) 6–26

1074. Ellis, M. de J. 'A new fragment of the Tale of the Poor Man of Nippur', *JCS* 26 (1974) 88–9

1075. Falkenstein, A. *Die Haupttypen der sumerischen Beschwörung* (Leipziger Semitistische Studien NF 1). Leipzig, 1931

1076. Falkenstein, A. and Soden, W. von. *Sumerisch-akkadische Hymnen und Gebete*. Zurich and Stuttgart, 1953

1077. Finkel, I. L. 'The crescent fertile', *AfO* 27 (1980) 37–52

1078. Finkel, I. L. 'A new piece of Babylonian libanomancy', *AfO* 29 (1983) 50–5

1079. Finkelstein, J. J. 'The so-called "Old Babylonian Kutha Legend"', *JCS* 11 (1957) 83–8

1080. Gadd, C. J. 'Two sketches from the life at Ur', *Iraq* 25 (1963) 177–88

1081. Geller, M. J. 'A Middle Assyrian tablet of Utukkū Lemnūtu', *Iraq* 42 (1980) 23–51

1082. Grayson, A. K. 'Assyria and Babylonia', *Or.* NS 49 (1980) 140–94

1083. Grayson, A. K. and Lambert, W. G. 'Akkadian prophecies', *JCS* 18 (1964) 7–30

1084. Groneberg, B. 'Untersuchungen zum hymnisch-epischen Dialekt der altbabylonischen literarischen Texte'. Dissertation. Munster, 1971

1085. Groneberg, B. *Untersuchungen zu Syntax, Morphologie und Stil der jungbabylonischen lyrischen Literatur*. Wiesbaden, 1987

1086. Gurney, O. R. 'Further texts from Dur-Kurigalzu', *Sumer* 9 (1953) 25ff

1087. Gurney, O. R. 'The Cuthean Legend of Naram-Sin', *Anat. Stud.* 5 (1955) 93–113, with corrections idem, *Anat. Stud.* 6 (1956) 163f

1088. Gurney, O. R. 'The Tale of the Poor Man of Nippur', *Anat. Stud.* 6 (1956) 145–62, with corrections idem, *Anat. Stud.* 7 (1957) 135f

1089. Gurney, O. R. 'The myth of Nergal and Ereškigal', *Anat. Stud.* 10 (1960) 105–31

1090. Gurney, O. R. 'The Tale of the Poor Man of Nippur and its folktale parallels', *Anat. Stud.* 22 (1972) 149–58

1091. Güterbock, H. G. 'Die historische Tradition und ihre literarische Gestaltung bei Babyloniern und Hethitern bis 1200', *ZA* 42 (1934) 1–91

1092. Hallo, W. W. and W. L. Moran, 'The first tablet of the SB recension of the Anzu-Myth', *JCS* 31 (1979) 65–115; references to earlier editions *ibid.* p. 65 notes* and 1

1093. Hecker, K. *Untersuchungen zur akkadischen Epik* (AOAT(S) 8). Kevelaer and Neukirchen-Vluyn, 1974

1094. Hirsch, H. 'Die Inschriften der Könige von Agade', *AfO* 20 (1963) 1–82

1095. Hofer-Heilsberg, A. 'Ein Keilschrifttext: der älteste Mimus der Weltliteratur und seine Auswirkungen', *Theater der Welt* 3/4 (1937) 1–15

1096. Hunger, H. *Spätbabylonische Texte aus Uruk* 1 (Ausgrabungen der Deutschen Forschungsgemeinschaft in Uruk-Warka 9). Berlin, 1976

1097. Kilmer, A. D. 'The first tablet of *Malku = šarru*', *JAOS* 83 (1963) 421–46

1098. Kinnier Wilson, J. V. 'Two medical texts from Nimrud', *Iraq* 18 (1958) 130–46

1099. Kinnier Wilson, J. V. 'Some contributions to the Legend of Etana', *Iraq* 31 (1969) 8–17

1100. Kinnier Wilson, J. V. 'Further contributions to the Legend of Etana', *JNES* 33 (1974) 237–49

1101. Kinnier Wilson, J. V. 'Medicine in the land and times of the Old Testament', in Ishida, T. (ed.) *Studies in the Period of David and Solomon and Other Essays*, 348–58. Winona Lake, Indiana, 1982

1102. Köcher, F. 'Ein akkadischer medizinischer Schülertext aus Bogazköy', *AfO* 16 (1952/3) 47–56

1103. Köcher, F. and Oppenheim, A. L. 'The Old Babylonian omen text VAT 7525', *AfO* 18 (1957/8) 62–80

1104. Köcher, F. 'Ein spätbabylonischer Hymnus auf den Tempel Ezida in Borsippa', *ZA* 53 (1959) 236–40

1105. Köcher, F. *Die babylonisch-assyrische Medizin* 1–VI. Berlin, 1963–80

1106. Kraus, F. R. *Die physiognomischen Omina der Babylonier* (*MVAG* 40/2). Leipzig, 1935

1107. Kraus, F. R. *Texte zur babylonischen Physiognomatik* (*AfO* Bh.3). Berlin, 1939

1108. Labat, R. *Commentaires assyro-babyloniens sur les présages.* Bordeaux, 1933

1109. Labat, R. *Le poème babylonien de la Création.* Paris, 1935

1110. Labat, R. *Traité akkadien de diagnostics et pronostics médicaux* 1–II. Paris and Leiden, 1951

1111. Labat, R. *et al. Les religions du Proche-Orient asiatique: textes babyloniens, ougaritiques, hittites.* Paris, 1970

1112. Labat, R. 'Hemerologien', in A 16, 4 (1975) 317–23 [In French]

1113. Laessøe, J. *Studies on the Assyrian Ritual and Series bît rimki.* Copenhagen, 1955

1114. Lambert, W. G. 'Three literary prayers of the Babylonians', *AfO* 19 (1959/60) 47–66

1115. Lambert, W. G. *Babylonian Wisdom Literature*. Oxford, 1960

1116. Lambert, W. G. 'A new fragment of The King of Battle', *AfO* 20 (1963) 161–2

1117. Lambert, W. G. 'The great battle of the Mesopotamian religious year: the conflict in the Akitu house (a summary)', *Iraq* 25 (1963) 189–90

1118. Lambert, W. G. 'The reign of Nebuchadnezzar I: a turning point in the history of Ancient Mesopotamian religion', in A 36, 3–11 (1964)

1119. Lambert, W. G. 'The Gula hymn of Bulluṭsa-rabi', *Or.* NS 36 (1967) 105–32

1120. Lambert, W. G. 'DINGIR.ŠÀ.DIB.BA incantations', *JNES* 33 (1974) 267–322

1121. Lambert, W. G. 'The problem of the love lyrics', in A 24, 98–135 (1975)

1122. Lambert, W. G. 'New fragments of Babylonian epics', *AfO* 27 (1980) 71–82

1123. Lambert, W. G. 'The hymn to the Queen of Nippur', in A 54, 173–218 (1982)

1124. Lambert, W. G. and Millard, A. R. *Atra-ḥasīs: The Babylonian Story of The Flood*. Oxford, 1969.

1125. Landsberger, B. 'Über Farben im Sumerisch-akkadischen', *JCS* 21 (1967) 139–73

1126. Langdon, S. 'The Legend of Etana and the Eagle', *Babyloniaca* 12 (1932) 1–56

1127. Leichty, E. *The Series Šumma Izbu* (TCS 4). Locust Valley, New York, 1969

1128. Lewis, B. *The Sargon Legend: A Study of the Akkadian Text and the Tale of the Hero Who Was Exposed at Birth* (ASOR Dissertation Series 4). Cambridge, Mass., 1980

1129. Mayer, W. R. *Untersuchungen zur Formensprache der babylonischen 'Gebetsbeschwörungen'* (Studia Pohl Series Maior 5). Rome, 1976

1130. Meier, G. *Die assyrische Beschwörungssammlung Maqlû* (*AfO* (Bh) 2). Berlin, 1937; with corrections *AfO* 21 (1966) 70–81

1131. Meier, G. 'Die Ritualtafel der Serie "Mundwaschung"', *AfO* 12 (1937/9) 40–5

1132. Meier, G. 'Ritual für das Reisen über Land', *AfO* 12 (1937/9) 141–4

1133. Moren, S. M. *The Omen Series Šumma Alu: A Preliminary Investigation*. Ph.D. thesis, University of Pennsylvania, 1978

1134. Müller, H.-P. 'Gilgameschs Trauergesang um Enkidu und die Gattung der Totenklage', *ZA* 68 (1978) 233–50

1135. Müller, K. F. *Das assyrische Ritual*, I: *Texte zum assyrischen Königsritual* (*MVAG* 41/3). Leipzig, 1937

1136. Myhrman, D. W. 'Die Labartu-Texte', *ZA* 16 (1902) 141–200

1137. Nötscher, F. *Haus- und Stadtomina der Serie šumma âlu ina mêlê šakin* and *Die Omen-Serie šumma âlu ina mêlê šakin* (*Or.* 31, 39–42, 51–4). Rome, 1928–30

1138. Nougayrol, J. 'Un chef-d'oeuvre inédit de la littérature babylonienne', *RA* 45 (1951) 169–83

1139. Nougayrol, J. 'Une version ancienne du "Juste souffrant"', *Rev. Bibl.* 59 (1952) 239–50

1140. Nougayrol, J. 'Aleuromancie babylonienne', *Or.* NS 32 (1963) 381–6

1141. Nougayrol, J. (ed.) *La divination en Mésopotamie ancienne et dans les régions voisines*. Paris, 1966

1142. Nougayrol, J. '"Juste souffrant" (R.S. 25.460)', in Nougayrol, J. *et al.* (eds.) *Ugaritica* 5, 265–73. Paris, 1968

1143. Nougayrol, J. 'L'épopée babylonienne,' in *La poesia epica e la sua formazione* (Atti Accademia Nazionale dei Lincei, Anno 367. Quaderno N. 139), 839–58. Rome, 1970

1144. Nougayrol, J. 'Einführende Bemerkungen zur babylonischen Religion', in Mann, Ulrich (ed.) *Theologie und Religionswissenschaft*, 28–45. Darmstadt, 1973

1145. Oppenheim, A. L. *The Interpretation of Dreams in the Ancient Near East with a Translation of an Assyrian Dream-Book* (Transactions of the American Philosophical Society NS 46/3). Philadelphia, 1956

1146. Oppenheim, A. L. 'A new prayer to the "Gods of the Night"', *Analecta Biblica* 12 (1959) 282–301

1147. Oppenheim, A. L. 'A Babylonian diviner's manual', *JNES* 33 (1974) 197–220

1148. Oppenheim, A. L. 'Man and nature in Mesopotamian civilization', *Dictionary of Scientific Biography* 15 (1975) 634–66

1149. Petriconi, H. 'Das Gilgamesch-Epos als Vorbild der Ilias (Der Tod des Helden I)', in Crisafulli, A. S. (ed.) *Linguistic and Literary Studies in Honor of H. A. Hatzfeld*, 329–42. Washington, 1964

1150. Pettinato, G. *Die Ölwahrsagung bei den Babyloniern* (Studi Semitici 21–2). Rome, 1966

1151. Pettinato, G. 'Libanomanzia presso i babilonesi', *RSO* 41 (1966) 303–27

1152. Picchioni, S. A. *Il poemetto di Adapa*. Budapest, 1981

1153. Reiner, E. Review of Köcher, F. *Pflanzenkunde, Bi. Or.* 15 (1958) 102f

1154. Reiner, E. *Šurpu. A Collection of Sumerian and Akkadian Incantations* (*AfO* (Bh).11). Graz, 1958

1155. Reiner, E. 'Fortune-telling in Mesopotamia', *JNES* 19 (1960) 23–35

1156. Reiner, E. 'A Sumero-Akkadian hymn of Nanâ', *JNES* 33 (1974) 221–36

1157. Reiner, E. 'Babylonian birth prognoses', *ZA* 72 (1982) 124–38

1158. Reiner, E. *Your Thwarts in Pieces, Your Mooring Rope Cut: Poetry from Babylonia and Assyria* (Michigan Studies in the Humanities 5). Ann Arbor, Michigan, 1985

1159. Reiner, E. 'Amulets and talismans', in Farkas, A., Harper, P. O. and Harrison, E. B. (eds.) *Monsters and Demons in the Ancient and Mediaeval World*, 27–36. Mainz, 1986

1160. Reiner, E. and Civil, M. 'The Babylonian Furstenspiegel in practice', in A 13, 320–6 (1982)

1161. Reiner, E. and Güterbock, H. G. 'The great prayer to Ishtar and its two versions from Bogazköy', *JCS* 21 (1967) 255–66

1162. Reisner, G. *Sumerisch-babylonische Hymnen nach Thontafeln griechischer Zeit* (Mittheilungen aus den orientalischen Sammlungen 10). Berlin, 1896

1163. Renger, J. 'Königsinschriften. Akkadisch', in A 16, 6 (1980) 65–77

1164. Rochberg-Halton, F. *Aspects of Babylonian Celestial Divination. The Lunar Eclipse Tablets of Enuma Anu Enlil* (*AfO* (Bh.) 21). Vienna, 1986

1165. Schott, A. *Das Gilgamesch-Epos.* Revised by Soden, W. von. (Universal-Bibliothek 7235[2]). Stuttgart, 1982

1166. Smith, S. *The Statue of Idri-mi* (British Institute of Archaeology in Ankara, Occasional Publications 1). London, 1949

1167. Soden, W. von 'Lexicalisches Archiv', *ZA* 43 (1935) 233–50.

1168. Soden, W. von. 'Bemerkungen zu den von Ebeling in "Tod und Leben" Band 1 bearbeiteten Texten', *ZA* 43 (1936) 251–76

1169. Soden, W. von. 'Das Problem der zeitlichen Einordnung akkadischer Literaturwerke', *MDOG* 85 (1953) 14–26

1170. Soden, W. von. 'Religiöse Unsicherheit, Säkularisierungstendenzen und Aberglaube zur Zeit der Sargoniden', *Analecta Biblica* 12 (1959) 356–67

1171. Soden, W. von. 'Das Fragen nach der Gerechtigkeit Gottes im Alten Orient', *MDOG* 96 (1965) 41–59

1172. Soden, W. von. 'Der grosse Hymnus an Nabû', *ZA* 61 (1971) 44–71

1173. Soden, W. von. 'Verschlüsselte Kritik an Salomo in der Urgeschichte des Jahwisten?', *We. Or.* 7 (1973/4) 228–40

1174. Soden, W. von. 'Die erste Tafel des altbabylonischen Atramhasis-Mythus', *ZA* 68 (1978) 50–94; for the SB recension see *ibid.* 86ff

1175. Soden, W. von. 'Untersuchungen zur babylonischen Metrik', *ZA* 71 (1981) 161–204

1176. Speiser, E. A. 'The case of the obliging servant', *JCS* 8 (1954) 98–105

1177. Stol, M. 'Le "roitelet" et l'éléphant', *RA* 65 (1971) 180

1177A. Sweet, R. F. G. 'A pair of double acrostics in Akkadian', *Or.* 38 (1969) 459–60

1178. Thureau-Dangin, F. *Rituels accadiens.* Paris, 1921

1179. Thureau-Dangin, F. 'Le Rituel pour l'expédition en char', *RA* 21 (1924) 127–37

1180. van Dijk, J. *Cuneiform texts of varying content* (TIM 9). Leiden, 1976

1181. Weidner, E. F. 'Ein Segensgebet für Assurbânipal', *AfO* 13 (1939/41) 210–13

1182. Weidner, E. F. 'Die astrologische Serie Enûma Anu Enlil', *AfO* 14 (1941/4) 172–95, 308–18; *AfO* 17 (1954/6) 71–89; *AfO* 22 (1968/9) 65–75

1183. Weiher, E. von. *Der babylonische Gott Nergal* (AOAT 11). Kevelaer and Neukirchen-Vluyn, 1971

1184. Weiher, E. von. *Spätbabylonische Texte aus Uruk* 2 (Ausgrabungen der Deutschen Forschungsgemeinschaft in Uruk-Warka 10). Berlin, 1983

B. ISRAEL AND JUDAH

1. Abbot, N. 'Pre-Islamic Arab queens', *AJSL* 58 (1941) 1–22
2. Absa Assaf, A. 'Untersuchungen zur ammonitischen Rundbildkunst', *UF* 12 (1980) 7–102
3. Ackròyd, P. R. 'Two Old Testament historical problems of the early Persian period', *JNES* 17 (1958) 13–27
4. Ackroyd, P. R. *Exile and Restoration. A Study of Hebrew Thought of the 6th Century B.C.* London, 1968
5. Ackroyd, P. R. and Evans, C. F. *The Cambridge History of the Bible* I. Cambridge, 1970
6. Ackroyd, P. R. and Lindars, B. (eds.) *Words and Meanings. Essays presented to David Winton Thomas.* Cambridge, 1968
7. Aharoni, M. and Y. 'The stratification of Judahite sites in the 8th and 7th centuries B.C.E.', *BASOR* 224 (1976) 73–90
8. Aharoni, Y. *Excavations at Ramat Rahel. Seasons 1959 and 1960.* Rome, 1962
9. Aharoni, Y. *Excavations at Ramat Rahel. Seasons 1961 and 1962.* Rome, 1964
10. Aharoni, Y. 'Arad: its inscriptions and temple', *Bi. Ar.* 31 (1968) 2–32
11. Aharoni, Y. 'Trial excavation in the "Solar Shrine" at Lachish', *IEJ* 18 (1968) 157–69
12. Aharoni, Y. 'Tel Beer-sheba', *IEJ* 19 (1969) 245–7
13. Aharoni, Y. (ed.) *Beersheba* I: *Excavations at Tel Beer-Sheba, 1969–1971 Seasons.* Tel Aviv, 1973
14. Aharoni, Y. 'The horned altar of Beersheba', *Bi. Ar.* 37 (1974) 2–6
14A. Aharoni, Y. 'Excavations at Tell Beer-sheba, preliminary report of the fifth and sixth seasons', *Tel Aviv* 2 (1975) 146–68
15. Aharoni, Y. *Investigations at Lachish: The Sanctuary and the Residency* (Lachish V). (Publications of the Institute of Archaeology, Tel Aviv University, 4). Tel Aviv, 1975
16. Aharoni, Y. *The Land of the Bible: A Historical Geography.* 2nd edn. Philadelphia, 1979
17. Aharoni, Y. *Arad Inscriptions.* Jerusalem, 1981
18. Aharoni, Y. and Amiran, R. 'Excavations at Tel Arad. Preliminary report on the first season, 1962', *IEJ* 14 (1964) 131–47
19. Albright, W. F. 'The date and personality of the Chronicler', *JBL* 40 (1921) 104–24
20. Albright, W. F. 'The seal of Eliakim and the latest preëxilic history of Judah with some observations on Ezekiel', *JBL* 51 (1932) 77–106
21. Albright, W. F. *The Excavation of Tell Beit Mirsim,* II: *The Bronze Age* (AASOR 17). New Haven, 1938
22. Albright, W. F. 'King Joiachin in exile', *Bi. Ar.* 5 (1942) 49–55, reprinted in *BAR* 1 (1961) 106–12
23. Albright, W. F. *The Excavation of Tell Beit Mirsim,* III: *The Iron Age* (AASOR 21–2). New Haven, 1943

23A. Albright, W. F. 'The son of Tabeel (Isaiah 7: 6)', *BASOR* 140 (1955), 34–5

24. Albright, W. F. 'Further light on synchronisms between Egypt and Asia in the period 935–685 B.C.', *BASOR* 141 (1956) 23–7

25. Albright, W. F. 'An ostracon from Calah and the North-Israelite diaspora', *BASOR* 149 (1958) 33–6

26. Albright, W. F. *The Archaeology of Palestine*. Revised edn. Harmondsworth, 1960

27. Albright, W. F. *The Biblical Period from Abraham to Ezra*. Revised edn. New York and Evanston, 1963

28. Albright, W. F. *Yahweh and the Gods of Canaan* (Jordan Lectures, 1965). London, 1968

29. Allen, L. C. *The Books of Joel, Obadaiah, Jonah, Micah*. London, 1978

30. Allrick, H. L. 'The lists of Zerubbabel (Nehemiah 7 and Ezra 2) and the Hebrew numeral notation', *BASOR* 136 (1954) 21–7

31. Alt, A. 'Die Weisheit Salomos', *Theologische Literaturzeitung* 76 (1951) 139–44, republished as *Kleine Schriften* II (1953) 90–9

32. Alt, A. *Kleine Schriften zur Geschichte des Volkes Israel* I–III. Munich, 1953–9

33. Alt, A. *Essays on Old Testament History and Religion*. Oxford, 1966

34. Amiet, P. *L'art antique du Proche Orient*. Paris, 1977

35. Amiran, R. 'The story of pottery in Palestine', *Antiquity and Survival* 2/2–3 (1957) 187–207

36. Amiran, R. *Ancient Pottery of the Holy Land*. Jerusalem, 1969

37. Amiran, R. 'The lion statue and the libation tray from Tell Beit Mirsim', *BASOR* 22 (1976) 29–40

38. Anderson, R. T. 'Was Isaiah a scribe?', *JBL* 79 (1960) 57–8

39. Avigad, N. 'The Jotham seal from Elath', *BASOR* 163 (1961) 18–22

40. Avigad, N. 'A seal of "Manasseh son of the king"', *IEJ* 13 (1963) 133–6

41. Avigad, N. 'Seal and sealings', *IEJ* 14 (1964) 190–4

42. Avigad, N. 'Seals of exiles', *IEJ* 15 (1965) 222–32

43. Avigad, N. 'Excavations in the Jewish quarter of the Old City of Jerusalem, 1971 (Third preliminary report)', *IEJ* 22 (1972) 193–200

44. Avigad, N. *Bullae and Seals from a Post-Exilic Judaean Archive* (Qedem 4). Jerusalem, 1976

45. Avigad, N. 'Baruch the scribe and Jerahmeel the king's son', *IEJ* 28 (1978) 52–6

46. Avigad, N. 'The seal of Seraiah (son of) Neriah', *Eretz Israel* 14 (1978) 86–7 [In Hebrew]

47. Avi Yonah, M. *A History of the Holy Land*. London, 1969

48. Avi Yonah, M. *Gazetteer of Roman Palestine* (Qedem 5). Jerusalem, 1976

49. Avi Yonah, M. *et al.* (eds.) *Encyclopedia of Archaeological Excavations in the Holy Land* I–IV. London, 1975–8

49A. Baldwin, J. G., *Haggai, Zecharaiah, Malachi: An Introduction and Commentary*. Leicester, 1972

50. Baldwin J. *Daniel, an Introduction and Commentary*. Leicester, 1978

51. Baltzer, K. *The Covenant Formulary in Old Testament, Jewish and Early Christian Writings*. Oxford, 1971

52. Barnett, R. D. 'Four sculptures from Amman', *ADAJ* 1 (1951) 34–6

53. Barnett, R. D. 'The siege of Lachish', *IEJ* 8 (1958) 161–4

54. Barnett, R. D. 'Layard's Nimrud bronzes and their inscriptions', *Eretz Israel* 8 (1967) 1*–7*

55. Barnett, R. D. *Illustrations of Old Testament History*. 2nd edn. London, 1977

56. Barr, J. Review of c 324 in *JSS* 14 (1969) 252–6

57. Barrois, A.-G. *Manuel d'archéologie biblique* I–II. Paris, 1939–53

58. Bartlett, J. R. 'The rise and fall of the Kingdom of Edom', *PEQ* 104 (1972) 26–37

59. Bartlett, J. R. 'From Edomites to Nabataeans: a study in continuity', *PEQ* 111 (1979) 53–66

60. Batten, L. W. *A Critical and Exegetical Commentary on the Books of Ezra and Nehemiah* (ICC). Edinburgh, 1913

61. Benoit, P., Milik, J. T. and de Vaux, R. *Les grottes de Murabba'at* (Discoveries in the Desert of Judaea II). Oxford, 1961

62. Bennett, C.-M. 'Excavations at Buseirah, southern Jordan, 1974: fourth preliminary report', *Levant* 9 (1977) 1–10

63. Ben Sasson, H. H. *A History of the Jewish People*. London, 1976

64. Ben Zvi, I. 'The origins of the settlement of Jewish tribes in Arabia', *Eretz Israel* 6 (1960) 35*–37*, 130–48

64A. Ben Zvi, I. 'Les origines de l'établissement des tribus d'Israel en Arabie', *Le Museon* 74 (1961) 143–90

65. Berger, P.-R. 'Zu den Namen ššbzr and šnᵓzr', *ZAW* 83 (1971) 98–100

66. Berger, P.-R. 'Der Kyros-Zylinder mit dem Zusatzfragment BIN II Nr. 32 und die akkadischen Personennamen im Danielbuch', *ZA* 64 (1975) 224–34

66A. Berman (Biran), A. 'Two Hebrew seals of the ʿebed class', *JBL* 55 (1936) 221–6

67. Betancourt, P. P. *The Aeolic Style in Architecture: A Survey of its Development in Palestine, the Halikarnassos Peninsula and Greece, 100–500 B.C.* Princeton, 1979

68. Beyerlin, W. *Near Eastern Religious Texts Relating to the Old Testament*. London, 1978

68A. Bickerman, E. J. 'The edict of Cyrus in Ezra 1', *JBL* 65 (1946) 249–75

69. Boecker, H. J. *Law and the Administration of Justice in the Old Testament and Ancient East*. London, 1980

70. Boraas, R. S. and Geraty, L. T. 'Heshbon 1974' (AUM 9). Michigan, 1976

71. Boraas, R. S. and Geraty, L. T. 'Heshbon 1976' (AUM 10). Michigan, 1978

72. Boraas, R. S. and Horn, S. H. 'Heshbon 1968' (AUM 2). Michigan, 1969

73. Boraas, R. S. and Horn, S. H. 'Heshbon 1971' (AUM 6). Michigan, 1973

74. Boraas, R. S. and Horn, S. H. 'Heshbon 1973' (AUM 8). Michigan, 1975

75. Bordreuil, J. *Revue d'histoire et de philosophie religieuses* (1979) 313–17

76. Borger, R. and Tadmor, H. 'Zwei Beiträge zur alttestamentlichen Wissenschaft aufgrund der Inschriften Tiglatpilesers III', *ZAW* 94 (1982) 244–51

77. Botterwick, G. J. and Ringgren, H. *Theological Dictionary of the Old Testament* I–IV. Revised English edn. Grand Rapids, 1977–80

77A. Bright, J. *Jeremiah* (The Anchor Bible). Garden City, New York, 1965

78. Bright, J. *A History of Israel.* Revised edn. London, 1972

79. Broshi, M. 'The expansion of Jerusalem in the reigns of Hezekiah and Manasseh', *IEJ* 24 (1974) 21–6

80. Brown, C. *The New International Dictionary of New Testament Theology* I. Exeter, 1975

81. Brown, F., Driver, S. R. and Briggs, C. A. *A Hebrew and English Lexicon of the Old Testament.* Oxford, 1907

82. Buccellati, G. *Cities and Nations of Ancient Syria* (Studi Semitici 26). Rome, 1967

83. Burrows, M. 'Jerusalem', in B 84, II, 843–66

83A. Burrows, M. 'The conduit of the upper pool', *ZAW* 70 (1958) 221–7

84. Buttrick, G. A. *et al.* (eds.) *The Interpreter's Dictionary of the Bible* I–IV and Supplement. Nashville and New York, 1962–76.

85. Chapman, S. V. 'A catalogue of Iron Age pottery from the cemeteries of Khirbet Silm, Joya, Qrayé and Qashmieh of South Lebanon', *Berytus* 21 (1972) 55–194

86. Charles, R. H. *The Apocrypha and Pseudepigrapha of the Old Testament in English* I–II. Oxford, 1913

87. Charlesworth, J. H. *The Pseudepigrapha and Modern Research.* Missoula, 1976

88. Childs, B. S. *Isaiah and the Assyrian Crisis.* London, 1967

89. Conrad, D. 'On zrw^c = "forces, troops, army" in Biblical Hebrew', *Tel Aviv* 3 (1976) 111–19

90. Coogan, M. D. *West Semitic Personal Names in the Murašû Documents.* Missoula, 1976

91. Cooke, G. A. *A Critical and Exegetical Commentary on the Book of Ezekiel* (ICC). Edinburgh, 1936

92. Cowley, A. E. *Aramaic Papyri of the Fifth Century B.C.* Oxford, 1923

92A. Craigie, J. C., *The Book of Deuteronomy* (NICOT). London, 1976

93. Crenshaw, J. L. 'Wisdom', in Hayes, J. H. (ed.) *Old Testament Form Criticism*, 225–64. San Antonio, 1974

94. Cross, F. M. 'Epigraphic notes on Hebrew documents of the eighth-sixth centuries B.C.: II. The Murabba^{c}ât papyrus and the letter found near Yabneh-yam', *BASOR* 165 (1962) 34–46

95. Cross, F. M. 'An ostracon from Hesbon', in B 72, 223–9 (1969)

96. Cross, F. M. 'Hesbon ostracon II', in B 73, 126–31 (1973)

97. Cross, F. M. 'Notes on the Ammonite inscription from Tell Sīrān', *BASOR* 212 (1973) 12–15

98. Cross, F. M. 'A reconstruction of the Judean restoration', *JBL* 94 (1975) 4–18

99. Cross, F. M. 'Ammonite ostraca from Heshbon: Heshbon ostraca IV–VIII', in B 74, Appendix 1–20 (1975)

100. Cross, F. M. 'Heshbon ostracon XI', in B 70, 145–8 (1976)

101. Cross, F. M. *et al.* (eds.) *Magnalia Dei: The Mighty Acts of God. Essays . . . in Memory of G. Ernest Wright*. Garden City, 1976

102. Cross, F. M. and Freedman, D. N. *Early Hebrew Orthography*. Baltimore, 1952

103. Cross, F. M. and Freedman, D. N. 'Josiah's revolt against Assyria', *JNES* 12 (1953) 56–8

104. Crowfoot, J. W. and G. M. *Samaria-Sebaste*. II: *Early Ivories from Samaria*. London, 1938

105. Crowfoot, J. W. and Kenyon, K. M. *Samaria-Sebaste*. I: *The Buildings at Samaria*. London, 1942

106. Curtis, E. L. and Madsen, A. A. *A Critical and Exegetical Commentary on the Books of Chronicles* (ICC). Edinburgh, 1910

107. De Geus, C. H. J. 'Idumaea', *JEOL* 26 (1980) 53–74

108. Delaporte, L. *Epigraphes araméens*. Paris, 1912

109. de Vaux, R. *Les institutions de l'Ancien Testament* I–II. Paris, 1958–60

110. de Vaux, R. *Studies in Old Testament Sacrifice*. Cardiff, 1964

111. Diringer, D. *Le inscrizioni antico-ebraiche palestinesi*. Florence, 1934

112. Diringer, D. *et al. Lachish*, III: *The Iron Age*. Oxford, 1953

113. Donner, H. and Röllig, W. *Kanaanäische und aramäische Inschriften* I–III. 2nd–3rd edns. Wiesbaden, 1969–73

114. Dothan, M. *Ashdod*, II–III: *The Second and Third Seasons of Excavations, 1963, 1965* (ʿAtiqot 9–10). Jerusalem, 1971

115. Driver, G. R. *Semitic Writing from Pictograph to Alphabet*. 3rd edn. London, 1976

116. Driver, S. R. *Deuteronomy* (ICC). 3rd edn. Edinburgh, 1895

117. Dunand, M. 'Nouvelles inscriptions phéniciennes de temple d'Echmoun à Bostan ech-Cheikh, près Sidon', *Bull. MB* 18 (1965) 105–9

118. Dunand, M. 'Byblos, Sidon, Jérusalem: monuments apparentés des temps achéménides', *VT* (Supp.) 17 (1969) 64–70

119. Dupont-Sommer, A. *The Essene Writings from Qumran*. Oxford, 1961

120. Eissfeldt, O. *The Old Testament. An Introduction*. Oxford, 1965

121. Eitan, A. *et al. Inscriptions Reveal. Documents from the Time of the Bible, the Mishna and the Talmud* (Israel Museum Catalogue no. 100). Jerusalem, 1973

122. Ellenbogen, M. *Foreign Words in the Old Testament, their Origin and Etymology*. London, 1962

123. Ellison, H. L. *From Babylon to Bethlehem: The Jewish People from the Exile to the Messiah*. Exeter, 1976

124. Finegan, J. *Handbook of Biblical Chronology*. Princeton, 1964

125. Fisher, L. R. (ed.) *Ras Shamra Parallels* I (An. Or. 49). Rome, 1972

125A. Fitzmyer, J. A. 'The Aramaic letter of King Adon to the Egyptian Pharaoh', *Biblica* 46 (1965) 41–55

125B. Fitzmyer, J. A. *A Wandering Aramaean: Collected Aramaic Essays* (Society of Biblical Literature Monograph Series 25). Missoula, 1979

126. Fohrer, G. *Introduction to the Old Testament*. London, 1970
127. Fohrer, G. *History of Israelite Religion*. London, 1973
128. Freedman, D. N. and Campbell, E. F., Jr. (eds.) *BAR* II. New York, 1964
129. Galling, K. 'Ein hebräisches Siegel aus der babylonischen Diaspora', *ZDPV* 51 (1928) 234–6
130. Galling, K. 'Beschriftete Bildsiegel des ersten Jahrtausends v. Chr. vornehmlich aus Syrien und Palästina', *ZDPV* 64 (1941) 121–202
130A. Galling, K. 'Kronzeugen des Artaxerxes? Eine Interpretation von Esra 4, 9f.', *ZAW* 63 (1951) 66–74
131. Galling, K. (ed.) *Textbuch zur Geschichte Israels*. 2nd edn. Tübingen, 1968
132. Gesenius, W., Kautsch, E. and Cowley, A. *Hebrew Grammar*. 2nd English edn. Oxford, 1910
133. Gibson, J. C. L. *Textbook of Syrian Semitic Inscriptions*, I: *Hebrew and Moabite Inscriptions*. Oxford, 1971. (For nos. of inscriptions see B 134, 163)
134. Gibson, J. C. L. *Textbook of Syrian Semitic Inscriptions*, II: *Aramaic Inscriptions*. Oxford, 1975
134A. Gibson, J. C. L. *Textbook of Syrian Semitic Inscriptions*, III: *Phoenician Inscriptions*. Oxford, 1982
135. Giveon, R. 'Two new Hebrew seals and their iconographic backgound', *PEQ* 93 (1961) 38–42
136. Glueck, N. *The Other Side of Jordan*. 2nd edn. Cambridge, Mass. 1970
137. Goedicke, H. 'The end of "So", king of Egypt', *BASOR* 171 (1963) 64–6
138. Gray, G. B. *The Forms of Hebrew Poetry*. London, 1915
139. Gray, G. B. and Paeka, A. S. *A Critical and Exegetical Commentary on the Book of Isaiah*. Edinburgh, 1912
140. Gray, J. *I and II Kings: A Commentary*. 2nd edn. London, 1970
141. Green, A. R. W. *The Role of Human Sacrifice in the Ancient Near East*. Missoula, 1975
142. Greenfield, J. C. 'Kittim', in B 84 III, 40–1
143. Grelot, P. *Documents araméens d'Égypte* (LAPO 5). Paris, 1972
144. Haran, M. 'The disappearance of the Ark', *IEJ* 13 (1963) 46–58
145. Haran, M. *Temples and Temple Service in Ancient Israel*. Oxford, 1978
146. Harris, Z. S. *A Grammar of the Phoenician Language*. Connecticut, 1936
147. Harrison, R. K. *Introduction to the Old Testament*. London, 1970
148. Hartman, L. F. *The Book of Daniel*. Garden City, New York, 1978
149. Hastings, J. (ed.) *Dictionary of the Bible* I–IV. Edinburgh, 1898–1902
150. Hatch, E. and Redpath, H. A. *A Concordance to the Septuagint* I–III. Oxford, 1897
151. Haussig, H. (ed.) *Wörterbuch der Mythologie* I. Stuttgart, 1962
152. Hawkins, J. D. 'Izrijau', in A 16, 5 (1977) 227
153. Hayes, J. H. *Old Testament Form Criticism*. San Antonio, 1974
154. Hayes, J. H. *An Introduction to Old Testament Study*. Nashville, 1979
155. Hayes, J. H. and Miller, J. M. (eds.) *Israelite and Judaean History*. London, 1977

156. Heltzer, M. 'Eighth century B.C. inscriptions from Kalakh (Nimrud)',
      PEQ 110 (1978) 3–9

157. Herr, L. G. *The Scripts of Ancient Northwest Semitic Seals* (Harvard
      Semitic Monographs 18). Missoula, 1978

158. Herrmann, S. *A History of Israel in Old Testament Times*. London, 1975

159. Herzfeld, E. *The Persian Empire*. Wiesbaden, 1968

159A. Hestrin R. 'The Lachish ewer and the ʾAsherah', *IEJ* 37 (1987) 212–23

160. Hestrin, R. and Dayagi, M. 'A seal impression of a servant of king
      Hezekiah', *IEJ* 24 (1974) 27–9

161. Hestrin, R. and Dayagi-Mendels, M. *Inscribed Seals from the Collections of
      the Israel Museum*. Jerusalem, 1979

162. Hoftijzer, J. and van der Koij, G. *Aramaic Texts from Deir ʾAlla*. Leiden,
      1976

163. Holland, T. A. 'A study of Palestinian Iron Age baked clay figurines,
      with special reference to Jerusalem', *Levant* 9 (1977) 121–55

164. Ibrahim, M. M. 'Two Ammonite statuettes from Khirbet El-Hajjar',
      ADAJ 16 (1971) 91–7

165. Iliffe, J. H. 'A Tell Fārʿa tomb group reconsidered', *QDAP* 4 (1935)
      182–6

166. Jakob-Rost, L. *Die Stempelsiegel im Vorderasiatischen Museum*. Berlin,
      1975

167. Jellicoe, S. *The Septuagint and Modern Study*. Oxford, 1968

168. Jidejian, N. *Sidon through the Ages*. Beirut, 1971

169. Kaiser, O. 'Die Verkündigung des Propheten Jesaja im Jahre 701',
      ZAW 81 (1969) 304–15

170. Kaiser, O. *Introduction to the Old Testament*. Oxford, 1973

171. Kaiser, O. *Isaiah 13–39: A Commentary*. London, 1974

172. Kaplan, J. 'The stronghold of Yamani at Ashdod-Yam', *IEJ* 19 (1969)
      137–49

173. Katzenstein, H. J. 'The royal steward', *IEJ* 10 (1961) 149–54

174. Kaufman, S. A. *Akkadian Influences on Aramaic* (AS 19). Chicago, 1974

175. Kenyon, K. M. *Archaeology in the Holy Land*. 2nd edn. London, 1965

176. Kenyon, K. M. 'Excavations in Jerusalem', *PEQ* 100 (1968) 97–111

177. Kenyon, K. M. *Royal Cities of the Old Testament*. London 1971

178. Kenyon, K. M. *Digging up Jerusalem*. London, 1974

178A. Kinnier Wilson, J. V. 'Medicine in the land and times of the Old
      Testament', in Ishida, T. (ed.) *Studies in the Period of David and Solomon and
      Other Essays*, 337–65. Tokyo, 1982

179. Kitchen, K. A. 'The Aramaic of Daniel', in B 341, 31–79 (1965)

180. Kitchen, K. A. *Ancient Orient and Old Testament*. London, 1966

181. Kitchen, K. A. 'Proverbs and wisdom books of the Ancient Near East',
      TB 28 (1977/9) 69–114

182. Kittel, G. and Friedrich, G. (eds.) *Theological Dictionary of the New
      Testament* i–x. Grand Rapids, 1964–76

182A. Klein, R. W. 'Studies in the Greek texts of the Chronicler [Summary of
      Th. D. disertation]', *HTR* 59 (1966) 449

183. Klien, R. W. 'Old readings in I Esdras: the list of returnees from Babylon,' *HTR* 62 (1969) 99–107
184. Koch, K. *et al. Das Buch Daniel* (Wege der Forschung). Darmstadt, 1980
185. Kochavi, M. 'The history and archaeology of Aphek-Antipatris', *Bi. Ar.* 44 (1981) 75–86
186. Koehler, L., Baumgartner, W. *et al. Hebräisches Lexicon zum Alten Testament* I–III. 3rd edn. Leiden, 1967–83
187. Kraeling, E. G. *The Brooklyn Museum Aramaic Papyri.* New Haven, 1953
188. Krahmalkov, C. 'An Ammonite lyric poem', *BASOR* 223 (1976) 55–7
188A. Kutscher, E. Y. 'Aramaic', *Current Trends in Linguistics* 4 (The Hague, 1970) 347–412
189. Lambert, W. G. 'A new look at the Babylonian background of Genesis', *JTS* 16 (1965) 287–300
190. Lambert, W. G. 'Nabonidus in Arabia', *Proceedings of the Seminar for Arabian Studies* 2 (1972) 53–64
191. Lance, H. D. 'Gezer in the land and in history', *Bi. Ar.* 30 (1967) 34–47
192. Lance, H. D. 'The royal stamp and the kingdom of Josiah', *HTR* 64 (1971) 315–32
192A. Landes, G. M. 'The material civilization of the Ammonites', *Bi. Ar.* 24 (1961) 65–86
193. Laperrousaz, E.-M. 'A-t-on dégagé l'angle Sud-Est du "Temple de Salomon"?', *Syria* 50 (1973) 355–92
194 Lapp, P. W. 'Late royal seals from Judah', *BASOR* 158 (1960) 11–22
195. Lebram, J. C. H. 'Perspektiven der Gegenwartigen Danielforschung', *Journal for the History of Judaism* 5 (1974) 1–33
196. Leiman, S. Z. *The Canonization of Hebrew Scripture: The Talmudic and Midrashic Evidence.* Hamden, Conn., 1976
197. Lemaire, A. '*Mmst* = *Amwas*, vers la solution d'une enigme de l'épigraphie hébraique', *Rev. Bibl.* 82 (1975) 17–23
198. Lemaire, A. 'Remarques sur la datation des estampilles "lmlk"', *VT* 25 (1975) 677–82
199. Lemaire, A. *Inscriptions hébraïques*, I: *Les ostraca* (LAPO 9). Paris, 1977
199A. Lemaire, A. 'Les inscriptions de Khirbet el-Qom et l'Asherah de YHWH', *Rev. Bibl.* 84 (1977) 595–608
200. Lemaire, A. 'Note sur le titre *bn hmlk* dans l'ancien Israël', *Semitica* 29 (1979) 59–65
201. Leuze, O. *Die Satrapieneinteilung in Syrien und in Zweistromlande von 520–320* (Schriften der Königsberger Gelehrten Gesellschaft 11/4). Königsberg, 1935. Reprint Hildesheim, 1972
202. Levine, B. A. 'The Netînîm', *JBL* 82 (1963) 207–12
203. Levine, B. A. 'Notes on a Hebrew ostracon from Arad', *IEJ* 19 (1969) 49–51
204. Levine, L. D. 'Menahem and Tiglath-Pileser: a new synchronism', *BASOR* 206 (1972) 40–2
205. Loretz, O. 'Die ammonitische Inschrift von Tell Siran', *UF* 9 (1977) 169–71

206. Luschan, F. von. *Ausgrabungen in Sendschirli* I. Berlin, 1893
207. Malamat, A. 'The historical background of the assassination of Amon, king of Judah', *IEJ* 3 (1953) 26–9
208. Malamat, A. 'Josiah's bid for Armageddon; the background of the Judean-Egyptian encounter in 609 B.C.', *JANES* 5 (1973) 267–79
209. Malamat, A. and Eph'al, I. (eds.) *The World History of the Jewish People: Ancient Times*, IV: *The Age of the Monarchies*: 1. *Political History*; 2. *Culture and Society*. Jerusalem, 1979
210. Martin, W. J. 'Dischronologized narrative in the Old Testament', *VT* (Supp.) 17 (1969) 179–86
211. May, H. G. *Material Remains of the Megiddo Cult* (OIP 26). Chicago, 1935
212. Mazar, B. 'The Tobiads', *IEJ* 7 (1957) 229–38
213. Mazar, B. 'The cities of the territory of Dan', *IEJ* 10 (1960) 65–77
214. Mazar, B. *et al.* ''Ein Gev, excavations in 1961', *IEJ* 14 (1964) 1–49
215. McCarthy, D. J. *Treaty and Covenant* (Analecta Biblica 21). Rome, 1963
215A. McCarthy, D. J. 'Covenant in the Old Testament: the present state of the enquiry', *CBQ* 27 (1965) 217–40
216. McCarthy, D. J. *Old Testament Covenant: A Survey of Current Opinion*. Oxford, 1972
217. McCown, C. C. *Tell en-Nasbeh* I–II. Berkeley and New Haven, 1947
218. McKane, W. *Proverbs: A New Approach*. London, 1970
219. McKay, J. *Religion in Judah under the Assyrians 732–609 B.C.* London, 1973
220. McKay, J. W. 'Further light on the horses and chariot of the sun in the Jerusalem temple', *PEQ* 105 (1973) 167–9
221. Meek, T. J. *Hebrew Origins*. 3rd edn. New York, 1960
222. Meshel, Z. *Kuntillet 'Ajrud. A Religious Centre from the Time of the Judean Monarchy on the Border of Sinai* (Israel Museum, Catalogue 175). Jerusalem, 1978
223. Millard, A. R. 'Baladan, the father of Merodach-Baladan', *TB* 22 (1971) 125–6
224. Millard, A. R. 'The practice of writing in ancient Israel', *Bi. Ar.* 35 (1972) 98–111
225. Millard, A. R. 'Assyrian royal names in Biblical Hebrew', *JSS* 21 (1976) 1–14
226. Mitchell, T. C. *The Book of Daniel*. London, forthcoming
227. Mittmann, S. 'Das südliche Ostjordanland im Lichte eines neuassyrischen Keilschriftbriefes aus Nimrud', *ZDPV* 89 (1973) 15–25
228. Momigliano, A. 'The Second Book of Maccabees', *Classical Philology* 70 (1975) 81–8
229. Montgomery, J. A. *A Critical and Exegetical Commentary on the Books of Kings* (ICC). Edinburgh, 1951
230. Moorey, P. R. S. and Parr, P. J. *Archaeology in the Levant: Essays for Kathleen Kenyon*. Warminster, 1978
231. Morgan, D. F. *Wisdom in the Old Testament Traditions*. Oxford, 1981
232. Moscati, S. *L'epigrafia ebraica antica, 1935–50*. Rome, 1951
233. Mullen, E. T. 'A new royal Sidonian inscription', *BASOR* 216 (1974) 25–30

234. Musil, A. *The Northern Hegâz. A Topographical Itinerary*. New York, 1926

235. Musil, A. *Arabia Deserta. A Topographical Itinerary*. New York, 1927

236. Myers, J. M. *Chronicles I–II* (The Anchor Bible 12–13). Garden City, 1965

237. Myers, J. M. *Ezra, Nehemiah* (The Anchor Bible 14). Garden City, 1965

238. Myers, J. M. *I and II Esdras* (The Anchor Bible 42). Garden City, New York, 1974

239. Naumann, R. *Architektur Kleinasiens von ihren Anfängen bis zum Ende der Hethitischen Zeit*. Tübingen, 1955

240. Naveh, J. 'Khirbat al-Muqanna' – Ekron: an archaeological survey', *IEJ* 8 (1958) 87–100, 165–70

241. Naveh, J. 'A Hebrew letter from the seventh century B.C.', *IEJ* 10 (1960) 129–39

242. Naveh, J. 'More Hebrew inscriptions from Meṣad Hashavyahu', *IEJ* 12 (1962) 27–32

243. Naveh, J. 'The excavations at Meṣad Hashavyahu, preliminary report', *IEJ* 12 (1962) 89–113

244. Naveh, J. 'Some notes on the reading of the Meṣad Hashavyahu letter', *IEJ* 14 (1964) 158–9

245. Naveh, J. 'The scripts of two ostraca from Elath', *BASOR* 183 (1966) 27–30

246. Naveh, J. *The Development of the Aramaic Script*. Jerusalem, 1970

247. Naveh, J. 'The ostracon from Nimrud: an Ammonite name-list', *Maarav* 2/2 (1979–80) 163–71

248. Naveh, J. Review of Herr, L. G. *The Scripts of Ancient Northwest Semitic Seals*, in *BASOR* 239 (1980) 75–6

249. Negbi, O. 'A Canaanite bronze figurine from Tel Dan', *IEJ* 14 (1964) 270–1

250. Neubauer, A. 'Where are the Ten Tribes?', *Jewish Quarterly Review* 1 (London, 1888–9) 14–28, 95–114, 185–201, 408–23

251. Newman, J. *The Agricultural Life of the Jews in Babylonia*. Oxford, 1932

252. Nicholson, E. W. 'The meaning of the expression '*m h'rṣ* in the Old Testament', *JSS* 10 (1965), 59–66

253. Nicholson, E. W. *Deuteronomy and Tradition*. London, 1967

254. Nielsen, E. *The Ten Commandments in New Perspective*. London, 1968

255. Noth, M. *Die israelitischen Personennamen in Rahmen der gemeinsemitischen Namengebung*. Stuttgart, 1928 and Hildesheim, 1966

256. Noth, M. *The History of Israel*. 2nd edn. London, 1960

257. Noth, M. *The Old Testament World*. London, 1966

258. Obermeyer, J. *Die Landschaft Babylonien im Zeitalter des Talmuds und des Gaonats*. Frankfurt, 1929

259. Oded, B. 'The historical background of the Syro-Ephraimite war reconsidered', *CBQ* 34 (1972)

259A. Olmstead, A. T. 'The fall of Samaria', *AJSL* 21 (1904–5) 179–82

260. Olmstead, A. T. 'Tattenai, governor of "Across the River"', *JNES* 3 (1944) 46

261. Olmstead, A. T. *The History of the Persian Empire*. Chicago, 1948
262. Pardee, D. 'Letters from Tel Arad', *UF* 10 (1978) 289–336
263. Payne, J. B. 'Eighth century Israelitish background of Isaiah 40–66', *WTJ* 29 (1967) 179–90; 30 (1968) 50–8, 185–203
264. Payne, J. B. *New Perspectives on the Old Testament*. Waco and London, 1970
265. Peckham, B. *The Development of the Late Phoenician Scripts* (HSS xx). Harvard, 1968
266. Petrie, W. M. F. *Beth-Pelet I (Tell Fara)*. London, 1930
267. Pope, M. H. "ʿAm Haʾarez', in B 84 1, 106–7
268. Porten, B. *Archives from Elephantine*. Los Angeles, 1968
269. Porten, B. 'The identity of King Adon', *Bi. Ar.* 44 (1981) 36–52
269A. Powis Smith, J. M. *et al.*, *Micah, Zephanaiah, Nahum, Habakkuk, Obadaiah and Joel* (ICC). Edinburgh, 1911
270. Purvis, J. D. *The Samaritan Pentateuch and the Origin of the Samaritan Sect*. Cambridge, Mass., 1968
271. Quinn, J. D. 'Alcaeus 48 (B 16) and the fall of Ascalon (604 B.C.)', *BASOR* 164 (1961) 19–20
272. Rainey, A. F. 'Private seal-impressions: a note on semantics', *IEJ* 16 (1966) 187–90
273. Rawlinson, H. 'Bilingual readings – cuneiform and Phoenician. Notes on some tablets in the British Museum, containing bilingual legends (Assyrian and Phoenician)', *JRAS* NS 1 (1865) 237–8
273A. Reich, R. and Brandl, B. 'Gezer under Assyrian rule', *PEQ* 117 (1985) 41–54
274. Ringgren, H. *The Messiah in the Old Testament*. London, 1956
275. Ringgren, H. *Israelite Religion*. London, 1966
275A. Robertson Smith, W. *Lectures on the Religion of the Semites*. Revised edn. London, 1927
276. Robinson, D. W. B. *Josiah's Reform and the Book of the Law*. London, 1951
277. Rogers, R. W. *Cuneiform Parallels to the Old Testament*. New York, 1912
278. Röllig, W. 'Gubaru', in A 16, 3 (1971) 671–2
279. Rosenthal, F. *Die aramaistische Forschungen seit Th. Nöldecke's Veröffentlichungen*. Leiden, 1939
280. Rowley, H. H. *Worship in Ancient Israel*. London, 1967
281. Saller, S. J. *The Memorial of Moses on Mount Nebo* I. Jerusalem, 1941
282. Sandars, J. A. (ed.) *Near Eastern Archaeology in the Twentieth Century (Essays in Honour of Nelson Glueck)*. New York, 1970
283. Sarna, N. M. 'The abortive insurrection in Zedekiah's day (Jer. 27–29)', *Eretz Israel* 14 (1978), 89*–96*
284. Sayce, A. H. 'Babylonian tablets from Tel El-Amarna, Upper Egypt', *PSBA* 10 (1888) 488–525
285. Schrader, E. *Die Keilinschriften und das Alte Testament*. 3rd edn. Berlin, 1902
286. Schürer, E. *et al. The History of the Jewish People in the Age of Jesus Christ* I–II. Revised English edn. Edinburgh, 1973–9

287. Segal, J. B. *The Jewish Passover, from the Earliest Times to A.D. 70*. London, 1963

288. Shaheen, N. S. 'The Siloam end of Hezekiah's tunnel', *PEQ* 109 (1977) 107–12

289. Shanks, H. *Judaism in Stone: The Archaeology of Ancient Synagogues*. New York, 1979

290. Shea, W. H. 'Adon's letter and the Babylonian Chronicle', *BASOR* 223 (1976) 61–4

291. Shea, W. H. 'The Siran inscription: Amminadab's drinking song', *PEQ* 110 (1978) 107–12

291A. Shiloh, Y. 'Iron Age sanctuaries and cult elements in Palestine', in Cross, F. M. (ed.) *Symposia* (AASOR, Cambridge, Mass., 1976), 157–8

291B. Shiloh, Y. *The Proto-Aeolic Capital and Israelite Ashlar Masonry* (Qedem 11). Jerusalem, 1979.

292. Simons, J. *Jerusalem in the Old Testament. Researches and Theories*. Leiden, 1952

293. Skinner, J. *Kings* (The Century Bible). Edinburgh, 1901

294. Smallwood, E. M. *The Jews under Roman Rule*. Leiden, 1976

294A. Snaith, N. H. *Leviticus and Numbers* (The Century Bible). London, 1967

295. Speiser, E. A. 'Background and function of the Biblical Nāśī', *CBQ* 25 (1963) 111–17. Republished in Speiser, E. A., *Oriental and Biblical Studies* 113–22. Philadelphia, 1967

296. Spycket, A. *La statuaire du Proche-Orient ancien*. Leiden and Cologne, 1981

297. Stamm, J. J. and Andrew, M. E. *The Ten Commandments in Recent Research*. London, 1967

298. Stern, E. *Greek and Latin Authors on Jews and Judaism* 1. Jerusalem, 1974

299. Stern, E. 'Israel at the close of the period of the monarchy: an archaeological survey', *Bi. Ar.* 38 (1975) 26–54

300. Sukenik, E. L. 'Inscribed Hebrew and Aramaic potsherds from Samaria', *PEQ* 65 (1933) 152–6

301. Tadmor, H. 'Chronology of the last kings of Judah', *JNES* 15 (1956) 226–30

302. Tadmor, H. 'A note on the seal of Mannu-ki-Inurta', *IEJ* 15 (1965) 233–4

303. Tadmor, H. 'Kronologiyah', in *Entsiqlopediyah Miqra'it* IV, 247ff

304. Tcherikover, V. A. *Hellenistic Civilization and the Jews*. Philadelphia, 1966

305. Teixidor, J. 'Bulletin d'épigraphie Sémitique', *Syria* 44 (1967) 163–95

306. Thiele, E. R. *The Mysterious Numbers of the Hebrew Kings. A Reconstruction of the Chronology of the Kingdoms of Israel and Judah*. Chicago, 1951; 2nd edn. Grand Rapids, 1965

307. Thompson, H. O. 'Cosmetic palettes', *Levant* 4 (1972) 148–50

308. Thompson, H. O. and Zayadine, F. 'The Tell Siran inscription', *BASOR* 212 (1973) 5–11

309. Thompson, H. O. and Zyadine, F. 'The works of Amminadab', *Bi. Ar.* 37 (1974) 13–19

310. Tomback, R. S. *A Comparative Semitic Lexicon of the Phoenician and Punic Languages*. Missoula, 1978

311. Torczyner, H. *Lachish*, I: *The Lachish Letters*. Oxford, 1948

312. Torrey, C. C. 'The letters prefixed to Second Maccabees', *JAOS* 60 (1940) 119–50

313. Tubb, J. N. *An Iron Age Tomb Group from the Bethlehem Region* (British Museum Occasional Paper 14). London, 1980

314. Tufnell, O. *Lachish*, III: *The Iron Age*. Oxford, 1953

315. Tushingham, A. D. 'The Western Hill [of Jerusalem] under the monarchy', *ZDPV* 95 (1979) 39–55

316. Unger, E. 'Altar: D. Palästina-Syrien', in Ebert M. *Reallexicon der Vorgeschichte* I, 109–12. Berlin, 1924

316A. Ungnad, A. 'Keilinschriftliche Beiträge zum Buch Esra und Ester', *ZAW* 58 (1940–1) 240–4

317. Ussishkin, D. 'The destruction of Lachish by Sennacherib and the dating of the royal Judean storage jars', *Tel Aviv* 4 (1977) 28–60

318. Ussishkin, D. 'Excavations at Tel Lachish – 1973–1977', *Tel Aviv* 5 (1978) 1–97

319. Ussishkin, D. 'The "Camp of the Assyrians" in Jerusalem', *IEJ* 29 (1979) 137–42

320. van den Branden, A. *Les inscriptions thamoudéenes* (Bibliothèque du Muséon 25). Louvain, 1950

321. Vattioni, F. 'I sigilli ebraici', *Biblica* 50 (1969) 357ff

322. Vermes, G. *The Dead Sea Scrolls in English*. 2nd edn. Harmondsworth, 1975

323. Vermes, G. *The Dead Sea Scrolls: Qumran in Perspective*. London, 1977

323A. Vriezen, Th. C. 'The Edomite deity Qaus', *Oudtestamentische Studien* 14 (1965) 330–53

324. Wagner, M. *Die lexikalischen und grammatikalischen Aramaismen im alttestamentlichen Hebräisch* (*ZAW* (Bh.) 96). Berlin, 1966

325. Watzinger, C. *Denkmäler Palästinas* I. Leipzig, 1935

326. Weinfeld, M. *Deuteronomy and the Deuteronomic School*. Oxford, 1972

326A. Weippert, M. Review of A 702, *Göttingische gelehrte Anzeigen* 224 (1972) 150–61

327. Weippert, M. 'Zum Präskript der hebräischen Briefe von Arad', *VT* 25 (1975) 202

328. Weiser, A. *Introduction to the Old Testament*. London, 1961

329. Weissbach, *Die Denkmäler und Inschriften an der Mündung des Nahr el-Kelb*. Berlin and Leipzig, 1922

330. Welten, P. *Die Königs-Stempel: ein Beitrag zur Militärpolitik Judas unter Hiskia und Josia*. Wiesbaden, 1969

331. Wenham, G. J. 'Legal forms in the Book of the Covenant', *TB* 22 (1971) 95–102

331A. Wenham, G. J. 'Deuteronomy and the central sanctuary', *TB* 22 (1971) 103–18

332. Wenham, J. W. 'Large numbers in the Old Testament', *TB* 18 (1967) 19–53

333. Wernberg-Møller, P. '"Pleonastic" *waw* in classical Hebrew', *JSS* 3 (1958) 321–6

334. Wilkinson, J. *Egeria's Travels to the Holy Land*. Warminster, 1971

335. Wilkinson, J. 'Ancient Jerusalem: its water supply and population', *PEQ* 106 (1974) 33–51

336. Williamson, H. G. M. *Israel in the Books of Chronicles*. Cambridge, 1977

337. Winckler, H. 'Aus einem Briefe des Herrn Dr. H. Winckler', *ZA* 3 (1888) 424–6

338. Winnett, F. V. and Reed, W. L. *Ancient Records from North Arabia*. Toronto, 1970

339. Winton Thomas, D. (ed.) *Documents from Old Testament Times*. London, 1958

340. Winton Thomas, D. *Archaeology and Old Testament Study*. Oxford, 1967

341. Wiseman, D. J. (ed.) *Notes on some Problems in the Book of Daniel*. London, 1965

342. Wiseman, D. J. (ed) *Peoples of Old Testament Times*. Oxford, 1973

343. Wright, G. E. *Biblical Archaeology*. 2nd edn. Philadelphia and London, 1962

344. Wright, G. E. *Shechem: The Biography of a Biblical City*. London, 1965

345. Wurthwein, E. *Der 'amm ha'arez im Alten Testament*. Stuttgart, 1976

345A. Yadin, V. 'The "dial" of Ahaz', *EI* 5 (1958) 91–6, 88–9*

346. Yadin, Y. *Hazor*, II: *An Account of the Second Season of Excavations 1956*. Jerusalem, 1960

347. Yadin, Y. 'Expedition D – the Cave of the Letters', *IEJ* 12 (1962) 227–57

348. Yadin, Y. *Bar Kokhba*. London, 1971

349. Yadin, Y. *Hazor* (The Schweich Lectures 1970). London, 1972

350. Yadin, Y. *Jerusalem Revealed: Archaeology in the Holy City 1968–1975*. Jerusalem, 1975

351. Yardin, Y. 'The historical significance of inscription 88 from Arad: a suggestion', *IEJ* 26 (1976) 9–14

352. Young, E. J. *The Prophecy of Daniel*. Grand Rapids, 1949

353. Young, E. J. *Studies in Isaiah*. London, 1954

354. Young, E. J. *Introduction to the Old Testament*. London, 1964

355. Zayadine, F. 'Recent excavations on the Citadel of Amman', *ADAJ* 18 (1973) 17–35

356. Zayadine, F. 'Note sur l'inscription de la Statue d'Amman J. 1656', *Syria* 51 (1974) 129–36

357. Zayadine, F. and Thompson, O. 'The Ammonite inscription from Tell Siran', *Berytus* 22 (1973) 115–40

C. PHOENICIA AND THE PHOENICIAN COLONIES

The bibliography of this section is based on that provided by Dr Culican before his death in 1984; it has been modestly updated.

I. GENERAL

1. Albright, W. F. 'Syria, the Philistines and Phoenicia', *CAH* II³.2, chapter 33.
1A. *Au pays de Baal et d'Astarte: 10,000 ans d'art en Syrie*. Musée du Petit Palais, Paris, 1983–4
2. Bisi, A. M. *La ceramica punica. Aspetti e problemi*. Naples, 1970
3. Bunnens, G. *L'expansion phénicienne en Méditerranée. Essai d'interprétation fondé sur une analyse des traditions littéraires*. Brussels and Rome, 1979
4. Cintas, P. *Manuel d'archéologie punique* I–II. Paris, 1970–6
4A. Culican, W. *Opera Selecta: From Tyre to Tartessos*. Gothenburg, 1986
4B. Gubel, E. *et al* (eds.) *Studia Phoenicia* I/2 (1983) et seq. (Orientalia Lovaniensia Analecta)
5. Harden, D. *The Phoenicians*. Harmondsworth, 1971. Revised edn, 1986
5A. *Les Phéniciens et le monde méditerranéen*. Brussels, 1986
6. Moscati, S. *The World of the Phoenicians*. London, 1968
7. Parrot, A., Chéhab, M. and Moscati, S. *Les Phéniciens*. Paris, 1975

II. SETTING AND HISTORY

8. Aimé-Giron, N. 'Un ex-voto à Astarté', *Bull. Inst. fr. Caire* 25 (1925) 191–211
9. Albright, W. F. *Yahweh and the Gods of Canaan*. London, 1968
10. Astour, M. 'The origins of the terms "Canaan", "Phoenician", and "Purple"', *JNES* 24 (1965) 346–50
11. Basch, L. 'Phoenician oared ships', *The Mariner's Mirror* 55 (1969) 139–62, 227–45
12. Basch, L. 'Trières grecques, phéniciennes et égyptiens', *JHS* 97 (1977) 1–10
13. Bisi, A. M. *Le stele puniche* (Studi Semitici 27). Rome, 1967
14. Brown, J. P. *The Lebanon and Phoenicia, Ancient Texts Illustrating their Physical Geography and Native Industries*. Beirut, 1969
15. Cintas, P. *Amulettes puniques*. Tuins, 1946
16. Cogan, M. 'Tyre and Tiglathpileser III', *JCS* 25 (1973) 96–9
17. Eiselen, F. C. *Sidon, a Study in Oriental History* (Columbia University Oriental Studies 4). New York, 1907
18. Frost, H. 'Ancient harbours and anchorages in the eastern Mediterranean', in *Underwater Archaeology: a Nascent Discipline*, 95–114. UNESCO, Paris, 1972
19. Glanville, S. R. K. 'Records of a royal dockyard of the time of Tuthmosis III', *ZÄS* 66 (1931) 105–21; 68 (1932) 7–41
20. Helck, W. *Die Beziehungen Ägyptens zu Vorderasien*. Wiesbaden, 1962
21. Katzenstein, H. J. *The History of Tyre*. Jerusalem, 1973
22. Kestemont, G. 'Le commerce phénicienne et l'expansion assyrien', *Or. Ant.* 11 (1972) 137–44
23. Leclant, J. 'Relations entre l'Egypte et la Phénicie du voyage d'Ounamoun à l'expédition d'Alexandre', in Ward, W. (ed.) *The Role of*

the Phoenicians in the Interaction of Mediterranean Civilization, 1–22. Beirut, 1968

24. Leclant, J. 'A propos des étuis porte-amulettes égyptiens et puniques', *Oriental Studies Presented to B. S. J. Isserlin*, 102–4. Leiden, 1980

25. Lipinski, E. 'The elegy on the fall of Sidon in Isaiah 23', *Eretz Israel* 14 (1978) 74–88

26. Martin, M. 'Re-examination of Byblian inscriptions', *Or.* 30 (1961) 46–78

27. Melena, J. L. 'Po-ni-ki-jo in the Knossos tablets', *Minos* 14 (1973) 7–84

28. Muhly, J. D. 'Homer and the Phoenicians', *Berytus* 19 (1970) 24–36

29. Muhly, J. D. *Copper and Tin* (Transactions of the Connecticut Academy of Art and Sciences 43). New Haven, 1973

29A. Muhly, J. D. 'Phoenicia and the Phoenicians', *Biblical Archaeology Today* (Israel Exploration Society) (Jerusalem, 1985) 177–91

30. Oded, B. 'The Phoenician cities and the Assyrian empire', *ZDPV* 90 (1974) 38–49

31. Peckham, B. 'Israel and Phoenicia', in Cross, F. M. *et al.* (eds.) *Magnalia Dei: The Mighty Acts of God. Essays . . . in Memory of G. Ernest Wright*, 224–48. Garden City, 1976

32. Quillard, B. 'Les étuis porte-amulettes carthaginois', *Karthago* 16 (1970–1) 5–32

33. Sethe, K. 'Der Name der Phönizier bei Griechen und Ägyptern', *MVAG* 31 (1916) 307–32

34. Scandone-Matthiae, G. S. 'Il problema delle influenze egiziane sulla religione fenicia', in *La religione fenicia: Atti del Colloquio in Roma, 6 Marzo 1979* (Studi Semitici 53). Rome, 1981

35. Speiser, A. 'The name Phoinikes', *Language* 12 (1936) 121–6

35A. Starcky, J. and Hours, F. (eds.) *Archéologie au Levant: Recueil à la mémoire de R. Saidah*. Lyons, 1982

36. Winter, I. 'On the problems of Karatepe: the reliefs and their context', *Anat. Stud.* 29 (1979) 115–36

37. Wiseman, D. J. 'A new stela of Aššur-naṣir-pal II', *Iraq* 14 (1952) 24–44

III. ARCHAEOLOGY, ARTS, AND CRAFTS

38. Aharoni, Y., Fritz, V. and Kempinski, A. 'Excavations at Tel Masos . . . 1974', *Tel Aviv* 2 (1975) 97–124

39. Amiran, R. *The Ancient Pottery of Erez Yisra'el*. Jerusalem, 1958

40. Anati, E. 'Excavations at the cemetery of Tell Abu Hawam', *ʿAtiqot* 2 (1959) 89–102

41. Anderson, W. 'A stratigraphic and ceramic analysis of the Late Bronze Age and Iron Age strata of Sounding Y at Sarepta'. Ph.D. dissertation, University of Pennsylvania, 1979. University Microfilms International, Ann Arbor and London

42. Astruc, M. 'Traditions funéraires de Carthage', *Cahiers de Byrsa* 6 (1956) 29–79

43. Baker, J. T. 'Tyrian purple; an ancient dye, a modern problem', *Endeavour* 33 (118) (Jan 1974) 11–17. New York

44. Barnett, R. D. 'Four Iron Age sculptures from Amman', *ADAJ* 1 (1955) 34–6

45. Barnett, R. D. *Catalogue of the Nimrud Ivories in the British Museum.* London, 1957

46. Barnett, R. D. 'Layard's Nimrud bowls and their inscriptions', *Eretz Israel* 8 (1967) 1–7

47. Barnett, R. D. 'The Nimrud bowls in the British Museum', *RSF* 2 (1974) 11–33

47A. Barnett, R. D. *Ancient Ivories in the Middle East and Adjacent Countries* (Qedem 14). Jerusalem, 1982

47B. Benson, J. L. *The Necropolis of Kaloriziki* (Studies in Mediterranean Archaeology 36). Gothenburg, 1973

48. Bikai, P. *The Pottery of Tyre.* Warminster, 1978

48A. Birmingham, J. 'The chronology of some Early and Middle Iron Age Cypriot sites', *AJA* 67 (1963) 15–42

49. Bisi, A. M. 'Une figurine phénicienne trouvée à Carthage et quelques monuments apparentés', *Mélanges de Carthage, Cahiers de Byrsa* 10 (1964–5) 43–53

50. Blinkenberg, C. *Lindos*, I: *Les petits objets.* Berlin, 1981

51. Boardman, J. *The Greeks Overseas, their Colonies and Trade.* 2nd edn. London, 1980

51A. Bordreuil, P. *Catalogue des sceaux ouest-sémitiques inscrits de la Bibliothèque Nationale, du Musée du Louvre et du Musée biblique de Bible et Terre Sainte.* Paris, 1986

51B. Bossert, H. T. *Alt-Syrien.* Tübingen, 1951

52. Bouni, A. and Lagarce, J. 'Rapport préliminaire sur la deuxième campagne de fouilles (1976) à Ibn Hani (Syrie)', *Syria* 55 (1978) 233–301

53. Braidwood, R. 'Report of two sondages on the coast of Syria south of Tartous', *Syria* 21 (1940) 183–226

54. Chapman, S. V. 'A catalogue of Iron Age pottery from the cemeteries of Khirbet Slim, Joya, Qrayé and Qasmieh', *Berytus* 21 (1972) 55–194

55. Coldstream, N. *Greek Geometric Pottery.* London, 1968

56. Courbin, P. 'Rapport sur la 5ème campagne de fouilles à Ras el-Bassit', *AAAS* 26 (1976) 63–9

57. Courbin, P. 'Ras el-Bassit, rapport sur la campagne de 1972', *AAAS* 23 (1973) 25–38

58. Courbin, P. 'Une pyxis géometrique argienne (?) au Liban', *Berytus* 25 (1977) 147–57

59. Crowfoot, J. W. and G. M. *Samaria-Sebaste*, II: *Early Ivories from Samaria.* London, 1938

60. Crowfoot, J. W., Crowfoot, G. M. and Kenyon, K. M. *Samaria-Sebaste*, III: *The Objects.* London, 1957

61. Culican, W. 'The iconography of some Phoenician seals and seal impressions', *The Australian Journal of Biblical Archaeology* 1 (1968) 50–103

62. Culican, W. 'Coupes à décor phénicien provenant d'Iran', *Syria* 47 (1970) 65–76

63. Culican, W. 'Some Phoenician masks and other terracottas', *Berytus* 24 (1975–6) 47–87
64. Culican, W. 'The case for the Baurat Schiller crowns', *Journal of the Walters Art Gallery, Baltimore* 35 (1977) 15–35
65. Culican, W. 'The repertoire of Phoenician pottery', in Niemeyer, H. G. (ed.) *Phönizier im Westen* (Madrider Beiträge 8), 45–78. Mainz, 1982
66. Dajani, R. W. 'An Iron Age tomb from Amman', *ADAJ* 11 (1966) 41–7
67. Dothan, M. 'Akko, interim excavation report, first season 1973/4', *BASOR* 224 (1976) 1–48
68. Dothan, M. 'Excavations at Azor, 1960', *IEJ* 11 (1961) 171–5
69. Dunand, M. 'A la recherche de Simyra', *AAAS* 7 (1957) 183–226
70. Dunand, M., Bouni, A. and Saliby, N. 'Fouilles de Tell Kazel', *AAAS* 14 (1964) 1–14
71. Elgavish, J. *Archaeological Excavations at Shikmona. Field Report No. 1.* Haifa, 1968
72. Fitzgerald, G. M. 'Tantourah (Dora)', *Bulletin of the British School of Archaeology in Jerusalem* 4 (1924) 35–45; 6 (1924) 64–73; 7 (1925) 80–98
73. Freyer-Schauenburg, B. *Elfenbein aus dem samischen Heraion.* Hamburg, 1966
74. Gjerstad, E. 'Decorated metal bowls from Cyprus', *Opuscula Archaeologica* IV, 5 (1946–8) 1–18
74A. Gjerstad, E. *The Swedish Cyprus Expedition*, IV/2: *The Cypro-Geometric, Cypro-Archaic and Cypro-Classical Periods.* Stockholm, 1948
75. Gjerstad, E. 'The stratification of Al Mina (Syria) and its chronological significance', *Acta Archaeologica* 45 (1974) 107–23
76. Goldman, H. (ed.) *Excavations at Gözlu Kule, Tarsus*, III: *The Iron Age.* Princeton, 1963
77. Grau-Zimmermann, B. 'Phönikische Metalkannen in den Orientalisierenden Horizonten des Mittelmeerraumes', *MM* 19 (1978) 161–218
78. Guy, P. L. O. 'An Iron Age cemetery near Haifa', *Bulletin of the British School of Archaeology in Jerusalem* 5 (1924) 47–55
79. Haevernick, T. E. 'Gesichtsperlen', *MM* 18 (1977) 152–231
80. Halbherr, F. and Orsi, P. 'Antichità dell'antro di Zeus Ideo', *Museo Italiano di antichità classica* 2 (1888). Atlas
81. Hamilton, R. W. 'Excavations at Tell Abu Hawam', *QDAP* 3 (1934) 74–80; 4 (1935) 1–69
82. Jensen, L. and F. *The Story of Royal Purple.* Champaign, Illinois, 1965
83. Johns, C. N. 'Excavations at ʿAtlīt (1930–1)', *QDAP* 2 (1933) 41–104
84. Johns, C. N. 'Excavations at Pilgrims' Castle ʿAtlīt', *QDAP* 6 (1938) 121–52
85. Kaoukabani, B. 'Rapport préliminaire sur les fouilles de Kharayeb, 1969–70', *Bull. MB* 26 (1973) 41–58
85A. Karageorghis, V. *Excavations in the Necropolis of Salamis* I–III. Nicosia, 1967–76
86. Lehrer, G. 'A Phoenician glass bowl from Nimrud', *Journal of Glass Studies* 16 (1974) 9–13
86A. Maass-Lindemann, G. 'Die Entwicklung der westphönikischen

Keramik im 7. und 6. Jahrhundert v. Chr.', *Madrider Forschungen* 6.3 (1982) 127ff.

87.   Macridey Bey, T. 'Caveaux de Tell er-Rechedieh', *Rev. Bibl.* (1904) 18–23, 561–8

87A. Markoe, G. *Phoenician Bronze and Silver Bowls from Cyrpus and the Mediterranean.* University of California, 1985

88.   Negbi, O. 'The continuity of the Canaanite bronzework of the Late Bronze Age into the Early Iron Age', *Tel Aviv* 1 (1974) 159–72

89.   Ohata, Kiyoshi. *Tel Zeror* 11–111. Tokyo, 1967–70

90.   Oren, E. D. *The Northern Cemetery of Beth Shan.* Leiden, 1973

91.   Prausnitz, M. W. 'A Phoenician krater from Akhziv', *Or. Ant.* 5 (1966) 177–88

92.   Prausnitz, M. W. 'Red-polished and black-on-red wares at Akhziv', *Praktikon tou protou Diethnous Kyprologikou Synedriou*, 152–6. Nicosia, 1972

93.   Pritchard, J. B. *Sarepta, A Preliminary Report on the Iron Age.* Philadelphia, 1975

94.   Quillard, B. *Bijoux carthaginois*, 1: *Les colliers.* Louvain, 1979

95.   Riis, P. J. *Hama: fouilles et recherches 1931–1938: les cimetières à crémation.* Copenhagen, 1948

96.   Riis, P. J. 'Sculptured alabastra', *Acta Archaeologica* 25 (1956) 23–33

97.   Riis, P. J. *Sukas* 1. (Publications of the Carlsberg Expedition to Phoenicia 1). Copenhagen, 1970

98.   Saidah, R. 'Fouilles de Khaldé: rapport préliminaire sur la première et deuxième campagnes (1961–1962)', *Bull. MB* 19 (1966) 51–90

99.   Saidah, R. 'Une tombe de l'Age de Fer à Tambourit', *Berytus* 25 (1977) 135–46

100. Shiloh, Y. *The Proto-Aeolic Capital and Israelite Ashlar Masonry* (Qedem 11). Jerusalem, 1979

101. Stern, E. *Excavations at Tell Mevorakh* (Qedem 9). Jerusalem, 1978

102. Stern, E. 'New types of Phoenician-style decorated pottery vases from Palestine', *PEQ* 110 (1978) 11–21

103. Stucky, R. A. 'The engraved Tridachna shells', *Dedalo* x, 19 (1974) 1–107. São Paulo, Brazil

104. Taylor, J. du P. 'The Cypriot and Syrian pottery from al Mina, Syria', *Iraq* 21 (1959) 62–92

105. Thalmann, J.-P. 'Tell ʿArqa (Liban Nord) campagnes 1–111 (1972–74)', *Syria* 55 (1978) 1–145

106. Torelli, M. 'Un uovo di struzzo dipinto, conservato nel Museo di Tarquinia', *Stud. Etr.* 33 (1965) 329–65

107. Uberti, M. L. 'Gli avori e gli ossi', *Anecdota Tharica* (1975), 93–108

107A. Vattioni, F. 'I sigilli fenici', *AION* 41 (1981) 177–93

107B. Wagner, P. *Der ägyptische Einfluss auf die phönizische Architektur.* Bonn, 1980

108. Ward, W. 'Three Phoenician seals', *JEA* 53 (1967) 69–71

109. Winter, I. J. 'Carved ivory panels from Nimrud', *MMJ* 11 (1976) 25–54

110. Winter, I. J. 'Phoenician and North Syrian ivory carving in historical context', *Iraq* 38 (1976) 1–22

111. Woolley, C. L. 'Phéniciens et les peuples egéens', *Syria* 2 (1921) 177–94
112. Young, R. S. 'A bronze bowl in Philadelphia', *JNES* 26 (1967) 145–54
113. Young, R. S. 'The 1961 campaign at Gordium', *AJA* 66 (1962) 151–68
114. Young, R. S. 'The 1963 campaign at Gordium', *AJA* 68 (1964) 279–92
115. Zayadine, F. 'Recent excavations on the citadel of Amman', *ADAJ* 18 (1973) 17–35

IV. COLONIAL PROBLEMS

116. Adamasteanu, D. 'Butera, Piana della Fiera, Consi e Fontana Calde', *Mon. Ant.* 44 (1958) 205–671
117. Albright, W. F. 'New light on the early history of Phoenician colonization', *BASOR* 83 (1941) 14–22
118. Bartolini, P. *Le stele archaiche del Tophet di Cartagine.* Rome, 1976
119. Berthier, A. and Charlier, R. *Le sanctuaire punique d'El-Hofra à Constantine.* Paris, 1955
120. Bisi, A. M. 'Aspetti e problemi della ceramica punica arcaica dipinta', *Studi Magrebini* 11 (Naples, 1968) 1–43
121. Chiappisi, S. *Il Melqart di Sciacca e la questione fenicia in Sicilia.* Rome, 1975
122. Cross, F. M. 'The interpretation of the Nora stone', *BASOR* 208 (1972) 13–19
123. Dothan, M. 'A sign of Tanit from Tell Akko', *IEJ* 24 (1974) 44–9
124. Fantar, M. *Escatologie phénicienne-punique.* Tunis, 1970
125. Fevrier, J. G. 'The child sacrifices', *Archeologia Viva* 1,2 (1968) 115–18
126. Garbini, G. 'Continuità e innovazioni nella religione fenicia', *La religione fenicia: Atti del Colloquio in Roma le Marzo 1979*, 29–42. Rome, 1981
127. Holm, G. *Storia della moneta siciliana.* Turin, 1906
128. Isserlin, B. S. J. 'Some common features in Phoenician town planning', *RSF* 1 (1973) 135–52
129. Krahmalkov, C. 'Notes on the rule of Softim at Carthage', *RSF* 4 (1976) 153–7
130. Lepore, E. 'Strutture della colonizzazione focea in Occidente', *La Parola del Passato* 25 (1970) 19–54
131. Peckham, B. 'The Nora inscription', *Or.* 41 (1972) 457–68
132. Polselli, G. Coacci, *et al. Grotta Regina*, 11: *Le iscrizione puniche* (Studi Semitici 52). Rome, 1979
133. Richard, J. 'Étude médico-légale des urnes sacrificielles puniques et leur contenue'. Unpublished dissertation, University of Lille, 1961
134. Stager, L. E. 'Carthage: a view from the Tophet', in Niemeyer, H. G. (ed.) *Phönizier im Westen* (Madrider Beiträge 8), 155–63. Mainz, 1982
135. Tamburello, I. 'Prodotti ceramici di Palermo arcaica', *Sicilia archeologica* 2 (6) (1969) 40–5
136. Teixidor, J. 'Bulletin d'épigraphie sémitique', *Syria* 50 (1973) 425–7
137. Whittaker, C. R. 'The western Phoenicians: colonization and assimilation', *PCPhS* 20 (no. 200) (1974) 58–70
138. Xella, P. 'Aspetti e problemi dell'indagine storico-religiosa', *La religione fenicia: Atti del Colloquio in Roma le Marzo 1979*, 17–25. Rome, 1981

V. CARTHAGE AND NORTH AFRICA

139. Aumassip, G. *et al.* 'Aperçu sur l'évolution du paysage quaternaire et le peuplement de la région de Ouargha', *Libyca (Anthropologie–Ethnologie)* 20 (1972) 206–57

140. Bakhuisen, S. C. *Chalcis in Euboea: Iron and the Chalcidians Abroad.* Leiden, 1970

141. Boucher, E. 'Céramique archaique d'importation au Musée Lavigerie de Carthage', *Cahiers de Byrsa* 3 (1953) 11–85

142. Camps, G. *Aux origines de la Bérbérie et rites funéraires protohistoriques.* Paris, 1962

143. Camps, G. *La nécropole mégalithique du Djebel Mazela à Bou Nouara.* Paris, 1964

144. Camps, G. 'Les Numides et la civilisation punique', *Antiquités africaines* 14 (1979) 43–53

145. Carter, J. H. 'Western Phoenicians at Leptis Magna', *AJA* 59 (1965) 123–32

146. Cintas, P. and Gobert, E. G. 'Les tombes de Jbel-Mlezza', *Revue tunisienne* 38–40 (1939) 135–9

147. Cintas, P. 'Deux campagnes de fouilles à Utique', *Karthago* 2 (1951) 5–79

148. Cintas, P. 'Nouvelles recherches à Utique', *Karthago* 5 (1954) 89–154

149. Cintas, P. *Éléments d'étude pour une protohistoire de la Tunisie.* Paris, 1961

150. D'Agostino, B. 'Pontecagnano, tombe orientalizzante in Contrada S. Antonio', *Not. Scav.* 21 (1968) 75–196

151. D'Agostino, B. 'Tombe della prima età del ferro a S. Marzano sul Sarno', *MEFR* 82 (1970) 571–619

152. Delattre, R. P. 'La nécropole punique de Douimès, fouille de 1893–1894', *Cosmos* (Paris, 1897) 1–31

153. Delattre, R. P. 'Fouilles de Carthage', *Bull. archéologique du Comité . . .* (1907) 443–8

154. Fantar, H. 'La tombe de La Rabta . . .', *Latomus* 31 (1972) 349–67

155. Fantar, M. H. 'Une tombe punique sur le versant est de la colline de Junon', *Antiquités africaines* 6 (1972) 17–27

156. Ferron, J. 'Le Médaillon de Carthage', *Cahiers de Byrsa* 8 (1958–9) 45–59

157. Gabrici, E. 'Cuma', *Mon. Ant.* 22 (1913)

158. Gauckler, P. *Nécropoles puniques de Carthage* 1. Paris, 1915

159. Harden, D. B. 'The pottery from the precincts of Tanit at Salammbo, Carthage', *Iraq* 4 (1937) 59–89

160. Hill, G. F. *Catalogue of the Greek Coins of Phoenicia.* London, 1910

161. Lambert, N. 'Tayadirt, une nécropole en Haut-Moulouya', *Libyca (Anthropologie-Ethnologie)* 15 (1967) 215–50

162. Lancel, S. 'Tipasitana III', *Bull. d'archéologie algérienne* 3 (1968) 85–166

163. Maiuri, A. 'Museo Nazionale di Napoli: Collezione Spinelli', *Boll. d'Arte* 39 (1954) 277–8

164. Merlin, A. 'Tombeaux de la colline dite "de Junon"', *Bull. archéologique du Comité . . .* (1918) 228–99

165. Morel, J. P. 'Kerkouane, ville punique du Cap Bon . . .', *MEFR* 81 (1969) 473–518

166. Napoli, M. 'Pontecagnano: problemi topografici e storici', *Stud. Etr.* 33 (1965) 661–70

166A. Niemeyer, H. G. 'Die Phönizier und die Mittelmeerwelt im Zeitalter Homers', *JRGZM* 31 (1984) 3–94

167. Novak, M. D. 'Notes sur la nécropole phénicienne de l'Henchir el Alia', *Bull. archéologique du Comité* . . . (1898) 314–50

168. Orsi, P. 'Le necropoli preeleniche calabresi', *Mon. Ant.* 31 (1926) 5–373

169. Ridgway, D. '"Coppe cicladiche" da Veio', *Stud. Etr.* 35 (1967) 311–21

170. Segert, S. 'Some Phoenician etymologies of North African toponyms', *Or. Ant.* 5 (1966) 19–25

171. Stager, L. E. 'Le Tophet', *Cedac Carthage Bull.* 2 (June 1979) 32–3. (Centre d'Etudes et de Documentation archéologique de la Conservation de Carthage)

172. van Compernolle, R. *Etude de chronologie et d'historiographie siciliotes.* Brussels and Rome, 1959

173. Vuillemot, G. *Reconnaissances aux échelles puniques d'Oranie.* Autun, 1965

VI. SICILY

174. Acanfora, M. O. 'Panormo punica', *Memorie dell'Accademia Naz. dei Lincei*, Ser. 8, 1 (1948) 197–248

175. Bisi, A. M. 'Testimonianze fenicio-puniche ad Erice', *Or. Ant.* 5 (1966) 238–48

176. Bisi, A. M. 'Erice. Saggi alle fortificazione puniche', *Not. Scav.* (1968) 280–92

177. Bernabò Brea, L. and Cavalier, M. *Mylai.* Novara, 1959

178. Buchner, G. 'Testimonianze epigrafiche semitiche dell'VIII secolo a.C. a Pithekoussai', *La Parola del Passato* (1978) 130–42

179. Cintas, P. 'La céramique de Motyé et le problème de la date de fondation de Carthage', *Bull. archéologique du Comité* . . . (1963–4) 107–15

180. De Miro, A. 'Heraclea Minoa', *Not. Scav.* (1958) 232–86

181. Gabrici, E. 'Rinvenimenti nelle zone archeologiche di Panormo . . .', *Not. Scav.* 2 (ser. 7) (1941) 261–71

182. Gabrici, E. 'Alla ricerca della Solonto di Tucidide', *Kokalos* 5 (1959) 3–8

183. Giustolisi, V. 'Nuovi elementi per le identificazione della Solonto di Tucidide', *Kokalos* 16 (1970) 144–65

184. Isserlin, B. S. J. and Taylor, J. du P. *Motya, A Phoenician and Carthaginian City in Sicily* 1. Leiden, 1974

185. Marconi, P. 'Tombe puniche a camera in Via Calatafimi', *Not. Scav.* (1928) 482–9

186. Marconi Bovio, J. 'Panormos. Necropoli punica', *Fasti Archeologici* 9 (1954) 219–20

187. [Motya, Mozia]. Ciasca, A. *et al.*, *Mozia* II (1966); *Mozia* IV (1968); *Mozia* V (1969); *Mozia* VI (1970); *Mozia* VIII (1973); *Mozia* IX (1978). Broncoli, I. *et al.*, *Mozia* III (1967). Bevilacqua, F. *et al.*, *Mozia* VII (1972). (Studi Semitici 22, 24, 29, 31, 37, 40, 45). Rome.

188. Schmiedt, G. 'Antichi Porti d'Italia', *L'Universo* 45/2 (Florence, 1965) 225–274

189. Tamburello, I. 'Palermo-Necropoli; l'esplorazione 1953–54', *Not. Scav.* (1967) 354–78

190. Tamburello, I. 'Palermo-Necropoli e sarcophagi', *Not. Scav.* (1968) 243–71

191. Tamburello, I. 'Palermo-Necropoli: rinvenimenti del Dicembre 1966', *Not. Scav.* (1970) 277–304

192. Tusa, V. 'Selinunte punica', *Rivista dell'Istituto Nazionale d'Archeologia e Storia dell'Arte* 18 (1971) 47–68

193. Whitaker, J. I. S. *Motya, A Phoenician Colony in Sicily.* London, 1921

VII. MALTA AND PANTELLERIA

194. Baldacchino, J. G. 'Punic rock tombs near Pawla', *BSR* 19 (1951) 1–22

195. Baldacchino, J. G. and Dunbabin, T. J. 'Rock tomb at Ghajn Qajjet, near Rabat', *BSR* 21 (1953) 32–41

196. Bonello, V. *et al. Missione archeologica italiana a Malta: Rapporta preliminare.* 8 vols. Rome, 1964–72

197. [Malta Museum] Reports on the working of the Museum Department. Government printing office, Malta.

198. Mayr, A. 'Pantelleria', *Röm. Mitt.* 13 (1898) 367–98

199. Mayr, A. 'Aus den phönikischen Nekropolen von Malta', *Sitzungsbericht der K. Bayerischen Akad. der Wissenschaften* III (1905) 467–509. Munich

200. Orsi, P. 'Pantelleria', *Mon. Ant.* 9 (1899) 450–540

201. Peet, T. 'Two early Greek vases from Malta', *JHS* 32 (1912) 96–9

202. Seltman, C. 'The ancient coinage of Malta', *Num. Chron.* (1946) 81–9

203. Swann, J. S. 'Description of ancient rock tombs at Ghain Tiffiha and Tal Horr, Malta', *Archaeologia* 42 (1870) 483–7

204. Verger, A. 'Ricognizione archeologica a Pantelleria', in Ciasca, A. (ed.) *Mozia* II, 121–41. Rome, 1966

VIII. SARDINIA

205. Acquaro, E. 'Tharros I', *RSF* 3 (1975) 88–119; 'Tharros II', *RSF* 3 (1975) 213–25; 'Tharros III', *RSF* 4 (1976) 197–227

206. Barnett, R. D. and Mendleson, C. (eds.) *Tharros: A Catalogue of Material in the British Museum from Phoenician and Other Tombs at Tharros, Sardinia.* London, 1987

207. Barreca, F. 'Tharros, scoperte a Capo S. Marco', *Not. Scav.* (1958) 409–12

208. Barreca, F. 'Nuove iscrizioni di Sulcis', *Or. Ant.* 4 (1965) 53–7

209. Barreca, F. *La Sardegna fenicia e punica.* Sassari, 1974

210. Bartolini, P. 'Fortificazioni puniche di Sulcis', *Or. Ant.* 10 (1971) 147–54

211. Bartolini, P. 'Gli amuleti punici del tophet di Sulcis', *RSF* 1 (1973) 182–203

212. Bartolini, P. 'Una oinocho-italo geometrica di imitazione fenicia a Bithia', *RSF* 8 (1980) 47–50

213. Bartolini, P. and Tronchetti, C. *La necropoli di Nora*. Rome, 1981
214. Bisi, A. M. 'L'apport phénicien aux bronzes nouragiques de Sardaigne', *Latomus* 36 (1977) 909–32
215. Bondi, F. 'Osservazioni sulle fonte classiche per la colonizzazione della Sardegna', *Saggi Fenici* 1 (Rome, 1975) 49–66
216. Cecchini, S. M. *I ritrovamenti fenici e punici in Sardegna* (Studi semitici 32). Rome, 1969
217. Cecchini, S. M. 'Per un'identificazione di Monte Sirai', *Or. Ant.* 10 (1971) 183–7
218. De Felice, E. 'La Sardegna nel Mediterraneo in base alla toponomastica Costiera antica', *Studi Sardi* 18 (1962–3) 73–112
219. Gouin, L. *Notice sur les mines de Sardaigne*. Paris, 1883
220. Gras, M. 'Céramique d'importation étrusque à Bithia (Sardaigne)', *Studi Sardi* 23 (1973–4) 131–9
221. Gras, M. 'Les importations du VIe siècle avant J.-C. à Tharros (Sardaigne)', *MEFR* 86 (1974) 79–139
222. Levi, D. 'Le necropoli puniche di Olbia', *Studi Sardi* 9 (1950) 5–120
223. Lill, G. 'Rapporti fra la civiltà nuragica e la civiltà fenicio-punica in Sardegna', *Stud. Etr.* 23 (1944) 323–70
224. Lilliu, G. 'Tripode bronzeo di tradizione cipriota della grotta Pirosu-su Benatzu di Santadi (Cagliari)', *Estudios dedicados al Professor Luis Pericot*, 328–44. Barcelona, 1973
225. Mingazzini, P. 'Resti di santuario fenicio in Sulcis', *Studi Sardi* 8 (1948) 73–83
226. Mingazzini, P. 'Resti di santuario punico . . . a monti di Piazza del Carmine', *Not. Scav.* (1949) 213–19
227. Mocci, A. *L'antica città di Cornus*. Bosa, 1897
228. [Monte Sirai] Barreca, F. and Garbini, G. *Monte Sirai* I (1964); Amadasi, M. G. *et al. Monte Sirai* II (1965); III (1966); IV (1967). Rome
229. Panedda, D. *Olbia nel periodo punico e romano*. Rome, 1957
230. Patroni, G. 'Nora, colonia fenicia in Sardegna', *Mon. Ant.* 14 (1904) 189–268
231. Pesce, G. 'Chia (Cagliari) – Scavi nel territorio', *Not. Scav.* 22 (1968) 309–45
232. Pinna, M. 'La peninsola del Sinis', *Studi Sardi* 9 (1950) 246–76
233. Puglisi, S. 'Scavo di tombe ipogeiche puniche', *Not. Scav.* 3 (1942) 92–115
234. Taramelli, A. 'Sulcis', *Not. Scav.* (1905) 152–6
235. Taramelli, A. 'Scavi e scoperte di antichità puniche . . . dell'antica Sulcis', *Not. Scav.* (1908) 145–62
236. Taramelli, A. 'La necropoli punica di Predio Ibba . . .', *Mon. Ant.* 21 (1912) 45–218
237. Tronchetti, C. 'Per la cronologia del *tophet* di S. Antioco', *RSF* 7 (1979) 201–5
238. Tore, G. 'Di alcune reperti dall'antica Bithia', *MEFR* 88 (1976) 51–5
239. Tore, G. 'Richerche puniche in Sardegna I', *Studi Sardi* 23, 1 (1973–4) 365–74

240. Uberti, M. L. *Le figurine fittili di Bitia. Collezione di Studi Fenici* 1. Rome, 1973

IX. THE SPANISH PENINSULA

241. Allan, J. C. 'A mineracão em Portugal na Antiquidade', *Boletim de Minas* (Lisbon, 1965)
242. Almagro, M. *et al. Huelva, Prehistoria y Antigüedad.* Madrid, 1975
243. Almagro Basch, M. 'A propósito de la fecha de las fíbulas de Huelva', *Ampurias* 20 (1958) 195–207
244. Almagro Basch, M. *Las estelas decoradas del Soroeste peninsular* (Bibliotheca Praehistorica Hispana VIII). Madrid, 1966
245. Almagro Gorbea, M. 'La necrópolis de Medellín (Badajoz). Aportaciones al estudio de la penetración del influjo orientalizante en Extremadura', *Noticiario Arqueológico Hispánico* 16 (1971) 162–202
246. Almagro Gorbea, M. 'Los dos jarros palaeopúnicos del Museo Arquelógico Nacional hallados en Casa de la Viña (Torre del Mar)'; *MM* 13 (1972) 172–83
247. Almagro Gorbea, M. 'El tesoro de Bodonal de la Sierra (Badajoz). Nuevo elemento de las relaciones atlánticas del Bronce Final en la península ibérica', *Rev. de la Universidad Complutense* 22 (86) (1973) 21–31
248. Almagro Gorbea, M. 'Pozo Moro y el origen del arte ibérico', *Cronica del XIII Congreso Nacional de Arqueología (Huelva 1973)*, 671–86. Saragossa, 1975
249. Almagro Gorbea, M. 'La epigrafía orientalizante en Extremadura', *Rev. de la Universidad Complutense* 25 (101) (1976) 45–59
250. Almagro Gorbea, M. *El Bronce final y el periodo orientalizante en Extremadura.* Madrid, 1977
251. Almagro Gorbea, M. 'Los relievos mitológicas orientalizantes de Pozo Moro', *Trabajos de Prehistoria* 35 (1978) 251–78
252. Alves Dias, M. M. *et al.* 'Duas necrópoles da Idade do Ferro do Baixo-Alentejo, Ourique', *O Archeólogo Portugues* 4 (1970) 175–96
253. Aranegui, C. 'La cerámica gris monocroma. Puntualizaciones sobre su estudio', *Papeles de laboratorio de arqueología de Valencia* 11 (1975) 332–79
254. Arribas, A. 'La necrópolis Bastitana del Mirador de Rolanda (Granada)', *Pyrenae* III (1961) 67–105
255. Arribas, A. and Arteaga, O. *La factoría fenicia de la desembocadura del río Guadalhorce (Málaga)* (Cuadernos de Prehistoria de la Universidad de Granada, Supp. 1). Granada, 1975
256. Arribas, A. and Arteaga, O. 'Guadalhorce, eine phöniko-punische Niederlassung bei Málaga', *MM* 17 (1976) 180–208
257. Arribas, A. and Wilkins, J. *La necrópolis fenicia del Cortijo de las Sombras.* Universidad de Granada, 1971
258. Arribas Palan, A. and Fajardo, F. M. 'La necrópolis ibérica del Molina de Caldona', *Oretania* 10–11 (Linares, 1969) 160–79
259. Arteaga, O. and Serna, M. R. 'Die Ausgrabungen von Los Saldares,

Prov. Alicante', *MM* 15 (1974) 108–23

260. Astruc, M. *La necrópolis de Villaricos* (Informes y Memorias 25). Madrid, 1951

261. Aubet, M. E. 'Los hallazagos púnicos de Osuna', *Pyrenae* 7 (1971) 111–28

262. Aubet, M. E. 'Materiales púnico-tartesios de la necrópolis de Setefilla en la colleción Bonsor', *Bol. del Seminario de Estudios de Arta y Arqueología* 39 (Valladolid, 1973) 5–27

263. Aubet, M. E. 'Excavaciones en las Chorreras (Mezquitilla, Málaga)', *Pyrenae* 10 (1975) 79–108

264. Aubet, M. E. 'La cerámica púnica de Setefilla', *Bol. del Seminario de Estudios de Arta y Arqueología* 42 (Valladolid, 1976) 19–48

265. Aubet, M. E. *et al.* 'Chorreras, eine phönizische Niederlassung östlich der Algarrobo-Mündung', *MM* 16 (1975) 137–78

265A. Aubet-Semmler, M. E. 'Die westphönizischen Elfenbeine aus dem Gebiet des unteren Guadalquivir', *Hamburger Beiträge zur Archäologie* 9 (1982) 15ff

266. Belen, M. 'Estudio y tipología de la cerámica gris en la provincia de Huelva', *Rev. Arch. Bib. Mus.* 79, 1 (Madrid, 1976) 353–88

267. Blanco, A. 'Origen y relaciones de la orfebrería castreña', *Cuadernos de estudios gallegos* 12 (36–7) (1957) 1–27, 137–59, 267–301

268. Blanco, A. 'El ajuar de una tumba de Cástulo', *AEA* 34 (1963) 40–69

269. Blanco, A. *et al. Excavaciones arqueológicas en el Cerro Salomón (Riotinto, Huelva)* (Anales de la Universidad Hispalense 4). Seville, 1970

270. Blázquez, J. M. 'Joyas orientalizantes extremeñas del Museo Arqueológico Nacional de Madrid', *Zephyrus* 14 (1963) 5–15

271. Blázquez, J. M. 'Fuentes griegas y latinas referentes a Tartessos', *Tartessos y sus Problemas, V Symposium internacional de Prehistoria Peninsular (Jerez de la Frontera, 1968)*, 91–110. Barcelona, 1969

272. Blázquez, J. M. 'Figuras animalisticas turdetanas', *Anejos de AEA* 7 (1974) (Homenaje a D. Pio Beltrán)

273. Blázquez, J. M. *Tartessos y los origines de la colonización fenicia en occidente*. 2nd edn. University of Salamanca, 1975

274. Blázquez, J. M. *et al. Huelva arqueológica: las cerámicas del Cebezo de San Pedro* (Instituto de Estudios Onubenses 'Padre Marehena'). Huelva, 1970

275. Blázquez, J. M. *et al. Excavaciones en el Cabezo de San Pedro (Huelva): campaña de 1977*. Ministero de Cultura, Madrid, 1979

276. Blázquez, J. M. *et al. Historia de Éspaña* 1. Madrid, 1980

277. Blázquez, J. M. and Luzón, J. M. 'La factoría púnica de Aljaraque en la provincia de Huelva', *Noticario Arqueológico Hispanico* 13–14 (1971) 304–31

278. Bonsor, G. 'Les colonies agricoles pré-romaines de la vallée du Bétis', *Rev. Arch.* 35 (1899) 126–59, 232–9

279. Bonsor, G. E. *Early Engraved Ivories in the Collection of the Hispanic Society of America*. New York, 1925

280. Cabré, D. J. and de Motos, D. F. *La necrópolis ibérica de Tútugi, Galera, provincia de Granada* (Junta Superior de Excavaciones y Antigüedades, Memoria 25 = Núm. 4 de 1918). Madrid, 1920

281. Carriazo, J. de M. *Tartessos y 'El Carambolo'*. Madrid, 1973

282. Carriazo, J. de M. and Raddatz, K. 'Ergebnisse einer ersten stratigraphischen Untersuchung in Carmona', *MM* 2 (1961) 71–106

283. Casal, L. A. 'Consideraciones en Torno a Tartessos y el origen de la cultura ibérica', *AEA* 52 (1979) 175–93

284. Cavaleiro Paixão, A. M. 'O recente achado de três escaravelhos na necrópole do Senhor Mártires em Alcácer do Sal', *Actas II Congresso Nacional de Arqueologia, Coimbra 1970*, 309–14. Coimbra, 1971

285. Checkland, B. *The Mines of Tharsis*. London, 1961

285A. Cirkin, J. B. 'Phönizier und Spanier', *Klio* 63 (1981) 411ff

286. Costa Arthur, M. de L. 'Necrópolis de Alcácer do Sal', *Cronica del II Congresso Nacional de Arqueología (Madrid 1951)*, 369–80. Saragossa, 1952

287. Cuadrado, E. *Repertório de los recipientes rituales metálicos con 'asas de manos' de la peninsula ibérica* (Trabajos de Prehistoria 21). Madrid, 1966

288. Cuevillas, F. L. *La civilización céltica en Galicia*. Santiago de Compostela, 1973

289. Culican, W. 'Almuñécar, Assur and the Phoenician penetration of the western Mediterranean', *Levant* 2 (1970) 28–36

290. Da Costa, J. M. 'O tesoro fenício ou cartaginês do Gaio (Sines)', *Ethnos* 5 (Lisbon, 1966) 529–31

291. Droop, J. P. 'Excavations at Niebla in the province of Huelva, Spain', *LAAA* 12 (1925) 175–95

292. Eogan, G. 'An associated find of gold-bar torques', *Royal Society of Antiquaries of Ireland, Proceedings* 97, 2 (1967) 129–39

293. Estachio da Veiga, S. P. M. *Paleoethnologia – Antigüedades Monumentales do Algarve* II. Lisbon, 1887

294. Fernández, M. *et al. Abdera, excavaciones en el Cerro de Montecristo (Adrá, Almería)* (Excavaciones Arqueológicas en España). Madrid, 1972

295. Fernández-Miranda, M. 'Horizonte cultural tartésico y hallazgos greigos en el Sur de la Península', *AEA* 52 (1979) 49–63

296. Ferron, J. 'L'urne cineraire d'Almuñécar', *Le Museon* 83 (Louvain, 1970) 249–65

297. Ferron, J. *et al.* 'Inscripción fenicia procedente del Cabezo de la Esperanza (Huelva)', *Trabajos de Prehistoria* 32 (1975) 199–211

298. Fletcher Valls, D. and Ballester, E. *El Museo del Servicio de Investigación... de Valencia* (1953) 16–17

299. Font de Tarradell, M. 'Dos peínes ibéricos de la Serreta de Alcoy y sus precedentes', *Papeles del Laboratorio de arqueología de Valencia* 10 (1970) 123–37

300. Freyer-Schauenburg, B. 'Kolaios und die westphönizischen Elfenbeinen', *MM* 7 (1966) 89–108

301. Gallo, G. N. 'Una sepultura del Cabecico del Tesoro con braserillo ritual', *AEA* 43 (1970) 62–88

302. Gamer-Wallert, I. *Aegyptische und ägyptisierende Funde von der iberischen Halbinsel*. Wiesbaden, 1978

303. García y Bellido, A. 'Hercules Gaditanus', *AEA* 36 (1963) 70–153

304. García y Bellido, A. 'II, Protohistoria: Tartessós; III, Colonización púnica; IV, La colonización griega', in Menéndez Pidal, R. (ed.) *Historia de España* I/2, 281–680. Madrid, 1952

305. Garrido Roiz, J. P. and Orta García, E. M. 'La tumba orientalizante de "La Joya", Huelva', *Trabajos de Prehistoria* 11 (1963) 7–36

306. Garrido Roiz, J. P. *Excavaciones en la necrópolis de 'La Joya', Huelva* I (Excavaciones Arqueológicas en España 71). Madrid, 1970

307. Garrido Roiz, J. P. and Orta García, E. M. *Excavaciones en la necrópolis de 'La Joya, Huelva* II (Excavaciones Arqueológicas en España 96). Madrid, 1978

308. Guerra, A. V. and Ferreira, O. da V. 'Inventário das estaçoes da Idad do Ferro nos arredores da Figueira da Foz', *Actas II Congresso Nacional de Arqueología, Coimbra 1970*, 297–303. Coimbra, 1971

309. Hibbs, V. 'A new view of two Carmona ivories', *Arch. Anz.* (1979) 458–80

310. Henig, R. *Terrae incognitae*. 2nd edn. Leiden, 1944

310A. Koch, M. 'Tarschisch und Hispanien', *Madrider Forschungen* 14 (1984)

311. Lafuente Vidal, J. *Alicante en la edad antigua*. Alicante, 1949

312. Leon, M. de P. 'Capitel ibérico del Cerro de las Virgenes (Córdoba)', *AEA* 52 (1979) 195–200

313. Lindemann, G. *et al.* 'Toscanos, Jardín und Alarcón, Vorbericht über di Grabungskampagne 1971', *MM* 13 (1972) 124–57

314. Lombard, M. 'Arsenaux et bois de marine dans la méditerranée musulmane, VIIe–XIe siècles', in Mollat, M. (ed.) *Le navire et l'économie maritime du Moyen Age au XVIIIe siècle principalement en Méditerranée*, 53–106. Paris, 1958

315. Luzón, J. M. and Ruiz Mata, D. *Las raíces de Córdoba. Estratigrafía de la Colina de los Quemados*. Córdoba, 1973

316. Maas-Lindemann, G. and Schubart, H. 'Jardin, Vorbericht über di Grabung 1974 . . .', *MM* 16 (1975) 179–86

317. Macineira, F. *Bares, puerto hispánico de la primitiva navegación occidental*. Santiago de Compostela, 1947

318. Malax-Echeverria, A. López. 'La necrópolis púnica "El Jardín"', *Tarshish-Malaka* III, 22–38. Malaga, 1969

319. Mesado Oliver, N. *Vinarragell (Burriana-Castellón)*. Valencia, 1974

320. Monteioro, R. and da Veiga Ferreia, O. 'Necrópole púnica(?) en Sessimbra', *Arquivo de Beja* 25–6 (Beja, 1968–70) 3–15

321. Muñoz, M. 'El tell púnico de Aljornó Herrera (Seville)', *Cronica del XIII Congreso Nacional de Arqueología (Huelva 1973)*, 809–18. Saragossa, 1975

321A. Negueruela, I. 'Zur Datierungen der westphönizischen Nekropole von Almuñécar', *MM* 22 (1981) 211ff

322. Niemeyer, H. G. (ed.) *Phönizier im Westen* (Madrider Beiträge 8). Mainz, 1982

323. Niemeyer, H. G. 'Zum Thymiaterion vom Cerro del Peñon', *MM* 11 (1970) 96–101

324. Niemeyer, H. G. 'Ein tartessisches Goldcollier aus Tharsis (Prov. Huelva)', *MM* 18 (1977) 116–29

325. Niemeyer, H. G. 'Toscanos. Vorbericht über die Grabungskampagnen 1973 und 1976', *MM* 18 (1977) 74–92

325A. Niemeyer, H. G. 'Auf der Suche nach Mainake', *Historia* 29 (1980) 165ff

326. Niemeyer, H. G. and Schubart, H. *Toscanes. Die altpunische Faktorei an der Mündung des Río de Velez, Grabungskampagne 1964* (Madrider Forschungen 6, Lieferung 1). Berlin, 1969

327. Niemeyer, H. G. and Schubart, H. *Trayamar. Die phönizischer Kammergräber und die Niederlassung an der Algorrobo-Mündung* (Madrider Beiträge 4). Mainz, 1975

328. Olonso, D. O. and Vila, R. C. 'Una estela funeraria con escudo de escotadura en U en la Provincia de Sevilla', *Trabajos de Prehistoria* 33 (1976) 387–95

329. Pellicer, M. *La necrópolis púnica Laurita del Cerro de San Cristóbal (Almuñécar-Granada)*. Madrid, 1962

330. Pellicer, M. 'Las primitivas cerámicas a torno pintadas hispanas', *AEA* 41 (1968) 60–90

331. Perez Diaz, M. C. 'Notas sobre vasos egipcios de elabastro procedentes de Torre del Mar (Málaga)', *Rev. Arch. Bib. Mus.* 79, 2 (1976) 903–18

332. Pingel, V. 'Zur Vorgeschichte von Niebla (Prov. Huelva)', *MM* 16 (1975) 111–36

333. Ponsich, M. *Implantation rurale antique sur le Bas-Guadalquivir* (Publication de la Casa de Velazquez, Série Archéologie 11). Madrid and Paris, 1974

334. Puech, E. 'L'inscription phénicienne du trône d'Aštart à Seville', *RSF* 5 (1977) 85–92

335. Remesal, J. 'Cerámicas orientalizantes andaluzas', *AEA* 48 (1975) 3–21

336. Ruiz Mata, D. 'Cerámicas del Bronce del poblado de la Valencina de la Concepcion (Seville)', *MM* 16 (1975) 80–94

337. Ruiz Mata, D. 'El Bronce final en Andalucia occidental', *AEA* 52 (1979)

338. Salkield, L. V. 'La minería hispana e iberoamericana. Estudios, fuentes, bibliografía, *VI Congreso Internacional de Minería* 103–24. Leon, 1970

339. Santos Rocha, A. 'Estações pré-romanas de Idade do Ferro nas vizinhanças da Figueira I (Santa Olaya) II (Crasto)', *Portugalia* 11 (Oporto, 1908) 310–58, 493–516

340. Sayans Castanos, M. *Los joyas célticas de Serradilla*. Plasencia, 1962

341. Schubart, H. *Die Kultur der Bronzezeit im Südwesten der iberischen Halbinsel* (Madrider Forschungen 8). Berlin, 1975

342. Schubart, H. 'Jardín, Vorbericht über die Grabungskampagne 1976 . . .', *MM* 18 (1977) 93–7

343. Schubart, H. 'Morro de Mezquitilla, Vorbericht über die Grabungskampagne 1976 . . .', *MM* 18 (1977) 33–61

344. Schubert, H. and Niemeyer, H. G. 'Untersuchungen zur west-

phönizischen Archäologie im Raum von Torre del Mar 1976', *Arch. Anz.* (1978) 230–49

345. Schüle, W. 'Der bronzezeitliche Schatzfund von Villena', *MM* 17 (1976) 142–79

346. Schüle, W. 'Las mas antiguas fibulas con pie alto y ballesta', *Rev. Arch. Bib. Mus.* 69 (1961) 339–75

347. Siret, L. *Villaricos y Herrerias* (Memorias de la Real Academia de la Historia 14). Madrid, 1907

348. Sola-Sole, J. M. 'Miscelánea púnico-hispana III', *Sefarad* 25 (1965) 27–32

349. Spindler, K. and da Veiga Ferreira, O. 'Der spatbronzezeitliche Kuppelbau von der Roça do Casal Meio in Portugal', *MM* 14 (1973) 60–108

350. Täckholm, U. 'Neue Studien zum Tarsis-Tartessos Problem', *Opuscula Romana* 10 (1974) 41–57

351. Tovar, A. 'El oscuro problema de la lengua de los Tartessios', *Tartessos y sus problemas. V Symposium Peninsular de Prehistoria, Jerez de la Frontera, 1968*, 341–46. Barcelona, 1969

X. THE BALEARIC ISLANDS AND THE NORTH-WEST MEDITERRANEAN COAST

352. Almagro, M. *Ampurias* I. Barcelona, 1953

353. Amorós, L. 'La cueva sepulcral preromana de "San Maímo" en el término municipal de Petra (Mallorca)', *Prehistoria y arquelogía de las Islas Baleares. VI Symposium de Prehistoria Peninsular, Barcelona 1974*, 137–70. Barcelona, 1976

354. Arteaga, O., Padró, J. and Sanmartí, E. 'El factor fenici a les costes catalanes i del Golf de Lió', *II Colloqui internacional d'arquelogía de Puigcerda*, 129–34. 1974

355. Astruc, M. 'Empreintes et reliefs de terre cuite d'Ibiza', *AEA* 30 (1957) 139–91

356. Aubet, M. E. 'Algunos aspectos sobre iconografía púnica: las representaciones aladas de Tanit', *Rev. de la Universidad Complutense* 25 (101) (1976) 62–82

357. Aubet-Semmler, M. E. 'La Cueva d'Es Cuyram (Ibiza)', *Pyrenae* 4 (1968) 1–66

358. Baqués, L. 'The foundation of Punic Ibiza from the Egyptian scarabs found there', *First International Congress of Egyptology, October 1976*, 154–5. Munich, 1976

359. Benoit, F. *Recherches sur l'hellénization du Midi de la Gaule.* Aix-en-Provence, 1965

360. Blazquez, J. M. 'Coroplastica preromana del Puig des Molins', *AEA* 37 (1964) 40–9

360A. Boardman, J. *Escarabeos de piedra procedentes de Ibiza.* Madrid, 1984

361. Camps Coll, J. and Vallepir Bonet, A. 'Cerámicas pintadas en Mallorca',

Cronica del XII Congreso Nacional de Arqueología, Jaen 1971, 283–94. Saragòssa, 1973

362.   Fatas, G. 'Une estela de guerrero con escudo escotado en V aparecida en las Cinco Villas, Aragon', *Pyrenae* 11 (1975) 165–9

362A.   Fernandez Gomez, J. H. and Padro, J. *Escarabeos del Museo arqueologico de Ibiza*. Madrid, 1982

363.   Fernandez Gomez, J. H. and Plantalamor Massanet, L. 'Cerámicas de tipología talayotica en el Museo de Ibiza', *Cronica del XIII Congreso Nacional de Arqueología, Huelva 1973*, 377–82. Saragossa, 1975

364.   Fernandez-Miranda, M. 'Jaritas ibericas de tipo Ampuritano en las Islas Baleares', *Trabajos de Prehistoria* 33 (1976) 255–90

365.   Frickenhaus, A. 'Griechische Vasen aus Emporion', *Anuari d'institut d'Estudis Catalans* (1908) 195–240. Barcelona

366.   Jully, J. J. 'Koine commerciale et culturelle phénico-punique et ibéro-languédocienne en Méditerranée occidentale', *AEA* 48 (1975) 22–94

367.   Llobregat, E. A. 'Las relaciones con Ibiza en la protohistoria Valenciana', *Prehistoria y arqueología de las Islas Baleares. VI Symposium de Prehistoria Península, Barcelona 1974*, 291–320. Barcelona, 1976

368.   Maluquer de Motes, J. 'Los Fenicios en Cataluña', *Tartessos y sus problemas. V Symposium Peninsular de Prehistoria, Jerez de la Frontera, 1968*, 241–56. Barcelona, 1969

369.   Murray, M. A. *Cambridge Excavations in Minorca: Trapucó I–II*. London, 1932–8

370.   Niemeyer, H. G. 'Archäologischen Beobachtungen aus Formentera', *MM* 6 (1965) 91–8

371.   Pericot-Garcia, L. *The Balearic Islands*. London, 1972

372.   Sanmartí, E. and Padró, J. 'Ensayo de aproximación al fenomeno de la iberización en las comarcas meridionales de Cataluña', *Monografies* 54, 157–75. Barcelona, 1978

373.   Solilier, Y. 'Céramiques puniques et ibéro-puniques sur le littoral du Languédoc . . .', *Rivista di Studi Liguri* 34 (1968) 127–50

374.   Tarradell, M. 'Ibiza púnica: algunos problemas actuales', *Prehistoria y arqueología de las Islas Baleares. VI Symposium de Prehistoria Península, Barcelona 1974*, 243–67. Barcelona, 1976

XI. MOROCCO AND THE ATLANTIC COAST

375.   Blázquez, J. M. 'Las Islas Canarias en la Antigüedad', *Anuario de Estudios Atlánticos* 23 (Madrid and Las Palmas, 1977) 35–50

376.   Callu, J.-P. *et al. Thamusida* 1. Paris, 1965

377.   Carcopino, J. *La Maroc antique*. Paris, 1947

378.   Cintas, P. *Contribution à l'étude de l'expansion carthaginoise au Maroc*. Paris, 1954

379.   Desanges, J. *Recherches sur l'activité des Méditerranéens aux confins de l'Afrique*. Ecole Française de Rome, 1978

380.   Germain, G. 'Qu'est ce que le Périple d'Hannon? Document, amplification littéraire ou faux intégral?', *Hesperia* 44 (157) 205–48

381. Gran Aymerich, J. M. J. 'Prospections archéologiques au Sahara Atlantique . . .', *Antiquités africaines* 13 (1979) 7–21
382. Jodin, A. 'Les gravures rupestres du Yagour, Haut-Atlas. Analyse stylistique et thématique', *Bull. archéologique marocaine* 5 (1964) 47–116
383. Jodin, A. *Mogador, comptoir phénicien du Maroc atlantique* (Etudes et travaux d'archéologie marocaine II). Tangier, 1966
384. Koehler, P. 'Une tombe punique au Cap Spartel', *Revue des Musées* 25 (Dijon, 1930) 18–21
385. Lonis, R. 'Les conditions de la navigation sur la côte atlantique de l'Afrique dans l'Antiquité: le problème du retour', *Colloque Afrique Noire et monde méditerranéen dans l'Antiquité*, 147–62. Dakar, 1976
386. Luquet, A. 'Ceramique pré-romaine de Banasa', *BAM* 5 (1964) 117–44
387. Mauny, R. *Les navigations mediévales sur les côtes sahariennes antérieures à la découverte portugaise.* Lisbon, 1960
388. Mvena, E. *Les sources grecs de l'histoire Nègro-Africaine depuis Homère jusqu'à Strabon.* Lille, 1972
389. Picard, G. *La vie quotidienne à Carthage au temps d'Hannibal.* Paris, 1958
390. Ponsich, M. *Nécropoles phéniciennes de la région de Tanger* (Etudes et travaux d'archéologie marocaine III). Tangier, 1967
391. Segert, S. 'The Phoenician background of Hanno's Periplus', *Mélanges de l'Université St Joseph de Beyrouth* 45 (1969) 502–18
392. Shaw, T. *Nigeria, its Archaeology and Early History.* London, 1978
393. Tarradell, M. 'Hipogeos de tipo púnico en Lixus', *Ampurias* 12 (1950) 250–3
394. Tarradell, M. 'Tres notas sobre arqueología púnica del Norte de Africa', *AEA* 26 (1953) 161–4
395. Tarradell, M. *Marruecos púnico.* Tetuan, 1960
396. Tarradell, M. 'Contribution à l'Atlas archéologique du Maroc', *BAM* 6 (1966) 425–43
397. Tarradell, A. and Font, M. *Eivissa cartaginesa.* Barcelona, 1975
398. Veny, P. C. 'Escorca (Mallorca) Cometa dels Morts', *Noticiario Arqueológico Hispánico* II (Madrid, 1975)
399. Villard, F. 'Céramique grecque de Maroc', *BAM* 4 (1960) 1–26
400. Vives, A. 'El Arte Egeo en España', *Rev. Arch. Bib. Mus.* 22 (1910) 397–420
401. Vives Escudero, A. *Esquema di arqueología cartagineza: La necrópoli de Ibiza.* Madrid, 1917

D. SCYTHIA AND THRACE

I. SCYTHIA

1. Alexandrescu, P. 'Les importations grecques dans les bassins du Dnepr et du Boug', *Rev. Arch.* (1975) 63–72
2. Alikhova, A. E. 'The ancient town-sites of the Kursk-Seim region', *MIA* 113 (1962) 134–41. Moscow [In Russian]

3.   Amandry, P. and Schiltz, V. (eds.) *Or des Scythes: trésors des Musées sovietiques*. Paris, 1975

4.   *The Ancient Thracians in the Northern Black Sea Region, MIA* 150 (1969). Moscow [In Russian]

5.   Anfimov, N. V. 'The Maeoto-Sarmatian burial ground near Ust-Labinskaya', *MIA* 23 (1951). Moscow–Leningrad [In Russian]

6.   Anfimov, N. V. 'The composition of the Maeotae culture and its links with the steppe cultures of the northern Black Sea region', *MIA* 177 (1971) 170–7 [In Russian]

7.   Anfimov, N. V. *The Kuban's Ancient Gold*. Krasnodar, 1987 [In Russian]

8.   Artamonov, M. I. *Treasures from Scythian Tombs*. London, 1969

9.   Bakay, K. *Scythian Rattles in the Carpathian Basin and their Eastern Connections*. Budapest, 1971

10. Barnett, R. D. 'The treasure of Ziwiye', *Iraq* 18–2 (1956) 11–116

11. Bashilov, V. N. (ed.) *Nomads of Eurasia*. Seattle and London, 1989

12. Berezovets, D. T. 'Excavations of kurgans near the village of Kut, Dniepropetrovsk region', in *KSIAK* 4 (1955), 81ff [In Russian]

13. Berezovets, D. T. 'Excavations at a Bronze Age Scythian period kurgan burial ground', *AP* 9 (1960) 39ff [In Ukrainian]

14. Berezovets, D. T. and Berezanska, S. S. 'Bronze Age settlement near Nyzhniy Rogachyk', *AP* 10 (1961) 40–5 [In Ukrainian]

15. Bergquist, A. K. 'The emergence of a state in pre-Roman Dacia: studies in the archaeology and ancient history of Transylvania, 800 B.C.–A.D. 106'. Unpublished Ph.D. dissertation. Cambridge, 1989

16. Bibikova, V. I. 'Fauna from the settlement near the village of Kirovo', in *Antiquities of the Ancient Crimea*, 97–109. Kiev, 1970 [In Russian]

17. Bittel, K. *Grundzüge der Vor- und Frühgeschichte Kleinasiens*. Tübingen, 1945

18. Boardman, J. *The Greeks Overseas*. 2nd edn. London, 1980

19. Boky, N. M. 'The Scythian kurgan near the village of Nederovo', *SA* (1974) 264–71 [In Russian]

20. Bukovsky, Z. *Scythian Influence in the Area of the Lusatian Culture*. Crakow–Gdansk–Warsaw–Wrocław, 1977

21. Chernenko, E. V. *Scythian Armour*. Kiev, 1968 [In Russian]

22. Chernenko, E. V. *Scythian Archers*. Kiev, 1981 [In Russian]

23. Chernenko [Černenko], E. V. *The Scythians – 700-300 B.C.* London, 1983

24. Chernikov, S. S. 'Eastern Kazakhstan in the Bronze Age', *MIA* 88 (1960) 105–17. Moscow–Leningrad [In Russian]

25. Chlenova, N. L. 'On the question of the origin of materials used for objects in the animal style', *MIA* 177 (1971) 208–17. Moscow–Leningrad [In Russian]

26. Cowen, J. D. 'The flange-hilted sword of bronze: was it first developed in Central Europe or in the Aegean?', *Bericht über den V. Internationalen Kongress für Vor- und Frühgeschichte, Hamburg 1958*. Berlin, 1961

27. Cowen, J. D. 'The Hallstatt Sword of Bronze: on the Continent and in Britain', *PPS* 33 (1967), 377–454

28. Dashevskaya, O. B. 'The Scythians on the northwestern coast of the

Crimea in the light of new discoveries', *MIA* 177 (1971) 151-5. Moscow–Leningrad [In Russian]

29. Debets, G. F. *The Palaeoanthropology of the USSR*. Moscow, 1948 [In Russian]

30. Dergachev, V. 'Neolithic and Bronze Age cultural communities of the steppe zone of the USSR', *Antiquity* 63 (1989) 793-802

31. Diakonov, I. M. *A History of Media*. Leningrad, 1955 [In Russian]

32. Dušek, M. 'Die thrako-skythische Periode in der Slowakei', *Slovenská Archeológia* 9 (1961) 155-74

33. Dyson, R. H. Jr., 'Problems of protohistoric Iran as seen from Hasanlu', *JNES* 24 (1965) 193-213

34. Ebert, M. 'Ausgrabungen auf dem Gute Marizin', *Prähistorische Zeitschrift* (1913) 1ff

35. Fettich, N. 'Bestand der skythischen Altertümer Ungarns', in D 173, 494-529

36. Foltiny, I. 'Zur Frage des "skythischen" Einflusses in Ostösterreich und Slowenien', *Arch. Austriaca* 33 (1963) 23-36

37. *From the Lands of the Scythians: Ancient Treasures from the Museums of the USSR*. New York–Los Angeles, 1974

38. Furtwängler, A. *Der Goldfund von Vettersfelde*. Berlin, 1883

39. Gaidukevich, V. F. *The Bosporan Kingdom*. Moscow–Leningrad, 1942 [In Russian] (Transl. as D 40)

40. Gaidukevich, V. F. *Das Bosporanische Reich*. Berlin, 1971. (German transl. of D 39)

41. Galanina, L. K., Domansky, Y. V. and Smirnova, G. I. *The Scythians. Exhibition Guidebook*. Leningrad, 1981 [In Russian]

42. Galanina, L., Grach [Grač], N., Kellner, H.-J. and Kossack, G. *Scythika: Vorträge zur Entstehung des skytho-iranischen Tierstils und zu Denkmälern des Bosporanischen Reichs*. Munich, 1987

43. Gallus, S. and Horváth, T. *Un peuple cavalier préscythique en Hongrie. Trouvailles archéologiques du premier âge du fer et leurs relations avec l'Eurasie* (Diss. Pann. Ser. II.9). Budapest, 1939

44. Ghirshman, R. *The Arts of Ancient Iran*. New York, 1964

45. Ghirshman, R. *Persia: from the Origins to Alexander the Great*. London, 1964

46. Ghirshman, R. 'A propos de la Nécropole B de Sialk', *JPEK* 24 (1974-7). Berlin–New York, 1977

47. Ghirshman, R. *Tombe princière de Ziwiyé et le début de l'art animalier scythe*. Paris, 1979

48. Goff Meade, C. *Iran* VI (1968) 105-34

49. *Gold der Skythen aus der Leningrader Eremitage*. Munich, 1984

50. Gorodtsov, V. A. 'Excavations at 'Chastye Kurgany' near Voronezh in 1927', *SA* 9 (1947) 13-28 [In Russian]

51. Grakov B. N. 'Scythian burials at the Nikolskoe barrow [*kurgan*] field', *MIA* 115 (1962) 56-113 [In Russian]

52. Grakow [Grakov], B. N. *Die Skythen*. Transl. by A. Häusler. Berlin, 1978

53. Grakov, B. N. and Melyukova, A. I. 'On ethnic and cultural differences in the steppe and forest-steppe regions of the European part of the USSR in the Scythian period', *VSSA* (1953) 39–93 [In Russian]

54. Grene, D. *Herodotus. The History*. Chicago–London, 1987

55. Griaznov, M. P. *Arzhan*. Leningrad, 1980 [In Russian]

56. Grinevich, K. E. 'New data on the archaeology of Kabarda', *MIA* 23 (1951) 125–30 [In Russian]

57. Gumilev, L. N. *Searches for an Imaginary Kingdom. The Legend of the Kingdom of Prester John*, transl. R. E. F. Smith. Cambridge, 1987

58. Hančar, F. 'Der "goldene Pflug" der skythischen Abstammungslegende in archäologischer Sicht', *Innsbrucker Beiträge zur Kulturwissenschaft* 14 (1968) 307–76

59. Harmatta, J. 'Darius' expedition against the Sakā Tigraxaudā', *Acta ant. Hung.* 24 (1976) 15–24

60. Hartog, F. *Le miroir d'Hérodote. Essai sur la représentation de l'autre*. Mayenne, 1980. (Transl. as D 61)

61. Hartog, F. *The Mirror of Herodotus. The Representation of the Other in the Writing of History*. Transl. by Janet Lloyd. Berkeley–Los Angeles–London, 1988. (Engl. transl. of D 60)

62. Ierusalimskaya, A. 'On the variant of the Catacomb culture in the foothills of the Caucasus', *SA* (1958) 2. 34–48 [In Russian]

63. Iessen, A. A. 'The Kuban region metalworking focus at the end of the Copper and Bronze Age', *MIA* 23 (1951) 72–124 [In Russian]

64. Iessen, A. A. 'On 8th–7th century B.C. sites in the south of the European part of the USSR', *SA* 17 (1953) 49–110 [In Russian]

65. Iessen, A. A. 'Some 8th–7th century B.C. sites in the North Caucasus', *VSSA* (1954) 112–31 [In Russian]

66. Iessen, A. A. 'The Azerbaijan Archaeological Expedition in 1956–1960', *MIA*, 125 (1965) [In Russian]

67. Ilinskaya, V. A. 'The bronze age Bondarikha culture', *SA* (1961) 1. 26–45 [In Russian]

68. Ilinskaya [Ilinska], V. A. 'The Basovskoe town-site', *AK* 18 (1965) 48–76 [In Ukrainian]

69. Ilinskaya, V. A. *The Scythians of the Forest-Steppe Left Bank of the Dnieper*. Kiev, 1968 [In Russian]

70. Ilinskaya [Ilinska], V. A. 'Androphagi, Melanchlaeni, Budini or Scythians?', *AK* 23 (1970) 23–39 [In Ukrainian]

71. Ilinskaya, V. A. 'Could the Belsk town-site be the town of Gelonus?', in Ilinskaya, V. A. (ed.) *Scythians and Sarmatians*, 73–95. Kiev, 1977 [In Russian]

72. Ilinskaya, V. A. and Terenozhkin, A. I. *Scythia, VII–IV Centuries B.C.* Kiev, 1983 [In Russian]

73. Jettmar, K. *Die Frühen Steppenvölker. Der eurasiatische Tierstil, Entstehung und sozialer Hintergrund*. Baden-Baden, 1964. (Transl. as D 74)

74. Jettmar, K. *Art of the Steppes. The Eurasian Animal Style*. London, 1967 (Engl. transl. of D 73)

75. Kastanayan, E. G. 'Earth cemeteries of the Bosporan towns', *MIA* 69 (1959) 257–95 [In Russian]
76. Kerashev, T. (ed.) *Treasures of the Adygeya Kurgans.* Moscow, 1985 [In Russian]
77. Khachatrian, T. S. *The Material Culture of Ancient Artik.* Yerevan, 1963 [In Russian]
78. Khalilov, Dzh. 'Archaeological finds of "Scythian" appearance and the question of the "Scythian kingdom" in Azerbaijan', in *Problems of Scythian Archaeology, MIA* 177 (1971) 183–7 [In Russian]
79. Khazanov, A. M. *A Social History of the Scythians.* Moscow, 1975 [In Russian]
80. Khazanov, A. M. *Nomads and the outside World.* Cambridge, 1984
81. Kiyashko, V. Ya. 'Excavations at the Konstantinovska settlement', *AO* (1968) 105f [In Russian]
82. Kiyashko, V. Ya. and Koreniako, V. A. 'An early Iron Age burial near the town of Konstantinovska-na-donu', *SA* (1976) 170–7 [In Russian]
83. Klejn, L. S. 'The origin of the royal Scythians according to archaeological data', *SA* (1963–4) 27–35 [In Russian]
84. König, F. W. *Älteste Geschichte der Meder und Perser* (Der Alte Orient 33). Leipzig, 1934
85. Korpusova, V. M. 'About the population of the hora of ancient Theodosia', *AK* (1972–6) 41–55 [In Ukrainian]
86. Kossack, G. 'Pferdegeschirr aus Gräbern der älteren Hallstattzeit Bayerns', *JRGZM* (1953) 111–78
87. Kossack, G. '"Kimmerische" Bronzen. Bemerkungen zur Zeitstellung in Ost- und Mitteleuropa', *Situla* (1980) 109–43
88. Kossack, G. 'Von den Anfängen des skytho-iranischen Tierstils', in D 42, 24–86
89. Kovpanenko, G. T. 'An 8th–7th century B.C. burial in the basin of the river Vorskla', *KSIAK* 12 (1962) 66–72 [In Russian]
90. Kovpanenko, V. P. *Tribes of the Scythian Period on the Vorskla.* Kiev, 1967 [In Ukrainian]
91. Krivtsova-Grakova, O. A. *The steppe region of the Volga and Black Sea in the Late Bronze Age, MIA* 46 (1955) Moscow [In Russian]
92. Krupnov, E. I. 'On the question of Scythian-period settlements in the North Caucasus', *KSIIMK* 24 (1949) 27–41 [In Russian]
93. Krupnov, E. I. *The Ancient History of the North Caucasus.* Moscow, 1960 [In Russian]
94. Krupnov, E. I. 'Towards a finer dating and periodization of the Koban culture', *SA* (1969) 1. 13–18 [In Russian]
95. Kuftin, V. A. *Archaeological Excavations in Trialeti* 1. Tbilisi 1941 [In Russian]
96. Kuklina. I. V. *Scythian Ethnogeography from the Ancient Sources.* Leningrad, 1985 [In Russian]
97. Kushnareva, K. Kh. 'Some Late Bronze Age sites in Nagorno-Karabakh', *SA* 27 (1957) 135–77 [In Russian]

98. Kuzmina, E. E. 'Ancient Iranian and Near Eastern elements in Scythian art', *Persica* 11 (1984). Leiden

99. Lang, A. 'Zur Chronologie frühskythischer Funde im Karpatenbecken und an der unteren Donau', *Actes du II Congrès International de Thracologie* I, 229–33. Bucharest, 1980

100. Leskov, A. M. *The Crimean Mountains* [Gorny Krym] *in the First Millennium B.C.* Kiev, 1965 [In Russian]

101. Leskov, A. M. 'Works of the Kerch expedition of the Institute of Archaeology of the Academy of Sciences of the USSR', *AIU* (1967), 30–5 [In Russian]

102. Leskov, A. M. 'The Kirovskoe settlement', in *Antiquities of the Eastern Crimea*, 7–59. Kiev, 1970 [In Russian]

103. Leskov, A. M. 'The pre-Scythian period in the steppes of the northern Black Sea region', *MIA* 177 (1971) 75–91 [In Russian]

104. Leskov, A. M. 'Die skythische Kurgane', *Antike Welt*. Special number (1974)

105. Liberov, P.D. 'Sites of the Scythian period in the basin of the Northern Donets', *MIA* 113 (1962) 5–84. Moscow–Leningrad [In Russian]

106. Lincoln, B. 'On the Scythian royal burials', in Skomab, S. N. and Polomé, E. C. (eds.) *Proto-Indo-European: The Archaeology of a Linguistic Problem: Studies in Honor of Marija Gimbutas*, 267–85. Washington, 1987

107. Lordkipanidze, O. D. 'Colchis in the early antique period and her relations with the Greek world', *Archeologia* 19 (Warsaw, 1968) 281–305

108. Makalatiya, S. I. 'Excavations at the Dvany burial ground', *SA* 11 (1949) 225–40 [In Russian]

109. Maksimova, M. I. 'A silver mirror from the Kelermes kurgan', *SA* 21 (1956) 281–305 [In Russian]

110. Mantsevich, A. P. 'A bull's head from a 6th century B.C. kurgan on the river Kalitva', *SA* (1958) 2. 196–202 [In Russian]

111. Mantsevich, A. P. 'A Kalitva Folyó Melletti Kurgan', *Archaeologiai Ertesítö* (1961) 77–81

112. Mantsevich, A. P. *The Solokha Kurgan*. Leningrad, 1987

113. Marčenko, K. and Vinogradov, Y. 'The Scythian period in the northern Black Sea region (750–250 B.C.)', *Antiquity* 63 (1989), 803–13.

114. Markovin, V. I. *The Culture of the Tribes of the North Caucasus in the Bronze Age (2nd Millennium B.C.)*, *MIA* 93 (1960). Moscow–Leningrad [In Russian]

115. Markovin, V. I. 'Scythian kurgans near the village of Goity, Checheno-Ingushetia', *SA* (1965) 2. 160–74 [In Russian]

116. Markovin, V. I. *Dagestan and Gornaya Chechnia in Antiquity*. *MIA* 122 (1969). Moscow [In Russian]

117. Martinov, A. I. and Molodin, V. I. (eds.) *The Scytho-Siberian World*. Novosibirsk, 1987 [In Russian]

118. Martirosyan, A. A. *Armenia in the Bronze and Early Iron Ages*. Yerevan, 1974 [In Russian]

119. Masson, V. M. (ed.) *Ancient Cultures of the Eurasian Steppe*. Leningrad, 1983 [In Russian]

120. Masson, V. M. and Taylor, T. F. 'Soviet archaeology in the steppe zone: introduction', *Antiquity* 63 (1989) 779–83
121. Melikishvili, G. A. *Nairi-Urartu*. Tbilisi, 1954 [In Russian]
122. Melikishvili, G. A. *On the History of Ancient Georgia*. Tbilisi, 1959 [In Russian]
123. Meliukova, A. I. (ed.) *The Scytho-Siberian Animal Style in the Art of the Peoples of Eurasia*. Moscow, 1976 [In Russian]
124. Meliukova, A. I. *Scythia and the Thracian World*. Moscow, 1979 [In Russian]
125. Meliukova, A. I. *The Krasnokutsk Kurgan*. Moscow, 1981 [In Russian]
125A. Meliukova, A. I. (ed.) *The Steppes of the European Part of the USSR in the Scytho-Sarmatian Period* (The Archaeology of the USSR 20). Moscow, 1989
126. Metzner, C. 'Some aspects of Early Iron Age pre-Scythian horse-gear and its contexts in the South Central Soviet Union', in Hodgson, J. and Taylor, T. (eds.) *The First Millennium B.C. in Europe: New Work*. Oxford, forthcoming
127. Miller, M. *Archaeology in the USSR*. London, 1956
128. Minns, E. H. *Scythians and Greeks*. Cambridge, 1913
129. Minns, E. H. *The Art of the Northern Nomads* (Proceedings of the British Academy XXVIII). London, 1942
130. Mongait, A. L. *Archaeology in the USSR*. Moscow, 1955 [In Russian] (Transl. as D 131)
131. Mongait, A. L. *Archaeology in the USSR*. Transl. by M. Thompson. Harmondsworth, 1961. (Engl. transl. of D 130)
132. Moruzhenko, A. A. 'New data on the Nemirov town-site', *AO 1966* (1967) 201–2 [In Russian]
133. Moruzhenko, A. A. 'The defensive structures of the town-sites of the Vorskli region in the Scythian epoch', *The Scythian World*, 133–46. (Kiev, 1975) [In Russian]
134. Mozolevsky, B. M. *Tovsta Mogila* [Tolstaya Mogila]. Kiev, 1979 [In Ukrainian]
135. Mozolevsky, B. M. *The Scythian Steppe*. Kiev, 1983 [In Ukrainian]
136. Munchaev, R. M. 'The Catacomb culture and the northeastern Caucasus', in *New Work in Soviet Archaeology*, *MIA* 130 (1965) 92–6. Moscow–Leningrad [In Russian]
137. Murzin, B. U. *The Northern Black Sea Region in the Archaic Scythian Period*. Kiev, 1984 [In Russian]
138. Muscarella, O. W. 'The tumuli at Sé Girdan: a preliminary report', *MMJ* 2 (1969) 5–25
139. Muscarella, O. W. 'The tumuli at Sé Girdan: second report', in *MMJ* 4 (1971) 5–28
140. Muscarella, O. W. '"Ziwiye" and Ziwiye: the forgery of a provenience', *Journal of Field Archaeology* 4 (1977) 197–219
141. Olmstead, A. T. *History of Assyria*. New York–London, 1923
142. Onaiko, N. A. *Ancient Imports in the Dnieper and Bug Regions in the 7th–5th Centuries B.C.* Moscow, 1966 [In Russian]

143. Otroshchenko, V. V. 'Decorative elements in the art of the tribes of the Srubnaya culture', *SA* (1974) 4. 71–81 [In Russian]

144. Párducz, M. 'Le cimetière hallstattien de Szentes-Vekerzug III', *Acta arch. Hung.* 6 (1955) 1–22

145. Párducz, M. 'Graves from the Scythian age at Ártánd (county Hajdu-Bihar, Hungary)', *Acta arch. Hung.* 17 (1965) 137–231

146. Petrenko, V. G. 'The region of the right bank of the Middle Dnieper in the 5th–3rd centuries B.C.', *SAI* D 1–4 (1967) [In Russian]

147. Petrovska, E. O. (Petrovskaya, E. A.) 'A 6th century B.C. kurgan near the village of Mala Ofirna on the Kievshchina', *AK* 21 (1968) 164–74 [In Ukrainian]

148. Piotrovsky, B. B. *Karmir-Blur* I. Yerevan, 1950 [In Russian]

149. Piotrovsky, B. B. *Karmir-Blur* II. Yerevan, 1952 [In Russian]

150. Piotrovsky, B. B. *Karmir-Blur* III. Yerevan, 1955 [In Russian]

151. Piotrovsky, B. B. *The Kingdom of Van (Urartu)*. Moscow, 1959 [In Russian]

152. Piotrovsky, B. B. *The Art of Urartu, VIII–VI B.C.* Leningrad, 1962 [In Russian]

153. Piotrovsky, B. B., Galanina, L. and Grach, N. *Scythian Art.* Oxford–Leningrad, 1987

154. Piotrovsky, B. B., Zavitukhina, M. P. and Barkova, L. L. *Frozen Tombs. The Culture and Art of the Ancient Tribes of Siberia.* London, 1978

155. Piotrowicz, L. 'L'invasion de Scythes en Asie Antérieur en VIIe siècle av. J. C.', *Eos* 32 (1939) 473–508

156. Pippidi, D. M. *I greci nel basso Danubio dall'età arcaica alla conquista romana.* Milan, 1971

157. Pogrebova, N. N. 'Some Transcaucasian weapon forms of the early Scythian period', *KSIAM* 89 (1962) 22–9 [In Russian]

158. Pogrebova, N. N. 'Some Iranian daggers in the Caucasus', *KSIAM* 103 (1965) 11–18 [In Russian]

159. Pogrebova, N. N. 'On the migration of Iranian-speaking tribes to eastern Transcaucasia in the pre-Scythian era', *SA* 2 (1977) 55–68 [In Russian]

160. Pokrovska, E. F. 'Pre-Scythian settlement in the basin of the river Tiasmin', *AK* 5 (1951) [In Ukrainian]

161. Popova, T. B. *Tribes of the Catacomb Culture.* Moscow, 1955 [In Russian]

162. Potratz, H. A. *Die Skythen in Südrussland.* Basle, 1963

163. Potratz, H. A. *Die Pferdetrensen des Alten Orient* (An. Or. 41). Rome, 1966

164. Puzikova, A. I. 'Two kurgans from the Scythian period burial ground at the village of Russkaya Trostyanka', *KSIAM* 102 (1964) [In Russian]

165. Raevsky, D. S. *The Scythian Culture's World Model.* Moscow, 1985 [In Russian]

166. Rice, T. T. *The Scythians.* London, 1957

167. Rolle, R. 'Urartu und die Reiternomaden', *Saeculum* 28 (1977) 291–339

168. Rolle, R. *Totenkult der Scythen.* 2 vols. Berlin–New York, 1979
169. Rolle, R. *Die Welt der Skythen: Stutenmelker und Pferdebogner: ein antikes Reitervolk in neuer Sicht.* Lucerne–Frankfurt/M. 1980 (Transl. as D 171)
170. Rolle, R. 'Der griechische Handel der Antike zu den osteuropäischen Reiternomaden aufgrund archäologischer Zeugnisse', in Düwel *et al.* (eds.) *Untersuchungen zu Handel und Verkehr der vor- und frühgeschichtlichen Zeit in Mittel- und Nordeuropa,* 460–90. Göttingen, 1985
171. Rolle, R. *The World of the Scythians.* Transl. by Gayna Walls. London, 1989. (Engl. transl. of D 169)
172. Rostovtseff, M. *Iranians and Greeks.* Oxford, 1922
173. Rostovtzeff, M. *Skythien und der Bosporus.* Berlin, 1931
174. Rostovtzeff, M. *The Animal Style in South Russia and China.* Reissued New York, 1973
175. Rudenko, S. I. *Frozen Tombs of Siberia.* London, 1970
176. Rybakov, B. A. *Herodotus's Scythia: Historico-Geographical Analysis.* Moscow, 1979 [In Russian]
177. Schmidt, E. F. *The Alishar Hüyük. Season of 1928 and 1929* II. Chicago, 1933
178. Shchepinsky, L. A. 'Burials from the start of the Iron Age near Simferopol', *KSIAK* 18 (1962) 57–65 [In Russian]
179. Shilov, V. P. 'On the resettlement of the Maeotic tribes', *SA* 14 (1950) 102–23 [In Russian]
180. Shramko, B. A. *Antiquities of the Seversky Donets.* Kharkov, 1962 [In Russian]
181. Shramko, B. A. 'Scythian period settlement in the Donets basin', *AK* 14 (1962) 135–55 [In Ukrainian]
182. Shramko [Šramko], B. A. 'Der Ackerbau bei den Stämmen Skythiens im 7.–3. Jahrhundert v.u.Z.', *Slovenská Archeológia* 21 (1973) 147–66
183. Shramko, B. A. 'The eastern fortification of the Belsk town-site', in Terenozhkin, A. I. (ed.) *Scythian Antiquities.* Kiev, 1973 [In Russian]
184. Shramko, B. A. 'The fortress of the Scythian epoch at the village of Belsk – the town of Gelonus', in Terenozhkin, A. I. (ed.) *The Scythian World,* 94–132. Kiev, 1975 [In Russian]
185. Silanteva, L. F. 'The Nymphaion necropolis', in *The Necropoli of the Bosporan Towns, MIA* 69, 5–107, Moscow–Leningrad, 1959 [In Russian]
186. Sinitsin, M. S. (Synytsyn) 'The population of the Dniester–Bug Black Sea region in the Scytho-Sarmatian period', *MAPP* 4 (1959) 13–43. Odessa [In Ukrainian]
187. Smirnov, A. P. *The Scythians.* Moscow, 1966 [In Russian]
188. Smirnov, K. F. *Sauromatian Weaponry, MIA* 101. Moscow–Leningrad 1961 [In Russian]
189. Sulimirski, T. 'Scythian antiquities in Western Asia', *Artibus Asiae* 17 (1954) 382–18
190. Sulimirski, T. 'The Cimmerian problem', *BIA* 2 (1959) 45–64
191. Sulimirski, T. *Prehistoric Russia. An Outline.* London, 1970

192.   Sulimirski, T. *The Sarmatians*. London, 1970

193.   Tallgren, A. M. 'La Pontide préscythique après l'introduction des métaux', *ESA* 2 (1926)

194.   Taylor, T. F. 'Iron and Iron Age in the Carpatho-Balkan region: aspects of social and technological change 1700–400 B.C.', in Sørensen, M.-L. S. and Thomas, R. (eds.) *The Bronze Age–Iron Age Transition in Europe*, 68–92. Oxford, 1989

195.   Taylor, T. F. 'An Agighiol-type beaker in the Rogozen hoard', in Cook, B. F. (ed.) *The Rogozen Treasure*, 91–100. London, 1989

196.   Tekhov, B. V. *Scythians and the Central Caucasus in the 7th–6th Centuries B.C. (Based on Material from the Tli Cemetery)*. Moscow, 1980 [In Russian]

197.   Terenozhkin, A. I. *The pre-Scythian Period on the Right Bank of the Dnieper*. Kiev, 1961 [In Russian]

198.   Terenozhkin, A. I. (Festschrift) *Bronze Age Sites in the South of the European Part of the USSR*. Kiev, 1967 [In Russian]

199.   Terenozhkin, A. I. 'The date of the Mingechaur horse-bits', *SA* (1971) 4. 71–84 [In Russian]

200.   Terenozhkin, A. I. 'Cimmerian swords and daggers', in Terenozhkin, A. I. (ed.) *The Scythian World*, 3–34. Kiev, 1975 [In Russian]

201.   Terenozhkin, A. I. *The Cimmerians*. Kiev, 1976 [In Russian]

202.   Terenozhkin, A. I. *Scythia and the Caucasus: Collected Works*. Kiev, 1980 [In Ukrainian]

203.   Terenozhkin, A. I. and Mozolevsky, B. N. [B. M.] *The Melitopol Kurgan*. Kiev, 1988 [In Russian]

204.   Todd, E. *The Explanation of Ideology*. Oxford, 1985

205.   Trapsh, M. M. 'A new archaeological find in Abkhazia', *KSIIMK* 53 (1954) [In Russian]

206.   Trippett, F. *The First Horsemen*. New York, 1974

207.   Troitskaya, T.N. 'Finds from the Scythian kurgans of the Crimea, in the regional local studies museum', in *The History and Archaeology of the Ancient Ukraine, 174–90*. Kiev, 1957 [In Russian]

208.   Van Loon, M. N. *Urartian Art. Its Distinctive Traits in the Light of New Excavations*. Istanbul, 1966

209.   Vickers, M. *Scythian Treasures in Oxford*. Oxford, 1979

210.   Vinogradov, J. G. 'Die historische Entwicklung der Poleis des nördlichen Schwarzmeergebietes im 5 Jahrh. v.Chr.', *Chiron* 10 (1980) 63–100

211.   Vinogradov, V. B. 'New finds of Scytho-Siberian animal-style objects in Checheno-Ingushetia', *SA* (1974) 4. 258–63 [In Russian]

212.   Vishnevskaya, O. A. *The Culture of the Saka Tribes on the Lower Reaches of the Syr Darya in the 7th–5th Centuries B.C.* Moscow, 1973 [In Russian]

213.   Waşowicz, A. *Olbia pontique et son territoire*. Paris, 1975

214.   Waşowicz, A. 'Les indices de la civilisation et de l'hellénisation des côtes de la mer noire dans l'antiquité', *Dialogues d'histoire ancienne* 6 (1980) 29–39

215. Wilkinson, C. 'More details on Ziwiye', *Iraq* 22 (1960) 213–20
216. Wiseman, D. J. 'The vassal treaties of Esarhaddon', *Iraq* 20 (1958) 1–14
217. Yakovenko, E. V. 'Ordinary Scythian burials in the kurgans of the eastern Crimea', in *Antiquities of the Eastern Crimea*. Kiev, 1970 [In Russian]
218. Yakovenko, E. V. *Scythians of the 'Skhidni' Crimea in the 5th–3rd Centuries B.C.* Kiev, 1974 [In Ukrainian]
219. Yalagina, G. 'A Scythian anthropomorphic stele in Nikolaev Museum' *SA* (1959) 2. 187–96 [In Russian]
220. Yatsenko, I. V. *Scythia VII–V Centuries B.C.* Moscow, 1959 [In Russian]
221. Yegorov, N. M. 'A burial ground of the Scythian period near the town of Mineralnye Vody', *KSIIMK* 58 (1955) 53–62 [In Russian]
222. Zamyatin, S. N. 'The Scythian cemetery at "Chastye Kurgany" near Voronezh', *SA* 8 (1946) 9–50 [In Russian]
223. Zavitukhina, M. P. *Ancient Art on the Yenisei: the Scythian Period.* Leningrad, 1983 [In Russian]

II. THRACE

A full bibliography will be found in Georgieva, S. and Velkov, V. *Bibliographie de l'archéologie bulgare (1879–1966)*. 2nd edn. Sofia, 1974; Velkova, Ž. 'Die thrakische Sprachreste, Bibliographischer Anzeiger 1852–1965', *Ling. Balk.* 12 (1967) 155–84; *idem*, 'Die thrakische Sprache, bibliographischer Anzeiger 1966–1970', *ibid.* 16, 1 (1972) 55–63; *idem*, 'Die thrakische Sprache. Ausgewählte Bibliographie 1955–1974' in D 228A; and D 231 and D 232.

224. Best, J. G. P. *Thracian Peltasts and their Influence on Greek Warfare.* Groningen, 1969
225. Boneva, M. 'Helmet of Corinthian type from Čelopečene, region of Sofia', in *Muzei i pametnici na kulturata* 3, 2–7. Sofia, 1963. [In Bulgarian with summaries in French, German and English]
226. Čičikova, M. 'Sur la chronologie du Hallstatt en Thrace', *L'ethnogenèse des peuples balkaniques, Symposium international sur l'ethnogenèse des peuples balkaniques Plovdiv 1969*, 79–92. Sofia, 1971
227. Danov, Ch. M. *Altthrakien.* Berlin–New York, 1976
228. Detschew, D. *Die thrakischen Sprachreste.* Vienna, 1957
228A. Detschew, D. *Die thrakischen Sprachreste.* 2nd edn with bibliography 1955–1974 by Živka Velkova. Vienna, 1976
229. Dimitrov, B. 'On the "arrow-coins" of the west and north coasts of Pontus', *Archeologija* (Sofia, 1975) 2. 43–6. [In Bulgarian]
230. Filov, B. *Die Grabhügelnekropole bei Duvanlij in Südbulgarien.* Sofia, 1934
231. Fol, A. *Political History of the Thracians (from the End of the Second Millennium to the Fifth Century B.C.).* Sofia, 1972. [In Bulgarian with summary in English]
232. Fol, A. *Thrace and the Balkans in the Early Hellenistic Epoch.* Sofia, 1975. [In Bulgarian with summary in English]

233. Gazdapusztai, G. *Beziehungen zwischen den präskythischen Kulturen des Karpathenbeckens und des Nordkaukasus* (Beiträge zum s.g. Kimmerierproblem). Szeged, 1963

234. Georgiev, V. 'Identification and etymology of some Thracian rivernames', *Bâlgarski ezik* 10 (Sofia, 1960) 511–15. [In Bulgarian]

235. Gerasimov, T. 'Staters of the region of Pangaeum, found near Sofia', *Bull. Inst. Arch. Bulg.* 15 (1946) 237, 242; 17 (1950) 318; 18 (1952) 403. [In Bulgarian]

236. Gerasimov, T. 'Donnés numismatiques sur la ville d'Odrysa (Odrosa) en Thrace', *Studia Balcanica* 10 (1975) 45–8

237. Gerov, B. 'Untersuchungen über die westthrakischen Länder in römischer Zeit, Teil I–IV', *Annuaire Univ. Sofia, Fac. philol.* 54, 3 (1959–60); 61, 1 (1967); 62, 2 (1968); 63, 1 (1969). [In Bulgarian, with summary in German]

238. Haas, O. 'Die phrygischen Sprachdenkmäler', *Ling. Balk.* 10 (1966)

239. Hammond, N. G. L. 'The Philaids and the Chersonese', *CQ* 6 (1956) 113–29

240. Hammond, N. G. L. *A History of Macedonia* I. Oxford, 1972

241. Kazarov, G. *Beiträge zur Kulturgeschichte der Thraker.* Sarajevo, 1916

242. Mihailov, G. 'On the *strategiai* in Thrace', *Annuaire Univ. Sofia, Fac. Lettres* 61, 2 (1967) 40–1. [In Bulgarian with summary in French]

243. Mihailov, G. *The Thracians.* Sofia, 1972. [In Bulgarian with summary in French]

244. Mihailov, G. 'Sur l'alternance occlusive: s + occlusive en thrace', *Philologia* 2 (Sofia, 1977) 3–16

245. Mihailov, G. 'Sur le nom des Thraces', in *Mélanges V. Beševliev*, 168–73. Sofia, 1978

245A. Mihailov, G. 'La ville de Satra à Crète et la tribu thrace des Satres', *Klio* 62. 1 (1980) 13–18

246. Mihailov, G. 'Processus d'urbanisation de l'espace balkanique jusqu'à la fin de l'Antiquité', *Pulpudeva* 5, 1982 (Sofia, 1986) 5–30

246A. Mihailov, G. 'Homère comme source historique et les études thraces', *Ling. Balk.* 28 3. (1985) 19–42

247. Mócsy, A. 'Die Vorgeschichte Obermösiens in hellenistisch-römischer Zeitalter', *Acta ant. Hung.* 14 (1966) 87–112

248. Papazoglu, F. *The Macedonian Cities in the Roman Period.* Skopje, 1957. [In Serbo-Croat]

249. Papazoglu, F. *The Central Balkan Tribes in Pre-Roman Times.* Sarajevo, 1969. [In Serbo-Croat with summary in French]

250. Papazoglu, F. *The Central Balkan Tribes in Pre-Roman Times.* Amsterdam, 1978. (Engl. transl. of D 249)

250A. Papazoglu, F. *Les villes de Macédoine à l'époque romaine* (BCH suppl. XVI). Athens, 1988 (New edn of D 248)

251. Pouilloux, J. *Recherches sur l'histoire et les cultes de Thasos* I. Paris, 1954.

252. Popov, R. 'Finds from tumuli at Endže (Carevbrod), Šumen region', *Bull. Inst. Arch. Bulg.* 6 (1930–1) 89–116. [In Bulgarian with summary in German]

253. Sarafov, T. 'Les Thraces Satres', *Annuaire Univ. Sofia, Fac. Lettres* 67. 1 (1973) 121–91. [In Bulgarian with summary in French]

254. Tončeva, G. 'Two tomb-monuments of Thracian chieftains', *Thracia, primus congressus studiorum thracicorum* I, 101–19. Sofia, 1972. [In Bulgarian]

255. Tončeva, G. 'Dagger of Cimmerian type from Belogradec, Varna region', *Arheologija* 3. (Sofia, 1976) 52–6. [In Bulgarian with summary in French]

256. Velkov, V. 'Über den antiken Namen des Flusses Arda', *Izvestija (Bulletin) de l'Institut de la langue bulgare* 16 (1968) 79–85

257. Velkov, V. 'Thraker und Phryger nach den Epen Homers', *L'ethnogenèse des peuples balkaniques, Symposium international sur l'ethnogenèse des peuples balkaniques Plovdiv 1969*, 279–85. Sofia, 1971

258. Venedikov, I. 'La campagne de Darius contre les Scythes à travers la Thrace', *Studia Balcanica* (1970) 25–32

258A. Venedikov, I. 'Thracian toponymy in motion. The population of south-eastern Thrace', in Fol, A. (ed.) *Trakijski pametnici, Monumenta Thraciae antiquae* III, 32–170. Sofia, 1982

258B. Venedikov, I. *The Vulchitrun Treasure.* Sofia, 1987

259. Venedikov, I., Fol, A. *et al.* 'Megalithic remains in Thrace', in *Trakijski pametnici, Monumenta Thraciae antiquae* I. Sofia, 1976. [In Bulgarian with summary in French]

260. Venedikov, I. and Gerasimov, T. *Thracian Art Treasures.* Sofia–London, 1975. (The numismatic section only by Gerasimov)

261. Wiesner, J. *Die Thraker.* Stuttgart, 1963

262. Wirth, G. 'Zum Volksstamm der Treren', *Klio* 49 (1967) 47–51

E. ANATOLIA

I. HISTORY AND ARCHAEOLOGY

1. Akarca, A. 'Beçin', *Belleten* 137 (1971) 1–37

2. Åkerström, Å. *Die architektonischen Terrakotten kleinasiens* (Acta Instituti Atheniensis Regni Sueciae, Series in 4°, XI). Lund, 1966

3. Akkaya, M. 'Kaynarca Tümülüsü Frig Çağı Bronz Eserleri', *Eski Eserler ve Müzeler Bülteni* 11 (1987) 31–6

4. Akurgal, E. *Griechische Reliefs des VI. Jahrhunderts aus Lykien.* Berlin, 1942

5. Akurgal, E. *Phrygische Kunst.* Ankara, 1955

6. Akurgal, E. *Die Kunst Anatoliens von Homer bis Alexander.* Berlin, 1961

7. Akurgal. E. *Urartäische und altiranische Kunstzentren.* Ankara, 1968

8. Akurgal, E. and Hirmer, M. *Die Kunst der Hethiter.* Munich, 1961

9. Albright, W. F. 'Cilicia and Babylonia under the Chaldaean ⸛ ⸢ *BASOR* 120 (1950) 22–5

10. Balmuth, M. S. 'Remarks on the appearance of the earlies⸗ *Studies Presented to George M. A. Hanfmann*, 1–7. Cambridge

11. Barnett, R. D. 'Early Greek and Oriental ivories', *JHS* 68 (1948) 1–25

12. Barnett, R. D. 'Phrygia and the peoples of Anatolia in the Iron Age', in *CAH* $11^3.2$, chapter 30

13. Bass, G. F. 'Mycenaean and Protogeometric tombs in the Halicarnassus peninsula', *AJA* 67 (1963) 353–61

14. Bass, G. F. 'Oldest known shipwreck reveals Bronze Age splendors', *National Geographic* 172 (1987) 693–733

15. Bean, G. E. *Turkey's Southern Shore*. London, 1968

16. Bean, G. E. *Turkey beyond the Maeander*. London, 1971

17. Bellinger, A. R. 'Electrum coins from Gordion', in Kraay, C. M. and Jenkins, G. K. (eds.) *Essays in Greek Coinage Presented to Stanley Robinson*, 10–15. Oxford, 1968

18. Birmingham, J. M. 'The overland route across Anatolia in the eighth and seventh centuries B.C.', *Anat. Stud.* 11 (1961) 185–95

19. Bittel, K. *Kleinasiatische Studien (Istanbuler Mitteilungen 5)* Istanbul, 1942

20. Bittel, K. 'Çalapverdi', *Istanbuler Mitteilungen* 8 (1958) 132–6

21. Bittel, K. 'Phrygisches Kultbild aus Boğazköy', *Antike Plastik* 2 (1963) 7–22

22. Bittel, K. *Hattusha. The Capital of the Hittites*. New York, 1970

23. Bittel, K. *Die Hethiter. Die Kunst anatoliens vom Ende des 3. bis zum Anfang des 1. Jahrhunderts vor Christus*. Munich, 1976

24. Bittel, K. and Neve, P. 'Vorläufiger Bericht über die Ausgrabungen in Boğazköy im Jahr 1969', *MDOG* 102 (1970) 5–26

25. Bittel, K. *et al. Boğazköy*, v: *Funde aus den Grabungen 1970 und 1971*. Berlin, 1975

26. Boardman, J. 'Ionian bronze belts', *Anatolia* 6 (1961) 179–89

27. Boardman, J. *Excavations in Chios 1952–1955. Greek Emporio* (Supplementary volume No. 6, B.S. Athens). London, 1967

28. Boardman, J. *The Greeks Overseas*. 2nd edn. London, 1980

29. Bockisch, G. 'Die Karer und ihre Dynasten', *Klio* 51 (1969) 117–75

30. Boehmer, R. M. *Die Kleinfunde von Boğazköy* (WVDOG 87). Berlin, 1972

31. Boehmer, R. M. 'Phrygische Prunkgewänder des 8. Jahrhunderts vor Chr. Herkunft und Export', *Arch. Anz.* (1973) 149–72

32. Borchhardt, J. 'Bericht über die Grabungskampagne in Limyra 1983', *VI. Kazi Sonuçlari Toplantisi*, 419–34. Izmir, 1984 (Pottery referred to on p. 420 and figs. 6–7)

33. Boysal, Y. 'A report on the 1969 Turgut excavations', *Anadolu* 12 (1968) 81–93

34. Boysal, Y. *Katalog der Vasen im Museum von Bodrum*, 1: *Mykenisch-Protogeometrisch*. Ankara, 1969

35. Brixhe, C. *Le dialecte grec de Pamphylie* (Bibliothèque de l'Institut français d'Etudes anatoliennes d'Istanbul XXVI). Paris, 1976

36. Buluç, S. 'Ankara tumuli', *AJA* 72 (1968) 135–6; 73 (1969) 214; 74 (1970) 167

37. Buluç S. 'Ankara Kabartmaları', *IX. Türk Tarih Kongresi* 1, 423–33. Ankara, 1986

38. Buluç, S. 'Patara yüzey araştırmasının ön verileri hakkinda', *I. Araştirma Sonuçlari Toplantisi*, 139–44, 287–92. Istanbul, 1983

39. Bürchner, L. 'Karer' und 'Karia', P–W x (1919) 1940–7
40. Butler, H. C. *Sardis*, 1: *The Excavations*. Part 1. Leiden, 1922
41. Caner, E. *Fibeln in Anatolien*, 1: *Prähistorische Bronzefunde* xiv.8. Munich, 1983
42. Carpenter, J. and Boyd, D. 'Dragon-houses: Euboia, Attika, Karia', *AJA* 81 (1977) 179–215
43. Çınaroğlu, A. 'Ein neuer schwarzer Stein aus Tyana', *Epigraphica Anatolica* 5 (1985) 5–7
44. Cogan, M. and Tadmor, H. 'Gyges and Ashurbanipal', *Orientalia* 46 (1977) 65–85
45. Cummer, W. W. 'Phrygian roof-tiles in the Burdur Museum', *Anadolu* 14 (1970) 29–54
46. Demargne, P. *Fouilles de Xanthos*, 1: *Les piliers funéraires*. Paris, 1958
47. Demargne, P. and Metzger, H. 'Xanthos in Lykien', P–W ix a 2 (1967) 1375–1408
48. Dörtlük, K. *et al. Antalya Museum* (ed. E. and I. Özgen). Ankara, 1988
49. Firatli, N. 'Finds from the Phrygian necropolis of Ankara', *Belleten* 90 (1959) 206–8
50. Friedrich, J. 'Phrygia. Geschichte', P–W xx (1941) 882–91
51. Gall, H. von. 'Zu den kleinasiatischen Treppentunneln', *Arch. Anz.* (1967) 504–27
52. Garstang, J. and Gurney, O. R. *The Geography of the Hittite Empire*. London, 1959
53. Garstang, J. and Myres, J. L. 'The Black Stone of Tyana. Midas beyond the Halys', *LAAA* 1 (1907) 10–16
54. Gimbutas, M. 'Timber graves in southern Russia', *Expedition* 3.3 (1961) 14–22
55. Gimbutas, M. *Bronze Age Cultures in Central and Eastern Europe*. The Hague, 1965
56. Goetze, A. *Kleinasien* (Kulturgeschichte des alten Orients iii.1). Munich, 1957
57. Greenewalt, C. H., Jr. 'Lydian vases from western Asia Minor', *CSCA* 1 (1968) 139–54
58. Greenewalt, C. H., Jr. 'Orientalizing pottery from Sardis: the Wild Goat style', *CSCA* 3 (1970) 55–89
59. Greenewalt, C. H., Jr. 'The Sardis campaigns of 1979 and 1980', *BASOR* 249 (1983) 1–44
60. Greenewalt, C. H., Jr. 'The Sardis campaign of 1983', *BASOR* Suppl. 24 (1986) 1–30
61. Greifenhagen, A. 'Schmuck und Gerät eines lydischen Mädchens', *Antike Kunst* 8 (1965) 13–19
62. Greifenhagen, A. 'Ein östgriechisches Elfenbein', *Jahrbuch der Berliner Museen* 7 (1965) 125–56
63. Güterbock, H. G. 'Kleine Beiträge zum Verständnis der Ankara Reliefs', *Bagh. Mitt.* 7 (1974) 97–9
64. Güterbock, H. G. 'Seals and sealings in Hittite lands', in De Vries, K. (ed.) *From Athens to Gordion*, Memorial Symposium for Rodney S. Young. Philadelphia, 1980

65. Hanfmann, G. M. A. 'Horsemen from Sardis', *AJA* 49 (1945) 570ff

66. Hanfmann, G. M. A. 'Lydiaka', *Harvard Studies in Classical Philology* 63 (1958) 65–88

67. Hanfmann, G. M. A. *Sardis und Lydien* (Abh. Ak. der Wiss. Geistes- und Sozialwiss. Klasse No.6). Mainz, 1960

68. Hanfmann, G. M. A. *From Croesus to Constantine. The Cities of Western Asia Minor and their Arts in Greek and Roman Times* (Jerome lectures, tenth series). Ann Arbor, Michigan, 1975

69. Hanfmann, G. M. A. and Mierse, W. E. *Sardis from Prehistoric to Roman Times. Results of the Archaeological Expedition of Sardis 1958–1975.* Cambridge, Mass., 1983

70. Hanfmann, G. M. A. and Ramage, N. H. *Sculpture from Sardis: The Finds through 1975.* Cambridge, Mass., 1978

71. Hanfmann, G. M. A. and Waldbaum, J. 'Kybebe and Artemis. Two Anatolian Goddesses at Sardis', *Archaeology* 22 (1969) 264–9

72. Hanfmann, G. M. A. and Waldbaum, J. 'New excavations at Sardis and some problems of Western Anatolian archaeology', in *Essays in Honor of Nelson Glueck. Near Eastern Archaeology in the Twentieth Century*, 307–26. New York, 1970

73. Hanfmann, G. M. A. *et al.* Sardis excavation reports in: *BASOR* 154 (1959) 5–35; 157 (1960) 8–43; 158 (1960) 1–11; 162 (1961) 8–49; 166 (1962) 1–57; 170 (1963) 1–65; 174 (1964) 3–58; 177 (1965) 2–37; 182 (1966) 2–54; 186 (1967) 17–52; 191 (1968) 2–41; 199 (1970) 7–58; 203 (1971) 5–22; 206 (1972) 9–39; 211 (1973) 14–36; 215 (1974) 31–60

74. Haspels, G. H. E. *The Highlands of Phrygia. Sites and Monuments* I–II. Princeton, 1971

75. Hawkins, J. D. 'The negatives in Hieroglyphic Luwian', *Anat. Stud.* 25 (1975) 120–56

76. Houwink ten Cate, P. H. J. *The Luwian Population Groups of Lycia and Cilicia Aspera during the Hellenistic Period.* Leiden, 1961

77. Houwink ten Cate, P. H. J. 'Kleinasien zwischen Hethitern und Persern', in *Fischer Weltgeschichte. Die altorientalischen Reiche*, III: *Die erste Hälfte des 1. Jahrtausends*, 112–34. Frankfurt/Main, 1967

78. Huxley, G. L. *The Early Ionians.* London, 1966

79. Kaletsch, H. 'Zur lydischen Chronologie', *Historia* 7 (1958) 1–47

80. Kjeldsen, K. and Zahle, J. 'Lykische Gräber', *Arch. Anz.* (1975) 312–50

81. Kohler, E. L. 'Phrygian animal style and nomadic art', in *Dark Ages and Nomads c. 1000 B.C.*, 58–62. Istanbul, 1964

82. Kohler, E. L. *The Lesser Tumuli: The Inhumations* (Gordion Final Excavation Reports II:1). Philadelphia, 1991

83. Körte, G. and A. *Gordion. Ergebnisse der Ausgrabung im Jahre 1900* (*JDAI*, Ergänzungsheft 5). Berlin, 1904

84. Koşay, H. Z. *Les fouilles de Pazarli entreprises par la Société d'Histoire turque.* Ankara, 1941

85. Kraay, C. M. *Archaic and Classical Greek Coins.* London, 1976

86. Kuniholm, P. I. 'Dendrochronology at Gordion and on the Anatolian

Plateau'. University Microfilms, Ann Arbor, 1979

87. *Labraunda. Swedish Excavations and Researches*, 1.1: Jeppesen, K. *The Propylaea*. Lund, 1955. 1.2: Westholm, A. *The Architecture of the Hieron*. Lund, 1963. (Acta Instituti Atheniensis Regni Sueciae v.1: 1 and 2)

88. Laroche, E. 'Lyciens et Termiles', *Rev. Arch.* (1976) 1. 15–19

89. Laumonier, A. *Les Cultes indigènes en Carie* (Bibliothèque des écoles françaises d'Athènes et de Rome 188). Paris, 1958

90. Mellink, M. J. 'Excavations at Karataş-Semayük in Lycia', *AJA* 68 (1964) 269–78; 69 (1965) 241–51; 70 (1966) 245–55; 71 (1967) 251–67; 72 (1968) 243–63; 73 (1969) 319–31; 74 (1970) 245–59; 75 (1971) 245–55; 76 (1972) 257–69; 77 (1973) 293–307; 78 (1974) 351–9; 78 (1975) 349–55; 79 (1976) 377–84

91. Mellink, M. J. 'The Early Bronze Age in southwest Anatolia. A start in Lycia', *Archaeology* 22 (1969) 290–9

92. Mellink, M. J. 'Local, Phrygian and Greek traits in northern Lycia', *Rev. Arch.* (1976) 1. 21–34

93. Mellink, M. J. 'Midas in Tyana', *Florilegium Anatolicum* (Mélanges E. Laroche), 249–57. Paris, 1979

94. Mellink, M. J. 'Comments on a cult relief of Kybele from Gordion', *Beiträge zur Altertumskunde Kleinasiens*. Festschrift for K. Bittel, 349–60. Mainz, 1983.

95. Metzger, H. *L'Acropole lycienne* (Fouilles de Xanthos II). Paris, 1963

96. Metzger, H. 'Fouilles du Létoon de Xanthos', *Rev. Arch.* (1974) 2. 313–40

97. Metzger, H. *Les céramiques archaiques et classiques de l'Acropole* (Fouilles de Xanthos IV). Paris, 1972

98. Mørkholm, O. and Zahle, J. 'The coinage of Kuprilli', *Acta Archaeologica* 43 (1972) 57–113

99. Muscarella, O. *Phrygian Fibulae from Gordion*. London, 1967

100. Neumann, G. 'Phryger', *Der Kleine Pauly* 4 (1972) 822–6

101. Neve, P. 'Hattusha in nachhethitischer Zeit', *Mélanges Mansel*, 873–91. Ankara, 1974

102. Neve, P. 'Boğazköy', *Türk Arkeoloji Dergisi* 22.2 (1975) 93–119

103. Neve, P. *Die Bauwerke von Büyükkale in Boğazköy* (Boğazköy-Hattuša XII). Berlin, 1981

104. Nougayrol, J., Laroche, E., Virolleaud, C. and Schaeffer, C. F. A. *Ugaritica* V (Mission de Ras Shamra XVI). Paris, 1968

105. Nylander, C. *Ionians in Pasargadae* (Acta Universitatis Upsaliensis, Boreas 1). Uppsala, 1970

106. Olfers, J. F. M. von. *Über die lydischen Königsgräber bei Sardes und den Grabhügel des Alyattes* (Abh. Ak. Wiss. Berlin 1858) (1859) 539–56

107. Oppenheim, A. L. *The Interpretation of Dreams in the Ancient Near East with a Translation of an Assyrian Dream-Book* (Transactions of the American Philosophical Society NS 46/3). Philadelphia, 1956

108. Orchard, J. J. *Equestrian Bridle-Harness Ornaments (Ivories from Nimrud* 1.2). British School of Archaeology in Iran, 1967

109. Özgüç, T. and Akok, M. 'Die Ausgrabungen an zwei Tumuli auf dem

Mausoleumshügel bei Ankara', *Belleten* 41 (1947) 57–85

110. Özgüç, T. *Kültepe and its Vicinity in the Iron Age* (Türk Tarih Kurumu v, 29). Ankara, 1971

111. Pedley, J. G. *Sardis in the Age of Croesus*. Norman, Oklahoma, 1968

112. Pedley, J. G. *Ancient Literary Sources on Sardis* (Archaeological Exploration of Sardis Monograph 2). Cambridge, Mass., 1972

113. Postgate, J. N. 'Sargon's letter referring to Midas', *Iraq* 35 (1973) 21–34

114. Pryce, F. N. *Catalogue of Sculpture in the Department of Greek and Roman Antiquities, British Museum*, 1.1: *Prehellenic and Early Greek*. London, 1928

115. Radt, W. *Siedlungen und Bauten auf der Halbinsel von Halikarnassos* (*Istanbuler Mitteilungen* Beiheft 3). Tübingen, 1970

116. Ramage, A. 'Lydian Sardis', in Guralnick, E. (ed.) *Sardis. Twenty-seven Years of Discovery*. Chicago, 1987

117. Ramage, A. and N. H. 'The siting of Lydian burial mounds', in *Studies Presented to George M. A. Hanfmann*. Cambridge, Mass., 1971

118. Roebuck, C. *Ionian Trade and Colonization* (Monographs on Archaeology and Fine Arts, Archaeological Institute of America). New York, 1959

119. Röllig, W. 'Gyges', in *Reallexikon der Assyriologie* III, 720–1. Berlin, 1957–71

120. Röllig, W. *Epigraphica Anatolica*, forthcoming

121. Şahin, M. Ç. *The Political and Religious Structure in the Territory of Stratonikeia in Caria*. Ankara, 1976

122. Sams, G. K. 'Phrygian painted animals: Anatolian orientalizing art', *Anat. Stud.* 24 (1974) 169–96

123. Schuler, E. von. *Die Kaškäer. Ein Beitrag zur Ethnographie des alten Kleinasien*. Berlin, 1965

124. Serdaroğlu, Ü. '1971–72 Hacibayramlar Kazisi', *Anadolu* 16 (1972) 77–84

125. Simpson, E. 'Reconstructing an ancient table', *Expedition* 25.4 (1983) 11–26

126. Simpson, E. and Payton, R. 'Royal wooden furniture from Gordion', *Archaeology* 39.6 (1986) 40–8

127. Temizer, R. 'Un bas-relief de Cybèle découvert à Ankara', *Anatolia* 4 (1959) 179–87

128. Tezcan, B. 'Göllüdağ', *AJA* 73 (1969) 213–14; *AJA* 74 (1970) 167; *Türk Arkeoloji Dergisi* 17.2 (1969) 211–35

129. Tezcan, B. 'Ikiztepe Kazisi', *VIII. Türk Tarih Kongresi, Ankara 11–15 Ekim 1976* I (1979) 391–7

130. Tezcan, B. 'Hacituğrul-Yenidoğan', *AJA* 77 (1973) 179–80; 78 (1974) 117; 79 (1975) 210; 80 (1976) 272

131. Thompson, M. 'Some noteworthy Greek accessions. Lydia', *Museum Notes* 12 (1966) 1–4 (American Numismatic Society)

132. Thureau-Dangin, F. and Dunand, M. *Til-Barsib* (Bibliothèque Archéologique et Historique XXIII). Paris, 1936

133. Treuber, O. *Geschichte der Lykier*. Stuttgart, 1887

134. Uçankuş, H. 'Emirdaği 'nda yeni bulunan bir Hitit kabartmasi', *Belleten* 139 (1971) 359–66

135. Uçankuş, H. 'Afyon'un Tatarli kasabasinda bulunan Phryg tümülüsü kazisi', *VIII. Türk Tarih Kongresi, Ankara 11–15 Ekim 1976*, I (1979) 305–33

136. Varinlioğlu, E. 'Eine neue altphrygische Inschrift aus Tyana', *Epigraphica Anatolica* 5 (1985) 8–12

137. Weissbach. 'Kroisos', P–W Suppl. 5 (1931) 457–8

138. Werner, R. 'Die Phryger und ihre Sprache', *Bi. Or.* 26 (1969) 177–82

139. Young, R. S. *Gordion* excavation reports in: *AJA* 59 (1955) 1–18; 60 (1956) 249–66; 61 (1957) 319–31; 62 (1958) 139–54; 63 (1959) 263–8 (by G. R. Edwards); 64 (1960) 227–44; 66 (1962) 153–68; 68 (1964) 279–92; 70 (1966) 267–78; 72 (1968) 231–41; 74 (1970) 167; 76 (1972) 177–8; 78 (1974) 117

140. Young, R. S. 'Phrygian furniture from Gordion', *Expedition* 16.3 (1974) 2–13

141. Young, R. S. *Gordion. A Guide to the Excavations and Museum.* Ankara, 1975

142. Young, R. S. 'Gordion', in Stillwell, R. (ed.) *The Princeton Encyclopedia of Classical Sites.* Princeton, 1976

143. Young, R. S. *Three Great Early Tumuli* (University Museum Monograph 43. The Gordion Excavations Final Reports I). Philadelphia, 1981

II. LANGUAGES

I. PHRYGIAN

144. Brixhe, C. 'Un ouvrage sur la langue phrygienne', *Rev. de Philol.* (1968), 306–19 (concerning E 157, below)

145. Brixhe, C. 'Problèmes d'interprétation du phrygien', *Le déchiffrement des écritures et des langues*, 65–74. Paris, 1975

146. Brixhe, C. 'Etudes néo-phrygiennes…', *Verbum* (Nancy), I/1 (1978) 3–21; I/2 (1978) 1–22; II/2 (1979) 177–82

147. Brixhe, C. in Young, R. S., *Three Great Early Tumuli = The Gordion Excavations*, Final Report I, 273–7. Philadelphia, 1981

148. Brixhe, C. 'Palatalisations en grec et en phrygien', *Bull. Soc. Ling.* 77 (1982) 209–49

149. Brixhe, C. and Drew-Bear, T. 'Un nouveau document néo-phrygien', *Kadmos* 17 (1978) 50–4

150. Brixhe, C. and Drew-Bear, T. 'Trois nouvelles inscriptions paléo-phrygiennes de Çepi', *Kadmos* 21 (1982) 64–87

151. Brixhe, C. and Lejeune, M. *Corpus des inscriptions paléo-phrygiennes* I: Texte, II: Planches. Paris, 1984

152. Brixhe, C. and Waelkens, M. 'Un nouveau document néo-phrygien au musée d'Afyon', *Kadmos* 20 (1981) 68–75

153. Calder, W. M. *Monuments from Eastern Phrygia* (Monumenta Asiae Minoris Antiqua VII), *passim.* Manchester, 1956

154. Friedrich, J. *Kleinasiatische Sprachdenkmäler*, chapter x, 'Phrygische Sprache', 123–40. Berlin, 1932. (With bibliography to 1932; texts cited as '1 F', etc.)

155. Friedrich, J. 'Phrygia (Sprache)', P–W 1941, 868–81

156. Gusmani, R. 'Studi Frigi', *Rendic. Ist. Lombardo* 92 (1958) 835–928 and 93 (1959) 17–49

157. Haas, O. 'Die phrygischen Sprachdenkmäler', *Ling. Balk.* 10 (1966) 1–260, with complements *ibid.* 19 (1976) 3, 49–82 and 4, 53–71.

158. Heubeck, A. 'Bemerkungen zu den neuphrygischen Fluchformeln', *Indogermanische Forschungen* 64 (1958) 13–25

159. Lejeune, M. 'Discussions sur l'alphabet phrygien', *Studi Micenei ed egeo-anatolici* 10 (1969) 19–47

160. Lejeune, M. 'Les inscriptions de Gordion et l'alphabet phrygien', *Kadmos* 9 (1970) 51–74

161. Neroznak, V. P. *Paleobalkanskije jazyki*, 66–155. Moscow, 1978 [Phrygian inscriptions and glosses]

162. Neumann, G. 'Bruchstücke alphabetischer Schriftdenkmäler aus Boğazköy', *Boğazköy* v, 76–84. Berlin, 1975

163. Neumann, G. 'Die altphrygische Inschrift von Firanlar Köyü', *Kadmos* 20 (1981) 143–9

164. Tuğrul, L. and Fıratlı, N. 'The Phrygian inscription of Germanos', *Annual of the Archaeological Museums of Istanbul* 13–14 (1966) 236–41

165. Young, R. S. 'Old Phrygian inscriptions from Gordion', *Hesperia* 38 (1969) 252–96

2. LYDIAN

166. Carruba, O. 'Studi sul verbo lidio', *Athenaeum* 38 (1960) 26–64

167. Carruba, O. 'Lydisch und Lyder', *MIO* 8 (1963) 383–408

168. Friedrich, J. *Kleinasiatische Sprachdenkmäler*, chapter ix, 'Lydische Texte', 108–23. Berlin, 1932. (With bibliography to 1932; inscriptions numbered as in the corpus by Buckler, W. H., *Sardis* vi, Part ii, Lydian Inscriptions. Leiden, 1924)

169. Gusmani, R. 'Studi Lidi', *Rend. Ist. Lombardo* 94 (1960) 275–98

170. Gusmani, R. 'Nuovi contributi lidi', *Rend. Ist. Lombardo* 95 (1961) 173–200

171. Gusmani, R. *Lydisches Wörterbuch*, Heidelberg, 1964, with Supplements 1, 2, 3, 1980, 1982 and 1986

172. Gusmani, R. 'Sulle consonanti del lidio', *Or. Ant.* 4 (1965) 203–10

173. Gusmani, R., 'Lydische Siegelaufschriften und Verbum Substantivum', *Kadmos* 11 (1972) 47–54

174. Gusmani, R. *Neue epichorische Schriftzeugnisse aus Sardis (1958–1971)* (Archaeological Exploration of Sardis Monograph 3), Cambridge, Mass., 1975. Teil A, Lydische Sprachdenkmäler, 1–62; Teil D, Die Inschrift der Synagoge, 113–32

175. Gusmani, R. 'Die lydische Sprache', *JAOS* (1975) 134–42 (with bibliography for 1964–75)

176. Gusmani, R. 'Lydiaka', *Or. Ant.* 14 (1975) 265–74
177. Gusmani, R. 'Zwei lydische Inschriften aus Sardis', *Kadmos* 18 (1979) 71–9
178. Gusmani, R. 'Ein Weihrauchbrenner mit lydischer Inschrift im Metropolitan Museum', *Kadmos* 22 (1983) 56–60
179. Gusmani, R. 'Zwei lydische Neufunde aus Sardis', *Kadmos* 24 (1985) 74–83
180. Heubeck, A. *Lydiaka, Untersuchungen zu Schrift, Sprache und Götternamen der Lyder.* Erlangen, 1959
181. Heubeck, A. 'Vermutungen zum Plural des Lydischen', *Orbis* 12 (1963) 537–50
182. Heubeck, A. 'Lydisch', in *Handbuch der Orientalistik,* volume *Altkleinasiatische Sprachen,* 397–427. Leiden, 1969
183. Heubeck, A. 'Ueberlegungen zur Entstehung der lydischen Schrift', *Kadmos* 17 (1978) 55–66
184. Heubeck, A. 'Zur lydischen Inschrift Nr. 62 (Tire)', *Kadmos* 19 (1980) 50–3
185. Heubeck, A. 'Lydische Marginalien', *Kadmos* 22 (1983) 61–8
186. Meriggi, P. 'Die erste Person Singularis im Lydischen', *RHA* 5 (1935) 69–116
187. Meriggi, P. 'Der indogermanische Charakter des Lydischen', *Festschrift H. Hirt* II, 283–90. Heidelberg, 1936
188. Ševoroškin, V. V. *Lidijskij jazyk,* Moscow, 1967 [In Russian]
189. Vetter, E. 'Zu den lydischen Inschriften', *Sitzungsb. Wien,* Phil.-hist. Klasse 232.3 (1959) 1–61
190. West, M. L. 'Lydian metre', *Kadmos* 11 (1972) 165–75
191. Zgusta, L. 'Lydian interpretations', *Ar. Or.* 23 (1955) 510–44

3. LYCIAN

192. Bryce, T. R. *The Lycians in Literary and Epigraphic Sources.* Copenhagen, 1986
193. Carruba, O. *Die satzeinleitende Partikeln in den indogermanischen Sprachen Anatoliens* (Incunabula Graeca XXXII). Rome, 1969
194. Carruba, O. 'Contributi al licio', *Studi Micenei ed egeo-anatolici* 11 (1970) 27–42, and 22 (1980) 275–96
195. Friedrich, J. *Kleinasiatische Sprachdenkmäler,* chapter VII, 'Lykische Texte', 52–90. Berlin, 1932. With bibliography to 1932; inscriptions numbered as in the corpus by Kalinka, E., *Tituli Lyciae lingua Lycia conscripti* (TAM I) Vienna, 1901
196. Gusmani, R. 'Concordanze e discordanze nella flessione nominale del licio e del luvio', *Rend. Ist. Lombardo* 94 (1960) 497–512
197. Gusmani, R. 'Zur Deutung einiger milyischer Wörter', *Ar. Or.* 36 (1968) 1–18
198. Gusmani, R. 'In margine alla trilingue licio-greco-aramaica di Xanthos', *Incontri Linguistici* (Trieste) 2 (1975) 61–75

199. Heubeck, A. 'Ueberlegungen zum lykischen Plural', *Incontri Linguistici* (Trieste) 2 (1975) 77–88

200. Heubeck, A. 'Zur lykischen Verbalflexion', *Serta Indogermanica, Festschrift G. Neumann*, 107–19. Innsbruck, 1982

201. Heubeck, A. 'Weiteres zur lykischen Verbalflexion', *Zeitschr. vergl. Sprachforschung* 95 (1981) 158–73

202. Houwink ten Cate, Ph. *The Luwian Population Groups of Lycia and Cilicia Aspera during the Hellenistic Period.* Leiden, 1961

203. Laroche, E. 'Comparaison du louvite et du lycien': [I] *Bull. Soc. Ling.* 53 (1957–8), 159–97; [II] *ibid.* 55 (1960), 155–85; [III] *ibid.* 62 (1967), 46–66

204. Laroche, E. 'La stèle trilingue récemment découverte au Létôon de Xanthos: le texte lycien', *CRAI* (1974), 115–25

205. Laroche, E. 'Les épitaphes lyciennes', in *Fouilles de Xanthos* V, 123–49. Paris, 1974

206. Laroche, E. 'Lyciens et Termiles', *Rev. Arch.* (1976), 15–19

207. Laroche, E. 'L'inscription lycienne', in *Fouilles de Xanthos*, VI. *La stèle trilingue du Létôon*, 49–127. Paris, 1979. (In the same volume, contributions by Metzger, H., Dupont-Sommer, A., Mayrhofer, M.)

208. Meriggi, P. 'Der Indogermanismus des Lykischen', *Festschrift H. Hirt* II, 257–82. Heidelberg, 1936

209. Meriggi, P. 'Su alcune strofe miliache della Stele di Xanthos', *Mélanges E. Boisacq* II, 143–54. Brussels, 1938

210. Meriggi, P. 'La declinazione del licio', I: *Rendic. Acc. Lincei* (1929) 408–50; II: *ibid.* (1979) 243–68

211. Mørkholm, O. and Neumann, G. 'Die lykischen Münzlegenden', *Nachr. Göttingen* (1978) 1.1–38

212. Neumann, G. 'Beiträge zum Lykischen': I: *Die Sprache* 7 (1961) 70–6; II: *ibid.* 8 (1962) 203–12; III: *ibid.* 13 (1967) 31–8; IV: *ibid.* 16 (1970) 54–62; V: *ibid.* 20 (1974) 109–14; VI: *ibid.* 30 (1984) 89–95

213. Neumann, G. 'Lykisch', in *Handbuch der Orientalistik*, volume *Altkleinasiatische Sprachen*, 358–96. Leiden, 1969

214. Neumann, G. 'Die lykischen Grabinschriften von Myra', in Borchhardt, J. (ed.) *Myra, eine lykische Metropole* (Istanbuler Forschungen 30) (1975) 150–6

215. Neumann, G. 'Neufunde lykischer Inschriften seit 1901', *Oesterreichische Akademie der Wissenschaften*, Denkschriften, 135 (1979) 5–57

216. Neumann, G. *Glossar des Lykischen.* In preparation

217. Pedersen, H. *Lykisch und Hittitisch (Danske Videnskabernen Selskab, Histor.-Filol. Meddelelser* 30.4), 1945

218. Pembroke, S. 'Last of the matriarchs: a study in the inscriptions of Lycia', *JESHO* 8 (1965) 217–47

219. Schmitt, R. 'Iranische Wörter und Namen im Lykischen', *Serta Indogermanica, Festschrift G. Neumann*, 373–88, 1982

220. Tritsch, F. J. 'Lycian, Luwian and Hittite', *Ar. Or.* 18, 1–2 (1950) 494–518

221. Tritsch, F. J. 'The Lycian bilingual in Stoichedon from Korydalla', *Kadmos* 15 (1976) 158–67

4. CARIAN

222. Brandenstein, W. 'Karische Sprache', P–W Suppl. VI (1935) 140–6
223. Deroy, L. 'Les inscriptions cariennes de Carie', *Antiquité classique* 24 (1955) 305–35
224. Friedrich, J. *Kleinasiatische Sprachdenkmäler*, chapter VIII, 'Karische Texte', 90–107. Berlin, 1932. (With bibliography to 1932)
225. Gusmani, R. *Neue epichorische Schriftzeugnisse aus Sardis* . . . (Archaeological Exploration of Sardis Monograph 3), 79–111. Cambridge, Mass., 1975
226. Gusmani, R. 'Zwei neue Gefässinschriften in karischer Sprache', *Kadmos* 17 (1978) 67–75
227. Jucker, H. and Meier-Brügger, M. 'Eine Bronzephiale mit karischer Inschrift', *Museum Helveticum* 35 (1978) 109–15
228. Kowalski, T. W. 'Lettres cariennes: essai de déchiffrement de l'écriture carienne', *Kadmos* 14 (1975) 73–93
229. Masson, O. 'Que savons-nous de l'écriture et de la langue des Cariens?', *Bull. Soc. Ling.* 68 (1973) 187–213. (With detailed bibliography for 1932–72)
230. Masson, O. 'Un nouveau fragment d'inscription carienne de Kaunos', *Anadolu – Anatolia* 17 (1973) [1975] 123–31
231. Masson, O. 'Le nom des Cariens dans quelques langues de l'antiquité', *Mélanges linguistiques offerts à E. Benveniste*, 407–14. Paris, 1975
232. Masson, O. 'Notes d'épigraphie carienne, I–II', 'III–V', *Kadmos* 13 (1974) 124–32; 16 (1977) 87–94
233. Masson, O. 'Un lion de bronze de provenance égyptienne avec inscription carienne', *Kadmos* 15 (1976) 82–3
234. Masson, O. *Carian Inscriptions from North Saqqara and Buhen*, with contributions by G. T. Martin and R. V. Nicholls, Egypt Exploration Society. London, 1978
235. Masson, O. and Yoyotte, J. *Objets pharaoniques à inscription carienne* (IFAO, Bibliothèque d'étude XV). Cairo, 1956
236. Meier-Brügger, M. 'Karika, I', 'II–III', *Kadmos* 17 (1978) 76–84; 18 (1979), 80–8
237. Meier-Brügger, M. 'Ein Buchstabenindex zu den karischen Schriftdenkmälern aus Aegypten', *Kadmos* 18 (1979) 130–77
238. Meier-Brügger, M. *Die karischen Inschriften* [aus Labraunda] = *Labraunda, Swedish Excavations and Researches* II.4. Stockholm, 1983
239. Meriggi, P. 'Zur neuen "para-karischen" Schrift', *Kadmos* 5 (1966) 61–102
240. Neumann, G. 'Eine neue Inschrift aus Chalketor', *Kadmos* 8 (1969) 152–7
241. Ray, J. D. 'An approach to the Carian script', *Kadmos* 20 (1981) 150–62
242. Ray, J. D. 'The Carian inscriptions from Egypt', *JEA* 68 (1982) 181–98

243. Ray, J. D. 'The Carian script', *PCPhS* 208 (1982) 177–88
244. Ray, J. D. 'The Egyptian approach to Carian', *Kadmos* 26 (1987) 98–103
245. Robert, L. 'Inscriptions inédites en langue carienne', *Hellenica* VIII (1950) 5–22
246. Şahin, M. Ç. 'A Carian and three Greek inscriptions from Stratonikeia', *ZPE* 39 (1980) 205–13
247. Ševoroškin, V. V. 'On Karian', *RHA* 22 (1964) 1–55
248. Ševoroškin, V. V. *Issledovanija po desifrovke karijskich nadpisej.* Moscow, 1965 [In Russian]
249. Ševoroškin, V. V. 'Zur Entstehung und Entwicklung der kleinasiatischen Buchstaben', *Kadmos* 7 (1968) 150–73
250. Ševoroškin, V. V. 'Zu einigen karischen Wörtern', *Münchener Studien zur Sprachwissenschaft* 36 (1977) 117–30
251. Zauzich, K.-T. *Einige karische Inschriften aus Aegypten und Kleinasien und ihre Deutung nach der Entzifferung der karischen Schrift.* Wiesbaden, 1972
252. Zgusta, L. *Kleinasiatische Personennamen.* Prague, 1964

F. EGYPT

1. Adams, W. Y. *Nubia. Corridor to Africa.* London, 1977
2. Aldred, C. 'The Carnarvon statuette of Amūn', *JEA* 42 (1956) 3–7
3. Aldred, C., Daumas, F., Desroches-Noblecourt, C. and Leclant, J. *L'Égypte du crépuscule.* Paris, 1980
4. Alexander, J. A. and Driskell, B. 'Qaṣr Ibrîm 1984', *JEA* 71 (1985) 12–26
5. Arkell, A. J. 'Varia Sudanica', *JEA* 36 (1950) 24–40
6. Arkell, A. J. 'An Egyptian invasion of the Sudan in 519 B.C.', *Kush* 3 (1955) 93–4
7. Baer, K. 'The Libyan and Nubian kings of Egypt: notes on the chronology of Dynasties XXII to XXVI', *JNES* 32 (1973) 4–25
8. Bakry, H. S. K. 'Psammetichus II and his newly-found stela at Shellâl', *Or. Ant.* 6 (1967), 235–44
9. Barguet, P. *Le livre des morts des anciens Egyptiens.* Paris, 1967
10. Barns, J. W. B. 'Egypt and the Greek romance', in *Akten des VIII. Internationalen Kongresses für Papyrologie, Wien 1955.* Vienna, 1956
11. Barta, W. 'Die Mondfinsternis im 15. Regierungsjahre Takelots II. und die Chronologie der 22. bis 25. Dynastie', *Rev. d'égyptol.* 32 (1980) 3–17
12. Basta, M. 'Excavations in the desert road at Dahshur', *Ann. Serv.* 60 (1968) 57–63
13. Beckerath, J. von. 'The Nile level records at Karnak and their importance for the history of the Libyan period (Dynasties XXII–XXIII)', *JARCE* 5 (1966) 43–55
14. Bierbrier, M. L. *The Late New Kingdom in Egypt (c. 1300–664 B.C.).* Warminster, 1975
15. Bietak, M. *Tell el-Dabʿa* II. Vienna, 1975
16. Bietak, M. and Reiser-Haslauer, E. *Das Grab des ʿAnch-Hor* I. Vienna, 1978

17. Bothmer, B. V. *et al. Egyptian Sculpture of the Late Period: 700 B.C. to A.D. 100.* Brooklyn, 1960

18. Breasted, J. H. *Ancient Records of Egypt.* 5 vols. Chicago, 1906

19. Bresciani, E., Pernigotti, S. and Giangeri Silvis, M. P. *La tomba di Ciennehebu, capo della flotta del re.* Pisa, 1977

20. British Museum, *A Guide to the Fourth, Fifth and Sixth Egyptian Rooms and the Coptic Room.* London, 1922

21. British Museum, *Ancient Egyptian Sculpture lent by C. S. Gulbenkian, Esq.* London, 1937

22. Brunner, H. 'Zum Verständnis der archaisierenden Tendenzen in der ägyptischen Spätzeit', *Saeculum* 21 (1970) 151–61

23. Budge, E. A. W. *The Mummy.* 2nd edn. Cambridge, 1925

24. Burstein, S. M. 'Psamtek I and the end of Nubian domination in Egypt', *JSSEA* 14 (1984) 31–4

25. Caminos, R. A. 'The Nitocris Adoption Stela', *JEA* 50 (1964) 71–101

26. Černý, J. and Groll, S. I. *A Late Egyptian Grammar.* Rome, 1975

27. Christophe, L.-A. 'Les trois derniers grands majordomes de la XXVIe Dynastie', *Ann. Serv.* 54 (1956) 83–100

28. Daressy, G. 'Stèle de l'an III d'Amasis', *Rec. Trav.* 22 (1900) 1–9

29. Davies, N. de G. *The Rock Tombs of Deir el Gebrawi* I. London, 1902

30. Davis, W. M. 'Egypt, Samos, and the archaic style in Greek sculpture', *JEA* 67 (1981) 61–81

31. Desroches-Noblecourt, C. 'Deux grands obélisques précieux d'un sanctuaire à Karnak', *Rev. d'égyptol.* 8 (1951) 47–61

32. Dixon, D. M. 'The origin of the kingdom of Kush', *JEA* 50 (1964) 121–32

33. Drioton, E. and Vandier, J. *L'Égypte (Clio. Les peuples de l'Orient méditerranéen,* 2). 4th edn. Paris, 1962

34. Dunham, D. *El Kurru.* Cambridge, Mass., 1950

35. Dunham, D. *Nuri.* Boston, 1955

36. Dunham, D. *The Barkal Temples.* Boston, 1970

37. Edel, E. 'Amasis und Nebukadrezar II', *GM* 29 (1978) 13–20

38. Edwards, I. E. S. *The Pyramids of Egypt.* New edn. Harmondsworth, 1985

39. Emery, W. B. 'Preliminary report on the excavations at North Saqqara, 1968–1969', *JEA* 56 (1970) 5–11

40. Faulkner, R. O. *The Book of the Dead.* 2 vols. New York (Limited Editions Club), 1972

41. Freedy, K. S. and Redford, D. B. 'The dates in Ezekiel in relation to Biblical, Babylonian and Egyptian sources', *JAOS* 90 (1970) 462–85

42. Gardiner, A. H. 'Piankhi's instructions to his army', *JEA* 21 (1935) 219–23

43. Gardiner, A. H. *Ancient Egyptian Onomastica.* 3 vols. Oxford, 1947

44. Gardiner, A. H. *Egypt of the Pharaohs.* Oxford, 1961

45. Gasm el-Seed, A. A. 'La tombe de Tanoutamon à el Kuuru (Ku 16)', *Rev. d'égyptol.* 36 (1985) 67–72

46. Gauthier, H. *Le Livre des rois d'Égypte* IV (Mém. Inst. fr. Caire XX). Cairo, 1916

47. Goedicke, H. 'Psammetik I. und die Libyer', *MDAIK* 18 (1962) 26–49

48. Goyon, G. C. 'La statuette funéraire I.E.84 de Lyon et le titre saïte *mr ḥwᶜ.w n swt*', *Bull. Inst. fr. Caire* 67 (1969) 159–71

49. Graefe, E. 'Die vermeintliche unterägyptische Herkunft des Ibi, Obermajordomus der Nitokris', *SAK* 1 (1974) 201–6

50. Graefe, E. *Untersuchungen zur Verwaltung und Geschichte der Institution der Gottesgemahlin des Amun von Beginn des Neuen Reiches bis zur Spätzeit.* 2 vols. Wiesbaden, 1981

51. Griffith, F. Ll. *Catalogue of the Demotic Papyri in the John Rylands Library Manchester.* 3 vols. Manchester, 1909

52. Grimal, N.-C. *Quatres stèles napatéennes au Musée du Caire* (Mém. Inst. fr. Caire CVI). Cairo, 1981

53. Grimal, N.-C. *La stèle triomphale de Pi (ᶜankh)y au Musée du Caire* (Mém. Inst. fr. Caire CV). Cairo, 1981

54. Gunn, B. G. and Engelbach, R. 'The statues of Ḥarwa', *Bull. Inst. fr. Caire* 30 (1931) 791–815

55. Gyles, M. F. *Pharaonic Policies and Administration 663 to 323 B.C.* Chapel Hill, 1959

56. Habachi, L. 'Psammétique II dans la région de la première cataracte', *Or. Ant.* 13 (1974) 317–26

57. Hall, H. R. *Catalogue of Egyptian Scarabs, etc. in the British Museum* I. London, 1913

58. Hall, H. R. 'The bronze statuette of Khonserdaisu in the British Museum', *JEA* 16 (1930) 1–2

59. Harris, J. R. (ed.) *The Legacy of Egypt.* 2nd edn. Oxford, 1971

60. Haycock, B. G. 'Towards a better understanding of the Kingdom of Cush (Napata-Meroë)', *Sudan Notes and Records* 49 (1968) 1–16

61. Helck, W., Otto, E. and Westendorf, W. (eds.) *Lexikon der Ägyptologie.* Wiesbaden, 1972– (in progress)

62. Iversen, E. *Canon and Proportions in Egyptian Art.* 2nd edn. Warminster, 1975

63. James, T. G. H. and Davies, W. V. *Egyptian Sculpture.* London, 1983

64. Janssen, J. J. 'The smaller Dâkhla stela', *JEA* 54 (1968) 165–72

65. Jeffreys, D. G. *The Survey of Memphis* I. London, 1985

66. Jelinková-Reymond, E. 'Quelques recherches sur les réformes d'Amasis', *Ann. Serv.* 54 (1956) 251–74

67. Junge, F. 'Zur Fehldatierung des sog. Denkmals memphitischer Theologie', *MDAIK* 29 (1973) 195–204

68. Kaiser, W. *et al.* 'Stadt und Tempel von Elephantine. Fünfter Grabungsbericht', *MDAIK* 31 (1975) 39–84

69. Kees, H. 'Zur Innenpolitik der Saïtendynastie', *Nachr. Göttingen.* Phil. Hist. Klasse, N.R. 1 (1934–6) 95–106

70. Kees, H. *Das Priestertum im ägyptischen Staat vom Neuen Reich bis zur Spätzeit.* Leiden–Cologne, 1953

71. Kees, H. *Ancient Egypt. A Cultural Topography.* London, 1961

72. Kees, H. 'Die priestliche Stellung des Monthemhet', *ZÄS* 87 (1962) 60–6

73. Kees, H. *Die Hohenpriester des Amun von Karnak von Herihor bis zum Ende des Äthiopenzeit.* Leiden, 1964

74. Kessler, D. 'Zu den Feldzugen des Tefnachte, Namlot und Pije in Mittelägypten', *SAK* 9 (1981) 227–51

75. Kienitz, F. K. *Die politische Geschichte Ägyptens vom 7. bis zum 4. Jahrhundert vor der Zeitwende.* Berlin, 1953

76. Kienitz, F. K. 'Die saïtische Renaissance' *Fischer Weltgeschichte* 4, 256–82. Frankfurt, 1966

77. Kitchen, K. A. *The Third Intermediate Period in Egypt.* Warminster, 1973 (for 1972); 2nd edn. 1986

78. Kitchen, K. A. 'Further thoughts on Egyptian chronology in the Third Intermediate Period', *Rev. d'égyptol.* 34 (1982–3) 59–69

79. Kitchen, K. A. 'Egypt, the Levant and Assyria in 701 B.C.', in *Fontes atque Pontes. Festgabe für Hellmut Brunner*, 243–52. Wiesbaden, 1983

80. Kuhlmann, K. P. and Schenkel, W. *Das Grab des Ibi, Obergutsverwalters der Gottesgemahlin des Amun* 1. Mainz, 1983

81. Lange, K. and Hirmer, M. *Egypt.* 4th edn. London, 1968

82. Leahy, A. 'Two donation stelae of Necho II', *Rev. d'égyptol.* 34 (1982–3) 77–91

83. Leahy, A. 'Tanutamun, son of Shabako?', *GM* 83 (1984) 43–5

84. Leclant, J. *Enquêtes sur les sacerdoces et les sanctuaires à l'époque dite 'éthiopienne' (XXVᵉ dynastie).* Cairo, 1954

85. Leclant, J. *Montouemhat, quatrième prophète d'Amon.* Cairo, 1961

86. Leclant, J. 'Une statuette d'Amon-Rê-Montou au nom de la divine adoratrice Chepenoupet', in *Mélanges Maspero* 1. iv, 73–98. Cairo, 1961

87. Leclant, J. 'Sur un contrepoids de menat au nom de Taharqa', in *Mélanges Mariette*, 251–84. Cairo, 1961

88. Leclant, J. 'Kashta, Pharaon en Égypte', *ZÄS* 90 (1963) 74–81

89. Leclant, J. *Recherches sur les monuments thébains de la XXVᵉ dynastie dite éthiopienne.* Cairo, 1965

90. Leclant, J. 'Les relations entre l'Égypte et la Phénicie du voyage d'Ounamon à l'expedition d'Alexandre', in Ward, W. (ed.) *The Role of the Phoenicians in the Interaction of Mediterranean Civilizations*, 9–31. Beirut, 1968

91. Leclant, J. 'Taharqa à Sedeinga', in *Studien zu Sprache und Religion Ägyptens* (Festschrift W. Westendorf), 2 vols., 1113–20. Göttingen, 1984

92. Leclant, J. and Yoyotte, J. 'Notes d'histoire et de civilisation éthiopienne. À propos d'un ouvrage recent', *Bull. Inst. fr. Caire* 51 (1952) 1–39

93. Lepsius, C. R. *Denkmaeler aus Aegypten und Aethiopen.* ed. E. Naville. 5 vols. Leipzig, 1897–1913

94. Lichtheim, M. 'The High Steward Akhamenru', *JNES* 7 (1948) 163–79

95. Lichtheim, M. *Ancient Egyptian Literature.* 3 vols. Berkeley – Los Angeles – London, 1975, 1976, 1980

96.   Lloyd, A. B. 'Triremes and the Saïte Navy', *JEA* 58 (1972) 268–79

97.   Lloyd, A. B. *Herodotus*, II: *Introduction*. Leiden, 1975

98.   Lloyd, A. B. 'Were Necho's triremes Phoenician?', *JHS* 95 (1975) 45–61

99.   Lloyd, A. B. *Herodotus*, II: *Commentary 1–98*. Leiden, 1976

100. Lloyd, A. B. 'Necho and the Red Sea: some considerations', *JEA* 63 (1977) 142–55

101. Lloyd, A. B. 'M. Basch on triremes: some observations', *JHS* 100 (1980) 195–8

102. Lloyd, A. B. 'The inscription of Udjaḥorresnet, a collaborator's testament', *JEA* 68 (1982) 166–80

103. Lloyd, A. B. *Herodotus*, II: *Commentary 99–182*. Leiden, 1988

104. Macadam, M. F. L. *The Temples of Kawa*, I: *The Inscriptions*. 2 vols. Oxford, 1949. II: *History and Archaeology*. 2 vols. Oxford, 1955

105. Maclaurin, E. C. B. 'Date of the foundation of the Jewish colony at Elephantine', *JNES* 27 (1968) 89–96

106. Malinine, M., Posener, G. and Vercoutter, J. *Catalogue des stèles du Sérapéum de Memphis* I. Paris, 1968

107. Masson, O. *Carian Inscriptions from North Saqqâra and Buhen*. London, 1978

108. Masson, O. and Yoyotte, J. *Objets pharaoniques à inscription carienne*. Cairo, 1956

109. Mauny, R. 'Le périple de l'Afrique par les phéniciens de Nechao vers 600 av. J–C', *Archéologia* 96 (July 1976) 44–5

110. Meeks, D. 'Les donations aux temples dans l'Égypte du 1er millénaire avant J.-C.', in Lipiński E. (ed.) *State and Temple Economy in the Ancient Near East*, 605–87. Leuven, 1979

111. Meeks, D. 'Une fondation memphite de Taharqa', in *Hommages à Serge Sauneron* I, 221–59. Cairo 1979

112. Meulenaere, H. De *Herodotos over de 26ste dynastie (II, 147–III, 15)*. Leuven, 1951

113. Meulenaere, H. De 'Trois vizirs', *Chron. d'Ég.* 33 (1958) 194–201

114. Meulenaere, H. De 'La famille des vizirs Nespamedu, et Nespakashouty', *Chron. d'Ég.* 38 (1963) 71–7

115. Meulenaere, H. De 'De vestiging van de Saïtische dynastie', *Orientalia Gandensia* I (1964) 95–103

116. Meulenaere, H. De 'La statue du général Djed-ptah-iouf-ankh (Caire JE 36949)', *Bull. Inst. fr. Caire* 63 (1965) 19–36

117. Meulenaere, H. De *Le surnom égyptien à la Basse Époque*. Istanbul, 1966

118. Meulenaere, H. De 'Die dritte Zwischenzeit und das äthiopische Reich', *Fischer Weltgeschichte* 4, 220–55. Frankfurt, 1967

119. Meulenaere, H. De 'La famille du roi Amasis', *JEA* 54 (1968) 183–7

120. Mitchell, R. M. 'Herodotus and Samos', *JHS* 95 (1975) 75–91

121. Müller, H. W. 'Ein Königsbildnis der 26 Dynastie mit der "Blauen Krone"', *ZÄS* 80 (1955) 46–68

122. Müller, H. W. 'Der Torso einer Königsstatue im Museo Archeologico zu Florenz', *Studi Rosellini* II 181–221. Pisa, 1955

123. Murnane, W. J. *Ancient Egyptian Coregencies*. Chicago, 1977
124. Otto, E. *Die biographischen Inschriften der ägyptischen Spätzeit*. Leiden, 1954
125. Parker, R. A. 'The length of the reign of Taharqa', *Kush* 8 (1960) 267–9
126. Parker, R. A. *A Saite Oracle Papyrus from Thebes in The Brooklyn Museum*. Providence, 1962
127. Parker, R. A. 'King *Py*, a historical problem', *ZÄS* 93 (1966) 111–14
128. Pelletier, A. *Lettre d'Aristée à Philocrate*. Paris, 1962
129. Pernigotti, S. 'Una statua di Pakhrof (Cairo J.E. 37171)', *Rivista* 44 (1969) 259–71
130. Petrie, W. M. F. *The Palace of Apries (Memphis II)*. London, 1909
131. Plumley, J. M. 'Qaṣr Ibrîm, 1974', *JEA* 61 (1975) 5–27
132. Plumley, J. M. and Adams, W. Y. 'Qaṣr Ibrîm, 1972', *JEA* 60 (1974) 212–38
133. Porter, B. and Moss, R. L. B. *Topographical Bibliography of Ancient Egyptia- Hieroglyphic Texts, Reliefs, and Paintings*. 7 vols. Oxford, 1927–1951. Edn. 2, vol. 1, 2 parts, 1960, 1964; vol. 11, 1972; vol. 111, 2 parts (ed. J. Málek), 1974, 1981
134. Posener, G. *La première domination perse en Égypte*. Cairo, 1936
135. Posener, G. 'Le canal du Nil à la Mer Rouge', *Chron. d'Ég.* 13 (1938) 259–73
136. Posener, G. 'Les douanes de la Mediterranée dans l'Égypte Saïte', *Rev. de Philol.* 21 (1947) 117–31
137. Priese, K.-H. 'Der Beginn der kuschitischen Herrschaft in Ägypten', *ZÄS* 98 (1970) 16–32
138. Ranke, H. 'Statue eines hohen Beamten unter Psammetich I', *ZÄS* 44 (1907) 42–54
139. Reisner, G.A. 'The Barkal temples in 1916', *JEA* 6 (1920) 247–64
140. Royal Academy, *5,000 Years of Egyptian Art*. London, 1962
141. Russmann, E. *The Representation of the King in the XXVth Dynasty* (Monographies Reine Elisabeth, 3). Brussels–Brooklyn, 1974
142. Sander-Hansen, C. E. *Das Gottesweib des Amun*. Copenhagen, 1940
143. Sauneron, S. (ed.) *Textes et langages de l'Égypte pharaonique*. 3 vols. Cairo, 1973 (1 and 2), 1974 (3)
144. Sauneron, S. and Yoyotte, J. 'La campagne nubienne de Psammétique II et sa signification historique', *Bull. Inst. fr. Caire* 50 (1952) 157–207
145. Sauneron, S. and Yoyotte, J. 'Sur la politique palestinienne des rois saïtes', *VT* 2 (1952) 131–6
146. Sayed, R. el- *Documents relatifs à Saïs et ses divinités*. Cairo, 1975
147. Schäfer, H. *Urkunden der alteren Äthiopenkönige (Urk. III)*. Leipzig, 1905
148. Schulman, A. 'A problem of Pedubasts', *JARCE* 5 (1966) 33–41
149. Segal, B. *Aramaic Texts from North Saqqâra*. London, 1983
150. Seidl, E. *Ägyptische Rechtsgeschichte der Saiten- und Persenzeit*. 2nd edn. Glückstadt, 1968
151. Smith, H. S. *A Visit to Ancient Egypt. Life at Memphis and Saqqara (c.500–30 B.C.)*. Warminster, 1974

152. Smith, H. S. *The Fortress of Buhen*, II: *The Inscriptions*. London, 1976
153. Smith, W. S. *The Art and Architecture of Ancient Egypt*. Rev. ed. Harmondsworth, 1965. 2nd edn rev. by W. K. Simpson, 1981
154. Spalinger, A. 'The year 712 B.C. and its implications for Egyptian history', *JARCE* 10 (1973) 95–101
155. Spalinger, A. 'Assurbanipal and Egypt: a source study', *JAOS* 94 (1974) 316–28
156. Spalinger, A. 'Esarhaddon and Egypt: an analysis of the first invasion of Egypt', *Orientalia* 43 (1974) 295–326
157. Spalinger, A. 'An Egyptian motif in an Assyrian text', *BASOR* 223 (1976) 64–7
158. Spalinger, A. 'Psammetichus, King of Egypt: I', *JARCE* 13 (1976) 133–47
159. Spalinger, A. 'Egypt and Babylonia: a survey (*c.* 620 B.C.–550 B.C.)', *SAK* 5 (1977) 221–44
160. Spalinger, A. 'The concept of the monarchy during the Saite Epoch – an essay in synthesis', *Or.* 47 (1978) 12–36
161. Spalinger, A. 'The date of the death of Gyges and its historical implications', *JAOS* 98 (1978) 400–9
162. Spalinger, A. 'The foreign policy of Egypt before the Assyrian conquest', *Chron. d'Ég.* 53 (1978) 22–47
163. Spalinger, A. 'Psammetichus, King of Egypt: II', *JARCE* 15 (1978) 49–57
164. Spalinger, A. 'The military background of the campaign of Piye (Piankhy)', *SAK* 7 (1979) 273–301
165. Spiegelberg, W. *Die sogennante demotische Chronik des Pap. 215 der Bibliothèque Nationale zu Paris*. Leipzig, 1914
166. Stadelmann, R. 'Das Grab im Tempelhof. Der Typus des Königsgrabes in der Spätzeit', *MDAIK* 27 (1971) 111–23
167. Terrace, E. L. B. 'Three Egyptian bronzes', *BMFA* 57 (1959) 48–53
168. Trigger, B. G. *Nubia under the Pharaohs*. London, 1976
169. Trigger, B. G., Kemp, B. J., O'Connor, D. and Lloyd, A. B. *Ancient Egypt. A Social History*. Cambridge, 1983
170. Vercoutter, J. 'The Napatan Kings and Apis worship', *Kush* 8 (1960) 62–76
171. Vernus, P. 'Inscriptions de la Troisième Période Intermédiaire', *Bull. Inst. fr. Caire* 75 (1975) 1–66
172. Vittmann, G. 'Die Familie der saitischen Könige', *Or.* 44 (1975), 375–387
173. Vittmann, G. *Priester und Beamte im Theben der Spätzeit*. (Beiträge zur Ägyptologie 1). Vienna, 1978
174. Waddell, W. G. (ed.) *Manetho* (Loeb Classical Library). London, 1940
175. Wenig, S. *Africa in Antiquity*. 2 vols. Brooklyn, 1978
176. Wilkinson, A. *Ancient Egyptian Jewellery*. London, 1971
177. Winter, E. 'Eine ägyptische Bronze aus Ephesos', *ZÄS* 97 (1971), 146–55
178. Winter, E. *Der Apiskult im Alten Ägypten*. Mainz, 1978

179. Yoyotte, J. 'Le martelage des noms royaux éthiopiens par Psammétique II', *Rev. d'égyptol.* 8 (1951), 215–39
180. Yoyotte, J. 'Quelques toponymes égyptiens mentionnés dans les "Annales d'Assurbanipal" (Rm. I, 101–105)', *RA* 46 (1952) 212–14
181. Yoyotte, J. 'Plaidoyer pour l'authenticité du scarabée historique de Shabako', *Biblica* 37 (1956) 457–76
182. Yoyotte, J. 'Néchao ou Neko', *Dictionnaire de la Bible.* Suppl. vi, fasc. 31, 363–93. Paris, 1958
183. Yoyotte, J. 'Sur le scarabée historique de Shabako. Note additionnelle', *Biblica* 39 (1958) 206–10
184. Yoyotte, J. 'Les principautés du Delta au temps de l'anarchie libyenne', *Mélanges Maspero* I, fasc. 4, 121–81. Cairo, 1961
185. Yurco, F. J. 'Sennacherib's third campaign and the coregency of Shabaka and Shebitku', *Serapis* 6 (1980) 221–40
186. Zeissl, H. von. *Äthiopen und Assyrer in Ägypten.* 2nd edn. Glückstadt, 1955

INDEX